*Praise for Robert Tombs's*

# THE ENGLISH AND THEIR HISTORY

"Robert Tombs's *The English and Their History* is history at its best. He gives a fluent, elegant and abundantly energetic narrative from the Bronze Age to the Scottish Referendum of 2014. . . . The final section of the book, covering the last half-century, is a triumph of precision and candour: I have not read history that is so important and exciting for years."
—Richard Davenport-Hines,
*The Times Literary Supplement* (Books of the Year)

"In his massive, engaging and persuasive new book, Robert Tombs speaks up for English history, and sometimes for England itself."
—*The Guardian*

"[A] work of supreme intelligence. In this vigorous, subtle and penetrating book . . . Tombs has done nothing less than narrate with rare freshness and confidence two thousand years of English history. . . . No history published this year has been of such resounding importance to contemporary debates. Tombs, who is both fearless and nonpartisan, deserves to be rewarded with a life peerage for this book. There can be no steadier, calmer and more informed adviser during the constitutional crises looming in the next two or three years."
—*The Observer* (London)

"Tombs has succeeded magnificently. Learned, pithy and punchy, with a laudable sense of narrative sweep and a bracing willingness to offer bold judgments, his survey is a tremendous achievement, and deserves to become the standard history for years to come. . . . [A] superb feat of compression and analysis."
—*The Sunday Times* (London)

"[A] compelling and intriguing analysis. . . . Vast in scope and full to the brim with scholarship that has been painstakingly absorbed only to be disgorged with an exhilarating mixture of conviction and lightness of touch."
—*Financial Times*

"Fascinating. . . . I found it especially strong on English-French relations, and early modern times. . . . Definitely recommended, I quickly became addicted to this book." —Tyler Cowen, *Marginal Revolution*

"Conducting a vast yet readable and sharply focused tour through the ages, and contrasting the English with their Celtic and continental neighbours, the thread is the evolution and paradoxical elusiveness of Englishness. . . . Jammed with succulent nuggets."
—*The Daily Telegraph* (Books of the Year)

"Robert Tombs's timely and magisterial *The English and Their History* . . . [is] a great achievement: You're in the hands of a learned and considerate guide whose judgments, whether you agree with them or not, you can be sure will be well-founded. A very good read and possibly the most important contribution to the subject since Trevelyan."
—Alan Judd, *Spectator* (Books of the Year)

"The perfect starting point for anyone who wants to grapple with the complexity of the English question. . . . [Tombs] writes beautifully; there isn't a lazy sentence in this text."        —*The Economist*

"Commanding. . . . [A] brilliant distillation of a vast tale and arguably the finest one-volume history of any nation and people ever written. . . . Comprehensive, authoritative, and readable to a fault, this book should be on the shelves of everyone interested in its subject."
—*Publishers Weekly* (starred review)

"Massive yet accessible. . . . Wonderfully reasoned and tidily structured . . . surprisingly approachable. . . . Lucid, engaging, and pleasantly nondidactic."        —*Kirkus Reviews* (starred review)

*Robert Tombs*

# THE ENGLISH
# AND THEIR HISTORY

Robert Tombs is professor of history at the University of Cambridge and a leading scholar of Anglo-French relations. His previous book, *That Sweet Enemy: The French and the British from the Sun King to the Present,* co-authored with his wife, Isabelle Tombs, is the first large-scale study of the relationship between the French and the British over the last three centuries.

*That Sweet Enemy: The French and British from the Sun King to the Present*
(with Isabelle Tombs)
*The Paris Commune, 1871*
*France, 1814–1914*
*Nationhood and Nationalism Before the Great War*
*Thiers, 1797–1877: A Political Life* (with J. P. T. Bury)
*The War Against Paris, 1871*

*Robert Tombs*

# THE ENGLISH AND THEIR HISTORY

VINTAGE BOOKS
A Division of Penguin Random House LLC
New York

FIRST VINTAGE BOOKS EDITION, NOVEMBER 2016

*Copyright © 2014 by Robert Tombs*

The Library of Congress has cataloged the Knopf edition as follows:
Tombs, Robert, author.
The English and their history / by Robert Tombs.
pages cm
I. Great Britain—History.   I. Title.
DA30.T656 2015   942—dc23   2014048390

Vintage Books Trade Paperback ISBN: 978-1-101-87336-6
eBook ISBN: 978-1-101-87477-6

*Author photograph © Blazej Mikuła*

www.vintagebooks.com

Printed in the United States of America
10  9  8  7  6  5  4

# Contents

# Illustrations

# Maps

# Figures

# The English and Their History

# Introduction: Who Do We Think We Are?

> In general, this only is allowed,
> They're something noisy, and a little proud.
>> Daniel Defoe, *The True Born Englishman* (1700)

> *Generally speaking, all the great events have been distorted, most of the important causes concealed, some of the principal characters never appear, and all who figure are so misunderstood and misrepresented, that the result is a complete mystification, and the perusal of the narrative about as profitable to an Englishman as reading the Republic of Plato or the Utopia of More.*
>> Benjamin Disraeli on the history of England[1]

The people who took the name "English," set up an English kingdom, and subsequently named their country England, and those who have lived there after them and thought of themselves as members of an English nation, are in two ways products of history: because of what happened to them and because of the constantly changing ways in which they remembered those experiences. This book explores these two connected themes. Though apparently simple terms, "nation" and "memory" raise questions that need to be considered briefly at the outset. What a nation really is has exercised thinkers over the last two centuries: whether nations are ancient or modern phenomena; whether they have some organic existence as cultural, genetic or geographical entities; whether they are political and ideological fabrications; or indeed various mixtures of these.[2] My view is that most nations and their shared identities are modern creations, the products of literacy, urbanization, and state-led cultural and political unification. But, as Ernest Gellner observed in an influential work emphasizing this "modernist" view, there are nevertheless some ancient nations.[3] Most of the oldest that still survive are on the western fringes of Europe, and one is England. The concept of an "English people" (*gens Anglorum*) emerged in the eighth century, an English kingdom with its own land ("eard") in the ninth, and that land acquired a name, England—or, rather, Englalond—around the year 1000. There are a few much older states in existence, particularly ancient empires and their successor states such as China or Iran. But there are few if any older "nation-states," a political form of which the English turned out to be pioneers—a sizeable political community with some sense of kinship, cultural similarity, participation in government and some representative institutions. The very idea that such peoples or nations have continuous histories over many generations, which we take so much for granted in Western culture, owes much to the pioneering writings of Anglo-Norman clerics in the twelfth century as they tried to make sense of the Conquest. Whether there really is a continuous and meaningful story of a place and its successive inhabitants over many centuries and through many changes is something this book attempts to explore, and we shall return to it in the concluding chapter.

The great labour over many centuries of recording, interpreting and narrating English history has created a splendid cultural treasure including some of our greatest poetry, drama, prose, painting and scholarship. History is not of course the only way of understanding a society: sociology, political science, economics and anthropology provide many insights, as in different ways do literature and art. But history has the particular quality of examining its subjects over time, proceeding by evidence-based narrative and argument, and it assumes that the past to some extent explains the present. It can thus help us to identify unusual aspects of our society and understand why we think about them in the ways we do.

Recently, many historians have consciously focused on phenomena that overflow national boundaries, and "transnational history" and "world history" have attracted much attention. This is welcome, as a basic fault of traditional national history (and most history ever written falls into this category) is insularity: writing consciously or unconsciously as if the history of a particular nation were self-contained, unique and incomparable, whereas it is inevitably part of much wider ebbs and flows. In the case of England particularly, some historians have come close to suggesting—sometimes with surprising vehemence—that it does not have, or should not have today, a meaningful history at all. The common argument is that it is subsumed into British history,[4] or even a history of "the isles"—"The old Anglocentric straitjacket is bursting at the seams."[5] This widespread view is expressed in major works of scholarship and reflected in the 2013 national history curriculum for England. The British perspective is most useful for the seventeenth century, when the island nations were entwined politically to a unique degree—though even then the insular view risks obscuring the fundamental importance to England of the Low Countries, France, Spain and Germany. Taking a longer view, it is evident that England has never been confined within a British shell. Not only was it, of course, a sovereign kingdom for most of its history; but no less importantly over the centuries, relations with Scandinavia, the Low Countries and France, and in modern times with the British Empire, the United States of America and Germany, have been even more important to England than those with the other island nations, even when these formed part of a more or less united kingdom.

Following the various Acts of British unification between 1536 and 1800* and colonial expansion in the eighteenth century, recounting the history of England certainly becomes more complex, especially in international contexts when England was not a separate actor, and historians of this period have often been criticized for using "Britain" and "England" interchangeably—as, indeed, many contemporaries did from the seventeenth century onwards. I hope I have avoided this. Nevertheless, the idea that England does not or should not have its own history is interesting and rather strange: it is unimaginable that the same argument could be made about Ireland, Scotland or France. A history of England seems to unsettle people: the past, it seems, is not dead; it is not even past.[6] This book attempts to tell the history of England, first as an idea, and then as a kingdom, as a country, a people and a culture, trying to begin at the beginning without assuming any inevitability in what occurred, and trying to explore what is proper to England, and what is shared with its various neighbours.

The second theme of the book is memory. Collective memory as a pillar of national identity was posited by John Stuart Mill in the 1860s and taken up in the 1880s by the French philosopher Ernest Renan, who placed "the shared possession of a rich heritage of memories" at its heart.[7] As a subject of academic study memory was first undertaken by French historians, whose term *mémoire* suggests not individual recollections but what is sometimes called "social memory"—a public culture, recorded in monuments, books, institutions and symbols.[8] This book pursues that idea: the history of England is not simply what happened, or what historians believe they can demonstrate, but what a vast range of people, for a great variety of purposes, have recorded, asserted and believed about the

* Acts of Union with Wales (1536 and 1543), the Union of the Crowns (1603), and the Acts of Union with Scotland (1707) and Ireland (1800).

past—a confused mass of ideas, emotions, words and images, often contradictory, argumentative and divisive.

Much "memory," individual or collective, is fiction, and no less powerful for that. This book is not a systematic analysis of English social
memory—such a thing would have to be a vast collective undertaking.[9]
Nor is it a study of English identity, of which there are several stimulating
examples.[10] It is a work of history, and thus of narrative. It does, however,
try to do something unusual: to make memory and its creation an inherent part of the story. Hence, it gives particular emphasis to important
creators and carriers of memory, such as language, literature, law, religious and political institutions, and of course historical writing itself,
from that by Bede, via Henry of Huntingdon, Geoffrey of Monmouth and
Shakespeare, to Macaulay, E. P. Thompson and many others. It discusses
widely accepted beliefs about the past—for example, concerning
Anglo-Saxon liberties, the common law, the significance of Magna Carta,
or the causes and consequences of the Industrial Revolution. For more
recent times, it looks at the ambiguities and consequences of the Victorian
age; at the reasons for taking part in the First World War and the divided
memories of that great disaster; and the "finest hour" tradition of the
Second World War and its legacy.

Four memory themes are given particular attention, however. Their
connections, spanning nearly all of our history, make up an arc of rise and
fall: the long and contradictory aftermath of the Norman Conquest; the
interpretation of the Civil War era and its ramification into a "Whig history" of progress; the history and conflicting memory of empire; and,
most recently, the sense of England and Britain as nations in decline. My
intention is to show how these ideas originated, what purposes they have
served, and how they appear in the light of modern research. The book is,
therefore, partly shaped by the stories and images that make up our collective memory. But I have also been concerned with things we have collectively forgotten and which I think we ought to remember. If this seems
contradictory, I hope nevertheless it constitutes a coherent story.

Every work of history reflects the experiences, beliefs and personality
of its writer. But every serious work of history is also a collective enterprise, drawing on the painstaking research and thinking of hundreds, even
thousands, of scholars today and far in the past. Historical novelists, playwrights or film-makers may feel free to tell the story however they wish;
but historians are guided and indeed constrained by this research, which
dictates much of what can and must be written. It has been an intellectual
adventure for me to explore the riches of English historiography, in constant renovation and expansion by historians of many nationalities.

Throughout I have tried to reflect the best modern scholarship, much of it hidden from the public gaze in the pages of learned journals and scholarly monographs and despite its inherent interest too often ignored.

My personal decisions are clearest in the broad shape of the narrative and in its emphases, though here too one can exaggerate the subjective element: in many ways I have not written the book I expected to write. Perhaps inevitably, the last 500 years have come to take up far more space than the previous 1,000. I have also given extra weight to what is unusual in England's history. One could describe a house by saying that it has walls, a roof, doors and windows; but generally more useful is to specify its distinctive style, situation, materials and colours. So with a nation: rather than those features that are shared with all the others, and certainly with those in north-western Europe—many economic and social practices, family relationships, property systems, gender roles, religious beliefs—I focus on specifically English experiences, including great political and international events. Also unique to England are cultural processes and economic innovations at certain moments in time: for example, the late-medieval expansion of written English and the eighteenth-century Industrial Revolution.

These are absorbing questions, not least for me, an Englishman with Irish connections who has spent most of his life studying France. So my approach to England's history has necessarily been without fixed preconceptions and, explicitly or implicitly, it is constantly concerned with wider historical perspectives. I believe it is meaningless to attempt any description of a society—that it was rich or poor, equal or unequal, free or oppressed, stable or unstable—except by comparison with other human societies. The philosopher Thomas Hobbes thought that "a writer of history ought, in his writings, to be a foreigner, without a country, living under his own law only,"[11] and this—despite occasional uses of "we," "us" and "our" in these pages—has been my watchword. Besides, had I been a lifelong English specialist, I doubt I would have had the nerve to try it.

# Prelude: The Dreamtime

*This, the noblest of islands . . . was first called Albion, then Britain, and is now known as England.*

Henry of Huntingdon, *Historia Anglorum* (c.1150)

The English occupy most of an island: this, we might think, sums up the essence of their history. But only if we add: a *unique* island. It is the main island of one of the three largest temperate archipelagos in the world—with Honshu in Japan and the South Island of New Zealand.* Unlike them, nearly all of it is habitable, suitable for various kinds of agriculture, with few natural barriers, and long fully settled. Most importantly, it is in sight and easy reach of a continent. These seas—between twenty and 400 miles of often rough but predictable water—have been from earliest times a highway for traders, settlers and invaders in both directions. The island overlooked the sea communications between the north and south of that continent and those that would eventually develop between it and the rest of the world. Scarcely less importantly, the English have only ever inhabited the mostly lowland part of the archipelago: they have coexisted with other island peoples. Nor have they inhabited it for long: of at least 11,500 years of continuous human settlement, only some 1,300 can be described as "English."

For all but the most recent fraction of time, the land now called England had no name that we know; nor indeed was it part of an island. The first signs of habitation by the predecessors of *Homo sapiens*—including their footprints in the mud—are as long as 800,000 years ago, when the land was a tropical peninsula and hippos swam in what we call the Thames.

---

* Great Britain measures 228,000 square kilometres; Honshu, 231,000, and South Island, 150,000. The only larger islands are tropical forest or semi-arctic tundra (New Guinea, Borneo, Greenland, etc.).

Several cycles of often rapid and extreme climate change swept human life away, then let it trickle back as the ice receded. For as much as 100,000 years, there seems to have been no human habitation at all, partly because a great river valley where the Channel is now made access difficult. But 60,000 years ago Neanderthals were present in what was still a peninsula, and 40,000 years ago the Cro-Magnons, who left flint tools and bones, including their own, some of which show possible signs of cannibalism. They were eliminated by the last ice age, when, about 25,000 years ago, the whole land was frozen over and remained uninhabitable for some 10,000 years. When the ice melted, the physical link with the Continent was worn away by a gigantic flood or floods, which scoured out the Channel when the vast lake that became the North Sea overflowed. The last land bridge—a narrow chalk ridge—may finally have been submerged only some 6,000 years ago, when the new island was already inhabited by people who are genetically the ancestors of most who live there today.[1]

The tiny population—a few thousand hunter-gatherers during the first few millennia—grew when from about 6,000 years ago they began burning and cutting down the forests, laid out fields for wheat, barley and oats, and shipped in cattle, pigs and sheep from across the Channel. In four centuries this transformed both the landscape and their own societies. Over several centuries from about 3000 BC, great ritual sites were built throughout the archipelago, the first being in the far northern islands. Large enclosed spaces were made both for ceremonial purposes and for defence, and their similarities indicate cultural homogeneity. There was eventually a particular concentration in the south-west, most famously in the sacred landscape round Stonehenge, built in several stages, and including great stones brought from far away to the north-west. Types of burials and monuments testify to changing cultural practices and beliefs.[2] As is common in other countries across the globe, the English incorporated these awe-inspiring remains into their national heritage, and first did so as long ago as the thirteenth century. But not until the late sixteenth century was an attempt made to survey ancient monuments and investigate their origins, in William Camden's *Britannia* (1586), and only in the early nineteenth century did serious archaeology begin.

During the Bronze Age (*c*.2500–1000 BC) the islanders engaged in tin-mining and metalworking, pottery, salt production, and leather and cloth manufacture, which they traded domestically and overseas. Most lived in small farmsteads, large enough for an extended family, with typical roundhouses inside a protected compound. Nothing disruptive seems to have happened over a long period from 2000 to 700 BC, when the climate was favourable and there was cultural continuity. By the time of the

Iron Age, from about 750 BC, the lowland areas had been cleared and settled, and every inch belonged to somebody or was expressly set aside for communal purposes. Some field boundaries are among the world's oldest constructions still in use.[3] The population grew to as much as 2 million, and coalesced into political groupings of rural settlements round a larger centre, dominated by a leader with a band of horse- and chariot-mounted warriors. Conflict between them was probably endemic. On the western fringes of the island, homesteads were designed for defence, and there was a central belt dominated by massive hill forts, which probably had a religious and political significance as well as providing storage for food and refuge in times of danger. Figures were carved into chalk hillsides, such as the White Horse at Uffington, the oldest. By about 60 BC several of the tribal polities were issuing their own coinage. An Italian writer described the natives of the coastal regions as "civilized" and "especially friendly to strangers" due to their frequent commercial contacts.[4] Their Druidic religion, however, did involve ritual torture and killing.[5]

A general name for the archipelago, "Pretannike," appeared in a work by a Greek explorer, Pytheas, who in about 320 BC sailed round the islands in a bold search for knowledge and trading opportunities.[6] The name, perhaps derived from a Celtic word for "the tattoed folk" (Caesar later described them as dyed with woad), evolved into "Bretannia" and "Britannia." The largest island became known as Albion or Alba, and the western island Ivernia or Hibernia. The only names we can give the island peoples—"Britons," "Picts" (in the remote unconquered north), "Scots" (in Hibernia), and southern peoples such as "Iceni," "Brigantes" or "Trinovantes"—are versions of the names given to them by the Greeks and Romans. Thus, through the words and ideas of Mediterranean writers such as Pytheas, Diodorus Siculus (*c.*60 BC) and Tacitus (*c.*AD 98), the islands and their peoples entered history. Linguistically and culturally they were little different from the Iron Age peoples of north-western Europe generally, known to the Romans as Celtae.

It is part of our national myth, thanks not least to Shakespeare, that the sea has been "a moat defensive" against invasion. In fact, there have been innumerable invasions over the centuries, some of them with profound effects, and very few of which could be prevented until recent times. The benefits of insularity had to be won the hard way.[7] The history of the island was transformed by Roman invasion in the first century AD, and by the movements of peoples that took place all over Europe for nearly 1,000 years from the third century to the twelfth. Unlike arrivals by land, whose usually slow and burdensome movements could be known, predicted, harried and blocked, seaborne incursions were swift and unpredictable, covering in hours what would take days on foot. If opposed they could sail on to find an undefended landfall, and if threatened they could retreat as easily as they had come. Their ships could bring goods to trade, and weapons and horses to fight; they could carry away booty and slaves. They could also bring women and children to settle. But if the sea facilitated the arrival of many small groups, it nevertheless made large-scale invasions difficult and hazardous, and rapid mass colonization impossible. Even the major conquerors—Romans, Saxons, Danes and Normans—were still relatively small bands of warriors, who took possession of the country and its peoples as overlords, but did not exterminate or expel them. Conquests caused huge political and cultural changes; and yet at the material level of land use and settlement life went on. New masters moved into existing communities, often built on existing sites, and interbred.

Much later, British writers invented heroic origin myths set in the mysterious centuries before the Romans came. The most popular and influential was by an Oxford cleric and Bishop of St. Asaph, Geoffrey of Monmouth, possibly of Breton descent. His *History of the Kings of Britain*, written in Latin in about 1136, popularized the story of "Brut," the Trojan hero Brutus, who landed in Albion, "uninhabited except for a few giants" including "a particularly repulsive one, called Gogmagog." After driving off the giants, Brutus renamed the island "Brutaigne," or Britain, after himself.[8] This story emulates that of the Franks and indeed the Romans themselves, who also claimed Trojan descent. Geoffrey's tales of warlike monarchs with unlikely names such as Gorboduc and Lud were read and believed across Europe and long remained popular. His stories were translated and readapted by later writers—above all the story of King Leir and his daughters, and of King Arthur and the magician Merlin. Geoffrey thus elaborated for the British a prestigious and exciting European lineage, and his narrative remained authoritative for over four centuries.

Before the dawn of the Christian era, the pagan peoples of the southern fringes of the island, far from being the woad-covered savages of legend, formed an old and sophisticated society with close economic and political ties with the Continent. Back and forth went mercenaries, traders, raiders, envoys and refugees. As the Roman Empire spread rapidly north during the first century BC, the island's rulers faced a dilemma. Some decided their interests lay in making treaties with Rome. Others prepared to resist and strengthened their old forts. Alliances were formed with kingdoms across the Channel, some of which may have been the overlords of southern coastal regions of the island. One reason Julius Caesar gave for his brief invasions in 55 and 54 BC was that warriors from the island were fighting against him as allies of the Gauls. With about 30,000 men, he landed in Kent and advanced north, crossing the Thames. At first the native kingdoms mounted a joint defence under the man the Romans called Cassivellaunus, but it was brief as some tribes changed sides. The historian Tacitus (c.AD 56–c.120) commented later that "nothing has helped us more in war with their strongest nations than their inability to co-operate. It is but seldom that two or three states combine to repel a common danger."[9] Yet Caesar withdrew, called away by the outbreak of revolt in Gaul.

The island's autonomy was thus preserved for nearly another century, partly by civil war inside the Roman Empire. But eventually, in AD 43, the Romans mounted perhaps the biggest invasion of the island in history, by some 40,000 men with a detachment of elephants, probably landing in several places simultaneously. The emperor Claudius took symbolic command.[10] Complete conquest took several decades. The process bore the Roman hallmarks of intimidation, ruthlessness and terror. For several years, Caratacus ("Caractacus"), son of the southern king Cunobelinus ("Cymbeline"), led a series of guerrilla campaigns as he was pushed further and further west, until he was captured and taken to Rome. Those still fighting, including Druids, retreated to Anglesey, which was stormed and its defenders massacred, in AD 60. But just as this resistance was being crushed, revolt exploded on the populous eastern side of the island—the devastating rising of the Iceni.

Rome's intention was annexation in the medium term: peoples that submitted without a fight would be allowed to keep most of their lands and for a time some autonomy as client states, but when their rulers died they would be taken over. This was applied to the Iceni, when following the death of their king his widow, Boudicca ("Boadicea"), was dispossessed. Tacitus adds that she "was flogged and her daughters raped"— presumably to make the point that there was no more Iceni royalty, just insolent natives.[11] The revolt spread south and west, towns such as Camulodunum (Colchester) were torched, and many of their inhabitants—especially the carpetbaggers who had followed the Romans in search of quick profits—were massacred, often with gruesome ritual. The Romans, some of whose military units had been wiped out, regrouped, and somewhere in the west-central part of the island their disciplined troops smashed the much larger rebel force and slaughtered as many as they could catch. Boudicca killed herself.

There was no further internal threat to Roman rule. In AD 77 the

renowned general Agricola arrived as governor, to extend Roman domination to the west and north, and this campaign formed the core of Tacitus's biography of Agricola, his father-in-law, and the source of the famous
jibe "They make a desert and call it peace." For fifteen generations Britannia, subdivided into provinces and districts, was part of the empire. Its
material attractions were the agricultural wealth of the southern regions,
tin and lead in the west and south-west, tribute, slaves and its strategic
importance as an offshore base that might otherwise shelter Rome's enemies. There was also political prestige among the Roman elite in occupying the very edge of the known world, lapped by the unexplored Ocean.[12]
Britannia would remain a final outpost, a road to nowhere.

The Romans did not attempt to govern the whole island. The remoter
western peninsulas were little touched. The far north was sealed off
behind a wide military zone of which Hadrian's Wall was the backbone.
Built on the orders of the emperor Hadrianus between 122 and 138 AD,
it was one of the great engineering projects of the ancient world, including
twenty forts and 300 smaller fortlets and towers. It would have taken a
workforce of 15,000–20,000 men some fourteen years to build.[13] Straight
paved roads transformed overland communications, and remained in use
for centuries. Trade with the Continent increased. Towns developed as
military, administrative and trading centres, most importantly the capital
at Londinium, the lowest bridgeable point on the Thames, and regional
capitals at Eboracum (York), Lindum (Lincoln) and Corinium (Circences-
ter). Many settlements developed from existing ones, as the native roots
of Latinized names such as Eboracum suggest. Most of Britannia remained
rural: 80 percent of the population lived in over 100,000 small settlements and some 2,000 villas, estates of varying sizes concentrated in the
south-east. Only 20–30 of these villas were palatial, belonging to a small
patrician class of serving and retired Roman officials and soldiers, and to
a Romanized native nobility who retained ancestral lands. Smaller villas
probably belonged to lesser native families who adopted Roman styles.[14]
Imperial links brought literacy, the Latin language and eventually Christianity. At first persecuted (giving Britain its proto-martyr, St. Alban), it
became the official religion of the empire during the later fourth century.
For the Romano-British elites, the empire conferred power and status,
and the sense of being part of a great if distant civilization—something
which, however dimly, outlasted the empire itself and deeply influenced
all its successor states.

The long decline and fall of the empire is one of the greatest and most
famous epics in history. From the third century AD, constant factional
conflicts, depositions and murders within the imperial elite; attempted

military coups (including several by the army in Britain); economic decline; epidemics; and above all uncontrollable movements of peoples caused the empire to fragment, until its western provinces became autonomous kingdoms under "barbarian" rule. Climatic fluctuations made parts of northern Europe less habitable and prompted migrations. Long-term events in Asia (such as conflict in the Chinese Empire and crisis in the Persian) caused steppe peoples to move west, among them the terrifying Huns, originally from the borders of China, who first appeared in the West in 376. To help defend themselves, the Romans recruited "barbarian" troops and brought them inside the empire, where they became political actors in their own right. The empire offered attractions to outsiders, and increasingly easy pickings to the boldest. The neighbouring northern provinces of Gaul and Britain were thus for several centuries exposed to incursions from peoples coming to trade, to raid, to settle and to offer their services as mercenaries in what became a vast protection racket.

Picts from north Britain and Scots from Hibernia raided the Romanized regions. From the third century onwards, those the Romans called "Saxons" (mostly peoples of north Germany and southern Scandinavia) harried both sides of the North Sea and the Atlantic coast of Gaul, taking loot and slaves, and drowning or crucifying one-tenth of their captives as a sacrifice to their gods.[15] The Romans reacted vigorously, stationing more troops in Britain than any medieval English monarch would ever command and building some of the largest fortifications in the empire, including the fortress at Eboracum and huge forts and naval stations on what came to be known as "the Saxon shore" (*litus saxonicum*), among them Porchester, Pevensey and Dover, and watch-towers as far north as the Tyne. Britain suffered less than many Continental provinces, which were exposed to mass overland invasions, but for that very reason, and because they became involved in the political factionalism of the empire, troops and money were drained away from the island to defend other provinces. In 367 there was an astonishing "barbarian conspiracy," when Picts, Scots and Saxons succeeded in coordinating their attacks on southern Britain. The attacks were beaten off, but danger remained ever-present.

In 408 came another major Saxon attack. The Roman connection was now more of a drain than a defence, and in 409, according to the Roman writer Zosimus, Britannia was "obliged to throw off Roman rule and live independently."[16] The following year, Rome itself was sacked by the Goths. No attempt was ever made to restore imperial rule to Britain. All over the Roman world, power and defence became increasingly localized, as peaceable landlords had to become warlords.[17] Villas and settlements close to the coasts or to navigable rivers were targets for shipborne raiders, brigands and rebelling peasants, and in such places the alternatives were to leave or die.[18]

An ancient story, recorded in a ninth-century *Historia Brittonum* and repeated by Geoffrey of Monmouth in the 1130s, is that the "King of Britain," Vortigern (the name is probably from a Brittonic term for "high ruler"[19]), engaged Saxon mercenaries led by the brothers Hengist and Horsa to take part in the defence against the Picts, but they tricked and corrupted him, especially through the gift of Hengist's ravishing daughter Renwein (Rowena), and opened a bridgehead for reinforcements and settlers. The story is evidently mythologized, and resembles similar accounts in other countries, but dangers from mercenaries were indeed common, and the legend may echo reality.

Over the fifth century, Saxons moved into the south-eastern and central parts of the island. The extent, timing and nature of this Germanization of Britain are disputed, especially by some archaeologists sceptical of ancient written accounts. Was it a rapid, violent invasion, resulting in the ethnic cleansing of the Romano-British population, exterminated or chased towards the west? So suggests the oldest surviving narrative (*c.*540), by the monk Gildas, which survives in only two medieval manuscript copies:

> The first wave landed on the eastern side of the island . . . and there they fixed their terrible claws, as if to defend the country, but in fact to attack it. Their German mother-land, seeing them successfully installed, dispatched a wonderful collection of hangers-on and dogs, who, arriving by the boatload, joined up with their misbegotten comrades.[20]

Or was it a less traumatic process, including gradual settlement in underpopulated areas and voluntary cultural emulation by the native majority, which left much of life undisturbed, as some archaeologists believe the material evidence shows?[21] The question is complicated even now because of its relation to various foundation myths: for example, that which saw the Saxons as the ancestors of the future English nation, which through them inherited liberties and customs brought from beyond the Roman frontier by free Germanic tribes. It is probable that many Germanic war bands—in all perhaps 100,000–200,000 people, equal to 10–20 percent of the native population—invaded the fertile lowlands of eastern and southern Britain.[22] They did not displace the existing population, though they certainly killed or drove out the relatively small Romanized elite. The hoards of treasure since discovered show that many failed to escape with their riches. Towns dwindled or were abandoned—Londinium became a ghost town. Trade collapsed, manufacturing ceased and coinage disappeared. Some Britons

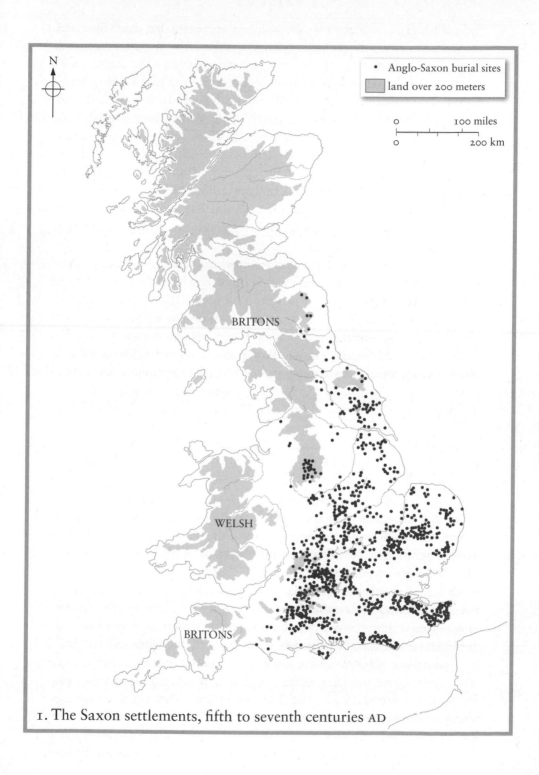

N

Anglo-Saxon burial sites
land over 200 meters

0        100 miles
0        200 km

BRITONS

WELSH

BRITONS

1. The Saxon settlements, fifth to seventh centuries AD

fled to refugee colonies in northern Iberia and what became "Brittany." Others held out for a time in the West Country, where Iron Age forts such as South Cadbury were reinhabited and strengthened. The remnants of Romano-British culture eventually found refuge in the very areas that had previously resisted imperial influence: the far west and north of the island, and across the sea in Hibernia, where an upper-class Roman Briton, Patricius (St. Patrick), began to convert the inhabitants to Christianity in about 450. The Saxons were powerful enough to eradicate Roman law and culture, including Christianity, and to impose new beliefs, customs and above all a new language—proof that the change had been a cultural cataclysm.

They settled as warrior lords, intimidating a leaderless and demoralized native population, moving into and exploiting existing peasant settlements, and taking British women as slaves or eventually wives. According to Gildas, they were "tyrants" who "plunder and terrorize the innocent," surround themselves with "many wives and whores," "wage wars civil and unjust . . . despise the harmless and humble but exalt . . . their military companies, bloody, proud and murderous men."[23] In time they became a nobility, distinguished from "the common stock" by "appearance, bearing and speech"—as one young Saxon warrior found to his cost when he tried unsuccessfully to escape death by pretending to be a peasant.[24] By the end of the seventh century, three main Germanic kingdoms had emerged, Northumbria, Mercia and Wessex, and several smaller kingdoms, including East Anglia, Essex, Kent and Sussex.

A grim insight into the realities of a life that was nasty, brutish and short is given by studies of Buckland cemetery, near Dover, in use from about the 480s to the 750s. At least 20 percent of the population died before the age of eighteen. Women's remains are far more numerous than those of men, as men died away from home in war or hunting. Yet, of those remaining, women had a lower life expectancy due to the dangers of childbirth. The average age of those who died at home was thirty-one; for men, thirty-eight. Only 6 percent lived beyond sixty. The lucky survivors commonly had dental problems, disabling damage to the joints, badly healed fractures and endemic diseases such as tuberculosis. Among the warrior nobility, the women stood a little more chance of surviving childbirth than among the common people, but the men were more likely to die violently.[25]

This dangerous and little-known age became the setting for an epic myth. Its origins lie in Gildas's account of heroic, doomed resistance by the Romano-British, led by the shadowy and possibly fictitious Ambrosius Aurelianus, "King of Britain," who won a great if temporary victory over Saxon invaders around the year 500 at Mons Badonicus—Mount Badon, perhaps Badbury Castle in Dorset. This won the British a generation of respite. Later writers, including the monk Bede at Jarrow in the eighth century and the authors of the *Anglo-Saxon Chronicle* in the ninth, tried to fill out the story. This is the context in which fleeting references to Arthur first appear in British annals—as a war leader, as a man who bore a cross as his standard at Mount Badon, and as a man killed in the battle of Camlann in 537. These are the meagre seeds of the later saga of King Arthur, largely invented by Geoffrey of Monmouth, who claimed to have found it in "a certain very ancient book" in Oxford. Geoffrey's account, in which "the fame of Arthur's generosity and bravery spread to the very ends of the earth,"[26] became the core of a glamorous pedigree for England's rulers. A generation later, in the 1170s, the French writer Chrétien de Troyes added to the mix the fashionable chivalrous themes of tournaments, amorous adventure, the knight errantry of Lancelot and Perceval, damsels in distress, and the story of the Grail. The Angevin kings audaciously claimed Arthur as their forebear. His body and that of Queen Guinevere were "discovered" in 1191 at ancient Glastonbury Abbey, soon the focus of a related myth concerning Joseph of Arimathea, bearer of the Holy Grail.[27] Moreover, Arthur's body established that he was safely dead: no longer could he return to chastise usurpers. Richard the Lionheart claimed to have Arthur's sword. Edward I, after defeating the Welsh in 1283, thought he had brought back his crown. Thus Arthur was linked with England—"Avalon" became Glastonbury hill, and "Camelot" perhaps Cadbury fort or Winchester. The legend of Arthur as overlord of all Britain provided a foundation for assertions of English hegemony—or hegemony by whichever Norman, French or half-French ruler sat on England's throne.

The great saga was further elaborated by Thomas Malory (around 1470), and much later by Tennyson, Wagner and even, in a reimagined form, by J. R. R. Tolkien and his many emulators, becoming one of the great and enduring European myths. Thus Arthur took on many meanings. He was the doomed Christian hero holding back the dark tides of barbarism, becoming the acknowledged king of all Britain, and aiming to restore the power of Rome. For early Welsh writers, he was a symbol of pre-Saxon civilization that would one day return, just as Arthur himself, grievously wounded in battle but magically healed and preserved on the Isle of Avalon, would return as "the once and future king." He was a symbol of the mystique of royalty, chosen as a boy because only he could draw the sword from the stone. He became the ideal king of the age of chivalry, an armoured warrior with a magic sword surrounded by an order of knights, but betrayed by his queen, Guinevere, and his greatest follower, Lancelot. In some stories, this is linked with a mysterious wound Arthur suffers, and some writers made him the symbol of a failing society. Religious significance is derived from a link with the legend of the Holy Grail. These stories[28]—which still inspire efforts to discover a "historic" Arthur somewhere in the islands—ascribed a unique significance to Britain as not merely a maltreated border province of Rome, but as the centre of a mystical epic. This contributed over the centuries to a sense of unique identity.

# PART ONE

# THE BIRTH OF
# A NATION

England had a troubled birth at a troubled time. During the fifth, sixth and seventh centuries, transforming events of human history were taking place far away: the great Chinese Empire was reunited under the Tang dynasty; the emperor Justinian struggled to re-establish the Roman Empire centred on Constantinople; the new monotheistic religion of Islam began its conquest of western Asia, the southern Mediterranean and Iberia. Britain, along with most of the former Western Roman Empire, had been transformed by an influx of marauding war bands. But, unlike most provinces, it did not come under the power of a single Germanic conqueror with a large army, able to set up an extensive kingdom[1]— such as Clovis, king of the Franks from 481, who dominated Gaul, or Theodoric the Great, who established an Ostrogothic kingdom in Italy in 493, or Clovis's Frankish successor, Charlemagne (r. 768–814), who created a vast if ephemeral empire from the Pyrenees to the Baltic, being crowned emperor by Pope Leo III in the auspicious year 800. Britain's insular position was largely responsible for its piecemeal conquest. Moreover, it lacked a Romanized native elite strong enough to Christianize and organize the invaders. Hence, it became the most fragmented and paganized part of the former Roman Empire.

Angles, Saxons and Jutes (as Bede called them) had arrived over several generations from the north-western fringes of the Continent. Like many of the groups on the move in Europe, they were not necessarily homogeneous ethnic units: it would be mistaken to imagine them as tribes, let alone nations. They were often polyglot armed bands which coalesced round a core group and a successful leader, recruited widely among the ambitious, the bold and the desperate, and were recognizable by some emblem or style of hair or dress. Only after they had settled into a territory under a stable power did some of them develop a distinct identity and a dialect that in some cases became a written language. Even then, group boundaries were loose. Languages were in flux, with Germanic and

Latin dialects coalescing and diverging in different ways. So conditions were not favourable for the development of homogeneous "peoples" or organized "nations." The identities that mattered were either wider—for example, to co-religionists—or much narrower: to family and kin-group, to local community, to a war leader. These overrode any larger loyalty, for they made life possible, giving protection, keeping order, dealing out punishment and reward. To be alone was likely to be fatal: even slavery might be better. So the conception of a single English nation was surprising, and its survival improbable. It would be an optical illusion of hindsight to imagine it waiting in the womb of history simply for the right moment to emerge.

# CHAPTER I

# This Earth, This Realm
## c.600–1066

By around the year 600 the islands were highly diverse in language, in religion and in the origins of their inhabitants. There were five main language groups: Germanic in the southern and eastern regions; Brittonic, Goidelic (Gaelic) and Pictish, in the northern and western regions; and later Norse, especially in the north-east. These categories—terms invented by other peoples or by later generations—are certainly not how they would have thought of themselves. In the northern and western parts of the archipelago were numerous predatory chiefdoms occupied with raiding, rustling and slaving. The more populous lowland areas were divided into several rival kingdoms, dominated by various north-European lineages, whose power and territory waxed and waned, often rapidly and catastrophically. The larger of them vied for overlordship. The most powerful came to be Northumbria, between the Humber and the Forth, with its main city York, which has been called the natural capital of Britain. Further south was the rising power of Mercia, expanding out from the Midlands, with its royal seat at Tamworth and later a religious centre nearby at Lichfield. It was protected against raids from the west by the huge defensive rampart known as Offa's Dyke—"the longest and, from an engineering point of view the most demanding earthwork known to European history,"[1] partly built under King Offa (r. 757–96), a man important enough to maintain relations with the emperor Charlemagne. The kingdom of the East Angles was protected from inland attack by the Fens and massive earthworks, and other great earthworks exist in the south-west. These huge constructions testify visibly to the power of regional rulers. The kingdom of Kent (the Roman "Cantium") probably had close ties with the Continent (Julius Caesar had believed that its people were Belgic immigrants). Wessex, the kingdom of the West Saxons, dominated the south-west. There were smaller kingdoms too, such as Lindsey in the east and Deira in the north. This was an unstable mixture, with warfare and raiding a constant feature of politics and culture. Kings and warlords increased their power and reputation by attracting foot-loose warriors to their service, whom they had to reward with treasure won by successful aggression.

Yet, from this turbulent mix, the English emerged as what some historians consider the world's first nation, marked out by common political and administrative institutions, wide political participation and a shared identity. They had no single ethnic origin, no common semi-legendary foundation event, no single ruler—and yet they all came to be called English.

## THE IDEA

The idea preceded the reality. It has been suggested, a little teasingly, that the inventor of the English was Pope Gregory the Great, in around 580—though he might have got the idea from the historian Procopius (c.500–565), who described one of the peoples of "Brittia" as the "Angiloi." Gregory, noticing fair-haired slaves for sale, was told they were Angles: "Not Angles, but Angels" was his famous pun. Whether or not the story is true, Gregory not only sent a mission of forty monks under the prior of a Roman monastery, Augustine, in 596 to convert these angels with dirty faces from their Germanic heathenism, but he firmly decided that they constituted a single people, and only ever referred to them as "Angli."[2] The organization of the Church that followed Augustine's mission was based unwaveringly on that assumption. There came to be a single Church of the *gens Anglorum*, with two provinces of Canterbury and York. This Church transcended the boundaries of the various kingdoms—the mighty Mercians were only briefly allowed to set up their own province based at Lichfield. No less important, the Church did not include all the islands, but excluded Ireland and nearly all the turbulent lands that would eventually become Scotland and Wales. The English Church would create its own distinctive culture. It adopted Roman practices in dogma and liturgy rather than older British and Irish traditions, as confirmed at the Synod of Whitby in 664. But it venerated British and English saints.

This story was given historical shape by Baeda, or Bede, a monk of the great Northumbrian monastery of Jarrow, who was "indisputably the greatest historian of the English Middle Ages, and arguably the greatest English historian of all time."[3] His *Ecclesiastical History of the English People*, written in Latin and finished in 731, gave an intellectual and religious significance to this still hypothetical nation, as one of the chosen Christian peoples, an instrument in God's plan to spread orthodox Roman Christianity. Widely circulated and authoritative, Bede's *History* first defined an English identity which has proved permanent.

In Bede's account, the "English people" derived their special significance from their conversion. Their Germanic ancestors, who worshipped several deities, such as Woden, were the longest-lasting pagan peoples in the former Roman Empire. Yet during the 200 years following Augustine's arrival they went from being pagan to being Christian. This is because conversion began at the top, with kings, queens and warriors. Christianity was a source of authority and status, a way of becoming part of that wider and prestigious Roman civilization now primarily embodied in the Latin Church, of leaving behind barbarism, and of drawing on a new source of ritual power. It was also a way of making allies, and of warding off the threat of powerful rivals: dynastic polities that converted early had a much better chance of survival.

So when in 597 Augustine had arrived in Kent, part holy man, part ambassador, he had been welcomed by King Aethelberht, and installed, significantly, in the half-deserted Roman town of Durovernum Cantiacorum—Canterbury. The king and several thousand of his subjects were baptized together, possibly in the Christianization of a pagan seasonal festival. The old gods were not forgotten, but downgraded: Woden was reinvented as a heroic human ancestor. Christianity proved an accommodating creed and a valued support for royal power. Since the time of Offa of Mercia, kings have been sacramentally anointed. The early English Church was uniquely keen on making them saints: some who were killed in the endemic wars were proclaimed martyrs, as long as some of their enemies had included pagans. The Church was happy to accept its share in the booty from successful wars, in the form of penitential offerings, such as endowment of religious houses. Princesses sometimes became their abbesses. Minsters (with functions similar to the later parish churches), monasteries and nunneries, such as Ripon, Hexham, Jarrow, Wearmouth, Whitby, Barking, Wimborne and Lindisfarne, became centres of political, economic and even military power, and the channels for spreading innovations in agriculture, wine-making, architecture and manufacture (textiles, pottery and glass). Some religious communities were comfortable annexes of courtly culture, and were criticized by the pious for excessive eating, drinking and fox-hunting. The English Church came to own about a quarter of all cultivated land—somewhat less than churches on the Continent, but more than enough to make it a great power in the land, and an important influence in Europe, as its missionaries helped to convert northern Germany.

Christianity brought back literacy. The stimulus of the written word produced a flowering of writing not only in Latin, but also in what was later termed Old English, as writing crystallized fluid dialects into a stable language, with a hybrid Latin and Germanic alphabet. English and Irish

Gaelic became the most developed vernaculars in Europe. Sermons and prayers were composed in English. So was poetry, adapting Germanic heroic style to religious use, notably *Caedmon's Hymn* (*c*.670) and *The Dream of the Rood* (*c*.700), which imagined the crucified Christ as a warrior dying gloriously in battle. Older sagas took written form, notably *Beowulf*, probably written down in the early 700s, one of medieval Europe's earliest surviving vernacular works. Roman learning was cultivated too, and Northumbria became one of Europe's main cultural centres. At its apex was Bede himself (*c*.672–735), who produced the greatest volume and quality of writing in the Western world since St. Augustine of Hippo in fourth-century Africa. At his monastery at Jarrow he had access to at least 200 books, mostly from Italy[4]—more books than the university libraries of either Oxford or Cambridge possessed 700 years later. Large parts of the Bible were translated into Old English between the seventh and eleventh centuries; it would be 300 years before they again appeared in the English language.

Other Germanic invaders of the Roman Empire, such as the Lombards, Visigoths and Franks—who had taken over most of Gaul in what eventually became the Carolingian empire—abandoned their vernaculars in favour of local variants of Latin. These later developed as the Romance languages. That the "Saxons" did not do so in Britain was long taken as proof that they had come in vast numbers and killed or chased out the previous inhabitants, who spoke Brittonic and Latin. As has been noted, archaeological evidence does not suggest an annihilation of the Romano-British population. That the Saxons did not adopt Latin is probably a sign that peripheral Britannia had not acquired a Roman culture strong enough to survive conquest. Brittonic, lacking the international prestige of Latin, was even less likely to survive the dominance of a Saxon warrior caste, whose language prevailed.

The Church did not aim to transform society, but was content to soften its edges. Slavery was accepted: but masters were taught that even the lowliest had souls, and the humble were consoled with promises of heavenly reward. The polygamous habits of virile pagan warriors were somewhat restrained, but the Church's acceptance of easy dissolution of marriage provided partial accommodation to custom. Penances prescribed for bestiality and "fornication with mother" perhaps show that old habits died hard. The feuding and warfare endemic among what Gildas called "bloodthirsty, proud, parricidal, warlike and adulterous enemies of God" were certainly not halted, but the Church provided some mediation and sanctuary.[5] Christianity could coexist with the warrior ethos. The body parts of defeated kings became relics: the head and hands of Oswald of

Northumbria, killed in battle and dismembered by the pagan Penda of Mercia in 642, were venerated. Even the soil from battlefields was believed to work miracles. *Beowulf*, not overtly pagan but not wholly Christian either, shows how Christianized warriors still relished strength, courage, generosity, comradeship and heroic death:

> They recited a dirge to declare their grief,
> Spoke of the man, mourned their king.
> They praised his manhood and the prowess of his hands . . .
> They said that he was of all the world's kings
> The gentlest of men and the most gracious,
> The kindest to his people, the keenest for fame.[6]

Thus, by the 700s, Christians in most of Britain were members of an English Church, which had taken on some of the territorial boundaries and the broad organizational form it was to retain for eight centuries, with its two provinces, its territorial bishoprics and a variety of religious communities, some including priests from Italy and North Africa. Whatever their earthly enmities, living in warring kingdoms, speaking different dialects, and calling themselves by a variety of names, these Christians knew that they were watched over by their own saints, including the seventh-century monk-bishops of Lindisfarne Aidan and Cuthbert; Chad, first bishop of the Mercians; and the abbess Werburga, daughter of a Mercian king. They knew they were a single people in the eyes of God—the *gens Anglorum*.

## THE KINGDOM

If English identity began as a religious concept, it took political form in response to a deadly external threat, which overturned the political structures of the island and the near Continent: the Vikings. The word means "sea adventurers" or "pirates," another variety of the war bands that ravaged Europe over several centuries. This new menace was engendered by the prosperity of the Carolingian empire and its neighbours, including Britain, which enriched Scandinavian warlords through trade, bringing about the consolidation of Denmark, Norway and Sweden as kingdoms, and then tempting them into a more predatory relationship with the richer countries to the south. Vikings soon menaced every coast and navigable river from the Baltic to the Black Sea, seeking money, treasure, cattle, and male and especially female slaves for the newly expanding Muslim world. Vikings (whom the English commonly called "Danes") first targeted the wealthy English Church—a reason why monastic chroniclers stressed the horrors of their depredations. The first big and shocking incursion into Britain was the looting of the holy site of Lindisfarne in June 793. News of the sacrilege echoed across Europe: "The blood of saints poured out around the altar . . . the bodies of saints trampled on . . . like dung in the streets," thundered Alcuin of York, Charlemagne's court theologian, who suspected it was divine punishment for monkish self-indulgence.[7] There came a lull during which there were only small sporadic raids until the 830s, when mass attacks began involving up to 100 ships. Recently the Vikings have to some degree been rehabilitated as successful traders. The old Roman Eboracum became one of their capitals, Jorvik (hence York). It recovered from its capture in 866 and even prospered by trade with Scandinavia. Vikings, keen traders though they were, undeniably had a "penchant for cutting up their potential customers."[8] A legendary ritual for defeated enemies was the "blood eagle"—chopping through the ribs and pulling out the lungs to be draped over the back like scarlet wings, said to have been the fate of King Ælla of Northumbria in 867.

The Viking attacks transformed the islands. The effects on the peasant population, exposed to violence and enslavement, were considerable, even if most were able to go on with their lives. The greater historic impact, however, was political. In some cases warlords and rebels thought they could use the Vikings as allies in factional struggles. They got more than they bargained for: in the far north, an aggressive Norse lordship took over in the Orkneys; other Vikings established a colony that became the kingdom of Dublin, the main base for raiding and slaving in Britain, and eventually part of a Viking kingdom including York. In 850–51, a Danish army tried to winter in Kent, and in 865 a "Great Army" came to stay for good. Vikings took over two of the four major kingdoms, Northumbria and East Anglia, and partitioned a third, Mercia. Wessex, the kingdom of the West Saxons, remained precariously the only intact Christian power. Its takeover of the remnant of western Mercia around 880 marked a geographical and ideological step towards creating a single English kingdom.[9]

That Wessex survived and expanded is bound up with the story of its king, Alfred—a story so like legend that it has often been debunked, but which nevertheless stands up to scrutiny. A twenty-three-year-old Alfred, slight in build, possibly suffering from some mysterious illness, inherited the throne in 871 to command the defence of his kingdom against a rampaging "Great Heathen Army" led by Guthrum, Danish king of East Anglia. Alfred forced them to retreat, but in 875 they launched a new attack, forcing him to flee into the marshes of Athelney in Somerset. Now the story becomes legend: the king, unrecognized, takes refuge with a peasant—a familiar story in many cultures, showing that the great are also human and vulnerable. In this version—told three centuries later, and popularized only eight centuries later—Alfred, left to keep an eye on the baking but understandably preoccupied, "burnt the cakes" or bread.[10] What is actually documented is no less gripping: Alfred summoned his men to meet him at "Ecgberht's Stone to the east of Selwood, and there came to join him all Somerset and Wiltshire,"[11] and at Ethandun (Edington) in 879 they attacked and defeated the Danes, who accepted baptism. But they remained formidable enough to be recognized as overlords of a vast tract of the east of the island—the Danelaw—up to the old Roman road known as Watling ("Waeclinga") Street, dividing the country from the Mersey to the Thames.

Danish armies, secure in their northern and eastern territories, could and did still invade whenever they felt strong enough. This menace was countered by an immense common effort: the economic and urban structure of Wessex was recast into a regular system of large fortified settlements, "burhs." Some were former Roman towns, some even older Iron Age forts, and some were new. Among them were Exeter, Bath, Bridport, Malmesbury, Shaftesbury, Porchester, Wallingford and Winchester. All were within twenty miles—a day's march—of each other, and controlled estuaries and river crossings. In times of danger the burhs were garrisoned by organized local defence forces, and there was also a field army, the "fyrd," and a royal fleet.

In 886 Alfred seized London. If we want a birth date for an English kingdom, this is as good as any.[12] So contemporaries seem to have thought: "All the English race turned to him," said the *Anglo-Saxon Chronicle*, "except what was in captivity to the Danish men."[13] So he seems to have felt himself, inspired by Bede's *History*. He referred to his people not as Saxons but as "Angelcynn"—"Englishkind"—a term first used in Mercia. Their language was "Englisc." Alfred, at first described in royal charters and on coins as *rex Saxonum*, duly became *rex Angul-Saxonum* in recognition of the union of Mercia and Wessex. He pursued a policy of what today we might term nation-building: "He sought to persuade [his subjects] that he was restoring the English, whereas, albeit following a model provided by Bede, he was inventing them."[14] He commanded a law code combining the customs of Wessex, Mercia and Kent and decked out with biblical teachings and Church laws—an important symbol of unity and status more than an instrument of rule, as in practice most law was oral and customary—"folk right." He sent English coins to succour the poor of Rome. He wanted to increase Christian piety so as to ward off divine

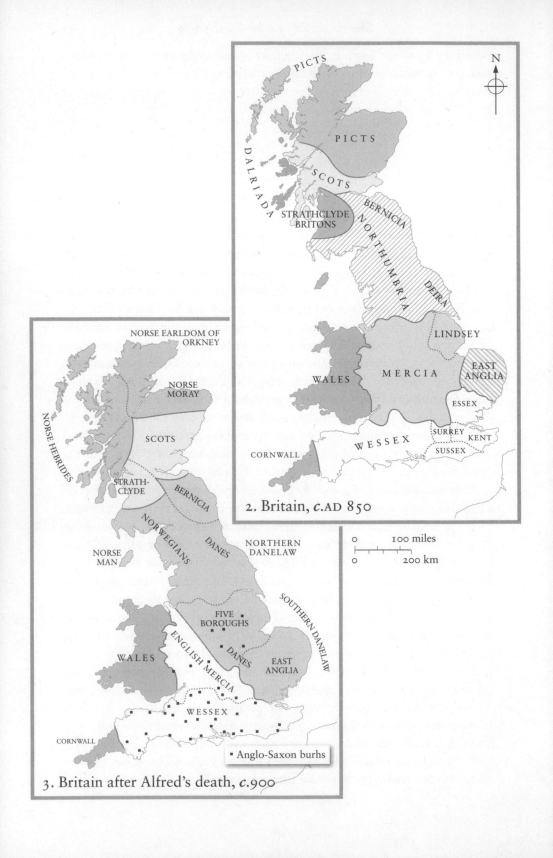

PICTS

PICTS

DALRIADA

SCOTS

STRATHCLYDE
BRITONS

BERNICIA

NORTHUMBRIA

DEIRA

WALES

MERCIA

LINDSEY

EAST
ANGLIA

ESSEX

WESSEX

SURREY

KENT

CORNWALL

SUSSEX

N

**2. Britain, *c*.AD 850**

NORSE EARLDOM OF
ORKNEY

NORSE
MORAY

NORSE HEBRIDES

SCOTS

STRATH-
CLYDE

BERNICIA

NORWEGIANS

DANES

NORTHERN
DANELAW

NORSE
MAN

FIVE
BOROUGHS

SOUTHERN DANELAW

WALES

ENGLISH MERCIA

DANES

EAST
ANGLIA

WESSEX

CORNWALL

■ Anglo-Saxon burhs

**3. Britain after Alfred's death, *c*.900**

0        100 miles

0        200 km

punishment in the form of Viking invasion, and believed this required literacy. He wrote to his bishop at Worcester:

> It seems better to me, if it seems so to you, that we ... should translate certain books, which are most necessary for all men to know, into the language that we can all understand, and ... that all the young freeborn men ... may be set to study ... until a time when they are able to read English writing well.[15]

He had Bede translated into English, and probably commissioned an *Anglo-Saxon Chronicle* written in English to record the national history. It was later copied and circulated, and added to separately in several religious houses, including Winchester, Abingdon, Worcester, Peterborough and Canterbury; and two versions continued well beyond the Norman Conquest.[16] English became the language of government, permitting more direct contact with the population. It was also the language of courtly culture: nowhere else in Europe except Ireland would have a vernacular high culture for another three centuries. Written English texts, often precious works of art, would become the property of whole communities, held in great churches, read out publicly on holy days, and also used to record important events, names of guildsmen and freed slaves, and legal decisions, which were written into the margins or on added pages.[17]

Alfred set himself the task of becoming not just a victorious warlord but a Christian philosopher-king, acquiring an unusual degree of learning for a layman. He translated (with assistance) some of the Psalms and several classical works, notably Boethius's *Consolations of Philosophy*, to which he added reflections of his own. In more than 1,000 years of European history between the emperor Marcus Aurelius and Alfonso the Wise of Spain, Alfred is the only European ruler we see reflecting personally on the moral duties of kingship.[18] As Father of the Nation he therefore has much to recommend him. He was first called "the Great" in the thirteenth century, and an unsuccessful attempt was made to canonize him in the fifteenth. But he later became a shadowy figure, except to antiquarians: even his burial place was uncertain, and did not become a site of pilgrimage. The Reformation, keen to explore the nation's origins, recovered him, and the eighteenth century celebrated him as a patriot-king: the song "Rule Britannia" comes from the masque *Alfred* (1740). In this work he was exalted by the "patriot" party as a symbol of Anglo-Saxon liberties (see p. 321), as well as founder of the navy and, thus indirectly, of future imperial greatness. The Victorians, not least in histories for children, hailed him as an ideal Christian ruler; and they erected monuments and statues to "the most perfect character in history."[19]

If Alfred was the first believable king of the "Angelcynn" and defender of their "eard," their land, were they really a nation? In fundamental ways, no. There was no word "England": the Angelcynn lived in Britain. Royal legal documents, charters, still referred to the kingdom as consisting of Anglo-Saxons, Northumbrians, Mercians, Britons and pagans. Aggrieved lords had few qualms about allying with invaders. The Danes in the north and east were unreconciled, and another mass invasion of Kent was beaten off in 892. After Alfred's death in 899 his nephew Aethelwold tried to enlist Viking support to gain the crown. Nobles and peasants (especially escaped slaves) were ready to run off to Viking bands. The interests of kin, lord and locality (especially former kingdoms such as Northumbria and Mercia, determined to preserve some autonomy) came first. The "English-kind" were not unusual in this lack of "national" solidarity: it was the norm.

Alfred's death led to multiple Danish invasions, and the beginning of a long grinding struggle to break their power. In the decade after the bloody battle of Wednesfield (Staffordshire) in 910, in which twelve Danish leaders were killed, Edward the Elder, Alfred's only son, conquered the Danish-ruled areas up to the River Humber, and fought off invasions from Dublin and Scandinavia. This was the first lasting setback suffered anywhere by the Vikings. Many of them crossed the sea to where the Frankish monarchy was falling apart, and in 911 established a colony of Northmen—Normandy. In 920, all the rulers of Britain submitted to Edward the Elder as "father and lord"—a term denoting status, not dominion. Edward's son Aethelstan succeeded him in 924. He conquered the Danish north-east, and he too was recognized as paramount king of Britain. A few years of peace ended with a joint invasion by Dublin Vikings, Scots and Britons, which might have shattered the new kingdom. But the invaders were crushed at Brunanburh (perhaps Bromborough, Cheshire) in 937, where "five young kings lay on the battlefield, put to sleep by swords."[20] This victory confirmed Aethelstan as *rex Anglorum*— the first to claim the title "king of the English," and the first who really ruled the whole people whose existence had been envisaged two centuries earlier by Bede.[21] Yet Aethelstan almost disappeared from the national memory, overshadowed by the prestige of Alfred, by the sainthood of Edward the Confessor, and, inevitably, by the mystical glamour of Arthur.[22]

Lack of evidence makes this one of the most obscure as well as disturbed periods of our history. No political settlement was permanent, or even outlived its author. Each king had to defend or re-create his inheritance. Aethelstan's brother Eadred, who reigned from 946 to 955, was proclaimed "emperor of the Anglo-Saxons and Northumbrians, governor of the pagans, defender of the Britons," and he maintained control in the north—the northern border reached broadly where it is today. On his death the kingdom briefly split. A short apogee came during the reign of Edgar (959–75), who succeeded as a child. In 973, he was finally crowned at Bath, in a religious ritual, elements of which have been used ever since; at Chester, British rulers met to accept peace and symbolically acknowledge his primacy by rowing him on the River Dee. There were no invasions. Great power was exercised by Dunstan, Archbishop of Canterbury, later canonized. He increased the power and wealth of bishops and monasteries, and weakened control over them by the nobility—a serious blow to the leading noble families. Combined with an effort to enforce Rome's restrictive marriage laws (couples sharing a common great-grandparent were considered incestuous), which threatened to make many heirs illegitimate, the result was dangerous discontent among the magnates of the kingdom, and even a confused succession to the crown.

But in appearance all was well. The English were prospering through agriculture and trade in conditions of peace and security unknown for centuries. In contrast with post–Carolingian Europe, England had no prolonged or general internal conflict in 200 years. Its kings ruled with an iron hand, punishing disobedient shires and nobles with hangings, ravaging, confiscation and exile. Enforcing law and custom was a job for the people themselves. Law, as was typical of lightly governed societies, aimed at compensation for injury ("If anyone strike another with his fist on the nose, iii shillings") and restraint of blood feuds, by regulating the "wergild" ("man money") paid by a killer to a dead man's kin or master. Wergild differed according to status: one king issued a proclamation to "all his people, whether men of a twelve-hundred wergild or of a two-hundred"—meaning nobles and peasants respectively. One of the concessions Alfred had extracted from Guthrum was that the price for killing an Englishman in the Danelaw should be the same as that for killing a Dane. Men were divided into groups of ten—tithings—to protect and police each other, and they bonded through eating and drinking. Ten tithings formed armed posses to ride after rustlers and escaped thralls (slaves) living as bandits, and if necessary attack their protectors. Thrall ringleaders were summarily hanged, and their followers were flogged, scalped and deprived of their little fingers—which marked them without destroying their ability to work. In the century before 1066 there was an increase in punishment (usually by death or savage mutilation) for crimes that were increasingly seen not merely as matters concerning individuals and families, but as offences against king and community by breaking "the king's peace." There were what now seem oddities: taking the king's wheat led to arrest, but braining one's mother with a candlestick brought only a religious penance.[23] Aethelstan commanded that free women harbouring thieves should be thrown from a cliff or drowned, and delinquent slaves stoned to death by other slaves ("And if any one of them fails three times to hit him, he shall himself be scourged three times").[24] Such harshness was not the whole story. Slaves could be freed as a religious act, as in the following case in the late tenth century of people who had voluntarily entered bondage in time of famine, and which suggests that human feelings could exist even in savage times:

> Geatfleda has given freedom for the love of God and the sake of her soul [to] Ecceard the smith, Aelstan and his wife and all their children born and unborn, and to Arkil, Cole, Ecferth [and] Aldhun's daughter and all the people whose head she took for their food in those evil days.[25]

The Angelcynn were becoming what we might recognize as an embryonic nation. Their boundaries were now broadly established. They had a distinct and fairly homogeneous system of customary law—even the "Danelaw" was little different—with the king's law over all. There was an English Church with English saints, which prayed for "the king of the English and his army," and which was beginning the long process of creating the hundreds of small parishes that would for a millennium provide the framework of English society. An opulent coinage was struck, millions of silver pennies bearing the king's head and title. An administrative system was gradually established over most of the country, based on the "scir" (shire), generally centred on a river port, governed for the king by an ealdorman and his deputy, the "scirgerefa" (sheriff), tax collector, judge and policeman. The shires would substantially retain their territories and names (such as Devenescire and Nordfulc) for over 1,000 years, with no major change until 1974. There was a regular system of participation in government. The warrior nobility, "thegns," and free peasants, "ceorls" ("churls"), met in shire courts and local monthly courts in every hundred (a subdivision of the shire). Tens of thousands of men took part in levying taxes, enforcing the law, hearing royal commands, and when necessary taking up arms. At the age of twelve, every freeman took an oath of loyalty to the king and obedience to the law—a practice that continued for many centuries.[26] To represent the whole kingdom, a gathering of thegns and prelates, the "witan" ("the councillors"), was summoned by the king at various places, sometimes traditional open-air sites, to take part in ceremonies, give advice, settle disputes, try cases of treason, or endorse royal acts. It was crucial at times of danger and of disputed succession. From the 970s it was called the "Angelcynnes witan," the council of the English people, and King Aethelred's 1008 law code was issued "on the decree of the English witan."[27] Though there were representative bodies in other parts of Europe, there were few if any national representative bodies like this.[28] The ability of English rulers to raise taxation and manpower was unequalled in Europe, and it required this unique degree of involvement and consent by local communities, including even relatively humble subjects.

The kingdom did not break down into warring principalities—unlike the collapsed Carolingian empire, from which many "Anglo-Saxon" institutions (such as national taxation, juries and oaths of loyalty) were originally copied.[29] Nor—most remarkably—did it descend into full civil war, despite blood feuds and factional conflicts. When civil war did threaten, in 1051, it was averted by protests that "it was hateful to men to fight their own kin . . . and they did not want to leave the eard open to foreigners by slaughtering each other."[30] Priests taught that the defence of the eard was a warrior's first duty. Loyalty to the eard survived conquests and changes of dynasty. Though there were regional identities and ethnic minorities (such as Brittonic speakers and Scandinavian immigrants), writers were now generally referring to the *Anglii*, and to the West Saxons, for example, as *occidentales Anglii*. In what may be the only surviving private letter from one ordinary member of the Angelcynn to another written some years before the Norman Conquest, "brother Edward" is reproached for "abandoning the English practices which your fathers followed" and copying Danish hairstyles, short at the back and with a fringe over the eyes, a sign that "you despise your *cynn*."[31]

By the year 1000, the eard had acquired a name, "Englalond," which began to be used in the *Anglo-Saxon Chronicle*—though it had various spellings and fanciful supposed origins. Its population was over 1.5 million, densest in the eastern and southern shires. An export trade in wool, an economic mainstay for centuries to come, was being established. The plentiful and uniform silver coinage promoted nationwide economic activity. Roads, bridges and harbours were publicly maintained under royal authority. Investment had accumulated: there were some 6,000 water mills, the most complex machinery of the time.[32] For all these reasons, the English kingdom emerged as probably the richest and one of the most powerful European polities, with effective control over the largest territory. It was ruled for more than a century by Alfred's descendants, who intermarried with Continental royalty, and claimed to be the oldest royal house in Europe, descended from the fifth-century Saxon invader Cerdic.

But the kingdom had a fundamental flaw: the inability to provide secure and orderly succession. In part this was accident: unlike the French Capetians, installed in 987, who managed to produce viable male heirs for centuries, after the death of Edgar in 975, at the age of thirty-two, the House of Cerdic was blighted by too many heirs or too few, by child heirs, and by several untimely deaths—not all from natural causes, as we shall see. The system for passing on the crown was a dangerous mixture of inheritance, bequest and election. Ideally, this would confer a triple strength: an adult and competent member of the royal family would be chosen by the existing king as his heir and recognized by the witan. But circumstances were not ideal, and then there could be several rival claimants (sometimes brothers, uncles, children) fighting for the crown, and often for their lives—or at least for their eyes, as blinding was one way of disqualifying contenders. The most catastrophic succession conflict, in 1066, led to the subjugation of England.

Such conflicts exposed weaknesses in the new kingdom: regional insubordination, political faction, the rivalry of ecclesiastical and lay rulers, and the discontent of powerful nobles. And this offered easy pickings to international predators, who now homed in on England's wealth to make it the most assaulted part of Europe. The late tenth and eleventh centuries, arguably the worst crisis in England's history, would see at least five attempts to conquer it. Two of them succeeded: first the Danes and then the Normans.

## CONQUESTS

When Edgar died in 975, only two years after his coronation and symbolic apotheosis on the River Dee, the new kingdom entered a vortex of political crises. Edgar had two young sons, the half-brothers Edward and Aethelred. They were backed by rival factions drawing on different kinship networks and regional power bases: "Strife threw the kingdom into turmoil, moved shire against shire, family against family, prince against prince, ealdormen against ealdormen, drove bishop against the people and folk against the pastors set over them."[33] The young King Edward was mysteriously murdered in 978, becoming St. Edward the Martyr—a shocking event, not least because nothing comparable had happened for generations. But now murder, and even blinding and mutilation, became more common. Edward was succeeded by the twelve-year-old Aethelred II (979–1016), who was to have one of the longest and most disastrous reigns in English history. He is universally remembered as "Ethelred the Unready" ("Unraed" meant "ill advised"). His big problem, Viking attack, was beyond advice, good or ill. The Vikings had been defeated, but they had not disappeared. They had been shut out of England and much of mainland Europe over the previous decades by stronger defences. From their bases in Dublin and the Isle of Man, as well as from Scandinavia itself, led by the kings of Denmark and Norway, they were seeking a softer target, which England's political turmoil now offered. After England had been free from Viking attack for nearly a century, and had let its defences decay, Aethelred's reign became a losing battle to fight or buy them off. It took them twenty years to conquer England.

Hundreds of raids followed Aethelred's succession: "Let us loyally support one royal lord," urged Aethelred, "and all of us together defend our lives and our country."[34] He took a fateful step in 991, making a treaty with Richard, Duke of Normandy, to deny a base to raiders who were using Norman harbours for shelter and the capital, Rouen, as a market for English loot and vast numbers of slaves. The Duchy of Normandy was autonomous, and its duke enjoyed personal power as great as any Continental prince, at a time when the disintegration of the Frankish kingdom had brought the rise of highly violent and unstable principalities. The Normans, descended from Vikings, had abandoned all but vestiges of their Scandinavian culture, but were proud of their aggressive military ethos and their berserk violence in battle. This would carry their young men as mercenaries, conquerors and finally rulers to southern Italy, Sicily and the British Isles. An English alliance with Normandy was both necessary and dangerous. It was cemented by the marriage of Aethelred to Emma, the duke's daughter.

In 991 came disaster, when a fleet led by King Olaf Tryggvason of Norway was confronted by an English army under ealdorman Byrhtnoth at Maldon in Essex.[35] Byrhtnoth allowed the invaders to come ashore to fight. He may have wanted to tempt them to land rather than letting them sail away elsewhere. His defeat and death became the subject of a long poetic lament, of which a substantial fragment survives. It contains an early expression of patriotism, when Byrhtnoth defies the Vikings:

> Listen, messenger! Take back this reply
> . . . that a noble earl and his troop stand here—
> guardians of the people and of the country, the home
> of Aethelred, my prince—who will defend this land
> to the last ditch.[36]

After Maldon, Aethelred's councillors urged him to buy the invaders off. This had often been done before, but it had never cost so much. Vast sums were raised by a universal land tax, the first of its kind in Europe, both to pay for soldiers and ships and to bribe the enemy: the Danegeld. Over the next twenty-seven years, over £250,000 was raised—an astonishing sum many times the king's normal annual income, and testimony to the unparalleled administrative efficiency of the English kingdom, with its local institutions and wide participation. The weight of taxation drove many free peasants into servitude. But the tax was also levied on the nobility— rare in Europe, and in the long term this was a considerable political unifier.[37] What happened was made proverbial by Rudyard Kipling as the archetypal act of weakness that makes the danger worse:

> And that is called paying the Dane-geld;
>   But we've proved it again and again,
> That if once you have paid him the Dane-geld
>   You never get rid of the Dane.

The Danes decided that if the English were so rich, they were worth conquering completely. Aethelred tried unsuccessfully to end the internal threat by ordering a massacre of Danes in England in 1002. There was a European-wide famine in 1005, which may have encouraged invasions. In 1006 the king of Denmark, Sveinn "Forkbeard," began a series of major raids with "plunder, burning and killing—and all England lamented and shook like a reed-bed struck by the quivering west wind."[38] In 1009 "all the nation" was called to pray and do penance. In vain: Canterbury was besieged and captured; Archbishop Aelfheah was taken hostage—"he who was earlier head of the English race and of Christendom was a roped thing"—and subsequently murdered during a drunken feast.[39] Aethelred, Emma and their three children fled to their allies and kinsmen in Normandy. Sveinn landed again in 1013, probably with help from residents of the Danelaw, took London, and thereupon died, as soon after did Aethelred. Their respective sons and heirs, Cnut and Edmund "Ironside," so called because he possessed "tremendous strength and remarkable endurance in warfare,"[40] fought each other to a standstill. But Edmund died or was killed in 1016 (by one account, "stabbed twice with a sharp knife in the private parts" while in the lavatory[41]). Cnut ("Canute") became king.

The kingdom of the English, after some 130 years of existence, thus became part of a North Sea empire. The Scandinavian influx into the British Isles over the whole Viking period was probably greater than any other population movement until that of the late twentieth century.[42] The Danish conquest, almost as bloody and disruptive in the short term as that of the Normans would be half a century later, was accepted by the conquered as inevitable. Cnut had the sense to make concessions in victory: he promulgated a code of laws "determined and devised by the witan," and sent a public letter written in English to "all his people . . . with friendship," promising to be a "gracious lord" and to espouse the laws "which all men have chosen and sworn to."[43] He buried the murdered Archbishop Aelfheah, regarded by the English as a saint, at Canterbury. He also (bigamously) married Aethelred's Norman widow, Emma. Cnut was now one of the most powerful European monarchs. In 1027 he went to Rome to take part in the coronation of the Holy Roman Emperor, Conrad II, a summit meeting of the greatest men of Europe, and he made sure the English knew that he had been treated with honour. His wisdom was proclaimed in one of the most famous of English historical stories, recounted a century later by Henry of Huntingdon: "King Canute" showed his flatterers that he could not hold back the waves, proclaiming that "the power of kings is empty and worthless," and that God was the only true king.[44] The main reason the English accepted Cnut was their hope that he could hold back the waves of Viking attacks through his simultaneous possession of Denmark and Norway.

In attempting to govern his unwieldy domains, Cnut made a major change in English governance. He created four regional earldoms (the Danish word "earl" replaced the older "ealdorman"). These great offices were sufficiently important for some of their holders to be remembered over the centuries. Siward of Northumbria appears in Shakespeare's *Macbeth*. Leofric, Earl of Mercia, was the husband of perhaps the most famous Anglo-Saxon lady, Godgifu—"Lady Godiva," who by tradition rode naked through the streets of Coventry to persuade him to forgo a tax increase. Godwine of Wessex, who had risen rapidly as Cnut's main English collaborator, fathered the last Anglo-Saxon king (though with a Danish name), Harold II. The danger, as the history of the Godwines showed, was to create over-mighty subjects whose power could challenge that of the king, and hence complicate an already unstable system of succession.

Cnut's death in 1035 began a struggle between two of his sons, Harold I, "Harefoot," and Harthacnut. Aethelred's two sons, Edward and Alfred, heirs to the Anglo-Saxon royal line, refugees with their Norman ally, tried to return. Earl Godwine—"a mighty earl and a ruthless traitor"[45]—is suspected of having simplified the succession problem with a brutality that shocked even contemporaries: the "aetheling" (prince) Alfred was seized when he landed in Kent in 1037, handed over to Cnut's son, Harold I, and maimed and blinded to destroy him as a potential king—an act from which he died. This seems to have been tacitly condoned by Godwine's fellow earls: it was above all necessary to avert civil war. In 1042, Aethelred's surviving son, Edward, became the undisputed king after the early deaths of Cnut's unlamented sons. Edward was far from ideal. He was little known, was far from being a heroic warrior, and was middle-aged, unmarried and without an heir. His only advantage—apart from the dubious one of unusual piety, hence his title "the Confessor"—was that he embodied the alliance with the Normans, now the main barrier against the Scandinavians. He had spent most of his life as an exile in Normandy, and was on excellent terms with the Norman dukes. In 1044 he married Edith, daughter of Earl Godwine, but, perhaps not to anyone's great surprise, produced no offspring. In retrospect, Edward's twenty-three-year reign (despite sporadic Welsh and Norwegian raids) seemed a golden age, the last flowering of the Anglo-Saxon kingdom and its culture, crowned by the rebuilding of the royal abbey of St. Peter, the "West Minster," consecrated in 1065 as the coronation site of English kings. Its Burgundian "Romanesque" style was entirely new for England, and the greatest architectural enterprise here since Roman times; its church was the biggest in northern Europe.[46] For future generations Edward's reign became a subject of nostalgia, and for future rulers a source of legitimacy, hallowed by his canonization in 1161.

The golden age had an obvious tarnish: the absence of an agreed successor. The heirs of Cnut would certainly assert their claims by force when the time came. Godwine's family—accumulators of vast estates in the south and Midlands, and now joined to the king by marriage—were emerging as possible claimants too. King Edward's closest allies and friends were the Normans. He had already appointed Normans to important bishoprics, and had granted land to Norman nobles. In about 1050 Edward seems to have decided to bequeath the crown to Duke William of Normandy: a logical outcome to the problem of succession, and perhaps the best available.

Edward's closeness to the Normans nearly led to civil war. In 1051 there was a violent clash between Norman knights and local people at Dover, and when Edward ordered Earl Godwine to punish the town, he refused. The king and Godwine both gathered troops, but few thegns were prepared to embark on civil war. The Godwines were briefly outlawed and forced into exile; but so powerful had they become that they found allies and hired a fleet, and were able to return triumphantly the following year. Again, there was no stomach for civil war. The king gave in, and his leading Norman supporters were banished. In 1053 Harold Godwineson succeeded to the earldom of Wessex, and his brothers became earls of Northumbria, East Anglia and Kent. They were now largely running the country on the king's behalf. In 1064 or 1065 Harold turned up in Normandy in obscure and endlessly debated circumstances. A plausible version is that he had gone to secure the freedom of his nephew, held hostage by William.[47] Harold arrived after a chapter of accidents (a shipwreck, capture by the Count of Ponthieu and rescue by the Normans). He was induced to swear solemn allegiance to William, and went off fairly amicably with him to wage war against the Bretons.

In December 1065, King Edward lay dying, muttering alarming prophecies. What actually happened is obscured by contemporary claims and counter-claims. Over the years, Edward may have considered bequeathing his crown to several possible candidates, including William of Normandy and the kings of Norway and Denmark. Now he decided, or was persuaded, to choose Harold Godwineson, the closest contender. Edward died on 5 January 1066. Harold was crowned the following day in the new Westminster Abbey, consecrated nine days earlier. He seems to have had popular support, and had been hastily elected by the witan. No doubt the pure ambition of the rapacious Godwine clan was a driving force: but also the kingdom was facing the imminent threat of a Norse invasion, as well as attacks by the Welsh and Scots, and it urgently needed an active leader. Harold's succession set in motion a Norman invasion too, as Duke William claimed to be Edward's rightful successor and accused Harold of breaking his oath. Securing the Pope's approval, he began raising an army.

So began King Harold's short and bloody epic of "forty weeks and one day." He led a forced march north, over twenty miles a day, to confront Norwegian invaders, led by King Harald "Hardrada" ("the Ruthless"), warlord and poet, who had sailed up the Humber. Harold's estranged brother Tostig had joined the invaders—a sign of how limited the idea of "national" and even family loyalty was among a cosmopolitan and factious nobility. Harold surprised them, many without their armour, at Stamford Bridge near York on 25 September 1066 in perhaps the most complete annihilation in medieval military history.[48] Hardrada and Tostig were both killed and their army of several thousand men was almost wiped out. This was an event of European importance, as it ended the era of great Viking invasions. Three days later Duke William, aged thirty-eight, ferried an army in hundreds of ships and boats the seventy miles from the Somme estuary to Pevensey in Sussex.[49] Harold rushed south with all the men who could keep up.

William's invading army—perhaps around 8,000 warriors—was made up of Normans and other adventurers tempted by a well-publicized speculative enterprise against a richer country, offering land, treasure and wealthy English brides. William's army was thus a bigger and better-led variant of the war bands that had ravaged Europe for centuries, and it formed part of what has been called an "aristocratic diaspora," in which ambitious warriors, mostly from the fragments of Charlemagne's Frankish empire, invested in horses, armour and weapons, and set out to con-

quer wealth and land round the periphery of Europe. By 1350, twelve of
the fifteen monarchs of Latin Christendom—including those of England
and Scotland—were of Frankish descent.[50] So England, and later Wales
and Ireland, shared the fate of Iberia, the southern Baltic and the Slavic
borderlands. What was unusual in the invasion of England, and to contemporaries shocking, was that it was not a pagan or heretical territory,
but a powerful and respected Christian kingdom. Hence it was important
that William could claim, fairly plausibly and possibly sincerely, to be its
rightful king.

The deciding factor was not right, but might, in the most famous battle
in English history. Yet little is certain about the precise unfolding of events
"at the grey apple tree"[51] seven miles from Hastings, on Saturday,
14 October 1066—not even whether Harold really was killed by an arrow
in the eye. Harold massed his men close together in what a French chronicler called "a human fortress"[52] and let the invaders attack him. The
battle was unusually hard fought and the invaders were suffering heavily
from the axes and spears of Harold's men. When William's horse was
speared and he was thrown to the ground, the Normans thought he was
dead and started to run. William rallied them by pulling back his helmet
to show his face and shouting unanswerably that "if you run you'll all
die."[53] What finally won for William were his armoured cavalry, the
close-range shooting of his archers—the two arms that were establishing
themselves as dominant in medieval warfare, neither of which the English
had—and the numbers and freshness of his warriors. According to another
French chronicler, Guy of Amiens, William sent four mounted warriors
through the fray to kill Harold, and they cut him to pieces; the embroidered Bayeux Tapestry seemed to show him with an arrow in the eye; and
later the Anglo-Norman historian William of Malmesbury combined the
stories to show him hit by an arrow and then dismembered on the
ground.[54] However it happened, Harold and his two brothers Gyrth and
Leofwine were killed, as were three of Edward the Confessor's nephews.
The English nobility was smashed: "Just as the forest is cut down by the
axe, so the English forest was destroyed."[55] Perhaps 3,500 English and
2,500 Normans were dead.

What happened after the battle was even more important. As we have
seen, the English kingdom had been in crisis, with several aggressive
claimants to the crown: civil war and invasion loomed over the country.
William had a plausible claim to be king, and the association with Normandy, already close, was the best guarantee of security. Harold and the
Godwine faction were not universally liked. So after Stamford Bridge and
Hastings, with Harold dead and his warriors slaughtered, the English

might have accepted William as king just as they had accepted Cnut half a century earlier, and for similar reasons. Quite quickly, influential Englishmen, including Archbishop Aldred of York, rallied to William, who was crowned on Christmas Day 1066 at Westminster Abbey. English soldiers joined his army. English officials kept their posts. Harold's sons, launching sea-borne raids from their refuge in Ireland, made little impact. By 1068 Edgar the aetheling (grandson of Edmund "Ironside") had made his peace with William, who was offering pardons and even marriage into his family for surviving English nobles.

If this had continued, the Norman Conquest might have had little more impact than that of Cnut, especially as the number of William's followers was fairly small—far fewer than in earlier Germanic and Scandinavian invasions. English society and culture might have been little changed. On the other hand, William had his greedy soldiers to reward, and they were hastily building wooden castles with forced labour to ensure their hold on the conquered territory—buildings never before seen in England and for which there was no English word. "When the castles were built, they filled them with devils and wicked men . . . they levied taxes on the villages . . . they robbed and burned."[56] Thousands of colonists followed in their wake. There was a prolonged free-for-all at local level as the victors advanced up to the still fluid and disputed northern and western marchlands. William's coronation itself provided an unfortunate and unintended symbol of ethnic division. When Normans and English in the audience shouted ritual acclamation of the king in their own languages, Norman soldiers outside, misunderstanding the English shouts as threatening, went on the rampage and set fire to several houses.[57]

It was probably determination to defend local power and property against Norman encroachment that caused scattered resistance in Northumbria, Mercia, Wessex and East Anglia. In 1069 Edgar the aetheling and surviving English earls, especially those from the north, where local autonomy was most jealously guarded, fought back, led by Earl Waltheof of Northumbria. So did local thegns such as Hereward in the fenland round Peterborough and Ely. The lack of options available to the English—and the limited extent to which this can be seen as a "national" uprising in modern terms—is shown by their alliance with the Danes, and their willingness to accept the Danish king, Sveinn Estristhson, as Cnut's heir. The Danes now launched their very last invasion, almost 300 years after their first. Welshmen too joined the northern rebels: "all the people of the land, riding and marching . . . greatly rejoicing."[58] York was taken and its Norman garrison slaughtered, Waltheof "cutting off their heads one by one" as they tried to escape.[59] The Danes, now welcomed by the local people, helped Hereward to capture Peterborough in 1070—but they then departed with the abbey treasure.

William acted ruthlessly to punish and eradicate opposition. What was remembered as "the harrying of the North"—a scorched-earth policy—left expanses of the Midlands and the north devastated, and many killed or starving. This was unusually brutal even by the harsh standards of the times. The monk-historian Orderic Vitalis some sixty years later described "helpless children, young men in the prime of life, and hoary grey-beards alike perishing of hunger."[60] Much of the land was still deserted a generation after.

William's own attitude seems to have changed. If he had ever intended to create an Anglo-Norman partnership, it was now abandoned. He gave up trying to learn English. He stopped using English in documents in 1070.[61] He spent little time in the country from 1072 until his death in 1087. He purged the English Church, and he dispossessed the English nobility wholesale: England was now to be ruled by Frenchmen. The monasteries—in which laypeople stored their wealth for safety—were plundered. William made the unprecedented claim that every acre of England now belonged to him by right of conquest, to be given as he wished to reward his followers and make them his dependants.

Where did this leave the Angelcynn, after the fourth great transforming invasion of the island? Why is 1066 the most famous date in our history? Because it caused the most traumatic political, social and cultural rupture. "No other event in western European history of the central Middle Ages can be compared for its shocking effects: the carnage on the battlefield, the loss of life and the consequent political upheaval."[62] Across Europe, writers recorded their shock and indignation at the bloodshed. Conquest meant wholesale national degradation. Before 1066, the English were widely regarded, not only by themselves, as "a glorious and splendid people."[63] Some might have considered them as a little too civilized: the Normans found English prisoners well dressed, long-haired and beautiful, much given to combing their locks—unlike the Normans' own shaven and crop-headed style. The English could claim to be "a people greater, richer and older" than their thuggish, illiterate conquerors.[64] English kings had probably been wealthier than most of their post-Conquest successors. But after 1066 the English as a whole—the "natives" (*nativi*), as they were generally known—would come to be considered a people of peasants using a crude vernacular, the butt of mockery. This influenced later views of the Conquest, even to the present day.

The Conquest annihilated England's ruling class, physically and genetically. Some 4,000–5,000 thegns were eliminated by battle, exile, or dispossession in the biggest transfer of property in English history. In the words of an English chronicler, "some were slain by iron, others placed in prisons . . . many were driven from their native land and the rest oppressed." Some fled to Scotland or Denmark; others became mercenaries as far afield as Byzantium, where they served in the imperial guard and set up a small English colony near Nicea. Harold's daughter married a Slavic prince. The last English earl, Waltheof, was beheaded in 1076. Most simply sank in society. English widows and heiresses were forcibly married to William's followers. Others entered nunneries "out of fear of the French"—including the future Queen Edith (wife of Henry I), "to preserve me from the lust of the Normans which was rampant."[65] As a later chronicler told it, "noble maidens were exposed to the insults of low-born soldiers, and lamented their dishonouring by the scum of the earth."[66] A generation after the Conquest, all significant power and wealth were in new hands.

We can dimly imagine the psychological effects of the sudden imposition of some 15,000 new masters with a foreign culture, whom the English called "French" or "Roman." English churchmen, the nation's spiritual and cultural leaders, were removed from the highest offices and replaced principally by French or Italian prelates. Within a generation, only one bishop was English, and only two great abbots. English saints, the highest symbols of local and national identity by whose merits God "adorned the island munificently,"[67] ceased for a time to be honoured. Lanfranc, former abbot of Bec in Normandy and now an imperiously reforming Archbishop of Canterbury, despised the English and had doubts about "the quality of the sanctity" of their saints—admittedly, not invariably dazzling. The new Norman abbot of St. Albans demolished shrines and burned relics.[68] When monks at Glastonbury resisted the imposition of Norman liturgy in 1083, soldiers killed or wounded several, shooting arrows down from the choir loft, and, relates the *Anglo-Saxon Chronicle*, "blood came down from the altar onto the steps and from the steps to the floor."[69] English libraries disappeared. The Church became the most visible channel for the cultural dominance of the new rulers, through endowments and vast new buildings. This was to atone for the sin of the Conquest, and literally to consecrate the new order: William had the high altar of his new Battle Abbey built on the spot where Harold fell. It was also an unparalleled way of showing off new riches, status and power.

All this might resemble cultural annihilation as well as political revolution. But fundamental elements of the past survived. Some of the greatest English saints were soon back in favour, and St. Edward the Confessor in time became the national and royal patron. This served the conquerors ideologically, maintaining a fiction of continuity, which insisted that the Conquest was the assertion of legitimate succession.[70] But it also helped to reassert the Englishness of the Church, the core of national culture in which English was still used and written. The system of government remained too, passed on to William by English clerics and office-holders clinging on to their jobs: the shires and hundreds with their officers and regular courts; and councils of nobles and prelates tenuously descended from the witan. The Normans added nothing to it because it worked, and helped them to rule. But it was a system that differed fundamentally from those on the Continent, including Normandy itself. This was so in two ways, both of which shaped England's future. First, it was fairly uniform and covered most of the country, and so tended to counteract the fragmentation of authority that had splintered European kingdoms and empires into a chaos of feudal principalities: "The sheriffs, though called vice-comites, were to be the king's officers; the shire moots might be called county courts, but they were not to be the courts of counts."[71] Second, it had a wide degree of participation, not only of noble magnates and great prelates, but of lesser knights, sheriffs and even free peasants in hundred courts—perhaps one man in twenty took part.[72] So ancient forms of representation that were snuffed out by kings and noble magnates on the Continent survived in England.[73] This was the reality behind the myth of "Anglo-Saxon liberty," for myths are rarely entirely fictitious. Institutions that had been born with the nation, and made the nation, survived. England under the Normans was still recognizably England.

# CHAPTER 2

# The Conqueror's Kingdom

*They built castles widely throughout this nation, and oppressed the wretched people, and afterwards it continually grew very much worse. When God wills, may the end be good.*

*Anglo-Saxon Chronicle, 1066*

Though the Conquest preserved many institutions, it yet changed the way England was ruled. Before, government had depended largely on consent; now it was dominated by force.[1] Unlike his predecessors, the Conqueror claimed to be the lord of all the land: this was the political revolution of the Conquest. Vast areas remained directly in the possession of the Crown, and all holders of land owed their rights and allegiance ultimately to him. The witan as the "council of the English people" soon disappeared, except perhaps in memory, and although assemblies were still summoned, they became gatherings of the king's main feudal tenants, usually called "concilia" (in French, *conciles*) or, later, "parlements." This word—which could simply mean "discussions"—came to denote formal meetings of the king and his magnates.[2] The four great earldoms set up by Cnut were abolished, and power was concentrated in the king's hands. The Conqueror claimed all the powers enjoyed by Edward the Confessor, and retained local administration under new management.[3] For all these reasons, kings of England were far more able to enforce the rights they claimed than were the other great monarchs, the kings of Francia and the German emperors, and this effective power of government was a fundamental characteristic of subsequent English history. That power is demonstrated by Domesday Book (1085–86), which set the seal on the Conquest by giving the king precise information on 13,400 named places he now possessed. The far north—Cumberland, Westmorland, Northumberland and Durham—were not included, as their possession was disputed and tenuous at best.

Domesday Book was so called, said a later royal treasurer, because "its decisions, like those of the Last Judgement, are unalterable." As a comprehensive survey of a country, it is "unrivalled, not only in medieval Europe, but anywhere at any time."[4] The aim was probably to sort out the chaos left by land-grabs that had followed the post-Conquest rebellions, to clarify the value and tenure of what the king owned, to facilitate taxation, and to bring the country under the rule of written law. Sworn juries were assembled to provide information on their districts (common practice in England and Normandy), and this information was recorded in Latin by royal commissioners, who often misunderstood English terms.[5] The king "sold his land on very hard terms—as hard as he could," recorded the *Anglo-Saxon Chronicle*,[6] and his harshness was passed down to the conquered English peasantry.

Domesday Book listed the different types of land and its use; minerals and manufactures; fisheries; 6,000 mills; productive people (nearly always only adult men) and their status, from earls to villagers, or "villeins" (109,000), and slaves (28,000); and animals, from plough-teams of oxen to bees. And it said how much all of this was worth. It shows England as a rich and developed agricultural country, with its forests already reduced to twentieth-century levels, nearly all today's villages already in embryo, and as much land under the plough as in 1900, using 650,000 oxen.

The royal family directly held 20 percent of the land, the Church had 25 percent, and a dozen magnates controlled another 25 percent—less concentration of wealth than under the Godwines. Effectively the country was controlled by about 250 people: the king, the great prelates (chosen by him), and about 170 barons with landed incomes of over £100 per year—practically all newcomers. Below them were the holders of the remaining 30 percent of the land: some 2,000 foreign knights, William's followers, and 8,000 other new settlers, some of them the rank and file of the conquering army, others who had followed in the conquerors' wake, and the surviving English free peasantry. Of nearly 2 million English, only four Englishmen (none of whose names are familiar today) were still major landowners, and only about twenty had incomes of over £20 per year.[7]

Despite political conflict and heavy taxation, much of England was prospering, and some credit must go to its post-Conquest rulers. Most fundamentally, they provided greater security against raids and invasion—the Norman Conquest was, of course, the last such. Their ambitious buildings created jobs and trade. Castles provided the focus of trading centres, and towns multiplied and grew. Exports—especially of wool to Flanders, and also of foodstuffs and minerals—flourished, and trade expanded with southern Europe. This expanded existing ports such as London and Ipswich, and created a string of new ones—Newcastle, Hull, Boston, Lynn and Portsmouth. In agriculture, the Normans introduced rabbits in carefully controlled warrens and fallow deer into the forests.

Social, economic and political control of the land and its people—what in the eighteenth century would retrospectively be termed the "feudal system"[8]—was given a more centralized and rigorous form after the Conquest swept away many existing rights and eliminated the English thegns. The Conqueror at once granted land—"fiefs," or "fees"—to his barons in return for their services, military and political, symbolized by the ceremony of homage, a public oath of allegiance. They in turn granted it to their own followers, for similar allegiance and services: England's 50,000 square miles could supply about 7,500 knights' fees of on average six or seven square miles. At the lowest level, "natives," "Anglici," "rustics," "serfs," "villeins" (the words overlapped) were allotted land and protection in return for rent, labour and other services. Many thousands of previously free English landholders became legally subject to the new lords. Recalled an early historian, "it was even disgraceful to be called English."[9] Over 70 percent of tenants were villeins, holding 15–40 acres, or "cottagers," with five acres or less; and many of the former employed paid labourers or slaves.[10]

All land and all men were now legally part of this hierarchy, which was buttressed by an ideology of lordship, duty and loyalty, of which the cult of chivalry and the Arthurian romances would later be the most idealized example. In theory, it gave rights as well as duties to all (even, to a limited extent, to villeins). "Glanvill" (the 1180s treatise on law traditionally attributed to Henry II's Chief Justice, Ranulf Glanvill) stated that "the bond of trust in lordship should be mutual."[11] However unequal the relationship, it did give some protection to dependants, and established a principle of reciprocity. The most unpopular landlords were not barons but monks: the monasteries were efficient and impersonal exploiters with long memories and clear consciences. The military foundation on which feudalism was supposedly based—service in arms was the prime duty owed—was never fully applied, and money was always a substitute. Towns and their inhabitants were always partly outside it.

The English version of this "feudal system" was unlike that elsewhere in Europe. The post-Conquest Crown recognized no powers or rights independent of the king. Nor did barons possess large continuous territories, but only scattered holdings. England escaped the trend that tormented the Continent: central authority did not fragment, but was strengthened. Great barons could never create autonomous and warring principalities. They had no jurisdiction over their vassals higher than that of the king's judges. A French historian comments that "the great success of medieval England was to combine an early centralization of justice with recognition of local liberties, buttressed by popular juries."[12]

What about the majority of the population? Pre-Conquest society was later idealized as embodying "Anglo-Saxon liberties," but it was nevertheless very violent, subject to heavy taxation and compulsory labour, and about 12 percent of the people were slaves—a status that the Normans gradually abolished in England, then in Wales and later in Ireland. It was also exposed to invasion and internal conflict. Even so the Conquest was disastrous for English peasants as a whole, through the direct effects of war, greater impositions, and the subjection of many thousands of freemen to serfdom. The luckier ones managed to remain as free tenants (14 percent of those listed in Domesday Book), or held subordinate positions as estate managers, foresters, huntsmen and minor royal officers. The Conquest may have increased a common sense of Englishness among the subject population: the old divide between Dane and Saxon seems to have disappeared. Many must have realized that their personal fate was linked with that of the country. When testifying about local affairs, jurors in the twelfth century sometimes spoke of "the Conquest of England" or referred to the time "before the Normans conquered England."[13] In some places, the customary rights of Anglo-Saxon days were successfully claimed, and long after 1066 peasants appealed to privileges granted by the Confessor, Canute or even Offa.

There were two groups of Englishmen, and some women, who retained power, wealth or status. The first group were townspeople. Although the Conquest led to an influx of urban immigrants, the English remained a strong presence, including among the most prominent groups—moneyers, goldsmiths, moneylenders (among whom there were also Jewish communities), merchants and royal officers. They were the only significant English group whose wealth and influence could approach that of the French landed magnates, with whom some of them mixed even at the level of the royal court. There were occupational hazards, however: in the 1120s many moneyers were castrated and had their right hands cut off by Henry I for debasing the currency. The second group were churchmen. As we have noted, the highest ranks of the clergy—commanding immense economic and political as well as spiritual power—were closed to Englishmen. But the lower levels—parish clergy, cathedral canons, archdeacons, monks, nuns, hermits and anchoresses—remained strongly and sometimes predominantly English in background and culture. Their oral teaching (mostly in English) and writings (in English, Latin and French) maintained English religious and cultural traditions. Some, notably William of Malmesbury (*c.*1090–*c.*1142), librarian of Malmesbury Abbey, and Henry of Huntingdon (*c.*1088–*c.*1157), hereditary clergyman-squire of Little Stukely and archdeacon of Huntingdon, both of mixed French and English parentage, were responsible, as we shall see shortly, for writing a new English history which helped to define the post-Conquest nation.

There were no more major revolts by the English after the harsh repression of 1069–70; but the heavy "murdrum" fine levied on local communities where a Norman was murdered (and any victim other than a serf was assumed to be Norman unless his "anglaiserie" was proved) is evidence of continuing localized violence by the English against their new lords, not least from outlaws in the forests.[14] The lack of larger conflict may have helped gradual reconciliation, or at least acquiescence. Among the aristocracy, if there was frequent political division, it was relatively restrained, and less violent than under the Anglo-Saxons, with the notable exception of the period of the "Anarchy" of Stephen's reign (see pp. 64–65), far worse than anything during the Anglo-Saxon kingdom. Nevertheless, not a single earl and hardly any barons were executed or murdered for political reasons for more than 200 years.[15] Political murders and mutilations practically ceased. By contemporary European standards, post-Conquest England was a haven of peace.

The Normans built the grandest, the most experimental, the most expensive buildings in a variety of styles, surpassing the greatest on the Continent. The new Winchester Cathedral (begun in 1079) was the longest in western Europe; London's White Tower (*c.*1080) was the biggest keep in western Europe; Westminster Great Hall (1097) was the largest secular covered space; Norwich castle (*c.*1100) was the most ambitious secular building in northern Europe; Christ Church priory, Canterbury, possessed the greatest glass windows in all Europe. Probably more cut stone than in the Pyramids was used in this, the most concentrated construction effort in England between the Romans and the Victorians, amounting to the greatest per capita investment ever seen in England until the Industrial Revolution.[16] Quite a lot, built in haste, fell down—some of it quite soon (towers at Winchester, Ely, Evesham, Bury St. Edmunds, Chichester). But what remained was stupendous, matched then only by Rome itself, Constantinople and Kiev, and it includes many of our greatest cultural treasures. But what the English at the time would have seen were "massive, stark, bright, uncompromising foreign structures, which transformed the English landscape."[17] Building also meant destruction, and this too was intentional. Down came the Old Minster and palace at

Winchester, seat of the kings of Wessex. Nearly all the great Anglo-Saxon churches, monasteries and minsters were demolished, and nothing of them remains aboveground in any English cathedral. By 1100, all were new or rebuilt in Romanesque ("Norman") style—Canterbury was modelled on Saint-Étienne, in Caen. The effort extended to buildings embodying a less spiritual form of power: about 500 castles were thrown up in fifty years—roughly one every ten miles—and at least ninety were of stone, serving both security and prestige. These were something new in England: the Anglo-Saxon nobility had not needed to live in fortresses, and the ramparts of burhs had protected the whole community. But Norman castles threatened as much as they protected, and they made the new rulers invincible: only one castle ever fell to an English rebellion, the temporary structure at York in 1069.

Buildings and land came to embody new family identities. Wealthy Anglo-Saxons had spread bequests widely among relatives to maintain the cohesion of an extended clan, very conscious of far-flung degrees of kinship. Norman wealth went into stones and mortar: according to William of Malmesbury, the Saxons had lived richly in "mean and despicable" houses, while the Normans lived frugally in "noble and splendid mansions." The practice grew of transmitting land where possible to a single male heir by primogeniture—a social revolution. The family became smaller and more vertical, and attached to a particular place. Names and titles reflected this change. Unlike in Anglo-Saxon and Scandinavian societies, which used Christian names and patronymics (e.g., Harold Godwineson) or identifying names based on characteristics or occupation (Thorkell the Tall, Eadric the Steersman), the Norman elite adopted permanent family names derived from land, castle or ancestor (Hubert de Vaux, Roger de Chateauneuf, Richard Fitzgerald). For the rest, individual nicknames (from place, job, physique—John Wood, Robert Smith, Thomas Becket) in time became permanent family surnames.

There was no greater cultural conquest than in language. Working shortly before 1066, a thousand writers and copyists of English have been identified. This may sound few, but it is several times the number writing Italian texts in Renaissance Italy.[18] The Normans eradicated written English as the language of government and undermined it as the language of literature, and spoken English ceased to be the language of elite society. This change was confirmed by England's attachment to the Angevin empire in 1154. It was long believed that English largely disappeared except as a peasant dialect. Walter Scott, in *Ivanhoe* (1819), made the famous point that English became the language of the farmyard (swine, ox, calf) and French that of the table (pork, beef, veal). But this does not mean that English was crude, and French sophisticated. As we have seen, Old English and Irish were the most developed of Europe's vernaculars. English had a standardized written form by the late tenth century, whereas French had no written literature at all until—ironically—it was pioneered in post-Conquest England, as we shall see, perhaps in imitation of Anglo-Saxon literature.[19] Replacing English required two languages: Latin, for legal, administrative, ecclesiastical, commercial and intellectual contexts; French for verbal communication among the new elites. The sophistication of English government drove a high level of lay literacy.[20] "Unless a man knows French he is little thought of," wrote the chronicler Robert of Gloucester in about 1290; "but low-born men keep to English and to their own speech still."[21]

Spoken English thus survived. Moreover, it soon predominated in everyday speech: the Normans needed it to communicate with the great majority of the population. Often within a generation, smaller landlords not only became bilingual in French and English, but English—except among the highest nobility and at court—probably became their first language. Knowledge of French remained an essential social attribute, but noble children had to be sent to France to learn it properly. Bilingualism became a mark of "English" identity among the descendants of the Normans. Trilingualism (with Latin) was the norm for the educated. In practice, there was a hybridization, or "creolization," with the languages being mixed together, creating huge changes in vocabulary and grammar. French and Latin words were imported into English, though more slowly than Scott's example might suggest. For example, in the popular verse history of Britain, Layamon's *Brut* (c.1200), a rare example of non-religious literature in English, there are only 250 French loan-words in 30,000 lines.

So written English too survived. It retained certain grass-roots legal functions. In important monastic outposts, notably Worcester, Hereford, Winchester, Canterbury, Peterborough and Exeter, which we can properly call patriotic, it was propagated as the way of teaching the people.[22] The monks of Peterborough Abbey were the last who continued to write the *Anglo-Saxon Chronicle*, until 1154; but they stopped using formal English in 1121, when it was replaced by local dialect—a sign of how quickly the old formal language was forgotten. By the end of the century, very few could still read it. In 1230, a monk at Worcester was trying to learn it—the West Midlands seem to have maintained a tradition—but by 1300 Old English had become an "ydioma incognita."[23] Yet English, in older and newer forms, continued to be written in religious centres such as Worcester and Hereford. Even after the Conquest, the production and use of vernacular texts was rarely paralleled anywhere in medieval Europe.

These were not luxury products, but were for everyday use in prayer, preaching and ritual, and hence for the mass of the people English remained the intimate language of belief and salvation. This is one of the things that prevented it, changing though it inevitably was, from becoming a dying peasant dialect. The French-speaking elite often mocked it as uncouth, and so using and writing it was somewhat subversive. One Worcester scribe left a list of the notable churchmen who "taught our people in English"; and he added, "not dim, their light: it fair glowed."[24]

English continued in place-names, though little in personal names. There is perhaps nothing that distances us more instinctively from the pre-Conquest English than names: Ealdgyth, Aelfgifu, Colswein, Eadric, Waltheof (even if a few were revived during the Romantic period—Karl Marx called one of his sons Edgar). Our names since the 1100s have been overwhelmingly Norman, a personal form of cultural conquest through snobbery: William (which became the most common), John, Richard, Robert, Margaret, Mary, Emma. In a significant conciliatory gesture, the sons of Henry III were christened Edward and Edmund, signalling a link with the pre-Conquest monarchy; and the former became King Edward I in 1272.

The Conquest thus began to transform much of English culture. But it is likely that Latin, the common language of Christendom, would in any case have been increasingly used in legal, devotional and intellectual matters, as was happening across Europe: even before 1066, despite the prominence of the vernacular, there was more writing in Latin than in English. Choices of names would also probably have changed, as elsewhere in Europe, as the Church encouraged more uniform devotions. French would have come into greater use among the educated and the fashionable, especially in courtly and chivalric literature. This was not only because of the Conquest; the peak of borrowing from French came three centuries after 1066, a consequence of the cultural magnetism of Paris and the other great French cities, which affected all of western Europe.

There was a dazzling literary revival in England in the century following the Conquest—but in Latin and French. It was probably the English tradition of vernacular writing that encouraged the development of writing in French.[25] Some of the earliest works of French literature came from England or had English connections. The famous *Chanson de Roland*, an epic poem of Charlemagne's battles against the Saracens, was first written down in England in the early twelfth century. The first historical work in French was Geoffroy Gaimar's history of the English, the *Estoire des Engleis* (c.1136–37), an accessible work in fashionable French verse based on the *Anglo-Saxon Chronicle*. English authors—or authors in England, often of mixed Anglo-Norman families—attained a European influence greater than ever before, and rarely equalled since.

Their most important works were histories or historical romances in Latin—the first major works of English history since Bede 400 years before. William of Malmesbury's *Gesta Regum Anglorum* (c.1126) was a continuous history of England from the arrival of the Saxons to Henry I, and Henry of Huntingdon's *Historia Anglorum* went from the mythical arrival of the Trojan hero Brutus to 1154, just before the author's death. The most extraordinary of these works went beyond English history, Geoffrey of Monmouth's *Historia Regum Britanniae* (c.1136), "one of the supreme achievements of the historical imagination," which transformed English visions of the past.[26] As noted earlier, Geoffrey and his emulators plunged into legend and fantasy to create a prestigious new common Anglo-British epic. It became one of the most popular historical works in the European Middle Ages, far more widely read even than Bede, and is the only historical work known to have been in the possession of great nobles.[27] It also produced popular spin-offs. The Jerseyman Wace, a monk in Caen, produced in 1155 a popular French version of the saga, called the *Roman de Brut* (Brutus), which, among other things, added the story of Arthur's Round Table. Significantly, he often translated *Britannia* as *Engleterre*. Layamon ("Lawman") prepared his English translation of *Brut* in the early 1200s—an oddity, as even patriotic writings (such as the *Roman de Waldef*—about Earl Waltheof) were usually in French. Walter Map, a Herefordshire priest at Henry II's court, wrote a French version of the Grail and Lancelot stories (c.1180). A later prose version of *Brut* was very widely read in Latin, French and above all English—more copies survive than of any other medieval manuscript, and it was repeatedly printed by Caxton after 1480.

Thus for more than two centuries English after 1066 almost ceased to be the language of secular literary culture, as the elite no longer commissioned major works in English. A rare exception, such as Layamon's *Brut*, was perhaps an early sign of a new appetite for literature in English. But especially in the religious sphere English writing—sermons, psalms, saints' lives, poetry, songs—continued as one element of a bilingual or trilingual culture. One of the most famous pieces of early music—"Sumer is icumen in / Lhude sing cuccu"—is a song written down in Reading Abbey in about 1250, using the same tune as a hymn.[28] English did not therefore decline into a merely spoken range of peasant dialects, as was traditionally thought. This was the basis of its later extension into political and literary uses, as we shall see.

## THE CONQUEST IN HISTORY

Early interpretations of the trauma of conquest testified to ideological confusion and a collapse of morale. Churchmen accepted that it must have been God's will that the English should lose "their safety and honour" and "should no longer exist as a people."[29] It had to be punishment for some heinous English sin: "slaughter and treachery" such as the murders of Edward the Martyr in 978 and Alfred in 1037; or Harold's oath-breaking; or just typical English depravity—the clergy's "drunkenness and the neglect of the Lord's house," and nobles making their slaves pregnant and then selling them abroad.[30] Stories circulated that Harold had survived Hastings and wandered off to live as a hermit—"the quietist literature of a defeated nation," picked up centuries later by Kipling.[31]

A more defiant tone appeared in the story of Hereward "the Wake"—perhaps meaning "the Watchful," though also perhaps a much later addition. The original *Deeds of Hereward*, written in English and translated into Latin (the version that survives), appeared roughly fifty years after the events described. The story, based on eyewitness accounts, focused on the Fenland uprising, and Hereward's defence of the Isle of Ely, which William in person finally captured by building a causeway across the marshes. This was the first heroic tale of English resistance, and it has survived some 900 years.

The twelfth-century works of William of Malmesbury and Henry of Huntingdon were more than simply a literary phenomenon: they were pioneering works that gave England a history.[32] Many details we piece together about the more obscure periods before the Conquest depend on their researches, using written chronicles (some now lost), traditions, songs and eyewitness accounts. They were writing at a time, says William himself, of vociferous disputes about the Conquest[33]—the first great historical debate in our culture. It permanently shaped the way we understand England's past, with the Conquest not an end or a beginning, but only an episode in a continuing story. William stressed that his history was written "for love of my country." He had been commissioned by the "English" queen, Matilda II, great-granddaughter of Edmund Ironside, whose marriage to Henry I in 1100 united pre- and post-Conquest royalty, and this obviously influenced his approach. He promised to be even-handed between Normans and English, and this too had a profound effect on later interpretations. William and Henry certainly did not write triumphal histories of the Normans (no English writer ever wrote a Norman-centred history), but nor were they vindications of the Anglo-

Saxons. Indeed, they marginalized Anglo-Saxon achievements, such as those of Alfred, which had to be rediscovered centuries later. As clergymen, these authors accepted the Conquest as God's punishment for English treachery, pride, lust, sloth and gluttony. In order "to wipe out the English nation," concluded Henry, God had chosen the Normans because "they surpassed all other people in their unparalleled savagery," which he amply documented.[34] However, he praised Norman religious reforms. William welcomed an influx of French culture brought by the Normans, but also described Hastings as "a day of disaster for our dear country" and lamented that "England has become the habitation of outsiders." Layamon wrote that "the Normans, with their evil power . . . harmed this nation."[35] Geoffroy Gaimar was critical of William the Conqueror, and praised Hereward as a hero.

These writers in their very ambivalence met a psychological and political need for a history of England that would transcend—even gloss over—the rupture of the Conquest, and construct a positive, unifying English identity for later generations. It would show "wretched England, long since destroyed" recovering its identity and pride: "England arise! Or rather, rise again!"[36] Thus, they helped to invent not only the notion of a continuous history of "England our island," but the very idea of national history as a single narrative of a place and its successive inhabitants reaching far into the past, and continuing despite successive invasions, changes of dynasty and transformations of culture.[37] In thus contributing to the way human beings conceive of collective national identities, their influence far beyond England was enormous and permanent.

The Conquest and its outcomes kept returning over the centuries as a crucial historical theme, and some of its ramifications will be seen in Chapter 6. The idea of a continuing "Norman yoke"—an oppressive legal, social and political system imposed by the Conquest and suppressing an "ancient constitution" embodying the rights of "freeborn Englishmen"—appealed to some of those resisting the prerogative claims initiated by the Tudor and Stuart monarchs. The idea also attracted religious radicals during the seventeenth century, among them the leader of the "Diggers," Gerrard Winstanley, who used it to attack the system of landownership. It was a strong element in the beliefs of supporters of the "Good Old Cause" of the Commonwealth after the Restoration in 1660, and it remained a feature of English and American Whig propaganda in the eighteenth century, famously in the writings of Thomas Paine. From this perspective, England's political history since 1066 was that of a struggle to regain the "ancient constitution" from the Crown, and even from Parliament, which some saw as the voice of Anglo-Saxon liberties, but others as merely another part of the "Norman yoke."[38] Late-eighteenth-century radicals claimed that the rights lost in 1066 had still not been restored, despite the revolutions of 1642, 1688 and 1776. In the nineteenth century, the demand for the rights of "freeborn Englishmen" appealed to democrats, Chartists and to romantic Tories such as Benjamin Disraeli, whose "two nations," the rich and the poor, originated as "the conquerors and the conquered."[39] There are echoes today: it was claimed in 2011 that people with Norman surnames such as Lacy or Glanville are wealthier than people named Smith, Mason or Shepherd.[40]

This view of history as rupture and continuous conflict had opponents, however. Many seventeenth-century parliamentarians and royalists equally downplayed the Conquest: neither wanted the Stuarts to be seen as the heirs of a conqueror, though for opposite reasons. Parliamentarians feared it might give legal grounds for absolutism, and royalists because it made the Crown seem tyrannical.[41] So they insisted that William and his successors had been bound by the ancient laws of the Anglo-Saxons—or, at least, that those laws had soon been restored by Magna Carta. The great nineteenth-century Oxford medievalist Bishop William Stubbs believed that the Anglo-Saxon witan, surviving as folk memory, was reborn as Parliament, and that Magna Carta showed that the nation "becomes one and realizes its oneness."[42] The idea that the trauma of the Conquest had rapidly been overcome had roots in the twelfth-century works of William of Malmesbury and Henry of Huntingdon. So did the view that conquest had cured Anglo-Saxon vices and brought cultural benefits. This appealed to later generations as part of a national history of continuity, reconciliation and progress: it had all turned out for the best. Thomas Carlyle asserted in 1858 that the Normans had forced "a gluttonous race of Jutes and Angles ... lumbering about in potbellied equanimity" to undertake "heroic toil and silence and endurance, such as leads to the high places of this Universe, and the golden mountain-tops where dwells the Spirit of the Dawn."[43] The idea that the Conquest had brought benefits fed British imperialism: conquest, while inevitably painful, could in the long run be good for the conquered. Stubbs argued too that the Conquest had saved England from the Europe-wide trend towards feudal fragmentation, which reduced France and Germany into warring statelets—a not implausible view, though it underestimates the cohesion of pre-Conquest England.

Another influential Victorian, Edward Freeman, believed that the conquerors were soon absorbed racially by the English—1066 meant only "the temporary overthrow of our national being ... in a few generations we led captive our conquerors."[44] Rudyard Kipling celebrated this idea in stories and poems for children:

I followed my Duke ere I was a lover
To take from England fief and fee;
But now this game is the other way over—
But now England hath taken me![45]

The most popular story of conflict and reconciliation is the saga of Robin Hood, the Sheriff of Nottingham, Prince John and King Richard the Lionheart. The link between Robin and the Lionheart was invented by a sixteenth-century Scottish historian, John Major, elaborated by Walter Scott in his enormously popular *Ivanhoe* (1819), and thence transferred to films and television. This version sets the story in the 1190s, makes Robin an outlawed Saxon yeoman and his merrie men the embodiment of Saxon freedom struggling against Norman oppression, epitomized by the cruel and decadent John and his henchmen. King Richard, though Norman, has somehow acquired Saxon virtues; and when he secretly returns from captivity, he is acclaimed by the loyal Saxons. Richard subsequently reconciles Saxons and Normans, who, says Scott, became "completely mingled."

These ancient questions long engaged historians, and still do. Was the Conquest a long-term subjugation making England an oppressed colony?[46] Or did Saxons and Normans quickly integrate to form a new English nation—and an aggressive one that soon began a "thousand-year Reich"?[47] Did fundamental institutions of Anglo-Saxon England survive? Would changes in language, law and government have happened anyway, as the whole of Europe evolved under the influence of Catholicism and French culture? How did conquest alter England's relationship with its island neighbours and with the Continent? How these events are interpreted has always affected the fundamental sense of what Englishness is. What recent scholarship tells us is that the rupture of conquest was traumatic but not complete. The principle governing institutions and the unity of the Anglo-Saxon kingdom survived, and were even strengthened by a powerful monarchy. The tradition of the witan and of a national community perhaps did survive or at least "re-emerged" to strengthen claims to rights and representation in Magna Carta and parliaments—though Roman law and the influence of the Church were also important.[48] The English were politically, economically and culturally subjugated, but their spoken and written language continued, as did their religious traditions. Though the conquerors soon began to pride themselves on being "English," lapping up patriotic English history and assimilating the few surviving English landowners, the majority of the "natives" long remained culturally distinct and politically unrepresented.

The Conquest further concentrated royal power: this was one of its historic consequences. But it could not provide stable kingship. It did not cure the problem of disputed succession: descent, bequest, election and coronation could still potentially conflict, and the death of every monarch posed a danger. The situation was further complicated as England and Normandy were at first considered separate inheritances. Every post-Conquest monarch for 150 years suffered rebellions, mainly due to family rivalry. Moreover, the unique power now claimed by the Crown led to attempts to bring the king under the rule of law, as enshrined in Magna Carta. Above all, the troubled link with Normandy and with other parts of France placed a recurring strain on English politics. English kings were often away pursuing Continental interests. Their use of England as an endless source of money for wars caused rumbling discontent, and was the greatest single reason why kings had to seek the consent of their subjects through parliaments. The gradual loss of French territories would also lead to conflict in England. For all these reasons, of the eighteen kings who reigned between the Conquest and the accession of Henry VII in 1485, only eight died peacefully—an unusually turbulent record by western European standards.* Yet, paradoxically, post-Conquest England as a whole, below the level of its rulers, was in general more peaceful than its neighbours, less ravaged by war between great nobles, by foreign invasion, or by general lawlessness.

## FROM NORMAN CONQUEST TO ANGEVIN EMPIRE

England, the richest part of the archipelago, had long been the target of raids and invasions, as we saw in Chapter 1. Both Hadrian's Wall and Offa's Dyke had tried to seal its land frontiers against attack. Alfred's successors had tried to reach a modus vivendi with their turbulent island neighbours. The Anglo-Saxon method was to claim a loose suzerainty, by alliances and ceremonies as well as by arms, as when in 973 Edgar was rowed on the Dee by a crew of kings (see p. 35). This assertion of primacy among the rulers of the islands did not imply an ambition to govern them. Until the Conquest, England's main political and cultural links had been with Scandinavia.

Geopolitically, the Normans wrenched England permanently onto a

---

* Henry I, Stephen, Henry II, Henry III, Edward I, Edward III, Henry IV and Edward IV. William the Conqueror, John and Henry V died of natural causes, but while on campaign. Four—possibly five—were murdered (Edward II, Richard II, Henry VI, Edward V and perhaps William Rufus); two died in combat (Richard I and III).

new course. Now it became a French colony, but one whose wealth and status (it made the Duke of Normandy into a sovereign monarch) made it a contender in western European power struggles. So it would continue, with brief intervals, for the whole of its history. This had an immense effect on domestic politics. England's relations with the other inhabitants of the British Isles were also changed forever. The Conquest, and its disturbed aftermath in the northern counties, provided an opportunity for repeated invasions across its northern and western frontiers. On the other hand, the Norman conquerors and those who followed in their footsteps soon spilled over into the Welsh and Irish principalities in a continuing quest for land and wealth.

England was relatively unified and secure. Its neighbours at that time and for long after were not. Ireland contained over a hundred "kings." The Welsh were split between clans grouped loosely into three main kingdoms. These feuded incessantly, resolving inheritance disputes by blinding, castrating and killing.[49] To the north were Brittonic, Scandinavian and Gaelic peoples, whose territories—Strathclyde, Galloway, Man, Argyll, Moray—were separate domains. They came gradually under the sway of the kings of Alba (the Gaelic name for Britain), descendants of the ninth-century Cinead mac Ailpin ("Kenneth MacAlpine"). "Scotland," in its modern sense, dates only from the 1200s.[50] These were warrior societies, violent even by Norman standards, which raided and traded in slaves.

The northerners invaded in 1070, profiting from the disorder of the Conquest—one of many occasions when Scots, English, Welsh and French would take advantage of each other's problems. A series of attacks from across the northern and western borders, aimed at establishing hunting grounds for loot and slaves, horrified the English and Normans:

> They slaughtered the sick in their beds, women who were pregnant or in labour, babies in their cradles or at their mothers' breast and sometimes they killed the mothers too. They slaughtered worn-out old men, feeble old women, everyone who was disabled . . . They carried off their plunder and the women . . . stripped, bound and roped together . . . Their fate was either to be kept as slaves or sold on to other barbarians.[51]

The conditions for future enmity were being established.

William the Conqueror died in 1087, while fighting against his neighbour the king of France. The dukedom of Normandy (the family patrimony) went to his eldest son, Robert "Curthose," and the crown of England to his second son, William "Rufus." He was killed in mysterious circumstances in the New Forest in 1100, and his younger brother hastily seized the throne as Henry I to forestall Robert. Henry, to win English support, promised in his coronation charter to restore and follow the laws of Edward the Confessor, and he at once married Matilda (a descendant of the House of Cerdic, originally named Eadgifu, or Edith). This was regarded by English writers as the restoration of the ancient line of kings; but some Anglo-Normans mocked the royal couple as "Godric and Godiva." Thus began a new cross-Channel conflict. Robert invaded England in 1101, and Henry invaded Normandy and captured his brother at the battle of Tinchebrai in 1106, on the fortieth anniversary of the battle of Hastings. Some regarded this as a kind of English revenge, but its real importance was to maintain England within a cross-Channel realm. Henry spent much time in Normandy, delegating the government of England to Matilda and Roger, Bishop of Salisbury.

Though Henry I had reunited England and Normandy, the number of potential claimants to the throne—brother, daughter, nephew, illegitimate children—was increasing. The situation was aggravated by the drowning in 1120 of the king's heir and only legitimate son, William Adelin (along with an illegitimate son and daughter, and many courtiers) in the *Blanche Nef* ("the White Ship"), which a drunken helmsman steered onto a rock in the Channel. The eventual outcome, following Henry I's death in 1135 in Normandy after eating a surfeit of lampreys,[52] was a prolonged civil war. The antagonists were another Matilda, Henry I's daughter (and dowager empress of Germany by marriage), and Stephen of Boulogne, grandson of William the Conqueror, who carried out a neat coup d'état while Empress Matilda was in France. Stephen persuaded the citizens of London to support him, the Archbishop of Canterbury to crown him, and the keeper of the royal treasury to hand over the keys. But Matilda and her supporters (backed by her new husband, Geoffrey, Count of Anjou) fought back. The Scots, as usual, took advantage of the political chaos in England to invade. They were defeated in 1138 in Yorkshire, at the Battle of the Standard, by a Norman and English army led by the Archbishop of York, carrying local religious symbols as their standard. This battle has been described as a catalyst of post-Conquest English identity in the face of the common enemy. Yet England was still facing a long civil war.

This sporadic conflict between Matilda and Stephen in Normandy and England from 1139 to 1153 brought to the fore the tensions of the rickety Anglo-Norman system, especially the difficulty of reconciling ambitious and resentful English, Norman and Angevin magnates. England, during what the *Anglo-Saxon Chronicle* described as "nineteen long winters," underwent a prolonged breakdown of royal authority such as was more common on the Continent, but which was unique in English history—a long-remembered ordeal known as "the Anarchy." "I do not know nor can I tell all the horrors nor all the tortures that they did to wretched men in this land." The warring barons "laid a tax upon the villages time and time again . . . When the wretched people had no more to give, they robbed and burned . . . you could well go a whole day's journey and never find anyone occupying a village, nor land tilled."[53] There were devastating invasions by the Welsh and Scots, killing and looting as far south as the Tyne. The Anarchy finally ended in 1153 when Matilda's son Henry was recognized by both sides as Stephen's future heir. That order was rapidly restored is testimony to the underlying strength of English governance.

Strictly speaking, Norman rule in England now ended: the House of Anjou, commonly called the Plantagenets,* succeeded in 1154 in the energetic person of Henry II, aged twenty-one, also descended from the Wessex House of Cerdic. He had already inherited the Duchy of Normandy and the counties of Maine and Anjou. Even more important—and a turning point in English and European history—three years previously he had taken the bold gamble of swiftly marrying the formidable Eleanor (Aliénor), heiress of the vast Duchy of Aquitaine and the counties of Poitou and Auvergne, whose marriage to Louis VII of France had just been annulled. She had to escape the French and elude two ambush attempts on her way to the altar. The marriage brought England into what has been called the Angevin empire, a vast agglomeration now stretching from Northumbria to the Pyrenees, and potentially the greatest power in western Europe.

This Continental connection, a French historian has recently suggested, made another history of Europe conceivable, with the British Isles politically integrated with the Continent.[54] In practice, however, what actually happened was that England was immediately drawn into an Angevin power struggle against the relatively new and still puny kingdom of France. Its Capetian kings had few powers and little money. But—even though this seemed merely theoretical—they were the kings to whom for nearly a hundred years the Plantagenets had owed feudal allegiance and homage for their various duchies and counties. On 5 February 1156, Henry, thirteen months after his coronation, met Louis VII of France at the border of Normandy and did homage to him for Normandy, Anjou and Aquitaine. There were subsequently several attempts at conciliation and at uniting the two dynasties by marriage. But eventually, from around 1170, the Capetians set out to undermine Angevin power. Henry and his troublesome sons Richard and John spent most of their time outside England resisting rebellion and encroachment. This rivalry with France would dominate English policy towards Europe for over 300 years. The ensuing heavy taxation

* From the family symbol, *planta genista*, a sprig of broom.

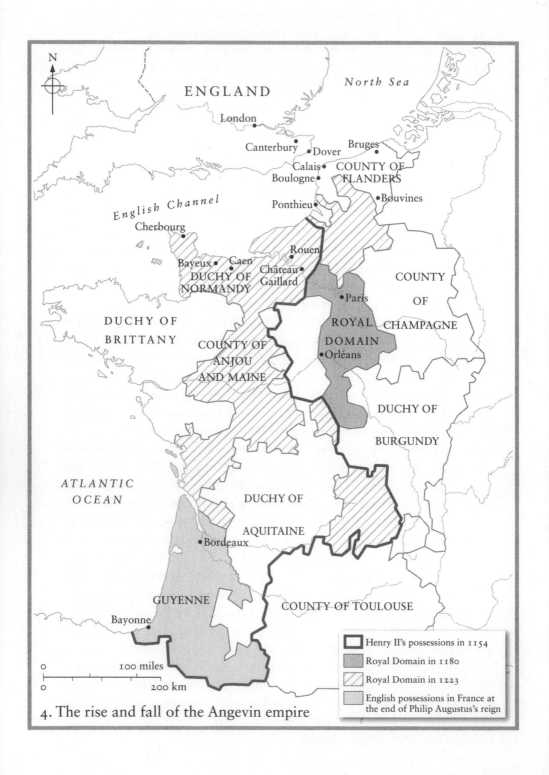

N

ENGLAND

North Sea

London

Canterbury
Dover
Bruges

Calais
COUNTY OF
Boulogne
FLANDERS

Ponthieu
Bouvines

English Channel

Cherbourg

Rouen

Bayeux  Caen
Château
Gaillard
DUCHY OF
NORMANDY

Paris
COUNTY

OF

DUCHY OF
BRITTANY

ROYAL
CHAMPAGNE

COUNTY OF
ANJOU
AND MAINE

DOMAIN
Orléans

DUCHY OF

BURGUNDY

ATLANTIC
OCEAN

DUCHY OF

AQUITAINE

Bordeaux

GUYENNE

COUNTY OF TOULOUSE

Bayonne

| | Henry II's possessions in 1154 |
| | Royal Domain in 1180 |
| | Royal Domain in 1223 |
| | English possessions in France at the end of Philip Augustus's reign |

0        100 miles

0        200 km

4. The rise and fall of the Angevin empire

would decisively affect England's domestic politics. And the Continental link would prolong the cultural pre-eminence in England of France and the French language,[55] while shifting its focus from Normandy to France itself, centre of the cult of chivalry and origin of Gothic architecture.

Henry II, "a stocky, strong, restless, energetic, passionate man,"[56] intelligent and well-educated behind a bluff exterior, capable of charm and good humour as well as dangerous rages, was one of England's most formidable and driven rulers. He was constantly on the move, to see and to be seen: he celebrated Christmas in twenty-four different places, crossed the Channel twenty-four times, and in all spent over fourteen years in Normandy, thirteen in England, and seven in Anjou and Aquitaine.[57] His consistent purposes were to reassert the legal authority of the English Crown and restore peace and order after the disastrous years of the Anarchy, to clear the Scots out of northern England, and to secure his Continental domains. But these tasks—above all the last—were too much even for him: thirty-five years of unceasing struggle wore him out, and he died a broken man at the age of fifty-six.

Arguably, his tendency to define and insist on the letter of his rights aggravated problems—admittedly, the bureaucratization and legalization of power was a European-wide tendency at this time, as both Church and lay princes began to employ university-trained administrators. In England, Henry's reign is usually seen as the genesis of the Common Law, a defining English institution. What actually happened, and what was later thought to have happened, is equally worthy of consideration.

Under the Anglo-Saxons, law had been fairly uniform in its main lines, and decentralized in its enforcement, through sheriffs, shire courts and collective self-policing through tithings, oath-taking and sworn local juries who identified criminals. After 1066 the Normans introduced complication—different laws for French and English, new forest law, Church courts using canon law, courts under the jurisdiction of local lords, and trial by combat. The Anglo-Saxon system continued too, including the sheriffs and county courts, the tithings, and the use of ordeals (by ducking in water or by carrying a hot iron) by which God signalled who was in the right. As before the Conquest, if locals could not cope, the king's men might intervene in a brief flurry of savagery: in Leicestershire, in 1124, "they hanged . . . more thieves than had ever been hanged before . . . in all forty-four men in that little time; and six men were blinded and castrated."[58] Usually, however, locals literally did it themselves: in one recorded case from the 1170s a Bedfordshire man got his next-door neighbour convicted (wrongfully) of stealing from his house, and did the blinding and castrating in person.[59]

Henry II's drive for law and order saw the introduction in the 1160s of travelling royal judges, who were increasingly professional lawyers, on "eyres" (journeys) to hear cases involving the Crown, and in the 1170s permanent royal courts began to sit at Westminster, developing standardized "writs" (court orders in the king's name) to initiate a range of procedures before royal judges. Writs were the basis of the system, and could be purchased for a modest sum by any plaintiff to summon an adversary before a royal court.[60] Thus originated in practice as well as in theory the universal primacy of royal justice: the "Common Law." It was gradually extended to cover every place and every free layman within the kingdom, irrespective of ethnicity. The unfree (serfs or villeins) did not have equal access to royal courts, particularly as concerned land tenure; but royal courts decided in disputed cases whether a man was free or serf.[61] In serious criminal matters, moreover, royal justice extended even to the unfree, because Henry extended "the King's Peace" to cover "all times, the whole realm, all men."[62] This contrasted with much of Europe, where what is commonly called the "feudal revolution" fragmented jurisdiction. A long-term divergence also began between English and Continental legal principles.[63] In Europe, law would either remain local, a patchwork of differing customs, or become transnational by borrowing Roman law enshrined in the Code of Justinian (AD 530). The English Common Law was the first national system of law in Europe. It was a hybrid of Anglo-Saxon and Norman customs and Roman theories, using French terms and concepts—debt, contract, heir, trespass, court, judge, jury—and (until 1731) keeping records in Latin. It was primarily concerned with land rights, based on the careful recording of precedents set by the decisions of judges who, to a large extent, laid down the law as they went along. This practice was formalized in the first great book of English law in use for at least three centuries, "Bracton"—traditionally attributed to one of Henry III's judges, Henry of Bratton (d. 1268), and based on the compilation of precedents. Thus the Common Law evolved over time, rather than deriving from a single code, as Roman law did.[64]

Henry's policy of asserting the legal rights of the Crown did not make him popular. Eyres were sudden, frightening descents that not only tried legal cases, but generally asserted royal power, including by aggressive imposition of higher taxes and feudal exactions. Mere suspicion brought ordeal by water or hot iron. Royal justice also led to a clash with the Church, when in the Constitutions of Clarendon (1164) Henry legislated for political control over the Church, including royal jurisdiction over those clergy (and bogus clergy) who committed crimes. This caused an angry breach with his close friend and trusted chancellor, Thomas Becket, whom he had made Archbishop of Canterbury in 1162, and who had unexpectedly become an intransigent defender of ecclesiastical privilege. Their trial of strength culminated in Becket's murder on 29 December 1170 in Canterbury Cathedral.

An archbishop's brains spattered across the cradle of English Christianity was an unparalleled sacrilege. It was also the exemplary martyrdom of a man who had played out in his life the Christian drama of repentance and salvation, abandoning wealth and power as the king's favourite to become an ascetic, an aggressive exponent of Church supremacy, and three years after his death a canonized saint. Yet this, one of the most famous and dramatic death scenes in medieval history, will always be surrounded by uncertainty. There is no firm evidence that Henry, in Normandy, uttered the notorious call to "rid me of this turbulent priest," though he probably said something similar.[65] It is not clear that the four knights who killed Becket premeditated his murder. It may be that Becket welcomed martyrdom, and his motives have inspired reinterpretation down to modern times: most poetically in T. S. Eliot's *Murder in the Cathedral* (1935) and Jean Anouilh's less subtle *Becket* (1959). The murder caused international outrage, from which the French court naturally tried to profit, urging the Pope to draw "the sword of St Peter."[66] But moderation prevailed: Henry was allowed to perform seemingly heartfelt acts of repentance in 1174, including being flogged by the monks of Canterbury. The capture the very next day of the king of Scots, who had invaded England, proved divine approval: William I "the Lion" was taken "shackled under the belly of a horse" to make formal submission to Henry. The dispute between king and clergy ended in a compromise that Becket's unbending sanctity had prevented: the clergy (and those claiming to be such) won certain legal immunities until the Reformation, and vestiges remained even until 1827.

Becket, although born of Norman immigrants, became England's favourite saint, a symbol of resistance to an alien Crown, in contrast with those countries whose national saint was a canonized monarch, such as the French St. Louis and the Bohemian St. Wenceslas. Thomas's shrine on the site of his martyrdom became one of the great pilgrimage centres of Christendom. Even Louis VII of France came to pray for his sick son in 1179, and doubtless enjoyed the embarrassment caused to Henry II. English kings had to bow the knee too, until Henry VIII vindictively destroyed the shrine in 1529. The cathedral expanded to accommodate the cult. Its new French style (which the seventeenth century dubbed "Gothic") was supervised by a French architect, Guillaume de Sens, until he fell off some scaffolding; it provided a model for English architecture for a generation. The Canterbury pilgrimage as a social phenomenon provided Geoffrey Chaucer with the central theme of the most famous work of medieval English literature.

In the 1170s began two decades of sporadic rebellions by Henry's sons, abetted by his wife, Eleanor, Louis VII of France, the Scots and discontented barons. Even more than personal resentments inside a seriously dysfunctional family, the basic reason was the inherent instability of the Angevin possessions. They were not really an "empire," but a collection of dynastic acquisitions intended in the course of time to be divided among the heirs. But how and to whom? Jealous neighbours were eager to profit from family dissensions. There was an even deeper problem. Henry was trying to preserve a multinational dynastic confederation straddling two kingdoms. But the kingdom of France was pursuing greater royal power: indeed, Henry was doing the same himself in England. So he and his sons inevitably came into conflict with the similarly ambitious Capetians. Within a generation of its establishment, the Angevin "empire" was being pulled apart.[67]

As John of Salisbury, Bishop of Chartres and Becket's biographer, noted, "The French fear our king and hate him equally." Henry's nemesis was France's most successful monarch, Philip II "Augustus"—"a cheerful face, a bald pate, ruddy complexion, given to drink and food, prone to sexual desire, generous to his friends, stingy to his foes, skilled in stratagems."[68] He dedicated his long reign (1180–1223) to increasing the power of his puny kingdom at the expense of his over-mighty vassals. At first, relations with England appeared friendly, with plans for a marriage alliance between Henry's son Richard and Philip's half-sister, Alix, but in 1186, when this failed to materialize, Philip became aggressive, and disputes over respective feudal authority turned into low-level conflict. He cut down the great elm tree where kings of France and dukes of Normandy traditionally met to negotiate. He cultivated Richard, even sharing a bed in token of friendship, and persuaded him that his father planned to disinherit him. This provoked a family civil war, in which Richard was aided by Philip. In 1189, Henry II, ill and exhausted, had to acknowledge defeat. In a final meeting with Philip, propped up painfully in the saddle, refusing to dismount and sit, he accepted all Philip's demands: for homage for his French lands, for money, above all to name Richard his sole heir; and two days later, on 6 July 1189, he died. Despite his thirty-four years of unrelenting effort, the Angevin "empire" was beginning to topple.

This was not at first evident. King Richard I, "the Lionheart," was crowned in 1189 amid scenes of popular rejoicing and vicious attacks on Jews—a usual by-product of Crusading fervour. Richard, who would spend only six months of his ten-year reign in England, was eager to join the Third Crusade, part of the widespread European reaction to the recapture of Jerusalem by the caliph of Egypt, Saladin (Saleh-ed-Din Yusuf ibn Ayub), in 1187. A fellow Crusader was his former accomplice and friend, Philip of France, but a series of personal, political and national disputes soon ended their always shaky alliance. As a Crusader, Richard won a brilliant if chequered reputation. He was a vainglorious product of the warrior culture and little else. Certain events of his life have entered legend: his chivalrous encounters with Saladin; his capture of Acre in 1191 followed by failure to retake Jerusalem; his secret journey back from the Holy Land and arrest by Duke Leopold of Austria, whom he had insulted; his discovery by his faithful minstrel Blondel de Nesle, who sang outside his prison (fiction, alas); his £100,000 ransom requiring an enormous tax levy on England (not fiction, and reluctantly paid); and his release in February 1194—"The devil has been let loose," warned Philip. His sudden arrival in England in March interrupted his intriguing brother John's attempt to usurp the crown, with the help of the French, who invaded Normandy. (This is the time of the legendary meeting of Richard with Robin Hood.) John fled to France, and Richard soon left England for good to pursue a long and at first successful struggle against Philip Augustus and his allies, which was cut short in 1199 by a crossbow bolt fired from the castle of a rebellious Aquitainian vassal. Richard, in a characteristic gesture, forgave the captured crossbowman from his deathbed—who after Richard died was flayed alive by his men.

Richard's international reputation, cultivated during his own lifetime, long remained potent. It combined glamour as a royal model of the new aristocratic culture of chivalry—he was "bold and courteous and bountiful," in the words of a French minstrel[69]—with his unique reputation as the only Christian warrior who could defeat Saladin. The "Lionheart" image also fed on the Arthurian legend, at this time attaining a Europe-wide circulation through the works of the French writer Chrétien de Troyes (see p. 19). It was in Richard's reign that the bodies of Arthur and Guinevere were "discovered" at Glastonbury, and he carried a sword called Excalibur when he went on Crusade. But the longest-living part of the Richard myth comes from his later association with the Robin Hood stories, in which his bravery, goodness and common touch personify an ideal English king, in contrast with the "Norman" vices of the cruel and duplicitous Prince John and his unscrupulous sheriff.

## THE COMMUNITY OF THE REALM

John became king in 1199. He has left a uniquely bad reputation, all the darker in contrast with his brother's gilded legend. He murdered, probably with his own hands, his young nephew, Arthur, who was supported for the throne by the barons of Brittany, Anjou and Touraine. John was detested for his efficient rapacity and unlovable personality. But his role in English history is enormous, largely through his failures. His nemesis was his former abettor Philip Augustus, who in 1202 used his legal authority to provoke a decisive conflict. John had arrogantly slighted one of his French vassals, Hugh of Lusignan, by marrying his betrothed, Isabelle of Angoulême, and Philip, as king and feudal overlord, summoned John to appear at his court to have the dispute judged. When John ignored the summons, Philip used feudal law to deprive him of all his domains in France. The resulting war forced many barons reluctantly to choose sides or lose their lands: they were obliged to be English or French— they could no longer be Anglo-Normans with lands on both sides of the Channel. In 1204, after an eight-month siege of the great Château Gaillard, built by Richard to dominate the valley of the Seine in Normandy, and which Philip's men finally captured after climbing in through the latrines, the French conquered Normandy. In 1205, they were threatening to invade England. The kingdom of France—its income 70 percent greater with the wealth of Normandy—became one of the dominant powers in Europe, and so it remained for six centuries. Of the Conqueror's duchy, only the Channel Islands remained to the English Crown, given legal autonomy to keep them loyal. The Angevin "empire" was reduced to England and turbulent Aquitaine, from the River Dordogne to the Pyrenees.

John was obsessed with regaining Normandy. He spent ten years travelling the length and breadth of England personally extorting money for war—a longer presence than any king since 1066, and not welcomed. Baronial families, the Church, Jews and the general population were all exposed to his use and violent abuse of the powers of the Crown: he more than doubled his revenue in England, the highest level of exploitation since the Conquest. Expedients included selling justice, seizing lands without process of law, imposing arbitrary fines, and ransoming widows by the threat of forcible remarriage. There was worse: the wife and eldest son of one recalcitrant baron were starved to death in the dungeons of Windsor; three sons of another were killed, two after being castrated, and a seven-year-old by hanging.[70] Meanwhile, the conflict with France had become a complex and extended European war, as both sides sought allies. John recovered Poitou, but when at last, in 1214, he invaded France, he had to turn tail when his German and Flemish allies were crushed by the French at the battle of Bouvines on 27 July 1214—almost as famous a date in French history as the battle of Hastings in that of England. John's hopes collapsed.

Had John been victorious in France he might have defied resistance in England, but after Bouvines there was a rebellion supported by great barons, lesser knights, clergy and town burgesses (London was the rebels' biggest stronghold). It was inevitably exploited by the French, the Welsh and the Scots. The revolt had many causes, but most important were John's methods of raising money. In the longer term, it could be seen as a crisis of the system: after 1066, as noted earlier, the Crown asserted rights that left all landowners vulnerable. The rebels wanted to bring the king within the law. The result was Magna Carta, the "great charter," sealed by John in June 1215 at Runnymede, a meadow beside the Thames near Windsor, one of the traditional meeting places of the pre-Conquest witan—a significant piece of symbolism. It addressed a miscellany of grievances against royal abuses: concerning inheritances, administration of justice, tenants' obligations, rights of widows, liberties of towns, privileges of the Church, protection of foreign merchants, and demands for labour to maintain ramparts and bridges. The Charter even called for uniform measures of ale. Most of it now seems quaint, if not incomprehensible ("In what case a Praecipe in Capite is not grantable"). Yet lurking among the thickets of legalese were glittering phrases: "We will sell to no man, we will deny or delay to no man, either Justice or Right"; "No Freeman shall be taken, or imprisoned . . . but by lawful Judgement of his Peers."

"Judgement of his peers" has come to be synonymous with trial by jury. But the link is coincidental. Nominating a group of men (sometimes but not always twelve) to give an opinion on oath was an ancient practice, Anglo-Saxon and Carolingian. But this was an instrument of authority, not a safeguard of individual liberty. Juries were there to provide information, as in the making of Domesday Book or by identifying suspected criminals. The inquest jury in Britain and the grand jury in the United States are existing examples. Shire court verdicts were given by everyone present—often over a hundred people—amounting to trial by public meeting. Criminal trials, as in other countries, were decided by various forms of ordeal, to which popular opinion remained attached (as in the ducking of suspected witches centuries later). It seems to have been the authorities who began to have doubts about trial by ordeal, as so many shady characters were getting off. The decisive change came not from Runnymede but from Rome, where in the same year as Magna Carta the Fourth Lateran Council banned priests from taking part in ordeals— prayers and blessings of the water and the iron were essential to the ritual. At first, the king and his judges did not know what to do, other than keeping suspects locked up indefinitely ("yet so that they do not incur danger of life or limb"), encouraging them to leave the kingdom, or taking securities for future good behaviour.[71] Eventually judges handed responsibility for deciding guilt or innocence to an already familiar institution: the jury.* *Vox populi* replaced *vox Dei*. Roman law was different: it required either two concurring witnesses—rarely practical—or confession of guilt, and so inquisitorial procedures were adopted, with routine use of torture, and juries became obsolete across Europe. Torture was something the Common Law neither needed nor accepted, as became a source of national pride. But suspects were at the mercy of jury prejudices, and trials were very summary, usually just a few minutes even in the nineteenth century. Yet the system gave the accused some safeguards—they could object to jurors, juries had to be unanimous to convict, the acquittal rate was quite high, and acquittal was final. Above all, the jury gave some protection against arbitrary judgement by the state—though only in 1670 were juries given immunity from punishment for bringing in the "wrong" verdict. So Magna Carta, the Common Law and the jury system together became accepted over the centuries as what was commonly termed "the palladium of our liberties."

Magna Carta has been called the first written national constitution in European history, though charters between rulers and ruled were not uncommon at the time in France, Catalonia, Germany, Normandy and indeed England. In important ways Magna Carta *was* unique, however. Its restraints on the Crown (though later claimed to be the "gode olde lawe" of the Anglo-Saxons) were unprecedented and profound. It took the form of a contract between the monarch and the "community of the realm"—"everyone in our kingdom"—and it ascribed permanent rights and powers to that community, even its humblest members. It made clear that the king was under the law, and it planned a system (a council of twenty-five barons) to force him to obey it, with the whole community being bound by oath to help them. Consent by "the common council of our realm" was required for taxation. Magna Carta was not, of course, egalitarian, but it was inclusive, granted to "all free men," and also giving to every man and woman without distinction the right to justice, protection from arbitrary demands for money, goods or labour, and protection against forced marriage. It was permanent, applying "in all things and places for ever."

Over the centuries, Magna Carta has been given both too much and too little importance. It was reaffirmed thirty-three times, and regularly read out ceremonially in public, acquiring status as fundamental law.

---

* Trial by battle persisted in theory—one ingenious murder suspect invoked it successfully in 1818, after which Parliament hastily abolished it.

After declining in significance in the fifteenth and sixteenth centuries, it was revived by seventeenth-century opponents of the Stuarts and by eighteenth-century American revolutionaries as the foundation of the rights of "free-born Englishmen"; the United States Supreme Court has frequently cited it in recent decades.[72] William Pitt the Elder described it as the "bible of the English constitution." Margaret Thatcher compared it favourably with the acts of the French Revolution's Declaration of the Rights of Man. On the other hand, it has been debunked as a narrow legalistic document defending only the privileges of the barons. In fact, it showed little concern with purely seignorial rights.[73] However narrow some of its detailed provisions, its broad principles (inspired by canon law, custom and earlier charters and coronation oaths) had open-ended implications. It guaranteed legal rights in phrases that became familiar watchwords. This confirmed its importance and enhanced its myth as the first great public act of the nation, a source of power and legitimacy in later political struggles. Its guarantees of essential liberties are still on the statute book 800 years later, and in recent English jurisprudence on the constitution it has come to be recognized as one of the fundamental laws of the land.[74]

John fought desperately with words and weapons, both before and after he was forced to seal the Charter. He proclaimed himself a Crusader to try to gain immunity, declared the Pope the feudal overlord of England and Ireland, and appealed to him to annul the Charter (which he did, proclaiming that it "shames the English nation" and was "null and void forever"). John hired foreign mercenaries and required all barons to take an anti-Charter oath. The rebel barons, facing defeat, promised Northumberland, Cumberland and Westmoreland to Alexander II of Scotland if he would intervene, and offered the crown of England itself to Louis, son of Philip Augustus. This was the first of several occasions, from 1216 to 1956, on which the possibility arose of England and France being politically joined. The Scots came south, and Louis arrived in May 1216 with a French army, promising to act "for the common good of England." He was welcomed into London as a liberator. Alexander paid homage to him as King Louis of England. His soldiers, however, were soon accused of being "wicked plunderers" who "set villages alight, did not spare churches or cemeteries, took and despoiled all kinds of men, and by harsh and hitherto unheard-of bodily tortures, compelled them to pay the heaviest ransoms."[75] Both sides in the civil war claimed to be defending England.

Then in October John lost his war chest and sacred relics in the Wash, and opportunely died of dysentery. His nine-year-old son, hailed by a contemporary poet as "a tiny spark of minute beauty, the sole hope of the torn kingdom,"[76] supported by the papal legate and England's most renowned knight, William the Marshal, was quickly crowned Henry III using his mother's bracelet—John had lost or sold the crown. He would reign for fifty-six years. Support for Louis, at first widespread among the barons, began to fade, and Henry's supporters proclaimed that they would "deliver England from the French."[77] The papal legate actually declared a Crusade against Louis and his partisans. The French were defeated at Lincoln, and fugitives slaughtered by English villagers. A French fleet with reinforcements was captured or sunk off Sandwich and its commander hanged. Louis wisely gave up, and was compensated with a large cash payment. As part of the deal, an amended Magna Carta was issued in the name of Henry III. It was issued again, along with a charter of forest rights, in 1225—this was its final agreed version, approved by former supporters and opponents of King John. "Here then," comments a modern historian, "was the final reconciliation."[78] Until, of course, the next time.

Henry III came of age and in 1232 carried out a coup d'état against his own officials. He had great visions, and wanted a government of his own men. He aimed to restore the personal power of the Crown and play a great role in Europe, and he called in like-minded administrators and soldiers from Poitou, his mother's home—soon notorious as "the Poitevins"—and also later from Provence (where his wife came from) and Savoy (home of his mother-in-law). These men were capable and tough. His Savoyard uncle, Boniface, whom he made Archbishop of Canterbury—the last foreigner ever to occupy the see—ended a disagreement with one prelate by felling him with his fist. Henry had no doubt of his right to appoint anyone he liked as his servants, reflecting a Europe-wide trend for career administrators instead of the traditional baronial officers and counsellors. Many were university trained: universities were established in many parts of Europe, including Bologna, Paris and Oxford, in the late twelfth and early thirteenth centuries. But to appoint foreigners to major offices reminded the English that they were a subject people: and subjection now extended to the nobility as well as the "natives." On the other hand, Henry named his sons after English royal saints, Edward and Edmund. He built a Palace of Westminster and a new Westminster Abbey, housing the shrine of Edward the Confessor, as the centre of English government. He forbade the English Church to introduce the Inquisition. All his judges—the men who had most contact with the people—were English. So his use of French ministers was purely pragmatic. English barons, led by Richard the Marshal, objected; when Richard was murdered in 1234 there was an outcry, and for a time the leading "Poitevins" were removed.

What brought on a crisis was Henry's European policy. He tried to win back Normandy, but was defeated by the French in July 1242 at Taille-bourg and Saintes. His attention turned south, where his domains in Gascony provided a link with potential allies against the kings of France (he had marriage links not only with Provence and Savoy, but also with Castile) and a stepping-stone towards the Mediterranean. The rulers of Savoy, who controlled access to Italy, recognized him as their overlord in 1246. He made deals with the Welsh and the Scots (who received part of Northumbria) to keep the borders quiet. But his activities in southern Europe grew ever more complex, far-reaching and expensive. In 1253, for the first time, each shire was ordered to elect two knights to attend a council in April, along with the magnates and prelates but meeting separately from them, to agree to taxation on behalf of the lesser landowners. This was later seen as another landmark in the history of Parliament, though nothing much happened as the assembly broke up without agreement.

England, although peripheral, was one of Europe's wealthier countries thanks to its agriculture, developed commerce and wool exports. Henry was eager to use these resources to exercise power at the heart of the European world, in Italy, Germany and even Jerusalem, to make the Plantagenets the greatest dynasty in Christendom. Pope Alexander IV encouraged this vaulting ambition as an instrument in the papacy's epic struggle with the imperial house of Hohenstaufen: "We wish to exalt the royal family of England," he wrote in 1255, "which we view with special affection, above the other kings and princes of the world."[79] Moreover, since King John had declared England a papal fief, its kings were theoretically his vassals. The Pope made Henry's son Edmund titular king of Sicily and southern Italy, and in 1257 arranged for his brother, Richard of Cornwall, to be crowned king of the Romans in Charlemagne's imperial capital of Aachen. This proclaimed him heir to the crown of the Holy Roman Empire, which, apart from its prestige, had powers in parts of Germany and Italy.

There were three huge problems with this European adventure. First, Henry had promised to pay the Pope the huge sum of 135,541 marks (so precise because it supposedly represented the money expended by the Pope to conquer part of Sicily), which of course would largely be paid by the English—and if not, Henry would be excommunicated and England placed under an interdict, both humiliating and inconvenient. Second, this was only the first instalment of what his European ambitions would cost, because he would have to fight to secure both Sicily and the empire—and he had also promised to go on Crusade. Third, Henry's megalomania would probably provoke a war with France and a French invasion; and the confusion provided another irresistible opportunity for the Welsh and the Scots to go on the warpath.

In April 1258 seven leading barons secretly took an oath to bring the king under control. Their leader was Simon de Montfort, Earl of Leicester, originally one of Henry's French entourage and his former governor of Aquitaine. He was the son of another Simon de Montfort, leader of the terrible Albigensian Crusade, which fifty years earlier had taken fire and sword to the Cathar heresy of southern France. Like his father, Simon II was a frightening figure: a great but impecunious and greedy *seigneur*, a renowned warrior, a man simultaneously racked by unbending religious fervour and rapacious personal ambition. Henry is supposed to have said to him, "I fear thunder and lightning terribly, but by God's head I fear you more than all the thunder and lightning in the world." The conspirators confronted the king at Westminster Hall and induced him to call a "parlemenz" at Oxford on 9 June to reform the state of the realm. From our viewpoint, both sides represented different mixtures of tradition and modernity. Henry stood for an ancient idea of absolute monarchy going back to the Romans—the barons consequently banned the teaching of Roman law. But his methods were "modern"—using a professional bureaucracy. The barons demanded to exercise their traditional duty of advising the king; but in doing so they adopted radical ideas of communal rights. Their motives of course were complex and diverse—from resisting tax increases to restoring the peace of Christendom—but all agreed that the king must be restrained by his subjects. Magna Carta had said this, but Henry had ignored it. Now the terms were to be tightened.

Those who came to the Oxford parliament in June 1258 were asked to take an oath in the name of "le commun de Engleterre." Communal oath-taking was an ancient practice. It had been done in 1205, when all males over twelve were ordered to take an oath to defend the kingdom against a possible French invasion, and in 1215, when an oath was taken to uphold Magna Carta. So *le commun* implied everyone, for all had a right and duty to take part in public affairs, at least in an emergency. This had sweeping consequences: the Provisions of Oxford, which Henry swore to accept, provided for elected committees to supervise the royal government, and for regular public "parlemenz." Moreover, Henry, as "king on Engleneloande," promised this in English to his "loandes folk," the people of the land—the first document issued in the king's name in English since the Conquest.[80]

But in 1261 Henry, supported by the Pope and Louis IX of France, renounced the agreement. Armed conflict began in 1263, and at the battle of Lewes on 14 May 1264 Henry was taken prisoner. The *Song of Lewes*[81] (a long Latin poem) asserted that "the community of the realm [*communitas regni*] should advise and let it be known what everyone [*universitas*] feels, for their own laws are most familiar to them . . . the customs of the realm passed down from father to son." The king's son Edward escaped and raised an army. Montfort found support in London, among the clergy, lesser knights and landowners, and even among peasants. But clashes of interest and political complexities wore down rebel support. The two sides finally fought it out at Evesham on 4 August 1265, and the rebel army was crushed. A phalanx of twelve knights had the task of killing Montfort. He watched them coming towards him through the chaos of battle: "How beautifully they advance," he said, "our bodies are theirs, our souls are God's." His body was castrated and dismembered, and his head carried off on a lance. Under his armour, he was found to be wearing a hair shirt, the penitential self-punishment of the Christian ascetic. He became a popular miracle-working saint.

Our understanding of the importance of the drama of the 1260s turns upon the interpretation of words. Later generations saw it as a landmark in the history of Parliament, a high point in the history of English freedom. Was "le commun de Engleterre" the beginning of "the Commons," a summoning of representatives of the people to take part in government? Many French and Italian towns had *communes*, which were civic governments. But this one concerned the whole of England. The nearest English expression was "loandes folk." However translated or interpreted, the sense was that everyone had some right and duty. For example, the villagers of Peatling Magna in Leicestershire fought their own little skirmish in the name of the "community of the realm" against a royalist band in 1265, just after the battle of Evesham, and later took the dispute to the king's court (they lost).[82] Perhaps we could take this as another birth of England, as a formally recognized, if embryonic, political community. Or perhaps a rebirth. The Conquest distorted what has been called a constitutional tradition begun with the "Angelcynnes witan": after 1066, when councils or parliaments met, they did so as the vassals of a foreign lord, not the representatives of a free nation.[83] But after 1200, these councils took tentative steps towards identifying themselves as representative of the whole community, in opposing the European priorities of their rulers and the heavy taxes required to finance them. After a gap of 200 years, a common English political identity began to re-emerge.

# Five Centuries After Bede

What was this political community of Engelonde—or Engleterre—and its people, 500 years after Bede's history of the *gens Anglorum*, and after 250 years of being ruled by Danes, Normans and Frenchmen?[1] Remarkably, the English still seemed a recognizable group (or so said foreign observers) who were rich, open-handed, convivial and rather vulgar—as a censorious French observer put it, "above all other peoples, drinkers, gluttons, and profligate wasters of all temporal goods."[2] There was a persistent story that Harold's men at Hastings had been suffering from hangovers. Continentals recognized the English by dress and manners; many apparently believed they had tails—a story that originated in a French history of St. Augustine.

We should not suppose, however, that this survival of an English identity was inevitable. As an American historian has recently remarked, "The tremendous strength of Englishness in our own world view can make the survival of that identity [seem] almost natural or foreordained."[3] But it was not. Bede's *gens Anglorum*, politically fragile, were repeatedly invaded and conquered. Much of eastern and northern England was ceded to invaders. The whole country briefly became part of a Scandinavian empire. It was soon after taken over by a Norman warrior class, incorporated into a large Continental conglomeration, and came close to being united with the kingdom of France. Its leaders were eliminated, its language lost status, and its new elite and those who aspired to join them primarily used Latin and French. In such circumstances, ethnic identities can disappear, just as Britons were replaced by, or grew into, Anglo-Saxons, and Gallo-Romans into Franks.

That Engelonde did not become Grande Normandie or France Occidentale argues that its identity had been strongly established well before 1066, and that the idea of Englishness had sufficient attractive power to persuade descendants of Danish and Norman conquerors that they were, and wished to be, English. That identity was in part based on a powerful sense of England as a place,[4] in which its island position was obviously important. Though the sea gave easy access to incomers and though the northern border was vulnerable, the boundaries of England were mostly recognized and fixed from the ninth century—more than a thousand years before those of most European countries. Its shires and many of its settlements are older still—Hampshire, for example, predates any of today's European states[5]—as are some of its fields, roads and even buildings. It also had distinctive cultural foundations—a language, of course, and an ancient Church with native saints—including Alban, Swithun, Dunstan, Neot, the miracle-working virgins Aethelthryth and Werburga, and Bede himself, all proudly listed by Henry of Huntingdon. Not coincidentally, it was the clergy who became the main transmitters of English identity through preaching and prayers, and not least through writing its prestigious, celebrated and partly invented history. Women too passed on language, arts and traditions, as marriage between Norman men and English women became common. The towns acted as melting pots for French immigrants and English burgesses, who retained wealth and influence after the Conquest, when the native nobility was eliminated. In rural society, there seems to have been integration in the middle ranks, where some English landowners and free tenants survived the Conquest, and were soon indistinguishable from the smaller French feudal tenants. People of English descent took French names; people of French descent spoke English. Three or four generations after Hastings, they were becoming harder and harder to tell apart. King John's loss of Normandy forced a choice: landowners who stayed in Normandy had their English lands confiscated.

For all these reasons, by 1200 at the latest the descendants of the victors of Hastings (with the exception of a small number of cosmopolitan aristocrats with lands in several countries) had become English, by speaking English, describing themselves generally as English, adopting what were thought of as English manners (including drinking), and expressing pride in their English lineage, gilded with the glories of Brutus and King Arthur. When the chancellor Thomas Becket was sent on an embassy to Paris in 1158, he was determined "to show and demonstrate the opulence of English luxury": this included bringing lavish presents, a choir singing English songs, and two wagonloads of ale, "that clear, salubrious drink, better in taste and colour than wine."

Much depended on context. Then as now, people had multiple identities. When consorting with or fighting the French the lords of England were "Engleis." They seem rather like Dutch colonists in South Africa calling themselves "Afrikaaners": they remained very different from the *nativi* or *Anglici*—the wholly English majority. When a legal treatise of 1179 commented that "nowadays . . . the nations are so mixed," it added significantly, "I speak of free people."[6] We cannot know much about what the natives thought of their newly minted "English" rulers. There are very occasional signs: outlaws in the forests; riots against French liturgy and against French visitors who denied that King Arthur was a real person; cheering for an "Englishman" (Anglus) to win a joust. Perhaps above all there is the veneration of two men of French origin who became popular English saints because they defied the king—Thomas Becket and Simon de Montfort.

The Englishness of the twelfth- and thirteenth-century elite was in any case very different from Englishness before 1066, whose culture there was no effort to rehabilitate or revive. Sir Lancelot replaced Beowulf as a literary hero. Relations with the outside world were transformed. England before 1066 had been on the defensive, and relations with island neighbours (despite their regular raids or invasions) had been generally cautious. The Norman Conquest made a crucial change. Before 1066 the kingdom served principally to defend the country, the eard. After 1066, England served to support largely absentee kings in their pursuit of external power. The Normans extended their conquest to the Celtic lands and entangled England in endless conflicts on the Continent. This was the real "Norman Yoke."

Its burden created the embryo of a national polity: the *communitas regni* appealed to in Magna Carta and then again in the barons' revolt of 1258. This "community of the realm"—ultimately everyone—united in asserting rights against their rulers, especially when those rulers treated England's interests as secondary. As the barons protested to the Pope in 1258, "a prince owes all his duty to God, very much to his country [*patria*], much to his family and neighbours, and nothing whatsoever to aliens."[7] Loyalty to the country could conflict with loyalty to the king, and a sense of foreign oppression became a feature of English identity.

What was unique about England lies in the realm of politics: the early development, in response to Viking invasions, of a powerful kingdom occupying a defined territory, with a system of government in which a large part of the population participated, whether they liked it or not—through courts and juries, through tithings, through labour, taxation and military service, through the use of royal coins, and, for the powerful, through royal councils and parliaments. Some historians have suggested that this made England the prototype of the nation-state.[8] Similar institutions to those of England had existed at times in other parts of Europe, particularly under the empire of Charlemagne, but they were swept away.

In England they survived. Being a powerful and yet vulnerable kingdom, able to raise taxes and impose law and order, and yet subject to disputed royal succession and foreign invasion, its kings needed the support of their people, and the people high and low needed to control the actions of their kings. Anglo-Saxon institutions, some of very ancient origin, were preserved and developed by the post-Conquest monarchy, which extended royal justice and created a Common Law. The country of Bede's *gens Anglorum* was never divided up into autonomous and warring feudal territories. Instead, the "community of the realm" imposed the rule of law on its powerful and rapacious post-Conquest monarchs to a degree unique in Europe.

The Common Law and Magna Carta were seen not as revolutionary innovations, but as restatements of ancient principles. The distinctness of the Common Law became a source of pride. The lawyer Sir John Fortescue's *De laudibus legum Angliae* (In Praise of the Law of England), written in the 1460s, even asserted that the Common Law was the most ancient in the world, unchanging custom that had survived all England's conquests.[9] But only from the sixteenth to the eighteenth centuries did this take on weighty ideological significance: the law was claimed to be above and beyond royal absolutism and hence the safeguard of liberty. This significance it has subsequently retained, at least subliminally. Moreover, by an unpredictable historical twist, "the insular and arcane learning of the small band of lawyers who argued cases in a corner of Westminster Hall became the law by which a third of the people of the earth were governed and protected, the second [after Roman law] of the two great systems of jurisprudence known to the world."[10]

Continuity is crucial in this story. Many of the jumbled ingredients of nationhood—beliefs, myths, institutions, customs, loyalties—that were already present in the ninth century were revived or reinvented in the twelfth. Thereafter they gained in potency because they persisted, deriving legitimacy from their ever-growing antiquity, enhanced by linking them with the real or mythical pasts of St. Edward the Confessor and King Arthur. England's laws and institutions came to seem untouchable and immutable, as if in the nature of things, dating from time immemorial. They could then be seen, in Edmund Burke's famous phrase of 1791, as creating "a partnership between those who are living, those who are dead, and those who are to be born." In such ways nations and identities are "constructed": that is, made by people, and not determined by geography, genes or blood.

# PART TWO

# THE ENGLISH UNLEASHED

The next three centuries saw the English unleashed: against their neighbours; from humiliating bonds of lordship; at times, against their monarchs; from the culture that had predominated since the Norman Conquest; against the Church; and against each other. Wars for defence and conquest were fought on every land border, and across the sea in France, Flanders, Ireland and Spain. The subject status of villeinage (see pp. 94–95), one of the targets of the 1381 Peasants' Revolt and a source of constant local resistance, largely disappeared, four centuries earlier than in most of Europe. Four kings were overthrown and killed, the nobility weakened, and ordinary people thrust their way into politics, claiming both ancient rights and a new voice. A modernized English language replaced French and Latin as the first language of politics, business, literature, law, even religion. The power and wealth of the Latin Church and its clergy were questioned. These upheavals coincided with—indeed, were connected with—devastating wars and social and economic catastrophe: population pressure, famine, plague and depopulation. Yet hardly, if ever, was the existence or unity of the nation, or the functioning of its institutions, seriously threatened. Despite everything, this was not a time of war of all against all. Revolts and civil wars aimed not to destroy but to restore what was believed to be the proper working of kingdom, Church and society. The worst civil violence was short, and the rule of law, however imperfect, was quickly restored.

Some of this history is linked with European and global changes: famine and plague, due to volcanic eruptions and microbes. England became briefly a great European power, though later outdistanced by a resurgent France and the new power of the Habsburgs. Geography distanced it from the mighty confrontations between Islam and Christianity in the Mediterranean world, the economic and intellectual focus of Europe.

Most of humanity was still fragmented by distance: great empires in China, India and Africa were shrouded in myth. Only at the very end of the period did Italians, Spanish and Portuguese begin epoch-making contacts with east Asia and the western hemisphere. England, shaken by internal conflicts, by then had been left on the margins.

# CHAPTER 3

# A Well Good Land

*Engelond his a wel god lond, ich wene ech londe best.*
Robert of Gloucester, *Chronicle* (*c.*1300)

The country recovered quickly from the civil war of the 1260s. Edward I informed the Pope in 1275 that he aimed at "bettering the state of the English Church and the reform of the kingdom, and . . . a general increase in the well being of the people."[1] This was a time of transforming growth, far beyond the control of rulers. The quantity of money in circulation tripled, due to commerce, credit, the spread of cash rents, the growth of towns, export earnings and growing population. Agriculture was becoming more commercial, with surpluses of corn, livestock, wool, timber and other raw materials being sold. All types of land were carefully used and managed for different purposes; even barren sandy heaths were "turned into gold" by large-scale rabbit warrens.[2] One of the biggest money-earners was wool, of which some twelve million fleeces were exported annually in the early 1300s, mainly from peasant flocks; and transporting this quantity—up to 6,000 tons—required tens of thousands of horses, large numbers of carts, and ships. There were now 800,000 oxen and 400,000 (much faster) horses, multiplying the muscle power of the male labour force six or seven times. The road system, expanding from the Roman roads still in use, was even denser than in the twenty-first century, and permitted quick and easy communications. There are many recorded examples of long journeys averaging twenty or thirty miles a day— Edward I's record was thirty-four miles in 1300 with court and household.[3] Speeds did not significantly improve until the railway age.

The most recent agricultural and social revolution, beginning before the Norman Conquest, was the spread of the collective open-field system, as populations grew into areas less densely settled and suitable for arable cultivation, and for example where heavier soils required more labour.[4]

Here each village's land was divided into two or three huge open fields, with cereals the main product, and with one field left fallow in turn for grazing, manuring and recovery of the soil. The great fields were often ploughed into a "ridge and furrow" pattern—the easiest way to use big teams of oxen—whose undulations are visible today under the pasture to which many fields were later converted. Households owned strips of land in each field, which they cultivated individually, but with the rules for ploughing, sowing, harvesting and grazing laid down collectively. Similar community agriculture also developed in parts of France, Scandinavia, Germany and eastern Europe.

The open-field system reached its peak in the 1300s, when it covered between a quarter and a third of England in a great belt descending from the north-east, through the Midlands, to Dorset and Hampshire. This central zone of "planned countryside" contrasted with the areas of "ancient countryside" to the west and east. The difference spanned the centuries, and still remains:

> On the one hand . . . the England of hamlets, medieval farms in hollows of the hills, lonely moats and great barns . . . ancient trees, cavernous hollo-ways and many footpaths, fords, irregularly shaped groves with thick hedges . . . an intricate land of mystery and surprise. On the other hand . . . the England of big villages, few, busy roads, thin hawthorn hedges . . . a predictable land of wide views, sweeping sameness and straight lines.[5]

"Planned" central England was a country of villages, each with a church, houses in uniform plots, and gardens along a street or round a green for common grazing. It was a stable system, economically and socially, with security being purchased by immobility: village boundaries lasted for centuries.

The "ancient countryside" to the west and east featured scattered farms and isolated settlements. In the west of the country there was more graz-ing land. In East Anglia and south-eastern England, densely settled regions, there was more intensive agriculture, using fields marked out by Iron Age or Roman settlers—some still extant today, bounded by hedges a thou-sand years old.[6] Already, large areas of wetlands had been drained and cultivated. Rural Norfolk in 1300 was as developed and populated as it would be in 1800.

Economic growth allowed more peasants to marry earlier, as they could support a family by combining a smallholding with wage-earning and trading—for example, women spinning and brewing ale (the most widespread village business), and men mining, woodcutting or weaving. Relatively prosperous peasants owned livestock, carts and ploughs, and lived in houses of improving quality—there are houses from the 1280s still occupied today. They bought furniture, pottery and clothes. They ate puddings and pies, bread and porridge, and drank ale. The population tripled in 200 years, reaching up to 6 million by 1300—also a level not attained again until the eighteenth century.[7]

People on average were taller than in the early nineteenth century (the low point) but slightly smaller than today: the average man was around 5 feet 7¼ inches (171 cm), and the average woman 5 feet 2½ inches (159 cm). This reflects diet and health throughout childhood. Girls and boys were cared for equally; there is no sign that girls were unvalued, as in parts of southern Europe. A significant proportion of people suffered from sinusitis, tuberculosis or anaemia (partly due to intestinal parasites) and almost everyone had toothache. Hard physical labour took a toll on limbs and joints. There were occurrences of leprosy and malaria. Diseases (including eye infections and blindness) arising from insanitary conditions, unclean water and vermin were endemic, though of course levels of immunity to infection were high and food allergies absent. Many monks, fitting popular legend, were obese. Agriculture was a dangerous occupation, as even relatively minor accidents—an infected cut, a kick from a horse—could prove fatal. So average life expectancy at birth for men was just over thirty, and for women just under—similar to several African countries today. But people who survived childhood, whether peasants or nobles, now had a good chance of reaching their forties, and those who reached fifty would probably live on to old age.[8]

Population expansion created new rural settlements, with farms won from woodland, heath and marsh. It also entailed new trades and migration to mushrooming new towns, of which there were over 800 in England by 1300, compared with eighty in Wales and fifty in Scotland. Towns were created more rapidly than at any other time in our history, with over fifty established between 1200 and 1320, including Weymouth, Salisbury, Leeds and Liverpool. Many were planned as an investment by lay or ecclesiastical lords. Houses and gardens were often built on uniform plots, held by rented "burgage tenure"; the pattern can still be seen in small towns today. By 1300, about 20 percent of the population lived in towns—similar to present-day Cambodia. By far the biggest town was London, the second-largest in northern Europe, after Paris, with perhaps 80,000 people. Next came Norwich, with 20,000. A few other important towns (Lincoln, Coventry, Oxford) had about 5,000; but most had under 2,000 people. Towns were above all markets, the main source of profit for their inhabitants and landlords. Some became centres of trades and manufacture, developing specializations maintained for centuries. Unlike in Flanders or Italy, English towns could not rule or coerce their hinterlands: they had to compete to offer services. Many held annual fairs, and the more important ones—St. Ives, Stamford, Boston, Winchester, Northampton— drew merchants from the Continent. The largest export items were wool (England was Europe's major source of fine wool), followed by other raw materials—hides, grain, tin and lead—and cheap cloth. England imported luxury goods, including woollen and silken cloth, furs, spices and wine— a peak of 5 million gallons in 1308 from Aquitaine.[9] The big towns, many of them sea or river ports, were international trading centres and powers in the land, especially London, which had salaried military forces, fortifi- cations and unequalled manpower, and controlled cash and credit.

A town—usually termed "borough"—was defined by having a charter from a lord or sometimes the king, giving certain privileges, such as hold- ing a market. Towns were attractive to the discontented, the desperate and the fugitive, as well as the enterprising and the ambitious. It was possible to make a start there as a servant or apprentice—roughly a quarter of the urban population. That towns were dirty, crowded, smoky and smelly goes without saying—Shitelane in Winchester was well named[10]—and their burgesses frequently ordered clean-ups. Stray pigs were a traffic haz- ard. Most buildings were wood and thatch, and vulnerable to fire. How- ever, these were not particularly medieval characteristics, and the general atmosphere must have resembled towns in poorer parts of the world today. Towns were also cultural and religious centres. They acquired prestigious origin myths and legends (the most famous being Coventry's Lady Godiva story; and Colchester claimed to have been founded by Old King Cole— one of Geoffrey of Monmouth's characters). They were not chaotic places: they had systems of government, and many confraternities and guilds with social, charitable, religious and political functions, which linked their settled inhabitants together. Religious festivals, processions and plays (such as the York and Wakefield mystery plays) displayed corporate unity and dignity—participation was compulsory.

The conception of legitimate power was that it came from above, ulti- mately from God. Disorder was due to sin and divine disfavour. Legiti- macy also came from the past: rights, status, property, laws—all were inherited. So desirable changes were conceptualized as a return to a pris- tine original. The ideal was of a stable, ordered hierarchy, in which all knew and accepted their position. This would be manifested in acts, sym- bols (including legally regulated differences of clothing and jewellery— knights were not allowed to wear gold rings), words of "affection and subordination," and deferential gestures. The servants of great lords would kiss objects before handing them to their master. One landowner ensured being treated with respect by giving a small grant of land to another in return for bidding him "welkeme" on public occasions.[11] Quarrels over precedence were common. To serve a superior—above all, the king—was honourable. No one contested this conception in theory, even if many preachers criticized those who were "prowde in lokyng, prowde in spekyng, prowde in heygh crying abov ynothere."[12] Great lords were also expected to make gestures of Christian humility: for example, washing the feet of the poor on Maundy Thursday.

Fulfilment came from conformity. Stepping out of line could attract sharp and rapid penalties, both informal and where necessary formal. Illicit sex was severely punished, as throughout Christendom, by both Church and civil authorities and by spontaneous popular action. Rebels, whether princes or peasants, were given short shrift. Social mobility was regarded with suspicion, and was extremely rare: the law was one way to rise quickly, and lawyers were widely detested; the Church was another, and the clergy were often resented too. Being different—as Jews, outsiders and heretics knew—was perilous. The Jewish community, introduced after the Conquest, in spite of playing an important economic role as moneylenders suffered repeated persecution. In 1190 in York, about 150 Jews either committed suicide or were slaughtered by a mob at Clifford's Tower. From 1218 they were ordered to wear a pair of white rectangular badges as an identifying mark. Oppression culminated in the Edict of Expulsion in 1290, when Edward I ordered all Jews to leave England.[13]

On the other hand, there was not the huge, excluded and abandoned "underclass" of modern times. It is unlikely that the lower orders had any systematically subversive aims, or any formed political ideas different from those of their superiors.[14] A slogan of the Jack Cade rebellion in 1450, "Every man should have his due," was not something that anyone would deny. Until the fourteenth century England was free of heresy, the form that subversive ideas took; and so it experienced none of the horrific persecutions that wracked parts of Europe—Henry III had forbidden the creation of an Inquisition as a public nuisance.

This is not to say that the mass of the people were either cowed or contented. Though they did not wish to subvert kingship, lordship or ecclesiastical authority, they demanded that they should be rightly exercised: they wanted good kingship and good lordship, which meant that it should be strong, effective, lawful and protective of their rights. For they undeniably had rights conferred by custom, which safeguarded their possessions and persons, and they were willing and able to assert them. Violence was rare: "over the entire period from 1200 to 1500 . . . many manors, estates and parts of the country appear to have been entirely untroubled by either popular protest or open confrontation."[15] Appeals to law and to customs which regulated land use, rents, services, prices and sharing of resources were the preferred way of acting, though strikes and passive resistance were also used. Establishing what the customs of a particular place actually were was a common source of dispute between peasants and lords, and it involved appeals to the memory of the oldest men and women, who could testify, sometimes on their deathbeds, to how things had always been done.[16] Even villeins were able to take legal action against their lords, or appeal to rights enshrined in Domesday Book, ancient charters, or customs dating "from time out of mind." English villagers have been described as "ungenerous, suspicious, highly . . . litigious, as well as downtrodden,"[17] but they were certainly not passive.

Society was a dense network of communities and associations, which gave it great resilience. This was often idealized in later centuries: for example, by nineteenth-century socialists such as William Morris. The patriarchal household was the fundamental economic, religious, social, legal and fiscal unit, and its head was expected to discipline its members, if necessary by force. Children were taught gender roles quite early, including by helping parents work; but they were also given considerable freedom to wander around and play—play that could include useful jobs such as scaring birds or collecting berries.[18] Most people lived in a village, worshipped in a parish, and worked in a manor. Village, parish and manor overlapped, in many cases being identical. The parish was the basic social and cultural institution. A manor was simultaneously an agricultural, geographical and legal entity, with a lord, a court, and on average about thirty male peasant tenants. A lord might possess many manors or only one. Work on a manor was to a large extent collective and remarkably participatory: the community regulated activity, rights and duties through juries, assemblies, by-laws and customs. Senior villagers held offices such as constable, churchwarden or ale-taster. The Anglo-Saxon tithings, responsible for mutual good behaviour (see p. 35), still existed. It has been suggested that village football emerged from all this group activity.[19]

About two-thirds of manorial tenants (more than in most of western Europe) were unfree in 1200—"villeins," "natives," "serfs" and "rustics" were equally pejorative terms, though without a precise or uniform significance due to large variations in local custom and frequent disputes about precise status.[20] Free and unfree tenants both owed various levies and fees (including on death and inheritance) and needed permission, on payment of a "fine," to marry. Unfree status—an ancient and fundamental feature of European society—probably dated back to slavery or had been acquired more recently due to economic hardship, such as inability to pay rent. It was hereditary through the male line: as the great legal commentator Bracton declared (*c.*1250), "A serf can only engender serfs." Villeins usually paid part of their rent in labour; in theory they could not leave the manor without permission; and they could be sold (usually along with the manor), though not evicted arbitrarily. For all but serious criminal matters, they came under the jurisdiction of their lord, not the king. The gradual extension of Common Law to all free men, and greater legal protection given to tenants against their lords, caused a fundamental change in the way society worked. Even unfree peasants could in practice pass on their land to their heirs and even sell it. It has been argued that by around 1300 most peasants had become effectively free, and that remaining labour services were more irksome than burdensome. Indeed, villeins generally paid lower rents, had larger holdings, and accumulated livestock, equipment and goods; and manorial custom could give them more security than was enjoyed by free wage labourers in later centuries.[21] Yet in extreme cases of conflict with powerful lords, their position was legally fragile, as the abbot of Burton, Staffordshire, showed his serfs in 1280, seizing goods and livestock on the grounds that they owned "nothing but what they have in their bellies."[22] Villein status was regarded by all as humiliating, and people were commonly sued for using it as an insult—still of course present in the language ("villainous," etc.). One tenant of the Earl of Gloucester, reduced to serfdom in 1293, drowned himself.

At a higher social level the beehive of groups continued: religious houses, colleges, borough corporations, shires, noble retinues. The wearing of badges and livery was a potent sign of belonging and hence of status. At every level the right and duty of self-regulation and the disciplining of members was crucial, by both formal and informal means. Expulsion from the group was a serious sanction. It might mean social ostracism. The ultimate expulsion was outlawry, known from Anglo-Saxon times as "bearing the wolf's head": "'Wolfshead!' shall be cried against him . . . and from that time forward it is lawful for anyone to slay him like a wolf."[23]

"Lordship" was the fundamental political fact: the possession of land, which also gave legal and economic power over men. What was later conceptualized as "feudalism"—a pyramid of power and duty based on the granting of land in return for service—lasted for only about a century after the Conquest. It was eroded by land tenure becoming in practice and in Common Law permanent, and increasingly paid for not by personal service but by money rents—the number of such tenancies roughly tripled in the two centuries after Domesday Book.[24] "Feudal" obligations were also complicated by land being held from more than one lord, who might be rivals, or held by women or children. So military services theoretically owed by knights and labour services by peasants were replaced by money rents or were just abandoned.

Yet lordship remained a central economic, political and cultural institution. Lords provided protection, justice (or, when advantageous, injustice), order and organization—including creating settlements and markets, building bridges, mills and churches, resolving disputes, and enforcing (or not enforcing) the law. In return they wanted obedience and deference, the greatest profit that could be extracted from land and labour, and when necessary armed force. A few magnates, especially in the Welsh and Scottish Marches, could raise several thousand men.

From the thirteenth century, the power of lordship came increasingly to be obtained not from feudal obligations, but from mutually beneficial political and financial arrangements. Great lords recruited paid retinues, men "retained" by contract for administrative, legal or armed service. Lords also paid annuities to selected gentry or professional men for occasional services. More broadly, they built up an "affinity" of lesser gentry, usually focused in regions of their major landholdings, in which protection, arbitration, representation at court and patronage would be repaid with support—for example, in the law courts, in Parliament, and if necessary on the battlefield, whether in the service of the king or in private conflicts. The affinity has been compared to a medieval joint-stock enterprise, but in some contexts it was a medieval political party—and sometimes a medieval mafia.

About 20,000 individuals and 1,000 institutions (mainly ecclesiastical) were England's landlords in the 1300s. The Crown, though the largest single landowner, directly held only 3 percent of the total, compared with William the Conqueror's 25 percent, most of which had been granted away.[25] There was a steep hierarchy among landowners. "Barons" were the king's main tenants. "Earl" was a purely honorific title with no legal significance. There was no defined nobility until the fourteenth century, when peerage was established as a political status, based on hereditary summons to Parliament. But English peers never enjoyed a distinct privileged legal status like that of their Continental equivalents: before the law, they were no different from any freeman. Throughout the fourteenth century, there were rarely more than a dozen earls or dukes (a title introduced by Edward III), including members of the royal family. In the early 1300s there were about seventy magnate families owning large, though invariably scattered, landed estates—as noted earlier, no English magnate ever possessed a large territorial domain, as was common on the Continent, nor did they have such extensive powers over their vassals. The nearest were the military "marcher" lordships on the Welsh or Scottish frontiers, which at times were indeed "over-mighty subjects."

The seventy or so magnate families had incomes between £1,000 and £4,000 a year. The Earl of Warwick in 1315 held at least 50,000 arable acres in 100 manors. Below the magnates came a cascade of about 10,000 lesser families, smaller tenants of the Crown or of the magnates, who together held roughly a third of all land. Of these about 1,500 in the early 1300s were knights (far fewer than immediately after the Conquest), usually the wealthier, with an average income of about £40. At this level of income, the Crown expected men to accept the onerous administrative and military duties of knighthood—for example, as members of commissions of the peace chasing bandits, as sheriffs, members of parliament, tax collectors, coroners and jurors, as well as soldiers in time of war. Below were "esquires" and what from the 1400s were termed "gentlemen" with £20 or less. Some of these were little different from "franklins" (prosperous free peasants) or "yeomen" freeholders, of whom there were at least 3,500 worth £5–10. These small freeholders constituted an important part of the local political community.

Noble or gentle status was defined not only by land and money, but by lineage, manners and a code of honour. There should be an "air"—appearance, gestures and language—though this might have to be learned from courtesy books or by copying superiors. In the chivalric poem *Sir Gawain and the Green Knight* (*c.*1376), the inhabitants of a remote castle are delighted by Gawain's arrival from King Arthur's court because they can copy his courtly manners, including "talkyng noble" and "luf-talkyng" (love language).[26] Despite its softer side, this was a trained warrior elite. Chivalric literature, tournaments and hunting marked its culture. It was not play-acting: barons and knights really did fight, and usually wanted to, some at an advanced age. Edward III's last expedition to France in 1359 included ten earls, and Henry V in France was joined by every able-bodied peer—there were not many "gentlemen in England now abed" on St. Crispin's Day, at least among the higher orders. In the civil wars of the fifteenth century, thirty-one peers or their heirs were killed in battle.[27] However, the number of knights actually declined as lesser gentry avoided the costs and duties of the military caste. This became increasingly professional, serving the king for wages and profit.

The Church, the *ecclesia Anglicana*, was the second most powerful institution after the Crown. Apart from its power over minds, as the focus of belief, common culture and supernatural power, it was an enormous economic and social force, having accumulated collectively half of all the land of England. Its bishops and great abbots were comparable in wealth and power with the earls—the Bishop of Winchester held sixty manors. They too could raise retinues and form affinities, though it was unusual for them to go into battle like Bishop Despenser of Norwich against rebelling peasants in 1381, "a wild boar gnashing his teeth, sparing neither himself nor his enemies."[28] By 1200 the basic territorial organization of the Church was fully established: the provinces of Canterbury (whose primacy was defined in 1353) and York; nineteen dioceses with their great cathedrals, law courts and bureaucracy; and 9,500 parishes. Much of this would last until modern times. The wealth of the dioceses—twelve of Europe's forty richest were in England—as well as the gifts of the faithful allowed huge spending on cathedrals, including the new one at Salisbury (c.1220–60). Sumptuous additions were made to existing buildings to provide space for saints' shrines and the pilgrims they attracted, in a new, exuberant and characteristically English variant of French Gothic developed in the later thirteenth century and afterwards called "Decorated."[29] Every great Decorated project was unique, characterized by dense sculptural displays and often bold engineering, as in the Ely octagon (1330s). The quality of workmanship, especially stone carving, as at Exeter Cathedral, rebuilt between 1275 and 1335, has never been surpassed.

The parish, with resident priest, predated the Conquest, but only became universal in the twelfth century. Within parishes there were confraternities and guilds, especially in towns, which with feasts, "ales" and charity provided sociability, status and entertainment, such as festivals, pageants and plays, as well as piety. There were elected churchwardens from the thirteenth century. There were many hundreds of chapels and chantries (set up to pray for the souls of their founders), and by about 1320, before the Black Death reduced their numbers, over 4,000 monasteries, nunneries and friaries. London had more than a hundred churches. Even a middling provincial town such as Gloucester, with around 4,000 inhabitants, had three abbeys, eleven parish churches, three hospitals and three friaries.[30] By 1300, about one in twenty town dwellers were clergy, and over the whole country there were about 50,000 male clergy of all varieties—a historic peak—and over 3,000 nuns.[31]

Monastic orders, both male and female, created great landed foundations, notably the ancient Benedictines and the Cistercians, branches of extensive international networks. The Cistercians arrived in 1128 and expanded rapidly, establishing rural monasteries such as Rievaulx (founded 1131) which were important agricultural producers, especially of wool. Some were involved in iron and coal mining. The Augustinians had many functions, including running hospitals such as St. Bartholomew's in London. The Crusading effort had inspired military orders, the Templars (from 1128) and the Hospitallers (from 1144). In the 1220s arrived the new preaching orders of friars, especially the Franciscans (Greyfriars) and Dominicans (Blackfriars), practising poverty and living in contact with the laity in towns. Some important towns were dominated by religious houses, such as the great monastery at Bury St. Edmunds, one of the biggest churches in Christendom. Similarly, Oxford and Cambridge were colonized by their new universities (founded respectively *c*.1170 and *c*.1210)—the only universities north of Italy and France. By 1300 Oxford was one of the intellectual powerhouses of Europe, producing some of the most original and radical thinkers of the age, several of them Franciscans— Robert Grosseteste, Duns Scotus, the controversial William of Ockham and Roger Bacon. Such ecclesiastical preponderance was not popular. Cambridge was founded by refugees from riots in Oxford. Bury and St. Albans had frequent disturbances. An extreme case in 1328, in the turmoil following the deposition of Edward II, was when the tenants of the abbey of Bury St. Edmunds kidnapped the abbot, smuggled him to the Continent, and held him prisoner for several months.[32] All these great centres would suffer in the Peasants' Revolt.

The royal administration, in which lawyers, clerics and lay administrators could make themselves useful to kings, was another focus of power. Its roots went back at least to Alfred, and it grew and developed new institutions during the twelfth and thirteenth centuries in response to the demands of wars in France, requiring money and men, and causing the frequent absence of the king. Law courts, a chancery (which handled, drafted and sealed documents), a treasury (which held and disbursed funds), and an exchequer (which accounted for them) were from the twelfth century based permanently in the rambling palace of Westminster, manned by professional lawyers and priestly administrators, often with local and family traditions of service.[33] In combination with increasing numbers of royal officials in the counties, it provided the bureaucratic bedrock on which the charismatic authority of the king could rest, and it enabled the Crown to police and tax probably more effectively than anywhere else in Europe.

Royal jurisdiction, the basis of the Common Law, gradually extended to every village, and however slow, partial and corrupt it had value as a last resort, when local procedures to keep order or resolve disputes were not working. It was widely used because it was cheap, and increasing demand led to a multiplication of royal courts, sitting at Westminster or travelling through the shires. Reports of cases were issued, and professional attorneys emerged. Writs ordering lower authorities to bring a person they had arrested before a royal judge began as an administrative convenience, but developed into a historic safeguard against arbitrary imprisonment in the form of the writ of habeas corpus, first recorded in the fifteenth century.[34] The extension of the Common Law during the twelfth and thirteenth centuries fundamentally reshaped the political values and practices of England.[35]

Parliaments (variously spelled) were a part of this growth of a state. Parliament is first mentioned in an official legal record in 1236, when it is hardly distinguishable from a meeting of the royal council, part of the feudal system by which vassals had the duty of giving advice to their lords. From the 1250s, a "parliament" had a higher status than a routine council meeting, and it convened at regular intervals; by the 1270s it was meeting routinely twice a year at Westminster.[36] Parliaments met briefly, mainly to consent to taxation and hear petitions as a quasi court of justice. But in times of crisis—such as war, financial urgency or disputed royal succession—Parliament became the focal point of the "community of the realm."

The Church, the towns and the royal administration were the only channels by which a few men—and even fewer women—of humble origin and extraordinary talents could rise in one generation to wealth and political influence. Two outstanding examples are William of Wykeham and William de la Pole, near contemporaries in a time of war and socio-economic upheaval. Wykeham, a farmer's son, became an administrator and confidant of Edward III, who in 1367 made him Bishop of Winchester (one of the wealthiest offices in Christendom) and chancellor of England. De la Pole (d. 1366), a Hull wool merchant, rose by providing loans for the Crown to be a knight and baron of the Exchequer; and his no less thrusting descendants became earls, dukes and members of the royal family—a unique achievement, though a perilous one, paid for by exile, death in battle, execution and murder.

At the apex of society was the greatest lord, the king, whose word was law, but who had a recognized duty to provide good government, to listen to advice, to defend the kingdom, to respect the rights enshrined in Magna Carta, and, as sworn at his coronation, to give equal justice to all. The king had to be judge, diplomat, politician, communicator, in some ways priest, often warrior, occasionally killer. Yet this—"O hard condition, Twin-born with greatness"[37]—was not an impossible task, even for men of ordinary ability. Indeed, it was "relatively easy . . . as long as you obeyed a few basic rules," such as respecting landed property and not showing outrageous favouritism.[38] This was because the political core of great nobles, prelates and officials was manageably small (around 100 people) and more broadly because the king's subjects wanted and needed him to succeed. His failure would be their danger. It is a later myth of "Whig history" (see pp. 264–73) that kings were constantly struggling with restive parliaments or against their "over-mighty subjects"—it was an "undermighty king" who was the real danger to society.[39] Kings did not meet systematic opposition from barons, parliaments or peasants. With no police force or standing army, other than the household retinue, they could keep order and enforce the law only because their subjects, from earls to villeins, provided the muscle to do so. Kings still travelled widely, to see and be seen, and for hunting, pilgrimages and campaigns, their belongings packed every few days into convoys of wagons, their table supplied, among other things, by venison ordered from the huntsmen of the royal forests. Edward I made 2,891 journeys during his thirty-five-year reign—a move every five days on average. Edward II made 1,458 moves—a similar frequency.[40]

The authority of kings came from God, derived from royal descent. England's French-speaking monarchs traced this back not just to the dukes of Normandy and counts of Anjou, but to the saint-kings of pre-Conquest England, and thence to Arthur and Brutus. There was no clean and avowable way for such sacred authority to be resisted, even by Parliament and the "community of the realm." When royal authority was overthrown—as it occasionally had to be—it was hard and often bloody to restore it:

> The woe's to come; the children yet unborn
> Shall feel this day as sharp to them as thorn.[41]

God's favour would be proved by success, so a usurpation that lasted would eventually cease to be one. Failure, of course, had the opposite implication. But no such success could be complete, and perilous doubts remained, or could resurface. From the deposition of Richard II in 1399 until the accession to the English throne of James VI of Scotland in 1603, the royal succession was never secure and was several times violently interrupted—the nagging worry of English politics. France provides a contrast: the succession was rarely in doubt, and so French kings did not continually have to seek the approval of their subjects as English kings did at crucial times. So English dynastic weakness nurtured an English constitutional tradition.[42]

The most successful kings—Edward III, Henry V, Edward IV—were men of exceptional ability who also understood the rules and played by them: namely, that they governed through consent and cooperation, and that this was not a limitation but a multiplication of their power. The kingdom could survive mediocrity, factionalism, error, corruption and military defeat. It was menaced with disaster, however, when a threat from foreign enemies encountered kings who would not or could not play their part—Edward II, Richard II and Henry VI. In such cases, the kingdom drifted into disorder and violence. Although some took advantage of the breakdown of authority to seize power or property, the social and political elites as a whole had a strong interest in restoring order; and moreover were no more lacking in a sense of duty or public spirit than their modern equivalents.

It is a much later myth—largely a product of politicized seventeenth-century history—that English medieval society was chronically lawless, marked by extreme oppression, violence, exploitation and rebellion. Many castles built by the Normans soon became obsolete and fell into disrepair. The homicide rate in the countryside in the 1200s was about one killing per year per twenty villages—much safer than parts of South Africa and South America today. Homicide in London between 1300 and 1350 approximated to that of modern Detroit.[43] Security relied on self-policing, including the famous "hue and cry," which called everyone out by shouts and trumpets to hunt down wrongdoers. Popular justice was harsh, especially against habitual criminals and outsiders. Order thus created was fragile: disorder and violence could suddenly erupt. If powerful local men, guarantors of law and order, themselves defied the law, it was hard to remedy except by the intervention of a magnate or, eventually, the king. If magnates feuded and royal government failed, general mayhem could ensue. The troubled 1320s to 1330s, for example, saw criminal gangs including clergy from Lichfield Cathedral terrorizing parts of the Midlands and the north.[44] But we should not confuse the abnormal with the normal: most people of all ranks wanted peace and order, and were willing to act directly to ensure it.

The kingdom, in short, is best seen as a loose hierarchy of self-governing communities—manors, parishes, guilds, boroughs, noble "affinities," shires—with royal authority to oversee its functioning. The affairs of parish, manor and shire usually came first for most of the elite as well as for the masses. They were aware of wide differences of region, dialect, family, gender, occupation and status; and it was not forgotten after more than two centuries—how could it be, when it was still expressed in differences of language?—that the rulers were descended from the conquerors, the ruled from the conquered. The English, wrote the chronicler Robert Mannyng in the 1330s, were held in bondage.[45] Yet they were also aware—painfully so when taxes were raised—of a central power and its institutions, king, courts and Parliament, and hence of a "community of the realm" to which all belonged, with a unique and distinctive law. England was unusual in being, and remaining, a single entity. This was something the French monarchy spent centuries of struggle trying to create and preserve—and which was finally brought about only by a revolutionary dictatorship.

By around 1300, England was, as we have seen, an economically dynamic country, a prosperous agricultural producer, though far less urbanized, industrialized and rich than Europe's economic powerhouse, Italy. Its GDP per head has been estimated at $727—above the average for Asia in the 1950s.[46] But there is evidence of strain on its capacities. Population reached its highest pre-industrial level. Demand for land to grow corn meant that the area cultivated was not equalled until the eighteenth century; indeed, some land then under the plough has never been cultivated since, including the East Anglian Breckland and parts of Dartmoor. One-third of England's remaining woodland was cut down; in the Weald after the Conquest it went at the rate of five acres a day for 260 years.[47] Agriculture was at full stretch; its best yields were not outstripped for another 500 years, and never since has agriculture formed so large a part of the national economy.[48] Demand for land pushed up rents. The number of tenancies multiplied, and their size diminished: by 1315 the average holding was only ten acres, and over half of tenant households could not feed themselves, let alone feed the towns, which may also have been reaching their sustainable limits—London was already having to bring coal from Newcastle. This was not a danger in good times, as there were many ways of supplementing incomes, and there was a ready market in food. But prices were inexorably rising, with a basket of consumables costing about 50 percent more in 1310 than a century before. Real wages fell by about 20 percent between 1290 and 1350. Those with little or no land, who depended on wages, suffered badly; those with much land and produce to sell profited.

Wars in Asia Minor from the 1250s and internal conflict in France in the 1290s disrupted Europe's international trade, causing a general commercial depression. England's cloth industry slumped. Commercial rents in London fell after 1305, as foreign merchants went bankrupt. England was less badly hit than more-developed countries such as Italy, as its agricultural and raw-materials exports held up, and were even stimulated by the demands of war.[49] But it was left all the more dependent on agriculture, and thus on weather.

Good weather and hence good harvests could sustain the situation. But in the second half of the thirteenth century a disastrous fall in global temperature began, whether due to a series of volcanic eruptions or changing solar activity. It caused extreme weather fluctuations and poorer harvests round the globe.[50] There was a succession of storms, frosts, droughts and floods. In 1250 wine production in England almost ceased for over 700 years. A "great storm" in 1289 ruined the harvest. In 1309–10 the Thames froze. Catastrophe came in 1315–16, when two years of continual rain and low temperatures ravaged successive harvests. This became the "Great European Famine": seven years of suffering during which virulent sheep and cattle disease also appeared, destroying food sources and decimating the draught animals that made cultivation and transport possible. It took twenty-five years to rebuild the herds. The plight of the north of England was seriously aggravated by several years of destructive Scottish raids following their victory at Bannockburn in 1314. These years saw by far the worst economic disaster in England's history: some half a million people died of hunger and associated diseases. Law and order temporarily collapsed as people struggled for food, and resisted the taxation to pay for war on three fronts. Yet despite being ruled by one of its most inept kings, Edward II (finally deposed in 1327), England survived.

A generation later, in 1349, came an even worse disaster: the "great pestilence," which later generations called the "Black Death," humanity's greatest recorded catastrophe. In a few months almost half the people of England were dead. The plague attacked four times in thirty years and then became endemic for over three centuries. We shall look later at its transforming effects on English society.

## THE ENGLISH AND THEIR NEIGHBOURS

> But there's a saying very old and true—
> "If that you will France win,
> Then with Scotland first begin."
>
>                     Shakespeare, *Henry V*, act I, scene ii

At least until these disasters, growing population and growing wealth, notably revenue from wool exports, gave England's rulers the power and opportunity to act beyond their borders. They fought in Wales and Ireland, attempted in the 1290s to conquer Scotland, intervened in Flanders and later Spain, and in 1338 claimed the throne of France. This, it has been plausibly argued, created a sense of embattled English identity. Was it also a manifestation of a characteristic English aggressiveness, the origin, as some historians suggest, of centuries of English "imperialism"—"a thousand-year Reich in the making"?[51]

That such a disparaging characterization of English history can be formulated is itself of historical interest, a reflection perhaps of post-colonial guilt in our own time. Moreover, medieval English policy, particularly that of Edward I, offends the nationalist assumptions that have shaped historical understanding and sympathy since the eighteenth century. The ambitions of English kings were justified in their time by appeals to divine will, law and inheritance—*"Dieu et mon droit"*—which are meaningless to the post-Enlightenment mentality. The policies of medieval French or Scottish kings, in contrast, have been justified anachronistically as contributing to nation-building, hence their attraction even today to Scottish nationalists. Yet all sides were engaged in predatory power politics using identical methods—indeed aggression came far more often from the Scots and French than from the English, and English attempts to create cross-border dynasties were meant as political solutions to intractable conflicts.

To understand these, we need to look back in time. The Norman Conquest had itself destroyed equilibrium. The Normans were part of the aristocratic diaspora that surged across Europe in search of new territories (see pp. 43–44). A flood of colonists followed the warriors, setting up tensions that lasted for centuries in East Prussia, Ireland and the Balkans. In struggles for power among Gaelic and Brittonic warlords, these interlopers could be useful but dangerous allies. Normans penetrated into Wales, creating semi-independent lordships, intermarrying with Welsh chiefs, and joining in their conflicts. Richard of Clare, nicknamed "Strongbow," the scion of an acquisitive family that arrived with the Conqueror, was recruited as an ally by the king of Leinster. David I, who became king of Scots in 1174 after being brought up at the Anglo-Norman court, invited Norman warriors to settle north of the border, both to fight for and to modernize his kingdom. They became great feudal lords, and in time Scotland's rulers. This created problems for kings of England, whose freelancing vassals were getting out of control. Henry II invaded Ireland in 1171 to try to prevent Strongbow and his heirs from setting up independent Norman-Irish principalities. The Anglo-Norman presence remained limited, and to some extent was absorbed. By 1300 the "English" lords were composing Irish poetry.

The king of England was naturally regarded as the leading king in Britain.[52] Norman and Angevin kings reinterpreted this old-established claim to primacy—backed up by fictitious inheritance from Arthur, king of Britain—in the new language of feudalism, asserting overlordship and demanding homage. In 1072 Mael Coluim (Malcolm) III made an act of submission to William the Conqueror, and this was in some form repeated by his successors. Nominal overlordship, like the older primacy of the Anglo-Saxon kings, was at first deliberately vague and made no claim to internal interference. Kings of Scots took over much of northern England during the "Anarchy" of the 1130s to 1140s, and after 1157 were also great English lords, until 1237 hereditary earls of Huntingdon, granted to them by Henry II in return for giving back northern England. As such they owed homage to the king of England.[53] This was a form of non-aggression pact, as war against an overlord was forbidden. Similarly, kings of England, as dukes of Normandy, counts of Anjou and dukes of Aquitaine, owed homage to the king of France. Great lords held lands in Ireland, Wales, France and Scotland: at one time, nine out of thirteen Scots earls held lands in England, and seven English earls in Scotland.[54] Barons such as Robert de Brus and Bernard de Bailleul (both ancestors of Scottish kings) fought on the English side in the Battle of the Standard in 1138, where de Brus conveniently captured his own son.

This web of interests and obligations sometimes inhibited aggression. But it also created uncertainty and ambiguity. Legal attempts were made during the twelfth century to remove uncertainty by reforming, defining and systematizing laws, rights and duties. But this created disputes over jurisdiction and sovereignty that were exploited both by kings and by their vassals. Thus, for example, French kings as overlords claimed jurisdiction over the English king's subjects in France, and French officials travelled English territory encouraging discontented vassals to appeal to Paris. The English king could be summoned before a French court, and if he refused to appear—as John did in 1202—his territories could be declared forfeit, as repeatedly happened. One brief war began between France and England after a French royal official went into disputed territory in 1323 to plant a post bearing the French royal arms, and a Gascon landowner strung him up on it.[55] Or an English king, as overlord, might demand military assistance from the Scots against the French, as Edward I did vainly in 1295.

These underlying tensions could lead to confrontation. No less important was circumstance: all the great wars fought by medieval England were marked by chance and unintended consequences. This is not a story of planned imperial expansion—not, anyway, on the part of England. Indeed, coexistence seemed probable. In 1237 the Scots formally gave up their claim to Northumberland, Cumberland and Westmoreland, thus removing a source of tension, to the satisfaction of regional landowners, who recognized both kings as their lords.[56] In 1247 the Welsh princes accepted Henry III's overlordship. France and England remained at peace for decades.

However, England's problems were always its neighbours' opportunity. The civil wars against King John in the 1200s encouraged Llywelyn ap

Iorwerth "the Great" of Gwynedd to overrun much of Wales; and in the 1250s Llywelyn II ap Gruffudd did a deal first with Simon de Montfort and then with Henry III, by which he was recognized as Prince of Wales under English suzereinty. But a further series of wars caused Henry's son Edward I finally to decide that conquest—not at first his aim—was the only solution. Huge castles were begun in the 1280s to dominate strategic points in Wales. The turbulent independence of the Welsh princes was ended. A new Prince of Wales was created in 1301—Edward, the eldest son of Edward I of England, and the title became that of the heirs to the English, and later British, throne.

In the thirteenth century, the idea of "Scotland" in its modern territorial and political sense had begun to develop. In 1230 the northern kingdom of Moray was conquered with "breathtaking savagery."[57] Alexander III, aged eight, was crowned in 1249 with new pomp, proclaiming his ancient Irish and English ancestry as a proof of full sovereignty, not subordinate status to the upstart Plantagenets. He married Henry III's daughter, and in 1278 paid homage at Westminster to Edward I—but specifically for the lands he possessed in England, not for Scotland. Relations were remarkably peaceful until in 1286 came two extraordinary accidents. Alexander, riding through the night in bad weather to his new French wife, rode over a steep bank and broke his neck. Then his successor, Margaret, his three-year-old half-Norwegian granddaughter, died on her way to Scotland. This left no undisputed heir. To avert civil war, Edward I was asked to arbitrate between no fewer than fourteen claimants. He seized the opportunity to assert his feudal supremacy, backed the pliable John Balliol, Lord of Galloway, as king—he had the best claim—and proceeded to treat Scotland as under his overlordship.

Ironically, what Edward was trying to do to Scotland, the king of France was trying to do to him—namely, exploit the power of overlordship. As we saw in the last chapter, the old Norman-Angevin "empire" had been the hapless target of successive kings of France, aiming to expand their effective possession of territories at first only nominally under their sovereignty. An important aim for the French kingdom was to gain unfettered access to the Channel, the Atlantic and the Mediterranean.[58] Languedoc was bloodily conquered. In 1259 Henry III had formally surrendered claim to Normandy and most other lost possessions, in return for retaining Gascony as a fief from the French Crown and becoming a peer of France. This had won three decades of peace, but it recognized the king of England as a vassal of the king of France, bound to give him military support, forbidden to aid any of his enemies, and ultimately under his legal jurisdiction. In 1294 skirmishes broke out, King Philip IV of France declared Gascony confiscated, and in 1295 the French raided Kent. When Edward demanded aid from his Scottish vassals, instead they signed an alliance with France. This famous and fateful "Auld Alliance" would shape the history of all three countries. Confident of French support, in 1296 the Scots crossed the Tweed, burning and killing. This was the beginning of the "Scottish Wars of Independence" and the prelude to the Hundred Years' War between England and France.

Edward I rapidly defeated the Scots that same year, putting Berwick to fire and sword in the process. He removed the symbols of Scottish kingship to Westminster, including the "Stone of Destiny" from the traditional place of coronation, Scone. The Scottish throne was left vacant. A knight, William Wallace, led an uprising in 1297 while Edward was away fighting the French, and launched a devastating raid deep into England, committing, according to English sources, sickening atrocities. Wallace's adventure ended after the French made peace with Edward, who then launched a series of massive invasions of Scotland. In 1298 Wallace was defeated at Falkirk, and later captured, tried at Westminster for treason, and executed at Smithfield. Many Scottish lords, including Robert Bruce (de Brus), a claimant to the throne, paid homage to Edward, and by 1305 it seemed the conflict was over. Scottish representatives attended a Westminster parliament.

But the following year Bruce unaccountably murdered a rival noble, John Comyn, and was forced to flee for his life. Bruce was a Francophone member of the Norman-Anglo-Scottish elite, with lands in both countries. He realized that his only chance of winning the crown—and saving his neck—was to rally support by leading an anti-English struggle and in doing so outflank his Scottish rivals. He proclaimed himself king of Scots. Pursued by English and Scottish enemies, he fled. Three of his brothers were executed and his sister was put in a cage. But helped by the death of Edward I in 1307, the incapacity of Edward II, support from the French and the Pope, and the beginning of the devastating famine in England, he was able to wreak savage vengeance on his enemies and raid south. An English army under Edward II was smashed at Bannockburn (24 June 1314)—in retrospect, the end of English ambitions in Scotland. Edward I's epitaph in Westminster Abbey is "the Hammer of the Scots," but it was the English who eventually took the hammering. Enjoying unchecked military superiority, the Scots for seven years launched repeated and devastating raids.[59] The north of England was practically defenceless: the 1315–16 famine was thus aggravated by destruction of crops and the removal of livestock by the invaders. Expeditions mounted by the chaotic government of Edward II all failed. Edward Bruce, Robert's brother, invaded Ireland, proclaiming himself king and calling for a Gaelic alliance against England. The result was devastation: rival armies "left neither wood nor lea, nor corn nor crop nor stead nor barn nor church, but fired and burnt them all."[60] In 1320 the Declaration of Arbroath was an unsuccessful appeal to the Pope, who had excommunicated Bruce for continuing the war. It asserted that the Scots, "a holy people" who had conquered the land by exterminating the pagan Picts, had a right to independence with Robert as king: "We fight not for glory, nor riches, nor honours, but for freedom."

England was meanwhile facing a new kind of crisis. Edward II, king since 1307 and "arguably the worst and ultimately the most dangerous king ever to rule England,"[61] had provoked mounting outrage, heightened by military failure against the Scots and the French, and by terrible economic disaster. He provides a perfect example of why kings were indispensable, and what it meant to be a bad one. He was irresponsible, lazy, vicious, politically reckless, somewhat eccentric, and indifferent to the interests of any but his personal entourage.[62] Discontent focused on his close friendship—its precise nature is unclear—with a Gascon knight, Piers Gaveston, whom he made Earl of Cornwall. Gaveston was captured and killed by opposition barons in 1312—the first political bloodshed for a generation, and the first earl killed since Waltheof in 1076. But in the next few years seven more earls would die. Following a period of turmoil, there emerged, as Edward's new favourites, the Despensers father and son, who proved as greedy as Gaveston but more dangerous. One of their enemies, Roger Mortimer, escaped from the Tower of London to France and became the lover of Edward's queen, Isabella, daughter of Philip IV of France, alienated from Edward, perhaps by too flagrant sexual infidelity. Mortimer and Isabella invaded England with about 1,500 men. A London mob beheaded the Bishop of Exeter, a royal supporter, with a breadknife, and the Despensers were executed in a particularly cruel and humiliating manner, being disembowelled on a high ladder, in sight of all. In January 1327 an unusually long seventy-one-day parliament deposed Edward with the support of the clergy, nobles, knights and representatives of the towns—what a chronicler called "the whole community of the realm," and "a great multitude of people, especially the Londoners," who attended sessions in Westminster Hall. Perhaps for the first time, the crowd was literally given a voice, shouting for Edward to be replaced by his son.

This unprecedented act by a parliament was needed to legitimize the change of king.[63] Edward was murdered soon after, possibly, as Christopher Marlowe's play relates, with a red-hot iron spit. But it was hard to substitute for a legitimate monarch. As usurpers, Mortimer and Isabella could only survive by self-aggrandizement, bribery and intimidation, which eventually made more enemies than friends. They made humiliating concessions to the Scots and the French, renouncing English overlordship of Scotland, while acknowledging French overlordship of Gascony. The crisis was ended on 19 October 1330 when Edward II's son, the seventeen-year-old Edward III, puppet king since 1327, led a handful of friends by night through secret tunnels into Nottingham Castle, seized Mortimer, and took power. Edward was to rule for fifty years. For most of that time, "England witnessed an extraordinary fulfilment of the potential of the medieval state founded on cooperation and trust between the king, the landed elite, and the church."[64]

Fortunately for England, France and Scotland had also been going through political and economic crises. Charles IV of France died in 1328, leaving his queen seven months pregnant. Robert Bruce, after another brief invasion of England, died in 1329, leaving only a five-year-old son, David II, who had just married Edward III's sister. France needed a regent; and if the widowed queen had a girl (which she did), that regent might become king. The practice of using royal marriages to cement peace settlements sometimes had dangerous consequences, and never more so than here: for the dead king's closest male relative was Edward III of England, heir, through his mother, Isabella, to the French throne. The French nobility, unwilling to contemplate the English king as their overlord, came up with the argument that succession through a woman was invalid, and chose his cousin Philippe de Valois as regent and thence King Philippe VI. But a powerful ideological weapon had been placed in the English armoury: a claim to the French throne. In Scotland, the old succession conflict had restarted. Edward Balliol (son of Edward I's protégé John) was crowned with tacit English assistance in 1332; Edward III helped him further by defeating a Bruce invasion of England at Halidon Hill in 1333. Balliol ceded Lothian and Berwick to England, and paid homage to Edward as overlord. The French backed the Bruce cause, gave shelter to David II, raided the English coast, and planned an expedition to Scotland.

France, England, Aquitaine and Scotland were thus locked in deadly embrace. There was another contender, Flanders. This province, with its splendid cities of Bruges, Ypres, Ghent and Brussels, was, like Aquitaine, nominally part of the kingdom of France—though, unlike Aquitaine, most of it eventually managed to elude France's grasp. To keep the insubordinate cities under control, Count Louis of Flanders depended on troops supplied by the king of France. But economically Flanders was linked with England, whose wool fed the looms on which Flemish wealth was based—a trade immensely valuable to both sides. Strategically, Flanders was to England what Scotland was to France: both an ally and a breach in the enemy's defences.

War began in earnest in 1337. In May, Philippe VI of France formally confiscated Aquitaine and Ponthieu on the grounds of Edward's disobedience and rebellion, and French forces invaded. In December an uprising began in Ghent, and the Flemish rebels appealed for English help. Edward and the Flemish were vassals of the king of France—the source of their problems. To make war against an overlord was a felony. The legal solution was epoch-making. Edward decided finally to renounce his feudal allegiance to the king of France and alleviate his allies' scruples by asserting his own claim to the French throne. He was pressed to do this by Flemish leaders, as it would make Edward their overlord and give his promises to them legal force. A new royal standard, bearing the lions of England and the lilies of France, was first flown in Antwerp, to popular acclamation. In May 1338 the Bishop of Lincoln carried a letter to "Philippe de Valois," which was read aloud to the French court, accusing him of usurping the throne and notifying him that "we intend to conquer our inheritance by force of arms." Philippe, seemingly unsurprised, declared that "no response is necessary."[65]

Thus began what was later termed the Hundred Years' War, which was soon under way from Scotland to the Pyrenees, with repercussions in Germany, Italy and even the Muslim world, as a projected Anglo-French Crusade was abandoned.[66] Neither France nor England was prepared for the spiralling demands of this war. Edward III attempted to organize a great alliance based in Flanders, but he soon started running out of money and amassing huge debts. He had to leave his wife, son and two earls in Flanders to guarantee payment, and pawned his crown to the Archbishop of Trier, who threatened to cut it up if he was not paid. French invasion plans were disrupted by an English naval victory at Sluys in Flanders on 24 June 1340—"a medieval Trafalgar" which annihilated the French fleet.[67] Edward's demands for unprecedented sums in taxation caused a popular and parliamentary crisis in England, and in December 1341 the king—an impulsive young man inclined to direct action—sailed up the Thames and carried out a near coup d'état against his own government. Parliament and the "community of the realm" united against him, and there was deadlock. However, the military situation across the Channel improved, when rival claimants to the autonomous Duchy of Brittany began a war. Edward, deploying his claim to the French throne, began supporting discontented vassals against Philippe—precisely what previous French kings had done to England. Soon he had allies in Brittany and Normandy as well as in Aquitaine and Flanders, and may have begun to take his own claim to the French throne more seriously.

Then came one of the greatest English success stories of the later Middle Ages.[68] Leading an army to aid his Norman allies and join up with the Flemings, Edward defeated the French at Crécy on 26 August 1346, capturing France's sacred battle standard, the Oriflamme of Saint-Denis, and decimating the French nobility. It was probably the first European battle at which guns were used. Among the dead were the French king's brother and nephew, eight princes of the blood, the Count of Flanders, the duke of Lorraine and the blind King John of Bohemia (whose three-feather coat of arms and German motto were assumed by the Prince of Wales as a tribute to his gallantry).[69] On 17 October another Scottish invasion was defeated at Neville's Cross, near Durham, by an army led by the Archbishop of York, and David II was captured. The English were then able to besiege and capture Calais—an invaluable gain, remembered for the story of the Six Burghers sent to surrender the town and threatened with death by Edward, then later hailed as patriotic heroes in France (and indeed England, as testified by their statue by Rodin outside the Palace of Westminster). The devastating onslaught of the Black Death in 1348–49 (see pp. 117–18) shook both countries, and the war staggered to a near halt for several years.

In 1355–56 began a new series of expeditions and deep raids. These *chevauchées*, or "rides," were a form of economic warfare, seizing valuables, extorting money, and deliberately destroying crops, buildings and mills, to discredit the French Crown and nobility, deprive them of revenue, and press them either to give battle or to seek terms. Raiding of this kind had been practised by both sides in the Scottish wars. The raids caused suffering to the civilian population, as was their intention, and French sources in particular stressed the looting, rape and massacre they involved. These formed the basis of a "black legend" of the English in France, still prominent in patriotic histories. Yet this was a standard form of medieval warfare, used by the French in Gascony and in raids on England's south coast during the 1330s, and prescribed by an influential classical text, Vegetius's *De re militari*.

On 19 September 1356, at Poitiers, a small raiding army under the Prince of Wales (later known as the "Black Prince," perhaps from the colour of his armour) crushed a badly commanded French army and captured 3,000 prisoners. This valuable haul included 14 counts, 21 barons, 1,400 knights, an archbishop, a marshal of France and, above all, King Jean II (who would only surrender to someone of sufficiently high birth—

as it happened, a French knight serving the English). Both the French and the Scottish kings were now prisoners, and the Tower of London contained the biggest assemblage of aristocrats in Europe.[70] France, under Jean's eighteen-year-old son, was in a state of chaos: there was an uprising in Paris, bands of mercenaries were on the rampage, and a peasant revolt, the Jacquerie, broke out. So Edward could make sweeping demands: a vast ransom and, in return for abandoning his claim to the throne, full sovereignty over a swath of western France from Calais to the Pyrenees.

But the French nobility fought back. The Jacquerie was suppressed by massacre, torture and the exemplary hanging of four men in every village. Paris was recaptured and the rebels slaughtered. English terms were rejected. So in 1359 Edward marched on Rheims, where French kings were anointed and crowned, with the intention of making good his claim to the throne. However, he failed to take the city, and his army was assailed by dreadful weather. Some, perhaps including Edward, took this as a Divine hint to moderate his terms—though pressure was maintained on the French by burning villages around Paris, and sometimes their inhabitants with them. Finally, at the Treaty of Brétigny (8 May 1360) a smaller though still enormous ransom was agreed for King Jean, and, in return for renouncing his claim to the throne, Edward was given full sovereignty (that is, he would no longer be a vassal of the king of France) over a considerably enlarged Aquitaine, Calais and Ponthieu. The victorious peace caused patriotic rejoicing and relief in England. The Commons thought that it meant "deliverance from the bondage of other lands and the many charges they had sustained."[71] It was called "the Great Peace," but contained the germs of an even greater war.

The prestige of the Crown and the unity of the elite, so damaged by the reign of Edward II, were restored by Edward III's victories. Embodying both was the Order of the Garter, which he created in 1348, after Crécy, to reward the prowess of his warriors, including poor knights, and to link great magnates with members of the royal family and household. The order met annually at Windsor for St. George's Day—a military saint whom Edward now made England's patron, with a red-cross banner—in its own chapel, a magnificent example of assertive English architecture. In 1358 the captured king of France was present, and three queens, in a ceremony, wrote a chronicler, "never held in England since the time of King Arthur." Edward was fascinated with chivalry, especially the Arthurian legends. He had planned to re-create Camelot at Windsor, with a Round Table of 300 knights meeting in a special building—never finished because of cost, though the table hangs in Winchester castle. Edward in his prime was the ideal leader for a military aristocracy—bold to the point of reck-

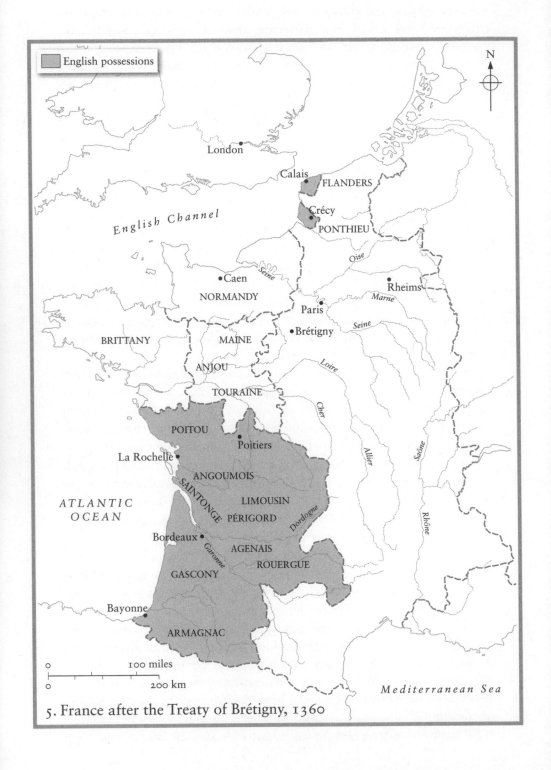

N

English possessions

London

Calais

FLANDERS

Crécy

PONTHIEU

English Channel

Oise

Caen

Seine

NORMANDY

Rheims

Marne

Paris

Seine

Brétigny

BRITTANY

MAINE

ANJOU

Loire

TOURAINE

Cher

POITOU

Poitiers

Allier

Saône

La Rochelle

ANGOUMOIS

SAINTONGE

LIMOUSIN

ATLANTIC
OCEAN

PÉRIGORD

Dordogne

Bordeaux

Garonne

AGENAIS

Rhône

ROUERGUE

GASCONY

Bayonne

ARMAGNAC

0          100 miles

0          200 km

Mediterranean Sea

5. France after the Treaty of Brétigny, 1360

lessness, athletic and gallant. In the tense moments before the beginning of a naval battle in 1350, he ordered his minstrels to play a dance and his knights to sing along. He practised the arts of courtly (and not so courtly) love. He had a sense of humour, as suggested by his attributed quip, *"Honi soit qui mal y pense,"* when he picked up a lady's fallen garter, and which became the motto of his new order. He forgave former enemies. In short, he enjoyed being king. For the qualities of an ideal knight were not only those of combat, but also of courtesy, comradeship, fidelity and piety. A "gentle knight" should be skilled in chess and song-writing. The incessant wars in Scotland and France exalted military culture and symbolism: the coat of arms became the sign of gentility, new buildings featured decorative battlements and heraldic symbols, and the tournament and the hunt were the most prestigious social activities. At times, knights tried to apply the idealized warfare of chivalry to the real wars in Scotland or France. Challenges to single combat or small-group encounters were common. There were even challenges to individual combat between monarchs—never accepted. Individual feats were celebrated. After the Treaty of Brétigny, there was even an abortive attempt at Anglo-French Crusading against the relentless Muslim advance in the Balkans, always the ultimate goal of chivalry.

But real war, while exalting chivalry, undermined it. One English knight, in a typical piece of chivalric bravado, rode up alone to hammer on the gates of Paris, no doubt to provoke a challenge: he ended up being knocked down by a butcher with an axe, and finished off by four peasants, who "hammered him like an anvil."[72] Common people were never included in chivalric warfare—its courtesies and restraints did not apply to them. But nor did they always apply to aristocrats: when the Oriflamme was unfurled, as at Crécy, it meant no quarter for prisoners; similarly, Henry V ordered the killing of prisoners at Agincourt. The great medieval battles bore little resemblance to Arthurian combats of knights on horseback. When the French nobility tried this, as at Crécy and Agincourt, it ended in humiliating carnage. The English had learned that lesson in Scotland. From the 1320s onwards, experienced armies fought on foot, knights alongside commoners, many of them archers; "feudal" service was abandoned. Routine activities of war—sieges, ambushes, raids, burning, looting, rape, slaughtering peasants—contravened chivalric codes. Richard II issued Ordinances of War in 1385 to try to limit the excesses. Yet, as a citizen of Paris admitted, where ill-treatment was concerned it was "much better to be captured by the English than by the Dauphin or his people."[73]

What most undermined the European-wide ideal of chivalry was that war became a political and national activity, and warriors became professionals. As wars lengthened, the costs became too high for fighting to remain a noble hobby: a warhorse could cost a knight a year's income, and capture and ransom could ruin the richest families. Under Edward III, even magnates were being reimbursed by the Crown, and the men they brought with them were paid retainers: an earl might recruit fifty men-at-arms and 100 archers; a knight, half a dozen esquires and a dozen archers.[74] The archers epitomize this professionalization: they were lightly armed commoners whose skill and strength with the longbow were practised from boyhood. Their arrows could penetrate the most expensive armour and bring the noblest knight crashing down long before he could use his lance or sword. The potential profits of war encouraged professionalization. Pay, ransoms and booty were worth the while of even the greatest: the Earl of Warwick netted £8,000 from ransoming the Archbishop of Sens, captured at Poitiers. Castles were built from such windfalls—Warwick, Bodiam, Caister. A lucky stroke could make a humble man's fortune: John de Coupland, who captured the king of Scots at Neville's Cross in 1346, received an annuity of £500 for life—he was later murdered by resentful neighbours. A great gainer was the chivalrous monarch himself, whose finances were transformed by royal and noble ransoms, which paid for enlarging and beautifying Windsor.

Literature both celebrated chivalry and hinted at its limitations. The stories of Arthur were retold and added to. *Gawain and the Green Knight*, written some time after 1350, is one of the most powerful late-medieval English poems. Only one early copy has survived, which suggests a small audience, but an elite one—the most likely owner of the manuscript was Sir John Stanley, head of a rising Lancashire dynasty. The poet celebrates courtly style, with details in French vocabulary of clothing, harness, armour, weapons—and hairstyle ("Fair waving locks tumbled around his shoulders / . . . And the full length of the noble hair of his head / Had been cut in a circle above his elbows"). The thrill of hunting is graphically described ("The shafts flashing through every break in the forest. / The broad heads bit deep into the brown hides. / Look! They cry and bleed, they die on the hillsides, / And always the hounds are racing at their heels"). Yet the hero, Gawain, is manipulated and in his own eyes humiliated, failing the test of knighthood. The poem ends with an enigmatic sting in the tail: what Gawain sees as failure is laughed off by Arthur's court, who decide to wear as their emblem what is to him a badge of shame—a lady's green sash. The poem ends "Hony Soit Qui Mal Pence," recalling the Order of the Garter, also a female token. So it may be in part a satire on the contrast between chivalrous ideals and earthy realities.[75]

A century later, Sir Thomas Malory wrote *Le Morte Darthur* (see p. 134), the most widely read and enduring Arthurian work.[76] Though the chivalrous saga ends in the destruction of an ideal, as the adultery of Guinevere and Lancelot leads to the breakup of the Round Table, there is hope through the repentance of the former lovers, and in the famous epitaph of Arthur as "the once and future king." Later generations both praised and condemned Malory's work—"the noblest Knightes [are those] that do kill most men without any quarell, and commit fowlest adulteries."[77] Only in the late eighteenth century and early nineteenth, amid the cultural revolution of Romanticism, with its powerful vogue for what became known as the "Medieval," was chivalry resurrected as an ideal "from the heroic age of Christendom"—and even as a model of gentlemanly conduct, though this was scoffed at by the more rational or less pious. The youthful Alfred Tennyson rewrote "Morte d'Arthur," close to Malory's narrative, but in verse of bleak perfection, conveying doubt and loss. Yet he hoped, tentatively, that chivalrous values might revive in "the modern gentleman": "Kind hearts are more than coronets, / And simple faith than Norman blood." Malory's action-packed tales had been moralized and become high art, exquisitely modulated and nostalgic.

## THE BLACK DEATH: AN END AND A BEGINNING

*I, as if amongst the dead, waiting till death do come, have put into writing truthfully what I have heard and verified . . . I add parchment to continue, if by chance anyone may be left in the future and any child of Adam may escape this pestilence and continue the work.*

A friar's testimony[78]

The bacterium *Yersinia pestis*, bubonic plague, originated in China and had long lived harmlessly in the burrows of marmots and gerbils on the Tibetan plateau. Highly unstable climatic conditions (see pp. 103–4), at their worst in the 1340s, caused changes in the disease and its hosts, and it spread to rats, rat fleas and humans.[79] It was carried to the frontiers of Europe by Mongol armies, whose attack on a Genoese outpost in the Crimea led to the first recorded outbreak of the plague in Europe in 1346, the year of the English victory over France at Crécy. The disease reached Constantinople in 1347, and arrived in Weymouth in a ship from Gascony in May 1348. It was probably now being carried by humans and their fleas and lice, and was thus readily transmissible between people, which explains its rapid spread along established communication routes: from Weymouth to Bristol, Ireland, and up the Severn into the Midlands; then in the autumn from the east-coast ports into East Anglia. During 1349 it crept across the whole island, averaging a mile or more a day. Soon after it arrived came the first deaths. Two weeks after that, the disease reached epidemic proportions: "Many died of boils and abscesses, and pustules on their legs and under their armpits; others frantic with pain in their head, and others spitting blood."[80] It was almost universally explained as a divine punishment for sin.

The disease was unknown in Europe, so natural immunity was low, and 80 percent of those contracting it died, some within hours. The mortality rate was highest for the vulnerable, already weakened by a succession of harvest failures. Children, pregnant women and the elderly were particularly hit. So were the poor, living in more verminous housing, badly fed and clothed, and without servants to look after them once they were ill. So were carers—women and priests. But no earls died, and only one of the royal family. Where entire households or communities were struck down, the direct effects of disease would be worsened by absence of basic care and by economic paralysis.

In England, as across Europe, perhaps half the population died.[81] Some communities were wiped out—in the manor of Wakefield it was noted that "the vill of Shelf is dead." In Winchester, six parish churches were abandoned. Crops remained unharvested, livestock wandered. Yet if society was shaken, it did not collapse. Even the dead were usually buried properly: although half the population of London died, excavations at the plague cemetery of East Smithfield show that bodies were not just thrown into pits, but were buried neatly in individual graves—proof that family, confraternity and Church carried on. Vacant tenancies and offices were filled. Even scaled-down war in France soon restarted, with its inevitable consequence, taxation. The unparalleled trauma left surprisingly few visible traces: England did not see the extreme religious reactions that appeared in places on the Continent. Though a large band of flagellants came to London from the Low Countries in 1349, whipping themselves and singing hymns outside St. Paul's, few joined in. Subjected to unimaginable horror, people carried on, and so the disaster was survived. This resilience even created the opportunity for greater freedom and prosperity.

# CHAPTER 4

# "The world is changed and overthrown"

Edward III and his parliaments acted vigorously to keep society running amid the plague. As they understood it, this meant requiring people to work, fulfil their obligations, and keep things as they had been before the catastrophe. This showed both an impressive willingness to take responsibility for a society in crisis, and also a stubborn determination to maintain the social hierarchy and hold back change. Royal courts acted to enforce agreements and payment of debts, and to maintain quality of workmanship. Flexible *ad hoc* decisions—what would develop into equity law, one of the characteristic features of English legal practice—began. Local knights were appointed as "Justices of the Peace" with the task of maintaining law and order and local administration, and they were ordered to meet regularly in "quarter sessions"—an institution that survived until the 1970s. An Ordinance of Labourers (made a statute by the first post-plague parliament) was immediately issued in 1349, followed by a Statute of Artificers. The aim was to fix wages and prices at pre-plague levels, requiring labourers on pain of imprisonment to work for those wages and forbidding employers to pay more; later, price controls were specified for various trades. Efforts were made to prevent serfs from leaving their manors and free men from changing jobs. People were forbidden by law to eat food or wear clothes above their station: ploughmen were only to wear cheap russet cloth; craftsmen and yeomen were not to have embroidery. Chroniclers endlessly decried fashions for daringly pointed shoes, tight hose and short tunics "cutted on the buttok [which] inflame women with lecherous desires." London guilds forbade apprentices to cut their hair "like a gallant or a man of court."[1]

These Canute-like efforts were in vain. The population had been reduced by famine and plague from about 6 million in 1300 to about 2.5 million in 1350. The pressure that had forced up rents and prices and depressed wages had gone. Surviving tenants threatened to leave unless rents were reduced and feudal obligations dropped. The new laws, though vigorously applied by local landowners as Justices of the Peace, were defied or evaded. There was an immediate leap in real wages as food prices fell. Employers had to supplement fixed wages with bonuses, free food, lodgings and allotments of land. Food traditionally given to harvest workers improved—even the poor refused "bread that had beans therein, but asked for the best white, made of clean wheat; nor none halfpenny ale in no wise would drink, but of the best and brownest."[2] Those who were denied better terms simply went elsewhere. In some districts, peasants tried to take legal action against their lords, or petition the king or Parliament. In 1377–88, at least forty manors in the southern counties asked the Crown to verify their entries in Domesday Book, which they believed showed that they had once been part of the royal domain, exempting them from labour services. At least one manor succeeded in establishing this freedom because it had belonged to the Anglo-Saxon kings.[3] On the Bishop of Lincoln's land at Sleaford, men

> hunted therein without his leave, trampled his growing grass, fished in his several fisheries, dug in his soil, carried away earth, fish, grass, hares, rabbits, pheasants and partridges, overwhelmed his bondmen with threats and insults, depastured his corn and grass with cattle and assaulted his servants.[4]

Moralists such as the poet William Langland (c.1330–c.1386) worried that society was growing unruly and materialistic. The Oxford theologian John Wyclif gained dangerous notoriety by urging in the 1370s that the wealth of the Church should be taxed. The struggle between the working population and its masters led to poisoned relations, with violence and intimidation on both sides, and a long crisis of authority. There was far greater violence from the 1350s to the 1380s in France, Flanders, Germany and Spain, however, marked by widespread urban and rural revolts, violent flagellant movements, and massacres of Jews and other minorities.[5]

In 1369, only nine years after the Treaty of Brétigny, the French had renewed the war by invading Gascony. A series of expensive counter-attacks proved ineffective. Edward III, in his sixties and ill, spent much time with his mistress, Alice Perrers, leaving government to ministers. There were inevitable complaints, part justified, that Perrers, her circle and ministers were abusing their positions. In 1376 the "Good Parliament" launched an extraordinary frontal assault on the Crown, for the first time led by the Commons. They elected a Speaker (a new office), who declared that the king "has with him certain councillors and servants who are not loyal or profitable to him or the kingdom," and they invented the process of impeachment, collective parliamentary prosecution of royal officers. The

Black Prince, Edward's heir, died in 1376, aged forty-six, and Edward III followed in 1377, leaving a ten-year-old king, Richard II. The French and their Castilian allies repeatedly ravaged the south coast, and encouraged a Welsh uprising and a Scottish invasion, further discrediting the government. This was probably the most serious foreign threat between the French attempt to seize King John's crown in 1216 and the Spanish Armada in 1588, and like all invasions it caused a furious popular reaction against those charged with the kingdom's defence.

Escalating discontent culminated in the "Peasants' Revolt" of June 1381—not only of peasants, but including many townspeople, craftsmen, village constables and other officers, substantial tenants, and some clergy and gentry. These were middle-aged, well-informed people, upwardly mobile and angry at the barriers placed in their way.[6] The poet John Gower had seemingly predicted such an outburst some four years earlier:

> He who observes the present time
> is likely to fear that soon . . .
> this impatient nettle [the people]
> will very suddenly sting us . . . [7]

The revolt was not an anarchic social upheaval. It was to some degree planned and coordinated, perhaps through local defence groups, and it had a set of clear political aims. The first outbreak, in May, was in Brentford, against collection of a heavy poll tax (a shilling a head) to meet the spiralling costs of the unsuccessful war with France. The other early centre of revolt was Kent, where there was particular anger with a government and nobility that had not prevented the most destructive raids for centuries by the French.[8] There, rebellion was sparked by the arrest of a man accused of being a runaway serf. The Kentish rebels marched on Canterbury and London, sporadically killing royal officers and "traitors." Violence against secular lords was normally very rare, and people were shocked by the violence that now occurred. The rebels showed political awareness as informed subjects of the Crown reacting to the events of the French wars and the divisions in Westminster.[9] When the fourteen-year-old Richard II sent to ask the rebels why they had taken up arms, they answered "to save him and to destroy traitors to him and the kingdom."[10] This echoed the complaints of the Good Parliament. Rebels had death lists, including the chancellor, Archbishop Sudbury of Canterbury, the royal treasurer, Robert Hales, and Edward III's son John of Gaunt, Duke of Lancaster, who had led court opposition to the Good Parliament. Other targets were lawyers and their documents—instrumental in holding down wages, collecting taxes, and enforcing seignorial dues; Flemish traders;

and ecclesiastical landlords, stubborn upholders of feudal privileges. Against all these there was serious violence. The most prominent demand was to end serfdom, whose breakdown the Black Death accelerated, making those still constrained by it all the more aggrieved. But few of the rebels were serfs, and this was not the only issue. Politically, the rebels were populist royalists, demanding "no lordship but that of the king," and expecting him to be on their side against corruption and oppression. They believed that the king needed them, and "traitor" was their worst accusation. Their watchword was "Wyth kynge Richarde and wyth the trew communes."[11]

London became the main focus of events. About 10,000 rebels arrived on 12 June, and king and government took refuge in the Tower. Londoners joined in the destruction of unpopular religious houses, prisons and the Savoy Palace of the hated John of Gaunt, built from the profits of earlier French wars. Lawyers and Flemings were hunted down and massacred. On 14 June Richard met rebels at Mile End, and conceded charters freeing them "from all bondage." Many then went home satisfied. Some rebels entered the Tower and executed Archbishop Sudbury and other royal officials. The next day, Richard again met rebels at Smithfield—now mainly Kentish men led by a certain Wat Tyler, one of the most famous unknowns in history. Their dramatic and confused meeting—the subject of many conflicting descriptions and explanations—ended with Tyler being stabbed to death by the mayor of London, the fishmonger William Walworth. The rebels in London, disheartened, soon dispersed.

Outside London, there were hundreds of outbreaks. The main targets were ecclesiastical landowners. There were violent disturbances against the abbeys of St. Albans and Bury St. Edmunds (where the prior's head was cut off and stuck on a pole), and against the university in Cambridge, where the urban elite supported the rebels. The chancellor was killed, the university archives and library were burned—a local woman shouting, "Away with the learning of the clerks!"—and Corpus Christi College, a large landowner patronized by John of Gaunt, was ransacked. Temporarily paralysed, royal government soon recovered, and by late June and July armed judicial commissions were travelling the country, arresting and trying rebel leaders. Dozens of men were hanged, including an excommunicated Colchester priest, John Ball, and the shadowy "Jack Straw," involved in the London riots. A man heard in a Cambridge pub lamenting the hanging of Ball and threatening vengeance was hanged too. Hundreds were imprisoned. But there was not the wholesale slaughter that had followed the French Jacqueries: "Nothing . . . became the English government more than the moderation with which it repressed a revolt it had helped to cause."[12] In November, the Parliament requested general pardons both for the rebels and for those who had used violence against them. All in all, bloodshed had been relatively rare.

This brief uprising had been more than just another rural disturbance. It had been a mass demand for rights and freedom, and had shown a striking degree of political sophistication on the part of the "trew communes." It was the first time that popular political and social ideas had been recorded in writing—England had an unusually high level of literacy thanks to its developed commercial activity. Political messages were transmitted in English through rhymes, sermons, handbills, posters, prophecies—and ministers of the Crown were killed by angry mobs because of them.[13] Understanding popular thinking is not easy, given fragmentary evidence, conflicting accounts (often by enemies trying to cast them as "rabidissimi canes," "the maddest dogs"), and the enigmatic nature of the sayings and writings themselves. The most famous rebel thinker was John Ball, whose supposed letters and sayings are a mixture of folk rhymes, prophecies and proverbs, such as "When Adam dalf and Eve span, Wo was thanne a gentilman?," on which Ball is said to have preached a sermon to the rebels at Blackheath. Or:

> John the Miller hath ground small, small, small
> The King's son of heaven shall pay for all,
> Beware or ye be woe,
> Know your friend from your foe,
> Have enough and say "Ho!"
> And do well and better, and flee sin
> And seek peace, and hold you therein.[14]

Interpreting such texts in full today is practically impossible, but popular ideas can to some extent be reconstructed from what the rebels said and what was said about them, and also by what they did. They conceived of a popular monarchy at the head of a free society, with law and order kept by the armed people, rather as in Robin Hood ballads. Tyler seems to have behaved to Richard II with the familiarity that Robin uses to his king—one of the things that got him killed. People everywhere burned seignorial records. At St. Albans and Bury they searched for charters given by Offa and Canute, proof of a belief in pre-Conquest liberties. They wanted fixed rents, and freely negotiated contracts between employers and workers. There would be no place for serfdom, corrupt officials, tricky lawyers, fat monks, greedy tax collectors or foreign merchants.

In the short term the rebels lost. The charters of emancipation were annulled, and Richard was reported to have said, "Rustics you were and rustics you are still; you will remain in bondage, not as before but incomparably harsher."[15] Similar was an assertion of authority by William Courtenay, the new hardline Archbishop of Canterbury: six of his unfree tenants, required to deliver hay and straw to him, had done so in secret, to avoid showing their servile status in public; so the archbishop forced them to parade publicly round the church carrying sacks of straw. But these were empty threats, and empty gestures. For the revolt was not erased from the memory of rulers or ruled. The Speaker of the House of Commons, Sir Richard Waldegrave, a critic of the government, even blamed the "riot" and "mischief" on excessive taxation, court extravagance and failure to prevent French raids.[16] The poll tax was dropped. No contemporary writers defended the rebels, but many conceded that the people had just grievances and that government must be improved.

The memory of 1381 inspired hope and fear. Other rebellions occurred in 1450, 1471 and 1497, literally following in the footsteps of Tyler and his followers by marching on London to petition the king. Seventeenth-century republicans and royalists too recalled 1381, though even radicals disapproved of what they thought of as mindless anarchy. When the French Revolution began, democrats such as Thomas Paine resurrected Tyler and Ball as proto-revolutionaries. Nineteenth-century democrats, notably the Chartists, agreed. Although orthodox Marxists were suspicious of peasants, heterodox Victorian socialists, including William Morris, admired them. Liberal historians were sympathetic to what they took to be a landmark in the progress of justice, liberty and even Christian Democracy. So after four centuries, Tyler and Ball were admitted to the progressive pantheon.

First impressions notwithstanding, the rebels eventually got their way. "The world is changed and overthrown," lamented Gower in the 1390s—not by a revolution, but by a multitude of small victories, aided by economic reality. After the great famine, and even more after the plague, labour was scarce and valuable. Serfs purchased their freedom ("manumission"), or simply refused to perform services, if necessary leaving to take land as free tenants elsewhere. Tenants of the Bishop of Worcester stated plainly in the 1430s that if he insisted on his legal rights "they would leave the lands, holdings and tenures . . . vacant to the great prejudice of the lord . . . and the final destruction of the . . . manors."[17] Lords gave way, or their land remained untilled. Some landlords paid tenants' building costs in order to keep them. By about 1450, servile tenures were largely extinct, replaced by "copyhold" tenure and money rents—"until the world is restored," hoped the Earl of Warwick's officials, vainly. John Paston (himself an upwardly mobile East Anglian lawyer) complained that his tenants were looking forward to "a new world."[18] Where ecclesiastical or lay lords were powerful enough to resist the tide, serfdom could linger into the next century, and with it the serf's burden of shame: in 1509 a Suffolk man, John Swan, was told by his betrothed: "John, I am sorry that ye can not . . . get your manumission, but sith it is so I woll not marry with you."[19] Yet overall the relative weakness of lords, the growth of a cash economy, and the legal rights of peasants under Common Law had already undermined servile status, so now it dissolved. Over much of the Continent, where these conditions did not apply, serfdom lasted another 400 years, and was even reinforced to compensate for the shortage of labour.

In England, tenants were increasingly free to use the land as they wished, including exchanging strips and dividing up or "enclosing" common fields. Significantly, manorial customs were now being recorded in English, not Latin or French, so that village communities could verify them.[20] They ran more of their own affairs—helping the poor, running the parish, passing by-laws. Food prices fell. Lords found it unprofitable to farm their "demesne" estates themselves for corn, and hence had less need for labour services. Instead, they let to farmers. The new term "yeoman" appeared, a substantial free peasant landowner or tenant. Much arable land was given over to pasture. Workers moved between jobs, and between country and town: many "abandoned villages" were not wiped out by plague, but simply deserted by people seeking better opportunities. Young people, particularly women, were able to earn a living independently of their parents, delay marriage, and choose their own partners—an epoch-making change creating what has been termed the "European marriage pattern." Society arguably became more restless and unstable, less dominated by family and community disciplines—in a word, freer. This was the time of "Dick Whittington," the poor boy who makes good, the most popular of late-medieval stories. The real Whittington became Lord Mayor of London in 1397—doubtless helped by being the son of a knight.

The terrible disruption caused by the Black Death, the subsequently rising level of per capita wealth, and the close connections with France and Flanders had contrasting effects on English high culture during the fourteenth and fifteenth centuries. Many craftsmen died in the epidemic, and building projects were interrupted or halted; and there is arguably a falling off in overall quality in stained glass, painting and stone carving, with a few exceptions such as the Black Prince's tomb at Canterbury, the celebrated Wilton Diptych and the magnificent Beauchamp tomb at Warwick. High-quality tapestry, illuminated books and paintings were generally imported from the more sophisticated urban cultures of Flanders, Paris and Italy, especially in the fifteenth century.

In music, this was a remarkable time. The late fourteenth century and the fifteenth are the first period from which names of many composers are known, and even some details of their lives and works. Their complex, delicate and tranquil choral music—including some probably by Henry V himself—expresses a highly wrought piety perhaps unexpected among these ironclad warriors.[21] It was an ephemeral art, thrown away and replaced, and it is largely by accident that many works escaped both the ravages of time and the purges of the Reformation, some by being conserved in Italy—and some at Eton College. Individual musicians could now gain an international reputation. Leading them was the astrologer, mathematician and musician John Dunstable, or Dunstaple (c.1380–1453). A recognizably English style of singing—mellifluous, even voluptuous—had been developed, combining high trebles and low basses. When English bishops took their choirs to the Council of Constance in 1417, the style was greatly admired, and during English rule in Paris during the 1420s and 1430s Dunstable, as the Duke of Bedford's household musician, set a musical fashion which became the first European international style.[22] Part of the attraction seems to have been a lively performance style: as a Venetian ambassador put it, "they didn't sing, they jubilated."[23]

Post–Black Death piety combined with growing wealth—especially in the small wool-producing towns of East Anglia and the Cotswolds, and the main ports such as Bristol and Hull—led to a great rebuilding and adornment of churches large and small: between 1380 and 1530, half of parish churches were rebuilt, some with ambitious towers and spires. Also built were chantries and family chapels where the dead were prayed for— perhaps an echo of post-plague bereavement—cloisters, almshouses, hospitals, schools for boys and girls, parish halls, and university and college buildings (in Oxford, on land confiscated from French religious orders). Wealthy and not-so-wealthy families gave to such public projects more than they gave the government in taxes. Guilds too were great builders of chapels and of their own meeting halls. The whole community contributed through "church ales" and "help ales," festivals sometimes lasting several days, eating and drinking together to raise money for buildings and for charity "in a convivial atmosphere . . . without emphasising social distinctions."[24] To this activity, England owes a lavish and unsurpassed architectural legacy, notably in its villages and small towns. There were now distinctive national styles, even if originally derived from France. The dazzling inventiveness of the "Decorated" style, up to the 1340s, was replaced by the more austere (and perhaps cheaper) "Perpendicular"—both terms coined by Thomas Rickman in 1817. Perpendicular, excitingly new with its cage-like stone tracery, vertical lines, great towers and spires, soaring vaults and growing expanses of glass, was developed at Westminster and London in the 1330s, elaborated at Gloucester Abbey for the shrine

Edward III had built for his murdered father, and fully applied at Windsor in the 1350s. Perpendicular remained the basic style for nearly two centuries, and has often been thought of as a response to the Black Death, though its beginnings just predated the epidemic. Yet the plague did indeed kill many older architects and perhaps provided the motivation, and in the longer term the wealth, for much new building, especially memorial chapels and chantries. The builders of these late-medieval masterpieces are the first English architects of whom we know some details, even their drawings and contracts. Many of them served in the royal office of works, overseeing a variety of projects as well as working for the Church and lay clients.[25] A leading figure is Henry Yevele (c.1320–1400), probably the son of a Staffordshire stonemason, who was responsible wholly or in part for the new nave of Canterbury Cathedral, for additions to Westminster Abbey, and for the remodelling of Westminster Hall.[26] The Perpendicular style had its Indian summer in the late fifteenth century: for example, in the great towers of Magdalen College, Oxford (c.1490) and Canterbury Cathedral (c.1490); and in St. George's Chapel, Windsor (1475), Henry VII's chapel in Westminster Abbey (1503), and King's College Chapel, Cambridge, a vast height of feathery fan-vaulting that unites walls, windows and ceiling, designed by Richard Ely and John Wastell, and only completed in 1515 after more than sixty years of delay due to dynastic upheaval. This style of refined magnificence was equally suitable to express the glory of God and the power and piety of kings; but it came to a sudden end both because "the dead hand of classic Rome" (as one historian puts it)[27] became the dominant European fashion, and because the Reformation took away the motive for ostentatious architectural piety. By the 1700s, the diarist John Evelyn could dismiss these buildings as "sharp Angles ... Narrow Lights ... and Crinkle-Crankle";[28] and many were lost, mutilated or destroyed until the Gothic Revival of the eighteenth and nineteenth centuries.

War booty from France as well as the profits from corn and wool paid for a rush of secular buildings in an exuberant variety of styles. All in a few decades, great castles in modern form were built by old or newly rich nobility near the northern and western borders, such as Raby, Warkworth, Bolton and Raglan. In more peaceful regions, castles were converted or built more for display of chivalric fantasies, such as battlements and portcullises, than for real defence—such were Windsor (modernized 1357–68), Warwick, Kenilworth and the fashionably brick-built Herstmonceux (1441). There were also new royal palaces, such as Henry V's Sheen (begun 1414); comfortable mansions, such as Penshurst Place (begun 1338) and elegantly modern brick, glass and timber houses, such as Ockwells Manor, Berkshire (1440s). Large numbers of smaller houses for gentlemen, merchants, millers, innkeepers and farmers were now better built and bigger, with the living quarters separate from the barns and byres, and with glass windows, parlours, kitchens and bedrooms. Many are still occupied, some 2,000 in Kent alone.

It was not only the rich who had money to spend. Wages rose and prices fell, increasing real incomes by 250 percent between 1300 and 1450, and reaching a level by 1500 that would not be permanently exceeded until the 1880s. GDP reached the equivalent of over $1,000 per capita (similar to China and India in the 1990s), and although for some time to come England would remain less wealthy than Flanders and Italy, unlike in most of Europe English wages stayed high even when population numbers slowly recovered.[29] The purchasing power of working people rose more steeply than at any time before the twentieth century.[30] This meant more and better food and drink—white bread, beef, mutton and fish. The Corpus Christi Guild at Bishops Lynn, for example, sponsored feasts in 1444 featuring mackerel, herring, whelks, crabs, chickens, capons, doves, geese, marrowbones, pork, beef, lamb and veal.[31] More ale was drunk, and beer (with hops) was introduced from the Low Countries. Brewing became more commercialized, with taverns and alehouses for drinking and playing games—the English pub was born. Consumption of all kinds increased: furniture, pottery, pewter (England's second most valuable export manufacture), clothes and fashion, ignoring the legal restrictions on dress. The booming trades in London were tailoring and brewing. People increasingly shopped for pleasure, as shops grew bigger and were better stocked, and streets such as London's Cheapside became famous for their variety. Industries began to recover from the post-plague slump, including metalworking, pottery and mining. Wollaton in Nottinghamshire was producing thousands of tons of coal a year and continued to do so until 1965. Miners reached productivity levels not surpassed until the nineteenth century. Yet people were also working less, and there were complaints about workers arriving late, spending too much time over meals, and taking siestas. Apprentices annoyed their elders by playing games. Morris dancing emerged around 1450. People took more leisure than at any time until the 1960s.[32] For most people (defeat in France, recurring plague and the "Wars of the Roses" notwithstanding) if ever there was a "Merrie England," this was it.

## A LANGUAGE FOR A NATION

Perhaps the most fundamental change in this time of changes was the sudden emergence of English as the first language of public life and modern literature. Since the Conquest, England had been the biggest multilingual and multicultural area in western Europe, with educated people bi- or tri-lingual—"not three cultures, but one culture in three voices."[33] Latin was the language of religion, scholarship and administration, and also (with a strong admixture of English and French words) of politics, business, law and everyday writing, even such things as household accounts. French, as well as having formal legal usage, was the language of fashionable culture. English remained as the everyday language, and also the language of religious piety. When it was useful, bits of the three languages were jumbled together.

The first English-language histories since the Conquest, both written in the 1320s and 1330s, were by Robert of Gloucester (possibly several authors) and Robert Manning, a Lincolnshire monk. Their narratives turn on the long struggle, after the Conquest "set us in serfdom," to restore the "gode olde lawe" of the Anglo-Saxons, with Becket and Montfort as national heroes. Previously, patriotic writing had been in French or Latin. Now English could be equated with national and social identity: the true people of "Inglande" were, wrote Robert Manning, "those who live in the country who know neither Latin nor French" but shared the "felawschip" of "Inglysch."[34]

Change came quickly from 1350, with the patriotism of the Hundred Years' War a catalyst. In the longer term, Norman French—more accurately "insular French"—had been losing ground to Parisian French, beside which it sounded provincial. But this made the metropolitan French culture maintained by the court and the high nobility as a badge of distinction seem increasingly alien, even the language of the enemy: Edward I accused the French of aiming to destroy the English language. French was decreasingly effective as a means of communication. When it was necessary to appeal to the public, English became attractive, practically and symbolically, as the language of the whole people.

Change came in an explosive burst, in hardly more than a lifetime, and it obliterated the remaining cultural divide dating from the Conquest. In 1362 law courts were ordered to use English. In 1363 Parliament was opened by the chancellor for the first time in English. From the 1380s parliamentary proceedings began to be recorded in English. In the "gramerscoles of Engelonde" children were abandoning French "and lurneþ an Englysch."[35] Wills and guild records began to appear in English, and during the 1400s the records of manorial courts, customary rights and by-laws changed to English. There was an appetite for religious and secular literature in English, as a source for sermons, for private and public reading, and for performance.[36] English Passion Plays and allegorical morality plays such as *Everyman* began to be staged. Henry IV accepted the crown in 1399 with a speech in English—perhaps the first king since Harold, whose mother tongue it was. Henry V used English to rally support for his war in France, on which official news bulletins in English were circulated. He also used English in personal letters. Shakespeare later made his halting use of French a sign of bluff English honesty.

This "Middle English" was very different from "Old English." The influx of a ruling class of non-native speakers after 1066 had led to simplification of the language, which lost much of its grammatical complexity—three genders, four cases, ten conjugations. The alphabet too became simpler, and more Latin-based. There was no common spelling, and there were differences of dialect and accent, though grammar was largely uniform. Alone of the Germanic tongues, it had received a massive influx of words from Latin and French, which doubled its vocabulary. Between 1250 and 1450, of 27,000 new words identified, 22 percent were derived from French, and most others from Latin. English often acquired several words for the same concept. They were sometimes used in tandem to make meaning sure, or just for rhetorical purposes, as in "aiding and abetting," "fit and proper," "peace and quiet." In due course they could acquire nuances of meaning, as with "kingly," "royal" and "regal," or "loving," "amorous" and "charitable," from English, French and Latin respectively. Linguistic flexibility was greatly enhanced by bolting together grammatical elements from each language. Prefixes and suffixes made word creation easy: for example, the Old English "ful" added to French nouns (beautiful, graceful); or French suffixes with Old English verbs (knowable, findable). It has been argued that this made it really a new language.[37] But the basics remained, and remain, Anglo-Saxon: in modern written English, the hundred most frequently used words are all derived from Old English.[38]

English as an advanced literary form was largely the creation of a generation of writers during the second half of the fourteenth century, the most famous of them Geoffrey Chaucer. Its origins were not in the court, but from the Midlands and north, with echoes of older literary styles. Popular Robin Hood stories, recited in verse by travelling minstrels, go back to around the 1330s—they were referred to (disapprovingly) in Langland's poem *Piers Plowman*, c.1377—and were first written down in the early 1400s. The stories traditionally originated in adjoining parts of Yorkshire and Nottinghamshire. It has been suggested that if there ever was a real Robin Hood—Robert Hod—he fought the sheriff in Yorkshire between 1226 and 1234. The ballads were soon so widely known that references to Robin and his band had become part of the language—one criminal priest in the 1400s took the nickname "Frere Tuck." The audience were probably yeomen and small "gentilmen"—a growing group, who shared Robin's dislike of greedy prelates and corrupt royal officials, who admired courage, physical prowess and generosity, and who were not averse to a bit of banditry themselves on occasion.

Robin Hood's 700-year survival into modern popular culture is unique. He was kept alive through a succession of popular reincarnations. First, as a prominent figure in summer festivities, along with maypole and morris dancing and popular plays (Maid Marian, from French stories, was now added). He re-emerged as a hero of street songs in the sixteenth and seventeenth centuries. The original medieval ballads were collected and republished by late-eighteenth-century antiquarians, especially Joseph Ritson—an admirer of the French Revolution, who turned Robin from picaresque bandit into fighter for justice and freedom. Scott's *Ivanhoe* (1819) brought medieval adventure and Robin Hood into modern literature. In moral and politically correct guise, Robin was for the first time a suitable subject for children's literature in Britain, France ("Robin des Bois," thanks to Alexandre Dumas) and America. The rest is Hollywood.

Sharing some of the same values, though at a higher level of sophistication, were poems of chivalry, such as *Gawain and the Green Knight*. This, in the Staffordshire-Cheshire dialect, preserved and revitalized the alliterative poetic style of the Anglo-Saxons, but in very different language, mixed with French and Latin. The greatest poetic work in modified alliterative style was *Piers Plowman*, by a West Midlands cleric, William Langland. He had links with the great monastery of Worcester, a traditional centre of English culture, and he was also associated with London intellectuals. The poem, which opens in the Malvern Hills, was written in about 1367–70 and repeatedly reworked. It was a complex and agonized allegorical meditation on the broken society—corrupt, selfish and in need of altruism. Langland's work, though by later standards conservative in its ideas and difficult in its style, appealed to political reformers. Making an ordinary peasant the prophetic, even Christ-like, touchstone of virtue could not but have disturbing implications. Langland may have hoped that writing it in English would reach a wider audience, and he became the first English poet to attain a national readership and influence, well enough known to be referred to by some of the rebels of 1381—proof that he was connecting with the preoccupations of his time.[39]

Very different was an entirely new literature at Richard II's court, above all that of Geoffrey Chaucer, royal official, diplomat and European intellectual. Though he also wrote in French, Chaucer's aim in his wide range of poetic, astronomical, philosophical and political writings was to bring English into European cultural life. As his fellow poet Lydgate saw it, he had taken a "rude" and "boistous" English, "of litel reputacioun," and began to "magnifie, And adourne it with his elloquence." In this, as for contemporary vernacular writers in French and Italian, there was a consciously patriotic ambition; Chaucer proclaims: "God save the king, who is lord of this language."[40] He was influenced less by earlier English writers than by Dante, Boccaccio, Petrarch, and the French poets Machaut and Deschamps (who wrote a poem in praise of "noble Geffory Chaucier"). His *Canterbury Tales*, begun in about 1387, often regarded as quintessentially English, were influenced by bawdy French *fabliaux* and by Boccaccio's *Decameron*—indeed, some of the *Tales* were translations— and he introduced hundreds of new words taken from French and Latin. Nevertheless, it is understandable that he should have been hailed over the centuries as "the father of English poetry," in a language so new it sometimes needed to be explained to his first readers in French or Latin glossaries. He single-handedly raised the cultural status of English, creating a sophisticated literature and language that is clearly an ancestor of modern English. The impact on a widening readership of a work as modern, witty and fashionable as the *Canterbury Tales*, portraying and satirizing a wide cross section of contemporary life, must have contributed to the creation of a sense of mutual recognition which is an ingredient of national identity. Finally, Chaucer helped to make London English, based on an East Midlands dialect, rather than the West Midlands dialects of Langland and *Gawain*, the dominant form of the literary language. Pronunciation was also about to change profoundly, a sign of new uses of the language, though older pronunciations survived, and still survive today, in the north and Midlands.[41]

However urbane, cosmopolitan, carefully enigmatic and seemingly lighthearted his most popular works were, Chaucer was inevitably involved in the intellectual and political tensions of his time. He was a courtier under Edward III and during Richard II's disastrous reign. He witnessed the Peasants' Revolt, though he referred to it only obliquely, and flippantly. He was a protégé, and eventually a relative by marriage, of the powerful and unpopular John of Gaunt. And the circle for which he primarily wrote was the royal household, which included the so-called Lollard knights, sympathizers with the ideas of John Wyclif, another crucial actor in the linguistic revolution of these years.

Wyclif was a prominent Oxford theologian (sometime Master of Balliol College) with court connections. He was brought to preach in London in 1376 by John of Gaunt in support of a campaign to increase Crown revenue by tapping the wealth of the Church: there were sweeping proposals circulating to use it to endow new earls, knights and squires, 15 universities, 100 almshouses, and 15,000 parish clergy. Wyclif was, among other things, a critic of Church corruption, which mainly meant its wealth. His advocacy of Church disendowment won approval in elite political circles and support in Oxford. His other ideas were even more far-reaching, including attacks in the 1370s on papal authority and on transubstantiation, the doctrine that the sacramental bread and wine really became the body and blood of Christ. This caused horror among the orthodox and denunciation of Wyclif as "the great heresiarch," the first major English heretic and the most subversive thinker of the later Middle Ages, who influenced the Bohemian Hussite movement and indirectly Martin Luther. Wyclif's writings were repeatedly condemned by the Pope, but he was sufficiently protected by his patrons to be allowed to retire unmolested to his benefice at Lutterworth, where he died in 1384. In 1428 his remains were exhumed and burned on papal orders.

A crucial part of the work of Wyclif and his followers—insultingly called "Lollards"; that is, mumblers—was to translate the Bible. This would, some thought, lead to a return to the golden age of Bede and Alfred, themselves biblical translators. A first word-for-word translation of the Latin Vulgate appeared in 1382, and a revised, slightly freer and more comprehensible version in 1388. As a cultural development, this can hardly be exaggerated: it was by far the most important body of English prose since the Conquest, and—mass-produced as far as manuscript-copying allowed—it had a much wider circulation than any other English writings.[42] It met a desire—so the Wycliffites hoped, and so their enemies came to fear—by laypeople, both nobles and "simple men" and women, to lead a more active and autonomous religious life. There was controversy about whether English ("not angelic," thought one chronicler) was an adequate or dignified medium for the divine Word: one English version translated biblical wine as "cider." "The pearled gospel," lamented one chronicler, was being "trampled by pigs."[43] But Lollards insisted that English was suitable, and perhaps even better than Latin.

Translating parts of scripture was far from new, and not necessarily controversial if it was a means of allowing "the lewd" (laity) to follow services and priests to prepare sermons. The pious and orthodox Henry IV had a vernacular Bible—the first king known to have had one.[44] But the combination of an English Bible and heresy was explosive, especially in the aftermath of the 1381 revolt, in which John Ball, suspected of links with Wyclif, had been so prominent. In 1401 heresy was made a capital offence for the first time in England, when a statute for the burning of relapsed heretics was passed. The 1409 Constitutions of Oxford instituted unprecedented policing of belief.[45] The translation into English of any passage or phrase from the Bible was forbidden without the permission of a diocesan council—stricter controls than anywhere in Europe, and which would in theory have condemned a large body of existing literature, including the *Canterbury Tales*. In 1413, Sir John Oldcastle, an active military and political servant of the Crown in the Welsh Marches, and a prominent Lollard, was condemned for heresy—the first influential layman so prosecuted. Oldcastle escaped from the Tower of London and led an abortive rebellion in 1414, expecting to win wide support. After three years on the run, refusing royal pardons, he was captured, hanged and burned in 1417. Henry V, who made political use of the English language, seems not to have been personally zealous in his opposition to Lollardy, but formal religious orthodoxy was necessary for a new dynasty, especially one also claiming the crown of France. The Oldcastle rebellion stained Lollardy with treason, and marked the end of open sympathy among the elite. He owes a kind of immortality to Shakespeare, whose Sir John Falstaff was partly a caricature of him.

The extent and significance of Lollardy have been much debated. It was traditionally considered a forerunner of the Reformation, but some recent historians have questioned its importance. Most opinion, however, sees its general influence as widespread and enduring, though forced underground.[46] The desire for an English Bible caused "Lollard Bibles" to be treasured and hidden, and the exquisite quality of some surviving copies proves it had an elite following.

The first major work of the new literature in a simple and colloquial English that is "all but modern"[47] was *Le Morte Darthur*, by a Warwickshire knight, Sir Thomas Malory (c.1417–71). He had served in Gascony and also been an MP for Warwickshire in the 1440s. As royal authority began to break down around 1450 (see p. 144), he was prominent in a local feud against the Duke of Buckingham, and was charged with extortion, rape, cattle rustling and robbery. There followed two picaresque decades of arrests, escapes, releases, banditry and political conspiracy, linked with the chaos of civil war. *Le Morte Darthur*, drawing on French versions of the saga supplemented by traditional English tales, was written in the 1460s, probably in the Tower of London (which had one of the best libraries in the country). It has been described as "troubled literature for a troubled time," and "not an exercise in nostalgia for a golden age."[48] Such was its popularity that it was one of the first books printed in England.

By the middle of the fifteenth century, there had thus emerged a body of widely known English literature and a substantial readership, as can be seen in the libraries of royal administrators, members of Parliament, lawyers and the gentry. Chaucer predominated. Other poets—Langland, Hoccleve, Gower, Lydgate—were also widely read. Chivalric romances, works of piety, histories and self-help books (on manners, medicine and hunting) accounted for the rest. Most were now in English. When William Caxton, a merchant who had spent much of his career in the Low Countries, where he had become involved in the new technology of printing, introduced it to London in 1476, this, along with much foreign literature, is naturally what he produced: Chaucer, Malory, Gower, Lydgate. To own—and perhaps read—the works of these authors was proof of intellectual and social status, and, as advised in Caxton's own *Book of Curtesye* (*c*.1477), a means of social education. This was especially true of Chaucer, whose work "enlumened hast alle our bretayne." But a century later this ambitious new literature could seem to the poet Sir Philip Sydney archaic—lost in "mistie time."[49] A musical culture too was systematically eradicated. Religious revolution would sweep all away.

## THE VASTY FIELDS OF FRANCE

The fall in population during the fourteenth century, which meant fewer hungry colonists, fewer soldiers and fewer taxpayers, encouraged a disengagement of England from Ireland, Wales, Scotland and to some extent France. The English "pale" in Ireland—the small region round Dublin under effective Anglo-Irish control—was less a bridgehead than a shrinking cul-de-sac. Though its rulers considered themselves "English," they played little part in English affairs, and England was only sporadically interested in theirs. Most of Ireland was left to itself. In Wales, a new Welsh elite was emerging (families such as the Twdurs—destined for an illustrious future) who usually accepted English overlordship but increasingly took control of local affairs. Edward I's brief ambition to unite the English and Scottish crowns had been abandoned, so there was no effective way of stopping Scots border raids. To defend the turbulent northern, western and Gascon borders, big militarized "Marcher" lordships had been created, with special powers and jurisdiction, ruled by families such as the Arundels, Mortimers, Percies and Greys, and with royal officers to command their forces. France was the most difficult problem. Disengagement there would mean not only the loss of Aquitaine, but also a threat to the Flanders wool trade, much of which flowed through the fortified English territory of Calais, and, through loss of influence in Normandy, Brittany and Flanders, make England vulnerable to French invasion.

Nevertheless, disengagement may have been what Richard II, from his teenage years, wanted. That, anyway, is one explanation of his disastrous and enigmatic reign. War demanded partnership and compromise with Parliament and the nobility, but peace would permit him to assert a personal authority he regarded as sacred, as shown in the Wilton Diptych, in which he is shown being presented to the Virgin and Child by St. Edmund the Martyr and Edward the Confessor. Richard's courtly magnificence included lavish patronage of arts and architecture, such as the wholesale modernization of Westminster Hall, with the creation of a new form of timber "hammer-beam" roof, making a unique throne room comparable with a great church. All this appealed to his "immature and self-centred personality,"[50] and it was encouraged by his immediate entourage. It led to friction with the nobility, who had not abandoned military ambitions in France, and to conflict with the Commons, who refused to agree to peacetime taxes at wartime levels, or to allow Richard to do homage to the king of France for Aquitaine, as in the past. That would, they said, place "every single Englishman . . . under the yoke of slavery."[51] The French took the opportunity to prepare a massive invasion and incited the Scots to do the same. In 1385 the "Wonderful Parliament" (so called because of its extraordinary actions), reminding the eighteen-year-old king of the fate of Edward II, forced him to accept a parliamentary commission to cut expenditure and safeguard the realm. Richard prepared to fight back, intent on having the commission executed for treason. He offered the French king, Charles IV, territory in return for support. But he was forced to give in by a military force mustered by five "Lords Appellant"— his uncle Thomas of Woodstock, Duke of Gloucester; Henry Bolingbroke, Earl of Derby; and the earls of Arundel, Warwick and Nottingham. Arundel added to their popularity by capturing fifty French ships laden with wine, and selling off the cargo cheaply. The "Merciless Parliament" then executed several of Richard's close friends and advisers, among them the Lord Chief Justice, Robert Tresilian, and forced others to flee, including the Archbishop of York, Alexander Neville.

After waiting and planning for ten years, Richard took his revenge. In 1396, a twenty-eight-year truce was signed with France, sealed by Richard's marriage to Isabella, daughter of Charles VI. In 1397 two of the Appellants, Arundel and Warwick, were arrested by surprise, the former executed and the latter imprisoned for life. A third, the Duke of Gloucester, was murdered. Their lands were confiscated and given to the king's supporters in the biggest such redistribution of the Middle Ages, effectively creating a new aristocracy.[52] A parliament met surrounded by the king's loyal Cheshire archers (motto: *"Dycun slep sicury quile we wake"* *).

* "Dickon, sleep securely while we wake."

Lords and Commons were forced to swear that all acts to restrain royal power were illegal—a renunciation of Magna Carta. Richard fantasized about a golden age of peace and unchallenged royal authority, which he announced triumphantly to foreign rulers. He insisted on the sacred nature of kingship—courtiers had to prostrate themselves, and he may have planned a re-coronation using the newly "discovered" holy chrism given by the Virgin Mary to Thomas Becket. He even dreamed of becoming Holy Roman Emperor.

His fatal mistakes, dramatized by Shakespeare, were in 1398 to banish Henry Bolingbroke, Earl of Derby and later Duke of Lancaster, the son and heir of John of Gaunt, confiscate his vast inheritance, and then to go off to Ireland, leaving England weakly guarded. Henry sailed in June 1399 from Boulogne with a few retainers and landed in Yorkshire. He found followers among those threatened by Richard's vengeful and unpredictable actions. Royal support collapsed, and Richard was intimidated into "resigning" the crown in September. Parliament assented to his replacement by Henry, on the grounds that Richard claimed that "he alone could alter and create the laws of his realm," and also because "no living person who came to know him could or wished to trust him."[53] He died—possibly starved to death—soon afterwards. Though he retained some popular support, he also inspired popular hatred—three of his earls were lynched.

Henry of Lancaster's coronation in 1399 as Henry IV (using the new holy oil) was both a counter-revolution and a new departure. It restored the old magnate families and confirmed the role of parliaments. But it changed the basis of kingship, for Henry, though Richard's cousin, was not his heir. He therefore claimed the throne by God's grace (proved by having succeeded), by necessity and, in Chaucer's word's, by "free election." His dubious legitimacy—seemingly confirmed when he was struck down from 1405 by a mysterious illness (rumoured to be leprosy, a quasi-biblical punishment for usurpation)—encouraged rebellions in England, a Scottish invasion and a formidable uprising in Wales, under Owain Glyn Dwr (Owen Glendower), supported by disaffected English magnates and of course the French, who raided Devon, invaded Aquitaine and threatened Calais. In England, "even harsher taxes were imposed . . . for they were hard pressed to hold their own in the wars against France, Scotland, Ireland, Wales and Flanders."[54] In 1405 Glyn Dwr and his English allies, Edmund Mortimer (who had married his daughter) and Henry Percy, Earl of Northumberland, agreed to divide England between them, with a large slice up to the Severn to go to an independent Wales. A French force landed in Wales in 1405 and got within sight of Worcester. But the French and Scots proved unreliable, and the

English Crown was militarily too strong for the Welsh, who were defeated, with difficulty, in 1408. The episode accelerated the long-term English disengagement from Wales, now dominated by an assertive Welsh gentry, who strengthened their position by fighting alongside the English in France—one such was Dafydd Gam, whose death at Agincourt, as "Davy Gam Esquire," was recorded in Shakespeare's *Henry V*. Ireland was left to its own devices. The Scottish border was secured (except for endemic raiding) for a generation by the fortuitous capture in 1406 of the twelve-year-old King James I by Norfolk pirates. For once, the English had only one enemy.

Events were now precipitated by civil war in France fought between factions led by two royal dukes, Burgundy and Orleans, and known as "Burgundians" and "Armagnacs." After Burgundy had Orleans murdered in the streets of Paris in 1407, both factions appealed to England for support. At first, in 1412, this went to the Orleans faction, who promised to recognize English sovereignty over Aquitaine—as the Treaty of Brétigny had done fifty years earlier. In 1413 the twenty-six-year-old Henry V succeeded to the English throne and began negotiations with all the parties. After customary haggling, his final demands boiled down to the Brétigny terms, and marriage with Catherine, daughter of the French king, Charles VI. When this was refused, he prepared for war. Who was the warmonger? For many (particularly French) historians, it was of course Henry: the son of a usurper aiming to consolidate his shaky throne; a brilliant but bloodthirsty warrior; a reckless adventurer; a pitiless religious fanatic, "Henry V lacked a sense of reality, and such a man is a calamity, because the strength of his beliefs ... makes him trample every obstacle under foot to attain his impossible dreams."[55] A modern English view is very different: Henry "envisaged England and France brought to a mutual peace through a common kingship,"[56] while retaining their own institutions and laws, and this vision was not impossible or even unusual. Previous wars had brought no lasting peace, and diplomatic agreements had failed because successive French kings had refused to respect English possessions on the Continent. In the nationalist tradition, this has been presented as France asserting its rights, even liberating occupied territory. In reality, English sovereignty (exercised with a light touch) was accepted by the inhabitants of Gascony, who showed no desire to be ruled by a king of France at least as foreign as the king of England. Henry's claim to the French throne was not just a bargaining ploy, as in the past. He may genuinely have intended a permanent political solution, "rather as the architects of the European Union sought to end the historical enmity of France and Germany."[57] He hoped that people on both sides of the Channel would accept it because of the benefits it would bring. But this political solution would first require force of arms.

His military strategy was new. He abandoned the scorched-earth tactics of the *chevauchée*—methods to be used against an enemy, not against those he wanted to be faithful, or at least acquiescent, subjects. So he besieged towns, brought territory under permanent control, restored order, and granted land to settlers in ancestral Normandy. He first captured the port of Harfleur after a siege that left many of his men sick. But he was determined to march with part of the army (about 6,000 men) "through his duchy of Normandy" to the English port, Calais. The main French army barred their way, and on 25 October 1415 they met at Agincourt, near Arras. The English, mainly archers, were tired, wet and demoralized. They were also greatly outnumbered, but (according to his chronicler) Henry boldly announced that "I would not have a single man more than I do; for these I have here with me are God's people."[58] The English archers and men-at-arms, fighting on foot as they had learned the hard way in Scotland and Wales, formed up between two woods, forcing the French to crowd together. When their mounted knights charged, bowmen shot them down. Panicking horses slithered in the mud; foot soldiers were trampled; fallen knights suffocated. Perhaps fearing that he was being surrounded, Henry ordered French prisoners killed—though more than 1,000, including two dukes and three counts, survived to reach England. As at Crécy and Poitiers, the battle was carnage for mounted knights: the French aristocracy was "decapitated."[59] It has been suggested that France's rulers could not trust their peasantry to bear arms, unlike the English, who depended on their archers. The six-foot longbow—even if many archers were Welsh, and yew bow staves came from Italy—became a symbol of England. In 1417 every goose in the southern counties was required to yield six feathers for the arrows.[60] The story of the two-finger salute (the bowstring fingers the French threatened to chop off) is too good not to be true. Agincourt was celebrated with pageants, popular verses and songs. Thanks to Shakespeare 160 years later, it acquired a permanent patriotic meaning.

Agincourt made Henry's prestige as king and warrior unassailable. God had tested him and vindicated his right to the French throne—a version immediately propagated by the English clergy. Many, even in France, agreed. Henry embarked on the methodical occupation of Normandy. Meanwhile, complex negotiations continued between English, Burgundians and Armagnacs. For the first time since 1066, a king of England refused to speak French, claiming that he and his council did not understand it.[61] When in September 1419 the Duke of Burgundy, Jean sans Peur, was murdered in the course of a meeting with the Armagnacs, the Burgundians appealed to Henry for aid and accepted him as future king. The Treaty of Troyes, in May 1420, agreed to the marriage of Henry to Catherine, daughter of Charles VI, and accepted him as Charles's regent and eventual heir. In December, he entered Paris. The dauphin, Charles's eldest son, was disinherited for his part in Burgundy's murder. But he fought on, and France descended into an appalling civil war, with England as a third party, beneficiary and—in the eyes of King Henry—potential saviour.

Henry V is considered by modern historians one of the ablest of English kings, with a "genius for conciliation," knowing intuitively how to unite and lead.[62] Could he have succeeded in uniting the French and British crowns? Many on both sides of the Channel were suspicious, despite assurances that the two countries would be governed independently, and they certainly disliked the cost. But in Aquitaine and Normandy many were willing to accept English sovereignty, and many elsewhere would welcome whoever brought peace and order. These included France's intellectual elite, the Sorbonne and many of the clergy, for whom the previous French dynasty had lost its legitimacy.[63] But Henry's vision was never to be tested, for he fell ill after besieging Meaux, east of Paris, and died on 31 August 1422 at the castle of Vincennes, near Paris, aged thirty-four—England's last real warrior king until 1688. His half-French baby son was heir to two kingdoms, and after the death of Charles VI in October he was proclaimed Henry VI of England and II of France. That he was accepted in England shows how much his father had consolidated the new Lancastrian dynasty; but France was another matter. For the next few years, Henry's able brother John, Duke of Bedford—"a subtle politician, knowing how to mix force and persuasion to create a pro-English party in France"—ruled as Regent of France in Paris.[64] Only a small English garrison—a few dozen men—was necessary, as Parisians hated and feared the Armagnacs. The Armagnacs and the dauphin Charles, now proclaimed Charles VII, ruled eastern France, precariously, from Bourges. The war attracted freelance bands from across Europe willing to offer their services to whoever paid best, and turning to brigandage when need or opportunity arose. A large part of the "French" army were Scots, whose motives were perhaps not wholly financial—before their crushing defeat at Verneuil in 1424, they told Bedford that "they would give no quarter and wanted none."[65]

In both countries, the demands of war, and its dynastic and legal complications, had produced a flood of propaganda to stimulate popular support—sermons, histories, ceremonies, writings, songs, news bulletins—for which the clergy were an important channel. Both sides claimed divine favour, and both emphasized the providential character of their histories. Edward III had begun this policy of deliberately and directly involving the population in supporting the war by acting as a truly national king. In France, the sacredness of the monarchy and "Holy France" were emphasized, the dead were "martyrs," and divine intervention was claimed: the episode of Joan of Arc and the consecration at Rheims would soon show how potent this could be. For both countries, the war seems to have increased a sense of national identity and participation. The victory at Agincourt and the subsequent capture of Rouen caused dancing in the streets of London. In France, where identity was less developed, the war accelerated it. The great patriotic historian Jules Michelet, looking back from the nineteenth century, declared that "the struggle against England did France an immense service. It confirmed and defined its nationhood. By uniting against the enemy the provinces discovered they were a people. In seeing the English close up they felt themselves to be France."[66]

The English seemed close to complete victory after Verneuil. But the "king of Bourges," as Charles was mockingly called, was saved by the River Loire and a farmer's daughter named Jehane—"Joan of Arc." The mighty Loire, France's eternal last defence against invasion from the north, could not be crossed until the bridge and fortress of Orleans were taken, and the English besieged it. Joan confronted Charles, claiming to have received orders from the saints to have him crowned and "chuck the English out of France." She was sent as a religious mascot with a relieving army to Orleans, and on 8 May 1429 the English retreated. She then accompanied the dauphin to France's coronation city, Rheims, deep in enemy territory, to be consecrated as Charles VII, formally breaking the Treaty of Troyes. As the English had the crown and regalia, they used copies; but fortunately they found the chrism brought by a dove from heaven in 981 for the coronation of Clovis, and used to anoint France's kings until 1825. In reply, the ten-year-old Henry VI was crowned at Notre-Dame in Paris: he had the right crown, but was in the wrong place. Parisians crowded in to watch and share the feast, but many were unimpressed: "The food was shocking . . . Most of it, especially what was meant for the common people, had been cooked the previous Thursday—the English were in charge . . . all they cared about was how soon they could get it over and done with."[67]

Joan's spell was broken when she was wounded and captured outside Paris. Soon after she was condemned for heresy, and burned at Rouen in 1431—"betrayed by her king and burnt by the Church," as left-wing French patriots would put it in later centuries with some justice, even though the English actually lit the fire. But she had served her purpose,

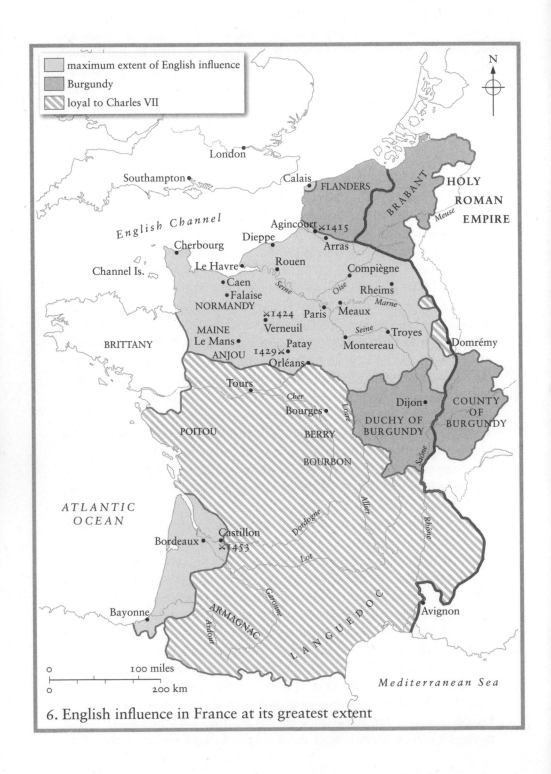

**Legend:**
- maximum extent of English influence
- Burgundy
- loyal to Charles VII

N

London
Southampton
Calais
FLANDERS
BRABANT
HOLY
ROMAN
EMPIRE
Meuse
English Channel
Agincourt ×1415
Dieppe
Arras
Cherbourg
Le Havre
Rouen
Compiègne
Channel Is.
Caen
Seine
Rheims
Falaise
NORMANDY
Marne
×1424
Paris
Meaux
MAINE
Verneuil
Seine
Troyes
Le Mans
Montereau
Domrémy
BRITTANY
ANJOU
1429×
Patay
Orléans
Tours
Cher
COUNTY
OF
BURGUNDY
Bourges
Dijon
POITOU
BERRY
Loire
DUCHY OF
BURGUNDY
Saône
BOURBON
ATLANTIC
OCEAN
Allier
Dordogne
Rhône
Castillon
Bordeaux
×1453
Lot
Bayonne
ARMAGNAC
Garonne
LANGUEDOC
Avignon
Ardour
Mediterranean Sea

0        100 miles
0        200 km

6. English influence in France at its greatest extent

and the English had not won. In 1435 the English position deteriorated disastrously when the Duke of Burgundy abandoned the alliance, and the statesmanlike Bedford died. Paris, with a garrison of only 400 English soldiers, fell in 1436, and English prisoners were drowned in the Seine.

In England, the enthusiasm aroused by earlier victories turned sour. Burgundy's defection led to attacks on Burgundian merchants in London. Henry VI's advisers—first his great-uncle Cardinal Beaufort and then William de la Pole, Duke of Suffolk—now wanted peace, and embarked on negotiations. Their authority to negotiate was questioned by "Good Duke Humphrey," Duke of Gloucester, the king's popular, bellicose, cultivated and quarrelsome uncle and heir. The negotiations, in effect, turned the clock back: the English accepted a perpetual truce and tacitly abandoned the claim to the French crown in return for guaranteed possession of Normandy and Aquitaine, and a marriage between Henry VI and Margaret of Anjou, the French king's niece. Truce and marriage notwithstanding, Charles VII's forces, realizing that the English were weakening, steadily reconquered the north. The internal situation became increasingly dangerous because of the personality of Henry VI, who came of age in 1447. For reasons that cannot now be diagnosed, he was incapable of governing: "Woe to thee, O land, when thy king is a child," wrote a contemporary. The king's pathetic vulnerability and passivity is expressed in a prayer he himself wrote: "Lord Jesus Christ, who hast created, redeemed, and preordained me to what I am; thou knowest what thou wouldst do with me; do with me according to thy will, with mercy." Ancient texts were searched for an elixir that would restore the king's health. Gloucester's wife commissioned a horoscope to see what was going to happen—she was arrested and died in prison. Gloucester himself was arrested and died, possibly murdered.

Normandy, the most prized of Henry V's acquisitions, where English settlers and an "English party" were strong, came under attack. Both the elite and the public in England were now in a dangerous mood. In January 1450 Bishop Moleyns, keeper of the privy seal, was lynched by unpaid sailors at Portsmouth. In April the English, suffering from indecision and lack of funds, were slaughtered at the battle of Formigny, in Normandy, many of them finished off as the battle ended by local peasants. Suffolk was impeached, accused of selling Normandy to the French. To save him, the king ordered him into exile, but he was recognized by the sailors on his ship. They rejected the king's safe-conduct and beheaded Suffolk, saying that "they did not know the king but they well knew the crown of England . . . and that the community of the realm was the crown of that realm." Violence spread in southern England, culminating in the "Jack

Cade" rebellion in June and July 1450, when Kentish rebels under Cade, a former soldier, marched on London, complaining that "the sea is lost, France is lost," and murdered Suffolk's ally the treasurer, Lord Say. The Bishop of Salisbury was murdered by his own flock. This was an unprecedented political attack by the people on the king's servants, going well beyond the Peasants' Revolt of 1381. They did not consider themselves rebels, but "true liege men" defending the "commynwele of the realme of Ingelonde."[68] The revolt was crushed and Cade killed in July. In August, word reached England that "Cherbourg is gone and we have not now a foot of land in Normandy."[69] Only the remnants of Aquitaine and the Flemish outpost at Calais (which was represented in parliaments) remained.

Profiting from the chaos in England, the French invaded Aquitaine by land and sea. English rule had many supporters, but most now switched to the winning side. On 14 June 1451 a herald stood on the battlements of Bordeaux and called symbolically and in vain for English aid. The city then surrendered. Bayonne followed. But French rule proved oppressive and rapacious. The Bordelais asked for English aid, and in October 1452 an Anglo-Gascon army re-entered Bordeaux as liberators. The French counter-attacked, killing all Gascons caught on the English side. On 17 July 1453 the veteran hero John Talbot, Earl of Shrewsbury, in his late sixties, launched an impetuous charge to try to surprise the invaders at Castillon. It was a bloody defeat for the English, mown down by cannon, a weapon now coming into common use. Talbot, without armour—which he had sworn when a prisoner never to wear against the king of France— was killed, his head split open and a sword stuck up his backside. So ended the last battle of the "Hundred Years' War," that great political and chivalric adventure which had caused so much devastation and suffering. The news caused Henry VI a complete mental breakdown: he no longer reacted to events around him, remaining "without any answer or countenance . . . and cast down his eyes again."[70] Coincidentally, at the other end of Europe, Constantinople fell to the Turks, ending a thousand years of Christian history. These two events arguably began an avalanche of political changes across Europe marking the beginning of modern European geopolitics.[71]

## THE WARS OF THE ROSES

Angered and divided by defeat, and with a helpless king, England was in a political crisis. All Henry's greatest subjects tried at first to act together to preserve order and peace. The problem was Henry VI himself. Unlike the earlier problem kings, Edward II and Richard II, whose depositions were generally welcomed, Henry had done nothing evil—his problem was incapacity, not vice, and admirers even thought him a saint. So he retained the loyalty of many of his subjects, and continued as a cipher for twenty-four years. This made the problem of governance insoluble and hence increasingly perilous.[72] Conflict finally broke out between the dukes of York and Somerset, both close relatives of the king, over who should take effective control of the kingdom. On 22 May 1455 the Duke of York attacked the royal forces at St. Albans, killed the Duke of Somerset and the Earl of Northumberland, and seized the king.

Possession of the king gave York power, and he called a parliament to try to restore unity. But he failed to command support in the country, and political factionalism and private feuding increased. The Scots and the French were threatening to invade. A rival coalition of magnates gathered round the queen, Margaret of Anjou. Many nobles did not want to join in the struggle, but they were involved willy-nilly. The gentry too were in a difficult position. Individuals commonly had relatives, friends and patrons on both sides, and often had to be tempted or pressured into making dangerous choices. It was hard to raise men and money when legal authority was contested, and interests and loyalties were so divided. So the rival forces recruited soldiers from the militarized Marcher lordships of the north and west, from the paid security forces of the towns, and from professional military units returning from France, many of whom were soon to die on English battlefields. These three decades of political instability from 1455 to 1487—whose romantic name was coined centuries later by Sir Walter Scott, inspired by a scene in Shakespeare—would see in all only a few weeks of intense and increasingly merciless combat, and sporadic local disorders. For most ordinary people, life went on fairly normally.

After a period of stalemate, the two sides fought in earnest at Northampton on 10 July 1460, and the Yorkists again won. The Duke of York then claimed the throne by superior hereditary right of descent from the second son of Edward III, his great-great-grandfather. This was his only viable strategy—but he was killed at the battle of Wakefield in December and his head displayed on a spike, wearing a paper crown. Queen Margaret's forces regained possession of the king, but London closed its gates against her, partly due to fear of what her army might do. Edward, Earl of March, the new Duke of York, aged eighteen, claimed the throne, marched north against the Lancastrians, and on 29 March 1461 won a hard-fought victory at Towton, near York, probably the biggest battle of the "Wars of the Roses," and often said (fancifully) to be the bloodiest battle ever fought on English soil.[73]

Towton made him King Edward IV; but Henry VI and his family escaped to Scotland. In 1465, brought south by his supporters in an unsuccessful invasion, he was captured and put in the Tower of London. In 1470 the powerful Earl of Warwick, "the Kingmaker," changed sides, thanks to an agreement with Queen Margaret brokered by the king of France. Henry VI, passive and uncomprehending, was restored, and Edward IV fled to Burgundy. Boldly returning in March 1471, and gathering supporters as he went, he was able to enter London and again imprison Henry VI. In battles at Barnet and Tewkesbury he finally defeated the Lancastrian forces: Henry VI's son Edward, Warwick and other Lancastrian magnates were killed or executed. Edward then returned to London, and had Henry VI murdered in the Tower.

Edward IV has been called "one of the greatest of English kings" because he rescued the kingdom from the shambles of civil war.[74] He was intelligent, conciliatory, lascivious and where necessary ruthless—his treacherous brother Clarence ended up drowned in a butt of Malmsey wine. He succeeded in restoring government to a remarkable degree. He also had time to build a new St. George's Chapel at Windsor, a monument to his dynasty in one of the last flowerings of native medieval architecture, and to fight campaigns against France and Scotland, regaining Berwick. But he died in April 1483 at the age of forty, the only one of four generations of his line to die of natural causes. His taste for women had led him into an imprudent marriage with the alluring widow Elizabeth Woodville, who bore him ten children, but whose rapacious relatives were hated by the established nobility. This precipitated the most infamous episode of this generation of violence.

Thanks to Shakespeare's portrayal of him as a twisted, clever, ice-cold cynic, Edward's thirty-year-old brother, Richard, Earl of Gloucester, is by far the most famous character of the period, whose reputation still arouses passions among zealous antiquarians. Recent research portrays him as a more banal character: he acted with "an ineptitude that beggars belief"[75] because he panicked when his brother the king died. The heir to the (arguably usurping) dynasty was only twelve: Edward V, who was under the control of his mother's family, the detested Woodvilles. This opened the prospect of violent factionalism, and Richard's desperate response was to try to safeguard himself by seizing the throne in July 1483, declaring his young nephews illegitimate, and then having them murdered in the Tower. He lasted two years, a time of intimidation, violence and rebellion, when unpopular courtiers "Ruleth all England under a Hog," in the words of a skit nailed to the door of St. Paul's. Few established families supported this patently criminal enterprise.

Hopes focused on Henry Tudur, Earl of Richmond, the surviving Lancastrian heir, descended in the male line from the scandalous marriage of Henry V's young French widow, Catherine, with one of her Welsh retinue, Owain ap Maredudd ap Tudur. At the centre of the web was his formidable mother, Lady Margaret Beaufort, aged fourteen at his birth. It was only through her, another descendant of John of Gaunt, that Richmond had a tenuous claim to the throne. She arranged his crucial marriage with the Yorkist heiress Elizabeth, the sister of the murdered "princes in the Tower." Moreover, Margaret's third husband was the northern magnate Thomas, Lord Stanley, a key supporter of Richard. The French court, to distract Richard from helping their enemies in Brittany, provided Richmond with money to hire an effective force of French, Breton and Scottish mercenaries to stiffen his few hundred English followers, and in August 1485 he sailed from France to Wales. Thus began the fifth successful invasion of England in a century. Richmond raised more men while marching east, profiting from his Welsh ancestry and flying the Red Dragon of Wales. He was still outnumbered when he met King Richard's army near Bosworth, in Leicestershire. But part of Richard's army—the Stanleys' 3,000 men—held back. Richard, "all influenced with ire . . . stuck his horse with the spurs"[76] and led a charge to try to kill Richmond. They got close enough to cut down his standard-bearer, but the French pikemen held them off—their commander was later rewarded with an earldom. The Stanleys then changed sides, and according to one account Richard was killed by a Welshman wielding a halberd. According to tradition, Sir William Stanley picked up the crown, placed it on Richmond's head, and proclaimed him King Henry VII. Richard's mangled body was slung across a horse and taken off to be displayed near naked in Leicester.[77]

Bosworth is often thought to have begun a new and more stable era:

> We will unite the White Rose and the Red . . .
> England hath long been mad and scarred herself;
> The brother blindly shed the brother's blood . . .
> Now civil wounds are stopped, peace lives again;
> That she may long live here, God say amen!

Was it really the beginning of a new age—the "Age of the Tudors"? In several obvious senses, it was not. Civil war did not end until the bloody defeat in 1487 at Stoke of a Yorkist rising using Irish and German troops, and even after that there were further plots and rebellions with Irish,

Spanish, Scottish and French links. The "Tudors" did not regard themselves, nor were they regarded, as a new dynasty. Henry's claim to the throne came from descent from the Conqueror via John of Gaunt, and his family considered themselves the royal house of Plantagenet reunited by Henry's marriage to Elizabeth of York. Their Welsh connection was not played up—apart perhaps from giving Henry's firstborn son a name with British resonance, Arthur, who was born in Winchester, considered the legendary Camelot. The name "Tydder" or "Tedder" was used only in scorn, and was never applied to Henry VIII, Mary or Elizabeth. Spelled "Tudor," and used as the label for a revolutionary political epoch, it was invented by the eighteenth-century Scottish historian David Hume.[78]

Henry VII felt insecure, with reason. He was unfamiliar with England, having spent most of his life in Wales, Brittany and France. He was isolated from much of the nobility, and so introduced new men and more bureaucracy into government, in the French style, using spies to sniff out opposition, creating a French-style personal bodyguard, the 300 Yeomen of the Guard, giving extra-legal powers to favoured men, accumulating money, and bringing the aristocracy to heel by forcing them into debt to the Crown by blatant abuse of legal procedures, imposing huge fines for trivial or non-existent offences. Thus traditional medieval government, based on cooperation between Crown and magnates, was changed not by design but by "crisis, error and misunderstanding."[79] Though the "Wars of the Roses" had had relatively little impact on most people most of the time, they had weakened the aristocracy, for whom they had been costly, demoralizing and lethal, especially between the battles of Wakefield (1460) and Tewkesbury (1471). Of the male descendants of Edward III, seven had been killed in battle and five executed or murdered; thirty-one peers or their heirs were killed in battle, and twenty executed. There had been savagery unusual between gentlemen, killing noble prisoners and letting ordinary soldiers go. Archaeology on the Towton battlefield suggests extreme violence against prisoners, even mutilation. Edward of Lancaster was allegedly involved in killing at the age of seven. Notorious was John Tiptoft, Earl of Worcester, a renowned humanist scholar, who tortured and impaled prisoners—a novelty picked up on his Mediterranean travels.[80] The war gave rise to armed feuding between neighbours—what we wrongly think of as typical medieval violence. This was what Thomas Malory got involved in (see p. 134), and as such is vividly recorded in the letters of the Paston family in East Anglia, whose legal dispute with the Duke of Norfolk over an inheritance now descended to sheep-stealing, shooting at tenants, and even a siege of their castle at Caister by the duke's miniature army, using cannon.[81] Worse than attrition and demoralization, insoluble conflicts of loyalty cost the magnates the support of the smaller landowners, the gentry, and without this their independent power dwindled. Though nobles remained important socially, economically and politically, superior power henceforth came from office under the Crown, which increasingly centralized authority in a much more opaque, unaccountable and frankly dangerous court—the world of the "Tudors." Local power was put increasingly into the hands of the gentry, as Justices of the Peace, rather than the nobility. But the Crown's long-established, efficient and conscientious financial and legal administration had suffered long-term damage, weakening the whole state; it was not fully restored until the eighteenth or nineteenth century.[82]

External circumstances helped the new king. The Scots and the French, tempted as usual to take advantage of England's problems, were soon halted: the Scots by chronic domestic conflict, and the French by the beginning in 1495 of three centuries of conflict against the Habsburgs. Henry VII, suspicious and fearful, was thus able to drag out a tense reign without major war, but in a perpetual state of emergency, shamelessly abusing his authority in a country very ill at ease with itself.[83] So great was the government's unpopularity that as soon as Henry VII died in 1509, his heir Henry VIII had his father's chief henchmen arrested, and two leading ministers, Sir Richard Empson and Edmund Dudley, were subsequently executed—an early foretaste from this tall seventeen-year-old of ruthlessness to come.

## THE END OF THE MIDDLE AGES?

The European world had been changing and expanding intellectually, economically and politically, and England, briefly one of its greatest powers, had been reduced almost to a backwater. If this had been due in part to domestic turmoil—no worse than elsewhere, however—there were greater reasons beyond its control. Cultural novelty and wealth were concentrated in the great cities of Italy, the Low Countries and Germany, to which England was only a supplier of raw materials. France, now consolidated and expanded, was becoming the most powerful state in Christendom. Christian Spain too had grown, in 1492 incorporating the remaining Muslim provinces in the south. That same year Christopher Columbus reached America, and the age of Spanish colonial power dawned. John, or Giovanni, Cabot, an Italian merchant settled in Bristol, reached "Newfoundland" in 1497, England's first attempt to keep up. In 1516, Spain became the core of the great, if dispersed, empire of Charles V, which by inheritance and marriage combined Spain, Portugal, their expanding empires, Burgundy (including the Low Countries), parts of Italy, the Habsburg domains in Austria, and the crown of the Holy Roman Empire, conferring prestigious if limited suzerainty over Germany and the traditional claim to be the secular leader of Christendom. Henry VIII briefly hoped to become Holy Roman Emperor, as a step to regaining the French territories and establishing England as a great Continental power. In fact, for the next three centuries, England would be on the defensive, needing to protect its security interests, even at times its independence, in the face of the new giant European powers.

So was the history of the fourteenth and fifteenth centuries a series of false starts and futile conflicts—in the opinion of the Victorian historian William Stubbs, "a worn-out helpless age, that calls for pity without sympathy"? Some false starts, certainly, most importantly the failures in Scotland and France; but an age hugely important for England and its people. Foreign and domestic conflicts increased a sense of national consciousness. In part this must have been based on a sense of shared threat from what Shakespeare called "the envy of less happier lands": invasions and military defeats caused furious popular reactions, such as the Jack Cade rebellion, not least because of the risk to trade with the Low Countries, Aquitaine and Normandy. Perhaps there was a shared sense of superiority over savage Scots, Welsh and Irish (though some of these were at times allies against the others), and there was certainly rejoicing over Crécy, Poitiers and Agincourt. But as the French were finally victorious at Orleans, Formigny and Castillon, and the Celtic neighbours irrepressible, any sense of English national superiority must have been a battered and confused one.

Identity is based not only on attitudes towards foreign "others," but on relationships within a political community. An English state structure had been created since the twelfth and thirteenth centuries, with permanent legal and fiscal institutions covering the whole country. Socio-economic change since the 1350s had altered the mutual relationships of its inhabitants, as serfdom ended, the living standards of ordinary people rose, and the English language became predominant. Compared with other medieval polities, England was unusually centralized under the Crown, which made it normally peaceful and well governed; but if things went wrong, they went terribly wrong. Parliament could in crisis oppose monarchs or even legalize their deposition, claiming to speak on behalf of all. This had brought into "the community of the realm" not only the barons, bishops and knights who sat in parliaments, but merchants, craftsmen and yeomen. The 1429 qualification for electing members of Parliament was freehold property worth forty shillings a year, which remained until the nineteenth century, and created an electorate running into tens of thousands.

War required manpower and taxation, and efforts were made to involve the whole country in campaigns in France through information and propaganda. The law not merely permitted, but required, yeomen to keep weapons and practice archery, to provide the Crown with a potent weapon. But, as the Robin Hood legend recalls, the bow was a great equalizer. The level of popular political involvement and awareness was different from the precocious "national identity" observed in Anglo-Saxon times, when there were huge divides of status, ethnicity and region, or at the time of Magna Carta, when the "community of the realm" were effectively Francophone landowners. Now it included in some sense every man, as we see from their actions at times of crisis, when ordinary people "acted as if they mattered, as if they were properly part of the political commonweal."[84] London was seized by popular uprisings in 1381 and 1450—both sparked off by military failures. Although these dramatic and violent actions horrified the elites, the fact is that ordinary people did matter, and their rulers needed their participation: as taxpayers, soldiers, jurymen, local officials and even parliamentary voters. Thus England had been transformed from "a feudally structured society to a politically integrated one."[85]

This did not of course mean that people were necessarily happy or secure: this was a hard and dangerous society, especially on its exposed borders. But the people of England in the 1400s—surely shockingly— were richer and safer than in many countries in the 2000s. Above all, this was because social and political structures never disintegrated, and there was never prolonged general disorder even during the Wars of the Roses. Economic change after the Black Death made it possible to throw off the bonds and humiliations of serfdom, destroying the old distinction between "free" and "unfree" and creating equality before the law.

Another great distinction also finally disappeared: between the "natives," who spoke English, and their masters, who spoke French. The language of England might have developed as an insular variety of French, with Latin additions and vestigial Germanic idioms. Instead, commerce, urbanization, political involvement and the wars against France catalysed an upsurge of English, which signified an end to the status of conquered people. This was not a return to pre-Conquest English, when an official language had stood above a multitude of regional dialects. Now English was simpler, Latinized and Frenchified. There were regional dialects, which amused Chaucer, but they were mutually comprehensible. English was again the language of law, government, poetry, thought and piety. The consequence was that such matters could enter the minds and mouths of everyone.

We are used to thinking of the late fifteenth century as the close of an era, "the end of the Middle Ages." All such ideas are of course based on hindsight, not on how people experienced their own times. Henry VIII would attempt to reconquer France, and in 1544 get within fifty miles of Paris, unaware that what historians later called the "Hundred Years' War" had long finished. The system of "medieval" government that had emerged over the previous two centuries—by which monarchs ruled, local notables cooperated, and parliaments met occasionally as required—had repeatedly proved itself resilient: not immune from disaster, but able to recover rapidly. It would, with substantial modification, last another two centuries, in contrast with the development of absolute monarchy in Europe. But hindsight is sometimes accurate: a world was indeed ending, and England was on the verge of its greatest intellectual and cultural upheaval since the Conquest.

# Writing the Middle Ages:
## Shakespeare and Lesser Historians

When subsequent generations have envisaged England in the later Middle Ages, Shakespeare's characters and language have shaped their vision—from the audiences of 2,000 or 3,000 in his own theatres to the many millions who have seen film and television productions, or studied the plays at school and university. No other country has had a slice of its past so dramatized, or exposed to such a large audience—except perhaps the United States through the Hollywood Western.

Shakespeare wrote his ten English history plays in a burst of activity in the 1590s, perhaps stimulated by contemporary interest in history, and the drama of the struggle against Spain, and perhaps by worries about Elizabeth I's uncertain succession. The plays were popular, both on stage and in print, as a way for ordinary people to learn their history.[1] Shakespeare drew on a range of sources and models: traditional mystery plays, with their mixture of tragedy and comedy; popular ballads; the political and moral allegory plays of the previous generation; classics, such as Ovid, Virgil, Seneca and Tacitus; other playwrights, such as Marlowe and Heywood; political writers, including Machiavelli and More; and recent historiography, notably Ralph Holinshed's *Chronicle* (1587).

It is unlikely that the plays from *Richard II*[2] to *Henry VIII* were conceived as a cycle. They were not written in chronological order, and were never performed in sequence in Shakespeare's time. Not until the Romantic period was interest shown in the histories as a whole. The first performance of a cycle of the plays was in Germany in the 1860s—and in England not until 1902. Perhaps Shakespeare's contemporaries could not miss the point about the perils of a breakdown in legal monarchical succession. But later generations were not given a connected story. Rather, certain scenes and characters became enduringly famous. Henry V inspired patriotic fervour in times of national danger, being performed to cheering houses in London when Napoleon was threatening invasion, inspiring Churchill's speech about the "few" in 1940, and being filmed, with tactful

excisions, by Laurence Olivier in 1944 as a celebration of an eternal
English, and indeed British, brotherhood in the face of danger. But the
most popular history plays over the centuries focused on a clown and a
monster—Falstaff and Richard III—relegating historical events to mere
scenery. Modern directors have extracted or introduced a range of meanings, from nationalist and imperialist to anti-fascist and pacifist, sometimes by modifying or parodying the plays, but also simply by emphasizing
certain of Shakespeare's own themes. Sometimes, such updating may simply show that we can no longer comprehend the original meanings.[3] But
modernized readings can also make Shakespeare's fifteenth-century saga
part of today's political sensibility: for example, by dressing Richard III
as a fascist dictator.

Shakespeare made England's recent history (and in a different way its
ancient myths, as in *King Lear* and *Cymbeline*) an artistic subject as great
as the history of Rome. France, in contrast, never had a single play about
its own history until 1765—a now forgotten work, *Le Siège de Calais*, on
its struggle with Edward III. Shakespeare's national self-dramatization
perhaps made the English regard themselves as special—perhaps to some
extent it still does.

His presentation of recent history is commonly dismissed as "Tudor
propaganda." There are passages and characters in several plays—most
obviously Richard III, but also Henry V, Hamlet, Macbeth and King
Lear—that justify the accession of the Tudors and even more so of the
Stuarts.[4] But most of Shakespeare's history is the opposite of propaganda:
always ambivalent, often amoral, rarely idealized, often derisive, sometimes cynical, with few heroes but many villains and inadequates, much
futility, no euphemism, little sign of the benign workings of Providence,
no edifying message, no "grand narrative," and at best a provisional
happy ending.

He presents England's history as bound up with monarchy, and this has
been described as "politically deferential."[5] But his vision also includes a
rural and popular England. His portrayal of royalty, moreover, is far from
reverential or idealized. Showing any monarch on stage in even slightly
controversial circumstances was taboo over much of Europe as late as the
nineteenth century; but Shakespeare not only lets daylight in upon majesty (in Walter Bagehot's 1860s phrase) but subjects it to a withering
glare, showing kings humiliated, deposed and killed. The plays are overwhelmingly political: the conflicts and decisions of people acting out of
ambition, lust, pride, fear, revenge, jealousy—and occasionally loyalty, faith
or honour ("a word," mocks Falstaff). Their efforts and aims are often
futile, absurd and meaningless. Even the most just or glorious war brings

waste, corruption, cruelty and death "stinking and fly-blown."[6] His kings and queens are as human as his peasants—selfish, cruel, doubting, incapable, lecherous, perfidious, but rarely very chivalrous, and sacred only by the grace of their subjects. Not surprisingly, there could be political trouble, and Elizabeth I remarked balefully after one performance, "I am Richard II, know ye not that?"

Shakespeare rarely preaches. His characters speak in many voices. Even his monsters have moments of humanity, courage or pathos. The audience decides. For a nation that was already politically aware and claiming the right to judge its rulers, this was pushing the door wide open. Shakespeare's own sympathies, as far as they are displayed, seem to be for peace, harmony and moderation, with England as a carefully tended garden—a task needing many hands, and never finished.

At the very least, the plays have left a memory of certain episodes, characters, words and phrases—"the winter of our discontent," "my kingdom for a horse," "once more unto the breach, dear friends," "uneasy lies the head that wears a crown," "Cry God for Harry, England and St George," "we few, we happy few, we band of brothers," "this other Eden . . . this precious stone set in a silver sea"—arguably the most famous eulogy of England. Such phrases, even when misapplied, create a sense of connection with the past.

Shakespeare's image of the fifteenth century is a grim one—perhaps grimmer than modern historians would warrant, certainly for the Middle Ages as a whole. Society and politics were not a conflict of all against all. England was normally a peaceful place, with occasional outbursts of mayhem. Its people were richer than at any time until the late nineteenth century. Social conflict was rarely violent, and there is no reason to believe that social relations, though steeply hierarchical and patriarchal, were more antagonistic than in modern times, once society had adapted to the growth of freedom and prosperity after the Black Death.

Other artists besides Shakespeare have contributed to our diverse images of the "medieval" period—the word itself invented only in the nineteenth century. The Romantic interest in national cultural tradition, popularized by Walter Scott, fostered a medieval craze across Europe and its overseas colonies. In architecture, art, literature and fashion, there was a vogue for medieval styles, symbolizing a harmonious, organic, Christian society. This led to the preservation and restoration of medieval buildings, and the creation of many new ones, from cottages to railway stations, in neo-Gothic style, often seen as native English—"Early English," "Decorated English," "Perpendicular English." Hence its adoption in 1835, in preference to neo-classical, for the new Palace of Westminster, a stupendous (and exaggerated) assertion of both the antiquity and the centrality of Parliament in English history.

But "medieval" could also be a term of abuse, as it has remained. The popular connotations of the word evoke violence, cruelty, oppression and ignorance. "Gothic" literature rather liked dwelling on the horrors. The cruelties of "medieval" punishments contrasted with eighteenth- and nineteenth-century campaigns to humanize treatment of criminals. Most of all, a dark picture of the Middle Ages fitted the historical narratives of Protestant and Enlightened Europe: they were seen as the backward, superstitious centuries between the collapse of ancient civilization and modern times when that civilization was rediscovered and surpassed. What became known as "Whig history"—essentially the view of history as political progress—necessarily saw the Middle Ages as an oppressive and barbarous prelude to "the sunlight that is to come." Many believed that Anglo-Saxon England had been free and happy, and saw the post-Conquest centuries as a struggle to recover lost rights, via Magna Carta and Parliament—a view originating during the medieval period itself. An even more negative view saw progress arising from modern urbanization and commerce, and dismissed as fiction the idea of ancient liberties or medieval progress. In this influential view, the Middle Ages could not be other than poverty-stricken, harsh and oppressive, and their politics merely the chaotic and selfish struggles of an over-mighty nobility. Our impressions of those centuries are still coloured and distorted by these now ancient cultural and historical traditions.

# PART THREE

# THE GREAT DIVIDE,
## *c.*1500–*c.*1700

England, precariously stable under the young Henry VIII (whose succession in 1509 was the first for a century to be undisputed), was living on the slopes of a European volcano. Geopolitical, cultural and ideological crises were shaking confidence in the authority of established Western civilization so severely that sensible people believed that the end of the world was nigh, or at least that God was punishing unfaithful Christians—the 1512 Lateran Council felt obliged to forbid preachers to touch on such subjects.[1] Muslim forces, having captured Constantinople, were advancing on land and sea. A devastating war began in Italy in 1494 between the two greatest Christian powers, France and the Habsburg Holy Roman Empire. The Dominican friar Savonarola established a theocratic dictatorship in Florence in 1495 to stamp out corruption, but he was overthrown and burned at the stake in 1498. In 1517, a German Augustinian friar, Martin Luther, nailed his own criticisms of the ecclesiastical authorities to a church door in Wittenberg. Popes had repeatedly been in conflict with Church Councils and had plunged into secular warfare and politics, and Rome itself was captured and sacked with appalling violence by Habsburg troops in 1527. Muslim armies overran Hungary, killing the king and slaughtering nobles and clergy, and they reached the gates of Vienna in 1530. Arab raiders took perhaps a million Europeans into slavery between 1530 and 1640, including some from Britain. A century of atrocious religious conflict began, leading to persecutions, civil wars and wars between states, culminating in the terrible Thirty Years' War (1618–48). England escaped the worst: but it could not avoid the seismic shocks, culminating in connected British civil wars, the last of the European wars of religion, which finally ended after a Dutch intervention only in 1691.

The intellectual roots of the upheaval, stretching back to fourteenth-century Italy, had given little hint of danger. A new interest in Greek and Roman antiquity, the core of what nineteenth-century historians dubbed the Renaissance, was further stimulated by large numbers of previously unknown texts rescued by refugee scholars from Constantinople. This inspired fashionable classical styles of literature, art and architecture. A fascination for Greek and Roman writings (taught by the *umanisti*— "humanists") made traditional philosophy and culture seem musty, even absurd: some mocked medieval theology as "debating how many angels could dance on the head of a pin." Controversial ideas circulating in the 1530s about the relative positions of the earth and the sun and the discovery of the Americas after 1492 showed that there were things in heaven and earth undreamed of in traditional teaching and even in the Bible. There was a desire to re-examine the sources of beliefs by studying original texts. In the 1450s, for example, philology had demonstrated that the supposedly fourth-century "Donation of Constantine," which the papacy had claimed as the origin of its temporal authority, was a forgery.

By far the most important new text was the Bible itself. Newly acquired knowledge of languages meant that humanist scholars could study the recently published Greek and Hebrew originals, even finding mistakes in the orthodox Latin "Vulgate," St. Jerome's thousand-year-old translation on which the Western Church had based its teaching. The most famous humanist, Erasmus of Rotterdam, in 1516 produced an edition of the Greek New Testament with a new parallel Latin translation giving changes of wording—significant because fundamental beliefs could hang on particular phrases, even words.[2] Humanists such as Erasmus, John Colet, the dean of St. Paul's, and Thomas More, lawyer, member of Parliament and in 1529 Lord Chancellor, had hoped that these intellectual advances would lead to religious reform and renewal. But they became weapons in an assault on authority.

Printing (from the 1430s) and cheaper paper meant that copies of ancient texts and modern translations could be made available outside the clerical and aristocratic elite, even to ordinary literate people—the gentry, merchants, yeomen, artisans. Printed Bibles appeared in German in 1466, and in Italian, Dutch, French, Spanish and Czech in the 1470s. Lay readers ceased to be dependent on the clergy to transmit the word of God. Instead of asking what God meant (which required experts to explain) they began to ask simply what God said, and decide on his meaning themselves. England was well behind in this because of strict anti-Lollard legislation.

Late-medieval Christianity, like most religions, invested enormously in mechanisms of salvation: ceremonies, rituals, chapels, chantries, shrines, relics, statues, pilgrimages and indulgences. This familiar, beautiful, mysterious and yet accessible form of worship provided comfort and hope.[3] Most people clung to it. Most of the cultural glories of Europe derived from it, as did the power and wealth of the Church. But it could become a squalid transaction between man and God by which favour, forgiveness and salvation were bought by performing a quasi-magical act, paying a fee, making a material gift to God or a saint, or bequeathing money for posthumous prayers. Intellectual scepticism could draw on traditional resentment of the clergy's wealth, as in the early example of Lollardy. "Jesus said, 'Feed my lambs,' not 'Shear my sheep,'" joked English reformers.

Luther's open challenge in 1517 was a denunciation of the "sale" of indulgences, by which punishment for sin could be remitted by a cash donation to the Church—currently, to build the magnificent basilica of St. Peter in Rome. Luther rejected the whole system of belief on which this kind of piety was based. Drawing on ideas of the fifth-century St. Augustine, he denied that merit or forgiveness could be gained by anything that sinful man could do: salvation depended solely on the mercy of God. Human beings could do nothing to deserve this mercy: God chose them to receive it. Though this idea had always been present in Western Christian teaching, the conclusions that Luther began to draw were that many of the activities of the Church, including most of its sacraments, were at best useless and at worst blasphemous, and that its ruling authorities were corrupt and oppressive, in effect perpetrating a huge confidence trick on Christians.

Luther's message appealed to many educated people, first of all in the German and Swiss cities, who were already emancipating themselves intellectually from the clergy by reading the Bible, which seemed to be the true way to faith, godliness and salvation. Luther also appealed, as Wyclif had done more than a century earlier, to nobles and princes for whom bishops, abbots and the Pope were powerful and wealthy rivals. Luther and his followers believed that religion and society needed authority, but that Christian princes, not the Pope, should wield it. It turned out that authority and order were not so easily preserved amid the moral and intellectual revolution Luther had ignited. Over much of northern Europe, crowds smashed statues in churches. In 1524, popular revolts, the so-called Peasants' War, began to sweep across central Europe from the Rhine to Poland. Ancient social tensions were inflamed by religious radicalism, despite Luther's furious denunciation of "thieving murdering peasants." Many thousands were eventually slaughtered, tortured and executed in the biggest ideological upheaval in Europe before the French Revolution. No one could doubt that religious dissension affected everything.

Amid this European turmoil, in 1526 a young former Oxford scholar,

William Tyndale, began to print copies in Cologne of his English translation of the New Testament from the Greek, undertaken in defiance of
English law. They were seized in a raid on his printer, but he began again
in Worms, and then again in Antwerp. Tyndale (to whom we shall return)
believed that biblical interpretation did not require clerical authority, for
it was simple and unambiguous: "The scripture hath but one sense, which
is the literal sense."[4] Perhaps 16,000 copies of his translation were smuggled into England over the next ten years (compared with the hundreds of
manuscript copies the Lollards had managed to produce). He is supposed
to have said to a critic that "ere many years I will cause a boy that driveth
the plough shall know more of the scripture than thou dost." This was a
truly revolutionary ambition.

# CHAPTER 5

# Reformation

*This realm of England is an empire . . . governed by one supreme head and king having the dignity and royal estate of the imperial crown.*

Act in Restraint of Appeals, 1533

It was at this very time, the mid-1520s, that Henry VIII concluded that his marriage was cursed. His consequent actions convulsed England for more than 150 years, opening a divide that has never entirely disappeared. His queen, Catherine of Aragon, daughter of Ferdinand and Isabella of Spain, had been married first in 1501 to his elder brother, Arthur, who had died soon after the wedding. Largely for diplomatic reasons, the Pope gave a dispensation for Catherine to remarry the teenage Henry in 1509, a month after he had succeeded to the throne. Royal marriages were for producing heirs, and here there had been disaster: a stillborn girl in 1510, a boy the following year who died after seven weeks, a miscarriage in 1513, another boy who died soon after birth in 1514, another miscarriage in 1517, and a stillbirth in 1518. A girl, Mary, born in 1516, survived, but female succession was risky, especially as the Wars of the Roses, a terrifying precedent, had shattered the certainty of royal succession. So the kingdom needed a boy. Otherwise, the king of Scots, the hereditary enemy, would be the closest male heir. In 1519 Henry promised to lead a Crusade in person if God gave him a son.

Henry was conventionally pious, and unusually interested in scholarship and theology—quite capable of drawing his own conclusions and convincing himself of their rightness. He had fathered an illegitimate son in 1519—Henry Fitzroy, Duke of Richmond, who lived into adolescence—which convinced him that the problem was his marriage. It may in fact be that a genetic abnormality explains both his reproductive problems and his later mental and physical decline;[1] but his own diagnosis was that his marriage to Catherine was against God's commandments, as laid down in the book of Leviticus. His advisers produced a tailored translation of chapter 21, verse 20, supporting this conclusion: "Who so marrieth his brother's wife doth a thing that is unlawful, he shall be without sons or heirs male"[2]—hence the stillborn boys. (The literal meaning was "they shall be childless," which of course did not fit.) He was, he decided, not validly married, and hence was free to marry again and produce an heir. At the opportune moment he fell passionately in love with Anne, the daughter of a friend and courtier, Sir Thomas Boleyn. She was vivacious and like the king interested in ideas. Although she was the sister of one of his earlier mistresses, they seem not to have become lovers: at first she resisted, and then he perhaps decided that, as future queen and mother of his heir, she must not become pregnant too soon.[3] Frustrated desire certainly spurred what became Henry's obsession: to get rid of Catherine and marry Anne, an outcome for which he had to wait for over five years.

Christianity was at that time unique among the major religions in not allowing divorce, hence the need for intellectual ingenuity. Henry's theological argument was weak, but not hopeless. His formidable chief minister, Cardinal Wolsey, began a diplomatic and legal effort in 1527 to resolve "the king's great matter" with Rome. Academics were recruited to draft arguments and assemble theological and historical evidence. The leading universities of Christendom were asked for their opinion, and several gave the desired answer. Making the issue one of international controversy was meant to put pressure on the Pope, but it raised the stakes dangerously. There existed less confrontational ways of arranging such matters. Catherine could have gone into a nunnery, like the wife of the French king, Louis XII, and there was even a suggestion of licensed bigamy. Where matters of state were concerned, such problems could normally be sorted out retrospectively, for example when Catherine died (which she did, of natural causes, in 1536). But Henry was self-righteous, impatient and indifferent to the beliefs, feelings or interests of others. His chosen argument was a challenge to the papacy: it had given permission for his marriage with Catherine, which Henry now denied its power to do. Any readiness by Pope Clement VII to be accommodating was inhibited by politics. Catherine appealed to her nephew, the Holy Roman Emperor, Charles V, who, having inherited the Habsburg domains in Germany and the Netherlands, the Spanish crowns and much of Italy, had become the dominant power in Europe. Moreover, as we have seen, the papacy, and indeed the whole of Latin Christendom, was facing an accumulation of crises built up over the previous century.

All this turned Henry's personal obsessions into the spark for the greatest revolution in English history, and one which contributed to the greatest fault-line in Christian culture for a thousand years.[4] Circumstances made the issues of principle—which Henry took very seriously—far more dangerous. Could the Pope interpret (or as Henry saw it, break) God's law expressed in the Bible? Was the Pope superior to a Christian king in his own realm? These were burning questions in the 1520s and 1530s. Moreover, Henry's clash with Rome ignited divisions inside England between evangelicals (those who stressed the importance of the Bible and faith) and conservatives (who held to existing ideas of worship, sacraments and Church authority). The former were increasingly attracted by reforming ideas from Germany and Switzerland. Henry loathed Luther, however. In 1521 he had published a powerful attack on Lutheran sacramental theories, which had won him the papal accolade *"Fidei Defensor"*—"Defender of the Faith"—a title English and British monarchs have subsequently retained, though not in the sense the Pope intended. Henry continued to have Lutherans burned as heretics throughout his reign. Yet with regard to papal authority he was following Luther's lead; and, as the first king to reject that authority, he amplified the European conflict. So his marriage and his conflict with the Pope, which in more normal times could probably have been solved by legal fiction and diplomatic negotiation, perhaps following a symbolic excommunication and period of interdict, in these abnormal times caused a breach that could never quite be repaired.

Henry was not a subtle man, and his attempt to persuade the Pope to annul his marriage took the form of pressure and threats. Cardinal Wolsey's attempt to use legal and diplomatic methods with Rome met with delaying tactics, so Henry dismissed the faithful Wolsey in 1529 and confiscated his property, most famously Hampton Court—a first warning to the English bishops and the papacy. He began to appoint to senior posts in the Church the Cambridge academics who had been advising him in his divorce case, most importantly Thomas Cranmer, made Archbishop of Canterbury (still with proper papal approval) in January 1533—just in time for Henry's marriage to Anne that same month. Eight months later, on 7 September, came the disappointing birth of a girl, Elizabeth.

In the 1530s came a rapid succession of parliamentary acts to remove the English Church from the jurisdiction of Rome, and to make Henry formally its head. The Act in Restraint of Appeals (1533) ended legal recourse to Rome, declaring England "an empire," drawing on arguments from "sundry old authentic histories and chronicles," including Geoffrey of Monmouth's imaginative saga. An Act of Succession (1534) declared Catherine's marriage void, confirmed that of Anne, and conferred the succession on her issue. Two Acts of Supremacy (1534) "confirmed" that

Henry was "the only supreme head in earth of the Church of England," and made it treason to deny it. Every man in the kingdom was required on demand to take a prescribed oath to accept the Act of Succession, and the clergy to accept the Act of Supremacy.

These great, but to most people remote, changes in jurisdiction and high politics caused little stir in England. Nearly all the bishops and most of the lower clergy accepted them, as did the nobility. But this did not make them evangelical reformers. The powerful Duke of Norfolk obeyed the king's will, but did not want meddling with traditional beliefs and practices, famously declaring "he had never read the Scriptures, nor ever would, and it was merry in England before this New Learning came up."[5] Conservative bishops continued to prescribe traditional worship and doctrine under the new authority of the king. Henry himself ferociously enforced orthodox theology and almost the whole Latin liturgy throughout his reign.

A few Observant Franciscan friars and Carthusian monks from the London Charterhouse refused to accept the new royal authority. So did two men of European reputation. John Fisher, pioneer of Greek learning, chancellor of Cambridge University, patron of St. John's and Christ's colleges, and Bishop of Rochester, was known as the most spiritual and austere, as well as the most intellectual, of the bishops. Sir Thomas More, lawyer and zealous Lord Chancellor, was the renowned author of an original product of humanist thought, the subtle and urbane parable *Utopia* (1516), describing an imaginary pagan island governed by equality and justice. Fisher had always been a supporter of Queen Catherine, whereas More, as Lord Chancellor, had officially presented Henry's divorce case to Parliament. But both believed that the king's rejection of papal authority and claim of supremacy contravened divine law. Fisher had gone so far as to propose that the emperor Charles V might intervene, though More firmly rebuffed any hint of treason. In April 1534, they both refused to take the required oaths, and were sent to the Tower. More had prepared his family by rehearsing his own arrest. Fisher believed in the supremacy of the Church over kings, and so would not accept the validity of Henry's divorce. More, like many humanists, was no exponent of papal theocracy, and he was willing to accept Anne as queen. But he would not endorse what he saw as Henry's split from the rest of Christendom.

A compromise would have been possible, as Cranmer urged, for both More and Fisher offered to swear to the succession itself, while remaining silent on papal authority and the royal marriages. But Henry insisted on complete public submission. In the Tower of London, both hoped that keeping silence would preserve their lives: they refused the oaths, but would give no reasons. "I do nobody harm, I say none harm, I think none harm, but wish every body good," protested More. "And if this be not enough to keep a man alive in good faith I long not to live."[6] Henry was not content with silence, and the unscrupulous and successful careerist Richard Rich, the Solicitor-General, was sent to entrap them. Fisher, old, ill and honest, was easy prey, and his fate was sealed when the Pope, trying to help, made him a cardinal—Henry commented that he would soon have no head to put his red hat on. More, an experienced lawyer, was probably not caught out, but nevertheless Rich testified that he had said that Parliament had no power to make the king head of the Church. He certainly thought this, but denied having said it, for thought was not treason: speech was. At show trials in 1535 both were found guilty. Henry's only mercy was to allow them to be beheaded, unlike recalcitrant Carthusian monks, more than a dozen of whom were hanged, drawn and quartered.

The consequences of Henry's religious revolution were even more dangerous in Ireland than in England, as from the 1530s English law and administration were for the first time effectively extended both to Wales and to Ireland. In Wales, this was to some extent beneficial, as it gave equality before the law, and Welsh culture and self-government were respected, for example with an official Welsh Bible and prayer-book. In Ireland, it was a different story. In 1534 the powerful Fitzgeralds took advantage of Henry's international isolation to rebel. Henry sent a small English army, which began bloody and indiscriminate repression. This initiated an escalation of violence and religious conflict that led to repeated atrocities during five wars over 150 years, and transformed the traditionally loose relationship of Ireland and England.[7] Seen from England, the strategic importance of Ireland as a base for possible invasion was greatly aggravated by sectarian and European conflicts, and any chance of reasonable Anglo-Irish coexistence disappeared. The conflicts of the sixteenth century would be transmitted into every succeeding century. The solution begun in 1546 of introducing armed English, Welsh and later Scottish settlers eternalized antagonism.

Henry's religious policy was now in the hands of two men, Archbishop Cranmer and Thomas Cromwell, the king's secretary. Cromwell has not been kindly treated by history, which casts him as a grim and amoral functionary, but he is one of the most remarkable men ever to have held high political office in England. The son of a cloth merchant and innkeeper, he began in his teens as a footloose soldier of fortune in Flanders and Italy, became a self-taught businessman, lawyer and intellectual, competent in French, Italian, Latin and Greek, and a man of sharp wit and sparkling conversation. He is said to have known Erasmus's translation of the New Testament by heart, and became a convinced evangelical reformer. He was the indispensable instrument of the king, and "vicegerent" of the Church. Cranmer and Cromwell have usually been seen as trying to push Henry further towards reform than he wished to go, with intervals in which the king swung back towards conservatism. But Henry was broadly determined to steer a middle course between tradition and reform: between "the usurped power of the bishop of Rome" and radical evangelists who "wrest and interpret" the Bible "to subvert and overturn as well the sacraments of Holy Church as the power and authority of princes."[8] Religion was too important to be left to the clergy: the political and social order was at risk.

This had been luridly demonstrated in the midst of Henry's reformation. In October 1534, France was swept by panic when posters were put up asserting that secret groups of heretics were planning to massacre the orthodox. Worse, in Münster, armed "Anabaptist" radicals had carried out a prototypical act of violent revolution, driving out the "godless" in February 1534 and setting up a terroristic Utopia under a messianic king, with all property in common, compulsory polygamy, all books banned save the Bible, and the death penalty for disobedience. In June 1535, after a terrible siege, an imperial army stormed the town and massacred the defenders; the "king" was torn apart with red-hot pincers.[9] In England, Henry did his bit by having a dozen Dutch Anabaptist immigrants burned.

Henry kept a close eye on doctrine. He insisted above all on "transubstantiation": that the bread and wine of the Mass were miraculously changed into the body and blood of Christ in a mystical participation in his sacrifice. This was the core of the idea of the Church and its priesthood as sacred and apart, unlike the radical belief that "the Lord's supper" was a commemoration ceremony performed by a group of believers. Henry insisted too that salvation came from good works, and not from faith alone—he thought it dangerous (as indeed sometimes it was) if people believed that they were "saved" however they behaved. So his convictions, which were apparently sincere, were also useful: they supported order and hierarchy and enhanced his own status as a divinely instituted monarch. Henry saw himself as a moderate. Those less moderate than himself—even those close to him—risked the stake or the block.

Henry's kind of moderation made conflicts between conservatives and evangelicals within the Church highly dangerous. Their labours to produce agreed liturgy and doctrine went far beyond academic debate. Conservatives were eager to bring charges of heresy, even against the highest—one said he "trusted to see the day that my Lord of Canterbury should be burned." Conservative JPs, supported by the cathedral clergy, were prosecuting evangelicals for heresy in Cranmer's own diocese. Even exile was no sure defence. In May 1535 Tyndale, halfway through his translation of the Old Testament, was tracked down in Antwerp by an agent of Bishop Bonner of London, and burned for heresy by the imperial authorities. The cautious evangelical Cranmer was lucky that Henry trusted him—on one occasion when he was accused of being "the greatest heretic in Kent," the king laughingly ordered him to investigate the charges himself.[10]

Henry backed reform where pilgrimages, monasteries and shrines were concerned. He wanted to forestall the dangerous likelihood of More and Fisher being considered by the people as modern Beckets, popular defenders of Church against king. This encouraged him to attack many aspects of traditional piety, including pilgrimages and monasteries. He destroyed the great shrine of the "traitor" Becket, and ordered all his images throughout the country to be destroyed. Moreover, monasteries were rich, owning about a tenth of the country's land. At least since John of Gaunt and Wyclif, there had been a notion that monastic wealth could provide a solid endowment for the Crown, which would no longer have to ask parliaments for constant taxes. Beginning in 1535, Cromwell rapidly organized "visitations" and inventories of religious houses, and began to close them down and confiscate their wealth—their land, their libraries, the jewels of their shrines and their sacred vessels. Henry accumulated chests of gold stored at the back of his bedchamber in Whitehall.[11] There was vast looting, and embezzlement: the reformers could profit from religion at least as well as the sellers of indulgences. The cultural losses are incalculable, including art, buildings and historical records. Tens of thousands of objects and works of art great and small were melted down, torn up, painted over or smashed. Matthew Parker, Master of Corpus Christi, Cambridge, saved ancient documents he thought proved the ancient autonomy of the English Church, and in doing so rescued swathes of England's early history from oblivion. Queen Anne campaigned for some of the proceeds to go to education and poor relief. Vast sums went on building or adorning palaces (including Richmond, Hampton Court and Nonsuch in Surrey) and on creating a navy; or it was squandered on an expensive and futile war with France in 1544.

In May 1536 Anne was convicted of treason in the form of multiple adultery and beheaded—the single act, perhaps, for which Henry is most widely remembered. Ironically, she lived less than a year longer than More and Fisher, and only weeks longer than Queen Catherine. They must have hoped that the king would tire of her, and so be reconciled with Rome. The former hope was realized; the latter, however, does not seem to have crossed his mind. Anne's fate remains an enigma. There have been many theories, some of them fanciful. It has long been believed that her fall was engineered by Cromwell, who thought her views on the wealth of the monasteries a threat to his position, or considered her a barrier to an alliance with Catherine of Aragon's nephew, Charles V (whose ambassador habitually referred to Anne simply as "the whore"). Henry was coming to regard her as another failure, as she had produced only a daughter and had suffered two miscarriages (most recently on 29 February—the day of Catherine of Aragon's funeral). He already had his eye on a younger replacement, Jane Seymour.

However, a careful examination of the evidence finds no indication of a plot against Anne, whose downfall was unplanned, unexpected and rapid.[12] The most likely explanation is that malicious gossip concerning Anne's relations with a young household musician, Mark Smeaton, and with Henry's friend and personal attendant, Henry Norris, reached the ears of Cromwell and the king at the end of April 1536, and they began an investigation. The gossip was unfounded.[13] Smeaton seems to have tried shyly to flirt with the queen; she had incautiously remarked that Norris would like to marry her if the king died; and she and her entourage had joked about Henry's impotence. All this was dangerous enough, but when Smeaton was arrested, he confessed to adultery with the queen— perhaps under torture (one account has Cromwell in person twisting a knotted rope round his head), perhaps after promises of mercy, perhaps even through some psychological fantasy. This single confession was sufficient, though all the others protested their innocence. Within three weeks, Anne, her brother, Norris, Smeaton and two other courtiers were tried, condemned and executed. If Henry had at first shown angry and tearful self-pity, he soon got over the execution of his wife and his closest friend. The cynical imperial ambassador reported that he had "shown himself more glad than ever since the arrest of the whore; for he has been going about banqueting with ladies."[14] Eleven days after Anne's death, he married Jane. What this shows is less a Machiavellian, faction-driven court than simply the perils of being close to a merciless and unpredictable tyrant.

Monasteries and nunneries were not universally popular as landlords, either with underpaid parish priests or with their long-suffering tenants— some monasteries were still trying to enforce serfdom. Yet it was their suppression, and what was feared might follow, that in October 1536 began the biggest popular uprising of the century in Lincolnshire and Yorkshire, calling itself the "Pilgrimage of Grace for the Commonwealth."

It was an orderly and organized movement, protesting its legality and loyalty, which prominent gentlemen and nobles were persuaded to join as leaders. The participants, who numbered over 30,000, carried religious banners, demanded an end to the closure of religious houses, which as they said provided aid to the poor, and demanded the summoning of a parliament. They repaired and reopened some monasteries that had been closed, and demanded prayers for the Pope. They were also angry at new taxes. Above all, they were determined to prevent the rumoured next step—merging parishes, closing churches, and seizing precious ritual objects, such as jewelled processional crosses. At stake were sacred places and things that belonged to and defined communities and ordered their collective rituals.

As in the Peasants' Revolt of 1381, the rebels knew their enemies: they had death lists, which included Cromwell, Cranmer and a long list of heretics, whom they wanted to burn along with their English Bibles. York and Hull were occupied by the rebels. Henry ordered the magnates of the north and east to raise forces to resist, but in the face of rebel strength the Duke of Norfolk negotiated, promising a free pardon, restoration of the monasteries, and a parliament. Henry acquiesced in the negotiations, even inviting one of the rebel leaders to meet him. When the danger subsided he renounced all concessions, and ordered summary executions of rebels. With characteristic vindictiveness, he instructed that monks who had returned to their dissolved abbeys should be "hanged upon long pieces of timber . . . out of the steeple."[15] The leaders tried and executed included two peers, several knights and the abbot of Fountains Abbey. In all, around 300 people were executed for religious reasons between 1532 and 1540. By 1540, all monasteries, abbeys and chantries had gone. Elements of their style of worship remained in the cathedrals, many of which had been in the hands of monastic orders, now transformed into cathedral chapters—including Canterbury, Durham, Ely and Winchester. The sale of monastic land was the largest such transfer since the Norman Conquest, and its buyers formed a powerful interest group against a return to the old establishment.

Queen Jane bore a son in October 1537, and died soon after. England at last had a future king, Edward. But other threats gathered. At last the Pope excommunicated Henry, and called for a crusade against him. France and Spain drew closer together, making a crusade possible, so the largest fortifications since Roman times were built to defend the main southern ports from Milford Haven to Essex, especially Portsmouth, Kent and the Thames estuary. Although Henry has long been considered one of the fathers of the English navy, seaborne activity was limited and unsuccessful.[16]

Henry continued to assert his conservative religious beliefs. In 1538, dressed all in white for purity, he presided personally over the trial and condemnation to the stake of John Lambert, who denied the literal bodily presence of Christ in the bread and wine of the Eucharist; and he ordered all foreigners holding such views to leave the country. At the same time, the danger of invasion led Henry and Cromwell towards a possible alliance with the Lutheran states of north Germany, an important step being another marriage—this time with Anne of Cleves. The story is famous: descriptions of her beauty, backed up by a portrait by Hans Holbein, tempted the king, but after he wedded "the Flanders mare" in 1540 he could not consummate the marriage. Henry—now an unhealthy fifty-year-old—was undoubtedly less rampant than in his prime. Anne, naïve and somewhat flabby, did not rekindle the dying embers. She backed out good-naturedly, with lavish financial compensation—a wise move. Also part of the story is that Henry blamed Cromwell, which brought about his downfall. There is little evidence for this view, as neither the diplomacy nor the wedding were solely Cromwell's idea, but it may have encouraged his many enemies.

On 10 June 1540, Cromwell, now Earl of Essex, king's secretary and holder of many other important posts, was brusquely arrested at a meeting of the Privy Council and his badge of office ripped from his neck. As with most of the sudden dramas of Henry's reign, the reasons are unclear. The most plausible explanations are that Cromwell had shown himself too favourable to religious reformers, forbidding "idolatry" in the form of statues and the cult of saints, pushing the provision of English Bibles, and favouring alliance with Lutheran states. Most dangerously of all, he had facilitated the circulation in "our maternal and English tongue" of a "great number of false erroneous books, whereof many were printed and made beyond the seas," promoting Lutheran beliefs forbidden by the king.[17] It has even been suggested that he was "as much a martyr to his faith as More and Fisher were for theirs," although his beliefs were ambiguous.[18] With the possibility of a *rapprochement* with France suddenly arising, Henry may also have acted for diplomatic reasons, as the French regarded Cromwell both as unfriendly and as a religious radical. Conservatives celebrated his fall by arresting 500 London evangelicals. He wrote to Henry: "I crye for mercye mercye mercye"[19]—in vain. He was beheaded on 28 July 1540, the day Henry married Catherine Howard, niece of the powerful and conservative Duke of Norfolk. Two days later, in unmistakable proof of his religious "moderation," Henry put on a grand show at Smithfield: three evangelicals burned for heresy, and three conservatives hanged and quartered for treason. No one could deny his sense of occasion.

With women, however, he was less adroit. The young Queen Catherine did not enjoy all aspects of life with her large and gloomy husband, and sought consolation by committing in reality what Anne Boleyn had been accused of, namely insanely reckless indiscretions with young men.[20] Though there seems to have been no evangelical plot against the Howard faction, it was an evangelical courtier who brought the story to Cranmer, and he informed the king, who was stunned. Inevitably, Catherine and her alleged lovers were executed, in November 1541.

The next few years were dominated by the usual war—though it turned out to be the last for more than a century—against a Franco-Scottish alliance, a ruinously expensive and unsuccessful adventure only remembered now because during a French attack on Portsmouth, in 1545, the great ship *Mary Rose* capsized, drowning 500 men. The war, bizarrely, was the last Crusade in English history, officially proclaimed by the Archbishop of Canterbury on the grounds that France had an alliance with the Turks. Like his tough medieval predecessors, the mild-mannered Cranmer found himself on horseback "with his dagger at his saddle-bow" defending the Kent coast.[21] The Scots were heavily defeated and James V killed at Solway Moss in December 1542, but they remained pro-French and hostilities resumed. A plan to march on Paris in alliance with the emperor Charles V was dropped when Charles pulled out. Henry, who led the army in person, was left with Boulogne, expensive to capture, fortify and garrison, and later sold back to the French at a loss. Thus was wasted much of the money raised from dissolving the monasteries. Perhaps the most lasting effect of the war was that it produced the first officially approved church service in English, written by Cranmer and issued in May 1544 to encourage prayers for victory. It became the litany in the Book of Common Prayer.

In a remarkable triumph of hope over experience, Henry got married yet again, in 1543, to an intelligent and cultivated thirty-one-year-old widow with evangelical tendencies, Catherine Parr. This time, despite the intrigues of religious conservatives, nothing untoward happened, and, importantly, Catherine exerted an intellectual influence on Prince Edward and Princess Elizabeth, whose upbringing she supervised. Such was the level of religious conflict that not even the queen was safe. The able and intriguing Bishop of Winchester, Stephen Gardiner, ambassador to Charles V, urged Henry to rein in religious change for diplomatic reasons. Powerful conservative politicians, including Norfolk and the Bishop of London, Bonner, rounded up and interrogated the usual suspects. In an example of the depths to which political life had sunk, in June 1546 a twenty-five-year-old evangelical, Anne Askew, was personally tortured in the Tower by the Lord Chancellor, Wriothesley, and Richard (now Lord) Rich, to try to make her incriminate wives of evangelical politicians, members of the queen's entourage, even the queen herself. "And because I laye styll and did not crye [they] toke paynes to racke me . . . tyll I was nygh dead"—an act that unsettled even those hard men, the members of the Privy Council. Crippled by the rack, Askew was burned at Smithfield.[22]

Henry maintained his religious balancing act to the end, and even after. He turned against the conservative faction before he died in January 1547, aged fifty-seven, and on his deathbed there were no last rites. Yet he preserved tradition in his will and the arrangements for his funeral. Dirges and requiems were chanted, and Masses were to be said in perpetuity for his soul. Thanks to Holbein's imposing portrait of him as a domineering physical presence, he is more familiar to later generations in appearance, as well as in deeds, than any previous monarch and most subsequent ones.

The succession of the nine-year-old Edward VI was inevitably the occasion of factional struggle. His uncle, Edward Seymour, later Duke of Somerset, governed from January 1547 as Lord Protector, with the support of Catherine Parr's family and other magnates. John Dudley, later Duke of Northumberland, ousted Somerset in October 1549, largely due to the latter's inept handling of rural rebellions in that year protesting against enclosure of common land, and his seizure of the king, which made things worse. If these political methods recalled bad memories of the previous century, this time there was no civil war: the conflict was contained within court and government. The time when great magnates could raise armies of retainers had ended with the Wars of the Roses. The Crown was acquiring a monopoly of military force.

In religious matters, there was consistency throughout Edward's reign. Both Somerset and Northumberland supported reforms far beyond anything Henry VIII would have countenanced. In London and the south-east, evangelicals were now numerous and active. The young king had been brought up and was still surrounded by evangelicals. Cranmer, whose beliefs had become steadily more reformist, was now properly in charge: he abandoned his priestly tonsure, grew a patriarchal beard and brought his wife out of hiding. The conservative bishops Gardiner and Bonner were locked up. Evangelical reform was pushed hard. There was further destruction or removal of church murals, statues, altars, precious books, vestments, vessels and memorials to the dead. The evangelicals (as all over Europe) were even more sexually censorious than the conservatives: Cranmer urged life imprisonment for adulterers, and punishment of sexual delinquents was made harsher.[23] The new official religion was too negative, thought the famous exiled theologian Martin Bucer (Regius Professor of Divinity at Cambridge): reform was being imposed "by means of ordinances, which the majority obey very grudgingly, and by the removal of the instruments of ancient superstition."[24] The most important innovation was the extension of services in English. Parts of the Mass were already in English. In 1549, a Book of Common Prayer, prepared by Cranmer, was made the compulsory liturgy of the Church, and in 1552 a more reformist version appeared. The theological messages in its phraseology and prescribed gestures were what counted—most importantly, the communion was no longer presented as a miraculous sacrament, but as a group commemoration.

To us today the cultural importance of the English liturgy may be more evident than its theology. Cranmer was eclectic in drawing on older texts—including the Sarum Rite (the Latin liturgy used in most of England) and Spanish Mozarabic prayers.[25] In modifying and adding to them, he fortunately turned out to be a writer of simple and limpid prose (his verse, as he realized, was poor), which stands out from the cluttered style common in the rapidly changing English of the time. The Prayer Book helped to shape the language, coining what became some of its most familiar phrases. For centuries to come people across the Anglophone world would pledge "to love and to cherish," be buried as "ashes to ashes, dust to dust," and pray for "rest and quietness," for "that peace which the world cannot give," and for God "to make thy chosen people joyful." Yet in 1550 this sensitive author had an intransigent religious radical, Joan Bocher, burned at the stake after failing to convert her—clearly not one of those chosen for joyfulness.

Edward, a serious, even rather fanatical boy, was not physically strong. By 1553 everyone, including himself, realized that a lung disease was killing him. He wanted to prevent his half-sister Mary, daughter of Catherine of Aragon and a staunch religious conservative, from succeeding him. In June he declared both Mary and Anne Boleyn's daughter, Elizabeth, illegitimate, and named his seventeen-year-old second cousin, Jane Grey, as his heir. She had been married in May to the Lord President Northumberland's son. However, Edward died unexpectedly on 6 July, before Parliament had enacted these changes. Mary escaped to East Anglia, where she and her household had large estates, and could call on armed support from relatives, neighbours and their dependants, especially religious traditionalists. She declared herself queen. Jane—"the nine-day queen"—warned publicly that Mary would bring "this noble, free realm into the tyranny and servitude of the bishop of Rome,"[26] but Mary was careful to base her appeal on right of inheritance, not her religious views. The attempt to oust her collapsed, as did a later uprising. Jane's father, her new husband and father-in-law, other leading supporters and finally Jane herself went to the block.

Mary wanted to bring England back to papal obedience and destroy heresy. This was not an impossible aim. Religious changes over the past generation had stemmed more from royal policy than grass-roots fervour. Evangelical movements certainly had their own dynamism, as events across Europe showed. But religious conservatism was also strong, and was rooted in popular culture. A period of determined royal counter-revolution might well have succeeded. Diplomatic as well as domestic issues were involved. Mary, daughter of a Spanish princess, consulted her cousin, Charles V, who urged her to marry his son and heir, Philip, regent of Spain—a man who has left a sinister image in the English memory as a fanatical persecutor of heretics and enemy of English freedom. She duly married him in 1554, at the age of thirty-seven, needing to produce the heir without which all her policy would be ephemeral. For Philip, who succeeded to the Spanish thrones in 1556, the marriage, which made him titular king of England too, was essentially diplomatic, to have England as an ally (or at least not an enemy) in the empire's rivalry with France.

Mary had at first been discreet about her religious aims, even promising not to "compel or constrain other men's consciences."[27] She hoped for a rapid and easy return to the papal fold. Her main instrument was to be her cousin, Cardinal Reginald Pole, who was to return to England from Rome as papal legate (which gave him supreme power over the English Church), absolve England from the sin of heresy, and take the reins of religious policy. This was hampered by those whom Mary must have expected to be the greatest enthusiasts—the emperor and the Pope. Charles would not allow Pole to return until after Mary had married Philip, which she did in 1554. After Pole's arrival in England later that year, it emerged that he was not trusted in Rome. In what came close to black comedy, his commission as legate was revoked by Pope Paul IV, and he was accused of being a Lutheran and summoned back to Rome to face the Inquisition. Mary refused to let him go, and thus found herself using her royal power over the English Church to defy papal jurisdiction, and in return the Pope refused to appoint bishops in England.

Mary also faced domestic political opposition and legal obstacles. Her marriage to Philip caused misgivings. He, to his great annoyance, realized that his kingly authority was restricted by statute, and so he left England in 1555 after a few months of marriage, spent most of his time in Brussels, and left the desperate Mary childless. Mary discovered that she could not simply ignore the vast amount of parliamentary legislation creating royal supremacy and transforming religious life—she was even forced to imprison (briefly) an old priest for illegally saying Mass. Parliamentary consent, which involved bitter debate, was required to change things back, though ironically Mary used the powers of the royal supremacy to purge hostile bishops and restore traditional worship. The question of what would happen to former Church land was crucial. Charles and Philip, wanting England as a stable ally, pressed Pole to recognize the rights of the new owners, but these were never solid, and the many buyers—a large part of the nobility and gentry—were suspicious.

The heart of the conflict was belief itself. The willing conformity Mary and Pole expected was indeed to be found all over the country, and especially in the north. But there were practical problems in returning to tradition. Religious objects had been disposed of. Buildings had been turned over to other uses—in one Kentish chapel "there was such a savour of hogg skynnes that no man could abide in the Chappell for stinck thereof."[28] In time hidden crucifixes and statues were brought back, and vestments and vessels obtained. Some parishes anticipated royal instructions by immediately resuming traditional ceremonies. In one Kent church, the evangelical vicar was pulled from the pulpit by his parishioners, imprisoned in a side chapel, and eventually burned for heresy. Church ales were held again to raise restoration funds, along with traditional entertainments—maypoles, morris dancing and plays. But elsewhere there was resentment (not least at the cost) or mockery. Evangelicals continued to meet and resist.

So Pole and Mary turned to force—the acts for which her reign is remembered. It was the most intense persecution of its kind anywhere in sixteenth-century Europe.[29] Possession of heretical or treasonable literature was made subject to the death penalty. The heresy laws were re-enacted in 1554, and at least 231 men and 56 women (compared with 2 under Edward VI) were burned, 85 percent of them in London, the south-east and East Anglia. Heresy was usually a very unpopular crime; culprits were denounced by neighbours, and at least one by his wife.[30] Some of those who turned out to watch the burnings displayed this detestation, encouraged by sermons preached from pulpits set up close to the pyres. But it was not so everywhere, and especially not in London, where some in the crowd showed solidarity with the victims. Eventually servants, apprentices and then "young folk" in general were forbidden to attend. Many of those burned were young too, and most were ordinary wage-earners—better-off targets escaped into exile.

The most famous victims, however, were senior churchmen—Bishops

Latimer of Worcester and Ridley of London, and Archbishop Cranmer, representing thirty years of the evangelical movement. Cranmer had played an important political and religious role since he had been recruited from Cambridge to advise on Henry's divorce. His views on predestination, justification by faith, and the sacraments—the central religious issues—had departed increasingly from tradition, as his Prayer Books showed. He had also been involved in the attempt to put Jane Grey on the throne, for which he was condemned to death for treason. But Mary wanted him tried for heresy, and this was done by a papal court in Oxford in 1555. On 16 October Latimer and Ridley were burned together in Oxford, and every household in the city was required to send a representative to watch. Latimer's traditional (but perhaps apocryphal) words were "Be of good comfort, Master Ridley, and play the man. We shall this day light such a candle by God's grace in England as I trust shall never be put out." With Cranmer, the government wanted a moral victory. He was subjected to long and heavy intellectual and psychological pressure, and signed several recantations of his heresies. The queen insisted that he should burn none the less, and he was led to the stake in Oxford on 21 March 1556 in what became the greatest propaganda disaster of her reign.[31] On the way, there was a crowded ceremony in the university church at which he was supposed to make a last edifying confession of guilt and repentance. But amid shouts and confusion, he disowned his recantations and affirmed his beliefs, before being hustled off to die. His right hand, which had signed the recantations, he himself thrust into the flames—"this hand hath offended."[32]

These dramatic accounts come from Foxe's *Book of Martyrs*, one of the great and now unread pillars of England's history. John Foxe's *Actes and Monuments of these Latter and Perillous Days* (1563), to give its full name, was a huge compilation with vivid and often shocking illustrations, and it was later made publicly available by law in every cathedral and in many churches. In various abridged forms, and even in Latin translation, it created not just a religious tradition but a national one, an inspiring collective saga of Protestant and English resistance to persecution and oppression. It was, and still remains, the basis of much that we think we know about this time, because Foxe is the best, and often the only, source for many of its most memorable episodes. He collected stories from eyewitnesses, which were subsequently told and retold down the ages, and which are now neither provable nor disprovable.

Mary's counter-reformation ended when she died of influenza in 1558 aged forty-two, internationally ridiculed for her phantom pregnancies and increasingly hated at home as a vindictive instrument of the Pope and the Spanish. She might have succeeded given time and an heir. Otherwise, nothing was sure, as her subjects well knew: one pious Suffolk man bequeathed silver for a new processional cross—but only "yf the laws of the realme will permit."[33] As it was, Mary's interests as queen of England were sacrificed to those of her husband, Philip, and the papacy.[34] This brought England into a disastrous war against the French, who in 1558 captured its last remaining continental possession, Calais—a devastating blow to Mary's remaining prestige. The danger of marital diplomacy was a lesson that her half-sister Elizabeth would take to heart.

What had been the cost of the Reformation in England? An unquantifiable extent of sorrow and anguish. A vast amount of vandalism of the artistic expression of centuries of piety in stone, wood, paint, cloth, metal and glass. A change in people's sense of the land itself, as healing wells and holy places, trees and stones were condemned as idolatrous. Yet some survived: Stonehenge proved too big to demolish; the Glastonbury thorn, cut down, grew back; some holy wells became health spas.[35] The cost in human lives, fortunately, was relatively small. Nearly 1,000 people were executed for heresy or for treason connected with religion—a substantial proportion of the 5,000 such executions estimated for the whole of Europe over the sixteenth century.[36] But far worse killing resulted—and was still to result over the next hundred years—from outbreaks of mass religious violence and war: for example, countless thousands in the German "Peasants' War" and 5,000 in the St. Bartholomew's Day massacre in France. This mass slaughter England was spared. Its religious revolution had come through the will of monarchs, who had the power to enforce changes and also to keep them in bounds.

This was nevertheless the most intense period of persecution in English history, in which overall about the same number of Catholics and Protestants died. It produced a celebrated band of martyrs: More and Fisher (both canonized), Ridley, Latimer and Cranmer (comparably venerated in Foxe's *Book of Martyrs*). Were they "men for all seasons"? Not entirely for ours. None of them defended the values we cherish—freedom of speech, pluralism and liberty of conscience. They died not for tolerance, but for truth. All had been to some extent persecutors before being persecuted. Fisher presided over book-burnings and thought the notion of freedom of belief absurd. More led raids on possessors of heretical books, advocated burning heretics lest they "wax bold," thought that evangelicals should have "an hot iron thrust through their blasphemous tongues," and was directly responsible for several burnings, including of a distributer of Tyndale's Bible.[37] Latimer preached at a burning, and Cranmer was personally involved in several. None of them believed—very few people did*—that intellectual freedom was a virtue or that religious persecution was wrong. They tried to save their own lives by silence, compromise, even recantation. Perhaps this helps us to sympathize with them, repelled as we are by fanatics thirsty for martyrdom. But despite their human fears and compromises, there was for each a line they would not cross, whatever the consequences, and this commands respect. It would be excessively optimistic to think that a revulsion against these killings sowed the first seeds of tolerance; but there was at least no return in England to large-scale execution for heresy. Elizabeth burned no one. The very last burnings (of two religious radicals) took place in 1612, under James I.

What had been the non-religious effects of the Reformation? England had been declared an "empire," whose monarchs claimed God-given religious powers comparable with those of the emperor Constantine. In reality, much of that power was exercised by parliaments, whose acts now regulated doctrine, worship, marriage, divorce, royal supremacy and royal succession. This further increased the role and prominence of parliaments, even, in the expression of the great legal historian F. W. Maitland, their "omnicompetence."[38] Society and the state became more laicized, and the number of prelates in Parliament declined. There had been a huge transfer of economic power from the Church to lay landowners. Although the Church remained a legal, political and cultural power in the land, it was no longer the mighty, semi-autonomous, international corporation of old.

The Reformation also modified national consciousness. As we have seen, the English had developed a sense of common identity relatively early. One of the difficulties—and part of the interest—is that historians differ profoundly on what national consciousness was and when it emerged. In England, as we have seen, unifying ideas and practices existed long before the Reformation—the Common Law, an ancient written history, the holding of parliaments, wide participation in government, and the use of a common language. Yet England was at the same time part of a Europe-wide religious culture, centred in Rome. Thomas More personifies this: a very English but also a very cosmopolitan figure, the last great popular English writer who used Latin as his natural medium, and who died rather than accept separation from the universal Church. The Reformation nationalized religion, asserting independence from Rome, enforcing an English Bible and liturgy, and praising the supposed purity of the native pre-Conquest Church.[39] Involvement in European religious wars,

---

* A partial exception was Foxe, who opposed the death penalty for matters of belief, though he approved of lesser punishments.

culminating in a struggle with Catholic Spain, identified Protestantism with patriotism—at least for Protestants. Constant use of the word "nation" by Wyclif, Tyndale and their successors in translating a variety of Hebrew, Greek and Latin terms reinforced the idea that nations were part of the divine order. The English came to see themselves as a chosen nation, a new Israel—though, like Israel, they knew that they often went astray. This was not new or unique—many peoples have considered themselves in various ways "chosen," including the Spanish, French, Dutch, Scots, Poles, Irish, Russians and Americans. These religious nationalisms deepened divisions between the island nations. Moreover, despite the efforts of its rulers, the Reformation, instead of uniting the English people in a national Church, divided it violently and in some ways permanently.

## THE AGE OF ELIZABETH

*I know I have the body of a weak and feeble woman, but I have the heart and stomach of a king, and of a king of England too.*
Elizabeth I, Tilbury, 1588

Elizabeth succeeded to the throne in 1558, at the age of twenty-five, around the time when the longest and perhaps the most devastating of three periods of extreme crisis in modern Europe's history began—the others being the French Revolutionary period and the years between 1914 and 1945. Heresy was regarded as a justification for deposing monarchs, and hence religious conflict crossed borders. England found itself in the middle of this maelstrom, cast as the leader and defender of a threatened Protestant cause. Fortunately, the country's fate would lie primarily in the hands of a "very vain and clever" (said the Spanish ambassador), cautious and circumspect woman—her loyal but often exasperated counsellors might have said an indecisive, parsimonious and procrastinating one. She controlled policy more than any other Tudor.[40] Her virtues, and vices, did much to keep the country safe throughout her long reign. However one describes them, these characteristics—caution, cunning, cleverness, procrastination—give her some claim to be considered England's greatest monarch.

Yet one crucial duty she refused: producing an heir. Here too her advisers were sorely tried by her apparent indecisiveness, until it was too late. There has been endless speculation about her avoidance of marriage and her strange hostility to marriage by members of her entourage. One suggestion (for which there is some possible evidence) is that she was assaulted as a girl by her guardian, Sir Thomas Seymour, and that this left her with an aversion to sex. On the other hand, Elizabeth's long and close relationships with trusted ministers—William and Robert Cecil, Christopher Hatton, Francis Walsingham—prove a marked ability to work closely with men. Her intense emotional relationships with others—most famously Robert Dudley, Earl of Leicester—suggest no lack of desire. But desire or aversion, especially for women, was rarely an issue in royal marriages. Lineage, politics and diplomacy obliterated personal sentiment. These gave Elizabeth weightier reasons for remaining the Virgin Queen, despite many suitors, including (briefly) her brother-in-law, Philip of Spain, Erik XIV of Sweden, two Habsburg archdukes and two successive dukes of Anjou. Marriage would make her husband king and potentially place her under his authority. Marriage to a subject risked jealousy and factional conflict at home. Marriage to a foreign prince, even though his formal powers would be legally restricted, risked pulling England into Continental conflicts, and would also cause dangerous religious complications. These were not merely theoretical considerations: the fates of her predecessor, Mary, married to Philip of Spain, and of her cousin, Mary, Queen of Scots, whose marriages were to entail murders, abduction, possibly rape, civil war, and finally exile and internment in England, provided the starkest of warnings. Elizabeth proved, for the first time in English history, that a woman could govern alone, and indeed her gender did not prove a dominating issue—though it was assumed that she would listen to male counsellors. But her childlessness, and her refusal to provide for or even discuss the succession, made her own life the thread from which England's political stability hung.

Elizabeth's early life had been an apprenticeship in caution, and her first act was, in effect, to call a halt to both the English Reformation and Counter-Reformation. She annulled Mary's policy. She was the daughter of Anne Boleyn, and her throne necessarily rested on royal supremacy, without which she was a bastard. Her beliefs were clearly reformist, she overrode Catholic sentiment, and her bishops were implacable in rooting out "superstitions" reintroduced under Mary. But she detested the subversive implications of radical evangelicalism, and cordially loathed the Scottish Calvinist John Knox, who had published a biblically based condemnation of government by women. She had no liking for theological disputes. Her taste was for ceremony and quiet mystery, not the emotive verbosity of evangelical preaching.[41] Her religious settlement was embodied in Acts of Supremacy (1558) and of Uniformity (1558), the Thirty-Nine Articles (1563), a summary of dogma largely drafted by

Cranmer and which had to be signed by all clergy and members of the universities, the hierarchy of archbishops, bishops, deans and archdeacons, and a liturgy in English based on Cranmer's 1552 Prayer Book, adapted to make it more acceptable to traditionalists.

This compromise has been described as "a monstrosity" that "nobody would deliberately have invented."[42] But Elizabeth insisted on it, forced it through a hostile House of Lords and maintained it throughout her forty-five-year reign. Like many hybrids, it proved durable, despite later attempts to prune it into different shapes. It was the foundation of the unique system later named Anglicanism. It "looked Catholic and sounded Protestant," as one historian has described it,[43] which means it pleased the compromisers and displeased the zealots of both camps. The halting search for consensus is one of the foundation stones of the spirit of compromise that has often been claimed as an English characteristic.

The Elizabethan Church also preserved two of the most evocative English sounds: the choral music of cathedrals and colleges, which the queen was determined to perpetuate, and the musical bell-ringing, regarded by purists as sinful, which became a uniquely English popular pastime.[44] The Whitechapel Bell Foundry, still working, was founded in 1570. Reformers, who only liked community psalm-singing, found the subtle sophistication of polyphonic music deplorably ornate, even idolatrous. On Cranmer's orders, books of "Popish ditties" had been ripped up and church organs wrecked, and the only approved music was to have a "plain and distinct note, for every syllable one."[45] The choir of King's College, Cambridge, for example, had been disbanded under Edward. Mary restored it and Elizabeth maintained it. She patronized the leading composers John William Byrd and Thomas Tallis, both religious conservatives. These last representatives of an ancient Catholic tradition thus became the founding fathers of Anglican church music.

Elizabeth had no sympathy with hardliners in either camp, and considered "what they disputed about but trifles."[46] Heresy trials were stopped and surviving prisoners released. She did not seek to "make windows into men's hearts," as the philosopher-politician Francis Bacon famously put it; and her judges were instructed that the queen wanted no "examination or inquisition of their secret opinions in their consciences for matters of faith."[47] Victims of over-zealous Church authorities were confident enough to appeal to Magna Carta. But the queen did insist that people should obey the law by at least a minimum of outward conformity, so as not to disturb "the common quiet of the realm."[48] Given her own impatience with dogma, she could not understand why some refused, whether traditionalists who refused to attend church occasionally or evangelicals who refused to wear ecclesiastical vestments. Gradually, Elizabeth's religion entered the minds and hearts of most people, as a generation grew up which thought of the Pope as Antichrist, the Mass as a mummery, and their Catholic past not as their own, but as "another country, another world."[49]

A religious middle way of this kind had become rare in Europe, and was running against the tide. The 1550s was a time of polarization across Europe, with the terms "Catholic" and "Protestant" for the first time becoming current. Until then, most people saw the situation as one of fluid schismatical and heretical turbulence within one Christian Church, and hoped that unity might be restored, perhaps by a General Council. But the Council of Trent, which met periodically between 1545 and 1563, deepened the divisions by defining Catholic doctrines (on faith, scripture, authority, the sacraments and papal supremacy) in a way that evangelicals would never accept, and instituting a "Counter-Reformation." On the other side, the fully reformed Genevan church of Jean Calvin represented an uncompromising model for evangelicals. The ideal of re-unifying Christianity still existed, but by victory rather than compromise. An age of religious wars had dawned.

These long-drawn-out religious, political and economic upheavals inevitably transformed secular culture. The suppression of traditional religious celebrations, the exaltation of the monarch as head of the Church, the secularization of monastic buildings and wealth, the rise of new families, Continental fashions, and the profits of trade and agriculture—all played a part in the painting, architecture and theatre that emerged during the sixteenth century.

A fashion for portraiture, which came later to England than to Italy, the Netherlands or France, was promoted by Henry VIII's patronage in the 1520s and 1530s of Hans Holbein, who also painted rising politicians such as Thomas More and Thomas Cromwell. Later artists adopted less subtle, even caricatural, ways of conveying the material power and status of their patrons, most famously in the official paintings of Elizabeth, allegories rather than likenesses, whose stridency reflects insecurity as much as majesty.[50] Individual and family portraits, whether on large canvases or as exquisite miniatures, were a way of recording and conveying an impression both of wealth and of culture.

Similar messages were carried by domestic buildings, of which this was one of the greatest and most adventurous periods in English history. Henry VII and VIII built palaces on an unprecedented scale—one way of establishing their own majesty and England's prestige. (Henry VIII was particularly competitive, as he had shown in 1520 when he met King

François I on the "Field of the Cloth of Gold" near Calais, and the two vied to outdo each other in a flamboyant display of opulence.) Under the parsimonious Elizabeth, the burden of cost fell on her great subjects, who built at vast expense in the hope of attracting a royal visit as she progressed round the country. Gentry families who had acquired monastic lands and buildings remodelled them as country seats. The fashion-conscious broke away in mid-century from medieval symbols (gate towers, battlements and great halls, of which Wolsey's 1520s Hampton Court was a late example), yet without adopting wholesale the fashionable classical styles of Italy and France. Instead came a striking modern vernacular style, seeking comfort, elegance, light (with bigger windows thanks to cheaper glass), privacy in individual rooms, and above all display. On a humbler scale, similar aspirations to comfort and privacy affected ordinary houses, where the replacement of open hearths by fireplaces and chimneys meant warmer and healthier interiors and permitted the use of a whole upper floor for bedrooms. In houses great and small, more light and less smoke meant a universal taste for decoration.[51]

In 1559, the year after Elizabeth's succession, the two great Catholic powers, France and the Habsburgs, made peace after half a century of devastating wars in Italy, Provence, Germany and Flanders. A grand Catholic alliance to destroy Protestantism thus became possible. The Pope duly urged Philip of Spain to invade England, to prevent Elizabeth from reversing Mary's religious policy, by which England had been the first Protestant kingdom to return to Rome. He offered to depose Elizabeth and make Philip king. The danger to England was in fact less imminent than it appeared. Spain and France still distrusted each other deeply. If either could master England, it would obtain a decisive advantage, even hegemony in Europe. But that would risk provoking the violent opposition of the other, and both shrank from renewing the war they had just ended. Moreover, if the Spanish did remove Elizabeth, the best hereditary candidate to succeed her was a protégée of France, Mary Stewart, since babyhood Queen of Scots and now wife of the dauphin François, heir to the French throne.[52] The French were already effectively ruling Scotland in her name, and plans were well advanced to annex it.[53] Spain had no wish to give them England too. Finally, Spain was confronting the Muslims in the Mediterranean—a reason to avoid adventures in northern Europe—and this conflict diminished only after the Spanish, Venetian and papal navies defeated the Turks at the great battle of Lepanto in 1571. So although religious conflict prevented England from being an ally, Spain hesitated to make it an enemy.

France, however, was on the verge of a series of disasters. Its king,

Henri II, was fatally injured in July 1559 in a joust in Paris to celebrate the marriage alliance of his daughter with Philip of Spain (widower of Mary Tudor). His teenage heir, François II (husband of Mary Stewart), died after a year and was succeeded by the ten-year-old Charles IX. The ensuing power vacuum permitted a sudden explosion of Protestantism in France, attracting a large part of the nobility and the urban population, especially in provincial towns in the south. In response came a popular Catholic backlash, whose leadership was assumed by the ducal family of Guise. The country divided into armed Protestant and Catholic factions. An indirect result was a Protestant and anti-French revolt in Scotland in 1559, with English help—the first successful Protestant overthrow of a Catholic government. When following her husband's death the nineteen-year-old Queen Mary returned to Scotland in 1561, it was in the throes of religious and factional strife.

These violent distractions gave England some respite. But in 1566, conflict came closer when Protestants in the Low Countries rebelled against their overlord, the ubiquitous Philip of Spain. This was the culmination of several years of unrest, combining religious dissent and resentment at foreign rule, during which Protestant England had been for the Dutch both a refuge and a source of encouragement. A Spanish army under the Duke of Alva crushed the revolt in 1567, executed 1,000 leaders, and sent refugees streaming into England, Scotland and Germany. England signed treaties with leaders of the French Protestants, with recovery of Calais in mind, and because French Catholics were supporting Spain. Similarly, because Scottish Catholics supported France, it supported Scottish Protestants—"with all fair promises first, next with money, and last with arms."[54] In 1568 Mary, Queen of Scots, had to flee to England, where she was interned in a succession of castles. Thus, religious conflict spread across frontiers, and eventually across the western hemisphere, when English naval raiders, most famously Francis Drake, were sent to harry the Spanish colonies both to weaken and to warn. In one of these expeditions, in 1577–80, he became the first captain to sail round the world and return alive—an extraordinary feat of navigation, and one that went far beyond the normal ambitions of English sailors, unused to southern oceans. He also seized large quantities of Spanish treasure on the way—a 4,700 percent profit, of which the queen's share was worth more than a whole year of Crown revenue.[55]

Elizabeth's life was the fragile bulwark against religious war in England. The Queen of Scots, half refugee, half prisoner, was the catalyst of danger, for if Elizabeth died, she, a great-granddaughter of Henry VII, would succeed as Catholic queen of England. (Even when queen of France, she had adopted the English royal coat of arms.) For Catholics, this would be a providential outcome, and some were ready to lend Providence a hand. Only months after Mary's arrival, a rebellion began in 1569 in the pro-Catholic north of England. Led by the earls of Northumberland and Westmoreland, it was connected with a half-baked plan to marry Mary without Elizabeth's knowledge to her cousin the Duke of Norfolk, England's premier nobleman. Elizabeth dealt unusually harshly with the rebels, over 500 being executed. In May 1570 a papal bull entitled *Regnans in excelsis*, excommunicating Elizabeth and declaring her a heretic, schismatic and bastard, was daringly nailed to the Bishop of London's door. This released Catholics from obedience to her. In 1571 the "Ridolfi plot" was uncovered—a vast labyrinth of agents, double agents, informers and provocateurs which featured bags of gold, codes hidden in Bibles, an Italian banker Ridolfi, Philip of Spain, the French, the Pope, Mary, Norfolk, and alleged plans for rebellion and Spanish invasion. The Privy Council, deeply alarmed, was willing to authorize torture of suspects, and the questioning of Mary herself—"haste, haste, haste, for life, for life, for life, for life," wrote the secretary, Burghley. The plot cost Norfolk his head; but Elizabeth would not proceed against Mary, or even allow legislation to disbar her from the throne. "The Queen's Majesty hath always been a merciful lady," wrote Burghley to his colleague Sir Francis Walsingham, "and by mercy she hath taken more harm than by justice."[56]

In 1572 the Netherlands revolt flared up again, and turned into a long war. England gave financial and finally military help, not least because it tied down a Spanish army which might otherwise invade England. Also in 1572 France lurched deeper into religious anarchy when the government ordered a wholesale massacre of Protestants on 24 August 1572—St. Bartholomew's Day. Several thousands were butchered by soldiers or mobs. Walsingham, on a diplomatic mission in France, witnessed it and sheltered fugitives. In France, as in the Low Countries, religious war now involved whole peoples in an apocalyptic atmosphere of terror. Governments struggled to keep some control, and realized that the rules of international politics had changed. People in England, of whatever faith, must have realized that they had so far escaped the worst, but that danger was approaching. Special prayers were ordered; and, on the principle that God helps those that help themselves, England's coasts and its small navy were prepared to resist invasion. Wrote one of the queen's officers, "We are left destitute of friends on every side, amazed and divided at home."[57] But nothing happened. The Dutch fought on. The French fought each other. Mary Stewart remained under guard. Elizabeth followed a cautious foreign policy. She refused the offer of the overlordship of the seventeen

Dutch provinces—another moment in English history when an attachment to the Continent did not materialize. She engaged in a long (and highly unpopular) diplomatic courtship during the late 1570s with a second duc d'Anjou, "her frog," without actually marrying him—yet she had the hand of a pamphleteer chopped off in 1579 after he criticized the idea.

Elizabeth was thus happy to play for time. But events accelerated. In 1580, a small papal-backed Spanish and Italian landing took place in Ireland to aid Irish rebels: the 500 men were captured and slaughtered—an act in which the soldier-courtier Sir Walter Raleigh and the poet Edmund Spenser were implicated.[58] In England Catholicism had by no means been eradicated: it survived under the protection of the gentry, especially in relatively remote rural areas—Lancashire, Monmouthshire, parts of Warwickshire—and even grew. The fear of internal subversion in England was increased by clandestine missionary activity by a new generation of Catholic priests, spearheaded from 1580 by a small number of the Jesuit order—"seedmen in their tillage of sedition," Burghley called them.[59] Trained in Rome, Spain or Flanders, the several hundred missionaries were hardened to the prospect of torture and death—grisly frescoes of martyrs adorned the walls of the English College in Rome. Their aim was not merely to minister secretly to uncompromising Catholics and prevent them from acquiescing in Elizabeth's compromise religion, but more ambitiously to make converts and prepare a general Counter-Reformation.[60] They brought a hardline message, backed up by the performance of exorcisms and proclamation of miracles: enemies of Catholicism were dying horrible deaths, outbreaks of disease were divine punishments, and those who attended Elizabeth's Church were doomed to hell. Priests insisted that their mission was religious, not political. The Jesuit Edmund Campion (one who did not, in fact, preach revolution) declared at his trial in 1581 that "if our religion do make us traitors, we are worthy to be condemned; but otherwise we are, and have been, as good subjects as ever the queen had."[61] But the distinction between politics and religion was often meaningless, as for example when a Winchester woman declared that she had had a vision of Elizabeth's imminent death, of Henry VIII and the Earl of Leicester in hell, and of Mary I and Mary Stewart in heaven.[62] In 1585 a group of Catholics petitioned the queen, protesting their loyalty: "Every priest and priests, who have at any time conversed with us, have recognised your Majesty their lawful and undoubted queen . . . And if we knew . . . of treason . . . we do bind ourselves by oath irrevocable to be the first apprehenders and accusers of such."[63] But Catholics were in fact faced with an insoluble dilemma of clashing loyalties.

Parliament responded with harsh laws to stem the missionary inflow, though the queen held back their application in most cases. In 1585, being ordained priest by papal authority after 1559 was made treason, and 123 priests were executed for this reason alone, out of a total of 146 executed between 1585 and 1603. A larger number not considered subversive—about 280—were imprisoned or simply deported.[64] Persecution reached a peak in the 1580s, when Spain was threatening invasion. Priests were hunted, so networks of safe houses with "priests' holes" were constructed. Enthusiastic hunters, such as the notorious Yorkshire MP Richard Topcliffe, who combined careerism, fanaticism and sadism, were licensed to use torture to extract the names of accomplices—he had a torture chamber in his house in Westminster. There were fifty-three cases in which torture was legally used—unique in English history. Torture was a sensitive matter: Topcliffe's nephew renounced the family name, and the playwright and pamphleteer Thomas Norton was indignant at being called the "rackmaster" by Catholics for his part in the interrogation of Campion. Norton insisted that torture was applied only with a Privy Council warrant, only to undoubted traitors to force them to reveal their accomplices, and that those who swore to tell the truth escaped it.[65] These sufferings and deaths became for English Catholics what the Marian persecutions and the Spanish Inquisition were for Protestants: a warning and an inspiration. The victims were at once regarded as martyrs, vindicated by many miraculous events—such as the Thames standing still as Campion died at Tyburn. Illustrated accounts of their sufferings were widely circulated across Catholic Europe. A counterpart of Foxe's *Book of Martyrs* was Bishop Richard Challoner's *Memoirs of Missionary Priests* (1741–42). The memory of persecution nourished a proud and bitter "recusant" tradition within English Catholicism, finally recognized with the canonization of the "Forty Martyrs" in 1970.

The official Catholic view, as expressed by the exiled Oxford don William Allen, founder of the English colleges at Rome and Douai, and later Cardinal, was that "by colour of contrived treason and conspiracy (the cause indeed being religion) the enemies of the Christian faith have shed . . . innocent blood to the infinite shame of our nation."[66] But treason and conspiracy there was, inevitably focused on Mary Stewart, the most dangerous woman in England. The hope of the papacy, France, Spain and influential exiles such as Allen and the Jesuit Robert Parsons (former Dean of Balliol) was that with the help of an invasion Mary could be put on the English throne with a suitable Catholic husband—a Habsburg or French prince—as king. Henry, Duc de Guise, Mary's cousin, was plotting invasion with the cautious assistance of Philip of Spain. He was in contact with powerful English Catholics such as Lord Henry Howard (brother of the beheaded Duke of Norfolk), the Earl of Northumberland, and the wealthy Throckmorton family, go-betweens with Mary. The secretary Walsingham's spies in the French embassy got wind of the plot in 1583, and after Francis Throckmorton was arrested and racked ("not much," said the government[67]) he confessed all.

The danger to Elizabeth was patent, especially after William the Silent, leader of the Dutch Protestants, was assassinated by a Catholic in July 1584. Her advisers took extraordinary measures: an "Instrument of Association," and then an Act for the Queen's Surety. What these meant was that if anyone "compassed or imagined" Elizabeth's death, then Mary could be tried for treason, or even lawfully killed by Elizabeth's subjects. An army under the Earl of Leicester was sent to help the hard-pressed Dutch, and a naval expedition under Sir Francis Drake attacked Spanish America and returned with a vast amount of loot.

Mary, desperate to escape confinement, continued secret contacts with her English and foreign allies. In 1586 she promised the English crown to Philip of Spain if he invaded. Philip's secret intention was to put Mary on the throne for her lifetime, but ensure that her successor as queen of England, Scotland and Ireland was his own clever daughter Isabel, with an Austrian Habsburg as king.[68] In July, in a letter to a young Catholic, Anthony Babington, Mary gave tacit assent to Elizabeth's assassination, while she herself was to be rescued by a small armed band. However, all this correspondence—smuggled in and out in beer barrels—was being intercepted and read by Walsingham's agents. When the fatal letter to Babington arrived, a copy was sent on to Walsingham marked with a gallows.[69] The conspirators mostly confessed. One, on the eve of execution, wrote his own wistful epitaph:

> My glass is full, and now my glass is run,
> And now I live, and now my life is done.

Pressed by her advisers, Elizabeth agreed to allow Mary to be tried for treason, but again resisted allowing her to be executed, despite demands from Parliament and her council. To spare Mary, they said, would encourage further conspiracy. But Elizabeth knew that to execute a fellow monarch—especially the queen and former queen of England's two closest neighbours and hereditary enemies—would have dire consequences. She hinted at a discreet assassination, but neither her councillors nor Mary's gaolers would agree. Eventually Elizabeth was induced to sign the death warrant, and her ministers then took the matter out of her hands, having Mary beheaded on 8 February 1587 at Fotheringhay Castle, Northamptonshire, the English stronghold of medieval Scottish kings.

Elizabeth was, or professed to be, horrified and angry. But her histrionics could not ward off one of the greatest dangers in England's history: a full-scale war with Spain. For several years, because of Spanish involvement in conspiracies against her, Elizabeth had been carrying out pre-emptive action—naval expeditions in the Americas, the establishment of a colony in Virginia, more help to the Dutch and French Protestants. But Philip II—quite as cautious a character as Elizabeth—was reluctant to embark on war, despite the urging of Pope Sixtus V. For one thing, even if he could conquer England, it was very unclear what he should do with it, for it would be hard to hold on to, and would arouse jealousy among potential enemies—a dilemma also faced by future would-be invaders, including Louis XV, Napoleon and Hitler. English exiles urged Philip to be bold: he had, Cardinal Allen argued, a claim to the throne as heir of the House of Lancaster—he was yet another descendant of the prolific John of Gaunt. Besides, Catholic princes could legally annex the lands of excommunicated heretics.[70] Philip finally took the decision to invade England around March 1587. The news of Mary's execution, which caused a sensation across Europe, confirmed him in his decision. There were good reasons to seize the moment. Elizabeth was isolated, the Turks were busy fighting the Persians, the Germans were preoccupied with Poland, and his Catholic allies the Guises had the upper hand in France. Spanish troops had invasion ports in the Netherlands. Not least, Elizabeth was repeatedly launching naval attacks. Drake's famous raid on Cadiz in April 1587, to "singe the king of Spain's beard," was intensely humiliating for Philip, and demonstrated the vulnerability of his sprawling domains.

So, in September 1587, Philip gave detailed instructions for a joint invasion by a "Gran Armada" from Spain and his army in the Netherlands. His main aim was "to see England—that great and ancient kingdom—once again within the Catholic fold and subject to the obedience of the Church of Rome."[71] England faced the danger not only of invasion, but also religious civil war and persecution, even annexation to a greater Habsburg empire—a danger comparable with 1066, 1805 and 1940. As Burghley saw it, Philip "is the mightiest enemy that ever England had, yea mightier . . . than any other monarch of Christendom these many years." Drake's advice was "Prepare in England strongly, and most by sea. Stop him now, and stop him ever."[72]

Burghley's foreboding was well founded. Philip's empire included Spain, Portugal, much of Italy, the Netherlands and European colonies in Asia and the Americas. The Holy Roman Empire was ruled by his cousin. France, dominated by the Guise faction, was supportive. His revenue was ten times that of Elizabeth, and it funded Europe's most effective army and largest navy—140 galleys and 60 or 70 sailing warships to Elizabeth's total of 40 ships.[73] The Spanish people backed a war to destroy English pirates and burn English heretics:

> My brother Bartolo is going to England
> To capture Drake and kill the Queen
> He will bring me back from the war
> A little Lutheran boy on a chain.[74]

But Philip and his commanders were aware of the difficulty and danger of the enterprise, which required bringing large forces together at the right place at the right time, and ferrying troops across the dangerous Channel in vulnerable boats. Both Parma, the army commander, and the Duke of Medina Sidonia, the naval commander, wanted to cancel or postpone the operation. But Philip pressed on, alarmingly reliant on "God, whose cause this is . . . He will not allow any misfortune." Public prayers, processions and flagellations were held, and soldiers and sailors were ordered to "avoid swearing and blasphemy." As one sceptical Spanish naval officer told a papal diplomat sarcastically, "God will surely arrange matters . . . either by sending some strange freak of weather or . . . just by depriving the English of their wits." Failing such a miracle, "the English, who have faster and handier ships than ours, and many more long range guns [will] knock us to pieces."[75]

The English ships were indeed more formidable. A permanent Royal Navy was a novelty for England, dating only from the 1540s, when it had absorbed a good part of the treasure of the monasteries. Permanent dockyards, stores and an administration had been set up. Ship design improved, and the casting of cheap iron guns was developed. Furthermore, as England, unlike Spain, had no trans-oceanic merchant trade, its fleet was designed solely for war, not for long-distance cruises and cargo-carrying. Its shipwrights had succeeded in combining speed and armament, enabling English ships to carry more and heavier guns than the Spaniards.[76] They were commanded by the likes of Francis Drake, John Hawkins and Martin Frobisher, hard-bitten West Country seamen who mixed buccaneering and politics, and to whom fighting the Spanish brought gold as well as glory. Their admiral, Lord Howard of Effingham, was rightly confident: "I think there were never in any place in the world worthier ships than these are . . . And few as we are, if the King of Spain's forces be not hundreds, we will make good sport with them."[77]

When the great battle actually came, it was an anti-climax. On 19 July 1588 the Armada—some 140 ships—was sighted. From the twentieth to the twenty-seventh, the two fleets sailed slowly up the Channel, with the 34 English ships firing constantly but doing no serious damage, until "our powder and shot was well wasted." On the twenty-seventh, the Armada anchored off Calais, hoping that Parma's 27,000 troops—Spanish, German, Walloon, Italian and Irish—would sail out to join them and cross to Dover. They learned that Parma would not be ready for six days, so the ships would have to wait, dangerously exposed to weather and the enemy. Even then, the troops, in barges, would be vulnerable to attack by Dutch Protestants in small inshore gunboats, before they could reach the fleet anchored out at sea. As with several other threatened invasions in English history, it might well have proved impracticable. The English did not wait to see. They sent in eight fireships during the night of 28 July, which scattered part of the Armada, and next morning were at last able to get close enough to do real damage with their guns. The Armada escaped into the North Sea, and struggled home, damaged, depleted and battered by storms, round the north of Scotland and the west coast of Ireland. The English fleet lost in all only about 100 men killed, though many more died of disease; the Spanish, from all causes, lost a third of their fleet and some 12,000 men.[78] Only on 18 August did Elizabeth go to join her troops at Tilbury:

> I am come . . . to live or die amongst you all, and to lay down for my God and for my kingdom and for my people, my honour and my blood even in the dust. I know I have the body of a weak and feeble woman, but I have the heart and stomach of a king, and of a king of England too, and I think foul scorn that . . . Spain, or any prince of Europe should dare to invade the borders of my realm.[79]

A cynical observer might only have seen a "spinster in her middle fifties perched on a fat white horse, her teeth black, her red wig slightly askew, dangling a toy sword . . . But that was not what her subjects saw."[80] Or what has remained in the national memory.

The failure of the Armada had consequences far beyond England and Spain, for it appeared to both sides to be a divine judgement: *"Flavit Jehovah et Dissipati Sunt,"* proclaimed an English celebratory medal—"God blew and they were scattered." For Protestants it vindicated their rejection of Romish superstition. For Catholics, and especially Philip and his people, it was proof of their sinfulness and unworthiness to fight in God's cause: "Almost the entire country went into mourning," wrote a Spanish friar. "People talked about nothing else."[81] In France, Henri III felt strong enough to have Philip's ally, the Duc de Guise, murdered; but this began a new round of civil war, and Henri himself was assassinated by a Dominican friar seven months later. His successor was the Protestant leader Henri of Navarre, as Henri IV, and despite converting to Catholicism he was

**Roman Catholic**
**Lutheran**
**Anglican** } Reformed
**Calvinist**
**Hussite**
**Orthodox**
**Muslim**

0      300 miles
0      500 km

NORWAY

Oslo

Stockholm

SCOTLAND

*Edinburgh*

SWEDEN

*North Sea*

DENMARK

IRELAND

Armagh

York

Copenhagen

*ATLANTIC OCEAN*

ENGLAND

London

Canterbury

Amsterdam

Wittenberg

Cologne

HOLY ROMAN EMPIRE

Prague

Paris

Strassburg

Munich

Vienna

La Rochelle

FRANCE

Basel

Geneva

Lyon

Trent

Milan

Venice

Toulouse

Genoa

PORTUGAL

Lisbon

Madrid

SPAIN

Rome

*Mediterranean Sea*

7. The divisions of faith in Europe, late sixteenth century

soon involved in war with Spain, with England as his ally. So France became the new focus of European conflict, diverting Spanish armies, relieving the pressure on the Dutch and English, and perhaps saving both from future defeat—for if the Dutch had been defeated, England would have been far more vulnerable to another invasion.

The war against Spain went on until 1604, with combats on land and sea in France, Spain, Portugal, the Netherlands, the Caribbean, Ireland and even England (in 1595 Spanish raiders burned Penzance). England cultivated friendly relations with another enemy of Spain, the wealthy Morocco. The 1590s were terrible years of economic distress, with four failed harvests and heavy war taxation. But the great danger had passed. Indeed, the English now took the offensive, seizing Spanish and Portuguese shipping and raiding their coasts (which is why the Bishop of Faro's collection of books is now in the Bodleian Library, Oxford). Ambitious sailors, soldiers and their backers grew eager, in Sir Walter Raleigh's words, "to seek new worlds, for gold, for praise, for glory."[82]

One such was Robert Devereux, the young and glamorous Earl of Essex, who provided the final tawdry drama of Elizabeth's reign. Stepson of her early favourite, the Earl of Leicester, he stepped into his shoes— now as a surrogate wayward son rather than a platonic lover. Seeing himself as the embodiment and defender of ancient nobility against upstart bureaucrats, he won a considerable following among dissatisfied nobles and unemployed officers—even some Catholics—by posing as the swashbuckling leader of a knightly brotherhood, a reincarnation of the age of chivalry. At the siege of Rouen in 1591 he challenged the governor to single combat to prove both that England's ally the king of France was in the right, and also that "my mistress is more beautiful than yours."[83] He demanded continuation of the war against Spain, and seems to have aimed at becoming the dominant political figure. His conceit fatally outweighed his ability. When at last given his chance at the age of thirty-three to lead an army in yet another bloody attempt to crush rebellion in Ireland, he proved both inadequate and untrustworthy. Dismissed from his offices and financially ruined, in February 1601 he attempted a half-baked coup or armed demonstration with a couple of hundred followers, including three earls, intending to force the queen to dismiss his rival, Robert Cecil, and restore him to favour. This collapsed when the City authorities resisted. Essex and his close associates were tried and executed. His ten-year-old son, four decades later, would lead another and far more formidable rebellion, commanding the parliamentary forces against Charles I.

This episode tells us much about English government at the end of the sixteenth century, albeit at a time of uncertainty when the queen obviously had not long to live. Although nobles such as Essex commanded a predominant place at court, especially when military service was required, and great influence in local politics through patronage, their power independent of royal favour had waned. It was again shown that a noble faction could no longer raise significant military forces from tenants and retainers. County militias were commanded by the lords-lieutenant, officers of the Crown. On the other hand, the force directly commanded by the central government was also negligible. Apart from the Yeomen of the Guard, there was no regular police or military force. The Crown had only 1,200 paid officials, compared with forty times that number in France.[84] Government depended on part-time local officials—sheriffs, lords-lieutenant, JPs, mayors—as well as relatives, friends and clients, to govern the country. Crown officials, MPs, courtiers and privy councillors might have to argue with mobs, raise and lead armed men, confront rebels sword in hand, arrest suspects, imprison them in their own houses, interrogate and even in extreme cases torture them—as well as conduct diplomacy, speak in Parliament, and administer finances. Even though there were institutions and practices that were by now being called a "State," government was still a small and personal affair. So rulers needed a broad measure of consent, and in emergencies depended on the active loyalty and energy of a small number of key men, and sometimes women.

Elizabeth enjoyed this broad consent. She had deliberately created an imposing image both majestic and popular, through pictures, propaganda, lavish spectacles and progresses round the country, in which she appeared as defender of the nation and preserver of peace. Her visit to the Earl of Leicester at Kenilworth Castle in 1575 took months to organize. Parliament functioned as a connector of Crown and country, and the Church reiterated the moral basis of government: "Such subjects as are disobedient or rebellious against their princes disobey God and procure their own damnation."[85] Religious violence had not, unlike in much of Europe, destroyed social and political cohesion. Elizabeth's willingness to allow some latitude in religious sentiment, her dislike of doctrinal meddling, and above all the justified perception that she protected the country from invasion and turmoil gave her a unique popularity.

After forty-four years on the throne she must have seemed eternal: her motto was *"Semper Eadem"*—"always the same." But she was clearly not immortal. Late in 1602, aged sixty-nine, she began her final illness, a bleak and steady decline marked by insomnia, lack of appetite and some mental confusion. She died at Richmond on 24 March 1603. Unlike her pious predecessors, she had refused to accept death, making no will, and doing nothing to arrange the succession. So she left many problems for the future. Her chief minister, Robert Cecil, Burghley's subtle and unsentimental son, had prepared for the future by discreet correspondence with James VI of Scotland, heir to the throne of England.

## A REVOLUTION OF WORDS

"In the beginning was the word," wrote William Tyndale in the 1520s, the first sentence of his translation of St. John's gospel. England was about to undergo a revolution of words. Protestantism was based on the interpretation of words, instead of the enactment of rituals, and the evangelical tide made the English into a nation of readers of books and listeners to sermons—preferably not much more than ninety minutes, as Archbishop Cranmer advised a colleague (enthusiasts relished three or four hours). The English became an increasingly literate nation of arguers about what words meant, and what they demanded. Less obviously, along with the rest of northern Europe, England was undergoing a profound cultural change: from a shame culture to a guilt culture,[86] from extroversion to introversion, from performance to emotion, from "charity" to "love." Battles were fought over words, and lives hung on them.

It was still unsettling when those words were English. Serious matters were expressed in Latin, and learned men often felt awkward using the "vulgar tongue." Erasmus never used any English during his long stays in the 1500s. Even a century later, the translators of the King James Bible thought primarily in Latin. Of the 2,000 books in Oxford's Bodleian Library in 1605, only fifty-eight were in English.[87]

English was about to be put to new uses: but how? Those dazzled by the riches of Latin and Greek, and by the elegant modernity of Italian and French, thought that English must shed its rustic manners and be enriched by emulating its betters: "The speche of Englande is a base speche to other noble speches, as Italion Castylion and Frenche."[88] This was nothing new. Chaucer, as we have seen, imported many words, and the flood of Latinate coinages reached a peak only in 1600. Caxton believed that the written language should leave the spoken language behind, both in vocabulary and in style, avoiding idioms and vulgar colloquialism. Sophisticated English would use long words, and lots of them, in complex sentences copied from the Latin classics—vast juggernauts of words and clauses, piled up and repeated like a verbal fugue. English, having lost its inflexions several centuries earlier, could not easily hold up the structure without collapsing into incoherence, as readers got lost in the labyrinth.

Education included training in rhetoric, and distinguished scholars, led by Erasmus, wrote books explaining the tricks. Latinized English could serve many purposes. In serious guise, it could be used in authoritative religious instruction, by masters like Fisher and More, to quench any possible doubts or fears. In a lighter mood, it could create elegant courtly literature, influenced by Italian styles, appealing to the collusive cleverness of an educated readership. It served very well for both flattery and display. Of course, this was widely mocked, not least by those who practised it, as in this parody of a letter asking for a job, from Thomas Wilson's *The Arte of Rhetorique* (1553):

> Pondering, expanding, and revoluting with my selfe your ingent affabilitie and ingenious capacitie for mundane affaires: I cannot but celebrate & extol your magnifical dexteritie above all other . . . There is a Sacerdotall dignitie in my native Countrey contiguate to me . . . which your worshipfull benignitie could sone impetrate.[89]

The greatest revolution in words, however, was inspired not by ancient Rome, but by ancient Israel, and its instrument was one man's pen—that of William Tyndale, whose cultural impact went far beyond the purely religious. In discussing Tyndale, superlatives come easily: "a writer whose influence was . . . possibly greater than Shakespeare's," who wrote "the most important book in the English language," which has "had more influence upon our literature and upon our general culture than any other," and was "England's greatest cultural contribution to the world for 500 years." Tyndale "made a language for England," "essentially the language which we use today."[90]

He was born in 1494 of a minor gentry family in Gloucestershire, about forty miles from Stratford-on-Avon, home of another writer with provincial and rural knowledge. Having learned Latin, Greek and Hebrew at school and at Oxford, and being refused permission to translate the Bible by the Bishop of London, he went to the Netherlands and Germany, and worked largely alone, often as a fugitive. Within ten years, he translated the New Testament and half of the Old, mainly from the Greek and Hebrew originals. How he came to "discover our language" in such circumstances "will always remain a mystery."[91]

Wherever it happened in sixteenth-century Europe, and later in other continents, providing the Scriptures in a readable vernacular was both a revolutionary and a transformative act, one that permanently changed politics, culture and identity. Thomas More was so aware of the danger that he thought that if an English Bible had to be available, it should only be distributed in sections to reliable men, and collected up again afterwards; and an act of Henry VIII (1543) forbade labourers and non-gentlewomen to read it. When the first licensed translation was placed in St. Paul's, a spontaneous public reading of the whole text began. Tyndale did for England, and ultimately the English-speaking world, what Luther had done for Germany a few years earlier—he unleashed an immense and unpredictable cultural and ideological force.

No less important is how he did it: the words he used. He recognized that many people thought that the Bible "can not be translated in-to our tonge, it is so rude." His answer was that if St. Jerome (*c*.400) had used Latin, the common speech of his day, "Why maye we not also?"[92] Tyndale would have none of the efforts to "elevate" English by Latinizing it—he insisted that common English was closer to Hebrew and colloquial Greek than Latin was. As a fervent evangelical, writing to be understood by the "boy that driveth the plough," he used everyday words and proverbs. Where there was no existing word for a Hebrew concept, he tried not to draw on Latin or French but to invent in English: "firstborniship" rather than "primogeniture," or (more successfully) "scapegoat," "castaway" and "granddaughter." He may have also have invented "busybody," "zealous" and "whoremonger." Overall, he used few neologisms or Latinisms. His lively style, using short, vivid phrases and simple words in relatively free translation, made the Bible a native work, and consecrated the language of ordinary people.[93] This shaped what standard English would turn out to be.

Tyndale's linguistic naturalness was a provocative challenge to the intellectual and institutional power of the Church. This partly concerned individual words, over which he was denounced by More, who said he was dishonest and mischievous to translate *presbuteros* as "senior" or "elder," not "priest"; *ecclesia* as "congregation," not "church"; and *agape* as "love," not "charity"—an emotion, not an action. Similarly, Tyndale's sinners were to "repent" (internally), not "do penance" (externally). Style became a weapon too. More's published attacks on Tyndale were not only ferocious, they were enormous, marshalling all the resources of Latinate prose, abandoning plain English to Tyndale, as if the language itself had been tainted by heresy. After More and Tyndale had both been killed because of words, the conservative Bishop Gardiner tried a last-ditch defence, listing 100 words that he demanded should be kept as close as possible to Latin.[94]

Tyndale long remained "the forgotten ghost in the English language," his achievement deliberately obscured in his own time, and thereafter barely remembered except by specialists.[95] After he was burned, his work was circulated under other names: in the "Great Bible," approved without knowing its real provenance by Henry VIII in 1539; in the Geneva Bible of 1560, which sold over 500,000 copies and which probably every literate Elizabethan owned and read;[96] and finally in the King James Bible of 1611, which remained the official Bible of Anglophone Protestantism for four centuries.

After James came to the throne in 1603, he held a Church conference at Hampton Court, at which he agreed to authorize a new version of the whole Bible. This may partly have been a unifying gesture, but was also because he disliked the Geneva Bible, which offended his elevated view of monarchy, "savouring too much of dangerous and traitorous conceits."[97] Six "companies" of scholars were recruited, based in Westminster, Cambridge and Oxford, some fifty translators, mostly prelates and senior dons. Sections of the Old and New Testaments were allocated to each. They were a group whose intellectual qualities were seasoned with not a little ruthlessness and worldly ambition. Their director was the Archbishop of Canterbury, the tough and political Richard Bancroft; also influential was the Dean of Westminster, the poetic and in some ways saintly Lancelot Andrewes (who could, however, turn his hand to persecuting the unorthodox when the need arose). They spent 350 comfortable and well-beneficed man-years between 1603 and 1611—while Shakespeare wrote a dozen plays, including *King Lear*, *Macbeth*, *Othello* and *The Tempest*; Guy Fawkes nearly blew up Parliament; and a colony was founded in Virginia—in producing what was largely a revision of what Tyndale had done practically single-handed. We should be grateful that they never considered a new translation: 80–90 percent of the New Testament and a large part of the Old remained Tyndale.

The king and Bancroft had drawn up a set of rules. The aims were to correct errors and obscurities, and, where possible, to nudge Tyndale's language in the direction of dignity, ceremony and poetry: "Whatsoever is sound alreadie . . . will shine as gold more brightly, being rubbed and polished."[98] The rubbing was carried out in committee meetings, by discussion and consensus, and with minute attention to detail. Their chosen style was somewhat archaic, and a more cautiously word-for-word rendering of the Hebrew and Greek, which at first seemed awkwardly un-English. A deliberately old-fashioned typeface was chosen for the publication. Tyndale's "thees" and "thous," normal in the 1520s, were rarer in ordinary speech by 1611, but now they added to the special quality of a sacred text: this was "not the English you would have heard in the street, then or ever."[99] Tyndale's dangerous words were polished away, and "ould ecclesiasticall words" restored: once more the Bible spoke of a "church" with "priests," and St. Paul's greatest virtue was "charity." Jewish and

Greek names were not translated in the annoying evangelical fashion—Timothy did not become "Praise-God." Many editions were rushed out over the next few years, full of misprints—among them "Thou shalt commit adultery," a typo that landed its printer in gaol.

The King James Bible has many admirers and a few detractors, who prefer the rough-edged integrity of Tyndale. The differences are small, and often insignificant. Where they count, they tend towards the dignified and poetic, for reading aloud. We can see this in the beginning of Genesis.[100] Tyndale was dramatically terse:

> In the beginning God created heaven and earth. The earth was void and empty, and darkness was upon the deep, and the spirit of God moved upon the water.

Lancelot Andrewes, in the Authorized Version, kept closer to the more incantatory Hebrew:

> In the beginning God created the Heaven, and the Earth. And the earth was without form, and void, and darkness was upon the face of the deep: and the Spirit of God moved upon the face of the waters.

One other book had a comparable effect on the English language, being for centuries communally read and heard: the Book of Common Prayer, largely the work of Thomas Cranmer in the late 1540s. Cranmer's words, like those of Tyndale and his revisers, became familiar to millions. His Collects—single-sentence prayers, short, clear and memorable—echo both old English and modern styles of rhetoric, with parallel clauses and doubling of words. But when compared with the bloated prose of contemporary fashion, Cranmer attains almost haiku-like elegance: "Lighten our darkness, we beseech Thee, O Lord; and by thy great mercy defend us from all perils and dangers of this night . . ."

Tyndale, Cranmer and the Authorized Version epitomized a Protestant "plain style," which shaped many aspects of the English self-image. In the words of the Cambridge don Roger Ascham, Elizabeth I's tutor, one should "speak as the common people do . . . think as wise men do." Thomas Wilson's widely read *Arte of Rhetorique* (1553) advocated "one maner of language" for court and country alike. Plain speaking came to be seen as a characteristically English virtue—along with freedom, unostentatious dress and dislike of elaborate bowing and gesticulation.[101] The long-term effect seems clear. The plain style is still comprehensible, because it has remained the language we use. The more pretentious style of fashionable "rhetorique," in contrast, became indigestible and opaque. Yet this took time to work through. For some hundred years, from around

1660 to 1760, the King James Bible (like Shakespeare) was considered barbarous and archaic. One eighteenth-century modernizer rewrote "Consider the lilies of the field . . . they toil not neither do they spin" as "Survey with attention the lilies of the field . . . how unbecoming it is for rational creatures to cherish a solicitous passion for gaiety and dress."[102] When the later eighteenth and nineteenth centuries rediscovered a taste for "noble simplicity," the Bible's language (like Shakespeare's) was hailed as sublime.

The Bible and the Prayer Book were the books that everyone heard, read and memorized—for many, the only books they possessed, a whole literature suddenly acquired and made universally available. Only Foxe's *Book of Martyrs* had comparable reach. A standard form of English became familiar across the country, without replacing spoken dialects. In France, in contrast, where most worship remained in Latin, French remained a foreign language in large parts of the country until well into the nineteenth century.[103] This had an importance beyond the linguistic, though we take it so much for granted that we overlook it. In countries from Wales to Ethiopia, where language, culture or statehood were inchoate or threatened, a vernacular Bible and liturgy could preserve or even create a sense of national identity and a common culture. In England, where such identity already existed, the effect must have been powerful as a constant reminder of belonging to what has been called the "imagined community" of nationhood,[104] now extended to all worshippers, men, women and children. As one historian has remarked with only slight hyperbole, for centuries to come it would be possible to check one's watch at 11:08 on a Sunday morning and know that at that moment everyone in the land was intoning the same psalm.[105]

England's greatest writer (1564–1616) appeared during its greatest revolution of words. The two are surely linked. That a man of outstanding intelligence should be stimulated to write by the political and cultural ferments of the time is easy to understand. But that a clever boy from Warwickshire should end up writing plays for the new London stage (the first public theatre was built in 1576), rather than works of theology in an Oxford college, is not so predictable. The professional theatre grew out of a widespread tradition of religious plays which from the 1530s onwards gradually fell victim to repression by the evangelical clergy, who considered them superstitious or blasphemous: God was not portrayed on stage in England between 1570 and 1951.[106] Travelling players were patronized during the 1550s by nobles and courtiers for reasons of prestige and propaganda as well as entertainment. From the 1560s they were performing regularly in London, and from the 1570s permanent theatres were built across the river from the suspicious City authorities—most famously the Rose (1587) and the Globe (1599). New kinds of plays were pioneered by the "University Wits," most notably Christopher Marlowe, Thomas Nashe and Thomas Kyd, and then by two friends and fellow actors, Ben Jonson and William Shakespeare. Like his contemporaries, Shakespeare was formed (in his case from Stratford Grammar School onwards[107]) by humanism, inspired by classical literature, particularly Ovid and Virgil, and concerned with rhetorical forms (of which "To be or not to be . . ." is a textbook example). The stories of his plays reflect many of the cultural and political concerns of his day, including treason, conspiracy, royal succession, war and the exotic.[108] But at deeper levels he is astonishingly not the product of his times, which is an evident reason for the continuing power of his work. Most obviously, he is not dogmatic; he displays a wide variety of cultural and religious influences, but is not defined by the religious conflict that shaped his time—hence continuing modern debate about his personal beliefs. He pays little respect to social and gender hierarchy. He writes of a "deep England," beyond London and the court. Women are always important and often dominant in his plays, and women came in large numbers to see them, scandalizing foreign visitors. It is often said that he conceals his opinions; it seems rather that the ideas he explores transcend the limits of contemporary polemics.[109]

Shakespeare was an innovator. He went far beyond Chaucer in linking English literature with contemporary European culture—an ambition that explains much of the brilliance of English literature at this time,[110] even though many contemporaries doubted that England could produce a great literature because the language seemed to be changing so rapidly. Eventually Shakespeare's writing became central to the whole history of European culture, placing the English literature of these few decades on an equal footing with the classics. But this could only happen long after his death, because English remained practically unknown outside the islands until the late eighteenth century. Unlike More, and later Bacon and Newton, who wrote for an international readership in Latin, he was unread abroad for at least 150 years after his death, and it took as long again before he was considered as more than an exotic English primitive.[111]

Like other English writers since Chaucer, he worked to stretch English into new forms for new uses—in his case, for all the genres of classical and Renaissance literature. So he was a great inventor of words— probably about 1,700, several times more than any other English writer at a time when word-making was at a peak. But he did not try to expand English simply by Latinizing it; he did not seek to create an esoteric language of high culture. Many of his new words are adaptations of existing ones—using nouns as verbs, adding "un-," or using familiar words in new senses. He mocks fashionable pretention in style, vocabulary and pronunciation, even though able to practise it himself. Indeed, he "repents of his own brilliance,"[112] coming to see rhetoric as a barrier to meaning and sincerity:

> Taffeta phrases, silken terms precise,
> Three-piled hyperboles, spruce affectation,
> Figures pedantical—these summer flies
> Have blown me full of maggot ostentation.[113]

Although he can do the fashionable Pastoral style, he ends with songs not about nymphs and shepherds named Amaryllis or Daphnis, but about Dick, Tom, Marion and "greasy Joan," who play not pan-pipes but "oaten straws." His most powerful writing is of piercing monosyllabic simplicity:

> Come, gentle night; come, loving, black-browed night;
> Give me my Romeo; and, when I shall die,
> Take him and cut him out in little stars,
> And he will make the face of heaven so fine
> That all the world will be in love with night
> And pay no worship to the garish sun.[114]

Later generations, in England and abroad, found much of his language embarrassingly crude, even obscene, which they saw as a consequence of his popular audience—in the words of the French philosopher Voltaire, "porters, sailors, cabbies, shop-boys, butchers, and clerks," whose coarse standards "revolt people of taste throughout Europe."[115] Such critics laboured to make Shakespeare more "poetic." John Dryden rewrote him; Nahum Tate in 1687 gave *King Lear* a happy ending. In French translations Othello's "old black ram . . . tupping your white ewe" became "a black vulture" and a "young white dove"; and it took a hundred years of successive translations before Desdemona's incriminating but commonplace handkerchief could be so called (rather than "a diamond headband") and another hundred before it could be described as "spotted with strawberries" (rather than "decorated with Asiatic flowers").[116]

Shakespeare's insistence on being colloquial and literary at once integrated the Germanic and Latinate elements of English into a single expressive language. Of course, there is a continuing tension, as perhaps in all languages, between the desire to communicate through simplicity, and to impress through elevation of style. Tyndale, Cranmer and Shakespeare aimed at simplicity, keeping the expanding literary and intellectual language close to the styles and forms of speech. They thus achieved the rare feat of being both popular and avant-garde.

One consequence is that the ideas, phrases and images they used, constantly repeated, adapted and learned by heart, have formed a common stock for people who may have no idea of where they came from. A very small sample includes:

> *From Tyndale:* "the salt of the earth," "the fat of the land," "the powers that be," "let there be light," "the spirit is willing," "signs of the times," "the apple of his eye," "a law unto themselves," "filthy lucre," "as bald as a coot," "the straight and narrow," "my brother's keeper," "blessed are the peacemakers," "let my people go," "eat, drink and be merry," "flowing with milk and honey," "a stranger in a strange land," "the flesh pots," "thou shalt not kill," "love thy neighbour as thyself";

> *From Shakespeare:* "fast and loose," "neither rhyme nor reason," "too much of a good thing," "the game is up," "dead as a door nail," "be all and end all," "one fell swoop," "bated breath," "truth will out," "the world's mine oyster," "mine own flesh and blood," "love is blind," "pomp and circumstance," "a foregone conclusion," "a tower of strength," "good riddance," "early days," "fair play"—and many more.[117]

Not only have these word-patterns enriched and enlivened for centuries the thoughts and speech of the vast majority of us who cannot invent our own, but being familiar, and known to be familiar, they help to create a common cultural identity. The closeness to speech of the greatest literature of the sixteenth century is surely a major reason why the written and spoken language has not fundamentally changed since: we can read most of Shakespeare with little effort and would have understood it had we heard it performed, whereas he would have found it as difficult to read Chaucer as we do.[118]

Shakespeare promised to confer immortality through his words:

> So long as men can breathe or eyes can see,
> So long lives this, and this gives life to thee.

Whatever may happen to England in centuries to come, its language, and Shakespeare's words, born in an age of revolution in words, will indeed have left an indelible trace on human experience.

# CHAPTER 6

# Revolution

*That great God who is the searcher of my heart knows with what
a sad sense I go upon this service and with what a perfect hatred
I detest this war without an enemy; but I look upon it as sent
from God.*

Sir William Waller, parliamentary general, June 1643.[1]

After two centuries of worry over royal succession, it is understandable that the son of Mary Stuart, the thirty-seven-year-old James VI, King of Scots since the age of one, was accepted with relief as Elizabeth's heir; and he reigned from 1603 to 1625. His Protestant upbringing, and the desire for a peaceful succession, made his Scottishness seem secondary, despite his mother's embarrassing execution and the long history of national enmity—the skull of one King of Scots was reportedly used as a flowerpot in the English royal household.[2] The lack of alternatives was an unanswerable argument. The union of the "three crowns," celebrated in many a pub sign, could be made to appear the culmination of a long process of history. Shakespeare changed from writing about England to writing about Britain—directly in *Macbeth* (*c.*1606), *King Lear* (1606) and *Cymbeline* (*c.*1610), for example, and indirectly in *Hamlet* (*c.*1601) and even *Henry V*, with its Welsh, Scottish, Irish and English stock characters (1600).[3]

But the link with Scotland, though long foreseen and practically inevitable, was to prove disastrous. In the House of Stewart (in England now spelled Stuart, in the French style affected by Mary, Queen of Scots) the country acquired Europe's most hapless dynasty. They had an incorrigible misunderstanding and dislike of English institutions, especially Parliament. James said in 1614 that he was "surprised that my ancestors should ever have permitted such an institution to come into existence. I am a stranger, and found it here when I arrived." The union of the crowns proved impossible to manage, largely because of the deep religious divisions it contained, and this was eventually to spread civil war throughout the islands. The union did not even ensure the most basic advantage, to protect England from a renewal of Scottish invasions: over the next 150 years these were more frequent and disruptive than ever. The outcome for Ireland was even worse, for James promoted large-scale immigration—"plantations"—of Scottish and English settlers in Ulster, fatally destabilizing an already fragile and oppressive system. These difficulties, however, all lay in the future.

## "GREAT BRITAIN": A DIVIDED REALM

*Hath not God first united these Two Kingdoms both in Language, Religion, and Similitude of Manners? Yea, hath he not made us all in One Island, compassed with One Sea?... What God hath conjoined then, let no Man separate. I am the Husband, and all the whole Isle is My lawful Wife: I am the Head, and it is My Body.*

James I and VI to Parliament, 1604[4]

James was delighted to have won the English jackpot, and set out to enjoy it—every day, he said, was like Christmas. His view of kingly status was breathtaking—"God calls them Gods," he declared. The Scriptures were censored: the word "tyrant," used over 400 times in the Geneva Bible, was expunged from the "King James" version. The king's ambition, shared by few of his English subjects, was to make Scotland and England one kingdom, "Great Britain." When this met parliamentary and legal opposition—"Being English we cannot be Britaynes"—James unilaterally introduced a union flag and common coinage, including a twenty-two-shilling piece called the Unite, bearing a motto from the book of Ezechiel: *Faciam eos in gentem unam* (I will make them one nation).[5]

The Common Law, based on judicial independence and precedent, was now marshalled against the encroachment of Roman law, used in Scotland, which buttressed James's absolutist pretentions. Using the history of English law as the test of political legitimacy was an "all but universal pursuit of educated men" during the seventeenth century.[6] The Common Law was asserted to be purely and uniquely English, embodying ancient unwritten rights—paradoxically, a new idea. One of James's most outspoken opponents was the choleric Chief Justice and MP Sir Edward Coke, who, wrote the great legal historian F. W. Maitland, "ranged over nearly the whole field of law, commenting, reporting, arguing, deciding—disorderly, pedantic, masterful."[7] Coke was dismissed in 1616, later imprisoned in the Tower, and had his papers confiscated in a vain attempt to shut him up. He proclaimed that Common Law was based "on the wisdom of those before us . . . in many successions of ages, by long and continual experience." It limited the royal prerogative, insisted Coke and his supporters, and it could even strike down Acts of Parliament. The then largely forgotten Magna Carta was, Coke declared, in its "great weightinesse and weightie greatnesse," the very "fountaine of all the fundamentall lawes of the realm" and a "restitution of the common law."[8] Thus an idea of ancient English uniqueness was identified with a tradition of law and political freedom. Coke set out the argument in his *Institutes of the Laws of England* (which began appearing in 1628) and in a series of controversial judgments, including a decision that the king had no power to legislate by proclamation. Similarly, Parliament's Petition of Right (1628) asserted that imprisonment without trial by royal order was illegitimate.[9] From this time originates our instinctive belief that law is, or should be, more than a collection of executive orders and directives, and that "law" and "rights" embody intangible and permanent values. "The rule of law" became central to English ideas of freedom and civilization.

Despite James I's elevated pretensions, his reign was marked by a personal eccentricity that clashed with—or perhaps was a consequence of— both a harsh upbringing and a high level of intelligence and cultivation (he was, for example, a considerable poet). His most notorious foible was his devotion to a series of male favourites, though neither in Scotland nor in England was this (probably non-sexual) infatuation of as much interest to contemporaries as it has been to later generations.[10] The handsomest and cleverest was George Villiers, whom he created Duke of Buckingham. Things had changed since Edward II and Gaveston. Noble families now hastened to ally by marriage with the parvenu, and although Buckingham was eventually murdered, it was by a religious fanatic, not a jealous aristocrat. James, one of the oddest occupants of the English throne—a crowded field—was widely mocked by his English subjects but rarely hated. He had a shrewd intellect, an active interest in ideas, a real generosity of spirit, and a genuine devotion to peace. He tolerated and even encouraged limited religious diversity. This was the world of Shakespeare's late plays, including *The Winter's Tale* (1611) and *The Tempest*, given at court in 1611; and of the emotional religious and sometimes erotic poetry of John Donne (patronized by James) and George Herbert.

James's position was threatened only at the very outset of his reign, by the most celebrated and dangerous conspiracy in our history: the Gunpowder Plot of 1605. The plotters were young Catholic gentlemen, some already implicated in the failed Essex coup four years earlier. They had hoped that James would fully restore Catholic freedoms. His willingness to turn a blind eye to discreet private worship was not enough: that would emasculate Catholicism, and end all hope of reconquering its old dominance. Despairing of foreign intervention, Robert Catesby, a Warwickshire squire, imagined a coup beyond the ambitions of any modern terrorist: to kill the whole governing elite, seize the king's ten-year-old daughter, Elizabeth (who was staying in Warwickshire), and in the power vacuum make her their puppet queen. The plotters collected gunpowder at their base in Lambeth and rented a store-cellar directly under the House of Lords. By night, they ferried in thirty-six barrels of powder, packed them with pieces of metal to increase lethality, and screened them with piles of coal and firewood. Their ability to do this undetected has led to allegations that they were being manipulated by Robert Cecil's spies, but the evidence is against this.[11] Rather, it demonstrates how little protected governments were. The opening of Parliament on 5 November would have crammed some 500 key men—the king, the Privy Council, peers, MPs and royal officials—into a confined space just above a ton of gunpowder, which would have destroyed the chamber, its occupants, and much of the palace and its surroundings.[12]

One of the plotters, Francis Tresham, wrote anonymously on 26 October to his brother-in-law, the Catholic Lord Monteagle, warning him to stay away from Parliament because "they shall receive a terrible blow . . . and yet they shall not see who hurts them." Monteagle took the note to the Privy Council. After some cogitation, they guessed what might be afoot—perhaps they recalled the attempt in 1567 in Edinburgh to blow up the king's father. A midnight raid caught "John Johnson" in the storeroom with flint, steel and kindling. Interrogated on the rack by the Privy Council themselves, he gave his name as Guy Fawkes, a Catholic soldier from Yorkshire, and admitted his intention, as he put it, of blowing King James and his courtiers back to the Highlands. Meanwhile, the other plotters, with servants and retainers, had assembled in arms in Warwickshire to seize Princess Elizabeth. When they realized that the explosion had not happened, and that she had been moved, the dwindling band spent 6 and 7 November riding from one Catholic house to another with a cartload of arms. They were caught next day by the sheriff of Worcestershire and his posse. Catesby and several others were killed and eight captured. They were hanged, drawn and quartered.

The government did not use this last and most spectacular Catholic plot to begin a general persecution. It did encourage, and indeed required, public rejoicing at the failure of the plot, and this became over the centuries England's only real, and certainly most enjoyable, national day. Most Catholics had turned away from conspiracy, tacitly accepting a government which generally left them alone. About 3 percent of the general population and 12 percent of the nobility and gentry remained Catholic, and the numbers were stable or even increasing.[13]

Fear of a "popish" threat was renewed by the outbreak in Prague in 1618 of what became one of the most devastating conflicts in European history, the Thirty Years' War. This combination of dynastic, sectarian, and geopolitical struggles drew in nearly all of Europe, from the Baltic to the Mediterranean. Though the war was never simply one of Catholics against Protestants, at times and in places it seemed like it—for example, Protestant Holland, Bohemia and the Palatinate were assailed by the Catholic Habsburgs, who steadily crushed their religious and political liberties. English opinion reacted strongly. Those who feared Catholics at home now had a greater worry: the onward march of "popery," a political as much as a religious concept. It revived age-old strategic worries about an enemy occupying Ireland or the Low Countries. Furthermore, Frederick, the Protestant ruler of the Palatinate and king of Bohemia, chased out of both by Catholic invaders, was now the husband of James's daughter, Elizabeth. English and Scottish Protestants enthusiastically supported their co-religionists, and over the next generation many, inspired by God, adventure and pay, volunteered to fight—we might recall the (much smaller) International Brigades in 1930s Spain. Thousands enlisted every year: in total perhaps 40,000 English and Welsh, and many thousands of Irish (on the Catholic side) and Scots. A considerable part of the gentry thus gained military experience in the Dutch, Swedish, French, Spanish and other armies. This was not merely the background to religious tension and political division in England, but a large part of their cause.

Public opinion supported Continental intervention, but did not want to pay for it. The chronic failure of English royal revenues to keep up with the increasing costs of governing and especially of fighting—one of the country's fundamental problems—paralysed it militarily. James, both personally and politically averse to a European bloodbath, tried to make a deal with Spain to restore Frederick and Elizabeth to the Palatinate peacefully. When in 1621 the Commons petitioned for a war with Spain, James dissolved them, imprisoned two of their members, and personally tore their protest from the journal of the House—a procedure that his son Charles would try with less success. James insisted that the privileges of the Commons depended solely on his will, which led the Commons to reply that their privileges were "the ancient and undoubted birth-right and inheritance of the subjects of England." Far from fighting Spain, James wanted an alliance, embodied in a royal marriage between his heir, Charles, and the Spanish Infanta. Charles and Buckingham tried to secure this highly unpopular but diplomatically desirable match by a bizarre adventure worthy of Alexandre Dumas, riding incognito across France (as Thomas and John Smith) and turning up unannounced at the Spanish court. When the Spanish under papal pressure demurred, James and Charles looked instead to France, Spain's enemy, and in 1625 Charles married Louis XIII's sister Henriette-Marie, or "Henrietta-Maria," by proxy in Cambridge. The seemingly unprincipled foreign policy of James (who died in 1625), Buckingham and Charles was detested at home. It was also unsuccessful, as they were fooled by Spanish and French statesmen more cynical still, most famously the masterful Cardinal Richelieu, who secretly played off the English against the Spanish, and used British ships lent to him to attack French Protestants. Naval expeditions, short of money and experience, repeatedly failed against the Spanish and then the French when an attempt was made to aid French Protestants besieged by Richelieu at La Rochelle. Buckingham became the scapegoat and was assassinated in September 1628. All was not lost: England stayed out of the Thirty Years' War and profited from trading with both sides.

As the Continent went up in flames, England was enjoying unparalleled political and social peace, and, ironically, it continued to do so until shortly before the outbreak of civil war. Violent religious persecution had been replaced by tacit toleration of diversity. While central government was strapped for cash, local government was flourishing. It was not democratic, but it was highly participatory: about one man in three took a turn in office, from aristocratic lords-lieutenant and gentlemanly JPs to farmers and craftsmen serving as churchwardens, constables or overseers of the poor. Local funds and local efforts were at last mastering food shortages, improving public health, and providing the best system of poor relief in Europe under Elizabeth's Poor Law Act (1601), brought in to replace monastic charity. In short, England managed to combine a ramshackle military system, a chronically impoverished central government, the most diverse religious culture in Europe and the highest level of domestic peace.[14]

Like his father, Charles, aged twenty-five at his accession, had difficulties with Parliament. Both considered it an archaic and time-consuming nuisance, and an infringement on their prerogatives. Their views may have been formed by Scottish experience, but, across Europe, Renaissance promotion of Roman ideas of law and government, which stressed untrammelled sovereign authority, left no place for medieval relics such as parliaments. The Reformation, by transferring the powers of the papacy to Christian princes, had further elevated their status. The Commons were warned that troublesome parliaments had been abolished all over Europe, "except here only with us."[15] Early in 1629, matters came to a head over the Commons' refusal to vote taxation and their criticism of Charles's religious policy, which we shall consider shortly. When the king ordered the Commons to adjourn on 2 March, members held the Speaker down in his chair and locked the door to keep a royal messenger out while they passed three resolutions criticizing Crown policy. This drama is decorously re-enacted at each State Opening, when the royal messenger, Black Rod, is made to knock on the slammed door to seek admittance. Thus the House of Commons mythologizes an independence from the executive power which it seldom exercises. At the time, many MPs found it shocking: "the most gloomy, sad and dismal day for England . . . in five hundred years." Another predicted accurately that "parliament doors [would be] sealed for many years"[16]—in fact, eleven, during which Charles ruled without summoning a parliament. The Crown's spokesmen and its critics used legal and historical arguments, scrutinizing the past for proofs of ancient liberties. Political antiquarians such as Sir Robert Cotton MP assembled the country's most important collection of ancient documents, including Magna Carta and Beowulf. His house and library next door to Parliament became not only a repository of national historical memory, but an armoury of precedents—so much so that Charles I shut it down in 1630. Official archives were also closed. Private collections and papers were searched or confiscated, including Coke's, who was suspected of writing a book about Magna Carta and was "too great an oracle amongst the people."[17]

Any seventeenth-century British ruler had to face three fundamental problems. Two were inherited from Queen Elizabeth: her Church and her fiscal system. The third had come with the Stuarts: the "three crowns" themselves. The Elizabethan Church, the least Protestant of all the reformed churches, was by contemporary standards fairly tolerant and intellectually diverse. James I permitted this, from a combination of laziness, pacifism and genuine intellectual curiosity,[18] and diverse elements were left alone if they did not make trouble. But hardly anyone wanted to keep the Church as it was, and opposing tendencies within it struggled to change it. The fiscal system, adequate until the 1550s, no longer provided sufficient funds for the central government, because it had not kept up with inflation, and especially because modern war—with artillery, fortresses, larger armies, bigger warships—was increasingly expensive. Elizabeth had bought peace for herself by leaving the unpopularity of raising taxes to her successors. So the English, observed the philosopher and sometime Lord Chancellor Sir Francis Bacon, were "the least bitten in the purse of any nation in Europe."[19] Parliament did not recognize this—

partly because of its mistrust of James and Charles—and so the Crown was forced into divisive means of raising revenue without parliamentary consent.

Finally there was the British problem: how to govern three kingdoms whose historic enmities were now aggravated by a widening religious gulf, especially between Counter-Reformation Catholicism spreading in Ireland and militant Calvinism in Scotland, the latter eager to conquer the whole British Isles. England's own religious and political quarrels were dangerously inflamed by developments in the other kingdoms. James had held the lid down by a characteristic combination of inactivity and shrewdness; Charles heated the pot by an equally characteristic combination of interference and clumsiness.[20]

Charles's eleven years of non-parliamentary rule—or "tyranny," as his opponents preferred it—is traditionally thought of as leading inexorably to civil war, as the rights of Parliament were denied and public opinion turned against the king. Modern research paints a different picture: a recent historian even calls them "halcyon days."[21] The absence of Parliament cooled the political temperature, and there is no evidence of widespread and serious public discontent. Charles was an earnest reformer. He worked to strengthen naval and military defences. His Book of Orders (a set of administrative instructions published in 1631) required local magistrates to report regularly on their activities to contain the recurrent plague, and to relieve poverty by job creation and poor relief. He ordered the protection of common rights against landowners' encroachments, for which Lord Saye and Sele (a leading Puritan and defender of parliamentary rights) was prosecuted. He also defended traditional games and festivities after church on Sundays—"such as dancing, either men or women; archery for men, leaping, vaulting, or any such harmless recreation [ . . . ] May-games, Whitsun-ales, and Morris-dances," because without them "the meaner sort who labour hard all the week should have no recreations at all to refresh their spirit." This order outraged the godly—it was required to be read out in churches, no doubt often between gritted teeth—and displeased many magistrates and employers. As one preacher put it, "Some scurvy popish bishop hath got a toleration for boys to play upon the Sabbath Day."[22]

With the country at peace, parliamentary taxation could be dispensed with: it accounted for only 7 percent of Crown income, the rest coming from a range of feudal dues, local rates, patents, fines and licences. So Parliament was not summoned. Revenue was increased by aggressive use of the royal prerogative. The extension of "ship money," theoretically an emergency levy to pay for naval defences, became a test case. Many stoutly refused to pay up, most famously John Hampden, MP for Buckingham-shire, who took his case to the courts, and whose resistance to "tyranny" became part of national myth. But, in fact, attitudes to ship money did not cause a decisive national split: many who opposed it later fought for the king. And few if any thought that civil war was looming over the rights of Parliament.

The truly serious issue, as it had been for a century, was religion, now the focus of cultural, social, personal and political life to an unparalleled extent. In the wake of the Reformation and the impact of the English Bible, most people felt more intensely about religion than all but the most fervent minority today. Furthermore, religion had an inescapable social and political impact that it has now almost lost in Europe—though not, of course, elsewhere. The ligament of society was the parish—on average, 500–600 people, of whom about a quarter were adult males. The parish was the spiritual embodiment of the community and also the basis of local government, responsible, for example, for roads and poor relief. All were required by law to belong—even Catholic "recusants" were required to show minimum participation. Most people believed that this was right: local and national communities had to be united in religion, for religious conflict could be deadly. "Men are governed in peacetime more by the pulpit than the sword," commented Sir John Eliot, a leading parliamen-tarian. Parishes, charities, Church courts and the Poor Law regulated indi-vidual and family behaviour, punished the unruly and cared for the vulnerable. The parish was meant to reflect the political and social hierar-chy, with clergy appointed by the Crown, local landowners or the bish-ops, and with respectable men taking turns as parish officers. So national religious politics affected every community in the land.

There were two sources of disruption. First, "Puritanism"—the name given by their opponents to those who thought of themselves as the "godly," and who wished in a variety of ways to purify the Church from every relic of "superstition." They were overwhelmingly Calvinists, believ-ing in Predestination—that God had chosen an "elect" for salvation. This was the orthodoxy of the Elizabethan Church, but there were different ways of interpreting it. The godly often did so exclusively: apart from the elect, the rest were irrevocably doomed to hell. They also believed that God controlled everything that happened, and sought evidence of divine favour or disfavour in every event—or, in what seemed inexplicable cases, looked for explanation to astrology or witchcraft. These beliefs caused psychological stress: some who feared they were damned despaired to the point of suicide. The conviction of being specially chosen by God often included the euphoric experience of being "born again." Believers were impelled to convince others and reassure themselves by their godly zeal that they were safely among the elect. The signs included sober dress, praying with sighs and groans, christening children with names like Hezekiah or Patience, household fasting, preaching the word, combating sin, and eradicating superstition from their own parishes. Puritanism thus covered a range of beliefs and practices, from helping the poor to smashing stained-glass windows. The godly were far from popular, for their aims included the suppression of traditional games and pastimes from bull-baiting to maypole dancing. "We had a good parson here before but now we have a Puritan," complained the daughter of a Wiltshire churchwarden, "a plague or a pox on him that ever he did come hither."[23]

Godliness could reinforce the existing hierarchy, when "elect" gentry, clergy and magistrates imposed stricter order on the idle, the drunken and the unruly. This, indeed, was part of its attraction: by the 1620s, Puritans included many of the socially influential, including leading magnates such as the Earl of Warwick, Lord Brooke, and Viscount Saye and Sele.[24] But the idea of the "elect" could also be subversive: the godly, women or men, poor as well as rich, had the right and duty to oppose and reprimand their ungodly social superiors, and break their power over the parish and the community. As Archbishop Bancroft feared, "half a dozen artisans, shoemakers, tinkers and tailors, with their preacher," might hope to "rule the whole parish."[25] Godliness could sometimes take in secular grievances, using graffiti and satirical verse to condemn selfish landowners or unworthy magistrates—a potent danger to men whose authority rested not on physical power but on respect and deference. So Puritanism also appealed to individuals and groups excluded from established hierarchies of rural or urban power—women, the lesser gentry, smaller merchants, educated craftsmen. An example is Oliver Cromwell, the landless younger son of a gentry family from Ely, whose relative poverty endangered his gentle status, who in his thirties suffered severe depression ended by a "born again" experience, found prosperity by obtaining preferential leases on cathedral property, and became a godly MP for Cambridge in 1640. But attempts to explain Puritanism as a socio-economic phenomenon have proved a dead end. It appealed to people of all regions, both sexes and all classes, from aristocrats to apprentices—just as Communism in the 1930s attracted both coal miners and Etonians. It also repelled a similar variety of people.

The second source of disruption was the theological opposite of the first: "Arminianism," especially as practised under Charles I's Archbishop of Canterbury, William Laud, appointed in 1633 during the "tyranny." Arminianism (which, like Puritanism, began as a term of abuse) was named after Jacobus Arminius, whose teaching had violently split Dutch Protestantism. Arminianism denied extreme predestination, teaching that free will had a role in salvation, and emphasizing the importance of the Church, its liturgy and its sacraments. This reassuring doctrine outraged Calvinists. For Puritans, godliness was a way of behaving in society, and a church was a building for preaching and spontaneous self-expression. For Laud, an Oxford academic as ascetic and unbending as any Puritan in his private life, a church should be a holy and beautiful place for formal prayer, regulated ceremony and the sacraments—what Puritans considered popery and superstition. Unlike Puritans, Charles and Laud did not regard Catholicism as the false religion of Antichrist. Arminianism reduced the status of the (self-identified) "elect" by bringing religious life firmly under the control of a powerful, obedient and properly appointed clergy. Moreover, Laud wished to recover at least part of Church lands and revenues lost during the Reformation by renegotiating leases and increasing tithes. This was far from welcome to the gentry and urban elites, whether godly or not. It weakened their control over their parishes by strengthening that of bishops and clergy, some of whom were made privy councillors and JPs:

> This upstart, plebeian priest [Laud] hoped to see the time, when ne'er a Jack Gentleman in England would dare to stand before a parson with his hat on. A fine scene truly! to see a gentleman of fortune and breeding, stand stooping, and bare-headed, to a small, ill-nurtured vicar; who had, perhaps, formerly cleaned his shoes, and lived upon the crumbs that came from his table![26]

This alarmed those who had acquired lucrative ecclesiastical land or revenues (not only the likes of Oliver Cromwell, but many of the established nobility). It also cost good money to restore and refurnish churches, many of which—including St. Paul's Cathedral—had become dirty and dilapidated. Across the country there were angry disputes about what might seem trivialities—whether the clergy should wear surplices, what the "altar" or "communion table" should be called, and whether it should be railed off from the congregation. The anger came from what these things represented. What was at stake in these religious tussles were power struggles, social upheavals and cultural intrusions comparable with the impact of Islamism today.

Discontent was raised to a shriller pitch by fears that Charles and Laud were drawing closer to "popery," the political as well as religious dangers of which seemed grimly demonstrated by the Thirty Years' War. Now the most immediate danger seemed to come not from outside, as in the past, but from subversion at the centre of power. The behaviour of Queen Henrietta-Maria seemed blatant proof. The marriage treaty of 1625 gave her the right to practise her Catholicism, and she did so ostentatiously. She had Inigo Jones design a sumptuous chapel in the Strand, staffed by Franciscan friars, which attracted the devout and the sycophantic. Catholicism seemed to be the court fashion, with prominent personages converting and Catholic peers being favoured. In 1640, peers and their households were exempted from the recusancy laws, and formed a prominent and powerful Catholic network. This affronted both the feelings and the pride of many powerful men, including peers such as the Earl of Warwick who were not extremely pious but who were leading critics of royal foreign policy. Even relatively sensible people could see official religious policy as a growing national danger:

> You shall see an Arminian reaching out his hand to a Papist, a Papist to a Jesuit, a Jesuit gives one hand to the Pope and the other to the King of Spain; these men having kindled a fire in our neighbour country, now they have brought over some of it hither, to set on flame this kingdom also.[27]

Laud enforced Arminianism, and made himself thoroughly hated as a persecutor. By the standards of the time it was mild, mostly admonitions and some sackings of recalcitrant clergy—fewer than under James I and minuscule compared with the later Commonwealth. The most offended Puritans could and did emigrate to the Netherlands or North America, and establish a godly "city on a hill" where they could persecute to their hearts' content. No one was burned for heresy in England during Charles's reign, and execution of witches was discouraged and in steep decline (it later revived sharply under the Puritans). When in 1637 three Puritan critics, William Prynne, Henry Burton and John Bastwick, courted martyrdom by publicly attacking religious policy in extreme language, and then behaving provocatively before the court of Star Chamber, they had their ears sliced off, but not their heads.[28] This became the most notorious act of the "tyranny," which aroused anger more than fear. But it was not a conflict between freedom and oppression: the oppressed were at least as determined as the oppressors to force their beliefs on others.

While there was religious and political discord by the late 1630s, there was no prospect of revolt, no discernible way by which the adversaries could have crossed the unthinkable gulf into civil war. England, with the important exception of those who had fought on the Continent, was a demilitarized and peaceful country by the standards of its time, or indeed those of our own day. Few people now owned weapons. Violence had greatly declined even in the formerly turbulent Scottish Marches, where there had been no large-scale Scottish incursion since 1513. Murder was rare—comparable with the rate today.[29] Political violence had never been lower. No peer was convicted of treason between 1605 and 1641—an unprecedented run. There was no rebellion between 1569 and 1642, tranquillity unequalled until the nineteenth century. There were more dead bodies at the end of a performance of *Hamlet* than after any political disturbance of these years. In short, for most of the 1630s, Charles's "tyranny" and abstention from European wars, far from provoking mounting resistance and unpopularity, meant for ordinary people in England a time of easing anxieties.[30]

Scotland was different: more turbulent, more militarized, and since 1603 left to govern itself. Neither James nor Charles liked Scottish Presbyterianism, a Calvinist model by which the Church was run by committees of lay elders and clergy, without the rule of bishops, and which thus eluded royal control: as James liked to put it, "no bishop, no king." The Stuart kings aspired to increase the unity of their domains. James had managed to reintroduce bishops, but without the powers of their English counterparts. His relatively benign neglect was replaced by Charles's unwelcome attention. In 1636, advised by Laud, he commanded the use of a prayer book in Scotland modelled on Cranmer's Book of Common Prayer. In July 1637, at its first use at St. Giles's in Edinburgh, the congregation rioted, shouting: "They are bringing popery in among us." Stools were thrown at the clergy. One man in the congregation who was imprudent enough to say "Amen" was hit on the face with a Bible by a woman who shouted: "Traitor, dost thou say Mass at my ear?" More riots and petitions followed, and in February 1638 a committee of lairds, burgesses and ministers drafted a Covenant to uphold the Scottish kirk and resist popery. It was subsequently sworn to by thousands, including some of the Scottish royal council, and "Covenanters" dominated the Scottish Assembly.[31]

Covenanters were seen by Charles as rebels, and he was determined to use English and if necessary Irish forces to reduce them to obedience, ignoring advice that he was "hazarding . . . your three crowns." Charles managed to raise 25,000 men in England solely by royal authority—the first time since 1382 that the country had gone to war without summoning a parliament. At all levels there was foot-dragging, even fear, over what were called "the Bishops' Wars." Wrote a Yorkshire MP, "These are strange, strange spectacles to this nation in this age that have lived thus long peaceably without noise of shot or drum."[32] The Earl of Northumberland, commander of the army, warned that "the People through all

England are generally so discontented . . . as I think there is reason to fear that a great part of them will be readier to join with the Scots, than to draw their swords in the King's service."[33] Some soldiers smashed "popish" symbols in churches and lynched officers suspected of being "papists." There were numerous allegations of Catholic conspiracies to murder politicians, blow up churches, or plan invasions. In 1639 there was a stand-off between the English and Scottish Covenanter armies.

Charles, needing money to pay his army and push back the Scots, was forced to call a parliament in April 1640, but it refused to vote taxes and was dissolved after three weeks. The worst riots for a century broke out in London in May, directed principally against Archbishop Laud, but also seeming to threaten Henrietta-Maria and her mother, Maria di Medici, resident at St. James's—never in real danger, though her carriage was pelted with carrots. An angry Charles personally wrote out a warrant to rack one of the rioters to discover ringleaders—the last legal use of torture in English history, as the following year Parliament abolished the prerogative court of Star Chamber, which, unlike Common Law courts, accepted evidence thus obtained.[34]

The collapse of royal authority was caused not by London rioters, but by the Scottish Covenanter army, which invaded in August 1640, commanded by a veteran of the Swedish army, Alexander Leslie. English defences dissolved, and the Scots for the first time in centuries occupied England as far south as Yorkshire. They began to play a weighty role in English politics, even demanding half the places on the English Privy Council. The ambition of the Covenanter leaders was to impose militant Protestantism throughout the islands. Charles had to agree to pay the Scottish troops' wages, and they forced him to call another parliament. This was also demanded by a petition of twelve leading peers, critics of royal policy, who included the earls of Essex, Bedford and Warwick. Parliament met, amid intense anxiety, on 3 November 1640. It was known later as the Long Parliament, as it met on and off for twenty years, the whole period of what would be the Civil War. The most influential opponent of Charles in the Commons was a Somerset Puritan, John Pym, who entered into contact with the Scots. Their presence in England gave Pym unprecedented leverage over the king, who was prevented from dissolving Parliament. The Scots insisted on radical action against popery and royal "tyranny," and the Commons duly targeted its two main bugbears, Thomas Wentworth, Earl of Strafford, in November 1640, and Archbishop Laud in December 1641. Strafford was the king's strongman in Ireland, and had made himself generally detested there, and was feared in Scotland and England too because of his readiness to bring over Irish troops to enforce royal authority. The Commons impeached him for treason—the procedure in which Parliament acted as a court of law with the Commons as prosecutor and the Lords as judge. He was guilty of many misdeeds, but not treason. But Parliament, whose own resentment was stiffened by Scottish pressure and threats from London rioters, voted his death by a Bill of Attainder, which required no evidence—one MP was expelled from the House after saying that he disliked committing murder with the sword of justice. The king reluctantly signed Strafford's death warrant—the only political execution of his reign, for which he felt both guilt and shame. This judicial assassination worried many, though not the jubilant crowd that turned out to see Strafford beheaded. His last words had weight: "I wish that every man would lay his hand on his heart and consider seriously whether the beginnings of the people's happiness should be written in letters of blood."[35]

The crisis in England, precipitated by invasion from Scotland, was fatally aggravated by events in Ireland, which left a suppurating wound on Anglo-Irish relations for centuries. In October 1641, another rebellion broke out. Strafford's fall had encouraged Catholic nobles to take up arms. Their well-founded fear was that the Scots and the Protestants in Ireland, in alliance with Pym's majority in Westminster, would insist on anti-Catholic measures and land confiscations.[36] But their limited uprising, with some rebels claiming to be acting on the king's authority, got out of hand due to popular hatred of Protestant immigrants in the "Plantations." Thousands were slaughtered, sometimes with unusual cruelty. Thousands of men, women and children were stripped of everything— sometimes literally stark naked—and chased out, many dying of hunger or cold. Protestants responded with violent reprisals. This orgy of ethnic and sectarian brutality between neighbours was unparalleled at the time in western Europe, and equalled only in the Ukraine, which saw comparable horrors. Accounts reached England and Scotland of mass rape, torture and mutilation, and the killing of children. It was rumoured that 150,000 and more had been killed; modern studies suggest that between 4,000 and 10,000 actually died in one of the bloodiest episodes in modern Irish and British history. Protestants across Europe were horrified. An individual example suggests the impact. Nehemiah Wallington, a godly London wood-turner, learned that his brother-in-law in Ireland had been killed in front of his children, two of whom had subsequently died, and that the widow had sex with an Irish Catholic to save herself and her surviving children. Gruesome atrocity stories were readily believed and permanently inflamed an existing stereotype of Irish savagery. The Thirty

Years' War, it seemed, had at last reached these islands, and "papists" in England seemed far more dangerous because they might call up an Irish invasion—a recurring fear in English politics for years to come. Wallington had heard that the rebels claimed to be obeying the king's orders: "If it be true . . . then surely the Lord will not suffer the king nor his posterity to reign, but . . . will requite our blood at his hands . . . And therefore these bloodthirsty papists do here among us in England plot what may be for our overthrow."[37] Such terrors were echoed across the country, fanned by the parliamentary opposition, who styled themselves "patriots" and claimed to be the true defenders of England.[38]

Political decisions in England had thus ignited violence in the other two kingdoms. That violence now made civil war in England thinkable, perhaps even inevitable. The king's opponents wanted an army raised to fight in Ireland, but they would not trust him to command it in case he used it against them and their Scottish allies. In the autumn of 1641 the Commons, led by Pym, drew up a Grand Remonstrance, a rambling, provocative and bizarrely paranoid attack on practically the whole of Charles's reign, down to its forest and fisheries policies. It accused "the malignant party" in Charles's entourage—"Jesuited Papists," bishops, treacherous courtiers—of undermining ancient liberties, weakening Parliament, tolerating popery, befriending Spain, fomenting the "bloody massacre" in Ireland—all part of a Europe-wide plot to destroy Protestantism. It demanded that the king should only appoint "such counsellors, ambassadors and other ministers . . . as the Parliament may have cause to confide in," or they would vote no money.[39]

The Remonstrance, after a twelve-hour debate, was passed by the Commons on 22 November 1641 by only eleven votes. Increasing numbers of people, including critics of the king, were becoming alarmed by the extremism of Puritan populists. Many MPs went home. There was a rallying to Charles in Parliament and the country. He was met by cheering crowds, and even made a triumphal entry into London on 26 November. This rallying of support encouraged Charles to try to snuff out opposition in Parliament, supposedly encouraged by the queen—"Go you coward, and pull those rogues out by the ears."[40] Lacking an army and a police force, on 4 January 1642 he went with his bodyguard and a couple of hundred armed courtiers to arrest a peer, Lord Kimbolton, and five MPs, including John Pym and John Hampden, for treason. Tipped off, they escaped by boat, but their rooms and belongings were searched. The threat of violence from the king's entourage ("many of them by wicked oaths and otherwise expressed much discontent") caused at least one MP to go home and make his will. The House declared that anyone arresting an MP without its consent was "guilty of the breach of liberties of the subject and of the privileges of parliament, and a public enemy to the commonwealth," and whoever had advised or agreed to it "are declared public enemies of the State and peace of this kingdom."[41]

Charles's attack on Parliament provoked a hostile reaction in the streets and among the City authorities: "The king had the worst day in London yesterday that he ever had, the people crying 'Privilege of Parliament' by thousands and prayed God to turn the heart of the king, shutting up all their shops and standing at their doors with swords and halberds."[42] Charles realized that he had lost control of London, and on 10 January he left. Many of his sympathizers in Parliament ceased to attend.

No one has ever doubted the importance of Charles's personality in the disasters that were to befall his kingdoms and himself, and many have ascribed the Civil War essentially to him. He was almost Puritanically strait-laced, uxorious and rather tight-fisted ("not in his nature bountiful"), except in acquiring art. The first English monarch since the Middle Ages to have travelled on the Continent, he became a genuinely enthusiastic patron, most famously of the work of Van Dyck and Rubens, and one of the great collectors in English history—he amassed hundreds of Titians, Raphaels, Leonardos, Caravaggios and Veroneses, mostly disposed of by the Puritans. The arts, including ceremonies, plays, masques and his own image, were always for him a means of conveying messages concerning order, virtue, dignity and majesty.[43] A natural reserve led to instinctive secretiveness, even duplicity. Sensitivity, even timidity, he sometimes compensated for by stubbornness, and occasionally violence. The sensitivity, however, was real. Probably no previous English monarch had been so hesitant to take life. His parliamentary opponents were more bloodthirsty, far more bigoted, and vastly more paranoid in their vision of the world.[44] But he was an inept politician, unable to understand or deal with opposition, detesting debate, and neglecting public opinion. Such "popularity" he despised, preferring authoritarian methods of doing what he thought right for his subjects. He could be persuaded to plunge into reckless actions, but repeatedly drew back "amazed" when things went wrong: "Very fearless in his person," wrote his great apologist Edward Hyde, Lord Clarendon, "but not enterprising; and had an excellent understanding, but was not confident enough of it."[45] In this he differed from his opinionated, garrulous, often foul-mouthed father, who relished argument and was less resentful of disagreement. Charles did, however, make a perfect martyr, because his enemies eventually made themselves far more hated than he was, and because he was ready to maintain his fundamental beliefs whatever the cost.[46]

## CIVIL WAR, 1642–51

Let the praises of God be in their mouth: and a two-edged sword in their hands;
To be avenged of the heathen: and to rebuke the people;
To bind their kings in chains: and their nobles with links of iron.

Psalm 149

Few wars can have broken out so untidily as this one did over the summer of 1642. England had no standing army. The militia existed largely on paper; even the Trained Bands (the portion of the militia that had received some drill and had some weapons) were far from constituting an effective army. Parliament and the king began raising men, not because both were bent on war, but to defend themselves and strengthen their bargaining positions. Who took the first provocative steps is debatable. Parliament dismissed the Privy Council and required an oath of allegiance from every man. Above all, it claimed control of the militia. On 12 July 1642 it voted to raise a force under the 3rd Earl of Essex, son of Queen Elizabeth's turbulent favourite, who had gained military experience fighting Spain and was a critic of royal policy. Charles dismissed hostile lords-lieutenant and issued "commissions of array" to prominent men authorizing them to raise recruits. On 22 August he raised his standard at Nottingham to rally supporters (worryingly, to the superstitious, it fell down). One MP later wrote that they had "slipped into this beginning of a civil war by one unexpected accident after another." Most of the country tried to hold back. Nearly every county petitioned for compromise. Some drew up neutrality agreements, especially where there were local divisions. Derbyshire refused to raise troops. Other counties, including Norfolk, Suffolk, Lincolnshire and Yorkshire, dragged their feet. In Staffordshire, the sheriff, JPs and grand jury agreed to raise a force to defend the county against "certain persons in arrays and warlike manner" whatever their loyalty.[47]

Committed and active minorities set the pace, forcing more and more people, from peers to farm labourers, to make a choice. There must have been much low-level individual conflict, as in Ludlow that June: as a godly gentleman, William Littelton, came out of church, "a man came to him and looked him in the fase and cryed 'roundhead'; he gaue the fellow a good box of the eare."[48] In Cheshire, a JP, Sir William Brereton, led a group originally formed to campaign against bishops and the Prayer Book, and now they raised a small but effective army. Near Preston, both sides tried to take command of the assembled militia, and MPs, the king's Commissioner of Array, deputy lieutenants and other county officials shouted angrily at each other, until the sheriff rode off ordering "all that were for the king" to follow him.[49] Two armed antagonists were hesitantly forming, but the country as a whole was not yet following.

Each side seized towns, strongpoints and military stores. The king was locked out of Hull, the biggest military depot, and also failed to take the main naval base at Portsmouth. Rival recruiters had some vicious little skirmishes, though both sides were eager not to fire the first shot in a major clash. At one stand-off in Warwickshire, the royalist Earl of Northampton was challenged by Lord Brooke to decide the issue by single combat, and when he declined because "gross and corpulent," it was suggested that twenty men from each side should fight it out.[50]

The biggest early outbreaks of violence were at Colchester in August 1642, when the royalist Lucas family were prevented by a crowd of citizens from raising an armed force for the king, had their weapons seized and their house just outside the city walls wrecked. Other noble and gentry families in the Stour valley (later the idyllic scene of Constable's greatest paintings) were also threatened or attacked. This has sometimes been seen as evidence that class conflict underlay the Civil War: the people of a cloth-manufacturing town were attacking the landed gentry. In fact, the attacks were carried out by socially diverse crowds, and were political and religious: the only targets were "papists" and their allies. Economic problems were blamed on papists, who provoked divine anger and fomented division.[51] Moreover, incidents such as these were extremely rare.

The first battle between what Kipling called "the raw astonished ranks" was fought on 23 October 1642, at Edgehill, in Warwickshire, an indecisive engagement which cost about 1,500 lives. A letter written on the eve of a later battle by Sir William Waller, a Presbyterian parliamentary commander, to his old friend Sir Ralph Hopton, who commanded the other side, expresses the revulsion caused by descent into this "war without an enemy": "We are both upon the stage, and must act such parts as are assigned us in this tragedy. Let us do it in a way of honour and without personal animosities."[52]

A war without an enemy, perhaps; but England's deadliest civil strife.[53] Ever since, people have tried to explain what it was about. There have been many attractively simple and all-embracing suggestions. That it was a struggle between liberty, embodied in Parliament, and tyranny, in the form of Stuart absolutism.[54] Or that it was a revolutionary class conflict, between feudal landowners and the industrious middle class of "artisans, merchants, yeomen" whose thrifty Puritanism shaped the values of democracy and capitalism.[55] "Cavaliers" and "Roundheads" were thus seen as clearly distinct in ways of life (including manners and appearance), ideologies and economic interests. Hence, the two sides were assumed to have been socially and regionally different, royalist support being concentrated in the relatively "backward" west of England and in ethnically distinct Wales and Cornwall; while parliamentary strength came from the socially and economically advanced areas of London and eastern England. Subtle variations have linked royalism with tightly controlled arable farming, and anti-royalism with forest and pasture.[56]

Such ideas have long been fundamental to our understanding of this period. But none of the simple explanations stands scrutiny. Religion was the clearest dividing line, but even that does not explain everything. Belief was a shifting spectrum. It is easy to identify the two poles—Catholicism and Puritanism—but both were small and unpopular minorities. Most people bunched towards the middle, suspicious of Laudian "popery" but also disliking Puritan "ranters." Nearly all were members of the Church of England. Not all believed extreme accounts of a "popish plot." All were monarchists, and most remained so throughout. Besides, political or religious disagreement is not the same as civil war, and explaining the first does not adequately explain the second. Previous attitudes did not simply carry over into the war, which for everyone was a new dilemma. We have already seen efforts to remain neutral. If one examines individual cases closely, it is often impossible to detect from earlier behaviour how people would react to the outbreak of war. Of 197 gentry families who can be identified as "Puritan" in 1643, one-third sided with the king.[57]

Some lines of division are counter-intuitive. Parliamentarian leaders were considerably older than royalists—a decade on average. Most of the ancient peerage, including non-Puritans, backed Parliament, but newer titled families largely supported the king. Parliament's forces for most of the war were commanded by peers and their sons; at Edgehill, the proportion of noble colonels on the parliamentary side was twice that on the king's. This reflected the nobility's dislike of the novelties of Stuart government, their exclusion from royal councils, and their support for an anti-Spanish foreign policy. Pym and Lords Brooke, Saye and Sele, and Warwick, for example, were all involved in a scheme to colonize the Caribbean with Puritan settlers, and thus were necessarily anti-Spanish.[58]

Rather than the country being pre-divided into two ideological and socio-economic blocks, it was suddenly wrenched apart from top to bottom. Every town and village was divided. Personalities and their influence, old friendships or quarrels, local history, local social and economic conditions, and of course religion all counted, but so did pay or other inducements. Most men who fought did so because they were conscripted, and it was common for prisoners of war to be encouraged to enlist on their captors' side: even Cromwell's New Model Army contained many turncoats. Though each side came to control certain parts of the country, this reflected military power more than popular support. Even in London and East Anglia there were many royalists, and neither side took for granted the loyalty of the counties it controlled. Royalist Wales and Cornwall are the only examples of solid regional loyalties, in reaction against a virulent new strain of English xenophobia on the parliamentary side.[59] The East Anglian cloth trade had affinities with godliness and supported Parliament, probably because of the custom of reading aloud and singing hymns at work, a tradition of petitioning Parliament through godly preachers, and trading contacts with the Low Countries. But Shropshire weavers, who traded with the Mediterranean, were royalist. Other industries reacted less predictably. Derbyshire miners backed the king in return for remission of the tax on tin. So the "middling" and "industrious" were divided like everyone else.[60] Traditional ties sometimes held, and sometimes did not. William Davenport called on his Cheshire tenants to join him in supporting the king, but while politely answering that they had "no disloyal thought," they said, "we dare not lift up our hands against that honourable assembly of parliament," and enlisted on the other side. Similarly, the Earl of Derby, Lord-Lieutenant of Cheshire, a generous and popular landlord, found some of his tenants turning against him, which embittered future relations.

Neighbours and friends chose opposite sides, and could feel confused and betrayed at meeting sudden hostility. A Herefordshire Puritan, Brilliana Harley, wrote:

> My thoughts are in a labyrinth to find out the reason why they should do thus to me . . . I can see nothing but love and respect arising out of my heart to them . . . I know not how those who I believe to be so good should break all these obligations.

On the other hand, war could also unite old enemies—in Herefordshire, "Sir William Croft, who once did not love Mr. Coningsby nor Mr. Scudamore, is now their mighty friend."[61] Former stern critics of the king's policies now fought on his side. Catholics rallied to the Crown, alongside those who had persecuted them.

Families split—perhaps one in ten of gentry families—with fathers, sons and brothers drawn, often with much heart-searching, to opposite sides, while mothers, sisters and family friends laboured to prevent an irreparable breach. Such was the Lilburne family: one brother eventually became the leader of the godly Levellers, another a royalist. Sir Edmund

Verney, a critic but also a friend of Charles, rallied with misgivings to his cause: "I have eaten his bread and served him near thirty years and will not do so base a thing as to forsake him." His eldest son, Ralph, an MP, chose the other side, and although Edmund was "much troubled" and stopped writing to him, he told a friend that Ralph "hath ever lain near my heart, and truly he is there still." Edmund, "infinitely melancholy" and expecting to be killed, died stoically as the king's standard-bearer at Edgehill. Ralph later withdrew from the parliamentary side, but never joined the king's.[62]

Each party was a shifting coalition. People held back or changed sides, both from self-interest and from principle. The country had stumbled into war, and it remained unclear what exactly each side was fighting for. The parliamentarian side denied that they were fighting against the king: rather they were trying to rescue him from evil counsellors, his true enemies. But some developed a new doctrine of the unlimited sovereignty of Parliament—an idea with a future. Charles claimed that he was not opposed to parliaments, made sweeping political concessions, and summoned loyal MPs to meet at Oxford in 1643. Over 40 peers and 137 commons attended—not far short of the number sitting in Westminster. A negotiated compromise always seemed in the offing. But the war itself widened the divide of anger and fear, and so made compromise increasingly difficult.

We should not exaggerate the social or cultural differences between the two armies, which we often derive from later literature, paintings and films. Officers on both sides were constantly complaining about the conduct and quality of their men, who ranged from "the committed and capable to the pathetic, reluctant and criminal."[63] Officers were mainly gentlemen. Even those on the parliamentary side whom Oliver Cromwell termed "plain, russet-coated captains" included many sons of the gentry and aristocracy. Yet both sides did tend to coalesce round certain values and ideas. These were encapsulated in the flags they carried into battle, which soldiers adopted as symbols of their common identity. At that time, commanders designed their own flags and mottoes, mostly in Latin on both sides. Far more parliamentarian banners—half as many again—had religious themes, and moreover were aggressively religious, bearing anti-papist designs and Old Testament mottoes such as "Aflame with love for Sion" or "Thou shalt break them with a rod of iron." Royalist religiosity was more subdued, even wistful: "May there be peace in your strength," "I hope for better things," even "I live and will die for these things"— Crown, Bible, sword, olive branch and land. Politics came after religion, with many references to Magna Carta on parliamentary banners, and to treason and rebellion on the royalist, along with some condemnation of social disorder—"Shall barbarians reap these crops?" Satire and humour were much more common among royalists, including a slogan referring to the Earl of Essex's notorious marital problems—"Cuckold wee come!" Soldiers' insults to each other carried similar if less elaborate messages: "papist dogs," "sons of a Puritan bitch," "traitors" and so on.[64]

There was doubtless pressure to conform to stereotypes of "Cavalier" and "Roundhead"—terms dating from 1640. Cavaliers "boast wonderfully and swear most hellishly," wrote a young Roundhead, and although they prayed too, they did so less ostentatiously, like Sir Jacob Astley before the battle of Edgehill—"O Lord, Thou knowest how busy I must be this day: if I forget Thee, do not Thou forget me." One godly royalist officer—who jokingly referred to himself as a praying captain rather than a swearing captain—was teased for taking his company to receive communion when he had been invited to a dinner: "Hang't, bully, thou mayst receive the sacrament anytime, but thou canst not eat venison at any time."[65] Cavalier officers tended to quarrel and fight duels. Royalists were more liable to "plunder" (a new word), partly because they were less well supplied, but also because of their commander Prince Rupert's readiness to apply harsh European methods of warfare. Roundheads went in for iconoclasm—cathedrals were their main targets, with fifteen of the twenty-six damaged—and for punitive pillaging of "papists," in practice not so different from simple plundering.

The uncertain divisions within the country were reflected in the early campaigns. For the first few months, both sides raised troops easily. The committed volunteered, and there was plenty of money to encourage the rest, including foreign mercenaries on both sides. After the battle of Edgehill, the king's army marched on London, but on 13 November 1642 it was halted at Turnham Green by the London militia behind eleven miles of entrenchments—a significant failure, and one which for the time being ended talk of a negotiated peace. Charles withdrew to Oxford, which was fortified too. Thereafter, there was no great strategic objective whose capture could decide the war. Several armies—eight by 1644—fought in fifteen regional theatres, particularly in the south-west, the north and the Midlands. Numbers waxed and waned. Advancing victorious armies held together, not least because they could live off new country and find loot—though this could be a problem too, as when parliamentary soldiers after their great victory at Naseby in 1645 disappeared to take their booty home. Armies shrank if they were stuck in one place, if they were marching hard with no result, or if, after a defeat, they were close enough to their home territory to facilitate running away—Parliament imposed col-

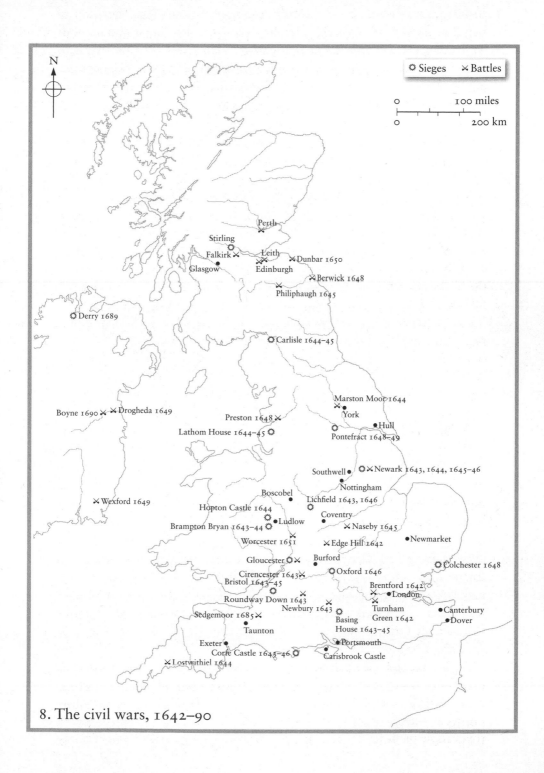

N

Sieges ✿   Battles ✕

| 0 | | | 100 miles |
| 0 | | | 200 km |

Perth ✕

Stirling ✿
Falkirk ✕ Leith ✕ Dunbar 1650
Glasgow ● Edinburgh
Berwick 1648 ✕
Philiphaugh 1645 ✕

Derry 1689 ✿

Carlisle 1644–45 ✿

Marston Moor 1644 ✕
Boyne 1690 ✕ ✕ Drogheda 1649    York ●
Preston 1648 ✕    ● Hull
Lathom House 1644–45 ✿    Pontefract 1648–49 ✿

Southwell ●    ✿✕ Newark 1643, 1644, 1645–46
Nottingham ●

Wexford 1649 ✕    Boscobel ●    Lichfield 1643, 1646 ✿
Hopton Castle 1644 ✿    Coventry ●
Brampton Bryan 1643–44 ✕ ✿ ● Ludlow    ✕ Naseby 1645
Worcester 1651 ✕    ● Newmarket
Edge Hill 1642 ✕
Gloucester ✿✕ ● Burford    ✿ Colchester 1648
Cirencester 1643 ✕    ✿ Oxford 1646
Bristol 1643–45 ✿    Brentford 1642 ✕
Roundway Down 1643 ✕    ✕ ● London
Sedgemoor 1685 ✕    Newbury 1643 ✕    Turnham ✕ Canterbury ●
Taunton ●    Basing Green 1642    ● Dover
House 1643–45 ✿
Exeter ●    ● Portsmouth
Corfe Castle 1643–46 ✿    Carisbrook Castle ●
✕ Lostwithiel 1644

## 8. The civil wars, 1642–90

lective fines for harbouring deserters. An important aim was capturing or relieving towns, and occupying territory to secure revenue, supplies and winter quarters. Another was to pursue and attack enemy forces—though regiments were often reluctant to stray far from home. The great battles—Edgehill, Roundway Down (1643), Newbury (1643), Marston Moor (1644), Naseby (1645)—were never planned in detail and were often unexpected.

More typical were hundreds of skirmishes—collisions between foraging parties, attacks on convoys, and over 300 sieges of country houses and castles, which dragged on because neither side had heavy artillery. Most casualties were suffered in such clashes, not unlike organized banditry or low-level guerrilla warfare in areas not securely controlled by either side. Women sometimes became famous defending their homes, for example Lady Derby at Lathom House and Lady Bankes at Corfe Castle. This was a wearing, nerve-racking business, as Brilliana Harley found to her cost. Her husband, a leading Puritan MP, was away at Westminster, leaving her in charge of a parliamentarian household at Brampton Bryan Castle in royalist Herefordshire, where her neighbours began a campaign of intimidation:

> I am used . . . with all the malice that can be. Mr. Wigmore will not let the fowler bring me any foule . . . They have forbid my rents to be payed. They drave away the yong horsess . . . and none of my sarvants dare goo scarce as fare as the towne . . . I am threatened every day to be beseet with soulders. My hope is, the Lord will not deliver me nor mine into theair hands; for surely they would use all cruellty towards me, for I am toold that they desire not to leave your father neather roote nor branch . . . [D]esire the prayers of the godly for us.[66]

She collected some weapons, and got a soldier experienced "in the Jerman wars" to take charge. Finally, in July 1643 there began a long sporadic siege, during which she died, and by March 1644 the castle was a ruin. Some house sieges became large military operations, but most remained small affairs between handfuls of men and women who might have known each other in peacetime. They had to decide how to behave to each other now they were enemies, and feelings of betrayal were common.

Countrywide, the royalists maintained military superiority during the first part of the war, despite Parliament's possession of London and the south-east, with their vast reserves of men and money. Cromwell famously put this down to the royalists being "gentlemen's sons," compared with Parliament's "broken-down tapsters." The difference was rather more substantial. The royalists had greater popular support and better military leadership, and adopted modern methods, including Swedish-style cavalry tactics and the latest artillery-proof fortifications. Charles appointed able commanders with Continental experience, including his nephew, the twenty-three-year-old Prince Rupert, son of the Elector Palatine, already a veteran of the Thirty Years' War. The royalists took Bristol, England's second port, in July 1643, cleared the south-west, and consolidated control of the north. Fighting in Ireland was interrupted in September 1643 by a truce between the rebel Catholic Confederation and King Charles's Lord-Lieutenant, the Marquess of Ormonde, which raised the prospect, terrifying for parliamentarians, that a royalist and "papist" Irish army might cross over into England, as indeed some of it did. Parliament ordered the killing of all Irish prisoners.

In desperation, Parliament appealed to the ruling Scottish Convention for help, offering in return to make England and Ireland Presbyterian. In September 1643, Parliament and the Convention drew up a Solemn League and Covenant to resist "the bloody plots . . . of the enemies of God" and eliminate "Popery, prelacy . . . superstition, heresy, schism, profaneness, and whatsoever shall be found to be contrary to sound doctrine and the power of godliness."[67] This brought the two countries closer than ever to union, and a Committee of Both Kingdoms was established as a joint authority. In January 1644, 21,500 Scots marched into England again under Leslie (now Earl of Leven). This was the largest army of the whole Civil War. Its intervention prevented a probable royalist victory and a compromise peace.

The Scots reversed the military balance in the north of England. Charles sent an army under Rupert to restore the situation. Rupert, with some 17,000 men to the allies' 27,000, manoeuvred successfully to force them to raise the siege of York. The two sides met on 2 July 1644 at nearby Marston Moor. As fighting had not started by early evening, the royalists relaxed. Seeing them preparing their supper, the allies launched a surprise attack at seven o'clock. Although the royalists recovered and drove back some of the attackers, they were in the end overwhelmed by the combination of stubborn Scottish infantry and disciplined East Anglian cavalry commanded by Cromwell. Over 6,000 died in probably the biggest battle ever fought on English soil.* A jubilant Cromwell wrote that "God made them as stubble to our swords." Parliament took control of northern England.

---

* Other candidates for this grim distinction are Towton and even Boadicea's last battle against the Romans. Marston Moor is the only one for which credible numbers exist.

The balance swung back the following month, however, when the Earl of Essex's army was surrounded at Lostwithiel in Cornwall by royalists led by Charles in person, and forced to surrender. Essex escaped humiliatingly in a fishing boat, but his men, allowed to march away unarmed, were decimated by hunger, disease and the attacks of local people. At the same time, a revolt started in Scotland, where Irish royalists led by the chief of the Macdonnells landed to support Catholic Highlanders in a devastating campaign against the Presbyterian Lowlands, forcing much of the Scots army in England to return home.

No end to the war was in sight. A significant peace movement surfaced. In the countryside appeared "clubmen"—local armed self-defence groups aiming to keep plundering troops of both sides out of their homes. Parliament's new and heavy taxes (including a direct "assessment" and the first excise duties) were a shock. Puritans created further discontent by attacking popular pastimes, and above all by trying to abolish Christmas, an occasion of "carnal and sensual delights"—not a wise political move. Leading figures on the parliamentary side saw no alternative to negotiations. Some even went over to the king. As their northern commander, the Earl of Manchester, famously put it, "If we beat the king ninety and nine times, yet he is king still, and so will his posterity be after him; but if the king beat us once, we shall all be hanged, and our posterity made slaves."[68] Compromisers clashed with hardliners both in Westminster and in Oxford.

Parliament offered peace terms in November 1644, but these included the "utter abolishing" of bishops and cathedrals, imposition of Scottish-style Presbyterianism, waging war in Ireland and Europe, savage measures against Catholics (including taking away their children—and possibly those of the king himself), permanently banning stage plays, and imposing a blacklist of royalists whom the king could not pardon.[69] When these terms were rejected, Parliament took decisive steps early in 1645 to intensify the war. An Act of Attainder condemned the imprisoned Archbishop Laud, the hated symbol of "popery," for whom a retroactive definition of treason was invented. "Is this the liberty that we promised to maintain with our blood?" exclaimed Essex. Laud was beheaded on 10 January.

The natural selection of war had produced a new officer corps, led by a new lord-general, Sir Thomas Fairfax, aged thirty-two, the son of a Yorkshire peer, and in his spare time a collector of art, church historian, and translator of poetry and philosophy. He had served with the Swedish army, the most efficient in Europe, and three of his brothers had been killed on the Continent.[70] A Self-Denying Ordinance (April 1645) removed members of Parliament from military command. At the same time a "New Model Army" of 22,000 men was formed under central, not local, control, directly paid by Parliament, and excluding foreign mercenaries— "there was not one man but of our owne Nation."[71] The infantry included royalist prisoners and impressed men from the south of England, who were quick to desert. But the cavalry, the decisive weapon, were volunteers from existing parliamentary forces, mainly the sons of yeomen and craftsmen. These "Ironsides" were better paid, better armed and equipped, and uniformed in red coats. Oliver Cromwell, an MP, was given command notwithstanding the Self-Denying Ordinance. Parliament was creating a professional standing army, more detached from civil society and accountability. It was an ideological force, officially described as "a rod of iron in Christ's hand to dash his enemies in pieces." Harsh discipline knocked it into shape, including humiliating and painful penalties for drunkenness and fornication; blasphemers had their tongues pierced with a hot iron. They could be equally brutal towards royalist prisoners. Conformity was reinforced by preaching and collective prayer—"no oaths nor cursing, no drunkenness nor quarrelling, but love, unanimity," wrote one observer.[72] They developed an ideological and psychological ruthlessness: for these men, backsliders and the lukewarm, even if a majority in Parliament or the nation, must not prevail against the will of God, who manifested his favour by granting victory.[73]

Victory indeed came quickly. On 14 June 1645 at Naseby in Northamptonshire, about 13,500 troops of the New Model Army under Fairfax and Cromwell decisively defeated 9,000 royalists under Rupert and Charles in person. "To see this," exclaimed Cromwell, "is it not to see the face of God!" Thereafter, royalist strength collapsed, as more than twenty strongholds fell. Parliamentary soldiers felt that they were living a continuous miracle: "Our enemies have perished (not by our valour, and weapons and strength) but at the rebuke of his countenance."[74] Charles's last hope were the royalists in Scotland, but they too were defeated in September at Philiphaugh. One of the last royalist positions was the huge fortified Basing House, in Hampshire, seat of the Catholic Marquess of Winchester. Its 400 male and female defenders had repelled two previous sieges. Cromwell's 6,000 men bombarded and stormed it on 16 October 1645, shouting: "Down with the papists!" As the defenders had refused to surrender, Cromwell, who had spent the previous night in prayer and meditation on the wickedness of idolaters, allowed about a hundred to be slaughtered, including six Catholic priests and a young woman who shouted angrily at the soldiers while trying to defend her father. "If the king had no more ground in England than Basing, I would venture as I did," said the marquess amid the charred ruins of one of the greatest houses in Europe. "Basing is called loyalty."[75]

As the fate of Basing and its defenders showed, vindictiveness had increased as the war dragged on. Bloody atrocities had been common during the fighting in Ireland and Scotland, and had taken place on a very large scale during the wars in Europe—the notorious sack of Magdeburg in 1631 had seen some 20,000 civilian deaths. Yet the war in England was fought with relative restraint. Most sieges ended through negotiation. In several cases, garrisons that refused a summons to surrender and forced the besiegers to storm them were refused quarter in accordance with the customs of war. The thirty-one defenders of Hopton Castle, Shropshire, for example, had their throats cut in March 1644, but this was rare. Though there was a vast amount of plundering and accompanying low-level violence, there seem to have been few cases of rape. Surrender terms were respected and civilian non-combatants were not harmed. Military prisoners were rarely ill-treated, and the wounded were cared for. The dead, when possible, were honourably buried. On occasions, the enemy's courage was praised, like the royalist Blue Regiment at Naseby, "like to a wall of brasse." There were often informal parleys between the two armies. Friendships and neighbourly relations sometimes survived being on opposite sides. The feeling persisted that this was a regrettable war, "a war without an enemy," fought within a nation that retained some sense of honour and community.[76] The limits of that community are shown by the very different treatment of Catholics, Irish and Scots, and sometimes women. Rupert's men killed 200 Scots when they took Leicester by storm in May 1645—a massacre said to have been carried out by his Irish troops. After Naseby, women found in the royalist camp—many of them Welsh soldiers' wives—were attacked by Roundhead soldiers. A hundred were murdered, and other "Harlots with golden Tresses" were marked as "whores" by having their noses slit or faces slashed—"just rewards for such wicked strumpets."[77] Although such atrocities were rare in England, these were alarming signs.

Simultaneously, a different kind of violence against women, though stemming from a similar mind-set, was happening away from the battlefield: England's only ever mass witch-hunt. This product of fear and political dislocation accounted during the summer of 1645 for a high proportion of all executions for witchcraft over the whole of English history. There were believers and sceptics on both sides, but the main believers in witches were, ironically, the self-proclaimed enemies of "superstition," especially those influenced by Scottish Presbyterianism. Many suspected Prince Rupert of using witchcraft, and seriously thought his poodle Boy, killed at

Marston Moor, was his familiar spirit. Some royalist women were lynched as witches after a skirmish at Brentford in 1642. Puritan East Anglia was the main centre of persecution, as it was of church vandalism.[78] The witch-hunt there was largely the work of an Essex man in his early twenties, Matthew Hopkins, fantasist son of a godly clergyman. This self-appointed "witchfinder-general" suddenly became active in the summer of 1645, and sold his consultancy services to several towns. His method was to ask for the names of suspects, and then "watch" them, keeping them without food, water or sleep, and interrogating them until some of them confessed. He probably had 100–200 people hanged, mainly elderly women. Accusers, witnesses and assistant witchfinders were also often women.

The king, having gradually run out of options following Naseby, arrived unexpectedly at the headquarters of the Scottish army at Southwell, in Nottinghamshire, on 5 May 1646. It soon became clear that the defeated monarch was in a surprisingly strong political position. The parliamentary coalition was divided and increasingly unpopular, and a large element of it wanted to negotiate with Charles. So did its Scottish allies. Public opinion was increasingly royalist, associating the king with peace and a return to normality. Crowds turned out to cheer him, and many people came to be "touched" for the "King's Evil," scrofula—a quasi-religious ceremony copied from the French monarchs and, like all faith healing, sometimes effective. In February 1647 Parliament paid the Scots army to go home. Charles was handed over to an English officer, and comfortably interned in Leicestershire. Over the next two years, he fatally overplayed his hand. The capture at Naseby of his correspondence and its subsequent publication showed him as duplicitous, as his behaviour confirmed. He was convinced of his own rightness, and saw no reason to deal frankly under duress with rebels. He thought he could play off the factions among his enemies; if not, he was prepared for martyrdom.

The factionalism of the parliamentary side was real enough. The religious gulf had widened, and had become entangled with struggles over power. Alliance with the Scots had required Parliament to make the English Church Presbyterian. This would have been an authoritarian system, tough on heresy and schism, requiring everyone to be a member of their parish church, and giving religious and hence much social and political power to committees of clergy and godly elders. To those fearing religious anarchy and social breakdown, this came to have attractions, at least as a lesser evil, and so Presbyterianism went from being seen as a means of subversion to being an ark of stability and authority. In contrast, "Independents" claimed the right to organize their own godly congregations outside a state Presbyterian Church. They demanded liberty of conscience for unorthodox beliefs—sects such as Brownites, Baptists, Congregationalists and even Quakers, whose strange beliefs and shocking behaviour meant that they were feared and detested by more orthodox Puritans. The sects allowed anyone to preach—not only educated and licensed clergy. All this alarmed a society that took it for granted that law, order and community could only be based on common religious belief and discipline. It therefore seemed possible that Presbyterian parliamentarians and royalists might come together in agreement.

Independency had many followers in the army. Godly soldiers came to see their own companies or regiments as religious brotherhoods, and the army as a collection of congregations. They were tolerant of exotic religious beliefs among their comrades, and liked spontaneous preaching and prophesying. We would get some of the flavour by imagining "Bible Belt" emotionalism backed by the ruthlessness of a revolutionary militia.

The New Model Army itself was a focus of financial and legal controversy. Its heavy cost, whether met through taxation or by direct exactions by troops on civilians, caused mounting resentment—"For the king and no plunder," shouted rioters. The army was coming to be hated, even by its own side. A petition from Essex lamented being "eaten up, enslaved and destroyed by an army raised for their defence."[79] Disbanding most of the army was the obvious solution. But many soldiers resisted being simply turned loose, especially as they were owed large arrears of pay—£3m in all, equal to more than three years of prewar state income. Many were fearful of being sent to Ireland, from where most soldiers never returned. Many too were preoccupied by the question of indemnity from prosecution. England had long been a litigious society, and, amazingly, officers and soldiers found themselves being sued by royalists for trespass, theft, burglary, assault or wrongful imprisonment for military actions taken during the war, and they faced ruin, imprisonment or worse from hostile juries and judges. One regiment feared that "we should be hanged like dogs" without a parliamentary law of indemnity. Finally, the army did not want its wartime sacrifices thrown away by a Parliament and a public backsliding towards royalism. These grievances turned the army into a political actor, debating and presenting collective demands, and eventually claiming the right of ultimate decision.

Amid this political imbroglio, the king appeared to be a key figure and a potentially decisive ally. Cornet Joyce took a force of cavalry in June 1647 to secure him and prevent his being used by Parliament. He was taken to the army's headquarters at Newmarket, and greeted by cheering crowds strewing green branches in his path. In July 1647 army commanders offered Charles a relatively conciliatory settlement, the "Heads of the Proposals," which included tolerance for Anglicans, moderate treatment for royalists, biennial parliaments, a redistribution of seats, and some popular reforms, including abolition of excise, monopolies and imprisonment for debt. The army and government were to be controlled by Parliament, but only for ten years, after which the Crown would resume authority. Charles made a conciliatory reply, accepting many of the army's proposals and promising to meet their arrears of pay. But many important matters were unresolved, and finally Charles spurned the deal, believing he could bargain for better terms: "You will fall to ruin if I do not sustain you."[80] The army marched on London, lodging Charles nearby at Hampton Court.

From this unstable politico-religious brew bubbled up revolutionary political debates and actions. These have fascinated modern readers because of their seemingly prophetic connection with some of our own ideas. Famous since their records were discovered in the late nineteenth century are the Putney debates, a series of discussions and prayer meetings held from October 1647 in Putney church between senior officers and regimental representatives usually known as "agitators." The very word evokes revolution, but the true term was the anodyne "adjutators"— assistants. The aim was to reach an agreed army position on the political future, to be embodied in an Agreement with the People, in effect a constitution for England. Discussions covered a range of issues concerning the army, but the debate that has fascinated later generations—though not a priority at the time—touched on political rights. Colonel Rainborowe, one of the delegates, ringingly declared:

> I think that the poorest he that is in England hath a life to live as the greatest he ... every man that is to live under a government ought first by his own consent to put himself under that government; and I do think that the poorest man in England is not at all bound in a strict sense to that government that he hath not had a voice to put himself under.[81]

This has become rightly famous, making Rainborowe a posthumous democratic hero. His motive in fighting for Parliament seems to have been mainly patriotic: he came from a prosperous family of sea captains and merchants, and had invested large sums in the colonization of Ireland.[82] It is hard to imagine anyone disagreeing that poor men in England had rights. Magna Carta had recognized some rights for all. Serfdom had disappeared nearly two centuries earlier. Parliament was considered the representative of the whole community, and its electorate was already large before the Civil War, including many urban householders and yeomen farmers.[83] The real problem for the army was elsewhere: any democratic election would favour the king.

Cromwell and other army Independents tried to form an alliance with the "Levellers," a name first given by their opponents to the radical fringe of Independent sects, largely London-based Baptists. This alliance, based on shared hostility to parliamentary Presbyterians, would prove short-lived. The Levellers' leader was John Lilburne, a pugnacious pamphleteer who combined reckless courage with a high degree of self-dramatization. His father was a Durham squire and his mother the daughter of a royal household official. He became a "born-again" Puritan in the 1630s, clashing repeatedly with a Church and state he considered idolatrous, and seeing his consequent sufferings as proof of righteousness. He had fought for Parliament, but left the army in 1645 in opposition to Presbyterianism. Though his views shifted markedly—at different times he inclined towards republicanism, royalism, democracy and military dictatorship—he denied wishing to "level all men's estates." He was consistent in demanding liberty of conscience for God's elect, the Independent sects. His other consistency was an acute mistrust of others' motives, assuming that all power corrupted. Hence, no form of government was perfect—the Bible specified none. So the Levellers wanted limited government—Lilburne extolled Magna Carta—with power decentralized and taxation low. But the army needed central authority to be strong and taxation high—anathema to the Levellers. For a time, soldiers and Levellers found common ground in blaming their troubles on parliamentary corruption.[84]

Some of the "prophetic" ideas and rhetoric of the radicals strike a chord today; yet they did not aim to be modern, but to return to an ancient purity. Their political action was at the service of godly religion struggling to defeat the Antichrist and make ready for a hopefully imminent Second Coming. The core of their radicalism was rejection of the Calvinist belief that many, or even most, human beings were sinners predestined to hell; instead they believed that many, if not all, could discover God's grace, and that they must therefore be free to seek it. Their problem was that most people were not seeking God in the way they approved. So papists, royalists and "prelatists" would have to be deprived of political rights indefinitely—which meant, in practice, excluding the majority of the country. The poor had to be helped by being moralized: swearing, drunkenness, adultery and sabbath-breaking would be harshly punished, with income from fines funding compulsory work projects. A pamphleteer lamented that

> the major part of the people do never move to any good work willingly
> before they are commanded; and the command must be on a penalty too,

else they will do little . . . [T]he godly and laborious poor may be countenanced and cherished, and the idle, and wicked, poor be suppressed.[85]

In short, radical ideas tended not towards democratic freedom, but towards godly authoritarianism resting on armed force.[86]

Charles slipped away from Hampton Court by night on 11 November 1647. His first thought was to make for France, but he ended up on the Isle of Wight, where he was politely interned at Carisbrooke Castle. There he was able to negotiate an alliance with important politicians in Ireland and with the Scots, who were promised a Presbyterian Church in England for a period, and a complete union of the two kingdoms. His escape from Hampton Court triggered royalist uprisings in several parts of England. The army leaders held an emotional three-day fast and prayer meeting at Windsor. All agreed to fight back, confident "in the name of the Lord only, that we should destroy them," and resolving to "call Charles Stuart, that man of blood, to an account for that blood he had shed."[87]

There was fighting in London, Kent, south Wales, the north and East Anglia in a "second civil war." The most important struggle took place at Colchester, held by 4,000 royalists commanded by the Earl of Norwich. Its siege tied down a large part of the parliamentarian army. This left the rest of the country vulnerable, and handfuls of royalists captured Berwick, Carlisle and Pontefract (where they held out for five months—long after Charles had been beheaded). A Scottish army invaded in July 1648, though they made themselves unpopular by plundering. Cromwell crushed them at Preston on 17 August, and marched into Scotland to force the removal of royalist sympathizers from the Edinburgh government. Colchester withstood a hopeless siege for eleven weeks, but surrendered after learning the news of Preston—flown in by the besiegers with a kite. The 300 royalist officers were given no guarantee of their safety, and two were executed. This was undoubtedly a sign of the anger that the resumption of fighting had caused.

Charles himself was to pay the price. Many in the army wanted him dead. They realized he could never be trusted to accept the system they wanted to impose. He was too popular, too slippery, and had support in all three kingdoms. But he might be even more dangerous dead, so some influential officers and the vast majority of MPs opposed regicide, and began another series of negotiations. After another long prayer meeting at Windsor in November, the army commanders—"never more politically dangerous than when they were wrestling with the Almighty"[88]—decided to bring Parliament to heel. They marched on London and sent troops to seize the king. On 6 December 1648 the Palace of Westminster was occupied by Colonel Pride's troops, who arrested forty-one MPs and confined them, singing psalms, in a nearby alehouse. "Pride's purge" reduced the House to a "Rump" of about 150 members acceptable to the army. They now asserted their right to try the king, because "the people," and hence the English House of Commons, "have the supreme power in this nation"[89]—a revolutionary step, and one unacceptable to the Scots. To objections that to try a king would be unconstitutional, Cromwell retorted, "I tell you, we will cut off his head with the crown upon it."[90]

Charles was tried by a special High Court of army officers and MPs. Peers and judges had refused to participate, as did about half of those first nominated. The trial began on a freezing 20 January 1649 in Westminster Hall. The atmosphere was tense; the president, John Bradshaw, wore an armoured hat. Charles was charged with unlawfully using "an unlimited and tyrannical power," having "traitorously and maliciously levied war" against Parliament and people, and thus being "guilty of all the treasons, murders, rapines, burnings" that ensued. He replied that "I do stand more for the liberty of my people than any that come to be my pretended judges."[91]

The trial was widely regarded as illegal, even sacrilegious; and worse than a crime—a mistake. Sir Thomas Fairfax, the popular lord-general of the army, stayed away. When his name was called, his wife commented loudly from the public gallery that "he has more wit than to be here." When Bradshaw spoke in the name of "the good people of England," she shouted, "not half, nor a quarter of the people of England," which caused an officer to threaten to fire into the public gallery, and there were some cries of "God Save the King!"[92] Even at this late stage, the intention of some involved in the trial may have been to force Charles to weaken himself politically by acknowledging the court and hence the supremacy of the Commons, and to accept a binding public agreement limiting his power and perhaps abdicating in favour of his son. But he refused to recognize what he accused of being an arbitrary and illegal court: "For if power without law may make laws," he said, "I do not know what subject he is in England that can be sure of his life, or anything that he calls his own."[93] He was engaging in a deadly game of bluff, encouraged by the evident hesitations and divisions among his judges. He was, however, prepared for death, having said years earlier that he was "resolved rather to shipwreck my person than . . . my beliefs." His apotheosis as a martyr was already being prepared. Both Charles and Bradshaw had been reflecting on precedents. The king had been reading Shakespeare and paraphrased *Richard II* in warning that "the child that is unborn" would repent a hasty judgement.[94] Bradshaw cited the precedents of deposing Edward II, Richard II and Mary, Queen of Scots. Charles's stubbornness pushed his judges into equal intransigence: Charles was not the only one astonished when he was brusquely condemned to death as a "tyrant, traitor and murderer"—indeed, disturbed members of the court itself were brought into line by a private tongue-lashing from Cromwell. It still remained uncertain whether he would actually be executed. Only 59 of the total court membership of 135 would sign the death warrant, drawn up in advance. No one would write out the order for execution, so Cromwell did it himself. A scaffold was erected outside James I's splendid Banqueting House in Whitehall. Fearing that as Charles had refused to recognize the court he might not meekly submit to execution, large staples were hammered into the timber so that he could if necessary be tied down. On 30 January 1649, Charles—wearing two shirts so as not to tremble in the cold— made his last speech: "Truly I desire [the people's] liberty and freedom as much as anybody whatsoever; but . . . their liberty consists in having government . . . It is not their having a share in the government . . . A subject and a sovereign are clear different things . . ."[95] He was beheaded by a heavily disguised executioner, and as the axe fell, soon after two o'clock, there was an anguished groan from the watching crowd, who were hustled away by the cavalry. His body was exposed "for many days to the public view" in Whitehall, "that all men might know that he was not alive."[96] Charles was more successful as a martyr than as a monarch. Even the parliamentarian poet Andrew Marvell thought that "he nothing common did or mean." A collection of his speeches and thoughts, the *Eikon Basilike*, published on the very day of his execution, rapidly went through thirty-six editions—far more than any Leveller writings.[97]

England became a republic by act of some 150 MPs of the Rump Parliament. On the morning of Charles's execution the proclamation of his successor was hastily forbidden; and in March the monarchy and the House of Lords were formally abolished. All adult males were required to take an "Engagement" to be "true and faithful to the Commonwealth of England, as it is now established." The Rump became sovereign, and its Speaker head of state. It was made high treason to deny its "supreme authority."[98]

Regicide stimulated millenarian fervour in preparation for Christ's imminent Second Coming. The "Diggers," at first a few dozen people planting beans and parsnips, appeared on a common in Surrey in April 1649, led by Gerrard Winstanley, inspired by voices and visions. Winstanley's writings condemned unjust land ownership as a consequence of the "Norman Yoke." An officer sent to investigate reported that they were a harmless "company of crack-brains." Two of them came to London and explained to Lord-General Fairfax that they did not intend to interfere with private property, but only use untilled land, and moreover that they were peaceful. Fairfax's officers were most concerned by their refusal to take off their hats in his presence. Soon, a few score Diggers had set up communities in eight counties. After a few months, following local complaints about their encroachment on common land—always a sensitive matter—the original Surrey group were prosecuted for trespassing and eventually forcibly dispersed on the orders of the local parson. Winstanley stayed, married into the local community, and eventually became a parish officer and chief constable. The Fifth Monarchists, led by Major-Generals Overton and Harrison but mainly drawn from London labourers, servants and journeymen, wanted the adoption of the Law of Moses in preparation for the Fifth Universal Monarchy. This, foretold by the prophet Daniel, they expected to begin in 1656, inaugurating the thousand-year rule of the Saints (themselves). Muggletonians (founded by the London prophet Lodowick Muggleton) also awaited the end of the world; the last surviving member of the sect is said to have died only in 1979. The notorious Adamites, whose biblical fundamentalism supposedly required them to hold prayer meetings naked, probably never existed. But some "Ranters" did claim that the "elect" could commit no sin, and a few denied the divinity of Christ. What became the largest group, the Quakers (another originally derogatory term), rejected all ecclesiastical structure and in their early years were seen as aggressively subversive. Such sects frightened many; and they could indeed be alarming—though the most radical tended to be the most peaceful and unworldly, and also the least numerous: the insurrectionary wing of the Fifth Monarchists had about twenty members.[99]

Power rested not with civilian sects, but with the army, which was again in a febrile state. In March and April 1649 there were petitions and scattered mutinies, mainly about obligatory service in Ireland and arrears of pay. These were encouraged and politicized by the Levellers, who attacked senior officers as "apostates . . . jesuits and traitors." Economic hardship was grist to the Levellers' mill, and they organized petitions to Parliament by women and youths. John Lilburne reported Cromwell as shouting, "You have no other way to deal with these men but to break them in pieces . . . if you do not break them, they will break you." Several mutinies, involving some hundreds of men, were sharply put down by a mixture of conciliation and force, with selected ringleaders being sentenced to corporal punishment or shot. The culmination came in Oxfordshire, in May 1649. Pursued by troops led by Generals Fairfax and Cromwell in person, mutineers tried to win popular support by declaring in favour of the royal heir, Prince Charles. After exchanges of fire at Burford, 350 mutineers were captured and locked in the church. Three were executed in the churchyard (bullet marks can still be seen on the wall), and Cromwell harangued the rest from the pulpit, seconded by a reprieved ringleader who confessed their collective guilt, "howling and weeping like a crocodile."[100] Such extreme changes of mood among the godly may be explained by their providentialism, ascribing failure to divine anger.

The Civil War was still not over. Charles II was proclaimed king in Edinburgh and in Dublin. Irish Catholics and Protestants had concluded a fragile coalition under the royalist Lord-Lieutenant, the Marquess of Ormonde, who hoped to invade England with 18,000 men. But Cromwell arrived in Ireland with a well-equipped and experienced army in August 1649, and began besieging royalist-held ports. First was Drogheda, defended by a mixed English and Irish garrison. After their artillery had blown breaches in the walls, the republicans stormed the town on 11 September. The royalists fought on, so Cromwell ordered no quarter: "Being in the heat of action, I forbade them to spare any that were in arms in the town." There was similar slaughter at Wexford in October, despite the defenders there being ready to surrender. In all, about 3,000 royalist soldiers were killed at Drogheda, and about 2,000 at Wexford. Also killed were hundreds of civilians, combatants or not, and every Catholic priest who was caught. The death toll at Wexford was swollen by the accidental drowning of 300 people trying to escape by boat.

These massacres have caused endless recrimination over the centuries between Cromwell's admirers and enemies, as well as being an emotive episode in Anglo-Irish history. Refusing quarter to garrisons that continued manifestly hopeless resistance was considered within the laws of war, with the aim of deterring futile loss of life, and it remained so up to the nineteenth century (the Alamo being a late and famous instance). The killings were not exclusively anti-Catholic or anti-Irish: part of the Drogheda garrison was Protestant and English, as was its commander, Sir Arthur Aston, said to have been brained with his own wooden leg. There was no general massacre of the Irish civilian population, there or elsewhere. Moreover, the scale of bloodshed at Drogheda or Wexford was small by Continental standards. Nevertheless, it is impossible to imagine anything like this happening in England. Basing and Colchester, vicious by English standards, were mild by comparison. Cromwell and his army acted with such ruthlessness because they saw the enemy as Catholic or Irish or royalist, or all three, who deserved punishment for resuming an immoral war. Cromwell was "persuaded that this is a judgement of God upon these barbarous wretches, who have imbrued their hands in so much innocent blood, and to prevent the effusion of blood in the future."[101] Far worse was to come. After the republicans had captured strongpoints across Ireland, they still had to fight a war against guerrilla bands of *tóraigh* ("tories"), and this wrought economic devastation, aggravated by epidemics. About 40,000 defeated Irish soldiers went to join the armies of Spain or France. An Act for the Settlement of Ireland condemned the Catholic gentry to full or partial confiscation of their land, to the benefit of 5,000 republican soldiers and investors, and this was only partly reversed after the Restoration. Ireland was by far the worst sufferer in the British civil wars, its population falling between 1649 and 1653 by perhaps 20 percent—many times the loss in England.[102]

Cromwell returned from Ireland to fight the Scots, now supporting the young Charles II, who had been invited back from Holland in June 1650. In September, Cromwell, outnumbered and seemingly trapped, outwitted and destroyed a Scottish army at Dunbar. In January 1651 Charles was crowned at Scone, and led his remaining Scottish forces into England. This was more a flight than an invasion, for the royalists, unable to face Cromwell in Scotland, hoped to rally support in England. Although royalism was widespread, and the parliamentary regime and army were far from loved, Scottish invaders were more detested still and found little aid—only 2,000 joined the 12,000 Scots, and the militia turned out against them. The royalists were forced to dig in at Worcester, where Cromwell, pursuing them with 40,000 men, attacked in September. The Scots were defeated, and Charles, who had been in the thick of the fight, fled.

His wanderings became part of royalist legend. He was harboured in Shropshire and Staffordshire by loyal subjects, Catholics prominent among them, in particular the Penderel brothers, one a miller and the others farm workers. He hid from searches at Boscobel House, Shropshire, in the boughs of a "royal oak" (commemorated in numerous pub names) and was taken down to Dorset disguised as a servant by Jane Lane, whence he escaped to France. He did not forget. When returning to England in 1660 he talked of his escape and the loyalty of ordinary people. When he lay dying thirty-four years after his adventure, a Catholic priest who had helped to hide him, John Huddleston, was brought to perform the last rites. A trust fund he set up for the Penderels continued for more than two centuries.

The Civil War was the most lethal conflict England had suffered since the Conquest. A recent estimate suggests around 86,000 killed in combat, nearly all soldiers; another 129,000, mostly civilians, succumbed to the diseases that accompanied war; and infant mortality reached the highest level ever recorded. These losses, in a population of 4–5 million, are proportionately much higher than those England suffered in the First World War, though they are far lower than those on the Continent during the Thirty Years' War or in Ireland.[103] Things could certainly have been worse. We have observed that the conduct of the war was mostly restrained. Violence, iconoclasm and looting were generally politically or religiously motivated and imported from outside, by the armies—something that reinforced local solidarity and passive resistance. There was no class war: looting and vandalism cannot be found on any scale; tenants and neighbours did not inform on royalists to pay off old scores or win advantages— the parliamentary authorities had to send in professional informers. There was little violence even inside divided communities, and the war did not give rise to later vendettas like the "White Terror" in post-Revolutionary France: former enemies were soon intermarrying, and split families made up.[104] This testifies to the solidity of English society and its local communities. It makes phenomena such as the "clubmen" (see p. 232) understandable, and also the survival of fervent popular royalism, identified with a return to normality.

## THE RULE OF THE RIGHTEOUS

The execution of Charles I and the defeat of his son postponed any prospect of such a return, and confirmed the country as a republic, the Commonwealth of England, the first British state, to which devastated Ireland was officially regarded as "belonging."[105] Scotland came under the military government of the Englishman General Monck. This was not, however, an end to England's political instability. One problem was still the army, which dominated the shrunken Rump Parliament (only sixty to seventy members met) and demanded that it should be both radical and popular—an impossible combination. Parliament merely reacted to events. Although much criticized for inertia, corruption and selfishness, not without justification, it had a genuine political problem—one that was to confront later revolutionary regimes in France and Russia: how could a revolution be preserved when most people disliked it? The revolutionaries had no means of creating a new political system because any attempt to do so would restore the old one.

This barren political landscape produced intellectual flowering. Thomas Hobbes, a royalist squire in exile in Paris in 1649, wrote *Leviathan*, in English and at great speed, which responded to the political breakdown of the 1640s with searing frankness. Its argument was that humans originally lived in a barbarous "state of nature" in which "every man is Enemy to every man . . . [in] continuall feare, and danger of violent death; And the life of man, solitary, poore, nasty, brutish, and short." They emerged from this by yielding individual rights of self-preservation to an all-powerful sovereign, individual or collective—"sovereign authority is not so hurtful as the want of it." The sovereign protects common peace and security, including by defining a minimum and non-threatening religious belief. Hobbes attacked political opposition as "destructive of the very essence of Government."[106]

*Leviathan* was intended to promote consensus, and Hobbes presented it to the exiled Charles II, whose tutor he had been. But it managed to upset all parties. Its minimalist religious view, and insistence that religious life must be subordinate to the civil power, caused Anglicans and royalists to reject it. Republicans condemned Hobbes as an apologist for tyranny and he was attacked as scandalously pessimistic, even atheistic. *Leviathan* was burned as heretical in Oxford. It is today widely considered "the masterpiece of English political thought, and a work which more than any other defined the character of modern politics."[107] This is because it based sovereignty on the state and on law, not on the person of the prince; and it based the legitimacy of the state on a secular idea of necessity, not on divine institution or patriarchal authority. After 1650 Hobbes accepted the Commonwealth as the de facto sovereign.

In the other political camp, a group of active republican intellectuals—including the poet and political pamphleteer John Milton (Latin Secretary to the Privy Council), Sir Henry Vane the younger (imprisoned briefly by Cromwell), and Algernon Sidney—drew inspiration from classical thinkers and from Machiavelli, and argued for an enlightened oligarchy to rule like the patricians of the Dutch and Venetian republics, in a "new Rome in the west," in Milton's phrase. Milton (1608–74), the son of a London scrivener, had been an active polemicist during the Civil War, advocating the right of husbands to divorce, and arguing in *Areopagitica* (1644) for "the Liberty of Unlicenc'd Printing." This has often been taken as a pioneering defence of press freedom; but Milton was arguing for freedom of discussion within the republican elite, and he did not of course favour extending this to royalists or Catholics.[108] James Harrington, in *The Commonwealth of Oceanea* (1656), produced a utopian blueprint critical by implication of the shoddy reality of dictatorship, and aiming optimistically to persuade Cromwell to institute a true Commonwealth. Milton saw it as a duty of poets to "deplore the general relapses of kingdoms and states from justice and God's true worship," though some of his most powerful and moving poems are personal meditations, including on his own blindness. His principal work, *Paradise Lost*, by far the greatest religious and philosophical work of poetry in the language, was begun as the Commonwealth neared its end, and through it "the self-destruction of the Puritan cause obtrudes" in Satan's fall from grace.[109] However, *Paradise Lost* was completed and published only after the end of the Commonwealth (when Milton briefly went into hiding), when it was acclaimed by political enemies as well as friends.

The army during the 1650s was thinking not of a new Rome, however, but of a new Jerusalem. It wanted the Rump out of the way so that it could anticipate Brecht's solution: if the people reject the government, change the people. But the Rump was not eager to dissolve itself. On 20 April 1653 General Cromwell, still an MP, attended the House "clad in plain black clothes" and with a military escort, and there took place one of the most famous, if least glorious, scenes in parliamentary history. After fidgeting through several speeches, Cromwell stood and made an increasingly angry one of his own, saying that some members were whoremasters and drunkards, "corrupt and unjust Men and scandalous to the Profession of the Gospel," adding, "I will put an end to your prating." He called in his soldiers to break up the debate: "The Generall, pointing to the Speaker in his chayre, said . . . 'Fetch him downe' . . . Then the Generall went to the table where the mace lay . . . and sayd, 'Take away these baubles.'"[110] The army installed the logical culmination of the Puritan revolution: a "Sanhedrin" of the godly, nominated by the Independent congregations, vetted by the Army Council, and nicknamed "Barebone's Parliament," after Praise-God Barebone (or Barbon), one of its members. Optimists hoped that it would be a prelude to the Second Coming. Cromwell expected the Assembly to "usher in things God hath promised."[111] It could hardly fail to disappoint. In fact, it was not wholly different from earlier parliaments, being largely made up of gentry, JPs and lawyers. It split over religious policy, and its moderate wing (profiting from the absence of the radicals at a prayer meeting) went to Cromwell and surrendered their powers to him, formally ending the Commonwealth. This seems to have forced an agonizing reappraisal: God, and godliness, had not shown the way, and saints had proved inadequate politicians. Senior army officers drew up a new constitution, the Instrument of Government, in December 1653, making Cromwell, aged fifty-four, a somewhat reluctant Lord Protector—an outcome greeted with general silence and indifference.[112] Like many republics, the Commonwealth had drifted into quasi-monarchy.

Cromwell's legendary instruction to Sir Peter Lely to paint him "warts and all" encapsulates his reputation for uncompromising integrity. Yet despite his fame he remains an enigmatic figure. In his own time and long afterwards he was notorious even among his followers for trickiness, even hypocrisy, a zealot for all seasons: "He will lay his hand upon his breast, elevate his eyes and call God to record; he will weep, howl and repent, even while he doth smite you under the first rib."[113] Yet his religious fervour was heartfelt. One explanation is that he had no fixed vision, and ascribed his changeableness to the promptings of Providence. His ideas and policies came from others: "Every man almost that talks with you is apt to think you of his opinion, my Lord, whatever he be."[114] This made him an effective conciliator: he sought consensus among the ruling group of officers and politicians, and turned out to be the only man who could keep them together. Similarly, he favoured freedom of conscience for the godly—"Scots, English, Jews, Gentiles, Presbyterians, Independents, Anabaptists, and all"[115]—as a route to eventual truth, unity and the Millennium. His distaste for "the raging fire of persecution," his desire to reconcile, and his respect for others' beliefs (not, of course, extending to Catholics, though even them he left alone) are his attractive qualities. His other great strength was in battle, when he was prompt, bold and decisive, and found an almost manic fulfilment; and it was his victories and standing within the army that ensured his political prominence. He ascribed these victories to God (playing down his usually superior numbers), thus proving his own righteousness. As a politician, he showed no long-term vision, and finally, like other disillusioned zealots (including his old friend and enemy John Lilburne), subsided into "pious resignation to the ways of providence," which had not seen fit to usher in Christ's kingdom—a judgement on their own unworthiness. Cromwell remains concealed rather than revealed by his voluminous letters and speeches, whose nineteenth-century publication founded the heroic reputation for which he "wrote and spoke the script."[116] For the nineteenth century, he became simultaneously a defender of popular rights, a moral exemplar and a patriotic hero (see pp. 269–70).

The Protectorate was a godly dictatorship, backed by the army, and justified by necessity. Like Charles I, Cromwell thought that "government is for the people's good, not what pleases them."[117] But he felt the need for parliaments, which he regularly hoped would be more worthy than their predecessors, and regularly dismissed when they were not. Niceties of law and procedure had to give way: "The throat of the nation may be cut while we send for some to make a law." Opponents were imprisoned without trial; the judiciary was purged to an unprecedented extent; awkward lawyers were arrested; rebels were sent into slavery. Cromwell attacked those who "cry up nothing but righteousness and justice and liberty."[118] It was he who was obeying God's will, not they, and to claim otherwise was blasphemy. Genuine blasphemy, however intended, was not advisable. When James Naylor, a radical sectarian, re-enacted Christ's entry into Jerusalem by riding into Bristol on a donkey, Parliament demanded his blood. Cromwell saved his life; but he was branded, pilloried, bored through the tongue, flogged twice, and sentenced to life imprisonment.

The dominance of the military and its religious assertiveness made the Republic a formidable enemy. Moreover, it had far more money than any of the Stuart monarchs—perhaps five times that of Charles I—due to punitive taxes on royalists and the sale of royal and Church lands. The Republic was enthusiastic for trade and colonies, and hence for ships, and both the merchant and war fleets grew rapidly.[119] In 1651 Parliament passed the epoch-making Navigation Acts, giving a near monopoly of trade to British ships. Perhaps due to Puritan frugality and devotion to duty, both the army and navy and their civilian administrators showed a professional efficiency against Dutch, French and Tunisians with few parallels in English history. Several monarchs from Alfred to Henry VIII have been hailed as "fathers of the navy"; but Cromwell has a better claim than most. In 1651 a Venetian envoy reported that "owing to the care of parliament they have 80 men of war, which are certainly the finest now afloat, whether for construction, armament or crews."[120] Making peace with the Dutch and the French, in 1654 Cromwell launched an attack on Spain in both Europe and the colonies, motivated by a mixture of religious zeal and opportunism. Spain was the perfect target for a holy war, the enemy of "whatsoever is of God," involving "all the wicked people of the world, whether abroad or at home."[121] To Cromwell's consternation, the forces of righteousness, although hanging on to Jamaica, were defeated at Hispaniola, forcing the conclusion that England had "provoked the Lord."

The remedy was compulsory national repentance. In 1655 eleven major-generals were appointed as provincial governors to oversee security and punish "all manner of vice." They were busily virtuous: "I cannot but please myself," observed one, "to think how greedily we shall put down prophaneness."[122] This was the most sexually repressive regime in our history, making adultery a capital offence. Swearing, fornication and drunkenness were also punished, "dens of satan" (pubs) were shut down en masse, and "loose wenches" rounded up for slave labour in Jamaica. Susan Bounty, convicted of adultery in Devon in 1654, was allowed to give birth to her baby, which was then taken from her and she was hanged.[123] Racehorses were confiscated. Fighting cocks, bears and dogs were slaughtered, inspiring Macaulay's quip that Puritans were concerned less with the pain of the animal than with the pleasure of the spectator. Banned were "revellings at country weddings" and traditional saints' days festivities—ending the miniature baby booms nine months after.[124] The deserving poor were succoured and the dissolute whipped and put to work. A "Decimation Tax" (10 percent of income) was imposed on former royalists. Willing helpers—usually minor gentry, former army officers and sectarian zealots—were recruited as "commissioners" and official "ejectors," and given sweeping powers to identify and remove ministers or schoolmasters guilty of lewdness, using the Book of Common Prayer, playing cards, encouraging traditional pastimes, or scoffing at the godly. One "ejected" clergyman described them as "oppressing, hungry, barking, sharking, hollow-bellied committee men [who] tyrannize . . . scratch and bite and test and worry the lives and estates of the peaceable subjects." As this outburst may suggest, they inspired more fury than terror. Despite their labours, "drunkenness and wickedness rageth in our streets,"[125] and parishes resisted orders to replace the now traditional Book of Common Prayer with a "Directory of Public Worship." When Cromwell had to call new parliamentary elections to get money for the Spanish war, there were shouts of "No swordsmen! No decimators!" and the major-generals had to be abolished.

In March 1657 Parliament offered Cromwell the kingship, and his refusal is usually seen as the triumph of principle over ambition. In fact, the intention was to limit his powers, as a king's powers were hedged about by charters, precedents and the Common Law of England, whereas a Lord Protector existed in a dangerous legal vacuum.[126] For this reason, and because the army disliked the idea, he declined after long hesitation; though so powerful was the culture of monarchy that at his funeral he was portrayed in effigy wearing a crown and holding a sceptre. After his sudden death in September 1658 the regime began to unravel. His son Richard, who succeeded as Lord Protector, was easily persuaded to bow out. The Army Council fell back on recalling the Rump Parliament in May 1659, but only forty-two turned up. Amid bitter wrangling between soldiers and politicians, and disturbances by both royalists and republicans, a Committee of Safety was set up to take control, but it soon ceased to meet. For a week, England had no central government, though few seemed to mind. "Boys do now cry 'Kiss my Parliament' instead of 'Kiss my arse,'" noted the young civil servant Samuel Pepys in his diary.[127] The highly competent General George Monck, commander of the army in Scotland, with whom royalist emissaries had been in contact, marched south, reaching London in February 1660 amid popular rejoicing at what would almost certainly mean a royal restoration. Monck called on MPs excluded in 1648 to resume their seats and summon fresh and free elections, and managed the delicate transition to monarchy. Charles II, from Holland, issued the conciliatory Declaration of Breda, promising pardons, religious tolerance, and payment of arrears to the army. On 8 May 1660 a "Convention Parliament"* unanimously declared Charles II king. The formerly republican fleet escorted him to Dover on 25 May, the flagship *Naseby* being renamed *Royal Charles*. Pepys was on board in a state of high excitement:

> By the morning we were come close to the land and everybody made ready to get on shore . . . I went . . . with a dog that the king loved (which shit in the boat and made us laugh and me think that a king and all that belong to him are but just as others are) . . . Infinite the Croud of people . . . A Canopy was provided for [the king] to stand under, which he did; and talked awhile with Gen. Monke and others . . . The Shouting and joy expressed by all is past imagination.[128]

In London, the celebrations were far more lavish, but the outburst of public rejoicing was the same. The diarist John Evelyn noted: "I stood in the Strand & beheld it, & blessed God: And all this without one drop of bloud . . . so joyfull a day, & so bright [was never] seene in this nation."[129]

## AFTERSHOCKS, 1660–89

It was too good to be true. A whole generation of resentments had accumulated. There were enemies and dangerous friends across the Channel. The Commonwealth had left huge debts, and there were unpredictable accidents. But Charles—"a prince of many Virtues, & many greate Imperfections . . . not bloudy or Cruel"[130]—held the country and the government together as long as he lived. This service he rendered as much through his "Imperfections" as his "Virtues." Those who like identifying prophets of modernity might see in him a prototype of contemporary politics. He was cynically realistic ("he had a very ill opinion of men and women," wrote Bishop Gilbert Burnet, and "thinks the world is governed wholly by interest") but concealed this behind an appearance of affability. He did not take religion too seriously—he was more or less Catholic, the clearest repudiation of Puritanism—and was indulgent to others as to himself: "God will never damn a man for allowing himself a little pleasure" (which in his case included fathering at least fourteen illegitimate

---

* So called because it met without a royal summons; the same occurred in 1689.

children). All this—which outraged Puritans—was politics as well as personality: he wanted to defuse religious conflict by favouring an inclusive Church of England, with tolerance for law-abiding Dissenters and a lessening of petty moral persecution. He worked hard at his image,[131] for example "touching" some 90,000 people for scrofula—"the King strokes their faces or cheeks with both his hands at once"[132]—a highly popular activity. He was determined to restore and maintain legitimate monarchy with hereditary succession, and believed that this required conciliation. The rest was subordinate to this: policies and ministers were secondary— "He lived with his ministers as he did with his mistresses," quipped the waspish politician George Savile, Marquess of Halifax; "he used them but was not in love with them." As one of Charles's friends put it:

> Restless he rolls from whore to whore
> A merry monarch, scandalous and poor.[133]

Notwithstanding inevitable disillusionment, few restorations have been so successful as what Daniel Defoe called "his lazy, long, lascivious reign."[134]

In August 1660 Charles pushed through an Act of General Pardon, Indemnity and Oblivion, which recognized changes in ownership of land and gave an amnesty covering the Civil War and republican period. Excluded were surviving regicides: nine were executed, and efforts made to hunt down the rest. Pepys went to Charing Cross to see General Harrison hanged, drawn and quartered—"he looking as cheerfully as any man could do in that condition." John Evelyn "met their quarters mangld & cut & reaking as they were brought from the Gallows in baskets."[135] Otherwise revenge was symbolic. Cromwell's body was dug up, hanged and beheaded (the head, by a long and circuitous route, is now somewhere in the chapel of Sidney Sussex College, Cambridge). There was no attempt to turn the clock back far: Charles I's anti-absolutist concessions of 1641 were kept; confiscated royalist lands were left with their new owners; former parliamentarians stayed in office—they made up nearly half of Charles's Privy Council and formed the majority of JPs. This, said disgruntled loyalists, was indemnity for the king's enemies, and oblivion for his friends. True, but safer and wiser than the attitude of the French Bourbons restored after the Revolution, who "had learned nothing and forgotten nothing."[136]

However, the king's friends were not willing to let go of everything: they would not let the detested Roundheads continue to run their parishes and towns. A series of statutes—an Act of Uniformity (1662), imposing the use of the Book of Common Prayer; a Corporations Act (1661), which excluded religious dissenters from town government; a Test Act (1672), requiring all public employees to take public oaths of allegiance and Anglican orthodoxy; and the Conventicles Act (1664), banning private Nonconformist worship. Thus, non-Anglicans were forced to conform to the Church of England or give up public office. About 1,000 ministers (one in six) gave up their livings, and about 2,000 clergy and teachers were ejected. Charles's attempts to circumvent this legislation were blocked. Intended to restore unity, these acts on the contrary created a permanent religious schism in England, the long-term legacy of the Civil War.[137] Disillusioned by the failure of the godly revolution, Dissenters went underground and turned inwards. This was the atmosphere in which John Bunyan, imprisoned for illegal preaching, wrote *The Pilgrim's Progress* (1678), one of the greatest and most popular works of Puritan piety— a work not of revolution but of individual salvation and stubborn righteousness. There was no attempt to silence Dissenters politically, however—they had the same right to vote and sit in Parliament. Some leading Anglicans were moving away from rigidity and compulsion towards what opponents called "Latitudinarianism"—a more tolerant and rational religion. Even in oppressed Ireland and divided Scotland there were signs of greater tolerance, for which the king deserves some credit.

Then came a series of unpredictable disasters. Ever since the Black Death, there had been sporadic recurrences of bubonic plague. But a devastating outbreak, the "Great Plague" in 1665, killed 70,000 people in London. The following year, in September 1666, the "Great Fire," which raged for five days, devastated a large part of the City of London, destroying 13,200 houses, 87 churches, the medieval St. Paul's Cathedral, four bridges and a vast quantity of goods, including a treasure of art, books and documents. Samuel Pepys

> saw the fire grow . . . upon steeples and between churches and houses, as far as we could see up the hill of the City, in a most horrid malicious bloody flame . . . one entire arch of fire . . . churches, houses, all on fire and flaming at once, and a horrid noise the flames made, and the cracking of houses at their ruine.[138]

It left 250,000 people homeless. The fire showed Charles, a big vigorous man, at his best, leading the fire-fighting in the streets, and reassuring people that there were no plots "by Frenchmen or Dutchmen or Papists . . . I have strength enough to defend you against any enemy."[139] Yet these disasters were a terrible psychological blow, especially when inevitably seen as divine punishments, if not popish plots. They darkened the optimistic beginning of the Restoration. The reeling country suffered another disaster, a humiliating defeat by the Dutch, the foremost commercial and naval power and a bitter rival, whose ships in June 1667 sailed up the Medway, piloted by republican exiles, sank most of the English fleet and towed away its flagship, the *Royal Charles*. There was a shock of panic and recrimination. "The dismay," wrote Pepys, "is not to be expressed."[140]

The fire produced benefits, for which Charles deserves some credit. The old insanitary wooden city was rebuilt, and Charles put Christopher Wren in charge. Wren's style of elegant plainness consciously drew on a tradition of English Protestant simplicity, as well as following a more general classically inspired trend against over-decoration. He left a magnificent heritage in the new St. Paul's Cathedral, fifty-two smaller City churches, Chelsea Hospital and the Monument to the fire. In other ways, Restoration culture was very un-English, and not very Protestant. Literary style, music and other cultural influences (including men's wigs) came from France. For the republican Algernon Sidney, this had political significance: "Those are most favoured at court, that conform to the French manners and fashions in all things."[141] For this reason, the French writer Voltaire later judged the Restoration to be the historic pinnacle of English culture. Poets such as Dryden agreed: wit, elegance and polish were the aims. The theatre was restored, and Restoration comedies by William Congreve, William Wycherley, John Vanbrugh and others outraged the godly by their cheerful amorality. For the last time, England had a court culture, which nurtured painters such as Sir Peter Lely, and at the tail end of Charles's reign Henry Purcell, its last great native-born composer for two centuries. But for even friendly critics such as John Evelyn, all this was the root of England's disasters, which were "divine judgments . . . highly deserved for our prodigious ingratitude, burning Lusts, dissolute Court, profane & abominable lives."[142]

A minor figure of this newly permissive culture was the naval administrator Samuel Pepys, the first Englishman intimately known in history. His secret diary, perhaps a development of the godly habit of daily self-examination, developed into a very different saga of triumphs, failures, amorous adventures (including sexual harassment verging on rape) and social climbing, occasionally with a tinge of Puritan remorse; but above all it was an anxious assessment of social, not spiritual, ascent from plebeian origins to gentlemanly status.[143] Not intended to be read by others, it is probably the most vivid and complete self-exposure in the language and a unique insider's history of the time.

In the early 1670s, as in the most dangerous times in England's past, European and domestic politics began to mix. This time, it began a process that would transform England, Britain and eventually the world. The connection, as over the previous hundred years, was "popery," the feared combination of religious and political oppression. Wars against the Dutch had caused a rapprochement with France, even under Cromwell (who had argued that the French were not really "popish," as their ties with Rome were loose). Charles, whose "mental map of Europe had its centre not in England at all, but France,"[144] where he had spent part of his exile, was eager to deepen the relationship. He admired the young Louis XIV, who after long civil wars had made himself a complete master, and he felt that his security ultimately depended on French support. The French, aware of England's commercial and naval strength, wanted a pliable ally on the British thrones, and offered support, including cash, sometimes brought to Charles by his valet[145]—precious when Parliament was difficult. Louise de Penancouët de Kéroualle, to whom Charles took a fancy in 1670, was ordered into his bed as an agent of influence. In 1662 Charles sold recently acquired Dunkirk to France. In 1672 he signed the Treaty of Dover, in preparation for a joint war against Holland. It contained a secret agreement that he would restore England to Catholicism with French military aid. It is most unlikely that he took this seriously. Yet, on the surface, such an enterprise looked plausible: Charles's mother, his wife, Catherine of Braganza, and his mistress, Louise de Kéroualle, were all Catholics, and he himself was sympathetic. So was his heir, James, Duke of York, and James's second wife, Mary of Modena. The attraction of Catholicism, as Charles remarked to the French ambassador, was that "no other creed matches so well the absolute dignity of kings."[146]

Catholicism was now in the ascendant in Europe, championed by France, whose population, armed forces and revenue far exceeded those of any other state. It no longer had serious rivals in Europe. Its monarch was absolute, its administration professional. Catholicism was being ruthlessly imposed on its once formidable Protestant community. Louis XIV was increasingly suspected of aiming at "universal monarchy"—what we might call being the sole superpower.

In 1672 a French army attacked the Dutch Republic, with English naval support—to royalists a natural alliance, and at first a popular one. But opinion shifted. "No one is able to explain," reported a Venetian diplomat, "why the people of England detest the French alliance so violently or why they wish for peace with Holland at any cost."[147] The reasons were that the French land invasion went worrying well, while their navy was accused of shirking battle so that the British and Dutch fleets would destroy each other. England, many suddenly thought, had been duped into abetting French aggression, with the connivance of a corrupt, Francophile and Catholic court. When Parliament refused finance to pursue the war, peace was signed in 1674. Charles prorogued Parliament and drew on French subsidies, assuring Louis that he was "standing up for the interests of France against his whole kingdom."[148] This was the context of a revival of anti-popery, which indirectly led to a second revolution and permanently transformed the state.

"Popery" was a political concept, as we have noted, not solely a religious one. When the Duke of York had planned to marry a Habsburg, this had been welcomed, although she was a Catholic. But his marriage with the Duchess of Modena in 1673 was unpopular, not because she too was Catholic, but because she was a protégée of France. The existence of an apolitical Catholic minority inside England was not the problem: "Our jealousies of Popery, or an arbitrary government, are not from a few inconsiderable Papists here, but from the ill example we have from France."[149] This atmosphere of international tension explains the panic over the Titus Oates "plot," which exploded in August 1678.[150] Oates was a fantasist and crook who had briefly trained as a Jesuit, which gave credence to his claim to know of a "popish plot" supported by France to assassinate Charles and place James on the throne. The story inevitably aroused echoes of the Gunpowder Plot and Mary, Queen of Scots. Its plausibility increased when the magistrate to whom Oates had told his story was mysteriously murdered that October. A former secretary of James and Mary of Modena, accused by Oates, was in fact found to possess letters from Louis XIV's Jesuit confessor, seeming to implicate James himself. There was a violent public and political reaction, and the last spasm of religious persecution in English history. At least twenty-four Catholics were executed for treason, and to be "proved" a Jesuit—even by public rumour—could be fatal. Following further accusations by Oates, five Catholic peers were impeached, and accusations were made against the queen herself. An aggrieved former diplomat, dismissed after a sex scandal, revealed to the House of Commons in December the details of Charles's financial arrangements with Louis—details that Louis had provided him with in order to punish Charles for contacts with the Dutch.[151]

The political storm was directed by the Earl of Shaftesbury and his able secretary, John Locke. Shaftesbury was a Presbyterian, and a former minister of both Cromwell and Charles. He now demanded the exclusion of Catholics from Parliament and forced Charles to agree to stricter enforcement of anti-Catholic legislation. James, on Charles's advice, left for Brussels. Parliament took a series of measures for "the better securing [of] the liberty of the subject" in case a Catholic became king: habeas corpus was made statutory by an Act of 1679, requiring prisoners to be charged within three days, and making it illegal to send them "beyond the sea" to escape English jurisdiction (governments had been sending suspects to Scotland, where they could be tortured). It is interesting that some of our most cherished civil liberties owe much to the paranoia of bigots. Paradoxically, however, when Parliament made the ancient Common Law practice of habeas corpus statutory, it made it less secure, because what Parliament could give it could also take away by suspending habeas corpus, and at times of war and rebellion it did so.[152]

Shaftesbury also aimed to exclude James from the throne. Two Exclusion Bills were presented to Parliament, one in May 1679, another in October 1680. This prolonged "Exclusion Crisis" of 1679–81 helped to define English political culture: the derogatory terms "Whig" and "Tory" (from *whiggamore*, Scottish Presbyterian rebels, and *tóraigh*, Irish Catholic rebels) were now applied to the king's opponents and supporters. Some of their fundamental ideas were taking shape—for the Whigs, theories about resistance; for the Tories, about legitimacy. In Scotland, an archbishop was lynched by a psalm-singing mob. Charles repeatedly dissolved or prorogued Parliament. He told the French ambassador that "his one and only interest was to subsist."[153] The French, however, were also funding the crypto-republican opposition to give themselves leverage over Charles.

Few could have missed the sense that the 1640s were being replayed, and hardly anyone wanted another civil war. It became increasingly clear that Oates's "Popish Plot," the catalyst of the crisis, was an invention. Parliament was summoned to Oxford in 1681, away from the London mob, and MPs arrived with armed bodyguards. The public began to rally to the king. The French ambassador, Paul Barillon, who was flirting with the Whigs, reported a dramatic scene when on 28 March 1681, as the Lords were assembling, Shaftesbury handed Charles a letter urging him to make his illegitimate but Protestant son James, Duke of Monmouth, his heir. The king publicly responded:

> My Lords, let there be no self-delusion. I will never yield, and will not let myself be intimidated. Men become ordinarily more timid as they grow old; as for me, I shall be . . . bolder and firmer, and I will not stain my life and reputation in the little time that, perhaps, remains for me to live. I do not fear the dangers and calamities which people try to frighten me with. I have the law and reason on my side. Good men will be with me.[154]

The Oxford crowds shouted, "Let the king live, and the Devil hang up all Roundheads."[155] Charles appealed publicly for loyalty: "We cannot but remember, that Religion, Liberty and property were all lost and gone when monarchy was shaken off."[156] Shaftesbury fled abroad in 1682, and

Locke drafted a *Treatise of Government* asserting the right to resist monarchs—a "scenario of civil war"[157] which later became a Whig sacred text. In the "Rye House Plot" in 1683, republicans planned to assassinate Charles and James as they returned from Newmarket races. In another half-baked conspiracy, the Earl of Essex (son of the Civil War commander), Lord William Russell (heir of the Earl of Bedford) and Algernon Sidney (son of the Earl of Leicester) planned to seize the king, take power with Scottish support, subjugate Ireland, and go to war with Holland. When they were caught, Essex committed suicide and the other two were executed. Algernon Sidney declared on the scaffold that he was willing to die for "the Good Old Cause"—a name that stuck. He was long revered as a Whig martyr.

Moderates, however, denounced Whig designs: "more wicked," said one MP, "than their malice could invent to accuse the papists of."[158] There was a grass-roots backlash against Whigs and Dissenters. So when Charles died suddenly on 6 February 1685, aged fifty-five, his brother's succession was assured. Charles has been much criticized, but one modern historian pays him a tribute that few British rulers could claim: "He was a king under whom most people in the three kingdoms were happy to live."[159] In the long run, the monarchy won the Civil War.[160] But the great divide had not been healed.

James II and VII ripped it open again. Yet his accession as the Catholic king of Europe's largest Protestant realm was welcomed by most people: "Never king was acclaimed with more applause," wrote the Earl of Peterborough. "I doubt not but to see a happy reign." Titus Oates, finally exposed as a liar, was branded and ferociously flogged. But religion remained the problem. Not James's personal Catholicism, which was known and, with misgivings, accepted. The problem was his ambition to turn England back towards being a Catholic state. This seems so unlikely an outcome that it is difficult to believe he meant it: but modern historians agree he did. His Catholicism was far more rigorous than that of Charles or Louis XIV. Like them he had mistresses; Charles joked that they were so ugly they must have been imposed on him as penances by his priests. Catholicism could accommodate such human frailty, especially among the great—a significant part of its attraction. But James agonized about his guilt. Catholicism also understood politics, being governed by a territorial prince who knew the world. But James, more Catholic than the Pope, challenged political reality, pushing on further and faster than his Catholic subjects and Rome itself thought prudent. He was more authoritarian than Charles, and more brutal than any of his Stuart predecessors, as he had already proved in crushing Presbyterian rebellion in Scotland.

Less intelligent than his brother, he was a formidable man of action. He must have thought that history was on his side. Catholicism and Catholic powers were rising. Protestantism was being eliminated in Italy, Hungary, Spain, France and Bohemia. The Treaty of Augsburg (1555) established that the religion of a state followed that of its monarch. James convinced himself that England would follow a strong lead, and that there would be massive voluntary conversions, which he would encourage by appointing Catholics to influential positions in the state: "patronage," he declared, "would make more converts than sermons." English history under the Tudors suggested the same. The Stuarts, of course, had been less successful, but James blamed "the yielding temper which had proved so dangerous to his brother and so fatal to his father."[161] Catholicism would restore the absolute power of monarchy: for James, these two objectives were inseparably linked.[162] So fears of "popery and arbitrary government," though shrill, were not groundless.

There was almost at once, in June 1685, a Whig-Protestant attempt on the throne, led by the Duke of Monmouth. Its pathetic weakness testifies to James's strength. Monmouth rallied 4,000 untrained men among the Dissenters of the West Country—farmers, cloth-workers and tradesmen. They were slaughtered at Sedgemoor in Somerset in July by 8,000 regular troops. Monmouth was beheaded shortly after. During nine days in September, Lord Justice Jeffreys heard 1,336 cases in so-called Bloody Assizes in Somerset. A woman, Alice Lisle, was burned at the stake for harbouring traitors; 800 men were sentenced to slavery in the West Indies, and 250 to death. After the first batch had been hanged, drawn and quartered, even Jeffreys assumed that the rest would be reprieved, as was customary. But James made all suffer the full bloody ritual, which left the execution ground awash with body fluids.

Politically, this tragedy strengthened the king: Parliament, alarmed at the renewal of civil war, voted him money and an army, making him the first monarch for more than a century with no financial worries. His first aim was to legalize Catholicism by statute, to make it more difficult to reverse when, as then seemed inevitable, his Protestant daughter Mary became queen. He began by trying to charm and bully Anglicans, meeting every MP personally. He thought that Anglicanism and French-style Catholicism ("Gallicanism," largely independent of Rome) had much in common and could form a common front against the detested Dissenters.

In October 1685, at the worst possible moment for James's policies— though he approved of the act itself—Louis XIV revoked the 1598 Edict of Nantes, which guaranteed French Protestants religious, civil and political rights. French Catholics joyfully demolished Protestant churches and desecrated cemeteries. There was some armed resistance, and troops were ordered to "take very few prisoners . . . spare the women no more than the men."[163] French troops also attacked Protestants in neighbouring Piedmont, where 2,000 were killed and 8,000 sent to the galleys. Fifty thousand refugees flooded into England, bringing harrowing stories of persecution. A French court preacher, congratulating Louis for the victory of Catholicism, urged him in a widely publicized sermon to be ready to do the same in England.[164]

James used the royal prerogative to exempt Catholics from discriminatory laws, and dissolved the protesting English and Scottish parliaments, which never met again during his reign. He began to run down the militia (embodying the citizen's right to bear arms) in favour of a large regular army, in which he began to commission Catholics as officers in all three kingdoms. Catholics also commanded the fleet and the Tower of London. Jeffreys was made Lord Chancellor; the Catholic Earl of Sunderland became Secretary of State; and other Catholics were appointed to the Privy Council, including a Jesuit priest, Father Edward Petre. In Ireland, James appointed the Catholic Earl of Tyrconnel as army commander and Lord-Lieutenant, ordering him to recruit Catholic soldiers—guaranteed to cause maximum alarm to all Protestants. By September 1686, 67 percent of soldiers and 40 percent of officers in Ireland were Catholics. The choice, as one peer saw it, was "whether I will be a slave and a Papist, or a Protestant and a free man."[165] Faced with Anglican opposition, James switched tactics and appealed to Dissenters to support repeal of the Test and Corporation Acts, to the benefit of both themselves and Catholics. He aimed to pack a future House of Commons with Dissenters and Whigs. Royal agents predicted a two-thirds majority.

James brought matters to a head in the early summer of 1688 by a Declaration of Indulgence, announcing that he would not apply discriminatory laws against Catholics and Dissenters but would allow them "the free exercise of their religion," and ordering this to be read out twice from the pulpit of every church.[166] Until now, Anglicans had not openly resisted: their royalist principles and fear of civil war held them back. But now the Archbishop of Canterbury, William Sancroft, and six other bishops petitioned James to withdraw his instruction, on the grounds that the Declaration was illegal. His response was to charge them with seditious libel for suggesting that the king could act illegally.

At this very moment, the political outlook was transformed. On 10 June 1688 a healthy son was born to James and Mary of Modena after fifteen years of marriage, their first five children having died young. He was baptized a Catholic. This meant, of course, that James's policy would not cease with his death, for the boy took precedence over his Anglican half-sisters Mary and Anne, born to James's first wife, Anne Hyde. The rumour was spread that the baby was not the queen's, but had been smuggled into her bed in a warming pan. This was a matter of European importance, because Princess Mary, now aged twenty-six, was the wife of Willem III van Oranje—"William of Orange"—grandson of Charles I, *stadhouder** of the Dutch Republic and leader of resistance against Louis XIV. Another war was looming between France and Holland, which would probably involve much of the Continent. England, thanks to James's interest in maritime and colonial affairs, had again become the strongest naval power in Europe. Would it join in? And on which side? James needed French money to pursue his Catholic revolution in England, and in April 1688 he had signed a naval agreement with France. The Dutch decided that they must at all costs prevent England from joining in a French attack on them. So foreign and domestic issues met.

On 30 June 1688 the seven bishops were acquitted of seditious libel by a London jury: "Bon fires made that night, & bells ringing, which was taken very ill at Court."[167] The same day, the Earl of Danby (a former minister of Charles II), Admiral Russell, Henry Sidney, Bishop Compton of London, the Duke of Shrewsbury, the Duke of Devonshire and Lord Lumley—five Whigs and two Tories, later known as "the Immortal Seven"—wrote to Willem promising support if he intervened to secure a free Parliament and to investigate the genuineness of James's new son. Willem had been waiting for this assurance—indeed, he had made it a condition of taking action. The Pope, the emperor and the king of Spain—Catholic enemies of France—tacitly approved, on condition that British Catholics were not harmed. The French were preoccupied by events in south-eastern Europe, where their Turkish allies were retreating before the armies of the Holy Roman Empire. So French ships concentrated in the Mediterranean, and troops were sent, not to attack the Dutch and protect James, but to help the Turks by launching a diversionary attack across the Rhine against the empire.[168]

The biggest seaborne invasion force in northern waters until D-Day 1944 first set sail from the Dutch Republic on 19 October 1688 but was driven back by high winds. At its second attempt to beat the weather on 1 November, it was blown down the Channel by what entered legend as

---

* The *stadhouder* was a partly elected and partly hereditary leader appointed in emergencies by the provinces of the Dutch Republic to direct the government and command the armed forces.

"a Protestant wind" that also kept James's navy stuck in the Thames estuary. The fleet reached Torbay on Guy Fawkes Day: 463 ships, 5,000 horses and 20,000 Dutch, German, Danish, French, English, Scottish, Swedish, Finnish, Polish, Greek and Swiss troops. No nation but the Dutch had the sea-going abilities for such a feat. Willem's army then marched on London. Facing it was James's much larger army of 53,000. People hesitated, frightened of another civil war. But "Hardly any one will voluntarily enter into the King's service," and spontaneous actions were for Willem. Armed meetings of citizens were called in the Midlands and north. "We count it rebellion to resist a king that governs by law," declared one such group in Nottinghamshire, "but . . . to resist [a tyrant], we justly esteem it no rebellion, but a necessary defence."[169] More and more towns and counties declared against James, who had some sort of breakdown, sent his wife and son to France, threw the Great Seal of the kingdom into the Thames, and—escorted to the coast by the Dutch—sought asylum from Louis XIV in December. Unlike Charles I and II, he did not try to raise popular support, and he left his troops leaderless and unpaid.

Riots had broken out, most seriously in London, where Catholic embassies and their chapels were attacked. It was rumoured that Irish Catholic troops had burned down Birmingham and were massacring Protestants. Disturbances persisted for weeks. Willem was welcomed in London as a saviour, and he tactfully let his English and Scottish mercenaries, commanded by General Mackay, lead the way into the city. Nevertheless, it was really the Dutch army and navy that had forced King James out of England without a fight in the most momentous invasion—part conquest, part liberation—since 1066. If this was a Protestant victory, it included what Willem called "our allies of the Roman communion," among them the Pope, who also opposed French hegemony.[170]

A Convention Parliament met in January 1689. It was composed of 319 Whigs and 232 Tories. What divided them now was how to define and justify what had happened. Whigs saw James as being deposed after breaking his "contract" with the people. Tories wanted to preserve the principle of monarchy as God-given, permanent and governed by lawful succession: James was "incapacitated," and Willem and Mary were regents. But Willem threatened to go home unless he was made king, and so he was, as co-sovereign with his Stuart wife, Mary. A Whig-Tory compromise emerged. James was declared both to have "broken the original contract between king and people" and also to have "abdicated" and left the throne "vacant." By leaving the country he had enabled divisive political questions to be fudged.[171] It could therefore be agreed that what had happened was that the existing constitution, which James had tried to destroy, had been preserved, not overthrown. These events, now often downplayed or forgotten,[172] were long extolled as the "Glorious Revolution," which, almost without bloodshed in England, ended monarchical absolutism, established the primacy of Parliament, and preserved the Protestant religion.

Thus England emerged—one of the last countries in Europe to do so—from two centuries of religious and political turmoil, after a unique succession of religious reformation and counter-reformation, conspiracies, civil war, regicide, republic, military dictatorship, restoration, renewed civil conflict, invasion and a second revolution. The outcome was an uneasy and ill-tempered compromise which soon included an unpopular union with Scotland. The possibility of a state and society based on enforced uniformity of belief and practice, whether Anglican, Presbyterian or Catholic, turned out to have gone for good. Pressure from Dissenters to reinstate republican moral sanctions (for example, by restoring the death penalty for adultery, abolished at the Restoration) was rejected, and England remained on the whole less repressive, for example, than Holland, Scotland and New England.[173] Disunity was institutionalized, both in religion, the dominant cultural arena, and in "Whig" and "Tory" political identities. This made England (together with the other island kingdoms) unique. Most of Europe moved towards confessionalization, the identification of a state and its people with a single religion; but England became legally divided. It would never recover religious, and hence cultural and political, unity or even consensus: it could never become like Scandinavia.

We like to think that liberty is fought for. Judging by occasional comments in the media and by politicians, a widespread belief is that liberty was won during the Civil War. The reality is different: the war almost destroyed liberty. Only when the country rejected fighting, and zealots had to abandon their visions of a compulsory New Jerusalem, was liberty possible. To the Whigs we owe the principle—Magna Carta restated in modern form—that rulers must obey the law and that legitimate authority requires the consent of the people. From the Tories came the principle—fundamental to any political order—that people have no right to rebel against a government because they disagree with it. Combining these seemingly conflicting principles produced characteristics of English political culture: suspicion of Utopias and zealots; trust in common sense and experience; respect for tradition; preference for gradual change; and the view that "compromise" is victory, not betrayal. These things stem from the failure both of royal absolutism and of godly republicanism: costly failures, and fruitful ones.

# The Civil War and "Whig History"

*We are Cavaliers or Roundheads before we are Conservatives or Liberals.*

W. E. H. Lecky, *The Political Value of History* (1892)

The great divide of the sixteenth and seventeenth centuries continues to shape our ideas of who and what we are. It has been enshrined in historical writing of unique importance, which more than any other historical narrative or political ideology shaped England's identity for at least two centuries, and still has echoes today. From the time of the Restoration onwards, royalist histories, memoirs, petitions and sermons defended Charles and attacked his enemies as power-hungry fanatics. Commonwealth histories, let off the leash by the 1688 revolution, dwelt on Stuart tyranny, Puritan sufferings, and Parliament's defence of ancient liberties.[1] Each side had its dead heroes. On one side "King Charles the Martyr," celebrated by the Church on 30 January. On the other, John Hampden and Algernon Sidney: the "Good Old Cause" was long summed up as that for which "Hampden bled on the field and Sidney on the scaffold."

The first monumental history was by a councillor of Charles I, Edward Hyde, 1st Earl of Clarendon. His *History of the Rebellion*, acknowledged as a masterpiece, was begun in the 1640s but published only in 1702. It analysed the conflict as a sudden and avoidable political crisis—remarkably close to today's scholarly consensus. What was later called "Whig history" took a more ideological view—declared the Whig pamphleteer and historian John Oldmixon in 1726: "The laws and customs delivered down to us from our British and Saxon fathers, justified the practices of those brave British heroes" who fought against the king.[2] The pioneer Whig history was by a French Protestant soldier in William of Orange's invading army, Paul Rapin de Thoyras—one of a line of French,

Scottish, Irish, Polish and German-born thinkers who have written so much of England's history. While recovering from his wounds, Rapin embarked on an *Histoire d'Angleterre* (1723–27). He wrote "uniquely for Foreigners," but was soon published in English. He was the first author for centuries to encompass the whole of English history in one continuous (and moreover clear and racy) narrative, including Alfred the Great, Magna Carta and the final struggle against the Stuarts.[3] Rapin's became the standard interpretation. It set out the Whig view of English history as a continuous struggle to defend ancient freedoms: "The English have been at all times extremely jealous of their liberties," but Charles I had tried to "enslave England."[4] The climax of the story was the Glorious Revolution, re-establishing Anglo-Saxon liberty. Parliament and its defenders were made the embodiment of the nation and its history.

David Hume, one of the greatest of Scottish Enlightenment philosophers, used history as a powerful weapon against what he considered pernicious political myths.[5] His *History of England* (1757) provided an accessible and "rapid" narrative for readers with only a six-volume attention span. His Scottish publishers, convinced that they had a best-seller on their hands, claimed that Hume was "truely imparshal." Some of the clergy condemned Hume as irreligious, not without reason; and he openly despised the religious quarrels of the Civil War period. He advised his readers that "extremes of all kind are to be avoided."[6] His core idea was that societies progressed through stages of development by improving education, government, law and economic organization. Hume wanted to efface the dangerous Whig-Tory "party rage," which celebrated conflict and was not in his view a basis for rational and peaceful politics. He went about this principally by demolishing every Whig shibboleth with grim relish. Saying that he would "hasten thro' the obscure and uninteresting period" of Anglo-Saxon England, he dismissed it as "extremely aristocratical," oppressive and violent. There was no "Norman Yoke": the Conquest had been beneficial, teaching the "rude" Saxons "the rudiments of science and cultivation." The medieval struggles of parliaments were the work of a "narrow aristocracy" and gave no benefit to the people; and Magna Carta brought "no innovation in the political or public law of the country." Anyway, freedom was not born in England: "Both the privileges of the peers and the liberty of the commons" were copied from France. As for the father of Parliament, Simon de Montfort, his "violence, ingratitude, tyranny, rapacity and treachery" made his death "the most happy event which could have happened to the English nation."[7] Thus Hume hoped to cut the umbilical cord connecting the English political imagination to an idealized past, which should be left in "silence and oblivion."[8]

Liberty, said Hume, came not from resistance to the Crown, as the Whigs maintained, but from its growing power: "It required the authority almost absolute of the sovereign . . . to pull down those disorderly and licentious tyrants [the barons] who were equally enemies to peace and to freedom." The Tudors (as he was the first to call them) had laid the foundations of a civilized absolute monarchy, for Hume the best form of government then available. In the Civil War, the royalists had been right to defend legal authority, on which true liberty depended. The ideas of Pym and Hampden were "full of the lowest and most vulgar hypocrisy." "Cromwel" [sic] had taken power by "fraud and violence." The Puritans "talked perpetually of seeking the Lord, yet still pursued their own purposes; and have left a memorable lesson to posterity, how delusive, how destructive that principle is by which they were animated." True liberty, he insisted, was not ancient but modern, a result especially of the growth of commerce and towns. It was not, therefore, an ancient Teutonic inheritance.[9]

Hume's boasted impartiality amounted to being scathing about everyone. But while claiming to be a "sceptical Whig" he trampled on the Whigs with particular gusto: their "pretended respect for antiquity" was only to "cover their turbulent spirit and their private ambition." Observing the political agitation of the 1760s (see pp. 346–47), he wrote that the English "roar Liberty, tho' they have apparently more liberty than any people in the World; a great deal more than they deserve."[10] History should teach them to be grateful for what they had, which was not the product of heroic struggle, but of "a great measure of accident with a small ingredient of wisdom and foresight."[11]

Hume claimed that he had been "assailed by one cry of reproach, disapprobation, and even detestation." Yet his book rapidly became the biggest-selling work of history to date, and it made him "not merely independent, but opulent"[12]—a reflection of most people's anti-Roundhead sentiments. Hume was indeed detested by Whigs, who accused him of being a Jacobite; he was even attacked in Parliament by Pitt the Elder. He retorted that "I have the impudence to pretend that I am of no party"; but it is hard to imagine a more effective Tory history than one that ascribes liberty to the power of the Crown.

Hume's version prevailed intellectually, to the frustration of Whigs, for nearly a hundred years. But it could not efface the political and religious divide. Grass-roots dislike of "Roundheads" and of Whig wars and taxes—almost certainly the majority view—meant that crowds at elections a century after the Civil War still shouted "Down with the Long Parliament!" and London street gangs in the 1750s called themselves

"Cavaliers" or "Tory Rory Ranter Boys." British and American opponents of George III claimed the liberties of the "ancient constitution," and were attacked as "Roundheads" by the king's supporters. The most provocative and popular radical, John Wilkes, produced a *History of England* (1768), copied from Rapin, insisting that "liberty is the character of an Englishman." Catherine Macaulay attacked Hume in her popular *History of England* (1763–83) and reaffirmed the eternal struggle for Saxon freedoms against the Norman Yoke—already an ancient idea. She was feted by radicals, Whigs and Dissenters, including Benjamin Franklin and George Washington, and later admired by French Revolutionary leaders. The 1780 Gordon rioters, pro-American and anti-popish, reminded Edward Gibbon of "forty thousand Puritans, such as they might be in the time of Cromwell . . . started out of their graves."

The 1789 French Revolution widened the existing division in England. Would it revive England's revolutionary spirit, dormant since the previous century, and begin a new era of radical change? The Whig Edmund Burke gave a provocatively negative answer in *Reflections on the Revolution in France* (1790), a book as much about England as France. Burke wanted to defend 1688—a unique "act of necessity" to preserve ancient laws and liberties—while attacking 1789 as a gratuitous assault on a legitimate government. His argument revived ideas about custom and Common Law, as in the writings of Sir Edward Coke, but using them to support, not undermine, the legitimacy of the state. England, he argued, had built up since Magna Carta an evolving "inheritance" of concrete rights and freedoms. Unless people willingly accepted that none had the right to "separate and tear asunder" this political partnership, government could depend only on force. He famously warned that this would be the fate of France until finally "some popular general [is] the master of your whole republic"[13]—a prediction perhaps recalling England's experience of Cromwell.

*Reflections* at first aroused indignation among opposition Whigs and began an angry debate (see pp. 385–86). But when France descended into terror and war with England, Burke's warnings seemed vindicated: the *Edinburgh Review* lamented that "it was thought as well to say nothing of Hampden or Russell or Sidney, for fear it might give spirits to Robespierre, Danton or Marat."[14] England's age of revolutions was indeed over, and Burke's book signalled its passing. The change was precipitated by the challenge of the French Revolution, which most of England, both rulers and people, finally rejected and fought against. Thus, in fact and in the perceptions of its own people and the wider world, England changed from being a byword for political change and turbulence into the defender and exponent of continuity and peaceful politics. Its modern political sensibility, with its respect for the law, pragmatism, and suspicion of "ideology" and "extremism," is closer to Burke than to his opponents.

This sensibility was translated into powerful historical form by Thomas Babington Macaulay. Hume still reigned supreme in narrative history despite the efforts of his eighteenth-century Whig critics. Macaulay picked up the Whig baton, and deliberately set out to replace Hume as the most influential modern historian of England. He centred the national story on resistance to the Stuarts, with 1688 beginning the modern age. Indeed, for Macaulay the seventeenth century *was* English history: five of the six volumes of his *History of England* (1848–55) were on 1685–1702; he disposed of the first thousand years in a few briskly dogmatic pages. He even pushed the Whig cause into the forefront of the history of humanity, declaring it "entitled to the reverence and gratitude of all who in any part of the world enjoy the blessings of constitutional government."[15]

Macaulay, like Burke, was an intellectual MP who harnessed history to politics. He was a literary celebrity of forceful personality and decided opinions—"I wish I was as cocksure of anything as Tom Macaulay is of everything," remarked the Prime Minister, Lord Melbourne. He was unashamedly partisan:

> When I look back on our history, I can discern a great party which has, through many generations, preserved its identity; [which] has always been in advance of the age, [which] steadily asserted the privileges of the people, and wrested prerogative after prerogative from the Crown . . . To the Whigs of the seventeenth century we owe it that we have a House of Commons. To the Whigs of the nineteenth century we owe it that the House of Commons has been purified.[16]

His response to Hume's philosophical model of progress was to ignore it. His strength was not analysis but narrative. He aimed at a large readership, to "supersede the last fashionable novel on the tables of young ladies." He applied literary narrative techniques to a major work of English history for the first time, concentrating on vivid descriptions of events and people, lauding heroism and denouncing vices (above all those of the Stuarts—"inconstancy, perfidy, baseness," etc.), and dwelling on heroic and pathetic ends; death scenes were a speciality. He was brilliant on memorable sayings and details, not least the gruesome: rebels hanged from a pub sign (the White Hart); a woman about to be burned at the stake arranging the straw herself so that she would die quickly. How much was true? Macaulay was not interested in testing evidence, but exploiting it. Popularity came: and a cheque for £20,000 from Longmans in 1856—worth several millions today—was preserved by the publishers as the relic of a prodigy.

Macaulay downgraded the idea of an "ancient constitution" inherited from the Anglo-Saxons—he considered it too democratic a notion. Progress was brought not by popular agitation but by the enlightened Whig elite, and it took the material form of trade, factories, libraries, public baths, "the effect of gradual development, not of demolition and reconstruction."[17] Other views of history he dismissed as "mythological fables for the vulgar." Macaulay defined the English not by race, religion or culture, but politically, as a free nation with parliamentary institutions, and as the world leaders of modernity.

Above all, Macaulay wrote a gripping national drama. He told the story of a victory of good over evil eventually won in the Glorious Revolution by ordinary men and women as well as by Whig grandees. The Liberal MP Robert Lowe summed this up in 1878: "The history of the English constitution is a record of liberties wrung and extorted bit by bit from arbitrary power." This Whig history was a powerful tool for the emerging Liberal Party and a stirring mythology for the politically aspiring and often Nonconformist middle classes. It became the national history, not only of England, but of Britain and the United States. It aroused admiration among Europeans envious that "the English Revolution" (a term coined in 1830 by the French historian and liberal politician François Guizot)[18] had, unlike its Continental counterparts, engendered peace, power and plenty.

Thomas Carlyle, like Macaulay (though they detested each other), helped to shape this version of the English past by publishing, almost simultaneously with Macaulay's *History*, *Oliver Cromwell's Letters and Speeches* (1845), with a long biographical commentary. This best-seller was said to have "reversed the verdict of history." It enabled Cromwell, previously considered a duplicitous and bloodstained dictator, to rewrite the story posthumously in his own words. He became a hero of progressive struggles, especially those of newly enfranchised Nonconformists waging a godly war on drink, vice, poverty, the Establishment and popery: "We have reigned with Cromwell," wrote *The Congregationalist* in 1873.[19] In 1875, when a memorial was raised on the battlefield of Naseby, the ceremony was attended by 2,000 members of the Agricultural Labourers' Union, recently founded by Joseph Arch, a Methodist lay preacher and later Liberal MP very proud of his Roundhead descent. Statues of Cromwell multiplied across the land. A Liberal proposal in 1899 to erect his statue with public funds outside the Palace of Westminster itself—the man who had used troops four times against Parliament reinvented as its defender—was defeated by Irish MPs mindful of Drogheda and Wexford. So the Liberal Prime Minister, Lord Rosebery, offered to pay for it out of his own pocket.

A scholarly seal was placed on the Whig account by S. R. Gardiner, a reclusive religious eccentric, descendant of Cromwell and professor at University College, London, who published the first thoroughly document-based *History of the Great Civil War* (1886–91): "He found the story . . . legend, and left it history," declared a contemporary. Gardiner characterized the conflict as "the Puritan revolution," for Puritanism "not only formed the strength of the opposition to Charles, but the strength of England itself"[20]—a remarkably audacious claim. J. R. Green had popularized this view in his *Short History of the English People* (1874), the first genuinely short and popular survey ever written. "Modern England began," he declared, "with the triumph of Naseby," and Puritanism made the English "serious, earnest, sober in life and conduct, firm in their love of Protestantism and freedom."[21] An 1860s political song proclaimed that "the cause that charged with Cromwell on Marston's bloody Moor" was still fighting the Tories.[22] Isaac Foot (1880–1960)— Liberal MP, leading Methodist, president of the Pedestrians Association, president of the Cromwell Association, temperance crusader and father of a future leader of the Labour Party—considered that to judge a man politically, he had only to ask himself on which side he would have fought at Marston Moor.

By this time, those who might have fought on the losing side at Marston Moor had long ceased to have an alternative history. Although many people disliked what Charles I had been against, few advocated what he had been for.[23] W. F. Yeames's famous painting *And When Did You Last See Your Father?* (1878) encapsulated dislike of Roundhead oppression, as did Frederick Marryat's children's novel *The Children of the New Forest* (1847), popular for a century. The Civil War inspired a torrent of nineteenth-century paintings, plays, novels, even operas. But such expressions of traditional royalism were only sentiment. Toryism, apart from scepticism about democracy and free trade, and loyalty to certain symbols— most obviously the Crown and the Church—had not had since Hume, and perhaps did not want, its own historical narrative. One of the most popular twentieth-century Tory politicians, Stanley Baldwin, boasted of his "Puritan blood,"[24] and one of the most historically aware Conservative ministers of the early twenty-first, Michael Gove, regularly proclaimed himself "a Whig."

Over the nineteenth century the Whig vision expanded chronologically and geographically. The Oxford regius professor E. A. Freeman identified embryonic Whigs and Tories as early as the eleventh century. The foundation of the empire, with Elizabeth I and Cromwell as oddly assorted heroes, became the apotheosis of the Whig saga, seen as the global spread of Protestantism, commerce, law and parliamentary government. John Seeley, the pioneer historian of the empire, concluding that "constitutional liberty [was] a completed development," proposed imperial expansion as now the "goal of English history."[25] A variant of this view became part of the national myth of America. A popular synthesis of British and American patriotism was Winston Churchill's best-selling *History of the English Speaking Peoples*, reflecting ideas going back to the 1860s, largely written in the 1930s, and published in the 1950s. In recent years Anglo-American "neo-conservative" history has revived a modernized Whig narrative.

So Whig history, in origin that of a party, became the national and imperial history, with pretensions to being the history of the world. In England and America it still permeates textbooks, political rhetoric and popular history. But its intellectual sinews have long since atrophied. The final flowering came with George Macaulay Trevelyan's *History of England* (1926), his *Shortened History* (1942) and his *English Social History* (1944). They were read by millions—he was, thought a colleague, "probably the most widely read historian in the world: perhaps in the history of the world."[26] Trevelyan, Macaulay's great-nephew, was the embodiment of the Liberal Establishment: a patrician family, regius professor and Master of Trinity College, Cambridge, and loaded with unsought and sometimes refused honours. His smooth Olympian prose suggests not a mind grappling with problems, but one dutifully reaffirming the Whig pieties—the familiar Parliament-centred story of continuity, freedom and progress, "the natural outcome, through long centuries, of the common sense and good nature of the English people," in a "sphere apart" from the Continent, where free institutions had "withered like waterless plants."[27] A French reviewer found these patriotic fanfares "xenophobic . . . complacent and self-satisfied."[28] Yet there was a whiff of nostalgia, even defeat: "I don't understand the age we live in, and what I understand I don't like."[29] The twentieth century had destroyed his faith in the happy endings that Whig history promised, and his mood was at best defiant rather than triumphant.

Intellectually, the Whig saga was moribund. The Cambridge historian Herbert Butterfield (later Master of Peterhouse) wrote a pugnacious pamphlet, *The Whig Interpretation of History* (1931), condemning it as a "caricature" of the past pandering to the "ideas and prejudices" of the present.[30] A real caricature had appeared a year before Butterfield's manifesto, *1066 and All That*, by W. C. Sellar and R. J. Yeatman, which made

Butterfield's point more amusingly and to a vastly wider readership: almost every episode in history was "a Good Thing" as it advanced Britain's progress to "Top Nation."

Another swipe came from socialist historians. R. H. Tawney saw the Civil War not as a fight for freedom, but for the replacement of feudalism with capitalism. Puritanism was a template for the hard-nosed businessman. Christopher Hill, Tawney's admirer, impressed by a visit to Russia in the 1930s, published *The English Revolution 1640* (1940), which described it as bourgeois revolution and "class war." "My virulence against Charles I," Hill later explained, "was I fear caused by conflating him with Neville Chamberlain."[31] The charismatic Hill, Master of Balliol College, Oxford, and his many disciples of the "New Left," wrote history that was emotionally as well as ideologically committed. They wanted "history from below," rescuing from oblivion the revolutionary "masses" blotted out of Whig history. The idea of a simmering English social revolution that never quite boiled over was now a source of regret. Hill turned the Whig saga upside down: "When we ask ourselves what has gone wrong with England in the past three centuries, one part of that answer is that the arrogant self-confidence of the ruling class ... was for too long unchecked."[32] The Levellers and the Diggers (rediscovered by Karl Marx's disciple Eduard Bernstein in 1908), their religious fundamentalism interpreted as social radicalism, were hailed during the 1960s and 1970s as "freedom fighters" and spiritual "founding fathers of the Labour Party." In this guise, they have inspired many books and at least one film.[33] Though discredited academically, such views still colour popular perceptions.

A preoccupation with "what has gone wrong with England" gave a body blow to Whig history as the national narrative. It had been a history of success: that is why the American version outlives the British original. It had shown England and its overseas offshoots as leading the world towards freedom, the rule of law and representative government. The First World War shook such confidence. The Second provided a last defiant flourish—Butterfield even wrote that it had made the myth true[34]— but the postwar torrent of "declinism" (see p. 767) gave the coup de grâce. The end of empire and the spread of democracy ended British exceptionalism. The successes of recently democratized states such as Germany negated the idea that long historical experience was a source of unique political wisdom. The prestige of ancient institutions dwindled. European integration pushed English and British law and institutions—now often presented as embarrassingly archaic and ripe for "modernization"— towards alignment with Continental norms. Anti-establishment historians could now recast the Whig story of centuries of noble political struggle

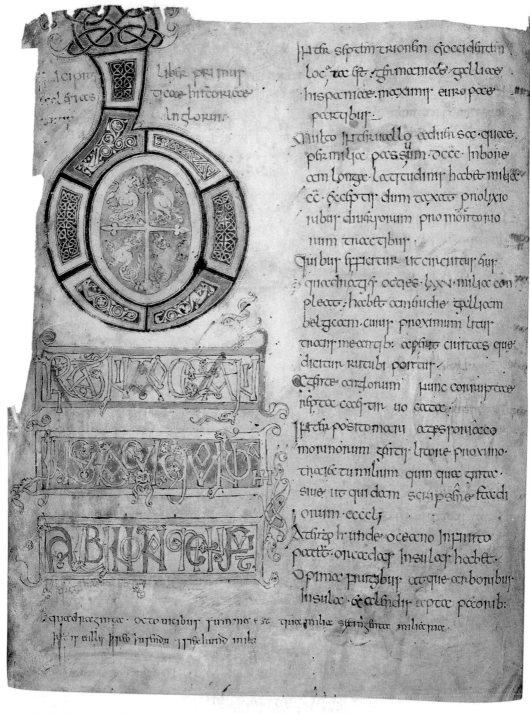

1. Bede, the most influential English historian of all time, finished his Latin *Ecclesiastical History of the English Church and People* in 731, giving an identity to the embryonic nation. The importance of the widely circulated and authoritative book is shown by the quality of this copy, probably written in Canterbury in the late eighth or early ninth century. It is the beginning of the book: "Britain, once called Albion, is an island of the ocean . . ."

2 and 3. The Anglo-Saxons were a wealthy and sophisticated society. This is reflected in the variety and quality of their art. Their language and literature were among the most developed in Europe: the importance of reading is shown by the Alfred Jewel (*left*), a pointer used to follow the words in manuscripts and a personal gift of the king; and this page from the *Aelfric Pentateuch*, showing Noah and his family leaving the Ark (*below*).

4 and 5. The Normans built the grandest, most experimental and most expensive buildings in Western Europe in the most concentrated construction effort in England between the Romans and the Victorians. Buildings were an instrument of domination: massive, stark and uncompromising, they transformed the landscape. Dover Castle (*above*) commanded the gateway to England, and was still used in the Second World War. Durham Cathedral (*below*) was a centre of spiritual and earthly power in the north.

6, 7 and 8. For most of its history England was a wealthy and populous agricultural society founded on wheat (*top left*) and wool. Domesday Book recorded its wealth in the 1080s, including 6,000 mills and 650,000 oxen. By then, forests were already reduced to twentieth-century levels; in 1300 as much land was under cultivation as in 1900. Ever since the Black Death, some of it has remained under grass, leaving visible medieval ploughing patterns in what were once great open fields (*top right*). Barns comparable with great churches and mansions, such as this twelfth-century example at Cressing Temple, testify to its productivity (*above*).

9 and 10. Medieval England was by contemporary standards a peaceful and strongly governed country. A crucial element was royal justice through the Common Law, represented in the image of Edward III in state surrounded by officials and judges (*left*). But the centrality of royal government meant that when things went wrong, they went very wrong. The legal dispute between King Henry II (*below*) and the Church led to the murder of Archbishop Thomas Becket in 1170.

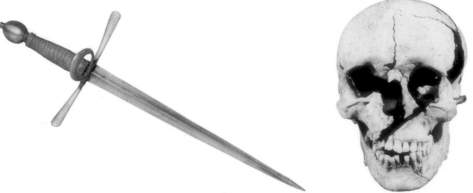

11, 12 and 13. The failings of Edward II and Richard II led to successive violent interventions by "the community of the realm." The Despensers, Edward II's favourites, were publicly disembowelled in 1326 (*top*). The rebel leader Wat Tyler was killed in 1381 with this dagger (*above left*), wielded by a fishmonger mayor of London, William Walworth, and preserved at Fishmongers' Hall. The most intractable royal failure, that of Henry VI, led to the Wars of the Roses, of which a skull from the battle of Towton (1461), the bloodiest battle of the Wars, is a grisly reminder.

14. Richard II's reign was also a time of cultural brilliance. Geoffrey Chaucer, courtier, diplomat and European intellectual, is shown in this early-fifteenth-century illustration reading his *Troilus and Criseyde* to the court. Chaucer created from the vernacular a sophisticated literature so new to his readers that it sometimes needed to be explained in French or Latin glossaries.

15 and 16. The fifteenth century was an end-point in politics and culture. The long connection with France, which had seemed at times destined to unite the two kingdoms, was broken with the loss of Normandy and Aquitaine. The Battle of Castillon in July 1453 (*top*) marked the end of the Hundred Years' War. The hapless Henry VI endowed a royal college at Cambridge, whose chapel is the last great flowering of the English "Perpendicular" style (*above*).

17. This title page of the first Bible in English given by royal command epitomizes the top-down English Reformation. Henry VIII, accompanied by Thomas Cromwell and Archbishop Cranmer (still beardless and tonsured), is giving the book to his grateful people; malcontents languish behind bars. This is one of only two surviving illuminated presentation copies, and probably belonged to Thomas Cromwell himself.

18 and 19. The English Reformation spared neither works of art nor human bodies. Vandalism against "superstition" ravaged the religious culture of centuries, such as this fifteenth-century Virgin and Child on the rood screen of the parish church of Great Snoring, Norfolk (*left*). Cranmer, intellectual leader of evangelicalism, fell foul of Mary I's Counter-Reformation and was burnt as a heretic at Oxford in 1556. Foxe's *Book of Martyrs* immortalized the scene, including Cranmer's gesture of thrusting his hand into the flames in atonement for having signed a recantation of his beliefs (*below*).

20. Elizabeth I was the keystone of security and domestic order, symbolized in icons of majesty and power, here showing the defeated Spanish Armada in the background.

21. New wealth, often acquired at the expense of the Church, led to the building of great houses such as Hardwick Hall in bold and lavish style, no longer with battlements but with great expanses of glass—testimony to confidence in civil peace.

22 and 23. Religious conflict under Charles I was primarily between the "godly" (Puritans) and official Anglicanism, personified by Charles and Archbishop Laud. The divide is shown by the contrast between Langley Chapel in Shropshire (*top*), purged of "idolatrous" decoration and with an ordinary table to celebrate "the Lord's supper," and the ornate chapel of Peterhouse, Cambridge (*above*), its sacramental altar railed off from the laity—later forbidden by Parliament.

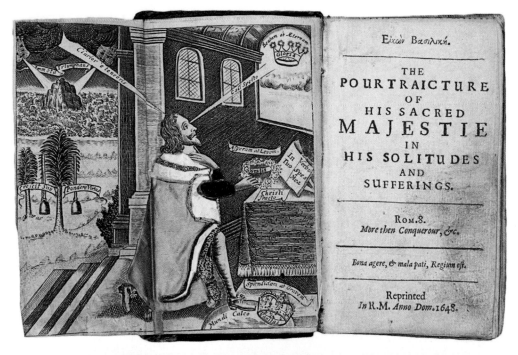

24 and 25. Charles I had prepared for martyrdom, as had his followers: they published the hagiographic *Eikon Basilike* ("royal portrait") (*top*) on the very day he was beheaded. The battle of imagery continued over succeeding centuries, with the parliamentary cause being claimed as that of religious and political freedom, as in this painting from the 1840s in the Houses of Parliament of *The Assertion of Liberty of Conscience* at a 1644 "Assembly of Divines" at Westminster (*above*).

26, 27 and 28. The Puritan republic was never popular, and in 1660 Charles II returned from exile in triumph (*top*). But the Restoration faced a series of disasters, including plague and the 1666 Great Fire of London.

This, as shown in these paintings by Jongh (1631 or 1637, *top*) and Canaletto (*c.*1746, *above*), helped to change London from a medieval to a modern city, stamped with the classical elegance of Sir Christopher Wren, architect of the new St. Paul's Cathedral and fifty-two smaller churches, whose spires dominate the cityscape.

29, 30 and 31. England's long political and religious crisis concluded with military intervention by the Dutch *stadhouder*, Willem III, who became William III and transformed England's politics and its role in Europe (*top left*). The "Glorious Revolution" of 1688–89 institutionalized party politics, whose first great practitioner was Robert Walpole (*top right*). The approval of Parliament became crucial to government, focused on this tiny Commons chamber whose members were elected under a bizarre variety of systems. Debate was an important aspect of politics: William Pitt the Younger, Prime Minister in 1783 at the age of twenty-four, who dominated English politics until his death in 1806, was a powerful performer (*above*).

ending in triumph into one of centuries of bitter class conflict ending in failure.

In the history of the Reformation, the old Protestant triumphalism has long gone, replaced by secularist indifference, ecumenical goodwill, and acceptance that Reformation was imposed by the Crown on a mostly Catholic nation. On the Civil War, a post-Marxist "revisionist" approach largely dominates serious history. Whereas Whigs or Marxists interpreted religious conflict as secondary to political or socio-economic struggles, revisionists took religious conflict as a reality; indeed, political and social tensions were often a consequence of underlying religious differences, not the other way round. This modern consensus shows some striking similarities to the interpretations of Clarendon and Hume. The Civil War was a political accident arising from Scottish, Irish and Continental, not solely English, causes—it was the last in the series of European wars of religion. England was not a revolutionary society: there was no class war, and the two sides were not socio-economically defined. Parliament and the Crown were not pursuing a centuries-old constitutional struggle of liberty against tyranny.

The disintegration of Whig history reflects the waning of an important English and British strain of self-confident Protestant Progressivism, which dominated in the nineteenth century and drained away during the twentieth. Is there still an underlying divide between "Cavalier" and "Roundhead"? In a culture and society secularized since the 1960s it is hard even to understand what the quarrel was about—a recent widely praised bodice-ripping Civil War television drama managed to leave out religion completely,[35] as did the 2013 proposal for a new National Curriculum in History. One distinguished historian nevertheless believes that "the self-conscious division of the modern nation into 'them' and 'us' has drawn, however distantly, on civil-war memories and civil-war stereotypes."[36] It was the Civil War that created the Whig-Tory divide moulding our deepest political identities, and it also bequeathed a sectarian bitterness that long enlivened and envenomed political culture. The tang remains as part of what it is to be English.

# PART FOUR

# MAKING A NEW WORLD,
## c.1660–c.1815

*Knowledge itself is power.*

> Sir Francis Bacon, *Meditationes Sacrae* (1597)

*Our ancestors, a few centuries ago, were sunk into the most abject superstition, last century they were enflamed with the most furious enthusiasm, and are now settled into the most cool indifference with regard to religious matters, that is to be found in any nation of the world.*

> David Hume, "Of National Characters" (1748)[1]

Between the late 1600s and the early 1800s, the English, like their neighbours, collectively drew back aghast from the extremism and dogmatism—"enthusiasm," as they termed it—that had disrupted life for two centuries. People in Europe learned to contemplate the universe and themselves in consciously new ways, entering what some called an "Age of Enlightenment" or "Age of Reason." Now other interests and ideas could be pursued, with more varied and less exclusive places to socialize, outside the church, the inn and the household. This stimulated new ways of getting and spending, which rewarded economic innovation, accelerated overseas contacts and conflicts, and eventually ignited a world-transforming technological and social revolution. Europe began its global ascendancy as the great Asian empires declined, and, more than ever before, contact with other parts of the world affected European life intellectually, economically and politically. England participated in these global changes, and eventually, for the first time in its history, led them.

From the political wreckage emerged those ideas, habits and institutions that we might dimly recognize as the origins of modern English and British "values." Influential voices began to preach rationality, tolerance, optimism, happiness, pleasure and politeness—even while practising adversarial party politics whose verbal violence was unparalleled in Europe. The ideas and practices of politics changed profoundly over the century. As one backbench MP observed in 1688, asserting that "kings are made by the people" would have been "high treason eighteen months ago"; but now it was being declared by a high-court judge.[2] Debate was less fettered, yet politics generally kept within peaceful limits, divided but stable.[3] The Stuart ambition of creating a United Kingdom of Great Britain was fulfilled.

For intellectuals and politicians observing from neighbouring nations, all this made post-revolution England seem a very unusual country, inspiring admiration, envy, and alarm.[4] It had apparently achieved at a stroke open government, religious toleration and relative peace. As Voltaire put it, "The civil wars of ancient Rome brought slavery, but the troubles in England have brought liberty."[5] Unexpectedly, this was also making it more efficient, powerful and wealthy, changing it rapidly from European laughing stock to global great power.[6] For the first time, the English language and English ideas, arts and fashions spread far beyond its shores, even inspiring "Anglomania" across Europe.

Britain fought a long series of wars and gained and lost immense territories. Was this a contradiction of Enlightenment ideas of tolerance and freedom? Not entirely. The wars were essentially fought against the superpower France, and were seen as a defence of English, European and Christian liberties against oppression and intolerance. They were also fought for trade and settlement, seen as progressive as well as highly lucrative, spreading the new rational, scientific, commercial and Christian civilization. This would broadly remain Britain's imperial ideology as long as the empire lasted. In the long run, the absorption of England into a British Empire would transform it as much as any of the other great changes of the Enlightenment.

But the financial costs and political disagreements arising from global expansion caused the violent break-away between 1775 and 1783 of much of what most people had thought of as trans-Atlantic England, ironically in the name of English rights and liberties. The crisis galvanized British and European politics and caused turmoil on the Continent. The French Revolution in 1789 began a new and greater struggle after which, in part by a process of elimination, England's political and cultural values became a global model, and its power was effectively unchallenged throughout the nineteenth century.

Progress is one of the Enlightenment ideas that has embedded itself at the heart of modern consciousness, as utopian fantasies about the future came to rival fantasies about a past golden age as sources of political and moral inspiration. At this time, England and Europe came to believe that they had discovered (or rediscovered from the ancient world) universal ideas and values which they hoped the rest of humanity would one day accept. It is still too early to say whether they were right.

# CHAPTER 7

# And All Was Light

*There is a mighty light which spreads itself over the whole world,
especially in those free nations of England and Holland, on whom
the affairs of Europe now turn.*

3rd Earl of Shaftesbury, 1706[1]

All Nature and its laws lay hid in night
God said: Let Newton Be: and all was light
Alexander Pope, *An Essay on Man* (1733–34)

For the first time since the decline of the Roman Empire, some Europeans of the late seventeenth and early eighteenth centuries began to think about the universe without instinctively deferring to the superior wisdom of ancient authorities, whether hallowed religious teachings, long-accepted philosophical and scientific principles, or immemorial laws, proverbs and customs. They were "the first intellectuals on record to express an entirely secular awareness of social and economic changes going on in their society."[2] Understanding should "begin with the Hands and Eyes," urged the scientific polymath Robert Hooke in 1665. This experimental method began its rise to become a dominant characteristic of Western thought.[3] Its authority of course has never been complete—religious scriptures and classical writings remained central—but it soon made the old ways of thinking a matter for mockery. One example which had an international impact was the novel written by an Anglican clergyman, Laurence Sterne, *The Life and Opinions of Tristram Shandy* (1759), which ludicrously parodied traditional religious, legal and scientific scholarship, epitomized by "the great and learned Hafen Slawkenbergius," who knew all there was to be known—about noses.

An intellectual avant-garde emerged in the comparative freedom of Holland and England. The relatively moderate Church of England was the "Mother of this sort of Knowledge."[4] Anglicans had become suspicious of "men of dogmas," or "reasoners," as Francis Bacon called them. Bacon (1561–1626), who combined a chequered political career with philosophical writing, is widely regarded as the father of modern scientific method. He rejected metaphysical speculation in favour of observation: "Men of experiment are like the ant; they only collect and use; the reasoners resemble spiders, who make cobwebs out of their own substance."[5] The Civil War deepened the desire to escape from the turmoil of religious subjectivity—what John Locke called "the ungrounded fancies of a man's own brain." Enlightenment was not intentionally anti-religious, though it had underlying anti-religious implications. Anglican intellectuals were confident that science clearly vindicated their beliefs, and long remained so.[6] Theology shaped Enlightened thinking, and clergy in all countries played a prominent role as transmitters of new ideas—80 percent of clergymen's libraries in England, for example, contained works by Voltaire.

To the pinnacle of the new intellectual endeavour rose an introverted and driven farmer's son from Lincolnshire, Isaac Newton (1642–1727), who began experimenting with optics by pushing pieces of metal into his own eye sockets. His *Principia Mathematica* (1687) remains one of the greatest achievements of the human mind,[7] proving that experiment and calculation could explain and predict natural phenomena. His fundamental insights into the forces holding the universe together prevailed until the twentieth century and are still used for many purposes. He became literally a legend in his lifetime, in the popular story (told by himself) that he conceived of gravity after the fall of an apple. English mathematics long remained under his shadow, and so it was in France that some of his major insights were pushed forward and his methods and old-fashioned notation improved. Newton also practised the older learning, fascinated by alchemy, the chronology of the Bible and the dates of future fulfilment of its prophecies: for him, science and religion were in search of the same ultimate reality.

Newton and his admirers—notably "Latitudinarian," or "Low Church," Anglicans, who had rejected Calvinism and prided themselves in being "free, moderate, rational, moral and new"[8]—believed that his insights demonstrated an ordered, benevolent Creation equally remote from the anarchic magical universe of Civil War sectarians and the dark vision of Thomas Hobbes's *Leviathan* (1651). They concluded that God intended social, political and religious relations to be as ordered and harmonious as the physical world. The Newtonians hoped that rational religion could reunite Christians and prepare for the Apocalypse, which Newton thought was on the distant horizon—the year 2000 seemed a likely date.[9] Although Newton quietly developed unorthodox ideas (he doubted the doctrine of the Trinity, and Charles II permitted him to hold his university posts without taking holy orders), he remained an Establishment figure: a pious Anglican Cambridge don for most of his career, MP for the University, President of the Royal Society, Master of the Mint, scourge of counterfeiters, and the first ever mathematician to be knighted—honours that impressed Europeans with the unique prestige of science in England.

Newton, despite Wordsworth's description of his "mind for ever voyaging through strange seas of Thought, alone," remained cautious. Nature was only God's "second book," after the Bible. He insisted that his discoveries demonstrated a universe continuously held in existence by God: for example, God made gravity operate. He shunned the Deist theories whispered in radical circles, by which a remote intelligence, having set the universe in motion (the famous "divine clockmaker"), played no further part in it. Newton's caution strengthened the Baconian empiricism that became a trait of English Enlightenment philosophy, and marks English habits of mind more than three centuries later. What was nevertheless revolutionary was that reason and science had become at least the equals of tradition and revelation: mathematics might demonstrate the wisdom of God; but theology could no longer invalidate scientific observation. "Faith," wrote John Locke, "can have no authority against the plain and clear dictates of reason."[10] This new readiness to test religious belief against reason and observation, opening the door to secular understandings of life, was new to Christianity—a Muslim attempt in eighth-century Iraq had eventually been suppressed as heresy, and the application of reason to religion permanently forbidden; and the polytheistic religions also kept faith and rationality in separate spheres.

No less significant were changes in philosophy and political thought, to which English writers now made their greatest contribution. John Locke (1632–1704) became almost Newton's equal in fame. An Oxford don, he was engaged in 1666 as political adviser by a Presbyterian peer, the 1st Earl of Shaftesbury, whose prominence in the "Exclusion Crisis" (see p. 257) forced them both into exile in 1682. This radicalized Locke's political views, which drew on French Calvinist arguments for a right to resist monarchs. His *Essay Concerning Human Understanding* and his anonymous *Two Treatises of Government* were published only in 1690, when he returned from exile after the Glorious Revolution, whose supreme intellectual apologist he became. In time he became an Enlightenment secular saint, hailed as the champion of religious, intellectual and political freedom, immortalized in bronze, paint and words—Samuel Johnson's *Dictionary* (1755) used more quotations from him than from any other author.[11]

The *Essay Concerning Human Understanding*, the seminal philosophical work of the Enlightenment, was immediately recognized as a new way of thinking—prescribed for study in Dublin, briefly banned in Oxford—and became the most widely read English work of philosophy, probably of all time. It was a comprehensive account in plain English of how human beings know and understand—the exotic word "idea" was one it brought into common usage. Locke wanted to foster a new critical attitude towards all knowledge, as an "under-labourer," as he put it, to scientists such as Robert Boyle (1627–91) and Newton, "removing some of the rubbish, that lies in the way." He argued that human beings are born with minds like "white paper, void of all characters, without any ideas." All they know comes through experiences and thoughts—"sensation and reflection." There are no innate ideas or principles imprinted on the mind—not even the idea of a God. So nothing is above or beyond reason and discussion, including faith: "He that believes without having any reason for believing [is] in love with his own fancies."[12]

Locke, like his contemporary René Descartes (whose belief in innate common ideas he rejected), considered that all were capable of reasoning: this was what made us human. So to become fully human meant learning to think for oneself, free from compulsion by authority or tradition. Locke believed in the unmediated message of the Bible. Yet his ideas were capable of more radical interpretation than he intended. Hume wrote that Locke "seems to have been the first Christian, who ventur'd openly to assert that . . . Religion was only a branch of Philosophy."[13] This was not so, but it is significant that it could have been thought.

Locke was equally celebrated as a writer on politics, and his prestige as a philosopher gave weight to his political writings. His influential *Letters on Toleration* (1689–92) provided an intellectual underpinning for the religious compromise that emerged from the 1688 revolution. He did not advocate complete toleration, because society had the right to protect itself from dangerous and damaging doctrines such as atheism or Catholicism. But beliefs that were not harmful should be free. This was representative of the developing European attitude: tolerance was necessary because intolerance was worse.[14]

The *Two Treatises* propounded a contract theory: government originated from an agreement among the governed. Contract theories were familiar. Hobbes had propounded a notorious version in *Leviathan* (1651). Locke shared the common revulsion against Hobbes, and he also argued, with copious biblical quotation, against traditional Tory theories that a king derived patriarchal authority from God. His *Two Treatises* denied the absolute authority of the Crown, and gave "the People" the right to "remove [an oppressive government] by force." Like Hobbes, Locke saw "civil society" as emerging by agreement of its members from the "state of nature." But he described that state as free, equal and governed by natural law, unlike Hobbes's predatory anarchy. So when men joined together to enhance the security of life and property, they did so as a "voluntary Union . . . freely acting in the choice of their Governours, and forms of Government." They did not permanently surrender their liberty, or set up an absolute sovereign: "There can be but *one Supream Power*, which is *the Legislative* to which all the rest are and must be subordinate, yet . . . there remains still *in the People a Supream Power* to remove or *alter the Legislative.*"[15]

The *Two Treatises* grew steadily in influence after Locke's death in 1704. Later interpretations gave them the prestige of a modern Magna Carta, not least in the United States, where conflict with the British Parliament in the 1770s gave Locke's ideas a relevance they had lost in England, and have caused them to be hailed as founding texts in modern political thought and the inspiration of the American Declaration of Independence:

> Men are naturally free . . . the *Governments* of the World . . . were *made by the Consent of the People* . . . whenever the Legislators endeavour to take away, and destroy the Property of the People, or to reduce them to Slavery under Arbitrary Power [the People] are thereby absolved from any farther obedience.[16]

Thus, a classic piece of Calvinist political radicalism was reinvented as the founding text of modern liberal democracy.[17] Locke—although neither a democrat, nor an egalitarian, nor an advocate of complete religious tolerance—became the prophet of modern intellectual, religious and political freedom.

## FROM ENTHUSIASM TO POLITENESS

> Know then thyself, presume not God to scan,
> The proper study of mankind is man.
>                      Alexander Pope, *An Essay on Man* (1733–34)

A surge of intellectual experiment, cultural innovation and public debate was made possible by political relaxation. Though capable of bursts of repression against religious minorities thought to be politically threatening, the Restoration was intellectually permissive, even encouraging, as shown by Charles II's patronage of the Royal Society. This was founded in

1660 to promote sociable intellectual discussion among the gentlemanly amateurs who were pioneering scientific experiment; and, although it long retained this general social function (Samuel Pepys, for example, was a member), it also brought together the leading scientific thinkers of the day, and constituted an important means of diffusing ideas, both in England and abroad. The Glorious Revolution went further, both by accident and by design. The Licensing Act controlling the press was inadvertently allowed to lapse in 1695 and was not restored (in contrast to France, which had 120 full-time royal censors).* William III favoured legal toleration of Dissenting sects, both because he himself had been in English terms a Dissenter, and more importantly because he wanted domestic harmony to further the war against France. The bishops discovered to their chagrin that they no longer in practice had the powers to prosecute heretics—on one occasion, Queen Anne kept deliberately losing the paperwork.[18] Moderates were appointed to vacant sees. Though blasphemy remained a crime, the need for trial by jury meant that prosecution of dissident views was chancy, and magistrates were usually unenthusiastic. So lax were controls that one Jacobite parson operated a printing press inside the King's Bench Prison.[19] As Locke put it, toleration "has now at last been established by law in our country. Not perhaps so wide in scope as might be wished for . . . Still, it is something to have progressed so far."[20]

This is not to say that complete domestic harmony broke out. The Glorious Revolution was far from initiating the smooth consensus that "Whig history" later celebrated. Religious antagonisms shaped political and cultural life throughout the eighteenth century and beyond. But they rarely caused violence, at least not in England. The struggle was waged with words—on paper, in Parliament, in pulpits, sometimes in the law courts, and in clubs and coffee houses. Moreover, there are many signs of a deliberate rejection of extremism—"enthusiasm," "fanaticism," "hypocrisy," "superstition"—whether "Popish" or "Puritan." It became common to praise the virtues of moderation, sincerity and rationality, so that differences of opinion would not (as one Anglican woman put it) "dissolve and deface the Laws of Charity and Humane Society." All parties claimed to practise politeness, plain speech, moderation and sincerity.[21] Dislike of intellectual extremism, and distaste for verbal violence, even within the adversarial party system, has remained powerful in English political discourse ever since.

The philosopher of politeness was a Whig intellectual, the 3rd Earl of Shaftesbury, whose widely read *Characteristics of Men, Manners, Opin-*

* A form of press control, legalized by Royal Charter, was proposed in 2013.

*ions, Times* (1711) asserted that human beings had an innate "sense of right and wrong," that "affection" for society and people was part of human nature, and that our own "happiness and welfare" depended on working for "the general good."[22] Shaftesbury believed that virtue was manifested in "good breeding," which meant being incapable of "a rude or brutal action." He thought that "good humour is not only the best security against enthusiasm, but the best foundation of piety and true religion," which would leave aside theological disputation in favour of "plain honest morals."[23] "Polite" culture was made fashionable by the enormously successful daily *Spectator* (1711–14), edited by Joseph Addison and Richard Steele. Its novel mixture of news, conversation, moral exhortation, literature and fashion was also published in book form, and translated for Continental readerships—in France, it became one of the most widely owned literary works.[24] Its fictional "club" (which attracted a quasi–soap operatical following) included the squire Sir Roger de Coverley and the City gent Sir Andrew Freeport, mellowed and slightly old-fashioned "Cavalier" and "Roundhead" characters ("a true Whig, arguing against giving charity to beggars," recalled Samuel Johnson disapprovingly of the latter[25]), but whose differences were now no more than courteous and even friendly banter.

Urbanity, civility and moderation—often called "the art of pleasing"—thus became ideals of eighteenth-century style, which people laboured to acquire. But there was a line to tread carefully. When the 4th Earl of Chesterfield's voluminous mid-century letters of advice to his son were published in 1774—stressing the need to work hard at perfecting polite (French-style) manners in order to please and manipulate others—they were condemned as "the morals of a whore and the manners of a dancing master," in Johnson's stinging summary.[26] Both morality and fashion now demanded emotional authenticity, naturalness and simplicity. This influenced the emerging ideal of the English gentleman, different both from the swashbuckling Cavalier and the humourless Roundhead, though absorbing sublimated elements from both—breeding and gallantry combined with benevolence and sincerity.

If politeness was an influential ideal, it was only part of the reality. Throughout the eighteenth century, and into the first decades of the nineteenth, there was a rumbustious, mostly male, counter-culture which deliberately flouted the rules of politeness (laughter was "ill-bred," decreed Chesterfield) with drinking, cruel and bawdy jokes, and raucous laughter—immortalized in the cartoons of James Gillray (1756–1815) and Thomas Rowlandson (1756–1827). Common language for bodily functions was uninhibitedly "Anglo-Saxon." The English laughed a lot, noted one foreign visitor, who took it as a sign of their liberty; even the House of Commons was sometimes convulsed with laughter.[27] Far from dying out under the onslaught of politeness, this non-polite culture developed new forms. There was a vogue for grossly scurrilous and erotic prints. Commercialized sports such as racing and boxing were regarded as quintessentially English. Fox-hunting became increasingly important in rural social life. Military service during the great wars against France—which at their culmination involved one man in six in uniform—encouraged a strongly masculine patriotic culture, scorning the "effeminacy" of politeness, French-style "foppishness," and the post-1740s cult of "sensibility," which embodied a very different idea of Englishness as soulful and romantic.

Polite society was one in which women, despite discrimination, mockery and sometimes brutality, could play a far more prominent public role than in other times and places, and women were important supporters and exponents of polite culture. Whereas in Italy and France upper-class women enjoyed certain freedoms and performed particular functions (most famously as French *salon* hostesses), in England women were more independently active in social and cultural life—so at least was the usually shocked opinion of foreign visitors. English ladies walked about unveiled and unchaperoned to visit friends, the theatre and coffee houses.[28] A few went much further. Aphra Behn (1640–89), a royalist and former secret agent, was a leading playwright and pioneer novelist, and one of the first professional women writers. Her popular *Oroonoko; or, the Royal Slave* (1688) was the story of a heroic African prince tortured to death by English slave-owners, and is often interpreted, among other things, as a royalist allegory. Mary Astell (1666–1731) was a redoubtable political philosopher, Tory polemicist and proto-feminist. Lady Mary Wortley Montagu (1689–1762) was famous for her travels, her wit, and for introducing vaccination, which she had observed in Turkey; and her posthumous letters showed her to be unusually open-minded. The "Blue Stocking" circle, an informal intellectual association led by women, began meeting in the 1750s. English women even took part in sports, and a few ascribed to masculine-style libertinism. A widely read French travel writer, the Abbé Le Blanc, was censorious:

> Our women who love the perfume of amber are little like the women of this country, who relish the scent of the stable . . . It is more graceful for women to speak of hairstyles and ribbons, the play and the opera, than of saddles and horses . . . She who has not the timidity of her sex more often replaces it by vice than by virtue.[29]

Women readers and writers helped to create the most characteristic literary form of the period, the novel, a new word for a new thing. There had been a long gap in popular prose fiction since Malory's *Morte Darthur*. What now appeared was writing about the present, focusing not on mythical heroes, but on fairly ordinary people. An important source was the Puritan practice of self-scrutiny and also the use of stories as parables, of which John Bunyan's *The Pilgrim's Progress* (1678–84), combining biblical and English visions, is the enduring masterpiece. Bunyan, a Cromwellian soldier and born-again Independent, was gaoled for illegal preaching under the Restoration, and there was clearly wish-fulfilment in his writings. *Pilgrim's Progress* ends with the godly triumphing after many tribulations, and his *Holy War* (1682) has sinners being hanged and crucified. He might be considered the godfather of the English novel, and the prolific Aphra Behn its godmother. But the most probable father was Daniel Defoe, over-ambitious businessman, political agent and spy. The novel as a fully formed genre seems to have appeared at his first attempt, at the age of fifty-nine, in *Robinson Crusoe* (1719). It is one of the most widely and enduringly successful books ever written, immediately translated and imitated across Europe. Defoe had perfected direct prose and vigorous narrative through years of journalism and pamphleteering—more than 300 titles earned him national celebrity and spells in gaol and the pillory. It was a defining parable of a new age: an ordinary man is cast adrift into a new world, and despite fear and loneliness masters it by reason, experiment and self-improvement, discovering God, himself and his fellow man. *Moll Flanders* (1722) is Defoe's fictional autobiography of a woman who, after years of vice, danger and crime, repents and ends contented—and prosperous. Defoe may have intended to write an exposé of the criminal underworld, but he also created an indomitable character, who belied the idea of helpless and submissive womanhood.

Novels worked through the individual imagination of author and reader, who chose when, where and how to read, whether silently and alone or aloud with family or friends. They created intimate quasi-knowledge of characters and situations, encouraging introspection and an interest in individual personality. Reading meant prolonged involvement, as eighteenth-century novels could be very long. They thus gave an unprecedented means of getting inside readers' heads—the reason why they were so often deplored, especially for their supposed influence on young women. For the first time, women authors were shaping public manners and morals. A hundred years after Aphra Behn, nearly all the most popular and prolific English novelists were women, including the most prolific of all, Elizabeth Meeke[30]—though those we now remember were mostly men. Many of the most significant fictional characters too were women, including those imagined by men: Moll Flanders (1722), Pamela Andrews (1740), Clarissa Harlowe (1748), Sophie Western (1749), even Fanny Hill (1749).

Many early novels took the form of letters, reflecting what seems to have been a genuinely popular craze for letter-writing, made possible by new, efficient and fairly cheap postal services—the London Penny Post made up to ten deliveries a day from the 1680s, and a national postal service grew from the 1720s. Ordinary people took increasing pride in learning to write with "Boldness and Freedom," seen as an English prerogative, epitomized by a simple "Round Hand" and increasingly informal style. Letters, for women and men, maintained family and social links in an increasingly mobile society, and more generally were a way of developing thoughts and communicating ideas.[31]

Another channel of self-examination and communication, where again women were prominent, was religious revival, equally a process of introspection, but combined with a compulsion to share and tell following the life-changing drama of conversion. This evangelicalism recalls the godliness of earlier generations, but it differed profoundly from Puritanism by rejecting Calvinist ideas of a small elect surrounded by the multitude of the damned, and by the fact that it was far less antagonistic to the Church of England. Hence, although it became a cultural revolution, its political and social radicalism was far less evident than a century earlier.[32]

The most important revivalist movement can be traced to Oxford undergraduates in the 1730s. Two of them, John Wesley and George Whitefield, proved to be communicators and organizers of genius, adept at using modern media—cheap print, popular magazines and music. Wesley was to edit or write more works than any other individual in eighteenth-century England. Influenced by Locke's philosophy of the mind, they developed a practical "method" of piety—hence Methodism—which respected rationality and refused authoritarianism. It thus grew out of aspects of Enlightenment and benefited from greater religious freedom. Methodism was to become not only national, but worldwide—"the most important Protestant religious development since the Reformation."[33] It grew within the Church, especially where the parish system was failing to cope with rapid change and dislocation: in remote rural areas in the north of England and Wales, among artisans in growing industrial towns, and in the colonies. Hence the importance of travelling preachers and open-air sermons and services. People on the move or in dangerous occupations where they depended on each other were strongly attracted, including miners, colonial slaves, sailors and soldiers—indeed soldiers did much to spread Methodism across the empire. Yet overall it became predominantly a women's movement—roughly three women to every two men.[34] It gave an important role to ordinary women and men as lay preachers and organizers. Its sociable practices of singing, "love feasts," "camp meetings" and "classes" (regular small meetings in people's houses) created social identity and powerful solidarities. Singing was the core of community worship and emotion. The Wesley brothers, John and Charles, produced some thirty hymn books, the first ever in the Church of England. They wrote many of the hymns ("Hark the Herald Angels Sing," "Gentle Jesus Meek and Mild" . . .), which embedded themselves in popular culture. Tunes were taken from many sources, including Handel, Purcell and folk tunes. Hymn-singing permanently affected English and American musical culture.

There was no attempt to suppress the movement, but the first generation of Methodists in the 1740s and 1750s met hostility from the authorities and the public. An erudite Archbishop of York told John Wesley that he would be better employed teaching "the morality of Socrates . . . than canting about the new birth."[35] Methodism was suspected of being another sectarian attempt to disrupt social and political harmony, break up families, contest masculine authority, stop traditional pastimes or alternatively to indulge in sexual licence under the guise of religious "enthusiasm"— new Ranters indulging in "weeping, roaring and agonies." Preachers were roughed up and humiliated, though rarely seriously hurt. But Methodists were not new Levellers: the importance of Methodism was that it was simultaneously subversive and conservative, a dynamic Revivalist movement but also a teacher of respectability, obedience and sobriety—in short, politeness.[36]

## NATURE AND IMPROVEMENT

Enlightenment thinkers aspired not only to understand the world but to improve it. This was an age away from the Calvinist belief, dominant half a century before, that God or the Devil controlled every event. Hobbes in the 1640s still spent part of *Leviathan* assuring readers that they need not fear fairies, ghosts, goblins and witches. Such fears declined gradually.[37] The last death sentence for witchcraft in England was in 1712—and Queen Anne pardoned her. A new optimism about the natural world saw it not as decayed, corrupted by sin, and nearing its providential end, with the Earth a "little dirty planet" to which mankind was condemned for the sin of Adam,[38] but instead as benign and beautiful.

There was therefore a new emotional and moral response to "nature" (a word whose modern sense dates from this time). Lord Shaftesbury proclaimed that "the wildness pleases." Nature poetry, influenced by classical models, especially James Thomson's *The Seasons* (1726), had a great vogue, and reached a literary and spiritual peak with Wordsworth in the next century. This new vision of nature has been called "the major English contribution to European aesthetics."[39] A pioneer was the innovative writer and architect Sir John Vanbrugh (1664–1726), who when building Blenheim Palace wanted to preserve ancient Woodstock Manor because it made a good "Landskip"—though the insensitive Duchess of Marlborough had it pulled down. A taste for paintings that embodied a "picturesque" ideal made the nostalgic Arcadian landscapes of the French painter Claude (1600–1682) a passion of wealthy English collectors. Paintings of picturesque real landscapes in Italy, of newly explored Pacific islands, and also of England itself became popular later in the century. The English "landskip" was pioneered by artists such as Paul Sandby and Richard Wilson in mid-century and reached its apogee in the early nineteenth century, the age of Turner and Constable. The latter, while regretting never having seen Italy, the inspiration of Claude, consoled himself that he "was born to paint a happier land, my own dear old England."[40] Although influenced by classical ideas, and by earlier French, Dutch, Italian and even Chinese art, landscape came to be considered a characteristically English genre. Watercolours became a polite accomplishment of ladies and gentlemen on their travels; and in the later hands of such as Richard Parkes Bonnington and J. M. W. Turner their flexibility enabled them to become an innovative medium for landscape painting in the spontaneous Romantic style.

The people of this rational age (unlike their Romantic successors) could not leave "nature" alone: they wanted to improve it, as with human society. They invented the "English garden," idealized nature in a small space, defined as "picturesque"—"that peculiar kind of beauty, which is agreeable in a picture."[41] Gardens were carefully planned to seem unplanned, and were thought to express English values such as freedom and simplicity. This period saw the birth of the English craze for visiting stately homes and gardens. Garden designers became rich and famous. William Kent, a Yorkshire apprentice who in the 1730s and 1740s became an all-purpose architect and designer, was considered the father of modern gardening, the exponent, according to Horace Walpole, of "an art that realizes painting and improves nature."[42] Lancelot "Capability" Brown (1716–83), a Northumbrian gardener, found fame and fortune in developing an opulent parkland style at Kew, Warwick, Blenheim, Chatsworth and many other prestigious locations. Humphrey Repton later developed a somewhat more ornamental style, as at Longleat and Woburn. "English gardens" were copied from Versailles to Vienna, from Rome to St. Petersburg. Sheep were put to graze picturesquely in the fashionable Crescent at Bath. Common and uncultivated lands—heaths, moors, marshes—were enclosed and improved. The English lowland landscape began to take its modern form as a huge garden, hedged, manured and commercialized. Here were Enlightenment principles in practice: the harmonization of man and nature, hierarchically organized as gentry estates and tenant farms, respectfully admired by foreign visitors awed by the wealth thus created. Even today, it can have a humane beauty that we feel to be "typically English."

Exploration now became not merely a commercial rampage, as in the days of Drake and Hawkins, but also a philosophical and aesthetic pilgrimage: it encountered natural peoples uncorrupted by civilization. Even cannibalism, Robinson Crusoe reflected, could not necessarily be condemned: "It is not against their own Consciences . . . How do I know what God himself judges?" Commissioning a voyage of exploration in 1768, the President of the Royal Society urged Captain James Cook to similar "patience and forbearance" towards native peoples who were "the natural [and] legal possessors . . . the work of the same omnipotent Author," and perhaps more "entitled to his favour" than "the most polished European."[43] Reports of Polynesian sexual freedom fascinated and titillated polite Europe—though John Wesley refused to believe them.[44] The Tahitian prince Omai, brought on a visit in 1774, was presented at court, given a royal pension, taken to see a parliamentary debate, and magnificently painted by Sir Joshua Reynolds. But, however respectful and admiring of "nature" Europeans might think themselves, they brought new diseases, unknowingly envenomed local power struggles, and infringed religious rules. When Cook was killed in a clash with Hawaiians in February 1779, it was shocking proof that contact between even the most Enlightened Europeans and "noble savages" was no idyll. Yet Cook had answered the big remaining questions about the southern hemisphere. For the first time in history, said one of his officers, "the Grand Bounds of the four Quarters of the Globe are known."[45]

There was a new optimism that reason could also discover the processes by which society advanced—"improvement" became a watchword, negating old ideas that humanity had declined from some remote golden age. What David Hume called the "science of man" could involve turning seventeenth-century vices—self-interest, acquisitiveness and pleasure-seeking—into eighteenth-century virtues. The Dutch-born Bernard Mandeville, satirizing Shaftesbury's idealism, wrote a scandalous *Fable of the Bees; or, Private Vices, Public Benefits* (1714), in which the hive prospered because of the ambition, greed and even dishonesty of its occupants:

> Thus every part was full of Vice,
> Yet the whole Mass a Paradise.[46]

Mandeville outraged moralists. Yet there was a growing tendency to recognize material gain as legitimate, and individual happiness and pleasure as proper objects of life.

Pleasure came into its own in the eighteenth century.[47] Religious toleration permitted greater variation in matters of personal morality, including sex. This was not straightforward: Dissenters demanded liberty for their beliefs, but these same beliefs generally involved sexual repression. John Locke, for example, did not see freedom of conscience extending to "adultery, fornication, uncleanness, lasciviousness [and] other such heinous enormities."[48] Nevertheless, Enlightenment turned gradually away from the body-hating asceticism that had been part of the Western tradition (at least in theory) since St. Augustine, and which the Puritans had taken to extremes, as in John Bunyan's tortured vision in which "Lord Lechery," "Mrs. Filth" and "Sir Having Greedy" contended with "Mr. Contrite" and "Mr. Penitent." Such attitudes now seemed—as Adam Smith put it— "disagreeably rigorous and unsocial."

The century and a half after the Restoration was a time of sexual "libertinism," at least for some. Libertines asserted that sexual indulgence was an irresistible natural need, and that women (commonly thought to have more powerful appetites than men) were equal partners in pleasure. Some even advocated homosexual freedom, though "buggery" was a capital offence. Sex became a theme in art, literature and even actual conduct to a degree unusual in historical terms, and comparable with our own day. This marked a new phase in Western culture.[49] Libertinism seems to have stemmed from Cavalier rejection of Puritanism both before and after the Restoration. It produced countervailing efforts to tame and repress natural instincts in the name of religion, politeness, "improvement," "reformation of manners" and public order. This struggle and its consequences— including frustration, concealment, "double standards" of male and female conduct, and clashes of elite and plebeian licence versus middle-class restraint—was a recurring subject of controversy. Adam Smith, for example, considered it inevitable that there should be "a 'strict' code for the common people and a 'loose' one for people of fashion."[50]

On the side of morality were Hogarth's great satirical paintings, such as *The Rake's Progress* and *Marriage à la Mode* (widely distributed as prints), and "sentimental" novels, such as Samuel Richardson's 1740s best-sellers *Pamela* and *Clarissa*. But other widely read novels, such as those of Henry Fielding and Tobias Smollet, were far more tolerant of what they regarded as (mostly male) human frailty, though they condemned cynical and vicious libertinism. Discreet or clandestine pornography in literature and art appeared on a significant scale for the first time. Some courtesans became celebrities, painted by leading artists. This has been seen as marking a sexual revolution: the end of the age-old consensus over sexual morality (accepted even when disobeyed), and the beginning of modern uncertainty about what was moral, permissible and natural.[51]

Commerce seemed the way to create a polite society in which the destructive characteristics of both Cavalier and Roundhead would become obsolete. As Samuel Johnson joked, man is rarely so innocently employed as in making money. The young French writer Voltaire praised the London Stock Exchange in the 1720s because men of all religions traded there peacefully; but his compatriot and fellow philosopher Baron de Montesquieu thought that in England "money is more important than honour or virtue and the people are coarse, unsociable and, worst of all, corrupt."[52] The great philosophers of the Scottish Enlightenment, so influential in England, saw balancing benefits. David Hume declared that "luxury when it is excessive, is the source of many ills, but it is in general preferable to sloth and idleness, which . . . are more hurtful both to private persons and to the public." What Hume termed "industry and the mechanical arts" made people more sociable: they "flock into cities . . . clubs and societies are every where formed . . . the tempers of men, as well as their behaviour, refine apace."[53] When Adam Smith turned Mandeville's cynicism into serious political economy in *An Inquiry into the Nature and Causes of the Wealth of Nations* (1776), the Enlightenment developed the nearest it got to a "science of man"—certainly that with the most durable influence. Smith believed that commerce promoted civilization, freedom, cooperation and equality: "The difference of natural talents in different men is, in reality, much less than we are aware of . . . a philosopher is not in genius and disposition half so different from a street porter, as a mastiff is from a greyhound."[54]

## COFFEE HOUSE CULTURE

*I have brought Philosophy out of the closets and libraries, schools and colleges, to dwell in clubs and assemblies, at tea-tables and in coffee-houses.*

Joseph Addison, *The Spectator*, 1711[55]

Both philosophy and less earnest kinds of literature did indeed come out of the closet and into the market place. Between 1660 and 1800, over 300,000 books were published in England, perhaps 200 million copies in all. They included best-sellers even by modern standards: Defoe's uninhibited verse satire *True-Born Englishman* sold some 80,000 copies.[56] England was wealthy and literate with many endowed schools even in rural areas teaching reading and writing free of charge.[57] Perhaps 10 percent of the population of London were significant consumers of culture.[58] With the end of press controls in 1695 (see p. 284) entrepreneurs and authors laboured to meet the demand. Access to books widened—circulating libraries were created, book clubs were set up, and book prices fell—permitting extensive reading of many works, instead of communally reading and perhaps learning by heart a cherished few. Yet the cherished few did not disappear: for many families their core reading was the Bible (selling perhaps 30,000 copies per year throughout the century) and some 50,000 other religious works, among the most popular being *Pilgrim's Progress*.[59] But now a farming or artisan household could buy or borrow a wider range of books for pleasure—"Tom Jones, Roderick Random, and other entertaining books, stuck up on their bacon racks." Reading became a source of pleasure, prestige and empowerment. Letters written in the 1740s by a Derbyshire wheelwright's apprentice, Leonard Wheatcroft, to his sweetheart, Elizabeth, a servant, were full of references to Shakespeare, Milton, Addison and Swift.[60] A mid-century Sussex grocer and parish officer, Thomas Turner, owned more than seventy books and periodicals, including works by Locke, Addison, Sterne, the nature poet Edward Young, Shakespeare and Milton; and he was reading several new books a year. He read sermons to his friends, and studied Locke in his shop between customers. Cheap editions appeared, of which the Methodists were great pioneers: John Wesley produced an abridged *Pilgrim's Progress* as a fourpenny booklet in 1743, and similarly abridged *Paradise Lost* and modern poetry for a mass readership.[61] Voluminous works—Johnson's *Dictionary* and Tobias Smollett's *History of England*—were sold cheaply by instalments. A wealthy reader could regard books as disposable. Lord Chesterfield advised his son to take a few torn-off pages of Latin poetry to the lavatory to read before putting them to practical use—"It will make any book you read in that manner very present in your mind."[62]

Newspapers and magazines boomed. The first successful London daily, the *Courant*, began in 1702, and soon there were about twenty papers, selling in all some 25,000 copies a week. The same happened in the provinces, led by the *Norwich Post* (1701). By mid-century thirty-five provincial papers were selling 200,000 copies a week, and many had larger circulations than the main papers in Continental capitals. Hundreds of towns had their own printers and booksellers, and the numbers were rising rapidly. It was commented in the 1770s that "this country is as much news-mad and news-driven as ever it was popery-mad and priest-ridden."[63] Magazines—the *Spectator*, the *Tatler* and the *Gentleman's Magazine*— were soon followed by a variety of more or less earnest (*The Free-Thinker*) and amusing (*Covent-Garden Journal*) emulators. The first magazine written by and for women, the *Female Spectator*, appeared in 1744.

For authors, dependence on royal or noble patrons gave way to a gamble on the market—another form of servitude, but a less demeaning one. Samuel Johnson, who famously described a patron as "one who looks with unconcern on a man struggling for life in the water, and, when he has reached ground, encumbers him with help," preferred to take his chances: "The World always lets a man tell what he thinks, in his own way."[64] His *Dictionary of the English Language* (1755) is a good example, for its production was financed by booksellers, who put up the equivalent of several million pounds in today's values.

This mix of commerce and culture produced what has been termed "the public sphere"—places and institutions for exchanging information and forming opinion, which lay between the purely private world and the official realm. Some were commercial establishments, such as the new and fashionable coffee houses, the first of which date from the middle of the seventeenth century. Over the eighteenth century some 130 types of society were spawned in the British Isles, totalling some 25,000 clubs in the English-speaking world.[65] Freemasonry spread rapidly from Britain to the Continent and the colonies. There were notoriously libertine groups such as the "Hellfire Club," businesslike agricultural improvement societies, or just informal groups of friends, including an "Ugly Club" for the ill-favoured. Debating, literary, philosophical and scientific societies multiplied, among them the Newcastle Literary and Philosophical Society; the Lunar Society, based in Lichfield and Birmingham, which included Erasmus Darwin, Josiah Wedgwood, the engineers James Watt and Matthew Boulton, and the Unitarian scientist Joseph Priestley; and Samuel Johnson's Literary Club. Such societies and their members participated in what came to be called "the republic of letters," crossing social, religious and national boundaries by reading, exchanging letters and visiting.

Samuel Johnson (1709–84) seems an archetypal figure of this world, yet at the same time a very unusual one: provincial, plebeian, ungainly, poor, politically unfashionable (a Whig-hating Tory with Jacobite sympathies), devoutly Anglican, respectful of rank yet notably undeferential— indeed often rude. Like others of similar views, he became a supporter of George III, and could be a pungent political pamphleteer, especially at the time of the 1760s and 1770s agitation of "Patriotism" ("the last refuge of a scoundrel"[66]) and the American rebellion. He stamped his mark on literary history by pure intellectual force and hard work, and also through the intimate biography written by his young friend and hanger-on James Boswell, published in 1791. A poor boy from Lichfield who had failed as a schoolteacher, Johnson went to London in 1737 to make a living by journalism, literary criticism, poetry and the theatre; but he always had to struggle against physical infirmities, periodic depression and a considerable degree of eccentricity. His life showed that talent could break through in eighteenth-century society—he acquired admiring supporters and a royal pension, and George III asked to meet him. But success in Grub Street was always precarious. As he himself said, "No man, however high he may now stand, can be certain that he shall not soon be thrown down from his elevation by criticism or caprice."[67]

Despite or perhaps because of adverse circumstances (including several arrests for debt), he was a literary pioneer and the author of works of astounding variety, from Latin poetry to travel writing. His *Dictionary* was the first to give examples (drawn from "polite writers") of the varying usages of words, and it remained the authoritative dictionary for more than a century. It showed language not as a static system, regulated by an official academy, but as created and changed by usage. He produced the first comprehensive scholarly edition of Shakespeare (1765), and a controversial *Lives of the English Poets* (1779–81), covering fifty-two authors, both landmarks in English literary criticism. Denied the security in domestic life he craved, he rooted himself in literary London society—famously declaring that anyone who tired of London was tired of life[68]—and this included meetings to eat and talk in London taverns, such as the Crown and Anchor in the Strand and the Turk's Head in Soho, with friends in his "Literary Club." This eventually (not entirely to Johnson's liking) expanded to become an unofficial British academy, whose thirty-five members were an unequalled galaxy of talent, including the painter Sir Joshua Reynolds, the actor David Garrick, the playwrights Oliver Goldsmith and Richard Brinsley Sheridan, the philosopher Adam Smith, the historian Edward Gibbon, the orientalist Sir William Jones, the naturalist Sir Joseph Banks, and the politicians Charles James Fox and Edmund Burke. Johnson's career and his circle can be seen as part of a conscious Enlightenment project to define and order knowledge, and to shape and influence emerging "public taste."[69]

Politics were affected by a comparable phenomenon now called "public opinion" with a claim to be heard. Parliament, although its debates were not published until the 1770s, was nevertheless connected with the public sphere because political discussion ran between the press, the pulpit, Parliament and any number of private clubs—"miniature free republics of rational society."[70] After 1660 English politics were uniquely open to public scrutiny and discussion, and politicians commonly directed their arguments to a large audience. Writers who overstepped the mark could still be prosecuted for seditious libel or even blasphemy—as in the case of John Wilkes (see p. 346)—but, still, matters that in other parts of Europe were state secrets (for example, public finances) were openly debated. The French philosopher Montesquieu, whose stay in London in 1731 contributed crucially to the most influential political book of the eighteenth century, *De l'esprit des lois* (1748), praised the English spirit of liberty, its toleration and (with reservations) its parliamentary system: "In Europe the last gasp of liberty would come from an Englishman."[71]

Of course, this "public" did not include everyone. Membership required a minimum of money, education and respectability. Yet its boundaries were permeable. Anyone with the price of an entry ticket could mingle with the aristocracy, even royalty—if usually at a distance. Foreign observers were startled: "Nothing is more common than to see in a tavern or café, Milords and Artisans sitting at the same table, talking familiarly about the public news and the affairs of the government."[72] Sport was equally shocking to Continental gentility: people of all degrees attended horse races, and cricket and boxing matches, and even took part. Late in the century François de La Rochefoucauld, observing modern agriculture in East Anglia, was amazed by the confidence of ordinary farmers—mere peasants!—who could talk knowledgeably about their methods, meet in clubs to exchange ideas, mix with gentlemen at fox hunts, and even spontaneously invite a duke's son like himself to lunch. Other visitors found it unsettling that in coffee houses, parks, theatres or pleasure gardens such as the famous Vauxhall and Ranelagh they could not judge status by outward appearance, and so risked encountering social inferiors.

There was some truth and some exaggeration in these observations. Politeness required affable mixing of different ranks: Steele had proclaimed that "the soul of politeness is equality"—but in practice there were limits: the well-born and fashionable did not normally hob-nob with the middle classes.[73] Masquerades—introduced from Italy and put on commercially from 1717 onwards—proved a scandalous and highly popular way of escaping convention and inhibition through disguise, which included cross-dressing and even "nudity."[74] There was a trend towards simpler dress for both sexes, influenced by fashionable ideas of "sensibility," and by notions of plain English masculinity rejecting foreign foppishness. Informal, outdoor, sporting styles became fashionable. Trends were sometimes set by the working classes, whose men, for example, first adopted "round" hats and abandoned wigs, followed by the upper classes.

Rustic straw hats became fashionable for women. Foreign visitors were disoriented: "In Paris, footmen and chambermaids often ape their masters in their dress. In London it is quite the opposite; it is the masters who dress like their servants and duchesses who copy their chambermaids—an almost inconceivable absurdity."[75] "Beau" Nash, the imperious Master of Ceremonies at Bath, refused admission in 1721 to the young Duchess of Queensberry on the grounds that her fashionably dressed-down apron was the attire of maidservants; but by the 1760s the queen herself wore one.[76] Nash more successfully forbade the wearing of swords in polite society—"a sword seen in the streets of Bath would raise as great an alarm as a mad dog"—and by 1780 this ancient mark of superiority had disappeared in England.[77] More subtle distinctions remained: "purity and politeness of Expression" were considered a mark of gentility—but, of course, this could be acquired with the help of grammar and elocution lessons.[78]

In short, social distinctions, though certainly maintained, were probably looser than on much of the Continent. "Everyone may choose his company according to his liking," wrote a German resident, who thought there was nowhere "where a man may live more according to his own mind, or even his whims, than in London." The Scot James Boswell agreed that in London "we may be in some degree whatever character we choose"[79]—a freedom he exercised with gusto.

The English public were highly interested in European peoples, their politics, and the ways their societies were affected by religious differences. Travel books were often critical of superstition ("mummery") and poverty in Catholic Europe ("Canvas Cloathes, Wooden Shoes and Straw to sleep"). They displayed a sense of solidarity with Protestant countries at times of danger from Catholic powers such as France, but they were not entirely uncritical of Protestants—particularly the "avaricious" Dutch when Holland was a national rival.[80] They tended to praise compromise and showed interest in how different religions coexisted. Those who could went to see for themselves. "It is certain that the English are the people of Europe who travel the most," declared a French writer in 1751. "Their island is for them a sort of prison."[81] The end of every war saw a rush to the Continent. Calais had hotels catering for British tourists, most famously the Hôtel d'Angleterre (with its own theatre and carriage hire), said to be the finest in Europe. The number of travellers increased: there may have been around 12,000 people visiting the Continent in the late 1760s, rising to over 40,000 in the mid-1780s. Many were young gentlemen, dispatched before or after university on a Grand Tour, usually through France to Italy, aiming to make useful contacts and acquire taste and good manners. "You are not sent abroad to converse with your own country-men," the Earl of Chesterfield told his son; "among them, in general, you will get little knowledge, no languages, and I am sure, no manners . . . Their pleasures of the table end in beastly drunkenness, low riot, broken win-dows, and very often (as they well deserve) broken bones."[82]

Foreign travel required money and some determination. "The multi-tudes of English in this country has [sic] made travelling as dear as in England."[83] Fleas and bedbugs, stomach upsets and road accidents were endemic. Books about travelling were a popular substitute for those who preferred to take their thrills vicariously. The published adventures of global travellers such as Bougainville and Cook made them national and European celebrities. Those who made the effort to cross the Channel themselves were relatively varied, from grandees to families of "the mid-dling sort" hungry for a taste of sophistication. English women were uniquely free to travel abroad. Hester Thrale, wife of a wealthy brewer, wrote that her family had "spent a Month [in Paris] of extreme Expence, some Pleasure and some Profit; for we have seen many People & many Things; and Queeny [her daughter] has picked up a little French & a good deal of Dancing."[84] Even the fun had a serious purpose: acquiring a cos-mopolitan sheen.

Cultural life was deeply influenced by the Continent. Many travellers brought back classical statuary (often fake) and portraits of themselves. The more studious and wealthy were a significant channel for importing artistic and architectural styles, mainly from Italy. Among the most influ-ential were the 3rd Earl of Burlington (d. 1753), collector, patron, archi-tect and energetic proselytizer for the classical Roman style; and the Society of Dilettanti, established in 1734 (famously dismissed by the ele-gant aesthete Horace Walpole as a club for which "the nominal qualifica-tion . . . is having been in Italy, and the real one, being drunk"[85]) but which nevertheless encouraged and even practised classical archaeology, created private and public collections, and contributed significantly to the British Museum (1759) and eventually the National Gallery (1824). The Latin and Greek classics retained the crowning intellectual prestige they had enjoyed for more than two centuries. The theatre staged or plagia-rized French drama and comedy, and the works of Molière and Voltaire were London staples.[86] The musical scene, after the death of Purcell in 1695, became increasingly cosmopolitan, without a lavish royal court to promote national styles, unlike in France. Thomas Arne (1710–78) was a considerable English figure, but musical fashions came increasingly from France, Italy and Germany. Handel from 1710 and later Johann Christian Bach ("the London Bach") were established in England, and at the end of the century Josef Haydn was a feted and highly paid visitor. These were European celebrities who practised an international style.

There was some reaction against European influence. William Hogarth complained in a letter to the press (signed "Britophil") about "foreign interlopers," and he tried to establish an English school of painting. Johnson's *Dictionary* was in part intended to rein in the "Gallick Structure and phraseology" fashionable among the elite.[87] He and the actor David Garrick, two friends from the same small town, Lichfield, promoted Shakespeare as the great national genius. At Stratford, Garrick organized an uproarious rain-soaked Shakespeare Jubilee in 1769, marking the birth of Bardolatry.[88] All had partial success, but fashionable England remained determinedly cosmopolitan—Horace Walpole "blushed" at Garrick's "insufferable nonsense about Shakespeare."[89]

## IMAGINING ENGLISHNESS

Novels, plays, poetry, songs, paintings and prints were powerful vehicles of ideas about Englishness. Characters and stories presented a range of models. Allegorical and moral themes were often pointed up by the names of characters: Allworthy, Random, Lovelace. In the late seventeenth century and early eighteenth, there were still echoes of the Civil War and the struggles of the Restoration, and Bunyan and Behn both created sometimes nightmarish visions of violence and revenge. A popular theme, whose first authors were ex-Cavaliers, features rogues and outsiders, particularly highwaymen, who wage war against the wealthy possessors, including the Roundhead leaders themselves—Oliver Cromwell and General Fairfax are portrayed as being robbed by gallant highwaymen, and in one story Fairfax's wife is raped.[90] The highwayman tale, modernizing the Robin Hood theme, became enduringly popular: Dick Turpin might be seen as the counterpart of Bunyan's Christian. These tales glorified Cavalier bravado, even to the foot of the Tyburn gallows. The crime story, one of the mainstays of Western literature, was conceived amid the political conflict and corruption of the late seventeenth century and the early eighteenth.

Two other typical story lines are the journey and the courtship, the latter a characteristic of the English novel—understandable in a society in which, unlike in much of Europe, marriages were not wholly arranged. Both story lines have some of the characteristics of a pilgrimage, with suffering and self-discovery leading to redemption and contentment. The Old Testament book of Job—in which God permits a righteous man to suffer before final vindication—provided a template for many authors, including Defoe. Samuel Richardson, a prosperous printer and the son of a Derby joiner, invented, aged fifty-one, the "sentimental" novel, which became an international craze. His *Pamela* (1740) and *Clarissa* (1747–48) were translated and copied across Europe. The Genevan Jean-Jacques Rousseau, perhaps the most influential European thinker of the century, wrote that "no one has ever written in any language a novel that equals or even approaches" *Clarissa*. "O Richardson!" exclaimed the French critic Diderot, "were I forced to sell all my books, you would remain to me on the same shelf as Moses, Homer, Euripides and Sophocles."[91] *Pamela* and *Clarissa* are explicitly Job-like stories of tormented but unconquerable female virtue, reflecting the increasingly accepted polite belief that women were superior to men in morality and conduct—a belief that has persisted to the present day. Both women personify puritanical godliness; their male would-be lovers are Cavalier rakes. Pamela reforms her admirer by her invincible chastity, and he marries her. But in *Clarissa* the heroine is drugged and raped by her obsessed admirer amid some 1,400 pages of tensely repressed eroticism which ends in the death of both main characters. "I heartily despise [Richardson] and eagerly read him, nay, sob over his works in a most scandalous manner," admitted Lady Mary Wortley Montagu.[92]

Usually, however, reconciliation, not tragedy, is the outcome of the novel: the journey reaches a destination; the courtship ends in happiness, or at least in marriage. Reconciliation and restoration of order are recurring patterns in English story-telling: Robin Hood is really the Earl of Huntingdon; Richard the Lionheart returns to claim his own; Dick Whittington becomes Lord Mayor of London; Tom Jones wins Sophie Western; Miss Elizabeth Bennet becomes Mrs. Fitzwilliam Darcy. And all live happily ever after.

The marriage of Tom and Sophie ends the most genial eighteenth-century combination of both the travel and courtship stories, *The History of Tom Jones, a Foundling* (1749), by Henry Fielding, playwright, journalist, lawyer, novelist and magistrate. The contrast between the roistering Tory, Squire Western, and the puritanical Whig, Mr. Allworthy, plays on both the political divide and the conflict of libertine and polite culture, between which Tom is disastrously torn. Conflict is resolved—amid mistaken identities, dastardly machinations, a duel, imprisonment, seeming incest, numerous seductions (including by a masterful woman) and even a Jacobite rebellion—by the redeeming love of Sophia. Tom abandons his libertine ways and harmony triumphs in the new polite and sentimental generation indifferent to the quarrels of the past. Half a century later, the courtship theme in the hands of its greatest exponent, Jane Austen, had moved on to include other issues: not the legacy of the seventeenth-century divide, but new problems of class and status (pride and prejudice) and the transition from rationalist to romantic values (sense and sensibility).

The eighteenth century coined the phrase "national character." David Hume defined it as "a peculiar set of manners" made "habitual [by] the nature of the government, the revolutions of public affairs, the plenty or penury in which the people live, the situation of the nation with regard to its neighbours, and such like circumstances."[93] Such "character" was reflected in songs, poems, fictional characters and images, of which one of the earliest is John Bull, invented by the Scot John Arbuthnot in 1712. Yet Hume believed that the English "of any people in the universe [had] the least of a national character; unless this very singularity may pass for such." He ascribed this to their "liberty and independency," which encouraged individuality, not uniformity.[94]

Defoe, who repeatedly brought up the question of nationality in his works, also thought the English "heterogeneous," but for less flattering reasons. In his sarcastic poem attacking critics of the Glorious Revolution, *The True-Born Englishman* (1701), he declared that the English, "a mongrel half-bred race," had inherited the worst elements of successive conquerors and immigrants:

> From this amphibious ill-born mob began
> That vain ill-natured thing, an Englishman . . .
> We have been Europe's sink, the jakes where she
> Voids all her offal out-cast progeny.[95]

Defoe's most famous characters, Robinson Crusoe and Moll Flanders, are contradictory half-outsiders, rootless semi-rogues but also vestigial Puritans, undergoing a Job-like ordeal. They represented a modern "mongrel" England of movement, the world's melting pot. Fielding, on the other hand—the author of the light-hearted patriotic song "Roast Beef of Old England," to a tune by Purcell—portrayed in *Tom Jones* a different England, sturdy, pluralistic and basically benevolent, where marriage brings a return to order: "There is not a neighbour, a tenant or a servant, who doth not gratefully bless the day."[96] Expressed in literature and imagery, this Arcadian vision of the permanence of rural England was beguiling as the country entered a traumatic period of change.

# CHAPTER 8

# A Free Country?

*England is at present the country in the world where there is the*
*greatest freedom. I do not make an exception for any republic.*

Baron de Montesquieu, 1748[1]

From a safe distance, the Glorious Revolution seems a turning point, the beginning of a calmer political world. But it did not take away memories of past violence, or fear of conflict: "The Fire of Contention, for at least an hundred Years, hath sometimes been kept smothering in, and sometimes Vesuvius like hath burst out."[2] To an already perilous domestic crisis, 1688 added new political and ideological complications and kindled foreign and civil war. England and its sister kingdoms now had rival claimants to the throne, each holding a different religion—neither of which was that of most Englishmen. On top of that, England found itself involved in the Dutch war against Louis XIV, who hit back by trying to ignite another British civil war in Ireland and Scotland (see p. 335).

While England's immediate future was being decided by European armies in Ireland, where James and William were fighting it out, its political elite was tying itself into ideological knots. Many who had welcomed William's intervention found his accession to the throne deeply troubling, for it flouted the principle of divinely sanctioned hereditary monarchy. Archbishop Sancroft, arrested by James II for resisting royal authority, now refused to crown William and Mary or swear an oath of allegiance to them, and, along with seven bishops and 400 lower clergy, was deprived of office in 1690. It is hard to imagine his medieval predecessors getting into such a pickle about deposing a monarch, but the Reformation had raised the status of the king to sacred levels. The Church had become the arch-defender of the Divine Right of the Stuarts. In principle all Tories agreed.

A Tory, as defined by Johnson's *Dictionary*, was "One who adheres to the antient constitution of the State, and the apostolic hierarchy of the church of England." Tories were reluctant to accept that Parliament, or the people, or armed force could impose and dismiss monarchs as they wished—the "king-killing" doctrine of the hated Roundheads. Worse still: though Charles had been beheaded, his son had eventually succeeded him; whereas James and his son were still alive and had simply been replaced. Did this mean the end of legitimate government and the rule of law? Whigs—political descendants of the Roundheads and sympathizers with "the Good Old Cause" of resistance to the Stuarts—were unambiguous supporters of the Glorious Revolution. The party division was to some extent bridged by fudging. Whigs, if they wished, could maintain that the people had dismissed James II because he had broken his contract. Tories could believe that it was an act of Divine Providence, or a legal hereditary succession on the grounds that James's son was an imposter (the "warming pan" story), or that James had abdicated, or bluntly that William was the conqueror who commanded obedience. To us, this may seem to be splitting hairs: but every political culture, including our own, needs its legitimizing myths.

Whigs were more sympathetic to Dissent and more suspicious of "popery." A later Whig intellectual, Joseph Priestley, remarked with satisfaction in 1772 that there was "so much of the old Puritanic spirit among us."[3] Whigs within the Church tended to be "Latitudinarians," and after 1688 they were appointed to many of its bishoprics. So religious differences mirrored secular rivalries. Both parties tried to use religion for political ends, and were denounced by their opponents for doing so.[4] Party division was embittered by memories of the Civil War and fears that Whig rule might lead to another republican despotism.[5] Whigs and Tories were evenly balanced within the elite, but Tories had greater support among the people. The majority of Englishmen clung to the stability embodied by monarchy, and took its religious character more seriously than did the new king himself—a Calvinist, not an Anglican, who described his coronation to a Dutch friend as "funny old Popish rites."

The Whig-Tory conflict, often called "the rage of party," rapidly became institutionalized. MPs and peers followed party lines. Pre-session meetings in pubs and coffee houses agreed tactics and policies, and the Whigs used Newmarket races for primitive party conferences. Party politics spread to counties and boroughs. News and propaganda circulated through coffee houses, pubs, churches and chapels. Parties clashed too over religion, or, more precisely, over the relationship between religion, state and society: politics was a branch of theology[6] rather as twenty-first-century politics is a branch of economics. Then, as now, more was involved than purely intellectual issues: interests, identities, traditions, memories and ramifying social consequences stemmed from different opinions on the nature of the Godhead or the functions of the Church, as from different opinions on the role of the market or the management of the National Health Service. In brief, devout Anglicans were likely to be Tory; Dissenters and Latitudinarians were likely to be Whigs.

The Church of England—to which 90 percent of the nation belonged—was a great political issue because it was so central to everyday life. Much of the cultural and administrative activity of communities passed through its hands, from feeding the poor to repairing the roads and punishing delinquents, and from scholarship in schools and the two universities to musical culture in the Three Choirs Festival (inaugurated in 1715). Even Vauxhall Pleasure Gardens, seeking to improve their raffish reputation, engaged two clergymen "who . . . are by their holy looks to keep decorum."[7] Anglicanism inculcated domestic peace and unity, deference, diligence, stoicism and "phlegm"—characteristics associated with a particular kind of Englishness.[8]

Most people still aspired to an inclusive national Church: but on whose terms? The idea of "comprehension," by which Dissenters (in majority Presbyterians) would join a looser Church, was supported by Whigs but refused by hardline Tories, who considered Presbyterians worse than papists, and feared that this was a Trojan horse for bringing religious radicalism and disorder into the Church. Instead of "comprehension," an Act of Toleration was passed in 1688, suspending the "pains and penalties" imposed on Protestant Dissenters and allowing them to worship separately in licensed meeting halls. However, toleration was not yet extended to Catholics, Jews or to Socinians (or Unitarians), an offshoot of Presbyterianism that denied the doctrine of the Trinity and hence the divinity of Christ. This challenged a basic tenet of the religious, political and social order: that Church and state were divinely ordained by Jesus; and Unitarians formed the intellectual core of religious and political radicalism later in the century.[9]

The post-1688 religious compromise was an uneasy resolution of England's wars of religion.[10] Dissenters could vote and be elected to Parliament, but the Corporation and Test Acts (1661 and 1672) required holders of public office and members of the universities to be communicant members of the Church. Many Dissenters got round the law by taking communion occasionally, but most resisted such subterfuges. The discriminatory laws if applied rigidly—usually they were not—constituted a severe burden, barring Dissenters from national and local office (for example, in town corporations), from many jobs, and even from doing business with public bodies. They were oppressive and humiliating:

Dissenters were required to pay church taxes, and marry in church. Demands by Dissenters for full equality were a chronic political grievance, not satisfied until 1828.

At a popular level, religious and political differences created two cultures: one festive, communal and royalist; the other puritanical, capitalistic and parliamentarian. Popular Toryism was a loose alliance of gentry, tradesmen and skilled artisans for whom "Church and king" symbolized traditional communal solidarity, in contrast to grasping individualism.[11] This solidarity was expressed through church festivities, with bell-ringing, food and ale: Christmas, 5 November, Oak Apple Day (29 May), church wakes, harvest homes, St. Cecilia's Day (for music) and many others. "I hear of one every Sunday kept in some village or other of the neighbourhood," wrote a newspaper correspondent in 1738, "and see great numbers of both sexes in their holiday clothes constantly flooding thither."[12]

Dissent catered to a sense of upward mobility both spiritual and worldly. Merchants and urban employers were often Dissenters and Whigs. The self-made manufacturer Jedediah Strutt, for example, moved to Unitarianism in the 1760s after concluding that "the Virtuous & good are [God's] peculiar Care & Concern."[13] A distinct Nonconformist society was perpetuated, with its own academies, meeting houses, clergy, regional strongholds and economic networks. The once-alarming Quakers would soon include extremely wealthy merchants and, in the Penn family, the patriarchal proprietors of a vast colony, Pennsylvania. Nonconformity would have an immense influence on cultural, political and economic life. In no other contemporary country was there such a recognized and powerful counter-society, some of whose purists denied the legitimacy of the state. This tended to liberalize England by keeping open the division that shaped its characteristically disputatious political culture.[14]

## A COUNTRY AT WAR

*Every man thinks meanly of himself for not having been a soldier, or not having been at sea . . . Mankind reverence those who have got over fear.*

Samuel Johnson, 1778

William had invaded England to bring it into the alliance fighting against Louis XIV's France, thought to be aiming at "universal monarchy." Louis retaliated by giving troops to aid James to recover his throne. Thus began a "Second Hundred Years' War," a titanic struggle to break French power that ended only in 1815 at Waterloo, and which we shall consider in its global dimensions in later chapters. During those 127 years, England fought in five of the eight bloodiest wars in world history: the Nine Years War (1688–97), the War of the Spanish Succession (1701–13), the Seven Years' War (1755–63), and finally the French Revolutionary (1792–1802) and Napoleonic Wars (1803–15).[15] And in addition to these was the American War of Independence (1775–83), less lethal, but extremely expensive. War created new institutions, new relationships, new demands, new powers, new ambitions, new dangers and new priorities, which crowded out the concerns with religious ritual and royal prerogative that had dominated previous decades. Thus war transformed England and Britain: "If there is a revolutionary change in the course of early modern British history it is to be found here; at least, this was the point at which observant contemporary intelligences became capable of saying that such a transformation was going on."[16]

Whatever the political alliances or concessions required to maximize the unity and commitment of England in that struggle, they would be made. Hence, religious toleration was necessary to maintain a broad anti-French coalition, and William insisted on it. He accepted a Bill of Rights (1689), which enshrined right of petition, free debate in Parliament, freedom of election, trial by jury, the right to bear arms and frequency of Parliament, and it forbade extra-legal royal action. A Mutiny Act (1689) made the existence of the army dependent on parliamentary consent. A Triennial Act (1694) required general elections every three years. In short, once again, but now more explicitly than ever, the Crown was made subject to law, and its powers, still extensive, were defined by agreement with the nation. This time, there was no going back on the deal, which sketched out a constitution for England. Parliament had placed itself at the centre of the state. But what made these changes effective was Parliament's ancient control of taxation. The pressing need created by war to have a parliament that would sanction ever-increasing taxation and debt changed it from a periodic event, called when the king needed it, to a permanent institution, which has met every year since 1689.[17]

Repeated wars changed the culture of politics. They focused attention overseas. The principal motive of fighting was to defend England's own liberties, originally against Louis XIV and James II, France's tool. Even most Divine-Right Tories could not stomach the return of a dynasty that rejected the Church of England, and whose fortunes depended on a French invasion: "Tis apparent how this poore Prince is menag'd by the French," noted the royalist diarist John Evelyn.[18] This acted as a unifying force, counteracting the centrifugal forces of religion and politics: there were limits beyond which all but a small minority would not go and a national cause that most acknowledged.

It was asserted at the time, and has been since, that the English were (and even remain) characteristically insular and xenophobic. It is true that resentment of the French, Dutch, Irish, Hanoverians and not least the Scots became at times political issues during these decades of conflict, especially when foreigners were seen as threatening English independence and interests—not unlike the Euroscepticism of modern times. They certainly believed that Englishness carried with it particular freedoms, rights and duties, of which they were jealous. Furthermore, popular prejudices were expressed less inhibitedly than in most other countries. There is, however, no yardstick to judge whether the English were more xenophobic than other nations, but some reason to think that they were not.[19] The upper classes were and remained admiring of French and Italian culture. Many people felt wider solidarities as Protestants and Christians, were fascinated by their neighbours and highly concerned by Continental affairs.[20] They believed England was fighting for the liberties of Europe— to defend the beleaguered Protestants of Germany, Holland, France and Italy from "popery" and persecution, and also to preserve Christendom itself, including Catholic Europe, from what was seen as the immoral and illegitimate hegemony of a Louis XIV willing to ally with Turks against Christians to extend his power.[21] Many English popular heroes were foreign, including several of their own monarchs and allied princes and generals; some were even Catholic, such as the imperial general Prince Eugene of Savoy.[22]

War required a bigger and more professional army, the origins of which went back to the New Model Army of the Civil War. Would it be maintained in peacetime or disbanded? This was a matter of great political and ideological significance. Politically, because with memories of civil war still fresh the control of military force seemed crucial. Ideologically, because the right and duty to bear arms was a defining part of free citizenship—as well as being cheaper. But the length and intensity of war after 1689 meant that the old idea that English freedom meant a society defended by its armed citizens and a monarch with no significant armed force became both unpopular and impractical. Hence, one of the characteristic vulnerabilities of the English state, its military weakness, disappeared. However, army service was widely shunned, and so England early became a country that relied on professional soldiers for serious fighting.

Lack of money had been England's other great weakness since the reign of Elizabeth, and it had caused recurring crises for the Stuarts. After the Glorious Revolution taxes spiralled, with parliamentary approval. By the end of the War of the Spanish Succession in 1713, tax as a proportion of national income had nearly tripled since 1688.[23] Taxation required collectors, and the revenue departments were expanded and professionalized under an Inspector-General (created in 1696) to levy customs and excise duties, notably on beer. The revenue service became one of the largest and most efficient arms of the state. The other main source of income, the land tax (created in 1688), was administered by Justices of the Peace—something that preserved local autonomy, but required local landowners to accept and pay a high rate of tax, which reached 20 percent of income. There is a popular idea of eighteenth-century England as grossly corrupt and incompetent, and although plenty of examples of private enrichment can indeed be found, research has shown that to take corruption as the norm is a caricature: by the European standards of the time, the administration was rigidly monitored, efficient, cheap, local and remarkably honest.[24] England and Holland became by far the most heavily taxed states in Europe—in itself a political revolution, because for a century Parliament had resisted taxation, even to the point of open conflict with the Crown. The result now was not mass revolt (though popular discontent was real, rioting not infrequent, and smuggling a major industry—Robert Walpole, for example, smuggled in his wines while a minister[25]) but rather acceptance by the Crown that Parliament was indispensable, and by the political class that national defence had to be paid for.

This acceptance was easier because England was a single political, legal and administrative unit: no regional or corporate tax privileges existed, unlike in most of Europe. So by comparison with states where taxation was arbitrary and unequal, expenditure was shrouded in secrecy, and war, peace and strategy were questions for monarchs alone, the English tax burden was generally regarded as fair, and the level of compliance was remarkably high.[26] The House of Commons, however, would only agree to grant funds for a year at a time. William and his successors had to accept its right to control how the money was spent, and thereby monitor government—the Commission of Public Accounts was established in 1690. The justification for war and the way it was conducted became more than ever subjects of parliamentary and public debate: so war and taxation, at least as much as the words, deeds and intrigues of philosophers, kings and politicians, revolutionized England's government.

Taxation, however, was not enough to meet wartime spending: governments had to borrow more than ever before. Public debt went from £3m in the 1680s to £100m in 1760, paying not only for Britain's navy and army, but contributing to those of its allies too. This required a sophisticated financial system, by which short-term liabilities—in effect, IOUs from government departments—could be replaced by long-term, low-interest bonds. During the 1690s, ministers, MPs and businessmen studied the methods of the Dutch and the Venetians, Europe's most sophisticated financiers. Experiments and mistakes were made with lotteries and life annuities. In 1694, William Paterson, a Scot, and Michael Godfrey, an Englishman, won approval from Parliament for a Bank of England, modelled on the Bank of Amsterdam: an event of truly historic importance. As Paterson put it, "The Wars of these times are rather to be Waged with gold than with Iron."[27] Immediately, in 1695, the Bank proved its worth by saving the government's credit from collapsing, and kept it afloat until peace came two years later. The intimate relationship between the Bank and war was dramatically shown when Godfrey was killed in the trenches at the siege of Namur in 1695. Financing wars against France transformed the City of London, which channelled international investment into interest-bearing bonds, and by the end of the century it was the world's financial centre.

Parliament underpinned credit. In contrast with absolutist states, its guarantee made default unlikely (many MPs were bondholders), and the Commons publicly voted taxation earmarked for interest payments. By 1715 fully half of tax revenue went to servicing what became a permanent National Debt. There were crises and panics about unsustainable debt levels. But "as long as land lasts and beer is drunk," declared the long-serving minister the Duke of Newcastle, England would never default.[28] Realizing this, domestic and foreign savers became eager to lend, keeping interest rates low. As confidence grew, the rate of interest fell from 14 percent in 1693 to 3 percent in 1731, meaning, of course, that Britain could borrow nearly five times as much money for the same outlay of interest, and so outspend its bigger and richer enemy France. The combination of the House of Commons and the City of London funded Britain's rise to world power.

But war brought new political controversies too. The rapid wartime growth of what has been termed the "fiscal-military state" altered the relationship of citizens and government. The state became increasingly intrusive and expensive. It also employed more people and created a larger number of beneficiaries, including "new men" such as bankers, lenders, contractors and bureaucrats, usually Whigs, who were both serving and profiting from its activities. Parliament, by placing itself at the centre of decision, was less clearly the defender of the citizen against the demands of the state: it was itself the demander, with many of its members benefiting personally from salaries, jobs, pensions and contracts.

There emerged new political alignments. In the 1690s a loose "Country

Party" was set up by Whigs led by the 3rd Earl of Shaftesbury (the theorist of politeness). Its ideas attracted many Tories. They claimed to be "Patriots," standing for the interests of the "country" against the selfishness of the "court" and the political and financial oligarchy. It found a fashionable ideology ready made, and which remained potent throughout the century—"Roman" or "civic humanist" ideas, derived from the prestigious writings of ancient patriots. Civic humanists thought politics should be the disinterested activity of a virtuous elite upholding the public good and combating corruption—for it was corruption, not the royal prerogative, that they now saw as threatening freedom: "What the French government does by despotism, the English government does by corruption." This was not a democratic creed: indeed, they feared democracy would facilitate corruption. The Country Party also appealed potentially to all who simply resented ever-higher taxes. War on the Continent seemed to many a cynical way of keeping the money flowing. Thus emerged a powerful but eclectic Patriot rhetoric, willing to lump together Roman republicanism, Magna Carta and Locke's contract theory. It came to permeate English political debate and was exported to America and France. Whenever we call for honest politics or high-minded leadership to combat self-interest, corruption and the self-absorption of "Westminster" or "Washington," we are echoing these ideas.

## STABILIZING THE STATE

An urgent political problem was the succession to the post-1688 throne. Queen Mary (James II's elder daughter and William III's queen and co-sovereign) died childless in 1694. It was assumed that William would never father a child. The heir was therefore his sister-in-law Anne, James II's younger daughter, a staunch Anglican acceptable to many who rejected William. Her adult life had been tormented by unsuccessful pregnancies, and her only surviving child died in 1700, aged eleven. William and Parliament acted swiftly to forestall a future in which the direct Stuart heirs would be James's Catholic descendants by his second marriage. The solution was the Act of Settlement of June 1701—an epoch-making measure. It excluded dozens of possible Catholic claimants to the throne* in favour of the closest Protestant, a granddaughter of James I, the Electress Sophia of Hanover, and her heirs, on condition that they were Protestants and married to Protestants. This demonstrated that the king and

---

* The Catholic "heir" today would be Duke Franz of Bavaria ("Francis II").

Parliament together had the power to choose a future monarch—similar to pre-Conquest practice, as some noted. The Act also safeguarded the independence of the judiciary, limited the powers of the Crown to make war, and required all business to go through the Privy Council—these last two clauses, perhaps unfortunately, were later repealed.

This Act remains in force. Now, its exclusion of Catholics may seem absurd or outrageous, and there are occasional pleas to change it. Then, it removed at a stroke the main cause of over 150 years of instability and bloodshed. It was a complete reversal of European practice by which states followed the religion of their rulers. In contrast, the Act of Settlement was the most fundamental assertion of the primacy of the nation over its monarch.

Soon after thus providing for the future, William fell from his horse in Richmond Park, and died in 1702, aged fifty-two. He has left little trace in England's national memory. He had a dour, taciturn personality and an uneventful and discreet private life. He rarely used artists to create a memorable image—he was in any case physically frail and unprepossessing. He spoke imperfect English, and reserved his confidence for Dutch advisers and soldiers, particularly Hans Willem Bentinck, whom he made Duke of Portland. He spent much of his reign outside England, and had little love for his adopted country or subjects, who returned his coolness—"I see that this people is not created for me, neither am I for this people."[29] Yet there is still a glaring mismatch between his historic role and the near oblivion into which he has fallen. He succeeded brilliantly in a perilous invasion of England, took control of the country almost without bloodshed, and began a new era in its internal history. Even more importantly, by enrolling England in his anti-French alliance, he prevented France from dominating Europe, and in doing so set England on the road to becoming a great power. So why is he not remembered as one of England's greatest rulers? Personality is the obvious reason: multiple spouses and lovers stick in the collective memory more easily than complex politics and diplomacy. Perhaps the very scale of the changes he brought about makes them hard to grasp, while there is no single dramatic event that encapsulates him or them—except, of course, the battle of the Boyne (see p. 335), so present in Irish memories. Perhaps too the English cherish those who embody continuity and defence against outside threats, such as Elizabeth I, rather than one who took them on new, and expensive, foreign adventures.

Anne was a popular queen, plump and unthreatening, proudly English and Anglican, the last of the true Stuarts, and arguably the last traditional monarch, who "touched" for scrofula (one beneficiary being the infant

Samuel Johnson). She was able to make important decisions about broad political orientations, and her wishes weighed with Parliament and the electorate. She even attended debates in the House of Lords to put pressure on its members, and was the last monarch to try to refuse consent to legislation (the Scottish parliament's Act of Security of 1703). But for reasons of personality, intellect and gender she could not be the head of the executive and commander-in-chief like William. Nor did she wish or attempt to have a brilliant court, like Charles II. So by choice and necessity William and then Anne hastened the transformation of the English monarchy towards being a symbolic, popular, even familiar institution.[30]

Relations between England and Scotland became critical. The Glorious Revolution had unleashed violent conflict between Calvinists, strongest in the Lowlands, and Episcopalians, strongest in the feudal Highlands. The wars with France had hit Scottish trade. The Scottish parliament had tried during the 1690s to establish a Central American colony at Darien—a reckless enterprise, disproportionate to the size of the Scottish economy, and which absorbed a dangerous proportion of Scottish capital. It involved Scotland in an attack on the Spanish Empire at a time when England was at peace, and following Spanish protests King William ordered English colonies to boycott Darien. The collapse of the colony in 1699 brought Scotland, already suffering from harvest failures and dearth, to the verge of financial collapse. Finally, the 1701 Act of Settlement, passed by the English Parliament for England, did not apply to Scotland, and some Scots saw this as a way of breaking the union of the crowns (by the above-mentioned Act of Security), or at least of extracting major concessions from Westminster.

The English government forced a choice: separation or union. It threatened to pass an Aliens Act, by which Scots would be treated as foreigners in England. Though the idea of union aroused no popular enthusiasm in either country, Whitehall had no desire, in the midst of a deadly struggle with France, to see the faintest possibility of Scotland being ruled by a Stuart under French protection, and so return to the days when Scotland was a dagger pointed at England's back. Daniel Defoe, journalist and pamphleteer, was sent to Edinburgh as an agent and propagandist. Inducements were offered to Scottish politicians, and a favourable financial settlement was prepared. Many Scots saw union as a way of stabilizing the country and modernizing its corrupt and archaic oligarchy.[31]

In 1706 and 1707 a Treaty of Union was signed and Acts of Union were passed by both parliaments. In Westminster, both Houses agreed without a vote. In Scotland, calculations of national interest were lubricated by English bribery. The Kingdoms of England and Scotland legally ceased to exist, being replaced—as James VI and I had wished a century earlier—by a United Kingdom of Great Britain, with a single "Parliament of Great Britain" in Westminster. Ireland remained a separate kingdom, with its own parliament (though subordinate to Westminster) and a Protestant government at Dublin Castle under a British-appointed Lord-Lieutenant. The lack of controversy in Westminster over the Union testifies to the expectation of the English political elite that for England nothing much would change. The immediate object had been achieved: preventing a breach over the royal succession. The future could look after itself.

There was no intention of changing the basic system of government, and so the creation of the United Kingdom was de facto a process of political attachment to England: its parliament was the existing English and Welsh parliament with Scottish (and after 1800 Irish) representation added. Consequently, the Union was tacitly unequal, given England's larger population and number of parliamentary seats, increasingly obviously as its population boomed from the 1730s onwards. Scots were expected to conform to the "ancient constitution" of England, and the new United Kingdom Parliament assumed the right to change Scottish laws and institutions predating the Union, even those considered by the Acts of Union to be "fundamental."[32] Queen Victoria's heir was Edward VII, not Edward I of the United Kingdom; and the present queen, despite a legal challenge in Edinburgh, became Elizabeth II. Scottish politicians and Scottish lawyers have sometimes questioned this English constitutional ascendancy, and the issue suddenly revived in importance after three centuries: whether the ancient Scottish nation, if independent, would legally be a new state or the revival of an old one became a subject with fundamental implications in 2014.

In popular memory, especially in Scotland, Union came to be regarded as a loss of liberty and an English "colonization." Many people in England at the time saw it the other way round. England was losing autonomy in the sense that policy at many levels had to take increasing account of the rest of Britain, Ireland, Hanover, and the Empire, and many non-English officials and politicians played a prominent role in its government. Scottish intellectuals and cultural luminaries—among them Hume, Smith, Adam Ferguson, Boswell, the novelist Tobias Smollett, the architect Robert Adam—were prominent in British and English cultural life and in the professions. The Scottish elites had for a century been active in English politics, sometimes sword in hand, and the Union now brought many more of them into the very centre of its political, legal, military, imperial and diplomatic functions. All this caused serious English resentment. At the same time, Scotland retained its separate legal system, its own religious establishment and its education system; and Scottish elites continued to run Scotland, a process in which the English took little part. Three centuries later, not much had changed, and so increasing Scottish self-government, further enhanced by the results of the September 2014 referendum, seemed to many on both sides of the border to be a less than earth-shattering development.

The most startling domestic crisis of Anne's reign shows that England had not transcended the religious and political tensions of the previous century. In November 1709, Dr. Henry Sacheverell preached a violent sermon attacking Whigs and Dissenters and their "hellish principles of Fanaticism, Regicide, and Anarchy," which when published sold 100,000 copies. He was impeached by the Whig Parliament, which banned him from preaching for three years. There were serious riots in his support across England, including in London, formerly a stronghold of Dissent, but where meeting houses were now attacked and "to the sound of breaking windows and burning pews, the capital . . . finally aligned itself with most of the rest of the country."[33] This episode showed dramatically how sensitive the Anglican majority were to anything that seemed to threaten the religious and social order, and that Whigs and Dissenters still carried the Roundhead stigma. It was also partly an anti-war outburst, blaming Whigs and Dissenters for "Continental entanglements." It showed that Toryism could spill over into Jacobitism, support for the exiled Stuarts. It was far from clear that the Act of Settlement would work, and that a Hanoverian succession was feasible. Queen Anne herself maintained discreet contacts with the exiled Stuart court—she referred to James II's son, her nephew, as "the Prince of Wales." The excitement of the Sacheverell affair, and the queen's Tory sympathies, led to a Tory landslide in 1710, and the appointment of Tory ministers.

The Tory government were much less committed to the wearisome Europe-wide struggles against France, which we shall examine in Chapter 9. There were brilliant military successes, particularly Marlborough's stunning victory at Blenheim in 1704 (see pp. 335–36). But by 1709 there had developed an expensive and bloody stalemate in Flanders. The Tories tended to take a "Country Party" view of the burden of taxation, and suspected their Whig predecessors of pursuing war unreasonably and profiting from it unscrupulously. So they were willing to respond to peace feelers from France, and would not allow their allies to stop them, even concluding a unilateral armistice. The Treaty of Utrecht was signed in April 1713. It required the French to recognize the Protestant succession and expel the exiled Stuarts.

The situation was transformed by Queen Anne's death in August 1714.

The Act of Settlement was now put to the test, and it took effect without a hitch: Georg Ludwig von Braunschweig-Lüneburg, electoral prince of Hanover, peacefully inherited two kingdoms and twelve colonies as King George I. He unhurriedly made his way over, taking six weeks to arrive with an entourage including cooks, mistresses and his court dwarf. "Better a prince from Germany than one from France," declared a leading Tory. George I brought about a further change in the role and status of the monarch.[34] He was far more foreign than James VI or William of Orange. A Lutheran, surrounded by a foreign entourage including two Turks acquired on campaign against the Ottomans, he had not bothered to learn English—his speeches from the throne had to be read by the Lord Chancellor. He played a limited role in domestic politics, even less in culture, and none at all in religion. He was very different both from crowned theologians like the Stuarts or a "Sun King" at the apex of elite culture and society like Louis XIV. A statue of the king put up in Grosvenor Square was defaced and eventually dismembered by passers-by.[35] He lived on a relatively domestic scale in the Dutch plainness of Kensington Palace, holding official court amid the ramshackle shabbiness of St. James's. Most of Whitehall Palace had accidentally burned down in 1697. No Hanoverian monarch had the money or the nerve to build an English Versailles, concentrating royalty, court and government in one magnificent setting, and this liberated English cultural life from the constraints, and perhaps benefits, of a dominant source of patronage. The low-key royal presence, scattered among various residences, including Hampton Court, Windsor, Kew and houses in London, must have seemed a great weakness compared with the overwhelming splendours of Bourbon Versailles; but by preventing royal isolation it turned out to be a strength.

No bill passed by both Houses of Parliament has ever been refused the royal assent since George I's accession. In practice Parliament, as the representative of the nation, was becoming the sovereign authority—or, to be precise, parliamentary statutes were becoming the highest form of law, able to replace or suspend elements of the Common Law or of the royal prerogative. The king still governed, though requiring parliamentary consent to be able to do so. Eighteenth-century theorists considered that there was a "mixed constitution," with a "balance" between the Crown and the two Houses of Parliament. Only over the nineteenth and even the twentieth century (in the Parliament Acts of 1911 and 1949) did the House of Commons become clearly predominant. Parliamentary sovereignty was by that time accepted as the fundamental constitutional principle, as defined by the great nineteenth-century constitutional lawyer A. V. Dicey: "Parliament . . . has, under the English constitution, the right to make or unmake any law whatever; . . . no person or body is recognized by the law of England as having a right to override or set aside the legislation of Parliament."[36] When it is said that the United Kingdom has no constitution, it really means that no entrenched fundamental text defines and limits the powers of the various branches of government, above all the legislative power of Parliament.

George I was far from being apolitical, however: he brought about a historic reorientation of England's domestic and foreign policy. He immediately threw out the Tories in what has been called a Whig "coup." He was angry both with the Tory peace of Utrecht, which he saw as a betrayal of European allies, and with the contacts several had pursued with the exiled Stuarts—though probably aimed at discouraging rather than encouraging Jacobite adventures. His new Whig ministers sent the former Secretary of State, Robert Harley, Earl of Oxford, to the Tower, and set about impeaching him and three others for high treason—Viscount Bolingbroke, the Secretary of State who had negotiated the Utrecht terms, the Earl of Strafford, another Utrecht negotiator, and the Marquess of Ormonde, commander of the army. This showed that traditional politics was not dead. Henry St. John, Viscount Bolingbroke, fled to France and joined the Stuarts as Secretary of State—an act which did huge damage to the Tory party. Oxford stayed and defended himself against impeachment so effectively that after two long years proceedings were dropped—an important landmark in political history, as he was the last minister of the Crown to face impeachment. Parliament could no longer treat the king's government as a separate power: Parliament itself was ultimately responsible for policy (unlike in the United States, where impeachment survives). As one of Harley's defenders put it, "If the command of the Sovereign, after mature deliberation in Council . . . followed by the approbation of two parliaments, be not sufficient justification for ministers . . . whose life is safe?"[37] Thus ended in England what would later be termed "the separation of powers": Parliament now combined executive and legislative powers in a single institution. A Septennial Act (1716) was passed, reducing the frequency of general elections from three years to seven—an important but long-resented step to lowering the political temperature. It provoked Jean-Jacques Rousseau's jibe that the English were free—but only once every seven years.

This ejection of the Tories—who represented majority feeling in the country—inevitably had repercussions. Government was now in the hands of a Whig oligarchy, which dominated the House of Commons. In many parts of the country, political life drifted into a coma.[38] Most Tories accepted the Hanoverian succession, because the Stuart "James III" refused to embrace the Church of England and remained a pensioner of France. But their acceptance of George I had been based on the assumption that he would keep a Tory government, protect the Church, maintain peace in Europe, and pursue purely English, not Hanoverian, interests. His coronation in October 1714 sparked off a wave of popular urban violence, destroying Dissenting meeting houses amid cries of "Down with the Roundheads!" and disrupting coronation festivities, with many shouted insults to King George—"There will be no good times 'till King James the 3rd come again ... you may kiss my Arse & King George too."[39]

As long as France supported the Stuarts, even discreetly, the cause of "James III" was not lost. In Catholic Ireland and Highland Scotland, Jacobitism was strong. In England, discontent with high taxes arising from wars in Europe, dislike of "Roundheads," and resentment of the Whig oligarchy ensured considerable popular Jacobite sentiment. Belatedly, hardcore Jacobites planned an uprising in Scotland and England. However, their staunchest champion, Louis XIV, died in September 1715. Before his death was known, the Earl of Mar had rallied a substantial Scottish army outnumbering government forces. But he delayed marching south. In the Catholic areas of Yorkshire and Lancashire, a few thousand gentlemen, their neighbours and dependants took up arms in the last Catholic uprising in English history. In both countries, the rebellion petered out in November 1715 with little bloodshed, and the repression was relatively mild—twelve English commoners were executed, thirteen gentlemen and one earl, and some Catholic estates were confiscated. The king was sufficiently untroubled to visit Hanover in July 1716 and stay for five months.

Only with foreign military intervention was a Jacobite rising credible. After a generation of warfare, England had accumulated enough enemies willing to try. The Spanish, Swedes and Russians all thought of taking a gamble on the Jacobites. But only the French could pose a real threat, and after the death of Louis XIV they wanted peace and time to recover. They even tipped off the British ambassador about a minor plot in 1722.

A more serious political threat was of a new kind: the speculative financial crash known as the South Sea Bubble. War had left both France and Britain with unprecedented public debts, widely feared at the time to be unsustainable. To find some way of reducing the burden without damaging future credit would confer a huge diplomatic and military advantage. A Scottish gambler and adventurer, John Law, persuaded the French government in 1717 that he had found the solution: to persuade creditors to swap their state bonds for shares in a new monopoly trading company, thus privatizing the Crown's debts. London followed, setting up the South Sea Company in 1719 to trade with the Spanish Empire, and likewise encouraging the exchange of bonds for shares. In both countries, this worked wonderfully. It was a time of naïve optimism concerning entrepreneurial innovation and global trade, and the share price of both companies rocketed (in London, by 700 percent), encouraging more bondholders to convert. A new French word, *millionaire*, was coined to describe the leading profiteers. But neither company had trading prospects adequate to support such euphoric expectations. The greedy and the credulous rushed to buy just as the more prudent and better informed (including the queen and a rising Whig politician, the Norfolk squire Robert Walpole) decided to cash in. The bubble burst in 1720 with a suddenness that has since become familiar, as have the panic and public outrage that ensued: "The directors are curst, the top adventurers broke." Suicides sharply increased. The Chancellor of the Exchequer went to the Tower, and the property of all the Company's directors was confiscated. Walpole, the new Chancellor of the Exchequer, played for time and protected as many politicians and bankers as he could—something that won him unpopularity, but limited the damage. He and the Bank of England saved the South Sea Company from bankruptcy: in later years it even returned a profit. This was the City's first "big bang," and regulation was introduced to make investment safer. English public finance came to be seen as more honest, as well as more efficient, than that of any other country in Europe.[40] In France the outcome was very different: Law's fiasco ruined its credit market for at least a century.[41]

## THE REIGN OF ROBIN

A major winner, politically as well as financially, was Sir Robert ("Robin") Walpole. He is traditionally considered "the first Prime Minister," and he was also the longest in office, as First Lord of the Treasury and Chancellor of the Exchequer, from 1722 to 1742. He was not the first great royal minister: his longevity, spectacular self-enrichment and social ascension might recall William Wykeham, Cardinal Wolsey or the Cecils, and like them he was able to build himself a palace, Houghton Hall in Norfolk. What was new about him was that, while he enjoyed the support of George II and his intelligent queen, Caroline of Anspach, he was not only a councillor dependent on royal favour, but also a parliamentary manager and a manipulator of the electorate, basing his power on a majority in the Commons.[42] It is this that makes him familiar despite his wig and knee-breeches. He spent much time in the Commons, unlike his immediate predecessors refused a peerage to remain an MP, cultivated members, explained policy in private meetings, and kept supporters happy with jobs and favours. There were usually about 100 MPs on the government payroll[43]—fewer than today—which made Walpole difficult to defeat. He expanded the Civil List (money voted by Parliament to cover Crown expenses, including salaries and pensions), the number of "placemen" (given jobs in return for political support) and the standing army. This "Robinocracy" caused outrage among his excluded opponents.

The first period of Whig-Tory conflict—"the rage of party"—was now over, with neither having won completely. The ideal Tory vision of a sacred paternalist monarchy and a Church monopoly of legal worship, their deep suspicion of "moneyed men," commerce and the growing state, and their dislike of European entanglements had been overcome by circumstances, most obviously the perennial threat from France and the inevitability of the Hanoverian succession. But clear Whig policies, including oligarchical rule, support for religious Dissent, a major role in Europe, and an unrestricted financial and commercial market, were unpopular and had been tarnished by the South Sea Bubble. Ideological and sectarian divisions faded, and under Walpole both government supporters and opponents became coalitions of interests. In short, though Whigs and Tories were descended from the two sides in the Civil War, politics was ceasing to be civil war by other means. Instead, Walpole gave the country what it now wanted—restrained taxation and public spending, and peace. He boasted in 1734 to the queen, "Madam, there are 50,000 men slain this year in Europe, and not one Englishman."[44]

If Walpole was the first Prime Minister, the brilliant and slippery Henry St. John, Viscount Bolingbroke, was perhaps the first Leader of the Opposition—albeit outside Parliament. After his impeachment and flight to the Stuarts in 1714, he made his peace with the Hanoverians and returned to England with a pardon in 1723. He had developed an eclectic doctrine that drew on "Country Party" resentments, criticizing Walpole and the Whig oligarchy as unrepresentative. He accepted the 1688 revolution, recast the idea of Divine Right to apply to the office of king, not to a person or dynasty, and espoused a Whig version of English history as that of a nation struggling for liberty—a useful creed for an opposition politician, even if a Tory. Drawing on civic humanist language of virtue and patriotism, his *Letters on the Spirit of Patriotism* (1736) and *The Idea of a Patriot King* (1738) called for "a patriot king" to rule in the national interest. He was also a pioneer theorist of empire, favouring seapower and overseas trade, not European commitments: "The sea is our barrier, ships are our fortresses."[45] He proved an able propagandist, reinventing Toryism as the expression of grass-roots resistance to a high-and-mighty oligarchy. But his greatest legacy was accidental: he suggested the concept of the "separation of powers" to Montesquieu, whom he had met when in exile, and whose *De l'esprit des lois* established the idea as the defining characteristic of a free government. As such it became the keystone of the future American constitution and those subsequently influenced by it.[46]

Attacks on "Robinocracy" and its times were headed by a phalanx of literary and intellectual talent unsurpassed in our history. The Tory Jonathan Swift's *Gulliver's Travels* (1726) mocked the selfishness, duplicity and pettiness of the political and financial elite. Alexander Pope, another Tory, excoriated the reign of "Dulness" in his mock heroic poem *The Dunciad* (1728). John Gay, in the first popular English stage musical, *The Beggar's Opera* (1728), lampooned politicians as criminals. Henry Fielding's novel *The Life of Jonathan Wild the Great* (1746) implicitly compared Walpole with the criminal mastermind Wild, hanged in 1725. William Hogarth, beginning his brilliant career as painter and satirist, created unforgettable images of decadence and corruption in *Gin Lane* and *The Rake's Progress*, widely circulated as prints. Walpole's opponents turned to Frederick, Prince of Wales, as their potential "Patriot King," and the musical spectacle *Alfred* (1740), written by the Scottish poet James Thompson and composed by Thomas Arne, was aimed to glorify him and exalt the ancient and modern spirit of patriotism, most enduringly in "Rule Britannia," thus drawing a pointed comparison with the debased government of Walpole and George II.[47] This tide of polemic colours later ideas of what the mid-eighteenth century was like—corrupt, cynical, criminal and gin-sodden.* Hogarth created many of these images. But he was a satirist and above all a moralist stigmatizing corruption, luxury and vice. He was not trying to be an accurate reporter. Moreover, he was using classical allegories familiar to his audience but lost on us. Others took a far less grim and judgemental view of London street life, as vital, exciting and fun: "The happiness of London," said Johnson a generation later, "is not to be conceived but by those who have been in it."[48]

Walpole did not suffer attacks patiently. He repeatedly used the Jacobite spectre to damage the Tories, and Tory families were excluded from local office. He used public money to bribe or buy newspapers and pay his

---

* England was far from leading the world in tippling. There was a surge in consumption in the 1730s, peaking at about six litres of spirits per head per year (far less than today's ten litres of pure alcohol per head). The Dutch, the Belgians and the French all drank more than the English; Americans put away more than twice as much.

own propagandists. He brought in a law to censor the theatre which lasted until 1969. Besides, there is a case to be made for Walpole and his supporters, known as the "Court Whigs": those who could govern England (Scotland remained largely autonomous) for twenty years in relative peace after a century of turmoil and a generation of war were more than mere crooks. They were realists: the country had to be governed, and they occupied the middle ground of politics. So much power had shifted to the Commons that they considered it legitimate to have some means of sustaining a working majority, and giving jobs to supporters was one. As for the rewards to ministers—whose salaries were many times higher than those of today—it was necessary to attract men of talent to do the thankless job of running the country. Walpole's party would be far more at home in twenty-first-century politics than their "Patriot" critics.

Walpole's downfall came when in 1739 he was reluctantly forced by an aggressive public reaction into a war with Spain—"the War of Jenkins's Ear"—following clashes between British merchant ships and Spanish colonial coastguards. This drew Britain into a general European war, the War of Austrian Succession (1740–48)—a conflict over territory between Austria and Prussia which dragged in most of the Continent and spread to the Americas and India. Early patriotic excitement turned against the government after naval failures, which united Walpole's many enemies, and he was pressed by his own supporters to leave office in February 1742 and accept a peerage. His fall was significant for what did not happen. There had been expectation that the supposedly corrupt system would be dismantled—for example, by barring MPs from receiving government jobs and pensions. Even one loyal Whig hoped that "the grand Corrupter" would be prosecuted: "May God grant [his opponents] honesty and resolution to pursue the Enemy of their Countrey to the Scaffold."[49] But Walpole was safe. The Whigs stayed in power. The war continued. A victory over the French at Dettingen in Germany in June 1743 caused rejoicing. George II commanded in person, the last king to do so—though it turned sour when the king was accused of mistreating his English troops, and when in May 1745 the French (with Irish Jacobite troops in the vanguard) won a major victory over the British at Fontenoy, in Flanders. Moreover, the war was causing the worst economic recession of the century. With Walpole no longer there to be blamed, critics looked for other culprits, not least the "German Hanoverian Usurper." They accused him of putting the interests of his ancestral dominion—that "despicable electorate," as the vocal Patriot William Pitt termed it—before those of England.

Prince Charles Edward Stuart, grandson of James II, decided to seize the opportunity to regain the United Kingdom for his family. He forced the hand of the dubious French government by landing on 23 July 1745 in the Western Isles of Scotland, accompanied only by a few dozen followers, then raising the Stuart standard at Glenfinnan on the mainland on 19 August. He had left a letter for Louis XV in his big childish hand pleading for help and promising to be "a faithful ally."[50] In a few weeks he was able to gather some 5,000 men, lairds and their feudal levies. Their inherited loyalty was fuelled by bitter Episcopalian hatred for the semi-democratic Presbyterianism of the Lowlanders and resentment of the pro-Hanoverian clans which ran Scottish government.

The plan was to march into England, raise rebellion among Jacobite sympathizers there—the north, the Midlands and Oxford University were thought promising—and trust the French to invade. As their military commander, Lord George Murray, put it, "certainly 4,500 Scots never thought of putting a king upon an English throne by themselves."[51] The campaign started amazingly well, however, when they surprised and routed a smaller Irish-British force at Prestonpans on 21 September. There was little now in their way, as most British forces were engaged in the Low Countries, and others had been ordered south to protect London from the French. Charles's boldness seemed to be working: the French decided to invade England in December, and asked Spain, Sweden, Switzerland, Genoa and the papacy to assist (without effect). The Scots crossed the English border in November. But English Jacobites, though fond of wrecking Dissenters' chapels and drinking rousing toasts to "the king over the water," were chary of risking their necks. Only the usual diehard Catholic squires from Yorkshire and Lancashire, and a pitiful 200 volunteers from Manchester, turned out.[52] The Scots had to requisition food and lodgings from a sullen and at best circumspect population. But they managed to keep advancing, causing mounting panic in London, and alarm as far away as the American colonies, where there were fears of a Catholic uprising. Benjamin Franklin feared forcible conversion to Catholicism if Prince Charles won.[53] England's southern counties made ready for a French landing by preparing warning beacons and driving off horses and cattle.

It was a flash in the pan. Dutch troops arrived at Newcastle. The king's second son, the Duke of Cumberland, brought reinforcements from the Low Countries and marched into the Midlands. The Scots reached Derby and, finding no significant support in England, decided, against the shrill protests of a rather petulant and drunken Charles, to withdraw to fight in the Highlands. They turned north on 5 December—an eternally controversial decision, for the Hanoverian troops were still few, and London was weakly defended. Cumberland followed them, and a rearguard skirmish at Penrith was the last ever fought on English soil. The French were finding it embarrassingly difficult to launch their invasion: assembling ships, men and equipment took time; then the wind was wrong; and then Boulogne proved too small and shallow to accommodate the necessary number of invasion barges. So they gave up.

At Culloden, near Inverness, on 16 April 1746, in a short and one-sided clash, the Franco-Scottish army of the twenty-five-year-old Charles was crushed by the Anglo-Scottish army of the twenty-five-year-old Cumberland, who became a popular hero, not least in the Scottish Lowlands. The conflict had turned vicious, with both sides accusing the other of atrocities. There followed 120 legal executions, a third of them army deserters, and including 3 peers. One Scottish peer was rescued romantically from the Tower by his wife. Prince Charles was equally romantically guided to the Western Isles by Flora MacDonald, and taken home in a French warship. Indeed, the whole episode was very rapidly romanticized in song and story, even by English writers who had no desire to see a Stuart restoration—a sign, perhaps, that they had not been very frightened, or had soon recovered. Only four years later, Henry Fielding used the invasion to add a comic twist to the plot of *Tom Jones*: Tom, a "hearty well wisher to the glorious cause of liberty and the Protestant religion,"[54] volunteers to fight the Jacobite "banditti," but soon abandons the cause in pursuit of love. Hogarth portrayed the defence of London as equally absurd in his *March to Finchley*. Only the grim fate of the Jacobite rank-and-file, whom nobody much cared about, resisted glamorization or comedy. Apart from those killed in battle (about 2,000 at Culloden), hundreds of others were summarily executed or died in prison. English Jacobite volunteers were also harshly treated. Several hundred were transported to America or exiled.

If "Bonnie Prince Charlie" acquired a kind of romantic aura, at least for later generations, the material victories were elsewhere. The French, helped by the diversion of Cumberland's troops, captured Brussels. The Whigs, thanks to an anti-Jacobite and anti-Tory backlash, won significant victories in snap elections in 1747. However much they grumbled, the English were loyal to the Protestant Succession. The best the Jacobites could manage by the 1750s were rags by drunken Oxford undergraduates (which almost provoked the government to end university independence), minor riots in the rough-and-ready West Midlands, and scuffles at Lichfield races.[55] Thus the English Civil War finally petered out.

## THE STATE OF THE NATION

*The true state of every nation is the state of common life. The manners of a people are not to be found in the schools of learning, or the palaces of greatness . . . nor is public happiness to be estimated by the assemblies of the gay or the banquets of the rich. The great mass of nations is neither rich nor gay: they whose aggregate constitutes the people, are found in the streets, and the villages, in the shops and farms; and from them . . . must the measure of general prosperity be taken.*

Samuel Johnson, 1775[56]

England had calmed down amazingly. When George I had died in 1727, nothing much happened. His son was crowned peacefully, the main excitement being the first performance of Handel's breathtaking "Zadok the Priest," sung at every coronation since. It celebrated a king who was both chosen by God and acclaimed by the people: the "funny old Popish rites" again meant something. The new queen, Caroline, ordered a bust of John Locke: the man who had made the case for civil war in the 1680s was now a political philosopher by royal appointment. Foreign admirers thought that England had somehow stumbled on a working political system which both encouraged and was sustained by science, commerce, reason and liberty.

If the political system seems remote from our experience, it may help to compare it with the modern United States, whose constitution preserves many of its features. The king was like an American president, at the centre of power, able to choose his Cabinet (Cabinet decision-making developed during the second half of the eighteenth century), but needing to have it approved by Parliament, and then often struggling with the legislature to have his policies accepted. Just as wealthy Americans from prominent families enter politics out of ambition and a sense of duty, so did Whig aristocrats. Their names and money ensure respect and influence, and enable them to employ clever staffers to feed them with ideas: a Kennedy, Rockefeller or Bush recall Shaftesbury, Newcastle and Rockingham. A local power base is built up using both economic influence and office holding— governors and senators in one case, JPs and lords-lieutenant in the other. Deference and patronage are vital in securing allies and funds, and important lobbies have to be cultivated and rewarded. A new president—as with George I or George III—can mean wholesale change, and a clear-out of office-holders high and low, eagerly replaced by a new party. Popular suspicion of "Washington" recalls the rhetoric of the "Country Party." And of course religious groups play a fundamental role.

Politics was an oligarchy, as in different ways it still is, with politics intermingled with social life. One January evening in 1765, for instance, Horace Walpole (son of Robert, MP and man of letters) attended the Duke of Cumberland's levée, visited a princess, went briefly to the House of Commons, then dropped in at the opera.[57] It was not at all democratic, but it was in many ways representative. Members of Parliament were mostly drawn from the landed gentry, with a significant element of lawyers, businessmen, and navy or army officers. Landed gentlemen were preferred as being independent and disinterested—unlike nouveau-riche "nabobs" from India, as unpopular as City bankers today. In many boroughs the electorate was small, and in "nomination" or "rotten" boroughs it was non-existent, corrupt, or effectively owned by a powerful landowner—about a quarter of all seats. These had a function like modern life peerages. Scotland retained its old system after Union: it had 45 seats, but only 428 electors in total. In England, however, most constituencies had genuine electorates. In London, all ratepaying householders had the vote, and in the counties owners of land worth forty shillings a year, giving an English and Welsh electorate of over 300,000—about a quarter of adult men, a proportion not exceeded until the 1867 Reform Act.[58] This made English government unique. Elections when held were often tumultuous, as voters announced their choice publicly and non-voters demonstrated. But MPs were often elected unopposed.

Most people wanted "independent" MPs who would scrutinize and debate financial and foreign policy, combat expense and corruption, and investigate popular grievances. They were expected to represent local interests near their homes, wherever their nominal constituencies happened to be. Large manufacturing towns regarded resident MPs and those sharing their economic interests as representing them, and saw no need to have parliamentary seats of their own, which could be a source of disorder, corruption and expense. Birmingham, Manchester, Leeds, Sheffield and other growing centres ignored the reform campaign of the 1780s. Besides, the Commons were supposed to represent the nation as a whole, by what was termed "virtual representation." As Edmund Burke, MP, told his Bristol constituents, "Parliament is not a congress of ambassadors from different and hostile interests [but] a deliberative assembly of one nation."[59] However, the Commons were divided into personal followings, interest groups and factions, and most obviously into government and opposition. Debates, bills and inquiries were given increasing publicity, culminating in John Wilkes's successful campaign in 1771 to remove controls over reporting.

The job of the Commons was usually seen as defending the interests of the "Country" against abuse by the "Court" and the government, most of whose senior offices were held by peers, and whose links with the Crown were shown by wearing court dress in Parliament. Reform efforts focused on reducing the government's ability to manipulate the Commons: so reformers later in the century demanded exclusion of office-holders and government contractors, or reduction of the electorate to lessen corruption. There was little popular demand to change the post-1688 system, but rather to make it work.[60]

Was this not a society of gross inequality, of degradation, of selfish materialism, of destructive self-indulgence? Yes, it was, not unlike our own. Did it not behave with a brutality that most of the world would now consider revolting? Yes, it did. People were executed for minor offences, and the number of crimes carrying the death penalty was even extended. There is a grotesque contrast—one that we have difficulty in understanding—between a level of civility higher than our own, and casually accepted brutality. On one hand, the emphasis on politeness, the cultural brilliance; on the other, ruthless treatment of criminals and the poor: this has left a deep mark on present-day memory, summed up colourfully as "the village cleared to create the deer park . . . the eviction, imprisonment, transportation or execution of those who lived there."[61] Does it not make a mockery of the idea of England as the "country of liberty" for any but the few?

The prevailing image of eighteenth-century England as a dirty, brutal, corrupt, chaotic and oppressive place has a number of sources. As already mentioned, the anti-Walpole polemic, Hogarth's moralizing imagery and the later caricatures by Gillray and his contemporaries—themselves heightened expressions of contemporary perceptions and polemics, including genteel disgust at the "mob"—have moulded all later visions of their time. Victorian historians wrinkled up their noses at the drink, violence and libertinism. Mid-twentieth-century historians condemned the cruelty, dirt and disease, and the callousness of those who went to laugh at the lunatics of Bedlam and watch the hangings at Tyburn.[62] Social historians highlighted the harsh punishment of innocuous crimes such as poaching—a perfect symbol of rural inequality in the age of enclosure, which deprived the poor of access to common land for pasture and fuel. They created an image of vicious class conflict, aggravated by rising capitalism: "The commercial expansion, the enclosure movement, the early years of the Industrial Revolution—all took place within the shadow of the gallows."[63] We perhaps find it comforting to contrast our own times with a past portrayed as chaotic and brutal—an image graphically shown in films and television programmes that linger on images of violence, filth and vice.

There are obvious questions about this lurid vision. Were conflict, violence and savage punishment in fact the norm—was there robbery in every byway, and were starving children hanged for stealing a loaf? Were cities filthy, and the poor living in degradation? Was it getting worse? And was it worse than in other contemporary, or even later, societies?

Accelerating urbanization, which made London the largest city in Europe, created social and environmental problems and often exaggerated perceptions of danger, reflected in crime literature. There was real organized crime, which alarmed the authorities. It included smuggling, poaching and housebreaking by violent armed gangs, which led to the notorious "Black Act" (1723), aimed at those who disguised themselves by blacking their faces. Dick Turpin, later romanticized, began as a gang member in Essex; he later turned highwayman and was hanged at York in 1739. Jonathan Wild, who organized crime in London in the 1720s while acting as a paid thief-taker, has been called "the world's prototype gangster."[64]

Despite these famous, but exceptional, examples, and despite the lack of organized law enforcement, the routine level of crime was not very high, or very serious. Henry Norris, a JP in the London suburb of Hackney, kept a record of his cases from 1730 to 1741: 207 offences—one every couple of weeks, mainly assaults, thefts (including digging up someone's turnips), domestic violence, drunkenness and swearing. Over a third he dealt with out of court, and a fifth under his summary jurisdiction. One case that went up to the Old Bailey and received a death sentence was the violent robbery of a woman, the knife-wielding attacker having been arrested by four local men. Most crime was of this kind, petty by modern standards. Homicide had fallen sharply since the late 1500s, and by the 1720s was comparable with that in England today. In Kent, it had fallen from an estimated 5.3 per 100,000 to 1.7—close to the 1.4 for England at the end of the twentieth century.[65]

The death penalty was extended, so that by 1800 there were 200 capital crimes, mostly against property—including shoplifting goods worth over five shillings (perhaps £200 today). This was a sign of weakness, an attempt to deter crime in a society which had few prisons, few police other than part-time parish constables, and no public prosecutors. Victims had to take the law into their own hands, make their own inquiries, arrest the criminals, and bring the prosecutions. Constables and passers-by joined in, as when Defoe's Moll Flanders tries shoplifting:

> There was a great Cry of stop Thief . . . upon which the Mob gathered about me, and some said I was the Person . . . I was brought back by the Mob to the Mercer's shop . . . so they kept me by force near half an Hour;

they had called a Constable . . . Some of the servants used me saucily, and had much ado to keep their Hands off of me.[66]

Despite the increase in the number of capital offences, actual executions were getting rarer: in the 1590s, 20–25 percent of accused felons were executed; by the 1730s, 10–12 percent.[67] Pardons (which commuted the death sentence to lesser punishments) were common. The cruelty of the law was also softened by juries and judges using time-honoured subterfuges, especially for women, children, family breadwinners and those with credible character witnesses. A high proportion of women convicted claimed to be pregnant, and this was usually accepted on little or no evidence. "Benefit of clergy," a relic of the medieval privileges of the Church, meant in practice relatively minor punishment for first time offenders claiming to be clerics.[68] Many accused were deliberately found not guilty of capital offences. This shows that the likes, dislikes and snap judgements of jurors after cursory trials—on average half an hour[69]—had power of life and death. Yet this personalized justice reinforced public belief that the law was fair. New charities and reform organizations—such as the Foundling Hospital, to which Handel gave the royalties from *Messiah*—addressed the roots of crime, such as neglect and drunkenness, and tried to improve treatment of criminals. Transportation to America seemed to provide one solution—on average, about twelve people per week in mid-century. But habitual and violent criminals or those of "bad character" were likely to be hanged, especially when the authorities were jumpy.

Public hanging remained common—probably about 100 people per year on average over the whole country. There had been a big decline in hangings since the fall of the Republic. The total number in London between 1703 and 1772 was 1,242[70]—18 people a year on average, with typically 5 people being executed on a "hanging day" every three or four months. In assessing the impact of executions on a society and its culture—the length of the "shadow of the gallows"—we might note that the frequency of executions in London was about the same as in Texas, and in England about half that in Iran, during the early 2000s.

How did England compare with its neighbours? It is impossible to say with precision, as statistics are rare. Foreign observers, though they thought its theatres showed too much violence, did not regard England as harshly ruled. Guidebooks warned of highwaymen, who were not deterred by the prospect of mere hanging—a view encouraged by the popularly admired effort of condemned men to "die game," meeting death with bravado before a cheering crowd. That was impossible in France, for example, where felons were tortured and then broken on the wheel, to die screaming in agony. Burning and drowning were still practised in many parts of Europe. The French mounted police had summary judicial powers, and could sentence without appeal and execute immediately. Nevertheless, England was probably near the harsh end of the European spectrum in numbers executed, if not in cruelty.[71] The lack of effective policing and, perhaps, popular participation through the jury system explain why. Absolutist regimes, more strictly policed and where criminals were useful as slaves or soldiers, sharply reduced executions; Russia and Austria even experimentally abolished the death penalty.

Apart from its fondness for the gallows, by the standards of its time eighteenth-century England was not a violent, brutalized or polarized society. This was a golden age for the aristocracy, yet it had no privileged legal status, unlike on most of the Continent, where feudal lordship and serfdom were the norm. Even the wealthiest in England had to bargain and submit to legal procedures. Local power relations depended on "deference"; but deference had to some extent to be earned, and could be withheld. Landowners had to pay attention to the views of their neighbours and dependants, which might include turning a judicious blind eye to certain customary practices:

> In every parish almost in the kingdom, there is a kind of confederacy . . . against a certain person of opulence called the squire, whose property is considered as free-booty by all his poor neighbours, who . . . look upon it as a point of honour and moral obligation to conceal, and to preserve each other from punishment.[72]

Attempts to enforce the letter of the ancient Game Laws (which reserved all game to the lord of the manor) could lead to serious confrontation with small landowners and tenant farmers.[73] Force was rarely available to maintain public order. Magistrates, mayors and constables had to rely far more than today on negotiating with angry people face-to-face. Draconian measures could only be used in what contemporary opinion regarded as extreme cases—for example, organized poaching by armed gangs of outsiders, but not the occasional taking of a hare by a local cottager.

Even the poorest had legal rights, including to economic assistance under the 1601 Poor Law.[74] This gave ordinary men and women, taking turns in their parish as Overseers of the Poor, the responsibility for assisting their needy neighbours who applied to them, the cost being met by a "poor rate" on the wealthiest members of the community. By the late eighteenth century it was unique in the world, "generous and successful enough to be termed a miniature welfare state."[75] In France—to put this in context—relief funds in 1790 averaged the equivalent of two or three shillings per year for each poor person, and in many regions were only enough to provide a pound of bread per year—just an emergency hand-out.[76] The beneficiaries of the English Poor Law were mostly the elderly, children, single-parent families, the sick and the unemployed, who could be given work—farmers could be required by magistrates to take on job-less labourers at a minimum wage. It was often wasteful, demeaning, open to abuse and in some circumstances cruel, but could also be generous and humane. At Erith in Kent, for example, overseers made grants not only for clothing, food, fuel, rent, medical care, cleaning and decent burial, but also "a pint of wine for Susan Ashton," "tobacco for Old Youngs," spectacles, money "to Samuel Jones to purchase a cow," "beer for Sterling's wife's burial," and marriage costs. In Yorkshire, grants or soft loans were made to set up small businesses: tools, machinery, even horses and carts were provided.[77]

This was possible because by the standards of its time—and indeed by the standards of parts of the world today—England was wealthy. Foreign visitors found ordinary English people visibly better off. The French writer Marie-Anne Du Bocage was impressed in 1750 to find that the rural population of Oxfordshire "have their houses well furnished, are well dressed and eat well; the poorest country girls drink tea, have bodices of chintz, straw hats on their heads, and scarlet cloaks upon their shoulders." Thirty years later a German pastor found Londoners "from the highest to the lowest ranks, almost all well looking people and cleanly and neatly dressed [with] not near so great a distinction between high and low, as there is in Germany."[78] Clothes were the manifestation of the material abundance that defined what it was to be English, and of which the English had long been proud: eating, drinking and dressing better than the downtrodden peoples of the Continent, symbolized by thin soup, skinny bodies and clogs. England's quality of life, as measured by the consumption of non-essentials and life expectancy, was "as high as could be expected anywhere on this planet."[79]

## ENGLAND AND BRITAIN

The creation of the United Kingdom in 1707 marked a new phase in an ancient history. As long as England had existed, the lands to the north had played an important part in its politics, never more so than during the Civil War, when Scottish armies had been decisive and Scottish Presbyterians had tried to impose their religion on England. Scotland still posed a threat to English security during the first half of the eighteenth century because of the Franco–Stuart alliance. Union was intended, after many previous efforts, to stabilize the political and strategic situation. Clear religious (and hence cultural and political) divisions remained within the United Kingdom: in Scotland, the Presbyterian Church was established by law; in Wales, Catholicism and then Methodism embodied cultural separateness; and eventual union with Ireland made religious conflicts and inequalities central to Westminster politics.

The Acts of Union created a common market and a single sovereign parliament, but the United Kingdom remained in legal and cultural terms multi-national, like several other contemporary states, most obviously the Habsburg Empire. There was no ambition, in that pre-nationalist and pre-democratic age, to create a single nation, or to inculcate a single feeling of British identity obliterating those of Scots, Welsh, Irish or of course English. The United Kingdom has never tried to become "united" in the sense understood at the end of the eighteenth century by France's nationalist republic, officially proclaimed "One and Indivisible," and which forcibly erased historic and ethnic identities. Once the danger of Scottish Jacobitism faded, the British state accepted and even promoted national differences, and hence the British army, a vehicle for ethnic pride, has had Royal Irish Hussars, Royal Welch Fusiliers, Royal Scots Greys, etc. But, significantly, no regiment is entitled "English," as if Englishness were the root-stock of Britishness onto which the others were grafted. Englishness similarly became in due course the lowest common denominator of American, Australian and other settler identities, invisible because pervasive.

This has led to considerable confusion. Many people, including many Scots and Irish and most Europeans, instinctively spoke of "England" to mean the United Kingdom; many still do. The English themselves soon began to mix up England and Britain.[80] Once they called Britain "England"; now they tend to call England "Britain." The idea of Britishness and even of a British nation gradually took substance during the eighteenth century.[81] It was applied mostly in external and imperial contexts—the empire and the army were "British," and Britannia ruled the waves: British nationhood was political, global and secular.[82] People in all the island nations began to think of themselves as having a dual identity. But all maintained, and knew that they maintained, very distinct cultural and political personalities. This has been lamented by some, and welcomed by others: Britishness was "voluntary and open, not essential or inherited."[83] As such, it could be extended across the globe; but it could also be reversed by the independence or autonomy of its constituent nations, even centuries later.

How does this affect our understanding of the subsequent history of England? Does it dissolve into the United Kingdom and its history stop?

Clearly not, no more than the histories of Ireland, Wales or Scotland do. Or must English history logically become a provincial history, like a history of Texas or Prussia, focusing on internal events, or on the processes of inter-reaction with the larger entity?[84] Such an approach would be evidently inadequate. Many historians of Ireland, for example, treat its history as that of a colony, but it would be absurd to treat England as a colony of Britain or the empire. Moreover, the United Kingdom was not a federal state, with new political institutions separate from and above those of England. These institutions, as we have noted, were those of Westminster. England after 1707 became the front legs of the pantomime horse, taking the main part in setting the common direction in domestic, foreign and imperial matters. Its history, to be meaningful, has to be written simultaneously at several levels: English, British, international and imperial. This inevitably means using different terms in different contexts. In the chapters that follow, some (for example on the Industrial Revolution or on Victorianism) essentially concern England. Those on the Empire or the two world wars necessarily show England operating within a larger entity. Thus England and its history continue, with a new flag, for some purposes a new name, and a rapidly changing world view.

# CHAPTER 9

# The Rise and Fall of the
# Atlantic Nation

*We are a small spot in the ocean without territorial consequence,
and our own power and dignity as well as the safety of Europe,
rests on our being the paramount commercial and naval power of
the world.*

Henry Dundas, secretary at war (1794–1801)[1]

The 1688 revolution was not only domestic in its aims and importance: it also reoriented foreign policy, committed England to play a
crucial part in European affairs, and, as is clear in retrospect, set it on the
path to world power.[2] The first act of Willem van Oranje, even before he
became king, was to dispatch troops to the Continent to fight the French.
While he lived, England was in a personal union not only with Ireland and
Scotland, but more importantly with the Dutch Republic. After Anne's
death, England was linked with Hanover. So for the first time since the
1450s it became a Continental power, its "horizons . . . delineated by two
German rivers, the Elbe and the Weser."[3] Within a single lifetime, what
had been a poor, weak, unstable and declining kingdom, well below Sweden in military terms, made itself a global empire. Its political institutions,
archaic, eccentric and seemingly doomed before 1688, were now compared favourably with those of the ancient world.[4] The English language,
hitherto known only in the islands and a scattering of outposts, and
English culture and manners, hitherto considered strange and provincial,
grew fashionable even in Paris and Versailles. Voltaire promised his friends
"to acquaint you with the character of this strange people . . . fond of
their liberty, learned, witty, despising life and death, a nation of philosophers."[5] England—London above all—became a global bazaar, insatiably
sucking in and spewing out goods, money, ideas, words and people. It
thus played an increasing part in the economic, demographic, social and
political transformation of the world, in ways that were unplanned,

largely uncontrollable and in many ways cataclysmic—a process in which England, both subject and object, master and slave, was itself transformed.

The 1688 invasion was an event of European importance. Trying belatedly to reverse it, the French in March 1689 sent a naval squadron, money, arms and 8,000 troops with James II to invade Ireland. They planned to gather support, invade Scotland, and march on London. But the Franco–Irish army failed to take the port of Derry (later renamed Londonderry), which withstood a siege from April to July 1689—a fatal delay. James and William met face-to-face at the River Boyne on 1 July 1690. This was a European battle. Both their armies were commanded by current or former officers of Louis XIV, and included French (on both sides), Dutch, Danish, German, English and Irish soldiers. James's army was defeated, but the war went on with French support for more than two years, and even then guerrilla war continued—another disaster for Ireland. The Dublin parliament passed "Penal Laws" to break the power of the Jacobite aristocracy, which further poisoned relations for generations. Thousands of Catholic Irishmen—the famous "Wild Geese"—were allowed to leave to join the French and other Continental armies, and for generations many young men followed the same path.

War between France and the Three Kingdoms continued for twenty-five years with only one pause. The Nine Years' War (1688–97), a coalition opposing the power of Louis XIV, was succeeded by the War of the Spanish Succession (1701–14), fought to prevent Spain and its empire falling into the hands of France, which would thereby have acquired southern Italy, much of South America and the Spanish Netherlands. These were wars of attrition, whose costs, as we have seen, transformed English government and politics. Huge armies fought hideously bloody, but rarely decisive, battles. Large areas of the Continent were ravaged to make them incapable of sustaining an enemy army. Long defence lines anticipated the trenches of 1914–18. Little of this gruelling fighting in Flanders, the Rhineland and Spain remains in the national memory—at most a few vaguely remembered names, above all Blenheim (the Anglicized name of the Bavarian village of Blindheim), fought on 13 August 1704. John Churchill, soon Duke of Marlborough, was a rare phenomenon: a brilliant English general. He had thrust into southern Germany to support the Holy Roman Empire invaded by the French. His largely German army arrived in a state to fight, thanks to painstaking organization and his ability to pay cash for food and fodder with wagon-loads of money provided by the City of London. For the first time for generations, a French army was smashed: half its men were killed, wounded, prisoners or dispersed;

its artillery, its regimental colours and its commander were captured. Blenheim caused elation in England, as its first great victory since 1588. It was interpreted as a Protestant and more broadly a Christian triumph over an immoral Louis XIV, religious persecutor and violent disturber of Christendom.[6] Two years later, in the Low Countries, Marlborough won the no less crushing victory of Ramillies, which excluded France from the Spanish Netherlands, and then Oudenarde, which led to the fall of the great fortress of Lille and opened the way for a possible march on Paris. Yet still no decisive result was reached. At Malplaquet (1709), in the Spanish Netherlands, the death toll was comparable with the terrible first day of the Somme in 1916, and it shocked all sides. As we have seen, suspicions were voiced that Marlborough and the Whigs were pursuing the war beyond reason for personal ambition and financial gain—Marlborough did indeed become extremely rich. A product of this polemic is the quintessential Englishman "John Bull," a character in a Tory tract by the queen's physician, Dr. John Arbuthnot. The "honest plain dealing fellow . . . very apt to quarrel . . . loving his bottle," is ruined by a crooked lawyer, "Humphrey Hocus" (Marlborough), in pursuing a lawsuit against "Lewis Baboon" (Louis XIV) over the inheritance of "Lord Strutt" (Charles IV).[7]

A war of such intensity had historic domestic repercussions. Most fundamental was the Act of Union (1707), cemented by the struggle against Louis XIV. In London, as we have seen, a pro-peace Tory government came to power, arguing (with Jonathan Swift and Daniel Defoe eloquent propagandists) that the time had come to create a balance of power and not weaken France too much. Marlborough was replaced and went into voluntary exile. The Treaty of Utrecht (1713) ended a period of extreme instability in European affairs. The union of the crowns of France and Spain was forbidden by the treaty, although Spain later became France's main ally against Britain. The Spanish Netherlands were ceded to the Habsburgs, safeguarding Holland. France again recognized Britain's Protestant succession and this time expelled the Stuarts, who sought refuge in independent Lorraine, then papal Avignon and finally Rome. Britain gained tracts of North America, strategically important naval bases at Gibraltar and Minorca, and a hopefully lucrative trading concession—the *asiento* (permission to supply slaves and send one annual trading ship to Spanish South America).

The link with Hanover long remained controversial, and crystallized a fundamental and long-lasting political division over participation in European politics. George I and II and their ministers, notably the Duke of Newcastle, with the support of Low Church Anglicans and Dissenters concerned with the defence of Protestantism, favoured a more European policy. Opposition Whigs (notably the Earl of Chesterfield and later William Pitt), High Church Anglicans and the remaining Tories accused them of sacrificing English blood and treasure for dynastic interests in Germany, and instead advocated a "blue water" strategy concentrating on naval, colonial and commercial interests. It seemed to many English people that they had lost all control over their destiny and their pockets. As a 1719 pamphlet put it:

> A Nation which hath stood its ground, and kept its privileges and freedoms for Hundreds of Years, is in less than a Third of a Century quite undone; hath lavishly spent above 160 Millions in that time, made Hecatombs of *British* Lives, stockjobb'd (*or cannonaded*) away its Trade, perverted and then jested away its Honour, Law, and Justice.[8]

Despite such grumbling, there was not much choice as long as France seemed to be aiming at "universal monarchy," and threatened to re-impose the Stuarts, "popery" and "arbitrary power." Unless the Stuarts could be persuaded to embrace Anglicanism and come back as constitutional rulers—an ever-receding prospect—the preservation of English liberties meant fighting for "European liberties" against France. There was, however, a long truce in the 1720s and 1730s, as both countries recovered from the effects of war and Walpole followed a peaceful policy. But both European and imperial tensions would cause a renewal of the struggle in the 1740s.

## BEYOND THE VAST ATLANTIC

> See, where beyond the vast *Atlantic* surge . . .
> Shores, yet unfound, arise in youthful prime . . .
> These stoop to Britain's thunder. This new world,
> Shook to its centre, trembles at her name:
> And there, her sons, with aim exalted, sow
> The seeds of rising empire, arts, and arms.
>
> James Thompson, *Alfred: A Masque* (1740)

Since Elizabeth I, in whose honour Virginia was named by Sir Walter Raleigh in 1584, England had begun acquiring transoceanic territories by settlement, force or even gift (Tangier and Bombay were part of Catherine of Braganza's dowry when she married Charles II). In the early eighteenth century its colonies were still less important than those of Spain, Holland or Portugal. There was nothing to suggest a great British imperial destiny.

Literary historians discern signs of incipient imperialism as early as Spencer and Shakespeare (*The Tempest* being a favourite example, as Prospero takes over Caliban's island). But most people in England, including those in power, seem to have remained little concerned about colonies until the mid-eighteenth century. Walpole was said to think that "it would be better for England if all the Plantations were at the Bottom of the Sea."

The priority in colonial policy was national security, and enhancing the financial and maritime power of the metropolis by trade. There was "a strong element of fear" in British thinking—fear especially of France—"and very little overt enthusiasm for the task of ruling."[9] Most territories were put in the hands of chartered trading companies, such as the East India Company (chartered in 1599), the London Company and the Plymouth Company (both 1606), and the Ohio Company (1747). The commercial nature of the British Empire (as it began to be called in the late seventeenth century) became a source of pride:

> Instead of Treasure robb'd by ruffian War,
> Round social Earth to circle fair Exchange,
> And bind the Nations in a golden Chain.[10]

Britain's American colonies were peopled in a multitude of ways during the early eighteenth century. Unpopular religious minorities were encouraged to seek new horizons, most famously the Puritan "Pilgrim Fathers," who sailed to Massachusetts in 1620. Jacobite rebels and reprieved criminals were offered transportation in preference to the gallows or the dungeon. African slaves formed a majority of the population in the West Indies and in some of the mainland colonies, and were present everywhere—there were 15,000 in New York: "slavery was a fundamental, acceptable, thoroughly American institution."[11] Voluntary emigration also boomed, especially after the Seven Years' War: there were English, Catholic Irish, Ulster "Scotch-Irish," Scots, Welsh, Germans (10 percent of the total population), Dutch, Finns, French and Jews. The impecunious could sell themselves into temporary bondage to pay their passage. Scots and Irish were particularly prominent in what was now a British, not an English, empire. The American population doubled every twenty-five years, and pushed west to find new land. Settlers were self-consciously British, and strongly attached to what they considered their rights as British subjects within a growing Atlantic nation.[12]

English exports and imports gradually shifted away from the Continent until by the 1770s more than half were to and from the wider world—a pattern that, with fluctuations, has continued ever since.[13] The consumption of new and fashionable commodities—sugar, cotton, tea,

Asian textiles, tobacco, coffee, chocolate—trickled down from the elite to an expanding market, and dynamized economic activity. England re-exported sugar and tobacco to Europe, and exported manufactures to the colonies. Its merchant marine, protected by the monopoly in colonial trade under various Navigation Acts, expanded, as did government revenues from customs duties. Men and money were thus available in time of war. A minister was stating a commonplace when he recalled that "Great Britain can at no time propose to maintain an extensive and complicated war but by destroying the colonial resources of our enemies and adding proportionately to our own commercial resources, which are, and must ever be, the sole basis of our maritime strength."[14]

Colonial policy was thus galvanized by European struggles, as statesmen began to realize the importance of maritime commerce. "Once, land forces made the destiny of states," reflected the French foreign ministry in 1779, "but since a century ago Neptune's trident has become the sceptre of the world."[15] Neither France nor Britain had begun with an ambition of expanding territorial empire. They wanted, as a French finance minister put it in 1752, "no victories, no conquests, only plenty of merchandise and some augmentation of dividends."[16] Conquest and government took place when there was direct competition between them, and where each was trying to restrain or exclude the other. This was most evident, and had the greatest consequences, in North America, the Caribbean and India.

The essential region was the Caribbean, the source of Europe's most profitable trading commodity, sugar. Heat and disease meant that cutting and processing sugar cane was lethal for Europeans. African slaves, who succumbed less quickly, were imported. Some 6 million people, plus the huge number who died in the process, were shipped from Africa in one of history's worst crimes against humanity. The British were by far the largest shippers, carrying over 3 million people between 1660 and 1807, when Parliament banned the trade; the French, and the Portuguese in Brazil, were their biggest customers. African rulers were eager suppliers. The trade expanded, reaching an all-time peak in the 1780s, when British slavers were transporting about 120 Africans per day.[17] Sugar flowed out and imports flooded back: linen from Ireland and Scotland, fish from Newfoundland, timber and rum from New England, and manufactured goods from England. This was the notorious "triangular trade": carrying manufactured goods to Africa to exchange for slaves, sold in the Caribbean to purchase sugar for Europe. By 1780 Liverpool was shipping one-third of Manchester's total cloth exports to Africa.[18] Britain and France were prepared to make unlimited efforts to seize and hold sugar islands, principally Jamaica for the British and Saint-Domingue (now Haiti) for the French. Tens of thousands of troops were repeatedly sacrificed to tropical diseases: officers resigned and men deserted when ordered there. But as George III put it to one of his ministers in 1779, "Our islands must be defended even at a risk of the invasion of this island"—Britain itself.[19]

The mainland colonies from Georgia to Nova Scotia, of growing significance because of their swelling populations, were less spectacular sources of wealth: societies of small towns and agricultural villages, they were mainly purchasers of manufactured goods from furniture to hair powder, and suppliers of commodities such as tobacco, rice, furs and indigo. But they were different from other colonies in being generally seen as extensions of Britain. There is no sign that they were growing apart from the mother country—indeed, there was increasing integration as colonists imported ideas and fashions as well as goods.[20]

The third great focus of overseas ambition was Asia, for centuries a source of luxury goods that Europe could neither grow nor make—spices, fine textiles and increasingly tea. The secretary of the East India Company told MPs in 1767, "We don't want conquest and power. It is commercial interest only we look for."[21] Europeans built fortified trading posts—the British at Calcutta, Bombay and Madras; the French at Pondicherry and Chandernagore; the Portuguese at Goa; the Danes at Tranquebar. Some grew into major ports, bigger than any town in the American colonies. Calcutta was founded in 1690 by Job Charnock, an agent of the East India Company who went out to India during the Cromwellian period, and showed his mettle by marrying an Indian widow, whom, according to tradition, he had snatched from her husband's funeral pyre. Calcutta had about 120,000 people by 1760—only a few hundred of them British—when New York had a mere 18,000. The support of the Indian merchant and administrative classes in these booming ports, closely involved in trade with Britain, was important in establishing British power.[22]

The European role in India was transformed by the conflict between France and Britain in Europe. Despite attempts to maintain profitable neutrality, the two East India Companies clashed. The local context is important. The Mughal Empire had originated in the 1520s with Muslim invaders from Central Asia, who conquered most of the subcontinent by the following century: this was their period of splendour, that of the Taj Mahal (c.1650) and the Great Mosque in Delhi (1656). Dynastic conflicts, religious and regional rebellions, and defeats inflicted by the Marathas (Hindu peasant warriors) and the Persians, who sacked Delhi in 1739, fragmented the empire into regional power centres, often ruled by former Mughal officials (such as "nawabs"—governors). European contemporaries—and earlier British historians of empire—portrayed an India in the grip of aggressive warlords, with peace eventually brought by British hegemony. The picture is mixed. More recent accounts present some post-Mughal powers as making viable efforts at state-building, and the Europeans as adding to the chaos.

The French raised local military forces—it was never difficult to recruit in India. They found that they could recoup some of their costs, and make huge private profits for their officials, by hiring troops out to Indian rulers, who became valuable allies in the Franco-British struggle. The British followed suit: by 1761 the East India Company had 2,000 European and 23,000 Indian soldiers. Europeans thus became involved in Indian politics, despite the caution of shareholders in London, concerned for their dividends, and ministers of the Crown, keen to limit their commitments. There grew up a symbiotic relationship of alliance, commerce, bribery, and debt involving Indian rulers and merchants, Company traders, and British and Indian soldiers.[23] Some Indian rulers had agents and lobbyists in London, and wealthy Company officials gained peerages or bought seats in the Commons. The established Mughal way of paying for military support was by making grants of land with the taxation revenue they commanded, and hence Europeans became involved in tax collection and territorial rule. In 1765 the Company received from the Mughal emperor the right to collect the taxes (the "diwani") of his richest province, Bengal: about £2m per year, equal to one quarter of the domestic revenue of the British Crown. This became the Company's main single source of income, and also a means of subsidizing British war costs outside India. Bengal— with a population of about 20 million people, far more than Britain and the American colonies combined—was the first place in which Company officials exercised quasi-sovereign authority. For mixed reasons of patriotism, security, personal profit and idealism, they seized the opportunity to found a territorial empire that had neither been envisaged nor desired in London.[24]

## THE FIRST GLOBAL WAR

The end of the War of the Austrian Succession in 1748 (see p. 322) left Britain and France in a state of cold war. The French wanted to halt the growth of the British colonies in North America, which had over 1,000,000 inhabitants to only 75,000 French in New France along the St. Lawrence valley and 6,000 in Louisiana, mostly in the Mississippi delta. The French also asserted a theoretical claim to vast tracts of the Great Plains. Though their numbers were small, they had an effective militia and important native allies, while the British colonists, grumbled the Duke of Newcastle, "don't seem to be able to defend themselves even with the assistance of our money."[25] The French pushed south along the Ohio valley, arresting or killing British traders and building forts, aiming to hem the British colonies into the coastal zone. A worried meeting of colonial representatives at Albany in 1754 concluded that the French intended to bring "the whole continent to [its] rule [in] a unified French plan [for] universal monarchy"[26]—this old bugbear being rather a colonial obsession.

The first direct clash took place in the Ohio valley in May 1754, when young Major George Washington, the son of a Virginia planter, and 100 Virginian militiamen and native allies attacked a French patrol of some 35 men, and subsequently massacred the wounded. Washington was accused in France of murder.[27] For the first time, both Britain and France sent regular forces to North America. A large British expedition to the Ohio valley was ambushed and slaughtered on 9 July 1755 by a French and native force near Fort Duquesne (now Pittsburgh). The British seized some 300 French merchant ships and 7,000 crewmen. The two countries were still formally at peace.

There took place in 1756 a "diplomatic revolution": the old enemies Austria and France allied against their new enemies, Prussia and Britain. Thus, the struggle that began on the Ohio became another great European war—the Seven Years' War (1756–63), often described as the true "First World War," involving Britain, France, Prussia, Austria, Sweden, and eventually Russia and Spain. But the greatest historic consequences of this European war were elsewhere: it changed the destinies of America and India.

The French took the offensive on three continents. Their ally the Nawab of Bengal captured the British post at Calcutta in 1756. Prisoners were crammed into a small cell (the "Black Hole of Calcutta"), where many died—a story propagated by Macaulay and once known to every schoolboy as a justification for subsequent British conquest. In south India, the Irish Jacobite General Lally, commanding French forces, promised to "exterminate all the English in India."[28] In North America the French and their native allies raided into New York and Pennsylvania. In August 1757 the garrison of Fort William Henry in New York were seized and many scalped. This episode, immortalized in James Fenimore Cooper's *The Last of the Mohicans* (1826), further poisoned relations. The French captured the British naval base at Minorca and invaded Hanover. Prussia was assailed from all sides. The veteran politician Lord Chesterfield lamented that "we are undone . . . at home, by our increasing debt and expenses; abroad by our ill-luck and incapacity . . . *We are no longer a nation. I never saw so dreadful a prospect.*"[29]

These defeats, combined with the worst harvest failures for generations, had dramatic repercussions. The biggest food riots of the century began in August 1756, drawing on existing discontent with enclosure of common land and enforcement of the game laws. By December, there had been 140 riots in thirty counties, mostly against what people saw as unjust and unpatriotic profiteering in grain. At least 20 people were killed, 200 prosecuted, and 4 hanged. Yet in every case the government was forced to make concessions. Juries would not convict printers prosecuted for publishing anti-government pamphlets. The governing class was accused of failing in its duty to the nation. Admiral Byng, accused of cowardice in failing to stop the French seizure of Minorca, had his house attacked by a crowd, who saw him as proof of corruption in high places—he "lolls at ease on his soft couch, and is supported by a court interest."[30] He was court-martialled in 1757 and shot, but this did not allay popular anger. Patriotic organizations were founded, such as the Laudable Society of Anti-Gallicans, the Society of Arts, the Marine Society and the Troop Society, which published propaganda, awarded prizes for services to the nation, and recruited paupers and boys for the armed forces. They gave an opportunity for men and some women from outside the elite to participate in political life and display their patriotism.[31]

William Pitt, a ruthlessly ambitious, brilliant and mentally unstable politician, revived Patriotic demands (see p. 311): opposition to "corruption," a militia instead of a regular army, and concentration on seapower and colonies rather than Continental war. This made him the darling of the City of London and the London populace, the seedbed of Patriotism. Pitt was appointed a Secretary of State* in 1756, and again from June 1757 to October 1761. "I know I can save this country," he declared, "and that no one else can." His presence had a galvanizing effect on colleagues and public—he "roused the antient spirit of this nation," according to the London Common Council, "from the pusillanimous state to which it had been reduced."[32] He was ready to devote vast sums and maximum effort to winning: this was important, because his Patriotic standpoint had been one of opposition to Continental involvement, and especially to spending money on wars in Germany. He promised the House in 1757 that he "would not now send a drop of our blood to the Elbe, to be lost in that ocean of gore."[33] But he did: supporting the Prussians with a few troops

---

* One of two senior ministers responsible for the overall direction of policy, including foreign affairs.

in Hanover and more importantly with a lot of money. This forced the French to concentrate their huge military forces in Germany, enabling Britain to strip home defences and send ships and men to North America, the Caribbean and India. In 1759 there were 32 battalions of redcoats in America, and only 6 in Germany; while of France's 395 battalions, only 12 were in America and 4 in India.[34]

After four years of largely fruitless effort, 1759 was to be the Year of Victories, all snatched from the jaws of disaster. At Minden (Hanover) in August the small force of six British battalions helped to rout the French, apparently after advancing by mistake. At Quebec in September, the young and neurotic General James Wolfe ("Mad, is he?" said George II. "Then I hope he will bite some of my other generals") captured the town by a death-or-glory night attack up steep cliffs, and was killed at the moment of victory. The French prepared a knock-out blow: to invade weakly defended England. But in November, in one of the most audacious naval actions in history, the British fleet under Admiral Sir Edward Hawke, in the midst of a storm, chased the French into rocky Quiberon Bay, Brittany, and sank or drove aground the core of the French navy. It was "akin to a Miracle," wrote Hawke, "that half our ships was not ashore in the pursuite of the Enemy, upon their own coast."[35] Had that happened, England would have been open to invasion, and history might have taken a very different path. As it was, Quiberon Bay ended France's last hope of victory.

The British had gained the upper hand in India too, defeating the Nawab of Bengal at the historical battle of Plassey in 1757 thanks to the daring and guile of a Company clerk turned soldier, Robert Clive. Madras withstood a French siege (its garrison church had prudently been built with a bomb-proof roof) and its army took the main French base at Pondicherry. Finally, after Spain had belatedly entered the war on the side of France in 1762, the British grabbed the rich colonial prizes of Havana and Manila—the latter by a scratch force from Madras of Indians, British, Germans and French prisoners, excited by the prospect of loot.

## TRAVAILS OF A PATRIOT KING

The approach of victory enabled the new young king, George III—one of our most high-minded, determined and disastrous monarchs—to sack his Whig ministers, led by veteran magnates the Dukes of Newcastle and Devonshire, in a policy that would begin to undermine the newly victorious empire. The first king since James II to be born in England and the first since Charles I to be devoutly Anglican, George announced on accession in 1760 that he "gloried in the name of Britain." He had described Hanover as "that horrid Electorate which has always lived upon the very vitals of this poor country." He yearned to be a Patriot King, which, he believed, meant ending partisan politics and welcoming all men of good will into the service of the nation—what one admiring Cambridge don called "his Majestys noble plan, the total abolition of all party distinctions."[36] In practice, this meant breaking the Whigs' forty-year near-monopoly on jobs and patronage. Members of traditionally Tory families—stigmatized by the Whigs as crypto-Jacobites—found themselves named Justices of the Peace and officers in the Militia. Lists of appointments were published with asterisks by the names of Tory appointees in case anyone missed the point. Whig grandees were humiliated by no longer ruling the roost in their "countries," seeing old enemies favoured, and being unable to reward or even protect faithful supporters, many of whom were sacked from government jobs in the greatest clear-out since the ousting of the Tories in 1714.

This was not a return of the old Toryism, which had ceased to exist as either a party or a programme, and remained at most a family tradition tinged with nostalgia.[37] Yet George's supporters were now attacked as Tories by displaced Whigs, though they did not use that name themselves, and had no party organization. Some were indeed Tories by John Wesley's definition: "one that believes God, not the people, to be the origin of all civil power."[38] Among them there were sentimental Jacobites such as Samuel Johnson, now however ready to acknowledge the Hanoverian monarchy as established "by the long consent of the people."[39]

Many Whig grandees and their followers soon accepted the new situation and were willing to take office. But there remained vocal and powerful unreconciled groups often known as the "Old Whigs" or "Revolution Whigs," who saw themselves as fighting to resist or restrain George III. At the most high-minded and dignified end of this heterogeneous opposition were the "Rockingham Whigs," a group round Charles Watson-Wentworth, 2nd Marquess of Rockingham, a prime example of the wealthy, cultivated and public-spirited Whig oligarchy: he was a Fellow of the Royal Society and the Society of Antiquaries, a member of the Society of Dilettanti, a trustee of Westminster School, vice-admiral of Yorkshire and Lord-Lieutenant of the West Riding (until George III dismissed him); he owned broad acres in Yorkshire, Northamptonshire and Ireland, and controlled several parliamentary seats; and he was a member of White's and the Jockey Club, a horse-lover and a patron of the arts who commissioned Stubbs's masterpiece *Whistlejacket*. Like other politically minded grandees, he supplemented his native abilities by hiring the best available talent, in his case Edmund Burke, his private secretary and political brains. Burke defined the Whig ideal: "Persons in your station of life ought to have long views ... You, if you are what you ought to be, are the great oaks that shade a country and perpetuate your benefits from generation to generation."[40] Rockingham believed that he and his kind ensured "the solid foundations on which every good, which has happened to this country since the Revolution, have [sic] been erected."[41] He deplored George III's effort to undermine these foundations, as he saw it, by abusing his prerogative and vast powers of patronage.

The king's opponents gained some satisfaction from the humiliation heaped on George and his former tutor and Secretary of State, the Earl of Bute, by John Wilkes, who stood at the least high-minded and dignified end of the opposition spectrum. Wilkes was a clever and charming rake, and a self-publicist and political mischief-maker of genius who stepped into the political limelight in 1762. His main target was Bute, a cultivated but pompous Scot with the unfortunate family name of Stuart, whose only qualification for appointment to office was the young king's favour. To his enemies, he personified both Scottish encroachment into English politics and the increase of royal influence. Wilkes began to launch scurrilous attacks on Bute (mockingly represented by the drawing of a boot) in his paper *The North Briton*, its title an anti-Scottish joke. He accused Bute of sleeping with the king's mother and negotiating a give-away peace with France after the Seven Years' War, the Treaty of Paris (1763). Bute, who had no stomach for a fight, resigned, and George III's first attempt to rule as a non-partisan Patriot King ended ingloriously, as Patriotism was hijacked by Wilkes. In no. 45 of the paper, in April 1763, the king himself was indirectly attacked for accepting the "odious" and "ignominious" peace treaty. Wilkes was deliberately raising echoes of the Civil War, extolling Hampden and Sidney and the "right of resistance."[42] The government prosecuted the paper for seditious libel under a general warrant directed at its unnamed "authors, printers and publishers." Wilkes astutely made this an issue of civil liberties and had general warrants declared unlawful (they were reintroduced in 1936). He even won damages for wrongful arrest. He was nevertheless convicted of seditious libel and expelled from Parliament. The government made public his ingenious if juvenile erotic poem *An Essay on Woman*, which brought further accusations of blasphemy and obscene libel. He was seriously wounded in a duel and, after fleeing to France, outlawed—a pretty comprehensive indication of the limits of English free speech. He enjoyed a happy four-year exile, being lionized in France, touring Italy, and acquiring an expensive teenage mistress.

The Treaty of Paris, though "odious" to Wilkes, Pitt and their Patriot admirers, has been described as the most favourable peace treaty for any victor in European history.[43] It left the British dominant in North America and eastern India. The Duke of Bedford, Britain's chief negotiator, had urged "moderation," and was willing to return some conquests: "We have too much already," he wrote, "more than we know what to do with."[44] He feared that France might seek revenge, with the help of other powers alarmed by Britain's rapid ascent. He was right. "England is the declared enemy of your power and your State," wrote the French foreign minister, the Duc de Choiseul, to Louis XV. "We must employ the genius and all the power of the nation against the English . . . only a revolution in America . . . will return England to the state of weakness in which Europe will no longer have to fear her."[45]

Wilkes, fleeing his French creditors, returned from exile in 1768 to face the courts and stand again for Parliament in the metropolitan constituency of Middlesex, where he was triumphantly elected in perhaps the most famous by-election result in English history.[46] There followed two days of rioting in London. Windows not illuminated in celebration of Wilkes's victory were smashed. The Austrian ambassador was pulled from his carriage and had "45" painted on the soles of his shoes. The supporters of this new and entertaining manifestation of Patriotism were the voters of the big, relatively democratic constituencies of London and its suburbs, whose thousands of freemen and ratepayers, from bankers to shopkeepers and craftsmen, had had their political appetites whetted by wartime Patriotism, and were kept on the boil by the political and financial turmoil of the postwar years. Wilkes's personal saga between 1768 and 1774 is too complex and farcical for easy summary: it includes imprisonment, release, voluntary re-imprisonment, riots in London in which several people were shot dead by troops (who were then charged with murder), and multiple elections to and disqualifications from Parliament. All this made Wilkes a popular hero and the government increasingly ridiculous. Leading opposition Whigs (including Rockingham, Pitt and Burke) held their noses and climbed gingerly onto the Wilkesite bandwagon. Eventually, the government and Parliament gave up in disgust, and in 1774 Wilkes was elected Lord Mayor of London and entered the Commons unopposed as member for Middlesex. He remained an MP until 1790. Wilkes's importance was that he brought new issues into the political arena, including parliamentary reform and the right to publish parliamentary debates, which he ingeniously asserted by using the privileged jurisdiction of the City of London to protect printers from arrest. He proposed the first ever motion for parliamentary reform (to shorten

parliaments and exclude placemen), supported greater religious toleration, and supported the newly inflammable topic of American colonial
rights.

Victory had created a ferment in American colonial politics too. It first
inspired imperialist euphoria, with fulsome expressions of loyalty to
Crown and nation. The journalist, philosopher and scientist Benjamin
Franklin, speaking proudly as "a Briton," predicted in 1760 that "the
foundations of the future grandeur . . . of the British empire lie in America."[47] That empire was potentially "the greatest political structure
human wisdom ever erected," which would "awe the world." James Otis,
later a rebel leader, wrote in 1764: "We love, esteem and reverence our
mother country, and adore our king."[48] But it became increasingly clear
that imperial visions in the two branches of the "British nation" were
very different. The king and his ministers wanted to stabilize, rationalize
and strengthen the enlarged empire in case of a war of revenge by France.
They regarded the colonies' contribution to the Seven Years' War as feeble. They also wanted to reduce the financial burden on Britain, whose
postwar debt was unsustainable—there were anti-tax riots in England
and Ireland, as well as in America. They planned to increase the power
of governors, enforce the widely flouted trade regulations, and induce the
colonies to contribute more in men and money to their defence—the
Americans were among the most lightly taxed people in the world, paying on average 1 shilling per head annually compared with 26 shillings in
England.[49] Stabilization also required limiting settler encroachment on
Indian lands so as to prevent bloody and expensive conflict—and to prevent the colonies growing too fast to be kept under British control. A
Royal Proclamation in 1763, which has been described as "the Indians'
'Bill of Rights,'" recognized indigenous land ownership and set a western
boundary to settlement. It was accompanied by treaties of alliance
between the Crown and "the American nations," who, tragically decimated over several generations by imported diseases such as smallpox,
were now recognized as having a right to protection against the violent
land-hunger of the colonists. The northern Indian superintendent, Sir
William Johnson, was an adopted member of the Mohawk nation, spoke
their language, and was married to a Mohawk princess, Gonwatsijayenni
(usually known as Molly Brant, or "the Indian Lady Johnson"). Their
son William became an officer in the British army. Their house, Johnson
Hall, which still stands in upper New York, was a centre of a genuine
British-Indian society. Delegations were received in London and some
met the king. A Mohican clergyman, Rev. Samson Occom, preached
some 300 sermons in England in the 1760s.[50] Just as important, the con-

quered French, in communities to the north and the west of the British colonies, would have to be integrated into the empire by parliamentary legislation to recognize their Catholic religious rights and their own legal system.

All this greatly displeased leading colonial citizens. They believed that they had shouldered their share of the war effort; indeed, they considered themselves its real heroes. They claimed full rights as "free-born Englishmen," and wanted the empire to be an association of self-governing communities. Colonial Patriots stressed their loyalty to the Crown: what they rejected was rule by the Westminster Parliament. But for British politicians Parliament's supremacy was fundamental to the post-1688 system, and to question it was considered Tory doctrine and treason against the constitution.[51] Colonial assemblies (which existed in most of the American colonies) wanted to set their own taxes and decide their own contribution to defence. They were avid to seize the fruits of victory over the French by taking over the vast formerly French territories to the west and north, and pushing out the French, Spanish and Indians. They were outraged that Redcoats—in however thin and porous a line—were barring their way. George Washington, sorely indebted, needed "the profits to be made from buying good land cheap" and with his partners in the Mississippi Land Company petitioned the Crown for a grant of 2.5 million acres—enough for many thousands of homesteads.[52] Such men—who included several "Founding Fathers"—were impatient with London not because it was too imperialist, but because it was not imperialist enough.[53]

Americans were further stimulated by Wilkes's guerrilla campaign for liberty during the 1760s and 1770s. He was sent many presents from the colonies (including forty-five Maryland hams) and several American counties subsequently bore his name. In return, two Americans were elected sheriffs of the City of London. The rhetorical extremism of Wilkes's campaign helped to convince American Patriots that they were facing a systematic assault on the liberties of "free-born Englishmen" on both sides of the Atlantic.

Wilkes's antics were only a small part of a current of political opposition strong enough to bring the Atlantic nation crashing down into civil war and revolution. The opposition Whigs—who included weighty and intelligent people such as Burke and Rockingham as well as cheeky populists like Wilkes—believed they were facing an absolutist plot led by the king himself to subvert the constitution won by their forebears in the Glorious Revolution. In retrospect, their fears—set out in Burke's *Thoughts on the Cause of the Present Discontents* (1770)—look like a severe case of political paranoia spiced with opportunism. But there seemed circumstantial evidence to support it. The growing army, navy and bureaucracy of the "fiscal-military state" had always been thought potentially dangerous if the Crown abused it. The wealth of India, channelled through the East India Company, could corrupt the political system and enable the Crown to bypass Parliament. There was public disquiet about abuses of power by the Company, many of whose officials, including Clive, had become obscenely rich through "private trade" (under highly privileged conditions) and "presents" from Indian rulers. Clive had rapidly accumulated a fortune worth several hundred million pounds in today's values, which he excused on the grounds that he could have had a lot more. The villain of Samuel Foote's popular satirical play *The Nabob* (1772) was described as rich with "the spoils of ruined provinces."[54]

One of those ruined provinces was Bengal, victim of a famine in 1769–70 that was widely blamed on Company exactions. A Commons select committee concluded that "the laws of society, the laws of nature, have been enormously violated. Oppression in every shape has ground the faces of the poor defenceless natives."[55] Samuel Johnson declared that the discovery of the sea route from Europe to India had been "disastrous to mankind." John Wesley anticipated divine vengeance for "such merciless cruelty." But despite a strong sense of guilt and disquiet about India—which to some extent continued throughout Britain's two-century involvement—most commentators felt there was no turning back. Even though Company rule was, as various critics put it, "a detestable tyranny," if Indian trade were lost "national bankruptcy" would ensue, and France would be handed "the empire of the sea" and "universal monarchy."[56] Power in India, if too valuable to relinquish, had to be made more accountable. Then, perhaps, it might become a benevolent autocracy legitimized by good government—essentially, the hope that prevailed until independence in 1947.

An East Indies Regulating Act (1773) tried to bring the East India Company's activities under control. But Whig critics suspicious of government power (and concerned for shareholders) feared that handing more power to the Crown was a remedy worse than the disease. In the American colonies too, new Crown courts and officials were bypassing elected assemblies. Moreover, the government planned to appoint American bishops—final proof, for Dissenters, of the Crown's monstrous aim of undermining the spiritual and moral independence of the colonies.

So Patriots in England and America believed that they were fighting a concerted threat to English liberties. This engendered a long and momentous debate over the respective rights of the British Parliament and the colonists, encapsulated in the slogan "no taxation without representation." Samuel Johnson contested this argument in a pugnacious and widely read pamphlet, *The Patriot* (1774): "He that accepts protection stipulates obedience. We have always protected the Americans; we may, therefore, subject them to government," and Parliament had the right to impose taxes "on part of the community for the benefit of the whole."[57] The first attempt to levy direct taxes had been the Stamp Act of 1765, which was violently resisted. Burke organized a repeal campaign, and Rockingham, briefly in office, favoured compromise. When a colonial congress called for a boycott of British goods, the Act was repealed, amid Patriotic rejoicing and fireworks on both sides of the Atlantic. But the trouble was far from over. John Wilkes's agitation reached a peak. William Pitt, now Earl of Chatham, also attacked the government: two of his followers resigned office, and one committed suicide under the strain. Yet even the most Patriotic Westminster Whigs—including Pitt, Rockingham, Lord Shelburne, Burke and even Wilkes—were unwilling to concede complete autonomy to the colonies, though they eloquently denounced the use of force in America. Rockingham passed a Declaratory Act (1766) stating that Parliament did have the right in principle to legislate for America, even if it prudently refrained in practice.

Successive governments were understandably eager to extricate themselves from the American morass without wholly losing face. Most colonists too had had enough. A new Prime Minister, Lord North, appointed in 1770, had the seemingly clever idea of abolishing existing duties, leaving only a light duty on tea from India to maintain the principle of Parliament's taxation power, but actually making tea cheaper. Such a duty would be difficult for the Patriots to oppose, and the income would help pay colonial governors, making them less dependent on the local taxes voted by their assemblies. But the crisis had gone beyond such political finesse. A range of public grievances and private interests—not always very avowable, such as smuggling and land speculation—had pushed influential colonial Patriots to the point of rebellion. At the same time, public opinion in England was growing impatient with what seemed selfish, unreasonable and lawless demands. So when in December 1773 a group of Patriots (including tea smugglers) threw a shipload of tea into the sea in the "Boston Tea Party," it was seen as a moment of truth: "whether we will govern America," North told the Commons, "or whether we will bid adieu to it."[58] London ordered the closure of the port of Boston as a punishment, and it abolished many Massachusetts political rights, believing that moderate colonial opinion would rally or at least acquiesce.

At least as serious—though far less remembered by history—was the Quebec Act (1774), which placed that new colony, with vast territories in

9. The Atlantic empire

the west, in the hands of a royal governor without an elected assembly. This placed a barrier in the way of the western expansion of the existing colonies, which they regarded as their right of conquest. If further proof of London's sinister aims were needed, the Act gave legal recognition and financial endowment to Catholicism, the religion of the overwhelming majority of the French-speaking population. This was a necessary step towards securing their loyalty, but to colonial Patriots it amounted to "popery and slavery." Consequently, "every tie of allegiance is broke by the Quebec Act," declared the Patriot Arthur Lee,[59] and it set the colonies on the path to outright rebellion. A Continental Congress of delegates from Patriot committees met in Philadelphia in September to coordinate resistance. In England, the Whigs were equally outraged. Moreover, there were many on both sides of the Atlantic who, whatever their political sympathies, feared sending "armed legions of *Englishmen* . . . to cut the throats of *Englishmen*." Chatham and Burke appealed for conciliation. The latter proposed a looser and more diverse empire "of many states":

> We must govern America, according to [its true] nature . . . and not according to our own imaginations; not according to abstract theories . . . The temper and character, which prevail in our colonies, are, I am afraid, unalterable by any human art . . . An Englishman is the unfittest person on earth to argue another Englishman into slavery.[60]

The North government offered compromise. Leading colonial politicians were reluctant to break with the mother country, on whose protection they ultimately relied. Benjamin Franklin, for example, hoped that another war with France and Spain would reunite the empire. A Second Continental Congress in 1775 still denied any intention of "separating from Great Britain and establishing independent states."[61] But Patriot hotbeds, especially in New England, no longer sought compromise, and shooting began at Lexington, in Massachusetts, in April 1775, followed by a pitched battle at Bunker Hill, outside Boston, in June. In August the Crown issued a Proclamation of Rebellion. The colonists hesitated until the following July before responding with a ringing Declaration of Independence:

> We hold these truths to be self-evident: that all men are created equal; that they are endowed by their Creator with certain inalienable rights; that among these are life, liberty, and the pursuit of happiness.

## THE END OF THE ATLANTIC NATION

*The "Great" will soon be gone from Britain . . . in a few years she*
*will fall to the second or third rank of European powers without*
*hope of ever rising again.*

French foreign-ministry report, 1777[62]

Loyalties on both sides of the Atlantic splintered in what was generally regarded as another British civil war. Perhaps a third of the country sympathized with the American Patriots—especially Dissenters, the Whig opposition and some transatlantic business interests. Bristol, the heart of Atlantic trade, had elected two pro-American MPs, Edmund Burke and a merchant from New York. All deplored the use of force. "If an arbitrary Military Force is to govern one part of this large Empire," warned Rockingham, "it will not be long before the whole . . . will be brought under a similar Thraldom."[63] Such views inspired the most famous Commons motion ever tabled, in April 1780: "The influence of the Crown has increased, is increasing, and ought to be diminished." Its passing caused the leading Whig orator, Charles James Fox, to exclaim that "if he died that night, he should think he had lived to a good purpose in contributing to bring about this second revolution." The Duke of Manchester (a descendant of the Civil War general) declared portentously that Charles I had been beheaded and James II deposed for "offences against the constitution of infinitely less magnitude."[64] Chatham warned the House of Lords that America could not be reconquered, and he deplored the use of German mercenaries against British subjects: "If I was an American, as I am an Englishman, while a foreign troop was landed in my country, I never would lay down my arms,—never—never—never!" Several senior military commanders in America took similar views, and were reluctant to adopt an aggressive strategy. But the rebellion also caused public resentment in England. The government—under the affable and moderate North, who claimed to be fighting "the war of the people"[65]—was supported by most Anglicans and by the dynamic new movement, Methodism. "Who would have imagined," lamented a Whig peer, "that the ministry would have become popular by forcing the country into a destructive war and advancing the power of the Crown to a state of despotism?"[66] The American conflict gave new clarity and meaning to the fading identity of Tory and Whig.

The clearest line was religious, replaying England's "great divide"—the colonial Patriots and their supporters were attacked by government supporters as "Roundheads." Their strongest partisans were indeed English Dissenters and Ulster Presbyterians, who identified with them on religious and political grounds. Dissenting ministers encouraged petitions by their congregations. Unitarians, the intellectual avant-garde of Dissent, to whom leading American Patriots, including Benjamin Franklin and the erudite Virginia planter Thomas Jefferson, were close, provided spokesmen. The Rev. John Horne Tooke, a well-connected ally of Wilkes, opened a subscription for the "widows, orphans and aged parents of our beloved American fellow subjects . . . FAITHFUL to the character of Englishmen . . . inhumanly Murdered by the KING'S troops."[67] Three other prominent Unitarian supporters were the Rev. Richard Price, an expert on public finance, the Rev. Joseph Priestley, a well-known experimenter with gases, and most influential of all Thomas Paine, who rose rapidly from obscurity to international celebrity through his tract *Common Sense* (1776), which made him an intellectual leader of the American Revolution. Born in Norfolk in 1737, he had had a picaresque career as corset-maker, sailor, shopkeeper, teacher and customs officer, and "reading and public-house conversation familiarized him with the scientific, political, and religious assumptions of Enlightenment Europe."[68] He possessed a gift for slick and pithy polemic, stuffed with biblical and historical citations, leading to attractively simplistic conclusions. Monarchy was unbiblical and popish. American independence was inevitable, and would permit prosperous and peaceful isolation from European quarrels: "England to Europe; America to itself." *Common Sense* reached a huge international readership—100,000 copies were quickly sold. Paine revived "Country Party" and civic humanist ideas familiar earlier in the century, and now spiced them with the Whig obsession with George III and what Paine called his "thirst for arbitrary power."[69] Ironically, it was an absolutist monarchy which gave the rebels decisive support: the French. They had been anticipating this opportunity for years, and secretly supplied money and shiploads of arms.

There was a strong Loyalist, or "Tory," party in America, including Episcopalians (Anglicans), people with strong cultural, political and economic commitment to the Atlantic nation, or those who simply feared taking the step into rebellion. It included German and Scottish settlers, who felt little kinship with the "Roundheads." This view was so strongly shared in Scotland—where volunteers for new regiments came readily from formerly Jacobite clans—that some Whigs denounced the conflict as "a Scotch war." A prominent North Carolina Tory was Flora MacDonald, saviour of Bonny Prince Charlie thirty years before. A much greater stake in the conflict was held by Shawnees, Creeks, Mohawks, Delawares, Cherokees, Iroquois and other nations, who feared invasion if the colonists could overturn the 1763 Proclamation. Their support for the Crown was the largest and most united native American effort the continent would ever see.[70] They sought an alternative within the empire to the prospect of long-drawn-out genocide which duly followed American independence, brought about by disease, armed force and forced relocation.[71] Loyalist ranks were also swelled by enslaved Africans, after freedom was proclaimed for any rebel-owned slave joining Crown forces. Whenever British forces approached, hundreds, even thousands of slaves would join them, seeking freedom in a British uniform. Up to 100,000 slaves joined this unique mass escape, including many belonging to George Washington.[72] British and American Whigs were outraged. Paine denounced "that barbarous and hellish power which hath stirred up the Indians and Negroes to destroy us"[73]—a comment that recalls Samuel Johnson's jibe that "the loudest yelps for liberty" came from the drivers of slaves.

At first, the war went fairly well for the Crown. Despite some incompetence, much jealous bickering over strategy, and early half-heartedness among senior commanders hoping for compromise, New York was occupied during 1776 and Quebec successfully defended. The dwindling "Continental Army" under General Washington limped away from New York towards Pennsylvania. British commanders, hoping to defeat the rebellion in 1777 before France could intervene, tried to isolate the rebel heartland in New England by sending 5,000 men under the urbane General Burgoyne—a writer of stage comedies in his spare time—south from Montreal towards New York to link up with General Howe. As Burgoyne's progress seemed assured, Howe marched south, defeated Washington's army in September at Brandywine, and took Philadelphia. But Burgoyne's force, now unsupported, was unexpectedly cut off at Saratoga with dwindling food, and was embarrassingly forced to surrender in October. The Whig leader, Charles James Fox, recalled this later as one of the happiest events of his public life. Saratoga raised morale in the rebel camp, enabling Washington to stick it out over the winter of 1777 with the hungry and ragged remnant of his army.

Most important of all, Saratoga emboldened the French—eager, like Dr. Johnson's patron, to encumber the Americans with help after their sudden and startling success. The French foreign ministry decided that "1778 will decide the fate of England and the predominance of France."[74] Speed was essential, as London began to put out peace feelers to the Americans. After a series of French provocations which the British tried to ignore—sending arms and money, sheltering American privateers, and giving diplomatic recognition to the Continental Congress—a French and a British frigate finally clashed in June 1778 off Brittany, and the colonial rebellion became another world war, with Spain joining in 1779 and besieging Gibraltar, and Holland extending the war to the Indies. For the first time, a Britain without allies faced a France with allies, able to concentrate all its forces on a maritime war. The war was popular in France, and also changed attitudes in England, bringing about an upsurge of patriotism.

The French and their allies planned a knock-out blow by landing 20,000 men on the Isle of Wight, destroying Portsmouth, crippling British naval power, and leaving England open to future raids and invasions. Instructions were issued for dealing with the natives: "The Englishman is puffed up when he is prosperous, but easily depressed by adversity . . . Money will all the more readily induce them to sell us their wares, since profit-making is the main interest of this nation."[75] Militia camps were established round London and became popular attractions. Bumbling preparations began for removing livestock, vehicles and grain from threatened areas. An optimistic military planner hoped that all male civilians would make "a Stand against the enemy," with "women and boys blocking roads and driving off cattle." The *Morning Post and Daily Advertiser* tried to cheer its readers up:

> Tho' *Monsieur* and *Don* should combine,
> What have true *British* Heroes to fear?
> What are Frogs, and soup-meagre and wine,
> To beef, and plum-pudding, and beer?[76]

The huge combined Franco-Spanish fleet—104 warships—outnumbered the Royal Navy. The Channel was open, as the British fleet retreated. The invasion force was ready and waiting in Normandy. Never had the French navy been so near the goal it had often dreamed of: invading England.[77] The third attempt in forty years this time actually arrived in sight of the Devon coast, on 14 August 1779. England was saved by a combination of Franco-Spanish incompetence, cold feet and disease, "a terrible plague that disarms our ships," without the Royal Navy firing a shot, and they returned forlornly to France in September with 8,000 sailors sick or dying. So many corpses had been thrown into the sea that the people of Cornwall and Devon were said to be refusing to eat fish.[78]

Half a world away, Britain's problems and France's encouragement brought together a formidable alliance of Indian states, including the powerful Maratha Confederation and Haider Ali, the indomitable ruler of Mysore in southern India. The Company's Bombay army was forced to surrender to the Marathas in 1779, and its Madras army was bloodily defeated by Haider Ali in 1780—the worst military setback ever suffered by the British in India. In Bengal, the ruler of Benares, a former ally, massacred a party of Company troops and forced the governor-general, Warren Hastings, to flee for his life.

Britain mobilized its peoples and resources more than in any previous war for what seemed a struggle to survive as a great power and a prosperous society. As George III emphasized to his ministers, "We can never exist as a great or powerful nation after we have lost or renounced the sovereignty of America," for "the West Indies must follow them," and "Ireland would soon follow the same plan," and finally "this island would be reduced to itself, and soon would be a poor island indeed."[79] So the navy was increased from a peacetime strength of 16,000 men to 100,000 by 1782; 250,000 men were in the regular army or the militia, many of them Irish and Scots, plus 60,000 Protestant Irish volunteers. These forces were not, as legend would have it, raised by "gaols [being] purged, and ye gallows defrauded," as one officer put it:[80] many were artisans and skilled craftsmen, led by a socially diverse officer corps. Taxes rose by 30 percent, and by the end of the war absorbed 23 percent of national income—more than in any previous war or in any other belligerent country. This was bound to cause socio-economic and political discontent, whether from those who opposed the war or those impatient that it was not being won. A Whig "Association Movement" began to press for parliamentary reform, and the most radical elements began to speak of annual general elections, manhood suffrage, a secret ballot and payment of MPs.[81]

For Loyalists, whether in America, Great Britain or Ireland, the struggle enhanced their "Britishness" and a grim pride in being alone against all comers. The army in America celebrated the feast days of "our brother saints," Andrew, David, George and Patrick. There was no longer a Jacobite fifth column in Scotland; but there was much doubt about how the Irish parliament and people would finally react. Large numbers had joined volunteer defence units, and this gave Dublin leverage over London. Concessions were made to Irish demands for greater commercial equality with Britain. An Irish Relief Act (1778) and a (British) Catholic Relief Act (1778) reduced legal disabilities against Catholics, with the support of Anglican bishops. Irish Catholic notables declared that "two millions of loyal, faithful and affectionate" Catholics were ready to serve the king—a manpower bonus that would buttress British world power for nearly 150 years. The British government was forced to acquiesce in a gradual assertion of greater autonomy between 1780 and 1782 by the Irish parliament, known as "Grattan's Parliament" after the brilliant orator and tactician Henry Grattan, who masterminded its strategy.

A pro-American and anti-popery backlash ensued, supported by prominent Dissenters, including John Wesley and Richard Price. "Shall these

[Catholic] vermin bask in the sun shine of court favour, while the honest amiable Dissenter is stigmatized as an enemy to the King and the Country?" asked a pamphleteer.[82] George III was caricatured as a monk. There were riots in Scotland. A Protestant Association was formed, strongest in Newcastle and London. The agitation culminated in the most destructive outburst of collective violence in modern British history. On 6 June 1780 a strongly pro-American Whig MP, Lord George Gordon—whose stepfather was from New York, who had spent several years there, and who had resigned his naval commission in protest against the "mad, cruel and accursed American war"—presented a petition to Parliament backed by a large crowd dressed, on Gordon's instructions, "in their Sabbath days cloaths" and led by a man in a kilt and two bagpipers.[83] The petition demanded repeal of the Catholic Relief Act. The palace of Westminster was invaded, Whig leaders cheered, and ministers, bishops and judges jostled and de-wigged. Five days of rioting ensued in London and some provincial towns.

The legend of the "Gordon Riots" as merely "frenzy, augmented by . . . fermented liquors," anarchy, primeval savagery and "infectious madness"[84]—as dramatized in Dickens's *Barnaby Rudge*—is misleading. The rioters were not vagrants or slum dwellers, and few had criminal records. They were mainly respectable journeymen, apprentices, labourers, small businessmen and craftsmen, including signatories of Gordon's petition. One who may have signed the petition and was certainly in the front row for the burning of Newgate was the engraver, poet and religious radical William Blake.[85] Many were from working-class Dissenting congregations—Baptists, Methodists, some Scottish Presbyterians, even descendants of Huguenots and a few Evangelical Anglicans.[86] They were well informed, and consistently targeted Catholic institutions such as schools and embassy chapels (one diplomat in vain offered the crowd 1,000 guineas not to wreck his new organ); also the houses of wealthy Catholics, politicians and judges, notably Sir George Savile, proposer of the Catholic Relief Bill, and the Tory Chief Justice Mansfield, whose houses were burned; and finally symbols of power—magistrates' houses, law courts, toll gates, several prisons (including Newgate) and the Bank of England. Other buildings were left untouched, as were working-class Catholics and their houses. Not a single person was killed by the crowds[87]—a striking contrast with the outbreak of the French Revolution nine years later. Samuel Johnson saw "the good Protestants" calmly wrecking the Old Bailey: "There were not, I believe, a hundred; but they did their work at leisure, in full security, without sentinels, without trepidation, as men lawfully employed in full day."[88]

This was because the City authorities refused to act, through either fear or political sympathy. Without their sanction—the law required a magistrate to read the Riot Act to the crowd, after which they had an hour to disperse—troops could not be used: soldiers had been charged with murder after the Wilkes riots, even when shooting in self-defence. The Cabinet had no idea what to do. After five days of mayhem, the Privy Council was advised that troops could lawfully prevent felony, and the king in person ordered the army to act, saying that at least one magistrate in the kingdom would do his duty. Soldiers patrolled the streets with orders to fire on groups that refused to disperse, and about 450 people were killed or wounded. Whigs denounced the king's action, Fox declaring that he would "much rather be governed by a mob than a standing army." Eventually, 160 rioters were put on trial, and 22 men and 4 women, most aged between seventeen and twenty-five, hanged near the scenes of their actions.[89] Gordon himself, charged with high treason, was acquitted.

It is difficult to say what this extraordinary episode tells us about late-eighteenth-century England, and about the world's most modern city. It has been seen as the last manifestation of an old-fashioned "mob" whipped up by part of the elite.[90] Or was England potentially on the verge of revolution at home as well as in America, as some contemporaries thought? The crowd that nine years later detonated the French Revolution by storming the Bastille was only a fraction of the size of that mustered by Gordon. Did the effectiveness with which the riots were finally suppressed show both the fear and the ruthlessness of the British state? Or was there in fact little "fear of the mob"?—immediately afterwards, there were exuberant popular celebrations of General Clinton's capture of Charleston.[91] The riots are marginalized in histories of British radicalism: their anti-popery does not fit comfortably into an idealized narrative of progressive popular struggle.[92] What the riots above all show is the continuing potency, especially in London, of militant religious Dissent galvanized by the American Revolution and which would remain the core of English political radicalism for generations. But because they had temporarily been so uncontrollable, the Gordon Riots seem to have ended the old tradition by which a degree of rioting had been condoned by opposition politicians as justifiable and tactically useful, as in the Wilkesite agitation. Now, John Wilkes personally took part in the defence of the Bank, and Whig politicians mostly disavowed the rioters. In future, political campaigning would be more polite and disciplined—as in the campaign against slavery.[93]

Otherwise, the political and military situation seemed to be stabilizing in 1780. North won a snap general election. There was no prospect of the French and Spanish trying another invasion. The Spanish navy was occupied in an epic siege of Gibraltar, which continued on and off for nearly four years. In America, English, Loyalist, Scottish, Native American and German troops advanced through the southern colonies. The Dissenting minister Richard Price lamented "the common expectation . . . that America will soon be ours again."[94] Washington's army was plagued by desertions and mutinies, and infiltrated by Loyalist agents. Wrote one congressman in 1780: "We are pretty near the end of our tether."[95] As the British war minister, Lord George Germain, saw it optimistically in December:

> So very contemptible now is the rebel force in all parts, and so vast is our superiority, that no resistance on their part is to be apprehended . . . and it is a pleasing . . . reflection . . . that the American levies in the King's service are more in number than the whole of the enlisted troops in the service of the Congress.[96]

So the likelihood arose again of a negotiated compromise. Some politicians had long considered abandoning New England—"not only no advantage but a considerable detriment"—and making "Hudson's River the barrier of our empire."[97] North assured Parliament in January 1781 that there was the prospect of "a just and an honourable peace."[98]

Washington implored more French help: without further money and supplies from France the rebellion seemed doomed, and without direct and substantial French military and naval help it would have been practically impossible to force the British out of those colonies they controlled.[99] France had provided money to pay for 15,000 American troops, and a French army of 5,000 men under the Comte de Rochambeau had been sitting in Rhode Island for months. In 1781 Versailles acted decisively. In March its Atlantic fleet was dispatched first to the West Indies, the main prize, and then, after failing to capture Jamaica, in July it sailed north to Virginia, to join up with Rochambeau and Washington. Fatally, the Royal Navy, intent on protecting the sugar islands, failed to stop them, and so the French navy and army were able to trap a small British force under General Cornwallis at Yorktown. Rochambeau's army besieged it, seconded by Washington's men and local militia. On 19 October, with many men sick or wounded and ammunition nearly exhausted, the British surrendered. They marched out playing a popular tune, "The World Turned Upside Down."

Yorktown was a fairly minor affair by the standards of European wars. Yet the choice of music was not inappropriate, for the psychological blow was severe: "Oh God! It is all over," exclaimed North. An MP wrote that "every Body seems really sick of carrying on ye American war."[100] A motion calling for peace was passed in the Commons. North insisted on resigning, for which George III, eager to fight on, never forgave him. The opposition Whig Rockingham returned to office in March 1782 and began to withdraw troops from North America, urging commanders to try to "captivate [American] hearts." The French fleet set sail for Jamaica to deliver the coup de grâce. The British fleet hastened westward to fight the only great battle it has ever fought outside European waters, and the only time the main fleet had been so far from home until it sailed to fight Japan in late 1944 and Argentina in 1982. The Battle of the Saints, in the Caribbean, on 9–10 April 1782, tilted the global advantage in Britain's favour, as the French and their allies ran short of money, men, ships and confidence. Admirals Rodney and Hood smashed the French fleet, using new tactics to break the enemy line. Rodney boasted to London, "You may now despise all your enemies." The Spanish failed to take Gibraltar in their final great assault in September, and the French, who had been hoping to effect another revolution in India, arrived with too little and too late: there was to be no Yorktown in Asia.

Some ministers wanted to do a deal with the Americans, and turn on France, Spain and Holland. But Rockingham and his successor, the Irish Whig magnate Lord Shelburne, were eager to end the war, against the express will of the king. This inaugurated several significant constitutional novelties: an opposition party came to office despite the opposition of the king, sacked nearly all the previous office-holders, and applied a programme adopted in opposition, which included measures to diminish the powers of the Crown—reducing the number of Crown appointments, bringing the Civil List under parliamentary scrutiny, disfranchising Revenue officers, and disbarring from the Commons men with state contracts (for example, to supply the armed forces). Ireland was given far wider autonomy. The new post of Foreign Secretary was created. So the British, as well as the American, constitution owed much to the American Revolution.

Peace negotiations were dominated by Shelburne. He had long sympathized with the American Patriots, and wanted to safeguard trade and political influence by a generous settlement. The French envoy was astonished at how "the English are buying peace ... their concessions with regard to boundaries, fisheries and loyalists exceed anything I would have believed possible."[101] Britain gave full independence to all the thirteen colonies involved in the rebellion, ceded to them all the territory south of the Great Lakes, and returned Florida to Spain. The Americans jumped at this, abandoning their allies—the preliminary peace agreement was signed without the French even being informed. Shelburne was little concerned about the Loyalists and the freed slaves, who at best were packed off to other colonies. The Native American allies he regarded with distaste, abandoning them to the new Republic, which "knew best how to tame their savage natures."[102] This has been called "a sentence of death for their civilization."[103] Shelburne's terms were attacked in Parliament, and he was forced out of office in April 1783. But Parliament could do nothing about a treaty that had already been signed, other than punish the government, and in September the treaties of Versailles and Paris were ratified.

American independence was a hammer blow to British prestige, and a triumph for France. The Habsburg emperor wrote England off as now "a second-class power, comparable with Sweden and Denmark."[104] French intervention had prevented the British from keeping much more of America than Canada and the West Indies. France, Spain and Holland had seized command of the seas for a crucial period, hampering British operations against the rebels and preventing the deployment of reinforcements. The fate of America was largely decided in the West Indies, which had first call on British troops and ships.[105] Despite the legend of lumbering Redcoats being defeated by straight-shooting frontiersmen, there is little doubt that the Crown forces, including many Americans—among them the native and the enslaved—could have defeated the half-hearted "Roundheads" had Britain not also been fighting a world war.

This, however, is not how we remember it. As in so much of our history, the Whig version, in both its English and American variants, has prevailed, and we have generally accepted the idealized vision of the American Revolution as a noble struggle for freedom and democracy. Here indeed is a case of history being written by the victors. America's flattering foundation myth is itself of immense historic importance. It drew on Enlightenment ideas, particularly those of Locke and Montesquieu, to give a universal significance to the traditional rhetoric of "free-born Englishmen," and so provided Europe with a new vista of optimism. We can see the difference if we compare the United States and Canada: the latter, however admirable, has never excited the world with the promise of "life, liberty, and the pursuit of happiness."

## FROM ATLANTIC NATION TO GLOBAL EMPIRE

*Nations, like mortal men, advance only to decline . . . We have read the most brilliant pages of our history.*

*Norfolk Chronicle*[106]

The Atlantic nation was no more: the future imagined by Benjamin Franklin and Adam Smith in which the capital of the British Empire might move to America had vanished.[107] The Crown had mobilized Indians, Africans, Germans, Catholic Irishmen, French Canadians and Scots against "true-born Protestant Englishmen" in America, and this left bitter divisions at home. The war had lasted eight years, from the first shots in Massachusetts to the last in southern India. Britain had been humbled, reduced and indebted. A quarter of the nation had seceded, worse than the loss of Normandy and Aquitaine in the 1450s. William Pitt the Younger, Chancellor of the Exchequer, told Parliament bluntly that "the memorable aera of England's glory ... is past."[108] Its political system, discredited by the Wilkesite agitation, the American Revolution, and the Gordon Riots, had disastrously failed; angry critics blamed excessive royal power, parliamentary corruption or the electoral system.

Then came another constitutional crisis. In December 1783 the king recklessly mustered every scrap of his influence and patronage to engineer the defeat in the House of Lords of a new ministry he abominated—an opportunistic coalition of the faint-hearted Lord North and the Whig leader, Charles James Fox, who attacked the king as the "infernal spirit which really governs." George then appointed as Prime Minister the strait-laced reformer William Pitt, aged twenty-four, relying on the prestige inherited from his father, "the Great Commoner," to rally Patriot forces to the Patriot King. This might have caused chaos, even revolution. George considered abdicating and retiring to Hanover, and the radical Duke of Richmond thought of moving to France for safety. But it became a royal triumph when Pitt won an early general election—the first time this tactic had been used so boldly—and set out to clean up and simplify the financial system, make public spending transparent, and reduce the huge national debt. Time-servers, moralists, taxpayers and modernizers rallied to Pitt's "Patriotic" policies of "oeconomical reform." This was a sign of fundamental change in the nature of the state, which would accelerate during the next gruelling round of war against France: state employment was ceasing to be a way of earning the highest income through fees and perquisites, and starting to become a salaried civil service with an ethos of public interest.[109] Pitt also proposed reforming Parliament, but few were interested: radicalism was essentially the old "Country Party" ideology, opposing corruption and high taxes. Altering parliamentary representation or extending the franchise were minority concerns. The king was now praised for having listened to "the voice of the people." Helped by his deserved reputation for dullness, domestic virtue and agricultural pursuits, "Farmer George" came at last to embody the Patriot King, guardian of the constitution. But in the late 1780s he suffered the first attack of severe mental confusion—the famous royal "madness"—due to a hereditary condition, porphyria. The public reaction seems to have been one of sympathy.

Even Ireland was relatively peaceful. Unrepresentative as it was, the Dublin parliament had taken advantage of the American war to achieve a greater measure of self-government. Power was in the hands of the "Protestant Ascendancy," making Ireland, like parts of eastern Europe, a country in which the rulers differed in religion from most of the ruled. Stirred by vivid memories of the rebellion of 1641, sectarian divisions remained, sometimes resulting in violence. However, both sides realized that a major uprising was unlikely, except in the event of foreign intervention. That none came was a missed opportunity for France and its allies, and testimony to their maritime failures. They would be somewhat more successful in the 1790s.

Paradoxically, defeated Britain emerged politically and economically stronger from the war than its victorious but exhausted enemies. It retained the West Indies, Canada, Gibraltar and its position in India. Trade with the United States—coveted by the French—was re-established with remarkable speed. Businessmen knew the market, could supply the world's cheapest manufactured goods, and offered unmatchable credit; moreover, the Americans rather ungratefully did not much like their papist and absolutist French benefactors. American demand became the most dynamic factor during a long trade boom beginning in 1783 and continuing for a generation, fuelling England's Industrial Revolution, as we shall see in the next chapter.[110] By 1821 the United States took 44 percent of its imports from Britain, and only 7 percent from France.[111] The ex-colonies remained sulkily part of the British world. Two centuries later, trade with North America remains a pillar of the British economy.

A new kind of British Empire was emerging, more racially and culturally diverse, more authoritarian, and also more paternalistic and—in British minds—more progressive. American independence relieved London of huge political burdens, including defence, the protection of native rights and the future of slavery. Defeat in America made the British public less willing to overlook the buccaneering immorality of the old colonial empire. There were more calls for redress of abuses in India. Slavery, epitomized by the notorious sexual debauchery of slave-owners,[112] now rapidly became a central moral and political issue. Criticism of the slave trade had been muted until the 1770s. There were many respectable participants, including King's College, Cambridge, philanthropic Dissenters and American Quakers. They had well-rehearsed justifications. Slavery was universal and immemorial; indeed, Britain and a few neighbouring countries were unusual in not having it at home. Africans bought by

Europeans were already captives in war or condemned criminals facing death or enslavement in Africa anyway. Above all, slavery was economically indispensable:

> I pity them greatly, but I must be mum,
> For how could we do without sugar and rum? . . .
> Besides, if we do, the French, Dutch, and Danes
> Will heartily thank us, no doubt, for our pains;
> If we do not buy the poor creatures, they will;
> And tortures and groans will be multiplied still.[113]

The trade had become routine, with slave-ships called *Charming Sally* or *Reformation* (owned by Quakers). One West African slaving post even had a golf course.[114]

Criticism of the trade had become audible in England in the 1760s. Laws were passed to give slight protection to slaves. A campaign against the trade began in the 1770s, and over the next century it was to become the most important humanitarian campaign in English history. It took off as American slave-owners were "yelping for liberty," and the loss of thirteen mainland colonies weakened the slavery lobby. In 1785 the vice-chancellor of Cambridge set as the subject for a prestigious essay prize "Is it right to make slaves against their will?" It was won by a St. John's undergraduate, Thomas Clarkson—surely the most important student activist in history—who began a life-long career as a propagandist and organizer. In 1787 the Society for Effecting the Abolition of the Slave Trade was set up, with many women members, whose role proved crucial. In 1789 a young Tory MP and Evangelical Anglican, William Wilberforce, encouraged by his friend William Pitt, the Prime Minister, began a long parliamentary campaign to ban the trade. In 1792 the government received 519 petitions, containing 390,000 signatures, and there was a large-scale boycott of slave-grown sugar. However, the beginning of another war with France took abolition off the political agenda for several years.

The loss of American colonies made India more important. A perceptive French diplomat predicted that its possession would decide the world balance of power for the next century, and some in Britain agreed in seeing it "as the salvation, as the wealth, the grandeur, the glory of this country."[115] Yet the rapacious conduct of the East India Company's officials was a long-standing scandal. The Whigs—with Burke the most determined—wanted to dispossess the "utterly incorrigible" Company. But the attempt in 1783 by the Fox-North coalition to create a political board of control in London had been attacked, not without reason, as an attempt to use

Indian wealth and patronage for party purposes, and George III, as we have seen, seized the opportunity to bring the government down.

The principal figure in Anglo-Indian politics in the 1770s and 1780s was Warren Hastings, the first governor-general. He was an intelligent autocrat who aimed to reform Company rule and eventually bring its territories under the Crown. Britain, thought Hastings, must rule in India "with ease and moderation," using Indian men, laws and institutions "according to their own ideas, manners and prejudices."[116] Hastings heard petitions in public like a Mughal nawab, supported Hindu and Muslim scholarship, and encouraged British "Orientalists" to translate Muslim and Hindu law and scriptures. He has thus been seen as embodying a respectful British approach to India in contrast with the aloof and superior attitudes of the next century. Yet the fundamental business of Company government, especially in times of war, was taxation and trade, and Hastings can equally be seen as continuing the unscrupulous traditions of an organization greedy to extend its power and make its servants rich. This was Burke's view. His outrage focused on Hastings, "the first Man of India . . . under whom all the fraud, all the peculation, all the tyranny, in India, are embodied, disciplined, arrayed, and paid."[117] Burke obsessively pursued Hastings's parliamentary impeachment for over eight years, from 1786 to 1795: "I know what I am doing, whether the white people like it or not."[118] But Hastings was finally acquitted in the context of another war against France. His high-handed methods, such as imposing large fines on Indian rulers and forcing them into alliances, were excused on grounds of necessity. If the moral and legal attacks of Burke and others helped to establish the idea that imperial government must be exercised as a trust, not as a means of plunder, the benevolent despotism of Hastings was accepted by later generations as the means to bring effective, modernizing government.

Over the eighteenth century the British interacted more than ever with the rest of the world, sometimes in extraordinary circumstances. Sir William Johnson, as we have seen, married into the Mohawk nobility. James Skinner, born in Calcutta in 1778 to an East India Company officer and an Indian mother, served in the Maratha army and later that of the Company as the colonel of "Skinner's Horse," and became the polygamous patriarch of an Anglo-Indian military dynasty. Eunice Williams, captured in a French-led raid into Massachusetts in 1704, aged seven, was adopted by the Mohawks, and lived among them for eighty years; indeed, a considerable number of English women and men, captured in war, made new lives with their captors. Less exotic but more typical was the fate of Essa Morrison, an East End whore who ended up in North America in 1765, sentenced to transportation for robbing a drunken sailor—one of a steady stream of convicts who peopled the colonies.[119] Trade, exploration, consumption, seafaring, migration, war, criminality, slave-trading, captivity, sexual relations and imperial power created a fantastic variety of experiences and responses, from near-genocidal hatred to integration. Imperial rule clashed with cherished ideas of England as a nation characterized by freedom and, as we have seen, this caused conflict over America. Advocates of empire insisted that they could have it both ways: the English were, wrote John Bruce, the official historiographer of the East India Company, "a free though conquering people,"[120] whose liberty at home fitted them for enlightened rule abroad. The impeachment of Hastings and the anti-slavery campaign showed growing sensitivity to the darkest sides of Britain's imperial aggrandizement. But, even when consciences were pricking, the profits of colonial trade had to be kept flowing, and the naval and military power that stemmed from empire seemed indispensable to the security and greatness of the nation. There seemed no way of staying rich and powerful while keeping clean hands.

# CHAPTER 10

# The First Industrial Nation

To crown his toils, Sir Industry then spred
The swelling sail, and made for Britain's coast.
A Sylvan life till then the Natives led,
In the brown Shades and green-wood Forest lost . . .
Then towns he quicken'd by mechanic Arts,
And bade the fervent City glow with Toil;
Bade social Commerce raise renowned Marts,
Join Land to Land, and marry Soil to Soil.
    James Thomson, "The Castle of Indolence" (1748)[1]

After the Restoration in 1660, there began in England economic changes that would, for better and worse, transform the life of humanity more than at any time since the prehistoric development of settled agriculture. Over the previous three centuries, total global per capita wealth had increased by less than 50 percent; over the next two centuries, it increased by more than 700 percent.[2] After nearly three centuries of trial and error, much of the world is still trying to follow in England's footsteps. Why did it happen? What were its consequences, good and bad?

The Industrial Revolution—a term from the 1820s—has left a mixed reputation in our national memory. If it made England what Disraeli called "the workshop of the world," it did so by means of William Blake's "dark, satanic mills," squalid towns, and a degraded and exploited workforce. That at least was the belief of many at the time and since. As England changed, it cherished a cult of unspoiled nature, and it has retained ever since a bittersweet nostalgia for Thomson's "Sylvan life," a pre-industrial arcadia. We see it in art, literature, music and politics; in England's lack of love for its big towns; in the protective passion for "picture postcard" villages; in the ersatz rusticity of the suburbs; and in the widespread taste for rural holiday homes and mass devotion to the

National Trust. Not least, we see it in the way English history is written. Yet while deploring their own ancestors' fate the English applaud the industrializing efforts of developing countries which have created cities far bigger, filthier, more unequal and more crowded than the worst Industrial England ever managed.

The Industrial Revolution is one of the most studied transformations in history. Yet it remains mysterious, inspiring contradictory and ever-changing accounts. This is partly due to competing economic theories and ideological sympathies, and partly because the data—pieced together from miscellaneous and often fragmentary sources—is rarely conclusive. So fundamental questions remain. Was the Industrial Revolution a rapid transformation, a sudden burst of technological innovation; or was it a process evolving slowly over generations, even centuries—not really a "revolution" at all? Was it a domestic English development, or was it brought about by external stimuli—most controversially, imperial conquest and slavery? Was it a result of Enlightenment ideas fostered by political liberty? Or just of big coal deposits? Did England's people choose this new way of living or were they forced into it by rapacious landlords, capitalists and rulers? Did it make them richer or poorer, with lives better or worse? Why did it happen when it did? Why in England, and not in India, China or Holland?[3]

## DAYDREAMS OF DESIRE

*The working manufacturing people of England eat the fat, and drink the sweet, live better, and fare better, than the working poor of any other nation in Europe; they make better wages of their work, and spend more of the money upon their backs and bellies, than in any other country.*

Daniel Defoe, *The Complete English Tradesman* (1726)[4]

Economic transformation did not begin with coal, steam and new machines. It can be traced as far back as the Black Death, and the rise in living standards that followed it, which made the North Sea region unique as an area of high wages, high consumption and capital-intensive production (see p. 126). In this part of Europe, even as population rose again in the 1500s and 1600s, the gain in living standards had to a large extent been maintained by intensifying agriculture and diversifying economic activity—in England, among other things, by manufacturing woollen cloth.[5] Consequently, although England had always been one of the world's more prosperous countries, for centuries richer than many developing countries in the twentieth century, by the eighteenth century it was one of the very richest, with a growing urban, manufacturing and service sector exceeded only by Holland. Its income per capita in 1760 was slightly above that of India in 2000.[6] Its workers' wages held up, while other countries, such as once world-leading Italy, were inexorably impoverished by rising populations. Although China and India were the world's main exporters of manufactured goods—cotton, silk, porcelain—and Asia had long enjoyed sophisticated commercial systems, average living standards there were much lower than in England.[7]

Then came something new, first seen in Holland and England in the late 1600s. People whose basic needs were fulfilled developed ever-increasing appetites for comfort, novelty and pleasure; and these appetites generated a widespread eagerness to earn more money to gratify them.[8] This is probably connected with the slackening of religious conflict, the growth of "politeness" (see p. 285), and the appearance of exotic imports from Asia and the Americas. People began acquiring more, and new types of, goods. They abandoned the uniform, unchanging, hard-wearing items that had satisfied most people since time immemorial—solid wood, tough leather, pewter, thick dark woollens. Household furniture was upgraded: in came wardrobes, comfortable chairs, clocks, mirrors, earthenware, even china. Old items were replaced with newer, more fashionable ones.[9]

There was a revolution in the clothing of ordinary people: in came white linen undergarments, white stockings, colourful outer clothes, ribbons, men's wigs, women's silk hats, neckerchiefs, silver buckles. The aim was to be neat, clean, modern and respectable, but not "flashy"—the look of Enlightenment England. Regional styles of dress disappeared. People were not aping their betters, but showing they were as good as anyone. Young working men and apprentices worked and spent—and sometimes stole—to look what they called "tight," "knowing" and "genteel." A sixteen-year-old Nottingham apprentice, William Hutton, was well aware in 1739 of what was at stake:

> I was arriving at that age at which the two sexes begin to look at each other . . . and a powerful mode to win is that of dress. This is a passport to the heart, a key to unlock passions . . . I envied every new coat . . . I made shift, with a little over-work, and a little credit, to raise a genteel suit of clothes . . . The girls eyed me with some attention; nay, I eyed myself.[10]

Clothing was the spearhead of the Industrial Revolution, because it began the mass consumption of machine-made goods. Cotton, adopted first by women for its brightness and cleanness, became the leading sector of industrialization. Buying goods became a form of enjoyment and self-invention. This was not a dour Protestant work ethic of thrift and saving, but a romantic work ethic based on self-expression, ambition and enjoyment—"daydreams of desire."[11] Fashion and novelty were the aims; and hence the appetite for goods was insatiable.

People began to consume more and more things that were merely pleasurable—and novel pleasures at that: tobacco, tea, sugar, coffee, fresh white bread, convenience foods and alcohol.[12] Harvest labourers in 1750s Hertfordshire were being fed not just beer, mutton and carrots, but tea, coffee, biscuits, chocolate, sago and rum. Many of these new pleasures had a social aspect—smoking, drinking, showing off new clothes—and this meant having more money to spend in taverns, gin shops, coffee houses and pleasure gardens, all characteristics of eighteenth-century society.

These new pleasures began to supplement, and even replace, the old unchanging pleasures of Merrie England: eating a lot, drinking a lot of beer, and taking plenty of time off (more leisure was taken before 1600 than would be taken again until the later twentieth century). Spending more required people to work longer and differently. People took fewer days off (facilitated by the Commonwealth's abolition of saints' days, not reversed at the Restoration). More married women took jobs. Working hours began a steady rise until they reached heights probably unprecedented in world history, on average 65–70 hours a week, compared with 40–50 hours in the developing world today.[13]

New habits of consumption reached not only the "middling sort," but trickled down to the poor, who acquired more goods than would have been available to a prosperous yeoman a century earlier: ownership of saucepans, dishes, clocks, pictures, mirrors, curtains, lamps, and tea and coffee utensils at least doubled between 1670 and 1730.[14] Watches, usually in silver cases—a new fashion item—become general among English working men in the second half of the century. They were a coveted means of display, with ribbons and seals dangling from the breeches pocket. They were also (as they could be pawned) an investment. By the 1790s there were an estimated 800,000 silver and 400,000 gold watches in England.[15]

What is termed proto-industry (rural, household-based production for non-local markets) supplied these new appetites to get and spend. This "industrious revolution" was powered more by perspiration than technological inspiration. Similar appetites fuelled the Asian "Tiger economies" in the late twentieth century, where meat, televisions, jeans, motor-cycles and mobile phones played the role of tea and sugar, watches, cotton clothes and crockery in providing incentives to earn and consume.

Women played a leading part in these changes, for girls and married women had unusual economic and social autonomy.[16] After the Black Death (again), when higher wages and social mobility increased socio-economic freedom, there developed in north-west Europe a characteristic marriage pattern. It had, and still has, profound cultural and social effects. In contrast to other continents (where marriage was and often still is universal, young and arranged, where new couples live within an extended family, and where young women occupy an extremely subordinate position) English women had more choice of partner and married much later, often their late twenties.[17] The Poor Law may have lessened the need to have lots of children, as parents were not solely dependent on their children in old age.[18] Moreover, English law, though it made married women subordinate to their husbands, recognized single women as independent of their male relatives. Late marriage gave young people several years of earning, spending and relative independence, often away from home. Among the consequences were rising premarital conceptions (from 15 to 40 percent over the eighteenth century) and illegitimacy (from 1 to 5 percent of births—nearly 1960s levels). In all, over half of first-born children were conceived out of wedlock, though usually with marriage the expected, if not the obligatory, consequence. Marriage and reproduction were responsive to economic opportunity: couples married when they could afford it, and set up households independent of parents and in-laws. Wives' and husbands' roles were increasingly similar and equal, with women often heads of families and owners of businesses. Family members were more willing and able to seek a variety of work—it was rare for fathers, mothers and children to work together in the same occupations. By the time of the Napoleonic Wars, two-thirds of married women were earning wages in such trades as retailing, lace-making, brewing and spinning—a much higher proportion than in most of the world today. Often it was the new earnings of young people and married women which enabled individuals and households to acquire new luxuries.[19]

## FROM AN "ORGANIC" TO A "MINERAL" ECONOMY

*It is impossible to contemplate the progress of manufactures in Great Britain within the last thirty years without wonder and astonishment. Its rapidity, particularly since the commencement of the French revolutionary war, exceeds all credibility. The improvement of steam engines, but above all the facilities afforded to the great branches of the woollen and cotton manufactories by ingenious machinery, invigorated by capital and skill, are beyond all calculation.*

Patrick Colquhoun, 1815[20]

This prosperous, hard-working, fun-loving and acquisitive society gave birth to what would become the Industrial Revolution. Precisely how this happened remains a matter of much theorizing and debate. One view sees it as the consequence of a complex of factors: the Enlightenment and its interest in science and experiment, literacy and education, the English political and legal systems, agricultural productivity, urbanization and increasing foreign trade, for example. Another view isolates a few key factors: high wages, coal, crucial inventions. The intuitive answer—one that we tend to apply to developing countries today—is that there are complex preconditions for economic growth.

If we take this view, there is much to say about England as an advanced economy, comparable only with Holland, and perhaps a few parts of western Germany, India and China. It had an unusually high level of literacy and education—probably higher, for example, than Pakistan today.[21] Some schooling for working-class children was not uncommon. Only in England and Holland could a majority of workers sign their names—something unprecedented in world history.[22] Two-thirds of English boys took long apprenticeships in the seventeenth and eighteenth centuries—impressive in the light of today's unfulfilled ambition to have half of young people in post-school education. Schooling and apprenticeship cost money, and required the prospect of high wages to make them affordable and attractive as investments, even to the poor: one Ealing gardener paid 6d a week to educate his two children—as much as he spent on beer. If there is a literacy threshold for economic development, England had probably passed it by 1700: there was practically universal literacy in high-level commercial occupations and close to universal in occupations where it was functionally valuable. England's economy was centred on what was now the biggest city in the western world. Its government kept order while permitting an unusual degree of liberty. It also gave protection against foreign competition. Its legal system protected property, but not so much as to prevent change: for example, by land enclosure. Its agriculture, already efficient and adaptable, could feed a growing and increasingly urban population.[23]

Did economic growth simply evolve from this mix? Some hard-headed economic historians, unwilling to believe what cannot be measured and tested, question these commonsense explanations.[24] Enlightenment science had little connection with industrial technology. Parliamentary government and civil liberty are not necessary for growth, as present-day China shows; and even in the eighteenth century absolutism may have produced slightly higher economic growth than representative government. Besides, a striking feature of eighteenth-century England was the unusually high level of taxes and trade regulations its governments imposed—not usually thought of as conducive to investment and growth.

This raises a controversial question. Over 80 percent of this tax revenue was spent on war over the eighteenth century, from which Britain finally emerged the biggest gainer. The Royal Navy alone received some 10 percent of national income—about twelve times its share today. So is the explanation of England's economic dynamism that it was a uniquely successful predator, beginning under Elizabeth with the buccaneering enterprises of Drake, Raleigh and Hawkins, taking further steps with the Republic's seizure of Jamaica and its Navigation Acts (1651), becoming global with the Hanoverian conquests in America and India, and culminating in nineteenth-century imperialism? Worse still, was England's economic development—as the Marxist historian and Caribbean politician Eric Williams asserted—crucially financed by the profits of slavery?[25] Was the Industrial Revolution thus tainted from its very origins, and the prosperity of the English—"aggressive, ruthless, greedy, unscrupulous, hypocritical"—built on the suffering of others—"happy, innocent, weak—waiting victims"?[26] Is that a root cause of the poverty in many parts of the world today? This is certainly the view of many from countries that found themselves at the receiving end of British power, and it produces feelings of guilt among sensitive English people two centuries later.

Here again, economic historians disagree. Some argue that foreign trade was a relatively small part of Britain's economic activity: exports were less than 10 percent of GDP in 1780, far less than today. The trade with Asia and the Americas was a small part even of that.[27] The slave trade and its offshoots were a small proportion of total foreign trade, and profits were economically negligible—around 1 percent of national income. A recent verdict is that overall "sugar cultivation and the slave trade were not particularly large, nor did they have strong growth-inducing ties with the rest of the British economy." Slavery certainly "did not by itself cause" the Industrial Revolution.[28] Hence, the Industrial Revolution was mainly driven by domestic demand—"the periphery was peripheral."[29] But other historians argue that although foreign trade was not the full explanation of economic growth, exports were crucial for those new industries that formed the leading sector of modernization—textiles, iron, engineering. These exported a rising share of their products: around 40 percent in 1801.[30] Slave-produced colonial products—particularly American cotton and Caribbean sugar—were at the heart of economic change. Part of the difference in interpretation depends on technical debate about economic growth models, hypothetical alternatives and financial statistics. But it is evident that industrialization as it actually materialized in England was shaped, even if not wholly caused, by overseas trade: how could the Industrial Revolution even be imagined without cotton? Whether there would have been other ways to achieve economic modernization at the time is a matter of debate.

Had England been decisively defeated between the 1740s and the 1810s by its European and colonial rivals—especially France, Spain and Holland—and its maritime power and trade thereby destroyed, then its economic growth and the Industrial Revolution could have been stifled. In that case, as George III feared at the time of the American war, it might have become "a poor island indeed," and France might have taken the lead in both economic development and global power.[31] Instead, England's finally successful struggle against French hegemony produced a secondary bonus: dominance of trade and communications between Europe and the world overseas, which consolidated and spread its trading strength in the nineteenth century. It was then that the Industrial Revolution really took off.

But this is not the same as saying that victory in war and the possession of foreign and imperial trade "caused" the Industrial Revolution. Other countries enjoyed important maritime and colonial commerce too. Holland remained a major Asian trader. Spain possessed the largest colonial markets. The biggest eighteenth-century import-export trade in colonial products was that of France, whose economic growth was built on West Indian products. But the Industrial Revolution did not take place in Spain, or France (not for want of trying), or even rich and commercially advanced Holland. So to explain English economic uniqueness we are led to what was different about England: technology, wages, consumption and energy.

During the eighteenth century there came an amazing succession of technological changes. Abraham Darby's iron-smelting with coke (1709) bypassed the need for charcoal; Thomas Newcomen's steam engine (1712) permitted the pumping out of deep coalmines; John Kay's flying shuttle (1733) speeded up weaving; James Hargreaves's spinning jenny (c.1765) multiplied the effectiveness of hand-spinning; Richard Arkwright's water frame (1769) used power for spinning with rollers; James Watt's condenser (1769) meant economical steam power; Samuel Crompton's mule (1779) began mass production of high-quality yarn; Henry Cort's rolling mill (1783) speeded up production of iron; Edmund Cartwright's loom (1787) enabled water and steam power to be used to make cloth. These transformed the productivity of workers and were continually improved. The focused ingenuity that produced them was found among the often self-taught artisans and businessmen who were already involved in the "industrious revolution." Ten "macro-inventers" have been identified: those mentioned above, plus John Smeaton (engineering) and Josiah Wedgwood (pottery). Three had been to grammar schools and one, Cartwright (the son of a landed gentleman), to Oxford. The others had little schooling, but had learned technical skills through apprenticeship, adult education and experiment. Newcomen, Hargreaves, Arkwright and Crompton were all of artisan background. Several had Dissenting connections.[32] Ordinary people thus changed history.

What made these ingenious labour-saving technologies worthwhile were the already high wages of English workers. Also, buoyant consumer demand ensured that new technology made profits. Cheaper products then further fed the growing demand for goods. Heavy investment in continuous technological development was thus viable in England. By contrast, spinning jennies were not taken up in France or India because labour was so cheap.[33] The French government was eager to obtain technology from England by industrial espionage and by offering inducements to British entrepreneurs and workers. Significantly, this did not always succeed. In 1785, with the help of the ironmaster William Wilkinson, a huge plant producing the Continent's first coke-blast iron was built at Le Creusot, in eastern France. It soon became a white elephant. Where wages and demand were low and skills rare, expensive prestige projects rusted.[34]

The epoch-making technological innovation was to harness energy generated from coal, marking the beginning of a transition from what has been termed an "organic economy" (wood-, wind-, water- and muscle-powered) to a "mineral economy." This permitted England to overtake Holland in wealth and India in manufacturing. It also did much to shape the country's economic, social and political geography, concentrating much of the new industrial activity near the coalfields of the Midlands and the north. England had very large coal deposits, which were indispensable to the Industrial Revolution. But so did many other parts of the world, including India. It was only in England that the mineral economy could take off, because it already had a sizeable coal industry (80 percent of Europe's production in 1700), principally to heat London, swollen by centuries of mercantile development. Early steam power—Newcomen's simple "atmospheric engine" (c.1712), which created a vacuum by heating and cooling steam—used so much coal that it was only viable at the pit head, where

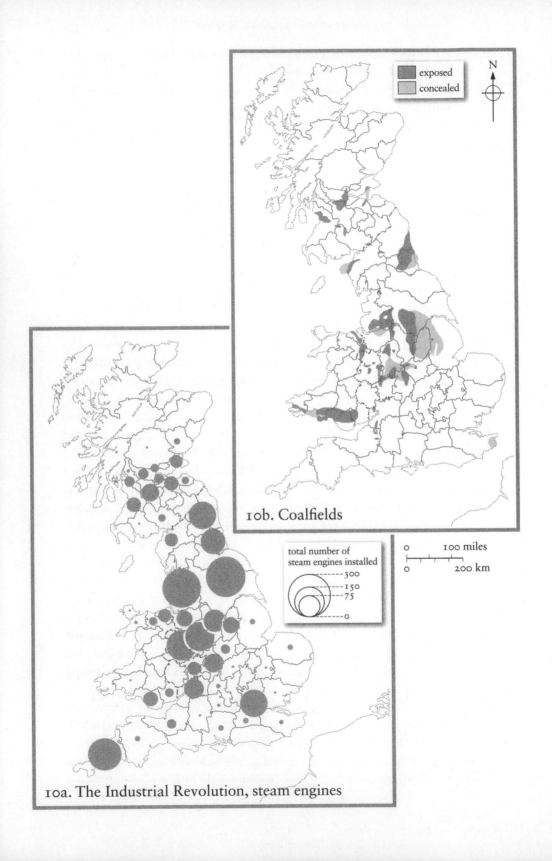

N

exposed
concealed

10b. Coalfields

total number of
steam engines installed
300
150
75
0

0        100 miles
0        200 km

10a. The Industrial Revolution, steam engines

fuel costs were negligible. Continual improvements in fuel economy (such as Watt's condenser) gradually extended the use of steam, though it took until well into the nineteenth century to produce a transforming effect on the English and then the world economy through powered machinery, railways, steamships and later electricity generation. It would be more than two centuries before the global spread of the carbon economy began to pose an environmental threat to the very well-being it had created.

## PROFIT AND LOSS

Though long term the global consequences, good and bad, of the Industrial Revolution are obvious, the immediate effects on England and its people are less so. This has long been a vexed question. From the beginning there were enemies of the new economy, who attacked it on moral, social, aesthetic and eventually ideological grounds. It was corrupting, encouraging luxury and vice; it was disruptive and ugly. Others had praised "commercial society," most famously the Scottish philosophers David Hume and Adam Smith, who asserted that the new economy remedied poverty and unemployment, and its "obvious and simple system of natural liberty" provided the basis for a peaceful, civilized, cooperative and stable society. Individual self-betterment would serve the general good as if by "an invisible hand": "It is not from the benevolence of the butcher, the brewer, or the baker, that we expect our dinner, but from their regard to their own interest."[35] So economic freedom was not only right, it was also productive. Oppression and slavery were not only wrong, but also inefficient. Pessimistic and optimistic interpretations have continued ever since, and have shaped English social and political ideas.

The fundamental question is whether the Industrial Revolution improved or damaged the lives of the English people as a whole. "Optimists" could point to the undeniable increase in living standards that took place—eventually. They inferred that technology and increased economic activity *must* have increased wealth. "Pessimists" argued that industrialization for many decades brought workers little but cost them much—loss of independence and self-respect, devaluation of skills, deteriorating health, high mortality, bad food, crushing labour (for men, women and children), and destruction of cherished customary rights and community traditions. In short, the Industrial Revolution created an impoverished, downtrodden and embittered proletariat, ground down by the power of money and the oppression of the ruling classes, and forced by long and bitter struggle to assert their meagre rights to a share in national wealth.

What is the evidence? Much painstaking investigation has focused on workers' wages and living standards. Perhaps surprisingly, real wages barely rose over the crucial period of the Industrial Revolution—by only 4 percent between 1760 and 1820. Over this period working hours greatly increased. Women and children worked more intensively, contributing about 25 percent of family incomes. Food prices rose and diet deteriorated. Health and hygiene in industrial cities worsened. Infant mortality was high and life expectancy low by present-day standards, and both actually deteriorated. People's physical condition as measured by their heights fell to one of its lowest ever levels and showed marked difference between classes—over five inches' difference between rich and poor boys in 1790.[36] It would seem that the pessimistic case is amply proved, and that industrialization amounted to stunted and damaged lives for generations of ordinary people.

Looked at closely, the picture is less stark. More optimistic views see economic changes, for good and bad, as linked to the aspirations and choices, however limited, of ordinary working people, who were not hostile to the market economy or indifferent to the goods it brought.[37] English wages did not rise partly because they were already very high by world standards: and they remained among the highest in the world over the period of industrialization. A sharp and continuous rise took place from the mid-nineteenth century onwards, when new industries and technologies had grown sufficiently to transform the whole economy. The average fall in height may have been due not to new factory conditions, but to increasing work in agriculture at a young age (the same fall can be seen in the nineteenth-century United States), and is therefore probably a consequence of the "industrious revolution" rather than of "proletarianized" labour in factories. Moreover, French, Italian and Austrian men were smaller still than Englishmen. English workers' attainment of a relative degree of prosperity brought what we now know to be unhealthy choices (more alcohol, tobacco, sugar and meat), health risks and family stress.[38] Similar things can be seen in the slums of Mumbai or Rio today: appalling and life-threatening conditions, but which also mean a chance to escape from age-old poverty and cultural and social immobility. Indeed, England's political stability must in part be due to many people being able to aspire to improvement, and even to attain it.[39]

There is, finally, a factor which most specialists now agree resolves the "optimist"/"pessimist" debate: England was experiencing a sudden demographic boom unique in its history. The population more than tripled in 150 years, from 5.2 million in 1701 to 17.9 million in 1851.[40] The reason is simple: increasing wages and job opportunities after the Restoration—

the "industrious revolution" again—which enabled people to marry several years younger on average than before, and which meant more children. The inevitable result of this process in other times and places was a sharp fall in living standards as numbers outran resources, reducing life expectancy, restricting births, or bringing even more severe consequences such as famines, epidemics or wars. These are the famous "Malthusian checks" first theorized by the Rev. Thomas Malthus in his *Essay on the Principle of Population* (1798). The consequences were visible in southern and central Europe, where living standards deteriorated sharply between 1500 and 1800, and real wages had dropped to a half or a third of those in England. Given its exceptional population explosion, eighteenth-century England was logically heading for a similar collapse in living standards and widespread misery.[41]

But it did not happen: "A basic feature of the human condition had changed."[42] There was certainly hardship, especially during and immediately after the Napoleonic Wars, in 1811–12 and 1816–21, when the whole country and its economic system were under strain. On top of that came a Continent-wide run of bad harvests, the worst of them due to a catastrophic volcanic eruption in the East Indies in April 1815, which disrupted global climate and caused widespread famine.[43] In England,

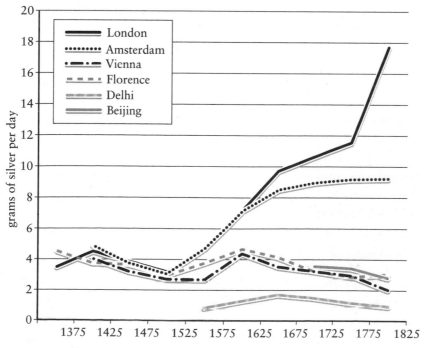

Figure 1: Labourers' wages around the world, 1375–1825

there was hunger and economic instability. But there was no economic disaster—as there might well have been had Napoleon won and wrecked British trade. And there was no political catastrophe. What was once seen as the "stagnation" or "decline" of English workers' living standards should properly be seen as their maintenance at a relatively high level. This stands out in comparison with disastrous increases in poverty in many parts of Europe since the seventeenth century.

How, in adverse circumstances, were English living standards maintained? By growing the towns, especially manufacturing and commercial centres such as London, Manchester, Liverpool and Birmingham. By creating new jobs in textiles, metalworking and commerce. By supporting incomes through the Poor Law. And by defending access to export markets by defeating Napoleon.

During several decades, things might still have gone badly wrong. But by the 1850s a "second stage" of industrialization was beginning. By 1850 Britain's GDP had overtaken that of the world's most populous country, China—a lead it maintained for more than 150 years. Productivity was transformed by the cheap energy of the "mineral economy," permitting what economists have called a breakout to permanent economic growth. This finally brought in the second half of the nineteenth century an unambiguous increase in workers' living standards. Thus was established, in difficult and dangerous circumstances, the prototype of a new society.

# CHAPTER II

# Wars of Dreams

When France in wrath her giant-limbs upreared
And with that oath, which smote air, earth, and sea,
Stamped her strong foot, and said she would be free,
Bear witness for me, how I hoped and feared! . . .
Forgive me, Freedom! O forgive those dreams!
> Samuel Taylor Coleridge, "France: An Ode" (1798)

*It appears possible that the whole world may go Mad, that all Governments may break to Pieces: that universal Frenzy may take place under the name of universal Fraternity, & that our Children may find themselves in the place & manners of the 8th century.*
> William Eden, Lord Auckland, 1792[1]

On 14 July 1789 a few hundred Parisians stormed the Bastille, France's Tower of London. The British ambassador reported that "the greatest Revolution that we know anything of has been affected with . . . the loss of very few lives: from this moment we may consider France as a free country."[2] England applauded. London theatres re-enacted the events. The House of Commons proposed a "day of thanksgiving for the French Revolution." The prime minister, William Pitt, commented that "our neighbours [were] an object of compassion, even to a rival,"[3] and he hoped for friendly relations and a joint abolition of the slave trade. Diplomats gloated over the downfall of the Bourbons only six years after they had humiliated Britain. The Foreign Secretary, Lord Carmarthen, anticipated "strutting about Europe with an Air of Consideration unknown to us for some Time."[4] Ordinary people rejoiced at the prospect of peace and wished the French well.

Most enthusiastic were Dissenters and the opposition Whigs. Charles James Fox exclaimed, "How much the greatest event it is that ever happened in the world! and how much the best!" France seemed to have adopted Whiggism, and Whigs hoped this would boost the flagging reform movement at home. France's Revolutionary leaders—gentlemen such as the Marquis de La Fayette, the Comte de Mirabeau and the Marquis de Clermont-Tonnerre, admirers of America and even of England—drew up a constitution and a Declaration of the Rights of Man and the Citizen. They consulted their friends Joseph Priestley, Thomas Jefferson, Tom Paine and a great patron of progressive intellectuals, the Marquess of Lansdowne (formerly Earl of Shelburne), who provided Mirabeau with a paid political adviser. The abolitionist Thomas Clarkson went to France in August 1789 to persuade them to abolish slavery—in vain. However, this "Whiggish" phase of the revolution soon gave way to peasant violence, religious conflict and struggles for power. More radical and impatient men began to demand greater democracy and national assertiveness.

English Dissenters, guardians of the ideological and institutional heritage of Puritan sectarianism,[5] interpreted the revolution as a providential blow against popery and superstition. This made them its active and invincibly optimistic supporters: "The French Revolution is of God," pronounced a Baptist minister in radical Norwich, "no power exists or can exist, by which it can be overthrown."[6] A Unitarian student at Cambridge, Samuel Taylor Coleridge, burned "Liberty" and "Equality" with gunpowder onto the velvety college lawns of St. John's and Trinity. Dissenting intellectuals scrutinized political events for their prophetic meaning, with "the Declaration of the Rights of Man in one hand, and the Book of Revelation in the other," as Joseph Priestley put it. Dr. Priestley, a renowned chemist and Unitarian minister in Birmingham (nicknamed "Gunpowder Joe" following his statement that "a train of gunpowder was being laid to the Church Establishment"), had since the American Revolution been prophesying "some very calamitous, but finally glorious events ... the downfall of Church and State together." This was "the commencement of the last great period, signified by the blowing of the seventh trumpet," which would soon end with the Second Coming of Christ—"It cannot, I think, be more than twenty years." The other leading Unitarian intellectual, Dr. Richard Price, was similarly expecting the arrival of the Messiah to "execute justice on the wicked and to establish an everlasting kingdom."[7]

The Dissenters' enthusiasm soon made the events in France a subject of ideological confrontation. On 4 November 1789 Price preached a sermon, "On the Love of our Country," to the reformist Society for Commemorating the Revolution, which was subsequently read out in the French Constituent Assembly. Price declared that "most" governments were "usurpations on the rights of men" and established churches were "priestcraft and tyranny." He ended with a stirring peroration: the French Revolution had "kindled into a blaze that lays despotism in ashes, and warms and illuminates EUROPE!"[8] Edmund Burke replied with *Reflections on the Revolution in France* (1790), denying that the events in France were comparable with 1688 or that there existed a right to overthrow governments, as Price asserted. Burke was angry that revolution was being treated as "a spectator sport for middle-class intellectuals, tempted to believe that they can proclaim governments illegitimate without anyone getting hurt"[9]—anyone who mattered, anyway. He insisted that 1688 had not tried to invent an ideal system from scratch—the dangerous French error. Every political community was slowly shaped by "the wisdom of unlettered men," in a permanent "partnership" of the living, the dead and the yet unborn. A free society relied on voluntary respect for its institutions, which "the longer they have lasted . . . the more we cherish them." He insisted that revolution entailed suffering and loss, and was "the very last resource of the thinking and the good . . . I cannot conceive how any man can have brought himself to that pitch of presumption to consider his country as nothing but *carte blanche*, upon which he may scribble whatever he pleases." Burke's position was historical and philosophical, not religious, unlike that of his opponents, whom he considered Puritan "bigots." Many were shocked that Burke, a leading Whig intellectual, supporter of American rights and religious tolerance, and nemesis of the East India Company, should attack the French Revolution. But his ideas were consistent. He had long dismissed abstract theory—"the fairy land of philosophy"—as the basis for social organization. Societies, he believed, grew organically, including by "sympathy" and "imagination." He denounced usurpations in which greed and intellectual arrogance (by people who "have no respect for the wisdom of others; but . . . a very full measure of confidence in their own") destroyed legitimate authorities, ancient rights, social relationships, and laws embodying the history and culture of unique societies. Hence he regarded oppression by the British in India and Ireland (he was a Dubliner) and oppression by the revolutionaries in France as morally identical. "I do not like to see any thing destroyed; any void produced in society; any ruin on the face of the land."[10]

*Reflections* met a chorus of denunciation. "Cursed Stuff," exclaimed his old friend and ally Fox. Pitt thought it too extreme. Young idealists such as Coleridge, Wordsworth and Keats continued to admire the French Revolution as a revival of the "Good Old Cause" of Sidney and "others who called Milton friend."[11] Dozens of rebuttals were written, including by Priestley, the historian Catherine Macaulay, and Mary Wollstonecraft, in her *Vindication of the Rights of Men* (1790) and *Vindication of the Rights of Women* (1792), maintaining that "God-given reason" was the only source of legitimate authority.[12] By far the most widely read reply to what he called Burke's "thundering attack" was Paine's *The Rights of Man* (1791), dedicated to George Washington. Paine's style was dogmatic reiteration. He did not engage with Burke's ideas, which he dismissed as foolish, incomprehensible ("all this jargon") or dishonest. His position was exactly what Burke rejected: judging political systems on ideological, not pragmatic, grounds. The new French constitution was "a rational order of things"; whereas the English system was tainted by originating in conquest in 1066 by "the son of a prostitute and the plunderer of the English nation," and it was stained by "the filth of rotten boroughs," where "every man has his price." Monarchy ("the enemy of mankind"), a hereditary peerage and an established Church were the roots of evil. The remedy was simple: "For a nation to be free, it is sufficient that she wills it."[13]

In arguing about France, Burke and Paine had reopened fundamental divisions about England—divisions echoing the Civil War. Paine's "rhetoric of radical egalitarianism," judged the historian E. P. Thompson, "touched the deepest responses of the 'true-born Englishman' [and] established a new framework within which Radicalism was confined for nearly 100 years." He was "the first to dare to express himself with such irreverence; and he destroyed with one book century-old taboos."[14] Radical societies circulated thousands of copies. A worried citizen informed the Home Office that "the book is now made as much a Standard book in this country as Robinson Crusoe and the Pilgrim's Progress."[15] In June 1792, Paine was summonsed for seditious libel, and escaped to Paris to sit in the National Assembly. But Burke's version of English history as a long collective "partnership" was no less influential, endowing its institutions with a powerful legitimizing pedigree.[16]

Though the revolution enthused the Dissenting elite, it provoked suspicion and hostility among others. The most dramatic manifestation came as early as 14 July 1791, when a dinner held to celebrate Bastille Day in a Birmingham hotel led to three days of rioting.[17] In all, three Unitarian chapels and one Baptist and at least twenty-seven houses were vandalized or pulled down in the customary ritual of popular protest. Joseph Priestley's house was gutted and his scientific instruments and papers destroyed. The victims were frightened and humiliated but not physically hurt. One was "hauled to a tavern . . . forced to shake a hundred hard and black hands," and buy 329 gallons of beer. The Dissenters targeted were the local plutocracy of bankers, merchants and manufacturers, doubly unpopular as killjoy Puritans. Their public espousal of a foreign revolution provoked the biggest and most tumultuous expression of popular feeling of the period. Radicals ascribed this "Church and king" reaction to drunken "mobs," stirred up by the authorities. In fact, the degree of popular support for the French Revolution was far less than its supporters had hoped; on the contrary, the events across the Channel galvanized popular conservatism.[18]

Paine's pamphlet had given many hostages to fortune. Convinced that the right ideas must produce the right outcomes, he had dismissed Burke's predictions of disaster—"he does not understand the French revolution."[19] But the gruesome "September Massacres" of 1792, when hundreds of men, women and children were butchered in the streets and prisons of Paris as suspected traitors, the execution of Louis XVI and Marie-Antoinette in 1793, and escalating Terror, war and economic disaster mocked Paine's confidence that "they order these things better in France." He himself, at first feted in Paris, was imprisoned and sentenced to the guillotine—a fate he narrowly escaped due to a change of government. These years fixed English "memory" of revolution, elaborated in nineteenth-century history and literature—especially Carlyle's vivid and tragic *History* (1837) and Dickens's *Tale of Two Cities* (1859), which emphasized the contrast between the Terror and English peace and security. Yet violence undesirable in England might be excusable in less happier lands. The liberal Tory J. W. Croker wrote that the revolution had "in the *ultimate issue of events*, proved beneficial," forcefully advancing progress in France and other nations. Macaulay agreed that the revolution had been a "purification," even though at "tremendous" cost.[20] The future English consensus that emerged over the next generation concerning the French Revolution, and by extension political change in general, was ambivalent: opposed to tyranny, in favour of moderate reforms, but hostile to violence.[21]

There were eventually some 2,000 Loyalist societies, such as the Association for the Preservation of Liberty and Property against Republicans and Levellers, founded in November 1792—the use of the term "Levellers" evoking negative popular memories of the Puritan revolution. Loyalists argued that rich and poor alike stood to lose from a French-inspired upheaval—a view reiterated in accessible language by the playwright and educator Hannah More, whose pamphlets flooded the country. At the sedate end of Loyalism were patriotic addresses, sermons, pamphlets and newspapers. Less sedate were bonfires, with Tom Paine as Guy Fawkes, fireworks, ox-roasting and drinking, often subsidized by local gentry.

Intimidating radicals was an important aspect of Loyalist activity: burning them in effigy, ejecting them from pubs and friendly societies, and privately prosecuting writers and publishers. Pitt did not like such disorderly activity. But Loyalism would prove unbiddable in years to come. It often sympathized with popular grievances, particularly over food shortages; and it did not guarantee unflinching support for a long war against France.

Radical societies were smaller, with dozens or at most a few hundred core members. The London Corresponding Society was started in January 1792 by a Scottish Dissenter, Thomas Hardy, who owned a shoe shop in Piccadilly. It began campaigning for manhood suffrage and solidarity with the French Revolution, and attracted several hundred members across the country. The largest provincial group, the Sheffield Society for Constitutional Information—probably England first working men's reform club—had about 600 active members in 1792. A high proportion were Dissenters, including Methodists and various Millenarians. Socially, these "English Jacobins," as they were sometimes called, were similar to the French Jacobins and Sans-Culottes they admired: a middle-class leadership, including both solid businessmen and sometimes marginal intellectuals (writers, artists, preachers, lawyers), and a rank-and-file of tradesmen and skilled workers.[22]

In the 1960s, left-wing historians turned to this period in a search for roots. E. P. Thompson's *The Making of the English Working Class* (1963)—the single most influential work of English history of the postwar period[23]—argued that the 1790s had been "crucial" in creating English class consciousness. Thompson had a nostalgic affection for a lost world of Bible-reading self-educated artisans—"the most distinguished popular culture England has known." He regretted that England had not managed to have a revolution, though it was some consolation that radicals had tried by propaganda, strikes, and occasionally conspiracy. In consequence, he thought, "everything" in English life subsequently became "a battleground of class."[24] Thus Thompson promoted small revolutionary groups, many of them religious sectarians more concerned with theology than economics, to the vanguard of popular working-class history. Paradoxically, these groups were little concerned with the practical problems of the poor, and sometimes they had a Puritanical objection to poor relief. They left social action to the Anglican establishment and the squirearchy. Indeed, far from creating new class divisions, during the turmoil of the Revolutionary Wars "the compassion and sensitivity with which magistrates handled poor law claims, food riots and other social problems in fact reinforced the status of the landed classes as social and political leaders of the nation."[25] What is most striking about England during this time of unparalleled change, danger and effort is the amazingly small amount of internal conflict.

Among the most intellectually daring, and posthumously famous, radicals of the 1790s were the circle that formed round the Unitarian publisher Joseph Johnson and Unitarian minister turned atheist William Godwin. They included Samuel Taylor Coleridge, Mary Wollstonecraft and William Wordsworth. Godwin's acclaimed *Enquiry Concerning Political Justice, and Its Influence on General Virtue and Happiness* (1793) and his political novel *Caleb Williams* (1794) imagined a robotic Utopia ruled by untrammelled reason and individualism. Irrational group activities such as concerts and the theatre would cease. Irrational emotions—such as partiality for one's own family—would become obsolete. Human imperfections, which engendered state institutions and property, would disappear. As Mind triumphed over Matter, all "infirmities of our nature" would be erased, including disease, sleep and sex ("mere animal function"), leading logically to immortality.

France's declaration of war on Austria and Prussia in April 1792 convinced English sympathizers that what they saw as a cosmic struggle was entering its critical phase. France's monarchical enemies were identified as "the *ten toes of Nebuchadnezzar*'s image, and the *ten horns of the beast*."[26] Clothes, blankets, boots and ammunition were collected for the hard-pressed French. When Prussian and Austrian invaders were turned back by a Revolutionary army at Valmy on 20 September 1792, Charles James Fox wrote that "no public event, not excepting Saratoga and York Town, ever happened that gave me so much delight." Horrors such as the September Massacres could be explained away as the consequence of aggression by Prussian and Austrian "Barbarians," as Fox called them. But although one Unitarian improbably described the rakish Fox as England's "angel of redemption,"[27] his support in Parliament dwindled.

The British government intended to stay neutral. The revolution was still regarded as "beneficial to our political interests." A Foreign Office official thought that for Britain, protected by its "salt-water entrenchment," intervention was "as unlikely a contingency as can well be foreseen." Pitt assured the Commons on 17 February 1792 that "unquestionably, there never was a time in the history of this country, when, from the situation of Europe, we might more reasonably expect fifteen years of peace."[28] But a year later Britain was at war. Military success had created euphoric ambitions in Paris. French victories—just after Paine's *Rights of Man* had appeared—stimulated radical activity in England as did bad weather, bad harvests and serious rises in food prices. Reports from French agents in England, and "fraternal greetings" sent to Paris by sympathizers, encouraged the French to overestimate the support they had in England, which some hoped was on the verge of revolution. But the Loyalist reaction gave the government confidence. The Foreign Secretary, Lord Grenville, wrote in December 1792, "Nothing can exceed the good dispositions of this country in the present moment. The change within the last three weeks is little less than miraculous . . . it will enable us to talk to France in the tone which British Ministers ought to use . . . and to crush the seditious disposition here." The execution of Louis XVI in January 1793 shocked the English public. The French envoy, Chauvelin, reported that he could not go out "without being exposed to the insults and ignorant ferocity of . . . the mob."[29] Both London and Paris dangerously exaggerated the weakness, and underestimated the resolve, of the other.

War finally came for the most traditional of reasons—the security of the Low Countries. London, fearful for the independence of Holland, sent pledges of support to the Dutch in the vain hope of deterring the French. But France's Revolutionary leaders were buoyed up by the euphoric belief that the revolution was spreading invincibly across Europe. Far from being deterred by the British action, the new French republic declared war on Britain and Holland on 1 February 1793, eleven days after Louis XVI had been guillotined. Paine drafted a call to the British people to revolt. Lansdowne accused the government of fighting a "war of metaphysics": "But who were the metaphysicians?" replied a minister. "They were 120,000 French soldiers, and their cannon and bayonets were the arguments they used."[30] Pitt's statement in the Commons placed the struggle on an elevated plane: "A free, brave, loyal and happy people" were fighting for "the tranquillity of this country, the security of its allies, the good order of every European Government, and the happiness of the whole of the human race."[31] War was to last with only a short break for twenty years.


## FIGHTING FOR THE FUTURE

*We must recollect . . . what it is we have at stake, what it is we have to contend for. It is for our property, it is for our liberty, it is for our independence, nay for our existence as a nation; it is for our character, it is for our very name as Englishmen; it is for everything dear and valuable to man on this side of the grave.*
             William Pitt, House of Commons, 22 July 1803[32]


Britain adopted its usual strategy of encouraging and financing a coalition against France, while concentrating mainly on naval operations and seizing colonial trade. The revolution's navy was weak, and the Royal Navy chased it off the seas. But the French proved unbeatable on land, as the revolution unleashed what has been called the first total war, raising huge armies by a mixture of ideological mobilization and terror, and supplying them by seizing money and material resources from "liberated" territories in Europe.[33]

War transformed English politics. It split the Whig Party and so strengthened the government—though even the most conservative Whigs hesitated to join Pitt, whom they considered the creature of George III. After Cambridge, Pitt had entered the Commons, for him a hereditary profession, at the age of twenty-one. He was reserved, stiff (except with women, went a common jibe) and shy, and had some irritating mannerisms. He had little life outside politics. He was not an ideal war leader, and colleagues were often frustrated by his tendency to delay awkward decisions. But he had reserves of strength and willpower: "I cannot permit myself to doubt." He was highly intelligent, listened to expert advice, was an effective arbiter among powerful colleagues, and, when he had made a decision, he had native toughness in carrying it out. He had a commanding knowledge of finance—essential in a war largely fought with money—yet he was careless of his personal interests and died in debt. By nature a reformer but also a cautious man, Pitt thought the European situation meant that parliamentary reform, concessions to religious minorities, and even action against the slave trade had to be postponed. Opposition Whigs inside Parliament and radicals outside condemned him as a traitor to reform, having abandoned his principles for the sake of office. Once war had begun, Pitt's more extreme opponents seemed—and some were—not only seditious but treasonable, aiding and encouraging the French, and unreliable in case of invasion. During 1793, eleven men were accused of sedition, of whom six were found guilty, and mostly punished with fines or short prison sentences.[34]

War also transformed French politics, but far more dramatically. Its new rulers had gone to war expecting quick victory. Instead, the revolution was soon on the verge of extinction, lashing out against supposed enemies and making convulsive efforts to raise armies. It threw back the invaders, and France's huge and unruly forces swarmed into Savoy, Germany, Belgium and Holland. Wavering aristocrat patriots such as La Fayette, hero of American independence, were forced to flee for their lives. A Revolutionary dictatorship took power, dominated by a young lawyer, Maximilien Robespierre. Counter-revolutionary forces resisted, including peasants, Catholics, and those who now felt that the old order had been less demanding and more protective of their way of life. By 1793 France

was in the grip of civil war and terror: 16,000 people died on the guillotine and many thousands more were slaughtered. Refugees streamed into
England. The British government set up an efficient secret service, often
using royalist refugees (including women and children) as agents, or
Englishmen posing as Americans. They gathered detailed information
about French naval forces and the state of French public opinion.[35]

Hardcore English supporters of the revolution were oddly unmoved by
the bloodshed in France. Paine, both before and after his imprisonment in
Paris, continued to urge an invasion of England. At the height of the Terror, Priestley "read with pleasure, and even with enthusiasm the admirable
Report of *Robespierre* on the subject of *morals* and *religion*."[36] He still
regarded France's enemies, including Britain, as the "ten horns" of the
Beast of the Apocalypse. Dissenters insisted that the revolution was a
providential struggle against popery, and many opposed what William
Blake termed "the English Crusade against France" caused by "State Religion." Blake is the best remembered of these visionaries because of his
sublime and incomprehensible *Jerusalem*—famous, ironically, because it
was made into a patriotic song during the First World War. His idea was
that the English Druids had been God's true Chosen People, though he
was uncertain about whether the "New Jerusalem" would eventually be
built in England's green and pleasant land or that of France.[37] Radicals
thus saw European events through an English religious prism, and the
loyalty of even politically conservative Dissenters was now at best qualified.[38] During late 1793 and early 1794, the London Corresponding Society and the Society for Constitutional Information held a series of public
meetings in London and Sheffield, calling for manhood suffrage, annual
parliaments, cheaper food, recognition of the "brave French republic" and
peace. They were not violent, but they used strong language and sang the
"Marseillaise." Ministers, for once, were alarmed. They knew hardcore
radicals were few, but also knew that ultimately public order relied on
broad consent and the actions of autonomous local authorities: "Our
laws suppose magistrates and Grand Juries to do their duty," noted Grenville, "and if they do not I have little faith in its being done by a Government such as the Constitution has made ours."[39] However, ministers had
more things to concern them than political discontent and spent surprisingly little of their time worrying about it.

More serious was the economic situation. The population, as we have
noted, was booming. Food output grew, but England was barely
self-sufficient. War made imports more precarious. More people than ever
before lived on manufacture and depended on overseas trade. Confidence,
credit and exports were affected by the war. Breadwinners were mobilized

for the militia and the navy. Many read Paine's accusation that the war was engineered by a reactionary and corrupt oligarchy to enrich themselves and take away France's freedom. But even more important was weather: the 1790s saw extreme climatic conditions across north-west Europe, and harvests were bad in 1791, 1792 and 1794, and disastrous in 1795, 1800 and 1811–12, in the later years possibly due in part to global volcanic activity. England, though better off than the Continent, was not spared. There were serious shortages in 1795–96, 1800–1801 and 1809–10.[40] People went hungry as wheat prices rose by 50 percent—not seen for 200 years. There were frequent riots, seizure by crowds of grain convoys and attacks on flour mills.

The response of central and local government was to combine relief and repression. Government agents bought hundreds of thousands of tons of foreign grain when they could find it: for example, from America, Canada, the Baltic and India.[41] Corn exports were stopped, and industrial uses (distilling, starch, hair powder) were forbidden. Attempts were made to cut consumption of fresh white bread, and promote brown bread and potatoes—much resented. Magistrates used old Common Law rules against profiteers. Soup kitchens were created. Poor Law payments increased. The other response, often called "Pitt's reign of terror," began in May 1794, when Hardy, secretary of the London Corresponding Society, the radical lecturer John Thelwall, the veteran Unitarian activist John Horne Tooke and others were charged with high treason—a grave charge chosen partly to "acquaint the country with the dangers." The accused, far from intimidated, mounted a spirited defence, even calling Pitt as a witness. All were acquitted by juries, to the jubilation of their supporters; judges and the Attorney-General were jostled. Eight other cases were then dropped. Nevertheless, these years saw a legislative onslaught on traditional liberties, including the suspension of habeas corpus.[42] After more big meetings and mobbing of the king and Pitt in London, the notorious "Two Acts" were passed—the Treason Act (1794) and the Seditious Meetings and Assemblies Act (1795)—which gave the government wide though temporary powers to hold suspects without trial and restrict or disperse meetings. They were rarely used. There was something restrained, even amateurish, about England's "Terror." The Home Office consisted of nineteen people—the Secretary of State, two under-secretaries and their clerks. The Home Secretary, the Duke of Portland, even took his wife and daughters to pay a courtesy call on one of the political prisoners.[43] Yet repression had an effect: the threat of the new laws, the financial costs of legal defence, arrests and detention of activists, and harassment by local magistrates and Loyalists wore radicalism down.

One event—comical in retrospect—showed Britain's vulnerability. In February 1797, 1,400 French, led by an American, and clothed in captured British uniforms, set out to burn Bristol, but landed in Fishguard, on the Pembrokeshire coast. They quickly surrendered after spotting a group of Welsh women in red cloaks whom they took for "a Ridgment of Soldiers": "The Lord took from our Enemies the Spirit of War and to him be the Prais."[44] This fiasco nevertheless caused a run on the Bank of England, forcing the government to end the convertibility of paper money into gold—just what the French had hoped to do for generations. Unexpectedly, paper currency turned out to be economically beneficial, by increasing the wartime money supply, and consequently buttressed Britain's war effort.[45]

More serious were the naval mutinies just afterwards. In April 1797 the Channel Fleet at Spithead refused to put to sea, though the mutineers promised to do so if the French left port. Serious violence was avoided by the mediation of an elected delegate of the mutineers, and a bargain was struck agreeing to better pay, food, leave and treatment of the sick, and it was celebrated with a banquet at Portsmouth of mutineers, admirals and civic dignitaries. These concessions encouraged further mutinies at the Nore and Yarmouth. The government now contemplated coercion, while offering to pardon men returning to duty. Much of the public, fearing invasion, turned against the mutineers, some of whom were mobbed on shore. Families wrote to urge submission. Seamen fought among themselves. By 13 June, after negotiations, all ships were in the hands of loyal sailors. Some 30 men were hanged, and over 300 received lesser sentences, including flogging and transportation. Alarmed contemporaries and some later historians have assumed that revolutionary groups were behind the mutinies, showing "how precarious was the hold of the English *ancien régime*," and threatening "to subvert the whole edifice of world power."[46] Yet the evidence for revolutionary intentions is slight. The mutineers made ostentatious demonstrations of loyalty. The Grand Duke of Württemberg, accompanied by the First Lord of the Admiralty, actually made a royal visit to the "mutinous" fleet, which punctiliously fired salutes on the king's birthday. The mutinies seem essentially to have been large-scale instances of traditional collective bargaining for seamen's rights which included petitions to the Admiralty and Parliament, and the violence at the Nore was partly due to a breakdown in communications. Admiral Nelson commented that "for a mutiny [1797] has been the most manly I ever heard of, and does the British sailor infinite honour." Three months later, the fleet defeated the Dutch at Camperdown. Thus patriotism and loyalism prevailed in the fleet as on shore. Yet discontented minorities existed, and it was impossible to be sure how far they extended.[47]

A truly revolutionary outburst came in 1798, not in England but in Ireland. Ulster Presbyterians founded a revolutionary society, the United Irishmen, in 1791, aiming at a French-backed Irish republic. A French expedition in support had only been prevented from landing in 1796 by weather. But the United Irishmen tried anyway in 1798, and the uprising was brutally crushed by both Catholic and Protestant forces, with perhaps 10,000 being killed: yet another bloodstained page was added to the history of British-Irish relations. The Act of Union of 1800 was a direct consequence of the French intervention: "The French will never cease to intrigue in [Ireland]," wrote Edward Cooke, a senior official in Dublin, and "as we wish to check the ambition of that desperate, and unprincipled power . . . we should be favourable to the principle of union."[48] But union made the "Irish question" a perennial issue in British politics, especially as the quid pro quo of full Catholic political rights was delayed indefinitely by George III, and finally conceded only in 1829. The impact of the French Revolution in Ireland arguably ended any chance of equitable Anglo-Irish coexistence, which since the 1780s had seemed a reasonable hope.

In England, support for war fluctuated. There was strong pressure to make peace in 1796–97 and 1800–1802. Opposition was predictably led by Dissenters, especially Unitarians and Quakers, and manufacturers—often the same people—whose dislike of the aristocratic and Anglican establishment was a major reason for opposing the war.[49] Popular unrest was of a non-revolutionary kind, provoked by food shortages, economic disruption and compulsory militia service. Disturbances were generally handled with sense and even sensitivity by central and local authorities. Exports (a significant share going to North and South America) recovered in the 1800s and remained generally buoyant. Big increases in taxation were digested, including the first income tax in 1799—10 percent on incomes over £200. The government was careful to place the main burden on the better off, and taxes on luxuries provided about 60 percent of total revenue.[50] Cash payments were made under the Poor Law to offset food costs, including to the families of men in the armed forces and those on low wages. In crisis years, such as 1801, around half the population received some aid.[51] All in all, the ordeal of war revealed a society accepting that its system of government was legitimate and its independence worth defending.[52] Ireland, and parts of Scotland, were a different story.

But the insoluble problem was how the war could be ended. Britain's main aim was the independence of Holland, but Holland had fallen in early 1795 and became a French satellite. British troops sent to the Low Countries under George III's son, the "Grand Old Duke of York," had soon been "marched back again." Prussia made a deal with the French.

Spain dropped out of the war. Austria continued the fight, supported by British loans, but was pushed back. So the "ten horns of the beast" were dropping off one by one. Maritime warfare was indecisive. Hopes of capturing France's West Indian colonies were ended by a great slave revolt in Saint-Domingue in 1791. The Royal Navy sailed into France's base at Toulon in August 1793 to support rebels there, but had to withdraw under the cannon fire of a young artillery officer, Napoleon Bonaparte, in December, after capturing or torching the French Mediterranean fleet. A landing at Quiberon Bay in July 1795 of a force of émigrés to help other rebels in western France ended in massacre. Financial aid by Britain to resurgent royalist parties in France, and the recruitment of agents at the heart of the republican regime—even its police and army—by British secret agents,[53] came to nothing when the same General Bonaparte crushed a royalist rising in Paris in October 1795. Corsican patriots threw out the French and asked to join the British Empire, but the island could not be held long and was evacuated in 1796. The dynamic Bonaparte marched into Italy in 1796 and crushingly defeated the Austrians, who were forced to yield control of northern Italy to France and accept French annexation of the Austrian Netherlands and the Rhineland. Britain's naval bases in Italy were threatened, and in 1797 the Royal Navy had to evacuate the Mediterranean. Pitt was willing to make peace with a reasonable French republic, if such emerged. As early as December 1795 the King's Speech had hinted at negotiations, but the French returned an "insolent" response demanding the return of all colonies and acceptance of its huge territorial expansion. Pitt was left hoping for "the return of reason in our deluded enemy." Though he won a general election in 1796, he and the Cabinet were close to despair over the war: "We shall be left to sustain alone the conflict with France and Holland, probably joined by Spain, and perhaps favoured more or less openly by the Northern powers," and though "with proper exertion we can make our party good against them all," victory seemed inconceivable.[54]

In 1798, hope suddenly dawned. Bonaparte led an invasion of Egypt, aiming to dominate the Mediterranean and perhaps march on India: "Truly to overthrow England," he argued, "we must occupy Egypt."[55] But his fleet was annihilated by Nelson at the battle of the Nile in August: eleven out of thirteen battleships were destroyed or captured, and Bonaparte abandoned his army in Egypt and escaped back to France. This gave a fillip to all France's enemies, and a "Second Coalition" of Austria, Russia, Turkey and Britain prepared a final effort. The revolution now seemed doomed: revolts erupted throughout the occupied territories and in western and southern France, while pro-French rebels in Ireland and Naples were bloodily crushed. In 1799 the Russians and Austrians advanced through Italy, Switzerland and Germany. British and Russian troops landed in Holland and captured the Dutch fleet. Bonaparte seized dictatorial power as First Consul in November 1799, telling his troops that the politicians were in British pay. He offered peace terms, which were promptly rejected. London thought he was playing for time: "The whole game is in our hands now, and it wants little more than *patience* to play it *well, to the end.*"[56] The final push was set for the summer of 1800, with coordinated invasions of France from several directions. But everything unravelled as the allies fell out and the French rallied. Consul Bonaparte showed himself to be more than just another ambitious general, when he ended internal rebellion by force and concession and then marched an army rapidly over the Alps to defeat the surprised Austrians at Marengo on 14 June. This effectively finished off the shaky Second Coalition. Bonaparte sent a letter to the Austrian emperor, supposedly written on the field of Marengo "surrounded by 15,000 corpses," offering peace and blaming the war solely on the greed of England—an explanation that many in Europe found plausible.

Now it was Britain that suddenly faced defeat. Austria and Russia sought peace. Bonaparte was preparing an alliance with Spain to attack Ireland, Portugal and India. Prussia occupied Hanover, the last British foothold in Europe. Russia, Denmark and Sweden were forming an "Armed Neutrality" and excluding British ships from the Baltic. Gold reserves dwindled and bread prices rose to three times their 1798 level. Oxford students were rationed; others less fortunate starved. A wave of riots tied down a large part of the army. Demands for peace became deafening. Pitt, on the edge of a breakdown, resigned in March 1801 when the king refused to extend equal rights to Catholics following the union with Ireland. The English now lived their recurring nightmare: an enemy dominating the Continent. This had to be pre-empted by what a minister called "one brilliant act of British enterprise [that] would intervene to check and soften the uniformity of calamity and defeat."[57] In fact there were two. In March 1801 General Abercromby forced a landing in Egypt and went on to defeat the larger French army—a remarkable success for the despised Redcoats. In April Nelson, at the first battle of Copenhagen, destroyed the Danish fleet, threatened to bombard the city, and forced Denmark to withdraw from the "Armed Neutrality," whose other members prudently did likewise. The pro-French Tsar Paul was assassinated, and Russian rapprochement with France halted.

So the unwinnable war could be ended. In November 1801, Pitt made

a frank admission to the Commons, if not of defeat, certainly of partial
failure:

> [Our] great object . . . was defence in a war waged against most of the
> nations of Europe, but against us with particular malignity . . . I had hopes
> of our being able to put together the scattered fragments of that great and
> venerable edifice [the French monarchy] in the stead of that mad system
> which threatened the destruction of Europe . . . This, it is true, has been
> found unattainable.[58]

Britain concluded the Treaty of Amiens in March 1802, in which it agreed
to return most overseas conquests except Trinidad and Ceylon, and effectively recognized the Continental hegemony of a much enlarged France,
including even control of the Low Countries. No agreement in our modern history, except that of Munich in 1938, has been so vilified and so
welcomed. Food prices fell precipitously and rioting subsided. A jubilant
Lambeth publican gave away all his beer. The London Corresponding
Society wrote an adulatory letter to Bonaparte declaring their devotion to
France and thanking him that "peace reigns on earth, and this is the work
of Frenchmen." Charles James Fox owned that "the Triumph of the French
government over the English does in fact afford me a degree of pleasure
which it is very difficult to disguise."[59] Tourists streamed across the Channel to see what post–Revolutionary France was like: they found ruined
churches and chateaux, and lots of soldiers. Politicians (eighty-two MPs
and thirty-one peers) went in the hope of sizing up the charismatic
Bonaparte. Dissenters identified him as God's latest instrument, in the
words of one radical MP, "the Great Man of the People of France, the
Liberator of Europe." Intellectuals admired him as a macho version of
themselves. Fox found him rather a bore, yet praised him in the Commons
as "the most stupendous monument of human wisdom."[60]

From most perspectives, France had won. "We are going fast down the
gulf-stream," wrote a British diplomat, "and shall never stop, I fear, till,
with the rest of Europe, we fall under the universal empire of the great
Republic."[61] Bonaparte was not content with a purely Continental hegemony. He ordered a naval building programme. He openly planned
another invasion of Egypt. A mission was sent to India, to build alliances
with local rulers and recruit troops. Territory was demanded in Australia.
Some 26,000 veteran soldiers sailed to reconquer Saint-Domingue and
reimpose slavery, planning then to land in Louisiana to re-establish France
in North America.[62]

These global ambitions explain why peace broke down after less than
a year over the seemingly minor issue of Malta. Its inhabitants had

requested British aid to expel the French. The Treaty of Amiens required Britain to evacuate the island. But Valetta's fortified Grand Harbour barred the way to Egypt and Asia, and the British stayed on. Negotiations came to nothing, and on 12 May 1803, after an ultimatum, Britain declared war. Ordinary people on both sides of the Channel were horrified, foreseeing years of hunger, taxation, conscription and impressment. Seamen sought safer jobs in coal mines and quarries. Landsmen rioted when ballots for militia service were ordered. In France, men married elderly widows to gain exemption, chopped off their trigger fingers, or headed for the hills. Both countries faced a deadly war of attrition. British ministers were remarkably confident that France would crack first.

## DEFEATING NAPOLEON

*[Until] there can be a final settlement that shall last, every thing should remain as unsettled as possible; . . . no usurper should feel sure of acknowledgement; no people confident in their new masters; no kingdom sure of its existence, no spoliator sure of his spoil; and even the plundered not acquiescent in their loss . . . [It] is our business to shew what England, as England, is: . . . it is only through us alone that they can look for secure and effectual tranquillity.*

George Canning, Foreign Secretary, 1807[63]

The political climate in England changed. Many who had supported the revolution in 1789 had been disillusioned, and had even less sympathy for Bonaparte's dictatorship. One minister actually appealed in the Commons for support from English Jacobins, "as men of spirit, of lovers of what they call liberty . . . [are they] content to be put under the yoke and crushed by France?"[64] France's invasion of peaceful Switzerland in 1798 had already turned Wordsworth against the revolution, even if his endorsement of England's cause was distinctly grudging: "Oh grief that Earth's best hopes rest all with Thee!"[65] Many—including Wordsworth and Coleridge—took a grim pride that the country stood alone. Most Dissenting congregations now supported a defensive war against a militaristic dictatorship. Not all, however. The hardline view was expressed by a Unitarian minister, Ebenezer Aldred, who had worked out that Britain—guilty of imperialism, slave trading and sodomy—was the real Beast of Revelation; and the Whore of Babylon was Britannia, shown on the new halfpenny piece "with wet drapery from the hips upwards . . . the feet,

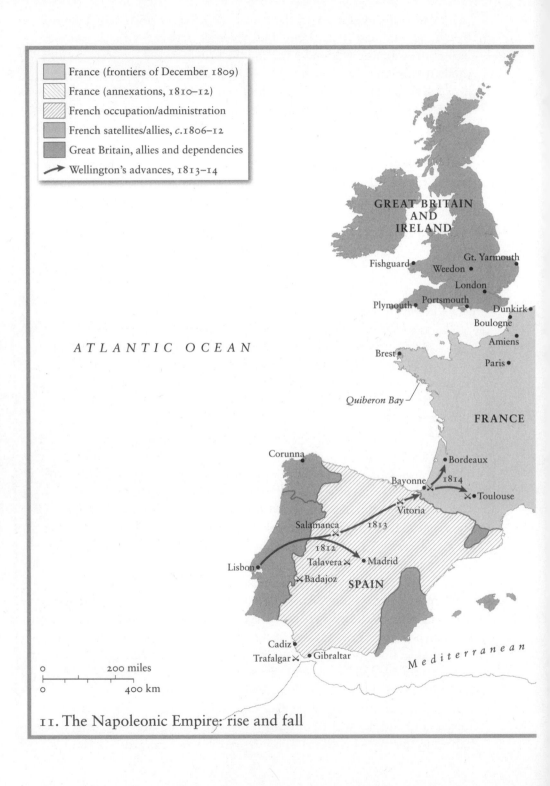

France (frontiers of December 1809)
France (annexations, 1810–12)
French occupation/administration
French satellites/allies, c.1806–12
Great Britain, allies and dependencies
Wellington's advances, 1813–14

GREAT BRITAIN
AND
IRELAND

Fishguard•          Gt. Yarmouth•
          Weedon•
                    London•
Plymouth•  Portsmouth•   Dunkirk•
          Boulogne•
                    Amiens•
Brest•              Paris•

*ATLANTIC OCEAN*

FRANCE

*Quiberon Bay*

Corunna•

                    •Bordeaux
          Bayonne•  1814
                    ×•Toulouse
          Vitoria
Salamanca        1813
      ×   1812
Lisbon•  Talavera×  •Madrid
   ×Badajoz    SPAIN

Cadiz•
Trafalgar×  •Gibraltar      *M e d i t e r r a n e a n*

0        200 miles
0        400 km

11. The Napoleonic Empire: rise and fall

arms, bosom . . . completely bare, and in the very attitude of invitation."[66] A tiny informal underground of activists, mostly in London, hoped that conspiratorial tactics might still work if coordinated with a French invasion.[67] But the country as a whole was increasingly united in support of the struggle.[68]

Like his predecessors in 1745, 1759 and 1779, the emperor Napoleon (as he became in 1804) decided on invasion: "The Channel is a ditch which will be crossed when someone has the boldness to try it." While still at peace he had started building 2,500 gunboats and landing craft, and he marshalled an Army of England of 165,000 men strung out between the Channel ports with its headquarters at Boulogne. He was confident that "foggy weather and some luck will make me master of London, of parliament and of the Bank of England."[69] Palpable danger—from Kent on clear days French troops could be seen drilling—caused a surge of patriotic excitement unparalleled until 1914 and 1939. When, one evening late in 1803, news came to Colchester that an invasion fleet had been sighted, there was instant turmoil, described by Ann Taylor to her sister:

> The volunteers were flying to arms. The officers at the play were scampering out to gallop home to their camps . . . all the horses, post chaises, etc., in the town were hired within half an hour, crammed full of red coats and even in some cases two or three upon one horse . . . Women running out of their houses screaming murder . . . However, in about half an hour signals were made to inform us that a mistake had been made . . . and of course we all recovered.[70]

By 1804, 380,000 men had joined the Volunteers in the greatest popular movement of the Hanoverian age.[71] This was above all *local* patriotism and often involved rivalry with other localities. In volunteer units, which were remarkably egalitarian and independent, men remained civilians in (often very elaborate) uniform, vocal in defence of their rights and their pay, able to go home when they had had enough, commanded by their neighbours, and with their own systems of discipline. The Piddletown Light Infantry, from Dorset, for example, decided that "Whoever Speaks, or Laughs in the Ranks, after the word attention is given . . . to be fined Sixpence." The Hackney Volunteers so resented being told to act as the French in a training exercise against the Islington Volunteers that they genuinely came to blows.[72] The regular army, in contrast with enthusiasm for local volunteering, was shunned by respectable English workers: between June and December 1803 recruiting sergeants scouring the country could induce only 3,481 men to enlist, and conscription was politically impossible.[73] So the army overseas was always short of men, depending disproportionately on Irish and Scottish manpower—not to mention Indian and Caribbean recruits. Still, the outcome is astonishing. By 1805 about 800,000 men were doing some form of armed service— 20 percent of the active male population, and up to 50 percent in threatened coastal counties. This is comparable with the total wars of the twentieth century and was a far higher proportion than in any other country—the government calculated that France had only 7 percent under arms.[74] But Britain could not and would not fight a total war like the French revolutionaries. Its effort depended largely on volunteering and traditional amateur local government: lords-lieutenant (at least one of whom relied on his wife as secretary), Justices of the Peace, parsons and parish officers. The system creaked under the strain, but its achievement testifies to the strength and initiative of local communities, which remained the bedrock of English governance until the 1940s. The needs of war, however, increased both the size and the efficiency of the central state.[75]

Propaganda emphasized national solidarity and common danger. It was reiterated that invasion would expose rich and poor alike to pillage and rape: "He promises to enrich his soldiers with our property," warned one pamphleteer, "to glut their lust with our wives and daughters."[76] Roast beef and even bread and cheese would be replaced by black bread and vegetable soup. *Henry V* played to patriotic audiences in London. Women were perhaps more engaged in public discussion than in earlier wars, thanks to the greater intensity of ideological and moral debate— even though one women's newspaper blithely continued to feature fashion news from Paris. Jane Austen's novels show the presence of war, however distant the fighting. Mary Wollstonecraft and Hannah More were leading polemicists on opposite sides. Women were particularly active in the mounting anti-slavery campaign.[77]

Defence preparations were orchestrated by the commander-in-chief, the able and energetic Duke of York, George III's second son. The navy surveyed every possible landing site from Cornwall to Scotland, with the main danger being Kent. Massive fortifications were begun at Dover. Round, squat "Martello towers" with cannon—168 in all—were built mainly on the shores of Sussex, Kent and Essex, but with some as far away as Dublin and the Orkneys. Dams were ready to flood the Lea Valley to protect London. Records of the 1588 defence against the Armada were dusted off. Volunteers were to slow the invaders down, while the country was "driven" of animals, vehicles and supplies, and roads broken up. Non-combatants would leave, taking "a change of linen, and one blanket for each person [and] all the food in your possession."[78] Meanwhile, 113,000 men would be hurrying to ten rendezvous points north

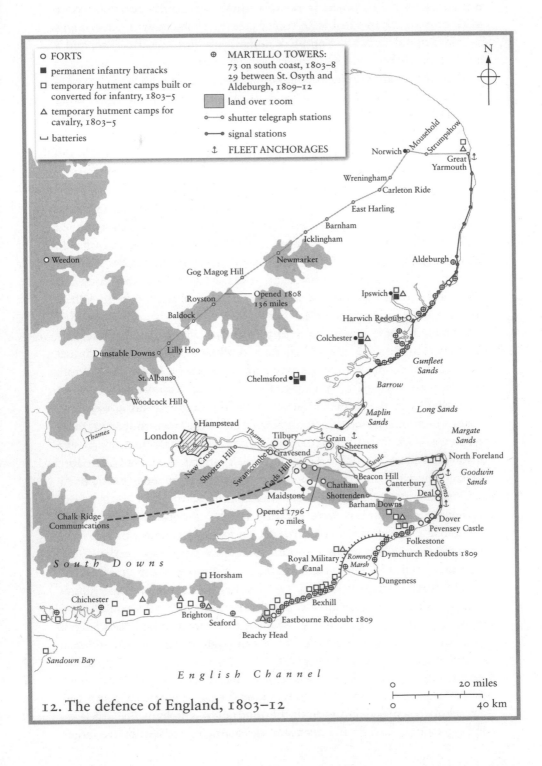

FORTS
■ permanent infantry barracks
□ temporary hutment camps built or converted for infantry, 1803–5
△ temporary hutment camps for cavalry, 1803–5
⌐ batteries

⊕ MARTELLO TOWERS:
73 on south coast, 1803–8
29 between St. Osyth and Aldeburgh, 1809–12

 land over 100m
◦—◦ shutter telegraph stations
●—● signal stations
⚓ FLEET ANCHORAGES

N

Norwich  Mousehold  Strumpshow
Great Yarmouth ⚓

Wreningham
Carleton Ride
East Harling
Barnham
Icklingham
Newmarket
Aldeburgh

Weedon

Gog Magog Hill
Opened 1808
136 miles
Royston
Baldock
Dunstable Downs  Lilly Hoo
St. Albans
Woodcock Hill

Ipswich
Harwich Redoubt
Colchester
Gunfleet Sands
Barrow
Long Sands

Chelmsford
Maplin Sands
Margate Sands

Thames
London  Hampstead
New Cross
Shooters Hill
Swanscombe
Cade Hills
Chalk Ridge Communications

Thames  Tilbury
Gravesend
⚓ Grain  Sheerness
Swale
North Foreland
⚓ Goodwin Sands
Beacon Hill
Chatham  Canterbury  Deal
Shottenden
Maidstone  Barham Downs
Opened 1796
70 miles

South Downs

Horsham

Chichester
Brighton
Seaford
Beachy Head

Royal Military Canal  Romney Marsh
Dover
Pevensey Castle
Folkestone
Dymchurch Redoubts 1809
Dungeness

Bexhill
Eastbourne Redoubt 1809

Sandown Bay

English Channel

0 ————— 20 miles
0 ————— 40 km

12. The defence of England, 1803–12

and west of London, which were stocked with coal and flour. Plans were made to carry on the fight if London fell: a vast fortified arms depot was built at Weedon in Northamptonshire with arms for 200,000 men, and a small Royal Pavilion for George III and his family.[79]

What did England really risk? Napoleon boasted that he would be "a liberator, a new William of Orange." Perhaps Tom Paine would have been brought out, as he kept hoping, as figurehead of a puppet republic. For Napoleon personally, invasion would be a life-and-death gamble, and for England a bloodbath whatever the outcome. A complete French victory—the only thing worth the huge risk—would probably have required crushing the people in arms, imposing long military occupation, dividing the United Kingdom, destroying its naval power, annexing colonies, massively confiscating property, and diverting its trade to France. "England was . . . bound to become a mere appendage of France," Napoleon later reflected.[80] This would surely have meant the implosion of the Industrial Revolution, economic collapse and catastrophic impoverishment of the booming population. So England was fighting not only for independence, but for existence.

Was invasion possible? Napoleon thought so: "If we control the crossing for twelve hours, England is dead."[81] But some French naval officers feared that many of his overloaded landing craft would sink even without the intervention of the Royal Navy. In August 1805, Napoleon summoned his battle fleet up the Channel to cover the invasion, but his naval commander, Admiral Villeneuve, shied away from what he considered certain disaster, and later committed suicide. Napoleon angrily abandoned the invasion and marched his army off "to fight England in Germany," defeating the Austrians and the Russians with chilling efficiency at Ulm on 20 October and Austerlitz on 2 December. Meanwhile, on 21 October, the French and Spanish fleets were no less efficiently destroyed off Cape Trafalgar. This long remained in the forefront of national memory as the victory that decisively ended the recurring threat of invasion. England had expected "that every man will do his duty," following the example given by its most charismatic sailor, Horatio Nelson, who gave his life and created a model hero for the age, combining audacity, vulnerability and pathos (and, though this was played down, a rather turbulent private life). Trafalgar was in reality a one-sided battle, as was now invariably the case when the totally dominant Royal Navy got to grips with its enemies, inferior in training, morale and physical health: two-thirds of the Franco-Spanish fleet of thirty-three ships of the line were captured or destroyed by the twenty-nine British at a cost of only 448 British lives. French casualties were appalling. The *Redoutable*, for example, battered by the larger

*Victory* and two other ships, had 571 of her 643 crew killed or wounded. Of 15,000 Frenchmen engaged, only 4,000 escaped.[82] Napoleon did not give up: he soon ordered the construction all over Europe of a massive fleet, with Antwerp chosen as the main base for future invasion.

"Roll up the map of Europe," Pitt is supposed to have said after Austerlitz, "it will not be wanted these ten years." Three months later, in January 1806, he died, aged forty-six, of an abdominal complaint aggravated by overwork, stress and drink. He had been Prime Minister, with a short interval, for nearly eighteen years, most of them at war. Little remembered today, this shy man's wartime leadership is approached in modern times only by that of Elizabeth I and Churchill. His young followers admired him, often extravagantly. Officials found him easy to work with and appreciated the "extreme quickness of his apprehension [and] the undivided and unprejudiced attention which he gives."[83] Some of his acquaintances found him an odd, sometimes infuriating, character. He was not religious, and so inhabited a different mental universe from most radicals, who hated him as a tyrant and warmonger. He was a powerful parliamentary orator, measured, high-minded, sometimes moving. The radical essayist William Hazlitt, who loathed him, scoffed that "posterity cannot find a single thing worth quoting." But one exception at least was his last public speech, at the Guildhall on 9 November 1805, soon after Trafalgar, when he was toasted as "the Saviour of Europe": "I return you many thanks for the honour you have done me: but Europe is not to be saved by any single man. England has saved herself by her exertions and will, as I trust, save Europe by her example."[84] Pitt's death opened a period of relative political instability: from 1805 to 1809 there were three prime ministers, four secretaries of state for war, and five First Lords of the Admiralty;[85] scandalously, two ministers, Castlereagh and Canning, fought a duel and had to resign. A coalition in 1806 including Fox as Foreign Secretary, known as the "Ministry of All the Talents," had no coherent strategy. So the war would go on without prospect of an end, with France dominant on land and Britain at sea.

The Royal Navy became over the course of the long conflict a uniquely effective force of over 600 ships and 135,000 men,[86] costing some £15m a year, equal to almost the total prewar state budget. From 1793 to 1815, it lost only one line-of-battle ship to enemy action, but captured or destroyed 139. This rise to supremacy had been a long process, with roots going back to the time of Pepys, Cromwell and the Tudors. It was the "most complex and expensive project ever undertaken by the British state and society," and had left few aspects of national life unaffected.[87] Large warships were the most complex artefacts in existence. Over her active lifetime, HMS *Victory* cost nearly £400,000—the annual budget of a small state. Wooden fleets needed highly skilled construction and constant maintenance, principally in the vast naval dockyards at Portsmouth, Plymouth and Chatham; and also in many private shipyards: for example, along the Thames but also as far away as Bombay. A medium-sized battleship of 1,900 tons required 3,000 tons of raw timber—the equivalent of 3,000–4,000 mature trees. The Royal Navy in 1790 had been built from well over half a million trees, and its wartime expansion drew on timber not only from English forests, but from the Baltic, the Mediterranean, North America, Asia and eventually Australasia (where a landing party were captured by Maori in 1809 while cutting kauri and eaten). Tree varieties were needed that would not shatter too badly under cannon fire, as splinters were the principal killer; teak, otherwise excellent, produced deadly splinters. Baltic pine was best for masts but the supply was vulnerable; and British development of Canadian pine eventually gave a great advantage. Capturing or destroying enemy timber supplies was an important object.[88] The navy had enormous workshops for rope and rigging using hemp from the Baltic. Copper-makers in Wales provided sheathing for the hulls to increase speed. Early steam-driven machine tools made millions of light, low-friction pulley blocks for the rigging, which saved manpower, weight and wear. A modest naval squadron had more artillery than both sides at Austerlitz, needing ironworks and cannon-makers, famously the Carron company in Scotland; the gunpowder required supplies of saltpetre from India. Brewers, butchers, bakers, salters and coopers had to provide safe food and drink that could survive long voyages and extreme climates. Probably the world's first assembly line made ships' biscuits.

Once ships were built and equipped they had to be manned; and, once manned, properly used. In the 1740s Admirals Anson and Hawke had pioneered a Western Squadron based at Plymouth to dominate the Atlantic approaches to Europe by long patrols at sea, and this control of crucial communications proved a decisive instrument of European and world power.[89] Blockades of French ports were progressively tightened as the navy learned how to spend long periods on station without its crews quickly falling sick—Admiral Collingwood, commander of the Mediterranean Fleet, had not set foot on shore for eight years when he died on board in 1810. Occasionally there were battles to destroy enemy navies or chase them from the seas. From mid-century—with 1776–82 an interlude—British confidence had grown and that of the French had waned. French admirals became justifiably frightened of the Channel, and pessimistic about the feasibility of invading Britain. Aggression became the hallmark of British naval culture, striving to force close action and inflict maximum damage, which demanded discipline, practice and confidence. The adoption in the 1780s of a large-calibre short-range gun, the carronade, reinforced these tactics. Stress was laid on gunnery practice, for speed of firing was decisive, and there was much experimentation with firing mechanisms and gun-laying systems. The effective firepower of the British by the 1790s has been reckoned as two or three times that of the French, and overall the Royal Navy inflicted about six times as many casualties as it suffered. French and Spanish sailors often abandoned their guns and lay down as British ships with fully loaded broadsides came within "pistol shot"—sometimes as close as twenty feet. The prospect of being boarded was equally intimidating, as the Royal Navy were formidable hand-to-hand fighters.[90]

Quality of manpower was decisive, because the British rarely had numerical superiority in battle: at Trafalgar, for example, the Franco-Spanish were more numerous. Warships needed big crews: 1,000 men for a line-of-battle ship, compared with twenty or thirty for an average merchant ship. So a navy required a large merchant marine to supply a pool of sailors, most of whom would be enlisted during a major war; and trade had given Britain the world's largest merchant navy. The Royal Navy had to compete with the merchant marine and privateers for men: the demand was two or three times the supply. Hence the Impress Service—the notorious "Press Gangs"—were as likely to be victims as perpetrators of violence. They were regularly attacked by mobs, and even imprisoned by local magistrates where there was a strong shipowning interest, Liverpool being notorious.[91] Prize money, on the other hand, was a powerful encouragement to volunteer. The profit made some officers very rich, and was an incentive for all ranks to be alert, enterprising and aggressive, although it sometimes distracted them from less lucrative duties. "You can't think how keen our men are," wrote Admiral Boscawen in 1756, "the hope of prize money makes them happy, a signal for a sail brings them all on deck."[92]

British sailors spent far more time at sea, giving the Royal Navy the advantage of tough and well-trained crews. They were led by a meritocratic and experienced officer corps expected to be able to administer a ship, navigate round the world, haul on a rope and lead a boarding party. Popular traditions about appalling conditions in the Royal Navy are partly myth: the navy's successes would be hard to explain if it had been "a sort of floating concentration camp."[93] Discipline was tough, but excessive harshness was frowned upon, and courts-martial were scrupulous and the same for officers and men.[94] Warships, though crowded, were safer, cleaner and less uncomfortable than merchant ships. Food and drink were good and plentiful—about 5,000 calories a day, including a pound of bread, a pound of meat and a gallon of beer—and if it ran short, officers too had to go hungry. Health was comparatively good. Fresh food was regularly issued to prevent scurvy, and in the 1790s lemon juice rations were introduced: in 1808, for example, the Swedish fleet had 1,500 men suffering from scurvy, while the large British Baltic fleet had only 4.[95]

By the last decades of the century, England was safe from invasion for the first time in its history, and so it remained. The French in 1779 had shown that a major landing might still have been possible (see p. 357), but Napoleon's failure in 1805 showed that it no longer was. At the same time, the Royal Navy extended its dominance round the globe. Sailing fleets in distant seas required roomy, deep and sheltered anchorages, stores of spars, rope, sails and ammunition, and a large hinterland for fresh food and water. The British secured bases round the globe—Gibraltar, Malta, Halifax, Bermuda, Jamaica, Antigua, St. Helena, Capetown, Mauritius, Bombay, Calcutta, Sydney—making a constant naval presence possible. As France and its allies lost their bases, they lost the very possibility of naval action. Domination of the European seas and the ability to project invincible power across the oceans, and hence to exert pressure over the world's commercial and economic life, was the foundation of a power which no other state or combination of states would seriously challenge until the fascist Axis of the Second World War.

But direct British power stopped at the Channel and North Sea coasts: strategically and politically, the French dominated the Continent, and the British could do nothing in Europe without allies. When Napoleon signed the Treaty of Tilsit with defeated Russia in 1807, Britain was alone. But there remained economic warfare. Britain's economy was doing rather well out of the conflict. Since 1790 overseas trade had grown by nearly 60 percent, and colonial re-exports, mainly sugar and coffee, by 187 percent. Domestic demand was strong. Agriculture had increased the acreage under the plough. The City had received a flood of capital and people seeking security and become truly international: rival financial centres, notably Amsterdam and Frankfurt, have never caught up since. Britain's finances seemed able to sustain a war indefinitely, and subsidize other countries willing to fight the French. The French resorted to the *guerre de course*, attacks on merchant shipping. This inflicted damage on British trade, but it could not defeat Britain, which lost only 2 percent of its merchant fleet during the Napoleonic Wars. The French themselves suffered far more: in 1803 they had 1,500 ocean-going merchant ships, but by

1812 only 179—compared with Britain's 24,000.[96] So Napoleon ordered a land blockade. In November 1806 his "Berlin Decrees" prohibited all trade with Britain from France and its satellites, declared all British civilians on the Continent prisoners of war, and ordered the seizure of all British merchandise. This "Continental System" aimed to wreck British trade and increase that of France: "England will end up weeping tears of blood."[97] London retaliated with Orders in Council in November 1807 forbidding any ship from any country to trade with Napoleonic Europe unless it first passed through a British port and paid a 25 percent duty.

One epoch-making consequence of the trade war was British abolition of the slave trade in 1806–7. The religious and humanitarian campaign against the trade had been growing for years. Such was the importance of the West Indies trade, especially in time of war, that neither Revolutionary France nor monarchist Britain would willingly contemplate any change in the slave economy. But after the French were deprived of most of their Caribbean trade by the great Saint-Domingue slave revolt in 1791, hard-headed English politicians could contemplate abolition not only as morally desirable, but as politically feasible. Appalling fighting in the Caribbean had highlighted both the atrocities and costs of slavery. Former and actual slaves (purchased by the War Office) had fought in the British army, challenging racial prejudices. As the Foreign Secretary, Lord Grenville, put it,

> Have we not ourselves made them soldiers? . . . Have we not employed them in every service requiring fidelity and courage, and all the intelligence and virtue which go to constitute a good military character? . . . But now . . . shall it be said that . . . they are unfit for trust and confidence, that slavery is their doom by nature?[98]

Slave soldiers were collectively emancipated. After slavery was reintroduced with horrific brutality by the French in 1803, anti-slavery became patriotic. The navy tried to blockade French, Spanish and Dutch Caribbean islands, but they evaded the blockade by exporting their produce under the American flag, which contributed to a war with the United States in 1812. But enemy production could be stifled by cutting off slave labour. Wilberforce and the abolitionists arranged that the government would introduce a bill to forbid British ships from carrying slaves to all foreign territories from where they could be re-exported to the enemy: "We should not give advantages to our enemies [and so] we should not supply their colonies with slaves." This 1806 Act—passed with huge majorities in both Houses—abolished two-thirds, perhaps even three-quarters, of Britain's lucrative and booming slave trade on the grounds of wartime necessity. The religious and humanitarian motives of the abolitionists could then come into the open, and Wilberforce and his allies extended the ban in 1807 to the remainder of the trade.[99] There was a less tangible patriotic motive too: to prove—not least to themselves—that the war against Napoleon was morally justified, and not simply the clawing of two cut-throat states.

Napoleon's Continental System required control of the whole European coastline to try to exclude British imports. But the result was vast organized smuggling to supply Europe's insatiable appetite for tobacco, cotton cloth, sugar, coffee, tea, chocolate, spices and manufactures. France's customs revenue collapsed. To close off access, Napoleon tried to take over Portugal and Spain in 1807–8, provoking resistance in both countries, notably the 2 May uprising in Madrid, immortalized by Goya's painting. Despite persistent Whig opposition, Britain gave swift financial, naval and military assistance, eventually under the highly capable control of the indomitable Arthur Wellesley, later Duke of Wellington, dismissed by Napoleon as the "sepoy general" as he had gained his military experience in India. The peninsula was reduced to bloody chaos, becoming in Napoleon's phrase an "ulcer" sapping French strength. Perhaps twice as many of his soldiers would die there as in the disastrous invasion of Russia in 1812.[100] For the first time since Marlborough, Britain exerted significant military power on the Continent, and five years of hard campaigning created an army eventually as good as the French. It was a very British army: only 20 percent were English, and there were large Irish and Scottish contingents.[101] But it was at first small—around 30,000 men— and depended on Spanish and Portuguese allies to divide enemy strength by constant guerrilla warfare. This enabled Wellington to sally forth in 1809 from his base in Portugal, where he was supplied by the navy, retreat back to it in 1810 when the French mustered superior forces, and then mount decisive advances into Spain in 1812 and 1813. The British army was, to put it mildly, hard-bitten, and it acquired a fearsome reputation for drunkenness, looting and rape. Fortunately, Wellington and his staff were capable administrators and usually maintained adequate supplies, because, as the adjutant-general put it, "A British army on short commons is no easy thing to govern . . . heroic in action . . . and when he is well fed, but in retreat where subsistence is short, [our soldier] becomes cross, unmanageable and too much disposed to give the thing up."[102] Some of its men were, in Wellington's words, the scum of the earth, but it also included adventurous or patriotic men of some education, whose letters and diaries left some of the earliest pictures of everyday campaigning. Victories in the peninsula, including at Talavera, Salamanca and Vitoria, raised the status of both the army and the aristocracy in public eyes.

Once Britain was their ally, exports to Portugal, Spain and their South

American colonies increased. Yet English textile industries were still inevitably affected by the barriers to trade imposed by the Continental System, and a peace campaign again drew support. As in the 1790s, it fed off economic distress, on a belief, strongest among Dissenters, that the war was futile and immoral, and on lingering admiration for the revolution and Napoleon. The crisis years were 1811–12, when bad weather ravaged harvests, further damaging the economy and government finances. Weavers, knitters and croppers in Lancashire, Nottinghamshire and Yorkshire, symbolically led by the folkloric "Ned Ludd," began selective breaking of new machinery, which was threatening their jobs. They were violently opposed by employers. Pitched battles took place. Thousands of troops were deployed. Some subsequent historians have seen this as an insurrection with revolutionary potential.[103] The Luddites' discipline and restraint suggest rather that it was a limited dispute about wages and conditions: they did not damage buildings or other property, but only the disputed machines, and they even left the machines untouched where employers paid better wages.[104]

The political system was also under strain. George III, having suffered periodic bouts of mental illness, became totally incapacitated in 1810 after fifty highly eventful years on the throne. He lived on in seclusion until 1820. His dissolute and unpopular son George was made Prince Regent in 1811. In February 1812, in "an uncharacteristic attack of common sense," he backed a government of Pitt's old supporters against the Whigs. Led by Spencer Perceval, it managed to keep the country and the war on course through the economic crisis.[105] But, in May, Perceval was assassinated in the lobby of the House of Commons by a deranged bankrupt businessman, causing temporary political chaos until he was succeeded by Robert Jenkinson, Lord Liverpool, already an experienced minister, who was persistent, prudent, discreet and trusted,[106] and who in November won a crushing election victory. He remained in office for most of the next fifteen years, presiding over final victory and then the difficult postwar period. Disputes with the United States about its trade with Napoleonic Europe led to an American attack in July 1812 and continual naval skirmishing. An invasion of Canada was beaten off by a British-Shawnee alliance. A small British force of 3,700 landed on American soil and burned Washington. The Americans made peace in 1814, but fighting continued for some time before the news arrived, and another small British force was defeated at New Orleans.

Napoleon's characteristically reckless invasion of Russia in 1812 because it refused to "act as my second in my duel with England,"[107] and in which his Grand Army of 220,000 was almost annihilated by Russian resistance, disease and weather, marked the beginning of the end of his brilliant and destructive career. Allies abandoned him and defeated enemies resumed the struggle, now fuelled by unprecedented amounts of British money. This was made possible by the new income tax, by trade with India and North and South America, by taxes levied in India, and by selling government bonds abroad. Money and weapons flooded onto the Continent: within a year £10m and a million muskets were distributed among thirty countries from Denmark to Sicily at around £1 per soldier per month—still vastly less than British armies cost. Russia, Prussia and Austria were enabled to field 700,000 men.[108] Between 16 and 19 October 1813, the multi-national armies clashed at Leipzig, the "Battle of the Nations," the biggest and bloodiest battle before the First World War. The French alone lost 60,000 men, and were forced to withdraw from Germany.

Britain's involvement in Europe was now more than merely financial. Many Europeans believed that Britain was indifferent to their sufferings while it made money: "we must not hide the fact from ourselves," wrote a British minister, George Canning, "we are hated throughout Europe."[109] Viscount Castlereagh, Foreign Secretary from 1812, wanted to show that Britain was no longer willing to leave the Continent in flames while it amassed colonial conquests and trading profits. This required more generous cash handouts. Castlereagh, moreover, built a partnership to guarantee a secure Europe after Napoleon's defeat. He persuaded the allies to pledge peace for twenty years—"a systematic pledge of preserving concert among the leading Powers," he wrote, and "a refuge under which all the minor states . . . may look forward to find their security."[110]

Allied armies converged on France in late 1813 and early 1814 and support for Napoleon dissolved. Wellington's army, now 100,000 strong, crossed the Pyrenees and were welcomed as liberators—not least because on Wellington's strict orders they paid hard cash for supplies, and he backed up those orders with the lash and the noose.[111] One British officer recalled a French landowner being so delighted at the price he got for his cattle that he "made us dance with his daughters, produced some of his best chateau margot [sic], sang half a dozen of his best songs, slobbered over us with his embraces, and was put to bed crying drunk."[112] Napoleon's faithful Marshal Soult, still trying to resist Wellington's advance, was "ashamed . . . that a town of 100,000 souls [Bordeaux] could get away with refusing to be defended and should greet a few thousand Englishmen with acclamation." He met the same problem at Toulouse: "Practically the whole city is against being defended."[113] But defend it he did, and the battle of Toulouse on 10 April 1814 was the last real battle in the south, costing 4,500 Allied casualties and 2,700 French. Soult marched away unpursued, and the British were greeted by the mayor, a band, and a crowd of citizens who gave them a banquet. Napoleon had already abdicated on 6 April. On the initiative of Tsar Alexander I, the ex-emperor was given as compensation the island principality of Elba, off the Italian coast.

In England people celebrated: "Bells Ringing Guns Firing and Tom Paines Quaking." Vast crowds in London "all went mad," with a funfair in Hyde Park and a miniature naval battle on the Serpentine. At Yarmouth, 8,000 feasted on nearly half a ton of roast beef, 1,800 plum puddings and 80 barrels of beer at a table three-quarters of a mile long, with Napoleon burning in effigy. A determined minority clung to different sympathies: when the radical journalist William Lovell was released from Newgate (from where he had been editing the anti-war *Statesman*), contributors to a fund for him included the leading Whigs the Duke of Bedford, Earl Grey and Fox's nephew Lord Holland, the radical MP Sir Francis Burdett, and "fifty-two Friends to Freedom, at the Green Man, Preston."[114]

## ENDGAME: LOUD SABBATH

> Again their ravening eagle rose
> In anger, wheel'd on Europe-shadowing wings,
> And barking for the thrones of kings;
> Till one that sought but Duty's iron crown
> On that loud sabbath shook the spoiler down.
>
>     Alfred Tennyson, "Ode on the Death of
>         the Duke of Wellington" (1852)

Napoleon left Elba with 600 men, landed in France on 1 March 1815, and almost single-handedly regained power in May. The allied states decided to put a final stop to the irrepressible ego of "the Corsican ogre" and formed another coalition—the seventh. He was proclaimed an international outlaw. The British government promised to finance a last campaign. Russian, Prussian, Austrian, Dutch and British armies mustered. Napoleon's only slight hope was a quick victory before the Austrians and Russians arrived on the scene. He hoped in particular that to defeat the British might bring down the Liverpool government, the paymaster of the coalition, and thus force the allies into negotiation.[115] So he marched against Wellington, commanding an allied army in Belgium, and the Prussians, who were marching to support him.

Napoleon's "more than human boldness" greatly impressed the teenage Macaulay, and many radicals cheered, including Lord Byron. They claimed (wrongly) that he enjoyed the support of the French nation, and was fighting for its freedom—he was, declared the radical writer William Godwin, "infinitely more dear to the people of France" than ever.[116] After half defeating the Prussians and Wellington's "Anglo-Dutch" army (which was also Irish, Hanoverian, Scottish, Welsh and Belgian) in early encounters, Napoleon crashed head on into Wellington's defensive position near Waterloo, south of Brussels, on 18 June 1815. This "near run thing," in Wellington's words, saw his troops stubbornly holding their ground and mauling the French frontal assaults until the arrival of the Prussians under Marshal Blücher brought a decisive end to Napoleon's last adventure.

The dramatic and bloody battle—Wellington's army suffered 15,000 casualties, nearly one man in four—gave rise to powerful legends, with echoes even now. Both sides thought the battle was more than just a physical struggle. The two commanders and their armies seemed to represent national and ideological opposites. Wellington's army embodied stoical resistance to Napoleon's bold aggressiveness: tradition against revolution, British phlegm against *furia francese*—"established character" against "angry and turbulent passions," as a British newspaper put it later. The great French romantic novelist Victor Hugo felt the same: "Never did God, who delights in antithesis, set up a more striking contrast . . . On one hand precision, foresight, analysis, prudence, a steady nerve . . . On the other hand, intuition, guesswork, military unorthodoxy, supernatural instinct."[117]

The British, outnumbered, fought defensively in thin lines or hollow squares against dense attacking columns of infantry and waves of cavalry. Their tactics were to wait impassive and silent: "'Steady, lads, steady' is all you hear, and that in an undertone." The yelling French masses came forward "vociferating . . . chaffing each other until they appear in a fury, shouting to the points of our bayonets."[118] At the last moment, the British fired disciplined volleys at point-blank range followed by rapid bayonet charges. Self-control, steadiness, mutual confidence, iron discipline, the sudden transformation from stillness to controlled aggression—this became the English ideal of masculine courage, epitomized in both naval and military tactics. Military fashions, virtues and vices—in clothing, education and behaviour (as in the revival of duelling)—became more common than for generations.

Wellington exemplified the gentlemanly virtues of calm, understatement and common sense.[119] In plain clothes, exposing himself to constant danger, giving only the occasional laconic order, he seemingly held the army together by presence and example. This was one of the greatest, and also perhaps the last, of historic battles in which such an immediate role was played by a commander-in-chief—"the last great Englishman," as Tennyson would later call him despite his Irish birth, "upon whose hand and heart and brain . . . the fate and weight of Europe hung."

What had a generation of war done? Why had it been fought? Britain had gone to war in 1793, as in the past, to protect its back door in the Netherlands, and prevent a hostile power from dominating the Continent. As in 1914 and even 1939, it could be argued that it should have kept out. But no British government has ever been willing to risk the domination of western Europe by a hostile power. As in 1914 and 1939, it expected a relatively short and limited war. When this proved wrong, and peace attempts repeatedly failed, there seemed no choice but to fight it out. Between 1793 and 1815, one estimate of British navy and army losses from combat, shipwreck and disease is 210,000 men—a death toll comparable with that of the First World War.[120] This proved to be the last decisive round in the long struggle against France that had begun in 1689, and which had cost an incalculable number of lives round the globe.

It was won thanks to acceptance by the country of heavy taxation and military service, strong commercial and agricultural growth, and great improvements in the efficiency of the state—"organization, management and control of resources had to be at the highest level, and they were."[121] The political and military leadership, many of them notable for "youth, intelligence and formidable industry," carried enormous workloads during years of war. Under pressure, the oligarchical system could identify and promote able men early. Pitt was not the only example—many ministers, commanders and key officials held important posts in their twenties and thirties. One was Viscount Palmerston, who became an MP and an Admiralty commissioner in 1806, the year after he came down from St. John's College, Cambridge, and he was Secretary at War two years later: "If [such men] had not worked as hard and competently as they did, Britain would not have survived the onslaught."[122] Impossible to defeat or conciliate, Britain had emerged as the leader of a grand coalition that finally brought Napoleon down. In doing so, it opened one of Europe's longest periods of peace. Admirers of Napoleon saw the price of this as a step backwards into Old Regime oppression, and some leading English radicals "grieved" at the outcome of Waterloo. Napoleon's subsequent packing off to St. Helena out of harm's way increased the fervour of his English admirers.[123]

Britain had emerged as the world's richest and most powerful state. One woman found this worrying: "I begin to be afraid, like the frog in the fable we shall all burst with national pride, for never, to be sure, did we stand so high before." But pride did not make it a happy or stable place, as we shall see in the next chapter. "What is it, after all, the people get?" rhymed a Whig paper, "Why! Widows, Taxes, Wooden legs, and Debt!"[124] The "fiscal-military state" had ballooned; condemnation of it as "Old Corruption" provided a rallying cry for the future.

Britain, in defeating the French Revolution in its various manifestations, had captured the future. No country until Lenin's Russia tried to copy the Jacobins, though vocal minorities were still excited by the memory of Robespierre or Napoleon. But nor did the reactionary ideologies of European counter-revolutionaries long prevail. Some form of English-style parliamentary government—Burke's "third option" between the "despotism of the monarch" and the "despotism of the multitude"[125]—was gradually accepted as the sensible replacement for absolute monarchy and the way to forestall revolution. English technology was also copied, albeit with misgivings, as the Industrial Revolution accelerated. England, admired, envied and resented, became Europe's principal template of modernity.

# PART FIVE

# THE ENGLISH CENTURY

*England will have to decide between national and cosmopolitan principles. The issue is not a mean one. It is whether you will be content to be a comfortable England . . . or whether you will be a great country—an imperial country—[and] command the respect of the world.*

Benjamin Disraeli, speech at the Crystal Palace, 1872[1]

The century that ran from the defeat of Napoleon to the First World War was the time in which the English, for good and ill, made a permanent impact on the common life of humanity. Sometimes they acted consciously, deliberately and en masse (for example, in anti-slavery and free-trade campaigns), though rarely with precisely the consequences they expected; and sometimes, as the historian Sir John Seeley famously put it, as if in a fit of absence of mind, following no apparent policy and showing little interest.

Their ability to have such impact, and the long-term consequences it produced, came from the fruition during the nineteenth century of economic, intellectual, political, social and religious processes that began in the eighteenth century and even earlier, creating the amalgam we think of as "Victorian England." Those running its affairs were not now for the most part buccaneers like Drake or adventurers like Clive. Though not averse to a healthy profit, many felt a moral responsibility to improve what they touched, or at least to persuade themselves that this was what they were doing. Fundamental to their motives and their power was the growth of England's coal-powered and mechanized economy and its worldwide commercial network, which continued to develop throughout the century. This development was possible, as we have seen, because of victory in the long struggle with France, which left England as part of an enlarged United Kingdom and a much expanded British Empire with unchallenged control of the oceans. England's economic dynamism both paid for and benefited from victory, and enabled it for a time to become (in Disraeli's famous expression) the workshop of the world. Yet this change, involving population growth, rapid urbanization and inevitable social upheaval, required a concerted effort to control and tame, making a turbulent and frightening society law-abiding and "respectable" to an extent it had never been before and has not been since.

Disraeli used the phrase "the empire of England."[2] It was common to talk of England, while meaning—as we would see it—Britain. Disraeli presumably meant that England was its economic core, its centre of decision, its predominant culture and increasingly its greatest body of people. England, like the other countries of the United Kingdom, remained a distinct entity, with particular social, political, economic and cultural characteristics. Just as England had an impact on the wider circles of the United Kingdom, the empire and beyond, so it was in return affected by them. It was moulded by increasing economic interdependence. Its political culture was periodically disrupted, even transformed, by external issues, especially those concerning Ireland. In writing England's history, perhaps more in this century than before or since, it is often necessary to see it as part of Britain, most obviously in international and imperial contexts. Yet many of the most important characteristics of this time—which I am treating under the thematic headings of "Dickensian" and "Victorian"— are peculiarly English. It is necessary, in short, to think not in terms of England or Britain, but England and Britain.

The world on which "the empire of England" was to have a multiplicity of political, economic and cultural effects was unusually open—or one might say vulnerable—to English influence. Europe had been traumatized and much of it ravaged by revolution and war, which explains why it was much less prone to inter-state war than it had been for centuries. Its stability was based on acknowledgement of British and Russian hegemony in their respective Western and Eastern spheres,[3] which lasted at least until the 1860s. Yet, internally, European societies were to be shaken up by the economic, technological and social processes in which England had led the way. So, rapidly, was the rest of the world, with the additional immense impact of mass European migration, and with direct and often violent interference by European states. Much of the world was already in a state of flux. In some regions, this was linked to the recent struggles in Europe, but in others it was happening independently of European or British intentions or actions. Thus, European empires in the Americas were collapsing or had collapsed, allowing new states to emerge; Asian empires were in crisis, exposing them to internal conflict and external, especially European, aggression; many new and often turbulent polities were emerging: for example, in Africa. Profitable contact with Europe was often desired, as a source of goods, money and weapons—though it brought a lot more than was bargained for.

These new and unpredictable circumstances gave British politicians, traders, investors, missionaries, soldiers and administrators both an opportunity and a motive for actions abroad that would benefit themselves and their country and—so most piously hoped—the world. It was now possible to exercise a light-touch hegemony over vast tracts of the globe, and dominate its communications to a degree that would have been unimaginable in earlier centuries and became impossible again after 1914. This hegemony, which now seems breathtakingly bold or arrogant, was bolstered by England's "soft power," stemming from its being the richest and most powerful country, which was proud to be—as its people repeatedly pointed out to others—at the forefront of modernity, the fulcrum of global power, and the exemplar of free and honest government.

"Dickensian," "Victorian" and "imperial": three of the most evocative and contested terms in the English historical vocabulary, and which seem to me a useful way of grappling with this complex and contradictory epoch in which the modern world was born.[4] Each of them carries with it a range of images and associations that shape and condition our responses to the nineteenth century. It is probably the period of our history about which we feel most ambivalent. As the French writer Alphonse de Lamartine said of the English of that time, it is possible not to like them, but impossible not to respect them.[5] We still struggle with the Victorians, and with reason.

# CHAPTER 12

# Dickensian England,
## *c.*1815–*c.*1850

*That we are moving in a right direction towards some superior
condition of society—politically, morally, intellectually and
religiously—. . . we humbly yet proudly . . . do fully recognise as a
great fact.*

Charles Dickens, 1851[1]

Dickensian: a word that since the 1850s has been colouring our view
of the early nineteenth century, and prevents us from seeing it with
our own eyes. The meanings are contradictory, like Dickens's own works:
jolly Christmases and failing NHS hospitals are both "Dickensian." His
most popular novels were *The Pickwick Papers* (1836–37)—Dickensian
jollity—and *Oliver Twist* (1837–38)—Dickensian horror. Oliver's "Please,
sir, I want some more" is one of the most memorable and devastating
satires in the language.[2] It fixes English society more than scores of reports
and monographs, even though workhouse inmates rarely went hungry,
and English public services were lavishly financed by international standards.[3] Readers of Dickens would never guess that the Poor Law he savaged was the biggest system of wealth redistribution in the world.[4] But
this weighs little alongside the story of Oliver Twist.

Dickens's writing colours his era at least as much as Bunyan, Fielding
or Austen colour theirs, creating a common stock of characters, situations, expressions and witticisms familiar to people of all classes, regions
and persuasions.[5] We still see England through his eyes. Charles Dickens
(1812–70) was a hard-working, self-made gentleman, the son of a feckless
Admiralty clerk (the model for Mr. Micawber), proud of his achievements, profoundly resentful of his childhood vicissitudes, and chippily
scornful of the ruling class, from whom he rejected all honours. He
emerged from a literary tradition which he acknowledged—Defoe, Hogarth, Richardson, Fielding, Smollett and Scott. He also emerged from but
rejected the low-life serial novels (often called "Newgate literature" or

"penny shockers"), which glamorized criminals: he wanted to moralize popular literature and create feelings of solidarity between social classes.

Dickensian England was a place of intense political and social debate. Not only was England rapidly becoming a new kind of society, it was doing so without any blueprint, without certainty that it was following a sustainable path. It was possible to be impressed by scientific and techno- logical modernity, but also fear that the country was heading for catastro- phe. Dickens, as writer and editor, was prominent in a literary and intellectual "post-romantic" group, including the philosopher and histo- rian Carlyle, Tennyson, and fellow-novelists Thackeray, Gaskell and Mar- tineau, all of whom were active in a process of analysis and introspection unsurpassed in our cultural history. Writers, philosophers, moralists and politicians shared an urgent concern with what Carlyle called the "condi- tion of England." Barely readable today, the splenetic Carlyle was then the conscience of the nation. Wrote George Eliot: "There is hardly a superior or active mind of this generation that has not been modified by Carlyle's writings."[6] Not all were convinced, including the philosopher James Mar- tineau (Harriet's brother), who thought his "power over intellectual men . . . not unlike that of Joe Smith the prophet over the Mormons, dependent on strength of will and massive effrontery of dogma."[7] But Dickens was a keen admirer, inspired by Carlyle's 1840 lecture "The Hero as Man of Letters," which called for "a Prophet or Poet to teach us"—a role Dickens was clearly taken with. These writers hoped to influence and manage social change, not least through propaganda. Unlike earlier social observers, such as Fielding, Austen or Scott, they were consciously writ- ing about a society that seemed suddenly unstable, dysfunctional and frightening.

Dickens's stance could be summed up as populist Christian radicalism: "I have very little faith in the people who govern us [but] I have great confidence in the People whom they govern."[8] His vision of his time revolved round his own personal history and obsessions. He detested the elite—including that of the churches—but had little sympathy with the criminal poor, and none with aggressive radicalism. He supported capital punishment, and the refuge for prostitutes he set up—"Urania Cottage"— was a strict institution which, he said, needed "the yoke of discipline."[9] He accepted social and economic inequality. He sent his eldest son to Eton—and withdrew him to avoid his being "pampered." His fictional characters he most identified with were gentle-born and visibly different from the plebeians. His ideal was leisured domestic felicity, with a wife who was virtuous, intelligent, beautiful, admiring and self-effacing, and an audience of adoring children. Living out this egocentric indulgence brought miserable consequences to his own large family: he dismissed the mother of his ten children as inadequate, despised his sons as unworthy of him, and reduced his daughters and his young secret mistress to economic and psychological dependency.[10] He applauded Progress (his God was certainly a modernizer), but rejected dogma and calculation which threatened generosity and love: "The Good Samaritan was a Bad Economist."[11]

Dickens was the first great modern writer to place working people and children at the centre of literature as individuals, making "washerwomen as interesting as duchesses"[12]—indeed, more so, as he did not write about duchesses. Poor people provided his models of human and moral values: they were not social problems, but happy, warm, cheerful, respectful and self-respecting, devoted to their families and satisfied with their jobs, making their way, in their own way, in the society in which they found themselves.[13] His ability to imagine larger-than-life yet believable characters—which even grudging critics saw as a kind of genius—explains the power of his vision, to which his illustrators, "Phiz" (Hablot Browne) and George Cruikshank, powerfully contributed. He used this power to be a "moral teacher," asserting what one critic called "the claims of the poor on the merciful sympathies of their fellows." His readers knew this was a novelty; some realized it was a cultural revolution. One reviewer asserted that Dickens's readers became "better men" through the "enlargement of sympathies." Another wrote that his "admirable portraits of the poor" had "rendered his name so truly dear to every lover of his country." Another observed with some bemusement that "it is a strange privilege . . . to have any—still more awful to have much—influence on men's souls."[14] Working people used Dickens's novels to illustrate their own lives, comparing people they knew with his characters, and their own experiences with his stories.[15]

Dickensian England was a place of exhilarating and frightening change. He was a dogmatic prophet of modernity—"a leader of the steam whistle party par excellence," as John Ruskin put it—but not without a backward glance and a streak of dread. He remembered the stagecoaches of his youth with nostalgia. Many novels were set in a never-never land drawing on childhood memories while also mixing in references to the present, and so giving posterity an entirely inaccurate image.[16] He was thrilled by the steam train, yet also identified it with destruction and death. But he angrily, intemperately, rejected anyone who questioned Progress or espoused tradition—Tories, "Young England," Catholics, Pre-Raphaelites (why not Pre-Newtonians, he sneered). He wrote the spoof Tory hymn "God bless the squire and his relations / And keep us in our proper stations." "Fine old English Tory times," he insisted, "were garnished well with gibbets, whips and chains."[17] He lavished the same contempt on "savages"—"cruel, false, thievish, murderous; addicted more or less to grease, entrails, and beastly customs," and ripe to be "civilised off the face of the earth."[18] In short, "The voice of Time . . . cries to man, Advance!" England, for him, was not advancing fast enough.

He was not uncritical of the new, however. He disliked America, commonly taken by Radicals as the embodiment of Progress. He loathed the influential theorists of Modernity, above all Malthusians and the Utilitarian, or "Philosophic Radical," followers of Jeremy Bentham, David Ricardo and James Mill, calculators of efficiency and profit, who taught that Civilization meant that "utility is the object of every pursuit," and that poetry was a primitive relic.[19] His quarrel in the early 1850s with his friend and colleague Harriet Martineau, a pioneer social novelist, feminist and prominent Utilitarian propagandist, is symptomatic. She attacked him as a "humanity monger" and a "pseudo-philanthropist" who opposed emancipation of women and Catholics, refused to look rationally at the costs and benefits of industry, and defamed "benevolent" employers and their wonderful new technologies. He saw her as turning people into robots.[20] In *Hard Times*, his main fictional excursion outside the south of England to "Coketown" (partly based on Preston), he drew a nightmarish picture of rationalized exploitation and a joyless materialist culture based on "Facts." He was not against factories, or even Coketown, in principle. But he feared Reactionaries and Utilitarians combined were risking disaster. The privileges of the former, as in pre–Revolutionary France, and the inhumanity of the latter, as in Coketown, risked creating the savagery he feared and stigmatized in *Barnaby Rudge* and *A Tale of Two Cities*. He warned in *Hard Times* that if the poor were deprived of "fancies and affections, [if] romance is utterly driven out of their souls, and they and a bare existence stand face to face, Reality will make a wolfish turn and make an end of you."

What was to be done? Not politics. He had been contemptuous of Parliament since working as a young reporter—even thirty years later he refused an invitation to sit for Birmingham. He espoused the party line of the Radical middle-class, lacking any tradition of public service and seeing the state as a parasitical encumbrance. Politicians and the state—except in its lowest manifestations such as workhouses, law courts and prisons—barely feature in his novels, at a time of great political fiction by Trollope, Disraeli and Eliot. His political satire was "tedious and ignorant."[21] His heart-rending exposures of social abuses contained no serious analysis. He despised militant philanthropists, especially women. So what were his remedies for England's ills? Benevolence, generosity, love—

what the contemporary critic Margaret Oliphant irreverently called "the immense spiritual power of the Christmas turkey."[22] A long line of critics attacked him for mawkish sentimentality, Oscar Wilde famously joking that one would need "a heart of stone not to laugh." Intellectuals, at least until the 1950s, generally despised him.

This little affected his popularity; perhaps the contrary. His non-sectarian Christian moralism made him seem "a kind of apostle of human goodness"[23] even to those who begrudged their admiration. One who did not begrudge was the young Queen Victoria, who found *Oliver Twist* "excessively interesting" and tried vainly to convert her cynical Prime Minister, Lord Melbourne. Her subjects agreed with her. *Pickwick* in serial form was selling 40,000 copies per episode, many of them read by several people, and in book form it sold 800,000 in forty years. The "penny edition" of *Oliver Twist* sold 150,000 in three weeks: "Scarcely ever had a tale such a wide circulation; scarcely ever did a tale take such firm hold on the popular mind."[24] Conservatives could relish the "Englishness" and cross-class solidarity. Radicals could applaud the withering denunciation of the status quo. All could approve his "tone of healthful morality . . . The good are rewarded and the bad are punished."[25] As George Orwell observed with some perplexity, he "attacked English institutions with a ferocity that has never since been approached. Yet he managed to do so without making himself hated [and] he has become a national institution."[26]

The novel became both popular and—as it was often read by parents to their children—far more strait-laced than in Fielding's time. Hence, Dickens's works are completely asexual. He strove to widen his readership, through serialization, illustrations, cheap editions, lending libraries and hugely popular public "penny readings." One critic conceded that *A Christmas Carol*—even if it was to blame for "the flood of terrible joviality and sentimentality . . . poured upon us with every Christmas"—had touched "the widest audience that is capable of being moved by literature."[27] Millions of every social class read Dickens or, if unable to read, listened to him being read—the only English novelist of his stature of whom that can be said. They long continued to do so, including, in Orwell's phrase, by Dickens being "ladled down everyone's throat in childhood."[28] Many more have absorbed his stories through pictures, plays, musicals and, later, radio, films and television—at least 180 adaptations since 1903. Consequently, his characters and the major episodes have maintained a unique familiarity.

His vision is pervasive: the 2008 film *Slumdog Millionaire*, for example, set among the poor of India, is a classically "Dickensian" story. Yet there is one profound difference. Dickensian England was consciously heading into the unknown. This made the slums of London or "Coketown" in the 1840s different from those of Mumbai or Chennai in the 2010s. The former seemed signs that England was becoming an uprooted dystopia, a warning to the world. The latter, however appalling, seem a transitional stage to a better future. The heirs of Martineau have routed the heirs of Dickens.

He has often been called the most "English" of writers, his characters embodying "the characteristic virtues, the typical shortcomings, of the homely English race."[29] What precisely these virtues and shortcomings might be, and whether they are characteristically English, is of course questionable. But people certainly believed that Dickens had shown them new varieties of Englishness, with ordinary people in the foreground. He thus made a unique contribution to creating the "imagined community" of the nation. We should not assume that Dickensian England is in every way unique: the "social question" was as much a preoccupation in France and Germany as in England, and authors such as Eugène Sue and Victor Hugo paralleled, even anticipated, Dickens's techniques, his rapport with his readers and his sentimentality. In Hugo's *Les Misérables*, Cosette is as ill-used and pitiful as Oliver Twist or Little Nell, Gavroche as indomitable as the Artful Dodger, Jean Valjean as selfless as Mr. Peggoty, Javert as cruel as Quilp or Bumble. Perhaps this is a reminder that we should not accept Dickens's highly coloured vision too trustingly, but look at Dickensian England through other eyes and with other perspectives too.

## THE TWO NATIONS

> *Two nations; between whom there is no intercourse and no sympathy; who are as ignorant of each other's habits, thoughts and feelings as if they were . . . inhabitants of different planets; who are formed by a different breeding, are fed by a different food, are ordered by different manners, and are not governed by the same laws . . . THE RICH AND THE POOR.*
> Benjamin Disraeli, *Sybil; or, The Two Nations* (1845)

After Waterloo, "Peterloo": troops charged a large peaceful crowd in St. Peter's Fields, Manchester, on 16 August 1819 and eleven died—a bungled episode when local magistrates ordered the yeomanry, amateur cavalry used for home defence and public order, to arrest a political speaker, causing general panic. It caused an outcry and remains notorious in our history because of its rarity. The early nineteenth century manages to be both unknown and infamous. Who but real experts know anything about Lord Liverpool, Prime Minister for fifteen years, the second-longest tenure in history? However vague our ideas—a sense of oppression by "rulers who neither see, nor feel, nor know," in Shelley's words; of hunger, rick-burning, the workhouse and transportation—this period plays a key role in our national narrative: the grim forces of Reaction are finally routed, and the age of Progress dawns. It is an inspiring and very English tale of progress through compromise. The reality is more complex, and more intriguing.[30] For example, reactionary "High Tory" beliefs—state intervention to defend the vulnerable, high spending on welfare, rejection of deflationary economics—chime more with modern sentiments than those of the progressive Whigs—rigid economic determinism, tax cuts, harsh welfare restrictions.

Between 1815 and 1850 England really did grapple with a combination of grave problems: explosive population growth peaking in the 1810s–1820s,[31] serious food shortages caused by climatic turbulence, uncharted economic and social change, unprecedented financial pressures and new epidemic disease. These gave rise to an incoherent political crisis, which included violent plots against the state (the Cato Street Conspiracy of 1820), riots in London in favour of the divorced Queen Caroline in 1820–21, as well as Peterloo, which encouraged Sir Robert Peel to contemplate "some sort of local force" more effective and reliable than unpaid JPs and the yeomanry.[32] That England emerged relatively unbloodied and unbowed is no mean achievement, and more than many at home and abroad expected. It might even suggest that some of those mostly forgotten rulers could see, and feel, and know.

The end of twenty-three years of world war in 1815 left Europe in a precarious state. The transition to peace would lead to years of economic and political upheaval. The lavishness of the "Regency"—epitomized for us by the Prince himself, the fastidious dandy Beau Brummell, the Europe-wide celebrity of Byron, the ambitious town-planning of Regent Street—was short-lived. The Prince was widely detested, Brummell died a dirty and penniless exile, and the Regent Street project was never finished. The war had left England with a paper currency, unprecedented tax levels (23 percent of GDP) and a huge national debt of some £800m, over 250 percent of GDP—a larger burden than that in 1918 or 1945. It was equal to over forty times prewar state income, around £40 for every person in Britain—the total annual earnings of a London labourer.[33] However alarming it seemed, this debt proved manageable through a combination of state frugality and economic growth.

In the short term, however, the "fiscal-military state" had become more expensive than ever, inevitably making politics of greater concern to more people. The idea of "Old Corruption"—extorting taxes to enrich a privileged elite—provided a potent rallying cry. The Radical Henry "Orator" Hunt, the speaker at Peterloo, saw this as the root of all evil: "What is the cause of the want of employment? Taxation. What is the cause of taxation? Corruption."[34] Some version of this blinkered view was the received wisdom not only in Britain but on the Continent, where intellectuals, economists and politicians waited with alarm or satisfaction for Britain to collapse under the weight of taxation, debt and pauperism. The leading French liberal economist Jean-Baptiste Say estimated that the government took 50 percent of British national income (more than double the real figure), and that this caused "distress" and required "perpetual labour" by ordinary people. So the pressure to cut was irresistible, and hasty demobilization of the armed forces and huge reductions in public spending were inevitable, leading to unemployment and slump. A Whig-Radical alliance in 1816 forced the government to abandon income tax, but this left the state more dependent on regressive indirect taxes, and so increased resentment. At the worst moment, the largest volcanic explosion known to history, in April 1815 in the East Indies, caused worldwide temperature falls, the worst American and European food shortages for more than a hundred years in 1816–17, a trail of disease and unemployment, and the steepest rise in crime of the nineteenth century. England coped relatively well, spending on poor relief rising from £5.4m to £8m between 1814 and 1818.[35] Nevertheless, there were riots and demonstrations culminating with Peterloo.

By far the biggest employer was agriculture, taking about a third of the male labour force. The booming wartime population and restricted imports had caused an extension of cultivation to common land and "waste." Despite occasional serious shortages, the country had been fed. Landlords and tenant farmers had made profits; but the poor had lost customary common rights as land was "enclosed," making them wholly dependent on wages, and creating a sense of injustice. Wartime conditions were clearly unsustainable, but again the solution was neither easy nor uncontentious. Should agriculture be encouraged to maximize production and try to feed the booming population? Or should cheaper overseas food supplies be sought, and some English land taken out of cultivation? In 1815 a notorious "Corn Law" was adopted, which gave some protection to domestic producers by excluding imports of grain until the price reached a certain level—for wheat, eighty shillings a quarter (sixty-four gallons).

Many, at home and abroad, thought that an overpopulated England was heading for famine. The most notorious and influential alarmist was an Anglican parson with radical connections, Thomas Malthus.[36] His *Essay on Population* (1798) mixed heterodox Christianity with what would now be called finite ecology, arguing that population growth inevitably tended to outrun food supply, and would inevitably be "checked" either by restraining births or by famine, hunger and war. In his own time and since he has been the object of controversy and denunciation—he himself apologized for his "disheartening" conclusions. Defended by political economists and attacked by a string of moralists, including Dickens, Carlyle, Coleridge, Byron, Cobbett and Disraeli, he had an immediate influence, for his argument seemed incontrovertibly logical, and it became, wrote one Utilitarian, "the fixed, axiomatic belief of the educated world."[37] Malthus's theories caused moral and intellectual turmoil, and the perception of the poor as a danger. Attempts to relieve poverty would encourage population increase, and so merely make the danger worse. His ideas retained a hold until the 1850s.[38] As late as 1852, the leading French radical Auguste Ledru-Rollin published a book prophesying gloatingly that England was doomed to mass starvation. The main target of such fears during the 1820s–1830s was the Poor Law, believed to encourage a feckless dependency culture and the breeding of too many children.

One way of escaping future hunger was to import food. This required secure control of the seas by maintaining the naval supremacy built up over the previous century (potential enemies looked forward to the day when England might be starved by a coalition of naval powers). It also meant exporting ever more goods and services to pay for imported food. These exports required increasing employment in manufacturing and commerce, and endlessly growing cities—an uncharted prospect. Was this just another road to disaster? Many thought so: only agriculture was "real," the rest was a house of cards. "Perish commerce!" declaimed the Radical William Cobbett. Many feared a future of ugly, polluted towns, crowded with degraded and lawless labourers. Could this be prevented, or must it be adapted to? Was more government intervention required, or should things be left to work themselves out under the rules of political economy and Divine Providence?

These questions reflected deep ideological and moral divisions. The philosopher and politician John Stuart Mill characterized it as "every Englishman of the present day [being] either a Benthamite or a Coleridgian."[39] This convenient labelling was derived from Jeremy Bentham (1748–1832), whose Utilitarianism gave a fresh ideological thrust to Radicalism, and the poet Samuel Taylor Coleridge (1772–1834), an enthusiastic revolutionary turned mystical conservative. The division covered politics, economics, science, social relations and not least theology—we must always remember that most of the political class, and most of the country, had religious beliefs now rare outside the deepest recesses of the American Bible Belt. Other voices called for a plague on both Benthamites and Coleridgians, including Dickens and Thomas Carlyle, denouncing all and sundry like a modern Jeremiah.

Benthamite Utilitarianism saw the universe as a self-regulating machine, with discoverable "axioms," such as the "Principle of Utility": "The greatest happiness of the greatest number ... is the measure of right and wrong."[40] Society should be reformed to work according to these axioms. This appealed both to political economists, who saw the rules as scientific, and to Evangelicals, who saw them as God's will. Individual choice was central—there was no such thing as society.[41] Coleridge once said to Martineau, "You seem to regard society as an aggregate of individuals." She replied, "Of course I do."[42] Government, professionally managed, must regulate individuals through a system of rewards and punishments, like intelligent laboratory rats. The virtuous man, taught Bentham, is an exact calculator.[43] Utilitarianism was authoritarian, epitomized by the "Panopticon," a prison (it could also be a school, hospital or factory) built so that inmates could be constantly observed by an all-seeing "inspector." Millbank (1816) and Pentonville (1842) prisons in London adopted some of these features.* Bentham, who considered the idea of natural rights "nonsense on stilts," had thought of having a million poor and potentially antisocial people confined in factory-prisons.[44] Not all his schemes were adopted, of course, but his fundamental maxims, his scorn for traditional thinking, and his bureacratic utopianism were widely influential among modernizers. His embalmed body still sits inspecting University College London.

The Coleridgian view—paternalist, interventionist, anti-liberal—saw the universe and human society not as machines but as complex organisms developing over time, under a Divine artist, not a celestial engineer. Society needed leadership and high-minded government to function. Coleridge advocated moral leadership by a "clerisy," a public-spirited cultural and intellectual elite. Such views of society appealed to those who saw the traditional landowning class as having that duty—as Edmund Burke had put it, like great oaks shading a meadow. However idealized this view, there was a wide acceptance of gentry leadership, and recognition of obligations to the "deserving" poor, through charity and the Poor

---

* Several other countries tried similar experiments, so appealing was the idea to administrators. The only true Panopticon prisons, however, were built in Cuba in the 1920s.

Law. Coleridge and Wordsworth, their youthful hopes of the French Revolution dashed, found consolation in the English countryside, and social relations based on what Wordsworth called "personal feeling" and "moral cement." Arguably, such a society could not survive population growth, urbanization and commercial expansion. Such was Wordsworth's fear: "Everything has been put up to market and sold for the highest price," he wrote to a friend in 1818. The only hope was for society's moral basis to be restored, but for that "they who govern the country must be something superior to mere financiers and political economists."[45]

This intellectual and moral divide was not party-political. For nearly half a century, from 1783 to 1830, England was almost a one-party state, run by William Pitt and his heirs, professional politicians who had built up an invincible body of support based on patriotic defence of country, king, Church, constitution and property, and a reputation for efficient and even (so far as war allowed) economical government. Pitt and his successors, the men who had led the war effort against Napoleon, including Castlereagh, Canning, Palmerston, Peel, Huskisson and Liverpool, enjoyed strong support among the country gentry who were the mainstay of the political class. Their opponents (as a term of abuse), and most historians (perhaps likewise), have called them Tories. But Pitt and his followers considered themselves Whigs or simply "ministerialists," and one Pittite minister, Palmerston (later a Liberal), referred to "the stupid old Tory party" as merely one awkward faction of their backbench support.[46]

Lord Liverpool had become Prime Minister in 1812 at a time of severe domestic and foreign crisis, following the assassination of his predecessor, Spencer Perceval, and at the height of the Napoleonic Wars. His long period of office, far from being blankly reactionary, saw moves towards freer trade, legal reforms, increases in religious toleration, streamlining of parliamentary procedures, the embryo of a professional civil service, the emergence of the idea of "His Majesty's Loyal Opposition" (as a distinct but not seditious government-in-waiting) and reforms in policing. The main opposition to some of these changes came precisely from some of his own backbenchers—the "stupid old Tory party." These Tories—often called "High" or "Ultra" Tories—condemned "liberalism" as "a system of letting loose all ties and bonds whatever, but that of selfish interest."[47] They also maintained their traditional loyalty to the Church, and resisted giving increased rights to Nonconformists and Catholics. This division, rather than attack from Radical or Whig opponents, eventually undermined Pittite ascendancy in the late 1820s.

Meanwhile, the Pittites' official opponents, Whigs and Radicals, were pretty feeble. The opposition Whigs—who had held office for only a few months since the early 1780s—were the aristocratic disciples of Charles James Fox (their secret, said one, was that they were all cousins), whose position rested on their wealth, status and ownership of parliamentary boroughs. They were led fitfully and ineffectually by Earl Grey and Fox's nephew Lord Holland, whose Jacobean mansion in Kensington, Holland House, was their social centre. They clung to a sense of themselves as the nation's true but misunderstood elite ("the ancient nobility, the great property of the Realm"), had deplored the war, often admired Napoleon (Lady Holland sent him books on St. Helena), and yet despised the meritocratic Pittites as parvenus—Grey dismissed Canning as "the son of an actress [and] *ipso facto* disqualified from becoming prime minister."[48] The Radicals were few in number—only three in Parliament in 1806, the most prominent of them the wealthy baronet Sir Francis Burdett—and although their numbers subsequently increased, and they could muster support outside Parliament at times of crisis, it was sporadic. Moreover, Radicals were divided. Some, such as the pugnacious journalist William Cobbett (who supported agriculture against industry) and the Birmingham banker Thomas Attwood (who opposed returning to the gold standard) had much in common with Tories. Other Radicals, notably the economist David Ricardo, who became an MP in 1819, supported economic laissez-faire. As a purely political cause, aiming at constitutional change, Radicalism seemed moribund. Its obsessive attacks on the state as corrupt, and its demands to reduce taxation and public spending, damaged many of the people Radicals claimed to represent. Whigs and Radicals combined held only some 150 seats in 1815, and the veteran "Orator" Hunt won only eighteen votes when he stood at Westminster in 1818.

As noted earlier, the fundamental economic and social fact was England's population growth, faster than anywhere in Europe. It rose from 8.6 million in 1801 to 17 million in 1851[49]—an increase of 98 percent, with the highest ever recorded growth in 1811–21 (16 percent in a decade). Around 40 percent of this population was under fifteen, comparable with much of Africa today. The total urban population, already the highest in Europe, tripled during the first half of the century. London's more than doubled, making it by far Europe's biggest conurbation. In the 1820s alone, Manchester grew by 47 percent, West Bromwich by 60 percent, and Bradford by 78 percent. Average life expectancy at birth was 41.7 years in 1841—also comparable with much of Africa in the 2000s. In the multiplying towns and among the poorest groups it was some ten years less than the national average. (Shamefully, there was still a nine-year gap between different parts of England in 2011.[50]) This corresponds to the darkest "Dickensian" images—of "Coketown" (1854), or the lawless and savage "Wodgate" in Benjamin Disraeli's novel *Sybil* (1845), where "swarming thousands lodged in the most miserable tenements in the most hideous burgh in the ugliest country in the world." A French visitor thought that "if the people [of Birmingham] go to hell, they won't find anything new."[51]

Yet this revulsion missed as much as it saw. Critics seized on the worst conditions, not the typical: there were horrible slums, but the vast majority of the people did not live in slums, the most notorious of which, investigated and later photographed, were often very small—a few streets or houses.[52] Working conditions in the new industries were horrifying by modern Western standards, but the deadliest trades were thoroughly traditional—file-making, chimney-sweeping and, worst of all, keeping a pub.[53] Moreover, England was in a considerably better state than elsewhere. In 1820 GDP per head was some 50 percent higher than in western Europe as a whole. Infant mortality in 1839 was 151 per 1,000 in England (comparable with that of Afghanistan in 2010); but in France it was 160, in Belgium 185 and in southern Germany 285. An unprecedented Europe-wide cholera pandemic in 1831, spread by infected drinking water, killed up to 7,000 in London—often taken as a symptom of the capital's archaic and decentralized governance (it had thirty-eight local authorities); but the same disease killed over 18,000 in centrally administered Paris. Cholera came to seem the nemesis of the growing city. The worst pandemic of the century, in the mid-1850s, killed another 11,000 in London and 23,000 across Britain—but 150,000 died in France.[54] London led the way during the 1850s in gradually improving public health, sewerage and drinking water in a joint effort by philanthropic campaigners, local-government bodies such as the Metropolitan Board of Works (1855), and parliamentary legislation.

Faced with new social problems, two very different communitarian remedies battled against the prevailing liberalizing current: "Owenism" in the 1820s and 1830s, and "Young Englandism" in the 1830s and 1840s. Robert Owen (1771–1858) was a brilliant young Welsh businessman who made a quick fortune in cotton in the 1800s. His textile mill at New Lanark (with Jeremy Bentham as a partner) aimed to provide an enlightened industrial model, and it drew thousands of visitors to see the houses and schools provided for workers, making its owner a celebrity—though some employees left because there was too much compulsory music and dancing.[55] Owen's ambition was no less than to change human society. In this he resembled a clutch of Continental utopian socialists, all sharing the idea of designing harmonious self-contained communities, which would spontaneously spread once their virtues (including gender equality) became apparent. Several, Owen among them, thought that pristine America would be the ideal site—a few Owenite communities there eventually merged into the wacky world of religious sectarianism, alongside the Shakers and the Mormons. Owen in England campaigned for cooperative societies (his most durable achievement), factory regulation, trade unions, gender equality and secularism, and he founded a hugely expensive model agricultural cooperative, Harmony Hall, in Hampshire. He was revered as one of the greatest philanthropists of the age.

"Young England" (its name reminiscent of movements on the Continent and in Ireland) emerged from the broad context of romanticism, the Gothic Revival and discontented Toryism. Fervent Gothic revivalists, such as the architect Augustus Pugin, aspired to a more humane and fraternal social morality, which they associated with medievalism and often Catholicism, of which their architecture was to be the material expression. Young England's most public manifestation, the Eglinton Tournament of 1839, was a mock-medieval festival held in reaction against Queen Victoria's rather subdued coronation (a result of Whig cuts). Rain did not deter the 100,000 spectators, and one armoured knight sported an umbrella. Its broader purpose was more serious, though equally fanciful: to resurrect the supposed paternalism of the medieval aristocracy. This prototype of "one-nation Toryism" achieved little in practice—it only ever mustered four MPs, and they broke up over the Corn Laws in 1846. But it provided a political debut for the brilliant young Benjamin Disraeli, whose novels, *Coningsby* and *Sybil; or, The Two Nations*, were expressions of Young England fantasies, and who, as some of his acquaintances noticed, was fond of dukes. But there was more to Disraeli than this. *Sybil*, one of the earliest "industrial novels," was the only one at the time to ascribe serious political motives to working-class characters.[56] His moral was that legitimate rule involved social responsibility, and that a divided England had to be reunited.

Paternalistic Toryism campaigned in the 1830s for legislation to limit hours, improve factory conditions, and protect child and women workers. It was led by a strange but determined group including Richard Oastler (a Leeds linen merchant turned squire), his friend Michael Sadler (another Leeds linen merchant) and the philanthropic aristocrat Lord Ashley, later 7th Earl of Shaftesbury. They had in common fervent Evangelical Anglicanism (opposing both slavery and Catholic emancipation) and were horrified by the moral and social effects of uncontrolled factory labour: "I heard their groans," wrote Oastler, "I watched their tears; I knew they relied on me."[57] Parliament enacted a watered-down Factory Act in 1833 and the principle of compulsory national labour regulation was established. Utilitarians and liberals deplored what they considered ignorant and damaging attempts to shackle the labour market and pile costs on employers.

Industrialists accused Tory paternalists—sometimes no doubt correctly—of being less solicitous about the farm labourers on great estates. It was also the case that Evangelical Tories were ultimately more concerned with souls than bodies, particularly those of women and children tempted by the money, drink, godlessness and sex supposedly inseparable from factories and mines. Sometimes they were right: factory work could give women sudden independence—sex without marriage, motherhood without a man and good wages. Many people found this deeply disturbing.[58] What was most alarming about Disraeli's Wodgate (based not on a new-style factory town, but on Willenhall, a Black Country lock-making centre of traditional craft workshops) was neither poverty nor oppression—its people he describes as highly skilled and prosperous. The problem was that it was ungoverned: "land without an owner . . . no parish . . . no meddlesome supervision . . . no municipality, no magistrate . . . no vestries, no schools."[59] Disraeli drew on reports from Ashley's Children's Employment Commission, but for "Wodgate"—usually cited as straight reporting—he both distorted and generalized. He left out the Sunday schools and chapels, ignored a report that, despite industrial pollution, "the inside of the poorest houses is [often] perfectly clean," and presented some exceptionally bad treatment of child apprentices as the norm.[60] Children often worked alongside parents or neighbours. Some mills and factories were hotbeds of prudishness, with loose morals and bad language "instantly rebuked."[61] Moreover, "lawless" places like Wodgate were unusual: most towns grew around old-established settlements. Even the "ungoverned" Wodgates were fairly peaceful: there were only fifty-six indictments for murder in the whole Black Country over the twenty-five years between 1835 and 1860.[62] Fundamental was mutual aid, in families, workshops, streets, chapels and pubs, where friendly societies and trade unions flourished, and where a new society and culture was being created which lasted 150 years.

Poor people themselves did not necessarily share the pessimism either of contemporary upper-class commentators or of later historians. The rural poor, especially young people underemployed in over-populated villages, found in towns and factories an escape from dependency, chronic poverty, and exclusion from adult life and marriage. However risky and accident-prone, a move to town meant more regular work, money in their pockets, freedom, the chance of family life and/or amorous adventure, and exciting new social and cultural opportunities. Judging from their own writings, many working people felt not only that they were living in a rapidly changing world, but that it was changing for the better. Typical was a Wiltshire carpenter, John Bennett, looking back later in life on his rural childhood in the 1790s: "what troublesome times we had during my bringing up," whereas today "the working classes in my opinion, was never so well off."[63]

## THE AGE OF REFORM

*All history is full of revolutions . . . A portion of the community which had been of no account, expands and becomes strong. It demands a place in the system . . . If this is granted, all is well. If this is refused, then comes the struggle between the young energy of one class, and the ancient privileges of another.*

Thomas Babington Macaulay in the House of Commons,
2 March 1832[64]

From the late 1820s to the early 1830s a chapter of accidents led to the unravelling of the Pittite majority and demands for parliamentary reform: these included a devastating international economic slump; the resignation in 1827 after a stroke of the Prime Minister, Liverpool, a unifying figure; European revolutions in Belgium and France in 1830; rural unrest in southern England; a series of sudden deaths (including those of George IV and a key politician, William Huskisson, the latter in one of the first ever railway accidents, both in 1830); and most importantly of all the concession of Irish and British Catholics' right to sit in the House of Commons by a Catholic Relief Act in 1829.[65] The last straw was a declaration on 2 November 1830 by the Prime Minister, the Duke of Wellington (in office since 1828), that he would oppose constitutional reform, and he resigned a fortnight later. The Whig leader, Lord Grey, suddenly popular, took office with the most blue-blooded and nepotistic Cabinet of the century—a coalition of Whig grandees, liberals and one Tory, the Duke of Richmond—with the aim of reforming the constitution. The traditional account of this famous episode owes much to political "spin" by the Whig MP Macaulay, and it still dominates popular history today.[66] Macaulay presented reform as the inevitable outcome of modernization: "While the natural growth of society went on," he told the Commons, "the artificial polity remained unchanged . . . Renew the youth of the State . . . The danger is terrible. The time is short."[67]

The constitution may well have been archaic and unjust—established systems often are—but this had not been a major issue: by the late 1820s constitutional reform seemed dead. The system worked not too badly, and perhaps people are rarely stirred by abstract constitutional debate. Even flagrant abuses, such as "rotten boroughs" (most notoriously the ruins of Old Sarum, whose seven "burgesses" elected two MPs), could be defended as allowing talent or unrepresented interests into politics, like twenty-first-century peerages. Bizarre voting qualifications (in "potwalloper" boroughs, everyone with a hearth to boil a pot could vote—so Preston had 50,000 largely working-class electors) arguably diversified the Commons. New industrial towns, not formally represented, were in practice represented by locally resident MPs. Non-electors made their voices heard through petitions, meetings and mayhem on election days—voting was public, and the crowd made its feelings unmistakably felt. As one reformer wrote to his wife, "We had a grand affair in the market place last night . . . flooring the fellows like ninepins . . . then mounted the Tory wagon! . . . We marched singing round the streets."[68] Popular disorder was a feature of elections at least until the 1920s, and was condoned by all parties as an expression of sturdy English liberty.

What had unexpectedly galvanized reform was the collapse of the stable Pittite majority, largely through a revolt over Catholic emancipation by the diehard "High Tories," those suspicious of liberalism and intransigently Anglican. Wellington and his most powerful supporter, Robert Peel, both of whom had much experience of Ireland, were convinced that Catholic emancipation—originally promised as a quid pro quo for Union in 1802—was politically necessary to prevent Ireland from becoming ungovernable. This was an argument that many Tories would not accept, and some opponents of Catholic emancipation now demanded a more representative House of Commons, which they believed would never have conceded emancipation. The government's supporters in both Houses of Parliament and among the electorate were angry, rebellious and confused, and Wellington's resignation in November 1830 seems to have been partly a gesture of impatience with the rebels.[69]

On top of this, the economic recession had sharpened perennial discontent over taxes and Church tithes, and petitions flowing into Parliament demanded cuts in both. Parliamentary reform, however, came only in third place in the number of petitions it inspired.[70] Simultaneously, the "Swing" disorders, a popular reaction to rural depression, peaked in November–December 1830. These have been called the "Last Labourers' Revolt," an outbreak of arson and riot, often featuring threatening letters signed "Captain Swing." Outbreaks happened mainly in grain-growing counties with chronic underemployment, most typically in larger villages

with big tenant farms, some artisans and shopkeepers, and some Dissenters. They were a protest against low wages, tithes, penny-pinching Poor
Law overseers and new mechanical threshing, which reduced seasonal
employment. Similar outbreaks in northern France and Belgium made the
situation seem more dangerously revolutionary than it was. Some landowners and magistrates sympathized with the rioters' demands, and urged
and sometimes even ordered an end to mechanization, which would
"leave the population born on the soil to subsist on a miserable pit-
tance."[71] But the landowning class as a whole were frightened, and some
saw both stern measures and parliamentary reform as necessary to restore
order.

The dramatic struggle for what would be hailed as the "Great Reform
Act" of 1832 was more significant that the details of the Act itself, for it
forced the political class to bow—a little—to popular pressure, and disposed of the idea that the Glorious Revolution settlement was untouchable. It also again redefined party identities. Those who opposed or tried
to limit reform were called, and now called themselves, Tory, or as their
leading figure in the Commons, Sir Robert Peel, preferred, Conservative—
wishing to conserve the 1688 constitution. Those elements of the old Pittite coalition who supported or at least accepted reform gravitated to the
Whigs, who would soon be termed Liberals.

Grey's first Reform Bill passed its Commons Second Reading on
23 March 1831 by a single vote—the MP concerned changed his mind
twice and later committed suicide—but it was defeated in committee.
Grey asked for a dissolution, and William IV, convinced of the necessity
of reform, overcame Tory resistance by dissolving Parliament in person—
"Damme, I'll go in a cab." The elections in April 1831 returned a
pro-reform majority. But a second bill was defeated in the Lords in October 1831, sparking serious riots: Nottingham Castle, seat of the anti-reform
Duke of Newcastle, was burned down, as was the palace of the anti-reform
Bishop of Bristol, in an outbreak of violence that cost up to 400 lives, the
bloodiest political episode in modern English history. When a third bill
was amended and delayed in the Lords, Grey resigned in May 1832, leading to a surge of protests known as the "Days of May." Wellington failed
to form a Tory government to pass a diluted bill, so Grey returned to
office with a promise from the king to create if necessary sufficient new
peers to overcome the Tory majority in the Lords. The Lords surrendered,
and the Act passed in June.

The Act itself has been the subject of debate and analysis ever since. A
prominent politician extolled it in 2010 as widening "the boundaries of
British democracy, for the first time extending the franchise beyond the

landed classes"[72]—wrong in every particular. It was the opposite of democratic—then a term of abuse. It removed the main democratic element in Parliament by abolishing the "potwallopers," explicitly disfranchised anyone receiving poor relief, and for the first time explicitly excluded women. It created uniform voting qualifications based solely on the ownership or occupation of property, strengthening the influence of landowners and the wealthy urban elites. Underpopulated and "rotten" boroughs lost 142 seats. But most were redistributed to the counties, with only 31 seats for the industrial cities, whose electors were qualified by occupying substantial property worth £10 per year. In the counties the Act added to the ancient electorate of "forty-shilling freeholders"* a new category of substantial tenants, likely to vote with their landlords. The total UK electorate increased by some 45 percent, from 497,000 to 811,000 (18 percent of adult males).[73] This was comparatively large—smaller than in Sweden and Holland, but much bigger than in the new post-Revolutionary regime in France.

The Whigs profited from their triumph by calling elections in 1832, winning a large majority. They slashed public spending by 10 percent to its lowest level of the century[74] and passed a remarkable string of reforming legislation, often along Benthamite lines. Slavery was abolished in 1833. Local government was modernized by the Municipal Corporations Act (1835), which it was hoped would be "poison to Tory-ism"; and it also disfranchised women who had qualified to vote in most parish and Poor Law elections.[75] The penal law—the "Bloody Code"—was transformed by Lord John Russell (of perhaps the greatest of Whig families): he in practice ended the death penalty for all but murder, so the number hanged annually fell from 178 to 26—around the European norm. This made juries more ready to convict for crimes such as rape, previously a hanging offence. The Prisoners' Counsel Act (1836) regularized the "adversarial" system of court procedure, begun in the eighteenth century, reducing the role and discretion of judges and juries, who had previously shown a high level of independence and/or capriciousness. With appropriate symbolism, in 1834 the ancient and rambling Palace of Westminster caught fire while it was being tidied—medieval exchequer tally sticks had been shoved into an oven—and it burned down.

The Poor Law was reformed (1834), slashing its cost; it was supplemented by an Anatomy Act (1832), which permitted the unclaimed corpses of paupers to be used for medical purposes—a quintessentially Utilitarian measure, but one which caused horror among its potential

---

* Resident freeholders of land worth £2 per year or more.

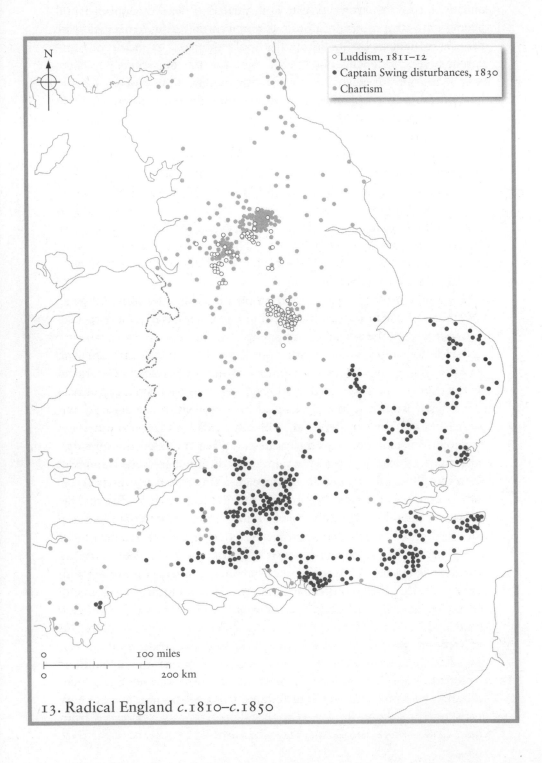

N

○ Luddism, 1811–12
● Captain Swing disturbances, 1830
● Chartism

100 miles

200 km

13. Radical England *c.*1810–*c.*1850

objects, and partly explains fear and hatred of the workhouse. Rural unrest was stamped on. In all 1,976 people in thirty-four counties were prosecuted in connection with the "Swing" outbreaks, some before a special commission as local magistrates were thought too lenient: 19 were hanged (mostly for arson), nearly 500 transported to Australia, over 600 imprisoned, and 800 acquitted or bound over to keep the peace. "From no other protest movement of the kind—from neither Luddites, nor Chartists, nor trade unionists—was such a bitter price exacted."[76] The "Tolpuddle Martyrs"—six men led by George Loveless, a farm labourer and Methodist preacher, who set up a legal agricultural trade union in Dorset—were prosecuted for illegally administering oaths to members and sentenced in 1834 to seven years' transportation. Immediately after sentence, Loveless wrote:

> We raise the watchword, Liberty
> We will, we will, we will be free!!!

A public outcry and mass petition brought them home. Most "Swing" transportees were also eventually pardoned, but preferred to stay in Australia.

Was this a contradictory mixture of enlightened humanitarianism and benighted reaction, of generosity and meanness? It was, rather, a logical application of the "mechanistic" principles of Utilitarianism and political economy. As Russell put it, "We are busy introducing system, method, science, economy, regularity, and discipline"—a process that left permanent marks on the British state.[77] The whole would be supervised, not by indulgent amateurs, but by a new breed of trained "inspectors" (a novel term). The prototype of Whitehall gentlemen who know best was Edwin Chadwick, a hardline Utilitarian and formerly Bentham's assistant. He became secretary to the Poor Law Commission (ministers considered his "station in society" insufficient for full membership). His role made him hated, but his reputation was restored by energetic work on public health and urban sanitation, culminating in his control of the General Board of Health (1848). He bequeathed to the nation the self-flushing narrow-diameter sewer and a more professional approach to administration.[78]

The New Poor Law (1834)—which fired Dickens's indignation in *Oliver Twist* (1837)—is the most notorious of the Utilitarian reforms, and that which most colours popular perceptions of this period. The old Poor Law, dating from Elizabeth I, had developed into a unique welfare system (see pp. 330–31). It had—or was believed to have—become increasingly unsustainable during the war years: total spending had increased from about £2m in 1784 to £6m in 1815, when around 15 percent of the population were receiving aid. In fact, the cost was pretty stable as a share of growing GNP (which contemporaries could not know)—around 2 percent. However, the rise in population, wartime inflation and postwar economic fluctuations made the old system of local financing unviable, imposing an open-ended commitment on ratepayers: in one small Yorkshire town, Newburgh, the annual bill to the thirteen ratepayers rose from £34 in 1817–18 to £130 in 1836–37.[79] Foreign observers thought it dangerous to give the poor a legal entitlement to assistance and commonly made the elementary error of assuming that because there were more "paupers" (i.e., benefit claimants) in England than in other countries, this meant that there were more poor people, and that the gulf between rich and poor was growing. Rather, it was because the Poor Law recognized relative deprivation: the richer society grew, the more the poor needed. So "the English poor appear almost rich to the French poor," observed the French liberal Alexis de Tocqueville. Paupers were quick to stand up for their rights by applying to Overseers of the Poor and, if dissatisfied, appealing to the magistrates: Tocqueville was scandalized to see old men, pregnant girls and unemployed labourers doing so unblushingly before the Justices of the Peace. This, he and many others thought, created a dependency culture that meant that "the number of illegitimate children and criminals grows rapidly and continuously, the indigent population is limitless, the spirit of foresight and saving becomes more and more alien to the poor," as truculent young men squandered their poor relief at the pub.[80] "Captain Swing" convinced many that the Poor Law was not even maintaining social peace.

Grey's government appointed a Royal Commission, which proposed a uniform, transparent and impersonal system, aiming to eliminate fraudulent claims and what it considered excessive generosity without removing the legal right to assistance. The New Poor Law (1834) had many Benthamite features. It prescribed ratepayer-elected Boards of Guardians, professional administrators, a central supervisory commission and national dietary regulations. The key idea was a self-acting "test" of genuine need: the traditional payments in cash or kind were forbidden (except in emergencies and for the sick); assistance was to be given only within workhouses offering a "less eligible" existence than the lowest wages could provide. So these "Whig Bastilles" were a deliberate deterrent, by monotonous (if usually ample) diet, unpleasant work and regimentation. The "respectable" poor were humiliated by wearing uniforms, being mixed with the unrespectable, and having their families split up between different day-rooms and dormitories. The press quoted one old man as vowing that "as long as I can arne a sixpence anyhow, they sharn't part me from my wife." Entry into "the House" was made a last desperate resort: thus, reported the Royal Commission on the Poor Law with evident satisfaction, "the line between those who do, and those who do not need relief is drawn, and drawn perfectly."[81] Spending on poor relief dropped from £6.3m to £4m, and the percentage of the population aided from 10.2 to 5.4 percent. Only some Tories and Radicals objected. Disraeli said that the Act "disgraced the country."[82]

Mr. Bumble and Mr. Gradgrind had thus arrived, ushered in by the Great Reform Act. Their sway was bitterly resented: "The ill feeling between the labouring people and those above them is very bad . . . more than is generally imagined," wrote an investigator. Many local authorities and ratepayers also disliked the new measures on grounds of humanity, practicality and cost, and stubbornly continued "outdoor relief"—for example, classing the unemployed or elderly as sick, and thus supporting them at home.[83] *The Times* ran a long campaign against the law. Periodic scandals—at Andover workhouse hungry men were reported in 1845 to be eating the marrow from the bones they were crushing for fertilizer—caused national outcry and lobbying for reform. For all these reasons, the New Poor Law was never fully implemented. In industrial towns, the problems were low wages and cyclical unemployment; it was absurd to think of interning thousands of laid-off workers and their families in workhouses. The Bradford workhouse could accommodate 260 people, but more than 13,000 were claiming benefits in 1848.[84] Thirty years after "outdoor relief" had supposedly stopped, 84 percent of "paupers" were receiving it. Moreover, payments were made in cash and with few strings—no curfews, compulsory labour, police surveillance or bans on alcohol as on the Continent. The stigma of the workhouse stayed, largely due to respectable claimants—often the elderly and children—being lumped in with drunks and vagrants. But, a generation after the Act, the Poor Law authorities began to diversify services: the workhouse remained, but was supplemented by infirmaries, schools, cottage hospitals, and "cottage homes" for children and old people. These did not carry the same stigma, and many are still in use. The Poor Law principle of universal legal right to assistance was so deeply engrained that it continued to influence English social policy long after the Poor Law itself was formally abolished in 1948.[85]

Poor relief—previously a source of social cohesion—had been envenomed and many lives blighted by Utilitarian reforms that were harsh, unworkable and counter-productive, for in trying to prevent the pauperization and demoralization of the poor, the reformers had in truth pauperized and demoralized them far more.[86] A shoemaker, Samuel Kydd, recalled that the reforms "did more to sour the hearts of the labouring population" than material hardship, and to "sap the loyalty of the working men, to make them dislike the country of their birth."[87] It did much to ignite arguably the greatest—if not the only—class war England has ever seen, the Chartist campaign.

Chartism was created in 1838, during an economic slump, when a People's Charter was drafted by an Owenite activist, William Lovett, and a veteran radical, Francis Place, for the London Working Men's Association. Disillusion with the reformed Parliament—"instead of RE-forming it has DE-formed"[88]—gave new life to a tradition of radicalism dating back to the eighteenth century. There was a bitter conviction that national and local government—now elected only by the propertied—had become more unfair and hostile to ordinary people, taxing their food through the Corn Laws and depriving them of their long-established Poor Law rights. The only remedy seemed to be to give the non-propertied the vote. The Charter demanded manhood suffrage, a secret ballot, annual general elections, equal constituencies, payment of MPs and no property qualification for sitting in Parliament. In 1839 a National Convention of the Industrious Classes met in London, Birmingham and Manchester, and a petition for the Charter bearing 1.2 million signatures was presented to Parliament. It was rejected, provoking an unusual intensity of conflict. There was a short-lived armed uprising in Newport, Monmouthshire, led by its former mayor, in which twenty-one people were killed. In 1842 there were waves of strikes and riots across the north and Midlands, including the "Plug Plot" riots, in which 50,000 strikers forcibly closed down factories by removing the plugs from their steam engines. "Slowly comes a hungry people, as a lion, creeping nigher," warned Tennyson.

Chartism, a loose alliance ranging from republicans to a few Tory radicals, brought together a range of causes: supporters of factory laws, temperance, trade unionism, Owenism, land reform, Corn Law repeal, Irish independence and popular education. Chartists kept up momentum by organizing lectures, dances, sports, sermons, poetry readings and plays. Many organized in "classes," on the Methodist model, and indeed many leaders were Methodist preachers. Yet some Chartists also used the language and threat of violence—collecting weapons (including bombs made from ginger beer bottles) and drilling. Some of its leaders had revolutionary affinities: Feargus O'Connor was the son of a United Irishman who had become a general under Napoleon, Bronterre O'Brien was writing a biography of Robespierre, and G. J. Harney was an admirer of the ferocious French revolutionary Marat. This caused disagreement within the movement, though some of the advocates of "physical" as opposed to "moral" force were surprising—the maverick Tory MP Richard Oastler called on fellow Chartists to arm in defence of "altar, throne and cottage,"[89] and Feargus O'Connor, praising "the great reformer" Peel, was elected MP for Nottingham in 1847 with Tory support.[90]

A simultaneous mass movement, the Anti–Corn Law League, was founded in 1839 by Richard Cobden and John Bright, promoters of what Disraeli called the "Manchester School" of economics. Cobden, elected to Parliament for Stockport in 1841, was a self-made Manchester cotton magnate, the son of small yeoman farmer who detested the landlord class: "We will grapple with the religious feelings of the people—Their veneration for God shall be our leverage to upset their reverence for the aristocracy."[91] Bright was a Quaker mill-owner from Rochdale, and MP for Durham from 1843. The league was to have a greater impact on politics and economics than any single-issue group before or since. In Britain and elsewhere, exporters were quick to see the advantages of freer trade and lower food costs, but there was far more to the league than merely business calculation.[92] It condemned trade barriers as pillars of war, poverty and aristocratic oppression, whereas free trade promised freedom, peace and prosperity for all. The league combined the organizational dynamism of a new business class with the campaigning fervour of Evangelicals and Dissenters: in one week it mailed some 9 million leaflets, and it organized saturation press campaigns. The campaign tapped into the anti-slavery movement, which had just succeeded in abolishing slavery in the empire. Cobden adopted the slogan "immediate abolition" because it was "the old anti-slavery *shibboleth*."[93] The league's optimistic message was the first effective answer to the Malthusian belief, so hated and so persuasive, that rising population would inevitably lead to poverty, starvation and conflict. What began as the campaign of a pressure group became the settled orthodoxy of the country until the 1930s and still influences English attitudes today.

Farmers led a counter-campaign in favour of continuing protection for agriculture, and a flood of rural support went to the Tories. This gave them a sweeping victory in 1841. The results show that a durable regional pattern was setting in. The Tories now dominated the English counties and smaller towns. The Whigs dominated the larger towns, especially north of the Trent, and were well ahead in Scotland and Ireland. These years set the scene for nearly half a century of Whig-Liberal hegemony once the Corn Law issue exploded, for the Whigs established an alliance with northern manufacturers and retailers, many of them Nonconformists, who dominated urban politics.

Sir Robert Peel became Prime Minister in 1841 as leader of what he called the "real old Tory, Church of England, protectionist, Protestant party." He popularized the name "Conservative," and is often credited with inventing the modern party, but if so he destroyed his creation. Tories had been elected to defend agriculture, which most believed was the very foundation of society and the state. But Peel accepted that Britain was destined to be an industrial nation: he thought one "might on moral and social grounds prefer cornfields to cotton factories [but] our lot is cast, and we cannot recede."[94]

Peel was an enigmatic character who, like Pitt, Canning, Palmerston and Gladstone, cannot fully be classified in party terms. He was certainly one of the most able and most consistent of modern politicians, and as such had little regard for backbench views—"the opinions of men who have not access to your knowledge . . . who spend their time in eating and drinking, and hunting, shooting, gambling, horse-racing and so forth."[95] He was the heir of a self-made textile magnate who had been the very first of the new industrial elite to sit in Parliament. He seems to have regarded himself as an outsider, despite his broad acres in Staffordshire, despite Harrow and Oxford, where he was the first man ever to take a "Double First" in both Greats and Mathematics. He was seen as cold and charmless, with "a smile like the silver plate on a coffin," according to the Irish leader Daniel O'Connell; but there is a story that one professional begging-letter writer had him (along with Dickens and Queen Adelaide) at the top of his list of soft touches. Yet, as Home Secretary, though he reduced the number of capital offences, he let more people actually hang.[96] Even his enemies never doubted his brains. "There were always great hopes of Peel, amongst us all—masters and scholars," recalled his schoolfellow Byron. "I was always *in* scrapes, and *he* NEVER; and *in* school, he *always* knew his lesson."[97] At Oxford, the Dean of Christ Church, Cyril Jackson, took a similar view of Peel's future importance: "Work very hard and unremittingly . . . Don't be afraid of killing yourself . . . I shall pursue you, as long as I live, with a jealous and watchful eye. Woe be to you if you fail me!"[98] From an early age (he entered Parliament at twenty-one from an Irish rotten borough) he saw himself as a realist. His mission was to steer England into safer waters, whatever the cost to himself—he had a taste for political martyrdom. A friend summarized his views:

> Peel considers a revolution at no great distance—not a bloody one and perhaps not one leading to a republic, but one utterly subversive of the aristocracy and of the present system of carrying on the government. He thinks we may get on quite as well after this change as before; but he considers it inevitable.[99]

He was seconded by another great defensive tactician, the Duke of Wellington, the Tory hero. Both had earlier agreed that it was necessary to try to pacify Irish Catholics by conceding political rights. In 1842 Peel slashed the corn and other tariffs and reintroduced income tax for incomes over £150—a fundamental step towards creating a system that was seen to be fair. It was equally important to show discontented workers that hardship was not due to restrictions on their food supply by the landed class. He came to accept—as did the "official mind" of Whitehall—that the Corn Laws would have to go. But as with the passage of the Great Reform Act, the drama surrounding abolition made it seem all the more historic.

The "Hungry Forties"—a term invented retrospectively during the anti-protectionist campaign of the 1900s—saw a Europe-wide economic slump of extreme severity. Beginning in 1846, this was a combination of the last of the age-old dearths caused by harvest failures and the first great global financial panic. Rising prices, a rush to import food, government borrowing and interest rate increases burst a speculative bubble based on railway-building. This gave rise to an acute sense of change and crisis, inspiring both utopian hopes and a sense of dread, as mass hunger and unemployment precipitated in 1848 a bloody cycle of revolutionary and counter-revolutionary conflict across much of Europe (see p. 562). The 1840s were also the climax of agonized English self-examination, the decade of several of Dickens's most popular works—including *The Old Curiosity Shop* (1840–41), *Barnaby Rudge* (1841), *A Christmas Carol* (1843), *Dombey and Son* (1848) and *David Copperfield* (1849–50); of Carlyle's *Chartism* (1840), famously denouncing the "cash nexus," and *Past and Present* (1843); of Disraeli's *Coningsby* (1844) and *Sybil* (1845); Charlotte Brontë's *Jane Eyre* (1847); Charles Kingsley's *Yeast* (1848); Thackeray's *Vanity Fair* (1848) and Elizabeth Gaskell's *Mary Barton* (1848); and impassioned poetry, including Thomas Hood's "Song of the Shirt," Elizabeth Barrett's "The Cry of the Children" and Tennyson's "Locksley Hall." Literature made metropolitan readers more aware of regional differences and problems, particularly those of the industrial north—though one reader declared that after reading the Brontës she would "rather visit the Red Indians than trust herself in Leeds."[100] The aim was to haunt readers' imaginations and prick their consciences.

Bad weather and the arrival of an unknown plant disease from America in 1845 began "an ecological catastrophe almost unparalleled in modern history"[101] by destroying potato crops. In 1846 wheat and rye harvests also failed from Spain to Prussia. Potatoes provided good and cheap nourishment across northern Europe, and the crop failures caused some 40,000–50,000 deaths in Belgium and similar numbers in Prussia. Far worse ensued in Ireland, whose population had risen to at least 8 million (compared with England's 15 million) and which was more dependent on potatoes than anywhere else, consuming some 7 million tons per year. The Irish famine, during which nearly a million people died and as many emigrated, has left a dark stain on English history, because of the overall responsibility of predominantly English governments. The tragedy has been described as "genocide," developing an accusation first put forward by Irish nationalists in the 1860s. It bred generations of hatred, not least among Irish-Americans. The genocide accusation, which can be found today on websites and in pop songs and was approved in the 1990s for teaching in schools in parts of the United States, alleges not merely that English aid was inadequate, but that the government deliberately blocked aid and created an artificial famine by extorting vast quantities of food from Ireland to feed England.

When the blight was first reported to Peel in September 1845—a potato merchant wrote warning him personally—he bought American maize for Ireland to feed 500,000 people for three months. In January 1846 he suspended the Corn Laws to allow untaxed imports. A Public Works (Ireland) Bill was introduced to provide employment. But the early potato crop was good, and disguised the peril. Irish nationalists minimized the problem and rejected aid: "No begging appeals to England . . . For who could make men and freemen of a nation so basely degraded?"[102] Peel's fall in June 1846, after repealing the Corn Laws, brought in a Whig government under Lord John Russell, which has long been condemned for dogmatic adherence to free trade. The traditional villain of the piece is Charles Trevelyan, Assistant Secretary to the Treasury, accused of dogmatism, racism and an Evangelical belief that the famine was the work of Providence. There is some truth in this, though Providentialist views were widespread, including in the Irish Catholic Church. The Whigs certainly believed in the beneficence of free trade, including exports from Ireland. They set up a public-works programme as a means of famine relief, though rejecting a large-scale plan of railway-building, aid to farmers and taxes on absentee landlords proposed by the Tory Lord George Bentinck. At the peak, over 700,000 people were being employed on public works—more than the total employment provided by Irish agriculture. But this was still insufficient. The potato crop failed disastrously again in 1846. Trevelyan wrote to a Catholic priest: "The famine is increasing; deaths become more frequent; and the prospect may well appal the heart." In January 1847 the government began direct food distribution through soup kitchens, which by July fed 3 million people daily, but this was considered only possible for a few months, and was cut back when the next harvest came. Trevelyan declared that "Absolute famine still stares whole districts in the face," and appealed for "a great effort [of] humane exertion"—voluntary contributions from the English people. A leading nationalist paper replied: "We scorn, we repulse, we curse all English alms."[103] The main collection in England, despite its own economic depression, raised £435,000—the equivalent of over £100m today—and smaller contributions came from the empire and America. The British Relief Association, a charity, was helping to feed up to 200,000 children. Another £9.5m came from public funds, equal to a sixth of total state spending and "probably unprecedented in famine history."[104] Yet it was nowhere near enough. People continued to die in their thousands, mostly from untreatable epidemic diseases worsened by hunger, movement and overcrowding at soup kitchens and workhouses, where many doctors and clergy also died. Trevelyan and Russell doubtless believed that everything possible had been done, and that the only long-term remedies were migration and agricultural reform. Palmerston, Foreign Secretary and an Irish landlord, himself chartered ships to take his impoverished tenants to Canada, and he supplied them with clothes and money.

In the conditions of the time—when the United Kingdom was economically at about the level of Cameroon today—famine could not have been wholly prevented. It was immense in scale and duration: there was a total overall shortfall of some 50 million tons of potatoes.[105] The food exported to England (a staple of the genocide accusation) accounted for only a fraction of what was needed to replace the potato and was "dwarfed" by government purchases of maize.[106] A measured judgement is that the Whig government "may have lacked foresight and generosity" and "may have been guilty of underestimating the human problems," but it was "not guilty of either criminal negligence or of deliberate heartlessness."[107] At the time, there was no clear demand within Ireland for a different policy, and the disaster made Irish independence seem unfeasible.[108] Yet British shortcomings, however they are judged, provided one of the pillars of Irish nationalism in future generations.

Aid from England, however substantial, had limits. Public opinion blamed rapacious Irish landlords for the problem, especially when they evicted impoverished tenants (here the English agreed with Irish nationalists): hence a general determination that they should pay their share. In Russell's words, "The owners of property in Ireland ought to feel the obligation of supporting the poor who have been born on their estates and have hitherto contributed to their yearly incomes. It is not just to expect the working classes of Great Britain should permanently support the burden."[109] Prosperous Irish tenant farmers also inspired little sympathy, in the light of reports that they were ignoring the crisis and even profiting from it. It was also reported that aid was being siphoned off to buy arms, while nationalists continued to collect political funds from the population. There developed a certain "compassion fatigue," aggravated by the hostile responses of Irish nationalists—"Thank you for nothing is the Irish thanks for £10 million."[110] But racial prejudice does not seem to have been a significant barrier to aid, and policies in Ireland were the same as those in Scotland, which was also suffering. Views for which English politicians were subsequently excoriated were shared by prominent Irish nationalists, one of whom, Justin McCarthy, a witness of the suffering, wrote later that "terrible as the immediate effects of the famine are, it is impossible for any friend of Ireland to say that, on the whole, it did not bring much good with it."[111] There was a bitter irony in the polemic, at the time and since. English politicians insisted on the permanence of the Union, yet thought of Ireland as a semi-foreign country; Irish nationalists rejected the Union and "appeals to England," yet later accused the English of lack of solidarity. The real English responsibility lies in the dysfunctional aspects of Irish society, in large part due to its long and troubled hegemony.

The Irish crisis had caused Peel to suspend grain tariffs as an emergency measure, and he then abolished the Corn Laws formally in January 1846 against the will of his own party. Passage through the Commons took thirty-two nights of angry debate, among the most dramatic in parliamentary history. The leading protectionist spokesmen were Lord George Bentinck, who obliquely accused Peel of "double-dealing with the farmers of England . . . deceiving our friends, betraying our constituents," and Benjamin Disraeli, who claimed to speak for "the cause of labour— the cause of the people—the cause of England!" The Conservative party was split: two thirds voted against Peel, typically those representing the counties and smaller boroughs, and holding local office as JPs, lords-lieutenant and sheriffs; they agreed with Disraeli that agriculture provided "the revenues of the Church, the administration of justice, and the estate of the poor."[112] Liberals and Radicals voted overwhelmingly— 95 percent—for repeal. Soon after, Peel was defeated on a secondary issue, and his career was over. In his resignation speech he said that the working class would have "abundant and untaxed food . . . no longer leavened by a sense of injustice." His followers, including young disciples such as William Ewart Gladstone, gravitated to the Liberals. He died in 1850, after falling from a horse. Factories closed as crowds of working people gathered to mourn. He was surely the most popular Conservative leader of all time with urban workers: 400,000 contributed a penny each for a memorial fund to buy books for working men's clubs and libraries.[113] He did much to convince them that the established order was not their enemy.

The repeal of the Corn Laws had little economic effect for a generation. But it had immense political and moral effect. It shattered the Conservative party and brought political divisions into private life to an unusual degree: for example, the Duke of Newcastle used all his influence to bring about his Peelite son's election defeat, and was only reconciled with him on his deathbed. More than material interests were at stake: there is no obvious correlation between Tory MPs' votes on repeal and their personal sources of income. Bentinck declared that repeal would save him £1,500 a year: "I don't care for that: what I cannot bear is being *sold*."[114] Disraeli's stance is usually dismissed as opportunism—the accusation of his political opponents, aggravated by snobbery and anti-Semitism, and repeated by historians afraid of being branded naïve.[115] In reality, he was a romantic English nationalist, a consistent supporter of protection against the cost-cutting commercialism of the "Manchester School." He also believed that Peel's betrayal of electoral commitments undermined the party system on which politics depended.

Symbolically, and in the long term really, the end of the Corn Laws marked the end of a governing order and a set of political ideas.[116] These ideas were of England as primarily an agricultural country, feeding itself, and governed by a paternalistic landed elite—the vision of Burke, Wordsworth and Coleridge. But by 1846 more than half the population lived in towns, and more people had worked in manufacturing than in farming since the 1820s.[117] The new urban mechanistic ideologies of Utilitarianism, political economy and free trade became the norm. All their opponents—from Tories to socialist Owenites—had lost the argument.

The economic crisis continued, straining every European state. In the spring of 1848 governments fell like dominoes in France, Germany, Austria, Hungary and the Italian peninsula. North-western Europe, including Britain, remained outside the epicentre, but felt the turbulence. Chartism had been quiescent since 1842, busy with a Land Company to promote rural resettlement, and building what are now desirable Grade II Listed cottages. But upheaval in France, and the torment of Ireland—which brought an influx of radical immigrants—saw a return to campaigning for parliamentary suffrage. The movement was held together by its principal leader, Feargus O'Connor, a charismatic Irishman from a wealthy nationalist family claiming descent from ancient kings. The immediate tactic was to present a third petition to Parliament. The ultimate aims were unclear, whether the petition were accepted or—as was likely—again rejected. The Chartist mayor of Birmingham vowed to Prince Albert, who seemed perfectly satisfied, that the movement was wholly loyal. But other Chartists' paramilitary drilling seemed proof that they aimed at revolution—some in the movement certainly did. One wrote later: "I believed more in fighting than I do now . . . I was for rebellion and civil war, and despaired of ever obtaining justice . . . save by revolution."[118]

The climax came in April 1848, as the revolutionary tide was in flood across Europe. A mass meeting was called at Kennington Common for the tenth from where, promised O'Connor, a monster petition weighing a ton and bearing over 5 million signatures would be carried to Parliament. Wrote one Chartist sympathizer to his wife: "London is in a state of panic . . . I expect a Revolution within two years: there may be one within three days." Not everyone was so excited. The novelist Thackeray "tried in vain to convince the fine folks at Mrs Fox's that revolution was upon us: that we were wicked in our scorn of the people." George Eliot had "no hope" of any good outcome: "Our working classes are eminently inferior to the mass of the French people [with] so much larger a proportion of selfish radicalism and unsatisfied, brute sensuality . . . Besides, it would be put down." The government, unlike many in Europe, was confident, despite expecting up to 500,000 Chartists in London. An army of 85,000 special constables had been sworn in, among them the more or less enthusiastic employees of large gas and railway companies. They were armed with wooden truncheons—"I often wondered what I should have done with it," recalled one. "I used to picture myself encountering a tall Irishman with a long spear."[119] The queen had been sent to the Isle of Wight. Royal Engineers partly sawed through the staircase to the British Museum's coin and medal room, so that it would collapse if a mob of looters charged up it. Police and troops blocked the bridges to protect Parliament. The senior boys of Rugby School offered their assistance—not required.

The Duke of Wellington, now seventy-nine, was in command of the forces of order. Ministers were determined to avoid another Peterloo, or indeed panicky shooting like that which had precipitated revolution in Paris six weeks earlier. The Kennington meeting would not be interfered with as long as it was peaceful, but no illegal march on Parliament would be permitted—never the organizers' intention. The Assistant Commissioner of the Metropolitan Police met O'Connor in a pub at Kennington and they agreed that a small party would be allowed to present the petition to Parliament. So, after rousing speeches, the meeting (on the size of which modern estimates vary from 15,000 to 150,000 people) broke up peacefully in a downpour—"the rain of terror," joked *Punch*.[120] The petition, taken to Westminster in a small convoy of cabs, was again rejected, and there was much mockery of the fact that it was smaller than announced, with many bogus or jocular signatures—Victoria Rex, Flat Nose, No Cheese, Mr. Punch, etc. This was not the end of Chartist activity—many leaders were arrested over the next few months for public-order offences—but it was the end of Chartism as a coherent political campaign.

As a movement it eventually faded in public consciousness. What was mostly remembered was the April fiasco. This was the version propagated by the popular Christian Socialist novelist Charles Kingsley (sympathetic to moderate Chartism) in *Alton Locke* (1850)—"the monster petition crawled ludicrously away in a hack cab, to be dragged to the floor of the House of Commons amid roars of laughter." The story was endlessly repeated.[121] Chartism was laughed out of standard history. Its leaders remained heroes for radical workers, however, and activism continued in non-political spheres, such as workers' education, anti-vaccination campaigns and temperance—working men's clubs were a Chartist initiative, and originally teetotal.

Why this eclipse of a vast and dynamic movement? The first, and most influential, answer was given implicitly by Macaulay: England had had its revolution in 1688, its fundamental liberties had already been won, and its ruling classes had realized in 1832 that timely concession was the price of domestic peace. Left-wing historians, perhaps exaggerating the strength of a radical tradition, emphasize that governments were willing and able to use force to break Chartism. Yet, all over Europe, more repressive states than the British had been brought down by popular movements, or only regained power through bloody repression. Why not in England? Let us forget any notion that there was an English tradition of exclusively peaceful politics: violence was a regular part of even electoral politics, and governments did not hesitate to use sedition laws and transportation to intimidate. However, it is noticeable that popular violence generally stopped short of killing, and governments were comparatively restrained in their use of force. There were at least twenty-two incidents in Europe between 1844 and 1914 in which more than twenty-five people were killed by government forces; none was in Britain.[122] This is not bad testimony to an absence of intense hatred and fear. Chartist extremism was criticized as alien to England. British governments, unlike many others, could rely on the support of both the upper and the middle classes—hence the 85,000 unused special constables in 1848.

There were other significant reasons for English stability. Several recent reforms were weakening the Chartists' belief that the state was their enemy—many of them admired Peel. The constant reduction of state spending (by 50 percent in thirty years), the shift from indirect taxes to Peel's income tax (1842), the Mining Act (1842), the Ten Hours Act (1847) and above all the repeal of the Corn Laws (1846) seemed to show that even an undemocratic Parliament could respond to popular demands.

Secondly, the Anti–Corn Law League's propaganda was dispelling Malthusian predictions of unremitting poverty. Many ordinary people—craftsmen, small businessmen, Dissenting preachers and women, all pillars of Chartism—were won over by Cobden's vision of economic justice, universal prosperity and peace through free trade. A third and simple explanation is that in 1849 gold discoveries in California and Australia, by increasing the world money supply, ignited a "mid-Victorian boom." The revolutionary storm thus passed England by. The free-trade journal *The Economist* (founded in 1843) congratulated its readers that "our disturbances, trivial and partial . . . only served to show . . . how thoroughly sound at core is the heart of our people,—how unlimited is our personal liberty,—and how unshaken and lofty our credit, even after so crushing a commercial crisis."[123]

Yet even without revolution, the old order, in Tennyson's phrase, was yielding place to new. The English "Old Regime"—based on throne, Church of England and gentry—had been abolished by the reforms of the 1820s and 1830s and the repeal of the Corn Laws.[124] The arbitrating role of the Crown had been ended by the party system, the House of Lords had surrendered in 1832 when the king consented to override it, and hence the old idea of a "balanced constitution" of separate independent elements was obsolete. The House of Commons was now predominant. Within it the weight of the industrial towns, the Dissenters, Catholics and the "Celtic Fringe" had increased due to redistribution of seats, religious emancipation and the influence of the urban middle-class electorate. The wealth, cultural confidence and prestige of the landed elite enabled it to continue to play a leading role for generations to come. But it was living on borrowed time, until the day when imported food was cheap enough to displace home production, and English agriculture and those who lived by it would inevitably decline.

## THE "BLEAK ERA" IN HISTORY

> Forget six counties overhung with smoke,
> Forget the snorting steam and piston stroke,
> Forget the spreading of the hideous town;
> Think rather of the packhorse on the down.
>     William Morris, "The Earthly Paradise" (1870)[125]

The suffering and dislocation experienced in England between 1790 and 1850 count among the worst in its history. In many ways the experience was not very different from that of developing countries in the later twentieth century: loss of status for some, sudden wealth and power for others, insecurity, disorientation, slums and disease; but also technological transformation, new opportunity and greater freedom. Except—and this makes it an English story, rather than just the English variant of a universal process—this was the first time it had happened, and no one knew whether it would end in wider prosperity or mass starvation. Fear and distaste vied with exhilaration and patriotic optimism—exemplified in the writings of Charles Dickens.

That ambivalence has remained in our historical memory ever since, shown lately in the 2012 Olympic Games opening pageant. One strand stresses the dark side of the Industrial Revolution. That term—coined in admiration by the French economist Adolphe Blanqui in the 1820s—became current in England only from the 1880s, through Arnold Toynbee's influential *Lectures on the Industrial Revolution in England*, in which he called it "a period as disastrous and as terrible as any through which a nation ever passed."[126] Toynbee, who first popularized the idea that England had become a new kind of industrialized capitalist society, was influenced by the writings of French and German observers half a century earlier, above all Friedrich Engels. Their understanding of an Industrial Revolution as the cataclysmic beginning of a new era was coloured by perceptions of the breakdown of feudal society at home. They projected their fears and hopes onto England: Engels prophesied revolution, and was annoyed that no one in England took him seriously. His *Condition of the English Working Classes* (written in the 1840s but published in English only in 1892) had a delayed impact on Toynbee and his contemporaries. Engels's harrowing denunciation of workers' suffering was largely a philosophical construct[127] based on the belief that England was beginning a proletarian revolution:

> The revolution must come; it is already too late to bring about a peaceful solution . . . The classes are divided more and more sharply, the spirit of resistance penetrates the workers, the guerrilla skirmishes become concentrated in more important battles, and soon a slight impulse will suffice to set the avalanche in motion.[128]

He seized on slums in Manchester as "the classic type of a modern manufacturing town"—although they were neither modern nor linked to manufacturing. He denounced as the "degradation" of the new industrial "proletariat" what was in fact the plight of a non-industrial, unskilled underclass, many of them newly arrived Irish immigrants, who had no connection with factory work.[129] Such slums in London, Liverpool and

Manchester illustrated not industrialization but the problems of rapid urbanization without manufacturing industry[130]—what England's booming population might have suffered had it *not* been for the Industrial Revolution, and which was being suffered in the ancient teeming cities of eastern and southern Europe, from Palermo to Moscow. In contrast to Engels's pessimism, an 1860s survey found 95 percent of houses in Hull and 72 percent in Manchester to be "comfortable."[131]

Following Engels and Toynbee, Barbara and Lawrence Hammond popularized a harrowing vision of what they called "the bleak era" which trapped the poor in "smoke and squalor" by means of a "class war" fought against them by the rich.[132] Tens of thousands of copies of their books, written in a vivid and dogmatic style from the 1910s onwards, had wide influence. The Hammonds, like Toynbee, were bourgeois liberals with socialist leanings—she had a private income, he wrote for the *Manchester Guardian*—who compared modern England unfavourably with ancient Greece. Their morality tales drew on poetry, novels and folk memory as much as documentary research. Their targets were the traditional landed elite and the new moneyed power, both of which they portrayed like the mustachioed villains of melodrama grinding down "the disinherited peasants that are the shadow of its wealth . . . the exiled labourers that are the shadow of its pleasures . . . the villages sinking in poverty and crime and shame that are the shadow of its power and pride."[133] In reality, as we have seen, the elites had shown considerable concern for the "condition of England," and the state, far from being the epitome of complacent and heartless "laissez-faire," was among the most efficient and probably the most interventionist in the world. Ironically, cuts in public spending were energetically pursued by Radicals, and the relatively humane pre-1834 Poor Law was condemned by both Toynbee and the Hammonds.

This "dark satanic mills" view, unforgettably labelled in Blake's stirring verses, became the dominant historical stereotype. The Hammonds aimed to "arouse doubt and shame . . . ; to anger, not to pacify." *Fabian News* praised their "formidable attack on the . . . prestige and self esteem" of the ruling classes.[134] Their stark historical vision provided a founding myth of the Labour movement. It was also acclaimed by nostalgic conservatives such as Hilaire Belloc, G. K. Chesterton and later the historian Arthur Bryant. It was dramatized by films and writings during the 1930s, when the sufferings of the Depression were ultimately blamed on the legacy of the Industrial Revolution.[135] As noted in Chapter 10, debate between "optimists" and "pessimists" continues, but with the old "catastrophist" view discredited among most scholars, though not among the general public. In no other country, surely, has such a bleak memory persisted of economic modernization. This is partly because in England there was no reassuring precedent to follow; because the English historical memory is so coloured by party polemic; and also because there were many voices lamenting the loss of "England's green and pleasant land."

# CHAPTER 13

# Victorian England

*It was an era of new ideas, of swift if silent spiritual revolution . . . All round us, the intellectual lightships had broken from their moorings . . . The present generation which has grown up in an open spiritual ocean . . . will never know what it was to find the lights all drifting, the compasses all awry, and nothing left to steer by but the stars.*

J. A. Froude, 1884

V
ictorian" is one of the most pungent words in our historical lexicon. It was in use in a purely chronological sense four decades after the eighteen-year-old queen ascended the throne in 1837, but in the more evocative sense that most of us understand it today "Victorianism" was invented from the early 1900s to the 1920s, by people who were starting to turn against it just as it appeared to have triumphed.[1] To them, and so to us, it generally conveys stifling convention, ugliness, humourlessness, hypocrisy, harshness and snobbery:

> Respectability was the thing: breeches were out and trousers came in; bosoms were being covered and eyes modestly lowered; politics was becoming sober . . . the odour of sanctity was replacing the happy reek of brandy, the age of the dandy was giving way to that of the prig, the preacher and the bore.[2]

One of the most influential critics, Lytton Strachey, in *Eminent Victorians* (1918) made his subjects seem odd, even laughable. It is rare indeed to hear "Victorian" used positively. Margaret Thatcher, never one to shirk controversy, invited it by praising "Victorian values." Does anyone else ever refer to themselves or their ideas as "Victorian"? In some ways we are still rebelling against Victorianism; and perhaps in some ways still living it.

The reality of the Victorian era, as opposed to our monochrome vision, was marked by complexity. One of the most acute observers of the age, G. M. Young, wrote in the 1930s that he "was constantly being told that the Victorians did this, or the Victorians thought that, while my own difficulty was to find anything on which they agreed."[3] Their own sense that they were living through a time of unprecedented change—"in our age, the transition is *visible*"[4]—was accurate. It would be easy to present Victorian England as a mass of contradictions. It rang with moral exhortation: listening to sermons was a popular pastime, even on honeymoon. Yet vices were not only secretly indulged but publicly flaunted. Politicians could show off their mistresses: for example, the Marquess of Hartington, Liberal MP and later holder of many ministerial offices, who openly took the well-known courtesan Catherine ("Skittles") Walters to the Derby in 1862.[5] Aggressive prostitution made parts of London's West End no go areas for respectable women, and the staff of the well-known Trocadero restaurant were so nervous about prostitutes that any unknown unaccompanied woman was shunted into a corner so that "in case of misbehaviour we can screen the table off."[6] Propriety and convention ruled, but emotion was constantly bursting out as men sobbed and women swooned, sometimes over things that even we would find embarrassingly sentimental: one elderly peer sobbed all night after reading one of Dickens's death scenes.[7] Modernity was lauded; but some of the most creative cultural impulses came from a reinvention of tradition in architecture, art and music. Religion exerted enormous power over people's lives. Yet never before had its power been so publicly questioned. Matthew Arnold's poem "Dover Beach" (1851), with its sonorous description of Faith ebbing with a "melancholy, long, withdrawing roar," is said to be the most widely reprinted poem in the language. It even became possible to regard religion as simply unimportant. It was doubt and contestation that inspired the vehemence of Victorian exhortation: "The virtues were flags to which men rallied in battle, not decorations for ceremonial parades."[8]

Yet Victorian England was not a time of chaos or incoherence. One thing impossible to overlook—for we live surrounded by it, on it, and often in it—is its stupendous effort in bricks and mortar: whole cities, roads, sewerage (most of London's hundreds of miles of sewers were built with remarkable speed in the 1860s), viaducts, telegraph wires, gas, water, schools, churches, hospitals, stations. Victorian energy and confidence transformed not only the physical environment, but every great institution in "the most striking example in our history of pacific, creative, un-subversive revolution."[9] The Victorians also created or maintained a degree of cultural unity. Upper class, middle class, and educated working class liked broadly the same things—horse-racing, cricket, even the same

books, poetry and paintings. They also laughed at themselves: much of
what we perceive as their oddities and foibles comes from their own satire: Dickens, *Punch*, Gilbert and Sullivan, Lewis Carroll, Oscar Wilde.

The woman who by accident of birth and longevity gave her name to a
society and a culture that extended well beyond even her long reign, was
in some ways an unfitting symbol of Victorianism. She was neither snobbish, nor racist, nor insular—one of the last causes she took up was that
of a persecuted French Jew, Alfred Dreyfus. She was not typically English:
she fully embodied the international nature of traditional monarchy. She
plighted her troth (she of course proposed) in 1839 to her handsome
prince, Albert of Saxe-Coburg-Gotha, in German (in which language she
wrote many private letters) and became the matriarch of a Europe-wide
royal clan. Her political influence—at first Liberal, later Tory—was often
"dissipated in reprimands and injunctions, often shrewd, always vigorous, but sometimes petulant and sometimes petty."[10] Albert, given the
unglamorous title of "Prince Consort," though having at first a rather
exaggerated notion of his role, was in many ways more sensible. He was
an intelligent, cultivated and very earnest man, and his influence was on
the whole salutary—though not in the over-strict upbringing of his eldest
son. Over her long reign, Victoria changed from the self-willed little Whig
of her youth, to the dutiful mother and wife, to the remote and indifferent
"widow of Windsor" following Albert's early death in 1861, and finally to
the grandmother of empire. She survived six assassination attempts—
mostly by madmen—against which almost no protection was provided by
her governments. She was at the centre of two of the great national
moments of the century: the Great Exhibition of 1851 (see pp. 472–73)
and her Diamond Jubilee of 1897, a popular celebration of imperial
power at which vast crowds cheered 50,000 troops from across the
empire, and the Queen-Empress reviewed at Spithead the largest naval
force ever assembled. Through her the modern monarchy was born as the
formal embodiment of the state, patron of a range of voluntary activities,
and symbol of unity in times of celebration or crisis.

"Victorianism" both preceded and survived Victoria. Its two main conflicting ideological forces, Evangelical religion and Utilitarian rationalism,
date from the mid-eighteenth century, as do galloping economic transformation and the accelerating global empire. Many Victorian manners and
conventions lasted at least until the 1960s. Its material infrastructure and
institutional framework, irksome as they often are, we still rely on. Victorian economic ideas are still with us—even the financial crash of 2008
has classic Victorian characteristics, including greed and infantile optimism, followed by penitential austerity. And the Victorians established an

almost universal faith in Progress, which, however threadbare, remains the foundation of the modern world view.

## VICTORIAN VALUES: RELIGION, PROGRESS, FREEDOM, RESPECTABILITY

### 1. Religion

> Oh yet we trust that somehow good
> Will be the final goal of ill . . .
> I can but trust that good shall fall
> At last—far off—at last, to all,
> And every winter change to spring.
>
> Alfred Tennyson, *In Memoriam* (1850)

Victorian England was a highly religious society; this was one of the best and worst things about it. But so had the country been in previous centuries, and so were all contemporary societies. *How* religious was it? Its favourite books included the Bible and *Pilgrim's Progress*. But when for the first and only time a census recorded religious practice on Sunday, 30 March 1851, the statistics shocked many. They showed a relatively high number "neglecting" religious services—estimated at 5.3 million people, 29 percent of the population. However, 7.3 million did attend church—41 percent of the population, about 70 percent of those able to do so. These levels are similar to those in the United States in the 2000s, though five times higher than the 8 percent attending Sunday worship in Britain in 2000.[11]

More than half of 1851 attendances were at Nonconformist chapels, not the Church of England. England had since the seventeenth century been unusually diverse and divided in its beliefs—"sixty sects and only one sauce," joked a French observer. Yet over the eighteenth century Old Dissent (Presbyterians, Congregationalists, Baptists, Quakers), legally tolerated in 1689, stagnated, and Anglican dominance seemed unchallengeable. The explosion of "New Dissent" (especially Methodism) from the 1770s to the 1840s marked one of the most dramatic social and cultural changes in the country's history.[12] English religion no longer consisted of a national Church with a few licensed dissenters, but of some ninety churches and sects. The omnipresent Church of England remained by far the largest—85 percent of marriages in 1851 were in church, and only 6 percent in chapel.[13] But the 1832 Reform Act had increased the voting power of

Nonconformists—about 20 percent of the new electorate. Many of them demanded outright disestablishment, some vehemently denouncing "the white-chokered, immoral, wine-swilling, degraded clergy, backed by debauched aristocrats and degraded wives and daughters."[14] To understand the continuing importance of the Church, and the vehemence of both its defenders and attackers, we would have to imagine an institution today combining the BBC, the major universities, parts of the Home Office, and much of the welfare, judicial and local-government systems.

Anglicanism was both strengthened and weakened by its ancient institutional structures. It was strongest in the Midlands and the south of England, and weak round the edges—the north, the south-west, the Scottish and Welsh borders, and Wales. This was originally for basic material reasons—scattered populations, low incomes and inability to support a resident clergy. But from the 1750s these areas boomed in population and industry. By the time the Church responded—building over 4,000 churches between 1820 and 1870, an effort unique in history—many people had been integrated into Nonconformist sects, especially Methodism: on "census Sunday" its chapels attracted about 2.25 million, over 20 percent of the total, and up to half of those in towns. John Wesley's flexible and even opportunistic methods (moving on when there was no response and consolidating where converts were made) proved highly successful: Methodism was the only denomination that positively thrived on socio-economic change—including population growth, industrialization, migration and social mobility. So, in its various forms, it became the most powerful catalyst of cultural dissidence in England. Chapels and their Sunday schools, often staffed by self-taught artisans and miners, became a channel of revolt against the squire and the parson,[15] providing an autonomous religious environment affording moral legitimacy, solidarity and self-confidence. In rural society, this might attract farmers who resented paying church rates and tithes, labourers in dispute with their bosses—even poachers. In short, all who detested parsons, who were often also Poor Law guardians or JPs: Radicals never forgot that it was a clerical magistrate who had read the Riot Act at Peterloo. The Primitive Methodists (the "Prims"), who doubled their numbers during the conflictual 1830s, remained a sect of the poor, preaching a lively message of "the 3 Rs": "ruin, repentance and redemption"; and their preachers provided a constant stream of trade union leaders. Mainstream Methodism attracted the hard-working, respectable and newly prosperous businessmen who now had the vote, and became one of the most dynamic forces in English politics.

Smaller older sects, such as Quakers and Unitarians, became the religion of urban and business elites, at least as much as the Church of England was that of the squirearchy. The Quakers, tiny in number, provide some of the most famous names in British business and finance: Cadbury, Fry, Rowntree, Barclay, Lloyd, Clark (shoes), Reckitt, Huntley, Palmer, Bryant, May, Swan, Hunter, Price, Waterhouse. Some were also influential philanthropists and campaigners: pious Dissenting families regarded their wealth and privilege as imposing a God-given duty to society.[16] Similarly, Evangelicalism, which influenced both Church and Dissent, was a call to public and political action in almost every sphere. It created vast numbers of charities and philanthropic lobby groups—many still in existence—largely depending on the voluntary labours of middle-class women.[17] Women as well as men were politically organized and powerful as lobby groups, despite lacking the vote. To their pressure is due much of what was "Victorian" in social and cultural life: anti-slavery, animal protection, Sunday Observance, prison reform, temperance, protection of women, and prosecution of obscenity and illicit sexuality. The so-called Nonconformist conscience was willing to use political action and law enforcement as a means of extending moral behaviour.[18] There were significant overlaps of members in the various societies. William Wilberforce, at the beginning of the century, in addition to anti-slavery, was also involved in support for missions, animal protection and religious education. At the end of the century, the prominent writer and campaigner Laura Chant was active in the Women's Liberal Federation, the Ladies' National Association and the British Women's Temperance Association, and was a founding member of the Women's Guardians Society (for Poor Law guardians) and the National Vigilance Association (for sexual censorship), whose journal she edited. Nonconformists and Evangelicals wanted to make people better: so they tended to disapprove of handouts to the undeserving, whether by the Poor Law or the Anglican Church. A challenge to Anglicanism from the other end of the spectrum was the Oxford Movement, an 1820s High Church dons' revolt led by the saintly poet John Keble, the Regius Professor of Hebrew Edward Pusey, and the vicar of St. Mary's, John Henry Newman. The rebels were determined, in Newman's words, to resist "Rationalism" and "Liberalism" in the Church which led to the subversive conclusion that "no theological doctrine is any thing more than an opinion." During the 1840s Pusey was banned from preaching and Newman censured by the University, "posted up by the marshal on the buttery-hatch of every College of my University . . . as a traitor . . . against the time-honoured Establishment."[19] This triggered his adhesion to Roman Catholicism in 1845.

The religious life of England thus grew ever more complex, ranging from Roman Catholic (against whom legal discrimination had mostly been abolished between 1791 and 1829) to Mormon: seventy new sects appeared in 150 years. A town such as Halifax had 7 religious buildings in 1801, and 99 in 1901—by then, the whole country had about 34,000 religious buildings, about one for every thousand people.[20] The various churches and sects created communities and hierarchies, from Anglican village churches where the squire occupied a special pew and the community displayed its pecking order, to the opulent chapels of the manufacturing cities where those who made the largest financial contribution occupied the places of honour. Most seats in all churches and chapels belonged to specific persons and families, showing how important membership was, and also how exclusive the smaller sects could be.

The main poles in this complex religious diversity are clear. On one hand, the core of Anglican and usually Tory England, where national and cultural identities were least ambivalent.[21] It was solid in prosperous agricultural areas of the south, the rural Midlands and parts of East Anglia, with small villages and parishes, resident clergy and large landowners who provided most employment. They had potential coercive power, but rarely needed it. The ideal Anglican village had a stable population, high employment, paternalistic labour relations, good housing, generous poor relief, Sunday schools, cricket on the village green, and, later on, church schools, mechanics' institutes, reading rooms, even in one case a pioneering village gas works. Squire and parson gave leadership, patronage and protection. Macaulay sneered that the Church of England was "the Tory party at prayers," but it would be truer to say that the Victorian Tory party was the Church at the hustings.

The other pole, Nonconformist and usually Liberal England, in the north, the south-west and the industrial Midlands, was where things were different: peripheral rural areas, with multiple land ownership, big parishes, non-resident clergy, more diverse and competitive economic conditions, non-agricultural employment, immigration (especially from the "Celtic fringe"), rapid population growth, industrialization and urbanization. There formed, especially in the north of England and Wales, what has been called "peripheral nationalism"; and if we adopt this term, then its opposite would be "core nationalism," expressed through Toryism. This is often imagined as a simple division between north and south—one of the fundamental ways of imagining England (and several other countries), though of course it overlooks the Midlands and East Anglia, neither one nor the other. The difference has become embedded in modern popular culture in immediately recognizable stereotypes: Coronation Street versus Ambridge.

Religious sectarianism alone did not create this division, which was also regional and socio-economic. Nor was the division watertight: there were Methodist Tories just as there were Anglican Liberals. But religion permanently fixed what might otherwise have been ephemeral divisions and tensions in a shifting and growing society. Sectarian rivalry created visceral identities and loyalties that carried over into politics. It was religion rather than class that decided how Victorians voted. Education further institutionalized the division in different school systems: Nonconformists opposed public subsidy of Church schools under the 1870 Education Act fearing that future generations would be brought up as both Anglican and Tory.[22] Victorians quarrelled about religion as we quarrel about the NHS or our own school system, transferring sectarian passions onto secular institutions. Their religious quarrels were never solely theological. Evangelicalism encouraged support for moral causes and hence to political activism. Nonconformists considered themselves the defenders of an old tradition of civil as well as religious freedom, and saw disestablishment of the Church as an essential step towards social and political improvement.[23] Defenders of the Established Church saw it, with the Monarch at its head, as the bedrock of social stability and national unity: in the words of the hymn, "One Church, one Faith, one Lord."

Fundamental intellectual challenges which gathered pace during the 1820s and 1830s shook the Christian world. One challenge came from within: a reaction led by Anglican intellectuals with Christian Socialist leanings against Evangelical hell-fire fundamentalism and its idea of a cruel and punitive God.[24] Another set of challenges came from geology, archaeology and astronomy. What John Ruskin called the geologists' "dreadful Hammers" ("I hear the clink of them at the end of every cadence of the Bible verses") split rocks and found fossils, proving that the book of Genesis was not literally true. Charles Lyell's *Principles of Geology* (1830–33) and Robert Chambers's anonymously published best-seller *Vestiges of the Natural History of Creation* (1844) brought these questions before a wide public. This discovery of hit-and-miss extinctions of species challenged the eighteenth-century belief that the universe expressed the harmonious Design of a loving creator. Tennyson expressed the anguished confusion of one

> Who trusted God was love indeed
> And love Creation's final law—
> Tho' nature, red in tooth and claw
> With ravine, shriek'd against his creed.[25]

Charles Darwin's *On the Origin of Species by means of Natural Selection* was written largely in the 1830s under the influence of Malthus's theory of "natural checks" on population and observations made on HMS *Bea-*

*gle*. He delayed publication until 1859 (the year of another kind of evolutionary tract, Samuel Smiles's improving book *Self Help*), when the socio-economic and political climate was calmer and the theory seemed less dangerous in its implications for belief in Divine creation, the main foundation of morality and social order as conventionally understood. There was still controversy, including a famous clash in 1860 at a meeting of the British Association in Oxford (embroidered in the telling) between T. H. Huxley, Darwin's pugnacious defender, and the Bishop of Oxford, "Soapy Sam" Wilberforce, essentially over whether Man was just another kind of animal. The greatest shock was felt by Evangelicals, whose faith was based on the literal truth of the Bible. Newman, in contrast, regarded Darwin's theory as compatible with his Catholic beliefs. Darwinism was soon being interpreted optimistically as the means used by God in creating a progressive universe. As the devout High Church Anglican Gladstone put it, "Evolution, if it be true, enhances in my judgment the proper idea of the greatness of God."[26]

Victorian Christians responded to these intellectual challenges. Evangelicals asserted the authority of Scripture, and a new Revivalist movement (to "revive" religious fervour), which began in America in the 1870s, drew crowds to large and emotional meetings. Catholics asserted the authority of the Church (whose bishops, controversially, were reintroduced into England in 1850), which was empowered, said Newman, to order its adherents "not to reason, but to obey."[27] Papal Infallibility was made an official dogma in 1870. "Broad Church" Anglicans, who eschewed both fundamentalism and authoritarianism, argued that Scripture had to be interpreted progressively as human understanding increased.

The other religious response to modern challenges was institutional: building churches, chapels, schools and missions, training clergy, publishing books, and getting involved in a range of social activities—Sunday schools, Poor Law administration, reform campaigns. More religious books and tracts were published than any other type: by the 1860s the Religious Tract Society was producing annually some 20 million tracts and 13 million copies of periodicals.[28] Free Sunday schools, mostly Anglican, staffed by hundreds of thousands of volunteer teachers, most of them women, attracted 425,000 children and adult pupils by 1818, 2.6 million by 1851, 6 million by 1911.[29] In England, as all over Europe, these efforts brought people into churches, schools, and ramifying networks of charities, sports clubs, Bible study groups, women's groups and youth organizations. The idea that modern life inevitably leads to secularization and unbelief, once taken for granted, is clearly wrong, as can be seen today in the United States, not to mention non-European societies. Religious practice remained high in England until the 1960s—one of the legacies of the Victorian age.

## 2. Progress

> Not in vain the distance beckons. Forward, forward let us range,
> Let the great world spin forever down the ringing grooves of change.
> > Alfred Tennyson, "Locksley Hall" (1842)

The Victorians believed in God. They also believed in Progress, and commonly linked the two beliefs. Technology and the infrastructure were changing with unprecedented speed and obvious effect. Railways, constructed with astonishing speed in the 1840s and 1850s, were a marvellous symbol of modernity. Wrote Thackeray in 1860:

> It was only yesterday, but what a gulf between then and now. Then was the old world. Stage-coaches, pack-horses, highwaymen, Druids, Ancient Britons . . . But your railroad starts a new era . . . We who lived before railways and survive out of the ancient world are like Father Noah and his family out of the Ark.[30]

But there was more to Progress than childlike wonder at new gadgets, however astonishing, and satisfaction at the visible increase in national wealth, however unprecedented. Ideas of Progress had burrowed to the centre of the Victorian world view. The Scottish Enlightenment had already elaborated the idea of successive stages of civilization: from the decline of savage and violent feudalism to the growth of peaceful and civilized "commercial society," which England seemed to epitomize. Historians wrote a saga of Progress: the Great Men of history, seen by Carlyle as crucial, were to be judged by progressive criteria: "Were their faces set in the right or wrong direction? . . . Did they exert themselves to help onward the great movement of the human race, or to stop it?"[31] Central to the "great movement" was the growth of freedom, associated in England with Protestantism and Parliament, and enshrined in the Whig interpretation of history by writers such as Macaulay (see p. 268). Not only in England was England's own history seen as showing mankind the way of the future by its long and ultimately successful struggle for freedom: the leading French historian and politician François Guizot declared in an influential history of European civilization that "the first clash took place in England . . . the effort to abolish absolute power in the temporal sphere and in the intellectual sphere, that is the meaning of the English revolution, that is its role in the development of our civilization."[32]

England's civil wars and violent revolutions were now in the past, for the lesson had been learned, as Macaulay put it during the debates on the Great Reform Bill in 1832, that "the great cause of revolutions is this, that while nations move onwards, constitutions stand still."[33] So the safe option was to embrace Progress, not resist it.

Science, a fashionable social as well as intellectual pursuit for Victorians, seemed itself an embodiment of Progress due to the huge strides in understanding it had made. As Carlyle joked in 1833: "Our Theory of Gravitation is as good as perfect ... Of Geology and Geognosy we know enough ... To many a Royal Society, the Creation of the World is little more mysterious than the cooking of a Dumpling."[34] We have seen the effects of geological and biological discoveries on religious belief, but they had a more general meaning—that the universe was not and had never been static, but was perpetually developing. The conception of time itself was revolutionized—a universe that had seemed a few thousand years old (and perhaps heading for a Providential end in the not too distant future) suddenly seemed incalculably ancient, and the human presence correspondingly reduced. At least as unsettling was the "Social Darwinism" of the pioneering sociologist Herbert Spencer. Coming from a typical Nonconformist Free Trade background, he extended Darwin's theory of natural selection to human society, asserting that races, nations and social classes, like biological species, were subject to the principle of "the survival of the fittest." This too was a theory of Progress, but a harsh and pessimistic one, based on conflict and struggle, and fearful of "degeneration." Far more optimistic variants of Progress coexisted: William Ewart Gladstone, while remaining a High Church Anglican, abandoned the pessimistic paternalism of his Tory youth in the 1830s, when he had believed that Church and state must impose morality on a wayward people, and became by the 1870s an optimistic Liberal prophet, believing that God's will for mankind could be brought about by "the great social forces which move upwards and onwards in their might and majesty."[35]

Political and economic circumstances in the 1850s made progressive optimism ascendant, indeed almost inescapable, in England:

> A land of settled government,
> A land of just and old renown,
> Where freedom slowly broadens down
> From precedent to precedent.[36]

The Great Exhibition of 1851, its organization presided over by the queen's cerebral German husband, Prince Albert, became a festival of reconciliation and hope, a visible embodiment of commercial, technological and political Progress, with England consciously leading the world in an unprecedentedly international festival of amity and trade, with 15,000 exhibitors from round the world displaying their wares. "Other nations have devised means for the display and encouragement of their own arts and manufactures," proclaimed the official programme, "but it has been reserved for England to provide an arena for the exhibition of the industrial triumphs of the whole world."[37] The astounding glass and iron Crystal Palace, designed by Joseph Paxton, the Duke of Devonshire's head gardener, was four times as long as St. Paul's, and "indescribably glorious," thought the queen, who opened it on 1 May amid massed choirs singing the "Hallelujah Chorus." She declared it "the *greatest* day in our history" and "the *happiest, proudest* day in my life." Few dissented, and an average of 43,000 people came every day for six months—the largest indoor crowds ever assembled. Macaulay concluded that "there is as much chance of a revolution in England as of the falling of the moon." A Manchester cotton merchant, Absolom Watkin, noted in his diary: "Our country is, no doubt, in a most happy and prosperous state. Free trade, peace, freedom. Oh happy England!"[38] Even the Crimean War and Indian Mutiny a few years later could be interpreted positively as showing that, despite the softening effects of peace and prosperity, "We have proved we have hearts in a cause, we are noble still."[39]

Over the next generation, the English wallowed in self-congratulation. School textbooks assured children that they belonged to "the greatest and most highly civilised people that the world ever saw ... The modern era of European civilisation receives its highest expression in the British isles"[40]—a happy condition in which the Scots and some of the Welsh were now generally included, but the Irish less so. This expressed a major Victorian tenet: Progress was not automatic, it had to be earned through work, thrift and "character." Samuel Smiles, a radical-leaning former Chartist, spread the message in a chatty collection of improving anecdotes, *Self Help* (1859), an international best-seller. It consisted largely of thumbnail sketches of self-made men, including businessmen, lawyers, artists, scientists, and "inventers and producers" as well as more conventional military heroes—including foreign ones such as Napoleon. Even he could be made to exemplify Smiles's main message: that "will ... patience, perseverance, and conscientious working, in elevating the character of the individual" led to "the most complete success"—a way of reconciling morality with inequality, and change with stability.[41]

Not everyone was so sublimely confident in Progress—at least, as epitomized by industrial society. Intellectuals such as the prominent art critic John Ruskin, originally an ultra-Tory, and the philosopher and school inspector Matthew Arnold were scathing in their contempt of the materialism, "philistinism" and ugliness of industrial society. Arnold's

"Philistines"—the middle class, especially the Nonconformists, increasingly important in politics and society—were "people who believe that our greatness and welfare are proved by our being very rich, and who most give their lives and their thoughts to becoming rich," hence condemning themselves and others to "the dismal and illiberal life."[42] But even the likes of Ruskin and Arnold saw themselves not as "reactionary" or "retrogressive" (newly coined terms), but as seeking a different and truer form of Progress, in which nostalgia overlapped with utopianism, creating visions in which the future in many ways resembled the past, most famously in William Morris's *News From Nowhere* (1891), an idyllic portrayal of a harmonious rural society of the future that was influential well beyond Britain. Morris, while at Oxford in the 1850s, was inspired by Ruskin's writings on Gothic architecture, which among other things criticized the inhumanity and chaos of industrialization, and by the medieval adventures of Malory's *Morte Darthur*, and he embarked on a life-long cultural and aesthetic battle "against the age," in association with the Pre-Raphaelite painters. He did this both in his prolific writings and in practice, by setting up in 1861 a firm producing craft-made furniture, wallpaper and other decorative objects, often inspired by natural forms, in conscious opposition to utilitarian mass-produced goods. Paradoxically, and to his own dismay, he was catering to the wealthy and fashionable, including royalty; and in 1883 he became a leading and very militant member of the Marxist Social Democratic Federation.[43] Ruskin, too, from the 1870s onwards combined writings on art and architecture with educational activities, social criticism, and a comparable combination of traditionalism, aesthetics and utopianism, and he also won many admirers, including Arnold Toynbee, the Webbs, Proust, Tolstoy and Gandhi.[44] Towards the end of the century, as we shall see (p. 531), more bleakly pessimistic views of modern society, often linked with Social-Darwinist fears of degeneration and decline, became common across Europe, and contributed to nationalist and socialist demands for radical change.

## 3. Freedom

*We Englishmen are Very Proud of our Constitution, Sir. It Was Bestowed Upon Us By Providence. No Other Country is so Favoured as This Country. This Island was Blest, Sir, to the Direct Exclusion of such Other Countries as—as there may happen to be.*
Mr. Podsnap, in Charles Dickens, *Our Mutual Friend* (1864)

Freedom was linked with religion (Protestantism being seen as freedom of belief and conscience), with new-found optimism over economic and political progress (seen as the fruits of freedom), and with national identity—the English saw themselves above all as traditionally free, a theme developed by a succession of great Victorian historians. There was soon near consensus over free trade, as much a moral as an economic policy. By the 1850s libertarian language dominated British political debates.[45] This owed much to the culture of religious Dissent, committed to dismantling the Anglican-Tory establishment. Nonconformity instinctively sympathized with struggles against oppression at home and abroad, whether Methodists forced to pay church tithes or Bulgarian Christians being massacred by Turkish *bashibazouk*s in the 1870s. This "popular front of moral outrage"[46] permeated Liberal, trade unionist and later Labour politics.

Freedom was not mere rhetoric. England developed perhaps the smallest central-government machinery ever found in an industrial society.[47] What was then called "grandmotherly government"—what we call "the nanny state"—was regarded as simply not English. There was agreement across parties and classes (for workers shared this view) as to what the state should *not* do: not squander taxpayers' money, not create or protect privileges (hence trade unions' persistent demand for "free collective bargaining" rather than state arbitration), and not throw its weight about at home.

The state, though small, was powerful and even authoritarian in areas where it did act, belying the image of laissez-faire inactivity created later by socialist writers such as Beatrice and Sidney Webb. In important areas it was far more intrusive and effective than the ramshackle European absolutist states condemned by English Liberals. For example, employers were gradually forced to accept liability for factory working conditions and safety in a long series of Factory Acts, of which that of 1833 instituted inspection and enforcement which, however inadequate, was far more extensive than in any other country.[48] The Poor Law had no parallel elsewhere as a means of social intervention. England was highly unusual in having an income tax, abolished in 1815 but as we have seen reintroduced by Peel in 1842. This required detailed declaration and inspection of private information—anathema in many countries. Despite an Englishman's home being proverbially his castle, it gave him no legal protection against arrest and interference. A series of Public Health and Sanitary Acts (beginning in 1848) took powers far exceeding those in authoritarian Continental states. Sanitary inspectors could enter private dwellings, order cleansing, stop nuisances, remove the sick to hospital, require notification of contagious diseases, even demand information concerning the state of people's bowels.[49] One health policy that the Liberal Nonconformist and progressive conscience could not stomach, as we shall see, was the regulation of prostitution under the Contagious Diseases Acts (1864), state connivance in vice.

One of the most effective Victorian lobbying organizations was the Society for the Prevention of Cruelty to Animals, founded in 1824 to prosecute those abusing working animals and engaging in rowdy blood sports. Bull-baiting was fairly easily suppressed, being associated with drunkenness, disorder and "rough" elements; though it took repeated use of troops in the late 1830s to stop bull-running in Stamford, where both townspeople and magistrates claimed it as an ancient right. "Royal" from 1840, the RSPCA helped to bring about a transformation of perceptions and behaviour. In the queen's words, "The English are more inclined to be cruel to animals than some other civilized nations are," and this was even taken as a sign of national toughness.[50] Campaigners distinguished between lower-class cruelty, seen as a social problem, and upper-class sport: the aim was not only to prevent cruelty to animals, but "to spread amongst the lower orders of the people . . . a degree of moral feeling."[51] By 1887, the RSPCA's annual general meeting of 7,000 activists in the Albert Hall, in the presence of the queen, could claim a "transformation [of] the national character" which put the English "at the head of all civilised peoples."[52] Another popular blood sport attracting respectable disapproval was attendance at public executions, and indeed there were campaigns to abolish hanging (removed from public view in 1868) and flogging in the armed forces (stopped in peacetime in 1867).

So is the idea of Victorian England as the home of personal freedom and *laissez-faire* a myth? In part, clearly so: it would be more accurate to describe it as the cradle of the nanny state, whose health-and-safety powers, and complaints about them, go back at least to the 1830s. But after parliamentary reform in 1832 and Corn Law repeal in 1846, the state was increasingly trusted to use power properly—it reassured Liberals, of course, that Liberal governments were usually in office. Moreover, if the central state remained small, it was because most powers were delegated to a complicated system of local government, "those ancient local institutions by which [the English] have been trained to self-government," as the constitutional historian Erskine May put it in 1861.[53] Local authorities were regarded as inherently less oppressive. They were often small bodies dealing with a particular task financed by a local rate: parish vestries, Poor Law guardians, elected school boards, elected health boards, and (from 1888) parish and county councils. Typical were the local School Boards, established by the 1870 Education Act, for which women as well as men were electors and eligible, and which ran all aspects of primary education. Justices of the Peace dealt with most offences. The police were under local watch committees. Much of this activity was concerned with the problems experienced by, and caused by, the "rough" lower classes, whose response was often fearful and resentful. But for educated Liberals and later socialists—for whom Bentham and Chadwick were heroes—liberty was not licence, and it was right to use compulsion where necessary to improve and moralize those who were not improving themselves. Increasing emphasis was placed on education, persuasion and outright moral blackmail: for example, in encouraging hygiene and providing health care. This battery of measures had considerable success in regulating, cleansing and indoctrinating what had seemed a dangerous urban society, while preserving and extending political freedoms.

## 4. Respectability

*The freer a country is from government interference . . . the more intolerant grows the mob: your neighbour, your butcher, your tailor, family, club, parish keep you under supervision and perform the duties of a policeman.*

Alexander Herzen[54]

There was another side to English freedom, as was observed by the sardonic Russian Herzen, in exile in London in the 1850s. If the state was in some areas remarkably unobtrusive, it was because civil society was active both alone and in partnership with the authorities in promoting self-restraint, civility, mutual aid and self-help. Respectability was a much broader process than merely compelling the working classes to accept middle-class standards of decorum. It meant working people themselves wishing to create security, cleanliness and safety for their families, asserting a social status, "keeping up appearances," and raising children according to various ideals of Progress, Christianity, manliness and femininity. Moreover, respectability was closely associated with political radicalism: it was not conservatives but Chartists, socialists and feminists who saw working-class respectability as the route to greater equality, and who campaigned against alcohol and sexual immorality. But people also wanted friendship, conviviality and fun in a society that would otherwise have been alienating and grim. Not all of these aims were compatible, and they gave rise to tensions, resentments, rebelliousness and mockery. But there was nevertheless genuine agreement on the virtues of self-reliance, self-control and the ability to look after a family: things that were "respectable."[55]

As men's wages rose in England and other wealthy countries, working-class mothers increasingly stayed at home. The Trade Union Congress, founded in Manchester in 1868, defined one of its aims in 1877 as "bring[ing] about a condition . . . where wives should be in their proper sphere at home, instead of being dragged into competition for livelihood against the great and strong men of the world."[56] The duty of men to respect and protect women was increasingly stressed, for if they were seen as weaker and perhaps less intelligent, they were also seen as morally superior, "the natural and therefore divine guide, purifier, inspirer of the man," as Charles Kingsley saw it.[57] Was this merely a male status symbol and did it strengthen "patriarchal" oppression? Were men demanding higher pay as "breadwinners," and then excluding women because they were cheap labour? Undoubtedly. But arguably there were benefits too, and it took a fairly serious family crisis to get married women back into the workplace.[58] More cohesive families in which mothers concentrated on domestic comfort, nutrition and health provided better living conditions than poor people had had for generations.[59] Even if men occupied a position of formal superiority, women commonly controlled the family budget, handing out pocket money to the wage-earners, and often directed the family's collective existence. "Fathers are regarded by the children as plain inferior to mother in authority, in knowledge of right and wrong, and above all of 'manners,'" wrote a leading social worker in 1906.[60] Men began drinking less from the 1870s onwards—a huge health benefit for all concerned. Death rates fell steadily after 1880. Children were better fed and stayed longer in the parental home. People worked hard to order their lives, care for their families, and keep themselves and their houses clean. Among the first mass-produced branded goods was Sunlight soap; in the 1880s the English each used over fourteen pounds of soap per year, and the French only six. "The English think soap is civilization," sneered the German historian Heinrich von Treitschke.[61]

Women played a key role outside the family too as organizers of mutual assistance in extended families and neighbourhoods—neighbouring housewives were the first recourse in cases of sickness or temporary hardship, even if only to provide a cup of sugar or a packet of tea. The Mothers' Union, by far the largest women's society, was founded in 1886. Working-class women policed behaviour in their neighbourhoods through mutual help, gossip and sometimes outright confrontation. Drunkenness, domestic violence and sexual irregularity were targeted: husbands were restrained; pregnant girls were sometimes viciously treated; errant boys were pressed to marry them. Where middle-class charity workers or officials did step in, they were increasingly likely to include women.

Self-help organizations were engines of respectability. Trade unions and friendly societies were tough on shirkers: benefit claimants were medically checked, often required to stay at home in the evenings, banned from drinking, and required to accept any suitable work. Errant members who drank too much or idled felt peer pressure to conform, including by "friendly visitation" from workmates. Trade unions prosecuted benefit cheats and published their names.[62] A declining minority resorted to Poor Law relief—about 2.6 percent of the population by the 1890s. It carried the stigma of failure for the able-bodied. Most recipients were elderly people living at home, not in institutions such as workhouses.[63] The attainment of respectability was a source of pride and the basis of political self-assertion. For example, mid-century Chartists and later Radicals demanded democratic rights on the grounds that they were respectable heads of households. A socialist orator in 1895 badly misjudged his East End audience when he summoned them to "come out of their bug-hutches and slums and fight for socialism," provoking an angry hearer to knock him off his soap box: "You lying ..., call my ... home a slum and bug-hutch!"[64]

The outward signs of increasing respectability from around mid-century can hardly be doubted. The temperance movement obtained regulation of access to drink and cast a long-term stigma on public drinking for the respectable. Alcohol consumption declined continuously from the 1870s, when it peaked at around a bottle of spirits and twenty-three pints of beer per month per head: consumption of spirits fell by 80 percent in sixty years, and beer by 40 percent.[65] Illegitimacy, which had been rising since the 1700s, fell sharply from 1850 and reached its lowest ever level in 1901, with dramatic effects on infant mortality, much lower than in France or Germany.[66] General attitudes to sex were a crucial aspect of respectability—for later generations almost a synonym for "Victorianism." However, while there were certainly changes, our stereotypes here are laden with myth and gross over-simplification derived from 1920s and 1960s denunciations.

In reality, Victorians' sexual beliefs and conduct varied widely and changed considerably over the decades. As a whole, they were little different from those of most human societies; by the standards of the time, Victorians were probably less prudish than Americans and in some ways (for example, the freedom given to young women of all classes) more permissive than the French. Victorians did not cover the legs of their pianos—this story seems to have originated as a joke about Americans, whose puritanism the English found risible. They tolerated nude bathing and public urination. They generally thought that sexual abstinence was damaging, and few believed that respectable women had no sexual feelings—on the contrary, they commonly believed that women could not conceive without orgasm.[67] There remained a libertine current: prostitutes and their clients were quite numerous though probably declining in number; a pornography trade existed; there were well-known risqué night-spots in London and other towns; in some upper-class metropolitan circles, there was toleration of discreet adultery and what in the 1890s was called

"fast" behaviour; and there occasionally emerged a few highly beleaguered sexual liberals urging free love. But, by the later decades of the
century, all such libertines knew themselves to be a deviant minority.[68]
Within marriage, however, sex could be respectable and even uninhibited.
The queen herself was a passionate lover of her husband and (reluctant)
producer of children. The parson and novelist Charles Kingsley exchanged
torridly religio-erotic letters with his wife, Fanny—but also whipped himself to stem his ardour for the "teaming tropic sea of Eros."[69] Dickens,
angry denouncer of Malthusianist restraint, fathered ten children.

Nevertheless, there was a disciplining of sexual and other behaviour
from early in the century, breaking with eighteenth-century libertinism.
Evangelical puritanism, radical ideas of self-improvement, the need to
reduce population growth, and the powerful urge to respectability all
played a part. Reports of debauchery in factories—probably always
exaggerated—disappeared after about 1855. Illegitimacy rates fell, as we
have noted, and did so especially in towns—sexual irregularity became
increasingly a rural pastime. Children per long-term marriage fell from
six to four between the 1860s and the 1900s.[70] The belief that women
who did not reach orgasm could not conceive must have encouraged
many to "lie back and think of England" in the hope of avoiding pregnancy. Contraception was to some extent available, but it was severely
limited by legal repression and moral revulsion. Delayed marriage, verbal
reticence, abstinence, repression of pleasure and even cultivated ignorance
("innocence") came to be the main methods of birth control. True sexual
Victorianism probably reached its peak well after Victoria's death.[71]

Repressed sexuality was not solely a matter of birth control. There was
also a strong and influential anti-sensualist tendency among progressives,
dating from the eighteenth century, which believed that lust was a primitive and destructive urge that as society became more rational and more
equal could and should be suppressed (if necessary with the aid of cold
baths and exercise). Such views appealed throughout the Victorian century to radicals and feminists, seeking to liberate women from male desire,
the burdens of reproduction and indeed their own appetites, which made
them (in the words of the pioneer feminist Mary Wollstonecraft) "the prey
of their senses." One Owenite socialist community in Surrey in the 1840s,
for example, believed that its married members should not have sex "more
than once in two or three years." The Chartist leader William Lovett opposed
alcohol, "unchastity" and divorce, and Chartist clubs, if they occasionally
permitted decorous dancing, forbade "suggestive hugging."[72] Similar in outcome, if not entirely in motivation, was Nonconformist puritanism, which,
while disliking celibacy (associated with Roman Catholicism) and approving of (moderate) sex within marriage, opposed anything that might inflame

erotic urges, whether in language, behaviour, the arts or dress. One Noncon-formist footman in the 1830s, for example, condemned the evening gowns of his employers as "disgusting": "They are nearly naked to the waist . . . the breasts are quite exposed except a little bit coming up to hide the nipples."[73]

New social-purity campaigns emerged in the 1860s with joint progres-sive and religious motives. The first targets were the Contagious Diseases Acts (1864–69), which, in eleven garrison towns, copied Continental prac-tice in permitting compulsory medical examination of suspected prosti-tutes and enforced hospitalization of those with venereal diseases. These Acts ran up against one of the most characteristic Victorian moral causes: the "rescue" and rehabilitation of prostitutes, in which both Dickens and Gladstone, for example, were personally involved. So they caused outrage: as the acts of an "aristocratic" state, as discrimination against women, as class oppression and as legal sanction for immorality: "Nothing is too filthy, nothing is too low, for the hands of an English gentleman," con-cluded a woman correspondent to the radical *Reynolds News*.[74] The cam-paign was a catalyst for English feminism. The leading figure was Josephine Butler, who combined opposition to state intervention (she also opposed sanitary inspection), feminism and austere Christianity—she detested laws that might lead prostitutes to forget that their trade was sinful.[75] But other important women—including the pioneer doctor Sophia Jex-Blake—sup-ported the Acts, as did some prostitutes, who petitioned to keep them, to the disgust of campaigners.[76] The Acts were repealed in 1886.

The campaign was whipped up by articles in the *Pall Mall Gazette* (July 1885), originated by Josephine Butler; the Salvation Army leader, Cath-erine Booth; and the journalist W. T. Stead. Entitled "The Maiden Tribute of Modern Babylon," they featured "The Violation of Virgins," and "How Girls are Bought and Ruined," and culminated in the "purchase" of a young girl for £5. The articles caused outrage: "An Earthquake has shaken the foundations of England," exclaimed one bishop. A petition of 400,000 signatures, two and a half miles long when unrolled, was brought to Westminster escorted by the Salvation Army, an organization in which women predominated. A rally in Hyde Park drew over 100,000 people, with feminists, socialists, clergy and trade unionists marching together.[77] Parlia-ment was forced to rush through the Criminal Law Amendment Act (1885), outlawing brothels and pimping, raising the age of consent from thirteen to sixteen, and, in a sweeping amendment proposed by the Radical MP Henry Labouchère, criminalizing "any act of gross indecency with another male person," as well as being party to it, procuring, and attempting to procure it.

A National Vigilance Association was created, including feminists, bishops, Nonconformist ministers and the Catholic primate, Cardinal Manning, with a trade unionist as secretary and its own journal, *Vigilance*

*Record*. It was soon energetically prosecuting rapists, paedophiles, homo-sexuals, pimps and pornographers—including a publisher gaoled in 1888 for translating Émile Zola's novels. This affair led to timidity and sullen self-censorship among British authors, who realized, in the words of Frank Harris (a leading editor and himself the author of a pornographic epic), that "grocerdom is organized in conventicle and church and rancor-ously articulate."[78] This was a period of moral panics. There had been serious riots in central London in 1886 and 1887. In 1888 there were eight gruesome murders, mainly of prostitutes, by "Jack the Ripper."[79] Feminists and morality campaigners fought from the 1880s to clean up London, supported by the Progressive Party, an alliance of Liberals, Fabian socialists and Labour organizations known as "Municipal Puri-tans," who controlled the London County Council until 1907. West End music halls, frequented by "wretched painted women plying their horrible trade" and "guilty foul-eyed men, seeking whom they might devour," were a particular target.[80] In 1894 the Empire, Leicester Square, was required to place a screen to separate the auditorium from the bar—a notorious pick-up place. But it was torn down by a gang of young bloods, among them Winston Churchill. The culminating act in these years of repression came in 1895, when Oscar Wilde was prosecuted and imprisoned under the Labouchère amendment—an episode which caused an international sensation. Josephine Butler felt sorry for Wilde personally, but lamented that "the Oscar Wilde madness is spread like a plague through London's fashionable and artistic society."[81]

Respectable Nonconformists and idealistic Progressives were the most "Victorian" element in sexual matters. Fear, ignorance, reticence, shame and censorship, policed by bodies such as the National Vigilance Associa-tion, though less universal throughout society than in later legend, were undoubtedly real. By the later decades of the century, as "respectability" and prudishness became more general, there is evidence of considerable female and some male ignorance about sex, along with diminishing mutual sexual pleasure.[82] Prostitution is the reverse side of the Victorian myth, our assumption being that sexual repression must have led to hypo-critical indulgence on a large scale. But though very visible in some places, as we have seen, the prevalence of prostitution has been vastly exagger-ated: a widely repeated estimate of 80,000 or more prostitutes in London should probably be closer to 5,000. A proof of the power of respectable Nonconformity to shape actual behaviour was the rarity of prostitution in the northern towns. We should be sceptical of the idea that hypocrisy was a Victorian hallmark: "As a matter of plain fact, sexual hypocrisy in the recorded lives of notable Victorians is rare."[83]

Respectability triumphed around the time of the queen's death, as shown, for example, by the plummeting statistics for drunkenness and domestic violence we have seen. But this victory contained the germs of its own slow decay.[84] The heroic age in which women and men of all classes struggled to impose peace, order and decency on a turbulent society came to a close. The epic battle between sin and salvation was over. With more money in their pockets due to a long period of economic growth and falling food prices, people began to relax. Church attendance began to fall, first in London as early as the 1890s. People did not go back to the debauchery of the Regency or the beer-fuelled rowdiness of the 1860s, but found new, more sedate and often family-friendly amusements in which fun did not outrage respectability—sport, light reading and by the 1920s a night out at the pictures, the wireless, the football pools (invented by Littlewoods in 1923) and perhaps the occasional moderate social drinking. Having vanquished Satan, Victorianism gradually began to melt.

## THE TRIUMPH OF THE TOWN?

*Our food, our clothing, the furniture of our homes ... the gas which illuminates our streets, our means of locomotion by land and sea, the tools by which our various items of necessity and luxury are fabricated, have been the result of the labour and ingenuity of many men and many minds.*

Samuel Smiles, *Self Help* (1859)

Into my heart an air that kills
From yon far country blows:
What are those blue remembered hills,
What spires, what farms are those?
That is the land of lost content,
I see it shining plain,
The happy highways where I went
And cannot come again.

A. E. Housman, "A Shropshire Lad" (1896)

The 1851 census uncovered a phenomenon new in history: England had become the world's first urban nation, with 54 percent of its population living in towns, compared with 19 percent in France. The census showed how far the economy had already gone towards what Smiles called "the career of industry." Coal, steam and machines were reshaping society by concentrating population around the mines, factories and workshops of the north and Midlands, which only in mid-century really did become the pillars of the economy. The sheer scale and rapidity of physical effort and financial investment were unprecedented, driven by growing domestic demand, technological innovations and world trade. During the two decades following the Great Exhibition total production nearly doubled. The length of railway line doubled, as did the number of passengers, while freight tripled. The tonnage of steamships increased nearly 600 percent. Nearly 1.5 million houses were built, and throughout the Victorian period housing kept ahead of population growth. The rate of income tax nearly halved—from 7d in the pound (2.9 percent) to 4d (1.6 percent).[85] There was destruction too: ancient buildings were swept away, and most large towns kept few, or even no, pre-1700 buildings apart from churches. The new town, smoking, noisy, often stinking and sometimes dangerous, but also creative of wealth, ideas and new experiences, became a characteristic of nineteenth-century existence.

The Victorian achievement, though undeniably immense, was uneven. On one hand, great civic and national monuments, public utilities, and streets of opulent or humble terraces which we still inhabit. On the other, rickety old slums in old city centres, and new and uniform red-brick boxes haphazardly covering great expanses of the Midlands and the north. Similar phenomena soon became familiar elsewhere: after Manchester, Birmingham and Liverpool came Lille, New York, Essen, St. Petersburg, Calcutta, Shanghai. Cities were exciting and liberating, alienating and hideous. The young French poet Arthur Rimbaud was "delighted and astonished" by 1870s London: the "energy," the tough but healthy life, the fog ("imagine a setting sun seen through grey crêpe"), the drunkenness and the sex.[86] Cities inspired a new literature, from the generation of Dickens to that of H. G. Wells and Arnold Bennett at the end of the century, and a new art, such as that of W. P. Frith, James Whistler and Walter Sickert; though arguably its greatest works were by a Frenchman—Claude Monet's 1890s views of the Thames in fog.

Everywhere, national governments, city administrators, businessmen, churches, charities and ordinary citizens laboured to sanitize, civilize and even beautify the new monsters. England was the first to plunge into mass urbanization—by 1850 roughly a quarter of the population lived in large towns of over 100,000 people, most of them the new industrial centres such as Bradford, Sheffield and Leeds—and hence it could make the first mistakes. It is regularly criticized for its chaotic and fragmented urban administration, the stinginess of its ratepayers, unwilling to pay for clean water and drains, the smoggy horrors of its factory towns, with their sickly infants and stunted adults—our vision of "Dickensian" and "Victorian" existence. How does England compare with other countries? Surprisingly well, despite our folk memories: far better than the other dynamic industrializers, Germany and America, better than prosperous semi-rural France, much better than poor rural Spain (traditional society was no paradise), and not far behind prosperous rural Sweden:

### Table 1: Death rates (per 1,000 population)[87]

|                    | 1840 | 1860 | 1880 | 1900 |
| ------------------ | ---- | ---- | ---- | ---- |
| Sweden             | 20.4 | 17.7 | 18.1 | 16.8 |
| **England and Wales** | 22.9 | 21.2 | 20.5 | 18.2 |
| Belgium            | 25.0 | 19.9 | 22.3 | 19.3 |
| France             | 23.7 | 21.4 | 22.9 | 21.9 |
| Germany            | 26.5 | 23.2 | 26.0 | 22.1 |
| Spain              | —    | 27.4 | 30.1 | 29.0 |
| Russia             |      | 35.4 | 36.1 | 31.1 |

### Table 2: Infant mortality (children under one year, per 1,000 live births)

|                    | 1850 | 1860 | 1880 | 1900 | 1910 |
| ------------------ | ---- | ---- | ---- | ---- | ---- |
| Sweden             | 146  | 124  | 121  | 99   | 75   |
| **England and Wales** | 162  | 148  | 153  | 154  | 105  |
| France             | 146  | 150  | 179  | 160  | 111  |
| Belgium            | 141  | 139  | 187  | 172  | 135  |
| Spain              | —    | 174  | 190  | 204  | 149  |
| Germany            | 297  | 260  | 240  | 229  | 162  |
| USA (white)        |      | 216  | 181  | 214  | 111  |
| (black)            |      | 340  |      |      | 170  |
| Russia             | —    | —    | 286  | 252  | 216 [1912] |

Infant mortality was twice as high in poor as in rich districts of London, but four times as high in comparable districts of Paris.[88] In an international Human Development Index comparison of ten western European and North American countries for 1870 (combining GDP, life expectancy and education) England was ranked first, and for 1913 was exceeded only by the United States, Australia and New Zealand. There were fewer poor people in England than elsewhere in Europe, even though there were still many of the rural and urban poor who were badly nourished.[89]

It seems that England's representative government, political liberty and participatory local authorities coped reasonably well, especially compared with the authoritarianism of Germany or the free-for-all of the United States. By 1880 England was far closer to attaining a national minimum standard of public health than any large Continental state.[90] English cities invested in water and sewerage. Sanitary officers worked to reduce over-crowding and control pollution. From the 1860s, all the main towns had by-laws laying down housing standards. As early as the 1840s, the average number of persons per house in London's East End was 6.4, and 30 per-cent of dwellings were "well furnished"—criteria for which included pos-session of such things as a piano.[91] The four- to six-room terraced house with front and back entrance and yard became standard working-class housing, unlike in Continental cities, where, noted a German observer, "people became imprisoned in giant, multi-storeyed barracks."[92] By the early twentieth century, there were eight occupants per dwelling on aver-age in London, compared with sixty in Berlin, where 60,000 people still lived in cellars, and rents were 23 percent higher than in England, despite wages being 17 percent lower.[93]

Industrialization made England temporarily dominant in production and trade, and it remained one of the world's leading economies, as basic statistics show:

## Table 3: Industrial production

|  | United Kingdom | France | Germany |
|---|---|---|---|
| Coal (millions of tons) | | | |
| 1820 | 17.7 | 1.0 | 1.3 |
| 1850 | 50.2 | 4.4 | 5.1 |
| 1880 | 149 | 19.3 | 47 |
| 1910 | 268 | 38.3 | 152.8 |
| Pig iron (millions of tons) | | | |
| 1820 | 0.374 | 0.198 | 0.095 |
| 1850 | 2.2 | 0.406 | 0.210 |
| 1880 | 7.8 | 1.7 | 2.5 |
| 1910 | 10.1 | 4.0 | 13.0 |
| Raw cotton consumption (thousands of tons) | | | |
| 1820 | 54 | 19 | — |
| 1850 | 267 | 59 | 26 |
| 1880 | 617 | 89 | 137 |
| 1910 | 740 | 158 | 383 |

So enormous was the expansion of output that it gushed through canals and railways to foreign consumers, despite efforts by many countries to protect their markets. Because England's non-agricultural population had increasingly to be fed from abroad, and because industry's appetite for raw materials was insatiable, the visible balance of trade in goods went regularly into deficit in the 1800s, and since 1822 has remained permanently in the red. It was more than balanced by the invisible earnings of banking, insurance and shipping, and buoyant returns on foreign investments, which grew hugely in the great age of globalization between 1850 and 1914.[94] The surplus financed even more overseas investments. England, along with parts of Belgium, southern Scotland, south Wales and northern Ireland, became the nucleus of a new manufacturing and trading system, which northern France and western Germany would quickly join, and to which producers of raw materials and food—Russia, North and South America, India, Egypt and Australasia—would be increasingly attached.

This brought new kinds of wealth, and new kinds of super-rich, such as the Rothschilds; Thomas Brassey, the railway contractor; and the Guinnesses. Yet until the 1860s land remained the predominant form of wealth. The very richest, such as the Dukes of Westminster and Bedford, were those who profited from economic growth by owning urban property and mineral rights:

Table 4: Millionaires and the sources of their wealth[95] (male, British, by year of death)

|  | 1809–58 | 1858–79 | 1880–99 | 1900–1914 |
|---|---|---|---|---|
| Land | 181 | 117 | 38 | 27 |
| Commerce | 3 | 16 | 23 | 38 |
| Manufacturing | 5 | 13 | 22 | 20 |
| Food, drink, tobacco | 0 | 1 | 14 | 14 |
| Professions and state service | 1 |  | 0 | 1 |

Disparities of wealth were great—92 percent of wealth was owned by 10 percent of the population in Britain just before the First World War. This is comparable with the world average in the early 2000s (85 percent), but much higher than the figure for Britain in the 2010s—some 44 percent.[96] In terms of income, in the 1860s some 4,000 people received more than £5,000 per year, and 1.4 million around £100, out of a total population of 20 million; a farm labourer might earn £20, and women workers half as much as men. In its distribution of wealth and income, Victorian England was probably comparable with Germany, but much less unequal than Russia and America, where both new and inherited wealth reached unique heights: in 1900 the richest American had at least twelve times as much money as the richest Englishman.[97]

Living standards for most people rose markedly in the second half of the century. As seen in Chapter 10, this question was long a subject of contention among historians, and is now largely resolved. During the "Industrial Revolution" wages stagnated—or held steady—despite the booming population, and however low by later standards were higher than in any other country. From mid-century real wages rose, and from 1873 rose sharply, boosted by a fall in food prices caused by cheap imports. The highest wages were in coal mining, factory industries and especially engineering. Competition for workers forced up all wages in mining and industrial regions. But in rural areas with no industry, and in towns with only traditional semi-skilled industries, wages lagged. Living standards were improved by a fall in the birth rate, meaning fewer hungry mouths to feed. People were able to consume more—literally, notably by eating more meat, and by acquiring many more goods, most obviously household furnishings and clothes. However, the steepest single increase in spending was on tobacco, especially fashionable cigarettes (supposedly copied from French soldiers in the Crimea). The mechanically produced Wills Woodbines at 1d for five were the workers' staple from the 1880s to the 1960s. Yet consumption of alcohol, as noted earlier, fell sharply from a peak in the mid-1870s. Rising wages (by about 50 percent, 1850–85) and improving living standards reduced vulnerability to disease, especially among babies and children. Less tangibly, people "consumed" more education, as children went to school, and belatedly, by the turn of the twentieth century, England had "something which could be called an educational system,"[98] with everyone having some degree of formal schooling.

The home (often said at the time to be an untranslatable English concept) became increasingly the focus of urban family life for all classes. As the journal *The Builder* put it in 1856: "The Londoner, when he has done his day's work, escapes the noise and crowds and impure air [with] his family removed from the immediate neighbourhood of casinos, dancing salons and hells upon earth which I will not name."[99] People spent more money on domestic comforts, including the ubiquitous parlour or front room, kept for special occasions. Living in an independent family house was a "chain which ran from the meanest cottage . . . to the grandest country mansion"[100]—a world of anxious gentility brilliantly and perhaps affectionately satirized in Mr. Pooter, proud master of The Laurels, Brickfield Terrace, Holloway: "I like to be at home. What's the good of a home if you are never in it? . . . There is always something to be done: a tin-tack here, a Venetian blind to put straight, a fan to nail up or part of a carpet to nail down."[101]

The industrial towns, which when Disraeli wrote *Sybil* seemed to be seething in anarchy, gave rise to their own social institutions. In Lancashire textile towns, workers at the same mill often played together, prayed together, sang in choral societies together, went on holiday together, and voted together—with employees of Anglican mill-owners tending to vote Tory, those of Dissenters Liberal.[102] Mining and other industries gave rise to similar sociability, of which brass bands are perhaps the most famous examples. Works outings were common well into the twentieth century. One given in the 1880s by Bass, the Burton brewers, involved nine special trains to Skegness. The Cadbury brothers gave enormous tea parties (no beer—they were Quakers) at their mansions near their Birmingham factory. Later, in the 1890s, came sports grounds and works teams. All this might be encouraged and subsidized by employers, but was not necessary controlled by them.

Neighbourhood clubs gave a fragile measure of economic security, collecting money for sick and unemployed members, for burial expenses, clothes, medicine, even Christmas—still common in the 1950s. They were often based in the local pub—the working man's labour exchange, trade union headquarters and social-security office—and some grew into permanent "friendly societies." Charities, extensive in the eighteenth century, greatly expanded: Charles Dickens described Victorian charity as "unexampled in the history of the earth." Some charities inculcated discipline: Octavia Hill's model dwellings for the poor, for example, begun in the 1860s, insisted on regular payment of rent and supervision of poor families by volunteer "lady collectors." Autonomous organizations multiplied, and some became major economic institutions—cooperative societies, savings banks and friendly societies, such as the Independent Order of Oddfellows or the Ancient Order of Foresters. These had their own social rituals, and were locally run, creating fraternity and solidarity. By 1901, friendly societies alone had 5.47 million members—more than half of adult men—and provided sickness benefits to about 40 percent of the adult male population. Trade unions also acted as friendly societies, collecting welfare funds for sick and elderly members. Medical insurance developed to cover most of the population. Half of all general practitioners were by this time contracted to insurance schemes to provide treatment for fixed fees, to the annoyance of the medical establishment. Voluntary hospitals, financed by donations, subscriptions and public collections, treated enormous numbers of outpatients, and made no charge to the needy.

Trade unions, which came to occupy a special role in English life, were part of this process of social organization, and they transformed work relations. Although "combination" by workers had been made legal in the 1820s, the Master and Servant Acts (1823 and 1867) continued until the 1870s to punish several thousand workers per year with fines or imprisonment for breaking contracts. Trade union organizers occasionally used violence against unpopular employers and blacklegs, even murder and blowing up a house in Sheffield in the 1860s. The situation was transformed by the Employers and Workmen Act (1875), a cross-party measure drafted by Liberals and enacted by Conservatives. Soon, unionization was regarded as a right, an aspect of social justice, and a pillar of industrial peace despite notorious exceptions, such as the London dock strike of 1912, in which both sides used organized violence. This contrasted with the relatively unfavourable legal circumstances for labour organizations prevailing in France, Germany and the United States, where strikes were violently combated. At the end of the century, the English workforce was about four times more unionized than the American, nearly one in five being fully paid-up members, compared with fewer than one in twenty.[103] The attitude of English unions was peaceful and yet adversarial towards employers, and the outcome was often a stalemate in which unions in effect controlled the workforce and working practices, and defended the interests of their members, including against other workers. This system was highly distinctive, and continued well beyond the Second World War. By all these means, the Victorian working class, at least its skilled and organized elements, established a recognized and independent place in the social order.[104] This relatively harmonious acceptance and institutionalization of class differences became a characteristic of England, and perhaps one reason for the common perception of it as "class-ridden."

Workers steadily obtained more leisure. Traditional local "wakes" (seasonal holidays, often with fairs) were grudgingly accepted by employers and local authorities. As early as the 1820s and 1830s East End artisans were going on trips to Gravesend and Margate, and in the 1840s Lancashire cotton workers took cheap excursion trains to Blackpool. Official Bank Holidays were introduced in 1871. Working hours fell steadily after 1850, establishing the five-and-a-half-day "English week" (as it was enviously known abroad). Some amusements were raucously indulged in by both the upper and the lower classes, who ignored or mocked disapproving do-gooders, and defended a measure of disorder and even violence as expressions of English freedom and masculinity.[105] The patronage of the gentry, and their influence on legislation, was an important reason why middle-class moralists could not impose a puritanical ideology of leisure, and this helped to avoid class friction and facilitate the development of an independent popular leisure culture. A Home Secretary in the 1880s ordered that there should be no interference with fairs just because they "gave trouble to the police"; they gave "a popular amusement for poor people."[106]

Such amusement grew more orderly, however, due less to law and the disapproval of the respectable and more to commercial interests: fairground operators, publicans, seaside landladies, music hall proprietors and football clubs did not want drunkenness, vice or violence. Commercialization meant quieter, more regulated behaviour. But it also meant that as people paid for what they liked and enjoyed, they were protected from the imposition of middle-class values by the power of the working-class purse.[107]

Urban leisure activities often included the public playing out of class rituals, a carnivalesque enactment without inhibition or hostility which persists, for example, in dressing up for Ascot. Native and foreign observers have been fascinated by this, for it contrasted with societies in which social differences were tenser and where classes maintained greater distance. A French political exile, Jules Vallès, was shocked to see London workers in the 1870s cheering the Lord Mayor's Show and disgusted that they wore frock coats and top hats instead of workers' dress. The French artist Gustave Doré painted scenes of packed and improbably orderly crowds of all classes watching horse races or the Boat Race. Horse-racing was the oldest and most durable example of cross-class entertainment, celebrated in Frith's painting *Derby Day*. The German chancellor, Prince Bismarck, supposedly told Disraeli in the 1870s that horse-racing meant there was no danger of revolution in England. Spectacle, betting and drinking were central to the fun. Boxing was equally disreputable, mercenary and popular with both nobs and plebs—George IV had eight boxing champions attending his coronation as pages. Jack Gully, a champion prizefighter, became an MP in 1832 and died a wealthy man in 1863, at the height of the Victorian age. Yet even boxing, considered a hallmark of English masculinity, began in the 1830s to be subject to prosecution imposing severe punishment if fighters died. The Queensberry Rules (1867) brought about a compromise, making the sport safer. Cricket and rowing similarly combined elite and popular enjoyment, though eventually the Oxford and Cambridge Boat Race and the Henley Regatta sidelined professional working-class rowers. The attractions of fox-hunting, which greatly expanded over the nineteenth century, brought gentry, farmers and increasingly the middle classes together, and there were also a few working-class packs; it was moreover the only sport in which some women participated on the same level as men. Leisure activities highlight an important aspect of Victorian society: different classes shared some pastimes, but often enjoyed them side by side in different stands or enclosures, without mingling, but without notable hostility.

Class and regional distinctions and changes were reflected in accent, long an English fascination (see Chaucer, for example) and a means of mutual identification. As early as 1589, would-be poets were advised not to use "any speech used beyond the river of Trent," even though it was "the purer English Saxon," but rather to use "the usual speach of the Court, and that of London ... and the shires within xl miles, and not much above."[108] Samuel Johnson and James Boswell found it an absorbing topic of discussion, observing that men of "the highest rank" disagreed on the proper pronunciation of simple words, and David Garrick teased Johnson for retaining "provincial sounds" from his native Staffordshire.[109] As Shaw put it in 1912, "It is impossible for an Englishman to open his mouth without making some other Englishman despise him."[110] But some gentlemen ignored metropolitan fashion well into the nineteenth century. Disraeli commented that the Earl of Derby, a landowner of ancient lineage and Tory Prime Minister, used a "Lancashire patois," and a Liberal MP noted Gladstone's "Lancashire twang"—proof of the continuing prestige of rural and provincial society.[111] But the Victorians developed a middle-class version of London speech, in 1869 dubbed Received Pronunciation, "the educated pronunciation of the metropolis, of the court, of the pulpit and the bar"—one sign among many of the rising status of the urban and especially the London professional elite. Although there was disagreement about what was in fact correct (the long *a* in *bath*, *laugh*, etc., was criticized as "drawling"), a largely standardized form spread through the public schools and their imitators.[112] What seems characteristic of England—still in the twenty-first century—is the coexistence of RP with a rich variety of ancient and modern regional accents in a complex and changing pattern of identity and status. This might be contrasted on one hand with France, where the Parisian equivalent of RP is so dominant as to have eliminated or marginalized most regional accents, and on the other with Germany, a country with no metropolis, and where no speech pattern predominates.

Rural society, in contrast with that of the towns, was on the verge of decline. Since the completion of enclosure between c.1720 and 1820, when most remaining common land was divided up, rural society and the agricultural system had been based on large-scale land ownership, tenant farming and wage labour. By around 1850 some 7,000 people and institutions—yeomen-farmers, squires, peers, Oxbridge colleges, the Church, the Crown—owned 80 percent of the United Kingdom. Some

360 estates of over 10,000 acres held 25 percent of the land of England. Over 200,000 tenants renting relatively large farms employed over 1.5 million people, nearly half of them women, and perhaps a third of the population was directly or indirectly dependent on agriculture for a livelihood.[113] Defenders lauded the system as an admirable balance of social stability and economic efficiency; its critics condemned it as an oppressive relic of the Norman Conquest—a view occasionally echoed today. The repeal of the Corn Laws had not brought the predicted apocalypse: the agricultural workforce peaked in the 1850s, and the acreage of wheat in 1869. "High Farming"—big farms, fertilizer, artificial feed, machinery and investment—kept producing large quantities of wheat, meat and dairy products for the booming urban population. But, once railways and steamships with efficient double-expansion engines carried wheat cheaply from the plains of North America after the Civil War ended in 1865, wheat prices fell steeply and steadily. Further mountains of grain arrived from Russia and India in the 1880s, from Argentina in the 1890s, and from Canada and Australia in the 1900s. The next step was refrigeration: the SS *Strathleven* arrived in London in 1880 with forty tons of frozen Australian beef and mutton, which was sold at Smithfield at 5½d a pound. Soon, chilled meat and butter flowed from Argentina, Australia and New Zealand: imports increased from 4 percent of consumption in the 1850s to over 40 percent in the 1900s. Cheaper food improved workers' living standards, as the Anti-Corn Law League had intended. Meat consumption increased from an average of 87.3 lb per year in the 1850s to 126.9 lb in the 1900s.[114] The availability of cheap and tasty processed food for a mass market (fish and chips are said to have been invented in Oldham in the 1860s)[115] is certainly part of the explanation for the characteristic quantity and quality of English popular cuisine.

These market forces, producing what was known at the time as the "Great Depression" because of their effect on agricultural prices across Europe, transformed the countryside. Farmers shifted from cereals to milk, meat, fruit and vegetables. They also increased mechanization: a typical farmer employed five or six people in 1851, but in 1901 only two or three. Rural England lost nearly 4 million people between 1851 and 1911, with 1.6 million moving to London and the industrial towns, 568,000 to coal-mining districts, and 1.5 million emigrating. Similar changes affected much of western Europe, but on a smaller scale, as import tariffs gave some protection to agriculture in France and Germany. Had similar measures been adopted in England, the agricultural sector might have been 20 percent bigger in 1913. The epoch-making decision taken in 1846 was only briefly and unwillingly reversed in the heyday of

new "Corn Laws," the 1962 European Common Agricultural Policy, to
which Britain acceded in 1973. The proportion in total consumption of
home-grown temperate produce (everything from oats to strawberries),
which was over 90 percent in the 1830s, had fallen to 40 percent by 1914;
the CAP put it back to nearly 90 percent in the 1980s, whence it has
again fallen due to CAP cuts pressed above all by British governments
following the original logic of Sir Robert Peel.[116]

Hard-headed economic historians regard cheap food and the shift away
from agriculture as economically beneficial. But it was also traumatic.
Common land, which had helped the rural poor to make ends meet, and
on which complex social relations were based, gradually divided and
fenced from the late Middle Ages onwards, had almost disappeared by the
early nineteenth century, and this left long and resentful memories of dispossession and injustice.[117] By the nineteenth century rural workers who
had not left agriculture were dependent on wages, and the downward
pressure on agricultural prices led to the "revolt of the field" in 1872–73—
an agricultural labourers' trade union movement led by Joseph Arch
(see p. 269). This alarmed landowners, but it soon dwindled, despite the
patronage of the radical-chic Countess of Warwick, sometime mistress of
the Prince of Wales. Farm workers who kept their jobs finally did earn
higher wages as their numbers dwindled. The landlords took the strain:
between 1870 and 1900 rents fell by a third and land values halved. "What
an infernal bore is landed property," expostulated the Lincolnshire peer
Lord Monson, "no certain income can be reckoned on."[118] From a strictly
economic viewpoint, landowners tried too hard to keep the system afloat,
using earnings from urban rents and business to subsidize their estates,
such was the prestige of land and the pull of old-fashioned paternalism. The
Earl of Derby, a magnate and leading Tory politician, in 1881 listed the
landowner's rewards as political influence, social importance and enjoyment. Four years later writing in his diary on "the four hundredth anniversary of Bosworth—the foundation of our family greatness," he reflected
that they still enjoyed political prominence and wealth, but wondered:
"Will either last?"[119] Large quantities of land and London mansions were
being sold off, if buyers could be found: the Duke of Marlborough commented in 1885 that "were there any effective demand . . . half the land of
England would be in the market tomorrow."[120] Pre-1914 governments still
contained many landed ministers, but the proportion was falling, as it was
in the civil service and the professions, in which gentlemanly amateurism
was no longer enough in an age of experts.[121] Ironically, a major ideological and political campaign against landlords began just as their fortunes
declined, culminating in a political and fiscal attack from the Liberal chan-

cellor, David Lloyd George, in the 1900s. The last newly created peer to live mainly on rental income was Lord Hesketh in 1935.[122] Despite a sentimental vogue for rural England there was no political will to protect the rural economy from cheap imported food, as elsewhere in Europe. Economically, Coronation Street conquered Ambridge.

Sentiment was another matter. As agriculture lost its economic centrality, the "countryside" (a nineteenth-century term) inspired a new devotion as the true essence of England. A range of organizations emerged to protect it and its culture, among them the Commons Preservation Society (1863), the English Dialect Society (1872), the Society for the Preservation of Ancient Buildings (1877), the Folklore Society (1878), the Lake District Defence Society (1883), the Society for the Protection of Birds (1889), the National Trust for Places of Historic Interest or Natural Beauty (1894), the Folk Song Society (1898) and the English Folk Dance Society (1911). The National Trust Act of 1907 allowed the Trust to declare land inalienable.[123] The Duke of Westminster perceptively remarked to Octavia Hill at its foundation that the Trust was going to be "a very big thing": now it is the largest heritage organization in the world, with nearly 4 million members, hundreds of miles of coastline, 4,000 historic buildings, and 235 gardens or parks.[124] Radicals who campaigned for the preservation of remaining common land from enclosure now thought of it as a weekend amenity for town dwellers, not a means for the rural poor to make a living—indeed, the two sometimes came into conflict.[125]

Smoky towns, it was hoped, could be humanized by the creation of parks, gardens and allotments—one of the most striking aspects of the Victorian town, copied across the world. New suburban districts of large and small villas with gardens were a peculiarly English creation intended to combine rural charm with urban amenity.[126] The ideal was democratized as from 1901 to 1911 the London suburbs absorbed 700,000 new people.[127] Gardening became a popular passion in all classes. Suburbia had several ancestors: the "model villages" created by aesthetically motivated landowners in the eighteenth century; the planned urban estates of Regency London; and communities for workers pioneered by Robert Owen, Titus Salt, and later Hartley's jam (Aintree in 1888), Lever Brothers (Port Sunlight), and Cadbury's (Bourneville) in the 1890s. The "garden suburb" was the brainchild of Ebenezer Howard, who founded the Garden Cities Association in 1899.[128] The aim was a "town-country," pioneered in Letchworth (1903), followed by Hampstead Garden Suburb (1907) and Welwyn Garden City (1920). All had in common vernacular architecture, influenced by William Morris's traditionalist "arts and crafts" movement, with village halls, low-density housing and greenery. "The houses themselves, among their trees and boscage, their gardens and greens, are a stirring picture of what our cities may be one day."[129]

All over Europe intellectuals and artists sought authenticity and the roots of national identity in rural life and culture, appropriated, adapted and sometimes invented. The interest now shown in rural England by middle-class townspeople of progressive bent had considerable cultural impact.[130] Examples are the novels of Thomas Hardy and *A Shropshire Lad* (1896), the hugely successful slim volume of morbidly nostalgic poetry by a Cambridge Classics don, A. E. Housman, evoking a "land of lost content." Folk music collectors, led by the indefatigable enthusiast Cecil Sharp, haunted pubs, village gatherings and workhouses. The Australian Percy Grainger went collecting with a phonograph in company with Lady Elcho, H. G. Wells, the society painter John Singer Sargent and the Tory politician A. J. Balfour in the latter's car. The fading tradition of Morris dancing revived with the foundation of the English Folk Dance Society in 1911. The thirst for authenticity had limits, however. "Realist" paintings of farm workers by George Clausen in the 1880s provoked sometimes rabid hostility: "Mr. Clausen has seen nothing but the sordid and the mean, and his execution . . . is as sordid and mean as his vision." Folk song collectors sometimes found that "the coarseness of the original words obliged me to re-write the song," and Grainger found Lincolnshire folk "nice people, big hearted and amusing, but (naturally) dirty handed and filthy."[131] Still, folk influence rejuvenated English music after two centuries of mediocrity. "Pastoral" tones inflected the music of Frederick Delius, Edward Elgar, George Butterworth, Gustav Holst, Ralph Vaughan Williams and later Benjamin Britten.

Yet English manifestations of "folk culture" were pallid compared with the ebullient and assertive popular nationalism of Hungarian, Czech, Finnish, and Russian art and music. Folk music and dancing remained a fad, the butt of jokes, an imposition on unwilling schoolchildren: prancing about in fancy dress never attained patriotic status. England (like France and Germany) had long had a cultural life that was both commercial and cosmopolitan, and it saw itself as a world culture. The English had no urgent need to discover their roots or throw off foreign influences, and were happy to buy in the good and the fashionable wherever it came from: those who wanted to hear "folk" music could listen to Dvořák (more popular in England than anywhere outside his native Moravia) or a generation later to American jazz, which deflated the English folk-music revival. Elgar, whose music is fancifully associated with the Malvern Hills, wrote in a mixture of European, "folk" and modern urban styles, such as the "Pomp and Circumstance" marches, the *Cockaigne Overture* (evoking London) and his symphonies.[132] Similarly, no poet straining to preserve rural dialects could rival the popularity of Kipling's cockney.

Influential commentators have seen attachment to a rural vision of England as a damaging rejection of industrial or capitalist values. For some people it definitely was a rejection, most famously for John Ruskin and William Morris. Stubborn emotional attachment to an idealized gentlemanly and rural culture and contempt for modernity was later diagnosed as the cause of long-term economic decline, as we shall see in Chapter 19. Worries about industrial decline appeared as early as the Great Exhibition itself. It became a source of alarm with the appearance of cheap ("Jerry-built") German manufactures in the 1880s, articulated in the best-selling book *Made in Germany* (1896). Politicians and leader-writers spoke of "defeat" by a German industrial "invasion," and of the "conquest" by America of British export "outposts."[133]

Was the economy really beginning a long decline? There were indeed some weaknesses. It was deeply engaged in industries, such as textiles, that were no longer in the forefront of technology. Hence it was weaker by 1900 than Germany, America or France in certain new industries—chemicals, electricity, aluminium, cars. So it is easy to see why there was concern. But belief in a general decline was an alarmist illusion. Although Germany and America had inherent advantages, such as larger domestic markets and tariff protection, Britain was still the world's biggest exporter of goods in the early 1900s—far ahead of Germany and the United States. The pre–First World War period saw buoyant production, exports and overseas earnings, through investments and through insurance and shipping, of which Britain maintained the overwhelming dominance established in the eighteenth century, controlling a third of total world tonnage. The main change in the English economy was modernization through a growing service sector, particularly financial services, always the high-productivity sector in the UK economy.[134] The idea that conservative English cultural values were holding the economy back thus has no substance. Moreover, there is no evidence of significant hostility between "old" and "new" elites, or of cultural dominance by snobbish anti-industrial or anti-scientific attitudes even in traditional institutions. Oxford and Cambridge started practical teaching of the sciences in mid-century, and pioneering work in nuclear physics was done in Cambridge at the Cavendish Laboratory, endowed in 1874 by one of England's grandest aristocratic families. By the last decades of the century, scientific education in English schools and universities had greatly expanded.[135] The English apprenticeship system continued to produce skilled workers. Studies have even suggested that a public-school education—"leadership qualities, a high level of self confidence, and connections"—was a business asset. Besides, most German businessmen received a classical, not a technical, education. In productivity England remained ahead even of Germany in most areas, and its overall skill level was slightly higher than in Germany or America.[136] The Victorian taste for the past and for preserving the countryside was not a barrier to change. It may well have served to make change acceptable by reassuring an increasingly urban society that its rural heritage was being preserved.

## THE GREASY POLE: POWER, PARLIAMENT AND PARTIES

> I often think it's comical
> That nature always does contrive
> That every boy and every gal
> That's born into this world alive
> Is either a little Liberal
> Or else a little Conservative.
>
> W. S. Gilbert, *Iolanthe* (1882)

The Victorians made politics into something we still recognize and inhabit, like the new Palace of Westminster itself: a system centred on what today is called "the Westminster village," on a non-partisan civil service, on disciplined government and opposition parties, and on winning elections by national bargaining between a professional political elite and a country whose diverse political loyalties are old, deep and instinctive. Victorian too was the origin of what can plausibly be described as democracy, albeit a male one. Westminster ceased to be simply the place where the powerful met and became the place where the powerful were made.

The psychology of politics changed around the years of the Great Exhibition: the "state" (still a slightly awkward word in England) and those who ran it became again generally trusted, and nearly a century of virulent radical attack on political institutions subsided. Victory in 1815 had begun a continuous period of retrenchment, dismantling what critics called "Old Corruption," and historians more prosaically term the "fiscal-military state." There had been a string of reforms, begun under Pitt in the 1780s and speeded up under Whigs and Peelites in the 1830s and 1840s: the Great Reform Act, abolition of slavery, reform of the Poor Law, reform of municipal government, and cuts in spending on defence, the Foreign

Office and the Crown. The 1834 Commons select committee on sinecures could not find any more to abolish, and in 1835 public spending reached its lowest point of the century. The 1846 repeal of the Corn Laws, low taxes and the decline of patronage meant that the "Old Corruption" rhetoric lost its potency.[137] Overall taxation was stable at just over 10 percent of national income (under a third of its level today). This was comparable with levels in Scandinavia and, despite the costs of empire, lower than in the Continental Great Powers. Nevertheless, because of the larger British economy, the sums raised in revenue were greater—around 10 percent more than in France, the next most powerful state.[138] The middle classes paid more, and non-voters, who had little say in government, paid little of its cost. Gladstone's Budget of April 1853 set the rules of this new era: it slashed import tariffs, announced a phased abolition of income tax, promised to be, in his own words, "cheese-paring" with taxpayers' money, and avoided redistributing wealth to any section of society. This became the Victorian consensus, and the budget speech, on the Gladstone model, became political theatre, with later chancellors using Gladstone's battered dispatch box.

In 1853–54 Gladstone, as chancellor, commissioned the Tory Sir Stafford Northcote and the Whig Sir Charles Trevelyan (who had experience of imperial administration) to report on how to eliminate patronage in the civil service in favour of open competition and merit—what Gladstone envisaged as rule by virtue. Since the late eighteenth century, under the influence of Pitt and the stresses of the wars against France, the civil service had become increasingly efficient and accountable (see p. 364). However, until the 1850s, and indeed for some time afterwards, there was no clear line between politics and administration, and appointments had often been based (as in many countries) on personal and family relationships and political patronage. A Civil Service Commission (1855) was created to oversee recruitment, and in 1870 an Order in Council required this to be by competitive examination. Robert Lowe, chancellor in Gladstone's government from 1868 to 1873, promoted this to create a civil service immune from popular and party pressure—the opposite of a democratic measure.[139] These reforms founded a system which, whatever its foibles, has remained largely disinterested and honest, a barrier against the scourge of corruption and an obstacle to favouritism. Even the lowest grades were banned from party politics.

The new civil service remained small: the Treasury, for example, had only ninety-six officials and the Foreign Office eighty-five—smaller than the press office at the Department of Work and Pensions today. An estimate for the whole United Kingdom in the 1860s arrived at 1,173 civil servants at "professional" grade, 1,801 at "superior" grade and about 10,000 general clerks, with salaries varying from around £800 at the top level to £100 at the bottom—about half as much again as a skilled worker.[140] Whether ministers controlled civil servants or vice-versa remains a perennial debate. As early as the 1850s the Prime Minister, Lord Derby, reassured the deeply non-economic Disraeli that he could easily be Chancellor of the Exchequer because "they give you the figures."[141]

In time state service was dominated (like the Church) by public-school-educated Oxbridge graduates. These two universities were mildly shaken up from the 1850s by a combination of royal commissions, legislation and internal reform, abolishing the Anglican monopoly and gingerly modernizing organization and teaching, including by introducing Modern History as a training in practical politics.[142] Balliol College, Oxford, under its Master, Benjamin Jowett (elected 1870), and his successors, consciously set out to train the nation's elite in the values of the civilized Christian gentleman, "to inoculate the world with Balliol," in Jowett's words. By 1914 four of Britain's ten ambassadors were Balliol men.[143] Senior officials were expected to be, and behave as, gentlemen, ideally with "the moral & physical training of the best public schools," believed to confer vigour and character that "young men of the middle and lower classes, indefatigable workers in grammar school" were unlikely to possess. This seemed particularly evident in elite departments such as the Foreign and Colonial Services: as the Parliamentary Under-Secretary for Foreign Affairs put it in 1890, "Less cram & book learning: and more saddle and *savoir faire* would serve the State better."[144] But book learning was taking over, even in the Foreign Office.[145]

This creation of a "neutral" state and a non-political and less patronage-based civil service drew much of the venom from politics, and there was never again the widespread anger and alienation that produced tension and even sporadic violence from the 1760s to the 1840s. The Crown, steadily deprived since George III of an active political role, could become the symbol and apex of this new vision of government: independent of private interests, subject to politics but not itself political, and "above party." Walter Bagehot (editor of *The Economist*) termed this in his *English Constitution* (1867) the "dignified" as opposed to the "efficient" part of the constitution. The rights and duties of the monarch he defined as to be consulted, to encourage, and to warn.[146] The queen continued to influence foreign policy, and military and church appointments, which many felt party politicians should keep out of. Republicanism— part of the traditional attack on "Old Corruption"—reached an all-time peak in the 1860s due to the widowed queen's self-isolation and to the

Prince of Wales's sexual and gambling peccadilloes. As Gladstone regretfully expressed it, "in rude and general terms, the Queen is invisible, and the Prince of Wales is not respected."[147] But the Crown benefited from the generally growing legitimacy of state institutions. Hence the long-term decline of English republicanism, which could no longer complain of the power of royalty, but only of its cost, and occasionally of its behaviour.

The new Palace of Westminster was completed in 1867. It proclaimed tradition in its Perpendicular Gothic extravaganza and its huge historical murals of historical, religious and chivalric themes. Not all were impressed: the French novelist Prosper Mérimée found it "a frightful monstrosity; before this I had no idea of what could be accomplished with an utter want of taste and two millions sterling."[148] During the 1840s and 1850s a Royal Fine Arts Commission, presided over by the new Prince Consort, had set out to shape the national memory and create a school of monumental history painting such as existed in Germany and France, but not hitherto in England. It was not one of Albert's happier inspirations. He insisted on the German style, and although he was not allowed to import German artists, he preferred those trained in Germany, notably Daniel Maclise and William Dyce. The well-known history painter Benjamin Haydon committed suicide after failing to win a single commission. Albert wanted to emphasize the royal element in history, with queens and their faithful consorts prominent, with a stress on harmony. Most artists engaged went for Anglo-Saxon themes, partly for romantic and picturesque reasons. When the Whigs came to power in 1846, the content was nudged in a Whiggish direction, stressing parliamentary tradition and especially the struggle against the Stuarts—the Commons' corridor features Alice Lisle sheltering fugitives after Sedgemoor (see p. 259). Albert insisted on giving "justice to the heroic virtues displayed by both sides" in the Civil War.[149] The only post-1688 subjects were the huge *Death of Nelson* and the meeting of Wellington and Blücher after Waterloo—completed in the 1850s, when relations with France were strained. When they were finished in 1856, the *Quarterly Review* pronounced the whole enterprise "vulgar in taste, poor in invention, commonplace in treatment," no better than "the walls of a French café"; and the frescos soon began to deteriorate.[150] They have not provided any icons of national history.

During the thirty years the palace was being designed to embody tradition, the activities of its occupants were transformed: like Pugin's Big Ben, Parliament was a modern mechanism adorned with pinnacles and a finial. It was streamlined, disciplined, democratized and yet in some ways made more remote from the millions outside. Public petitions, an ancient practice, had multiplied to 30,000 a year by 1840 (120 times more than in

1800), becoming a paradise for cranks, and so debates on them were abolished. Ministers took control of business from backbenchers, and in the 1880s, in response to Irish obstruction, copied a French procedure dubbed "the guillotine" to cut debates short. Inquiries into matters of public concern and preparation of legislation were transferred to royal commissions or officials. The House thus became more party political— less absorbed by local affairs and grass-roots petitions, and more with national issues. MPs, especially those from the new urban constituencies, were seized, said one, with "a rage for speaking," and adopted a more emphatic "preaching" style than the composed classical oratory of the past. This verbosity further increased the need for procedural control by governments.[151] The House of Lords, despite its surrender over the Great Reform Act, retained its powers. Few members attended regularly, but many did so for great political and constitutional issues, such as Catholic emancipation, the Corn Laws, Irish home rule and electoral reform. The Lords' legal functions as the supreme court were exercised from the 1840s by the "law lords" (judges who were peers), a small and elderly group who for practical reasons were supplemented from the 1850s by specially appointed judges, the first non-hereditary "life peers," a new species that in the twentieth century would transform the Upper House.[152]

Who were these Victorian politicians? They were all rich. There was a solid contingent of lawyers, as in every parliament in the world. But the largest group were landowners, many the sons of peers: Liberal MPs during the 1860s and 1870s included 198 large landowners (40 percent of the party), among them Lord F. C. Cavendish, the Hon. G. H. Cavendish, the Hon. W. G. Cavendish, Earl Grosvenor, Lord Richard Grosvenor, Lord Robert Grosvenor, Lord A. H. Paget, Lord C. E. Paget and so on. They often started young, and some soon attained junior office: they were the equivalent of the young professional politicians of today produced by think-tanks and adopted in safe seats, and like them they did much of the hard work—hence the high proportion of scions of the nobility in governments of both parties at least until the First World War. Their prominence was decreasingly the result of old-fashioned economic and social dominance. It could happen as late as the 1868 elections that an East Anglian landowner, Edward Fellowes (later Lord de Ramsey), would ride ceremoniously to the hustings accompanied by his 150 mounted tenants, who waited quietly in a semicircle while he was returned unopposed.[153] But rather than crude intimidation this was ritual acquiescence in political representation by a prestigious elite who enjoyed a tolerably favourable image throughout most of the nineteenth century[154]—and who could pay their own expenses. Many elections were uncontested because the outcome was too one-sided to justify an expensive contest. It was not easy to find men willing to spend large sums of their own money to fund election campaigns, cultivate constituencies, and sit in Parliament—a position, thought Lord Willoughby de Broke, that ranked in county society between the Colonel of the Yeomanry and the Dean of the Cathedral, but well below the Master of Foxhounds.[155] Often a sense of religious obligation, family tradition and noblesse oblige combined to impress his public duty on some less-than-willing victim, who would resign himself to electioneering— as Lord Cranborne (later Prime Minister) put it, to "screwed-up smiles and laboured courtesy, the mock geniality, the hearty shake of the filthy hand, the chuckling reply that must be made to the coarse joke."[156]

The Liberal Party, as it was officially called from the 1860s, contained, in addition to landowning "Whig" notables and a sprinkling of Radicals, a large minority of businessmen (about 30 percent in the 1860s, of whom a fifth have been described as "militant"), who were its most effervescent feature. They included the religious Dissenters, the moral crusaders and the social reformers. Their energy, money and popular influence made the great employers far more formidable than the old-style Radicals, and they were willing to get to grips with public affairs to a remarkable degree. Moreover, this political role seemed perfectly natural both to themselves and to their employees.[157] In the small West Country textile town of Westbury, both party candidates in the 1860s and 1870s, Laverton and Phipps, were mill-owners—the only large employers in the town—who nursed a keen reciprocal hatred. Some industrialists occupied a position in their urban constituencies as prominent as that of any landed magnate in the shires—a Liberal candidate for Oldham in 1868, John Platt, a Nonconformist, employed 7,000 people in the town. (He won.)[158]

The great statesmen often expressed impatience with, if not contempt for, their rank and file. Disraeli complained that his MPs "could not be got to attend to business while the hunting season lasted . . . they never read . . . they learnt nothing useful, and did not understand the ideas of their own time"[159]—admittedly, many of the ideas Disraeli considered modern were extremely odd. Some foreign observers were more impressed. The French philosopher Hippolyte Taine, visiting in the 1860s, saw "peers, MPs, landowners whose manners and faces are those of men used to authority and action . . . expressive, decisive . . . creating a feeling of respect."[160] Their party identities were strong, if unorganized. The Corn Law issue fractured the Tory Party for a time, but gut beliefs re-created a Whig-Tory divide, and most members defined themselves in party terms and voted accordingly. Only a dozen of the 654 MPs elected in 1852 did not adopt party labels at all, and those who really behaved as Indepen-

dents probably numbered under forty.[161] What were their gut beliefs? For
Tories, a lingering attachment to agricultural protectionism, and the
paternalist, hierarchical, Anglican society that lay behind it. For old-style
Whigs, "past historical reminiscences," according to one of them: memories of Fox, attachment to liberty and reform, and the aim of dismantling
the Tory *ancien régime*.[162] For the Radical and later Liberal tendency, dogmatic devotion to free trade, cheap government and Nonconformity. But
parties needed brains as well as guts, for it was far from inevitable that the
ancient Whig and Tory factions would evolve into mass electoral forces.
Disraeli laboured to find a new purpose for Conservatism, as protectionism was "not only dead, but damned," and the party survived and began
to gather new support from the 1870s. Whigs, Radicals and Dissenters
too had to go beyond ancestral pieties. Espousing progressive causes, and
with a solid bloc of Nonconformist activists, at first they succeeded far
better, attracting and organizing the new and aspiring urban electorate to
become a broad national Liberal Party. During the 1850s and 1860s they
formed the natural party of government, presiding over the "high Victorian" age.

The rejuvenation of the old parties is rightly associated with two
professional politicians, Benjamin Disraeli (from 1876 Earl of Beaconsfield) and William Ewart Gladstone (always "Mr. Gladstone"), both
highly unusual men to remake traditional parties, indeed highly unusual
men by any standards. In some ways both were characteristically but
differently "Victorian"—Gladstone in his agonized and introspective
religiosity, Disraeli in his romantic devotion to aristocratic leadership
and grandiose patriotism. For this very reason both inspired more than
usual animosity, and they disliked each other intensely. In other ways they
were unusual, even eccentric. Both had chronic money problems and
resorted to financial expedients that today would seem scandalous. Disraeli (1804–81) was by birth a middle-class Jew, a nominal Anglican with
no real religious belief, a dandified bohemian intellectual who admired
Byron and Napoleon, a romantic philanderer, an early supporter of votes
for women, and a successful writer ("when I want to read a novel I write
one"). Yet he became leader of the party of Church, land and tradition.
Gladstone (1809–98) was a High Church Anglican of deeply conservative
instincts who became the personification of the "Nonconformist conscience" and democratic radicalism. Other important Whig and Tory
prime ministers, much more typical of the political class, have left far
less trace: Lords Grey, Russell, Aberdeen, Derby, even Palmerston and
Salisbury.

Disraeli, the main talent in the Commons of a party whose natural

leaders were in the Lords, by skill, luck, masterly inactivity, waspish oratory and propaganda (some of it posthumously attributing to him
far-sighted visions he never had) managed to give the Tory party a more
or less coherent Conservative creed as the non-reactionary promoter of
national cohesion, defending Burkean traditional influences against ideological abstractions, unwanted interference and democratic enthusiasm.[163]
Abroad, Conservatism would be the exponent of the nation's will and
character, ready to use its power to play a leading and responsible world
role. Disraeli and the queen agreed to proclaim her "Empress of India" in
1877, a controversial innovation which critics dubbed "imperialism." The
climax of his world policy came in 1876–78 (see pp. 578–79), when he
warned the Russians off Constantinople—an event largely remembered
for a popular song ("We don't want to fight, but by jingo if we do") and
the new notion of "jingoism." Gladstone and the Liberals demonized
Disraeli—"Dizzy"—as an irresponsible and irreligious charlatan bereft of
ideas and principles, a view coloured by anti-Semitism. But "that Jew," as
Mrs. Gladstone called him, was neither an unprincipled opportunist nor
a jingoistic imperialist. He rather resembled one of the improbable characters from his own novels, inspired by English history and noblesse
oblige to re-create an undivided nation—"Society has a soul as well as a
body." But he was often contemptuous of the shortcomings of the political
elite in practice. This included an ambivalent attitude to the queen, which
combined courtly flattery and private exasperation: he told Derby that
she was excessively demanding and sometimes "very mad." He acquired
the trappings of a country gentleman, but liked rural life in small doses.
He was fascinated by the arcane wisdom of Judaism, believing himself
destined to wield British power, "to sway the race that sways the world"
in an epic global chess game for world civilization against the forces of
revolution, nationalism, militarism and pan-Slav imperialism.[164]

Disraeli was an old-fashioned politician at home (though he advocated
votes for women), intent on parliamentary manoeuvres, rarely involved in
public campaigning, and inattentive to details of policy. Most of his career
was in opposition. He briefly became Prime Minister at the age of
sixty-four in 1868, when the Earl of Derby resigned due to gout, and
again after an election victory in 1874, when his ministers promoted a
series of important social reforms. His election defeat in 1880—mainly a
consequence of the agricultural depression—was followed shortly after
by his death in April 1881. He declined a deathbed visit from Victoria,
who genuinely admired him—"She would only ask me to take a message
to Albert."[165] He became posthumously a Tory icon, inspirer of the Primrose League, the first mass party organization in our history, and one in

which women were prominent. He was hailed, rather fancifully, as the inventor of Tory democracy from his "Young England" days, and became remarkably popular, as shown in affectionate music hall songs: he had, said *The Times*, discerned "the Conservative working man, as the sculptor perceives the angel prisoned in the block of marble." He was also by some way the wittiest Prime Minister in our history, with only Churchill comparable. (Why is it that the only memorable, let alone amusing, remarks made by prime ministers are all from Tories?)

Gladstone was a perfect foil: a different species of Victorian who featured thinly disguised as "Joseph Toplady Falconet," a sanctimonious and scheming villain in one of Disraeli's novels: "essentially a prig, and among prigs there is a freemasonry that never fails. All the prigs spoke of him as the coming man."[166] Scion of a wealthy Liverpool-Scottish mercantile and slave-owning family, Gladstone was far more an Establishment figure than the bohemian Disraeli, making an early reputation for intellectual brilliance and unusual piety at Eton and Oxford, where he was president of the new Union and, like his mentor Peel, took a rare double first. He was marked out as a Tory defender of the Established Church as "a conscience, in the state." The free-trade issue moved him towards what would become the Liberal Party, which he came to dominate while never being fully part of it—one thing he shared with Disraeli was a cavalier attitude to party organization. Christianity was his emotional core, and like many Liberals he saw economic and political freedom as generators of moral behaviour. Unlike the languid Disraeli, he was one of those driven nineteenth-century monsters of energy:[167] in politics for over sixty years and still prime minster in his eighties; chopping down trees for relief in a perfect symbol of radicalism—"A wild man will go at trees" was Lewis Carroll's anagram of his name. (Disraeli loved planting them, tokens of permanence.) He scrutinized his daily conduct for seventy years in voluminous diaries he called "an account-book of the all-precious gift of Time."[168] A typical entry (9 Feb. 1876)—a relatively leisurely time when out of office—reads:

> Wrote to Mr. C. B. Waring—Mr. J. Rawlinson—Helen G.—Mr. G. Ellis. Worked on arranging papers &c. Saw Mrs. Dalton: heard sundry things X.*
> Saw Ld Granville—M. Neville—Mr. Gurdon—Mr. Knowles—Mr. Godley. Family party to see Rip Van Winkle: good scenery and acting, play most immoral *re* drink. Read Youatt on the Horse—M. Harvey on Irish Finance.[169]

Intellectually ravenous ("He reads as other men breathe," said one acquaintance), he recorded reading over 20,000 books, including Homer's

---

* Mrs. Dalton was a prostitute; X meant "rescue work."

*Iliad* thirty-six times; he wrote reviews, pamphlets and major works on classics, theology, contemporary literature and politics; he was involved with universities, charities and the arts; he knew several languages, speaking in French from the top of the Eiffel Tower on the centenary of the revolution, and once in Corfu in classical Greek, which unfortunately none of his audience could understand. He was liable to embark suddenly on one-man political crusades ("inebriated by the exuberance of his own verbosity," said Disraeli), and obsessively "rescued" prostitutes and whipped himself to exorcize the temptations they aroused.[170] In short, he was the most wide-ranging, intelligent, unpredictable, dynamic and psychologically odd of our great modern politicians, a group lacking neither neuroses nor abilities—"a *considerable* screw loose somewhere," commented a Whig lady after one intense conversation.[171] His feverish moral temperature rallied the Nonconformist masses: one Middlesborough Baptist congregation hailed him as "a prophet of the most high God." This was no bar to political scheming: as the Radical MP Henry Labouchère commented, he played with an ace up his sleeve and considered that God had put it there. Religion made the conservative Gladstone a democrat when he discerned morality in the masses. His "Midlothian Campaigns" from 1879 to 1892 were the first mass election speeches ever made by a leading politician in Britain: "I have hammered with all my little might at the fabric of the present Tory power . . . the triumph grows & grows: to God be the praise."[172] Many disliked the spectacle of a leading statesman, in Disraeli's words, "spouting all over the country like an irresponsible demagogue."[173] Huge audiences—sometimes several in a day—were riveted by his preaching style of oratory and what one later recalled as "a great human personality, under whose spell . . . I felt lifted into a holy region of politics, where Tories cannot corrupt."[174] This gave the German sociologist Max Weber his concept of "charismatic" leadership, as Gladstone reached a level of vehemence equalled in Europe only by the socialist left. The keynote of "Gladstonian Liberalism" was moral fervour, often moral outrage: targets included political interference in the Church of England; the wealth and privilege of the Church of Ireland; Bourbon and papal government in Italy; the Turks, who massacred Christian rebels in the 1875–76 "Bulgarian Horrors" (p. 579–80); Disraeli and the Tory government for complicity; and finally the Union with Ireland. Gladstone built up strong Scottish and Welsh connections, and his staunchest supporters were non-Anglicans, who gave him their prayers and votes: "Our three *corps d'armée* . . . have been Scotch presbyterians, English and Welsh nonconformists, and Irish Roman Catholics"—groups whose mutual antagonisms were balanced by their shared hostility to the Anglican Establishment. This helped to consolidate Conservatism as the defender of national institutions.[175]

What was Victorian politics about? Not the same things as ours. Parties claimed to have "principles," although they were never entirely sure what they were, and there were no election manifestos in the modern sense. It did not much matter who the nominal party leader was, as he was not the designated future Prime Minister. Mid-century consensus meant that the great twentieth-century issues—economic policy, public spending and wealth redistribution—did not exist as party matters. All agreed that the cost of government should be as low as possible, that individual self-reliance was morally beneficial, that generally the state should interfere as little as possible with people's choices, but that where necessary practical measures to promote welfare were desirable. So measures concerning housing, sanitation and welfare were usually non-partisan, originating with backbenchers or departmental ministers, and were enacted under both Conservative and Liberal governments. Foreign and imperial policies were periodically major issues, because of cost and morality, and because they were supposedly being made to serve the interests of the privileged—hence Radicals tended to assume that Britain was always in the wrong.[176] The most powerful issue—really, a constellation of issues—was religion, which involved education, taxation, symbols such as MPs' obligation to take an oath, the proper role of the state, social policies on prostitution and alcohol, the rights of women, and foreign-policy matters such as support for Italian nationalists against the Pope or Balkan Christians against the Turks. As the electorate widened, single-issue groups became more active in the Liberal Party, tending to make the Conservative Party the resort of those who wanted to be left alone.

Moral and social concerns were combined in all the most significant campaigns of the century. Perhaps the longest running and most political—it came to be identified with the Liberal Party—was temperance. Drink was seen as the core of the moral, social and economic problems of the lower orders—"a traffic in misery and death [which] weakens the power and impedes the progress of the people," declared a leading prohibitionist in 1856.[177] In the 1850s well-known reformers campaigned against "BEERHOUSES and low ALE-HOUSES ... the chief direct causes of crime." Other places of popular entertainment were targeted, such as "singing rooms": one, in Preston, which attracted large audiences, was attacked as a "manufactory ... of thieves and prostitutes" due to its "gross and open immorality ... gross innuendos ... heavy cursing, emphatic swearing, and incitement to illicit passion."[178] Temperance built up a large organized following in which practically every church, chapel and Sunday school played a part, with societies such as the Band of Hope, songs ("My drink is water bright ...") and ceremonies ("taking the pledge" not to drink). Yet so central to social life was drinking culture and the public house that the temperance movement never had more than local successes in controlling the sale of drink—it never came close to imposing major restrictions on the scale of those in Wales, and even less to attempting outright prohibition as in the United States. The identification of the movement with the Liberal Party in fact hobbled it, as electoral concerns inhibited its freedom. Gladstone was only partly exaggerating when he blamed the Liberals' 1874 election defeat on an anti-temperance reaction—"We have been swept away, literally, by a torrent of beer & gin."[179]

Popular Toryism was in part a reaction against the barrage of largely Liberal and Nonconformist campaigning. As noted earlier, it had long been associated with less censorious Anglicanism and with willingness to accept the people as they were, championing their right to play rowdy traditional games such as mass Shrove Tuesday football matches, often linked with Church and gentry patronage. Late-nineteenth-century Tory populists made a point of defending "the pleasures of the people" at the pub, the racetrack or the music hall against Liberal disapproval.[180]

Constitutional questions could be deeply divisive, as in the Irish Home Rule controversy of the 1880s, not least because of connections with sectarianism. But democratization, however fundamental it may seem to us, never generated great excitement. Victorians did not claim that the British constitution was "democratic," a word suggesting extreme Continental ideologies and American vulgarity; but they thought it provided effective government, guaranteed liberty, and was broadly representative of society.[181] Voting was not seen as an individual human right, but a way of ensuring that local communities and shared interests were represented: hence, landowners and businessmen could represent their employees, and male householders their dependants. Although the 1832 Reform Act had been proclaimed a final settlement, its illogicalities were glaring—for example, huge inequalities in the distribution of seats and in the proportion of people qualified to vote in different constituencies. Electoral reform became a matter of commonsensical tidying up combined with avid party calculation. Gladstone thought that emancipating "a select portion" of the working class, distinguished by "self-control, respect for order, patience under suffering, confidence in the law, respect for superiors," would buttress his policy of cutting expenditure and maintaining peace.[182] In 1864 he asserted that "every man who is not presently incapacitated by some consideration of personal unfitness or of political danger, is morally entitled to come within the pale of the constitution." But it was not a burning issue. Opposition within the Liberal Party came from high-minded elitists such as Robert Lowe and John Bright, and non-party intellectuals such as Carlyle and Matthew Arnold, who feared the corrupting effect of uneducated voters, "impulsive, unreflecting and violent people."[183] A reform rally in Hyde Park in July 1866 trampled flower beds, broke some railings, and caused an exaggerated level of alarm—testimony to how uneventful popular politics had become.

The Tories took little part in the debate and came into office in the middle of the process, with Lord Derby as Prime Minister and Disraeli Leader of the House and chancellor. Disraeli aimed, under the slogan "Household Suffrage," to get an Act passed that would keep the Tories in office, please as many people as possible, split the Liberals and do the minimum of harm to Tory electoral strength. In this the Representation of the People Act (1867) was largely successful: householders (under a variety of property qualifications) were given the vote in borough constituencies, but not in the counties, so most new voters were in larger towns that were mostly Liberal already, and there was little effect on the Tory counties and small towns. Some 30 percent of adult men now had the vote, taking the electorate from just over one million to just over 2 million. There was even some parliamentary support for women's suffrage, notably from Disraeli; some women were given the vote in local elections in 1869 and for the new county councils in 1888. In the general election of 1868, the widened electorate made no significant difference in party terms, and the composition of the political class was unaffected. But the 1867 system introduced unexpected consequences that made further changes inevitable. The 1884 Act—one of the least remembered great events in our history—applied the borough "household franchise" to the counties too, a change that was logically impossible to resist. The Bill was introduced by the Gladstone government, and after a delay it was allowed through the Lords by the Tory leader, the Marquess of Salisbury, in return for a redistribution of seats to favour his party. This Act gave nearly two-thirds of adult men the vote.* The Radical John Bright proclaimed that power "has been given henceforth and forever to the people . . . we have no longer charges to bring against a selfish oligarchy."[184]

Widening the franchise in 1867 began several decades of extravagant electoral corruption, perhaps giving bitter satisfaction to Robert Lowe: the golden age of Victorian politics was also the gilded age of bribery.[185] English elections had never been models of civic virtue, with drunkenness and low-key violence normal, but now venality reached shocking, or per-

---

* The Act created an electorate equal to 16 percent of the total population, compared with 27 percent in Republican France (Europe's only large democracy), 14 percent in Denmark and 9 percent in Norway; the German Reich had male suffrage for the Reichstag, which had little power, but not for the crucial Prussian parliament.

haps comic, depths—certainly it was widely regarded as rather a jape, and those involved faced little reprobation. Between a third and a half of English boroughs experienced corruption serious enough to draw attention, including Oxford, Cambridge, Durham and a high proportion of ancient cathedral cities. The commonest form was hiring "committee rooms" in public houses and providing "party workers" (in effect all comers) with free "refreshments" and the cash payment of "expenses." Consequently, electoral turnout could reach 90 percent. The Liberal candidate in Bradford in 1868 hired rooms in 158 pubs and spent over £7,000 (well over £1,000,000 today). Some Liberals had scruples about using such dens of iniquity and so paid bribes in the street. Even scrupulous candidates had to "nurse" their constituencies between elections, which meant generous donations to local causes, gifts of food and fuel to the elderly, paying for party organization, and even endowing a local library or park. The MP who held Windsor between 1890 and 1906 (being then succeeded by his nephew) was described in the local press as

> personally so popular . . . that whatever his politics he would have retained
> the seat as long as he cared to do so. [He] has been a benefactor to Windsor
> in many ways, notably in support of the local infirmary, and is regarded as
> the personal friend of every inhabitant of the borough.[186]

Politics was thus an expensive game: the average cost to a county MP was over £1,000 a year (hundreds of thousands today) and to a borough MP half that sum. Perhaps the highest-spending MP was Sir George Elliot, Tory member for North Durham, the self-made son of a coal miner, who reckoned that twenty-four years in politics—excluding charitable donations—cost him £124,000. Legal petitions for corruption were fairly common. In Macclesfield in 1880 one led to the disqualification from office of both Liberal MPs, both party agents, four magistrates, three aldermen and thirty-one local councillors. The Ballot Act (1872), making voting private, had little effect other than assisting some voters to take bribes from both sides. The Corrupt Practices Act (1883), which limited the amount that could be spent, had greater long-term consequences for the decency of English politics. Decisive action came with the permanent disfranchisement of constituencies where corruption was most habitual, though cases persisted into the early 1900s. Public attitudes gradually became less tolerant of corruption, though there was a minor resurgence in the early 2000s, facilitated by the relaxation of rules on postal voting. During the heyday of corruption both parties were making these costly investments in democracy, thus cancelling each other out, and allowing other factors—most obviously religious loyalty and economic interest—to prevail.

The widening of the electorate in 1867 and 1884 had, if not immediate

impact, fundamental long-term effects. It removed grievances, strengthened traditional institutions, and, as promoters hoped, gave governments
more legitimacy to do what they wanted.[187] The larger electorate was
harder to manage, and more elaborate party organizations developed.
These needed new sources of funding: large gifts from supporters, fund-
raising by activists and the quasi-sale of honours practised by both parties
from the 1880s[188]—arguably a more anodyne form of corruption than the
"pork-barrel politics" of dispensing economic favours, which caused
repeated scandals in the other large democracies, France and the United
States. Politics became more professional, with permanent central and
local organizations, yet also required the involvement of far more amateurs to canvass, put up posters, and distribute leaflets, because paying or
bribing was no longer legal. The Liberals relied on religious and single-issue
groups, often restive with the party leadership. Conservatives were more
successful in recruiting obedient volunteers, particularly through the
Primrose League, which by 1900 included half a million women. The
number of uncontested elections fell: in those rural constituencies, for
example, where (Anglican) landowners and their tenants had long formed
a solid Tory bloc, the enfranchisement of (often Nonconformist) farm
labourers, voting Liberal, made a contest more feasible. As important as
any of these changes was the revolutionary restructuring of parliamentary
constituencies insisted on by Salisbury, which established the framework
of modern British politics: relatively uniform constituencies became the
norm, breaking up the ancient county and multi-member borough structure into single-member constituencies. This ensured the representation of
what might otherwise have been minorities lost in a mass electorate—
which for Salisbury meant middle-class supporters in the residential districts of big cities, which with lordly condescension he dubbed "Villa
Toryism." These changes lessened the importance of local issues and local
personalities, whether big Tory or Whig landowners or Liberal employers.
New politicians appeared. The most famous were "Radical Joe" Chamberlain (who began as mayor of Birmingham in 1873) and "Tory democrat" Lord Randolph Churchill, an MP from 1874. What was new was
not their origins or allegiances—a Unitarian Liberal businessman and the
Tory son of a duke representing a family-controlled borough were hardly
novelties—but their calculated publicity-seeking and espousal of controversial issues attracted a national following that enabled them to force
themselves to the forefront of national politics.

The changes also made people, including politicians, think differently
about the right to vote. Traditional ideas were that Parliament represented
interests and communities, whose representatives were elected by a lim-

ited number of supposedly worthy citizens who were voting not just for themselves, but in the common interest. This they did publicly at the hustings so that all knew how each had voted—and non-voters could make their feelings felt, often rudely. But the extension of the franchise, and the secret ballot, made this idea untenable: voting had become private and individual, a personal right, not a public trust. So, logically and ethically, how could any honest citizen be refused the vote? How could women, often better educated than male voters, be refused the parliamentary suffrage, especially when so many were politically active as party workers, essential for electioneering? The 1867 and 1884 Acts did not introduce full democracy, but they made it, in the view of many, inevitable.[189]

More immediate in its effect on English and British politics was the question of Ireland.[190] Ireland had been acquiescent enough since the turbulent days of Catholic emancipation, revolution and famine to have been largely forgotten in England. But the European agricultural depression of the 1870s inflamed the perennial friction between landlords (largely Protestant) and tenants (largely Catholic), leading to rent strikes, forced evictions, "boycotting," cattle-maiming, arson and the occasional murder, orchestrated by a Land League demanding greater rights for tenants. London replied with "Coercion"—detention without trial. Mayhem was injected into British politics through the large and disruptive Irish representation at Westminster, especially a Home Rule Party led by the fox-hunting, cricket-playing nationalist squire, Charles Stuart Parnell. Gladstone had believed for some time that "my mission is to pacify Ireland," and he made a long visit there in 1877. A Land Act (1881) created a land court to arbitrate rents and increased tenants' rights. The Land League was banned and Parnell interned before he made an informal agreement with the government to stop the violence in return for the cancellation of rent arrears. But hardline nationalists responded in 1882 by stabbing to death the Chief Secretary for Ireland and his deputy in Phoenix Park, Dublin. In 1884–85 Gladstone was faced with electoral reform and crises in the Sudan and Afghanistan as well as the Irish question, and he came to believe that the 1800 Act of Union had been "a gigantic though excusable mistake."[191] After the November 1885 general elections (with the enlarged electorate), the 86 Irish Home Rule MPs just held the balance of power between 334 Liberals and 250 Conservatives. Gladstone, with his seamless combination of messianic altruism and low politics, announced his conversion to Home Rule, and so became Prime Minister for the third time in January 1886 with Irish support. He thought a self-governing Ireland would drop extremism, outgrow popery, and develop into "a healthy society" governed mainly by "the leisured class."[192]

He introduced an expensive Land Bill (in effect buying out the landowners) and a complex and cautious Government of Ireland Bill for an Irish assembly, with ample safeguards for Protestants and for British unity: it was, he told the Commons, "one of the golden moments of our history . . . which rarely return."[193]

But this golden moment opened a breach in English political life far more significant than the widening of the electorate.[194] For the Liberal Party split: Home Rule was opposed by the saintly Nonconformist John Bright, the thrusting Radical Joseph Chamberlain, the Whig aristocrat Lord Hartington and over ninety others, and the Bill was defeated in June 1886. Gladstone went to the country and was decisively defeated by a "Unionist" electoral alliance of Tories and the dissident "Liberal Unionists." Scotland, Wales and Ireland all produced Home Rule majorities, but England voted against. Yet Gladstone's Liberals re-emerged as the largest party at the 1892 general election, with 49 percent even of English votes, and he again became Prime Minister at the age of eighty-three, despite being hit in the eye while campaigning and assaulted by a mad cow. He mustered the energy to fight for another Home Rule bill, but it was defeated in the Lords, with Salisbury claiming that the government had no mandate for such fundamental change. Gladstone finally resigned in 1894. The combined Unionists won a large majority in the 1895 general election.

The opponents of Home Rule, the most determined of whom were the Presbyterians of Ulster, feared that it would begin the unravelling of Britain and its empire, threatening its international position, its global prosperity, and its domestic peace and security—fears in which ancient anti-Catholic and anti-Irish prejudices played a part. So another chance of settling Irish politics was lost. "What fools we were," said King George V later. A sizeable part of the Liberal electorate moved to the Tories. Salisbury became Prime Minister and held office four times between 1885 and 1902, marking the beginning of more than a century during which the Conservative Party (officially "Conservative and Unionist") would be the predominant political force.

"Whig" and "Tory," and the more modern "Liberal" and "Conservative" (terms borrowed from Spanish and French politics in the 1830s): are they now just archaic labels with no significant relationship to their origins in a society in which political choice is thought to follow individual opinion and socio-economic interest? The prudent answer would be yes. And yet: in 2010 the Tories still won in the English counties and small towns, as in the 1840s; the anti-Tory parties were stronger in larger towns, especially in the north, areas where Nonconformity is or used to be strong. London, today as in the 1880s, is different from the rest of the country, divided primarily along plain socio-economic lines; but for most of the country, the old religious divisions remain as a ghostly presence influencing instinctive loyalties. Some Nonconformist sects are still unusually disposed to vote for the Liberal Democrats. Anglicans are far more likely to vote Conservative: in the 2010 elections, twice as likely as Catholics.[195] Furthermore, Tories are still attracted by Disraeli's and Burke's "one nation" ideal of unity and harmony, and would doubtless agree with the former that "the Tory party . . . is the national party; it is the really democratic party of England."[196] They retain a "Country Party" suspicion of expensive state bureaucracy and of ideology, regarding their own opinions as simple good sense. They are attached to traditional ideas of liberty, at least for people like themselves. If they love lords a little less than Disraeli and Burke did, they are relatively deferential, aspire to social ascension, and are not averse to the idea of a public-spirited elite, even to Old Etonians in government. That elite is often said to possess a complacent sense of "entitlement." Tories often idealize the past, celebrating a triumphalist version of English and British history, and clinging to ancient symbols such as monarchy. Many retain a fondness for the Church of England, at least as an aesthetic and social, if not necessarily a spiritual and political, presence. Finally, of course, the Tory party is predominantly an English party: even in the 1860s it had only two seats in Scotland; in 2010 it had only one—on the English border.

By contrast, the anti-Tory traditions, Whig, Liberal and Labour (and more recently Scottish and Welsh nationalist), have a different myth of England and Britain. They reject the Burkean vision of harmony in favour of one of conflict—"the rich story of the people of these islands who fought for and defended our rights," in which the populist royalists of 1381, the hell-fire fundamentalists of the 1650s, ambitious opportunists such as Wilkes and Paine, strait-laced suffragettes, and tight-fisted social engineers such as Beveridge are transformed into a torch-bearing relay of Progress.[197] There is too a streak of Whiggish elitism: leaders of the "left" (a term not applied to English politics until the twentieth century) have usually been of comfortable, even wealthy, backgrounds, sometimes with a family tradition of politics, and a sense of intellectual, moral and even social superiority over plebeian and provincial Tories ("the stupid party," "the nasty party"), including lofty disdain for popular royalism and today a cosmopolitan distaste for "Euroscepticism." Alternatively, even simultaneously, comes identification with proletarian, ideally northern, roots. The Nonconformist tradition bequeaths campaigning militancy, a self-image of anti-Establishment rebellion, a view of politics as moral struggle (as opposed to "the art of the possible"), a taste for shibboleths (from Church disestablishment to fox-hunting), and sectarian suspicion of the motives of opponents ("lower than vermin"[198]). Both traditions are very different from the mainstream European right and left, which are based on clearer ideological differences or plainer socio-economic interests that simply do not match English politics.* The origins of the English divide can be traced far beyond Gladstone and Disraeli: to the wars against Revolutionary France, to the American Revolution, and ultimately to the religious conflicts of the sixteenth and seventeenth centuries: "The really important attitudes [in Victorian politics] had nothing to do with the Industrial Revolution, much to do with the English Civil War."[199]

Geographical voting patterns, magnified by the first-past-the-post system, make these deep continuities visible: the Ambridge versus Coronation Street polarity. The pattern is even reflected in our genes,[200] though its reappearance at every national election seems always to astonish us. The areas of strength of the Anglican Church uncovered in the 1851 census are strikingly similar to the electoral strongholds of the modern Conservative Party. In every election since the introduction of democracy, predominantly Anglican areas have voted Conservative. Conversely, there was long a clear correlation between Methodism and Liberal and Labour loyalties.[201] (In Scotland, Wales and Northern Ireland, the influence of religion has been, and remains, more marked than in England.) Those who saw themselves as nineteenth-century heirs of the Commonwealth men, whatever their social background, provided the leadership of the Liberal Party, trade unionism and the Labour Party.[202] Nonconformity was the closest predictor of voting Liberal ("the party of Christ") and then Labour well into the twentieth century. Labour voting was also strongly associated with Catholicism, with its strong links to Irish immigration. The expansion of the electorate strengthened this pattern, in which community identities shaped individual political choices, and it has been strong enough to outlast political changes such as the middle-class shift to Toryism at the end of the nineteenth century and the rise of Labour, the cuckoo in the Liberal nest. In some places today, the mosque is replacing the chapel in this respect, with Muslims now the most strongly left-voting group in the country, despite commonly holding "right-wing" views.[203]

Enduring geographical and religious patterns are found in many countries. In France, Catholics and anticlericals battled for two centuries; the Protestant north/Catholic south divided Germany; and there was long a regional pattern to Republican and Democratic loyalties in the United

---

* The most obvious examples today are controversies over health and education, which dominate English politics but have little or no echo on the Continent.

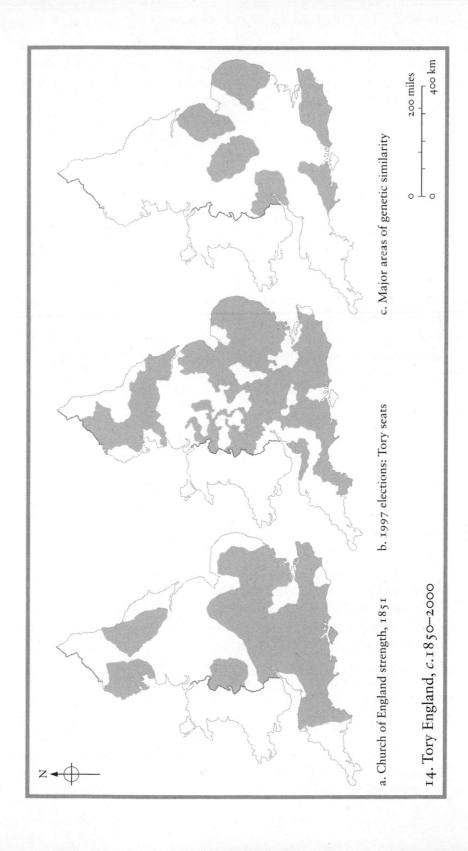

N

a. Church of England strength, 1851          b. 1997 elections: Tory seats          c. Major areas of genetic similarity

14. Tory England, c.1850–2000

0 _____ 200 miles

0 _____ 400 km

States dating back to the Civil War. One long-debated question about the English experience is whether the influence of Methodism—proverbially judged more important to the English left than Marxism—restrained extremism and class conflict. Élie Halévy, in one of the many influential histories of England by non-Englishmen, thought so: Methodism explained "the miracle of modern England, anarchist but orderly, practical and businesslike, but religious, and even pietist."[204] E. P. Thompson rather agreed, but deplored its "self-effacing and apologetic" tone, "forever professing their submission" to the established order.[205] There are doubtless several reasons why English politics has long been unusually peaceful, at least to the extent that it is very rare for people to kill or even hurt each other; but it seems plausible that the shared Christianity of rival parties was one of the causes. When we combine this restraint with a visceral and unrelenting partisanship eager to see the worst in the other party's actions, an imperviousness to argument, a sanctimonious relishing of moral scandal, a taste for tub-thumping and an aversion to coalition government, we see the legacies of Victorian sectarianism in a political culture strikingly different from that of other Western democracies.

## PLAYING THE GAME

The sand of the desert is sodden red,—
  Red with the wreck of a square that broke;
The Gatling's jammed and the Colonel dead,
  And the regiment blind with dust and smoke.
The river of death has brimmed his banks,
  And England's far, and Honour a name,
But the voice of a schoolboy rallies the ranks:
"Play up! play up! and play the game!"

Henry Newbolt, "Vitaï Lampada" (1898)

*We have witnessed a great change in manners: the substitution of words without blows for blows with or without words; an approximation in the manners of different classes; a decline in the spirit of lawlessness.*
Criminal Registrar's Report for 1899[206]

The Bolsheviks failed to create a "Soviet Man"; but "Victorian" woman and man were more durable products. The English took at least until the

1960s to "cut Queen Victoria's umbilical cord," as a radical Labour politician, Tony Benn, put it.[207] To create order after a period from the 1780s to the 1840s of rising disorder—illegitimacy, drunkenness, domestic violence and political unrest—required a long collective effort which, as we have noted, began to bear fruit after around 1870, as shown by diminishing drunkenness and crime. This effort involved powerful organizations: churches, Parliament, the courts, the new police, schools and universities, and a multitude of voluntary bodies aiming to "improve" society, especially the morals and well-being of its lower orders. The philosopher John Stuart Mill wrote in 1853: "Whatever else may be included in the education of the people, the very first essential of it is to unbrutalise them; and to this end, all kinds of personal brutality should be seen and felt to be things which the law is determined to put down." Respectability, as we have seen, was the admirable but rather depressing watchword; "playing the game" a widely shared value. Sport itself, and the idea of "fair play," was seen both as a means of inculcating desirable behaviour and as a metaphor for social virtue. The common English use of sporting phrases in political and social contexts, noticed by many foreign observers, implied an increasing acceptance of social conventions—"playing by the rules" in individual, family and public life. The "stiff upper lip" of the public-school hero, and the self-improvement, self-education and responsibility of the trade union leader both reflected and propagated these values.

The Victorian age moralized sport as a creator of manly Christian virtue. In part this was a way of keeping schoolboys, students and workers out of mischief: "Wherever cricket is widely practised, crime is very light," the Lancaster Assizes were told in 1851.[208] Previously, educators had disapproved of such activities. The Master of Balliol tried to interfere in the first University Boat Race in 1829. In 1834 the headmaster of Westminster School ("cowardly, snivelling, ungentlemanlike, treble damnable shit," in the view of one of his pupils) forbade the annual boat race against Eton. This changed completely within a generation: in the 1850s the schools and in the 1860s the universities enthusiastically took up games. "Muscular Christianity," as Disraeli called it, is associated with the writings of Charles Kingsley, Thomas Hughes and other "Christian Socialists." Hughes's *Tom Brown's Schooldays* (1857), described by *The Times* as a book that "every English father might well wish to see in the hands of his son," immortalized Dr. Thomas Arnold's Rugby School of the 1830s. Arnold had set out to moralize the large elite boarding school ("public school") and use it to create a Christian ruling class marked, as he put it, by "religious and moral principle . . . gentlemanly conduct . . . [and] thirdly, intellectual ability."[209] Hughes made Arnold a hero and pioneered the school story as a new literary genre. Hughes was also a herald of the new cult of games, especially "rugby," the variety of football practised at the school, though Arnold himself had in fact not been interested in such unspiritual pastimes. But Hughes set an adventurous and yet Christian "manliness" against an older rakish masculinity represented by the drunken and lecherous bully Flashman. Team games became lessons in courage, fairness, comradeship, leadership—in short, "playing the game." There was another advantage in encouraging—indeed compelling—sport: "the strong athletic boy" was less interested in sex than "the intellectual bookish boy," and was less likely, optimists thought, to be "hopelessly besmirched and befouled."[210]

Crucial to the myth and reality of the public school was the relative autonomy of boys, who themselves organized discipline (including fagging and caning) and sport: what began as neglect by schoolmasters in chaotic institutions came to be seen as training for adult life. Grammar schools (cheaper and non-boarding) and later the publicly funded Board schools copied the ethos. Foreign observers were sometimes impressed. "Boys who learned to command in games were learning to command in India," declared the headmaster of an elite French school after visiting Eton in the 1870s.[211] The emphasis on games, toughness, schoolboy independence and a code of silence often meant tolerance of bullying, ubiquitous corporal punishment and a preference for physical over intellectual pursuits—characteristics maintained at least until the 1960s. In inculcating a certain masculine culture, this was a somewhat gentler equivalent of the universal military service that became the norm on the Continent.

Spawned by Tom Brown, school stories in novels and new children's papers such as *Boys of England* (1866), *Boy's Own Paper* (1879), and later *Magnet* and *Gem* reached a mass readership of all classes over the next century. Stories for and about children appeared in all Western countries at this time, but the boarding-school story, with echoes of Thackeray, Dickens and Hughes, was an English speciality. It attracted some serious writers—Kipling's *Stalky and Co.* (1899) was, according to George Orwell, the "main origin . . . with immense influence on boys' literature."[212] But the biggest vector was the comic. Frank Richards's first Greyfriars story, featuring Billy Bunter, appeared in 1907, and remained almost universally popular among boys, girls and young adults of all classes for half a century. The influence was huge, varied, even contradictory: a childhood code of honour, pride in the school, a set of moral taboos (especially telling tales to adults), an ethos of fair play, chauvinistic patriotism and an early form of mildly subversive youth culture.[213]

The school story grew out of the new experience of nearly universal schooling, first among upper-class boys at boarding schools and finally among all children, notably later than in most of northern Europe due to the obstacle of sectarianism. The 1870 Education Act initiated a national system of Elementary schools, run by elected School Boards, and in 1880 attendance became compulsory, and, for the needy, free—though a sizeable minority did not attend regularly. The new Act was bitterly opposed by Nonconformists, as it also gave financial support to voluntary Anglican and Catholic schools. The effect of the Act is debated. Some historians regret that the Board schools drove cheap, user-friendly private schools for working-class children out of business. Others criticize them for narrow curricula and harsh discipline. But working-class parents and children were often enthusiastic: "I now see Board Schools almost equalling the colleges of some of the older universities," wrote a worker in the Potteries in the 1890s; "poor children now receive a better education than what I once heard Tom Hughes say he received when a boy."[214] Most remembered the schools and their teachers positively, as teaching not only the "3 Rs," but also English literature—though history, geography and science were often sketchy. Literacy had been rising steadily since the 1830s, especially for women, and did so very sharply from the 1850s (55 percent) to the 1890s (around 90 percent), catching up with Europe's leading countries, Prussia, Scotland and the Netherlands.[215] Elementary schools did not play games, however. At most the boys did gym; girls, one educationalist suggested, "might find a little wholesome exercise in cleaning out the school."[216]

Since time immemorial local games—often rowdy and violent, as we have noted, with cash prizes and betting—had been sporadically played on holidays. Urbanization, shorter working hours, higher incomes, newspaper publicity and improved transport created an appetite for more regular games, clubs and competitions—croquet, badminton, football, rugby and tennis were all developed between about 1850 and 1870. They required agreed rules and organizations. Some (for cricket, bowls, golf) predated the Victorians; but the Victorians generalized the new practices of the schools and universities. The Football Association, founded in 1863 by old-boys' clubs, adopted Cambridge University rather than Rugby School rules, forbidding "hacking" (i.e., kicking an opponent) and carrying the ball. But largely due to the prestige of the school, Rugby rules (adopted by the 1871 Rugby Football Union) remained predominant for a generation, including within the empire, where soccer never caught on, and in countries influenced by the "Tom Brown" ethos, including France and the United States, the latter adopting its own armoured variant.[217]

Thousands of sports clubs appeared, based on pubs (including Man-

chester United and Tottenham Hotspur, at the White Hart), churches (perhaps a quarter of all clubs, including Aston Villa, Everton, Fulham and
Wakefield Trinity), temperance societies and factories (West Ham, Arsenal). By the end of the century, Liverpool had 212 football clubs and
224 cricket clubs. In the 1900s one in twenty males aged fifteen to thirty-
nine participated actively in football, and a million watched each Saturday. Local clubs gave identity and pride to industrial towns and working-
class districts of cities. The crowd, not the players, created this, as professional teams recruited widely. The Tottenham side that won the FA Cup
in 1901, for example, contained no Londoners.[218] International matches
and tours began in the 1860s, including by an Australian Aboriginal
cricket team in 1868. The FA Cup (1871), open to all clubs, helped to
spread soccer, and crowds for the final rose from about 5,000 to 80,000 by
1914. A symbolic milestone in the transition of football from schoolboy
pastime to urban spectator sport was the defeat of the Old Etonians by
Blackburn Olympic, a professional working-class team, in the 1883 Cup
Final—a significant step in the formation of modern working-class culture.[219] No less symbolic was the split within rugby, when working-class
clubs from the north of England were excommunicated by the Rugby
Football Union in 1893, because gentlemanly amateurs refused to play
against semi-professional working-class players, who were dominating
the county championship. The amateurs intended to preserve rugby as
what the *Yorkshire Post* called in 1886 "an honourable pastime—one
which gentlemen can indulge in and ladies patronize." So in 1895 a professional "Northern Union" was set up—the beginning of what became
the Rugby League, with which the RFU fought a bitter and snobbish
feud for a century.[220] Boxing was similarly divided between amateur and
professional.

Cricket was the most morally sublimated game: "playing a straight
bat" was more than a mere technical expression. It retained cross-class
participation and appeal, making it the real national game, and fostering
virtues claimed to be quintessentially English, such as team spirit, fair play
and coolness under pressure. Its emotional home was the village green,
and the first serious history of the game was written by a vicar, the Rev.
James Pycroft, in 1861.[221] It was supposed to bring different classes
together in a uniquely English way, before they went back to their separate social worlds. It kept an upper-class element, with high-level school
and university teams, amateur "gentlemen" players and government by
the Marylebone Cricket Club. County and Test cricket retained leisurely
pre-industrial timetables, making the game deliberately unsuitable as a
mass spectator sport. Yet here too there was a characteristic divide, with
professional club cricket having a quite different, and northern, style.

Gentlemanly amateurs, advocates of "muscular Christianity" and inter-class fellowship, deplored commercialization, were shocked by rowdy and partisan crowd behaviour, and accused professional players of cheat-ing and violence. Socialists tended to agree—this was for them a symptom of the degeneration of the working class, and another opiate of the masses. There developed two cultures of sporting manliness. On one hand, an upper-class ideal of participation rather than spectating, of amateurism, self-restraint, ostentatious good sportsmanship (when the elite football club the Corinthian Casuals conceded a penalty they always allowed their opponents to score) and aristocratic effortlessness—"the Corinthian of my day never trained," claimed one of its captains, "the need of it was never felt."[222] On the other, a working-class focus on professionalism, physical aggression, spectating and winning—even by breaking the rules. But there was often hypocrisy in amateurism, including secret payments and generous "expenses." Perhaps the most famous English cricketer of all time, a hero to all classes, was Dr. W. G. Grace (1848–1915), a throw-back to the raffish pre-Victorian sporting world of gamesmanship and betting, who made some £120,000 (many millions in today's values) as an "amateur."[223] Some of the worst violence occurred in the gentlemanly Rugby Union, while plebeian professional football retained an ethos of fair play as long as the Victorian spirit lasted—at least until the heyday of Stanley Matthews and Tom Finney, perhaps of Gary Lineker. Although some contemporaries worried about crowd misconduct, before 1914 soc-cer spectators were generally well-behaved and were never considered a threat to public order.[224]

Organized sport was the great cultural invention of late-Victorian England, carrying a characteristic whiff of moralism tempered with hypoc-risy. Idealists believed that it would foster character, teamwork, and inter-class and even international amity. No doubt it often did. It taught that fair play, perseverance and bravely doing one's best were virtues: this was the spirit of the "good loser." But sport could also produce violence, contempt for intellectual activity, and local and national chauvinism (rugby caused serious friction between Britain and France in the 1920s, and cricket similar resentment between England and Australia); and, as we have seen in rugby and cricket, it institutionalized class differences for a century or more. Moreover, with the sole exception of suburban tennis, it increasingly excluded women. It also became big business: one rough contemporary estimate is of 3 percent of GNP by 1895,[225] which if true would be higher than today. Other countries copied: one sign of England's prestige as the model of modernity, and surely its greatest contribution to global popular sociability.

"Playing the game" came to imply a much wider acceptance of rules and conventions. An important way of measuring this is the degree to which Victorian society became law-abiding. Recorded crime fell steadily from the 1860s to 1914. Violence fell sharply from the 1870s, as drinking diminished, and it reached a low point in the Edwardian period. Homicides, already few, halved from 1.6 per 100,000 in 1860 to 0.8 per 100,000 by 1914—at least one-third lower than today, and indeed lower than any populous country today.[226] As always, a high proportion of killings—roughly a third—took place within families. Much domestic violence—"in which women's weapon of the tongue was met by men's weapon of the fist"[227]—had been regarded as minor, even legitimate, a private matter that rarely reached court. Yet even this was increasingly investigated, censured and punished by law. Many other homicides resulted from fights among men, especially after drinking—a result of wide acceptance of a "fair stand-up fight" as a manly way of settling disputes. Such assaults were rarely prosecuted, or resulted in nominal punishment, as long as "fair play" was respected, with no "un-English" kicking, brutality or "cowardly use of the knife."[228] Despite periodic scares, violent robbery declined—the last highwayman is recorded in 1831. Riot and arson almost disappeared. Weapons were decreasingly used. Duelling had begun to fall out of favour over the eighteenth century, earlier than in most countries, and was frequently stopped by passers-by; and from the 1830s duellists and their seconds were prosecuted for murder or attempted murder—seen abroad as an extreme example of English respect for law.[229] Although owning and carrying weapons, including thousands of cheap pistols, had long been uncontrolled and indeed regarded as a civil right, as still in the United States, using them for robbery or attacks on the police was very rare. By general agreement, legislation began to be adopted from 1903 to limit ownership and carrying of guns: a remarkable example of willing self-disarmament, and hence of trust in both the state and one's neighbours. An important aspect of these changes was a different ideal of manliness, based on self-restraint and fair play.[230]

Property crimes too fell steadily from the 1880s, especially the pettiest sort—small quantities of food and clothing stolen from the poor by the poor, previously a common feature of life. Female criminality diminished, possibly due both to reduced need and to reduced opportunity. The proportion of the population involved in crime narrowed—"weakness, not wickedness is their great characteristic," wrote the secretary of the Howard Association for Penal Reform in 1908. The number of hardened professional criminals was small.[231] The old "rookeries," criminal slums where outsiders feared to tread, were steadily demolished—though interestingly, and rather shamingly, they left a long shadow, visible in London today: when pulled down, they were replaced by social housing, so even in opulent Chelsea, the poorer areas today were also poor in the nineteenth century.[232]

One expanding crime, certainly in the value of what was stolen, was embezzlement and fraud. This, due to the growth of the financial sector, could reach stupendous levels, ruining masses of small savers. The chief cashier of the Shropshire Bank stole £200,000 in the 1850s—many millions today, and far from unique. Embezzlement caused the collapse of the Liberator Building Society in 1892, reducing nearly 3,000 people, many of them elderly women, to destitution. There were many larger cases only partly discovered, and no doubt many more that never were. Law enforcement grew tighter for ordinary people, but put few obstacles in the path of white-collar criminals. Even financial crashes in the 1850s to 1870s, investigated by Parliament, had little result in legislation, and many activities now regarded as criminal, such as insider trading, were normal.[233]

The increase in public order is often ascribed to the police—Sir Robert Peel's 1829 innovation, influenced by his experience in Ireland, and confirmed by the Police Act (1839). The very small, unpopular, impecunious and sometimes rather comical forces set up hesitantly over the next quarter of a century are unlikely to be the sole explanation, at least in their early decades. Early police forces were a barely literate and often drunken body of ex-labourers, with rapid turnover owing to the gruelling physical and psychological demands of the job. The Metropolitan Police had only 13 detectives in 1868, compared with some 3,000 today. The introduction of police forces into provincial towns in the 1830s and 1840s ignited riots, in which angry crowds fought the police, and sometimes chased them out—at that time a town of 20,000 people was likely to have only around 10 policemen, and the whole of Herefordshire had only 5. They were rarely armed, and the Home Office refused to allow military training. Particularly unpopular were police actions to suppress popular amusements. Policemen were both perpetrators and victims of frequent violence. Isolated rural constables especially risked serious assault, and in London attacking a policeman was seen as an act of pluck. Fourteen-hour days and twenty-mile foot patrols were common. Policemen could be forbidden to drink, smoke or gamble, and required to attend church in uniform; in some forces, beards were banned, and in others they were compulsory; family life was regulated. Perhaps unsurprisingly, many policemen, even senior officers, fell spectacularly short of these exacting standards. Superintendent Joseph "Jack the Lad" Young, of the East Riding Constabulary, for example, was allowed to retire in 1872 after a career featuring drunkenness, withholding information, forgery, and serving in his son's butcher's shop while in uniform. In Ipswich and the East Riding of Yorkshire whole police forces were sacked, mostly due to drunkenness and neglect of duty.[234]

The police improved in the last quarter of the century, when career prospects and "perks" improved, a professional force emerged, and men had an incentive to stay on, behave themselves, and win extra pay and promotion. Promotions took place from the lower ranks, with no "officer corps" as in the army. Policemen's reputation, and self-respect, began to improve. They rescued people from fire, flood and runaway horses. The middle classes, at first suspicious on grounds of civil liberty, came to see them as protectors. Poorer people were more exposed to theft and violence than the wealthy: farmers losing sheep, shopkeepers pilfered, workers robbed of their wages. They began to seek the protection of the law and the police, of whom they began to form a somewhat more favourable image.

Eventually, the police and the courts had an impact. According to a select committee report in 1853, people "feel more safe . . . there are districts now where it is well known that doors are left unbolted, and clothes left out now without fear, which could not have been done in former days."[235] Magistrates' summary jurisdiction took over increasingly from jury trials. New national model prisons were opened, inspired by utopian ideas of reforming prisoners through confinement. Prison regimes were harsh, as they were in other liberal states such as France and the United States, with hard labour and the solitary "silent system" as at Pentonville (1842), loosely modelled on the Benthamite Panopticon (see p. 434), which drove many inmates insane. Juvenile institutions such as "reformatory schools" (1854) and "Borstal Institutions" (1908) were built, and seem to have had some success in preventing reoffending. Surprisingly, violent crimes by children were sometimes treated less severely, and with far less public alarm, than today.[236] Schools kept more children off the streets and out of trouble. Police numbers rose steeply after 1860: by 1891, there was in London one policeman for 421 inhabitants—comparable with the national average today of one for 410. They adopted what might now be termed "zero tolerance," making very large numbers of arrests for offences such as loitering, drunkenness and minor assault, and the courts gave short prison sentences for offences for which in earlier times offenders would have been bound over, fined or discharged. The impact of these changes was magnified because criminals—whether poor people who committed occasional petty crime or gangs of thieves, pickpockets and fences of the Dickensian type—were used to no organized policing at all. They fell easy prey to the new activism of the Victorian state, armed with the camera, the fingerprint and the telegraph.[237]

Law-abiding behaviour was not only a matter of repression, but reflected changing ideas about violence, masculinity, individual rights, public behaviour and the proper workings of society. As a result of the growth and stabilization of the economy, the exhortations of reformers and churches, socialization by schools, newspapers and the whole network of civil society, from friendly societies to brass bands and sports clubs, acts once regarded as acceptable or merely inevitable (such as drunkenness or domestic violence) become objects of public disapproval. The semi-democratized political system had, or seemed to have, both the power and the legitimacy to regulate society in a manner that seemed permanent and unchallengeable—a rare, even unique, state of affairs, which survived until the 1960s. Its dark side was the persistence, unusual in liberal Europe, of relatively frequent capital punishment (more than one every month in the 1900s) and some corporal punishment—a cause of public debate from the 1830s to the 1970s, but accepted by the majority. This seemingly contradictory acceptance by an increasingly non-violent society of an unusual level of violence on the part of the state and by private persons (such as schoolmasters) probably has several explanations. It was often argued that exemplary severity—whether by hanging murderers or caning schoolboys—was a necessary condition of more general peacefulness: England's unarmed police force needed the threat of the gallows. Some kinds of controlled violence, whether in sports or in the punishment of boys, were believed to inculcate an English brand of masculinity. Finally, traditional practices seemed to work, and a self-confident, even arrogant, nation seems to have been uninterested in comparisons with other countries.[238] This has often been seen as the triumph of middle-class hegemony; but it should be remembered that among the main beneficiaries of this long process of pacification were the most vulnerable—working-class women, children, even animals.[239]

If this seems a dull story, worthy but conformist, there was another side to playing the game: laughing at it. "English humour" came to be seen at home and abroad as an arcane national characteristic. The English had long been well-known for laughing—irreverently, cruelly, obscenely. This was part of their much-vaunted freedom, exploited by Hogarth, Gillray and Rowlandson. The Victorians wanted their jokes more restrained and polite—at least when the targets were themselves. The genial cartoons of Sir Edward Tenniel set an approved standard. Cruelty in humour became bad taste, and whimsy replaced the belly-laugh. An increasingly organized, rational and rule-bound society discovered a taste for nonsense, and invented a new kind of literature: the quietly insane poems of Edward Lear (they first appeared in 1846) and the stories of Lewis Carroll, with *Alice's Adventures in Wonderland* published in 1865. W. S. Gilbert, also during the 1860s, began writing "topsy-turvy," turning Victorian sense into nonsense and presenting English society as a pantomime in a series of popular operettas in the 1870s and 1880s. Oscar Wilde delighted the upper classes in the 1880s and 1890s by teasing them: "Never speak disrespectfully of society. Only people who can't get into it do that." Music hall songs expressed a working-class humour of fatalism, political scepticism, the evasion of tragedy or anger, and a stance of comic stoicism.[240] Parody, irony and absurdity, often impenetrable to outsiders, became and remain the essence of "English humour," both laughing at and celebrating its own foibles—what has been called "the importance of not being earnest."[241]

## SECOND THOUGHTS: THE STRANGE DEATH OF LIBERAL ENGLAND?

In a brilliant, tendentious and influential work of 1935, a young journalist, George Dangerfield, created a long-lasting image of *The Strange Death of Liberal England*, in which a façade of peace and prosperity is undermined by political hatreds, working-class militancy, the revolt of the Suffragettes and incipient civil war in Ireland. "Fires long smouldering in the English spirit suddenly flared up, so that by the end of 1913 Liberal England was reduced to ashes. And a very good thing too." The First World War was the coup de grâce: "On the splendour of Imperial England there falls, at last and forever, an inextinguishable dark."[242] There is some truth in this description, although the picture was hugely overdrawn, reflecting the pessimism of the 1930s.

The 1884 Representation of the People Act had made Britain something like a male democracy, as we have seen; and nearly everyone qualified actually voted—turnouts were regularly over 80 percent. Working men were being elected to School Boards, as Poor Law guardians, and as local councillors. There was a wide supposition that politics would inevitably become more populist, and more directed towards improving the lot of the masses. It did this rather little: but the expectation was important. Ideas for improving society were shifting away from moralism, and towards economics, sociology and biology. Concepts such as "unemployment" and "unemployability" appeared. As a worker for the Howard Association, aiding prisoners, put it of one of his charges, "As soon as I let him go, back to his misery, and what we call his sin, he certainly goes. Pathological and social causes are too powerful."[243] The agricultural depression and a 10 percent spike in unemployment led to riots, widespread vandalism and looting in Trafalgar Square and the West End in February 1886 and on "Bloody Sunday" (13 November 1887), when two people were killed. Although small by European standards this marked the end of complacency about the unemployed urban poor.[244]

The Poor Law relieved poverty but did nothing to prevent it. On the contrary, thought critics, it spawned a growing underclass with a culture of dependency. It was also criticized for treating drunks and criminals the same as the respectable poor. Octavia Hill's Charity Organization Society (which aimed to coordinate charitable activity "scientifically" and coined the phrase "the undeserving poor") wished only to "help those persons who are doing all they can to help themselves."[245] Quasi-Darwinian theories of "degeneration" or "regression," which became fashionable across the Western world, assumed that social conditions could cause a deterioration in an individual or even a whole "race." This seemed to explain the "residuum" of feckless slum dwellers simply "unfit" for modern life—the very opposite of chapel-going, trade-unionized, law-abiding factory workers. "The foul and fetid breath of our slums is almost as poisonous as that of an African swamp," wrote "General" William Booth, founder of the Salvation Army, in 1890. "A population sodden with drink, steeped in vice, eaten up by every social and physical malady, these are the denizens of Darkest England."[246] Charity workers, trade unionists and socialists agreed that policy should not perpetuate this underclass but rather aim to eliminate it. Many deserving Poor Law claimants agreed, for they detested being classed with vagrants and "roughs." Experts were impressed by discriminatory and coercive systems: for example, compulsory labour colonies in Germany, France and the United States. Sidney and Beatrice Webb (a formidable and dedicated intellectual team who spent part of their honeymoon at the Trade Union Congress) urged "treatment and disciplinary supervision," with obligatory labour or training, and detention centres for the "defective."[247] The Labour MP Will Crooks told the Commons that "a man unwilling to work should be made to work," if necessary by "keeping him short of food for a time."[248] Charles Booth, in a massive study of *Life and Labour of the People of London* (1891–1902), found a persistent level of poverty, which he blamed on idleness and criminality among an underclass who should be "harried out of existence." William Beveridge's *Unemployment: A Problem of Industry* (1909) ascribed unemployment to the inefficient working of the labour market. The need, it seemed, was for a more "scientific" approach.

Respectable workers become more assertive. The 1884 Act had enfranchised better-off workers, including coal miners. Serious trade fluctuations and foreign competition since the 1880s had encouraged the extension of trade unionism to less skilled workers. Union membership, already high by international standards, doubled between 1906 and 1914. Some union leaders were excited by revolutionary "Syndicalism" from France and America, whose main idea was revolution through a general strike. Even moderates sought alliances between unions to multiply the effectiveness of strikes. Increasing union membership, low unemployment and a rising cost of living provided the conditions for an increase in labour militancy from 1910 to 1914, with most strikes in 1913, the year of lowest unemployment (2.1 percent), when workers' bargaining power was highest.[249] As well as these major strikes, there were some turbulent demonstrations, especially in Dublin, Liverpool and Wales, and even—extremely rare events—the use of troops. At Tonypandy, a meeting of miners in November 1910 led to looting of Jewish-owned shops and a striker being shot.[250] There were four deaths the following year in Liverpool and Wales.

This later led some historians such as Dangerfield—and a few people at the time—to assume that Britain was in the grip of a class revolt, and that Liberalism, with its cross-class support, was doomed to make way for socialism and a Labour Party. Few historians think this now: the Liberal Party (not to mention the Tory party) still attracted workers and trade unionists. England's first Marxist party, the Social Democratic Federation, founded by a cricket-playing, Old Etonian revolutionary, Henry Hyndman in 1883, remained a doctrinaire sect. The Fabian Society (1884), the prototype think-tank, was politically moderate, for all its authoritarian social blueprints. The Independent Labour Party, set up in Bradford in 1893, was a non-Marxist socialist party; it attracted male and female enthusiasts, including the Pankhursts and future politicians such as James Keir Hardie and James Ramsay MacDonald—but not many voters. In the 1895 general election all its candidates came bottom of the poll. Various socialist groups, whether Marxist or "ethical socialist" (drawing on religious and romantic ideas of fellowship and community, and best represented by William Morris and Edward Carpenter, the prototype sandal-wearing vegetarian who campaigned for rural life and sexual freedom), attracted young skilled workers and intellectuals. They typically read John Ruskin's denunciations of greed and competition, subscribed to Robert Blatchford's newspaper, *The Clarion*, handed out pamphlets, formed bicycling clubs, and won some seats on local councils, School Boards, and as Poor Law guardians. But their often condescending attitudes towards "the mob" and "slummites" went down badly: middle-class activists encountered indifference, if not downright hostility, from the very people whose interests they claimed to represent.[251] Most unions and most workers remained Liberal. So-called New Liberalism developed social-welfare policies favourable to workers; indeed the twentieth-century "socialism" of the Labour Party is largely a continuation of New Liberalism.

An important catalyst to social reform was the Boer War against the independent South African Republic, which began in 1899 (see p. 584–85). Not only were British regular troops defeated in the early stages of the war, but nearly one-third of army recruits were rejected on grounds of physical unfitness—taken as a sign of the biological deterioration of the urban lower classes. This was misleadingly alarmist: recruits were relatively unfit because fitter young men found better-paid jobs than the regular army, but the overall physical level of the population was higher than ever before and compared favourably with Continental European countries.[252] Yet an official investigation advocated "dealing drastically with a class that, whether by wilfulness or necessity, is powerless to extricate itself from conditions that constitute a grave menace to the community by virtue of [its] permanent taint."[253] Salvation was vested in a campaign for "National Efficiency." The fashionable stress on pseudo-biology as an explanation of social problems led to some extreme ideas being voiced across the political spectrum for dealing with the "residuum" and the "unfit": internment, sterilization (the young and modern-minded Winston Churchill briefly thought of using X-rays) and compulsory labour. "Eugenics," a form of Social Darwinism developed by Darwin's son-in-law, Francis Galton, attracted a galaxy of celebrities, including politicians, clergymen, feminists and intellectuals such as George Bernard Shaw, the Webbs, J. M. Keynes and H. G. Wells. They exhorted the middle classes, nature's fittest, to reproduce more—especially educated women who seemed to be neglecting their racial duty to breed. Sidney Webb, luminary of the Fabian Society, feared that "children are being freely born to the Irish Catholics and the Polish, Russian and German Jews . . . and to the thriftless and irresponsible."[254] A series of official commissions studied the birth rate, divorce, "inebriates," venereal disease, the "feeble-minded" and the Poor Law. The more radical ideas (for example, sterilization of the "unfit") were never applied in England, nor were compulsory labour colonies created. But there was strong pressure to do something.

The political landscape began to change because of an unexpected legal decision, the Taff Vale judgment of 1901, described by Dangerfield as a gratuitous "attack by Capital upon Labour." The Taff Vale Railway Company successfully sued the prestigious Amalgamated Society of Railway Servants for damages for breach of contract after a sudden strike. Fabians, who favoured compulsory labour arbitration as in New Zealand and Australia, approved. But politicians were alarmed. As the Conservative Prime Minister, A. J. Balfour, put it, "There is no party which does not recognise to the full all that trade unions have done . . . trade disputes in this country have been carried on with a wisdom and a moderation on both sides which cannot be paralleled in another industrial country."[255] Ramsay MacDonald, secretary of a new Labour Representative Committee (LRC), appealed to the trade union movement to seek direct representation in Parliament: the deadly threat to trade unions raised by the Taff Vale case, he declared, urgently required the creation of a Labour Party. Although Parliament quickly passed a Trades Disputes Act (1906) giving unions legal immunity (a status otherwise held only by the monarch), more than 120 unions with over 800,000 members had already affiliated with the LRC, which became the Labour Party in 1906, under the leadership of the former Scottish miners' leader, Keir Hardie. However, most trade unionists had no desire to destroy the Liberal Party: their aim was to achieve favourable legislation through alliance with the Liberals, with whom the LRC concluded an electoral pact. This would contribute to a landslide Liberal electoral victory in 1906. These early Labour politicians were working-class Liberals in all but name, sharing the core values of free trade, temperance and Dissent; their favourite reading was John Ruskin, Charles Dickens and the Bible.[256]

The political situation was further shaken up by the resurgence of two old and divisive issues: education and free trade. Balfour's Tory government passed the 1902 Education Act, creating a national system based on Local Education Authorities, but this provoked bitter Nonconformist-Liberal opposition because it subsidized Church of England, Catholic and Jewish schools. Then in May 1903 the Colonial Secretary, Joseph Chamberlain, split his party and galvanized the Liberals by proposing import tariffs with "imperial preference," aiming simultaneously to strengthen the empire, protect domestic industry and agriculture, and raise the money for old-age pensions. This caused a political sensation: "All the old warhorses [were] snorting with excitement," wrote the Liberal leader, Campbell-Bannerman.[257] The Liberal Party marshalled the arguments familiar since the 1840s. Free trade meant peace and brotherhood; tariffs meant conflict and oppression. In a rather unscrupulous campaign, they poured out propaganda about the 1840s—the "Hungry Forties"—before the Corn Laws were repealed, when people had supposedly been starved by a heartless squirearchy. The campaign was effective, and influenced twentieth-century views of "the bad old days."

The "bread tax," educational sectarianism and a touch of racism over the immigration of Chinese labourers into South Africa brought a Liberal landslide in 1906, with 400 seats to the Conservatives' 157; 29 Labour MPs were elected, 24 of them with Liberal support. Sir Henry Campbell-Bannerman as Prime Minister, and then after his death in 1908 H. H. Asquith, introduced the most important rush of reform since the 1830s. Lloyd George, as chancellor, and Churchill, president of the Board of Trade, took the lead over school meals, accident compensation, child protection, labour exchanges, town-planning, old-age pensions (1908) and "national insurance" (1911). Churchill said in old age that it was the best government he had ever been in. Their programme was meant to be planned and rational, treating poverty as an economic rather than a moral problem, pre-empting both authoritarian socialism and Tory tariff reform, and safeguarding traditional Liberal values of independence, self-reliance and economy.

Lloyd George's old-age pension scheme was for five shillings a week for those over seventy. John Burns, the trade union leader, told the Prime Minister that five shillings meant "a great deal to the honest and provident poor" (the weekly rent of a room was around a shilling). Some thought a non-contributory scheme bad in principle: it "sets up the State . . . as a source of free gifts," wrote William Beveridge, who considered that even the poorest "waste more than twopence a week on drink, let them contribute that."[258] As well as a means test, beneficiaries were required to have a record of good behaviour—a reflection of the desire of "scientific" reformers not to indulge the underclass, even in old age. In practice the law was generously and intelligently administered through local post offices. Those without birth certificates, for example, were allowed to prove their age otherwise—as by inscriptions in family Bibles; one old lady proved her age by bringing along her seventy-two-year-old son. The impact was enormous, and arguably made poor people regard the State—traditionally an object of suspicion—as a benevolent entity with unlimited resources. A Sheffield newspaper reported that "the vast majority . . . would not believe until the money was handed over to them that the Government had made such a generous provision for their old days."[259] "Pension Day," 1 January 1909, was celebrated with flags and bonfires. Liberal, Labour and Tory parties all tried to claim credit, but obviously the Liberals had the best claim.

Churchill's National Insurance scheme provided health insurance to contributing workers, and unemployment benefit for certain occupations, aiming to tide over families in temporary difficulties not of their own making, thus saving them from destitution and the Poor Law. It seemed fraught with economic and political danger.[260] No other country, even much-admired Germany, had dared to introduce compulsory unemployment insurance. One Swiss canton had tried it, but its scheme went bankrupt in two years. Unlike the Poor Law's unlimited non-contributory benefits, the insurance scheme would give defined benefits in return for contributions (for example, seven shillings a week for up to five weeks of unemployment, with requirement to accept suitable work if available). Unlike in charity systems, being "deserving" was no longer the touchstone. As Churchill put it, "If you are eligible, we shall pay. If not, go away . . . I do not like mixing up moralities and mathematics."[261] The principle of insurance would create automatic discipline. Workers dismissed for misconduct were penalized. But there were to be no labour camps: Churchill "refused to let the State use its power over those in distress for any purpose except to relieve distress."[262] Existing institutions were incorporated into the new systems: the friendly societies, the insurance companies, the trade unions (whose membership in consequence boomed) and the doctors—the British Medical Association now began its rise to influence.

Politically, the reforms were explosive. In order to pay the costs both of old-age pensions and expensive new battleships due to a naval arms race with Germany (see p. 587) Lloyd George introduced a "People's Budget" in 1909, with a range of new or increased taxes, including a "super tax" on incomes over £5,000, increased death duties and a new land tax, popular among Liberals and Labour, and of course particularly unwelcome to landowners. Conservatives flouted a 150-year-old convention by defeating the Budget in the Lords, causing a new general election in 1910. Lloyd George, a Manchester-born Welshman, saw himself as the scourge of the "feudal" aristocracy (though Churchill, an aristocrat himself, was nearly as tough) and proclaimed a struggle between "Peers" and "People."

The ensuing general election, in February 1910, left Liberals and Tories neck-and-neck, making the Liberals dependent on the Irish Nationalists to pass a Parliament Bill to overcome the Lords' veto. The price of this support was Irish Home Rule. There were political intrigues on all sides, and the floating of many ideas (electoral reform, an elected House of Lords, devolution, "grand committees" for the British nations and—Churchill's idea—the splitting up of England into regions) that remain weirdly familiar over a century later. A second general election in December gave Liberals and Tories exactly the same number of seats. The Irish Nationalists again held the balance. The new king, George V, agreed to create if necessary enough Liberal peers to overturn the Tory majority in the Lords, and all but the Tory "Diehards" gave in. The Parliament Act (1911) limited the obstructive powers of the Lords over legislation: they no longer had a veto over "money bills" or bills passed three times by the Commons.

Democratization and social reform ignited the question of women's rights. Women, particularly the educated and religiously motivated, had long played a more prominent part in English public life than in most European countries, not least since the long anti-slavery campaign from the 1790s to the 1830s. Florence Nightingale's struggle against male incompetence had made her a household name. Women had been deeply involved in protests against the "Bulgarian Horrors" in 1876, horrified by sexual violence and enslavement of Christian women—a significant moment in the political mobilization of women, following their prominence in the campaign against regulated prostitution. Women—sometimes the same ones—were outspoken critics of British policy towards Boer women and children. More routinely, women were leaders in so-called social purity campaigns and in the temperance movement. Middle-class women were also increasingly involved in local government by the end of the century as Poor Law guardians (more than 800), as professional and volunteer charitable workers (perhaps 500,000), as members of School Boards and as teachers (over 170,000 women taught in the Elementary schools), and from 1907 as voters and members of county and borough councils. Hundreds of thousands of women were volunteer Tory or Liberal Party workers. Educational opportunities had increased: though Oxford and Cambridge resisted giving women equal status, women's colleges were established there in the 1870s; and other universities, led by London, admitted women on equal terms. The British Medical Association admitted women in 1892.[263]

These activities did not necessarily challenge the "separate spheres" idea of gender difference, and so the granting of the vote in local elections, and membership of women on School and Poor Law Boards was not controversial—for some, this did not seem really "political." No more controversial were the growing professional opportunities for women in teaching, medicine and social administration. But there remained strong taboos. Even croquet, badminton, tennis and especially bicycling—"a dawn of emancipation"—raised controversy about what women could and should do, and whether they could decently wear the simplified and practical clothing style termed "Rational Dress." "Few would believe how insulting and coarse the British public could be," complained a correspondent of the progressive *Clarion* in the late 1890s, "unless they had ridden through a populated district with a lady dressed in Rationals." In 1899 the editor of *Rational Dress Gazette* was struck with a meat hook while she was cycling through Kilburn.[264]

There was deeper controversy in two areas: that of the family and that of Parliament. There were several family issues: married women's control over their own property; conditions of divorce; married women and work; rights over children; and intimate questions of sex and childbirth. Some of these issues were solved by legal reform (for example, the Married Woman's Property Act, 1882, which gave married women the right to own and manage property independently of their husbands). Others were less amenable to legislation. As Christabel Pankhurst wrote, "There can be no mating between the spiritually developed woman of this day and men who in thought and conduct with regard to sex matters are their inferiors." She believed that most men were infected with venereal diseases, and that this was leading to "physical, mental and moral degeneracy and race suicide."[265]

Votes for women did not raise universal male opposition. As early as 1848 Disraeli had said in the Commons that if a woman could be head of state, a landowner and a churchwarden, she could certainly exercise the vote.[266] In a few small countries and provinces women received the legislative vote in the 1890s, principally New Zealand (1893), South Australia (1895) and a few U.S. states, such as Wyoming. But it was still a daring idea for national parliaments in large states. In Britain, Lord Salisbury, the antithesis of a progressive, regarded it as logical that educated and property-owning women should have the parliamentary vote. Moreover, many of them would vote Tory. During the 1890s a majority of Conservative and Liberal MPs came to support some degree of women's suffrage.[267] Trade unionists and socialists were divided. Some opposed the vote going to middle-class women while many working-class men remained unenfranchised as non-householders. Some working men feared women would vote to close down pubs. But these were hardly insoluble problems: in 1904 in reply to a petition from 66,000 women mainly in the Lancashire cotton industry (where women and men were used to fairly equal treatment), the House of Commons passed a pro-suffrage motion by 184 votes to 70. There would sooner or later have been some sort of compromise, the usual mixture of principle and electoral calculation. The practical obstacle was the Liberal government, which controlled the parliamentary timetable, and had other things than women's suffrage on their minds—principally the battle with the Lords, their shaky majority and a growing crisis in Ireland. But some women refused to wait on male politicians or make compromises. Rather than push on a slowly opening door, they preferred to throw a brick through the window. In 1903 the Manchester socialists Emmeline Pankhurst and her daughter Christabel had set up the Women's Social and Political Union, and in 1906 they moved to London to form a small, determined, largely middle-class organization, relying on direct action. Not all sympathized with what one socialist woman called the "Society Woman's Political Union," and some working-class feminists refused to be "mixed up with ... educated and upper class women who kick, shriek, bite and spit."[268] The Suffragettes, as the *Daily Mail* nicknamed them, set out to create the maximum embarrassment for the government by public acts of defiance (in January 1908 two women chained themselves to the railings outside 10 Downing Street) and petty but sensational acts of violence. They were ready, even eager, to suffer for the cause: they seem to have been the inventors of the hunger strike, and were often roughly treated by policemen and members of the public. In short, the Suffragettes raised the profile of the suffrage issue, but made its opponents more intransigent, and sometimes more brutal.

In 1909 the Liberal Home Secretary, Herbert Gladstone (son of "the People's William"), authorized force-feeding of Suffragette hunger strikers—an act that recalled the bodily intrusions of the Contagious Diseases Act, and even torture, and it caused widespread repugnance. A cross-party private member's bill giving women the parliamentary vote was backed by 299 to 189, but then Parliament was dissolved amid the crisis over the Budget. Two similar bills failed in 1911–12, as did a compromise "Conciliation Bill" offered by Asquith which would have given some women the vote. These failures were due to a hostile reaction to Suffragette violence, to opposition from Irish Nationalists, and to Liberal reluctance to support an "undemocratic" measure which, said Lloyd George, would add "hundreds of thousands of votes ... to the strength of the Tory party."[269] The Suffragettes again went on the rampage, smashing the Orchid House at Kew, bombing Lloyd George's house and setting various buildings on fire. Another private member's bill was defeated. The voluptuous bottom of Velasquez's *Rokeby Venus* was slashed. Attempts were made by male sympathizers to horsewhip Liberal MPs. Fortunately, no one was killed. But in 1913 Emily Davison, for no clear reason—possibly to attach a banner—walked in front of the king's horse in the Derby and was fatally injured. The Suffragettes' campaign had arguably become counter-productive. Their membership collapsed, whereas that of the moderate suffragists shot up. Were the Suffragettes, as the leading feminist Millicent Fawcett said, "the most powerful allies the antisuffragists have"?[270] In some ways they were, though paradoxically by focusing attention on suffrage they had given moderate feminists a new determination, and won them the support of many politicians and even the TUC. It was clear that women's suffrage was not far off; but whether the Suffragettes hastened it or delayed it is a matter of speculation, as war suspended normal politics.

Suffragette prisoners were then released, and most devoted themselves energetically to the war effort. The war swept away the parliamentary obstacles to women's suffrage and altered the public mood. When peace returned English women got the vote—at the same time as in Austria, Czechoslovakia, Sweden, Poland, Germany, Holland and Luxembourg—and there was also a string of legislation improving women's social rights. The Suffragettes are commonly cited as ultimate vindication of illegal direct action. They still inspire many attracted by intransigent assertions of principle, or excited by a touch of (not very serious) violence in politics, in what was the first deliberately violent English political campaign since the 1840s—one in which those injured were mainly Suffragettes themselves, and nobody was killed except Emily Davison.

Lloyd George's victorious battle over the "People's Budget" with the House of Lords had required the support of the Irish Nationalists. In return, they wanted Home Rule. In April 1912 a Home Rule Bill was introduced. Ulster Protestants resisted and demanded autonomy—"Home Rule within Home Rule." In January 1913 the Bill passed its Third Reading, and the Liberal government was resolved on pushing it through, while trying to get a compromise that would exclude Ulster, at least temporarily. Also in January a paramilitary Ulster Volunteer Force was created, soon reaching 85,000 men, and illegally and openly importing weapons. In September leading Unionists, led by Sir Edward Carson and the Marquess of Londonderry, proclaimed that an Ulster provisional government had been chosen to resist nationalist rule and govern Ulster "in trust for the British nation," and that it would take power "when it shall be deemed expedient."[271] The following month, a nationalist Irish Volunteer force was set up in Dublin and by March 1914 reached 20,000 men. There were well-founded doubts whether the regular army, disproportionately officered by Irish Protestants, would be reliable if ordered to use force against the Ulster Volunteers: in March 1914 several officers threatened to resign their commissions in the so-called Curragh Mutiny. In May the Commons passed the Home Rule Bill. By the summer, as the swelling rival volunteer forces greatly outnumbered those of the Crown, the United Kingdom seemed threatened by another civil war in Ireland. The nationalist Patrick Pearse looked forward to it as "a cleansing and sanctifying thing."[272] Arguably, all this was really "an extreme form of the politics of theatre . . . the danger of civil war was always more apparent than real."[273] Be that as it may, the onset of the First World War postponed it for two years. When in September 1914 the Irish Home Rule Act formally became law, war had broken out, and Home Rule was suspended for the duration.

So was Dangerfield right? Was Liberal England dying? It had some alarming symptoms which were certainly linked. Democratization and tough economic conditions demanded social reforms. So did seeming failings during the Boer War. The latter also required higher defence spending, further increased by the naval arms race with Germany. The combined costs meant a "People's Budget" and a clash with the Tory House of Lords. Constitutional crisis reopened the Irish question and led to the threat of civil war. Democratization raised the question of women's suffrage, but the constitutional crisis, especially the Irish question, scuppered legislation and ignited the Suffragette campaign. Economic instability and political turbulence led to the formation of the Labour Party and an unprecedented wave of strikes when a return to full employment strengthened workers' bargaining power. But Liberal England's underlying state was nevertheless robust. The socialist intellectual G. D. H. Cole diagnosed a revolt against "parliamentarism" in the name of "direct action," but this seems disproved by the fact that the turnout for the general election of December 1910 was the highest in history—86.6 percent.[274] The real threats came from outside England's borders: in Ireland, and far more dangerously from conflicts in the Balkans in which it had little influence and little interest, but which would change it forever.

# CHAPTER 14

# Imperial England, 1815–1918

There's a little group of isles beyond the wave—
So tiny you might almost wonder where it is,
That nation is the bravest of the brave,
And cowards are the rarest of all rarities.
The proudest nations kneel at her command;
She terrifies all foreign-born rapscallions,
And holds the peace of Europe in her hand
With half-a-score invincible battalions!
*Such at least is the tale which is born on the gale*
*From the island that dwells in the sea*
*Let us hope, for her sake, that she makes no mistake*
*That she's all she professes to be!*

W. S. Gilbert, *Utopia Ltd.* (1893)

The end of the titanic struggle with France in 1815 left Britain the first global hegemon in history, a position only otherwise occupied by the United States after 1989. Its naval power maximized its strength, enabling some 45 percent of its forces to be deployed overseas at the end of the war.[1] Yet there were limits to its power, some self-imposed. Policy after Waterloo was defensive: "It is not our business to collect trophies," wrote the Foreign Secretary, Lord Castlereagh, to the Prime Minister, "but to try [to] bring the world back to peaceful habits."[2] An unwitting tribute was paid by Napoleon: "Castlereagh had the Continent at his mercy . . . And he made peace as if he had been defeated. The imbecile!"[3] As we saw in Chapter 13, there was irresistible pressure to reduce taxation and debt. The navy was rapidly cut back to a peacetime footing, with nearly 90 percent of its officers unemployed, and the number of ships in commission falling from 713 in 1814 to 121 in 1818.[4] All governments throughout the century were as parsimonious as they could be, pressed by lobbies that combined equal devotion to peace and cheap government. Gladstone's Liberal government in the 1860s, for example, was so keen to reduce the costs of empire that it was happy to contemplate "friendly relaxation" of links with the colonies, or even "separation," and it shrugged off the queen's complaint that Britain was being reduced to "a second-rate power."[5] Military spending was generally 2–3 percent of national income—about the same as today—but Britain's wealth meant that this represented more money than in any other state except sometimes France.[6] Yet it often seemed (as a senior officer minuted in 1899) that Britain was "attempting to maintain the largest Empire the world has ever seen with armaments and reserves that would be insufficient for a third-class Military Power."[7]

With limited material forces, it had to deal with robustly independent and relatively powerful European states. The navy, master of the oceans, had 40,000–50,000 men in mid-century, about the same as today. Its reach, as was often wryly observed, depended on there being water. The army was never more than a sizeable colonial police force by comparison with those of the other Great Powers. In 1857, on the eve of the Great Mutiny, there were only 23,000 British soldiers in the whole of northern India from the Khyber Pass to Rangoon, fewer than in Northern Ireland in the 1980s; and there were more British troops in Afghanistan in 2012 than in any of the Victorian Afghan wars. So the army was often over-exposed, sometimes disastrously so: 700 British troops, 3,800 Indian and 12,000 civilians were massacred in Afghanistan in 1841, another 1,700 men wiped out at Isandlwana in Zululand in 1879, and half a brigade lost at Maiwand in Afghanistan in 1880. The Foreign Office in the 1820s had a staff of 36, and the separate Diplomatic Service remained unchanged between the 1860s and the 1910s at under 150 men, compared with a combined total of over 6,000 today. The Colonial Office numbered 113 clerks in 1903—half the U.K. Ministry of Defence's press office today—to oversee an empire that consisted of over 100 separate political units (not including some 600 Indian princely states).[8] The Indian civil service in the late nineteenth century numbered no more than 2,000— smaller than Ofsted, the school inspection service, today. Many, at the time and since, have emphasized the fragility and even the illusory nature of British power during the once-vaunted "Pax Britannica."

Yet if we look from the outside, as if from Paris, St. Petersburg or Constantinople, the picture is different. Britain was effectively invulnerable: all other major states, including the United States and Japan, were invaded during the nineteenth century, some several times. But no potential enemy since Napoleon has ever seriously prepared an invasion of Britain, and he

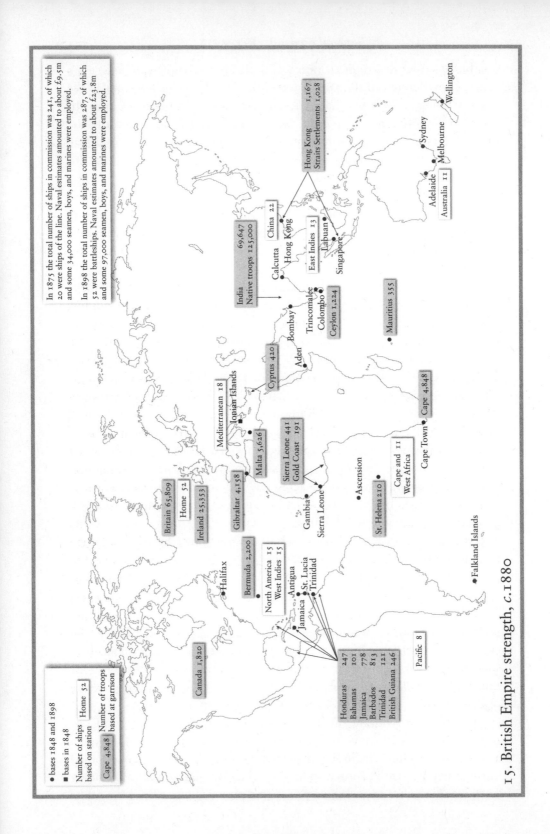

In 1875 the total number of ships in commission was 241, of which 20 were ships of the line. Naval estimates amounted to about £9.5m and some 34,000 seamen, boys, and marines were employed.

In 1898 the total number of ships in commission was 287, of which 52 were battleships. Naval estimates amounted to about £23.8m and some 97,000 seamen, boys, and marines were employed.

Hong Kong 1,167
Straits Settlements 1,028

China 22
Hong Kong
East Indies 13
Labuan
Singapore

India 69,647
Native troops 125,000

Calcutta

Bombay
Trincomalee
Colombo    Ceylon 1,224

Aden

Mauritius 355

Cyprus 420
Ionian Islands

Mediterranean 18
Malta 5,626

Cape 4,848

Sierra Leone 441
Gold Coast 191

Cape and
West Africa 11

Cape Town

Britain 65,809
Home 52
Ireland 25,353

Gibraltar 4,158

Gambia
Sierra Leone

Ascension

St. Helena 210

Halifax

Bermuda 2,200

North America 15
West Indies 15

Antigua
St. Lucia
Jamaica    Trinidad

Falkland Islands

Canada 1,820

Honduras 247
Bahamas 101
Jamaica 778
Barbados 813
Trinidad 121
British Guiana 246

Pacific 8

Wellington

Sydney
Adelaide    Melbourne
Australia 11

● bases 1848 and 1898
■ bases in 1848

Number of ships
based on station    Home 52

Cape 4,848    Number of troops
based at garrison

15. British Empire strength, c.1880

would probably have failed had he mounted it; Hitler got no further than aspiration. No one between 1815 and 1914 dreamed of threatening its security in Europe. No major state until Japan in 1941 calculatedly attacked its empire. All were deterred by its naval power, its huge financial and economic capacity, and its ability to strike without being struck. Its dominance of the seas made any repetition of the global conflicts of the eighteenth century impossible, and restrained the imperialist ambitions of European powers. Simon Bolivar, the early-nineteenth-century South American revolutionary leader, declared that "only England, mistress of the seas, can protect us against the united force of European reaction."[9] Despite continual complaints about excessive naval spending over the century, the Royal Navy maintained overwhelming superiority: in the 1880s it had thirty-eight large battleships, while all other navies combined had only forty; and although its numerical superiority declined later in the century as other countries built, it still maintained a "two-power standard," a navy larger than those of the two next strongest naval powers combined.[10] A striking sign of power is that in major areas Britain got its way, and even got more than it wanted. It had not wanted to rule Egypt, for example, but eventually did; the French did want it, but could not get it. It obtained practically all it wanted economically in South America without needing major political intervention. The most important international consequence of British naval power was to provide a guarantee of open international trading conditions for everyone, fostering an economic globalization in many ways more complete than in the twenty-first century, and, unlike previous periods of partial globalization, driven more by technology than by violence.[11]

British power and influence in the century following Waterloo—vastly more extensive than those of the United States since 1945—are explicable in large part by the fluidity and fragility of much of the globe.[12] The fragmentation of the Mughal Empire following Persian and Afghan invasions in the early eighteenth century was the condition of British power in India. The Chinese Empire entered into a crisis in the mid-eighteenth century. The Persian Empire collapsed in the 1720s. The Ottoman Empire began its long agony after defeat by Austria and Russia in the late eighteenth century and Napoleon's invasion of Egypt in 1798. The Napoleonic Wars also finished off the Spanish Empire, fragmented the Portuguese, and enfeebled the Dutch. New and sometimes aggressive polities were appearing in Africa and Asia, such as the Asante and Zulu kingdoms, the caliphate of Sokoto, the Sikh and Maratha confederations, and the kingdom of Siam. In other parts of the world, organization and identity were still local: there were 150 "nations" west of the Mississippi; over 200 language groups in Australia; hundreds of polities and thousands of language groups in Africa.[13]

In these circumstances, resistance to British power was weak, and its hegemonic position could be maintained on a shoestring. Many of the inhabitants of a pre-nationalist world were more or less acquiescent, and even cooperative. The British saw themselves as having duties as well as interests, and, like other powerful peoples, saw their interests as the interests of all: spreading Christian civilization, breaking down vested interests, encouraging toleration, opening communications, and promoting international commerce.[14] Governments upheld what they saw as the national interest and very rarely allowed themselves to be dictated to by lobbies: they manipulated business interests rather than being manipulated by them.[15] The broad aim was to project a favourable image of Britain as embodying constitutional freedoms, humanitarian rights and the rule of law.[16] British politicians often felt moral pressure to intervene where states were failing or non-existent, most extensively in India and Africa. Inaction was seen as a shameful dereliction of duty. It was strongly felt to be an obligation to provide leadership and assist the forces of progress, preferably by peaceful means, but by force if necessary against "barbarity." The moralizing, missionary aspect of nineteenth-century politics should not be underestimated,[17] despite Cecil Rhodes's cynical quip that empire was philanthropy plus 5 percent profit. So Britain was diplomatically very active and at war somewhere most of the time. There was lethal arrogance here, combined with naïvely optimistic generosity, believing that the freedom and prosperity England had recently secured should be spread.

The ideological foundations of foreign policy were above all Whig ideas of English history as the triumph of Progress. This led Charles James Fox to commit the Whigs to supporting "civil and religious liberties all over the world." Tories—often accused from Castlereagh onwards of complicity with reactionary regimes—did tend to be less assertive and "ethical," though these were differences of degree. For generations, much of the energy came from evangelical Anglicans and the Nonconformist conscience—what we might call the "religious left." Radicals, both secular and Christian, believed in the universality of progressive values, which they considered Britain had a duty to uphold. The most pugnacious exponent of this muscular liberalism was Henry John Temple, 3rd Viscount Palmerston (1784–1865), whose career spanned six decades. He was Secretary at War as early as 1809, Foreign Secretary from 1830 to 1841 and 1846 to 1851, and Prime Minister from 1855 to 1858 and 1859 to 1863—the zenith of British power and overseas activity. Palmerston was a cosmopolitan Anglo-Irishman who liked to play John Bull: he could say unashamedly that inferior states needed to feel his stick across their shoulders from time to time; and also say that the extinction of the Atlantic slave trade was the greatest moment of his career. The brutality and the humanitarianism emerged from the same frame of mind.

Europe was always the centre of the plot even when the action took place somewhere else.[18] Treaties in 1814 and 1815 to maintain peace and restrain France were largely a British achievement.[19] Britain and Russia were the dominant European powers during the first half of the nineteenth century, and both wanted in different ways to stabilize the Continent. The "Holy Alliance," Tsar Alexander I's visionary attempt to create a permanent international organization on religious principles (which Castlereagh privately described as a "piece of sublime mysticism and nonsense" and did not sign[20]), was criticized for prioritizing stability over liberty. British governments—Castlereagh quietly, and his successor George Canning more stridently—saw it as in the national interest to promote liberal reform as a safeguard against both absolutist aggression and the dangers of revolution.

Britain exercised a quasi-protectorate over western Europe and the Mediterranean, which persisted, unevenly, until the Second World War. Countries think twice about—or do not think at all about—challenging the hegemonic power and tend to adopt policies that it favours. They may request more protection than the protector wants to give. The Portuguese government repeatedly asked for British assistance against internal enemies, and the Swedes asked for patrols in the Baltic in the 1860s. Britain discouraged Russia and Prussia from intervention in France at the time of the 1830 and 1848 revolutions. It helped to bring about Greek independence from Turkey in the 1820s. It protected newly independent Belgium during the 1830s and guaranteed its future independence. It aided liberal movements in Spain and Portugal during the 1830s and 1840s, though with limited success, and restrained French interference. It promoted Italian independence and unification in the 1850s and 1860s. It repeatedly defended the Ottoman Empire from France, Egypt, Austria and Russia. Britain used its influence to restrain Scandinavian quarrels and was ready in 1864 to send a fleet to counter Prussian and Austrian moves into Denmark. Overt influence was most easily exercised where seapower could disrupt economic activity by blockade, prevent or facilitate the transport of troops, or even take direct action by bombardment or amphibious landing. Even the hint of these possibilities might be effective. Muhammad Ali, the ambitious ruler of Egypt in the early nineteenth century, thought that "with the English for my friends I can do anything: without their friendship I can do nothing."[21] In Europe and the Mediterranean, by means of diplomatic pressure, investments or loans, and occasionally military force, Britain favoured, and sometimes protected, representative government, economic development and trade. Western Europe, with misgivings, followed its lead.

Britain—considered by Gladstone to be "the centre of the moral, social, and political power of the world"[22]—had other kinds of influence in Europe too. We can detect its "soft power" in the near universalization of English styles of men's clothing, of social customs such as clubs and sports, of English literature and increasingly the English language, which began to rival French. As John Bright declared in 1865, "England is the mother of parliaments," for the two-chamber parliament became the standard form. So did constitutional monarchy, the accountability of ministers to parliament, parliamentary control of the national budget, collective Cabinet responsibility, freedom of expression, legal political parties, trial by jury and independence of judges. It was impossible to copy exactly a system that was as idiosyncratic, uncodified and rapidly evolving as that of England, yet its domestic history seemed to show that it had found a way of giving some rights to all without guillotining the elite. This was not democracy or egalitarianism—those on the left continued to take inspiration from the French Revolution. But France itself, in its constitutional Charters (1814 and 1830) and, after a painful interval, in its Third Republic (1875) came as close as it could to the arcana of Westminster. Belgium (1832), the Netherlands (1848), Denmark (1848), Italy (1860), Sweden (1867) and Spain (1874) also tried English-style systems. Absolutist states such as Austria and Russia eventually found a House of Lords a useful device for neutralizing even a timid elected chamber.

English economic developments too provided the model to be followed with enthusiasm or trepidation. Technology, institutions and legislation were copied—railways, steam power, machinery, stocks and shares, limited-liability companies, factory acts. Manchester and Birmingham were visited by foreign industrialists, who bought English machines, raised English capital, and hired English workers—sometimes with alarming results when they got drunk, demanded wage increases, and caused trouble with the locals. After 1860 the British creed of free trade inspired the first short-lived European common market.[23] But jealousy of English economic dominance, and revulsion at the social and political consequences of industrialization—cities, smoke, nouveau riche vulgarity, working-class assertiveness, social change, visible poverty—were as marked as admiration of the wealth and power it yielded. "The English," pronounced the French novelist Théophile Gautier in 1856, "can forge iron, harness steam, twist matter in every way, invent frighteningly powerful machines: [but] despite their stupendous material advances, they are only polished barbarians."[24]

## DOMINION OVER PALM AND PINE, c.1815–1880

*Never certainly did any nation, since the world began, assume anythiug like so much responsibility.*

J. R. Seeley, *The Expansion of England* (1883)

During the Napoleonic Wars the number of Britain's overseas possessions had increased from twenty-six to forty-three,[25] and there then followed a century of expansion, averaging 100,000 square miles per year. Paradoxically, there was little or no appetite in London for adding to the empire, and some conquests were handed back. Parts of Indonesia were returned to Holland in 1824. The Ionian Islands were ceded to Greece. There was no attempt to regain Corsica, which had previously asked to join the empire, after its reoccupation by France in 1796. Later requests from inhabitants of Ethiopia, Mexico, Uruguay, Sarawak, Katanga and Morocco to join the empire were firmly turned down, and there was reluctance and delay in absorbing Fiji, New Guinea and Basutoland. Occupying new territory usually turned on some combination of strategic interests, local responses, economic importance, lobbying by interested parties, sudden emergencies and the wish to keep other European states out.

English opinion was by no means sure that it wanted an "empire," which implied authoritarian rule and, some feared, threatened liberty at home by augmenting the power of the state, especially its military institutions. A *British* Empire should at least be a free association, and many believed, even hoped, that its constituent parts would gradually become independent, like the United States. Empires also cost money: England had been and continued to be the most heavily taxed nation in the world in cash terms, with the heaviest burden falling on the middle classes.[26] Cheese-paring governments wanted colonies to be self-supporting. This was rarely achieved, and Britain paid most of the defence costs, as well as subsidizing administration and communications. It is worth recalling the context of Disraeli's famous phrase about India: "There never was a jewel in the crown of England that was so truly costly."[27] Yet England was rich enough to afford it. As a proportion of GDP taxation and spending were slightly below the European average between 1870 and 1913: central government revenue *c.*1870 was 8.7 percent of GDP in Britain, compared with 15.3 percent in France, 11.6 percent in Belgium, 9.5 percent in Sweden, 7.4 percent in the USA, 4.3 percent in Norway.[28]

Many in England felt uncomfortable about India, less the jewel in the crown than the cuckoo in the nest. As we saw earlier, the British presence there had originally been commercial, through the chartered Honourable East India Company (HEIC). Over the second half of the eighteenth century it had increasingly become a territorial ruler, originally under nominal Mughal sovereignty and then as an agent of the British government—the greatest ever quango. But expansion had taken place haphazardly, often driven by the ambitions of men on the spot, months away from the restraining and parcimonious hands of Whitehall and Westminster. British actions had always aroused controversy as well as pride. "How can the same nation pursue two lines of policy so radically different . . . despotic in Asia and democratic in Australia? . . . Why do we . . . involve ourselves in the anxiety and responsibility of governing two hundred millions of people in Asia?" asked Sir John Seeley, the pioneer Cambridge historian of empire, in 1883.[29] Yet this view of the empire as a confederation of settler colonies ignored the immense economic and strategic importance of India, both directly as a market for British goods and as the source of the Indian army that made Britain an Asian power from the Persian Gulf to Shanghai, and also indirectly, as Indians were the producers, merchants and labourers who constructed a vast economic network. As one historian sums it up, "Across a large part of the world East of Suez, it would have been more accurate to talk not of a British, but of an Anglo-Indian empire."[30]

Those driving the extension of power in India between the middle of the eighteenth century and the middle of the nineteenth had a potent mixture of motives: the ambition to make a name and a fortune; a growing belief in Britain's destiny to rule as a "new Rome"; and a confident belief that they could "improve" India, encouraged in some cases by Christian zeal, and in all cases by the belief that Britain was in the vanguard of human Progress. Intervention and often annexation took place in what the British considered failing states, where there was internal conflict, disputed succession, serious human rights abuse or the danger of inter-state conflict.[31] Where there was, or seemed to be, a military threat—from the Marathas (whose cavalry were ferocious raiders), the Afghans or the Sikhs in the Punjab—they were fought and eventually defeated or at least checked. By 1850 the HEIC directly governed most of northern, central and south-eastern India, and states under Indian rulers were subordinated. This security-led expansion of what has been called the "imperial garrison state" was more important than trade or settlement in pushing forward the boundaries of empire.[32]

Perhaps the most notorious cultural imperialists were the Utilitarians James Mill and Thomas Babington Macaulay, who in 1835 drafted a Minute on education in India, arguing that money should be spent on teaching English and European science, philosophy and history, rather than "medical doctrines which would disgrace an English Farrier—Astronomy, which would move laughter in girls at an English boarding school—History, abounding with kings thirty foot high . . . and Geography, made up of seas of treacle and seas of butter."[33] This is often quoted as an egregious example of racial arrogance; in fact, it was Utilitarian arrogance towards all traditional culture, English as well as Indian—Mill considered all poetry a relic of barbarism. Not all shared Mill's sweeping modernism: Benares College, founded in 1791, preserved, even re-created, a supposedly traditional Indian culture. The British were often torn between admiration and impatience, pride and guilt. One of the most influential voices of the age, Richard Cobden, regarded Britain's record in India as one of "spoliation and wrong" and hoped for the "happy day when England has not an acre of territory in Continental Asia."[34]

Many humanitarians, however, were eager to use British power to do good, and they constituted a significant lobby. Anti-slavery was the most urgent cause. When in 1814 Castlereagh successfully pressed the French to agree to abolish their slave trade in five years' time, this delay was denounced as the "death warrant of a multitude of innocent victims" and a huge national campaign was organized, claiming 750,000 supporters. Wellington tried to renegotiate the treaty, and the government put pressure on its allies Spain and Portugal, the main slave-buying nations, to stop the trade. Castlereagh wrote: "You must really press the Spanish . . . there is hardly a village that has not met and petitioned."[35] London even asked the Pope for support. Castlereagh persuaded the reluctant Great Powers to attach to the Treaty of Vienna (1815) a condemnation of the slave trade—the first such "human rights" declaration in a major international treaty.[36] This began a long effort to end slaving, against the resistance of the slave-trading and slave-holding nations and their African suppliers.

Campaigning peaked in 1833 with more than 5,000 petitions, containing nearly 1.5 million signatures. One, more than a mile long, was signed and sewn together by women, who played an unprecedented part in the campaign, among them Elizabeth Heyrick, author of *Immediate, Not*

*Gradual Abolition* (1824). Parliament responded in 1834 by emancipating 800,000 slaves in the empire, paying a huge £20m in compensation to the owners—equal to a third of the state budget—and requiring a four-year "apprenticeship" by slaves. This was thus a compromise measure, but still its anniversary was publicly celebrated annually by American abolitionists as a great achievement.[37] In 1843 British subjects were forbidden to own slaves anywhere in the world. The abolition of slavery in the empire in practice applied to slave ownership by whites. Greatly affected was the Cape Colony, one of the most rigid and oppressive slave societies in history. The "Boers" (Dutch-speaking settlers) responded by trekking out of British territory, outraged that black people were "placed on an equal footing with Christians, contrary to the laws of God."[38] Traditional forms of servitude remained endemic in Africa and Asia, however, and in places still remain; and colonial authorities were very cautious about tackling them.

Even when other states agreed to outlaw slave trafficking—sometimes (as with Spain and Portugal) with compensation paid by Britain—they commonly winked at evasion. So the Royal Navy placed a permanent squadron from 1808 to 1870, at times equal to a sixth of its ships, to try to intercept slavers off West Africa. It was based at Freetown, the capital of the colony for freed slaves at Sierra Leone, which had the first African Anglican bishop, Samuel Crowther, rescued as a boy from a slave ship by the Royal Navy. Patrolling was a thankless and gruelling effort, exposing crews to yellow fever, hardship and even personal legal liability for damages; it also cost a large amount of taxpayers' money. France and the United States refused to allow the Royal Navy to search ships flying their flags. There was continual diplomatic friction with slave-trading states. British officials there were often threatened with violence. During the 1830s and 1840s several American ships forced by bad weather into British colonial territory had the slaves they were carrying released.[39] In 1839 in the famous case of the slave ship *Amistad*, when captives rebelled and killed the captain, British testimony proving illegal action by American officials helped to secure their freedom. A serious dispute with the United States occurred in 1841 when American slaves on the ship *Creole*, being taken from Virginia to be sold in New Orleans, seized the ship and killed a slave-trader. They were given asylum in the British-ruled Bahamas, where they were acquitted of any crime and declared free.[40]

Britain signed forty-five treaties with African rulers to stop the traffic at source. They were very reluctant to give it up, even threatening to kill all their slaves if they were prevented from selling them. In several cases, Britain paid them to abandon the traffic. Abolitionists urged that Britain should maintain a territorial presence in West Africa, to combat illegal trafficking and promote legitimate commerce, such as palm oil, to wean African rulers and Liverpool merchants away from slaving and towards soap manufacture—a good example of cleanliness being next to godliness. By 1830 palm oil exports were worth more than the slave trade. But the trade continued, and the Royal Navy adopted more aggressive tactics, including blockading rivers and destroying slave pens on shore, even when these were foreign property. In 1861 it occupied Lagos, deposing the ruler who refused to stop the trade, and thus blocked one of the main slave routes. Over sixty years the navy captured hundreds of slave ships off the African coast and freed some 160,000 captives. As one recalled it:

> They took off all the fetters from our feet and threw them into the water, and they gave us clothes that we might cover our nakedness, they opened the water casks, that we might drink water to the full, and we also ate food, till we had enough.[41]

Several hundred thousand more were prevented from being shipped from Africa by naval and diplomatic pressure.[42]

Palmerston, as Foreign Secretary, was prepared to put pressure on slave-buyers too. In 1839 he simply ordered the seizure of Portuguese slave ships, and in 1845 his successor, Lord Aberdeen, declared Brazilian slave ships to be pirates, and 400 were seized in five years. In 1850 the Royal Navy even forcibly entered Brazilian ports to seize or destroy hundreds of slave ships—decisive in forcing Brazil, the biggest slave-buyer of all, to end one of the largest forced emigrations in history. Palmerston said this had given him his "greatest and purest pleasure."[43] Cuba, supplied by fast United States ships, came under similar pressure. But American ships were treated more cautiously, as searches of suspected slave ships carrying the Stars and Stripes caused threats of war from Washington. As Palmerston expostulated, "every slave trading Pirate" could escape by simply hoisting "a piece of Bunting with the United States emblems."[44] The American Civil War caused a reversal in American policy in 1862, when Abraham Lincoln's government signed a secret treaty allowing the Royal Navy to intercept American slavers. The Spanish and Cuban authorities bowed to circumstances, and the Atlantic slave trade was effectively ended. Slavery itself remained legal in the United States until the 1860s, and in much of Latin America until the 1880s. As late as 1881 the Royal Navy arrested an American slave ship off the Gold Coast.[45]

The British campaign against the slave trade has often been debunked. French and American slave-traders accused Britain of using it as a pretext to try to gain control of West Africa, Cuba, even Texas. Some later historians claimed that slavery ended only because it was no longer profitable. But recent research is practically unanimous that slavery was booming, and it would have been in Britain's economic interests to expand it, as the United States did. But Britain was rich enough to let its powerful humanitarian and religious lobby get its way.[46]

Did Britain—another accusation at the time and since—use the slave trade as a pretext for colonial expansion in Africa? In fact, successive governments were reluctant to rule inhospitable and relatively profitless territory, and movement inland was negligible until the late-nineteenth-century "scramble for Africa." The exception, which involved campaigns against the aggressive slaving kingdom of the Asante (Ashanti)—a magnificent and exceptionally cruel warrior society—was done at the request of Africans on the coast, who were subject to repeated attack from the 1820s onwards and requested British protection. Central Africa meanwhile was being devastated by Muslim slavers supplying the Middle East. The Foreign Office estimated that they were taking 25,000–30,000 people per year during the 1860s, and the nineteenth-century total has been estimated at between 4 million and 6 million people, huge numbers dying as they were dragged across the Sahara or to the coast, and many others being killed in the violence of capture.[47] British anti-slavery groups— inspired by the adventures and writings in the 1850s and 1860s of one of the most revered Victorian heroes, the working-class missionary and explorer David Livingstone—demanded government intervention in what Livingstone had rightly called the open sore of the world. He hoped optimistically that a "Christian colony" of "twenty or thirty good Christian Scotch families" would lead to moral and commercial improvement and would put an end to slavery.[48] Instead, a long diplomatic effort was required to throttle the trade, by persuading African rulers to stop supplying and Muslim states to close the great slave markets of Egypt, Persia, Turkey and the Gulf. Britain had far less power to act directly in the Muslim world, where slavery had ancient social and religious sanction, so action had to be discreet. The consul-general at Cairo in the 1860s, Thomas F. Reade, spied out the Egyptian slave markets disguised as an Arab. He estimated that 15,000 Africans were sold in Cairo annually, and reported on "the cruelties and abominations" involved. Other diplomats were active in helping escaped slaves, including by purchasing their freedom with official funds, and the consul in Benghazi maintained a safe house for escapers at his own expense.[49] British interference in the slave trade— however cautious Whitehall tried to be—could cause serious tensions and even led to mass uprisings in Egypt and the Sudan (see pp. 582–83). However, careful but persistent high-level pressure on the Egyptian, Turkish and Persian governments to forbid the trade, backed up by naval patrols, treaties and even bribes to officials to apply the law, eventually had considerable effect. Pressure and financial inducements to the sultan of Zanzibar (a vast slaving entrepôt) shut its slave market in 1873. Pressure on Egypt resulted in an Anglo-Egyptian Convention of 1877 to end the trade, and in 1883 a similar convention was signed with the Ottoman government.[50] Further afield, the navy even patrolled off Australia to stop "blackbirding" (bringing quasi-slaves from Fiji and other Pacific islands) for the sugar plantations of Queensland.

Britain pressed for the insertion of an anti-slavery agreement in the 1885 Berlin Act on the partition of Africa, though it was notoriously unequally applied. As a Foreign Office official noted in 1896, Britain, "with small military means," could only govern "countries full of Arabs . . . with the assistance of the Arabs."[51] Moreover, the partial abolition of slavery was no panacea—indeed, it gave rise to other social and economic problems. There was a huge multiplication of indentured labour, particularly of Indians shipped to the Caribbean and Africa, who were also highly exploited. Suppressing the slave trade meant at first unsaleable slaves being held by African rulers, and treated even more cruelly. Generally, the British stopped slave trading and abolished slavery as a legal status in territories they controlled in Africa and India (often with financial compensation to the slave-owners), so that slaves could free themselves— which many did. The colonial official Frederick Lugard claimed that 55,000 became free without violence in northern Nigeria between 1902 and 1917.[52] Gradual abolition weakened the brutal hierarchies of slave-owning societies, indirectly benefiting women and the young. The fact that emancipation was supervised by "alien and disinterested authorities" smoothed the process.[53]

Humanitarian pressure also played a part in the annexation of Natal, the Gold Coast, New Zealand and Fiji. The case of New Zealand illustrates the process. Maoris first visited London in the 1820s. They encouraged white settlers of various nationalities in the 1820s and 1830s to trade and provide technology. Some settlers were innocuous, even benevolent. Others were unscrupulous predators who sold guns and alcohol, fuelling internecine wars. Under pressure from missionaries, and with French annexation imminent, a hesitant naval officer, Captain William Hobson, signed the Treaty of Waitangi in 1840 with Maori rulers, several of whom had previously requested British protection. The intentions were to control increasing white settlement, regulate land sales, prevent inter-racial conflict, and forestall the French. As so often in imperial history, the future was strewn with unintended consequences: British troops ended up fighting wars in 1845 and 1860 against the Maori to defend settlers whose aggressive behaviour the British government deplored. The Fiji islands were made a protectorate in 1874 after several requests by Fijians, who were victims of slaving and other depredations by white interlopers.

## THE WHITE TIDE

> Here we had toil and little to reward it
> But there shall plenty smile upon our pain,
> And ours shall be the mountain and the forest,
> And boundless prairies ripe with golden grain.
>
> Charles Mackay, "The Emigrants" (1856)[54]

The vast migrations of European and Asian peoples, which began in the 1500s and peaked in the nineteenth and twentieth centuries, destroyed and remade large parts of the world. There were remarkable achievements. New South Wales, which had been a tiny, starving and violent convict settlement in the 1790s, in a few decades had a beautiful convict-designed church, a grammar school, a university college, a cathedral and a parliament, and within a century was one of the richest communities in the world. But for indigenous populations, especially hunter-gatherers and traditional rulers, in the Americas, southern Africa, Australasia, Siberia and the Pacific, mass immigration was the end of their world, a living nightmare from which many of their descendants have not woken, and may never wake. For many settlers on the "frontier," lured by dreams of self-betterment, even wealth, life was not much better—a struggle against nature, poverty and often violence.

Wherever outsiders arrived, indigenous populations collapsed. Diseases to which they had no immunity wrought devastation: smallpox, measles, tuberculosis, influenza. Microbes were even-handed: when thirty-six emigrants from the isolated Scottish island of St. Kilda (a third of its population) sailed for Australia in 1852, half died of measles on the way. A quarter of the population of Fiji also died of measles.[55] In North America, the native population fell from perhaps 10 million to less than 500,000; in New Zealand, from around 100,000 to 40,000. In parts of South America, the Caribbean, southern Africa and Australia, peoples became extinct, culturally and even physically. Perhaps the most notorious case today is Australia, where the aboriginal population fell from perhaps 750,000 to 60,000 during the nineteenth century. This is usually blamed on Europeans, who did indeed wreak havoc; but the deadliest killer, which probably wiped out around half the population in a few decades, was smallpox brought by Asian fishermen in the late eighteenth century.[56]

Disease was the main but not the sole scourge, as waves of settlers occupied land and seized resources. "Undeveloped," sparsely populated land was profitable for grazing, farming, mining and forestry for European and especially British markets. Most vulnerable were stateless hunter-gatherers in the Americas, Australia and parts of Africa, who were assumed to be able to "move on" as Europeans displaced them. But, as in Australia, "nomads" were spiritually and economically dependent on intimate knowledge of a territory, and to be forced out was both demoralizing and dangerous, as they became liable to attack by other native peoples. Europeans used sustained violence to expand their settlements and defend their new property. Settlers, scientists and politicians commonly regarded the extinction of "savages" as progress. After a few generations, the best that most survivors could hope for was to work as labourers for the new masters, or eke out an impoverished, demoralized and despised existence in "reservations" and shanty towns on the margins of American, Australian and African settler society—a position that many still occupy.

British and Irish settlers played a major part in this catastrophe, totalling more than a third of some 50 million emigrants from Europe between 1815 and 1930. The disproportionate number of British subjects (11.4 million from Great Britain and 7 million from Ireland, compared for example with 4.8 million from Germany) who went far overseas was partly because the way was opened by British world power and global commerce. Mass emigration provided new opportunity for millions and relieved social problems. The typical migrant, from mid-century onward, was young, male, unmarried and semi-skilled. Most British and European emigrants, however, went not to British colonies, but to the United States—if "Westerns" were accurate, their cowboys would have Scottish and Irish accents. Enthusiastic colonialists welcomed this global propagation of "the race," creating "great British cities" such as New York, Boston, Sydney, Auckland and Toronto.[57] Later perspectives damn the enterprise as "genocide." Yet the British Empire did not deliberately promote genocide. Parliamentary committees from 1814 onwards began to consider the plight of "the Aboriginal Peoples of the British Empire" and enacted laws to restrain British subjects even outside British territory. In countries such as the United States, Argentina and the Boer republics that had thrown off imperial controls, partly to have a free hand in dealing with natives (see p. 349), aggressive settlement was deliberately condoned and assisted by governments and their armed forces. As President Theodore Roosevelt saw it, "The most ultimately righteous of all wars is a war with sav-

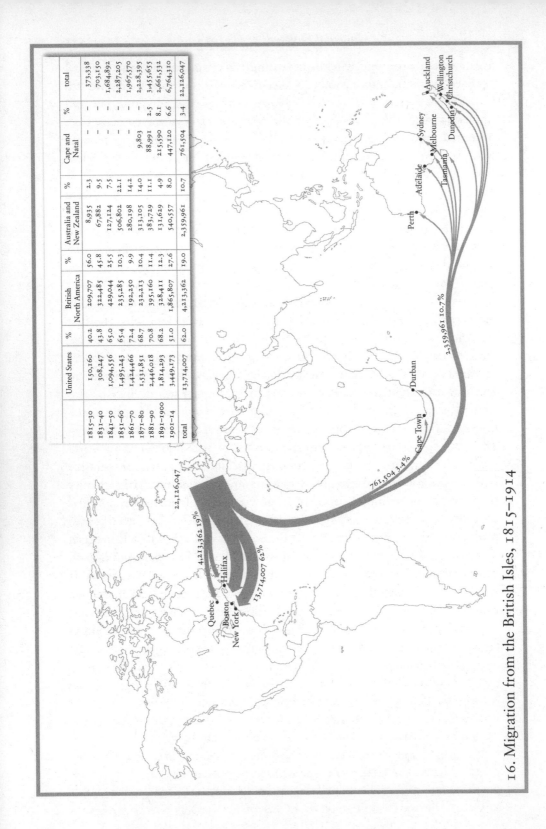

| | United States | % | British North America | % | Australia and New Zealand | % | Cape and Natal | % | total |
|---|---|---|---|---|---|---|---|---|---|
| 1815–30 | 150,160 | 40.2 | 209,707 | 56.0 | 8,935 | 2.3 | – | – | 373,338 |
| 1831–40 | 308,247 | 43.8 | 322,485 | 45.8 | 67,882 | 9.5 | – | – | 703,150 |
| 1841–50 | 1,094,556 | 65.0 | 429,044 | 25.5 | 127,124 | 7.5 | – | – | 1,684,892 |
| 1851–60 | 1,495,243 | 65.4 | 235,285 | 10.3 | 506,802 | 22.1 | – | – | 2,287,205 |
| 1861–70 | 1,424,466 | 72.4 | 192,250 | 9.9 | 280,198 | 14.2 | – | – | 1,967,570 |
| 1871–80 | 1,531,851 | 68.7 | 232,213 | 10.4 | 313,105 | 14.0 | 9,803 | – | 2,228,395 |
| 1881–90 | 2,446,018 | 70.8 | 395,160 | 11.4 | 383,729 | 11.1 | 88,991 | 2.5 | 3,455,655 |
| 1891–1900 | 1,814,293 | 68.2 | 328,411 | 12.3 | 131,629 | 4.9 | 215,590 | 8.1 | 2,661,532 |
| 1901–14 | 3,449,173 | 51.0 | 1,865,807 | 27.6 | 540,557 | 8.0 | 447,120 | 6.6 | 6,764,310 |
| total | 13,714,007 | 62.0 | 4,213,362 | 19.0 | 2,359,961 | 10.7 | 761,504 | 3.4 | 22,126,047 |

16. Migration from the British Isles, 1815–1914

ages . . . the fierce settler who drives the savage from the land lays all civilized mankind under a debt to him."[58]

British colonial authorities, under pressure from missionaries and humanitarian bodies such as the Society for the Protection of Aborigines, accepted a duty to native peoples. But there was also a contrasting belief that all peoples had a duty to "the human species" to develop the territories they occupied, or else make way for others who would do so.[59] Hunter-gatherers were seen as failing in this duty by not making full use of resources. Some attempts were made in South Africa, Australia, Canada and New Zealand to protect native land rights and stop violent attacks. This protection was never effective, and sometimes little more than symbolic—for example, forcing the trial and execution of seven New South Wales settlers in 1838, despite protestations that it was "hard for white men to be put to death for killing blacks." This was one of only two cases of whites ever being executed for the murder of Aborigines. At least 20,000 blacks and 5,000 whites were killed in more than a century of conflict in Australia, where periodic massacres continued into the 1920s.[60]

Humanitarian concerns ran up against "progressive" pressures to encourage settlement and welcome colonial self-government. British ministers such as Gladstone hoped that political responsibility would make settlers moderate their actions—an over-optimistic hope—and in New Zealand and southern Africa Britain delayed self-government to persuade them to do so. But in both regions its troops fought wars against native peoples to try to secure frontiers largely destabilized by settlers. Would any conceivable government action have prevented or significantly moderated the effect of mass immigration, most of which, of course, was to non-British territory, namely the United States? Could any authority without modern technology have policed long and distant frontiers of settlement? Would the Maori and others have been better off facing a settler free-for-all if London had followed its initial preference to decline responsibility? We rightly criticize colonial authorities both for what they did and for what they failed to do. But probably nothing made much difference in the long run: the ambitions of 50 million people were uncontrollable.

## "GOD'S DIPLOMACY"

O ye, the wise who think, the wise who reign,
From growing commerce loose her latest chain,
And let the fair white-wing'd peacemaker fly . . .
Till each man finds his own in all men's good,

And all men work in noble brotherhood,
Breaking their mailed fleets and armed towers,
And ruling by obeying nature's powers.

Alfred Tennyson, "Ode Sung at the Opening of the
International Exhibition," 1851

From the 1820s onwards there developed a visionary programme to transform the world by means of free trade—the closest modern England ever came to a national ideology.[61] Its prophet was Richard Cobden, co-founder of the Anti–Corn Law League, who, not content with the success of his cause in England, toured Europe and America as self-appointed "ambassador of the People." He declared free trade to be "the greatest revolution that ever happened in the world's history" and "the only human means of effecting universal and permanent peace."[62] As a children's book put it, the aim was that "everybody may . . . be joined together in love and trade, like one great family; so that we may have no more wicked, terrible battles, such as there used to be long ago."[63]

Contemporary critics and later writers often dismissed this as a cloak for economic self-interest: Britain had an economic dominance unique in history with 20–25 percent of total world trade, 30–40 percent of world shipping, 38 percent of world trade in manufactured goods, and 50 percent of total foreign investment, and so profited from removal of trade barriers. This is at best a half-truth. Over the whole period in which it operated, c.1850 to c.1930, free trade probably made Britain slightly poorer.[64] It meant that no British government could use its economic bargaining power to force other governments to accept free entry of British goods, which, in spite of the confident hopes of idealists and economists, few ever did. Britain simply allowed free access to its domestic market to all, including to countries such as the United States that limited British access to theirs. Free trade was maintained even when it seemed to be damaging the British economy: for example, due to German import penetration in the 1880s, when German industry was protected by tariffs from British competition. It may be that this was done partly by miscalculation and for party reasons, but there is no doubt that free trade seemed genuinely altruistic, and was unconditionally supported by religious groups, the anti-slavery movement, trade unions, women's associations and peace campaigners in the hope that all would eventually see the light. The dogma was that commercial freedom would inevitably bring political freedom and international harmony, and hence the dissolution of empires, the liberation of serfs and slaves, the end of the "antagonism of race, and creed, and language," and the abolition of "gigantic armies and great navies"[65]—which states would no longer need or, in the absence of revenue from tariffs, be able to afford.

There were indeed some real benefits. As we have seen, workers got cheaper food. More widely, Britain's commitment to free trade stimulated world trade for more than half a century. Cheaper British manufactured goods raised the living standards of overseas consumers.[66] Britain's "terms of trade" (the relative price of its exports compared with that of its imports) greatly declined after 1800, as the prices of its manufactures fell and the prices of the raw materials and food it bought abroad rose, thus further sharing the fruits of industrial revolution with the world. This, it has been suggested, is "surprising" to those who conceive of Britain as the industrial core "brutally exploiting a helplessly dependent primary producing 'periphery'" or as "a hegemonic imperial state wringing tribute from its colonial territories."[67] Other countries—often using British capital and machinery—were able to import the latest techniques and hence catch up. If this was an overall benefit to the world's economic well-being, there were also those who lost, sometimes catastrophically: peoples whose land was taken for agricultural development, and who went hungry while their countries exported produce—most disastrously, in the Indian famines of the 1870s and 1890s.[68]

So beneficial did free trade seem to its disciples that they believed that no government, and particularly not archaic and reactionary regimes such as those of China and Japan, had the right to deny its benefits to their own people. Free traders were universalistic: all mankind was morally and intellectually the same, human values were transnational, racial or ethnic differences were irrelevant, and civilization and progress were the right and destiny of all. However, some nations were more advanced than others—with England economically and politically in the lead. This could mean, as one Englishman put it tartly in 1863, that his countrymen thought that "all men were morally and intellectually alike" and all "equally inferior to himself."[69]

Unquestioned belief in the morality and civilizing influence of commercial freedom explains how a country that was striving to stop the African slave trade was also striving to export opium to China. Some of the same people were involved, notably Palmerston. Although he believed that "Her Majesty's Government cannot interfere for the purpose of enabling British merchants to violate the laws of the country to which they trade," he equally believed that "Commerce is the best pioneer of civilization," making mankind "happier, wiser, better."[70] The grotesque tragi-comedy of Anglo-Chinese relations, marked by reciprocal arrogance, incomprehension and racism, had begun in the 1790s, when a diplomatic mission bear-

ing gifts of British products was told (in reality, rather duplicitously) that
China wanted nothing that Britain could provide. The Chinese insisted
that the British and all foreigners were barbarians who could on no
account be treated as equals. The British regarded the "Tartar" Empire as
archaic, cruel and corrupt, having no right to refuse diplomatic relations
or ban beneficial commercial contacts. Opium grown in India was one
commodity Chinese consumers were certainly eager to buy, but the Peking
authorities insisted that Britain and other foreign governments should
prevent the trade. Opium—though in Gladstone's view a "most infamous
and atrocious trade"[71]—was extremely valuable to the East India Company and merchants such as Jardine & Matheson and their Chinese partners. They argued that opium had long been grown and used in China and
was no more harmful than whisky, but there was much criticism in Britain
of the "immoral" trade. Whether opium was the cause or the pretext for
conflict, it is likely that a clash would have occurred in time, as happened
with Japan. For the Qing Empire, much was at stake. The court and the
scholar-bureaucracy foresaw that contact with the outside world would
destabilize the empire, and feared that a rise of mercantile wealth in the
coastal regions would undermine their authority. The First Opium War
(1840–42) began when the authorities in Canton destroyed opium stocks.
The British government, already involved in serious disputes in South
America, Syria and Afghanistan, and with Chartist agitation at home, was
reluctant to get involved, but felt it had to uphold its credibility. The
United States and several European countries followed suit—the first time
the British and American navies fought on the same side. Foreign luminaries, including the French political philosopher Alexis de Tocqueville and
the American John Quincy Adams, applauded the British action as progressive.

   The Chinese were astonished by British power, as Royal Navy frigates
sailed up the Pearl River, sinking war junks and bombarding and occupying
Canton. The British were astonished by Chinese resistance—some Manchu
soldiers killed their families and committed suicide rather than surrender.
Both were shocked by what they saw as the cruelty of the other. "How false
was [our] idea that we were coming among a people who only waited for
the standard of the foreigner to throw off a detested and tyrant yoke,"
recalled the military secretary to the mission, Lord Jocelyn.[72] The Chinese
signed the epoch-making Treaty of Nanking (1842), ceding to Britain the
sparsely inhabited Hong Kong island with its excellent anchorage, accepting diplomatic representation, opening five "treaty ports," including
Shanghai (the number later greatly increased), to foreign residents, and
conceding "extraterritoriality," by which foreigners were placed under the

legal jurisdiction of their consuls—a flagrant breach of Chinese sovereignty necessitated, in Western eyes, by the barbarities of Chinese law.

A devastating indirect consequence was chronic rebellion across China, which marked the beginning of the end of the ancient Chinese Empire. The Taiping rebellion (1850–64), one of the bloodiest in history, led to perhaps 50 million deaths. Its first stirrings began in the 1830s among the minority Hakka people near Canton, led by a visionary schoolteacher, Hong Xiuquan, who founded a new religious sect. Though driven by social and economic discontents, the movement legitimated itself by creating an idiosyncratic version of Christianity—the God-Worshipping Society—which worshipped Hong as Jesus's younger brother. An attempt to suppress it led to a rapidly spreading revolt. At first the rebels' quasi-Christianity won some sympathy from the West. British naval officers were officially sent fifty theological questions: "Does any one among you know 1. How tall God is, or how broad. 2. What his appearance or colour is. 3. How large his abdomen is. 4. What kind of beard he grows," etc., to which they gave "courteous and thorough" answers, but also said that they "think it right to state to you distinctly that we . . . can subscribe to none of your [dogmas]."[73] There emerged a nightmarishly violent and puritanical communistic theocracy in which the rank and file were in absolute subjection to the divinely chosen elite. Their capital at Nanking fell in 1853 with appalling carnage, but the revolt continued. Britain found itself simultaneously defending the Qing Empire against the Taiping revolutionaries and attacking it to enforce the terms of earlier treaties.

## THE MID-CENTURY CRISIS AND ITS AFTERMATH, c.1840–80

*I may say without any vainglorious boast that we stand at the head of moral, social and political civilization. Our task is to lead the way and direct the march of other nations.*

Lord Palmerston, 1848

*The English piously believe themselves to be a peaceful people; nobody else is of the same belief.*

W. E. Gladstone, 1859

Overseas, as at home, the 1840s were a time of emergencies: the First Opium War, the annexation of New Zealand, the occupation of Kabul in 1842, the First Sikh War in 1844. Closer to home, there was an angry dispute with France over respective influence in Spain. Yet Europe, despite sporadic tensions, seemed acquiescent in the aftermath of the Napoleonic Wars, with governments holding down democratic and nationalist malcontents and minimizing international conflict. It was enjoying an economic boom. Railways, only fifteen years after the first line opened in England, were being hastily built across Europe, many using British capital, entrepreneurs, workers and equipment. All this suddenly changed, when in 1846 Europe and the world entered a catastrophic economic crisis. After first stirrings in Switzerland and Naples, on 24 February 1848 a sudden uprising in the streets of Paris installed a democratic republic, sending out shockwaves of fear to rulers and hope to radicals. Political exiles in London were jubilant: "Frenchmen, Germans, Poles, Magyars sprang to their feet, embraced, shouted and gesticulated in the wildest enthusiasm . . . great was the clinking of glasses that night in and around Soho and Leicester Square."[74] A landslide of revolutions spread across Germany, the Habsburg Empire and Italy. As exiles went off to join revolutions at home, ejected European politicians came in the other direction—the defeat of a generation that had fought a long rearguard action against change and now sought asylum in England.

But within months the "springtime of the peoples" turned chilly, as revolutionary alliances unravelled, middle-class liberals confronted hungry workers, rival nationalisms collided, and ousted conservatives rallied. In June 1848 a workers' uprising in Paris was crushed, and over the next two years counter-revolution regained Berlin, Vienna, Prague, Venice and Rome. Hungarian nationalist forces were defeated with the help of the Russian army, and Italian nationalists by the Austrians. Prince Louis-Napoleon Bonaparte, Napoleon's nephew, was elected president of the French republic by a landslide in December 1848. In 1851 he carried out a coup d'état to stay in power, and proclaimed himself the emperor Napoleon III the following year.

People in England reacted in three main ways. First, the fact that England had escaped revolutionary violence caused relief and self-congratulation (see p. 473). The second reaction was sympathy with the victims of repression. A naval squadron was sent to support the Turks in their refusal to hand over 4,000 Hungarian refugees. The Hungarian leader, Lajos Kossuth, was given a hero's welcome in England in 1851, addressing crowds of up to 200,000 and making the "Kossuth hat" a fashion item. The Italians Giuseppe Mazzini and Giuseppe Garibaldi enjoyed similar adoration. They were seen in England not as dangerous revolutionaries, but as fighters for English-style liberties—an impression they willingly confirmed. When the Austrian General Haynau, who had been involved in the Hungarian repression, visited London in September 1850, he was beaten up by workers—an episode for which Palmerston refused to apologize. These public sympathies were to affect Britain's European policies over the next decade.

The third English reaction was suspicion towards France, which had succumbed first to unstable republicanism, then to Bonapartist dictatorship. "God bless the narrow sea which keeps her off," wrote Tennyson in 1850, "I wish [it] were a whole Atlantic broad." Had the coup d'état carried out by Louis-Napoleon Bonaparte in December 1851 ended conflict or destroyed liberty? Was he the saviour of France or what Prince Albert called "the walking lie"?[75] When Palmerston immediately expressed approval of the coup, he was forced to resign. There was recurring fear about what a Bonaparte might do. The Foreign Office was unhappy when in 1852 he revived the Napoleonic empire, forbidden by the 1815 Treaty of Paris. Consuls in French ports were instructed to watch out for preparations to invade. This was a grave political blow to Cobdenite internationalists and the peace lobby, and Britain increased its naval expenditure. Napoleon III (as he had now become) was genuinely dangerous, but not in fact to Britain—he was relatively Anglophile, and had learned from his uncle's experience that France must never risk British enmity. But imperial France did not inspire trust, and so Britain ended up following Palmerston's habitual strategy—cooperating as closely as possible with the country that seemed its most dangerous potential enemy.

Thus began two decades of rapid and uncontrollable change in Europe and the world—a linked global crisis.[76] China was still in turmoil. There was serious unrest in British settler colonies, sparked off by tax increases for defence thought necessary due to the international tension. To calm the unrest, London hastened local self-government.[77] This began what soon seemed the natural, inevitable and even desirable policy by which dependent colonies would be consolidated and given autonomy. It was first formalized in Canada, which became a "Dominion" by the British North America Act (1867), a pattern followed in due course in Australia, New Zealand and South Africa. The next great tremor was the Crimean War, from the British point of view fought to prevent Russian domination of the Ottoman Empire, whose Christian Danubian provinces Russia had invaded. The crisis might have been solved diplomatically had not British public opinion been so hostile to Russia and Austria, which tried vainly to mediate, and had not Napoleon III been ready for action against Russia. British and French progressives saw this as a struggle against tyranny, and hoped to weaken Russia permanently and destroy its hegemony over eastern Europe, liberating Poland, Hungary and even Italy. However, it was difficult to do any damage at all to that vast empire. Naval operations in the Baltic and the Pacific were barely a pinprick. The main Anglo-French effort was aimed at destroying the Black Sea naval base at Sebastopol, to remove the amphibious threat to Constantinople. This proved more difficult than expected, though it was an achievement to be able to transport armies to the Black Sea and support them through a long and finally successful campaign. But the campaign became a byword for incompetence by British generals and politicians. Thanks to the press (especially the pioneering war reporting of the *Times* correspondent William Howard Russell), early photography and Alfred Tennyson, the war provided battles and heroes whose names still adorn streets and pubs throughout the land. But as even Tennyson's epic "Charge of the Light Brigade" admitted, "someone had blundered." The stoical sufferings and courage of the troops, decimated by diseases far more than by bullets, created a new public sympathy for the army. Florence Nightingale became a national heroine for her labours in improving the care of sick and wounded soldiers. Another woman, the warm-hearted Mary Seacole, who sold food and drink, was celebrated posthumously.[78] Britain's military weaknesses—small numbers, inadequate leadership, lack of military infrastructure—were patent, while the French army proved that it was again the world's strongest. The gainer from the war was Napoleon III, who dominated the peace negotiations in Paris and astutely made up with the Russians. He had broken up the anti-French solidarity of the other Great Powers created by Castlereagh in 1814. Russia felt betrayed by Austria. Britain had become France's ally. So Napoleon had the opportunity to remodel Europe, and over the next fifteen years he would set off a political avalanche which eventually carried him away.

The first aftershock for Britain came in India, when mutinies in the East India Company's Bengal army in February, April and May 1857 turned into a revolt across north-central India, involving both peasants and princes. The causes were many and have been debated ever since. The withdrawal of British troops from India for the Crimea, the exposed failings of the British army—dangerous for a regime so reliant on prestige—and expectation of Russian or Persian intervention created a sense of opportunity among discontented Indians, and perhaps fed prophecies that the British would be defeated one hundred years after Clive's 1757 victory at Plassey. There were political, military, economic and religious grievances among the Company's subject peoples and its troops. The Bengal army, largely high-caste Hindu gentry, resented deteriorating conditions of service for what had been the most attractive employer in India, but which now seemed to bring social degradation.[79] Peasants resented taxation and changes in land tenure. Princes, dispossessed princes,

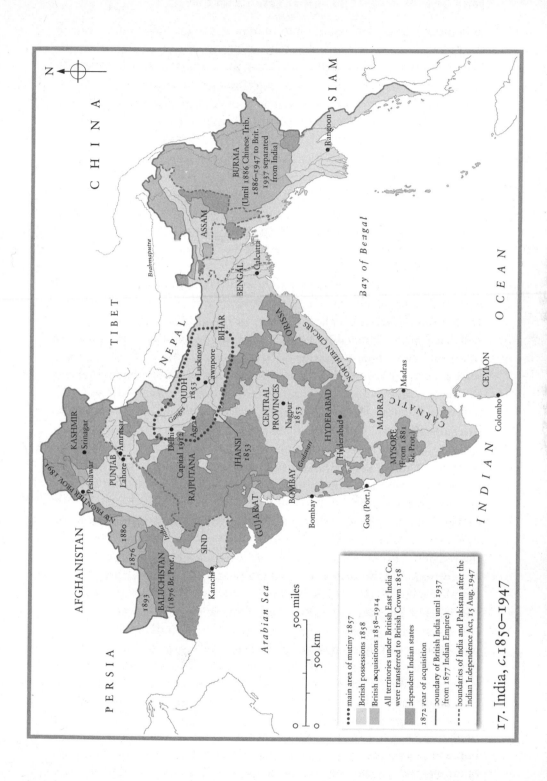

17. India, c.1850–1947

N

CHINA

SIAM

Rangoon

BURMA
(Until 1886 Chinese Trib.
1886–1947 to Brit.
1937 separated
from India)

ASSAM

Brahmaputra

TIBET

Calcutta

BENGAL

Bay of Bengal

NEPAL

BIHAR

OUDH
Lucknow
1853
Cawnpore

ORISSA

NORTHERN CIRCARS

KASHMIR
Srinagar

Delhi
Capital 1912

Agra

Ganges

JHANSI
1853

CENTRAL
PROVINCES
Nagpur
1853

HYDERABAD

Hyderabad

Godavari

MADRAS

Madras

CARNATIC

CEYLON

Colombo

PESHAWAR
Peshawar
PUNJAB
Lahore
Amritsar

RAJPUTANA

NW FRONTIER PROV. 1891

1880

1876

Indus

SIND

GUJARAT

BOMBAY

Bombay

Goa (Port.)

MYSORE
(From 1881
Br. Prot.)

INDIAN

OCEAN

AFGHANISTAN

1893

BALUCHISTAN
(1876 Br. Prot.)

Karachi

Arabian Sea

PERSIA

•••••• main area of mutiny 1857

British possessions 1858

British acquisitions 1858–1914

All territories under British East India Co.
were transferred to British Crown 1858

dependent Indian states

1872 year of acquisition

boundary of British India until 1937
(from 1877 Indian Empire)

boundaries of India and Pakistan after the
Indian Independence Act, 15 Aug. 1947

500 miles

500 km

would-be princes and their military retainers bitterly resented British takeover of "lapsed" states, when there was no direct heir, or when the British considered them badly governed, as in the Muslim-ruled Awadh (Oudh), just annexed. Nana Sahib, who became the most notorious rebel leader, had been refused recognition as adopted heir of a Maratha prince. The Rani of Jhansi, later a heroine to both Indian nationalists and feminists, was alienated by British rejection of her similar claim. The British later liked to think that it was their modernizing reforms, such as railway-building, that were resented by reactionaries. Some reforms certainly had caused resentment—for example, banning the burning of widows, "suttee" (also "sati"), legalizing their remarriage, and permitting (against sharia law) inheritance by Muslim converts to Christianity. The abolition of suttee caused one of the first major campaigns against British rule and stimulated the creation of Hindu newspapers.[80] Christian missionary activity (which the Company traditionally disliked as a nuisance) was a further aggravation. These resentments were expressed in an anonymous manifesto sent to all the princes of India: "The English are people who overthrow all religions . . . the common enemy of both [Hindus and Muslims, who] should unite in their slaughter . . . for by this alone will the lives and faiths of both be saved."[81] The final spark for the mutiny was the introduction of new rifle cartridges, supposedly greased with pork and cow fat, polluting for both Muslims and Hindus and seen as a plot to force mass conversion to Christianity.

This inextricable confusion about causes illustrates a fundamental problem of foreign rule: the difficulties of understanding and communicating with the ruled. The British were horrified and enraged by the savage violence suddenly inflicted not only on supposedly popular army officers, but on any British person (other than converts to Islam), on women and children, and on Indian Christians—an unmistakable sign of the religious hatreds British rule had aroused, and of the absence of basic human solidarity between them and many of their subjects. Though there were several vicious episodes, the most notorious took place at Cawnpore (Kanpur) in June and July 1857—a traumatic event constantly retold in British accounts. A few hundred British and loyal Indian soldiers, civilians, women and children withstood a three-week siege in harrowing conditions. They were persuaded to surrender by promises of safe conduct by river, but as they tried to embark, they were ambushed and several boats set alight. Few men escaped. Nearly 200 captured women and children were subsequently butchered and thrown down a well, some still alive. British troops arriving soon after found their prison "ankle deep in blood, ladies' hair torn from their heads . . . poor little children's shoes lying here and there, gowns and frocks and bonnets . . . scattered everywhere."[82]

The British and their Indian supporters fought with savage desperation first for survival and then for revenge. Men whose families had been killed often took the lead. Villages suspected of harbouring rebels or mistreating British fugitives were burned. Suspected mutineers were indiscriminately massacred. At Cawnpore, condemned men were forced to clean the blood-stained floor—polluting to Hindus, who, wrote General James Neill, "think that . . . they doom their souls to perdition. Let them think so."[83] Some were forced to eat pork and beef before being killed. Another notorious punishment—copied from the Mughals and Marathas—was to be tied to a cannon and "blown away": "His head flew up into the air some thirty or forty feet—an arm yonder, another yonder, while the gory, reeking trunk fell in a heap beneath the gun."[84]

The governor-general, Lord Canning, a former Peelite and son of the 1820s Foreign Secretary George Canning, tried to rein in the reprisals and was mocked as "Clemency Canning": "As long as I have breath in my body . . . I will not govern in anger." He was supported by some of the government in London. Palmerston called a National Day of Fast, Humiliation and Prayer on 7 October 1857. The day inspired calls for clemency and criticism of misgovernment. Radical newspapers expressed sympathy with the Indians. There was a wider conviction that rule in India had to be reformed: the mutiny, thought the Earl of Elgin, proved "the scandalous treatment the natives receive at our hands."[85] The queen wrote that "for the perpetrators of these awful horrors no punishment can be severe enough . . . But . . . the native at large . . . should know there is no hatred of brown skin."[86] But for many British in India there certainly was. Wrote one young officer, Edward Vibart: "These black wretches shall atone with their blood for our murdered countrymen,"[87] and he and others like him made sure they did.

The revolt did not spread beyond the north-central provinces. Large princely states and the traditional elite stayed aloof or supported the British, as did much of the business class. The Madras and Bombay armies stayed obedient. Part of the Bengal army, particularly Sikhs and Gurkhas who had no links with the mutineers, fought for the British. The rebels were disorganized and had no strategy. They concentrated their forces at a few urban centres, especially Delhi, whose elderly king, Zafar II, grandson of the last Mughal emperor, provided a uniting symbol, especially for some Muslims. British accounts portrayed tiny imperial forces defeating vast hordes of the unrighteous, but the effective numbers were usually pretty equal. Delhi contained many turbulent, disorganized sepoys, mainly Hindus, erratically supported by volunteer Muslim jihadis, many seeking martyrdom; but perhaps only 10,000–12,000 could ever be mustered. Besieging them from Delhi ridge, just north of the city, were 3,000 British and 8,000 Indian troops, who finally stormed the city walls on 14 September. A third of British soldiers and half the officers became casualties in six days of bloody stalemate in the narrow streets: "For the first time in my life," wrote an eye-witness, "I have lived to see English soldiers refuse repeatedly to follow their officers."[88] Finally they captured Delhi by sheer stubbornness as the rebels fled. Suspected mutineers, passive bystanders, even some supporters of British rule, were slaughtered. Wrote one soldier to the *Bombay Telegraph*: "They were not mutineers but residents of the city, who trusted to our well known mild rule for pardon. I am glad to say they were to be disappointed."[89] Officers and men, in customary search for drink and "prize money," looted the city, especially the Red Fort, palace of the Mughals, which still bears the scars. Many women of the court were raped. The aged king was imprisoned; most of his sons and grandsons were summarily executed—in several cases, simply murdered. Tracts of the city were systematically vandalized and demolished, their inhabitants left destitute and without shelter. The great Urdu poet Mirza Ghalib, a Mughal nobleman and a friend of the British, mourned those on both sides "laid low in the dust": "My face is pale; only the tears of blood / Bring colour to the cheeks whence colour fled."[90]

Fighting continued for nearly two more years, during which time the East India Company was abolished and its possessions in India transferred to the Crown; some 600 princely states continued as semiautonomous dependencies. The proclamation was accompanied by a pardon to all rebels not involved in murder. A "State of Peace" was not formally declared until July 1859. The death toll is unknowable. This "Great Mutiny" or "First War of Independence" has always seemed a watershed. It arguably transformed not only institutions but attitudes, making the British more pessimistic, politically more conservative, more distant, perhaps more racist. The ruined Residency at Lucknow, which had withstood a siege, was kept as a memorial, the one place in the empire where the Union Jack was not lowered at dusk. The well at Cawnpore became a shrine. Indians remembered savage conflict and repression, which entered nationalist tradition. A troubled British official felt this while watching a game of badminton years later on an old battlefield:

> Near me a Musalman, civil and mild,
> Watched as the shuttlecocks rose and fell;
> And he said as he counted his beads and smiled,
> "God smite their souls to the depths of hell."[91]

Yet some believed that direct rule would bring better government and reconciliation. The new imperial government was ambitious, at least in intentions.[92] But British rule has long been accused of deliberately devastating Indian industry in the interests of British exporters. More broadly, economic imperialism, taxation (though often lower than under the Mughals) and government negligence are blamed for India's de-industrialization and impoverishment. The basic fact seems plain: India, in the eighteenth century, was the main manufacturer of cotton cloth for the world, but by the mid-nineteenth it was the largest importer of Lancashire cottons, England's leading export; moreover, its own considerable export earnings from third countries helped to balance Britain's own trading deficit.

Given the size of India (20 percent of the world population in 1820) and its centrality to the empire, it is a devastating accusation to say that it was deliberately or even accidentally impoverished by British policy. What is the verdict? Asian living standards had begun to fall relative to Europe long before imperialism, partly due to political instability; and British rule did not see a further fall, but a slow rise. Asia's export successes had depended on cheap skilled labour: and the low cost of Indian labour made early technology unviable (see p. 377). Rapid early-nineteenth-century improvements in technology meant that English cotton goods suddenly became both cheaper and better than those of India, which consequently lost its global markets. In the space of a generation (roughly from the 1830s to the 1850s) India thus became "de-industrialized," as did China. However, modern mechanized cotton mills began to be built in the 1850s, and by 1876 India reached the "one million spindle mark"—twenty years before Japan and thirty before Brazil. Famous names appeared at this time: J. N. Tata visited Lancashire in 1872 and six years later opened modern cotton mills at Nagupur; his son, Sir Dorabji Tata, established a huge steelworks in 1911. By 1900 India had the fourth-largest cotton industry in the world, after England, the USA and Russia. It also had the fourth-largest railway system in the world (paid for by Indians but with British technical direction and aided by cheap British capital), with three-quarters of Asia's total track—thirty-five times more than China. Agricultural export growth in India was comparable to Brazil's. Indian industry began competing successfully with British imports—especially as the imperial government gave preference to Indian-produced goods. The colonies, including India, were very lightly taxed—probably less so than if they had been independent: Indian taxes were 20–40 percent lower than in the non-European world in general, and lower in British India than in the semi-autonomous princely states.[93]

But, even if all this is accepted, the worst accusation is that colonial rulers, by encouraging export-oriented commercial agriculture and building railways, destroyed traditional subsistence farming, using free-market economics as a "mask" for "holocaust" and "colonial genocide."[94] The worst famines in 1876–79, 1889–91 and 1896–1902, caused by severe droughts connected with variations in the "El Niño" current, were world-wide, but particularly deadly in India, China, Brazil, Russia and east Africa. To what extent was Britain responsible? A popular view—propagated today in a range of American universities and radical websites—blames it for every disaster from Brazil to China because it fostered a globalization that brought political, social, economic and ecological catastrophe. Imperial government failed disastrously to prevent a terrible death toll. Yet the Famine Codes drawn up in India in the 1880s were the world's first modern anti-famine policy, still consulted today. They proclaimed that "the object of State intervention is to save life . . . all other considerations should be subordinated to this." Nor did colonial authorities refuse funds—the spending on famine relief in India in 1873–74 and 1896–97 was equivalent to over £700m in today's values, and tens of millions of people were assisted.[95] But the authorities did fear that mass relief would encourage dependency and prove financially unsustainable, and so they cut relief too quickly. They also over-estimated the ability and willingness of the market to mobilize resources in these unprecedented crises, and were too hierarchical, complacent, dogmatic and finally parsimonious.[96] Was this "genocide"? Imperial government did not do enough in the face of mass hunger, and this is widely accepted as an intrinsic failing of unrepresentative governments, colonial or other. Did British policy of encouraging commercial agriculture aggravate natural disaster? The answer is not simple. It depends on whether one assumes that traditional agriculture could have averted similar famines at a time of exceptional climatic disturbance.

The great Indian Mutiny was not the only extra-European preoccupation of the overstretched British during the highly eventful 1850s–1860s. There was a minor conflict with Persia in 1856–57. Then came another spasm in the trial of strength with China, the "*Arrow* War," which had begun in 1856 when the Chinese authorities arrested the crew of a British-registered ship, the *Arrow*. British troops would soon be involved in another Maori war in New Zealand, in 1860. Above all, in Europe Britain faced the danger of conflict with France and the consequences of sudden revolution in Italy.

On 14 January 1858 Italian nationalists threw bombs at Napoleon III in Paris, leaving him unscathed but killing or injuring over 150 people. When it became known that bombs and bombers had come from England, there was a furious reaction in France. The British ambassador in Paris urged with timeless political wisdom that it did not matter "*what* is done provided *something* is done," so the government introduced a Conspiracy to Murder Bill. But this aroused a public outcry and was defeated in the Commons, forcing Palmerston to resign again, though he returned to office the following year. When one of the conspirators was put on trial in London, his defence counsel urged the jury to defend the "cause of freedom and civilization throughout Europe . . . though 600,000 French bayonets glitter in your sight," and they duly acquitted the accused.[97] There was another French invasion scare, and even fears that India might have to be abandoned and troops brought home. But Napoleon did not want war and late in 1858 invited Victoria and Albert to the gala opening of a naval base at Cherbourg—an ambiguous compliment, as it would be the base for any invasion, a knife pointing directly at Britain's jugular.[98]

Napoleon III did plan war, but against Austria, to destroy its power over the various states of Italy. In 1859, in alliance with Piedmont-Sardinia, he defeated the Austrians in a campaign in northern Italy. This was a climactic moment for Victorian liberalism.[99] Italians were seen as engaged in an epoch-making struggle for liberty against political and religious oppression. "I side with those who are at war with Russia and Rome, with earthly and spiritual despotisms," wrote one of Gladstone's friends.[100] The Royal Navy did nothing to hamper the transport of French troops to Genoa.

Napoleon suddenly agreed, partly to strengthen relations with Britain, to a commercial treaty, negotiated secretly between Richard Cobden and the French free-trade economist Michel Chevalier and signed in January 1860. The treaty opened the French market to a range of British goods. It became the core of a short-lived European economic community, extended by other treaties to the whole of western and central Europe, with free movement of population, certain rights of citizenship and an embryonic single currency, which became the Latin Currency Union. This was the apogee of the free traders' vision, and Europe became for a time Britain's main trading outlet.[101]

The mood changed when later in 1860 Napoleon, as a reward for fighting in Italy, annexed the Sardinian territories of Nice and Savoy, albeit with the consent of the Sardinian government and the inhabitants. It caused alarm because it seemed to show he was set on territorial expansion. Victoria bemoaned a future of "bloody wars and universal misery."[102] When also in 1860 France launched the world's most powerful warship, the ironclad *Gloire*, Britain prepared for the worst. Huge fortifications—"Palmerston's follies"—were hastily built to defend England and the empire, with the biggest forts protecting Portsmouth and Plymouth in case of a surprise French invasion. An even bigger warship than the *Gloire*, HMS *Warrior*, was quickly launched, the first large warship to be built wholly of iron, and a naval arms race began. Men flocked to join the Volunteers: there were university units, factory units (the initiative often coming from the workers), the famous Artists' Rifles and the London Scottish, and also teetotallers, cricketers, freemasons and some radical units dressed in Garibaldian red shirts. The Volunteers literally changed the face of Britain by helping to popularize military-style beards, a hallmark of late-Victorian masculinity. Their shooting matches and field days provided the spectator sport of mid-Victorian Britain.[103]

London did not want to see Napoleon dominant in Italy, so in August 1860 the Royal Navy permitted Garibaldi to land a tiny army in Sicily, and then invade Naples. There were some English volunteers with him—merely tourists visiting Mt. Etna, announced Palmerston with characteristic effrontery. The small Italian states collapsed, and the British encouraged the Sardinian government, under King Victor Emmanuel and his liberal and pro-British prime minister, Cavour, to unite the whole peninsula as a single Kingdom of Italy. This was a cheap success for Britain and a boost to its people's self-confidence: a popular cause had triumphed and the possibility of French domination had receded, with Britain using only diplomatic influence and a peaceful naval presence. Garibaldi declared that "England was the representative of God" in the battle against "tyranny and evil priests."[104] Italy, said Gladstone, had adopted "the English way." The English reciprocated enthusiastically. Garibaldi visited England in 1864, and was feted by all parties and sections of the population. Thomas Cook began taking tourist parties to Italy. Both the Foreign Office in Whitehall and the Free Trade Hall in Manchester were built in Italianate style.

Britain and France despite these recurring tensions remained awkward allies outside Europe. In China, the *Arrow* War had been deliberately escalated by the governor of Hong Kong, Sir John Bowring, a free-trade fundamentalist, founder member of the Anti–Corn Law League and former Radical MP for Bolton. Believing that "Jesus Christ is Free Trade" he acted in November 1856 to try to compel the Chinese by force to concede greater commercial access, and ordered the navy to shell the Canton defences—an enterprise denounced both by Tories and more pacifically minded free traders. In retaliation, the Chinese governor of Canton offered $100 for every English head, and attacks on foreigners multiplied. The Earl of Elgin—who deplored imperial expansion as merely "increasing the area over which Englishmen . . . exhibit how hollow and superficial are both their civilisation and their Christianity"—was, ironically, sent to negotiate with the Chinese by force, though his arrival was delayed by the Indian Mutiny. Elgin confided to his diary that the "wretched" *Arrow* case was "a scandal." He loathed the Hong Kong merchants who were "for blood and massacre on a great scale," and who "for the most selfish objects, are trampling under foot this ancient civilization." But he nevertheless permitted a fairly minor bombardment and occupation of Canton in December 1857. The French, determined not to be left out, contributed troops. After sporadic skirmishing, multi-national diplomatic wrangling and broken agreements, it was decided to mount an expedition to Peking. An Anglo-French force landed in August 1860, simultaneously negotiating and looting with gusto as they marched. Elgin grumbled that he was earning "a place in the Litany, immediately after 'plague, pestilence and famine.'"[105] In the confusion, several British, French and Indians— soldiers, diplomats, a *Times* journalist—were taken prisoner. Private Moyse, of the Buffs, was beheaded for refusing to kowtow to a Chinese officer, and his defiance was celebrated in a once-famous patriotic poem:

> Last night among his fellow roughs,
> He jested, quaffed and swore;
> A drunken private of the Buffs,
> Who never looked before . . .
> And thus with eyes that would not shrink,
> With knee to man unbent,
> Unfaltering on its dreadful brink,
> To his red grave he went.[106]

Other prisoners were tortured, some to death; a few may have been eaten alive by animals. As a reprisal targeted at the imperial court, a furious Elgin in October ordered the destruction of the vast Summer Palace, some 200 buildings in a park outside Peking—a unique cultural monument, though of varying taste. Thus Elgin, sneered Lytton Strachey, "in the name of European civilization, took vengeance upon the barbarism of the East."[107] A mountain of loot ended up in auction rooms in London and Paris, and even now *objets d'art* found in attics occasionally confer undreamed-of wealth on lucky heirs.

The Convention of Peking (1860) confirmed and extended concessions to foreigners, ceded Kowloon to Britain, accepted foreign diplomats at Peking, and opened ports to foreign trade. The British were determined to prevent the Chinese Empire from collapsing and either becoming "another India" or being partitioned by rivals, particularly Russia and France. So they treated China as an informal protectorate, preventing other states from obtaining more than minor commercial footholds. The Royal Navy tried to suppress piracy, sometimes at Chinese request. British and French troops defended Shanghai against the indomitable Taipings, and a young officer, Major Charles ("Chinese") Gordon, commanded an international mercenary force, the "Ever Victorious Army," against them. Shanghai was developed by British business and remained largely under British control until 1937. The British consular service in China was the largest in the world, and the key Chinese Imperial Maritime Customs Service, a major source of state revenue, was run for forty-five years by the incorruptible Sir Robert Hart, who saw himself as a disinterested servant of China: "I want to make China strong, and I want to make England her best friend."[108]

Japan was a comparable but simpler prospect. Its feudal *shogun* government, ruling in the name of a powerless emperor, forbade foreign access to the country. In 1853 an American naval squadron had made an intimidating appearance, followed closely by Russian and British ships. Foreign diplomats were reluctantly admitted, but were subject to threat and actual violence—the British legation was repeatedly attacked. Foreign ships were fired on in 1863, and so a British squadron bombarded the port of Kagoshima. This sparked off a restoration of the emperor in 1867, and a civil war which destroyed the old shogunate and initiated rapid modernization as the best form of self-defence. Soon, Samuel Smiles's *Self Help* was a best-seller; and Japan managed to combine economic Westernization with national independence, an example to Asian nationalists.

The British and French continued wary cooperation in the Americas. The French invaded Mexico in 1862, later installing a puppet government under the cricket-playing Habsburg Archduke Maximilian—an adventure which Palmerston refused to join. The French wanted to profit from the American Civil War, which had begun in 1861, to secure Mexico by agreement with the Confederacy, the rebellious slave-owning Southern states. Despite their inferiority in numbers and industrial capacity, the Southern armies were at first successful: they were better led, and their soldiers were motivated by determination to maintain the harsh racial hierarchy on which their society depended. They needed to be able to buy ships and weapons abroad, especially in Britain. Anti-slavery feeling was strong in Britain. Harriet Beecher Stowe's anti-slavery novel *Uncle Tom's Cabin* (1852), also produced as a stage play, had had a stunning emotional impact on working-class audiences.[109] So there was potential sympathy in England for the Northern states, and certainly reluctance to give active help to the South. President Abraham Lincoln, however, repeatedly declared that he was not fighting to end slavery, but to preserve the Union, and this confused matters for the British government and public. If they condemned slavery, they also had mixed feelings about the Union—not least because of the threat its expansion posed to Canada—and thought that perhaps the Confederate states had the right of self-determination. The Southern states, moreover, were the main suppliers of raw material to England's huge cotton industry. Disruption of the supply by a Northern naval blockade of the South caused social and economic damage, especially in Lancashire, where it caused mass unemployment; consequently, the labour press (such as *Reynold's News* and the *Working Man*) sided with the South. Volunteers from England and other European countries, whether as adventurers or idealists, fought on both sides in the war,[110] which some saw as having parallels with social and political divisions at home. As a Stockport weaver who fought for the North put it, "I detested slavery of every kind whether among the white factory operatives at home or among the negroes of America. I always went with the dog that was down."[111]

With opinion thus divided, there was a possibility that Britain might recognize the Confederacy and sweep away the Union blockade, allowing the South to equip itself freely from European shipyards and arsenals, and cotton supplies to flow. Palmerston, now Prime Minister, was, however, cautious: as he observed to the Foreign Secretary, Lord John Russell, "They who in quarrels interpose, Will often get a bloody nose."[112] But a serious dispute with Washington in 1861 might easily have tipped the balance towards intervention. In November, a British ship, the *Trent*, was stopped on the high seas by a Federal warship and two Confederate diplomats on their way to Britain were arrested. In Friedrich Engels's view, as he wrote to Karl Marx, "To take political prisoners by force on a foreign ship is the clearest casus belli there can be. The fellows must be sheer fools to land themselves in a war with England."[113] Prince Albert helped to calm down the British government's response—the last official act of his life— and Abraham Lincoln's government sensibly backed down and handed the diplomats over.

Then, in the summer of 1862, with North and South deadlocked in an increasingly bloody and destructive struggle, Napoleon III suggested joint mediation by France, Britain and Russia to end the war, which could have resulted in a break-up of the United States. Gladstone, Chancellor of the Exchequer, reflected in September that:

> the case of Lancashire is deplorable, but even this is a trifle . . . compared with the wholesale slaughter that is going on, and its thoroughly purpose-less character, since it has long been (I think) clear enough that Secession is

virtually an established fact, & that Jeff. Davis [the Confederate president] & his comrades have made a nation.

—an opinion he later repeated in a sensational public speech in November, and later still regretted as a grave error. Abolitionists strongly disagreed with Gladstone, whose views the leading Liberal John Bright explained as due to the "taint" of coming from a slave-owning family.[114] But part of the public, including many suffering Lancashire workers, thought Gladstone might be right. Palmerston, as well as being cautious, was, as we have seen, strongly opposed to slavery and considered that "slavery . . . was from the beginning the obvious difficulty in our way as mediators." To impose a two-state settlement would mean giving "the guarantee of England" to the perpetuation of Southern slavery, which was unthinkable.[115] The Cabinet decided for the time being against mediation. Lincoln's sudden cooperation with London in 1862 over suppressing the slave trade (see p. 551), his belated proclamation of abolition in January 1863—though many thought this mere opportunism—and a change in the military situation marked by a Union victory at the bloody battle of Gettysburg in July decided the issue. Without Britain, France could not act. British reluctance to support the Confederacy caused disappointment and anger in the South, and attempts to foment conflict between Britain and the North, including by minor violations of Canadian neutrality.

A second dispute came over the clandestine construction in England of warships for the Confederacy, especially the steam sloop *Alabama*, which wrought havoc with United States merchant shipping from 1862 to 1864 before finally being sunk off the French Channel coast. This time the dispute was solely diplomatic. Washington demanded huge financial compensation on the grounds that the British government should have prevented the ship from leaving its Liverpool shipyard, and that not doing so had prolonged the war. Britain in 1871 agreed to international arbitration and subsequently paid some compensation for sunken ships. Both disputes, despite much transatlantic huffing and puffing, were thus settled peacefully. Despite mutual ill-feeling, another war, present or future, between the United States and Britain was a prospect from which both sides finally recoiled.

As well as its economic effects on Lancashire, the American Civil War also hit Jamaica, sparking one of the most notorious episodes in colonial history, the Morant Bay rebellion of October 1865. The former slave population was impoverished and dependent on a white and mixed-race landowning class. Protest, articulated by revivalist Baptist preachers, led to a small uprising in which twenty people were killed and several plantations looted. The leaders insisted on their loyalty to Queen Victoria and hoped that she would send "fresh gentlemen from England and we and those gentlemen will quite agree." But there was panic among the white and mixed-race minorities, and rumours of atrocities. The governor was Edward Eyre, the son of a clergyman, who had previously been a humane and successful Protector of Aborigines in South Australia. He saw Jamaica very differently and declared martial law. This permitted local militia and regular British and West Indian troops and sailors to go on a looting and killing spree. Houses were burned and people were shot, flogged and hanged indiscriminately or after derisory courts-martial. Nearly 500 were killed. They included a prominent local politician and a Baptist minister. A senior official wrote to the Colonial Secretary: "No one will ever believe the things that were done here in that mad, bad time. And very few will hear of the tenth part of them—including some of the worst."[116] There was an outcry in England, led by the Anti-Slavery Society, and Eyre was removed. He was prosecuted, unsuccessfully, for murder and abuse of power by a committee led by John Stuart Mill and supported by Charles Darwin. But another committee supported Eyre, and included Thomas Carlyle, Charles Dickens, John Ruskin, Charles Kingsley and Alfred Tennyson. These advocates of progress and civilization identified it with the imposition of imperial rule, however brutal the means.

Meanwhile, a political avalanche in Europe was gathering speed. In 1864 Prussia and Austria invaded and annexed the largely German-speaking provinces of Schleswig and Holstein, ruled by the King of Denmark. In 1866 Prussia declared war on Austria and the smaller German states, and won an amazingly rapid victory. It dissolved the German Confederation (created in 1815 by the Treaty of Vienna) and established its own North German Confederation, effectively a Greater Prussia. In July 1870 France and Prussia went to war after a diplomatic dispute manipulated by the Prussian prime minister, Otto von Bismarck. Napoleon III's armies were overwhelmed, he himself was captured, northern France was invaded, and a republic took power in September. Paris was besieged and bombarded by the German armies. In January 1871 a German Empire, with the king of Prussia as emperor, was proclaimed in Louis XIV's great palace at Versailles. This new state was composed of all the German states except Austria and it also annexed a large slice of north-eastern France. Its victory showed it to be the greatest power on the Continent, and its creation began a new era in European history. In none of these momentous events had Britain played a significant role, and this is often cited as proof of the narrow limits of its real power. Wrote a Frenchman bitterly to an English friend: "The influence of Britain in Europe is down; England is now a merchant's country, as America is."[117]

However, none of these changes directly threatened British interests or created any desire to intervene. Italian unification had created a friendly liberal state, seen as adopting British principles. Sympathy for German unification was also widespread. The Foreign Office considered the Schleswig-Holstein dispute a "petty squabble," and although the Cabinet agreed to send a fleet to the Baltic if Copenhagen were threatened—an unlikely possibility—it was realized that British intervention might make things worse.[118] In 1870 most people thought that the French were the aggressors as usual and sympathized with what Carlyle, in a much-noted letter to *The Times*, called "noble, patient, deep, pious and solid Germany." Queen Victoria (whose eldest daughter was married to the heir to the Prussian throne) expressed the general view in characteristically emphatic prose: "We must be neutral *as long as* we can, but *no one* here conceals their opinion as to the *extreme iniquity* of the *war*, and the *unjustifiable* conduct of the French!"[119] Britain's most direct concern was Belgian independence, and this was better secured by a German than by a French victory. But the completeness and ruthlessness of Germany's victory caused a change in sentiment. The Foreign Secretary, Lord Granville, wrote that his "heart bleeds for the misery of France—I lie in bed thinking whether there is nothing to be done."[120] The Lord Mayor of London raised a relief fund, which when starving Paris surrendered sent in shiploads of supplies, including 1,000 tons of flour, 7,000 live animals and 4,000 tons of coal.[121]

Britain's world position was weakened by France's prostration, worsened by the Paris Commune insurrection from March to May 1871, because it lost a valuable auxiliary, as had been shown in the Americas and China. The ambassador in Berlin, Lord Odo Russell, was soon to write an alarmist report that Bismarck was aiming at the "supremacy of Germany in Europe and of the German race in the world."[122] He was not the only one to worry. A best-selling novel, *The Battle of Dorking*, written by an army officer and later MP, G. T. Chesney, imagined a successful German invasion of England. The success of what Gladstone termed "Bismarckianism, militarism and retrograde political morality" in uniting Germany was another blow to liberal hopes that in the era of free trade and Progress war was obsolete.[123] But no British government dreamed of trying to undo what Bismarck had done.

Gladstone made the best of the situation, writing that Britain's role in Europe was one of "moral" influence, but his insistence on cutting defence spending to abolish income tax was one cause of his fall from power in 1874. Disraeli (from 1876 Earl of Beaconsfield) declared that Britain now "almost systematically" kept clear of Continental conflicts, because it was "really more an Asiatic power than a European."[124] Where Asian and

European interests met, in the Near East, he was ready to take strong action, however. When Russia invaded Turkey in 1877, as we shall see, he threatened war. He was angry at being drawn into expensive, distracting and potentially humiliating little colonial wars in Afghanistan and against the Zulus, which saw the military disasters of Isandlwana in 1879 and Maiwand in 1880. Though Zulus and Afghans were subsequently defeated, largely to restore prestige, Disraeli worried that such episodes "reduce our Continental influence and embarrass our finances." Whatever he said about Asia, Europe remained his main preoccupation.

## THE SCRAMBLE FOR EMPIRE

*Our Western civilization is perhaps not absolutely the glorious thing we like to imagine it.*
                J. R. Seeley, *The Expansion of England* (1883)

*The days are for great Empires and not for little States.*
                Joseph Chamberlain, 1902

The "New Imperialism" of the last quarter of the century saw European countries competing to create empires in Africa and Asia. As a leading French politician saw it, "It is through expansion, through influencing the outside world, through the place that they occupy in the general life of humanity, that nations persist and last."[125] The "Great Depression"—a period of Europe-wide economic slow-down between the 1870s and late 1890s—undermined free trade and made colonial markets seem essential, with glowing predictions of undeveloped wealth, accessible now that the adoption of quinine as a remedy for malaria made entrepreneurial ventures less likely to end in rapid demise. Imperialists in France, Germany, Belgium, Russia, Japan and the United States as well as in Britain prepared for a future of competing colonial trade blocs defended by armies and navies paid for by tariffs.

The first pebble in the landslide, unpredictably, was a Christian uprising in Turkish-ruled Bosnia and Bulgaria in 1875, which was ferociously crushed, killing between 4,000 and 15,000 men, women and children. Gladstone, in opposition, denounced the "Bulgarian Horrors" in a widely read pamphlet and vehemently demanded that the Turks get out. Russian armies invaded Bulgaria and marched on Constantinople, forcing the Turks to surrender. But Disraeli took the traditional position of defending the Ottoman Empire against Russia, sending a naval force to Constantinople, and bringing Indian troops to Malta. Liberals denounced this "Beaconsfieldism" as a noxious mixture of "jingoism" (see p. 505) and *Realpolitik*, which made Britain complicit in Turkish atrocities. A Congress met at Berlin in 1878, chaired by Bismarck. It brokered a compromise, agreed in advance between Britain and a disappointed Russia, which seemed a triumph for Disraeli and his cerebral Foreign Secretary, the Marquess of Salisbury. It shored up the core of the Ottoman Empire, reduced the territory seized by Russia's protégé, the newly independent Bulgaria, placed Bosnia and Herzegovina under Austrian administration, and gave Britain Cyprus as a naval and military base to support the Turks against Russia. British influence grew in Turkey (which was required to adopt reforms, including banning the slave trade) and in Egypt. Disraeli concluded that "the virtual administration of the East by England was the only hope for the prosperity of those Countries and Peoples."[126]

The "scramble for Africa" began along the southern Mediterranean, where nominal Ottoman sovereignty was swept aside in the wake of Turkey's defeat and humiliation. The French claimed a protectorate over Tunisia in 1881. In 1882, with Gladstone again in power, British troops, to general surprise—not least in Britain—occupied Egypt after anti-Western riots and violence against Europeans. French resentment at Britain's takeover of what they coveted themselves envenomed relations for a generation. Without Britain's occupation of Egypt, "there is no reason to suppose that any international scrambles for Africa, either west or east, would have begun when they did."[127] Bismarck summoned another conference in Berlin in 1884–85 to discuss Africa. There followed what now seems the nadir of imperialist avarice. At the time, optimists saw it as progressive, with European states taking responsibility for a long exploited and victimized continent, which was suffering a paroxysm of violence caused by gunrunners, slave-traders, ivory-hunters, greedy concessionaires, aggressive explorers, treaty-extorters, importunate missionaries and Islamic fundamentalists.[128] Britain pressed for an agreement to abolish slavery in territories taken over by European states. France laid claim to a vast area of western and central Africa. Italy (which, sneered Bismarck, had a large appetite but poor teeth) joined in, with ambitions for Libya and Ethiopia. Germany too wanted to enter the race. So did independent or semi-independent African states, including Ethiopia, Egypt, Liberia, Transvaal, the Orange Free State, and the Muslim Sokoto caliphate, the world's last great slave society,[129] all of which expanded their territories. So did individuals, notably King Leopold of the Belgians, who set up a private empire in the Congo, and the freebooting mining millionaire Cecil Rhodes, who in 1889 set up the chartered

British South Africa Company, which took over territories that later became "Rhodesia."

Whitehall's vain preference was for as little change as possible in the very limited European presence in Africa. It had long restricted its own possessions to strategic points on the coasts, and even then periodically thought of abandoning them. But it went along with the general movement, laid down at Berlin, to make formal claims to vast inland territories and attempt to govern them—an enterprise described by the Tory Prime Minister, Lord Salisbury, who took office in 1885, as "drawing lines on maps where no white man's foot ever trod" (newly acquired Uganda, about the size of Britain, had only twenty-five British officials). He complained that his advisers would have liked to "annex the moon in order to prevent its being appropriated by the planet Mars."[130] But the alternative seemed exclusion by France, Belgium, Germany and Italy.

Britain's real motives in setting the "scramble" in motion in Egypt have been much debated, but it seems, as usual, to have reacted to events, intending its intervention to be short. It began under Gladstone, fervently opposed both to imperialism and to spending money. Egypt, ruled by a Khedive (originally an Ottoman viceroy who had become a hereditary prince), faced financial problems aggravated by a fall in world cotton prices. The Suez Canal, built by French engineers in the 1860s, had greatly increased Egypt's already important strategic significance as a link in the fastest route from Europe to Asia. Disraeli had bought the near-bankrupt Khedive's shares in the canal in 1874. In order to ensure that Egypt's foreign debts were honoured, an international commission had been installed in 1876 to manage the state finances—a prototype IMF. But anti-foreign riots broke out in June 1882, in which fifty Europeans were killed. A British naval squadron shelled Alexandria's fortifications as a warning. The bombardment provoked further violence and a military coup by nationalist officers led by Colonel Ahmed Urabi ("Arabi Pasha"), backed by slave-traders and the Muslim religious establishment.[131] It was defeated by a British military force in September. William McGonagall hymned the triumph:

> Arabi's army was about seventy thousand in all,
> And, virtually speaking, it wasn't very small,
> But if they had been as numerous again,
> The Irish and Highland brigades would have beaten them, it is plain.[132]

Gladstone, at first sympathetic to Egyptian independence and determined not to extend British commitments, now convinced himself that this was "an upright war, a Christian war," which if necessary "the single power of England" must undertake to "convert the present interior state of Egypt from anarchy and conflict to peace and order." He felt that "in being party to this work, I have been a labourer in the cause of peace."[133] He considered hanging Arabi if it could be done "without *real* inclemency," but instead he was exiled to Ceylon where the (Tory) governor gave a dinner in his honour.[134] Evelyn Baring, a soldier and colonial administrator, was appointed as "Agent and Consul-General" in 1883 to sort out the Egyptian administration and end British involvement as quickly as possible. He remained for twenty-four years, effectively as governor. He and the British were long proud of his achievement in promoting social and political reform, free trade and low taxation. This had something of the characteristics and disadvantages of an IMF intervention today: cutting costs, and pushing resources towards exports.

During the 1880s Britain also claimed and occupied (usually with very small forces) the large hinterlands of its existing West African coastal outposts to keep the French out: Sierra Leone, the Gold Coast, and what became the vast colony of Nigeria, originally governed by a chartered company. In East Africa, where there was no significant economic interest and where the main activity had been the suppression of the slave trade, there was a similar desire to limit the incursions of others and keep potential rivals well away from the sea route to India. The former slaving island of Zanzibar, long dependent, was formally made a protectorate; large mainland territories further north became British East Africa (later Kenya) and the Uganda Protectorate. Burma was conquered in 1885 and Siam given informal protection for a characteristic mixture of motives: to keep the French out, to safeguard the frontiers of other British territories, and to protect commercial interests.[135]

Though intervention in Egypt was meant to be short—a leitmotif of British imperialism—it enmeshed Britain in a struggle in the Sudan, Egypt's turbulent southern colony. Tribes in Darfur and Kordofan, traditional large-scale slave-traders, joined in an anti-Egyptian uprising led by Muhammad Ahmad, whose followers proclaimed him the Hidden Imam, the Mahdi, leader of a new "jihad." In 1883 they annihilated an Egyptian army of 10,000 men commanded by a British officer, Hicks Pasha. The Gladstone government, unwilling to get involved, sent General Charles Gordon to extricate Egyptian troops and administrators—a bad choice. Gordon—"Chinese Gordon" since his combat against the Taiping—was one of those tortured Victorian Christian warriors who sought earthly glory or martyrdom on the fringes of empire—mad, good and dangerous to know. He was as fatalistic about death as any jihadi, having once written to his sister: "I died long ago . . . I am willing to follow the unrolling of the scroll."[136] He refused to evacuate Khartoum, intending to oblige the government to fight the Mahdists. Public opinion (backed emphatically by the queen) eventually forced their hand, and British troops slowly fought their way across the desert. They arrived at Khartoum two days after it had fallen in January 1885. Gordon's death caused public excoriation of Gladstone. The Sudan imbroglio, unwanted and unnecessary, gave rise to some of the most celebrated patriotic imagery—including a romanticized Death of Gordon—and verse, including the exhortation to "Play the Game" (see p. 519). But attention was drawn away to a bigger crisis: a Russian threat to Afghanistan (the "Penjdeh incident" of March 1885) which caused Britain to threaten war—another round in what Kipling was to call "the Great Game" of central Asian rivalry with Russia.

It was only eleven years after Gordon's death, in 1896, that General Kitchener, acting as commander of the Egyptian army, led an Anglo-Egyptian force against the Mahdists, who had in the meantime proclaimed a new jihad, reinstated slavery, and launched bloody attacks against Christian Abyssinia, as well as against disobedient Sudanese tribes. The Mahdists were slaughtered at Omdurman in September 1898, mounting suicidal frontal attacks: 11,000 were killed, at a cost of forty-eight Egyptian and British—proof both of religious fervour and of a sudden if short-lived disparity in military technology not seen again until the end of the twentieth century. A more romantically archaic aspect of the battle received much publicity: the last full-scale cavalry charge in British history, in which the twenty-three-year-old Winston Churchill rode. Kitchener then politely evicted a small French force from Fashoda, on the Sudanese Upper Nile, where France had hoped optimistically to establish a presence in order to put pressure on the British to relinquish control over Egypt. French nationalists were outraged at the Fashoda retreat, and there was even reckless talk of war.

Britain's other main African concern was in the far south. It had taken the Cape as a naval base during the Napoleonic Wars. Subsequent history is a textbook example of usually reluctant imperial expansion mostly driven by local problems: to control settlers (in this case mostly Dutch "Boers"); to restrain them from attacking natives; to defend them from reprisals when they did; to secure frontiers by pushing outwards, thus replacing existing problems with new ones; to fight wars against neighbouring polities seen as a threat—most famously, the militaristic Zulus, temporarily triumphant over a small British force at Isandlwana in 1879; and to secure valuable assets—in this case, diamonds and gold. The Boers, as annoyingly intractable as the Zulus, decimated an even smaller British force at Majuba in February 1881—"Sad Sad news from South Africa," lamented Gladstone, "is it the Hand of Judgement?"[137]

Southern Africa by the 1890s posed a unique set of difficulties. The "Boers," essentially patriarchal and racist farmers, longer established and even more disobedient than settlers elsewhere, had established an autonomous South African Republic (ZAR). The discovery of gold and diamonds had turned Johannesburg and its region into a turbulent and corrupt Wild West, a magnet for the usual hopefuls, crooks, tarts, lunatics and adventurers from around the world. The income from mining, warned a Colonial Office official in 1896, enabled the Boers to buy "arms and ammunition enough to shoot down all the armies of Europe."[138] Their rejection of nominal "suzereinty" was a challenge to Britain, especially as they attracted support from France and Germany. The latter annexed the adjoining South-West Africa in 1884, where it soon fought a genocidal war against the inhabitants.

In Capetown and London appeared a new breed of ideological imperialists—they had counterparts in Berlin, Washington and Paris—convinced that the future prosperity and security of Britain and the "race" depended on unifying the empire. Their leader was the popular former radical Joseph Chamberlain, now Conservative Colonial Secretary. He was seconded by Cecil Rhodes, a ruthlessly successful diamond millionaire with megalomaniac political ambitions who had become prime minister of Cape Colony, and Alfred Milner, a partly German and highly educated social reformer and imperialist, who was High Commissioner. For them, the challenge was fundamental: "What is now at stake is the position of Great Britain in South Africa," Chamberlain told the Cabinet in September 1899, "and with it the estimate of our power and influence in our colonies and throughout the world."[139]

Their first plan had been to foment an uprising among the foreign population of the ZAR, who had no political rights, by secretly encouraging the "Jameson Raid" into the Transvaal by an armed group in December 1895. The raiders were immediately rounded up by the Boers, and no uprising ensued. This fiasco drew world attention. Kaiser Wilhelm II sent a telegram of congratulation to the ZAR president, Paul Kruger. When Britain began to build up forces in the Cape, the Boers declared war in October 1899 in a self-proclaimed "struggle against the new world tyranny of Capitalism."[140] This may seem in retrospect a remarkably bold or reckless act, but the Boers hoped that early successes would force the British to compromise, as after Majuba in 1881. Britain and the world were respectively shocked and delighted when a weak British invasion force was repulsed, and border garrisons at Ladysmith and Mafeking (commanded by Colonel Robert Baden-Powell) were besieged. Relief forces were badly mauled during the "Black Week" of December 1899. This provided a thrilling saga for newspaper readers at home and a new roll-call of heroes. When the sieges were finally lifted in 1900, uninhibited popular rejoicing—"mafficking"—shocked progressives.

Opinion at home was divided. Mainstream Liberals held to the belief that war in general was immoral and expensive, especially this one, which many believed had been brought about by the machinations of capitalists and Jews. Some ultra-conservatives agreed. So did some socialists, tinged with anti-Semitism. But others, including the Fabian Society, supported British imperialism as progressive, while the popular socialist writer Robert Blatchford robustly declared that "England's enemies are my enemies."[141] This was the majority view, and it led to a Conservative victory in the "khaki election" of October 1900. But the war required more effort than anyone had imagined, and it became the most difficult since the Crimea and at £270m the most expensive since that against Napoleon. Not for the first time, the British had underestimated their enemy, who were highly mobile, familiar with the country, skilled marksmen, better armed and more numerous. British soldiers were picked off by a concealed enemy with Mauser rifles and smokeless ammunition. One such defeat, at a hill called Spion Kop, gave a name to rising terraces at football grounds—imperial culture was not always serious.

The Boer cause enthused all who loathed the English, especially if they also hated capitalists and/or Jews. At the 1900 Paris Exposition, one of the most popular exhibits was a Boer farmhouse. Volunteers from across Europe and from Ireland went to fight for Boer freedom. Facing them, British regulars and volunteers were joined by men from Canada, Australia and New Zealand, eventually totalling 250,000, now competently commanded by a veteran of the Indian Mutiny and Afghanistan, Lord Roberts of Kandahar, and the conqueror of the Sudan, Sir Herbert Kitchener. Once these forces could be supplied and moved—which required the assistance of a large number of Africans, who preferred a future under the British than the Boers—the ZAR was invaded, and by June 1900 had fallen. But some Boer "commandos," small groups of mounted infantry, continued a guerrilla war, their exploits applauded across the white world.

Kitchener countered the guerrillas by a scorched-earth policy, burning 30,000 farms, and criss-crossing the country with barbed-wire fences protected by blockhouses and armoured trains. Civilians were compulsorily evacuated to "concentration camps," where dirt and overcrowding led to some 40,000 deaths and international outrage, in which the "pro-Boer" minority in Britain joined. Leading Liberal politicians such as Campbell-Bannerman and Lloyd George denounced these "methods of barbarism." Barbarism worked, however, and the Boers surrendered in 1902. The empire had rallied to an unprecedented extent. Other countries, especially France and Germany, had been indignant but impotent in the face of the Royal Navy. The Boers accepted British sovereignty and the ZAR formed a federation with the British colonies of the Cape and Natal. The main British strategic and political object—control of the Cape and overlordship of southern Africa—had been preserved, and was to last through two world wars. However, the Boers, having lost the war, largely won the peace, for the British, as in all the settler colonies, gradually conceded self-government, formally established in 1909. The losers were the Africans within the union, left under a racist government. Swaziland, Bechuanaland and Basutoland had the relative good fortune of remaining under imperial protection.

The war had profound effects. Chamberlain, convinced that this was the historic opportunity to consolidate the empire, launched a campaign for Imperial Federation based on "preference" in trade, and which would he hoped move towards true political federation under an imperial Parliament in which all the white colonies would be represented. But Britain could give no "preference" as long as it practised unconditional free trade with everyone. So Chamberlain campaigned for import tariffs, arguing that they would also create "fair trade" by protecting British industry against (protected) German and American competition, as well as raising revenue for welfare. For Chamberlain's supporters, this fiscal revolution would solve economic, social and strategic problems at a stroke. But free trade, seen by most voters as meaning cheap food, was too deeply ingrained in British political culture, and the Conservative government was crushed by a Liberal-Labour landslide in 1906. The second consequence of the war was to convince many that the empire needed a friend. It was, in Chamberlain's phrase, a "weary titan," the "object of envy and greed to all the other Powers," lamented the Secretary of State for India.[142] Lord Salisbury, Prime Minister until 1902, had refused to panic: "We know that we shall maintain against all comers that which we possess, and we know, in spite of the jargon about isolation, that we are amply competent to do so."[143] His successors were less sanguine, and pessimism about the future became a dangerously pervasive characteristic of official thinking.[144]

Russia was by far the biggest worry. It was industrializing very rapidly, with the world's highest economic growth rates. It was expansionist in China, the Near East, Persia, and central Asia, from where it seemed poised to influence Afghanistan, and from there threaten the north-west frontier and the plains of India—whose population, it was feared, might not be wholly averse to a Russian invasion. And "compared to our empire

[Russia was] invulnerable," observed the First Lord of the Admiralty; there was "no part of her territory where we can hit her."[145] Russia's alliance with Britain's other mischievous colonial rival, France, had increased the danger, made palpable when in 1892 a Russian naval squadron had paid a much-trumpeted visit to the French fleet at Toulon. In 1898 Britain could only protest when Russia and Germany extracted monopoly trading rights in regions of China. In 1900 France and Russia had agreed on mutual support in case of war with Britain. In 1901 Russia began building a railway line to Tashkent, a possible means of supplying an invasion of India. The United States, although considered by optimists as an "Anglo-Saxon" cousin, inspired chronic suspicion and had embarked on aggressive colonialism, which included making open threats against British Guiana in 1895 and attacking Spain in 1898 to seize the Philippines and make Cuba a satellite. Germany seemed the natural partner for Britain, but approaches in the 1890s were disappointing. The Kaiser, Queen Victoria's grandson, was erratic, the German public seemed Anglophobic, and in 1900 the German navy began building battleships designed to operate in the North Sea.

Fear of a European war, hardly an issue for a generation, began to return. Since the 1860s Britain and the empire had been semi-detached from European politics (see pp. 577–78). The Boer War showed that this "Splendid Isolation" could be maintained—just. Futuristic war fantasies, serialized in new mass-circulation papers such as Alfred Harmsworth's *Daily Mail*, reached large readerships. In the 1890s the French and Russians were always the fictitious enemy. But in the 1900s the line-up changed, due to fears about German naval expansion. In the prototype spy novel, Erskine Childers's best-selling *Riddle of the Sands* (1903), the German navy plots a surprise invasion one misty morning across the North Sea, and is thwarted by a plucky yachtsman. Public opinion demanded a big naval programme, and spending on the navy increased by 50 percent between 1899 and 1905.[146] It focused on building expensive new "Dreadnought" battleships, heavily armed and turbine driven—"We want eight and we won't wait" was the popular cry.

Salisbury's government had sought to strengthen its strategic position by improving relations with the United States and—an unusual act in peacetime—signing a treaty with Japan in 1902. This encouraged the Japanese to resist Russian expansionism in north China in the epoch-making Russo-Japanese War in 1904–5. Japan wanted Britain to prevent France from aiding Russia. Neither Whitehall nor the Quai d'Orsay wished to find themselves at war because of conflicts over Manchuria or Korea—something that seemed perilously close when Russian warships fired on British trawlers in the North Sea in October 1904, claiming they were Japanese torpedo boats. A rapprochement between Britain and France seemed urgent. The so-called Entente Cordiale was signed by the Conservative Foreign Secretary, Lord Lansdowne, in 1904. The ground had been prepared in 1903 by a brave royal visit to Paris by Edward VII, who adroitly used his known Francophilia—not least his reputation as a ladies' man—to flatter the French public. Behind the scenes was a colonial deal: Egypt for Morocco. Whitehall, long the protector of Moroccan independence, now backed a French and Spanish takeover to forestall possible German naval bases on its Mediterranean or Atlantic coasts threatening Britain's imperial communications—proof of how seriously London took Germany's naval building, which by 1914 made it the world's second naval power.[147] German protests led to two diplomatic "Moroccan crises" in 1905 and 1911 (when the dispatch of a German warship to Agadir led to a war scare), and these strengthened Anglo-French solidarity. A comparable agreement with Russia was signed in 1907 over Persia, though by 1913 relations were again tense. These "ententes" were not alliances, but rather deals with the two countries with which Britain had most difficulties—"For purposes of ultimate emergencies," noted a Foreign Office official, an entente "may be found to have no substance at all." Britain's policy, said a senior Foreign Office official, should be to "keep up strength, and keep your eyes open; trust no one, except yourself."[148] So when war suddenly appeared imminent in July–August 1914, over an event in a far-away country of which the British knew nothing, it was by no means clear that they would join in. Only three months earlier, a Foreign Office official had noted that "should war break out on the continent the likelihood of our dispatching any expeditionary force is extremely remote."[149] What happened, and why, are subjects for Chapter 15.

It was to be a global imperial war, declared on behalf of the whole empire, including the self-governing Dominions, who did not demur. Over 2 million soldiers from the empire served. War began early on the oceans: a German cruiser was sunk by an Australian ship, HMAS *Sydney*, and a German squadron was annihilated near the Falkland Islands. Over 800,000 Indian troops fought on the Western Front, in the Middle East and in Africa. Australians and New Zealanders fought in Turkey and Palestine, and also, with Canadians too, in France. A long and devastating campaign took place in Africa, in which British, Indian, South African and West African troops laboriously overran the German colonies. Armies of Indian and Chinese labourers built railways and dug trenches in France. The Mesopotamia Campaign, which ended in disaster for the Indian and

British troops involved, showed the empire at its worst, incompetent, arrogant and callous. Yet final victory was also an imperial victory. The Dominions and India took part in the peace conference. The former, as well as Britain, obtained colonial territory, in the form of mandates from the new League of Nations. It was in 1920 that the empire attained its greatest size, and Britain remained, as after Waterloo, the greatest global power. However, the weariness of the titan and both its ruthlessness and its weakness in adversity were soon to become painfully clear. The vast armed forces were rapidly demobilized. There was serious unrest in Egypt and India, and in 1919 the Afghans actually launched an invasion. Ireland tumbled into civil war. Egypt was recognized as independent in 1922. India soon took the first steps towards self-government. The Dominions, not for the first time, proved self-assertive. So victory in 1918 did not, unlike that in 1815, begin a new period of hegemony. The world was no longer controllable.

# Englishness in the English Century

*Why is it that an Irishman's, or Frenchman's hatred of England does not excite in me an answering hatred? I imagine that my national pride prevents it. England is so great that an Englishman cares little what others think of her, or how they talk of her.*

Thomas Babington Macaulay, diary, 1849[1]

If England was what England seems
   An' not the England of our dreams,
But only putty, brass an' paint
   'Ow quick we'd chuck 'er! But she ain't!

Rudyard Kipling, "The Return" (1902)

Victorian England was a pioneer: in its economy and technology, its social conditions and living standards, its political organizations, its ways of thinking about man, nature and religion, and its role as the core of a global empire. None of these characteristics was unique to England, but the combination of them probably was: no country became so early and so rapidly urban, industrial, rich, (semi-)democratic and intellectually pluralist. But other nations soon followed: much of what we consider "Victorian" was common to the modernizing Western world. What did it mean to be English in this century of power and wealth? On the whole, self-satisfaction: at a time when bombastic patriotism was universal from Chicago to Vladivostok, English "jingoism" was part of the common culture. The Great Exhibition, and later the queen's jubilees, were genuinely popular festivals; and "mafficking" crowds showed that imperialism was not confined to the wealthy. But there was also, and always, dissent (often linked with Dissent): admiring Napoleon at the beginning of the century, deploring vulgar "jingoism," sympathizing with the Boers, disowning many of the symbols of state nationalism, and adopting an Englishness with a different history, morality and sensibility. Englishness, as always, was characterized by diversity of belief, opinion and loyalty.

England's history, drawing on eighteenth-century ideas, was generally understood as Progress. England was a leader, whether through Protestant Christianity, historical luck, native virtue, inheritance, hard work or even bracing climate. By the 1850s and 1860s it seemed evident that England was leading mankind towards the future. But from the 1880s, or even earlier, something seemed wrong: it was as if England's apogee had come and gone without anyone noticing. Perhaps when Palmerston died in 1865? Or some time in the 1870s, when it was still the Workshop of the World and without enemies? Had "Beaconsfieldism" started the rot with its demagogic "jingoism"? Or Gladstone's radicalism—his "gorgeous and reckless optimism," as Salisbury put it? Even, perhaps, democracy, which some of the high-minded found disappointingly materialistic, immoral— and Tory. Now intellectuals praised French culture (perhaps they always had) and denounced English "philistinism." Democrats and Dissenters envied the United States its seeming egalitarianism and religious free-for-all. Businessmen, scientists, social reformers, academics and trade unionists admired Germany. Mr. Gladstone even spoke highly of Russia. But England itself, and the English people, seemed to be stagnating, economically, politically, socially, even racially. Kipling's poem "Recessional," published on the front page of *The Times* (17 July 1897), expressed a sober view at the time of Victoria's diamond jubilee:

> Far-called, our navies melt away;
> On dune and headland sinks the fire:
> Lo, all our pomp of yesterday
> Is one with Nineveh and Tyre!

What did it mean that England was part of a world empire and the centre of a global economic system? During the nineteenth century, it was probably more outward-looking than any nation before, more involved in its everyday life with more of the world.[2] Travel, trade and migration from the seventeenth century onwards had meant an infinity of exchanges involving "scholars, administrators, travellers, traders, parliamentarians, merchants, novelists, theorists, speculators, adventurers, visionaries, poets, and every variety of outcast and misfit."[3] A Parsee merchant, Sir Mancherjee Bhownaggree, was Tory MP for Bethnal Green from 1895 to 1906. The results of being "outward-looking" were by no means all positive, whether for the lookers or the looked at. Huge attention—over 20,000 historical studies—has been directed at "imperialism" as the core of Britain's engagement with the world, although the empire was less politically important to England than was Europe, and in some ways (for example, as a destination for emigrants) less important than the United States. The empire, a recent study suggests, probably meant less to most English people than to its admirers and critics abroad.[4]

Economically, England was more globally connected than any Continental country. It exported to distant markets, imported food and raw materials from distant producers, provided financial services to the world, and sent people round the globe. Colonial trade and investment was about one-third of Britain's total.[5] However, economic historians mostly agree that having an empire on balance made little economic difference, either good or bad.[6] Free trade neutralized imperial possession, and Whitehall would not privilege British companies. Even in the most notorious case of force being used to obtain commercial access—China—Britain did not seek exclusive privileges. Its object was to bring China into the global system. The big gainers from globalization were the countries supplying British and European markets, whether inside or outside the empire, including the United States, Argentina, Siam, Canada, Australia, New Zealand, Malaya, Burma, Ceylon and the Gold Coast. All had rapid growth rates and some enjoyed the world's highest living standards. Their security and communications were protected by Britain (permitting lower taxation), they had a buoyant market, cheap capital, orderly immigration and stable institutions: "They paid for little and received a great deal."[7] India is a different and more contentious story, as we have seen. Yet after 1880 Indian industrial production grew by 4–5 percent per year—comparable with Germany.[8]

Influential scholars have argued that "the imperial experience . . . entered into the cultural and aesthetic life of the metropolitan West."[9] They insist that the unprecedented power of the British Empire, both for its subject peoples and for its rulers, in some way touched every aspect of life. An "imperial map of the world" pointing the way to future conquest has been detected in English literature as early as *Othello* and *The Tempest*; *Robinson Crusoe* is "unthinkable without the colonizing mission"; allusions to slavery in Jane Austen's *Mansfield Park* show "a broad expanse of domestic imperialist culture without which Britain's subsequent acquisition of territory would not have been possible."[10] Empire, some believe, left its mark of Cain on English culture, explaining its racism, violence, inequality, militarism, "masculinism" and misogyny. But other historians point, on the contrary, to the weakness of empires, their inability to fulfil their own intentions, their dependence on the acquiescence and cooperation of those they (sometimes nominally) ruled, and their limited impact at home, where ideas about empire were diverse and changing.

32 and 33. The Enlightenment in England saw practical ideas applied to everyday life, and craftsmen (*below*) were as indispensable as philosophers. Computing longitude—for which a huge prize of £20,000 was offered by Parliament—required time-keeping of unprecedented accuracy. A Yorkshire carpenter turned clockmaker, John Harrison, devoted years of tireless ingenuity to making chronometers (*left*), the most complex manufactured objects in existence, which by 1760 could function in the harshest sea-going conditions.

34 and 35. Bristol, well situated for trade with the Americas, southern Europe and Africa, was England's second port after London and was a centre of the "triangular trade" in manufactures, slaves and sugar (*top*). Over the seventeenth and eighteenth centuries, trade and domestic consumption stimulated an "industrious revolution" based on commerce in traditionally made goods, followed by an "industrial revolution" powered by coal and steam. This scene (*above*) is by a self-taught artist, James Sharples, a worker in a large Blackburn factory.

36. Between 1660 and 1800, more than 300,000 books were published in England, perhaps 200 million copies in all. Public libraries were created, book clubs were set up and book prices fell. Women readers and writers helped to create the most characteristic literary form of the period, the novel.

37. New habits of consumption were reaching the poor, who acquired more goods than would have been available to a prosperous yeoman a century earlier: ownership of saucepans, dishes, clocks, pictures, mirrors, curtains, lamps and tea and coffee utensils at least doubled between 1670 and 1730, as reflected in William Biggs's 1793 painting *Poor Old Woman's Comfort*.

38. A radical pro-American backlash in 1780 culminated in London with the most destructive rioting in modern English history, the Gordon Riots. The rioters targeted Catholic institutions, pro-government politicians and buildings symbolic of authority, including Newgate prison and the Bank of England. Yet not a single person was killed by the crowds.

39. Plymouth Dockyards. The immense power of the Royal Navy was based on a huge and expensive infrastructure, the biggest industrial organization in the Western world, with roots going back to the time of Pepys, Cromwell and the Tudors.

40. In the summer of 1781, General Cornwallis and a small army marched from South Carolina to Virginia but were cut off by the French navy at Yorktown and besieged by a much larger Franco-American force. On 19 October 1781 they laid down their arms, with a band playing "The World Turned Upside Down."

41. Wellington's performance at Waterloo was as much a triumph of nerve as of tactics. Wearing civilian clothes and exposing himself to enemy fire, he managed throughout to give his troops an impression of imperturbable confidence, and after a long and very bloody day, with a wave of his hat gave the final order to advance.

42. The empire always depended on the political, economic and military participation of local elites, none more so than the Skinner clan, whose service to the East India Company and the Crown made them hybrid Anglo-Indian gentry. Colonel James Skinner is pictured here at a regimental durbar. Indian troops helped make Britain a great Asiatic power from the eighteenth century until the end of the Second World War.

43. Imperial power was stretched thin, sometimes disastrously so. An armed intervention in Afghanistan ended in the retreat of a small Anglo-Indian force from Kabul during the winter of 1841, during which nearly all were massacred. This painting of 1896 imagines the last moments of the 44th Foot before it was overwhelmed.

44. England had been deeply involved in the slave trade, and it was deeply involved in its abolition, in one of the first mass political campaigns. Here Thomas Clarkson, a tireless abolitionist organizer, addresses the Anti-Slavery Society in 1840. Visible in the audience are a liberated slave, Henry Beckford, the Quaker social reformer Elizabeth Fry, and the Irish Catholic leader Daniel O'Connell.

45. This photograph, one of the earliest of an English crowd scene, shows the great Chartist meeting at Kennington in April 1848, after which a petition was presented to Parliament demanding democratic reform. Some hoped or feared that there might be a revolution, and the government had prepared for violence. But it passed off peacefully.

46. Since the eighteenth century, England, Ireland and Scotland have sent millions of migrants round the globe, creating what has been called the Anglosphere. Similar people, activities, associations and buildings rapidly took root in North America, South Africa and Australasia, as in this busy scene in 1850s Melbourne.

47. Organized sport was one of the great Victorian cultural innovations, with a truly global impact. Its organizers thought of it as a moral training; its spectators, as a source of excitement. The two often clashed. The FA Cup helped to spread interest in the game. This 1892 final, between Aston Villa and West Bromwich Albion, was won 3–0 by West Brom.

48. The novelist Samuel Butler's naïve painting of family prayers records a crucial aspect of Victorian life, combining family, hierarchy, patriarchy—and tedium. The 1851 census, the only one that ever recorded religious practice, showed Victorian England to be about as religious as the United States today.

49. It was a source of national pride that politicians were treated as ordinary people. When Lord Morpeth went to Windsor in the 1850s for an audience with the Queen, he travelled in an omnibus, as Mr. Gladstone is shown doing here. A contemporary wrote in the 1860s: "Even the Prime Minister must pick his way along Parliament Street, an errand boy with a blue bag at his side and a burly coal-heaver before him—no ceremony—no exclusiveness."

50. The new Palace of Westminster was completed in 1867. Its extravagant Perpendicular Gothic made an architectural claim to the centrality of Parliament in English history. During the thirty years it was being built, the activities of its occupants were streamlined, disciplined, even democratized, yet in some ways became less responsive to the millions outside.

51 and 52. English women were active in many spheres, and often in conflict with nineteenth-century propriety. Elizabeth Halliwell of Wigan was one of those who, in the 1880s, insisted on their right to work at the colliery pithead, which both main political parties were trying to ban. Daisy, Countess of Warwick, could afford to brave convention by supporting agricultural trade unionism—and by being the Prince of Wales's mistress.

53. The First World War was an industrial war, dependent on factory workers as much as soldiers. The preliminary bombardment for Passchendaele (1917) used up a year's output of 55,000 munitions workers. The huge investment in arms manufacture appears in this photograph of the workforce of one giant Vickers plant in Kent assembled on Armistice Day, 1918.

54. This mural in Walsall Town Hall celebrates the crossing of the St. Quentin canal, the strongest point in the Hindenberg Line, by a local regiment—once a source of civic pride, but later overtaken by memories less of victory than of suffering.

55. The artist Henry Tonks drew and painted men with facial injuries as part of a medical exercise. Even now these are a disturbing reminder of the price paid by many thousands who survived the war but never recovered from its effects.

56. Britain had the strongest peace movement in interwar Europe, campaigning for "collective security" through the League of Nations and for disarmament. This made it politically difficult for governments to rearm after the Nazis took power in Germany, though they did so with increasing speed after 1936—the year of this demonstration.

57. The "Jarrow Crusade" of 1936 marks our memory of interwar England. The staple industries of the north—textiles, coal, shipbuilding—had lost world markets, largely a consequence of the war. But elsewhere in England the early 1930s saw rapid economic recovery—a difference that entrenched the north–south divide.

58. The Battle of Britain, fought under the gaze of millions, created an epic, rendered into Shakespearean language by Churchill. Paul Nash's painting evokes the strange beauty of aerial combat in blue skies.

"LET US GO FORWARD TOGETHER"

59. Women were for the first time in the front line as the Luftwaffe attacked RAF bases. Corporal Josephine Robins was one of six members of the Women's Auxiliary Air Force to be awarded the Military Medal for "gallantry in the field."

60. Churchill's appointment as Prime Minister on 10 May 1940 alarmed many insiders, but boosted public confidence. His image, oratory and personality did much to create the drama of the "finest hour" and his own legend within it.

A TIMBER, PLASTER AND THATCH VILLAGE

61. As England became more and more urbanized, the village became an ideal—a trend going back at least to the nineteenth century. This romanticized picture, for a popular 1950s children's book on architecture, epitomizes the "Picture Post-Card" scene.

62. The postwar reality, with massive house-building, was more likely to be a housing estate or a block of flats. This utopian vision of modernity soon turned sour.

63. This dramatic landscape epitomizes another pole of English life: the industrial city, created a century before this photograph of Halifax was taken in 1958. Though few realized it at the time, this scene and the patriarchal working-class society with which it was associated were on the brink of extinction.

64. For nearly two centuries, England's history was marked by emigration. Since the 1940s, continuing a long tradition, it has been increasingly affected by incomers, at first from the Commonwealth. Here, men, women and children from the Caribbean take their first steps onto the streets of London, having arrived at Waterloo station from Southampton docks.

65. Dreaming spires and huge laboratories: Cambridge embodies English intellectual and social tradition, yet it is a global institution with researchers coming increasingly from overseas. Its success, like that of England itself, demands continuing ability to juggle dynamic change and rootedness in history.

66. The Queen's position in national and international affection was presumably thought sufficiently unassailable for an astonishing bit of "British humour" in the 2012 Olympic opening ceremony, when she "parachuted" into the arena accompanied by James Bond—fictitious naval officer and secret agent. He has become another global symbol of Britishness, and Britain's ambition to "punch above its weight" with often slender material forces.

Not all English ideas about the outside world were connected with imperialism. Long the most popular novel set outside Europe—indeed, the fastest-selling novel in England of the whole century—was *Uncle Tom's Cabin* (1852), proof of the enduring power of anti-slavery.[11] The great popular heroes, David Livingstone and General Gordon, were seen as humanitarian and religious martyrs, not imperial conquerors, while foreign liberators such as Kossuth and Garibaldi enjoyed comparable popularity in England. Colonies of settlement had bigger impact than any other part of the empire, and were almost universally regarded as beneficial—to England, to the colonists, even to indigenous populations. Liberals, and in later decades trade unionists and the Labour Party, shared these views—by the end of the century there were important links between trade unions in Britain and the colonies. Remittances of money, cheap postage and returning migrants spread the benefits and channelled experience of the outside world to millions still at home. Yet, as we have noted, migration was not in most cases an "imperial" experience, as the largest number of migrants went to the United States.

The English thought of themselves as Christian Europeans. This was reinforced, not weakened, by the experience of empire, shared with other Europeans. England was seen as a leader of European civilization, and in areas such as economics and politics, clearly pre-eminent. Elsewhere, the superiority of others was accepted: in general culture and the arts of living, the French; in art and music, the Germans and Italians; in philosophy and scholarship, the Germans; and in almost everything, the ancient Greeks. Many in England thought of themselves (or at least their compatriots) as what Matthew Arnold called "philistines." Compared with European influences, the cultural impact of the rest of the world, including the empire, was tiny. Probably the greatest late-nineteenth-century impact of a non-Western culture was that of Japan, from the Japanese exhibition in London, which drew a million visitors in 1862, to Gilbert and Sullivan's *The Mikado* (1885). Non-European items were rare in the press, however, and only occasionally appeared in political debate. Neither schools nor universities taught the geography or history of other continents, or of the empire.

The truly "imperialist" group in English society were those who ruled the empire, often inter-related families with a tradition of colonial service. They were few: those with direct experience of the empire, including soldiers, missionaries and families, were around 1.5 percent of the English population, considerably more in Scotland and Ireland. Arguably, their influence on culture and "identity" was limited and superficial[12]—such as the thick curling moustache, an Indian virility symbol made compulsory for European officers in the East India Company's army, and thence the badge of the English gentleman in the early twentieth century. It is often assumed that English education, through the public schools and Oxbridge, was fundamentally shaped by the demands of empire, concentrating on "character building" for future proconsuls. There is some reason to be cautious. "Muscular Christianity," the desire to keep boys out of mischief and the established prestige of the Classics may sufficiently explain educational eccentricities.

During the last quarter of the century efforts were made to stimulate imperial fervour. Disraeli made a controversial gesture by proclaiming Victoria Empress of India in 1876—the origin of the term "imperialist" in the English context. Intellectual analyses were provided by a Liberal MP, Sir Charles Dilke, in *Greater Britain* (1868), and by a Cambridge historian, John Seeley, in his influential *Expansion of England* (1883), which argued that empire, now that political liberty at home had been achieved, had become the goal of England's history. Both were trying to prepare their ignorant and apathetic countrymen for a future of Darwinian struggle. But imperial policy remained a minority interest, little reported in the press. Parliamentary debates were sparsely attended. Seeley quipped that it was as if they had "conquered and peopled half the world in a fit of absence of mind."[13] Dilke and Seeley saw the real empire as the settler colonies, which they hoped could be consolidated. India and the rest were an embarrassment—even, as Disraeli had put it when Chancellor of the Exchequer, "a millstone round our necks." By the end of the century, as Africa, Asia and the Pacific became arenas for Great Power rivalry, imperial issues became more prominent. The crucial figure was "Joe" Chamberlain, the most charismatic late-Victorian politician, whose role in promoting imperial federation and precipitating the Boer War we have noted. But the 1906 general election was a decisive defeat for his vision of imperial federation, proof of the political weakness of imperialism at its apogee. Moreover, the white colonies had been given increasing self-government since the 1840s (see p. 564) and saw no reason to give it up. The six Australian colonies federated in 1901, and those of South Africa in 1909. An enthusiast, Lord Meath, campaigned for an "Empire Day" (adopted in 1902), but he had to pay for it from his own pocket, and many teachers and local councils disliked introducing it into schools. The suggestion of a school flag-raising ceremony was dismissed as un-English. Respectable workers despised soldiers, and, though patriotic, their love of England stopped at Dover.[14]

A semi-imperial popular culture appeared. Henry Rider Haggard's *King Solomon's Mines* (1886) sold 650,000 copies. Children's adventure literature—G. A. Henty's novels, the *Boys' Own Paper* and girls' adventures too—sometimes used imperial themes. But "Westerns" and spectacles like Buffalo Bill's Wild West Show outweighed imperial derring-do. There was little serious literature of empire—only Rudyard Kipling bears comparison with contemporaries such as Hardy, Henry James, Zola and Proust.[15] He wrote mostly about India's un-heroic side. Joseph Conrad wrote grimly of "the horror" of (Belgian) white men in Africa, though he cautiously approved of the British Empire. There was little serious imperial art: plenty of cigarette cards and biscuit tins, but little or no painting other than battles—a genre despised by intellectuals, and in the hands of its most famous exponent, Lady Butler, often about failure. The stand against the Zulus at Rorke's Drift in 1879 was painted by the famous French artist Alphonse de Neuville—military painting was more fashionable there—and the picture ended up in a Sydney museum, where it remains (somewhat to the embarrassment of the curators) the most popular work. Far more important was the impact of Japanese paintings and prints, African sculpture and Javanese music, which avant-garde Europeans hastened to imitate. This could be seen as an offshoot of imperialism, but it was a different form from that of rule.

Englishness was thought to have a distinct "character."[16] Disraeli declared in 1832 that "nations have characters, as well as individuals." Dr. Thomas Arnold, headmaster of Rugby School, coined the term "national identity," and John Stuart Mill, in *The English National Character* (1834), tried to analyse it, concluding that it was created by race, language, religion, geography and above all "the possession of a national history . . . [a] community of recollections; collective pride and humiliation, pleasure and regret." But what *was* Englishness, and where should it be going? Was it essentially rural and needing urgently to be preserved? This was a view of radicals and socialists such as William Morris and Robert Blatchford, for whom the Industrial Revolution had been a disaster; and many conservatives could agree. Or was England a new urban society, urgently needing further modernization of its educational, social and political systems so as to keep up with Germany and America? Were the English now subsumed into an "imperial Anglo-Saxon race"? Was England great and invincible, or was it decadent and in decline? There were writers and politicians of all parties—Liberal imperialists, Unionists and socialists, for example—for whom England was simply too small for the modern world. Its history had to be extended, to make William Wallace, Robert the Bruce and George Washington heroes of a more inclusive Anglo-Saxon saga to promote racial unity. Or should "little England" be unchained from the world imperial juggernaut? So thought some who admired the Boers, sympathized with the Irish, and wanted the English too freed from the burdens of history. These dilemmas were clear in much of its culture. Kipling, who had lived in India, South Africa and America, settled in 1896 in rural England, his "favourite foreign country," and tried to pull the different strands together, with the land itself containing and reconciling centuries of change: but this could only be done by the magic of Puck, in a fantasy for children.[17] What if, despite Kipling's strenuous assertion, England *was* only "what it seems"? As he remarked privately, it was "a stuffy little place," and he seems to have been happier in France.[18]

Two dramatic events in 1912 crystallized such confused feelings: the failure of Captain Robert Falcon Scott's expedition to be the first to reach the South Pole, and the death of its members in March; and the sinking of the great liner *Titanic* a few days later in April with the loss of some 1,500 lives. Even after a century, these tragedies retain astonishing resonance. The fatal collision of the "unsinkable" ship with an iceberg on its maiden voyage seemed to symbolize the hubris of modern society. The ship has been seen as a microcosm of Britain's tensions and inequalities, embodied in the hierarchies among passengers and crew, issues emphasized in modern fictionalized accounts, but controversial at the time too. For conservatives, the disaster provided a moving vindication of traditional moral values—of gentlemanly chivalry and the qualities of "the race," calmly "playing the game" in the face of death, and putting women and children first. But many feminists rejected such chivalry as an excuse for gender inequality and a cloak for the White Star Line's "essentially masculine passion for record-breaking and money-making at any and every cost!"[19] Moreover the official British inquiry discovered that women and children travelling first class had been put first far more than those in third class: only 3 percent of the former had died, but 60 percent of the latter.[20] *Titanic*'s captain, Edward Smith, went down with the ship: a hero, or the man whose negligence had caused the disaster?

Scott's fate, and that of his companions, news of which reached England only the following year, was another gentlemanly saga: heroic failure to be first to reach the Pole, the self-sacrifice of Captain Oates, going deliberately to his death with only a laconic farewell, all stoically recorded by Scott as he lay slowly dying: "Had we lived, I should have had a tale to tell of the hardihood, endurance and courage of my companions which would have stirred the heart of every Englishman. These rough notes and our dead bodies must tell the tale." Later, Scott's story, like that of the *Titanic*, was given other meanings—arrogance, snobbery, amateurish incompetence—expressing a negative view of Englishness.

Both tragedies—in large part, unpredictable accumulations of mishaps—have been interpreted retrospectively as heralding the end of an English age, whether in heroism, pathos or folly.

Scott represented in his personality and in his prose an extreme form of the late-Victorian concept of the English gentleman: "manly," straightforward, stubborn, unimaginative, and gentle. He sensed his iconic role, and his death in 1912 was soon felt strangely to have foreshadowed the fate of many of his class in the First World War.[21]

# PART SIX

# THE NEW DARK AGE,
## 1914–1945

*The most striking outward feature of the history of the last generation is the shrinkage of the world . . . As the world contracts, the human race grows more conscious of its unity . . . We can now look forward with something like confidence to the time when war between civilized nations will be considered as antiquated as the duel.*

G. P. Gooch, *The History of Our Time* (1911)[1]

Most Europeans in the 1900s, with the English prominent if not pre-eminent among them, imagined themselves at the constantly advancing crest of a civilization greater than any the world had known. One feature of civilization was a conscious turning away from war: by 1914, 194 treaties included provision for international arbitration of disputes; there were over 400 peace organizations in the world, forty-six of them in Britain and seventy-two in Germany, and a Palace of Peace to house their conferences was opened in The Hague in 1913.[2] A much remarked book, *The Great Illusion* (1910), by Norman Angell (later a Labour MP and Nobel Peace Prize winner), demonstrated that economic interdependence made war economically self-defeating—how could he imagine that "total war" would ignore economic rationality, the rights of property, international law and the most basic rights of humanity?

There were dissenting voices from this progressive consensus, loudest in France, Germany, Italy and Russia, but present everywhere. They believed that "civilization" was rotten, and would have to be killed or cured by violence. There were also polemics about which nation or race best represented civilization. Some of these dissenting voices—nationalist or socialist or both at once—would eventually become dangerous. But this could only happen because of another level of conflict: between states simultaneously ambitious and fearful. Many agreed with the late Lord Salisbury that the world was divided into living and dying nations: but which were which, and how could nations ensure that they were among the former?

The violent collision of 1914 was the shattering event, still controversial in its nature and causes, that began four decades of violence, hatred and cruelty which the peoples of 1900 could not have foreseen in their sickest nightmares. England, the United Kingdom and the empire were deeply engaged in these events. Indeed, the jealousy and resentment they inspired were among the underlying causes of the conflict. Much of their wealth and power, accumulated over two centuries, was expended. Britain's net overseas investments in 1913 had been twice its GDP; 43 percent of all the world's foreign investments belonged to Britain, twice as much as America and Germany combined. After the First World War, they were half that; after the Second, there was little left. This diminished the flow of income that had previously cushioned living standards, paid for imports, and buttressed defence spending.[3] The country's wealth hardly increased over thirty years, leaving it by 1945 shabby and tired. By comparison with most of the other belligerents—Germany, France, Russia, Japan, Austria, Poland, Italy—England had survived enviably unscathed. But it was no longer the centre of world wealth and power. The United Kingdom had broken up. The empire soon disintegrated. But defeat would have been infinitely worse.

# CHAPTER 15

# The War to End War

If any question why we died,
Tell them, because our fathers lied.
                Rudyard Kipling (whose son was killed),
                          "Epitaphs of the War"

But with the best and meanest Englishmen
I am one in crying, God save England, lest
We lose what never slaves and cattle blest.
The ages made her that made us from dust:
She is all we know and live by, and we trust
She is good and must endure, loving her so:
And as we love ourselves we hate her foe.
          Edward Thomas (killed 1917), "This is no case of
                                petty right or wrong"

The "Great War" haunts the English and British memory as horror and futility, blundered into for incomprehensible reasons, and pursued blindly for unknown ends at unimaginable cost—750,000 lives, and money that could have paid for thousands of hospitals and schools, and a university for every city.[1] Across Europe, 9 million soldiers died; one in three of all British males aged nineteen to twenty-two in 1914 were killed.[2] The war is taken, as in Kipling's searing lines, as condemnation of the old society, its morality and its values: "the supreme and tragic climax of Victorian cant,"[3] and "the old Lie: Dulce et decorum est pro patria mori."[4] But today's collective memory distorts the experience of those who endured the war. They saw it as a struggle for freedom and for a better world—"the war that would end war," as the socialist novelist H. G. Wells declared. Most still believed it in 1918, and many would continue to believe it as long as they lived.[5] Were they deluded, or are we uncomprehending? We struggle to understand why the war was fought, but can clearly see with hindsight that it failed.

## LIGHTS OUT

*The lamps are going out all over Europe; we shall not see them lit again in our lifetime.*

Sir Edward Grey, 3 August 1914

On Sunday, 28 June 1914, an open-topped car took a wrong turning in Sarajevo, the capital of Austrian-ruled Bosnia, and slowly reversed. So a Bosnian Serb student had an easy target in its passengers, Archduke Franz Ferdinand, heir to the thrones of Austria and Hungary, and his wife Sophie. Two bullets killed both.[6] On 23 July Austria-Hungary delivered a stern ultimatum to Serbia, which had armed and trained the assassin, and on the twenty-eighth declared war and bombarded Belgrade. On 4 August German troops attacked Belgium, and the British Empire declared war. The connection between these events still causes controversy and confusion, as it did at the time. Big, easy and interesting explanations—that the war was due to capitalism, colonialism, "war psychosis" of mass societies, secret alliances or a predetermined conspiracy—do not work. At best they are unhelpful, like explaining a car crash by the invention of the internal-combustion engine. There may simply not be an all-embracing explanation. But neither is it enough to call it an inevitable accident—that Europe slithered into war, as David Lloyd George later said. What happened was deliberate. As Wilfred Owen retold the story of Abraham and Isaac, the angel tells Abraham not to sacrifice the boy:

Offer the Ram of Pride instead.
But the old man would not so, but slew his son,
And half the seed of Europe, one by one.

For several years, tensions between states had been increasing, and generals, diplomats, politicians and writers began to plan for the possibility of war. For Whitehall, the main danger at first seemed a familiar one: imperial rivalry with France in Africa and with Russia in Persia, central Asia and China. The situation was complicated by Germany's decision in 1900 to double the size of its navy and build up a battleship fleet to challenge British dominance of European waters. The First Lord of the Admiralty, Lord Selborne, warned in 1902 that this fleet "is very carefully built up from the point of view of a war with us," alarming if Germany joined a hostile coalition with Russia and France.[7] In fact, Germany's strategy, as the British Foreign Office realized, was not to attack but to threaten Britain in the hope of forcing it to acquiesce in German colonial expansion, and scare it into neutrality in case of a European war.[8] Britain signed an "Entente Cordiale" with France (1904) and a less cordial entente with Russia (1907), which seemed to reduce the possible threat posed to Britain. The government, following a press campaign in 1909, pledged to outbuild Germany in fast, heavily armed Dreadnought battleships, which thanks to superior shipbuilding and financial strength (due in part to Lloyd George's "People's Budget") it was able to do, doubling naval expenditure, which rose to a quarter of the state budget in 1912.

British politicians, diplomats, service chiefs and public came to see Germany as a potential threat—dramatically underlined by the two Moroccan crises (see p. 588)—and France as a potential ally, although plans were still being considered for the possibility of war against France and Russia. Tentative military "conversations" took place between British and French generals. The Foreign Secretary, Sir Edward Grey, tried to explain it all in 1911 to the Prime Minister, Herbert Asquith:

> Early in 1906 the French said to us "will you help us if there is a war with Germany?" We said "we can't promise our hands must be free." The French then urged that the Mil[itar]y Authorities should be allowed to exchange views—ours to say what they could do—the French to say how they would like it done, if we did side with France—Otherwise, as the French urged, even if we decided to support France, on the outbreak of war we shouldn't be able to do it effectively. We agreed to this.[9]

Germany, despite financial pressures, increased its battleship programme in 1912. Churchill, now First Lord of the Admiralty, told Parliament that Britain faced "a very powerful, homogenous Navy, manned and trained by the greatest organizing people of the world . . . and concentrated within easy distance of our shores." The Admiralty responded by a naval agreement with France: France would defend the Mediterranean, allowing Britain to concentrate its ships in the North Sea; by implication, it would protect France's west coast and shipping. Churchill wrote that if war came and Britain defeated Germany's fleet, "we can put everything else straight afterwards"; otherwise, "there will not be any afterwards."[10] Nevertheless, Germany and Britain remained each other's biggest trading partners, and the two had extensive social and cultural contacts, from socialists who were partners in the Second International, to cavalry officers who came to hunt with the Quorn. The head of the German navy, Admiral von Tirpitz, Anglophobia notwithstanding, sent his daughters to

Cheltenham Ladies' College, and his officers bought their dress uniforms in Savile Row.[11]

By 1913 relations with Germany were improving hesitantly, encouraged by shared worries in London and Berlin about growing Russian power, and about the danger of serious conflict in the Balkans. Germany quietly scaled down its naval plans (which for the time being it could no longer afford), but much damage had been done: as the German foreign minister observed, tensions "had gone too deep for a speedy improvement." Yet by June 1914 Grey was hoping that improving relations with Germany might make London "the connecting link" between the European Powers, able to calm tensions.[12] War was not seen as inevitable. But when the fatal crisis came, the rapprochement with Germany was too recent to make a difference.

War, of course, did not begin in Morocco, the North Sea or the Channel, but on the Danube. The British ambassador in Vienna, Sir Fairfax Cartright, had predicted the crisis with astonishing prescience in January 1913: "Servia will some day set Europe by the ears and bring about a universal war on the Continent . . . [T]he Serbs may lose their heads and do something aggressive against the Dual Monarchy [Austria-Hungary] which will compel the latter to put the screws on Servia."[13] The Balkans had become the arena for growing antagonism between Austria-Hungary and Russia, implicitly involving their respective allies, Germany and France.[14] From 1908 Germany, France and Russia all began to build up gold reserves in case of war.[15] In 1912–13 there was war between their protégés, Serbia, Bulgaria, Romania, Greece, Montenegro and Turkey. Security, prestige and political stability seemed at stake, above all in multinational Austria-Hungary, whose survival was threatened by Slav nationalism, and in Russia, committed to "protect" the small Slav states. France saw its security as dependent on its 1893 defensive alliance with Russia. Even Germany, the most powerful Continental state, felt it needed its ally Austria against a rising Russia, which, said the chancellor Theobald von Bethmann Hollweg, "weighs on us like an ever-deepening nightmare."[16] The German general staff, a law unto itself, had developed the "Schlieffen Plan" in 1908 for simultaneous war against France and Russia: to invade Belgium, launch a devastating attack across France's unprotected northern frontier, defeat the French within a month, and then turn on Russia. Civilian politicians were not told the details.[17] Speed and surprise were crucial, so the complex plan to mobilize the army (involving 300,000 telegraph and telephone operators transmitting the orders, 30,000 locomotives and over 800,000 railway wagons) was also a plan to begin hostilities. For other countries, mobilization could be a means of leverage in negotiations—what has been called "armed diplomacy"—but for Germany it would launch a war, scheduling an attack on the Belgian city of Liège on the third day of mobilization.[18] The only way for Belgium and France to avoid a war would be to allow the Germans to invade their territory without resisting.

By 1914, although most people were blithely unaware of it, European peace was a house of cards. But someone still had to topple it.[19] There was a window of opportunity for war, because all four Continental powers felt they could win. France and Russia (humiliatingly defeated by Japan in 1905) would not have felt this as recently as 1910. The confidence of German and Austrian military commanders, however, was ebbing: they believed that Russia and France, both modernizing their armies, would be too strong for them by 1917. Helmut von Moltke, the German chief of staff, considered that "today we should still be a match for them." The Austrian chief of staff used an appropriate gambler's metaphor: "In 1908–9 [victory] would have been a foregone conclusion, in 1912–13 it would have been a game with decent chances, *now* we play *va banque*."[20] Both high commands had repeatedly been urging war while there was time,[21] and after the Sarajevo assassination Vienna and Berlin resolved to destroy the Serbian threat—"Now or never," commented the Kaiser.[22] Hence the ultimatum to Serbia. If they could intimidate Russia or France into backing down, and limit conflict to Austria and Serbia, as they continued to hope, so much the better: the predominance of Germany and Austria would be cemented without a major struggle, and the Franco-Russian alliance be destroyed. But, when the Russians began hesitant military preparations with the intention of deterring or if necessary fighting Austria, the German army, and hence Germany, had only left itself the choice of backing down or of launching the Schlieffen Plan, with its unprovoked attack on Belgium and France. So, notwithstanding diplomatic to-ings and fro-ings and agonized hesitations on the brink, Germany's rulers steeled themselves to fight a European war while they thought they could still win it. France and Russia were equally resolved to stand by Serbia and each other. None grasped what war would cost either in human or in material terms.

Where did Britain come in? The Foreign Office at first thought "the storm will blow over."[23] The *Manchester Guardian*, voice of Liberalism, declared: "We care as little for Belgrade as Belgrade for Manchester." Asquith told the Archbishop of Canterbury that Serbia was "a wild little state [that] deserved thorough thrashing."[24] Norman Angell recalled that Germany was "racially allied to ourselves." A group of Oxford, Cambridge and Aberdeen academics declared that "we regard Germany as a nation leading the way in the Arts and Sciences, and we have all learnt and are learning from German scholars. War upon her in the interest of

Servia and Russia will be a sin against civilisation."[25] Leading politicians were more concerned with the danger of conflict in Ireland than with distant rumblings in the Balkans, which the government hardly considered. The day after Austria's ultimatum to Serbia, 24 July, Asquith and Grey mentioned the Serbian crisis in Cabinet, though only after an involved discussion of Irish matters. This was the first time they had discussed foreign affairs for a month, and they agreed that Britain would try to mediate. Asquith reflected that the crisis opened the prospect of "a real Armageddon, which would dwarf the Ulster and Nationalist Volunteers to their true proportion." But he was confident that "there seems no reason why we should be anything more than spectators."[26] The ruling Liberal Party and its Labour allies were overwhelmingly opposed to war: "A good ¾ of our own men in the H. of Commons are for absolute non-interference at any price," wrote Asquith to a close friend.[27] Several members of the Cabinet threatened to resign rather than support British intervention. Bankers and businessmen, the Cabinet was told, were "all aghast" and predicted general ruin leading to "violence and tumult" as workers starved.[28] Pro-neutrality declarations were issued by churches, trade unions and the press: "We see no reason," wrote one Tory paper, "why Great Britain should be drawn in."[29] So on 24 July Grey duly invited the other powers not directly involved—Germany, France and Italy—to a conference in London to find a peaceful solution.

Grey was convinced that British security, and indeed honour, required that France should not be crushed by Germany. He also feared making an enemy of Russia—"If we fail her now," wrote the ambassador in St. Petersburg, "we cannot hope to maintain that friendly cooperation with her in Asia that is of such vital importance to us." On 28 July Austria declared war on Serbia, and on the twenty-ninth Russia ordered the mobilization of its forces. When King George V informed Asquith on 28 July that he had told Prince Henry of Prussia that Britain would try to remain neutral, Asquith pointed out the dangers: "Russia says to us: 'If you won't say you are ready to side with us now, your friendship is valueless, and we shall act on that assumption in the future.'" The desperate French ambassador warned that if Britain let France down "those in favour of an alliance with Germany at the expense of Britain could feel justified"—France would watch the future ruin of the British Empire "without a movement of sympathy."[30] On 30 July Germany refused to attend Grey's conference, asking instead that Britain should promise neutrality in return for a pledge that Germany would make no territorial changes after its victory. Sir Eyre Crowe, head of the Foreign Office's Western Department, thought this "cynical and dishonourable," proving that "Germany wants this war."[31]

Amid these pressures from all sides, the British government tried to dissuade the other states from taking fatal actions. Grey confided to a friend that he had "not lost all hope of a settlement,"[32] and he warned Paris on 31 July that Britain might have to remain neutral because its involvement could bring down the European economy. On 1 August, George V on Foreign Office advice sent a personal telegram to the tsar (addressed to "Dear Nicky" and signed "Georgie") urging the Russians to stop their mobilization. Later that day Grey told the German ambassador that if Germany promised not to attack France, Britain would remain neutral and try to keep France neutral. As German troops were already entering neutral Luxembourg, this news gave the German chief of staff a mild stroke. On 2 August the British Cabinet reluctantly consented to defend the French coast and French shipping from possible German attack. On 3 August Germany declared war on France. That afternoon Grey made a statement in the Commons asserting that if Britain stayed neutral it would "sacrifice our . . . reputation before the world, and [we] should not escape the most serious and grave economic consequences." Both the king and the social reformer Beatrice Webb recorded in their diaries the impact of Grey's speech on public opinion: Webb thought that now "even staunch Liberals agree that we had to stand by Belgium."[33] Both Lloyd George and Churchill, however, thought that if the Germans marched through only a small part of its territory, no British action would be necessary. But on 4 August the German army smashed its way into the heart of Belgium, and the Belgians fought back. "This simplifies matters," commented Asquith. The German ambassador in London reported to Berlin that "the Government will have behind it the overwhelming majority of parliament [for] the protection of France and Belgium."[34] Britain declared war at midnight on the fourth. A month later, it signed a pact with France and Russia not to make a separate peace.

Could the British government have prevented the war? Grey has long been condemned for failing to make the country's position clear. What should he have done? Promised intervention, so as to deter Germany? Or neutrality, so as to deter Russia and France? In fact, having no power to promise anything with the Cabinet and Parliament deeply divided, he tried to finesse, warning the Germans that Britain would not allow France to be crushed, telling the French and Russians that it would not support Balkan adventures, and announcing to all that it would not support any aggressor. He also pressed unsuccessfully for a conference, urged a delay in hostilities, and even promised, completely unrealistically, to keep France neutral if Germany did not attack. Probably what he actually did, and anything he might have said or done, could not have averted catastrophe.

The prospect of war with Britain caused only momentary hesitation in Berlin, while the Russian foreign minister assumed Britain would have to join the war sooner or later. Although Britain with its empire was the world's greatest power, its strength was potential—ships able to impose a blockade, money, untrained manpower, but not boots on the ground. Berlin hoped that the war would be decided, perhaps finished, before Britain could effectively intervene.

Should Britain then have stayed neutral, as most people at first wanted, limiting the war to the European Continent? Was Belgium—as the German government alleged—merely an excuse for the interventionists led by Grey and Churchill to embark on a conflict that they misunderstood and whose costs they disastrously underestimated? Plans assumed a war of three to eight months, and the government first intended to limit Britain's role to naval action.[35] Given the terrible permanent damage the war did, it is natural to feel that Britain should have stayed out at all costs. What would these costs have been? The Foreign Office feared both possible outcomes:

> (a) Either Germany and Austria win, crush France and humiliate Russia. With the French fleet gone, Germany in occupation of the Channel, with the willing or unwilling cooperation of Holland and Belgium, what will be the position of a friendless England? (b) Or France and Russia win. What would then be their attitude towards England? What about India and the Mediterranean?[36]

As Bethmann Hollweg put it, "the English policy of the Balance of Power must disappear" and "a new Europe" be created. This, feared Grey, would expose Britain and its empire to subsequent German aggression, perhaps abetted by an embittered Russia and France—which the German government did indeed intend. "[I]f we must bleed to death," said the Kaiser on 30 June, "at least England must lose India."[37]

A few historians have taken an optimistic view of the likely consequences of a German victory. It would merely have brought about "the Kaiser's European Union," a German-led common market "eight decades ahead of schedule . . . with which Britain, with her maritime empire intact, could . . . have lived." Besides, Germany might meanwhile have become a democracy.[38] Such optimism rests on two assumptions. First, that the hegemonic war aims formulated by Germany soon after war began would not have emerged had Britain not intervened. Second, that the Kaiser's government is comparable with those of post-1945 Germany: mellowed by victory, it would have introduced democracy, handed power to its domestic enemies, and devoted itself to friendly relations with its defeated foreign rivals. It is true that Germany (like other belligerents) had no list of war aims when war broke out: not surprisingly, as all were claiming to be fighting in self-defence. In the hope of preventing or delaying British intervention, Germany offered not to annex any Belgian territory if the Belgians did not resist—a significant condition—and not to annex any French territory—though French colonies were fair game.[39] But relative restraint promised before war had begun rapidly disappeared once battle was joined.

So a far less optimistic vision of German victory is plausible. Even if Britain had remained neutral, war would still have broken out, Germany would have invaded Belgium and France, and the French and Belgians would have resisted—as of course they did irrespective of British action. Germany would probably have been victorious eventually without British intervention, but that victory would not have been quick or painless. As it was, the French army bloodily threw back the German invasion with minor help from the British, and the French and Russians were capable of resisting for many months at least on their own. As early as September 1914, Bethmann Hollweg (a relative moderate) laid out his vision of the "Kaiser's European Union" when imposed by force. Belgium would be taken over completely as a "vassal state" with its ports "at our military disposal," and this became the core of Germany's war aims in the west.[40] The German navy wanted to establish bases directly threatening England— something that the English had fought against for centuries. This aim was supported by nationalist politicians and newspapers, and backed by an upsurge of Anglophobia.[41] To ensure "security for the German Reich in West and East for all imaginable time," Bethmann envisaged annexing large parts of northern France, including the Channel coast, imposing a crippling financial indemnity, making France "economically dependent on Germany" and excluding British commerce. Holland would become "dependent." A "European economic association" would be imposed to "stabilise Germany's economic dominance"; Germany would subsequently set up a continuous "Central African colonial empire." Finally, Germany would detach vast territories from Russia to "thrust [it] back as far as possible"—precisely what it did after defeating Russia in 1917.[42]

Germany's rulers came to see the war as a struggle against democracy, with victory the way of finally establishing their authoritarian power, which by the end of the war was practically a military dictatorship. The Kaiser, when he thought Germany had finally won in March 1918, said that "if an English delegation comes to sue for peace it must kneel before the German standard for it was a question here of a victory of monarchy over democracy."[43] Democracy would have had a bleak future in a Europe dominated by triumphant military monarchies in Berlin and Vienna. It seems unlikely that French democracy would have survived—it did not in

1940. Other vassal states would plausibly have come under harsh puppet dictatorships. What German soldiers and governors actually did is telling: over 6,000 civilians in Belgium and France were massacred in the first weeks of the war by invading troops; Belgium and occupied northern France were subjected to harsh military rule, semi-starvation, mass forced labour and systematic economic devastation in many ways worse than in the Second World War. In short, England in 1914 faced a prospect not so different from those in 1803 and in 1939. Perhaps in all three cases it could have survived as a cowed and impoverished satellite state, and it is possible to consider that a lesser evil than the carnage of war. But in 1914 government and people chose overwhelmingly to fight against "militarism" and aggression, defending law and order in Europe and even hoping that this would be the war to end war. They were probably right to fear what a victorious Germany might do, but they underestimated—like everyone else—the cost of preventing it.[44] Most of them always thought it was worth the immense sacrifice. It is possible to disagree. But it was not a frivolous cause or a senseless decision.

Nor was it taken lightly. One of the hoariest and most disdainful myths of 1914 is that politicians and people vacuously welcomed war as a thrill. In no country was this so. Everywhere it was greeted with foreboding and alarm. "The whole thing is a gigantic nightmare," wrote the British envoy in Berlin, Sir Horace Rumbold, "and I keep on wondering whether I am in a sane world."[45] "We must fight," wrote Ada Reece, a doctor's wife. "But all are agreed that it will be more terrible than any previous war [and] the ultimate consequences . . . none can foresee."[46] Rupert Brooke, later famous for his romantically patriotic poem "The Soldier," felt "depressed" about the "war business," and thought it would be "Hell to be in it; and Hell to be out of it."[47] The *New York Times* reported "no flag waving, no demonstrations, no music-hall patriotism."[48] Once war had begun, people rallied and gave their troops a good, and sometimes festive, send-off—this is what the photographs and newsreels of cheering crowds that have entered popular memory usually show. But few expected quick or easy victory: indeed, the notorious phrase "over by Christmas" appeared in the press only in late 1917. Those most likely to believe in a short war were enlightened readers of Norman Angell, and, as he had predicted, the 1914 crisis brought the world economy to the verge of collapse.[49]

But support for the war, especially among Liberals and socialists, grew in response to German actions, particularly the invasion of Belgium. Kate Courtney, an active Quaker and pacifist (and Beatrice Webb's sister), recalled that this was "the rock on which all anti-war feeling was shipwrecked," including her own.[50] Reports of the German atrocities, brought by refugees, began to appear late in August. The young artist Stanley

Spencer felt that "the more beastly the stories become, the more I feel I ought to go or do something."[51] Mrs. Pankhurst declared that "Prussianism is masculinity carried to the point of . . . obscenity." Suffragettes became enthusiastic propagandists, adopting the slogan "For King, For Country, For Freedom," and campaigning against those Mrs. Pankhurst called "conscientious objectors, passive resisters and shirkers."[52] The destruction of Louvain, including the burning of its ancient library, had a galvanizing effect on intellectuals, and many leading artists and academics subsequently worked to support the war effort, including Conan Doyle, Kipling and Galsworthy, and musicians such as Elgar, Stanford and Parry, who turned Blake's "Jerusalem" into a stirring patriotic anthem. The shelling of Scarborough and Hartlepool by German warships in December made clear that this was no longer a distant conflict.

Not all were convinced. In contrast both with their leaders and with their followers, some Liberal and Labour politicians and intellectuals remained opposed to British involvement. Charles Trevelyan (who resigned from the government), the MPs Arthur Ponsonby, Ramsay MacDonald and Philip Snowden, the Cambridge mathematician and philosopher Bertrand Russell, and Norman Angell set up the Union for Democratic Control, financed by wealthy Quakers such as the Rowntrees and Cadburys. It aimed to combat what they saw as the causes of the war—alliances, "balance of power" ideas, armaments, popular "jingoism" and "herd mentality"—and replace them with an "International Council," and in time a "federalised Europe."[53]

## DREADFUL SERVICE

*I adore war. It is like a big picnic without the objectlessness of a picnic. I've never been so well or so happy.*
> Julian Grenfell (killed 1915), letter to his mother,
> 24 October 1914[54]

> Little did I dream, England, that you bore me
> Under the Cotswold hills beside the water meadows,
> To do you dreadful service, here, beyond your borders
> And your enfolding seas.
>> Ivor Gurney (wounded 1917), "Strange Service"

On 6 August, the government, after much hesitation, agreed to dispatch a British Expeditionary Force, the "BEF," to northern France, comprising all the regular troops in the United Kingdom supplemented by reservists.

Using 1,800 special trains, 240 requisitioned ships, 165,000 horses, London buses and delivery vans (some proclaiming HP Sauce to be "the World's Appetiser"), it was in place in France only sixteen days after war was declared. But it was small: some 110,000 men, of whom 75,000 were combat troops; there were 1.7 million Germans and 2.4 million French in the field. Lord Kitchener (the new Secretary of State for War) warned the BEF's commander, Sir John French, to expect few reinforcements and to avoid heavy casualties. Even so, it was expected that 75 percent of the force would be killed, wounded or captured within six months.[55]

This proved an underestimate. The BEF found itself in the path of 580,000 Germans advancing by surprise through central Belgium. They fought defensive battles at Mons at 23 August (the first British battle in western Europe since Waterloo, thirty miles away), inflicting heavy casualties on the packed German ranks, and at Le Cateau on the twenty-sixth. They were forced into headlong retreat, losing up to 20,000 men killed, wounded, captured or left behind. It was this crisis, with the BEF facing destruction, not a boyish thrill of adventure, that caused the famous rush of volunteers: its all-time peak was from 25 August to 5 September.[56]

By 5 September the German armies had reached the River Marne, east of Paris, their nearest units only twenty miles from the city ramparts. The great battle of the Marne, involving over a million men on a hundred-mile front, halted the German advance at the cost of 80,000 French and 1,700 British casualties. The BEF's role, largely symbolic, was significant: the exhausted Germans decided to retreat if the British crossed the Marne, which they did on 9 September. Moltke resigned as hopes of a rapid German victory collapsed. The rest of 1914 saw the two sides manoeuvring to outflank each other to the north-west, until both reached the sea. From then on, the lines were largely fixed, from the Channel to the Swiss frontier. The BEF was redeployed on the left of the Allied line, close to its supply ports. In October and November French, British, Indians and Belgians fought for Ypres—the first of four ever-bloodier battles over its ruins. These were the deadliest months of the whole war. By the end of 1914, the French had lost 528,000 men killed, wounded or captured, the Germans 800,000, and the old BEF had been largely wiped out, having lost 90,000 men, two-thirds of them at Ypres.[57] The Territorials were sent out to reinforce them. On the Eastern Front, the much-vaunted Russian "steamroller" had been halted by smaller German forces, and the Austrians had suffered reverses in Serbia and Poland.

The war then became a harrowing test of endurance, blood and treasure (it would eventually cost on average some £7,000—perhaps £350,000 in today's values—for every one of the 4 million enemy soldiers killed).[58] The Allies had to force the Germans out of occupied France and Belgium, and hence to attack, but with inferior equipment and without benefit of surprise,[59] inevitably at a heavy cost in life and limb. Kitchener realized that the war would be long and that Britain would have to send a mass army overseas for the first time in its history. He appealed for 100,000 volunteers: by the end of September there were 761,000. Time would be needed to turn them into soldiers, as "to send untrained men into the fighting line," said Kitchener, "was little short of murder." One of his colleagues was blunter: the new army was "the laughing stock of every soldier in Europe . . . under no circumstances could these mobs take the field for two years."[60] Consequently, "no very important supply of British effectives could be looked for until the late spring of 1915," concluded Kitchener, and "the British army would only reach full strength . . . during the Summer of 1917."[61] Until then, the death toll would fall mainly on the French and Russians.

Britain relied on volunteers until 1916.[62] Conscription was traditionally unpopular, but in any case there was no system for applying it. By the end of 1915, 2,466,000 men had joined, about one in three of those eligible, making it the second-largest volunteer army in history (slightly smaller than the Indian Army in the Second World War), and probably the largest proportion of any nation ever to volunteer to fight overseas. Women too volunteered: eventually 100,000 served in uniform and some were killed in action. This was not an exact cross-section of British, or English, society. Most likely to volunteer, and to be killed, were the upper and middle classes, from peers to clerks. Many were officers, leading from the front. A high toll was paid by public schools (Etonians were five times more likely to be killed than the average) and Oxbridge colleges. The peerage suffered heavier losses than in the Wars of the Roses.[63] Some less obvious groups— sons of Church of Scotland ministers, City bankers (80 percent enlisted, 16 percent killed), Elementary school teachers, fishermen (used in mine- sweeping) and cab-drivers—also suffered disproportionately. Asquith lost a son, as did the leader of the Labour Party, Arthur Henderson; the Leader of the Opposition, Bonar Law, lost two; and the leader of the Irish Nation- alists, John Redmond, lost a brother; twenty-three MPs were killed, aged between twenty-eight and fifty-six (15 Conservatives or Unionists, 7 Liber- als, 1 Irish Nationalist). Industrial workers (including miners and railway- men) formed more than half the army, reflecting their majority position in society; yet proportionately they served less, held back by the need to main- tain production. Agricultural workers—in contrast with Continental armies—suffered least, partly for the same reasons, and also because they tended to be older, a consequence of the prewar rundown of agriculture.

Paradoxically, the volunteer system produced a fairer distribution of risk than conscription. French and German conscription systematically excluded valuable workers, while in Britain many of them volunteered. So England did not experience such sharp inequalities as those in France or Germany between the casualty rates of different occupations, ages and classes, and which caused festering political division. Volunteering also gave time to adjust to war, and gave men control over the nature and style of their military service: for example, by joining local regiments.

If this caused manpower inefficiencies, it was of incalculable benefit to morale. In London, more men may have served as volunteers than would have been conscripted.[64] Volunteering ensured a quality and enthusiasm that partly made up for inevitably short and inadequate training; wrote a regular officer who had commanded the peacetime Guards brigade: "The quality of the men is undoubtedly of a higher standard than that of the old Army"; raw young officers showed "a zest and fearlessness which augurs well."[65] Strikingly, these civilian-soldiers, often with a discipline founded more on friendship, "with an arm across one's shoulder" (appalling slackness to regular soldiers), proved more resilient than the rigidly drilled regulars of 1914, who were more likely to desert, surrender or even wound themselves to escape combat.[66] Recruitment was not only military. The war effort required volunteer commitment by men and women of all ages. The subsequently famous "King and Country" poster of Kitchener's mustachioed face seemed old-fashioned at the time and was not widely circulated. Recruitment publicity concentrated on the rights and duties of citizenship in a range of activities: a nurse with bandages, a female munitions worker, a boy scout delivering mail.[67]

England was proportionally neither the most nor the least engaged in the war of the British nations: though differences were small, Scotland was the most (it had the highest level of casualties of any part of the empire, comparable with Germany) and Wales the least. Feeling in Ireland was mixed, yet there was much support for the war throughout: over 210,000 Irishmen (about 11 percent of military-age men) volunteered for the army, including Catholics and Protestants, Nationalists and Unionists.[68] The empire made an enormous contribution, often to the surprise of its rulers: 1.3 million troops from the settler Dominions, 827,000 from India, 57,000 from Africa. Volunteers from Canada, Australia (30 percent of military-aged men) and New Zealand (40 percent—the highest) approached the level of Britain (60 percent, including later conscripts).[69] Numerically, however, the empire's forces were predominantly English: of seventy-four divisions deployed in the main theatres of the war, sixty-four were British, and of these 80 percent were English.[70]

There were notable differences within England, as within the other countries of the United Kingdom: big cities and their suburbs yielded most volunteers, rural areas least. Much depended on the enthusiasm of local notables and the existence of prewar military links, weakest where there was a strong heritage of Gladstonian Liberalism and Dissent—"the chapels held soldiering to be sinful."[71] Perhaps, too, city populations felt more involved in outside events. Farmers, pressed to plough up pasture for cereals, found it easier to hold on to their labourers—and their sons. Lady Ottoline Morrell (purple-haired patroness of the arts and half-sister of the Duke of Portland) turned Garsington Manor into a refuge for artistic conscientious objectors, nominally farm workers.[72] Those who did not volunteer needed positive reasons not to do so in the face of considerable moral pressure. They were often men with dependants. Sometimes pressure to enlist was crude; but this should not be exaggerated—Suffragettes handing out white feathers were unpopular. There was less pressure in communities where lots of other men stayed back, due to vital industries such as mining. But we should not neglect the importance of genuine choice: if there were conscientious objectors (mostly religious—the biggest group were Christadelphians[73]), there were far more conscientious volunteers. Historians in all the combatant countries have recognized the importance of commitment by men who were not merely slaves to compulsion or community pressure, but believed that they had a duty to their families, communities and country. The typically English irreverence, particularly towards military pomposity—"We are Fred Karno's Army," etc.—should not mislead us. Recruitment drew on local attachments. "Pals' Battalions" (a phrase coined by the Earl of Derby in Liverpool) were a well-known example, drawing on neighbourhood, church, class and even political identity—there was a company of "socialist comrades" in the Cheshire Regiment. The Liverpool Scottish (a territorial unit which before the war was associated with the Birkenhead Dramatic Society, the Birkenhead Rugby Football Club, the Methodist Church and the Conservative Club) was commanded throughout the war by Liverpool's social elite. Mrs. E. Cunliffe-Owen (a well-known sportswoman) raised a "sportsman's battalion," which included two England cricketers and a boxing champion.[74] Class differences did not dissolve in the trenches, but, as in peacetime activities such as sport, were incorporated. Different units had class affinities: smart territorial units such as the London Rifle Brigade had a substantial entrance fee. Military ranks reflected social differences. This seems to have had some advantages: a sense of gentlemanly duty towards subordinates and the obligation of courage and leadership were "firmly ingrained in the country's social elite through the paternalism—

deference exchange characterizing peacetime class relations ... with excellent results for unit cohesion and combat performance"—one of the British army's few advantages over the German.[75] By the end of the war, a third of officers were from lower-middle- and working-class backgrounds, but (unlike in other armies) they were expected to emulate traditional standards by fellow officers and soldiers too, who liked their officers to behave (as one NCO told his German captors) like "brave lads and real gentlemen."[76]

Conscription was introduced in 1916. By this time it was widely supported as fairer, given growing public hostility to "shirkers." It did not greatly change the composition of the army—it may even have increased its middle-class component, as many workers were exempt. Uniquely, Britain adopted a system of local appeals tribunals, and many men did appeal, usually on economic or family grounds. The tribunals have a bad name, largely due to the postwar self-dramatization of conscientious objectors, who formed only about 2 percent of cases. Generally, the tribunals (which deliberately included trade unionists and socialists) were thorough and humane, and agreed to large numbers of at least temporary exemptions, usually for family reasons; and 80 percent of conscientious objectors were given exemptions.[77] Eventually, nearly 60 percent of military-age Englishmen served, compared with some 80 percent of French and Germans.

The first units of Kitchener's New Army sailed in the summer of 1915, and all thirty divisions were in the field by the summer of 1916. This huge expansion of the army faced handicaps in a country with no great military infrastructure like those of Continental states—barracks, stockpiles, medical services. As one general noted, "It took the Germans forty years of incessant work to make an army." Continental conscript armies reckoned on about a year's basic training; the British now hoped that six months would suffice, and when under pressure only three. Early volunteers drilled with wooden rifles and gunners practised with drainpipes on carts. A vast increase in officers was needed—from 28,000 to eventually 230,000. These were not just young men from school and university to lead platoons and companies (among them Siegfried Sassoon, Robert Graves, Rupert Brooke, Wilfred Owen, Harold Macmillan and J. R. R. Tolkien, whose experiences influenced his *Lord of the Rings*[78]). Also vital were men capable of organizing and commanding brigades and armies, and analysing and reacting to new conditions of warfare—massed artillery (responsible for over 70 percent of casualties), aircraft, chemical weapons. Elderly regular officers and NCOs were rarely capable of managing such a transformation. The British army was experienced in colonial campaigns. It took time to learn, digest and pass on the new skills of industrial warfare.[79] There was an inevitable cost in lives. It also took time to design and produce adequate weapons and enough ammunition. In 1914 the BEF had only 24 heavy guns; by 1918, 2,000. By 1916 fifty times the prewar annual output of TNT was being used every week. The preliminary bombardment for the third battle of Ypres (1917) lasted nineteen days, using 321 train-loads of ammunition totalling 4.3 million shells—a year's output of 55,000 munitions workers, costing £22m (almost the whole army budget in 1914). Britain would manufacture over 200 million shells, 15 for every German soldier, and by the end of the war its aircraft industry had reached three times the size of the German.[80]

It was unclear how the war could be fought and won. Assumptions that a modern war could only last a few months were quickly confounded. One conclusion, that of "Westerners," was that the decisive struggle was the Western Front, where the British and French must defeat the main German armies. Few generals believed in a "breakthrough" to decisive victory—though a disastrous exception was the commander-in-chief, General Sir Douglas Haig. Numbers and firepower would have to bleed the enemy to death, at the inevitable cost of the blood of one's own soldiers. The first big battles in France were costly, chaotic and inconclusive attacks in 1915: an attempt to take some of the weight off the French (who lost another 500,000 men in 1915), and to test the new army. All sides started to run out of shells. In Britain this became a "shell scandal," which forced Asquith to establish a coalition government in May 1915 and opened what would become a fatal split in the Liberal Party.

Those who baulked at the deadly quagmire in France, most famously Churchill and Lloyd George, sought other strategies: naval blockade to strangle German trade and the opening of new fronts in the Balkans or the Turkish empire. These "Easterners" hoped, as Lloyd George put it, "to get at the enemy from some other direction, and to strike a blow that would end the war."[81] Their big idea, pressed by Churchill as First Lord of the Admiralty, was to sail a fleet into Constantinople and force the Turks to surrender, thus aiding the Russians, assailed by the Turks as well as by the Germans and Austrians. The plan was adopted enthusiastically by the government, desperate for a way to shorten the war. Controversy long continued over whether it was a brilliant strategic idea from Churchill's fertile brain or a half-baked fantasy. On 18 March 1915 an Anglo-French fleet tried to force the narrow straits of the Dardanelles. They drew back in the face of mines and shore batteries. British, French, and Australian and New Zealand (ANZAC) troops landed to clear the shore defences on the Gallipoli peninsula. They too were fought to a standstill. British and

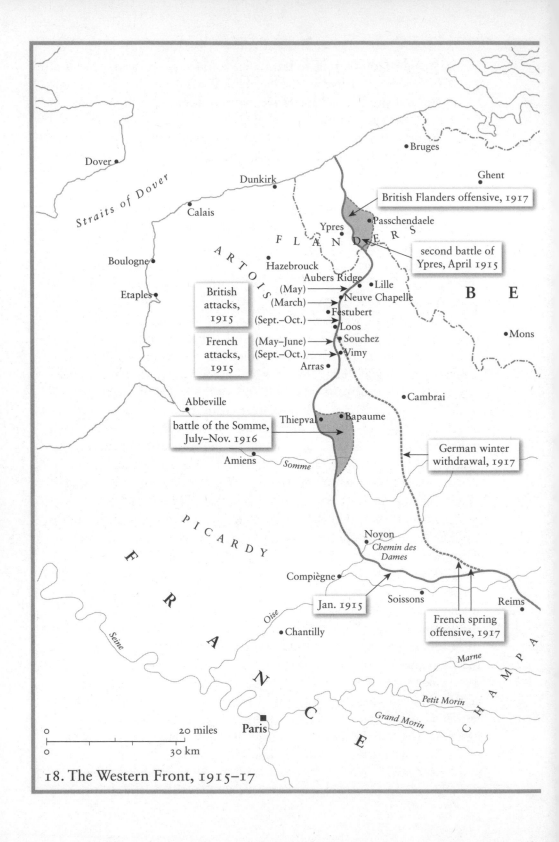

Dover •

Straits of Dover

Dunkirk •

Calais •

• Bruges

Ghent

Boulogne •

Etaples •

A R T O I S

FLAN D E R S

Ypres •

• Passchendaele

British Flanders offensive, 1917

second battle of
Ypres, April 1915

Hazebrouck •

Aubers Ridge •

B E

British
attacks,
1915

(May) ⟶

(March) ⟶

(Sept.–Oct.) ⟶

• Lille

Neuve Chapelle

• Festubert

• Loos

• Mons

French
attacks,
1915

(May–June) ⟶

(Sept.–Oct.) ⟶

Arras •

• Souchez

• Vimy

Abbeville •

battle of the Somme,
July–Nov. 1916

Thiepva.

Amiens •

Somme

• Cambrai

• Bapaume

German winter
withdrawal, 1917

P I C A R D Y

F

R

A

N

C

E

Seine

Noyon
• Chemin des
Dames

Compiègne •

Jan. 1915

Oise

• Chantilly

Soissons •

Reims •

French spring
offensive, 1917

Marne

C H A M P A

Petit Morin

Grand Morin

0        20 miles

0        30 km

■ Paris

18. The Western Front, 1915–17

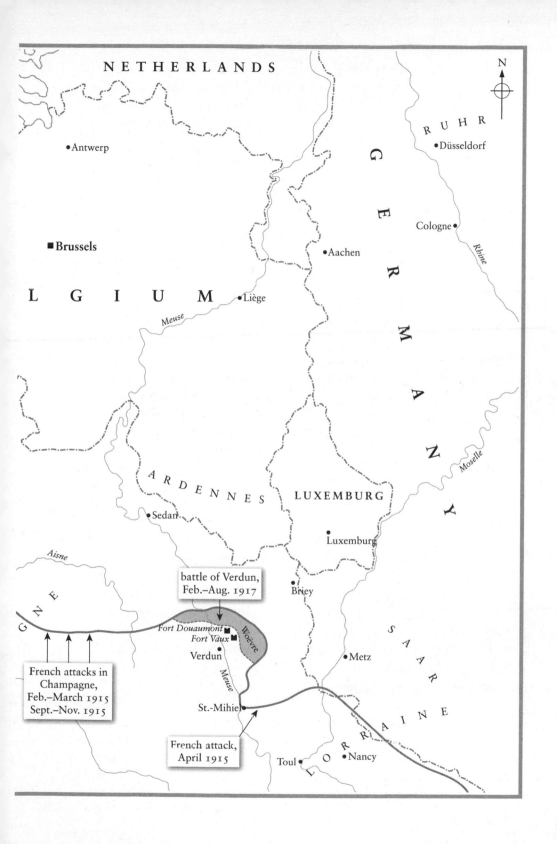

N

NETHERLANDS

•Antwerp

RUHR
•Düsseldorf

Cologne•

■Brussels

•Aachen

GERMANY

L G I U M

•Liège

Meuse

Rhine

A R D E N N E S

LUXEMBURG

•Sedan

Luxemburg•

Moselle

Aisne

battle of Verdun,
Feb.–Aug. 1917

G N E

Briey•

Fort Douaumont■
Fort Vaux■

Woëvre

French attacks in
Champagne,
Feb.–March 1915
Sept.–Nov. 1915

•Verdun

SAAR

Meuse

•Metz

St.-Mihiel•

French attack,
April 1915

L O R R A I N E

Toul•

•Nancy

Indian reinforcements brought no more success. All troops were finally evacuated in December and January 1916. Conditions had been appalling and casualties heavy: 71,000 British, 33,000 Anzacs, 23,000 French, 5,000 Indians and about the same numbers of Turks. Including the sick, total Allied casualties may have reached 390,000—in a campaign that had aimed to avoid the slaughter of the Western Front, not replicate it. A casualty of a different kind was Winston Churchill, who was forced out of the Cabinet and went to fight in the trenches. He later claimed that the operation had almost succeeded: "All the time, clear and simple solutions existed which would speedily have produced the precious element of victory."[82] But a recent study argues that it never had any chance of success, because it is unlikely the Turks would have surrendered even with Allied battleships in the Bosphorus, and even if they had it would have changed little.[83] So defective were the planning and execution, this was never put to the test. The British underestimated the determination and ability of the Turks, who had for most of the nineteenth century been their despised protégés. After Gallipoli came another disaster: in 1916 the Turks forced a whole British-Indian army in Mesopotamia to surrender.

A "Western" strategy for breaking the stalemate was agreed at a conference of Allied commanders in December 1915. French, Russians, British, Serbians and Italians (who had entered the war that May) would launch simultaneous offensives in the summer of 1916 with the maximum of troops.[84] This would force the enemy to fight everywhere at once, "wear out"—i.e., kill—their reserves, and finally overwhelm them. The biggest effort would be a joint Franco-British attack astride the River Somme. But the Germans struck first, before "the balance of numbers" deprived them, in the words of their commander, General von Falkenhayn, "of all remaining hope." He saw no chance of a military breakthrough, even less of invading "the arch-enemy," Britain. He decided instead to "bleed the French army to death," destroying French morale, and forcing the inexperienced British to attack to help their ally, thus suffering huge casualties too. France and Britain might then see the war as hopeless and sue for peace. The chosen killing ground was the exposed fortress town of Verdun. Beginning on 21 February 1916, the German and French armies embarked on a vast and hideous mutual slaughter, each eventually losing over 300,000 men.[85]

Two months later, in April, there were an uprising in Dublin and small disturbances in Wexford and Cork. Home Rule within the United Kingdom had been voted by the Commons in May 1914, but subsequently suspended until the peace. The moderate nationalist John Redmond, leader of the Irish Parliamentary Party, supported the war effort, hoping that a common patriotic struggle would unite Catholics and Protestants. The *Irish Times* extolled "the spectacle of Irish Unionists and Nationalists fighting side by side in Flanders . . . little more than a year ago they were preparing to kill one another. Today many of them have died for one another."[86] This policy was widely supported, including by volunteering for the army, supporting the Red Cross, and sheltering Belgian refugees.[87] But it was utterly rejected by radical nationalists, who feared they were losing ground to the moderates: "Home Rule was in the air. The over-whelming majority of the people supported Redmond . . . There were reports of the success of recruiting [for] the British Army . . . Our dream castles toppled about us with a crash . . . The Irish people had recognized themselves as part of England."[88] To disrupt this, radicals sought German assistance for an insurrection: a glorious revolt which, even if defeated, would inflame nationalism, and reap its reward when Germany won the war. On 24 April, Easter Monday, some 1,500 insurgents seized the General Post Office and other buildings in the centre of Dublin. In the ensuing conflict, 116 soldiers, 16 policemen and over 60 rebels were killed, as were a considerable number of civilians. Some 400 rebels were imprisoned in England and released after a few months; but 15 of the leaders were court-martialled and shot. Comparable punishment—and probably with greater severity—would have been inflicted in any of the belligerent countries. Yet it was a political disaster, tipping much Irish opinion towards sympathy with the rebels. Nevertheless, Irishmen, including Catholic Dubliners, continued to volunteer for the British army through-out the war; and no Irish regiment ever mutinied.[89] The well-received visit of the Irish Canadian Rangers (a predominantly Catholic regiment recruited in Quebec) to Dublin, Belfast and other Irish cities in January 1917 demonstrated that many Irish Catholics still supported the war effort eight months after the execution of the rebel leaders.[90] However, the war polarized opinion. Sinn Fein began to win by-elections at the expense of Redmond's moderate nationalists, exploiting fears (never realized, but seemingly imminent during the crisis of the great German offensives of 1918) that the military conscription recently adopted in Britain might be extended to Ireland.[91]

On 4 June 1916 the Russians launched a long and costly offensive to take the weight off Verdun, and the Italians followed suit on the fifteenth. The British commander-in-chief, Haig, refused to advance his Somme attack painstakingly planned for July: six months of preparation were under way and included laying 50,000 miles of telephone cable and build-ing eight new railway lines to carry supplies (every yard of front would require about a ton per day). But he did agree to go ahead on schedule, although the planned French participation was greatly reduced due to the haemorrhage at Verdun. Instead of the original joint campaign by more than twenty-five British and forty French divisions (a million men in all), the British would now take the lead, with twenty-four divisions to eighteen French.[92] This would be the first great test of Kitchener's army. As the head of military intelligence, General Charteris, summed it up:

> We do not expect any great advance . . . We are fighting primarily to wear down the German armies and the German nation, to interfere with their plans [and] prepare for the great offensive which must come sooner or later . . . The casualty list will be long. Wars cannot be won without casualties. I hope people at home realize this.[93]

On 1 July the British army began the biggest and bloodiest battle in its history. At 7:30 a.m., after an unprecedented artillery bombardment of 12,000 tons of shells, 55,000 British and French soldiers went "over the top," with another 100,000 following. The French and some British units made rapid progress. "It all seemed so easy—much easier than when we had practised it," wrote one soldier to his family. Another said: "We have done better than expected, and the Germans are putting up a pretty poor fight . . . we feel that the end of the war is now near." Siegfried Sassoon noted in his diary that men were "watching the show and cheering as at a football match," and he later described it as "great fun."[94] But elsewhere there was disaster: the artillery, partly through inadequate shells, partly through faulty planning, had failed to destroy the barbed wire; German dugouts and strongpoints had survived; so machine-gun and artillery fire decimated the attacking wave, killed many who had reached their objectives, and even hit those moving up from the rear—in one notorious example of men killed advancing in line, as if on parade, they were still half a mile behind their own trenches. One soldier saw his comrades "mown down like meadow grass. I felt sick . . . and remember weeping." Another described a noise like "wet fingers screeching across an enormous plate of glass"—the screams of thousands of wounded men. Many had "crawled into shell holes, wrapped their waterproof sheets round them, taken out their bibles and died." By the end of the day, there were 19,240 dead and 37,646 wounded or missing, including 75 percent of all the officers engaged, among them two generals. One battalion, 10th West Yorkshires, lost 90 percent of its strength. The French apparently lost only 1,600—the Germans had prepared for a British, but not for a French attack. The French commander-in-chief concluded that "the British do not yet have the skill . . . their artillerymen were less skilful than ours and their infantry less experienced." German assessments agreed: sometimes young officers "just stood there perplexed and paralysed" amid the carnage; "the officers and NCOs . . . lacked experience of war and the ability to react swiftly to new, changing and unexpected situations."[95]

But the battle was not over in one day: it continued as a four-and-a-half-month campaign with successive British and French offensives, including the first use of tanks, major use of aircraft and vastly increased artillery. Wrote one German soldier: "The strain was too immense . . . the English . . . surprised us in a manner never seen before. They came on unstoppably." German aircraft and artillery were "as good as eliminated," units were bled "like lemons in a press," and lost large numbers of officers and NCOs—their army would never be the same again. The Germans lost heavily due to their policy of defending every foot of ground and immediately counter-attacking every British advance—proof that German professionalism could be as prodigal of men as British amateurism. There were blatant instances of desperate German soldiers killing their own officers. Total casualties defy the imagination: some 420,000 British, 200,000 French, 465,000 German.[96] From a strategic viewpoint, the campaign helped to save Verdun and preserve the French army, and it forced the Germans onto the defensive. The Somme, wrote one young German officer, had been "the muddy grave" of the German army. After the Somme campaign, German soldiers showed somewhat less determination to fight on than the British.[97] German officers who interrogated British prisoners were impressed by their confidence in final victory: "Again and again we hear from prisoners the self-satisfied question: 'Don't you think we have done very well?' "[98]

The Somme, especially its first day, has taken on emblematic meanings. First, of the inhuman logic of the First World War: huge battles fought not to capture or liberate countries, or even seize resources or vital strategic objectives, but to kill enemy soldiers. After the disaster of Gallipoli, no one in any country could come up with any other way of fighting. The Somme—like its ghostly twin Verdun—epitomizes this implacable war of attrition. Does it epitomize anything else: the particular stupidity or inhumanity of the British army, or the officer class, or English society? Mistakes were certainly made, some of them stupid or wishful, which destroyed thousands of lives. The terrible losses on 1 July 1916—the worst the British have ever suffered in a single day—were aggravated by a series of human errors, stemming from the attempt to do too much too quickly. The British were still mostly amateurs—clerks, students, teachers, workers, farmers. They had not had time—in many cases they had not survived long enough—to learn the deadly specialized skills of a war of machines. There was some resistance to free discussion and new thinking at the highest level, for which Haig, who commanded from December 1914 to the end of the war, bore much responsibility. He had, judges a recent biographer, "an excitable temperament (which a carefully controlled exterior merely masked) combined with an intellect that offered him a fairly limited penetration into the fog of war," and this repeatedly led him to over-optimism, grandiose expectations and a refusal to listen to unwelcome views.[99] But similar criticisms were made of the German high command.[100] It is telling that although other generals and politicians (especially Lloyd George, who detested him) were painfully aware of Haig's shortcomings, there seemed no one better to replace him. "Haig . . . just squanders the lives of these boys," said Lloyd George.[101] He even tried repeatedly to put him under French direction.

Some senior British officers were indeed ill equipped to cope with war on an industrial scale. Yet the "lions led by donkeys" image (a phrase never used at the time but popularized in a 1960s book[102]) is at best a half-truth. They were not all heartless old men miles behind the lines: by 1918, the average age of a British major-general was forty-seven, and one brigade commander was twenty-five; and 232 generals were killed or wounded in action.[103] The traditional officer corps (public-school sportsmen, etc.) produced some effective commanders, such as Sir Horace Smith-Dorrien, who saved the BEF in the first battles of 1914; the 10th Earl of Cavan, one of the best Corps commanders on the Western Front, who went on to win a great victory against the Austrians in Italy; and Sir Ivor Maxse, prewar commander of the Brigade of Guards, recognized as the best trainer of troops and "one of the finest generals in the war."[104] New men, such as the able Australian General John Monash, a civil engineer before the war, could be at least as prodigal with soldiers' lives as the blimps; and by 1918 he had pushed the Australian Corps past breaking point, aggravated by his high degree of isolation from his men, which led to a refusal to go into action unique among the British Empire forces.[105]

Overall the British coped as well as the better-trained French and German high commands, despite the former's broader recruitment and the latter's greater intellectualism.[106] British military orthodoxy (stressing character, boldness, patriotism and the offensive spirit) was little different from that of other armies, even if the British used sporting metaphors much more: "playing the game," being "in at the Final," sometimes beginning attacks by "kicking off"—booting footballs into no-man's-land, which the Germans, once they had realized this was not a secret weapon, condemned as shockingly unmilitary. The British played more sport too: the French "could not understand the reason why the English spent so much of their life on football . . . instead of practising warfare."[107] The British did not have a system for learning and applying lessons systematically, as the Germans did; but sometimes the lessons the Germans applied were wrong. So finally "British pragmatism trumped German rationalism."[108] Every army and society, grappling with an unprecedented situation, sacrificed hundreds of thousands of lives: the French army, for example, lost more men in one day (22 August 1914) than the British did on the notorious first day of the Somme.[109] Technological limitations meant that "generals were like men without eyes, without ears, without voices."[110] The fundamental cause of the carnage, however, was not military or social, but political and ideological: few in England, or any other country, were willing to surrender or even accept semi-defeat. The loss of life increased the determination to win, to justify the sacrifice. Only when the whole fabric of society began to unravel in some countries did resolve evaporate.

The Allies agreed to try again in 1917. In March the French army launched a huge, scientifically planned and, it hoped, decisive offensive in Champagne. It began more successfully than the first day of the Somme, but over the next few days the French suffered 130,000 casualties. A large part of the army mutinied. Consequently, the French postponed major offensive operations: as its new commander, General Pétain, put it, they would wait for the Americans and the tanks. At the same time, a revolution in Russia overthrew the tsar, though the new provisional republic tried to continue the fight. The British were under pressure to attack the Germans somewhere, to take pressure off the French and the faltering Russians and Italians, and produce some dramatic effect. In July 1917 they began another campaign, which was to become as notorious as the Somme: the third battle of Ypres—"Passchendaele." This began successfully by the standards of the Western Front by seizing some ground, and the British showed that they had vastly improved their military skills. German intelligence reported the British troops confident of victory. Their advances convinced Haig that "the critical moment of the war" had arrived, with the German army weakening and a successful peace in sight. "If we can keep up our effort, final victory may be won by December." But unseasonable rain in August slowed progress, and a deluge in October turned the battlefield into an ocean of mud. One young officer recalled: "I felt myself sinking, and struggle as I might I was sucked down . . . The leg of a corpse was sticking out of the side, and frantically I grabbed it; it wrenched off . . ."[111] He managed to wriggle out, but many were not so lucky:

From the darkness on all sides came . . . long, sobbing moans of agony, and despairing shrieks. It was too horribly obvious that dozens of men with serious wounds must have crawled for safety into new shell-holes, and now the water was rising round them and, powerless to move, they were slowly drowning ... And we could do nothing to help them.[112]

Haig insisted on continuing attacks in October and November in impossible conditions, incurring thousands of British, Canadian and Australian casualties in vain. During the whole Third Ypres campaign, the British lost about 275,000 men and the Germans about 200,000.[113] Meanwhile, the Bolsheviks had seized power in Russia and rapidly dropped out of the war.

It is widely believed that the Somme and Passchendaele (both bloodier than the Second World War battle of Stalingrad) split and crippled English and British society, perhaps permanently. In the short term they did little to shake the military or civilian leadership. The army emerged from the Somme campaign with astonishingly good morale, convinced, as one letter put it, that "they can beat the Bosche when and where they like." But the army was decimated and shaken by the futile horrors of the last weeks of Passchendaele, which made it dangerously vulnerable, in both numbers and morale, to the great German offensives launched in 1918. Yet, as the Germans concluded from interrogating British prisoners, although "war-weariness and a lack of confidence are voiced quite openly," they were "still ready to hold out ... The Englishman considers a German victory impossible."[114]

The war was testing every army and society to breaking point. In all, 1 in 4 of British infantry would be wounded; 1 in 8 killed.[115] Yet human beings—soldiers and civilians—endured. The more integrated and politically developed countries, Britain, France and Germany, were more resilient than Russia, Austria-Hungary and Italy. The Russian army and state fell apart during 1916–17; the Austrians had mass surrenders and desertions; the Italian army collapsed at the battle of Caporetto in October 1917, losing 700,000 men, most of whom surrendered or went home. Part of the French army, as we have seen, had mutinied in 1917. Yet the German army too was showing signs of disintegration—10 percent of men being transferred from the Eastern to the Western Front late in 1917 deserted on the way.[116] Trench warfare, though less deadly than war in the open, was psychologically more stressful because of the feeling of helplessness it created (gas, for example, was terrifying but rarely fatal). It caused many kinds of breakdown, especially in exhausted men (highly religious teetotallers were thought most fragile). As a pioneer American psychiatrist observed of British combatants in 1917, "Neurosis provides a means of escape so convenient that the real source of wonder is that ... so many men should find a satisfactory adjustment without it." Only about 6 percent of British troops became psychiatric casualties, compared with 28 percent of Americans.[117]

Men were not constantly in the trenches. They typically spent about fifteen months on the Western Front, with about one-third of that time made up of short periods in the line; they might be in action four or five times. Siegfried Sassoon—"Mad Jack," winner of the Military Cross, warrior, poet and protestor—spent less than a month at the Front.[118] All soldiers discovered ways of relieving stress—superstitions, trench folklore, religion, poetry, diaries and letters, sport, drink, sex (there was a high rate of venereal disease among troops in France), and black humour (songs, jokes, cartoons and cheerfully satirical trench newspapers such as *The Wipers Times*). This was something of an English speciality, a humour of comical stoicism:

> If the Hun lets off some gas—
> Never mind.
> If the Hun attacks in mass—
> Never mind.
> If your dug-out's blown to bits,
> Or the C.O.s throwing fits,
> Or a crump your rum-jar hits—
> Never mind.[119]

Trench warfare was constant drudgery and discomfort punctuated by moments of extreme stress. As one officer put it, it also included "relaxation and jollity and mere boredom."[120] A subaltern of the Warwickshires noted in his diary in April 1917:

> We routed the company out and played football near the cemetery before lunch and in the afternoon a crowd of us turned out with revolvers and potted at bottles. Of course we had money on it and I was glad to find my hand was still steady enough to rake in a few francs.[121]

Quite a number enjoyed front-line service, or said they did, both for the excitement and for the chance to prove themselves as men. A young soldier at the Somme wrote that he could "look the rest of the lads in the face and claim to be one of them."[122] Sassoon, author of ferociously anti-war poetry, wrote to a friend that "I chased 40 Bosches out of a trench . . . all by myself. Wasn't that a joyous moment for me? They ran like hell and I chucked bombs and made hunting noises."[123]

The British army became remarkably cohesive and increasingly efficient. This is not because its training, disciplinary or morale-building methods were enlightened or effective. Notoriously, it executed far more of its own men (nearly 400) than the German army (about fifty), though British harshness was about the same as the French, and considerably less than

the Italian, Austrian or Russian. Of those shot, 75 percent were for desertion, though desertion was extremely low—less than 0.5 percent, about
the same as in the less punitive German army.[124] Keeping soldiers busy
when out of the front line (including with parades and spit-and-polish)
and pressing for constant "aggressiveness" in the trenches may have been
less sensible than giving soldiers more rest and better training—though the
same could be said of the Germans. On the other hand, the solicitude of
junior officers for their men's welfare (backed up by chaplains and the
YMCA), the loyalty inspired by locally recruited battalions, and the strong
motivation (including religious) of a largely volunteer army proved a resilient
mix. Here, arguably, the British army was superior to the German. Reasonable
food, regular leave, a degree of rest and letting off steam by "grousing" were
essential to soldiers' morale, which was more stable than in the German
army.[125] The proportion of prisoners was low, indicating willingness to fight,
as shown in Table 5.

Table 5: Proportion of prisoners within total losses[126]

|         | Total losses, millions | Prisoners, millions | Percentage |
|---------|------------------------|---------------------|------------|
| Russia  | 6.8                    | 3.5                 | 52%        |
| Austria | 6.9                    | 2.2                 | 32%        |
| Italy   | 2.0                    | 0.53                | 26%        |
| France  | 3.8                    | 0.45                | 11.6%      |
| Germany | 6.9                    | 0.62                | 9%         |
| Britain | 2.6                    | 0.17                | 6.6%       |

The explanations for British soldiers' ability and will to endure are
straightforward: they accepted the rightness of their cause, they blamed
(at times loathed) the Germans; they broadly trusted their own institutions; they were of high average physical and mental quality; they were
under less extreme conditions of privation than other armies; and they
were sustained by comradeship, esprit de corps and good regimental officers. Perhaps above all, as every army showed, support and encouragement from home, and a feeling that home was being protected, were
fundamental. Wrote one soldier to his girlfriend in February 1918: "it's
just the thought of you all over there—you who love me & trust me to do
*my* share in the job that is necessary for your safety and freedom . . . that
keeps me going & enables me to 'stick it.'"[127] In this new kind of mass
industrialized warfare, paradoxically, morale and commitment were all
the more important, as little groups of soldiers now acted independently
amid the lunar landscape of the trenches, unlike in the great set-piece

battles of the past when troops marched in formation under the eyes of their commanders.

## KEEPING THE HOME FIRES BURNING

*Is there any man, woman or child who does not think of the men in the trenches? Most people are so impregnated by the war, that they live with it, they sleep with it and eat with it.*

Civilian diary entry, March 1918[128]

Keep the home fires burning
While your hearts are yearning
Though the lads are far away they dream of Home.

Song by Lena Gilbert Ford, 1914
(killed in an air raid, 1918)

A widely accepted cliché is of a civilian population unable or unwilling to face the reality of modern war, and thus of an alienation of civilians from soldiers unable to communicate their dreadful experiences. This stereotype owes something to the anti-civilian venom of Siegfried Sassoon's writings; but in reality contemporary civilian accounts demonstrate a fairly high degree of knowledge about conditions in the trenches. Home leave and frequent letters—in 1916 some 11 million letters and 875,000 parcels were being sent to the troops every month—maintained close contact, and civilians were painfully aware of the dangers and sacrifices of the soldiers.[129] A film, *The Battle of the Somme* (1916), which gave a fairly realistic view of the trenches, was seen by 20 million people in six weeks. One of them was Lloyd George's secretary, Frances Stevenson, whose brother had been killed. She wrote in her diary: "I have often tried to imagine myself what he went through, but now I *know*, and I shall never forget."[130]

In December 1916 the German government declared its willingness to negotiate, but this was dismissed, rightly, as a propaganda ploy. Berlin, still confident of victory, had no intention of giving up conquered territories. But no British government would permit it to keep them, especially Belgium and northern France. However, some prominent intellectuals, including Bertrand Russell, argued that a negotiated settlement was possible. They had sympathizers in the United States, including President Woodrow Wilson, who in January 1917 called for "peace without victory . . . a peace between equals." They found in Siegfried Sassoon, a decorated serving officer, an ideal mouthpiece in a public protest in July 1917 against the war being "deliberately prolonged [as] a war of aggression and conquest."[131]

No significant anti-war movement ever emerged, however, despite real hardships. An important reason was popular anger against the Germans, which began in 1914 and reached a peak in May 1915, after the torpedoing of the liner *Lusitania*, in which 1,200 civilians, including children, were drowned. This gave rise to the biggest anti-ethnic rioting in twentieth-century England, with attacks on German-owned shops. Feeling was further inflamed by the execution in October 1915 of Edith Cavell, a British nurse living in Belgium who had helped Allied troops to escape. Attacks on the Asquith government grew shriller, accusing it of not prosecuting the war with sufficient vigour. In December 1916 Asquith was replaced by Lloyd George, leading a coalition government of Tories, Liberals and Labour, but excluding Asquith and other former ministers. This proved to be the beginning of a new political era: the divided Liberal Party began a permanent decline, after having been the predominant force in British politics since the 1830s.

Lloyd George, the first leading politician since Thomas Cromwell of plebeian origins, was a life-long professional politician in a modern mould, not a member of the gentry, or a wealthy businessman, or an intellectual. He had risen from Welsh provincial roots by intelligence, hard work, ruthlessness and ambition. He came from the world of Nonconformist Liberalism, which gave his politics its democratic bite and its echoes of the chapel, without his being too heavily burdened by the proverbial Nonconformist conscience. Unlike other great war leaders—the Pitts and Churchill—he did not have to dominate a crisis, but ran a collective effort, at which he proved adept, and he was good at maintaining Home Front morale. However, his reputation for trickiness weakened him, especially with regard to the army leadership. His wish to spare soldiers' lives was sincere, but he did not know how to do it and at times made things worse.

The most consistent domestic resentments were of "profiteers" and "shirkers." These were central issues of wartime grass-roots politics. The former included bosses, shopkeepers, farmers and civilian workers on high wages. The latter could include all those who were not in uniform or otherwise seen as not "doing their bit." Similar phenomena emerged in all the belligerent countries, often with greater bitterness than in England. The basic causes were everywhere similar: tension between those actually risking their lives and their families, and the rest (including more or less blatant "shirkers"); wartime price rises and shortages, especially of food, often blamed on profiteers; working conditions and wages; and government regulations and controls, those on beer-drinking being particularly resented.

Strikes were a worry and a cause of class tensions. Many thought it akin to treason that workers should strike over pay and conditions while soldiers were risking their lives. In France and Germany, key factory workers were put under military discipline. Workers often justified strikes on the grounds of "fair play" and exploitation by "profiteers." Wages, although rising in cash terms, were not keeping up with inflation, and workers in war industries were often working long hours in dangerous conditions. Consequently strikes were frequent, especially in the Welsh coalfields and for a time on Clydeside. Britain, indeed, had far more strikes than Germany. But Germany was effectively under martial law, and strikers could be sent to the front or court-martialled. At times of military emergency, as in the spring of 1918, strikes in Britain completely stopped. Strikes were many, but short, and were rarely if ever political, let alone revolutionary. There were no anti-war strikes—indeed, the seamen's union refused to carry delegates to a Stockholm peace conference in 1917. Productivity was higher than in Germany, and "Red Clydeside" was the best of the lot. Even the most suspicious of the intelligence services agreed that workers were loyal.[132]

The British government could shield its people from the worst effects of war. This was partly because it was a rich country, able to buy on world markets, and because Britannia ruled the waves, enabling food to be imported despite the vastly exaggerated menace of U-boats. Moreover, the liberal British state proved reasonably adept at creating a centralized war economy. The size of the civil service doubled; twelve new ministries were created, of which five remained after the war; and public spending rose from £184m in 1913 to £2.7bn in 1918. By 1918, 85 percent of all British food supplies were administered by the state. Uniquely among the European belligerents, bread was never rationed. Shortages, though trying, were nothing like those in Germany, Austria or Russia. In Germany, for example, from July 1916 onwards the normal ration (black bread, meatless sausage, potatoes and turnips) was 60 percent below subsistence, sapping support for the government and the war, and culminating in a collapse of public health and mass death.[133] There were no food riots in Britain. Indeed, the diets and health of poor children and women markedly improved, due to full employment, the opening up of new occupations to women, and measures such as the Maternity and Child Welfare Act (August 1918), which gave local authorities broad powers to "make such arrangements as they may see fit" for improving the health of expectant and nursing mothers and young children under the auspices of special committees including at least two women.

The number of women in jobs increased by nearly a quarter; by the end of the war 947,000 were working in the munitions industry alone. Some thought this was creating "a new type of girl." But two-thirds had left their jobs by 1920, and by 1921 fewer women were working than in 1911. There was some increase in juvenile crime (other types of crime fell), probably due to absence of fathers in the army. There was a jump in illegitimacy from 4.3 to 6.3 percent of births—what one commentator called "war nymphomania."[134]

Rent control, introduced in 1915, was one of the most enduring legacies of the war and perhaps the most significant piece of social and economic legislation in the first half of the twentieth century. By making private letting less profitable and so reducing the supply of rented accommodation, it had the unintended long-term consequence of turning the English middle classes from renters to homeowners—a change of enormous long-term social and economic importance.[135] Also long lasting in their effects were limits on alcohol: the strength of drinks was reduced, prices were increased, and opening hours were limited, which cut consumption by half[136]—fully reversed only in the 1990s.

Those feeling the economic pinch were the middle classes: they had more wage earners in the army and disproportionate casualties, and their cost of living was rising fast at home—even if some middle-class women found work financially and personally rewarding. By 1917 discontent was being expressed through a number of eccentric populist movements such as the National Party and the "Vigilante" group, some of them winning substantial votes at by-elections. They attacked the government for feebleness at best, and at worst accused traitors, aliens, Jews, profiteers and socialists of undermining the war effort. Among the biggest long-term losers, however, were the traditional landowning class, with rents held down by law and costs and taxes spiralling; and if both fathers and sons were killed, repeated 40 percent death duties amounted almost to confiscation. There were vast sales of land from 1917, estimated at a quarter of England. This was a change in individual land ownership not seen since the Norman Conquest; and one who sold up was Sir Hereward Wake.[137]

The war brought historic political changes too. An all-party Speaker's Conference in 1916 decided that those serving the country must be given the vote. This was effected by the Representation of the People Act (1918), enfranchising 12.9 million men over twenty-one (mostly non-householders) and 8.4 million women over thirty. Politicians were glad to have a face-saving way of resolving the issue of votes for women, complicated before the war by the Suffragette campaign. Thus, Britain came close to full democracy by consensus and due to circumstance.[138] In 1918 a Sex Disqualification Removal Act opened jury service, the magistracy and the legal profession to women. The Speaker's Conference also recommended creating multi-member constituencies in the cities, using the Single Transferable Vote; and for other constituencies it recommended the Alternative Vote. The House of Lords wanted to go further, with Proportional Representation throughout. In the absence of agreement, the "first past the post" system remained almost by default, and by chance spared Britain some of the turbulence soon to afflict countries with multi-party systems. The Labour Party distanced itself from the divided Liberal Party and called on discontented Liberals to join them—according to the party's leader, Arthur Henderson, Labour had been "too short of brains." Thousands of activists from the Union of Democratic Control and the Council of Civil Liberties (both embodying suspicion of the war in the Nonconformist-conscience tradition) gravitated to Labour, despite the suspicion some old-style patriotic trade unionists felt for middle-class "cranks" and "psalm-singing hypocrites."[139] In January 1918 the Labour Party adopted a new constitution, whose Clause 4 (carefully drafted by the Fabian Sidney Webb) pledged to secure for "the producers by hand or by brain [i.e., white-collar workers] the full fruits of their industry . . . upon the basis of the common ownership of the means of production"—a commitment abolished, amid much furore, in Tony Blair's "Clause 4 moment" in 1994.

Domestic stresses of all kinds—strikes, food shortages, air raids, xenophobia—reached their nadir in late 1917 and early 1918, with the Bolshevik Revolution, the collapse of the Italian front, the Passchendaele disasters, the height of the German U-boat campaign causing serious food shortages at Christmas 1917, aerial bombing (up to 300,000 Londoners were sleeping in the Tube), and the beginning of new German offensives in March 1918. The royal family even changed its name from Saxe-Coburg to Windsor. Elsewhere things were worse. In France, there were strikes and mutinies. Russia was descending into an abyss of defeat and civil war. Austria was falling apart. Germany was freezing and starving, and wounded soldiers begging in the streets were even subject to violence. American entry into the war in April 1917 gave hope to the Allies, but it was unclear that help would come in time.

Could the English and British people have endured suffering on the level of their Continental allies and enemies? Why doubt it? They were far less divided in terms of class, politics and ethnicity than Russia, Austria or Germany, and less in terms of politics than France. But their postwar politics and social relations would have born deeper scars than they did. And had they lost the war, that would have "ripped the nation apart." Victory mattered, as the history of Germany shows so dramatically, "and in the end, nothing else mattered so much."[140]

## THE PRICE OF VICTORY

*Many of us are now tired. To those I would say that victory will belong to the side that holds out the longest . . . there is no course open to us but to fight it out. Every position must be held to the last man: there must be no retirement. With our backs to the wall and believing in the justice of our cause each one of us must fight to the end.*

Field-Marshal Haig, "Order of the Day,"
11 April 1918

*No Englishman would ever admit it [but] there have been times in the war when the paralysing thought has flashed through our minds that we were going to get—well, that we were not going to win!*

Woman's diary, October 1918[141]

The war had spread a very long way from Sarajevo. It ignited all the Balkans and brought in Turkey, Italy, Japan (which seized German outposts in China) and the United States. Russia, following an ancient politico-religious ambition, coveted Constantinople (which Britain and France now agreed to), and fought the Turks in the Caucasus, the context for the first twentieth-century genocide, that of the Christian Armenians. A British and Indian army marched from Basra towards Baghdad in 1915, but part of it was forced to surrender after a siege at Kut the following year, and many soldiers died in captivity. An Arab revolt in 1916 was given support, involving a young Oxford archaeologist, T. E. Lawrence, the only romantic hero of the war. British, Indian and ANZAC forces eventually took Jerusalem, Damascus and Baghdad in 1917, where they were greeted as liberators from Turkish rule. The British government signed a secret agreement with the French dividing most of the Turkish empire into "spheres of influence" between them. Also, the Balfour Declaration in November 1917 committed Britain to a "National Home for the Jewish people in Palestine," though without prejudicing "the civil and religious rights of existing non-Jewish communities"—who, it was assumed, would be grateful for economic development.[142] This had seemed a clever idea, pleasing Jewish opinion thought to be influential in Russia and America. Britain thus blundered insouciantly into what would turn out to be an intractable and damaging problem with long-term ramifications unimaginable at the time.

The war at sea was crucial, perhaps decisive. The Germans, at the beginning of the war, had cruisers which attacked British shipping, and most, after doing some damage, were caught and sunk. Two-thirds of Germany's small merchant fleet was seized or interned itself in neutral ports. At least three-quarters of the world's ocean-going merchant shipping belonged to Britain, which also dominated credit, insurance and communications, and so it had extensive control over world trade.[143] It was clear from the start that Britain would use its commercial and naval power as a weapon: the Germans had respected Dutch neutrality to have a "windpipe" for imports and exports. The Royal Navy did not have a free hand to throttle enemy commerce. In optimistic prewar days, the Declaration of London (1910) allowed seizure only of military goods ("absolute contraband"), and excluded food, fertilizers, cotton, etc. The development of mines and submarines made traditional blockade (posting ships at the entrance of enemy ports) impossible; so the navy imposed a "distant blockade," closing the exits from the North Sea. This was arguably illegal. But it began to affect German food supplies as early as the winter of 1914.[144]

Control of the North Sea depended ultimately on the two battle fleets. The German High Seas Fleet had at its core sixteen dreadnought battleships and five faster, more lightly armoured battlecruisers. The British Grand Fleet, at Scapa Flow and Rosyth, had twenty-eight dreadnoughts and nine battlecruisers. The Germans had successes, including the hit-and-run bombardments of Scarborough and Hartlepool. But German commanders never imagined they could defeat the Grand Fleet. Their hope was to ambush smaller forces and so wear away British superiority, which on one occasion they nearly did. The British hoped to catch the whole German fleet at sea and bring it to battle, and so wireless interception and codebreaking became an important activity of the Admiralty in tracking German movements. On 31 May 1916, in mid-afternoon, the German fleet thought they had caught the British battlecruiser squadron about seventy-five miles off the Danish coast, but found the whole British fleet, under Admiral Sir John Jellicoe, bearing down on them. The ensuing battle of Jutland, involving some 250 ships, was the biggest concentrated naval battle in history, and the only great clash of the dreadnought age, the epitome of mechanized war in which massive armoured battleships, with screens of cruisers and destroyers, fired long-range salvos of huge shells capable of destroying ships and their crews literally in a flash. The main action lasted little more than two hours. The outcome was disquieting for the Royal Navy and disappointing for those expecting a new Trafalgar. Partly due to poor communications between Jellicoe and the Admiralty, the German fleet escaped as darkness fell, having inflicted heavier casualties than it received (some 6,000 to 2,500): it sank three battlecruisers (which blew up, killing some 3,000 men) and eleven smaller ships, and lost one battleship, a battlecruiser and eight smaller ships. This has often been diagnosed as another symptom of pervasive British decline even where it seemed strongest, with a complacent, hidebound Admiralty overtaken by a modern rival. But the differences were small. German ships were more heavily built, not being designed for long voyages. British gunnery was better and inflicted much damage, but their shells were less penetrative and so sank fewer German ships. Worst of all, British battlecruisers proved vulnerable to catastrophic explosions when plunging shells smashed though their thin armour, exploding ammunition brought up for the heavy guns, which then ignited the ships' magazines.[145] But strategically it was a British victory: the battered German fleet fled back to port, and never risked action again. An American newspaper put it well: the German fleet had assaulted its gaoler, but was still in gaol.

Thanks to control of the seas, Britain and France (whose economies became closely integrated) were able to draw on global resources—at a cost. Between August 1914 and October 1916, their trade with the United States quadrupled, and 40 percent of British government war purchases were made there.[146] Britain was the biggest spender of all the belligerents. It subsidized its allies and paid 90 percent of the empire's costs. It was also the biggest lender, advancing £1.6bn to its allies, principally Russia and France, much of which was never repaid. It raised domestic funds by a mixture of taxation and selling war bonds to the public. To raise foreign exchange, about a quarter of its huge foreign investments were liquidated and over £800m was borrowed from the U.S. government. In all it spent over £9bn—more than the total for the previous forty years of public spending. It increased its national debt by £6.6bn, ten times the prewar total.[147]

Britain's blockade of Germany at first proved indecisive. Neutral countries, particularly the United States, demanded freedom of navigation and trade, and the Foreign Office was extremely sensitive to their demands. Moreover, British firms were themselves trading on an increasing scale with Holland, Switzerland and Scandinavia, which in effect were German proxies: one Zeppelin shot down over England proved to have a fabric covering made in Lancashire. It was not clear that Britain could destroy German commerce without wrecking its own financial institutions and devastating its economy, which was paying the costs of the war. In 1915 German exports, via the neutrals, recovered to 60 percent of their peacetime figure.[148] Only as the war lengthened and intensified was the blockade of Germany tightened. An Order in Council of 7 July 1916 allowed European neutrals only to import and export on their own behalf, to prevent them acting as German intermediaries. Britain used its financial strength to buy up neutral goods to deprive Germany. More and more were declared "contraband," liable to seizure by the navy, including cotton, wool, fertilizers (devastating for agriculture), and animal feed vital both for meat production and for transport horses, whose requisition by the army and subsequent destruction in battle caused huge economic disruption. Wool prices in Germany rose by 1,700 percent. Meat consumption fell on average from 1,050 grams per week to 135 grams. The milk supply was halved. In 1916 even potatoes ran short. Oil, petrol and domestic fuel became chronically scarce. Germany's capture of Romanian oilfields in 1916 was sabotaged by a buccaneering Tory MP, Colonel J. Norton-Griffiths, who wrecked the installations. Germany began to suffer universal shortages—aggravated by the devastation of eastern Europe—and introduced thousands of *ersatz* (substitute) products, including acorns, nettles, powdered hay, flavoured salt and even insects.[149] A vast black market appeared. The whole economy and the structures of society came under increasing pressure. Rickets, dysentery, scurvy and hunger oedema appeared. The death rate rose: that of women by 51 percent, while in England it was falling. The German economy shrank by 30 percent, whereas the British grew throughout the war. The blockade required a huge effort by the Royal Navy, which lost over 43,000 men. It was a step towards "total war," resulting in perhaps 500,000 German deaths.[150] But the blockade depended not only on the Royal Navy's warships: it also reflected Britain's control of the world's telegraph communications, commercial networks, merchant shipping and insurance.[151]

The Germans retaliated with the submarine: "England wants to starve us into submission," said Tirpitz, "we can play the same game."[152] Its naval staff had high hopes of submarine warfare and made glowing promises. But, to work, it had to be "unrestricted"—torpedoing without warning any ship in a declared "prohibited region" round the British Isles. This was regarded by the British, and most others, as a war crime. In 1914, an admiral had declared that "no nation would permit it, and the officer who did it would be shot."[153] But when the *Lusitania* was sunk in May 1915, the officer who did it became a hero. American anger caused the Germans to suspend such attacks, but in January 1917, accepting the likelihood of war with America, they again declared unrestricted submarine warfare, believing that if they could sink 600,000 tons of shipping per month it would starve Britain into surrender and so win the war by November 1917. The Admiralty and the British government were very alarmed early in 1917 by large-scale sinkings (885,000 tons in May), and the decision of neutrals, except the Norwegians, to stay in port. The submarine threat passed into national folklore. Churchill described it as "among the most heart-shaking episodes of history . . . a turning point in the history of nations."[154] Seizing German submarine bases in Belgium was one motive for the 1917 Passchendaele bloodbath. In all, 6.7 million tons of British shipping were sunk—roughly equivalent to 1,000 medium-sized ships. But Germany's submarine strategy was a pipe dream, based on absurdly optimistic assumptions about British shipping, finance, politics and the economy. All coped. Home cereal production shot up. The poorest people in Britain actually ate better during the war. Even racehorses continued to eat, rather than be eaten. After convoys were introduced in 1917, finally involving 4,000 Royal Navy vessels and 140,000 sailors, sinkings amounted to only 393 of the 95,000 ship-crossings of the Atlantic. The American army was convoyed across without loss—largely in confiscated German liners. At any one time, there were only about twenty German submarines in the Western Approaches. German shipyards were unable to increase the numbers significantly. Half the U-boat fleet was sunk—178 out of 345.[155] So control of the sea proved literally vital: Germany tried to starve Britain, and failed; Britain tried to starve Germany, and succeeded.

America declared war in April 1917. The last straw was a German proposal to Mexico that if the United States entered the war, Mexico should attack to recover Texas, Arizona and New Mexico—an offer intercepted by London and passed on to Washington. There followed a series of tentative peace initiatives during 1917, mainly originating in Germany for propaganda reasons. This encouraged some Allied citizens to believe that peace was on offer, and that their governments were refusing it for unavowed reasons. This suspicion was strengthened when the Bolshevik regime in Russia disclosed "secret treaties" by which Britain had agreed to Russian annexation of territory. Lloyd George and Woodrow Wilson responded with moderate—or "sanitized"—statements of peace aims, to influence both their own and enemy civilians. The reality was that the German government, now effectively a military regime, would not give up its conquests. Some of its military planners were thinking not only of this war, but of the next, with Britain the main enemy.[156]

Germany's last possible chance of victory came early in 1918. The war in the east ended when the Bolsheviks sought peace, and in the Treaty of Brest-Litovsk (March 1918) Germany gained all it had hoped for since 1914. Vast territories were detached from Russia, containing 90 percent of its coal mines, 50 percent of its industry, and 30 percent of its population, which became nominally independent but under German occupation. Food supplies were to be diverted to Germany and Austria. Troops could now be concentrated on the Western Front—including even a few unhappy Austrians. The aim was to win a decisive victory by defeating the British army before Germany's economy, or its allies, collapsed, and before American troops could swing the manpower balance. The German commander, Field Marshal von Hindenburg, concluded that "we have to defeat the Western Powers in order to secure the political and economic position in the world that we need." The Kaiser agreed: "Someone has to cop it—and that one's England."[157] Germany's battered army was to mount its last offensive, its soldiers' spirits raised by the thought that they were fighting to finish the war.

They aimed the main blow against the BEF, which they hoped still lacked the skill to improvise in the face of a huge surprise attack: "Our toughest and most stubborn, but at the same time our clumsiest opponent is the Englishman," wrote the German army's head of operational planning. The intention was to break through towards the Channel ports, winning a decisive victory: "The British must be knocked out of the war," declared General Ludendorff, Chief of the General Staff and effectively Germany's military ruler.[158] The chosen weak point was where the British and French armies met, and where the British Fifth Army had just taken over thirty miles of front from the French. This point, east of the River Somme, had been quiet; the trench system was weak, and the defenders were stretched thin. Moreover, the government was holding men back in England, for fear that Haig would waste them in useless attacks. So there was no way of stopping the German attack, codenamed "Michael," launched on 21 March with a barrage of 3 million shells. Led by storm troops armed with flame-throwers and machine guns, and cloaked by thick fog, fifty-nine German divisions fell on twenty-six British. In places, the British were outnumbered 8:1. Fifth Army was later criticized, and inquiries made about its morale and discipline; but in the circumstances it resisted as well as it could. The Germans took 13,000 prisoners—the largest number ever taken from a British army in a day—but advanced less than three miles, only halfway to their objectives.[159]

Gaps opened in the British line, and between the BEF and the French, with the danger that the Germans would achieve their aim of sweeping north to cut the BEF off from its supply ports. Communications broke down, and there was panic on the ground and at British headquarters. From 23 to 26 March the British army faced one of the greatest crises of the whole war: "we had to make a hasty retreat with all our worldly possessions," wrote a soldier on the twenty-third; "every road out of the village was crowded with rushing traffic—lorries, limbers . . . wagons, great caterpillar tractors with immense guns behind them, all were dashing along in an uninterrupted stream." Their retreat angered many French civilians and soldiers, who accused them of running away "like rabbits." However, the men streaming rearwards or wandering about lost were often support troops or non-combatants. According to the military police, combat troops on the road "were chiefly those who were genuinely lost and anxious to rejoin their units." Those surrendering had usually been surrounded by superior forces, including a lone general who manned a machine gun until overrun. If the morale of Fifth Army really had collapsed, the Germans might have won the war. But the soldiers, if critical of their leaders, were far from feeling beaten: as German intelligence reported from interrogating prisoners, "in the English army the opinion is widespread that under German leadership English soldiers could conquer the entire world."[160]

The Germans finally advanced up to forty miles on a front fifty miles wide. The Kaiser exulted that "the battle is won, the English have been utterly defeated." The German fleet was ordered to prepare to disrupt a possible British evacuation from Dunkirk.[161] The Belgian government considered withdrawing to Tunbridge Wells. Haig urgently needed French help, and it came, forty-seven divisions in all, although relations were cool with the pessimistic General Pétain, no admirer of the British (they had "run like the Italians at Caporetto"). The British government, to coordinate the Allied effort, supported the appointment of the French General Ferdinand Foch as "generalissimo," but relations between the two allies, and particularly between Haig and Pétain, remained chilly.

By 28 March the BEF with French help was stopping the German advance, slowed by exhaustion, resistance on the ground, unprecedented British air attacks, the loss of thousands of its horses, the devastated ground of the old Somme battlefield it had to struggle across, and, last but perhaps not least, the discovery by the hungry troops of vast British supply dumps. While they gorged on bully beef and rum, they also realized the hollowness of propaganda claims that submarines had made the British as hungry as they were. They had committed ninety divisions to the attack and lost 240,000 men (to 178,000 British and 77,000 French). But they had not won decisively. Above all they had not taken the vital rail-

N

NETHERLANDS

•Dover

Straits of Dover

•Bruges       •Antwerp

Dunkirk

Ghent•  *Lys*

Calais•

Ypres •Passchendaele

Cassel•  F L A N D E R S

■ **Brussels**

Boulogne•

•Lille  B E L G I U M

Étaples•  A R T O I S

Mons•

*Front line, 11 November*

Arras
27 Sept.

•Cambrai

Abbeville

Bapaume•  •Flesquières

27 Sept.

Amiens•  •Albert

29 Sept.

Villers-Bretonneux•  •Hamel  •Saint-Quentin

8 Aug.  *Somme*

P I C A R D Y

Montdidier

Noyon

Mezières•

*Chemin des Dames*

F  *Aisne*

Compiègne•

Beauvais•  *Oise*

Soissons•

•Reims  C H A M P A G N E

R

Chantilly•  Villers-
Cotterêts

A  18 July  26 Sept.

*Seine*  N  *Marne*  Châlons-
sur-Marne

**Paris**  C  *Petit Morin*

E  *Grand Morin*

*Seine*

| | Somme offensive ("Michael"), 21 March–5 April |
| | Lys offensive ("Georgette"), 21–29 April |
| | Aisne offensive ("Blucher-Yorck"), 27 May–4 June |
| | Matz offensive ("Gneisenau"), 9–12 June |
| | Champagne-Marne offensive ("Friedenssturm"), 15–17 July |

- - - "Hindenburg Line"
→ British counter-attacks
→ other allied counter-attacks

0       30 miles
0       50 km

19. The Western Front, 1918

way hub of Amiens, seven miles beyond their furthest advance. This would have completely disrupted the BEF's supply of munitions, food and reinforcements, possibly forcing a wholesale British evacuation. Senior Allied generals feared this might force them to consider offering peace. But German commanders failed to realize it and so spared the Allies the stark choices they were to face in 1940.[162] Half the French army had now joined in the battle. By early April, the German attack had stuck, under heavy British artillery and air attack.

The Germans then launched another major offensive against the BEF further north, in Flanders, with thirty-one divisions against thirteen. This also made early advances, with many British soldiers surrendering. Haig issued his "backs to the wall" order. Both Germans and British were suffering heavy casualties. The emergency seems to have increased determination among British troops and at home, where strikes completely stopped. Well-supplied British soldiers, galvanized by the sight of refugees and burning towns, held on in the face of the severe but temporary pressure.[163] The British 55th Division held Festubert and Givenchy in what has been called one of the most impressive defensive battles of the war.[164] The confidence of German soldiers, who knew this was the last throw of the dice, began to plummet. By the middle of April, both attackers and defenders were exhausted. The German army had lost huge numbers of men; its generals realized that they had not won and began to consider an armistice. So did some British. But the Germans' idea of an acceptable peace was far from that of the Allies, and their hope of a propaganda campaign to encourage a peace movement in Britain was unrealistic. On the contrary, Britain's effort intensified when in April a new Military Service Act extended conscription to all men between 17½ and 50.

The Germans shifted their attack to the French front, to force the French army to suspend its support of the BEF, still Germany's main target. At the Chemin des Dames, seventy miles north-east of Paris, a devastating surprise assault began on 27 May—just at a point where five exhausted British divisions had been sent to "rest" and were almost wiped out. Again the initial German onslaught was irresistible, and the French feared that Paris and Verdun might fall. The British started planning an evacuation of the BEF if the French were overwhelmed, and the embassy in Paris began to pack. Lord Milner, a member of the War Cabinet, warned Lloyd George of the danger of France and Italy being defeated, leaving "the German-Austro-Turko-Bulgar bloc" dominating most of the Eurasian land mass, with Britain the "exposed outpost" of a free world based on the empire and America.[165] But despite local successes the Germans were still not in sight of victory, and their efforts became increasingly desperate. The battle-hardened French hung on. American troops were at last beginning to enter the fight. The success of a surprise French counter-offensive on 18 July on the Marne, also involving British, American and Italian troops, showed that the German army had shot its bolt. As one German general wrote, this was "the sharp turning point in the conduct of the war."[166]

Then, on 8 August, the Germans were completely surprised by a well-planned offensive east of Amiens by 552 British tanks leading Canadian, Australian, British and French infantry. Massed tanks had a stunning impact, and the attack pushed forward eight miles, one of the longest one-day advances of the whole war. Thousands of Germans surrendered. Ludendorff later called it "the black day of the German army . . . [It] put the decline of [our] fighting power beyond all doubt [and] opened the eyes of the staff on both sides."[167]

The biggest and most decisive campaign of the war was fought in the autumn of 1918. For the first time the British proved markedly superior in skill, tactics, leadership, ideas, organization and equipment, including tanks, intelligence-gathering, air support and artillery. A Canadian soldier wrote home: "I guess we can boast of the best morale the world has ever known, especially among the British and their Colonials."[168] The Germans were dug into the Hindenburg Line, six layers deep. The main defence ran along the deep Saint-Quentin Canal, impassable to tanks and fortified with masses of barbed wire and machine-gun emplacements. General Rawlinson's Fourth Army assaulted it at the end of September. The 46th (North Midland) Division attacked where the Germans assumed it was impossible: across the canal itself. On 29 September they stormed across equipped with life-jackets and rafts from Channel ferries, at a cost of only 150 casualties.[169] From then on, under continual British attack which gave them no chance to reorganize, the Germans fell back along the whole front. Ludendorff and several other generals collapsed under the strain. Eventually the Central Powers as a whole began to disintegrate. This final struggle was bloody and exhausting. Warfare in the open cost 260,000 British casualties at the highest daily rate of the whole war—nearly two-thirds of soldiers in the front line in August had become casualties by November.[170] Among them was Wilfred Owen, who, having won the Military Cross capturing a German machine-gun nest, was killed leading his men across the Sambre–Oise canal. But the result was decisive. The French, Americans and Belgians combined took 193,000 prisoners during the culminating four months of combat; the British and imperial forces, less than half their number, took 200,000.[171] There were mass surrenders and desertions by German troops, often led by their officers, who realized that there was no longer any hope of victory.

Yet few on the Allied side realized the end was imminent. The British expected to be fighting until 1920. But the German army, state and society were collapsing. On 5 October, hoping to divide their enemies, the German government asked President Woodrow Wilson for an armistice based on his "Fourteen Points" announced in January 1918, which specified withdrawal from occupied territory and national self-determination, but included no punishment for Germany. French and British politicians and generals were ready to agree. They baulked at the prospect of invading and governing Germany, whose army was still on French and Belgian soil. They also feared that if the war continued American power would increase and their own diminish, weakening their ability to influence the peace terms.[172] On 11 November at eleven o'clock, fighting stopped. The BEF—now 1,859,000 men, half of them teenagers—halted just north of Mons, where it had begun.

## HOW WE REMEMBER THEM

*They went and saved something and never came back. What it was they saved I cannot exactly tell, but I do know that I have never seen anything since 1918 that was worth their sacrifice.*
              J. B. Priestley, *The Lost Generation* (1930)[173]

The First World War is remembered in England as a uniquely poignant and traumatic tragedy, bearing many meanings. In no other European combatant country does it occupy this place in national culture, even though most suffered more severely. Some of the reasons are plain. England has never made another military effort on this scale; the only events that approach it are the Civil War and the Napoleonic Wars, which also left long memories. Western Front battles caused repeated and cumulatively unprecedented bloodbaths in appalling conditions. They involved the whole nation: unlike in earlier wars, the middle classes and respectable working classes served en masse, and many wrote about it. One household in three suffered a casualty; one in nine a death. England and Britain are unique among the European combatants in never having undergone a subsequent trauma—revolution, civil war, tyranny, defeat, foreign occupation—devastating enough to push 1914–18 into the background, or even efface it from popular consciousness. For England the First World War remains the most appalling event in three centuries.

The ways in which the war was publicly commemorated,[174] with the emphasis not on victory but on death, helped to fix a certain memory for later generations: the dignified Cenotaph, which Kipling called "the place of grieving" (seven miles of wreath-laying mourners came to its inauguration); the Tomb of the Unknown Warrior in Westminster Abbey (visited by a million people in its first week in 1920); the vast war cemeteries with their uniform headstones conferring "equal honour" (at first controversial, but soon visited by more than 100,000 people per year); and Armistice Day, with its funereal ceremony of remembrance led by the monarch. All emphasized collective mourning, sacrifice and irreparable loss, recalled during the two-minute silence:

> For those minutes, tell no lie:
> (Grieving—grieving!)
> Grave this is your victory;
> And the sting of death is grieving![175]

Although only a minority had suffered directly, the whole nation felt it should share their grief. Celebrations—for example, Victory Balls—were stopped as inappropriate. The contrast may be seen in France, which suffered double the losses, but where the war was one of national liberation, and so the Armistice has always been celebrated with a victory parade, and the Unknown Soldier rests under Napoleon's Triumphal Arch. The war has taken on other meanings in England, some of them very different from the predominant experience of those who actually lived through it. The subsequent creation of this common "memory" has become a historical subject in its own right.[176] Scholars have laboured to counteract myths and restore historical accuracy; but a few lines of Wilfred Owen outweigh a shelf of monographs.

First, this memory is marked by incomprehension: we have no narrative of the First World War as we have of the Second, which we idealize as a crusade against fascism. But we cannot conceive of any political, ideological or military aim which could redeem the horror of the trenches, a perfect symbol of the futility of war. This is very different, again, from France, where to describe the war as futile would cause bafflement.[177] Most English people who lived through the war saw it as a struggle against German "militarism," worthwhile because it would create a better world. What undermined this were not the events of 1914–18, but what happened in the 1930s, when the very idealism of the war turned on itself in bitter disillusion, as victory collapsed into economic disaster and renewed conflict.

This disillusion grew in several stages. The Versailles treaty failed to match idealistic hopes of reconciliation: the Independent Labour Party considered it "a capitalist, imperialist and militarist imposition [which] aggravates every evil which existed before 1914."[178] Later, powerful attacks were made on the military leadership, first by Winston Churchill, in his *World Crisis*,[179] which implicitly blamed British generals for failure on the Western Front—partly self-defence against criticism of his own Gallipoli disaster. More pointed criticism came from Lloyd George in his memoirs[180]—one index entry reads: "Military mind: regards thinking as a form of mutiny." Until then, the generals had been undisputed heroes: Haig's funeral in 1922 brought out crowds of mourners on the same scale as for Churchill himself, or for Princess Diana.[181] The German and Soviet governments peddled the view that all imperialist and capitalist states had been equally guilty of causing the war, and this was accepted by many as a necessary part of postwar reconciliation. Some went further. Arthur Ponsonby, a Germanophile Liberal MP, pacifist, member of the UDC and later Labour minister, published the influential *Falsehood in War-Time* (1928), marked by contentious interpretations and even fabrications.[182] He asserted that Britain and France had lied about the causes of the war, and that reports of German atrocities were myths or deliberate falsehoods. His aim was to show "the blatant and vulgar devices [used] to prevent poor ignorant people from realizing the true meaning of war," and he concluded that "none of the common herd . . . will be inclined to listen to the call of their country once they discover the polluted sources from whence that call proceeds."[183] Such assertions fed the "Appeasement" current, and fostered a cynicism that later dismissed reports of the Holocaust as propaganda. Only in 2001 did historical research decisively prove that accounts of German atrocities in 1914 had been based on fact.[184]

During the late 1920s peace, disarmament and security through the League of Nations seemed at last to have hopes of succeeding. The majority who had supported the Great War as a stern necessity, and the minority who had opposed it, had equal reason to emphasize its horrors, to advocate a world united in consigning war to "a dead past"—the words of George V when he opened the Imperial War Museum in 1920.[185] In the 1930s, as Europe was racked by economic disaster, with Nazism in power in Germany, there seemed even more urgent reasons to reject war. Both left- and right-wing newspapers published gruesome photographs of trench warfare to "make the blood of the most bigoted war-monger run cold."[186] This was the context of a succession of powerful artistic works, including plays, novels, memoirs, films and paintings, expressing the horrors of the war. R. C. Sherriff's play *Journey's End* (1928) showed large theatre and radio audiences the inhuman stresses of the trenches and, set in a dugout, created one of the stereotypes of the Western Front—though the author, who had served in the trenches, denied any propagandist intention. The memoirs of Robert Graves (1929) and Siegfried Sassoon

(1930), the German Erich Maria Remarque's novel *All Quiet on the Western Front* (1929), an international best-seller that became the first major "talkie" war film (1930), and the poetry of Edmund Blunden, Graves, Sassoon, Owen and others (edited in the late 1920s and early 1930s by Blunden[187]) appeared alongside an already vast and diverse popular literature of the war, both romanticized and realistic, including songs, adventure stories, love stories, spy thrillers (for example, those of John Buchan), plays, children's stories and films.

The war had inspired in every country floods of verse from romantic patriotism to black despair: some 2,225 poets were published in Britain alone. Some of the most powerful poetry came from established writers far removed from the trenches, including Thomas Hardy, W. B. Yeats and Kipling, and continued after the war in modernist works by Ezra Pound and T. S. Eliot. Even A. E. Housman's 1890s elegies took on a poignant retrospective meaning ("And there with the rest are the lads that will never be old"), and were set to music by George Butterworth (killed 1916). Verse was a natural medium for educated young English officers— *The Wipers Times* joked about the "insidious disease" of poetry: "Subalterns have been seen with a notebook in one hand, and bombs in the other absently walking near the wire in deep communion with the muse."[188] The Germans and French made a greater mark with novels, able to record more complex experiences, ideas and emotions; but poetry created simple memorable images which, more than novels or plays, have retained immediacy and power, not least because they used accessible traditional forms. The soldier-poets were not pacifists: they accepted the justification of the war—"the foul tornado, centred at Berlin," in Wilfred Owen's words.[189] But some wanted to thrust its horrors before civilians, impelled by agonizing survivors' guilt and sometimes guilt at killing. Sassoon, on the same day he described his "joyous" feelings in combat, wrote a poem about a dead German he had found in a trench—"No doubt he loathed the war and longed for peace / And cursed our souls because we'd killed his friends."[190] All this contributed to the "war to end war" resolve. It can be seen in Owen's sonnet to an artillery piece—a necessary evil to be renounced once victory was won:

> Reach at that Arrogance which needs thy harm
> And beat it down before its sins grow worse [ . . . ]
> But when thy spell be cast complete and whole,
> May God curse thee, and cut thee from our soul![191]

Some of these poems provided defining images for later generations. Similar image-makers were war artists, both modernists such as Richard Nevinson or Paul Nash and traditionalists such as John Singer Sargent and William Orpen. Their images too were often later reinterpreted as "anti-war" statements, even though the artists, and their first audiences, saw them rather as tributes to the sacrifices of British soldiers in a terrible but just war.[192] Wilfred Owen, the most famous of the war poets today, was only widely discovered in the 1960s—his work had been excluded in the 1930s from the *Oxford Book of Modern Verse* by its editor, the Irish poet W. B. Yeats, who considered it "unworthy of the poet's corner of a country newspaper."[193] The modern canon of war poetry was created from the 1960s onwards, selected to reflect modern beliefs and sensibilities. It became part of the school curriculum, as in no other country.[194] Those who served in the Second World War are by comparison ignored: their poetry unknown, their letters unread, their novels unstudied, their sufferings and struggles overshadowed. We cherish the memory of those we think died for nothing.

For all these reasons the Great War retrospectively changed its meaning. Unanswerably, it had not "ended war." Many came to see it as the fault of lying diplomats, blundering generals and ignorant civilians, compounded by a political and social elite that was callous, incompetent and exploitative—"hard-faced men who . . . have done very well out of the war," in John Maynard Keynes's famous phrase.[195] These messages, mixing indignation, mockery and pathos, fitted the anti-Establishment 1960s, whether for left (such as the socialist Joan Littlewood, director of the satirical musical *Oh What a Lovely War*) or right (the proto-Thatcherite Alan Clark, author of a military history, *The Donkeys*, one of Littlewood's sources), and including long-time pacifists such as Bertrand Russell and Benjamin Britten, whose *War Requiem* (first performed in 1962 by German, Russian and English singers) chose texts from First World War poets. The fiftieth anniversary BBC television series *The Great War* (1964) used archive footage and sound effects to bring the obscenity of trench warfare to a vast audience. But, significantly, the war also became the subject of mockery. *Oh What a Lovely War* (1963), filmed in 1969, made it a pantomime. The Oxford historian A. J. P. Taylor, in *The First World War: An Illustrated History* (1963), dedicated to Joan Littlewood, combined satire and scholarship. The 1989 television series *Blackadder Goes Forth* features endless attacks aimed to "move [Haig's] drinks cabinet six inches closer to Berlin." This use of black comedy seems to be uniquely British—it would be unthinkable in France, and probably meaningless elsewhere. In England, as a reviewer of *Oh What a Lovely War* commented, 1914-18 has become "a sitting target for anyone who wants to deliver a bludgeoning social criticism without giving offence."[196] The war still inspires emotion, fanned by the popularity of family history and by "a bizarre aspiration to misery."[197] It shows no sign of losing its potency, constantly reinterpreted in novels, plays and films ever more fanciful and sentimentalized, and ever more remote from lived reality. As the approach of the 2014 centenary demonstrated, even to discuss the question of whether the war might have been justified could arouse strong feelings.[198] The years 1914–18 now represent a timeless, mythical quintessence of "War," which helps us to juggle our own ambivalence about war and violence, because it can be heartily deplored without implying pacifism. But while lamenting their fate, must we reduce those who really did fight and suffer, mostly by choice and in the belief that they were doing right, to deluded victims or simpletons?

# CHAPTER 16

# The Twenty-Year Truce

*It will all be useless.*
Georges Clemenceau, French prime minister, 11 November 1918[1]

The armistice brought quiet only on the Western Front. The defeated and even the victorious empires were racked by revolution, civil strife and ethnic violence: in Russia and its western marches, where far more people would soon die than in the world war; in the former Austria-Hungary; in Slovenia, where Italy, attempting to seize more territory, hazarded its own liberal regime; in Ireland, which saw its most vicious fighting since 1798; in the former Ottoman Empire, its capital under Anglo-French occupation, soon at war with Greece; in Armenia, the Kurdish lands, Iraq and Palestine; in Africa; and in India, where at Amritsar in 1919 a British general carried out a notorious massacre. In China the first sparks of a terrible conflict were struck when the Japanese seized the former German concession ports. An influenza pandemic in 1918–19, unconnected with the war, killed three or four times as many people worldwide as the war itself. The victors of 1918, including Britain, the leading global power, had not solved all their prewar problems. On the contrary, the war had unleashed a generation of violence, which the victors would struggle in vain to contain.

## THE PEACE TO END PEACE?

*This is not a peace, it is an armistice for twenty years.*
Marshal Foch[2]

A peace conference met in Paris from January to May 1919—"I never wanted to hold the Conference in his bloody capital," complained Lloyd

George, "but the old man [Clemenceau] wept and protested so much that we gave way."[3] He installed himself in a comfortable flat with his secretary and mistress, Frances Stevenson, his teenage daughter, Megan, and his assistant, Philip Kerr. Twenty-seven national delegations took part, including India and the Dominions. The British Empire delegations were quartered at the Hôtel Majestic, near the Arc de Triomphe. For security reasons the French staff were replaced by Britons, and the food deteriorated to the level of "a respectable railway hotel." Drinks were free for the Dominion and Indian delegates; the British had to buy their own.

The most intractable problem was that Germany remained potentially the strongest state on the Continent and, with Russia gripped by revolution, relatively more powerful than before the war. When the armistice came, it was not clear—certainly not to the Germans—that they had really been defeated, rather than tricked into surrender and "stabbed in the back" by revolutionaries. German troops were still on foreign soil. Only small border areas were occupied. The Allies' military strength was melting away—Britain's citizen-soldiers, convinced the job was finished, were clamouring to go home. With the eclipse of Russia and Austria, Germany towered over central and eastern Europe. Britain's particular fears had been removed, however. The German navy had sailed to Scapa Flow to surrender and had scuttled itself. Its colonies had been seized. Belgium was liberated. So early on differences emerged between British (and similar Dominion and American) views and those of France and other Continental states, who remained worried about a resurgence of Germany. The British Cabinet decided that it should throw in its lot with the Americans, and Woodrow Wilson's new world order, rather than relying on a close alliance with France to maintain European security. Lord Robert Cecil, the former Minister of Blockade, drew up plans for a League of Nations, for the time being excluding Germany.

The French wanted more concrete guarantees of security, focusing on the Rhine barrier. They wanted the west bank turned into an independent buffer state to block future aggression and, by making Germany vulnerable to invasion, to act as a ring through its nose. Wilson and Lloyd George, hopeful of reconciliation with Germany, refused. Deadlock was broken when Britain and America offered France an indefinite security guarantee: Lloyd George even suggested building a Channel tunnel to facilitate military aid. Clemenceau gave in and settled for permanent demilitarization of the Rhineland frontier zone by Germany and a fifteen-year Allied occupation. Germany was to be allowed an army of only 100,000 men, with no tanks and no air force, and a small navy with no submarines, monitored by an Allied control commission. A hostage to fortune was given by a declaration that this was a step towards "a general limitation of the armaments of all countries."[4]

The real decisions were taken in private by Lloyd George, Clemenceau, Wilson and sometimes the Italian prime minister, Vittorio Orlando. Said one participant: "No four kings or emperors could have conducted the conference on more autocratic lines."[5] They negotiated in haste, confusion and not a little emotion: Wilson, the Presbyterian college professor, perorated; Clemenceau, a veteran political bruiser described by Lloyd George as a "disagreeable and rather bad-tempered old savage," growled and sometimes wept; and Lloyd George deployed his considerable talents as a fixer. He bore the responsibilities of power lightly. In the evenings, in holiday mood, he went out to cafés and restaurants, or led sing-songs round the piano.[6] The conference spadework was done by fifty-two specialist committees and hastily thrown together in a 200-page draft treaty which the "Big Three" had no time to read, and which the official delegations saw only a few hours before it was handed to the representatives of the new German Republic.

The Germans had been excluded from the negotiations and on 7 May 1919 were summoned to receive the draft treaty. In an angry scene, their chief delegate rejected responsibility for the war—"a lie"—and accused the Allies of killing "hundreds of thousands" of German civilians "with cold deliberation" by continuing the naval blockade despite the armistice.[7] The Germans were given two weeks to make written comments. These, when they came, rejected practically the whole treaty. Finally, threatened with invasion, they signed the "diktat" Treaty of Versailles under protest in the Hall of Mirrors, the very room where the Reich had been proclaimed in 1871 as German armies starved Paris. British officers saluted the German delegates—the only ones who did. The Germans and their sympathizers insisted that they had been tricked: the "Fourteen Points," the basis on which they had requested an honourable armistice, had been flouted; instead, a harsh "Carthaginian Peace" annexed territory and resources, imposed ruinous "reparations" and unilateral disarmament, demanded punishment of war criminals, and saddled the German people with "war guilt." And still the British naval blockade continued—condemned today by some historians as a war crime.

The indignation was less than justified. The blockade indeed continued until the treaty was concluded, but no longer applied to food.[8] The Allies never seriously considered breaking up the German Reich, deciding only to occupy the strategic Rhineland for fifteen years. Little of the territory permanently transferred was "German"—most was conquered French, Danish and Polish land now restored, and several disputed areas were left to Germany after plebiscites. Besides, the disintegration of the German Empire (like that of the Austrian, Russian and Turkish) had been spontaneous, and it was impossible, as well as unthinkable, for the Allies to reverse it. The treaty broadly respected self-determination. Critics of the treaty were strangely contemptuous of the new states, such as Poland and Czechoslovakia, but showed intense concern for the rights of German minorities incorporated into them.

The notorious Clause 231—the so-called War Guilt Clause or *Kriegsschuldfrage* (and similar clauses for Germany's allies)—in English specified "responsibility," not guilt, though the German word *Schuld* means both "debt" and "guilt." Allied governments insisted that Germany and Austria-Hungary were indeed mainly responsible for the war—a view broadly endorsed by most modern historians.[9] This was bitterly contested by the new German government in a propaganda campaign (orchestrated by a special section of the Foreign Ministry) which tried to shift the blame onto the Russians and the French. Nearly a century later, the terms of the debate have changed little; and, while infinitely less impassioned, it still has political implications.[10] Whatever the causes of the war, during its course the Germans had proved harsh occupiers, exploiting forced labour, pillaging conquered territories (for example, removing most of the northern French textile industry to Germany lock, stock and barrel), and systematically wrecking everything as they retreated. In the words of the Allies' blunt official statement, "Somebody must suffer the consequences of the war. Is it to be Germany or only the peoples she has wronged?"[11] They hoped that financial liability might deter future aggressors. They were also determined to recoup some of their own losses, obtain security, and satisfy their electorates. Much attention focused on the vexed question of "reparations" (a politically correct neologism), the most criticized aspect of the treaty, commonly blamed later for economic depression, the rise of Hitler, even the Second World War. Yet the demand for reparations was understandable and politically unavoidable. Germany had suffered negligible damage; but in France alone 15,000 square kilometres of territory had been devastated. It seemed just that Germany should help to "repair" the damage, for without reparations the European victors would have been economically weaker than the vanquished.

The English public, as the 1918 election had shown, was keen to "make Germany pay": all candidates opposing punishment of Germany were defeated, and Lloyd George, sensitive to the public mood, advocated putting the Kaiser on trial. But the political and intellectual elites had misgivings, most on practical, some on moral grounds. The Foreign Secretary, A. J. Balfour, thought that as Germany was such a powerful state, the only way of preventing it from again being dangerous was "a change in the international system of the world," not mere "manipulation" of frontiers.[12] His younger officials were outraged at the terms of the treaty: "This bloody bullying peace is the last flicker of the old tradition . . . we young people will build again," wrote Harold Nicolson.[13] At the Hôtel Majestic they set up an Institute of International Affairs to express their disquiet. The Archbishop of Canterbury voiced unease. Lloyd George began to urge concessions to Germany. J. M. Keynes, a Cambridge don, businessman, Bloomsbury intellectual and principal Treasury adviser at the conference, resigned to write *The Economic Consequences of the Peace*, which appeared in December 1919. It quickly sold over 100,000 copies, becoming a best-seller in Britain and America, and it was translated into eleven languages.

Keynes denounced the treaty as the moral equivalent of Germany's invasion of Belgium, marked by "imbecile greed . . . and hypocrisy [imposing] demands on a helpless enemy inconsistent with solemn engagements on our part on the faith of which this enemy had laid down his arms . . . reducing Germany to servitude for a generation . . . her children starved and crippled." He echoed the protest of the German delegation: "Those who sign this treaty will sign the death sentence of millions of German men, women and children."[14] Much of the book's impact came from Keynes's insider status. Kingsley Martin, a Cambridge undergraduate attending Keynes's lectures, found it "wonderful for us to have a high authority saying with inside knowledge of the Treaty what we felt emotionally."[15] Keynes was a recognized expert on the fraught and opaque subject of reparations. But although he used technical arguments and many statistics, they were enlivened by his eyewitness account of a battle between "two rival schemes for the future polity of the world" in which Wilson, a "blind and deaf Don Quixote," the crafty Lloyd George and the cynical Clemenceau were on the wrong side, thinking in terms of "a perpetual prize-fight" of national interests and rivalries, not of "humanity and of European civilization struggling forwards to a new order."[16]

Keynes had written what many were saying: his very vocabulary can be found in the letters and diaries of British Empire and American delegates in Paris, and he had been urged to write by General Jan Smuts, a South African delegate and member of the Imperial War Cabinet. These ideas stemmed from prewar Liberal pacifism, temporarily muffled in 1914, but which revived as the war lengthened and grew more atrocious. They were expressed by the Union for Democratic Control, godparent of the League of Nations. Woodrow Wilson's vision of a "peace without victory" and of reconciliation offered hope of "escape from what was swallowing up all we [Keynes and fellow progressives] cared for." War would truly be ended only by destroying what progressives regarded as its true causes: "secret diplomacy," the arms industry and the old ruling class. As that class had, it seemed, already been swept from power in Germany, there was no reason for harshness and suspicion—on the contrary. Old-style power politics should give way to the League of Nations, which would guide the destiny of the world, believing, wrote Keynes, that "the solidarity of man is not a fiction."[17]

Keynes's influential denunciation of reparations as cruel and irrational was questionable. Hugely varying estimates were made of what Germany should and could pay. Most economic historians now consider that reparations could have been paid. The crux for Germany was not economic but political: reparations signified defeat. It was realized that reparations might actually benefit the payer, by stimulating production and exports, and damage the recipients (confiscating German merchant ships did nothing for the struggling British shipbuilding industry, and free German coal to France and Belgium undercut British mines). America favoured reducing German reparations, but unhelpfully insisted that the former allies repay American loans—which would have loaded most of the huge cost of the war onto English taxpayers. Reparations finally demanded totalled £6.6bn to be paid over thirty-six years. To put this sum in context, the Allies' full military costs were some £12bn in 1913 prices, not to mention civilian losses: damage to buildings in France alone was estimated at $17bn.[18] Moreover, less than half the sum demanded of Germany was considered by the Allies to be actually recoverable.[19] During the 1920s reparations and eventually debts were repeatedly scaled down, and Germany in reality paid very little—about £1bn over thirteen years of wrangling, less than one-third of it in cash.[20] As the former Minister of Blockade, Lord Robert Cecil, saw it, reparations caused "the maximum of financial disturbance with the minimum of result."[21]

More than any other work, Keynes's book discredited the Versailles settlement and highlighted—and exaggerated—differences between the former allies. His assertions shaped opinion for generations. Many still believe them. Rejection of the treaty became one of the fundamental principles of the Labour Party, but it extended far beyond the left.[22] German economic revival was regarded as in Britain's economic interests, and its political revival desirable to balance French ambitions. As the Foreign Office put it, "From the earliest years following the war, it was our policy to eliminate those parts of the Peace Settlement which, as practical people, we knew to be untenable and indefensible."[23] Thus was born "appeasement," which dominated interwar British policy, made enforcement of the Treaty of Versailles impossible, and encouraged British and American disengagement from Europe.

The League of Nations was formally established by the Treaty of Versailles, with its headquarters and secretariat in Geneva, run by Sir Edward Grey's former private secretary, Sir Eric Drummond. It provided hope of a better world, and sometimes a way of avoiding difficult decisions. A League of Nations Union spread nationwide in Britain and attracted cross-party support, including former conscientious objectors and former war heroes, Tory grandees and TUC leaders. By 1927 it had 654,000 members and many affiliated organizations. Stanley Baldwin, the Tory leader, was a vice-chairman, and the chairman, Lord Robert Cecil, son of the former Prime Minister Lord Salisbury and a former Tory minister, became one of the most active peace campaigners, winning the Nobel Peace Prize in 1937. The Labour Party called in 1928 for "whole-hearted support of the League of Nations as the arbiter of international peace and order, in preference to the basing of peace upon separate pacts, ententes and alliances."[24] Disarmament became the league's chief preoccupation.

The problems of postwar Europe were many and profound. Germany was largely surrounded by new, relatively weak states whose very existence many Germans resented. Many of its politicians and people were unreconciled to defeat; resentment of the Treaty of Versailles was the one tie that bound the deeply divided nation together.[25] The victors were disunited: America and then Britain reneged on their promise to guarantee France's security after the American Senate (in a debate in which Keynes was repeatedly cited) refused to ratify the Versailles treaty or join the League of Nations, despite Woodrow Wilson having been one of its moving spirits. The best chance of lasting peace would have been continuing Allied solidarity, a British alliance with France, and compromise over reparations and debt. This sounds simple; it proved impossible. The fundamental flaw of the treaty was not (as a leading British newspaper stated recently) that its "harsh terms would ensure a second war," but rather that (as a contemporary French critic put it) it "was too gentle for what is in it that is harsh."[26] The victor powers would not, perhaps could not, either fully conciliate Germany or fully dominate it.

## WIDER STILL AND WIDER

*We are only at the beginning of our troubles.*
Lord Balfour, Foreign Secretary, 1919

Outside Europe, the British Empire emerged from the war more powerful—certainly bigger, with 500 million people—than ever. It had acquired major tracts of Africa and much of the Middle East under League of Nations "mandates": theoretically, the league was placing former German or Turkish possessions under the care of benevolent British administration. Its main global rivals, Germany and Russia, had been eliminated. A simplified "Basic English" was created to be the new world language. Many foreign observers regarded the empire as by far the greatest world power. In terms of population and resources, it clearly was. But those resources were controlled by a complexity of governments and peoples. In war, they might cooperate. In peace, they did not. The war effort, furthermore, created expectations of reward. The Dominions themselves took German colonies—South Africa took German South-West Africa, Australia took part of New Guinea. White settlers in African colonies were constantly insubordinate.[27] The Statute of Westminster (1931) formally recognized the legal independence of the Dominions within a "Commonwealth" in which they were as independent as they chose to be. When new global dangers appeared, the Dominions proved even more inclined to isolation, cost-cutting, appeasement and wishful thinking than Britain, and the need to defend them was an extra burden.

Following the solidarity displayed during the war, the empire commanded general approval in Britain. There were practically no absolute anti-imperialists, including within the Labour Party. The public considered it a beneficent and largely willing association, notwithstanding widespread unrest. The empire could only be justified in England by the belief that it was a "family" based on loyalty—a vision that the monarchy did much to support—and was bringing general progress. The term "Commonwealth" became popular well before it was officially adopted. This view of empire required considerable wishful thinking, but it was not wholly false. There were now some subsidized development projects, and with the onset of the Great Depression imperial trading preference became a reality. As new dangers arose from states motivated by totalitarian and racist expansionism, the empire provided some protection for its more exposed elements.

But the barbarism of the war had shaken the psychological bondage of the empire's subjects. European superiority was no longer intellectually or physically unchallengeable. The economic shockwaves of the war and a postwar slump affected the colonized peoples. There was unrest in Nyasaland, Ceylon, Somaliland, Sudan, Egypt, Iraq and the West Indies. India was in a state of sporadic rebellion, in which regional and religious tensions were accompanied by rising political support for the nationalist Congress Party. Palestine saw increasing friction between Jewish settlers and the native population. The Russian Revolution and conflict in Ireland created apprehension of "a world movement," as Balfour put it, "plainly discernable on every continent . . . We are only at the beginning of our troubles." A senior general warned of being "spread all over the world, strong nowhere, weak everywhere."[28]

Ireland was racked by vicious and futile conflict. Here too the Great War had hammered open existing political fractures. Although Home Rule had been agreed in 1914, fear of conscription during the war and repression after the Easter Rising had undermined the pro-war Irish Parliamentary Party and replaced it with the republican Sinn Fein, which set up its own symbolic parliament in January 1919. Westminster legislated in 1920 for two Irish parliaments, in Dublin and Belfast, with a joint Council of Ireland. Sinn Fein rejected this "partition," denied Westminster's right to legislate for Ireland, and began killing policemen and miscellaneous others, seemingly to prevent compromise by provoking conflict. Conflict duly came with retaliatory killings of Sinn Feiners and anti-Catholic violence in Ulster. The British government, trying to extricate itself from Ireland, and lacking the resources, the will and the wisdom to defuse the conflict, tried to snuff out the violence by interning activists. The weakened and demoralised Royal Irish Constabulary, mostly Catholic, was reinforced by auxiliary police, including the 10,000 "Black and Tans," mostly British former soldiers. Nationalist killings were met with a semi-official policy of reprisals, including shooting to kill and burning houses. Death squads operated on both sides. The most notorious single incident was "Bloody Sunday," 21 November 1920, when fourteen supposed British intelligence officers were assassinated and vengeful "Black and Tans" shot fourteen dead at a Gaelic football match in Dublin— "Dublin's Amritsar."[29] In May 1921 the two Irish parliaments were elected, one dominated by Sinn Fein, the other by Ulster Unionists. A conference in London sought a solution based on an independent Ireland, with autonomy for Ulster, membership of the Commonwealth and safeguards for Britain's security. On 6 December 1921 a treaty established an "Irish Free State" within the Commonwealth. But worsening political and sectarian murders in both Ulster and the Free State, and a refusal by many nationalists to accept the treaty, led to a three-way civil war in the summer of 1922 when Dublin government forces raided Ulster and also attacked anti-treaty rebels of the Irish Republican Army (IRA) in Dublin. The Dublin government sent more rebels to firing squads than the British had in 1916, and the civil war petered out in 1923. It had cost some 2,000 lives—relatively few compared, for example, with the 36,000 killed in the simultaneous civil war in Finland, or the large number of Irishmen killed in the Great War.[30] The outcome was a grudging compromise: the Irish Free State attained independence and remained nominally a member of the Commonwealth and "six counties" centred on Protestant Ulster became a self-governing province of the United Kingdom; but hopes of a gradual reunification of north and south and friendly relations with Britain had evaporated. It took until 1998 to return to the outcome available in 1920.

The Middle East was a great prize. British paramountcy seemed assured following the disintegration of the Ottoman Empire—an illusion soon dispelled. Friction ensued with France, which demanded Syria and Lebanon under league mandates. This forced Britain to reduce the territory it had offered to the leaders of the Arab Revolt, the Sherif of Mecca and his sons Abdullah and Faisal. Britain stood by when the French bombarded Damascus in 1920 and ejected Faisal. He was willing to accept British protection, and Britain made him king of Iraq (important for its oil) and Abdullah king of Transjordan, both under British supervision by league mandate. In 1922 Britain found itself on the brink of an unwanted war with Turkey. Palestine was taken by Britain under league mandate, in the belief that it would secure communications with "the Southern British world" from Cape Town to New Zealand. Its first administration consisted of a cashier from a bank in Rangoon, an actor-manager, two assistants from Thomas Cook, a picture dealer, an army coach, a land valuer, a bo'sun from the Niger, a Glasgow distiller, an organist, an Alexandria cotton broker, an architect, a junior London postal official, a taxi driver from Egypt, two schoolmasters and a missionary. The ambiguous Balfour Declaration of 1917 had paid lip service to the interests of both Jews and Arabs, but by encouraging Jewish immigration and land purchase, it inevitably fuelled conflict. By the late 1920s the governor of Palestine had concluded that the Jews were ungrateful, the Arabs impertinent, and the Balfour Declaration a "colossal blunder." Arab uprisings in the 1930s were treated with harsh but ineffective repression combined with a promise to limit Jewish immigration and create an independent two-state Palestine, which satisfied neither side.[31]

In India, a capital worthy not merely of a global but of a galactic empire had been in preparation since 1911, aiming "to rival Paris and Washington." It was to be a garden city in a hybrid neoclassical cum Mughal style, with as its centrepiece Sir Edwin Lutyens's stunning viceregal palace.[32] But in the far south there was sectarian violence; and in the north rioting was met with massacre. In April 1919, at Amritsar, some 400 people were coldly shot down in what Churchill called a "monstrous" and "sinister" act; the army imposed what the Secretary of State for India condemned as "terrorism" and "racial humiliation." The Government of India Act (1919) conceded some provincial self-government and a wider franchise, and in

1929 the Viceroy, the moderate Tory Lord Irwin (later Lord Halifax), offered talks to Indian nationalists with a view to India attaining future "Dominion status,"[33] like Canada, Australia, New Zealand and South Africa. Although Churchill insisted in 1930 that Indian independence could not happen in "any period which we can even remotely foresee"— the usual reasons being that India was too big, too diverse, too backward, too divided and too turbulent to exist without a firm but fair British umpire—in fact rapid steps towards self-government were being taken, under unrelenting political, moral and economic pressure from the embarrassingly peaceful Mohandas Gandhi, a hero to many in England, and whose popular campaigns undermined the deference to British authority on which imperial rule depended. The Baldwin government passed the Government of India Act (1935), against the impassioned opposition of backbench imperialists led by Churchill. It established relatively democratic self-government at provincial level, in the hope of maintaining imperial control of the whole—a doomed compromise.[34]

The empire seemed to insiders "a brontosaurus with huge, vulnerable limbs which the central nervous system had little capacity to protect, direct or control."[35] Postwar economic problems made it even more than usually short of resources. Little more than a decade after its great victory, it would face the most dangerous predators in its history.

## A LAND FIT FOR HEROES

Peace at first brought a world economic boom. There was a widespread determination to ensure that the postwar world would indeed improve the lot of ordinary people, the "heroes" (in Lloyd George's word) who had made sacrifices for victory. People put the privations of the war years behind them as rationing and controls ended. Those who had increased their savings could spend. Companies borrowed to rebuild their stocks and invest. In England workers who had pushed up their wages during the war were determined to keep them, even though working hours were substantially cut—estimated to have raised unemployment by 4 percentage points. Unemployment benefits became arguably more generous than ever before or since: benefits for a family of four rose by 240 percent between 1920 and 1931, and for a substantial proportion of men and women equalled over 80 percent of their previous wage.[36] A house-building programme started. There was major improvement in public health largely due to improved treatment of infectious diseases such as tuberculosis: the average life expectancy of women, for example, increased between the wars from fifty-two to seventy-one years, much of this due to new drugs preventing postnatal infections. State medical insurance now covered 40 percent of the population (compared with 6 percent in France).[37] The state had greatly increased its size and scope during the war, and much of this remained: spending and taxation had roughly tripled in four years and income tax had quintupled. During the 1920s public expenditure was around a quarter of GDP (double that in 1913), and for the first time social services became by far the largest item.[38] The wartime state had controlled a large part of the economy, and this seemed a power that should be used in peacetime for general betterment—a change (further accelerated by the Second World War) that affected British economic performance for good and ill for some sixty years.

The "coupon election" of December 1918 (the "coupon" being the endorsement given by the leaders of the coalition government to its approved parliamentary candidates) had produced a big gain in seats for the Tories. Although Lloyd George remained Prime Minister until 1922, the Liberal Party was in near-terminal decline. The war had made many of its shibboleths obsolete: peace, free trade, cheap government. It had been split by the rivalry between Lloyd George and Asquith. Many prominent activists had shifted to Labour. What now became the two main parties, Conservative and Labour, to a large extent reproduced the geographical, ideological and social patterns of the prewar Conservative and Liberal parties. Tory governments held office under Andrew Bonar Law and Stanley Baldwin between 1922 and 1924. Then came the first brief minority Labour government, under James Ramsay MacDonald, Britain's first working-class Prime Minister, from January to November 1924. He came to power in a reaction against Baldwin's support for tariff reform— the issue that had wrecked the Tory position in 1906. MacDonald and Baldwin alternated until 1931. Both were centrist politicians, MacDonald having moved a long way from his socialist roots. Baldwin gave women the vote on the same basis as men in 1928, making them the majority of the electorate, and so completing Britain's long transition to democracy.

The First World War is often considered a cultural watershed, breaking down old orthodoxies and social hierarchies and engendering new ideas, morals and artistic styles. There is some truth in this view, but there are also many exaggerations. The 1920s saw a gradual decline in institutional religion, especially Nonconformity.[39] Women had fulfilled new roles, and many had the vote; but this had been emerging before the war, and the armistice saw a deliberate retreat, reaffirming gender differences and returning women to domesticity. It is true that the upper classes, particularly landowners, had been hit hard by taxes and death duties, while wages (most obviously of servants) had risen. From *Lady Chatterley's Lover* via *Brideshead Revisited* to *Right Ho, Jeeves*, the vicissitudes of the gentry became a literary theme. Modernism in the arts—again with pre-war roots—attained prominence, including in some war art, notably by Richard Nevinson and Paul Nash, and some artists associated themselves flamboyantly with an avant-garde in politics and morality. But all over Europe the war also caused a revival of traditional cultural forms and a desire to nurture national traditions.[40] In England too there was this trend of national rediscovery which reached its culmination during the Second World War. Some artists who had previously sought inspiration in France now developed an English form of modern art, and could be found on English beaches "sheltering their watercolours from the drizzle"[41] or painting landscapes and churches. Among them were Paul Nash, Stanley Spencer and John Piper, who wrote of artists being "pilgrims in their own country." Some of their work reached a wide audience through illustrated Shell guidebooks. A similar rediscovery was taking place in literature—for example, in the works of such very different writers as T. S. Eliot, Virginia Woolf and John Betjeman—and in widely read travel writing, such as H. V. Morton's *In Search of England* (1934) and J. B. Priestley's much grittier *English Journey* (1933). There was even an attempted revival of tradition in food and cultivation, through the English Folk Cookery Association (1928). Occasionally these cultural interests produced eccentric lifestyles and no less eccentric political affinities.[42]

Cultural novelty was clearest in popular entertainment: the cinema became a mass phenomenon, along with the gramophone and, soon, the wireless. There was, as all over Europe, Americanization. It had begun shortly before the First World War, but American participation in the war accentuated it: ragtime, jazz (first performed in England in 1917) and their offshoots transformed popular music and dancing.[43] It is this, of course, that has left a strong image in popular memory of the "Roaring Twenties," the Jazz Age, the Charleston (1925), and flappers with bobbed hair and (relatively) short skirts. Hollywood quickly established its pre-eminence as the source of new cultural phenomena, not least the creation of global celebrities. But English entertainers could produce plausible home-grown equivalents, whether in modified American style (by bandleaders such as Bert Ambrose and Jack Hylton) or native (for example, the working-class Lancastrians Gracie Fields and George Formby in music and comedy films, and the quintessentially English gentleman star, the mild-mannered and un-muscular Leslie Howard, of Hungarian stock). Many were also stars overseas in the 1930s, including Howard and Hylton, described by a BBC broadcaster as "the most important unofficial ambassador of England on the Continent."[44] The cinema also became a powerful news and propaganda medium through newsreels and documentaries, and indirectly by feature films, which whether British- or American-made tended to be patriotic and conservative, especially when treating popular historical subjects such as monarchs or statesmen—there were, for example, popular films featuring Disraeli (1929), Henry VIII (1933), Elizabeth I (1936 and 1939) and Victoria (1937 and 1938). The wireless was supervised by a paternalistic elite of whom the archetype was the strait-laced John Reith, general manager and then director-general of the British Broadcasting Company from 1922 to 1938. It propagated a broad, rather puritanical and improving national culture—"Giving the public slightly better than it now thinks it likes." Consequently the BBC joined—and eventually replaced—the Church of England as the voice of the nation. George V made the first royal Christmas broadcast in 1932. Stanley Baldwin was the first politician to appreciate in the 1920s that radio was not for making speeches, but for "talking to you in your own homes, as if I were with you there"; and his ability to do that won him considerable popular affection, especially among new voters and women.[45]

However significant these cultural and social phenomena, it was economic upheaval, most dramatically symbolized by the Wall Street Crash in 1929, that dominated domestic life between the wars, affecting its culture and still shaping our memory of it, as in other countries. The international postwar boom at first disguised Europe's underlying weakness, but it was fuelled, like all booms, by a mixture of greed and wishful thinking. The appearance of prosperity rested on a façade of cheap money, because European governments had largely paid for the war by printing banknotes while holding down prices. It became increasingly clear that postwar Europe was suffering from fundamental economic problems. A short but severe depression came in 1920–21, leaving a ruinous trail of bankruptcies and debt. Hyperinflation in Germany in 1923 reduced the mark in a few months from 7,000 to the dollar to 4 trillion.[46]

The war had cost Britain the financial and economic pre-eminence built up since the eighteenth century, undermining its foundations as the world's greatest creditor, exporter and financial centre. Its long-established deficit in "visible" trade (goods, including food and raw materials) had previously been balanced by "invisible" earnings from banking, insurance and shipping, and pushed far into surplus by overseas investment earnings. The war cost Britain more than any of the Allies (see pp. 638–39) and its national debt had risen to 126 percent of GDP. (In 2014 it was around 60 percent.) Its old financial strength had ebbed and its balance of payments was in the red.[47] Worse still, Europe's overseas markets had shrunk.

In 1913 Britain had been the world's biggest exporter of manufactured goods, principally to India, Germany, South America and the Dominions. During the war, production had been diverted to the war effort, cutting deliveries to overseas customers. They had found other suppliers or built their own factories. America and Japan had moved into British markets in South America and Asia, tripling their exports during the war years. India, the biggest customer for England's biggest export, cotton cloth, was being lost: the war boosted India's own textile industry, and political boycotts of British goods increased. China followed the same path. Total exports of cotton cloth fell by 71 percent between 1913 and 1937. The war had stimulated frenetic production of coal, ships, metals, aircraft, motor vehicles and chemicals. Some new industries survived and helped to transform the economy; but others depended on wartime demand—for example, replacing merchant ships sunk by submarines. The end of the war saw a collapse of both overseas and home demand in staple industries: 60 percent of the steel industry was idle; total exports fell by half between 1913 and 1937.[48] This was the economic death of Victorian England.

Problems were compounded by understandable but nevertheless damaging policies. Working hours were further cut. Wages remained high,

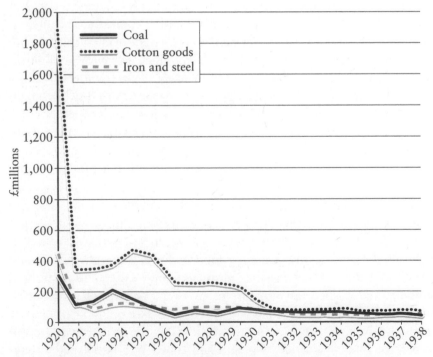

Figure 2. Value of UK exports at constant prices, 1920–38

arguably 10 percent above competitive levels, pricing British workers out of employment.[49] Prices fell, but attempts to cut wages to keep pace were resisted by the unions. There were miners' strikes, and a nine-day General Strike in 1926, which caused considerable alarm and disapproval among Labour and Liberal politicians as well as Tories. It was cut short before it could seriously disturb the peace—an American reporter had seen "more fighting in one night of a local steel strike in Pittsburgh than there has been in all England this week."[50] A theoretical remedy would have been investment to increase productivity; but with markets depressed and firms short of funds this was unfeasible—contrary to popular belief about "profiteers," company profits as a whole had fallen sharply during the war, due to controls, taxes and rising costs. Moreover, most people hoped that the problems were temporary and that markets would return to pre-war normality. Instead, British goods became increasingly uncompetitive in foreign and domestic markets. By 1929, even before the Wall Street Crash, exports were still 20 percent below the 1913 level.[51] It is a bitter irony that after a war that had killed so many young men the great inter-war scourge was unemployment. The number killed was in fact slightly lower than the rate of prewar emigration: over 200,000 a year emigrated before 1914, whereas the war years saw more returning than leaving.[52] Emigration was now restricted, as the United States imposed limits, and in the Dominions jobs were few. So many workers stayed unemployed, and their skills and perhaps motivation declined. It has been argued, con-troversially, that high unemployment benefit may have encouraged this.[53] However bleak our view of interwar England—powerful in literature and popular memory—its economic situation was closer to that of Scandina-via than of France, Germany or central and southern Europe, let alone Russia, all of which fell further behind England in their standards of living.

An attempted economic cure was returning to the gold standard—fix-ing the value of the pound in terms of gold. This system had been sus-pended as a wartime measure, but was due to resume in 1925. The aim was to restore international price stability, which export-oriented British industry sorely needed. Before 1914 the gold standard had facilitated trade and investment, and so most countries, like Britain, returned to gold if and when they could, including the United States, Germany, Australia, New Zealand and Scandinavia. Moreover, gold was popular in England, being associated with cheap food. Economic historians now generally agree that the return to gold was a fundamental cause of economic disas-ter. Yet the decision was not taken lightly. In Britain, Churchill, the chan-cellor, who is commonly blamed, was painfully aware of the dangers, most obviously of raising the value of sterling too high. The decision was made only after thorough expert discussion; moreover, the alternative of allowing unstable exchange rates risked damaging the world economy further, and hence also harming British export industries.[54]

It was hard to gauge the correct value of a currency, and Churchill's decision to fix the pound at the prewar rate against the dollar ($4.86 to £1) proved too high, making exports more expensive. The system had worked before 1914 because the main financial centres—London, Paris, Berlin, New York—had cooperated to try to ensure stability, and the keystone of the system, the Bank of England, had been at the centre of a global free-trading economy willing to buy goods from countries in difficulty and invest in their growth. The Bank had when necessary provided bail-outs to foreign countries as "lender of last resort." After 1918 the City was no longer the world's banker—Wall Street was. But the Americans lacked the will to manage the world economy and, moreover, America was not a free trader.[55] After the war Europe owed America money: the Allies owed what they had borrowed; the defeated Central Powers owed reparations. But protectionist America did not buy enough European goods to enable them to earn the money to pay their debts, and even imposed a 30 percent import tariff. Hence, Europeans depended on America lending them more money to repay what they already owed. A final problem was that America and France had deliberately undervalued their currencies, creating trade surpluses which drew in gold from other countries—by 1929 40 percent of the world's gold was in Fort Knox. Other countries, losing gold, the guarantee of their currency, were forced to raise interest rates to halt the loss, which further slowed their economies.

The first international tremors were banking crises in Austria and Germany in 1928. But the trigger of disaster was the Wall Street Crash of 24 October 1929, the classic bursting of a speculative bubble, familiar from the eighteenth century to the twenty-first. Its consequences were so devastating because of the fragility of the postwar economic and financial systems, and because of the subsequent actions taken by governments. America had already reduced its lending to Europe to finance its own boom; the bust, by ruining banks and destroying credit, caused America to stop lending altogether. The worst consequences were in America itself, and in Germany, where banks and businesses failed, jobs disappeared, and people went hungry. The reaction everywhere was self-protection at the expense of trading partners, some of whom were of course former enemies or imperial masters, which made cooperation and solidarity at best grudging. Countries raised tariffs against foreign imports to protect home producers, with the result that world trade collapsed. This was a further blow to struggling English export industries; and it also damaged the crucial services sector—shipping, insurance and banking.

Ramsay MacDonald's 1929 Labour government made attempts to improve relations with Germany and Ireland and give greater autonomy to Egypt and India. But it was bereft of a policy for coping with the financial crisis. One minister, Sir Oswald Mosley, urged huge job creation, but most feared financial strain. The Cabinet fragmented when a run on the pound forced it to seek financial support in Wall Street, which insisted on a cut in public spending. So in August 1931 MacDonald suddenly resigned and formed a National Government, with Tory and Liberal support. Most of the Labour Party opposed and was consequently decimated in the ensuing 1931 general elections, causing MacDonald to be reviled in Labour folklore as a traitor. The National Government tried to cut public-sector wages, leading to the "Invergordon Mutiny"—a strike in the navy—and another run on the pound. So after hanging on for nearly two years, Britain abandoned the gold standard in September 1931, and the pound lost 30 percent of its value—a milestone in modern economic history. But the decision was less tortured than in some countries. Britain had suffered far less from inflation in the 1920s than France or Germany: the latter had suffered the traumatic experience of hyperinflation in 1923, when people had needed barrow-loads of banknotes to buy groceries and savings had become worthless. So British politicians and public opinion were less fixated on gold, and devaluation happened without a political outcry. Not for the last time, the economy benefited from a currency debacle, followed by a cut in interest rates from 6 to 2 percent. English goods became cheaper, winning back home and foreign markets. Fifteen other countries followed suit. By 1932 the economy was starting to recover, growing by 4 percent per year, with average unemployment over the 1930s (9.8 percent) roughly half that in the United States (18.2 percent).[56]

In Europe, new and fragile democratic governments seemed impotent to halt the economic crisis. Many were hamstrung by proportional representation, which gave no clear majority to govern. Communists, radical nationalists or authoritarian conservatives were threatening to take or actually taking power in Poland, Germany, Austria, Hungary, the Balkans, Portugal and Spain. Even in traditionally stable countries, including Belgium and Norway, extremist populist parties emerged. In France, Europe's oldest large democracy, a Communist party and several fascist-style movements threatened the parliamentary republic. Most seriously of all, in Germany the National Socialist German Workers' Party began winning the votes of people desperate for some way out of the slump, blamed on reparations and the Treaty of Versailles.

Ramsay MacDonald, showing his age (seventy-one), retired in 1935 and was replaced by the reassuring Stanley Baldwin, who had twice before been Prime Minister. Baldwin continued to lead a mildly reforming National Government, mainly Conservative, but with "National Liberal" and "National Labour" participation. Baldwin defended this coalition as a moderate bulwark against extremism—including that of his critics in the Tory party, among them Winston Churchill. Baldwin had been a successful businessman running a large family firm, a West Midlands steelmaker, and he cultivated a relaxed and relaxing consensus style of unthreatening, Christian, pipe-smoking, very English patriotism; he once told his children he would have refused to choose between Cavaliers and Roundheads in the Civil War. Although he began rearmament he was viscerally opposed to war, saying in 1936 that he was "not going to get this country into a war with anybody for the League of Nations or anybody else or for anything else."[57] This was not just talk: he had given away his firm's war profits as tainted. He was a reassuring leader for a new democratic electorate facing persistent unemployment, divisions over partial self-government in India, controversial decisions over rearmament and the tawdry Abdication Crisis of 1936. The determination of the popular young king, Edward VIII, who succeeded in 1936, to marry the louche American Mrs. Simpson and make her queen seemed to Baldwin, and much of the public, to undermine the modern justification of monarchy: as a dignified symbol of unity and duty, and a "moral force" serving as a "guarantee," as Baldwin put it to the Commons, "against many evils that have afflicted other countries."[58] Contrary to myth, the king's supposed political beliefs, whether left or right wing, seem not to have been an issue for the government, though one Labour MP warned of a "fascist monarchy," and Baldwin was certainly annoyed by the emergence of a loose "king's party," including Churchill, Lloyd George, Oswald Mosley and several press barons. Baldwin soon formed a dim view of his new monarch, told him firmly that he could not marry Mrs. Simpson and keep the throne, and steered an Abdication Bill swiftly through Parliament. The crisis evaporated when the uncharismatic, dutiful and suitably married Duke of York succeeded as George VI in December 1936. Baldwin thereupon retired.

The rowdiest political novelty of these years was the photogenic former Labour minister and baronet Sir Oswald Mosley, who at first attracted a range of support, including the young Welsh socialist Aneurin Bevan and John Maynard Keynes. As in similar Continental movements, Mosley attempted to draw on the comradeship of the trenches, hence the uniforms and taste for violence which appeared in quasi-military political movements in many countries. This dynamic political style, attempting to bypass old left-right divisions in a "third way," appealed to many newly enfranchised voters, not least women. Mosley's British Union of Fascists (1932) seemed able to win support across the political spectrum, including two Labour MPs, Independent Labour Party militants, Communists, former Suffragettes, working-class Tories and trade unionists attracted by "Socialism plus Patriotism," as well as a right-wing fringe. However, violence at its meetings was seen as going beyond the traditional tolerance of low-level violence that was seen as a healthy English tradition. As one Tory MP, William Anstruther-Gray, told the Commons, "I am not against interrupters being ejected . . . [or] seeing a man knocked down in a scuffle, but when it comes to seeing eight or ten men kicking and beating a man on the ground, then everything British in me swells up on the side of the fellow who is not getting fair play."[59] Although it provoked street violence and anger, the BUF had a limited following: parliamentary politics and the established parties were strong and the Depression was lifting. Its notorious East End march in October 1936 saw 7,000 "Blackshirts" confronted by several hundred thousand angry opponents.[60] The Public Order Act (1936) banned political uniforms and gave the police wider powers to regulate political meetings, ending the age-old electoral mayhem. But in those countries defeated in the war, newly created by the Treaty of Versailles, devastated by the Depression, threatened by Communism, or where democracy was new and often corrupt, fascism was a real and growing menace.

We remember the 1930s in England not as a time of political stability and robust economic recovery, when unemployment fell by 30 percent and which had one of the most developed welfare systems in the world,[61] but as a time of helpless misery and pessimism. The Jarrow hunger marches in 1936 made a lasting impression. George's Orwell's *The Road to Wigan Pier*, commissioned and published by the Left Book Club in 1937, became a classic. Walter Greenwood's *Love on the Dole: A Tale of the Two Cities* (1933), about the sufferings of a family doomed by the Depression, became an international best-seller, a play seen by over a million people, and eventually a film, transforming its author from unemployed Salford clerk to celebrity. Even the *Daily Telegraph* praised him for stirring "the public conscience," and the socialist *New Clarion* thought he showed that "capitalism is utterly condemned."[62]

Much of the reason for this pessimism was a belief across Europe that Western civilization was nearing collapse: moral, social, political and above all economic. As Sidney and Beatrice Webb put it with grim relish in their *Decay of Capitalist Civilization* (1923), "Capitalism need not

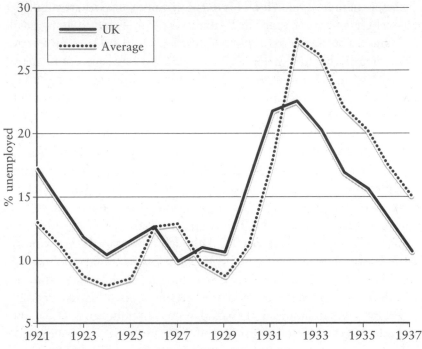

Figure 3. Unemployment in Britain and Europe, 1921–37

hope to die quietly in its bed; it will die by violence, and civilisation will perish with it." Their book, wrote the editor of the *New Statesman*, shaped the beliefs of British socialists for twenty years. For some on the left, any form of radicalism was welcome. The prominent playwright George Bernard Shaw, a celebrity socialist gadfly of sometimes surpassing silliness, thought both Communism and Fascism showed the way to the future. "Who can blame Signor Mussolini," he asked a BBC audience in 1929, "for describing [democracy] as a putrefying corpse?" Lenin and Stalin ("a good Fabian") had begun a "great Communist experiment" which would prevent the "collapse and failure" of world civilization; while "the Nazi movement is in many respects one which has my warmest sympathy."[63]

Most English people, however, disliked and suspected Nazism from the beginning. Communism, on the other hand, especially after the Wall Street Crash, attracted many intellectuals, not a few with public-school, Tory and Oxbridge backgrounds, dazzled by the contrast between a "successful" Soviet Russia and a faltering capitalist world. The Communist Party never attracted more than a few thousand full members in England, but progressives—led by an elite of economists, political scientists, composers, actors, artists and writers—hailed Moscow as the New Jerusalem. H. G. Wells, though admitting its "permanent Terror," considered that the USSR "remains something splendid and hopeful." Many were convinced of the need for a "planned economy" and a Soviet-style remedial prison system. A stellar group of metropolitan intellectuals centred on the Hampstead Ethical Institute, including Vera Brittain, Leonard Woolf, the Huxleys, Bertrand Russell, H. G. Wells and Rebecca West, published the succinctly titled journal *Plan*, urging "socialization of the collective economic affairs of mankind." At the height of the Great Terror in 1936, Victor Gollancz, director of the Left Book Club, named Stalin his Man of the Year. Many visitors to Russia, including Shaw and the Webbs, saw only happiness, prosperity and freedom; even some who admitted the regime's tyranny accepted that omelettes required broken eggs. The Webbs showed their growing confidence by removing the question mark from the title of the 1937 edition of their *Soviet Communism: A New Civilization?* "All I know," wrote Beatrice, "is that I *wish* Russian Communism to succeed," and she angrily dismissed the view of her more perceptive nephew, the journalist Malcolm Muggeridge, that it was based on "the most evil and most cruel elements in human nature."[64] The Webbs imagined the Soviet Communist Party as a combination of charitable organization and religious order, "a remarkable companionship" with a "vocation of leadership" over many "voluntary organisations" forming a "multiform democracy"—certainly not a dictatorship, and Stalin was not "the sort of person to claim or desire such a position."[65] The Wykhamist Labour MP Dennis Pritt thought that if Soviet Interior Ministry officials had been sent to prison, it was just to make sure that conditions were comfortable. Not only Communists, but many in the centre and on the right of politics too, not least prominent businessmen and MPs, were becoming convinced of the necessity of state economic intervention—a view most authoritatively expounded by Keynes in his *General Theory of Employment, Interest and Money* (1936).

The most obvious visible reason for pessimism was that economic suffering was intense in certain regions, particularly in the north of England, home of the old staple industries. Interwar decline and the Great Depression accelerated problems already detectable before 1914. Whole communities were now blighted: the north-east went from 2 percent unemployment in 1913 to 30 percent in 1932. At the depths of the slump, in 1932, there were 3.5 million registered unemployed and many more on short time. The existing north–south divide now acquired a new dimension: the once mighty but now depressed industrial north contrasted with growing new industries in the south and the Midlands, which by 1936 had only half or a third their level of unemployment. While the shipbuilders of Jarrow went hungry, workers in the motor vehicle, chemical and electrical-goods industries of Coventry, the Black Country and the outer-London suburbs were prospering.[66] The Labour Party and trade unionism became entrenched in these old Liberal Nonconformist heartlands of the north, but made only partial inroads in the Midlands and the south.

The 1930s recovery was largely based on the domestic market, as those with jobs benefited from falling prices and greater purchasing power. The results are still visible in the rows of 1930s houses (3 million of them), often with a tasteful hint of timbering or stucco, that line arterial roads into southern and Midland towns: house-building accounted for 30 percent of new jobs between 1932 and 1934 as costs fell and building societies offered up to 95 percent mortgages. There was buoyant demand for building materials, furniture and household gadgets. The car industry took off: exports in 1938 equalled those of Germany, France and Italy combined. Revival was assisted by protection from foreign imports and privileged access to empire markets. In 1931 a tariff of 10 percent—introduced by Joe Chamberlain's son Neville, the chancellor—was imposed on foreign manufactures. The Ottawa Conference (1932) created a system of "imperial preference" (internal free trade): by 1934 the empire was taking 44 percent of British exports, a pattern that continued until the 1960s. A "sterling bloc," using sterling as its exchange medium, was created: it included not only the empire, but also Scandinavia, much of the Middle East, Argentina and Japan. This marked the eclipse of the globalizing free-trade orthodoxy established in the 1840s. It had long been defended by Liberals and Labour, which in 1924 had scrapped wartime tariffs with the old Liberal slogan of the "free breakfast table." But by 1930 even the Manchester Chamber of Commerce, high priests of free trade, backed tariffs. The difference was soon felt: imports had risen by 66 percent between 1920 and 1929; between 1929 and 1937, they fell by 18 percent.[67]

The Prince of Wales famously remarked that "something must be done" to find people work. Things were done, but not always the right things. The relative success of the Yorkshire woollen industry, which found niche markets for high-quality goods, shows that the old staples were not dead. But elsewhere the response, shared by governments, employers and unions, was defensive: "rationalization," minimum-wage agreements, regulating tribunals and boards, controlled rents, mergers, price-fixing, market-sharing, import tariffs and subsidies. This put off the inevitable, and delayed the shift of investment and labour from declining to expanding industries. It also had an impact on attitudes and policies towards competition lasting at least until the 1980s, creating an environment in which one economist could declare in 1937 that "free competition has nearly disappeared from the British scene."[68] Employers and workers hung on, hoping for improvement. But real improvement, restoring demand to old industries, came with rearmament, which began in 1936. Recovery was "due more to Mr. Hitler than to Mr. Keynes."[69]

## TO THE DARK GULF

*We are all members of the human race ... There must be something in common between us, if only we can find it, and perhaps by our very aloofness from the rest of Europe we may have some special part to play as conciliator.*
            Neville Chamberlain, Prime Minister, speech 1938[70]

*I have watched this famous island descending, incontinently, fecklessly, the stairway which leads to a dark gulf. It is a fine broad stairway at the beginning, but after a bit the carpet ends. A little further on there are only flagstones, and a little further on still these break beneath your feet.*
            Winston Churchill, House of Commons, 24 March 1938[71]

As the 1920s wore on, the passions and dangers that had seemed so real at the Paris peace conference were fading. In 1923, after Germany repeatedly refused to make reparations deliveries, its industrial Ruhr district was occupied by French and Belgian troops, and the German currency rocketed into hyperinflation. But the franc too nearly collapsed, and France's uncompromising action damaged its relations with Britain and America, more inclined to concession. The experience left everyone chastened. The Americans and the British Labour government called for discussions. The Dawes Plan (1924) reduced the reparations bill and abandoned enforcement. A conference at Locarno in 1925 between Britain, France, Germany and Italy produced diplomatic conviviality. The new Tory Foreign Secretary, the well-meaning Austen Chamberlain, waxed lyrical: "I rub my eyes and wonder whether I am dreaming when the French foreign minister invites the German foreign minister and me to celebrate my wife's birthday, and incidentally talk business, by a cruise on the Lake."[72] Germany joined the League of Nations. A Locarno treaty jointly guaranteed Germany's western border and renounced military aggression. Nothing, deliberately, was said about its disputed eastern border. The vestigial organization for monitoring German disarmament was abolished and a blind eye was turned to its evasion of the Versailles limitations, which many in Britain regarded as a dead letter. Whitehall hoped its Continental entanglements were ended. Churchill, Chancellor of the Exchequer, voiced a common opinion when he argued that Britain should concentrate on defending the empire. But he resisted naval expansion— "Why should there be a war with Japan?" he demanded in 1924; "I do not believe there is the slightest chance of it in my lifetime."[73] In 1928 the highly publicized Kellogg-Briand pact (initiated by the American and French foreign ministers) was an international renunciation of war, signed with a gold pen by statesmen who privately regarded it as an empty gesture, a "pious declaration against sin."[74] But it was very popular and revived public optimism. In 1929–30, the Labour government slashed naval strength, stopped work on the Singapore naval base, and in 1930 limited warship-building by treaty with the United States and Japan. This was the time when powerful literary works appeared exposing the horrors of the Great War. Churchill assured an audience in Montreal in 1929 that "the outlook for peace has never been better for fifty years."[75]

But a large part of the German public was not reconciled. Even the relatively moderate Weimar Republic was evading arms limitations by tank training with the Red Army in Russia, developing civil aircraft that could be converted for military use, and building "pocket battleships" just inside the tonnage limits. Its politicians invoked the "spirit of Locarno" to press for a reduction of the French army and immediate evacuation of the Rhineland, garrisoned by Allied troops. Prominent German politicians also demanded union with Austria, forbidden by the Versailles treaty. The French rather desperately urged a federal "European Union," and began building the Maginot Line of fortifications to defend their eastern frontier.

The international peace movement, in its multifarious forms, was probably strongest in Britain.[76] It spread across ages, classes and parties, and attracted unparalleled mass involvement in which women were particularly prominent. Vast quantities of literature were disseminated. Schoolchildren were taught that "collective security" through the League of Nations was like the whole class standing up against a bully. A World Disarmament Conference of fifty-nine states met in Geneva in February 1932, the object of hopes, prayers and millions of petitions. But disarmament was a dangerous issue. It caused disagreement among the democratic states, which all claimed to have special security needs and wanted disarmament to be led by others. Worse, it gave a platform to Germany, which although it was secretly rearming was legally under restraints, and it demanded "equal treatment," for which MacDonald's government thought it had "strong moral backing." In effect, this would mean Germany rearming and everyone else disarming. Churchill raised a rare warning voice: "When they have the weapons, believe me they will ask for the return . . . of lost territories." But he too urged that "the just grievances of the vanquished" should be redressed.[77]

In January 1933, while the Disarmament Conference was in session, Adolf Hitler, supported by some 40 percent of the electorate, became head of a coalition government. The Nazis soon seized sole power. At first there was no change in German foreign policy. The new regime continued to press for "equal rights," and Hitler put on a convincing show of being a man of peace. But on 14 October Germany walked out of the conference, left the League of Nations, denounced the Versailles disarmament clauses, reintroduced conscription, and began to triple the size of its army. One of Hitler's constant themes had been the iniquity of the Versailles treaty, and many thought that this explained his rise. As the *Manchester Guardian* saw it, "the Nazi revolution" was an outcome of "brooding over the wrongs of Germany." The Labour *Daily Herald* even welcomed his reintroduction of conscription as "bright with hope," a sign that "the poison of Versailles is at last draining from [Europe's] blood."[78]

So Hitler's arrival did not precipitate a change of heart in Britain. On the contrary, "collective security," appeasement and disarmament seemed ever more urgent. "There was no sense in rushing into alliance," thought the Prime Minister, MacDonald, in March 1933, "and making Germany feel that she was being threatened."[79] The Oxford Union—the undergraduate debating society, traditionally a nursery of politicians—voted in a much-reported debate a month after Hitler came to power to "refuse under any circumstance to fight for King and Country." The successful proposers argued that "the war to end war" had produced only unemployment and spending on armaments. In October 1933 the Labour Party conference supported a similar motion to "take no part in war and to resist it with the whole force of the Labour Movement." At a by-election in East Fulham on 25 October, just after Hitler had walked out of the disarmament conference, the Tories were beaten by a peace candidate— "a nightmare" to Baldwin. He nevertheless pledged air parity with Germany in 1934 and campaigned for a major increase in armaments in 1935 to keep up with Germany and Japan. "Our desire to lead the world towards disarmament by our example of unilateral disarmament has not succeeded," admitted the Defence White Paper. The Labour Party condemned it as "the merest scaremongering . . . to suggest that more millions of money needed to be spent on armaments," and for most of the decade Labour's views were confused and contradictory, though they were not alone in that.[80] Churchill hoped unrealistically that Hitler could be contained by a mixture of deterrence and concession—muscular appeasement rather than the flaccid kind—and that a strong Britain could "stand aside" from European conflicts: "I hope and trust that the French will look after their own safety, and that we shall be permitted to live our life in our island . . . we have to be strong enough to defend our neutrality."[81]

During the 1930s the hope that the League of Nations could police the world by moral influence collapsed. It began to unravel because of the unsatisfied ambitions of two of the victors of the First World War, Japan and Italy, as well as the resentment of one of the vanquished, Germany. In 1928 Japanese forces in northern China began to take control of Manchuria, a process which the league (in effect Britain) and the United States were unable to contain. In October 1935 Benito Mussolini, the Italian Fascist dictator, attacked the ancient and archaic African monarchy of Abyssinia (Ethiopia). Its emperor, Haile Selassie, appealed to the League of Nations, to the embarrassment of France and Britain. France considered Italy a potential ally in case of war with Germany. Ethiopia, and its gallant and picturesque monarch, came to embody all the ideals and hopes of peace and security through the league. The British League of Nations Union had recently held a "Peace Ballot" in which over 11 million people participated (30 percent of the eligible population) showing strong support for collective security, for disarmament, for stopping the arms trade, and for acting "by economic and non-military measures" against aggression (90 percent supported) and even "if necessary by military measures" (over 50 percent supported, though 26 percent definitely rejected this). The league did impose economic sanctions against Italy (including foie gras, but crucially not oil). The Royal Navy sent a fleet to the Mediterranean. But the outcome combined the worst of all worlds. Britain and France secretly arranged a deal to give Mussolini most of what he wanted while preserving a vestige of Abyssinian independence. When this became known in December 1935, there was a public and parliamentary outcry in Britain, and the deal was abandoned. Mussolini was now determined to conquer all of Abyssinia and also took the first steps towards alliance with Hitler. The League of Nations proved impotent: it was effectively the end of collective security, and the repercussions were felt round the world. Many smaller countries now retreated into strict neutrality. The British and French governments were unwilling to take effective measures against Mussolini: no one wanted a European war over Abyssinia, but Britain was amply strong enough to stop Mussolini by closing the Suez Canal. That it did not do so proved to the world, and most importantly to Hitler, that Britain, the world's greatest power, was not willing to take risks to defend international law.

Hitler seized the opportunity to send troops illegally into the Rhineland on 7 March 1936. He also denounced the Locarno Treaty. It began as a cautious dipping of the jackboot toe: a mere 3,000 troops crossed the Rhine, with orders to withdraw if the French reacted. This was the moment at which, legend has it—a legend encouraged by Hitler himself—the Nazi adventure could have been snuffed out: the *Führer* would have been humiliated, and the army might have overthrown him. But Hitler had adroitly accompanied his move with various peace offers, using the usual moral equivalence tactic of demanding that the Belgians and French demilitarize their frontiers too. No one in Britain or France—public, politicians or generals—wanted to pick up Hitler's gauntlet. Even Churchill hoped for a "peaceful and friendly solution."[82] For appeasers, the Rhineland was a hangover from the Versailles treaty and of French "militarism." MacDonald hoped that Hitler's bold action had taught the French a "severe lesson." The former Labour chancellor Philip Snowden muttered that the "damned French are at their old game of dragging this country behind them in the policy of encircling Germany."[83] Anthony Eden, the Foreign Secretary, proclaimed that it was "the appeasement of Europe as a whole that we have constantly before us," and that the government was eager to take up Hitler's peace offers—which never actually materialized. A government appraisal of the strategic situation concluded that Britain had too many commitments and could not contemplate going to war with any chance of success before 1939, or even 1942.[84]

Four months after the Rhineland invasion, in July 1936, a military uprising began in Spain. It turned into a three-year civil war between Nationalists and Republicans, and a pawn in a much larger strategic game. Mussolini, for reasons of prestige and strategic advantage, gave military help to the Nationalist rebels. For Hitler, it was a way of distracting the other powers from his own plans, and strengthening links with Mussolini. It also provided a live training ground for his new army and air force. The French socialist-led Popular Front government sympathized with its Frente Popular counterpart in Madrid, but the French right strongly supported the rebels. The Soviet Union cautiously gave some aid to the Spanish Republicans, largely to defend its reputation as leader of international progress. Stalin was beginning to "purge" his real or imagined enemies and this murderous paranoia was soon extended to Spain, where non-Communist Republicans were slaughtered. The Nationalists slaughtered even more, on a scale and with a degree of savagery unseen in western Europe since the French Revolution. Whitehall had little sympathy for either side, and all parties in Britain wanted to contain the conflict. Paris and London agreed on a policy of non-intervention, which

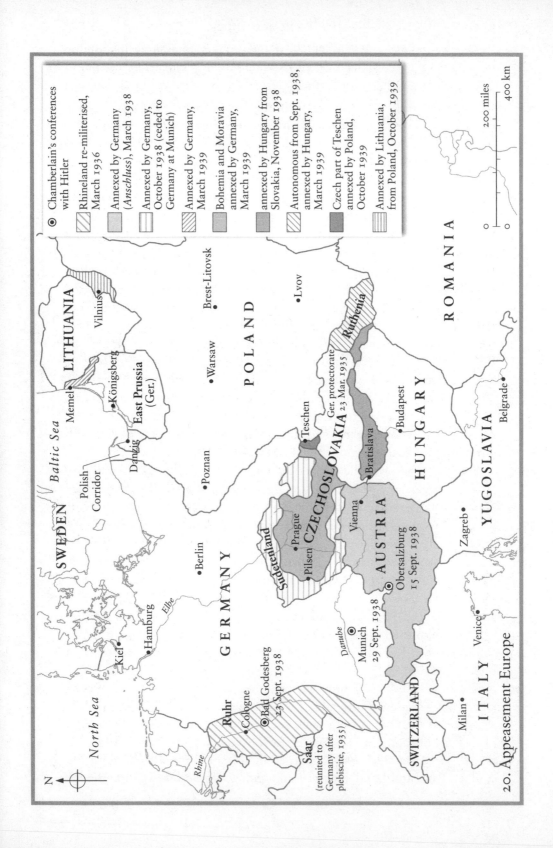

N

*North Sea*

SWEDEN

*Baltic Sea*

LITHUANIA

Vilnius •

Memel

Königsberg •

**East Prussia** (Ger.)

Danzig

Polish Corridor

• Poznan

• Warsaw

Brest-Litovsk •

POLAND

• Lvov

Teschen •

Ruthenia

Hamburg •

*Elbe*

• Berlin

GERMANY

Sudetenland

Prague •

CZECHOSLOVAKIA

Ger. protectorate 23 Mar. 1935

HUNGARY

Budapest •

Bratislava •

Kiel •

*Rhine*

Ruhr

Cologne •

◉Bad Godesberg 23 Sept. 1938

**Saar** (reunited to Germany after plebiscite, 1935)

*Danube*

◉ Munich 29 Sept. 1938

23 Sept. 1938

SWITZERLAND

Pilsen •

Vienna •

AUSTRIA

Obersalzburg 15 Sept. 1938 ◉

Milan •

**ITALY**

Venice •

Zagreb •

YUGOSLAVIA

Belgrade •

ROMANIA

◉ Chamberlain's conferences with Hitler

⧄ Rhineland re-militerised, March 1936

▨ Annexed by Germany (*Anschluss*), March 1938

▥ Annexed by Germany, October 1938 (ceded to Germany at Munich)

⧄ Annexed by Germany, March 1939

▨ Bohemia and Moravia annexed by Germany, March 1939

▨ annexed by Hungary from Slovakia, November 1938

⧄ Autonomous from Sept. 1938, annexed by Hungary, March 1939

▨ Czech part of Teschen annexed by Poland, October 1939

▥ Annexed by Lithuania, from Poland, October 1939

0        200 miles

0    200    400 km

20. Appeasement Europe

twenty-four other states accepted. A monitoring committee in London became an international bear-garden, and non-intervention became a sham, which only the British adhered to—even the French quietly shipped arms to the Republican side. But it provided a fig leaf of respectability and prevented open confrontation between the Great Powers. "Where humbug is the alternative to war," said one British diplomat, "it is impossible to place too high a value upon it."[85]

But outside worldly-wise diplomatic circles, the conflict acquired powerful emotional and ideological significance. Some 60,000 men from fifty countries, 80 percent of them Communists, volunteered for International Brigades to defend the Republic; 2,300 were from Britain, of whom 500 were killed. They were there, said one statement reminiscent of the First World War, "to defend our own homes, the homes of Britain" against "the aggressors"; and on their return they placed a wreath at the Cenotaph.[86] The whole English political spectrum was affected by what most saw as a struggle of democracy against dictatorship. Some, especially young intellectuals, saw it more starkly as a choice between Communism and Fascism, with old-style parliamentary liberalism irrelevant. But humanitarian concern for Spain crossed party lines and included Tories such as the Duchess of Atholl, who chaired the National Joint Committee for Spanish Relief.

The Abyssinian and Spanish crises created the sense of a Europe already gripped by conflict. Nearly everyone in England had supported peace and collective security, assumed to be a painless option. What if goodwill and disarmament did not work? The League of Nations Union lost members and influence, and faced painful choices. How far was it necessary, when faced with aggression, to apply economic sanctions, which might lead to war, or even to threaten military action? Peace activists split, often angrily. Many became more determinedly pacifist, some rather oddly advocating quasi-military training in non-violent resistance or psychological exercises including knitting, silence and folk-dancing. Some groups campaigned for unilateral British disarmament. The pacifist Peace Pledge Union, set up in May 1936 by Canon Dick Sheppard, quickly attracted 120,000 members, including prominent intellectuals such as Bertrand Russell, Aldous Huxley and Vera Brittain, who criticized "so-called peace lovers" who were not absolute pacifists.[87] The anti-war position united old-style humanitarian or religious idealists such as Arthur Ponsonby and the much-loved Labour leader, George Lansbury, socialists such as Harold Laski and Stafford Cripps, who blamed war on capitalism, and a variety of campaigners, including Great War veterans. Having rejected the Germanophobic propaganda of 1914–18, well-meaning progressives refused to see Hitler's Germany as truly evil. Like the generals, they were preparing for the last war.

Resistance to fascism was still only thought conceivable through collective security, and was assumed to be a common act by decent "like-minded countries." When Churchill organized a cross-party public meeting in October 1936 to back rearmament, it flopped.[88] But, although many countries participated enthusiastically in the League—Luxembourg, Czechoslovakia, Switzerland and Belgium were assiduous—collective security really meant Britain and France. Supporting collective security and rejecting British rearmament were not as complementary as idealists insisted. Although the tough-minded trade union leader Ernest Bevin attacked Lansbury at the 1935 party conference for "hawking his conscience round . . . asking to be told what to do with it," Labour politicians and newspapers adamantly opposed increased defence spending until 1937: "Not a single penny for this government's rearmament programme."[89] The new party leader, Clement Attlee, attacked the government for putting the country "permanently on a war basis" and having "absolutely no policy for peace." He declared: "Do not compete with the fascists in arms and they will not rearm." The *Manchester Guardian* attacked the government's programme as "£400 million for death."[90]

The peace movement and appeasement were galvanized by fear, which crossed political boundaries. Aerial bombardment with poisoned gas—"the rain of death"—was the recurring nightmare. Baldwin had warned "the man in the street" in November 1932 that "there is no power on earth that can protect him from being bombed . . . the bomber will always get through." The Left Book Club sold 100,000 copies of books on protection against air raids. Extreme fears were encouraged by an odd combination of propagandists. Advocates of air force expansion—most famously the Italian Giulio Douhet, who had keen disciples in the RAF—stressed the potency of air attack. A few tons of gas, experts claimed, could wipe out a whole city. They urged the need for a big air force independent of the army and navy (whose own commanders were sceptical). The message was taken up in many lurid works of fiction and cinema in several languages, such as *The Poison War, Chaos, War Upon Women, Empty Victory* and most famously H. G. Wells's *The Shape of Things to Come* (1933), which predicted a war over Danzig in 1940 and was filmed with striking music by Arthur Bliss. In *The Black Death* (1934) poison gas kills everyone in England except a few holidaymakers in the Cheddar Caves. Pacifists and disarmers hammered the message home.[91] Bertrand Russell predicted in 1936 that "London . . . will be one vast raving bedlam, the hospitals will be stormed, traffic will cease, the homeless will shriek for help . . . the government . . . will be swept away by an avalanche of terror."[92] The wealthy Labour MP Stafford Cripps financed an anti-rearmament film in 1936, seen by over 2 million people, reiterating, with a stressful musical score by the young pacifist Benjamin Britten, that "there is no defence against air attack," and urging people to write to their MP to demand that "the governments of the world should get together to make war impossible."[93] The British government's Joint Planning Committee warned in 1936 of an immediate knock-out blow from the air in case of war with Germany, with 20,000 casualties within hours.[94] Daylight bombing, mainly by German aircraft, of the undefended Basque town of Guernica in April 1937, which killed several hundred people, showed these horrors in action and seemed to justify the most pessimistic assumptions.

Despite the vehemence of the peace movement, the mainly Conservative National Government, nominally headed by MacDonald, announced expansion of the RAF in 1934, and his successor, Baldwin, began major rearmament in 1936: war, he said, was not "inevitable," but it was "a ghastly possibility and it is our duty to fight it in every way we can." Planning also began for rationing, mass evacuation, and a national hospital service to deal with millions of expected casualties—the first steps towards a national health service.[95] Britain had to face the possibility of simultaneous war with Germany, Italy and Japan—"something greater than we have ever done before."[96] A shipbuilding programme aimed at a "two-ocean fleet": five battleships were laid down in 1937 to Japan's one, and the world's first purpose-built aircraft carrier, *Ark Royal*, was begun in 1938. The same year the navy introduced ASDIC (an echo-sounding submarine detection system). The chancellor, Neville Chamberlain, shifted spending and strategy towards the RAF, whose budget overtook the army by 1937 and the navy by 1938. Bomber Command, a deterrent force, was set up in 1936 and heavy-bomber designs were commissioned, including the Wellington and the Lancaster.[97] The government then shifted funding towards air defence. This was partly because fighters were cheaper and produced more impressive statistics of RAF expansion, but also because a revolution in aircraft technology (epitomized by the Supermarine Spitfire, based on a racing design, and the Rolls-Royce Merlin engine—neither of which was originally expected to amount to much) combined with the invention of radar (successfully tried in 1935 and rapidly developed) made it more feasible to detect and intercept bombers. Fighter Command was given clear priority in 1938.

The shift in spending to the RAF had serious consequences. Though it still outbuilt every navy, including the United States and Japan, the Royal

Navy's ability to deter or oppose Japan while simultaneously dominating European waters was reduced. The army was downgraded—there was to be no repetition of the Western Front, and even the term "BEF" was officially avoided. The RAF and the Royal Navy had some of the best equipment in the world; but the army did not, and its weakness in vital weapons such as tanks would be felt throughout most of the Second World War. Experts said that the French army could cope with the Germans unaided. The priority was to defend "our own Empire or Flanders." But the true aim was not to fight at all, and to negotiate a general settlement with Hitler, backed up by a deterrent air force and sweetened with economic and colonial concessions.

How would Hitler respond? Baldwin thought that "none of us know what goes on in that strange man's mind," but *Mein Kampf* suggested that he wanted to "move East, and if he should move East I should not break my heart."[98] The Foreign Office lost its single copy of the original unexpurgated edition of *Mein Kampf*, but working out Hitler's mind had become a preoccupation well outside Whitehall. Books purporting to explain him (and Stalin too, for that matter) had become big sellers: *Mein Kampf* in translation was selling 50,000 copies a year in the late 1930s. But Hitler (unlike Stalin) was rarely even grudgingly admired, except by a few eccentrics such as Unity Mitford. He was overwhelmingly disliked, feared, and also (like Mussolini) mocked, as a house painter and even a clown—a way of relieving fear: he was just "a stubby little Austrian," wrote the *Daily Herald* in 1933, "with a flabby handshake, shifty brown eyes, and a Charlie Chaplin moustache."[99]

Nevertheless, a procession of progressive notables went to sound him out in 1936. Arnold Toynbee pronounced him "sincere" and passed on his offer to send troops to help defend Singapore.[100] Lloyd George was much impressed by "the greatest German of the age." Lansbury was delighted to find Hitler "a total abstainer, non-smoker [and] vegetarian [who] likes children and old people," and he wrote fulsomely of his desire for peace— "Germany needs peace . . . Nobody understand this better than Herr Hitler." If given a fair share of "the world's resources and markets" he would cooperate in "discussions on how to abolish war by abolishing armaments."[101] Hitler was adroit at playing up to such wishful thinking. Though Lansbury expressed them naïvely, similar ideas were at first not uncommon and were also echoed in the policies of successive Conservative ministers. Anthony Eden, the Foreign Secretary, thought Hitler "sincere" in wanting disarmament. Labour favoured a "constructive policy of appeasement." Few in Britain could take Nazi ideology seriously, assuming that *Mein Kampf* was largely bombast.[102] Many sought to find out what Hitler "really" wanted. He had told them: but a mixture of decency, prejudice, fear and self-deception stopped most ears.

Two men who shared the general deafness were Neville Chamberlain, who became Prime Minister on 28 May 1937, and the pious and gentlemanly Lord Halifax, who became Foreign Secretary in February 1938. Chamberlain, afflicted with an unimaginative brass-tacks kind of rationalism combined with a social reformer's aversion to arms spending and a sincere loathing of war, was convinced that he must and could do business with Hitler and Mussolini. What was needed was to obtain a list of Germany's real demands—rabble-rousing aside—"run through their complaints and claims with a pencil,"[103] and strike a deal for a "general settlement" of Europe, including disarmament. Halifax was sent in November 1937 to sound the Nazis out. He met Hitler, who advised him to sort out India by shooting Gandhi and a few hundred nationalists, and made it perfectly plain that he was not interested in anything Britain could offer. Halifax noted that "we are not talking the same language." But he—like Chamberlain—was incapable of drawing the unpalatable conclusion: Hitler inhabited an alien mental and moral universe in which it was possible to want war, not peace. Halifax decided that a policy of "reassurance" was needed. Chamberlain wrote to his sister (his principal confidant) that we should say to Germany: "Give us satisfactory assurances that you won't use force to deal with the Austrians and Czecho-Slovakians and we will give you similar assurances that we won't use force to prevent the changes you want."[104]

Having sized up his opponents, Hitler invaded Austria in March 1938 and proclaimed its union with Germany, breaking the Versailles treaty. Chamberlain hoped that things would "settle down" so that he could "start peace talks again." Hitler began to make barely concealed preparations to attack Czechoslovakia, the last democracy east of Switzerland. The Treaty of Versailles, mainly to give it defensible frontiers, had included the largely German-speaking Sudetenland, whose ethnic nationalists had been a pernicious nuisance since Habsburg days. They were happy to provide Hitler with a pretext to rescue them from Czech oppression by "always demand[ing] so much that we cannot be satisfied." The British, including Churchill, were taken in, thinking that ethnic grievances were the cause of the crisis and that the Germans had an arguable case. But the real reason, Hitler told his generals, was to "clear the rear for advancing against . . . Britain and France," as the Czechs, who had a large and well-equipped army, were France's allies. He envisaged taking the Low Countries, knocking out France, and expelling Britain from the Continent. In the meantime he was accelerating military, naval and air preparations.[105] The French prime minister, Édouard Daladier, came to warn Whitehall that Hitler was far more dangerous than Napoleon—"awful rubbish," thought the Foreign Office.[106]

Whitehall had always deplored France's various east-European alliances as a provocation to Germany. It regarded as madness action on behalf of Czechoslovakia, widely regarded as one of the Versailles treaty's mistakes, "a country which we can neither get at nor spell," and which, thought the Permanent Under-Secretary at the Foreign Office, Sir Alexander Cadogan, "is not worth the bones of a single British Grenadier."[107] Moreover, a simultaneous crisis began with a new Japanese assault on China in 1937. Chamberlain and Halifax easily convinced themselves that a way must be found to let the Sudeten Germans have autonomy, even if they joined Germany and made Czechoslovakia indefensible. The mainstream Foreign Office view, expressed by Cadogan, was that "as long as Hitler could *pretend* he was incorporating Germans in the Reich we could *pretend* that he had a case."[108] Halifax confided to a German envoy that his dearest ambition was that "one day the Führer will be seen entering Buckingham Palace at the side of the King," amid cheering crowds.[109] Chamberlain invited himself to Berchtesgaden on 15 September 1938— only the second time he had ever flown, and the only time a Prime Minister has ever embarked on such a dramatic personal peace mission—to tell Hitler that he could have the Sudetenland in return for a four-power guarantee of the new Czech borders. The *Daily Herald*, the popular Labour paper, declared that he had "the sympathy of opinion everywhere, irrespective of Party." On 22 September he again met Hitler (whom he found "entirely undistinguished"[110]) to seal the bargain.

To his surprise and irritation, Hitler began tearing away the diplomatic fig leaves by threatening an immediate invasion. Not only Churchill now, but Robert Cecil and even Labour Party leaders favoured a stronger line.[111] The French began mobilization. Whitehall informed Berlin that Britain "would not guarantee that they would not do the same"—almost a clarion call by Chamberlain's standards—and the navy and air force prepared for action. But it was made clear to the French—while trying not to "offend France beyond what was absolutely necessary"—that Britain could give negligible military aid.[112] French and British intelligence grossly overestimated the German army and air force, claiming that it could cause 50,000 civilian casualties in Britain within twenty-four hours, while the RAF "would have been wiped out in three weeks." Air raid shelters were dug and gas masks distributed. Over half a million people volunteered for Air Raid Precautions. "Everyone is calm, resolute and cheerful," wrote Vita Sackville-West. "One hears more jokes than ever, although they all realize quite well what it means. I do respect the English, for all their faults." Not all were so stoical: Virginia and Leonard Woolf sat gloomily discussing death, despair and "the inevitable end of civilisation" with Kingsley Martin, editor of the *New Statesman*, who hinted at suicide (poison pills had become a fashion item).[113] On 27 September Chamberlain made his characteristically disheartening broadcast lamenting the "nightmare" of war over "a far away country of which we know nothing" and "a quarrel which has already been settled in principle." When Hitler suggested a conference of himself, Chamberlain, Mussolini and Daladier at Munich on 29 September, Chamberlain leapt at it. His constant hope was that "the longer the war is put off the less likely it is to come at all."[114]

"Munich" and "appeasement" are now potent insults in our political vocabulary, synonyms for myopia, betrayal and cowardice. At the time, Munich seemed the only chance of saving the world from catastrophe, and "appeasement" was a very positive term in diplomatic vocabulary.[115] People cheered, from the benches of the House of Commons to the streets of Munich, where they threw flowers and shouted "Heil Chamberlain!" Even Churchill wished him well, as did the Labour and Liberal leaders. Mussolini produced a "compromise" plan (drafted by the Germans), which was accepted after a few cosmetic concessions by Hitler—notably that he would take over the Sudetenland in stages under international supervision. Chamberlain ignored Daladier throughout. After the deal was done, he asked for a private meeting with Hitler and produced a declaration of "the desire of our two peoples never to go to war with one another again," and promising "consultation . . . to remove possible sources of differences [and] ensure the peace of Europe." This was his longed-for "general settlement." A surprised Hitler signed. He was later ashamed at having flinched at the threat of war and angry at having been deprived, as he saw it, of the prestige of a military victory—"that fellow Chamberlain has spoiled my entry into Prague." Ironically, his popularity and prestige benefited enormously, for he had triumphed without the war the German people and the German army feared. Thereafter he would act without constraint: "Our enemies are small worms. I saw them in Munich."[116]

Could Hitler have been stopped in 1938? Would his critics in the army, alarmed by his recklessness, have overthrown him? If war had actually begun, could Germany have been defeated? Czechoslovakia was not the ideal issue for making a stand. It is surprising that Daladier and even Chamberlain contemplated going to war at all. The transfer of the Sudetenland, arguably an act of self-determination, had already been agreed, so the dispute was only over procedure—"a few days one way or other in a time-table!" protested the Canadian High Commissioner.[117] Could such a conflict have rallied opinion in Britain, the Dominions and France, let alone America? Hitler, dismissing his generals' pessimism, would not have backed down; and France and Britain would have had to fight. Chamberlain's intervention, the Munich conference and Hitler's loss of nerve really did prevent war. Could Chamberlain reasonably have opted for war when there appeared a peaceful alternative? Arguably, September 1938 was either too late or too early for a confrontation. Too late because the Rhineland, the jumping-off point for invasion, had been lost, so the French army had no strategy for invading Germany. Too early, because appeasement had not yet been discredited: Hitler insisted that the Sudetenland was his last territorial claim in Europe, and many wanted to believe him. Also too early because British and French rearmament on land and in the air was in its infancy: only in April 1938, sweeping aside Treasury objections, had Chamberlain's government launched a plan to build 12,000 combat aircraft by 1940. At the time of Munich, radar defence was incomplete, there were few Hurricanes and no Spitfires in service, and few bombers capable of damaging, or even reaching, Germany.[118] All believed that they could do little or nothing to help the encircled Czechs.

The idea of British and French weakness and vulnerability is ingrained into our ideas of this period, and was certainly in the forefront of the minds of many politicians, military leaders and the public. But from the German viewpoint the situation looked very different, as Hitler was being emphatically told by his military and civilian advisers.[119] The Czechs had a powerful modern army and the Russians were willing to give them at least some help. The Czechs could have done serious damage to the German army and air force, making it impossible to launch a rapid attack in the west. The French army was still by far the largest in Europe, backed up by the financial and material resources of the British Empire protected by the world's most powerful navy. The German army in 1938 was not capable of inflicting a decisive defeat on the French. Despite fears of a devastating knock-out blow from the air, the Luftwaffe was outnumbered by the combined forces of Britain, France and Czechoslovakia, and its aircraft could not even reach England from German bases. In short, Nazi Germany was risking a long, unwinnable war without allies against a coalition with access to the world economy. Hitler accepted the "extraordinarily generous settlement" offered at Munich and "almost certainly saved his regime from disaster."[120] The Allies were better armed by 1940. But so were the Germans: much better.

Waving Hitler's signature presaging "peace for our time," Chamberlain returned to England as perhaps the most popular man in the world, mobbed by cheering crowds, and receiving 40,000 mainly congratulatory letters and hundreds of presents. He was suggested for a Nobel Peace Prize. Portugal erected a statue on behalf of "Grateful Mothers." Blackpool Football Club offered to build twelve houses for ex-servicemen in his honour. The peace activist Lord Ponsonby spoke of "the unspeakable relief of millions." There were some dissenting voices, most famously Churchill's: "This is only the first sip, the first foretaste of a bitter cup." Events soon confirmed this grim prediction, pricking the Chamberlain bubble. *Kristallnacht*, organized mob violence against Jews in Germany, took place on 9 November 1938. "I must say Hitler never helps," grumbled one Tory MP.[121] Early in 1939 the Spanish Republic finally succumbed, and on 13 March the German army occupied Prague, violating the Munich agreement. A Gallup poll showed 87 percent now favoured an alliance of Britain, France and Russia, though 55 percent still trusted Chamberlain.[122] Much of the press continued to favour appeasement, though it was probably lagging behind public opinion. Only the *Daily Telegraph* had consistently opposed, earning its proprietor a dressing down from Chamberlain.

The left too was far from resolute, despite Bevin and a growing anti-fascist current. Kingsley Martin thought that Britain "cannot stand up to Germany . . . We must be prepared to sing smaller in the world." The Labour frontbencher Herbert Morrison thought that it might be wise to let Germany "have a run in South East Europe"; and an editor of the *Daily Herald* admitted being "prepared to eat a lot of mud to avoid war."[123] In April 1939, 87 percent of Labour MPs, with Attlee "shaking with rage,"[124] opposed the Military Training Act as a step towards conscription—anathema even to those who had reluctantly accepted rearmament.[125]

Chamberlain told the Commons, however, that "we must arm ourselves to the teeth,"[126] and the government doubled defence spending from 1938 to 1939, further fuelling economic recovery. Although weakened by the Depression and by earlier defence cuts, the aircraft, engineering and shipbuilding industries were among the strongest in the world.[127] Production for export was slashed. Air defences took shape, with a chain of radar stations being built covering the southern and eastern coasts, and by the summer of 1939 nearly all biplanes had been replaced by monoplanes, mostly Hawker Hurricanes. The navy was outbuilding every other in the world, and by 1939 it had more battleships, aircraft carriers and cruisers than any other country.

Intelligence reports arrived early in 1939 that Germany was planning imminent surprise attacks on Holland and even Britain. This was false information, fabricated by conservative anti-Nazi elements in Germany in the hope of goading the West into action. They certainly galvanized Whitehall, strangely confident as rearmament accelerated. The Prime Minister surprised the Commons on 6 February with a sudden pledge of support to France—"Really Chamberlain is an astonishing and perplexing old boy," sighed the MP Harold Nicolson.[128] "We have at last got on top of the dictators," wrote Chamberlain to his sister on 19 February. "Of course, that doesn't mean I want to bully them."[129] Joint military planning belatedly began, and it was decided to expand the army's Field Force from two to nineteen divisions. Offers of support were showered on eastern Europe, especially Romania (important for its oil) and Poland. Poland was the crux, as the Nazis repeated their Sudetenland tactic, using as a pretext for aggression Danzig (an international city) and the corridor through German territory connecting Poland with the sea. On 31 March 1939 Chamberlain told the Commons that Britain and France would aid Poland if its independence were endangered.[130] This did not mean that he was resolved to face an inevitable war. He still hoped to maintain peace by combining deterrence (building bombers and finding allies) with appeasement (offering large slices of Africa and economic favours).

Deterrence was also the aim of the unenthusiastic Franco-British attempt in August 1939 to explore alliance with the Soviet Union, even today a controversial issue. The left had long been keen to cooperate with what it considered "this most peaceful Great Power," and so was Churchill. Neither Chamberlain nor Stalin had any reason to trust the other. It was not clear—and is still not—what the crafty and paranoid Stalin really wanted and whether he would or could have provided effective aid in case of war, having recently slaughtered his senior military commanders. Moreover, for obvious reasons neither Poland nor Romania wanted the Red Army on their soil. Stalin seems to have been keen on promoting a war between Germany and the Western Powers, and on 24 August the Soviet Union astonished the world by announcing a non-aggression pact with Nazi Germany: all the "isms," quipped a Foreign Office official, had become "wasms." This may be what Stalin had intended all along: negotiations with France and Britain being bargaining counters to get a good deal from Hitler, promote a destructive war among the "imperialist" states, seize territory, and gain time to prepare for war with Japan. Soviet exports of food and raw materials to Germany rose by 2,000 percent. This set the seal on Hitler's war.

It began when he attacked Poland on 1 September. Mussolini tried to repeat the Munich ploy by proposing another conference, and Chamberlain and the French vacillated. A furious House of Commons, in an exceptionally stormy session, pressed the flustered Prime Minister (sounding to one witness like "a dithering old dodderer"[131]) to act. When Labour's deputy leader, Arthur Greenwood, began by saying "Speaking for the Labour Party . . . ," the Tory Leo Amery shouted: "Speak for England!" Greenwood did: "I wonder how long we are prepared to vacillate at a time when Britain, and all that Britain stands for, and human civilization are in peril." The left-wing pacifist James Maxton called for peace and was shouted down. Greenwood told Chamberlain quietly that unless he sent an ultimatum to Germany "neither you nor I nor anyone else on earth will be able to hold the House of Commons."[132] The ultimatum was delivered at 9 a.m. on 3 September demanding an immediate German withdrawal from Poland, and at 11 a.m. the country was officially at war. Most London children had already been evacuated, as had the animals from the Zoo.

When Chamberlain admitted mournfully to the Commons—rallying calls were not in his nature—that "everything that I have worked for, everything that I have hoped for, everything that I have believed in during my public life, has crashed into ruins," he could have been speaking of the whole country's experience since 1918, and especially that of its political and intellectual elites. The peace movement was the largest popular mass movement in Britain between the wars.[133] Reconciliation with Germany had been seen as morally and materially necessary. War had been rejected as dooming civilization, and rearmament as barbarity. It seemed impossible that anyone, even the most brutal dictator, did not, deep down, share these sentiments. "Appeasement" was this belief in practice: seeking the reasons for German discontents and working together to resolve them peacefully. This might have worked—or at least conflict might have been contained or limited—had it not been for the Great Depression and the rise of the Nazis. Hitler crystallized and gave direction to all that was sick in German society. Wishful thinking and fear—not admiration for or sympathy with Nazism, which hardly existed in England—then caused "appeasement" to continue until Hitler's repeated aggression made it irrelevant and finally contemptible.

Chamberlain and Baldwin, recently so popular and trusted, were made scapegoats. The public mood was soon to be articulated in one of the most influential political tracts of modern times, *Guilty Men* (July 1940), by Michael Foot and others, which sold 200,000 copies, many from barrows in the street. It did much to shape retrospective memory of the interwar period. Appeasement was repackaged as a squalid sell-out by a few cowardly and scheming (mainly Tory) politicians—"the MacDonald–

Baldwin ascendancy ... this regime of little men." Baldwin (who had bravely initiated rearmament) and Chamberlain were the main villains. The unpreparedness of Britain for war was exaggerated and the huge rearmament programme dismissed as Tory misinformation. The peace movement was minimized as a few "half-baked ... fools and fanatics," and the Labour and Liberal politicians who had been passionate opponents of rearmament—who included Foot himself—were absolved.[134] This view of the 1930s served both Churchill and Labour, and it became the consensus view. It marked a fundamental change in Labour's positioning— putting itself forward as the party of the nation and of resistance to Hitler. "Attlee's victory in 1945 owed a lot to the fact that the left constructed a myth of betrayal around which the British could unite."[135]

The collapse into war of the hopeful vision of international reconciliation to which most English people had clung since 1918 inevitably raises the question of whether different choices might have succeeded in averting the catastrophe. A closer relationship with France, bedevilled throughout the interwar period by mistrust and misunderstanding, might have deterred Germany—rulers, people and army—from embarking on aggressive adventures: but Lloyd George had backed out of alliance in 1920. A tougher policy of deterrence would necessarily have been part of such a policy: but enlightened opinion strongly opposed it, and no one advocated a new alliance with France until 1939, when it was too late to head Germany off. Once Hitler had embarked on a plan of aggression deliberately aiming at war, conquest and genocide, he could only have been stopped by force. Politicians, pundits and public in Britain and France grossly overestimated German strength and underestimated Hitler's monstrous ambitions—an enfeebling combination of errors. They wanted to believe that he was a normal human being and, despite his bombast, a politician who had rational aims, with whom a deal could be reached, and who would keep his word. Hitler encouraged this illusion by astutely seizing on issues arising from the discredited Versailles treaty—the Rhineland, Austria, the Sudetenland, the Polish Corridor—that well-meaning people took a long time to recognize as only pretexts for aggression.

Britain was militarily, economically and politically far stronger than many of its politicians and intellectuals recognized, but thanks to them we have been conditioned by a conventional historical narrative to think of interwar Britain, the greatest world power, as weak and vulnerable. As we have seen, the Czech crisis of 1938 brought war close while the Nazi regime and its military power were still shaky. An authoritative opinion is that "in 1938, it is highly doubtful whether Germany would have achieved the kind of victory won in 1940."[136] Well-meaning determination to avoid war only delayed it and increased its ultimate cost. So "appeasement" became a dirty word: but only hindsight makes it possible to distinguish it from things we today approve of—"engagement," negotiation, peaceful compromise. At the time, there was a marked lack of agreement or consistency in suggesting alternatives to Chamberlain's policy.[137]

By 1939 most people in England, Britain, the empire and France had come to accept the fearful necessity of war. Only 2.2 percent registered as conscientious objectors. Some even felt a kind of relief: "We've been waiting a whole year, not knowing if there'll be a war or not. I want a knock at Hitler," said a young Lancashire woman.[138] "Whatever status Britain has in the world today," wrote one historian five decades later, "stems ineluctably from the course of action she followed in 1939, and from the revolt in the House of Commons and Cabinet on September 2 . . . which stemmed in turn from the degree to which British opinion accepted that . . . pride, self-respect, honour and very existence were bound up with the fulfilment of Britain's guarantee."[139] On the first day of war, Churchill, brought into the Cabinet, struck a different note from Chamberlain's lamentations: "We are fighting to save the whole world from the pestilence of Nazi tyranny and in defence of all that is most sacred to man."[140] And so they were.

# CHAPTER 17

# The Edge of the Abyss, 1939–1945

*Hitler knows that he will have to break us in this island or lose the war. If we can stand up to him, all Europe may be free and the life of the world may move forward into broad, sunlit uplands. But if we fail, then the whole world . . . will sink into the abyss of a new dark age . . . Let us therefore brace ourselves to our duties, and so bear ourselves that, if the British Empire and its Commonwealth last for a thousand years, men will still say: "This was their finest hour."*

Winston Churchill, House of Commons, 18 June 1940

## THE LAST EUROPEAN WAR

*Either the German Reich or this country has got to go under, and not only under, but right under.*

Sir Robert Vansittart, Foreign Office memorandum,
6 September 1940[1]

When war began, London, Paris and Berlin thought they knew what to expect. There might be an attempt at an aerial knock-out blow, so warning sirens sounded in London as Chamberlain announced war, and two RAF planes accidentally shot each other down. Mountains of sandbags appeared; pillar boxes were smeared with gas-detecting paint; papier-mâché coffins were stockpiled; cities were blacked out. Prisoners were released, and the sick sent home to release hospital beds. Family pets were put down as 3.5 million people moved house in a few weeks, half of them under the government's official evacuation scheme, codenamed "Pied Piper." Children clutching gas masks, labelled with their names and schools, and supposedly equipped with a change of underwear, a warm pullover, soap, flannel and toothbrush, handkerchiefs and a pencil, were evacuated from the industrial cities—more than a third of their children in total[2]—a vast and often fraught upheaval that has entered English folklore (though French and German children went through similar or worse experiences too). The paintings were removed from the National Gallery and stored in slate mines in north Wales. Billingsgate fish market was dispersed, spreading stinking fish and profane language widely over the nation.[3] But no bombers appeared: Britain was out of range. Poland, as all except perhaps the Poles knew, was lost. The French had no intention of attacking Germany's western frontier, which was defended only by middle-aged reservists with three days' ammunition and no air cover: the Allies had a superiority of 3:1 in men and 5:1 in artillery, and all the German tanks were in Poland.[4] But the Allies sat tight. They had digested the bloody lessons of 1916–17: the Maginot Line, the West Wall (or Siegfried Line) and strong Belgian fortifications ruled out breakthroughs. In September, after crushing Poland, Hitler offered a compromise peace, which was refused.

If the Germans attacked, all were confident they would be held: neutral Belgium and Holland were the obvious targets, and when the Germans invaded, the French army and the BEF (as it was popularly called, echoing the First World War) would rush in to block them. A stalemate would ensue, favouring the Allies. Chamberlain proclaimed that "Hitler has missed the bus" and even told his sister that the war might be over by spring 1940.[5] "Economic warfare" was the watchword. The Royal Navy dominated the oceans—the German naval commander, Admiral Erich Raeder, said that if forced into action his fleet could only "go down with dignity."[6] Seapower gave Britain access to world resources, while cutting off Germany. German strength would decline as it was deprived of food and raw materials. Its imports were duly cut by two-thirds.[7] Precision bombing by the RAF, if and when used, would multiply its problems. Allied strength would meanwhile grow: the British army was swelling with conscripts, the forces of the two empires would rally, and the rearmament programmes begun in 1936 would reach completion in 1941–42. Italy and Japan had not joined Germany. In time, the United States might join the Allies. So Germany would be defeated no later than 1943 or 1944—unless Hitler fell earlier (a revolution in Germany was the great hope of the left). The French propaganda slogan "We shall win because we are the stronger" was not as absurd as it later seemed. In total population and economic resources, France and Britain outweighed Germany: their combined populations were 90 million, compared with the German-Austrian 76 million; their GDP totalled $470m, compared with $375m. And in addition to this they had their two empires, rich in food, oil, metals, rubber and manpower. Thanks to hasty rearmament, the Allies were more than a match for Germany on land, both in quantity and in quality:

they had some 3,000 tanks to the Germans' 2,500, and French tanks were more powerful. The Luftwaffe, however, was markedly superior to the Allies in total aircraft, with twice the number of bombers.[8] But combined Allied aircraft production quickly overtook that of Germany. In both Britain and France, public opinion seemed resolute—almost certainly more so than in Germany.

Both sides considered trying to break the stalemate—nicknamed the "Bore War" (later "Phoney War"). Russia's pact with Germany upset Allied calculations, and the French even urged the demented idea of bombing Russian oilfields—Chamberlain, who thought the Hitler-Stalin friendship would not last, said no. Scandinavia seemed crucial: about a third of Germany's total iron-ore supply came from Sweden, via the Norwegian port of Narvik, which the Allies were preparing to block. So on 9 April 1940 the Germans, to everyone's surprise, invaded Norway by sea and air. Allied counter-attacks started badly on land, though a large part of the Germany navy was sunk and 200 of their aircraft destroyed. After parliamentary criticism on 7–8 May Chamberlain decided to form a National Government; but the Labour Party refused to serve under him. The situation was transformed overnight by a sudden German attack on Holland, Belgium and France beginning at 5:35 a.m. on 10 May. Churchill (ironically, largely responsible for the Norwegian operation) became Prime Minister that same afternoon at the age of sixty-five.

This now seems providential. "I felt as if I had been walking with destiny," Churchill famously wrote later, "and that all my past life had been but a preparation for this hour and for this trial."[9] But Churchill was a highly divisive figure who inspired strong feelings—negative as well as positive—inside the political class and in the country. There had been a real possibility of the Foreign Secretary, Lord Halifax, being appointed: Chamberlain and the Conservative Party preferred him, so did the Labour leadership, so did the king, and so did the senior civil service—"the mere thought of Churchill as Prime Minister sent a chill down the spines of the staff at 10 Downing Street . . . and throughout Whitehall."[10] But Churchill tacitly refused to serve under Halifax, who backed out. Two-thirds of the new government had served under Chamberlain, who remained as quasi–Deputy Prime Minister; Halifax remained at the Foreign Office, and the Labour leader, Clement Attlee, became Lord Privy Seal. Foreign diplomats noticed that many Tory MPs, unlike Labour, were not cheering Churchill in the House—when Chamberlain (still party leader) was told, he ensured that they did. A Home Intelligence Report on 21 May 1940 concluded that "the belief that Britain will triumph eventually is universal."[11]

The German surprise attack on France was an act of desperation. Hitler and his commanders shared the Allied view that Germany would lose a long war and so decided they must shorten it "even if the operation had only a 10 percent chance of success," said their chief of staff.[12] The plan was to thrust through the wooded Ardennes to cut behind the Allied armies advancing into Belgium. The Germans too had learned lessons from the First World War, but those of 1918: the power of surprise, rapidity, tanks and aircraft. The Allied air forces, committed further north, did not detect or attack the fifty-mile traffic jams in the narrow Ardennes lanes, created by 134,000 marching soldiers, 1,200 tanks and thousands of horses and carts. By the time the Allies realized this was more than a feint, it was too late: the Germans, supported by 1,000 aircraft, had seized bridges at Sedan and on 13 May crossed the wide River Meuse. The Allied air forces tried to bomb the vital bridges, but their slow light bombers were easy meat: forty of the seventy-one RAF bombers were lost, among the highest casualty rates it has ever suffered.

By 15 May seven armoured "Panzer" divisions were on the loose in France. The French army's mobile reserve had previously been rushed north into Holland, so there was nothing in the Germans' way. The French prime minister, Paul Reynaud, rang his friend Churchill at 7:30 a.m. saying, "We are defeated; we have lost the battle." Churchill promised to fly over to "have a talk," thinking at first that Reynaud was exaggerating— "it was ridiculous to think that France could be conquered by 120 tanks."[13] In Paris the next evening, wreathed in cigar smoke, he tried to "revive the spirits" of French ministers by promising that Britain would fight on, and would bomb German towns and burn their crops and forests. Indeed, he had already ordered bombing of German cities. But he also quietly ordered preliminary planning for a possible evacuation of the BEF.[14]

The Allied armies, trained for static warfare, lacking information and effective leadership, sometimes panicky, their communications and supply lines disrupted, could not halt the German rush. Hundreds of tanks and aircraft ran out of fuel and ammunition. "This is like some ridiculous nightmare," wrote a British officer in his diary. "Our communications have gone . . . The Germans have taken every risk—criminally foolish risks—and they have got away with it."[15] Hitler too was panicking: General Heinz Guderian, too bold in pressing ahead, was temporarily sacked.[16] The Panzers were vulnerable to a pincer attack from the north and the south, which would cut them off as they were trying to cut off the Allies. The French wanted the BEF, as yet less involved in the fighting, to take the lead by attacking from the north. But the British were now fighting in Belgium, making an about-turn dangerous, especially as the Belgian army was flagging. The best the BEF managed was on 21 May near Arras, when an armoured brigade gave General Erwin Rommel's Panzer division a fright by tearing into its supply columns and slaughtering some poorly

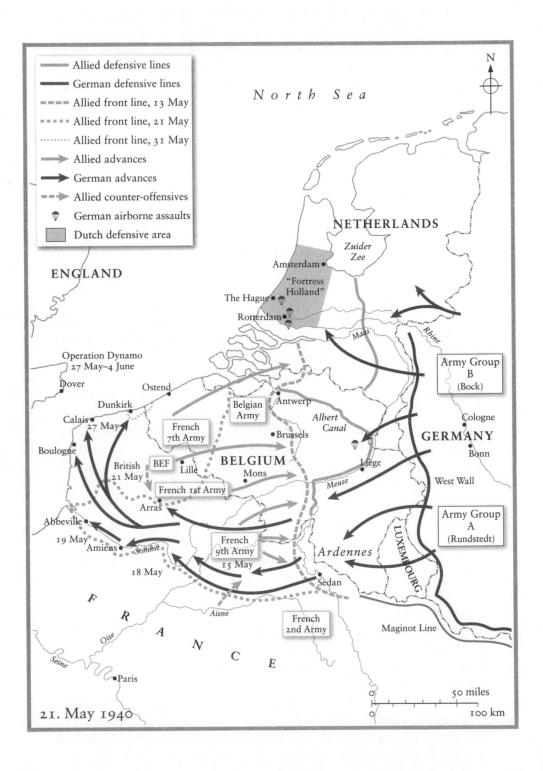

Allied defensive lines
German defensive lines
Allied front line, 13 May
Allied front line, 21 May
Allied front line, 31 May
Allied advances
German advances
Allied counter-offensives
German airborne assaults
Dutch defensive area

North Sea

N

ENGLAND

NETHERLANDS

Zuider
Zee

Amsterdam

"Fortress
Holland"

The Hague

Rotterdam

Maas

Rhine

Army Group
B
(Bock)

Operation Dynamo
27 May–4 June

Dover

Ostend

Dunkirk

27 May

Calais

Boulogne

British
21 May

BEF

Lille

Arras

Abbeville

19 May

Amiens

Somme

18 May

Belgian
Army

Antwerp

Albert
Canal

French
7th Army

Brussels

BELGIUM

Mons

French 1st Army

French
9th Army

15 May

Ardennes

Liège

Meuse

Sedan

Aisne

French
2nd Army

Cologne

GERMANY

Bonn

West Wall

Army Group
A
(Rundstedt)

LUXEMBOURG

Maginot Line

F

R

A

N

C

E

Oise

Seine

Paris

21. May 1940

50 miles

100 km

trained SS infantry. But it lost most of its tanks and withdrew, short of fuel, food and ammunition.

The BEF kept fighting, and largely maintained its cohesion, but its weaknesses were patent. Most of its men were raw territorials, and the regulars had mostly been in Palestine trying to deal with Arab unrest. So it was untrained in large-scale operations. Although certainly modern—the masses of equipment abandoned at Dunkirk "we poor wretches can only gaze at with envy," wrote a German officer[17]—some artillery dated back to the Great War and its tanks were of varying quality. This was not conservatism: the British Army had been a world leader in tanks. But it had been behind the RAF and the Royal Navy in the queue for new equipment (see pp. 683–84), and indecision and teething troubles had meant unsuitable models being rushed into service.[18] One of its divisional commanders, General Bernard Montgomery, thought the BEF "totally unfit to fight a first-class war on the Continent of Europe."[19] But its main problem was size: on paper, it had 14 hastily assembled divisions, compared with 141 German divisions, 104 French, and 22 Belgian.

Its commander-in-chief, Lord Gort, VC, concluded that evacuation was the only way to save it. As early as 18 May, only a week into the German offensive, planning began. The BEF carried out a fighting withdrawal on Dunkirk, but hampered their allies by blowing up bridges with abandon and destroying the Lille telephone exchange, which deprived the French First Army of most of its communications.[20] On 19 May the Germans reached the coast, cutting communications with Calais and Boulogne. A small force held out in Calais with what their German besiegers called "unheard of obstinacy"[21] and won several days' respite. But by 23 May another divisional commander, General Alan Brooke, thought that "nothing but a miracle can save the BEF now and the end cannot be very far off! . . . [B]eginning to be short of ammunition, supplies still all right for three days but after that scanty."[22] The BEF's survival depended not only on its own resolve, but on the actions of the Germans and the French. The German troops, tired and short of ammunition, were ordered on 24 May to halt their advance. This was confirmed by Hitler, still alarmed at the risks being taken. Soldiers and tanks needed rest and repair before moving south to complete the conquest of France. German caution was confirmed by a French counter-attack on 25 May, and French troops fought desperately from 23 to 29 May to hold the Germans away from Dunkirk.[23] Hitler probably did not believe the BEF could escape, and he might have considered it a bargaining counter in future armistice negotiations, which now seemed likely.

The last week in May was the low point: the only moment at which the government seriously contemplated giving up the struggle. It is hard to think of any time in our history—not Harold's actions in 1066, or those of Elizabeth and Burghley in 1587–88, or the decision to fight Bonaparte in 1803—in which the thoughts and personalities of a few individuals had such momentous consequences not only for England, but for the world. Above all one individual: Winston Spencer Churchill. His personality, partly through his own writing of history (which, as he said with characteristic humour, he would ensure was kind to him), has rightly become entwined with the British, and indeed the Western, memory of the war. But his leadership, and hence Britain's fighting on, was far from secure. Hitler was dropping hints of a deal. Voices inside and outside the government urged negotiation and muttered criticisms of Churchill. Halifax thought Germany had won and that the government must "safeguard the security of our Empire." He told the Italian ambassador on 25 May that they would "consider any proposals . . . provided our liberty and independence was [sic] assured." On 26 May Reynaud flew to London to suggest either a joint request for an armistice or British consent to a French request.[24] He urged making concessions to Italy (still at peace) in the hope that Mussolini might mediate. The inner War Cabinet—Churchill, Chamberlain, Halifax and two Labour ministers, Clement Attlee, the party leader, and his deputy, Arthur Greenwood—met secretly the same day. Churchill argued that Britain, unlike France, could still resist and should not be dragged by France into accepting "intolerable terms." Halifax replied that it was not "in Herr Hitler's interest to insist on outrageous terms."[25] For the time being, of course, this was true. That evening, Churchill felt "physically sick."[26] He was an imperialist, who stressed that he was fighting for the empire; and, logically, preservation of the empire required a deal with Hitler. But he knew there was more at stake even than the empire, and for several years had been trying to rally anti-Nazi opinion, including Jews and trade unionists.[27] His position in the Cabinet was fragile. Halifax was supported by Chamberlain. Attlee and Greenwood, understandably hesitant in the face of the disaster, nevertheless backed Churchill's refusal to negotiate. Now a forgotten figure, Greenwood, MP for Wakefield and a former economics lecturer at Leeds, thus helped to make history.[28]

Meanwhile, on 26 May, the Dunkirk evacuation—Operation Dynamo—had begun. It was thought impossible for more than a small number of men to escape. French and North African soldiers were sacrificed "holding the Wehrmacht noose open" as British troops embarked.[29] On 27 May the War Cabinet met twice. The Chiefs of Staff advised that Britain, if it had air superiority, could hold out. Churchill argued strongly that "our prestige in Europe was very low," but could be won back by fighting on.

"Even if we were beaten, we would be no worse off than we should be if we were now to abandon the struggle"; but to be lured into negotiation was a "deadly danger." Halifax threatened to resign, noting in his diary that "Winston talked the most frightful rot . . . I despair when [he] works himself up into a passion."[30] Churchill had to concede that if peace terms were offered to France "he would be prepared to consider them."[31] The danger was that Britain might be drawn into another, far more traumatic, re-enactment of Munich: Churchill warned on 28 May that if "we got up to leave the conference table, we should find that all the forces of resolution which were now at our disposal would have vanished."[32] That same day, Belgium surrendered. Churchill met all twenty-five ministers, telling them that successful resistance was still possible, while nothing could be hoped for from Hitler: "If this long island story of ours is to end at last, let it end only when each one of us lies choking in his own blood." This was not bombast: he had accepted the likelihood that he would die.[33]

Operation Dynamo was ably organized by Admiral Bertram Ramsay's staff at Dover from 26 May to 3 June. The French mounted a stubborn house-to-house defence of Lille, which held seven German divisions at bay for four vital days until 1 June. A broadcast appeal for small craft on the twenty-ninth was not universally answered—some south coast fishing boats and lifeboats refused. But the Port of London sent barges, tugs and lighters, and many weekend sailors turned out—one man ferried 200 men off the beaches in his own boat. In all, around 900 ships and boats took part. The rescuers were shelled from shore, bombed, and attacked by submarines and E-boats. On 1 June 3 destroyers and a passenger ship were sunk, so daylight sailings stopped. In all, 250 ships and boats were sunk. The RAF lost 177 planes protecting the beaches and shot down 244 of the Luftwaffe. Dunkirk, in flames, surrendered on 4 June. There had been friction with the French, who wanted to keep fighting, and inevitable incidents of panic and indiscipline. Yet more than 300,000 British and Allied troops were finally rescued—vastly more than anyone had thought possible. Another 130,000 were evacuated later from ports in French hands. But some 64,000 vehicles and 2,500 artillery pieces were abandoned, and 68,000 men had been captured, wounded or killed.[34]

Wars are not won by evacuations, as Churchill reminded the Commons; but defeat was avoided by this one. Without the intrepid professionalism of the Royal Navy, the bravery of civilian boat crews, and the tenacity of the French troops defending the perimeter, most of the BEF would have had to surrender. The pressure on Churchill to seek peace would then have been tremendous. His skill and determination—aided by the survival of the BEF—had enabled him to prevent his colleagues from clutching at negotiations, and the perilous moment passed.

Dunkirk is, surely, the most moving saga in our history, and "the Dunkirk spirit" epitomizes the united and stoical determination we like to think we are capable of. A doomed army was brought home from under the enemy's nose by the quiet courage and spontaneous ingenuity of their countrymen, sailing unarmed in fishing boats, yachts and pleasure steamers, braving bombs and shells in a mission of rescue. It has profound meaning for an island people wary of Continental dangers. The writer and broadcaster J. B. Priestley, one of the most famous voices of wartime England, put it into words on the BBC on 5 June, speaking of the ferry *Gracie Fields*, built to carry "children sticky with peppermint rock" and now sunk in the Channel:

> This little steamer, like all her brave and battered sisters, is immortal. She'll go sailing proudly down the years in the epic of Dunkirk. And our great grandchildren, when they learn how we began this war by snatching glory out of defeat, and then swept on to victory, may also learn how the little holiday steamers made an excursion to hell and came back glorious.[35]

Thoughts of evacuating the Royal Family and treasures from the National Gallery to Canada were now dropped: "None must go. We are going to beat them," said Churchill.[36] On 4 June he could make his defiant promise: "We shall fight on the beaches, we shall fight on the landing-grounds, we shall fight in the fields and in the streets, we shall fight in the hills; we shall never surrender."

The Battle of France ground on. The French demanded that the RAF should be fully committed: they had always believed that the main British contribution to the fighting would be in the air. But the RAF had already lost 959 aircraft and 435 pilots and had only 331 modern fighters left. The force based in France had lost half its strength in ten days. Its ground attacks (unlike in 1918) had been entirely ineffective, for interwar planning had deliberately rejected support for the army in favour of strategic bombing and homeland defence—not until 1941 were Hurricanes equipped with bombs to assist the Eighth Army in the desert. Air Marshal Sir Hugh Dowding, head of Fighter Command, put the issue starkly: "If the Home Defence Force is drained away in desperate attempts to remedy the situation in France, defeat in France will involve the final, complete and irremediable defeat of this country."[37]

On 7 June the Panzers began to pierce the rapidly improvised and overstretched French defensive line. On the tenth Mussolini declared war. On the twelfth the French army began a general retreat. The Germans marched into Paris on the fourteenth, and that same day the last British troops left France. The French increasingly felt abandoned. On 16 June they again asked for British consent to an exploration of armistice terms. The British reply, as before, was that France should fight on, with a government in exile in England or North Africa. Hoping to encourage French resolve, Churchill made the famous offer "that France and Great Britain shall no longer be two nations, but one Franco-British Union."[38] This, however, precipitated the collapse by splitting the French cabinet: Marshal Philippe Pétain, the Anglophobic deputy prime minister, dismissed it as an invitation to "marry a corpse." Reynaud resigned, and Pétain became prime minister on 17 June. He at once broadcast to the nation that "the fighting must cease" and asked for an armistice. Over a million soldiers began to lay down their arms. Against all expectations, Britain found itself without European allies, with all its strategic assumptions overturned, facing for the first time since Napoleon the peril the English had fought to prevent for centuries: an enemy dominating the Continent and poised on the Channel and North Sea coasts. Yet talk of negotiation had ended: by 16 June the Cabinet had accepted Churchill's view that "in no circumstances whatever would the British Government participate in any negotiations for armistice or peace . . . We were fighting for our lives and it was vital that we should allow no chink to appear in our armour."[39]

## HISTORY IS NOW AND ENGLAND[40]

At last the push of time has reached it; realer
Today than for centuries England is on the map
As a place where something occurs, as a springboard or trap.
                              Roy Fuller, "August 1940"

*With a fixed smile, England hopefully begins the hopeless struggle . . . France is beaten. We'll win. We can't use bases in Ireland. We'll win. Hungary joins Germany. We'll win. We're beaten in Greece, in Libya, in Crete. We'll win. English towns are destroyed. We'll win. Ships bringing food and arms are sunk. We'll win . . . So childishly confident in the future that they make you shed tears of pity, admiration and faith.*
                              Albert Cohen, refugee[41]

We are a little frightened, we who have been happy,
We are not frightened enough to become what you want.
                              London woman's diary[42]

The prospect of having to fight, in Churchill's words, "if necessary for years, if necessary alone" seemed to leave the English oddly unmoved.

George VI thought like many: "I feel happier now that we have no more allies to be polite to & to pamper." People stopped carrying their gas masks. Evacuees drifted back home. The war seemed far off. An American journalist noted "the English habit of considering war as a series of small personal affronts," such as tea rationing; but "of the prospects for survival and victory, nothing."[43] Katharine Moore, close to the danger in Kent, observed on 1 June that since Dunkirk "I feel that for the first time Hitler has not had it all his own way." On the twenty-sixth she thought the future "looks immensely black," but "I have recovered from the shock of the French capitulation and keep cheerful, making jam, gardening and doing odd jobs."[44] George Orwell, in "The Lion and the Unicorn" (1940), his exasperated love letter to England, praised its "gentleness," "private-ness" and loathing of bullying, and he trusted that "a certain power of acting without taking thought" meant that "in moments of supreme crisis the whole nation can suddenly draw together."[45]

The danger had not, of course, gone away. The Germans were indeed making preparations to invade England, in Operation Sealion, scheduled for late September 1940. A "Black Book" had been drawn up of 2,820 British subjects and exiles to be arrested. Their English targets were a motley collection, including writers, bankers, the public schools ("calculated to rear men of inflexible will and ruthless energy"), the Boy Scouts and, for some reason, the Rossendale Union of Boot, Shoe and Slipper Operatives. Amateurish and even comical though this may seem, the Nazis, and later the Russians, showed in Poland that they were perfectly capable of murdering a nation's elite in order to reduce it to slavery. They envisaged a mass deportation of men. England's Jewish population, the largest in western Europe, faced annihilation. Ireland—ironically, considering its neutrality and the sympathy of some Irish nationalists for the German cause—was to be merged with Britain.[46]

When France fell, not a few in Britain believed that the war had to stop and a deal be done with Hitler or preferably a more rational Nazi leader. For these, Churchill's broadcast "Finest Hour" speech was nonsense—"a few stumbling sentences to the effect that the situation was disastrous, but all right."[47] Some fled to America. There was still a pro-appeasement and pro-negotiation current composed of uncompromising pacifists, the far left, the revolution-fearing right, those terrified of airborne Armageddon, and some prominent progressives who for whatever reason baulked at continuing the fight. They included Lloyd George (ready to take power and make peace when the moment came),[48] H. G. Wells, George Bernard Shaw, a clutch of Anglican prelates, the prominent feminist Vera Brittain and the Peace Pledge Union (which increased its membership), some

Bloomsbury aesthetes, artistic and show business celebrities, eccentric pro-fascists, the Independent Labour Party, the Communists and their fellow-travelling intellectuals, and a few dozen MPs and peers, notably the mostly Labour parliamentary Peace Aims Group, with about twenty-five members, which had even made contact with the Germans. The National Council for Civil Liberties attacked wartime restrictions as a "reactionary step towards real totalitarianism."[49] Keynes mocked the "intelligentsia of the Left . . . loudest in demanding that the Nazi aggression should be resisted" but who after a few weeks of war "remember that they are pacifists" and "leave the defence of civilization to Colonel Blimp and the Old School Tie." But their support soon dwindled: by December 1940 only three Independent Labour MPs still called openly for peace.[50]

We rarely ask seriously whether the anti-war lobby, and politicians such as Halifax, might have been right: whether a negotiated peace in 1940 might not only have respected British independence and preserved its global power, but also have spared the world the then barely imaginable horrors of genocide, race war, mass bombing and nuclear weapons, none of which had begun in the summer of 1940. The problem with making peace in 1940, as with appeasement earlier, is that it assumed the ambitions of Hitler and the Nazi movement to be conventional and limited—territory, colonies, natural resources, security. We now know—as readers of *Mein Kampf* might have realized had they been able to believe it—that Hitler's central aim was unlimited racial conquest in eastern Europe, to win a vast new "living space" for the German people, turning Germany into a leading world power and making it impervious to another British naval blockade, if necessary by starving or exterminating the peoples presently occupying this "living space."[51] The stunning victory of 1940 made Hitler's fantasies possible, but they had taken shape much earlier, born of the transforming experience of the First World War, the trenches and the devastating effect of the British blockade. He had mostly fought against British and imperial forces, and this had marked him with a conviction of the power and ruthlessness of the British Empire, and more broadly of the "Anglo-Saxon race." He admired Britain's power, the breeding of its upper class, its "determination for victory," its "racial quality." He intended to make Germany at least the equal of the British Empire and the United States, by force and cunning. He hoped that once "the English" (as he thought of them) had been overcome or intimidated into making peace, they might be used as subordinate allies in his global struggle, ultimately against the United States, and if necessary come under complete German control.[52] Even late in 1941, he still hoped that Churchill would be overthrown and that the "peace-loving" English would cooper-

ate with Germany.[53] It was not his primary aim to attack and destroy
Britain, its empire or the United States, about which he had ambivalent
views. But this ambivalence included hatred of London and New York as
the centres of "Jewish" capitalism, and by 1942 he had come to see the
English as an enemy that had to be destroyed. In the summer of 1940,
however, he was far from this point. The immediate problem, as the Bourbons and Napoleon had found, was that invading England was a desperately difficult and dangerous gamble, and Hitler and his military
commanders did not get far in their plans for it. Britain could, therefore,
have made terms with Hitler in 1940—even the reasonable terms for
which Halifax had hoped. Though no one outside Hitler's circle knew it
fully at the time, the price of peace would have been for Britain to acquiesce in a merciless and ultimately genocidal Continental domination by
an inhuman and reckless totalitarianism. Peaceful coexistence and cooperation with such a regime, as many intuitively felt, was unthinkable and
would have meant a moral degradation worse than military defeat. The
British public and its leaders had taken a long time to accept this; but at
last the penny had dropped.

"The English," concludes one historian, "who had not been conquered
by an invader for nearly one thousand years, knew in their bones that
their defeat would mean a kind of death for England, that its effect would
not be temporary."[54] A poll showed that 75 percent (85 percent of men)
expected Britain to fight on, and 50 percent were confident about fighting
alone. They were a cantankerous and contrary lot: highly critical of politicians, officials, the armed forces and the BBC (not least the accents of its
announcers); disliking censorship and shocked by prosecutions of grum-
blers for "defeatism." Much of this stemmed from a perceived lack of
determination and effort by those in authority. People wanted strong,
decisive and even fairly authoritarian action. Intelligence reports showed
general impatience with half-hearted leadership. Churchill gave such people what they craved: tough talking, pugnacity, determination, bravado—
"he's the fellow we can follow."[55]

The importance of Churchill's leadership, despite criticisms then and
since, remains undeniable. Attlee once said tartly that Churchill's main
contribution to the war was talking about it.[56] Churchill himself said
modestly that it was "the nation and race dwelling all round the globe
that had the lion heart," and he only "had the luck to be called upon to
give the roar."[57] There was truth in both remarks. Churchill was above all
a master of words, prepared and memorized, inspired by Shakespeare,
Gibbon, Macaulay—over 2,000 speeches, over 4 million words during his
career. He said that "words are the only things which live for ever," and

many of his phrases became part of the language—the only English statesman of whom this can be said. In the 1930s his words had seemed
old-fashioned, overblown, repetitious and worse still misapplied to bad
causes, a symptom of lack of measure and judgement—the cartoonist
David Low had satirized "the Winstonocerous," which "Destroys Imaginary Enemies With Great Fury."[58] But in 1940 reality caught up with
rhetoric, as his grim predictions came true. Not everyone was convinced—
especially left- or right-wingers—but most of the country was. In July
1940 his approval rating was 88 percent, and even in the worst period of
the war, in early 1942, it never fell below 78 percent—though "satisfaction" with Churchill as expressed to Gallup did not always mean unqualified admiration, or agreement with his conduct of the war. He led Britain
into total war without much thought for the morrow: he said he had
"only one single purpose—the destruction of Hitler—and his life was
much simplified thereby." His speeches and later writings did much to create the drama of the "finest hour" and his own legend within it.[59]

Enemy propaganda attacked his idiosyncrasies, but most people
accepted them, even liked them, as a sign of common humanity. He,
grandson of a duke, was the first of that small group of prime ministers to
be generally referred to by their Christian names. But his idiosyncrasies
were real, including meddling, stubbornness, sometimes bullying and chaotic methods of working, aggravated by advancing age, years of stress,
alcohol and failing health. General Brooke, Chief of the Imperial General
Staff and his closest military adviser, sometimes found working with him
almost unbearable:

> He knows no details, has only got half the picture in his mind, talks absur-
> dities and . . . the wonderful thing is that ¾ of the population of the world
> imagine that Winston Churchill is one of the great strategists of history, a
> second Marlborough, and the other ¼ have no conception what a public
> menace he is and has been throughout this war! It is far better that the
> world should never know, and never suspect the feet of clay of that other-
> wise superhuman being. Without him England was lost for a certainty, with
> him England has been on the verge of disaster time and again.[60]

Churchill's strategic judgements were often questionable and sometimes
capricious—most famously over Greece, Singapore, bombing and the
"Mediterranean strategy"—and his ruthlessness with commanders struggling against the odds was not only unjust but damaging. But as was said
of an earlier charismatic war leader: "Oh! but this does not derogate from
his great, splendid side."[61] Wars cannot be fought without mistakes;
indeed, it is rarely clear, even with hindsight, what *were* mistakes. Wars do

demand inspiration, direction, dynamism and someone who fully accepts, in President Truman's phrase, that "the buck stops here." Who could have filled this role during the crisis years of 1940–42? Not Chamberlain, Halifax or Eden; not Attlee, Cripps or even Bevin (whom Churchill regarded as a possible replacement in an emergency); not Lloyd George; not the king. Only Winston Churchill.

In England, and throughout the United Kingdom and the empire, millions of ordinary people prepared for a fight. There was a rush of marriages. Even before war had begun, 300,000 men and women had volunteered for the armed forces reserves, and 1.5 million for the Auxiliary Fire Service, Air Raid Precautions, the Special Constabulary and other civilian services, including the soon omnipresent Women's Voluntary Service, generally run by middle-class housewives. Local self-defence groups started to form even before the government appealed in May 1940 for Local Defence Volunteers. In one Sussex village, Wilmington, a meeting in the pub drew "shepherds, farm hands, gardeners, village shopkeepers, a retired civil servant from India, a retired schoolmaster, and one or two folk who worked in London and had cottages"; they elected the pub landlord, "the best rabbit shot in the neighbourhood," as corporal. Churchill soon invented a more stirring title—Home Guard. There were over a million volunteers by the end of June, many of them veterans of 1914–18, with armbands for uniforms, preparing to resist invasion with shotguns, pick-handles and the occasional rifle. Soon they were guarding beaches, factories and roadblocks, demanding identity cards, stopping and even shooting at mysterious nocturnal vehicles (courting couples were much harried). Training schools were set up by private initiative, one of them staffed by veterans of the Spanish Civil War. A few select units were preparing for post-invasion guerrilla warfare and sabotage.[62]

Volunteering was backed up by conscription. The 1939 Military Training Act had required young men to undergo six months' training, and on the first day of war the National Service (Armed Forces) Act had extended it to all men between eighteen and forty-one, though universal registration of men and their occupations took until June 1941. By the end of 1939 over 1.5 million men were in the regular armed forces; 43,000 women, all volunteers, were in the auxiliary services. Personal hardship gave grounds for exemption, as did "conscientious objection"—only 0.6 percent actually claimed it.[63] Key occupations serving the war effort were "reserved," and employers could ask for "deferment" of crucial staff, but civilian life too was to become increasingly organized and directed. This was the beginning of unprecedented national mobilization, never equalled in any democratic country.

Exactly how much danger was Britain facing in the summer of 1940? The German navy, already weak, had been mauled in Norway. The army had no plan with any prospect of success for a cross-Channel invasion. If invasion were possible at all, the first requirement was control of the air, to force the Royal Navy out of the Straits of Dover and the southern North Sea. The Luftwaffe had suffered losses in France and had available about 750 long-range bombers, 250 dive-bombers, and 750 fighters. RAF Fighter Command had lost many aircraft in France, and its strength, which had risen to about 600–800 fighters, was only half what was ideally needed. But it had growing numbers of the solid and dependable Hurricanes, and a third of the force were Spitfires, the only equal in performance to the Messerschmitt Bf 109. In 1938–39 a system of control stations had been completed, integrating radar, spotters, radio links and geographical sectors—the best air-defence system in the world, so new that the Germans did not know how to counter it. Here women were in the front line, helping to plot and direct the battle—arguably the first time that women had been so active in operations, directly under fire when stations were attacked. In 1941 women were deployed in anti-aircraft and searchlight batteries, though (as in Germany) they were not allowed actually to fire guns—the public did not want women "in combat," though in fact over 300 were killed or wounded.[64]

What Churchill named the Battle of Britain was the first, and still the only, decisive battle in history fought entirely in the air. It began in August with a German plan to overwhelm the RAF, attacking fighter stations and engaging in aerial combat with British fighters. Fortunately, the onslaught was not always focused on what mattered, and there was no concerted attack on the radar system. Flying from airfields in France, the Germans could seize the initiative for basic technical reasons: the limited range of radar meant that it gave only a few minutes' warning of an attack; but it took about four minutes for the warning to reach RAF fighter stations, then thirteen minutes for a Spitfire to reach a combat height of 20,000 feet.[65] As the Germans would have arrived at or near their targets by this time, available fighters had to engage them at once, even if outnumbered by German fighter escorts. Moreover, while fighters were in combat, other German raiders might attack their undefended airfields. In late August and early September, the German tactics were having an impact, though far less than they thought. The RAF too had advantages: they were receiving more new aircraft than the Germans, they could repair or salvage many damaged over England, and get shot-down pilots back into action. Though the RAF, and particularly its pilots, was under extreme pressure, it was not being destroyed.

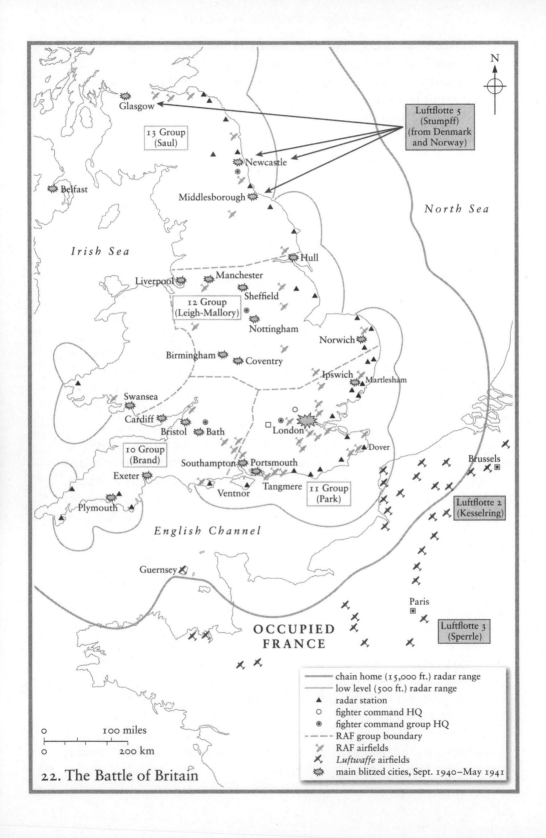

N

Luftflotte 5
(Stumpff)
(from Denmark
and Norway)

13 Group
(Saul)

Glasgow

Belfast

Newcastle

Middlesborough

*North Sea*

*Irish Sea*

Hull

Liverpool    Manchester

12 Group
(Leigh-Mallory)

Sheffield

Nottingham

Norwich

Birmingham    Coventry

Ipswich    Martlesham

Swansea

Cardiff

Bristol    Bath

London

Brussels

10 Group
(Brand)

Southampton    Portsmouth

Dover

Exeter

Ventnor    Tangmere    11 Group
(Park)

Luftflotte 2
(Kesselring)

Plymouth

*English Channel*

Guernsey

Paris

**OCCUPIED
FRANCE**

Luftflotte 3
(Sperrle)

——— chain home (15,000 ft.) radar range
——— low level (500 ft.) radar range
▲ radar station
○ fighter command HQ
◉ fighter command group HQ
– – – RAF group boundary
✈ RAF airfields
✕ *Luftwaffe* airfields
✺ main blitzed cities, Sept. 1940–May 1941

100 miles

200 km

22. The Battle of Britain

Daylight aerial combats were most intense during August—with a mass attack on the fifteenth—and September. Both sides believed they were inflicting far higher losses on the enemy than was the case. Dogfights were described by the press and the BBC, sometimes in tones reminiscent of sports commentaries. This did not please all listeners, especially women: "A battle isn't a Boat Race . . . his callous Oxford accent made it worse." Despite official warnings, adults and children insisted on watching, "thrilled by spectacle of air raid; not nervous at all."[66] Fighter pilots, with their casual style and language, now became heroes. This had not previously been so: the "Brylcream Boys" had been resented as undisciplined and pampered, and soldiers accused them, unjustly, of leaving the Dunkirk beaches unprotected—cinema newsreels featuring airmen were often booed. Pilots were young and two-thirds were volunteers, often having joined the prewar RAF Volunteer Reserve from an interest in machines—including fast cars—and many came from a grammar school or technical background. A sizeable contingent were Poles or Czechs. There were not many in total: about 3,000, of whom one in six would die. On 20 August Churchill, echoing Shakespeare's Henry V before Agincourt, gave them their title in history: the Few.

On 5 September, Hitler switched the weight of the attack from airfields to cities, especially London—what soon became known as "the Blitz." Birmingham and Liverpool were hit before London received a massive surprise daylight raid on 7 September by 300 bombers and 600 fighters, which started huge fires in the East End, a beacon for more bombers that night and subsequent nights. London was practically undefended for several days. But on 15 September—"Battle of Britain Day"—attacks on London were met by massed fighters. The RAF claimed to have shot down 185 planes. The real number was about 60—a still considerable figure which brought German losses in a week to some 175, an unsustainable rate of loss and a blow to their belief that they were on the verge of victory. Operation Sealion was postponed. The great daylight battles of 15 August and 15 September showed that German fighter strength was inadequate to gain air superiority. In the view of one historian of Germany, it was "an extremely one-sided affair"—for the RAF.[67] Between July and October the RAF lost about 790 planes and the Luftwaffe about 1,300. Britain was producing more aircraft than Germany (15,000 during 1940 to Germany's 10,800), including twice the number of fighters; it had also ordered another 10,000 planes and 13,000 aero engines from the United States.[68] The success boosted public confidence: "At any rate, we have won the first round."[69] An official pamphlet, *The Battle of Britain*, reached millions, and created a legend.

The Germans switched to night attacks against cities, hoping optimistically to destroy the aircraft industry, shatter civilian morale, and generally disrupt the infrastructure. London was regularly hit by about 200 German and Italian bombers for seventy-six nights. Massive raids on London, Birmingham and Bristol on 15 October by 400 bombers hit the railway stations, Battersea Power Station and BBC Broadcasting House, and started hundreds of fires. Buckingham Palace was hit three times: "I'm glad we've been bombed," commented the queen. "It makes me feel I can look the East End in the face." That the king and queen stayed and visited bombed areas of London and other towns, and that their two daughters stayed too, despite widespread rumours that they were being sent to Canada, had a big effect on public opinion.[70] By mid-November the Luftwaffe had dropped 13,000 tons of high explosives and a million incendiaries on London. They then switched their attacks to other ports and industrial towns, most notoriously the engineering centre of Coventry. Here, on the night of 14–15 November, 450 bombers guided by radio beams[71] destroyed twelve factories and much of the town centre, killing 380 people. There had been some warning, partly from detecting the electronic beams, partly from decoding radio signals, but available fighter cover was insufficient. The story that the raid was allowed to proceed by Churchill to prevent the Germans from realizing their codes were breakable is now recognized as a fable.

The German high command was becoming impatient that England was not collapsing, and the navy persuaded Hitler in February 1941 to order attacks to be concentrated on the great ports. London was thereafter largely spared. Defences against night bombers were only beginning to be effective, and Luftwaffe losses throughout the Blitz were low—about 1.5 percent of sorties flown. Radar-guided guns and searchlights, and special night-fighters also with radar, began to come into service in 1941. But what really ended the Blitz was the diversion of the Luftwaffe to Russia. Over eight months, for the loss of 600 bombers, the Germans had killed over 43,000 civilians, wounded 139,000, and done huge material damage, making over 2 million homeless. But the effect on both the war economy and on civilian morale had been limited. A Gallup poll of Londoners early in 1941 found that the weather depressed them more than the bombing.[72]

Indeed, in terms of morale and politics, the Blitz was counter-productive. It greatly affected world and most importantly American public opinion. Across Europe, resistance to German occupation often began with small gestures of Anglophilia: placing flowers on war memorials, attending funerals of RAF crewmen, wearing a rose on the king's birthday. The English, rather like the Spanish republicans a few years earlier, were seen as defying the forces of tyranny on behalf of freedom everywhere: "The image of England had entered the minds of millions of people in Europe to whose great-grandparents the word 'England' meant but a vague blur."[73] A Swiss Jewish writer and diplomat, Albert Cohen, recorded impressions in which astonishment and emotion, seasoned with slightly ambivalent stereotypes, pay tribute to a certain idea of Englishness:[74]

> I watch them in the carriages of their luxurious London Underground . . . elegant uniforms, little plumes, kilts, green pompoms, golden badges . . . The officers, like advertisements for electric razors . . . The shy young soldiers . . . soft-eyed, ready to blush, huge determined little boys, well-dressed, well-polished . . . Well-brought-up girls in soft wool . . . cross their thoroughbred legs with the confidence of a people used to mastery and sure of tomorrow . . . They smoke continuously, these fresh English girls, with empty eyes, calm chins, sure of being in the right . . . All sit decently silent and still . . . sleepwalkers in a fog of tobacco and antiseptic soap . . . The Germans kill them with bombs every night, and the next morning one hears Schubert in German on the BBC.

The events of 1940 retain a powerful if vague place in English memories. They show us as we would like to be: cheerfully stoical ("mustn't grumble"), "pulling together" across class and party, with the king and queen braving the bombs just like the East Enders, everyone living on the same rations, helping neighbours and even complete strangers, "carrying on" and "doing their bit" irrespective of danger. In June 1940 tenants of an estate in Stockwell were "busy making shelters comfortable with carpets to sleep on, furniture, beds for children, pictures of King and Queen, artificial flowers, Union Jacks etc. Women scrubbing floors and laughing: 'Wish Hitler could see us now!' " "Noticeable friendliness everywhere among all classes and types of people," said an intelligence report at the height of the Blitz. "Townswomen's Guilds report jam-making going strong."[75]

It is easy to point out that reality fell short of the ideal, and many have done so:[76] panic, looting, family breakdown, youth crime, a black market, government incompetence, snobbery, class resentments, anti-Semitism, strikes—all these existed in England as in all combatant countries. Soldiers and their wives resented highly paid civilian workers and strikers. Non-stop air raids created fear, exhaustion and resentment. Civil-defence arrangements were chronically inadequate. Yet what remains impressive is how much people really did "pull together" and "carry on" in circumstances of danger, often doing far more than the minimum:

Choosing to run life-and-death risks at work for no financial gain, and giving money away to the government [through "Spitfire funds"] were two of the most extraordinary aspects of wartime life. People were actively forging a quintessentially wartime relationship between themselves and the nation; it was a bond of their own making, and the result of their own direct choices.[77]

The Blitz was the first test: hammering AA guns, howling dogs, the tearing crash of bombs ("as if someone was *scratching* the sky *with a broken finger nail*" . . . "We heard it coming and had covered the children and were standing over them"), the bells of ambulances and fire engines ("'Are you all right?' people kept asking me"), chemical smoke, sewage and leaking gas: "The whole of the smell was greater than the sum of its parts. It was the smell of violent death itself." And tea: "We were all awash with tea . . . That's one trouble about the raids, people do nothing but make tea and expect you to drink it." The fear of bombing, fostered during the 1930s, was at first acute—"suffered agonies of fright at the time of Munich."[78] But for most people the reality was less than the expectation: "One is relieved to find how little bombs can do as compared with the mental picture one had"; "If anyone had told me I *could* have felt so unconcerned when an alert—or guns—sounded, I would not have believed it." Some people felt bravado, even exhilaration, at surviving and keeping their nerve: "Feeling indescribably happy and triumphant . . . 'I've been bombed—me!'" A Southampton librarian "enjoyed the raid . . . I felt keyed up and kind of happy like when you're pretty drunk. I met some pals after the raid . . . and made a party of it." Local pride was stimulated by raids: people were annoyed when the BBC, for security reasons, gave no details. "We're in the news—but why don't they mention the street by name. It's not *fair!*"[79]

Most people, despite repeated disruption and accumulating tiredness, stubbornly carried on. In early raids, the sirens sent everyone to shelters, sometimes for hours, including factory and office workers. Some civil service departments prided themselves on the speed and universality with which their staff went to ground at the first alert. Many hours of working time were thus lost. "You can waste a lot of time on this air raid lark if you want to," commented one working woman. Gradually it became a matter of pride to work "after the siren," and spotters, often young, went up to the rooftops to look out for the actual arrival of bombers before giving the final warning to shelter. In private life it was a similar story. "I'd just got into bed and I heard [the siren], but I thought to myself, Well, I want to get the house tidy tomorrow and you can't keep going properly can you with all this popping up and down," wrote a London housewife. "I'm just going to put the Yorkshire pudding in the oven," protested another when the sirens went, "what about the Sunday dinner?" Daughters would go out and listen for bombs while mothers cooked, only giving the alert if absolutely necessary. Having responsibilities, whether to family or community, was a prophylactic against fear. A sense of personal achievement was strong, especially in London, and perhaps especially among ordinary people, who "felt a great sense of pride, achievement and importance that was unrelated to the yardsticks of wealth, family relationships and a successful career . . . people felt that they were playing a part in their nation's history." For the first time, "the East Ender became an icon of British values."[80] "Cockney feet mark the beat of history," wrote Noël Coward in a popular 1941 song. Home Intelligence observers found ordinary people "express gratification that Government wants to know what they think because 'this is a people's war.'"[81]

In the course of the war, 60,000 civilians were killed, half of them in London; perhaps 250,000 were injured and 2 million made homeless. In central London, 90 percent of houses suffered some damage, and in the whole country 250,000 were destroyed and 4 million damaged; 20 percent of schools and hospitals were damaged.[82] Popular memory, today fostered by "The Blitz Experience" at the Imperial War Museum, is of sheltering in the Tube. There was reckoned to be enough shelter of some sort for 20 million people. But most even in London did not use shelters, and only 4 percent used the Tube—which still meant over 100,000 people. For various reasons, of which longing for a reasonable night's sleep was one ("I'd die in my sleep, happily, if only I *could* sleep"), more than 90 percent slept at home: in "Anderson shelters" in the garden (essentially a hole with a corrugated iron roof), under the stairs or just in a downstairs room.[83] In the East End, the first area to be hit, shelters were inadequate, insanitary and dangerous—the authorities had prepared for a quick "knock-out" attack, not for months of bombing. Local councils were often not up to the job. Some shelters were disorderly, filthy, noisy and unpleasant, with rowdyism and drunkenness. But as in all aspects of the Home Front, improvisation, often by well-meaning and sometimes bossy volunteers (such as the committee set up in the Swiss Cottage station, with its own news-sheet), had considerable effects. The clergy got involved— "From what I can see the parsons are having the time of their lives," noted one London woman.[84] Bureaucracy was badgered, sanitary conditions improved, order created. Soon, Tube trains circulated with food and drink. Medical services appeared. Some people actually came to like shelters, some of which acquired reputations for gentility or conviviality: the lonely went for company, the young for fun. Censorious elders disapproved. One described a Liverpool shelter in October 1940 as "most revolting" being "packed" with "very young girls, generally accompanied by foreign or British seamen, many under the influence of drink." The notorious Tilbury shelter in London—a chaotic unofficial shelter in a vast warehouse—was after a few weeks attracting people to "a companionable evening and a cheap Salvation Army meal" with music and dancing.[85]

ARP wardens, policemen and firemen, often out in the bombing, coped well with repeated danger, trauma and fatigue. Contrary to prewar expectations, very few people suffered psychological breakdown. On the contrary, being involved in important work was therapeutic. Suicides fell by nearly a third. The birth rate (both inside and outside marriage) rose. There is no evidence of class or gender differences in ability to cope with stress, but the young, including children, were most resilient. Least resilient seem to have been those who, whether due to education or lack of it, did not share the sense of national purpose or trust the government, or who for other reasons felt helpless and passive—reports often mentioned elderly women. Being with others was important. It was not fear but bravery that proved contagious.[86]

## BLOOD, TOIL, TEARS AND SWEAT

*It is necessary that the Government should be given complete control over persons and property, not just some persons of some particular class of the community, but of all persons, rich and poor, employer and workman, man or woman, and all property.*
                    Clement Attlee, Labour leader, June 1940[87]

Toil and sweat were as important as blood and tears—and so was a leavening of fun and laughter. One enduring consequence was to change the country from a predominantly free-market economy into a centrally managed economy.[88] The market could not sustain the war: most obviously, the diversion of industry to armaments meant that as early as 1938 exports had to be cut, and by 1943 they had fallen by 71 percent, whereas import costs had risen by 30 percent. War expenditure rose from 7 percent of net national expenditure to 55 percent. Taxation rose steeply. Overseas investments were requisitioned and sold. Non-essential imports were reduced— food imports fell by 55 percent. Millions of acres of grassland, heath and fen went under the plough, some for the first time since the Black Death. Golf courses and ancient lawns and meadows were sacrificed. Windsor

Great Park became the largest cornfield in England. The number of allotments nearly doubled as people "dug for victory." Clubs were set up to keep pigs. Diets had to change, requiring control of food supplies. Inflation had to be checked. The mobilization of 4.5 million men and 467,000 women into the armed forces required new workers to take their places in industry and agriculture, including many women (1.8 million in the munitions industries alone) who had never before had jobs. Women between twenty and thirty without children were conscripted for civilian labour or service in uniform. Many older people, including at least a million women, volunteered for a range of tasks. Nearly three-quarters of teenagers between fourteen and seventeen were engaged in some kind of war work.[89] This was a great social and psychological upheaval—there were 60 million changes of address during the war. But at the time the disturbances were seen as temporary. There was disapproval of overt alteration of gender roles, most obviously if it seemed to mean—as it often did[90]—greater social and sexual freedom.

Chamberlain had realized in 1938 that normal economic rules had to be suspended, and the Dunkirk crisis brought further huge steps. The Ministry of Labour and National Service was held by the tough, able and patriotic union boss Ernest Bevin, surely England's greatest working-class politician. Child of a single mother, sometime farm worker, van driver, Baptist lay preacher and co-founder of the Transport and General Workers' Union, Bevin held a key position in the government and the war effort, far more than simply as a symbol of cross-class unity. Though autocratic, even egotistical, he was capable of utter loyalty and was respected and trusted by both Churchill and Attlee. The Emergency Powers Act (1940) permitted him to direct any person to perform any service he saw fit, and set their wages, hours and conditions. He wrote, "Immediately a nation is involved in a great crisis . . . it is bound to become collectivist,"[91] and he used his powers over more than 8 million workers both to prosecute the war and to extend collective agreements, unionization and regulation of working conditions. The "Bevin Boys," drawn by lot among conscripts to work in coal mines, are widely remembered, but this was only a small part of Bevin's empire.

There were five major constraints on the wartime economy: gold and foreign-currency reserves, raw materials, shipping, industrial capacity, and manpower. These constraints could in various ways be pushed back. But several of them needed American help: America could supply financial credit, raw materials, ships and industrial capacity. Congress, however, had passed laws forbidding loans and restricting the supply of armaments. By the end of 1940 Britain's foreign-currency reserves were nearly exhausted, and its accumulated foreign investments were being sold off as fast as possible in Wall Street. In March 1941 the United States passed the Lend-Lease Act, removing restrictions on purchases and deferring payment until after the war. The contribution this made to Britain's war effort is evident: in all, more than half its tanks came from America, and one-fifth of its aircraft. Churchill declared later that Lend-Lease was "the most unsordid act in the history of any nation." It was also good business. The American economy boomed, growing by 50 percent during the war years (that of Europe fell by 25 percent). Washington extracted trade and strategic concessions, denuding Britain, its greatest trade rival, of postwar economic power: London had to agree to abolish all forms of discriminatory treatment—i.e. imperial preference—and to reduce tariffs and other trade barriers.[92] Keynes, who went to Washington to negotiate, complained that the American government waited until Britain was "more or less bankrupt before any assistance was given," aiming to "leave the British at the end of the war . . . hopelessly insolvent."[93]

Manpower was the greatest constraint. Much was done to use all available workers, and millions accepted long hours, hard conditions and dangers. The Ministry of Labour recognized the plight of those, especially women, working "for long hours, week in week out [with] two or three hours a day or even more in . . . a crowded bus or train and in all weathers [and] with homes and young children to look after." "Normal" working hours were set at 8 a.m. to 7 p.m., seven days a week, but people exceeded them, often sleeping at the office or in a corner of the workshop, until Bevin had to tell them to take reasonable time off. Workers making radar equipment at the Metropolitan Vickers factory in Manchester during the 1940 crisis kept going for forty-eight hours without stopping. In 1941 the government introduced compulsory "national service" for everyone—the first time any country had conscripted women. Their mass adoption of trousers was a minor revolution, deplored by some as immoral. Families and neighbours assembled aircraft components in their front rooms. MPs too spent spare time making munitions. Children collected salvage and aluminium saucepans for Spitfires, and they were officially urged to join youth organizations. Later, prisoners of war—130,000 Italians and 90,000 Germans—were put to work. Men and women were directed, in addition to their full-time jobs, into extra part-time work in civil defence, the police and the Home Guard. Consumer industries were run down: the cotton industry, the great staple of the Industrial Revolution, saw a third of its mills close. The "manpower budget," by which the government allocated workers to different industries, became the main means of economic planning and ultimately determined every part of the war effort, from the number of bombers raiding Germany to the size of the clothing ration.[94]

This mobilization of the population into various forms of national service—eventually including over 90 percent of men aged fourteen to sixty-four, and 40 percent of women (90 percent of single women aged eighteen to forty)—matched or exceeded levels in totalitarian states, yet direct powers of compulsion were used sparingly. It was, in Bevin's words, "the voluntary submission of a free people to discipline."[95] Germany, whose Nazi regime feared opposition at home, instead ruthlessly exploited occupied countries, slave labour and foreign workers—more than 7 million in Germany in 1944. Yet British industry performed better than those of Germany, Japan and Russia, being outpaced only by the USA. In the key area of aircraft, Britain out-produced Germany every year except 1944, when the latter was forced to turn out a vast number of fighters to counter the bombing campaign. Britain also built more battleships and aircraft carriers than any country except the United States.[96] The performance of its products was generally as good as and often better than those of enemies or allies: for example, the Spitfire, the Mosquito, the Lancaster, the Merlin engine, the jet fighter and new types of radar.

But no amount of effort and ingenuity could circumvent the fact that Britain had 48 million people, compared with 79 million Germans, 70 million Japanese, 140 million Americans and 180 million Russians. Britain's armed forces wanted more manpower. So did its factories. The 1942 Manpower Survey showed that all would have to accept limits. Bevin declared in 1943 that "the standards and amenities of the civil population cannot be further reduced."[97] The culmination was 1944: thereafter war production, and the size of the armed forces, had to be limited, and even diminished.

People got used to rationing, queuing and shallow baths—which shocked Mrs. Roosevelt when staying at Buckingham Palace. Indeed, rationing was welcomed as necessary and equitable.[98] Petrol was rationed from the beginning; many staples—butter, meat, tea—from 1940; cheese and clothing in 1941; sweets and soap in 1942. Two-thirds of all food came under government control, and the Ministry of Food had 50,000 officials by 1943. People were prosecuted for waste—including one elderly lady for feeding crumbs to birds. Basics (bread, potatoes, vegetables, fish) remained unrationed, and their consumption greatly increased. New foods (famously Spam) and old (horsemeat) appeared and were unevenly appreciated. Food prices were kept down. Huge numbers ate in canteens or "British Restaurants." The "Rural Pie Scheme"—delivered by WVS ladies to workers in the fields—provided more than a million lunches a week. The average diet was healthier than normal, if less enjoyable: workers in one Birmingham factory canteen rejected salads and demanded fish and chips and cream cakes.[99] Beer (though much weaker due to wartime regulations) and tobacco were unrationed—the war effort seems to have been fuelled by Woodbines and tea. Despite U-boat attacks, Britain never went very hungry, certainly not on the scale of Europe, where some 5 million people died, or Asia, where perhaps 20 million died, including some 2 million in Bengal. The average British daily calorie intake fell from 3,000 to about 2,800 in 1940–41, compared with a civilian ration of 2,570 in Germany, 1,600 in Norway, 1,300 in France, and deliberate famine in eastern Europe.[100] Clothing was also rationed (it worked out at a pair of underpants every two years, a pullover every five). Simple "Utility" goods of many kinds were designed to save materials, with "fripperies" prohibited. Despite grumbles, this was widely supported, and a department store magnate, Lord Woolton, the Minister of Food (patron of the all-vegetable "Woolton Pie"), was probably the most popular minister.

Voluntary acceptance of these wartime conditions was essential. Bevin brought trade union leaders into partnership as "labour directors." Often there followed advantages in wages and conditions, and trade union membership rose by over a third, to 8 million in 1943. With labour scarce, shop-floor workers and shop stewards were in a strong position, not always controllable by the leadership. Strikes, though fewer than during the First World War, increased sharply in 1944 as victory approached: there were over 2,000 strikes and 3.7 million lost days, mostly in coal mining. But there was only ever one significant strike throughout the war in the huge munitions industry. Most stoppages were short and local. Although strikes were made illegal in 1940, prosecution of strikers was rarely attempted, and even then often unsuccessful.[101]

Entertainment and morale-building both for soldiers and for civilians were important government concerns. Sports suffered from the mobilization of players and takeover of grounds (the Oval became a prison camp), but did their best to continue in truncated form. The BBC multiplied in size and scope, adding a "Light Programme," and attracting vast audiences. Its newsreaders, such as Alvar Liddell and Bruce Belfrage, became celebrities. It created a range of highly popular programmes, from serious panel discussion ("The Brains Trust") to variety. A great success was a new kind of lunatic comedy, *ITMA* ("It's That Man Again"), which invented universally familiar catchphrases and stock characters—"Mrs. Mopp," "Colonel Chinstrap"—and took a mildly satirical view of the war. It was part of a culture that was "not collectivist but anarchic, celebrating not the unity of mankind but its absurdity; not the rightness of the national cause but the fallibility of all in authority."[102] War was thus the seedbed for future generations of "British humour." Classical music widened its appeal in broadcasts and live performances. The Proms for the first time attracted mass audiences, as did the pianist Myra Hess, who organized daily lunchtime concerts throughout the war in a National Gallery stripped of its paintings: the most popular composers were the great Germans and Austrians, who, unlike during the First World War, were moral allies, not surrogate enemies. Once, a bomb exploded during a performance: neither audience nor players missed a beat. ENSA (Entertainments National Services Association) took travelling shows of varying quality to military units and factories, sometimes with leading popular entertainers such as Gracie Fields, Vera Lynn and George Formby, and also classical musicians, including Benjamin Britten and Peter Pears, who had returned from America in 1942. CEMA (Council for the Encouragement of Music and the Arts) organized theatre, ballet and opera in army camps, churches and canteens; it developed into the postwar Arts Council.

Cinema attracted up to 30 million attendances weekly, and like the wireless constituted a shared wartime experience that both reflected and created a sense of unity.[103] The Ministry of Information encouraged morale-boosting films, many promoting behaviour implied to be typically English, in the hope, as Orwell put it, that what people think they ought to be they tend to become. But the ministry did not control the industry. In the famous case of *The Life and Death of Colonel Blimp* (1943)—part of a more general debate about whether traditional English values were adequate to total war[104]—the film could not be stopped despite Churchill's hostility, and its makers, Michael Powell and Emerich Pressburger, continued to work with the ministry. Producers, writers, actors and composers threw themselves into the cinematic war effort, even though their ideas did not parrot official views, and indeed might criticize the authorities or social inequality. The central theme was that of a "people's war," in which ordinary men and women were vital, and in which class and gender differences were superseded by comradeship. The preferred style was realistic, even documentary, and "human," based on believable characters (for example, firemen and women factory workers) coping quietly with everyday hardships and personal tragedies, with pomposity deflated by humour, and eschewing showy "heroics" or emotionalism. Audiences often preferred films that were both more patriotic and more sentimental than critics and professionals liked, such as the American film *Mrs. Miniver* (1942). The Royal Navy was the most admired of the services, and the most cinematic; a ship could symbolize both the hierarchy and unity of society, as in Noël Coward's *In Which We Serve* (1942), the most successful wartime film, showing upper-class officers and working-class ratings united by danger, duty and suffering (the authorities at first disliked it, as the ship is sunk). Its popularity motivated attempts to produce similar films on the army and the RAF.[105] Historical films were another staple, evoking a half-timbered rural England whose unchanging character was invincible, or celebrating historic victories (Churchill's favourite was on Nelson). The most enduring was Laurence Olivier's *Henry V* (1944)—a play that had also been popular during the war against Napoleon. Its emotional climax is Henry's speech to "we few, we happy few, we band of brothers." It was the first Shakespearean film to be a great popular success. A left-wing American journalist wrote after seeing it: "I am not a Tory, a monarchist, a Catholic, a medievalist, an Englishman [or] a lover of war, but the beauty and power . . . was such that . . . I wished I was, I thought I was, and was proud of it."[106] Yet there was much soul-searching about what English character and values really were, or what they ought to be; and also a wish to see the war as more than a nationalist conflict— echoing the anti-war feeling of the 1930s—but rather as a struggle for democracy and civilization, which Churchill himself put powerfully into words.

So it was widely accepted that an essential part of maintaining national cohesion was to improve the lot of the mass of the population. The queen wrote to her mother during the Blitz: "The destruction is so awful, & the people so *wonderful*—they *deserve* a better world."[107] Making this better world—belatedly fulfilling the promises made during the First World War but dashed by the Depression—became an important part of British domestic and foreign propaganda, which the Nazi government tried to drown out. Social welfare in Britain was already "probably more comprehensive than in any other democratic country,"[108] but there were gaps and these had been shown up by the strains of war, including by evacuation (of which there was another, smaller, wave during the Blitz, and a third during the V-weapon attacks in 1944). Evacuation brought the rural and middle classes into close contact with deprived city children, with results that received sensational, and rather exaggerated, press coverage, especially concerning "problem families" (a new term), lice, scabies and bed-wetting.[109] Wartime needs had already brought about important increases in national welfare benefits in 1940 and 1941. Sir William Beveridge, austere social scientist, eugenicist, Whitehall mandarin, former director of the LSE and an Oxford don, was commissioned in 1941 by Arthur Greenwood, Labour Minister of Reconstruction, to report on welfare policy, which he did the following year. He had been advising on this since the 1900s and many of the ideas he produced were familiar— essentially, contributory insurance and a stern refusal to give "something for nothing." An exception was his support for family allowances, with the eugenicist aim of encouraging good-quality babies to ensure "the adequate continuance of the British race." Allowances were at first opposed by the TUC, which feared they would "dig at the roots of a virile trade unionism," in which a man should earn enough to support his family.[110]

What Beveridge called in Victorian language "the five giants" of "Want, Disease, Ignorance, Squalor and Idleness" would be attacked through "a comprehensive programme of social progress." He aimed to create "incentive, opportunity, responsibility," by providing a "national minimum" safety net (£2 per week) in return for "service and contribution." He favoured austerity: "no allowance for beer or tobacco or cinemas [or] high rents," and compulsory training for the long-term unemployed. Everyone, rich and poor, would pay the same level of contribution and receive the same level of benefit, regardless of means. This would encourage people to work to provide "more than that minimum" for themselves and their families through extra insurance and private pension schemes. Inherent to Beveridge's vision was a National Health Service to maintain breadwinners' health and so keep down costs.[111]

The Beveridge report (December 1942), was a best-seller despite its resolutely boring title: *Social Insurance and Allied Services*. A Barrow-in-Furness housewife, after hearing him on the radio, felt "a bit more hopeful about the 'brave new world' now."[112] An opinion poll showed 86 percent in favour of its recommendations, including big majorities among those who felt that they themselves would not gain from them.[113] This popular reaction spurred a startled government to act, or at least to promise. Churchill committed himself to a postwar "Four-Year Plan" to implement compulsory national insurance "from the cradle to the grave," a National Health Service, increased welfare (for "putting milk into babies"), equal opportunity in education, full employment, house-building and "a broadening field for state ownership and enterprise."[114] But Tory hesitations over Beveridge, and their lack of an alternative vision, meant that they "slithered haltingly and unpersuasively towards collectivism, but without gaining any credit."[115] Labour's contrasting enthusiasm for "Beveridge Now!" opened a political division that would contribute to their landslide victory in 1945, and the rapid implementation of the plan.

The other major reform was aimed at Beveridge's "Ignorance": to extend compulsory secondary education to fifteen, rising to sixteen. There was also discussion about incorporating the independent public schools into the system—Churchill wanted 60–70 percent of their places filled by bursaries awarded by "the counties and the great cities"[116]—and many other politicians and non-party voices urged greater equality. Leading the change was the young Tory R. A. Butler (relegated to the then minor role of president of the Board of Education in part for his pro-appeasement record). The Act of 1944, a historic landmark, bore the marks of its time: greater uniformity and central supervision. A new Ministry of Education reorganized the existing mix of local-authority schools, church schools and independent foundations. Hundreds of small Local Education Authorities disappeared. Fees for publicly funded schools were abolished. The new model was for three types of state secondary provision: grammar, technical and "secondary modern," providing academic, technical and vocational instruction, to be given "parity" of resources and esteem. Children would be directed into one of these types by a single aptitude test (based on quasi-scientific IQ testing) at the age of eleven. But this was not meant to create a rigid divide: it was urged as crucially important that there should be easy subsequent transfer between these schools, and it was officially hoped that they might all be located together, as "multilateral" schools—the germ of the later comprehensives. Butler spoke of his aim of "welding us all into one nation . . . instead of two nations as Disraeli talked about." But the system never worked as intended: technical education was not developed by Local Education Authorities, and transfer between schools rarely happened, leaving a divide between grammar and secondary modern schools drawn by the "11 plus" examination.[117] This created enduring resentments which have bedevilled debate about education in England ever since.

The idea of state planning, around since the 1920s, had been boosted by the war, even among Tories such as Churchill. The successes of Britain's war socialism, and the example of the now widely admired USSR, seemed unambiguous. More broadly, the war had created a general desire for improvement, for fairness, for an end to the unemployment and instability of the 1930s, and for organized national efficiency. These aims seemed achievable through central direction. The war had given the state vastly greater resources of manpower, money and expertise. A senior civil servant saw this in January 1941:

> The war is moving us in the direction of Labour's ideas and ideals, and the planning for a new "national order" will be more towards the left than may generally be imagined . . . it will be fatal for officials to formulate their ideas in any spirit of timidity . . . Planning on bold and generous lines is what is looked for, and it may well be necessary to free our minds from conceptions that . . . seem almost sacred.[118]

In things that mattered, wrote Attlee's economic adviser, Douglas Jay, "the gentleman in Whitehall really does know better what is good for people than the people know themselves."[119] This was an important part of a political, intellectual and above all an emotional swing to the left, which has become a significant part of our memory of the war.

But the New Jerusalem had limits. The cost of the war, and of postwar military spending during the Cold War, restricted social spending. Important interests set boundaries. Doctors wanted a centrally funded health service, but only if their private contracts were preserved. Trade unionists wanted full employment, but no controls over labour. Employers wanted state aid, but no state interference. People's sentiments and expectations were ambivalent: there was certainly a widespread desire for improvement in health care, employment prospects and prosperity, but at the same time almost universal hostility to official interference in private lives. Many people felt they were fighting for a better world; but were also defending the untidy and unregimented pluralism of British social life, which intellectuals such as Orwell saw as the best protection of freedom. Victory, most people hoped, would allow them to return to normal, and be left alone by officialdom.[120] This ambivalence partly explains the swings in postwar politics.

## THREE CORNERS OF THE WORLD IN ARMS

> Come the three corners of the world in arms
> And we shall shock them! Naught shall make us rue
> If England to itself do rest but true!
> Shakespeare, *King John*: a popular wartime quotation

> Peter was unfortunately killed by an 88;
> it took his leg away, he died in the ambulance.
> I saw him crawling on the sand, he said
> It's most unfair, they've shot my foot off.
> How can I live among this gentle
> obsolescent breed of heroes, and not weep?
> Keith Douglas, Tunisia, 1943[121]

Suspension of the war on the Continent in 1940 was arguably the best available alternative for Britain and the world, for it made eventual victory possible.[122] A clear-sighted U-boat officer thought that "the English can hold out under existing conditions for years . . . The U-Boat arm will not [break them] nor airmen either. Time is on the side of the English and we cannot afford to give them time."[123] Britain, the world's greatest arms manufacturer,[124] was indeed unlikely to lose but it was not clear that it could win. Germany could not win, but it was not clear how it could lose. Britain was fighting two major enemies, with a third, Japan, threatening on the other side of the globe. The possibility of having to negotiate a compromise one day with Germany hung in the air. Yet the Chiefs of Staff were optimistic: a Future Strategy Paper (4 Sept. 1940) predicted that an oil shortage would force the Germans into a decisive battle in the Middle East, and, following that, Britain should aim to "pass to the general offensive . . . in the spring of 1942." Churchill hoped the new Special Operations Executive (SOE) would "set Europe ablaze"; and equally great and unrealistic hopes were placed in bombing. An eventual British invasion of the Continent, it was hoped, would simply give the coup de grâce to a bomb-shattered and reeling Germany.

Behind these hopes lay the resources and manpower of the empire: as well as Britain's own armed forces, 2.6 million in 1940 and rising to over 5 million in 1945, they included the largest volunteer army in history, 2.5 million strong, from India; 500,000 from Africa; over a million from Canada; over a million from Australia; and over 300,000 from New Zealand, which had a proportion of battle casualties second only to that of the Soviet Union.[125] This total manpower was comparable with that mobilized by the United States (about 12 million by 1945), much greater than that of Germany (which peaked at some 9.5 million in 1943), though smaller than the vast but incalculable total for the Soviet Union, which lost about 10 million men killed or permanently missing during the war against Germany.[126] British Empire forces would serve in Britain, East and North Africa, Madagascar, Egypt, Syria, Iraq, Palestine, Hong Kong, Malaya, Burma, Greece, Italy and eventually France and Germany—a wider deployment than those of any other combattant.[127] Part of the English myth of 1940 is of fighting "alone." In fact, this was the last great imperial struggle, the fourth great war in which Britain was victorious by being able to mobilize global resources against a European hegemon.*

Across Europe and the world, people judged the combatants, made their calculations about who would win, and chose sides or temporized, influenced by pre-existing attitudes to what they thought of as "England." Many Nazis viscerally detested England, sometimes for the very things Hitler professed to admire, such as its supposed haughty and aristocratic character—Luftwaffe pilots called the RAF "*die Lords.*" Opinion surveys in Germany reported "Sentiment strong against England": "People wish, sometimes openly, that Churchill wouldn't give up" so that they will

---

* The others being the Seven Years' War (1756–63), the Revolutionary and Napoleonic wars (1793–1815), and the First World War.

"really get it in the neck."[128] One German U-boat officer predicted glee-fully in 1941 that "they'll get such a bellyfull! There'll be air-raids day and night! They'll have no rest. Then they can creep away into their rabbit-holes in England and eat grass. God punish England and her satellite states."[129] But some young Germans, "Swing Kids," copied "the English style" (including rolled umbrellas) as a sign of dissidence, and Nazi party authorities threatened harsh punishment on "yid-Eton style girls and boys" who affected "all the bits and pieces of being a *gentleman* . . . the English style, the stupid, phoney magic . . . typical of the island."[130] People round the world came to like the Germans because they disliked the English; and vice-versa. Anglophile (and Germanophobe) and Germano-phile (and Anglophobe) sympathies often corresponded with the upper and lower-middle classes. Anglophiles in many countries, including Ger-many, were often conservatives who admired what they saw as English respect for tradition and disdain for vulgar demagoguery, and they shared Churchill's detestation of Nazism as a mixture of barbarism and techno-cratic modernity—a view not very different from that of its admirers, who saw it as the creator of an exciting, powerful and profitable "New Order." Wrote a prominent French intellectual, the novelist Pierre Drieu la Rochelle: "Someone who today believes in the victory of England is like someone who in 1900 prophesied the victory of China, with its manda-rins and pigtails and jade buttons, over the European empires with their motors and cannons." Many saw Hitler's "New Europe" as inevitable. Both Vichy France and Franco's Spain would contemplate joining the war on Germany's side against Britain. A former Dutch prime minister, Hen-drik Colijn, although he abominated Nazism, proclaimed in June 1940: "One fact dominates everything: Germany will now lead Europe."[131] But Britain's continuing fight denied that Germany had won, and also denied that Europe was decisive. General Charles de Gaulle had got the point at once, when on 18 June 1940 he appealed to the French nation not to despair: "Must hope disappear? Is defeat final? No! . . . [We] can make common cause with the British empire, which commands the seas and is continuing the struggle."[132] Hitler's propaganda minister, Joseph Goeb-bels, a leading Anglophobe, was disturbed by reading reports of a House of Commons debate on the war in June 1941: "Churchill's speech [con-tained] excuses and very little information. But no sign of weakness . . . England's will to resist is still intact."[133]

But the global extent of Britain's empire was a cause of vulnerability as well as of strength. In the Middle East and Asia, the war gave an oppor-tunity to all those who resented British power and colonial rule. Many hated Jewish settlement in Palestine, grudgingly permitted by the British.

Some actively cooperated with the Nazis, who tailored their anti-Semitism to attract Arab support. In Egypt, King Farouk was forced in June 1940 to appoint a pro-British government literally by tanks on his lawn. In Iraq, a pro-Nazi nationalist, Rashid Ali, seized power in 1941, launched anti-Jewish violence, and began hostile preparations with German aid until he was removed by a mainly Indian expedition. In India itself, the war had disrupted moves towards self-government, causing conflict between the Congress Party, the main political movement, and the British authorities, who crushed riots and interned opposition politicians, including Gandhi and Nehru. An Afghan diplomat assured a German colleague that "Germany has many friends in the world, more than she thinks. They wait for her to show the way to a new order of the globe." But another German diplomat lamented "the hardly comprehensible aura which still enveloped England [and] continues to delude some countries even now."[134] For both friends and enemies, being "pro-English" would encompass many things: "liberal, democratic, humanist, pro-Jewish, even *Catholic* on occasion, anti-Nazi in every case."[135] Despite Germany's dizzy triumphs of 1940, many people remained sceptical that it could win in the end. They were right: Hitler, looking back a few weeks before his suicide, admitted he had "underestimated one factor . . . the extent to which Churchill's Englishmen were influenced by the Jews" and so denied Germany its ultimate victory.[136]

A tangible feature in Britain of the globalization of the war was the presence of foreign troops: European, Commonwealth (including 500,000 Canadians) and American (up to 2 million). The English were more than ever exposed to the delights of American culture—chewing gum, nylons, films, music, dances. Reactions were mixed, and Anglo-American relations became a romanticized subject of later books and films. At the time, some disliked American "bragging" and their seeming indifference to everything in England except girls.[137] Another cause of friction was racial segregation in the American army. In one Warwickshire Women's Institute, for example, a local organizer was "really astonished at depth of feeling against any discrimination against blacks . . . dislike of white Americans really bitter, but none of darkies."[138] The period before D-Day saw an erotic explosion: "I won't describe the scenes or sounds of Hyde Park or Green Park at dusk or just after dark," wrote a Canadian soldier—"a vast battlefield of sex."[139] Over 40,000 British women married Americans and emigrated, often in rather demeaning circumstances. Many foreign soldiers stayed, including Poles and West Indians.[140]

Seapower, for both defence and attack, was the key to victory, as it had been against the Kaiser, Napoleon, Louis XV and Philip of Spain. It determined all Allied strategic decisions: "If we lose the war at sea, we lose the war," observed the First Sea Lord. In 1940 approximately one-third of the British war effort relied on imports.[141] The Atlantic routes to Canada and the United States were the principal lifeline. The Mediterranean was the embattled route to North Africa, the Suez Canal and, with the safer but long route round the Cape, to the Arab oilfields, Asia and the Pacific. The United States and Canada were essential suppliers. South America too was a source of vital meat and grain. The Royal Navy's blockade of Germany and occupied Europe cut off or reduced essentials for the Axis war effort—oil, fertilizer, animal feed, rubber, copper, nickel, cotton, wool—forcing the laborious manufacture of synthetic oil and rubber, causing chronic food and fuel shortages and strangling production. Consequently, the German conquest of western Europe was giving them far less benefit than expected: for example, by the end of 1941 Britain had shipped in over 5,000 American aircraft; Germany had received, from France and Holland, a grand total of seventy-eight. The same disparity extended across the board: Germany had at most 8 million tons of oil per year, and from this it had to try to supply Italy and the economies of the conquered territories; whereas Britain imported over 10 million tons in 1942, despite the submarine campaign in the Atlantic, and 20 million tons in 1944.[142]

Germany was much weaker at sea than in 1914. It was outclassed on the surface, and Britain's ruthless seizure or destruction of most of the French fleet in 1940 deprived it of the possibility of rapid reinforcement. But it could still inflict serious damage on merchant shipping by stealth and speed. The first British success came when the pocket battleship *Graf Spee* was cornered and tricked into scuttling itself in December 1939 in Montevideo harbour. The fast battlecruisers *Scharnhorst* and *Gneisenau* sank twenty-two ships in a two-month Atlantic sortie early in 1941— their one major success. One of Germany's two powerful battleships, *Bismarck*, managed only one six-day sortie in May 1941. Intercepted by the battlecruiser *Hood* and the battleship *Prince of Wales*—so new that civilian shipbuilders were still on board—*Bismarck* sank *Hood* (of her crew of 1,400 only 3 survived), but was damaged by shells from *Prince of Wales*. Forced to head for shelter in Brest, the German ship was hunted down, disabled by air attack, quickly put out of action by the heavy guns of the battleships *Rodney* and *King George V*, and finished off with torpedoes, with the loss of 2,000 crewmen. Thereafter, Germany's remaining capital ships lurked in Norwegian fjords. The havoc that even their threat could wreak was shown in July 1942 when Ultra codebreaking (see pp. 732–33) indicated that the battleship *Tirpitz* was about to put to sea with a powerful squadron to attack convoy PQ 17, thirty-seven ships taking supplies to Russia. To avoid total destruction, the convoy was ordered to scatter—a controversial, harrowing, but justifiable decision. But twenty-six ships were then picked off by aircraft and submarines, with the loss of 153 seamen and their cargo of 2,500 aircraft, 4,000 trucks and 430 tanks. Yet, overall, Germany's surface fleet was contained, not least by lack of fuel, and all its major ships were eliminated by a combination of the Royal Navy and the RAF. *Scharnhorst*, its movements disclosed by Ultra intelligence, was caught and sunk by the battleship *Duke of York* after trying to attack a convoy in December 1943. *Tirpitz* was eventually sunk by RAF bombers in November 1944 after twenty-two air attacks.

The Mediterranean was a vital but vulnerable link. Italy's most effective force was its navy, larger than that of its German ally. It was met head-on, with a successful air attack by twenty Swordfish torpedo bombers at Taranto in November 1940, which disabled three battleships, and by a fleet action at Cape Matapan (based on signals intelligence) in March 1941, which sank three cruisers. The Italian army was defeated in Abyssinia and eastern Libya by smaller British forces between September 1940 and April 1941. The Italians invaded Greece unsuccessfully in October 1940, but in April 1941 the Germans joined in, attacking Greece and Yugoslavia. Churchill felt obliged to aid the Greeks with aircraft, ships, and then British and Australian troops drawn from North Africa. German intervention tipped the balance against them, and they had to be hastily evacuated to Crete, and then, after a German airborne attack, evacuated again to Egypt. The fall of Crete in May 1941 was a damaging humiliation, and its evacuation cost the navy three cruisers and six destroyers sunk, and 2,000 sailors killed. The Germans also aided their Italian ally in North Africa, sending the dynamic General Erwin Rommel's Afrika Korps in February 1941. The victorious British forces in North Africa had been seriously weakened by the expedition to Greece and Crete. They were also distracted by the need to control Iraq and its oilfields and to secure their rear in Lebanon and Syria (controlled by the Vichy French, who were offering airfields to the Luftwaffe). They could not cope with Rommel's small Panzer force—he became a legend to his enemies as the "Desert Fox"—and all their previous gains in Libya were lost by July 1941. The Italians sank two British battleships by midget submarine in Alexandria. All these losses badly weakened the Royal Navy, and for a time it lost control of the Mediterranean. But it may be that Greece and Crete caused Hitler to delay his attack on Russia by several weeks, leaving insufficient time for a decisive victory before the onset of winter in 1941.

The Mediterranean remained bitterly contested by sea and air until 1943, and so most British communications had to be routed round the

Cape, which required far more ships. Malta, for centuries the key to the Mediterranean, remained an exposed and vital outpost for the Royal Navy, especially its submarines. The island was constantly attacked by Italian and German bombers from Sicily and North Africa, and precariously supplied by convoys from Gibraltar, which were themselves prodigies of determination as they braved constant sea and air attack. Malta was probably (along with Dover) the most damaged place in the empire and its population the most tested: at the height of the attack, the first half of 1942, about 7,000 tons of bombs fell on the area of the Grand Harbour in six weeks; twenty-one Royal Navy warships were sunk, and 75 percent of the houses in Valletta were destroyed or damaged.[143] The unique award of the George Cross to the whole island in April 1942 was a symbolic recognition of its extraordinary fortitude. It was largely British submarines based there which decimated Italy's merchant navy and blockaded Rommel's forces in North Africa.

But the Atlantic was Britain's lifeline and the artery of the whole Allied war effort. As President Roosevelt put it to Churchill, if Hitler could not win there, "he cannot win anywhere in the world in the end."[144] Germany's best chance of controlling the sea, defeating Britain, and winning the war was during nine months between June 1940 and March 1941, when over 2 million tons of British shipping were sunk, the peak of losses. Conquest of Norway and France had transformed the strategic situation, giving naval and submarine bases with easy access to the Atlantic, and air bases covering the Western Approaches to Britain—long-range bombers sank over 1.5 million tons of British shipping in 1940–41. The German navy adopted the same tactics and objectives as in the First World War: unrestricted submarine warfare. The Kriegsmarine calculated that if it sank 600,000 tons of shipping monthly for twelve months—the same calculation as in 1917—Britain would starve. But the Royal Navy too had learned from 1917, and at once adopted what would be a highly efficient global convoy system, though the delays inherent in convoy organization equated to a major loss in shipping capacity. Some 9,000 convoys were escorted to and from Britain during the war, roughly one every two days for over five years. Most were not even attacked, and over the whole war 99 percent of ships sailing from North America to Britain arrived safely. But this success required unrelenting effort. "Wolf packs" of several dozen U-boats were assembled to attack convoys and they had a formidable advantage—the Kriegsmarine could decipher British merchant-navy codes and so could track convoy movements from a control room in France, whereas the British ceased to be able to read a new German naval code in February 1942, and only broke it in December. Early in 1941 the

Germans were almost sinking their target figure, and occasionally exceeded it during 1942. Overall, however, as in the First World War, they failed to take account of the world total of shipping that could be drawn on to service British trade, and also the country's ability to replace lost ships and reduce imports by home production (including by "digging for victory" and greater efficiency). Britain launched more than 1.2 million tons of new ships in 1941, and only briefly in 1942 and 1944 did it have to run down its reserves of key materials: otherwise, imports always exceeded consumption. Germany struggled to maintain the submarine campaign, hampered by shortages of copper and rubber imposed by the British blockade: the number of U-boats operating in the Atlantic fell to only twenty-two in February 1941. In the second half of that year, sinkings fell sharply to below 100,000 tons per month, and there was no hope of fulfilling the plan of defeating Britain by the autumn.[145] Britain's biggest problem was the 600-mile "Atlantic gap"—the mid-ocean area beyond air cover. In short, the U-boats could slow, but not halt, the flow of food, materials and men. Nevertheless, sinkings were grievous: 1,299 ships in 1941, with over half their crews drowned. U-boats also sank a huge amount of American shipping when the United States entered the war—easy pickings due to American inexperience.[146]

Britain had a priceless secret, "an energizing vein that runs through the whole conduct of the war."[147] This was its growing penetration of secret enemy communications. These used versions of a commercially produced encoding machine, Enigma, developed in Germany in 1923 and then costing about £30. It was simple to use, easily portable, capable of encoding a message into trillions of random combinations, and regarded as indecipherable. It was used by all the German armed forces, at all levels from the high command to units in the field. The Polish intelligence service tried for years to find a way into the system, and began to succeed in the early 1930s. In July 1939 they shared their knowledge (including Enigma machines and the design of an advanced electronic calculator) with the French and British. The British took over the work and based it at Bletchley Park, in Buckinghamshire, where during the Phoney War intense efforts were made to create a system to penetrate and exploit Enigma. By April–May 1940 they began to decipher messages—too late to influence the 1940 disasters. Neither the Poles nor the French ever told their German conquerors that Enigma was vulnerable.

The Bletchley staff, 150 in 1939, rose to 3,500 women and men by late 1942 and over 9,000 by 1945, plus overseas outposts. Many of the staff were academics or students, mostly from Cambridge and Oxford, in mathematics, history and languages. They deciphered often fragmentary messages, assessed their importance, and distributed the resulting information securely to the right people in a system codenamed "Ultra"—the highest level of secrecy. They developed new computing technology as well as relying on native cunning in deducing the meaning of incomprehensible messages. When, for example, young Harry Hinsley, a working-class Walsall boy recruited while a history undergraduate at St. John's, Cambridge, guessed in June 1940 that the German navy was planning a sortie, the Admiralty ignored him and the aircraft carrier HMS *Glorious* was sunk by the *Scharnhorst*. After that they listened, including when he told them he thought the *Bismarck* was heading for France—and she was caught.

Amazingly, the Ultra secret was kept throughout the war and for thirty years afterwards, such was the cohesion of the large Bletchley team. Allied commanders had to be careful to conceal from the enemy when they knew his plans in advance. The most valuable information was often of a routine nature—numbers of enemy tanks and aircraft, location of U-boat "wolf packs," movement of supply convoys, and shortages of fuel or ammunition. Several times, the secret was nearly disclosed (the worst offenders being indiscreet Americans and careless New Zealanders), but it was saved by luck, and by the refusal of the Germans and Japanese to believe that Enigma could be broken. For agonizing periods, it did remain unbroken—as we have noted, between February and December 1942 U-boat codes were impenetrable, at a cost of merchant seamen's lives and millions of tons of shipping. But in the end the impossible was done: by brilliant mathematics in which two Cambridge dons, Max Newman and Alan Turing, were prominent; by ingenious technology (the first electronic digital computer, Colossus II, was largely designed by a Post Office engineer, Tommy Flowers); by informed guesswork, such as that by Hinsley; and by daring military actions hundreds of miles from Bletchley. The guesswork—which the English have liked to see as a victory for certain of their national traits over those of their enemy—came for example by noticing that German radio operators were addicted to routine phrases (though not, contrary to popular myth, "Heil Hitler") and working back from there. The daring actions were capturing lists of Enigma key settings from German ships or submarines. On one crucial occasion, 30 October 1942, these were snatched from a sinking U-boat in the Mediterranean by three young sailors, two of whom, Lieutenant Anthony Fasson and Able Seaman Colin Grazier, drowned and were posthumously awarded the George Cross. Their coup was equal to a major naval victory, for it enabled Bletchley Park again to penetrate German communications and greatly reduce convoy losses.[148] From 1942 the amount of information took off and by the end of the war nearly 100,000 decrypted messages, and over 500,000 short German naval signals, had been supplied to Allied forces abroad. Ultra intelligence eventually gave the Allies a huge, increasing and at times incalculable advantage, and while it could not guarantee, it did certainly advance Germany's defeat.

The fateful decisions that turned the last European war, principally Anglo-German, into the Second World War were taken as early as the summer of 1940. "England" stubbornly refused to see what was plain to Hitler: its only hope of remaining an imperial power was to choose "Europe" against America.[149] After losing the Battle of Britain and abandoning Operation Sealion in December 1940, Germany had no obvious way of defeating Britain, except by the slow and uncertain submarine campaign, which (as in 1917) risked dragging in America. Among Hitler's plans was indeed a war with the Anglo-Americans, featuring "Plan Z" to build by 1948 a huge battle fleet to intimidate or defeat Britain and a long-range bomber force (initiated in 1937) to attack America. But, although a giant aircraft carrier was laid down, this was far off, even for fantasists. The reality was that Germany, despite its conquest of much of Europe, lacked the oil, raw materials and manufacturing capacity to win a long war against Britain, backed by its empire and America. So as early as July 1940 Hitler talked of bringing forward an attack on his accomplice Russia, and in September he concluded a pact with Japan. The fixed point in his world view was to conquer "living space"—*Lebensraum*—in eastern Europe. This had been postponed pending the defeat of France and Britain, but the latter's resistance changed the calculation: "Britain's hope lies in Russia and the United States," Hitler told his generals in July 1940. "If Russia drops out of the picture, America, too, is lost for Britain, because elimination of Russia would tremendously increase Japan's power in the Far East."[150] Conquest of Russia, assumed to be easy, would gain for Germany the resources that would neutralize the British naval blockade. An inevitable, even desired, consequence would be the removal and likely starvation of 20–30 million Slavs and Jews. "Efforts to save the population from death by starvation," decided the high command, "diminish the staying power of Germany in the war and resistance . . . to the blockade."[151] Then would come global victory, beginning with an attack on the British in the Middle East and India, if they had not seen sense and become Germany's pliant ally. Late in 1941, with Russia's defeat seemingly imminent, attention shifted back to the naval and air war against Britain. Later, in 1943, facing stalemate in the east, Hitler talked of making peace with Stalin and concentrating on the destruction of "England," now seen as the perversely implacable enemy.[152]

From December 1940 onwards, detailed plans were made for Operation Barbarossa. Stalin, who had taken advantage of his pact with Hitler to invade Poland, Estonia, Lithuania, Latvia, Finland and Romania and slaughter opponents there, disregarded warnings from Churchill (derived from Ultra) and from his own spies that a German attack was imminent. So when it began on 22 June 1941 the Red Army and Air Force were taken by surprise and crushingly defeated. By July the German army was celebrating victory. Special units—*Einsatzgruppen*—began the systematic slaughter of Communists and Jews. Within months, hundreds of thousands of mainly Jewish men, women and children, and hundreds of thousands of Russian prisoners, had been murdered and a secret order had been given to annihilate all the Jews in Germany's hands.

The Japanese had been hesitating about whether, or when, to start a war against Britain and America. Hitler was eager to bring them into the struggle and promised his support. In December the Japanese launched nearly simultaneous attacks against the somnolent American naval base of Pearl Harbor, Hawaii, and against British colonies. On 11 December, Hitler, as promised, declared war on the United States. Thus, thanks to its enemies, the British Empire was no longer alone: first the Soviet Union and then the United States were forced to fight. "So we had won after all!" wrote Churchill later. "England would live; Britain would live; the Commonwealth of Nations and the Empire would live." The Russians, recovering remarkably, temporarily stopped the German advance in December 1941, inflicting and receiving huge casualties.

For the time being, the new allies were no help to Britain: the Russians were again on the verge of defeat as the Germans resumed their advance; the unprepared Americans were "dazed," Air Marshal Harris discovered, "hardly able to speak," and cancelling promised aircraft deliveries to the RAF.[153] From late 1941 until the summer of 1942, Britain faced its worst and most demoralizing setbacks. Malta was under unrelenting air attack, the Royal Navy in the Mediterranean was decimated, and the weakened army in North Africa was under severe pressure. The effective closure of the Mediterranean route made it impossible to send rapid reinforcements to Asia. On 8 December 1941, the day after Pearl Harbor, the Japanese attacked the Philippines, Malaya and Hong Kong, on the fourteenth they entered Burma, and on the twentieth attacked the Dutch East Indies. British forces in Burma began a demoralizing 900-mile retreat into India. In Libya, after pendulum-like advances and retreats, Rommel's forces tipped the balance: in June 1942 they took the key port of Tobruk, and went on to threaten Egypt.

The Royal Navy had long planned as best it could for a simultaneous war in Asia as well as the Atlantic and the Mediterranean. During the interwar period, Singapore had been designed as a fortified naval base, but never completed due to British and Australian defence cuts: Ramsay MacDonald had condemned it as "wild and wasteful."[154] Nevertheless, it seemed one of the most heavily defended pieces of territory in the British Empire,[155] at least to non-experts, including Churchill. Heavy guns covered its sea approaches, and though they were not, despite legend, pointing only out to sea, they were designed to engage large ships, not aircraft, tanks or soldiers on bicycles. Malayan forests and terrain had been supposed to make a land attack unfeasible, but by 1941 Malaya had some of the best roads in Asia. It was also far more vulnerable due to Japanese presence in the nearby French colony of Indo-China. The Chiefs of Staff knew that air defence was the key. But Churchill gave priority to the Middle East and Russia: there were only 158 aircraft in Malaya, less than half the required number, while 445 modern aircraft had just been shipped to the Soviet Union.[156] The battleship *Prince of Wales* and the battlecruiser *Repulse* had been sent out to Singapore in October to deter the Japanese, impress Stalin, and calm Australian nerves. They sailed from Singapore to disrupt Japanese landings on the Malayan coast, but on 10 December both were sunk by land-based aircraft from French Indo-China. This stunned Britain's Asian empire and presaged disasters to come.[157] The British and Americans had lost ten battleships in three days—as many as in the whole Japanese navy—adding to recent serious British losses in the Mediterranean of four battleships and an aircraft carrier seriously damaged or sunk by torpedoes or midget submarines.[158] General Brooke, the newly appointed Chief of the Imperial General Staff (CIGS), noted that "from Africa eastwards to America through the Indian Ocean to the Pacific, we have lost command of the sea. This affects reinforcements to Middle East, India, Burma, Far East, Australia and New Zealand!"[159]

The Japanese occupied Hong Kong on 25 December, and went on a spree of rape and killing. In Malaya, they advanced with ruthless efficiency, bombing and machine-gunning everything that moved. Japanese radio mocked "you English gentlemen," asking, "Isn't [our bombing] a better tonic than your whisky soda?" The Indian, Australian and British forces, hastily rushed in, numerically superior but poorly trained, without air cover, tanks or anti-tank weapons, weakly commanded and low in morale, fell back on Singapore, where many arrived after weeks at sea just in time to surrender. The British civilian administration, frightened by what the Japanese might do to Europeans, especially women, fled, destroying everything of value they could. This abandonment and destruction had a devastating psychological effect on the people of Malaya, long reliant on British protection. At the end of January, Singapore island was besieged. The British headmaster of the elite Raffles College asked one of his boys what was happening—"the end of the British Empire," replied the boy, Lee Kuan Yew, later the Cambridge-educated first prime minister of independent Singapore.[160] The Japanese attacked on 8 February, with heavy shelling and bombing. Churchill ordered a fight to the last man, for the honour of the empire and the army—and to reassure Australia, India and America. The Japanese themselves were nearing exhaustion and running out of ammunition. But on 15 February the whole British Empire force, 85,000 men, surrendered to 30,000 Japanese, whose commander could hardly believe it. Prisoners and civilians suffered cruelty of a kind already seen on a far more horrific scale in China.

The fall of Singapore—which Churchill called "the worst disaster and largest capitulation in British history"[161]—is often plausibly seen as marking the end of British prestige in Asia, exposing the psychological ascendancy on which imperial rule had been based as mere bluff. As one Indian officer put it, "The Fall of Singapore finally convinced me of the degeneration of the British people and I thought the last days of the British Empire had come."[162] In India, Gandhi and the Congress party called in the summer of 1942 for a massive campaign of civil disobedience, the "Quit India" movement. This was a formidable threat to British rule in the face of the Japanese advances, and the colonial authorities suppressed it by banning Congress and gaoling thousands of its activists.

The primary causes of the Asian disaster were more material than psychological: a naval base without ships and airfields without planes. The Japanese conquered the scattered British Empire in the Far East—Hong Kong, Malaya, Singapore, Burma and North Borneo—for the loss of 5,000 men.[163] With it came a significant proportion of the world's rubber, tin and oil. The loss of Burmese rice, combined with severe flooding, inept, timid and selfish policies by Indian and British administrators, and local profiteering, led to a terrible famine in Bengal in the summer of 1943. World food shortages and transport problems, including lack of shipping (due to U-boat sinkings, the multiple demands of war, Churchill's indifference and American commanders' refusal to lend ships), greatly aggravated it. The nationalist leader Jawaharlal Nehru, from his prison cell, lamented "the misfortune of India . . . not only to have a foreign government, but a government which is incompetent and incapable of organising her defence properly or for providing for . . . the essential needs of her people." Perhaps 2 million died; and only the drive of a new viceroy, Field Marshal Viscount Wavell, and an improved harvest alleviated the crisis.[164]

A dispassionate explanation for Britain's early reverses is simple. The country and the empire were fighting, almost unaided, three formidable enemies spread round the globe. It had never before faced such a combination. It had to react to the unexpected with military forces that had been rapidly expanded and armed with new weapons developed only in the previous four or five years—and some of them, including early bombers and a succession of tank types, did not work very well.[165] The army, the Cinderella service between the wars, had to be built up in months from a small imperial gendarmerie into a mass conscript army—the recurring English problem for three centuries. Its needs had to wait on those of the navy and the insatiable RAF. An obvious reason for not seeing weaknesses of the army as a symptom of national decline is that the navy and the RAF were clearly unaffected: they were ruthlessly efficient in sinking submarines, shooting down bombers, dropping bombs, and accepting—and inflicting—high levels of casualties.

But dispassionate analysis was nigh impossible in 1942. The public, politicians and military commanders were angry, worried, and seeking scapegoats. Churchill had to deal with criticism in the Commons and a vote of confidence in January—finally won by 146 votes to 1 (an Independent Labour member). In private, his mood fluctuated between sturdy confidence and despondency. Behind the scenes, insiders were shaken. "Why is it that we can never win any battle at all?" lamented one MP in his diary. "A whisper is going around that our troops do not fight well."[166] The CIGS, Brooke, wrote in his diary: "Cannot work out why troops are not fighting better." Churchill himself burst out in private that "in 1915 our men fought on even when they had only one shell left . . . We have so many men in Singapore . . . they should have done better." Brooke meditated gloomily that "I have during the last ten years had an unpleasant feeling that the British empire was decaying and that we were on a slippery decline!! . . . I wonder whether we shall again bring off a comeback?"[167] We see here the fear of decline that was to scar English elites for generations, and still clings to our view of ourselves like pitch. In August, Churchill made a dangerous and tiring flight to Moscow only to be asked by Stalin, "Why we were so afraid of the Germans . . . if the British army had been fighting the Germans as much as the Russian army it would not be so frightened of them."[168] Many in Britain took a not dissimilar view. Admiration for Stalin and the Red Army reached enormous heights.[169]

Worries about the performance of English soldiers have caused much subsequent cogitation among military historians. Generals and politicians were indeed set against repeating the slaughter of the First World War, and adopted tactics with that aim, such as using concentrated artillery fire to prepare the ground for infantry. Citizen armies of liberal states certainly did not fight like the Nazis or Soviets, comparatively indifferent to casualties and enforcing discipline by thousands of executions (though these could not prevent large-scale desertion). English soldiers were said to "lack enthusiasm and interest in the war" and when questioned had "few, if any, ideas" of the issues. Lectures were provided, but may not have counteracted what one paratrooper summed up as the men's "three basic interests: football, beer and crumpet." English soldiers came from a civic culture that, as we have seen, had over the Victorian period become decreasingly violent: Orwell thought that "in no country inhabited by white men is it easier to shove people off the pavement."[170] They were largely apolitical and identified most strongly with their families and their homes.[171] A Wolverhampton boy expressed this in a farewell letter to his parents which, like many soldiers, he had written to be sent if he was killed:

> England's a great little country—the best there is—but I cannot honestly say that it is "worth fighting for." Nor can I fancy myself in the role of a gallant crusader fighting for the liberation of Europe . . . No, Mom, my little world is centred around you and including Dad, everyone at home, and my friends . . . *That* is worth fighting for [and] worth dying for too.[172]

Motivation was often expressed as a wish to "get the job done" and go back home; and the strongest everyday loyalty was to comrades and unit.[173] Not everyone lacked confidence in the British army, however. As they retreated though Athens in April 1941, "clapping crowds lined the streets . . . Girls and men leapt onto the running boards to kiss or shake hands with the grimy, weary gunners . . . crying: 'Come back—You must come back again—Goodbye—Good luck.'" Far away in Belgium, "the smallest English success is greeted by nine tenths of the Belgians as if it were their own national triumph."[174] The best placed to judge British soldiers were the Germans who fought against them: they considered them "tough guys . . . like us," who at Dunkirk, in Greece and in North Africa had proved themselves "tough and brave opponents"—"Put a British soldier in a German uniform and you won't notice the difference."[175]

The British Chiefs of Staff had early worked out a grand strategy to defeat Germany, and when the Americans entered the war and agreed to make the defeat of Germany their first aim, it began to be put into effect. General Brooke claimed authorship: "I am positive that our policy for the conduct of the war should be to direct both our military and political efforts towards the early conquest of North Africa. From there we shall be able to reopen the Mediterranean and to stage offensive operations against Italy."[176] This strategy, which the Americans broadly accepted though with considerable misgivings at a conference in Casablanca in January 1943, has often been criticized, at the time and since.[177] It dissatisfied insistent voices at home—not to mention Stalin—who demanded a "Second Front Now" in Europe to help the Russians. It dissatisfied later historians who observed that what Churchill called "the soft belly of the Axis" in southern Europe proved exceedingly tough, requiring a bloody slog up the Italian peninsula—not the original British intention. Moreover, these hard and costly campaigns were far from the centre of German power, as Stalin was well aware. It is hard to see a realistic alternative, however. Churchill was keen for a time on sending British troops to Russia, and he insisted on dispatching precious weapons and supplies—a total of some 4 million tons, a quarter of all the foreign supplies the Soviets received. This meant nearly 700 shiploads, sailing round the north of Norway in appalling weather to Archangel and Murmansk, exposed to sea and air attack, and requiring the protection of nearly 900 warships and 260,000 men in all. Most cargoes arrived safely, and the Germans suffered serious naval losses—a striking demonstration of British seapower.[178] It is hard to conceive of any additional moral obligation to "send a drop of our blood . . . to be lost in that ocean of gore,"[179] by launching a premature and potentially suicidal invasion of northern Europe. Above all, the British and Americans lacked the men and the ships for a cross-Channel invasion of France in 1943 (as some powerful American voices urged); but their armies were already on the spot in Tunisia, in easy reach of Sicily and Italy. Another and deadly kind of Second Front was open, however: bombing Germany.

## THE END OF THE BEGINNING

*Let victory go to those who made war without liking it.*
André Malraux, writer and politician[180]

The tide of war turned rapidly from the middle of 1942. On 30 May the RAF launched its first "1,000 bomber raid." On 4 June the Americans caught a Japanese fleet at Midway and sank four aircraft carriers, the spearhead of the imperial navy. A mainly Canadian raid on Dieppe on 19 August, though ill-conceived and costly in lives, brought Allied troops briefly back to France. Also in August, a large convoy fought its way through to Malta, raising the siege. Rommel's advance was halted at the Egyptian border at the end of August. The Axis forces in North Africa were handicapped by shortages of food, fuel and ammunition imposed by

British naval power, by air inferiority, and by Ultra intelligence affording knowledge of their strength and movements. When Rommel sent Hitler his plan to attack Egypt, it was immediately decrypted and sent to General Montgomery, his opponent, and the navy and RAF redoubled their attacks on Axis supply convoys. Consequently, when Rommel tried to break through at Alam Halfa in September, he was blocked by Montgomery's Eighth Army, then ran out of petrol, and was exposed to heavy RAF bombing.[181]

The battle of El Alamein in October was the first major land defeat suffered anywhere by the Germans, and Churchill ordered church bells rung for the first time since 1939. The victorious Eighth Army included British, Australian, New Zealand, South African, Indian, Polish, French and African soldiers. In November 65,000 American and British troops landed in Morocco and Algeria. In January 1943 came the first great German disaster on the Eastern Front, when the survivors of their Sixth Army, originally some 250,000 men, surrendered at Stalingrad. At "Tunisgrad" 290,000 men surrendered in May,[182] trapped by a mixed American, British and French First Army from the west, and by the Eighth Army from the south-east, while escape was blocked by the Royal Navy. In July–August 1943, Sicily was invaded; the Germans, fooled by a corpse carrying bogus papers planted by the British, had reinforced Greece. A big amphibious Anglo-American landing at Salerno in September was almost repulsed, and the Italian campaign, intended to be marked by surprise and speed, became painfully slow and costly, marred by inter-Allied jealousy, mistrust, lack of coordination and downright incompetence. On 2 December the first atomic chain reaction took place at Chicago University.

The strategic artery for the whole effort was still the Atlantic. During the summer of 1943 the Battle of the Atlantic was won, largely by the Royal Navy, through a combination of traditional seamanship, clever intelligence, technological advances and new tactics. The mastermind was Admiral Sir Max Horton, the unsung commander-in-chief of the Western Approaches, based at Liverpool. He trained "support groups" of anti-submarine ships and aircraft carriers coordinated with long-range shore-based patrol aircraft—a mere few dozen of which closed the "Atlantic gap." Airborne searchlights, radio direction-finders, better depth charges, special anti-submarine torpedoes and new centimetric radar (developed at Birmingham University), able to detect sea-level targets, gave the submarine hunters sudden and devastating advantages. Rather than relying on avoiding the wolf packs, from April 1943 Horton sent escorted convoys to take them on. The convoy ONS 5, sailing that month, was attacked by

39 U-Boats, which sank 12 of its 43 merchant ships; but 7 U-boats were themselves sunk, and another 5 badly damaged. In May, June and July the U-boat fleet was shattered, with 10 a week being lost.[183] In all, 700 U-boats were sunk, 70 percent of them by British and empire forces; and three-quarters of their crews were killed. After 1943, less than one ship per 1,000 in North Atlantic convoys was being lost.[184] This hastened victory in the west, and saved vast numbers of lives across Europe.

Italy collapsed over the summer of 1943, and Japan faced inevitable defeat, however protracted and bloody, due to its lack of natural resources and its industrial inferiority. The focus of the war was more than ever Germany. Despite its dispersal of forces and losses of men from Leningrad to Tunisia, and the attrition of the Anglo-American bombing campaign, it remained a formidable enemy. It was leeching on the whole of occupied Europe: food, resources and labour—nearly 8 million conscripted workers and prisoners in Germany, and 20 million working for the German war effort in occupied countries.[185] Hitler maintained an extraordinary hold over Germany, and was determined at all costs to fight on and continue the genocide against the Jews.

The British and American governments and peoples have been accused of indifference to, or culpable ignorance of, the fate of European Jewry. Before the war began, Britain had been "relatively generous"[186] in admitting Jewish refugees, giving both official and private aid. Baldwin had launched an appeal fund, and Harold Macmillan MP sheltered forty refugees in his own home. But even as late as 1944 most people in Britain had not realized the full enormity of Nazi genocide, and many remained sceptical of "atrocity stories" as propaganda.[187] There is evidence too that some British officials were unsympathetic, even anti-Semitic. Nevertheless, when accusations are made that the Allies could have done significantly more by warning Jews of their fate, making threats to the Nazis of later retribution, bombing Auschwitz or the railways used to carry victims to the death camps, or somehow bringing about the escape from Nazi clutches of a large number of their victims, such courses of action invariably prove on examination either to have been in fact undertaken, or else to have been impossible, or useless, or never thought of by anyone at the time.[188] All that could be done was to defeat Germany as fast as possible.

Bombing had always been envisaged by the RAF as the way "to defeat the enemy nation" by destroying its will to fight, as its commander, Air Marshal Hugh Trenchard, had argued as long ago as 1923.[189] But the onset of war had shown prewar predictions to have been fantasy or bluff. Gas, of which both sides had stocks, was never used. Nearly all countries' bombers were small or slow or both. They had difficulty in reaching, finding, let alone hitting, targets, as the RAF found when, amid the desperate crisis of May 1940, Churchill ordered attacks on Germany. In daylight, bombers proved highly vulnerable, and at night accuracy was impossible. There were heavy losses from enemy action and accident. The idea— which persisted in propaganda—that bombers were capable of pinpoint attacks on military or industrial targets was disproved by an official investigation of the results of RAF raids in June and July 1941. It showed that only two-thirds of bombers actually arrived, and of these only one-third dropped a bomb within five miles of the target—in the foggy Ruhr, only one in ten. The only target that could feasibly be hit by night bombing was a large town: "area bombing" was the only available tactic.

Bombing was Britain's most visible offensive weapon against Germany. As Stalin said to Churchill, the British were going to "pay their way by bombing."[190] Churchill had been disillusioned by the early bombing effort, but thought it was "better than doing nothing."[191] In February 1942, Air Chief Marshal Arthur ("Bomber") Harris took over Bomber Command. He at once launched "fire raids" on Lübeck and Rostock, ancient towns with many wooden buildings vulnerable to incendiaries. The Germans retaliated with "Baedeker raids" against historic English towns, including Canterbury, York, Norwich and Bath, which did considerable artistic and human damage. Harris escalated the campaign with attacks on the Ruhr industrial region, and on 30 May 1942 used every available aircraft for a propaganda coup—the first "1,000 bomber raid" against Cologne, which did massive damage and was followed two nights later by a similar raid on the steel town of Essen. This was the beginning of a strategy that would eventually fulfil, if not exceed, the apocalyptic fears of the 1930s.

Harris's aim was to "de-house" industrial workers and destroy their productivity: a logical pursuit of total war in which the whole economy served the war, and male and female workers were as much part of it as soldiers. The consequences were foreseen from the beginning: the RAF staff in 1942 predicted "a scale of bombardment which would far transcend anything in human experience," involving the destruction of 8 million houses, 900,000 deaths and 1,000,000 serious injuries.[192] Perhaps around 350,000 Germans were in fact killed. Bombing inevitably condemned non-workers, including children, to hideous deaths. Millions of children and non-workers, on the other hand, left or were evacuated from industrial cities, as had happened in England at the beginning of the war—though in the German case official preference was given to the racially and socially approved. Churchill put it rather brutally in May 1942: "All they have to do is to leave the cities where munitions work is being carried on—abandon their work, and go out into the fields, and watch their home fires burning from a distance." But the Air Ministry privately accepted that deliberately bombing civilians was "contrary to the principles of international law," and in public it was strongly played down.[193] When a survey in 1944 asked Londoners if they approved of bombing Germany, some 60 percent gave unqualified approval; but 75 percent were convinced that it was aimed only at military targets. The most prominent critics were the Labour MP Richard Stokes (a constant critic of the war) and George Bell, Bishop of Chichester, an embarrassingly saintly opponent, a prewar peace campaigner, defender of interned enemy aliens, and critic of "the propaganda of lies and hatred," who asked in the House of Lords in February 1944, "How can the War Cabinet fail to see that this progressive devastation of cities is threatening the roots of civilization?"[194]

The British bombing campaign was one of the most terrible acts of war in European history. Critics, then and now, have usually denied the material and psychological effectiveness of bombing: slaughter was doubly indefensible if it was futile.[195] The fact that German industry continued to produce and Nazi power did not collapse seemed to prove that futility. Moreover, building and supporting huge bomber fleets weakened the Allied effort in other spheres—a view many admirals and generals shared. The real moral position, however, is more disturbing: bombing did work. It was inhuman *and* effective, devastating the economy, diverting crucial resources, and destroying German morale.

From 1942, Bomber Command pursued a systematic campaign of devastation. A huge investment was made in aircraft, new electronic navigation and bomb-aiming, sophisticated tactics and crews, who received, said Harris, "the most expensive education in the world."[196] Another 850,000 workers were deployed in the aircraft industry.[197] A new generation of four-engined heavy bombers, ordered in 1936, was now entering service and eventually 16,000 of them would be built. The Lancaster, operational from March 1942, could carry up to ten tons of bombs—five or six times the load of the biggest bombers in service in 1940, and more than any other aircraft anywhere. In March 1943 the "Battle of the Ruhr" was launched, four months of sustained attacks on the core of Germany's war economy. Between 24 July and 3 August 1943 the port city of Hamburg was devastated. A calculated mix of high-explosive and incendiary bombs succeeded in unleashing a huge firestorm, which incinerated, suffocated or baked alive those within it, even inside shelters: 900,000 people were made homeless, 125,000 injured, and nearly 40,000 killed—the most lethal single action in the whole European war, killing in a few days roughly as many as in the eight-month Blitz on England.[198] In November the Battle of Berlin began: a four-month attack comprising sixteen major raids by an average of 500 bombers. The Americans were not involved. They could not fly at night, and believed that the German economy could be hamstrung by daylight precision attacks on a few key installations. Harris dismissed these as "panacea" targets, and they proved at best indecisive and too costly in casualties. A rare British venture of this kind was the "Dambuster" operation (Operation Chastise) against the Ruhr water supply in May 1943. Harris had reluctantly accepted it ("tripe of the wildest description"), and it confirmed his suspicion of "panaceas" that cost his crews' lives: an ingenious plan requiring a specially made weapon, intensive training, and a high level of coolness and determination destroyed two out of three targeted dams, disrupted water and electricity supplies to Ruhr factories, and was a propaganda coup; but it cost 40 percent of the aircraft and half the crews involved.[199] How much damage was really caused has remained a subject of debate. In the long run, the sledgehammer had more effect than the scalpel. The 1943 Battle of the Ruhr, in which the RAF dropped over 30,000 tons of bombs on Germany's industrial heartland (twice the power of the Hiroshima atomic bomb), shocked the Germans. Goebbels noted in his diary: "We find ourselves in a situation of helpless inferiority." The devastation of Hamburg and the mass exodus of over 800,000 of its people cost two months of the city's total production, pulverized its shipyards and nearly 600 other industrial plants, and stopped work on twenty-five U-boats.[200] These raids permanently stopped increases in armaments production. This was a turning point in the war, grossly underestimated by historians and by Allied analysts at the time.[201] Bomber Command, suffering heavy losses, shifted the focus of its attack from the Ruhr to Berlin. Although terrible damage was done to the capital (400,000 people were made homeless in a single night in November), this was not Germany's main industrial core.

Bomber Command's losses were approaching the unsustainable. The Germans put immense resources into a complex of radar, control systems, searchlights, night-fighters and guns. The RAF tried counter-measures, including singing rude or funny songs over the German radio frequency to drown the voices of ground controllers, employing German speaking WAAFs to send fake instructions, and by the brilliantly simple device of jettisoning quantities of metal foil to blind radar. But the defence systems always caught up. In the 1943 Ruhr campaign 640 bombers were lost, and in the Berlin campaign another 492 aircraft, out of Bomber Command's average front-line strength of about 890. The aircraft were quickly replaced, but thousands of crew members were being killed or captured. The repeated stress was gruelling: one veteran remembered men vomiting before taking off—"but they still went."[202] The moral pressure to carry on was powerful.[203] Resistance networks in occupied Europe helped some thousands of downed airmen to evade capture, at extreme risk to themselves: British intelligence reckoned that every airman who escaped cost the life of a helper.[204]

Although 90 percent of German battle casualties from 1941 to D-Day were inflicted by the Red Army, far more damaging to Germany's total war effort was the bombing campaign, which also starved the Eastern Front of men and weapons, facilitating the Red Army's victories by ensuring their vast superiority in tanks and artillery. The skies were "the real front line," as the German Air Ministry saw in 1943; "the mass of fighters must go for home defence . . . to meet the British and American threat."[205] Bombing forced a large part of German industry, most of the air force and much of the army into air defence. Germany could have built far more tanks, artillery and ground-attack aircraft for the Eastern Front: but that would have meant exposing its homeland to the bombers. Over 2 million workers were engaged in the aircraft industry, which in 1943 absorbed over 40 percent of German war production, compared with only some 6 percent for tanks. In July 1943, for the crucial battle of Kursk, the Wehrmacht could muster only half the number of tanks of the Red Army and one-quarter the artillery. There were 55,000 anti-aircraft guns defending Germany, including nearly 9,000 of the dual-purpose 88 mm guns— deadly tank-killers, of which Rommel's Afrika Korps had had only thirty-five. Around 70 percent of all Germany's fighter planes were in the west in 1943-44, not fighting the Russians: by April 1944 the Germans had only 500 planes on the Eastern Front, facing 13,000 Russian. The home air defences absorbed over 900,000 men—far more than defended Stalingrad in 1943 or Normandy in 1944. Even more labour was used in struggling to patch up the damage.[206]

It is a tenacious belief that bombing failed to undermine civilian determination, and even strengthened it. This is very far from the truth. From 1942, RAF raids were disrupting life, progressively overwhelming the Reich authorities' ability to cope, destroying public confidence, and causing increasing flight from the cities. Many demoralized workers were absentees from their jobs. From 1943 the Nazi party was losing control: members were no longer wearing their badges, were avoiding the Hitler salute, and were shirking their administrative or policing functions. The Gestapo reported that no leading industrialists any longer believed in victory. In August 1943 the Luftwaffe chief of staff, General Hans Jeschonnek, shot himself. Ordinary people were blaming the Nazis for their sufferings, and the regime resorted increasingly to violence and terror to maintain its grip. It encouraged the lynching of downed airmen. From 1943 a hundred Germans a week, including senior officials, were being sentenced to death for defeatism or "sabotage." Looters in the bombed cities were summarily executed from 1944, and some, especially conscripted foreign workers of whom hundreds of thousands went on the run, formed armed gangs and fought back. From the autumn of 1944 there were mass public executions.[207] The German Home Front was falling apart.

## VICTORY

Actors waiting in the wings of Europe
we already watch the lights on the stage
and listen to the colossal overture begin ...
Everyone, I suppose, will use these minutes
To look back, to hear music and recall
What we were doing and saying that year
During our last months as people, near
The sucking mouth of the day that swallowed us all.

Keith Douglas, Sherwood Rangers Yeomanry,<br>killed in Normandy, 9 June 1944[208]

Far away on the border of India, the Japanese army suffered the biggest defeat in its history[209] in the four-month battle of Imphal (March–July 1944) at the hands of General William Slim's Indian, British and African Fourteenth Army. The Japanese had attacked to pre-empt a British offensive, and to commit their "Indian National Army" in the hope of starting a revolt in India. Some Indian prisoners of war had been induced by the Japanese and Germans to form pro-Axis army units, usually with the promise of Indian independence, but most soon realized these promises were hollow. The Japanese failure at Imphal eventually became a rout, in which they lost 60,000 men—two-thirds of their total force—and all their heavy weapons.

Victory in Europe required an invasion of Germany itself. Roosevelt had, seemingly spontaneously, spoken of "unconditional surrender" at the press conference that followed his Casablanca meeting with Churchill in January 1943; but the phrase did not appear in the official communiqué. Whatever was said or not said by politicians, there was probably no alternative. Statesmen remembered the ambiguous outcome in 1918. Any hint of negotiation risked disrupting the Grand Alliance, especially given Stalin's suspiciousness—though, ironically, at times he probably contemplated negotiation himself.[210] So no one in the Allied camp was much interested in plots by anti-Nazi German patriots, who, realizing that Hitler was going to destroy Germany, would have liked a deal with the Anglo-Americans which would leave Germany many of its eastern conquests and let it keep fighting the Bolshevik threat. They were several years behind the times, or ahead of them. The Allies all agreed that Germany and the Germans, good and bad, must be crushed.

In January 1944 the 900-day German siege of Leningrad was lifted. The Red Army began moving ponderously forward. The British and Americans combined carried out a major escalation of their bombing campaign. The Americans built swarms of P-51 Mustang fighters whose Rolls-Royce engines and extra fuel tanks enabled them to escort daylight raids, forcing outnumbered German fighters into battle until there was hardly a German air force left. In February came "Big Week," a concerted attack on aircraft factories and on the Luftwaffe. By March Germany was losing a fifth of its fighter pilots every month. This facilitated RAF night and day raids, which, thanks to new tactics (such as "Pathfinder" aircraft identifying targets) and equipment (such as ground-scanning radar) were now accurate enough to destroy small targets. Germany's war economy was being inexorably smashed.[211]

A land invasion of Europe, the long awaited Second Front, was the great enterprise—Operation Overlord—for which Britain and America had been preparing since the Casablanca conference, at which Churchill had persuaded the Americans that the invasion should not be hurried. The Channel had rarely been crossed by an invading army in either direction. The last successful attempt had been that of William of Orange in 1688, aided by weather and a non-hostile reception in England. William the Conqueror had succeeded in 1066, but Harold's army had been elsewhere. Napoleon, after energetic preparation, had given up: he had boasted that the Channel was only a ditch, but the ditch proved too wide. The Kaiser had decided not even to try, and Hitler cancelled his plans before they began. It was too risky: an invading army had to win completely, or face disaster—there was no easy retreat. Napoleon, the Kaiser and Hitler had tried instead to defeat England by attacking its potential Continental allies, ultimately Russia.

Despite changes in technology, the basic problem remained logistics. Even if defence was weak (which it was emphatically not in 1944—Rommel, in command of the defence, had fifty-eight divisions), transporting and then supplying an army across the Channel required a huge quantity of coordinated shipping. Had Napoleon invaded in 1805, his soldiers could have carried their ammunition supply, and his food and transport needs could have been met from English barns and stables; but modern armies and navies, though they had vastly greater resources, also had vastly greater needs in ammunition, food and fuel (for example, 500 train-loads of petrol for D-Day itself). Ships, munitions, food stores and landing craft had to be accumulated for what would be by far the biggest seaborne invasion in history—850,000 men in three weeks—and this took time. During June 1944 more than half a million tons of supplies would be landed, and Channel storms caused shortages of fuel and ammunition that stopped the invaders in their tracks.

The Dieppe raid in 1942 had been a disaster, and this time nothing was left to chance by the mainly British planners. Normandy was chosen as the site—more or less where William the Conqueror had sailed from. There were wide beaches and a nearby harbour, Cherbourg, which it was hoped to capture quickly to facilitate the flow of supplies. Moreover, as Normandy was not the most obvious place to land, the Germans, and Hitler personally, could be persuaded by elaborate and ingenious subterfuge—including the use of double agents and the creation of phantom armies in Scotland, Essex and Kent—that after feint attacks elsewhere the main landing would come across the narrow Straits of Dover.[212] So security had to be absolute. Minute details of the beaches and their defences were plotted on a large wall map concealed under guard behind the ladies' underwear department of Peter Robinson, in Oxford Circus. The English coast from the Wash to Land's End was closed. No embassies or governments-in-exile in London were allowed to send messages in cipher, apart from the American, the Soviet and the Polish (whose messages the British could not decode and hence considered the Germans could not either). Ultra showed that the Germans had taken the bait: large forces were kept guarding the Pas de Calais for weeks after D-Day. The French Resistance, armed, trained and directed largely by SOE, disrupted German movement and communication. In one picturesque but important sabotage, two schoolgirls drained the oil (which they then sold on the black market) from German tank transporters and substituted abrasive oil supplied by SOE which wrecked the engines—one act in a succession of guerrilla operations that held a whole SS Panzer division away from Normandy for a fortnight.[213] The last-minute problem was the weather: only three days gave suitable tidal and full-moon conditions, and D-Day had to be delayed from 5 to 6 June because of storms. The invasion, under the supreme command of the American general Dwight D. Eisenhower, was commanded by Montgomery, Air Chief Marshal Sir Trafford Leigh-Mallory and Admiral Sir Bertram Ramsay—poetic justice, as the latter had organized the evacuation from Dunkirk.

The first Allied unit to land in France in the early hours of 6 June

1944 was a company of the 2nd Oxfordshire and Buckinghamshire Light Infantry, followed shortly afterwards by thousands of British and American airborne troops, and then the huge seaborne landings. Nearly 7,000 ships and landing craft, including 1,200 warships, three-quarters of them British or Canadian, were manned by 113,000 Royal Navy personnel, 53,000 Americans, and Canadian, Norwegian, Polish, Dutch, French and Greek sailors. Protected by over 11,000 aircraft, they carried onto the beaches 62,000 British troops, 57,000 Americans and 22,000 Canadians, supported by intense naval and aerial bombardments. The landings have rightly become an epic of history and of (particularly American) popular culture, which shapes our ideas of "the longest day" as particularly gory. In fact, the landings proceeded smoothly, given the heavy fortification of the coast. Though the Americans met some opposition, all the beachheads were captured at a cost of 10,000 casualties—roughly 7 percent of the force, fewer than expected. This was largely due to careful planning, overwhelming naval and air superiority, and, for the British, superior tactics, enabling them to deploy ninety-six tanks on Gold Beach (where the 50th Division suffered only 413 casualties), compared with only five tanks on the American Omaha Beach.[214]

A week after D-Day, on 13 June, secretly developed V1 "flying bombs" began falling on London, and continued in fluctuating numbers thereafter. In all, 10,000 were launched; about a third crashed prematurely; a third were shot down; and 3,500 hit England, mostly London, killing over 6,000 people. On 23 June the Russians launched a massive offensive. On 20 July anti-Nazi officers failed to kill Hitler and seize power, and brave Germans, some bearing famous names, were shot or hanged with piano wire. The war went on.

In Normandy, the battle inland was far tougher than D-Day itself. Allied generals used their material superiority to limit human losses: according to a German view, "The English, and even more the Americans, have . . . sought to avoid a very large sacrifice of lives."[215] Nevertheless, over 200,000 Allied soldiers became casualties, including some three-quarters of the British infantry. German skill and determination, enforced by Hitler's refusal to allow withdrawal, was aided by severe bad weather, which stopped the flow of ammunition and blinded Allied aircraft, and by a landscape of steep banks and hedges—a problem the British had first met in an earlier landing in Normandy in 1758. "This country is perfect for defence," wrote a British tank commander. "Must be a Paradise for Jerry's A[nti] T[ank] gunners. Also excellent for booby traps, snipers, etc. . . . Advances are literally made field by field."[216] The British, Canadians and Poles fought a ten-week battle of attrition with the main German

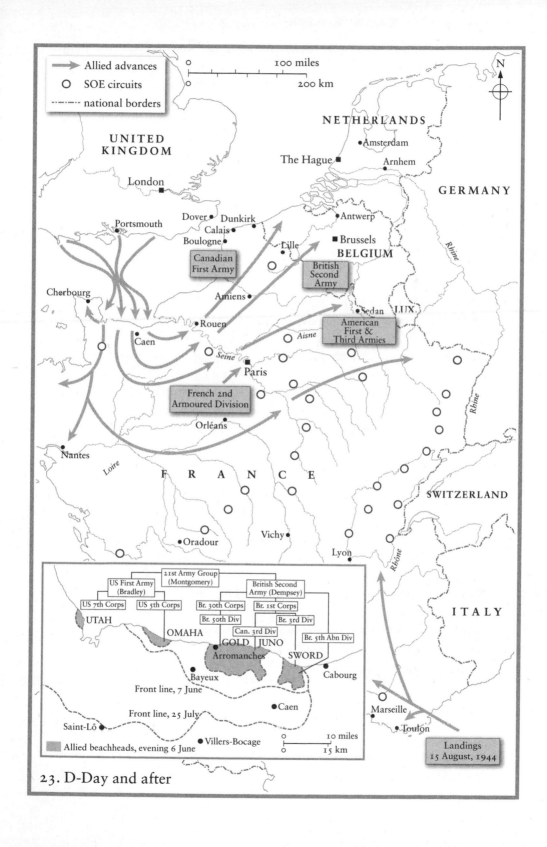

UNITED
KINGDOM

NETHERLANDS

Amsterdam

The Hague

Arnhem

GERMANY

London

Dover    Dunkirk
Calais
Boulogne
Lille

Antwerp

Brussels
BELGIUM

Rhine

Portsmouth

Canadian
First Army

Amiens

British
Second
Army

Cherbourg

Sedan    LUX

American
First &
Third Armies

Caen

Rouen

Seine

Paris

Aisne

French 2nd
Armoured Division

Orléans

Rhine

Nantes

Loire

F R A N C E

SWITZERLAND

Oradour

Vichy

Lyon

Rhône

ITALY

21st Army Group
(Montgomery)

US First Army
(Bradley)

British Second
Army (Dempsey)

US 7th Corps    US 5th Corps

Br. 30th Corps    Br. 1st Corps

Br. 50th Div

Br. 3rd Div

UTAH

OMAHA

GOLD   JUNO

Can. 3rd Div

Br. 5th Abn Div

Arromanches

SWORD

Cabourg

Bayeux

Front line, 7 June

Marseille

Caen

Toulon

Front line, 25 July

Saint-Lô

Villers-Bocage

Allied beachheads, evening 6 June

10 miles
15 km

Landings
15 August, 1944

23. D-Day and after

forces, including seven of their ten armoured divisions, which cost some 65,000 British casualties—a proportion similar to that at Passchendaele in 1917. "Survival now seems to me more a matter of luck than anything else: we are being fired at in the tanks by A[rmour] P[iercing] . . . machine gunned from the air: shelled by artillery: mortared: sniped at: machine gunned by ground forces . . . and then there are the countless mines and booby traps."[217] From 18 to 21 July alone, Second British Army lost over 6,000 men and a third of its tanks.[218] The Allies called down carpet bombing of German positions, notoriously those by the RAF in and around Caen, the ancient Norman capital. It was left, wrote one British soldier, "a waste of brick and stone . . . The people gazed at us without emotion of any kind; one could hardly look them in the face, knowing who had done this."[219] Despite shattering air attacks, it took until late August to destroy, capture or throw back the German forces, most of whom fought their way out of Allied attempts to trap them. "We have to attack everything: trees, shrubs, hedgerows, woods, haystacks, sheds, houses: all are strongly defended: held by an invisible enemy."[220] The Americans eventually broke out further south into open and hardly defended country, much of it already in the hands of over 30,000 Resistance fighters, where they made rapid progress. Meanwhile, on 15 August 1944 a mainly Franco-American force, with British naval and air support, had landed in Provence and marched rapidly up the Rhône valley, aided by Resistance forces armed and trained by SOE.[221]

The Battle of Normandy, and the months of hard fighting that followed, led to misplaced polemics between generals at the time and national historians since. These have often turned on the alleged over-cautiousness of Montgomery (criticized by the Americans, with whom he had very bad relations, and taken up by Churchill, to the extreme annoyance of General Brooke), and the slowness of the British army, supposedly intimidated by memories of its losses during the First World War, and lacking in commitment. This, following on from earlier criticism of British—especially English—troops, caused unfavourable comparisons with American enthusiasm or German professionalism. It has interacted with the "declinist" theme in writing about England: their "limited success" in Normandy reflected a wider failing, concludes a recent French historian; it "anticipated [England's] relative decline."[222]

Some criticism is doubtless founded. Mistakes were certainly made, as in all wars and on all sides. Most English and other Allied soldiers were fighting a big battle for the first time; on the other hand, some units that had already fought in North Africa and Italy felt they had already "done their bit." One German report claimed that "the conduct of the battle by the Americans and English was . . . very methodical. Local successes were seldom exploited . . . The British infantryman is distinguished more by physical endurance than by special bravery. The impetuous attack, executed with dash, is foreign to him. He is sensitive to energetic counter attack."[223] One of those infantrymen put the same thought rather differently: "The frightened country boys were facing troops who, man for man, were craftier and better trained, who had been reared as warriors; they were outfought at every turn; but they managed, somehow they managed, heaven only knew how they managed, to stay where they were."[224] And eventually it was the Germans who gave way, losing more men in a shorter time than ever before, in a bloodbath equal to Stalingrad.[225]

The belief that British, and particularly English, soldiers fought poorly, probably coloured by earlier failures in Singapore and North Africa, influenced by rival patriotisms, and linking in with ideas of national "decline," is a good example of how historical myths are built up. Careful research shows that the evidence usually cited is highly selective and misleading, focusing on a few units that had suffered very heavy casualties in a short time. German soldiers generally considered the British tougher opponents than the Americans. Those Germans who criticized lack of "dash" did not realize that since the 1920s the British army had successfully developed tactics aimed to minimize casualties.[226] The British took on by far the strongest opposition in Normandy, and so, despite these careful tactics, their loss of life was twice that of the Americans, whose subsequent advances were facilitated by the British army's decimation of the main German forces.

Thereafter, the British advance through cheering crowds along the familiar roads of Picardy and Flanders, via Amiens, Arras and Lille, to the vital Channel ports and into Belgium and Holland, was one of the fastest in military history—430 miles in nine days—"on the whole," wrote one of its officers modestly, "more tiring than dangerous."[227] This has been pushed into the shade by the American advances across France and the thrilling and highly publicized liberation of Paris in August by the French 2nd Armoured Division, brought from England specially for that purpose and spared the Normandy bloodletting. Even less remembered is the gruelling and strategically essential three-month battle by the Canadians and British to liberate the Scheldt estuary and Antwerp, beginning in September. Despite serious errors by Montgomery, this brought about a complete revolution in the supply situation of the Allied armies in November, making an invasion of Germany possible.[228]

Allied governments and generals thought the war was now practically over. They received several shocks. On 8 September 1944 the first V2 rocket, carrying nearly a ton of explosive, was launched from the Netherlands and fell on Chiswick, killing three people. There was no defence against these rockets and no warning. Over the next five months, an average of five rockets hit England daily, most of them aimed at London, where 2,700 people were killed; most of the V2s, however, were fired at the advancing army in Belgium. A few days after the first V2 landed, Operation Market Garden culminated in a brave but bungled attempt by British airborne troops to seize a bridge over the Rhine at Arnhem, a failure that ended hopes of a thrust into Germany to end the war by Christmas. As logistical difficulties and the approach of winter slowed the Allied advance, on 16 December the Germans launched Hitler's last-gasp offensive against the Americans in the Ardennes, the "Battle of the Bulge." German tanks, with only a minimum of fuel, aimed to break through to Antwerp, capture its huge petrol stocks, and cut off Allied supplies. The attack was a complete surprise, but never attained its objectives due to determined American resistance, and it used up Germany's last reserves of tanks and aircraft.

Meanwhile, Allied bombing was further increasing in scale: not just hit-and-miss bombing of workers' houses, but the systematic devastation of everything—as Harris said, "to be certain of destroying anything it was necessary to destroy everything." This included the now accurate obliteration of canals, railway junctions, tunnels, oil refineries, power stations, aircraft factories, and sites for launching V-weapons. The area bombing of cities also continued. From June 1944 until the end of the war, Anglo-American bombers dropped a million tons of bombs on Germany. Amid the spreading devastation, the Germans maintained a stubborn and hopeless resistance.

From 4 to 11 February, the "Big Three" Allied leaders and some 700 advisers met at Yalta, in the Crimea, to strike a deal on the division of the postwar world. On 13–14 February 1945 Dresden was attacked and destroyed. It was targeted as a transport hub by nearly 800 Lancasters, in response to Russian requests to support their advance—and because Dresden was still relatively undamaged and hence a worthwhile target. Perhaps 25,000 people were killed, provoking international protest and private criticism from Churchill. Arguably, the bombing campaign was continued too long, at least in part to punish the German people. On the other hand, Allied planners were still far from sure that the war was nearly over and were worried by the appearance of the V-weapons. A German diarist wrote early in 1945 that "fear and panic rule among the public."[229] This apocalyptic aversion therapy—91 percent of Germans said that bombing was the hardest ordeal of the war—seems to have had a long-term effect on German culture, making it one of the least militaristic in Europe. The only possible justification for the horror of bombing is that it served the overriding purpose of destroying the Nazi regime and shortening the war which every day killed tens of thousands of people: concentration and death camp victims, Allied soldiers and civilians, and the Germans themselves—3.2 million German soldiers died from January 1944 to May 1945. Had the war continued, even worse escalation was under consideration: poison gas and the atomic bomb.[230]

Throughout the war, the RAF flew over 370,000 sorties against Germany and dropped nearly 1,000,000 tons of bombs. Losses were heavy: 10,000 aircraft were destroyed; 55,000 RAF airmen (from seventeen countries) and 26,000 Americans were killed. This was a higher proportion of losses (51 percent) than among the infantry in the First World War.[231] Doubts and soul-searching about both its morality and effectiveness still continue. Harris was denied an honour by the postwar Labour government, and there were protests when his statue was erected in the Strand in 1992; though by 2012 a prominent memorial to Bomber Command could finally be built in Green Park with little controversy.

While British and American generals and politicians bickered (the British were as inclined to criticize American failures as vice-versa), in March 1945 their armies crossed the Rhine and flooded into western Germany. The V-weapon sites were captured or bombed. In April British troops liberated the Bergen-Belsen concentration camp, where 50,000 people were dead or dying: BBC staff in London refused to believe the first reports, but newsreel cameras soon showed a horrified public for the first time the real nature of what they had been fighting and what they had escaped. The BBC reporter Richard Dimbleby told a colleague that "you'll never wash the smell of it off your hands, never get the filth of it out of your mind."[232]

The Red Army had slowed its advance while "liberating" Poland, Hungary, Romania, Czechoslovakia, Austria and the eastern fringes of Germany. When the Anglo-Americans finally advanced into Germany, it rushed at Berlin, losing more men killed than the Americans suffered in the whole war,[233] and pouring 40,000 tons of shells into the city. Hitler shot himself on 30 April, and Berlin fell on 2 May. On the third the German forces in Italy surrendered; on the fourth the whole of northern Germany, Holland and Denmark surrendered to Montgomery; on the seventh German delegates signed an unconditional surrender at Eisenhower's headquarters at Rheims; and on the eighth another for Stalin's benefit in Berlin.

In Burma, Japanese control was collapsing. Neither the "Indian National Army" nor the "Burma Independence Army" retained whatever enthusiasm they had once had for Japanese hegemony. The Burmese nationalist Aung San, made a major-general by the Japanese, changed sides, and his men joined the British in making the reconquest of Burma a war of liberation. The final Japanese counter-attack in August 1945 cost them 17,000 casualties to 95 British—perhaps the greatest disproportion of casualties of any battle in the war.[234] Nevertheless, the Humpty Dumpty of European empire was in pieces. British troops found themselves unwillingly involved in resisting rebellion against French and Dutch colonial rule in sometimes bloody conflicts.

But in Europe war was over, and so was the wartime political truce in Britain. Labour left the coalition immediately. In July 1945 perhaps the most famous general election in British history took place. Churchill remained popular—so popular that most, including some Labour leaders, assumed he must win. The Conservative Party was less favoured. They were in poor organizational condition, with a far higher proportion of their party agents and MPs in the armed forces (135 MPs compared with 14 Labour).[235] The party had campaigned less during the war than its opponents, and it had developed few postwar policies—Churchill had not been interested in distractions. But Labour leaders from 1941 onwards had skilfully built up their claim to be the party of modern Britain, with a sophisticated campaign about building the postwar world.[236]

It has often been thought that 1945 showed a historic shift in opinion. This is at first sight plausible. The Tories struggled under the weight of the 1930s, both economic and political, and opponents continued to play on the "Guilty Men" theme. The Labour leadership were well-known and respected, and shared the prestige of victory. The vista of a brave and planned new world was opened by the successes of wartime economic mobilization, the Beveridge report (though Beveridge, a Liberal, failed to win a seat) and boundless admiration for the Soviet Union—"more freedom there for more people than anywhere else, from what I hear," noted a middle-class Women's Institute organizer.[237] Yet this affected a minority of politically active people: the Labour share of the vote had only increased by 10 percent since 1935. Many ordinary voters had been turned off party politics by the war, and many were politically confused and apathetic following the long political truce. Their hopes for the postwar world were at best vague, and often sceptical. Most saw no point in an election while the war with Japan was continuing, and the sudden return to sour party polemic seemed shocking. So when Churchill began some belated and notoriously intemperate campaigning in 1945 (asserting that socialism meant "some sort of Gestapo"), he probably did more harm than good. One voter found it "very disturbing . . . that a national hero should stoop to make such public utterances." Yet the Labour lead dropped from 20 percent in the polls during the spring of 1945 to 8 percent on polling day in July. All politics was unpopular—"they're like a lot of old fish wives . . . bawling and screaming insults."[238] Half the armed forces did not vote at all—but those who did mainly voted Labour. This was still ample for a landslide. When votes from around the world were counted, Labour had 48 percent to the Tories' 40 percent. They gained 250 seats, including 79 they had never won before in the suburban south of England. The Liberals gained votes but lost seats. Labour had their first clear majority: 393 to the Tories' 213. In England, Labour had won 331 seats to the Tories' 167. It was the latter's worst defeat since 1906.[239]

It is tempting to interpret this as one symptom of deep social and cultural changes caused by the war. Illegitimate births had risen by 25 percent. Divorces had increased from one to five per hundred. Youth crime among boys and even more among girls appeared to have soared, doubtless due to the closure of many schools, the absence of fathers, and greater opportunity; but also due to severe enforcement of often new offences: for example, minor black marketeering. But in Britain as on the Continent the war in many areas had less than revolutionary consequences, and many of its effects cut both ways, with a powerful general yearning for a return to normal. For example, far more women had jobs; but they were mostly unskilled and badly paid. Moreover, there was an almost universal expectation that married women would give up work when peace returned, and many did so by choice. Perhaps surprisingly, the overall outcome was to reinforce the traditional family, which emerged from the war "stronger, more tightly knit and more home-centred than it had ever been before."[240]

English troops were more widely spread across Europe and the world than at any time in the country's rather warlike history, from Denmark via Germany, Austria, Italy and Greece, to Africa, India, Burma, Malaya, Vietnam, Borneo and China. A large part of the fleet was being sent to the Pacific, and there were plans for a British army to take part in the invasion of Japan. The atomic bombs dropped on Japan in August 1945 forestalled this possibility—the climax of an American aerial assault on Japanese cities that had gone far beyond the deadliest European raids. The idea of an atomic weapon had originated in England as early as 1904, when Frederick Soddy (subsequently a Nobel Prize winner) informed the Royal Engineers of its possibility.[241] Work in physics in several countries in the late 1930s convinced scientists that it was feasible. In 1940 work began in earnest in England, spurred by fears that Germany was working on a bomb. In fact, work there was less advanced and was abandoned. Early British research was transferred to America and developed into a huge scientific and engineering programme beyond the means of any other country. The decision to use atomic bombs as soon as they were available (agreed by Roosevelt and Churchill) had both military and political motives. The atomic bombing of Hiroshima and Nagasaki ended the Second World War, and began a new age.

# Memory, History and Myth

How important was Britain's part in defeating Fascism? It has become the orthodoxy to minimize it, by comparison with the United States (whose alliance was emphasized in Churchill's later carefully crafted portrayal of the war[1]) and the Soviet Union. We are accustomed, in contrast, to an impression of Britain's weakness, vulnerability and strategic failures, creating an uneasy sense of inferiority that has never quite gone away. Admiration for the Red Army, and the cultural influence of America—including what has been called "the Americanization of memory" by Hollywood—have contributed to this picture. One seemingly affected by it was the Prime Minister, David Cameron, who announced to American television viewers in 2010 that "we were the junior partner [of the USA] in 1940 when we were fighting the Nazis."[2] It is certainly true that Britain could not have defeated the Axis powers alone; but neither could the USSR or the USA.

The empire, as we have noted, was both a weakness and a strength, and had always been so, for it required a dangerously wide dispersal of force. At times and in certain places this meant defeat, or the narrowest of victories. Yet empire and Commonwealth manpower, resources and money, when mobilized, helped to turn the tide against Japan, Italy and Germany—a fact overlooked in the idea of Britain "standing alone." The war changed the expectations and widened the horizons of imperial populations: they realized that the British were not invincible, and mixed with ordinary British sailors and soldiers on more equal terms.[3] This was both the apogee and the twilight of the empire, for three years the main barrier against the global triumph of Fascism.

Britain's effort was indispensable to victory. Had it made peace with Germany in 1940, Nazi dominance of Europe for the foreseeable future would have been unchallengeable, and American isolationism confirmed. This would truly have been "a new dark age." Germany would have held the global initiative, with free access to oil, food and raw materials. The subsequent defeat of an isolated USSR, simultaneously assailed by Japan, would have been inevitable, accompanied by a planned genocidal depopulation of much of eastern Europe. As it was, Soviet survival depended on the ability of Britain and America to supply it, to tie down Axis forces, and to force the Germans to divert their industrial and military strength away from the Eastern Front into naval and aerial warfare. The Allies' victory was impossible without control of the seas, which for most of the war rested principally on the Royal Navy, the main victor of the Battle of the Atlantic, the eventual controller of the Mediterranean through which a "Second Front" was opened, and the main support of the D-Day landings, primarily a British operation in both planning and the forces engaged. The Royal Air Force, however controversial its area-bombing strategy even now, from May 1942 was the only force, as the Russians admitted, able to "[take] the war onto Germany's own territory";[4] and from 1943 onwards, with the U.S. air force, it gradually destroyed Germany's ability to make war, as evidence from German sources has recently made clear.[5] In a nutshell: the defeat of Japan was overwhelmingly American; American economic power made it possible to crush the Axis in under four years (it had taken twelve to defeat Napoleon); the evisceration of the German army was mainly due to the Russians; but the strategic defeat of Germany as a whole and that of Italy were primarily due to Britain.

It has become a commonplace in historical writing, television and other media to contest the "finest hour" story of unity, solidarity, commitment and victory by stressing domestic social and political tensions, economic weaknesses and military failures. Memory of the war soon became a subject both of broad comedy (often by those who had lived through it) and of political satire.[6] Some historians of both left and right have consciously aimed to "demythologize" the "layers of nostalgia" of a "complacent" patriotic memory.[7] This was sometimes explicitly a reaction against much later events, such as "Thatcherism" at the time of the Falklands war,[8] and, more broadly, to remove a supposed psychological barrier to radical change or to acceptance of European integration. Wartime propaganda did accentuate the positives and censor the negatives. War in reality was a terrible strain, a disruption of lives, an inevitable cause of tragedy for many, and of unhappiness, exhaustion and constraint for most. Prewar social and political tensions did not disappear and could even be aggravated. There were indeed deserters, profiteers and black-marketeers. Yet despite every qualification, the evidence is overwhelmingly of general commitment to the national war effort.[9] For many people—not only those doing glamorous and exciting jobs—participation formed the most purposeful, intense and exciting years of their lives. The wife of a Birmingham mechanic noted in her diary in 1944: "I have read and heard of emancipation but I have never experienced it myself until these war years. I am a totally different person now to the person I was in 39 ... I am today steadily happy for I run my own ship."[10] This experience, on a national scale, heralded a postwar cultural revolution.

The economy, too, as has been shown in recent research,[11] was far stronger and more efficient than is conventionally realized: it out-produced Germany in aircraft, and the rest of the world (except finally the United States) in ships. It matched totalitarian levels of mobilization without using totalitarian methods—a unique achievement. The military failures on land that so alarmed Churchill and his advisers as symptoms of decadence, and have exercised some historians, have prosaic explanations, including inferior equipment, lack of training and inexperience. The final British victories in Europe and Asia are less, if at all, remembered.

Britain was certainly at the limits of its strength as constituted by population, size of economy and accumulated wealth. It was undoubtedly able to defend itself against Germany and control the Atlantic, but to be forced simultaneously to hold the Mediterranean and the Middle East, and protect South-East Asia, India and Australasia, was more than it had ever had to do in the past, and more than any state in history has ever tried to do.* From 1938 it became increasingly clear that Britain would have to throw everything into the effort, regardless of consequences. The normal trade by which it earned its living had to be suspended. Exports of manufactures were slashed in favour of arms production, while imports of war materials rose. Gold reserves and overseas investments were largely spent. By 1944 Britain's export trade was a mere 31 percent of the 1938 total. It had also adopted a system of state control of much of the economy which it took forty years to unscramble.

The war, even as fighting continued, became an absorbing cultural theme, taken up in literature, cinema (it was the first war to be related mainly by film, and the English were the world's keenest filmgoers[12]), music, art, history (above all, Churchill's own six-volume history), games, hobbies, later television and recently computer games. For years afterwards, peaking in the 1950s, the war remained an inexhaustible subject with a huge audience. The memory thus transmitted to later generations is a fragmentary one. An obvious reason is the unparalleled extent and complexity of Britain's war. For Russians, arguably, the war can be encapsulated by the sieges of Leningrad and Stalingrad, the core of Vasily

---

* The only comparison would be the American War of Independence, a global struggle against France, Spain, Holland and the thirteen colonies—which Britain of course lost.

Grossman's great 1960s novel *Life and Fate*. For Americans, memory seems to focus on Pacific islands and D-Day. For the French, on the "syndrome" of occupation, collaboration and resistance. But for Britain, the only European country to have fought the whole war, it cannot easily be abbreviated: Dunkirk, the Battle of Britain, the Blitz, the "Desert Rats" in North Africa, the Battle of the Atlantic, Arctic convoys, "Dambusters," the Burmese jungle, SOE agents, prisoner-of-war camps, D-Day, Arnhem, and lately codebreaking and deception—all these have powerful resonances both reflected in and created by historical writing, fiction and works of art, above all film. So the war has become a bewildering kaleidoscope of episodes. One of the most important war novelists, Evelyn Waugh, set action in Norway and Crete—both defeats, and both of secondary importance. The most popular war writer, Alistair Maclean, used a fictitious Mediterranean episode for the best-selling *Guns of Navarone*. A widely read popular history, Paul Brickhill's *The Dam Busters* (1951)—which became the most popular war film (with the most famous music, and a screenplay by the First World War playwright R. C. Sherriff)—commemorated a real but highly unusual operation. The more realistic themes of wartime films disappeared after 1945: the involvement of ordinary people in and out of uniform, the prominent role of women, and the down-to-earth solidarity of the nation.

Instead, films of the 1950s—such as *The Wooden Horse* (1950), *The Cruel Sea* (1953) or *The Cockleshell Heroes* (1955)—concentrated on small-scale historically based episodes emphasizing the strains of war on a few stoical but sensitive individuals. These films were easily mocked, but few were "exploitative or xenophobic"; many were "enlightened, honourable and moving."[13] They showed little groups, all male, predominantly officers—prisoners of war, commandos, ships companies, air crews—triumphing over superior forces by characteristically British/English ingenuity and courage, sometimes in the face of official obstruction. This stiff-upper-lip "David and Goliath" theme, though flattering, creates an impression of a Britain far weaker and more marginal to the main events than it really was. In the 1960s English cinema dropped this kind of film, though frequent television repeats keep the 1950s imagery familiar. Reasons included criticism of "old-fashioned" productions, cost (as cinema audiences shrank), and the consequent importance of an American market which disliked "guys with limey accents acting as if they were saving the world."[14] War films during the 1960s and 1970s were mostly fictional Anglo-American adventure stories, neither real nor realistic. Some films—American or Anglo-American—excluded or marginalized British participation; sometimes the English appeared only as women or children in the presence of North American males.[15]

Despite a commonplace view that the English are excessively interested in the war, it rarely figures as an important theme in post-1960s culture. Its literature is largely forgotten. Films and television serials may occasionally be set during the war years—*The English Patient* (1996), *Charlotte Grey* (2001), *Enigma* (2001), *Atonement* (2007) and TV series such as *Foyle's War* (from 2002)—but they are not about the war, which provides merely a backdrop for costume drama. This sets England apart from most of the countries involved, for which the war remains important as epic or as trauma. No English film is comparable with, for example, *Lacombe Lucien* (France, 1974), *Come and See* (USSR, 1985), *Au revoir les enfants* (France, 1987), *Stalingrad* (Germany, 1993), *Saving Private Ryan* (USA, 1998), *Band of Brothers* (USA, 2001), *The Pianist* (Poland-France, 2002), *Downfall* (Germany, 2004), *Black Book* (Holland, 2006), *Indigènes* (France, 2006), *Katyn* (Poland, 2008) or *In the Fog* (Belarus, 2012).

What "memory" of the war remains? A mass of ageing popular representations; little familiar literature or art; an Americanized film culture; computer games (also Americanized); a theme in the school curriculum as an adjunct to Hitler; some nostalgic and sanitized museum re-creations of "the Blitz" purporting to let people share wartime "community experiences" ("try on the clothes . . . join in the songs"), and occasional awkward official ceremonies.[16] Is it consensus over the war that explains this in part: that it raises no great problems that still confront us? Nothing with the concreteness and power of First World War poetry remains in our culture from the Second. It seems that we, unlike the other victor countries, prefer a "bad" war to lament, rather than a "good" war to celebrate. Or is it that memory of the war has been distorted by "backward projections of what post-war Britain was thought to have become: a welfare state, a craven satellite of the US, a decrepit industrial basket-case"?[17] Be that as it may, the Second World War is the most enduringly important event in modern English and British history, and it has left a multitude of fragmentary memories, some proud, some querulous: a vague belief in Britain's rightness; a feeling that this was "perhaps the only period in the whole of British history during which the British people came together as a metaphysical entity";[18] but little appreciation of the full extent and significance of what England, Britain and the Empire really did.

Yet postwar England was, and is, affected by the war and its memory more than it realizes. Institutions, both ancient and modern, that had "a good war," that were associated with resistance, unity and victory, acquired a popular prestige and affection that sustained them in the postwar years, and in varying degrees sustains them still. The monarchy, shaken by Edward VIII's abdication, became in George VI and his family a symbol of duty and unity, "probably more universally popular than at any other time in its history of nearly a thousand years."[19] Parliament, previously derided as ineffective and irrelevant, became the nation's rallying point and the stage for Churchillian oratory. The armed forces, despite grumbling and mockery of "bull" and "Blimps," were the people in arms against invasion. The BBC earned lasting national and international prestige as the voice of truth and freedom, and as creator of a shared national culture embracing both high art and low comedy. The National Health Service, rooted in wartime policy, came to embody the solidarity that had been the highest aspiration of the Home Front. The Labour Party and the trade unions, epitomized by the close relationship of Clement Attlee and "Ernie" Bevin, became national institutions, pillars of wartime mobilization and partners in government. Even Whitehall, with its personnel doubled, despite being the butt of discontents of all sorts, had become credibly the place which "knew best," as England changed "from one of the most localised and voluntaristic countries in Europe to one of the most centralized and bureaucratic."[20] Much of postwar politics concerned this heritage: how to administer it, or dismantle it, or pay for it.

# PART SEVEN

# AN AGE OF DECLINE?

*England is sticky with self-pity and not prepared to accept peacefully and wisely the fact that her position and her resources are not what they once were.*

John Maynard Keynes, 1946[1]

*In the immediate aftermath of the war we continued to rank as one of the great powers ... A quarter of the world's population did after all still belong to the British Commonwealth and Empire ... [However,] today we are not only no longer a world power, but we are not in the front rank even as a European one ... You have only to move about Western Europe nowadays to realize how poor and unproud the British have become ... It shows in the look of our towns, in our airports, in our hospitals ... In many public statements, Britain is referred to as a model not to follow ... [W]e are surely capable, unless our national character has undergone some profound metamorphosis, of resuming mastery of our fate. But a considerable jolt is going to be needed.*

Sir Nicholas Henderson, ambassador to France, 1979[2]

Few terms have more frequently been applied to postwar Britain than "decline." Henderson's lament, leaked to the press at the time of Margaret Thatcher's first election victory, said eloquently what had become a commonplace. Decline and the desire to "manage" or more ambitiously to "reverse" it have shaped political language and motivated a host of often contradictory domestic and foreign policies. Although reference was commonly made to "Britain," in practice discussion was focused on England, and for many people, from Tory radicals to left-wing journalists, decline has shaped their vision of England as a decaying relic, and the English as "distressed gentlefolk keeping up appearances, making ourselves ridiculous and obnoxious."[3] Things once regarded with affection or pride were reviled or mocked. "Declinism" became a set of ideas and assumptions that were widely taken as self-evident, and they retain some influence even today.[4]

The idea of decline rests on two assumptions. First, that England/ Britain has experienced a collapse in international power and economic dynamism. Second, that this results from long-standing failures of the nation as a political, economic, social and cultural organization. Some historians made declinism an intellectually credible story going back into the nineteenth century and beyond. The conclusion has been that major policies, institutions, even fundamental aspects of English culture were ill adapted to a modern nation—a potent weapon for radicals of left and right.

Loss of world hegemony was at the root of declinism. An early manifestation was a 1956 television series, *We the British: Are We in Decline?*, which was entirely about decolonization.[5] Certainly, the world changed over the twentieth century, and all overseas colonial empires (including that of the United States) dissolved. But declinism, ignoring the experience of other countries, focuses on a deeply pessimistic view of postwar England's weakness contrasted with a grossly overblown image of its earlier power. Victorian hegemony, real though it was, always had limits (see

p. 542)—there was something in the complaint that Britain had been a third-rate power with a great empire. Except at sea, it had slender means, and was shaken by frequent disasters, as we saw in Chapter 14. If Mrs. Thatcher could not delay German unification in 1989–90, neither could Mr. Gladstone in 1870–71. Loss of empire was the most spectacular face of "decline," but the empire as a whole was ceasing to be (if it ever really had been) the bedrock of wealth and power, and its winding up has not weakened or impoverished England—rather the contrary, for what was a liberation for the colonies was also a liberation for England. The fact is that the power of the empire, real when it could be mobilized, had been mostly taken up by defending itself. In military terms (even leaving aside technology such as aircraft and the atom bomb) Britain in the 1950s was far stronger in sheer numbers of men than at the height of Victoria's empire. The obvious response is that decline was relative and that Britain had been overtaken by others. In one sense this is obviously true, but even so it can be misleading. Britain was overtaken in the 1940s only by America and Russia, but it had itself overtaken its old rivals France and Germany; whereas at the height of Victorian power, its armed forces had always been smaller than those of France, Russia, Germany and even some lesser states, and only at sea had it been predominant. Moreover, Britain's former hegemonic and imperial position was not taken over: no country has been able (or perhaps wished) to exercise comparable sway. Of the two "superpowers" (a 1943 coinage) that seemed to dwarf Britain in the 1950s, one proved to have feet of clay. The other, whose huge economic and military expansion constituted the real change in the postwar structure of power, has found in Vietnam, the Middle East and Afghanistan that the very different ideological and political state of the world no longer permits the light-touch hegemony formerly exercised by Britain.

If we take a longer view, distribution of power and wealth in the modern world has been remarkably stable. When Britain emerged as a significant force, after the War of the Spanish Succession in 1713, it was the smallest and yet most global of the world's half-dozen or so most powerful states, alongside China, India, Russia, Germany (the Holy Roman Empire) and France. It occupies a similar position three centuries later. The change in the world has not been the decline of Britain, but the post-1941 rise of America, which in wealth and military power outdistanced not only Britain, but every other state.

Nor has England declined economically: by the late 1950s and 1960s it was of course richer than ever. The change has been that a few other countries have caught up. This is not a quibble, but a fundamental difference of analysis, as catching up with the pioneers is a normal feature of

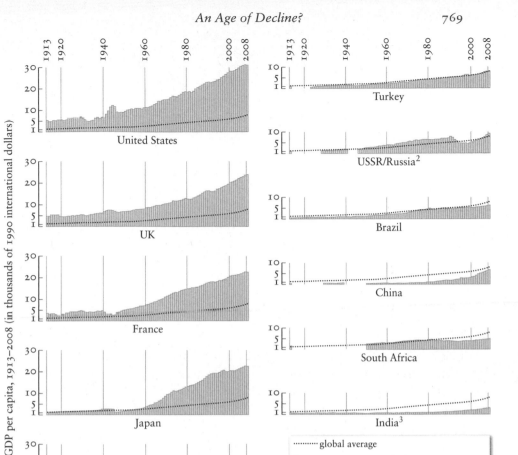

Figure 4. The illusion of economic decline

economic modernization, as developing countries attract foreign investment and import the latest technology. England remains, as in 1713,
among the richest countries in the world—in 2008, among populous
countries, the United Kingdom was second only to the United States in
gross per capita income.[6]

Declinism has been our national narrative for several generations, a
chorus of lamentation in a lucky country where life is safer, longer and
more comfortable than ever in history. What would happen to our view
of the past, and the present, if we abandoned this historical fit of the
vapours? Surely it would permit a calmer, more rational analysis of our
situation and our needs.

# CHAPTER 18

# Postwar

*It must be realized that Great Britain was not part of Europe; she was not simply a Luxembourg.*

Ernest Bevin, August 1950

*I am always astonished when people refer to that period as a time of repression, dullness or conformity—the Age of Anxiety etc. The 1950s were, in a thousand different ways, the reawakening of normal, happy life.*

Margaret Thatcher, 1995[1]

The Labour government of 1945–51 was an impressive and experienced ministry. It needed to be. It was faced with an even more testing situation than that in 1918: chaos in Europe; cataclysm in India; the beginning of the Cold War; and the spectre of national bankruptcy. It had to meet expectations that victory would mean improvement in housing, employment and living standards. It is mainly remembered as the creator of the Welfare State (a phrase coined in the 1930s), but its efforts in foreign, imperial and economic policy, if less remembered, are no less important. Its two leading members were Clement Attlee, a public-school-educated former social worker and veteran of Gallipoli, and Ernest Bevin, a pillar of the trade union movement. Both were models of late-Victorian probity, Attlee being perhaps the nearest to secular sainthood of any modern politician. He was driven around by his wife in the family's old car, and was the last Prime Minister who unaffectedly used public transport, like many of his distinguished predecessors. The clear difference between parties led to an unprecedented, and unrepeated, identity of class and party: in the 1945 general elections 75 percent of the middle class voted Tory; 66 percent of the working class voted Labour. But this was rarely openly discussed, and political feelings were not very strongly expressed—certainly less so than in the nineteenth century.[2]

Europe was in a state unknown since the Thirty Years' War. Many cities were piles of rubble. Some 20 million Germans were homeless, up to 2 million women had been raped—often gang-raped and tortured—by Russian soldiers; many were afterwards beaten to death or shot, and countless survivors were left infected or pregnant. Across Europe some 30 million people had been "displaced," and huge numbers were in camps or just existing amid the ruins. Britain was a paradise by comparison, as it would soon show the world with the 1948 London Olympics and the 1951 Festival of Britain. Yet it did face what Keynes called "a financial Dunkirk." During the war its export trade had fallen by two-thirds as production was skewed towards armaments, leaving "far too many teeth, far too little tail, for economic survival."[3] Two world wars had turned it from the world's biggest creditor into its biggest debtor.[4] Overseas assets had been spent, reducing foreign income by two-thirds. Lend-Lease was terminated one minute after peace returned, leaving Britain with a bill of $650m.[5] In return for a dollar loan—finally paid off in December 2006—it had to agree to dismantle imperial trade preferences.[6] This concession, which one MP called "an economic Munich," was needed to prevent having to live on "bread and potatoes," as the chancellor put it. Income tax was at a 50 percent basic rate, double its prewar level, with surtax rising to 95 percent. There were 2 million men in uniform, adding to a labour shortage; and yet an export drive was required to pay for imports, which meant further cutting home consumption. By 1951 exports had duly increased to 75 percent in volume above their prewar level, but real wages were lower than in the 1930s.[7] In 1947–48 came a terrible winter that slowed the whole economy and forced Labour into public-spending cuts. The British zone in Germany was on the verge of famine, on a weekly ration of a loaf of bread and half a herring, plus a tiny quantity of sugar, butter and skimmed milk. It was costing £100m a year to sustain even this level, forcing the government to tighten food rationing at home: bread had to be rationed in 1946 and potatoes in 1947—something that had not happened during the war itself. The government even drew up a precautionary "famine food programme" for Britain, with powers to conscript labour for agriculture.[8] British forces resisting a Communist takeover in Greece were too expensive to maintain and had to hand over to the Americans.

In these circumstances, the creation of the "Welfare State" in 1946–48 was an achievement for which the Labour government is rightly remembered. Inevitably, given the constraints, there was rather less than met the eye. The plan was not to create new welfare services, but to nationalize and universalize those already existing unevenly.[9] The complex Victorian mix—including private insurance, friendly societies, charities, state insurance benefits, local poor relief, self-governing hospitals, and local-authority clinics and homes—was to be replaced by a uniform national system, which is what the Welfare State (summarized by the Beveridge report as "social insurance and allied services") amounted to. The greatest beneficiaries were working-class housewives, not covered by existing insurance schemes, and the middle classes, who had previously had to pay for their doctors' services.

Beveridge had considered that wartime economic controls would continue indefinitely to ensure full employment, necessary to make his scheme solvent—this would, he said, take the country "half way to Moscow."[10] Keynes too thought "Russian methods" might be necessary. Beveridge assumed that demand for welfare would be limited in a society of stable nuclear families whose male breadwinners would be kept fit for work by the NHS. Moreover, he considered poverty an absolute, not a relative, condition, which could therefore be eliminated by a minimum subsistence payment. These miscalculations meant that the National Insurance scheme was never what its name suggested: it was never funded from contributions (only around 24 percent in the early years), and it became decreasingly so. Open-ended benefits on the basis of need, inherited from the Poor Law and renamed "National Assistance," marked out British practice from Continental insurance systems. The ancient Poor Law principle of indifference to personal morality probably contributed to "the moral relativism, pluralism and privatism" of postwar British society,[11] in strong contrast to countries such as Germany, where entitlement to benefits was conditional on behaviour. Spending was held down: the biggest jump in welfare spending in our history was not in the late 1940s but in the early 1920s.[12] So Britain's Welfare State was in time overtaken by most of western Europe, partly because of Britain's postwar burden of defence spending.

The new National Health Service was built on the foundations of the Emergency Medical Service and the National Blood Transfusion Service, conceived in 1938 to accommodate expected mass casualties from bombing. The NHS was established by law in November 1946 as universal and free, though some charges were introduced as early as 1951. Given the centralizing urges of the time, it aimed at top-down control, with a hierarchy of regional and local boards appointed by the ministry, similar to nationalized industries. As the Health Minister, Aneurin Bevan, put it in a phrase that became part of official folklore, "If a bedpan is dropped in a hospital corridor in Tredegar the reverberations should echo round Whitehall." However, this led to unresolved tensions with the medical profession. Bevan had to compromise with the British Medical Association, the doctors' professional body, which had voted 8:1 to boycott the service. He said he had "stuffed their mouths with gold"—not the last time this would happen. He agreed to abandon the socialist vision of primary-care centres (local clinics) with salaried staff. Instead, the new system perpetuated the dominance of large hospitals, run in practice by their consultants, who retained independent professional status as private contractors. General practitioners too retained some independence as contractors receiving fees. The system, which came into effect in July 1948, was very popular, but was not copied by other countries, where its austere virtues (egalitarianism, limited patient choice, and relative cheapness compared with America, France or Germany) had less appeal as symbols of national solidarity.

The Welfare State was part of a wider strategy of state planning. Coal, rail, steel, electricity and gas were nationalized and placed under autonomous boards. It was assumed that these, controlled by the "public-minded expert," would act harmoniously and for the public good. The New Towns Act (1946) and Town and Country Planning Act (1947), energetic slum clearance, the creation of "green belts," and the building of large housing estates and New Towns initiated two or three decades in which English towns were reshaped. Around a third of all houses in the country had been damaged or destroyed during the war, and gleeful demolition of hundreds of thousands more became part of postwar culture: "a sense of shame about the industrial past, a visceral and blinkered rejection"[13] caused much unnecessary destruction. Huge house-building programmes began, mainly of council estates—a British invention. Bevan hoped that these "modern villages" of family houses would re-create the "living tapestry" of traditional village life.[14] Some did. But the 1950s and 1960s universalized a cheap all-purpose modernism combining banality of design and poverty of execution, epitomized in multi-storey car parks, shopping centres and tower blocks, at best bland and at worst dystopian, obliterating identity and memory. They were presented by their defenders as excitingly modern, inspired notably by the Swiss architect Le Corbusier, who had advocated demolishing central Paris and covering it in giant uniform towers. Popular resistance, especially to tower blocks, eventually stemmed the tide of glass and concrete—for a time.

Despite financial pressures, which it hoped were temporary, the government was adamant in maintaining Britain's status as one of the "Big Three," being "certain [the Russians] will not be able to resist advancing into any vacuum we may leave."[15] Hence the decision in December 1945 to build an atom bomb (first tested in 1956) to maintain security, prestige and leverage over American strategy. As Bevin put it, "We've got to have this thing whatever it costs. We've got to have the bloody Union

Jack on top of it."[16] Bevin, a forceful man of fertile imagination, aimed to create a mighty "Third Force"—a British-led Western European Union, centred on a Franco-British alliance, bringing in the Benelux countries, Scandinavia and eventually a democratic Germany, and incorporating British, French and Belgian African colonies whose economic resources would be developed to mutual benefit, and associating independent Commonwealth countries too. He hoped in four or five years, "if we only pushed on and developed Africa," to have the Americans "eating out of our hands."[17]

But commitment to Europe was to be one of "limited liability" in case the fragile Continent collapsed. Britain would not surrender sovereignty and go down "paths along which there is no return." As Bevin put it:

> The people in this country were pinning their faith on a policy of defence built on a Commonwealth-USA basis—an English-speaking basis. People here were frankly doubtful of Europe. How could he go down to his constituency—Woolwich—which had been bombed . . . and tell his constituents that the Germans would help them in a war against Russia?[18]

Partial decolonization was not seen as the end of world power. Britain, like France, had drawn on its empire during the war, and, also like France, hoped a modernized empire would be a means of maintaining its wealth and power in the world of the "superpowers." Labour and Tory governments continued to envisage a global role as leader of a post-imperial Commonwealth linked by strategy and trade. Only in retrospect is it clear that the war had accelerated fundamental changes in the world affecting Britain's position:[19] it had been financially ravaged; it no longer appeared as the main military defender of the Commonwealth, which was now the United States; and it was about to lose power in India, and hence its position as a major Asian-Pacific power. Above all, the onset of the Cold War and the permanent military and political competition of the two superpowers over the next four decades would make all other countries to varying degrees their satellites, hastening general decolonization, and leaving little room for lesser states, such as Britain or France, to act as credible Great Powers.

The first and most dramatic change was Indian independence. Internal self-government had been conceded in practice by the Government of India Act (1935); and by 1945 there remained only some 600 British officials in the entire Indian civil service. Formal independence had been promised during the war. British rule could not in any case be maintained by force. In the Central Provinces, bigger than England, there were only seventeen British officials, nineteen British police officers and no troops.

The Viceroy, Lord Wavell, concluded in 1946 that "we have no longer the resources, nor I think the necessary prestige and confidence in ourselves." The unique economic importance of India as a market for Lancashire textiles had long gone: the Cabinet was told that "we should not be sacrificing anything that mattered."[20] The aim was to hand over to a government that would remain in the British sphere of influence, and avoid what Churchill called "scuttle." The British wished to establish a united India from the imperial mosaic of provinces and princely states, but the stumbling block was Hindu-Muslim division, manipulated by the Congress Party and the Muslim League. The British reluctantly accepted partition, rather than attempting to broker a confederation. This was to end in horrific violence and permanent tension. How much British policy was to blame continues to arouse controversy. Britain no longer had the power or the will to dictate—"the sawdust was running out of the doll hour by hour," as the viceroy's chief of staff, General Ismay, summed it up.[21] A new viceroy—the last—was appointed: Lord Mountbatten—"a left-wing patrician with royal connections and an ego to match"—who sympathized with the Congress Party.[22] He accepted a face-saving mission, and he and the Attlee government set an early date for independence in the hope of forcing a compromise between Hindu and Muslim politicians. But continuing intransigence forced partition. A British barrister presided over the hasty drawing of a frontier between India and Pakistan, kept secret in the vain hope of limiting conflict and then suddenly announced in June 1947. An Indian Independence Act was hastily passed by Westminster in July. The prospect of partition ignited mass sectarian violence, looting, rape and ethnic cleansing, with up to a million deaths in atrocious circumstances. This was "probably less than would have occurred if the process had been significantly slower," in the view of one historian. But in the view of another the haste made it "the most contemptible single act in the annals of the empire," even though "the ultimate drivers of the split were indigenous."[23] Both may be right.

India had been the heart of the Asian empire, with much of the rest an appendage: Ceylon and Burma were duly given independence in 1948, the latter leaving the Commonwealth. But some remaining colonies and the Dominions in the "Sterling Area" (those countries that used sterling for international payments) now had an important role in relieving postwar Britain's financial distress. As Bevin told the Commons in 1946, "If the British Empire fell . . . the standard of life of our constituents would fall considerably."[24] Their raw materials (including rubber and tin from Malaya and copper from Northern Rhodesia) could earn vital dollars, which were pooled in London. They also provided a privileged market for

British exports and supplied British consumers with much-needed products (tea, sugar, chocolate, butter, lamb), for which they were paid in sterling. Economic development was forcefully pursued in Africa. British emigration to East Africa and to the Dominions was encouraged. Immigration from the Caribbean began, despite the foot-dragging of officials and the hostility of trade unions: as British subjects, West Indians had the right to travel freely to Britain, where they had legal equality and the vote. The *Empire Windrush* sailed into Tilbury on 22 June 1948 with 492 job-seekers, mostly young men. Colonial Office officials met them and accommodated some in an old air raid shelter, whose nearest labour exchange was at Brixton, where many settled—the seed of a new community. Eleven Labour MPs wrote to Attlee warning that "an influx of coloured people" might damage "harmony, strength and cohesion." By the later 1950s over 20,000 people per year were arriving from the Caribbean, and smaller numbers from India and Pakistan.[25]

The Middle East was now the fulcrum of British strategic ambitions: a bulwark against Soviet expansion and a vital source of oil—some 60 percent of Britain's consumption.[26] The desire to maintain relations with the Arab world, and forestall Soviet interference, was a major reason for withdrawing from Palestine. Here again, British policy was and remains controversial. The 1917 promise of a "Jewish homeland" created irreconcilable tensions (see p. 637). The Second World War and the Holocaust made conflict impossible to contain. The United States, the Soviet Union, and progressive opinion across Europe and in Britain (including in the Cabinet) wanted Holocaust survivors and other Jewish emigrants from Europe to be able to settle in Palestine. President Truman demanded that 100,000 should be admitted at once, to which Bevin retorted sharply that the Americans did not want too many Jews in New York, and insisted that "I don't want the Arabs to be dismissed as if they were nobody."[27] British officials and soldiers, trying to limit Jewish immigration, became targets of Zionist terrorists, many trained in the Soviet bloc.[28] Their biggest coup was the blowing up of the King David Hotel in Jerusalem, used as the British headquarters, in July 1946; and although in the view of a recent Israeli historian "British officials and troops by and large displayed restraint and humanity,"[29] there was a spiral of vicious reprisals and counter-reprisals. Attlee and Bevin decided to give up a hopeless, expensive and thankless burden—there were more British troops policing Palestine than had been needed for the whole Victorian empire—and relinquish the League of Nations Mandate to the United Nations. London suggested a two-state solution, but this was rejected by both sides, as were less realistic plans by a United Nations committee to divide Palestine into seven parts, which sparked off violent protests and attacks on Jews across the Arab world. British troops and officials—around 100,000 in all—began to leave in June 1947, and all were gone and the Mandate formally ended by the following summer. The Zionists and Arabs were then free to square up for what became the first Arab-Israeli War of 1948–49.

Bevin's lasting success—far from his original intention—was to help to create an Atlantic security system in response to the onset of the Cold War. Churchill, Leader of the Opposition, had already warned in a speech at Fulton, Missouri, on 5 March 1946, that "an iron curtain has descended across the Continent." Bevin had hoped at first that a Labour government could maintain reasonable relations with the Soviet Union, but in 1948 its takeover of Czechoslovakia, pressure on Scandinavia and eleven-month blockade of West Berlin, which required a huge U.S.-British airlift to supply it, convinced him that his vision of a European "Third Force" was unviable: America had to be linked indefinitely into the defence of western Europe. Hence the North Atlantic Treaty of April 1949, creating a military alliance of the United States, Britain, France, Canada and several other European states, eventually including Germany (1954), with a permanent headquarters near Paris. Britain's prominent military role in NATO and elsewhere in the world demanded a large defence budget of around 10 percent of gross national income: this was very high in historical terms, and it only fell to late Victorian levels (2–3 percent of GDP) in the 1990s.[30] Britain maintained an advanced arms industry, large conscript armed forces until 1960, and a determination to assert a partnership as equal as it could make it with the United States. This led in 1950 to participation in the Korean War—a costly involvement which damaged recovering national finances and the economy: but "we could not afford to lose America's support in Europe," decided the Cabinet, "and on that account we must . . . accept American leadership in the Far East."[31]

The Conservatives returned to office under Churchill in 1951 after two successive general elections in 1950 and 1951, which had the biggest electoral turnouts (84 and 82.5 percent, respectively) since the introduction of full democracy.[32] The narrow Tory victory, aided by the eclipse of the Liberals, was probably due mainly to their promise to end austerity and rationing—which happened gradually between 1952 and 1954[33]—and get the economy back to normal. This meant cutting defence spending. The end of the Korean War improved Britain's trading position, as did the recovery of the Continental economies. The early 1950s were a hopeful time. The Festival of Britain in 1951—the centenary of the Great Exhibition—was a series of hundreds of nationwide events promoting music, theatre, film, architecture, science, technology, industrial design and simple amusement, with its main focus London's South Bank. It was followed

shortly after by the coronation on 2 June 1953 of a pretty young queen—
the first global television event and the last great aristocratic and imperial
flourish, where ermine and coronets mingled with turbans and slouch
hats, with Churchill in the silks and feathers of a Knight of the Garter. A
1953 study by two sociologists (a Labour Party research officer and a Chicago academic) concluded that the coronation brought out "a degree of
moral unity equalled by no other large national state."[34] Just on cue, a
carefully planned "British" (or "Commonwealth"—New Zealand and
Sherpa) expedition was the first to climb Everest. The following year, the
first four-minute mile was run by an Oxford medical student, Roger Ban-
nister. The first jet airliner, the De Havilland Comet, had entered service in
1952. The world's first commercial atomic power station, Calder Hall,
opened in 1956, and that same year the Fairey Delta 2 (later cancelled,
but pirated by the French for their Mirage) was the first aircraft to fly at
1,000 mph. In 1957 the D-Type Jaguar won five of the top six places in
the Le Mans twenty-four-hour race. All seemed to show that, despite the
grime and the bombsites, a rejuvenated country had entered a "New Elizabethan" age, and that wartime efforts had placed it in the forefront of
technological innovation. Although the parties were still sharply distinct
in class terms, there was by later standards little difference in their broad
economic policies, which assumed state controls, nationalized utilities,
Keynesian demand management to maintain high employment, and
attempts at harmonious consultation with management and trade unions,
which was christened "Butskellism."* We now tend to recall the postwar
years as a time of grim "austerity"; but the early 1950s were a time of
unprecedented prosperity, improving housing, family stability, full
employment, low crime—a paradise for children. "Britain was still best:
that was so deeply part of how citizens thought, it was taken for granted.
Education, food, health, anything at all—best."[35]

Whitehall's ambitions to retain preponderant influence in the Middle
East and a degree of leadership in South Asia depended on the military
presence in Egypt conceded by a 1936 defence treaty. This gave Britain
military bases in the Suez Canal Zone—a territory the size of Wales, with
stores, maintenance facilities and airfields, from which they could even, if
necessary, bomb southern Russia. Britain had treated Egypt shamefully:
not even a colony or member of the Commonwealth, it was a nominally
independent country bullied into submission and used as a mere convenience. In July 1956 the nationalist military ruler, Colonel Gamal Abdel
Nasser, nationalized the Suez Canal, 40 percent owned by the British govern-

---

* Coined by the *Economist* (13 Feb. 1954) after the centrist politicians R. A. Butler (Conservative chancellor, 1951–55) and Hugh Gaitskell (Labour chancellor, 1950–51).

ment, in an open challenge to Britain. Nasser was also helping Algerian nationalists in their fight against French rule. The French and British governments persuaded themselves that they faced another Munich, with Nasser as Hitler—the first time that "Munich" became a rhetorical standby. Whitehall believed British power in the Middle East was at stake, and with it their Great Power strategy and their supply of cheap oil paid for in sterling, for the Middle East was in the Sterling Area. Whitehall estimated that if Middle Eastern oil had to be bought in dollars, it would cost the economy another $500m–$700m annually. Gold reserves would disappear, the Sterling Area would disintegrate, and the defence budget would be unsustainable—"a country that cannot provide for its own defence is finished," warned the Permanent Under-Secretary at the Foreign Office.[36] Churchill's successor, Anthony Eden, leapt at a plot suggested by the French and the Israelis, who had their own reasons for wanting to get rid of Nasser: the Israelis would invade Egypt, and the French and British would send an expedition to "protect" the canal, and, at the same time, remove Nasser. Eden, increasingly unstable and possibly ill (the easiest explanation), ignored advice and took key decisions in secret. This was not only a crime, it was a blunder: Eden convinced himself that the Americans would acquiesce. In October 1956 Israel invaded. On 5 November the Anglo-French force, commanded by a New Zealander, reached Port Said. But the crisis caused a run on sterling and the Bank of England's reserves dwindled alarmingly: $50m was lost during the first two days of the Suez operation. A loan in dollars was urgently needed from the Americans to stave off a sterling crisis—even the possible collapse of the Sterling Area and the ruin of Britain's commercial position. President Eisenhower let it be known that "he did not see much value in an unworthy and unreliable ally and that the necessity to support them might not be as great as they believed"; and a British diplomat concluded that the Americans "seem determined to treat us as naughty boys who have got to be taught that they cannot go off and act on their own without asking Nanny's permission."[37] The British government, duly chastened, agreed to a cease-fire without even consulting the French.

The Suez debacle is commonly interpreted as the end of British imperialism, of Great Power pretensions, even of national self-confidence. This is somewhat exaggerated: Anglo-American relations were swiftly restored, most of the blame was placed on Eden (who retired on health grounds), the Tories under Harold Macmillan remained in power, and politicians' desire to play a great role in the world remained undiminished. Suez did, however, provide a dramatic symbol of longer-term changes in Britain's policy and power.[38] The question was, did imperialism help or hinder either policy or power? Attlee had previously concluded that "an attempt to maintain the old colonialism would, I am sure, have immensely aided Communism," and the Cold War now dominated policy.[39] Britain's general object now was not to maintain colonial rule, but to consolidate friendly independent states, including through economic, security and intelligence links.[40] Malaya (the most valuable remaining colony, independent from 1957, and renamed Malaysia in 1963) was successfully defended from 1948 to 1971 against Communist insurgency and Indonesian threats. A vicious conflict in Cyprus from 1955 to 1960 was ended by independence with Britain continuing to hold two large "sovereign" military bases. Yet the importance of Suez should not be underestimated in its effect on public and official perceptions. The divided Commonwealth had not provided the hoped-for support. The entente with France, Bevin's key to leadership of Europe, had been unceremoniously jettisoned. A defence review concluded in 1957 that "in the Mediterranean or in the Far East the UK would only act in cooperation with the US."[41] Britain's leaders had been shown to be both inept and dishonest, and had been humiliated before the world and, perhaps more importantly, before their own people.

The end of empire then came quickly. There were general causes: the economic, political and psychological effects of two world wars both in European states and in their colonies; the Cold War and Soviet-backed anti-colonialism; American ambivalence; pressure from the UN; and not least white-settler extremism, which led South Africa to leave the Commonwealth in 1961 and Southern Rhodesia to declare illegal independence in 1965. There seemed only unpalatable choices: as the Colonial Secretary, Alan Lennox-Boyd, put it in 1957, "to give independence too soon and risk disintegration . . . ; or to hang on too long, risk ill-feeling and disturbance, and eventually to leave bitterness behind."[42]

Wartime demand for food, postwar demand for dollars and the political fashion for top-down capital-intensive development proved destabilizing in what was assumed to be the most long-lasting part of the empire: Africa. One notorious example was the "ground nuts scheme," begun in 1947, aiming to cultivate 3 million acres in Tanganyika to produce vegetable oil. It was a fiasco—only 46,000 acres were completed. More generally, colonial administrations now pushed forward economic modernization and increased production for export, which meant cajoling, or forcing, African peasants into new methods and often laborious improvements for which they received little reward. New white farmers were arriving to direct the process. A growing population of landless men grew increasingly resentful. Attempts to create new political structures made things worse: the abortive 1953 Central African Federation, including the two Rhodesias (later Zambia and Zimbabwe) and Nyasaland (Malawi), aimed to preserve British influence by keeping disproportionate power in the hands of white settlers. But this strengthened nationalism, led by educated urban Africans, and the federation had to be abandoned ignominiously in 1963.[43]

Macmillan tried to make a virtue of necessity, in a famous speech in South Africa in 1960 proclaiming that "a wind of change" was blowing through Africa. The French and Belgians were feeling the same draught, with bloody conflicts in Algeria and the Congo, and this added to pressure on Britain—"other people's empires were crumbling all around," explained a senior official.[44] Some colonial officials feared granting independence too fast, but the British did not want their own Congo or Algerian war. So between 1960 and 1966 twenty colonies became independent.* Most remained in the Commonwealth, and for a time preserved Westminster-style politics. But they were not the pliant satellites that Whitehall had hoped for.

The worst episode in British decolonization was the "Mau-Mau" uprising in Kenya, mainly between 1951 and 1957. Mau-Mau was a highly violent movement of young Kikuyu, both landless farm labourers and men from the Nairobi shanty towns, some of whom had fought for Britain in Burma. It was directed against landowners, both Kikuyu and white. It practised intimidation, murder, mutilation, and secret oath-taking with traditional magic—believed to include bestiality and the consumption of menstrual blood, fresh semen and human flesh.[45] This brought out European horror of the "heart of darkness": the Colonial Secretary, Oliver Lyttelton, detected "the horned shadow of the Devil himself."[46] Massacres by Mau-Mau led to revenge killings by anti–Mau-Mau Africans and panicky repression by the settler Home Guard, with the authorities trailing in their wake. Ill-treatment amounting to torture was used to convict suspects or to extort confessions prior to "rehabilitation." More people were formally tried and sentenced to death, mainly for murder, than at any other time or place in British imperial history: 1,090 men went to the gallows.[47] Tens of thousands were interned. A scandal occurred when eleven detainees were beaten to death in Hola camp in 1959, an episode vehemently denounced in the Commons by the Tory MP Enoch Powell. In the short term, the Mau-Mau horrors were a setback to progressive African nationalism. Yet they equally marked the moral collapse of British rule, and a new Colonial Secretary, Iain Macleod, thought the episode meant "inexorably a move towards African independence."[48] In June 2013 the Foreign Secretary, William Hague, expressed regret for "torture and other

* Cyprus, Nigeria, Sierra Leone, Tanganyika and Zanzibar (Tanzania), Western Samoa, Jamaica, Trinidad and Tobago, Uganda, Kenya, Nyasaland (Malawi), Northern Rhodesia (Zambia), Malta, Singapore, Gambia, the Maldives, British Guiana (Guyana), Bechuanaland (Botswana), Basutoland (Lesotho) and Barbados.

forms of ill-treatment at the hands of the colonial administration"; the British government agreed to pay nearly £20m to over 5,000 surviving victims, and to contribute to building a memorial in Nairobi.[49]

Recent writers have stigmatized "Britain's gulag" and "Kenya's Belsen." Some assert that the violence was as bad as or worse than the atrocious Algerian War. The British have been accused of genocide, with up to 300,000 Kikuyu people unaccounted for.[50] This widely repeated accusation is based on comparing the actual population in 1962 with an estimate based on extrapolating earlier demographic trends. Closer analysis shows that lower population growth had various causes, including improved education for women. Infant mortality did increase, but far less, for example, than in Iraq due to the First Gulf War and United Nations sanctions. The official figure for Mau-Mau deaths was 11,503, and that for the victims of Mau-Mau about the same.[51] Terrible though this was, comparison with Algeria is misplaced: loss of life there was at least ten times greater. Even without such exaggeration, the Mau-Mau conflict marked a grotesque and sinister end to postwar visions of progressive colonialism. British ideas of compulsory progress were at the root of the problem, for the background to rebellion included resistance to campaigns against female genital mutilation (campaigns which outraged traditionalists, the pillars of colonial rule) and resentment at heavy-handed agricultural modernization.[52] "Development" (meaning commercialization of agriculture) and "partnership" (in practice white-settler supremacy) involved dispossession and displacement of peoples. It made a mockery of the idea that well-meaning colonial rule could lead to a harmonious and mutually beneficial long-term association.

## REMEMBERING THE AGE OF EMPIRE

> Set in this stormy sea
> Queen of these restless fields of tide,
> England! what shall men say of thee,
> Before whose feet the worlds divide?
> Oscar Wilde, "Ave Imperatrix" (1887)[53]

*As with so many of the world's problems, we are responsible for the issue in the first place.*
David Cameron in Pakistan, 5 April 2011

Thus a Tory Prime Minister gave an answer to Wilde's question: a negative one. Many countries in the world think of Britain—perhaps especially of England—in terms of the empire, the aspect that figures in their own national histories. It also affects ways we think of ourselves. David Cameron's comment contrasts with the view expressed by Tony Blair to the French National Assembly in 1998: as former empires "our two nations understand power. They are not afraid of it; they are not ashamed of it either." But *should* we, on the contrary, be more afraid of using our power? Should we be ashamed, and try to root out what many critics think has been ingrained into our culture by imperialism: arrogance, insularity, racism? The empire, one distinguished historian has even said, is "our Holocaust."[54]

English justifications of the empire from the early nineteenth century until the mid twentieth drew on Enlightenment ideas of civilization and the Whig idea of progress.[55] Imperial apologists, from celebrated writers such as Macaulay and Seeley to junior district officers, were predominantly "culturalist," believing that Europe embodied a more advanced stage of civilization whose values were universal and could and should be introduced into less developed societies. There was certainly racism too, in the sense of believing that certain races were not merely "backward," but inherently inferior. This was a minority view, however, at least among the educated, and was usually considered un-Christian. Authoritarian rule over India and other dependent colonies justified itself by the claim that backward peoples—"half devil and half child," in Kipling's notorious phrase—were being protected, including from themselves, and advanced. This claim involved some hypocrisy, notably a deep ambivalence about advancement in practice. Those among the subjects of the empire who accepted its claims and cooperated, whether by clinging to approved traditional cultures (for example, Indian princes or Sikh soldiers) or by embracing certain English values (most obviously Christianity), were to varying degrees privileged and respected: there was no objection to the sons of native potentates going to Eton, and the Gurkhas still command wide public affection. Those who were most disliked and despised by colonial authority were those who in fact genuinely embraced British values and used them against the empire, of whom the greatest example was Gandhi, meaningfully dismissed by Churchill as "a seditious Middle Temple lawyer."

Law and order, honest government, free trade, and the suppression of slavery, internal warfare and barbarous practices—these were the justifications, and pretexts, for colonial rule. The logic was that in due course the whole empire would follow the white settler colonies towards self-government, though this was seen as remote. When hasty decolonization did come in the 1950s and 1960s, it was presented as a successful change from empire to Commonwealth. A generally positive view of the empire and its history—that it included crimes and flaws but was well-meaning and on the whole politically and economically beneficial both to colonizers and to colonized—remained the orthodoxy in England until at least the 1960s.

The historical boot is now on the other foot: recent opinion emphasizes the violence of conquest, the universality of racial disdain, the destructiveness of settlement, the harshness of imperial government, the arrogance of its practitioners and the sterility of its legacy. There have always been many critics of imperial rule, from Edmund Burke onwards (see p. 367). William Pitt apologized for England's involvement in slavery two centuries before Tony Blair did so, and in far more heartfelt terms, calling for "an atonement for our long and cruel injustice."[56] Recent historians emphasize the injustice and uncover the cruelty, as in the case of the Mau-Mau. When many former colonies shed Westminster-style government, the idea of a progressive legacy seemed hollow. More fundamentally, critics rejected the "progressive" history of empire root and branch: the means could never be justified, and the ends were never achieved. Hence, Niall Ferguson's argument that the British Empire created the modern world provoked an outcry.[57]

This transformation in attitudes has several sources. One is a desire to focus on the history of the poor and oppressed. Another is nationalism, the main impulse for anti-imperialism in all colonies and former colonies, democratic or dictatorial, non-white or white: rejection of empire is the core of many national foundation myths. Another source is anti-capitalism, one of the oldest and newest forms of anti-imperialism. Another still is moral revulsion against all pretentions to racial or cultural superiority. The influential work of Edward Said,[58] powerful in argument and brilliant in presentation, accused European imperialism, unlike earlier empires, of imposing intellectual and cultural domination, and spattered European culture in general with the mire of imperialism.

The empire and its rulers have thus come under withering scrutiny by highly motivated historians from every continent; perhaps only Nazi Germany has been subject to comparable investigation. Moreover, "fabulously detailed" colonial archives leave every blemish exposed: "You would be hard pushed to get similar evidence of fierce internal debates, admissions of failure or even hard statistics from, say, United Nations organisations' records today."[59]

The British Empire is too recent to be regarded by most commentators with the detachment that can be applied to older empires such as the Ottoman or the Mughal. When the latter used violence against their subject peoples, they can be said to have carried out "stabilizing operations"; but when the British did so, they committed "war crimes," even "genocide." This may be poetic justice for people who prided themselves on spreading civilization, but it makes their record difficult, if not impossible, to assess. Perhaps no one really wants to assess it, because comparison with preceding or succeeding regimes is taboo, especially when independent states are more oppressive and incompetent than the British were. Few today are interested in assessing "good quiet work" in forestry, or in combating locust swarms or the tsetse fly.[60] By what criteria could one judge the effects, for example, of missionary education on headhunters in Borneo? If the empire is regarded as "wholly without any redeeming features,"[61] only denunciation is required. It is therefore possible to denounce both imperial strength and imperial weakness, both what it did and what it failed to do. Some established practices that the British tried to stop— the slave trade, female infanticide, genital mutilation, widow-burning, cannibalism, headhunting, tribal warfare, witchcraft, human sacrifice, systematic sexual abuse—cannot easily be defended today. They can, however, be played down, their existence minimized or dismissed as colonialist fantasy. Alternatively, the sincerity and effectiveness of British policy can be criticized: they had ulterior motives, failed to make much difference, and anyway had no right to interfere. The question of whether outsiders have the right to intervene by force in the name of "universal" humanitarian principles is no less controversial today.

It is true that humanitarian aims were only one part of the complex motivations for empire, that they often camouflaged political ambition and financial greed, and that they often went hand in hand with cultural and racial arrogance and hypocritical double standards.[62] And yet there *was* slavery; there were human sacrifices; there was endemic warfare; and to ignore this is to belittle the humanity of those who suffered in pre-colonial societies, which were not idyllic Gardens of Eden spoiled only by the imperial serpent. It is common to stress the humiliations imposed by colonial rule, and the damage it did to indigenous cultures. But the rule of conquering Mughals, Asante or Zulus was violent and humiliating for their subordinates too. Should we sympathize, for example, with the humiliation of those Zulu elders who lamented in 1900 that under British rule they had "practically lost control over their girls and women"?[63] The weakening of traditional elites and cultures was for many a liberation. The adoption of Christianity brought by missionaries often meant self-emancipation, especially for the young, poor and female.[64] What did freed slaves, women escaping forced marriage, or people spared from human sacrifice feel about their colonial masters?

Imperial rule was not—it simply could not be—all powerful. It was "a global mosaic of almost ungraspable complexity and staggering contrasts"[65] made up of literally hundreds of units, including self-governing Dominions, internally autonomous protectorates, dependent territories linked by treaty and directly administered Crown Colonies. Its total military manpower was usually less than the United States recently found insufficient to control merely Iraq. As George Orwell (an anti-imperialist former colonial policeman) put it, over "nearly a quarter of the earth, there were fewer armed men than would be found necessary by a minor Balkan state."[66] So the acquiescence of most and the cooperation of many was essential for it to work at all. This too can be criticized, because the empire often ruled by confirming the power of existing elites or creating new ones, and hence was often a force not for progress but for conservatism. Even then, there were gainers. Sometimes the experience of empire was "essentially one of sympathy and congruence."[67] There emerged dynamic processes of economic, cultural and social change, which the British sometimes facilitated, sometimes failed to stop, and often simply acquiesced in. In such new metropolises as Calcutta, Bombay, Madras, Toronto, Shanghai (much of it run by British officials), Cape Town, Singapore, Sydney and Hong Kong, people took what advantages they could from the empire—travel, trade, education, employment, law and order.

The empire was thus a bargain, or a series of bargains and accommodations, sometimes unspoken, sometimes formal (as with treaties of protection), and always changing. One party to the bargain was to provide protection, security, honest government, arbitration between conflicting groups and access to global trade. The other parties were to give obedience, taxes, labour, even loyalty, and many exercised subordinate authority as princes, chiefs, officials, soldiers and policemen—many of their descendants today govern the independent successor states. Neither side ever really fulfilled the bargain, and it worked out better in some places than others: better in Malta than Jamaica; better in New Zealand than Australia; better in Malaya than India. Not all colonial subjects were included in the bargain, or not to the same extent. For some people it offered more: to princes more than to peasants; to settlers more than to aboriginals; to slaves more than to slave-owners. Some lost more than they gained. Some lost everything.

But this could be said about many systems of rule. What can we say specifically about the *British* Empire, and the English part in it? To draw up a balance sheet, weighing the destruction of aboriginal lives and cultures against the creation of wealthy modern states, would be morally repulsive, above all for an English writer. To try to compare its performance with other empires or with non-colonial states is interesting but not necessarily meaningful. For example, taxes were lower in colonial India than in independent Siam; British rule in India was more authoritarian but less corrupt than Russian rule in central Asia. Indian nationalists are convinced that India would have been richer and happier without the British, and would have developed modern political institutions; British imperialists used to argue that India would have been prey to war and disorder between its post-Mughal states. Both arguments are speculative. Even if we tried to guess alternative histories, it would not take us far. Corsica, for example, had it remained British (see p. 396) would surely today be an independent EU state like Malta: who is to decide whether that would have been a better outcome than as part of France?

Comparing the empire with its successor states is particularly sensitive and uncertain. Where there have been improvements after independence, does this show that colonial rule was holding back progress? Or do such improvements owe something to the infrastructure created under colonialism? The answer to both questions may be yes—or indeed no. When things have deteriorated after independence, does this prove the merits of colonial rule or simply demonstrate its toxic legacy? That legacy can be used to excuse or justify later oppression, as in Mugabe's Zimbabwe.[68] It is also a means for shrugging off responsibilities: it is not unknown for Australians today to blame the plight of Aboriginal people on "the British." Finally, ascribing cynical and selfish motives to imperial politicians makes it easier for present-day politicians to present their own (neo-imperialist?) actions in a favourable light: "We don't do empire." If we accepted that nineteenth-century imperialists also had good intentions, we might today be more alert to the dangers—which they too experienced—of unintended consequences, "collateral damage" and political failure.

What then should we think about our imperial past? Inevitably it leaves a mixed and ambivalent memory, for it had contradictory consequences that include the bad, the good and the indifferent. The early empire was entwined with slavery. It facilitated mass migration, which had devastating human and ecological effects, as well as good ones. It vandalized and often despised other cultures. It could be ruthless and sometimes savage. It dictated to other peoples how they should deal with the challenges of an integrating world, and, to add injury to insult, the solutions it dictated were sometimes disastrous. It also combated slavery worldwide and did more than any other power to try to stop it. It tried to palliate the effects of migration—inadequately and ambivalently, but the consequences of a free-for-all would surely have been worse. It preserved and strengthened aspects of indigenous cultures: for example, by creating written forms of languages and preserving monuments which are now regarded as part of world heritage. The devotion of its often lonely and exposed officials and missionaries is undeniable, even if that devotion was sometimes unwelcome and misplaced. It attempted to found viable successor states. And finally, towards the end of its life, the empire and its peoples did much to save the world from Fascist and hyper-nationalist domination.

Even this last consideration would not excuse the English, many Scots and Irish, and some Welsh "in all their multifarious guises: fresh-faced district officers, hymn-singing missionaries, eccentric engineers, elegant diplomats, drunken sailors"[69] from having rampaged round the world gratuitously seizing control of other peoples' countries—if that were the whole story. Britain's rulers in the eighteenth century believed that their safety required them to struggle against French power, including commercial power beyond the seas. They succeeded in preventing a quite likely outcome: French world hegemony, in many ways a natural development, given France's greater territory, population and cultural prestige. When Britain emerged victorious in 1815, its intention was not further expansion, but stability. Indeed, British world policy after 1815—perhaps from much earlier—was a long defensive action marked by repeated "mission creep." The nineteenth-century world was far more unstable than the label Pax Britannica suggests: the great empires of the Mughals, the Ottomans and the Manchus were all in crisis, as were smaller polities.[70] British governments were reluctant to take on ever more commitments. But it was scarcely possible for the only global power to keep out of global affairs, and if it had, it is not clear that the world would have been less vulnerable, unstable and violent. The real alternatives to British hegemony would probably have been conquests by others, or perhaps global anarchy.

There have been many suggestions, some fanciful, about what it did to the English to have been possessors of power and empire, among them "economic enfeeblement" and "tortured" relations with Europe.[71] Historians argue about whether the country was deeply affected by both the possession and the loss of empire, or whether in fact most English people were indifferent to empire and little touched by it.[72] In either case, few English problems and foibles today can seriously be explained as consequences of empire or post-imperial nostalgia. In the past, empire sporadically diverted English resources, energies and attention far outside its borders, forcing its affairs to be run in a way that was certainly very different from that required by a medium-sized offshore nation.[73] Empire had many superficial effects on England's culture: for example, in diet and sport. It encouraged individual and national arrogance, expressed with

fulsome self-satisfaction that today makes us laugh or squirm. It sometimes demonstrated the force of Lord Acton's dictum: "Power tends to
corrupt, and absolute power corrupts absolutely." It is often said that part
of this corruption was racism and xenophobia: it certainly produced
plenty of crass and vulgar racists and xenophobes. But it also had the
opposite effect, simply by making more of the English accustomed to a
variety of peoples and cultures. Even slight experience of Europe and the
world today suggests that the English have become one of the least racist
and least xenophobic of peoples. One obvious sign is the absence, fairly
rare in Europe, of a significant racist political party. Another may be the
globe-trotting propensities of people of all ages. More than ever we have
become what Defoe called "a mongrel half-bred race," and are generally
quite happy to be so. Some aspects of post-imperial immigration into
England have caused political and social problems. But those problems do
not arise from the imperial legacy, which makes integration easier, as the
successes of people from East Africa or Hong Kong demonstrate. England
(like France) has inherited from imperial days a relatively high degree of
engagement with the outside world, in giving aid and in trying to play
a forceful role in world affairs. This could be seen as "a continuing, in
some respects remarkably unchanging, imperial story."[74] It sometimes has
good and sometimes has dire results. But it is hard to see indifference
to the outside world, as practised by some European countries, as a moral
virtue.

Perhaps our general judgement on the whole period of British and
English world power from the 1750s to the 1950s should be that it was
an improvised set of responses to an unprecedented global situation,
marked by political upheaval, technological revolution, and huge movements of peoples. British governments and their agents made some terrible mistakes and committed some shocking crimes. They were often
arrogant and hugely over-confident, though much of this was bluff by
people ruling through prestige rather than force—as Orwell saw it, by
being a "hollow, posing dummy, the conventionalized figure of a sahib"
obliged to "spend his life in trying to impress the 'natives.'"[75] Was there
always something a little absurd in the spectacle? As Noël Coward put it
in "Mad Dogs and Englishmen" (1931):

> It seems such a shame
> When the English claim
> The Earth
> That they give rise
> To such hilarity
> And mirth.

But they did bring substantial periods of relative peace and order to large tracts of the globe—in the view of the same Orwell, "the Empire was peaceful as no area of comparable size has ever been."[76] Free trade was intended to benefit all, and arguably on balance it did: "By abandoning protection Britain magnanimously chose not to exploit its unique position of mid-century market power."[77]

Most English people were little interested in imperial matters most of the time—less so than their Scottish and Irish neighbours, who played a disproportionate part in running the empire.[78] Nevertheless, English influence over global developments was immense, and some of the consequences were permanent and valuable. They tried to implant their own traditions of parliamentary government and the rule of law; and, even in those countries where these traditions faltered after independence, they still remain a widely held aspiration. Perhaps most important of all has been the emergence of English as the first global language. In important ways still unfolding, the British Empire "made the world one."[79]

# CHAPTER 19

# England's Cultural Revolutions

So life was never better than
In nineteen sixty-three
(Though just too late for me)—
Between the end of the "Chatterley" ban
And the Beatles' first LP.

Philip Larkin, "Annus Mirabilis" (1974)

An era seems to have ended *circa* 1960. But which? Of the war and
the postwar? Of the New Jerusalem and the brief "New Elizabethan
Age"? Of empire? Of Victorianism and "the nation's last puritan age"?[1]
An end is also a beginning. Again, of what? Of breakdown? Of liberation?
Of decline? Of rejuvenation? Or all of these? The changes are not just an
English story: they affected the whole Western world and beyond, and
this gives us a starting point. But there were English patterns in this kaleidoscope, which we also need to identify. Indeed, England was often
regarded as setting the pace of change.

Transnational elements can be briefly listed. The war itself, both uniting and dividing, which left a legacy of social disturbance and ideological
controversy. An unprecedented postwar economic boom—what the
French call "the Thirty Glorious Years"—which shifted populations from
country to town, provided better-paid jobs and new housing, dissolved
communities, extended secondary and university education, created more
jobs for women, gave money to young people, and brought new aspirations and impatience with restricting conventions. Struggles against European colonialism and American racism, which mobilized people in pursuit
of greater freedom and equality. Communist victories in China, Cuba,
Vietnam and Cambodia, which gave radicals the thrill of participating in
a global revolution. The Cold War, which by threatening nuclear destruction inspired new anti-war movements. The contraceptive pill, which gave
women control of reproduction, reducing their dependence on men and
parents.

England experienced every element in this upheaval, though in some important ways less than elsewhere. Its great transformation from agriculture to industry, and from country to town, had happened a century earlier. It had won two world wars and was proud of itself. It was richer than all its neighbours and growing richer still. Its politics were moderate, with no great Communist Party, and no reactionaries nostalgic for the stamp of the jackboot. But still it changed with dizzying speed: it may even be that "the generation that grew up in the 1960s was more dissimilar to the generation of its parents than in any previous century."[2]

This change contrasted vertiginously with the stable elements of 1950s society: full employment, the Welfare State, the mass building of new family houses, the biggest increase in church-going for a century, continuing low crime, record levels of marriage, a baby boom with falling infant mortality and "marital stability without known historical precedent," of which the 1945 film *Brief Encounter* is an icon. It was a respectful, indeed deferential, time: the BBC did not permit anything "derogatory to political institutions," including impersonation of "leading public and political figures." Magistrates ordered the destruction of more than 1,500 works of fiction considered obscene, among them Flaubert's *Madame Bovary* (1857), and a bookseller was gaoled for two months for selling D. H. Lawrence's *Lady Chatterley's Lover* (1928). In short, the 1950s saw the triumph of Victorian values, and finally a wide distribution of their fruits[3]—the basis of Tory ascendancy. But those fruits contained seeds of destruction. For example, the Welfare State assumed social conformity and economic stability, but it tended to undermine them by lessening the penalties for nonconformity. Mass slum clearance and the building of new towns and housing estates promised a better life—on the assumption that neighbourliness and respectability would continue, indeed increase, despite the disruption of communities and the alienating scale and uniformity of much of the architecture.

In the vanguard of change were the young (whose wages rose 83 percent in the 1950s[4]) and especially educated young women, who went away from home to attend universities and art schools (on the Continent they usually lived with their parents), and who led a move away from mainstream culture and morality. The popular press, a unique element of English culture, increased its coverage of sex, ostensibly to educate, and increasingly to titillate, breaking down post-Victorian reticence and making sexual gossip and pleasure a central part of popular culture.[5] Pop songs and new girls' magazines reinforced the message. Sixth-form girls who believed that premarital sex was "always wrong" fell from 55.8 percent in 1963 to 14.6 percent in 1970; and the percentage of girls losing their virginity before the age of sixteen rose sharply from around 5 percent in the early 1950s to over 20 percent in the early 1970s.[6] A series of events not only symbolized, but actually created and propagated change, and to look at them chronologically shows how they cumulatively created a cultural revolution.

In 1953 the Kinsey Report on *Women, Sexual Behavior in the Human Female,* received wide press coverage in its statistical analysis and open discussion of the sex lives of Americans. "Teddy Boys," flamboyant and sometimes violent, appeared. From 1956, the year of Suez, all indices of religiosity—such as church attendance, religious marriages, infant baptism, Sunday school enrolments—began to decline after a postwar rise, though this was the resumption of a trend observable from the 1920s, as Victorianism slowly melted (see p. 483).[7] That same year, rock 'n' roll arrived with the film *Rock Around the Clock*, and John Osborne's play *Look Back in Anger* symbolized the revolt of the "Angry Young Men." In 1957 the Wolfenden Report urged decriminalizing private homosexual acts between consenting adults. In 1958 the teenage playwright Shelagh Delaney's *A Taste of Honey* brought the story of a working-class unmarried mother into mainstream theatre. The Campaign for Nuclear Disarmament, uniting veteran pacifists and young activists, staged its first protest march to the weapons laboratory at Aldermaston. Also in that year the Liberals had their first by-election success for thirty years, when Asquith's grandson, Mark Bonham Carter, won Torrington from the Conservatives; and there were serious race riots in Nottingham (sparked off by a pub brawl) and Notting Hill.[8] *Boyfriend*, a new kind of girls' magazine, appeared in 1959, as did the most original postwar car, the Mini—designed in response to the petrol shortage caused by Suez. In 1960 the prosecution of Penguin Books under the new Obscene Publications Act for publishing *Lady Chatterley's Lover* generated public fascination. When the prosecuting counsel asked the jury whether it was a book "you would . . . wish your wife or your servants to read," he showed a pompous old hierarchy at bay. Penguin won the case, as famous authors, critics, politicians and, perhaps most significantly, teachers and Anglican prelates asserted the book's moral value: "What Lawrence is trying to do," explained the Bishop of Woolwich, "is to portray the sex relationship as something essentially sacred . . . in a real sense an act of holy communion."[9] By the end of 1960 the book had sold 2 million copies. In 1961 "the Pill" appeared, and in three years, despite restrictions, was being used by 500,000 women and talked about by many more. In 1961 the Cambridge student review *Beyond the Fringe* opened in London, in which Peter Cook, Dudley Moore, Alan Bennett and Jonathan Miller mocked a range of authority figures. Sir Hugh Carleton-Greene became director-general of the BBC, and turned it in a progressive direction. In 1962 it launched a late-night satire show, *That Was the Week That Was*, introduced by David Frost, which delighted and scandalized a large audience. That same year saw the last time a prisoner was flogged. Also in 1962 Dean Acheson, the former U.S. Secretary of State, caused a furore by declaring that "Great Britain has lost an Empire and has not yet found a role." The first James Bond film, *Dr. No* (based on a 1958 novel), appeared.

The year of sensations was 1963. The Telstar satellite made world television news possible. The Beatles became famous, screamed at by crowds of teenage girls. The MI6 and Foreign Office insider "Kim" Philby (Westminster and Cambridge) was exposed as a Russian agent—one of several traitors whose Establishment connections had averted suspicion. The Tory war minister, John Profumo, resigned in June after lying about his affair with a call girl, Christine Keeler, soon one of the most famous women in Britain: the scandal exposed sex, drugs, hypocrisy and espionage in high places, and received titillating mass press coverage—"Last week the Upper Classes passed unquietly away," declared one journalist.[10] *Oh What a Lovely War* (see p. 650) opened, as did a sexy film version of *Tom Jones*. The Bishop of Woolwich (now famous as a *Chatterley* witness) published *Honest to God*, criticizing traditional religion and morality: "Nothing can of itself always be labelled as 'wrong' . . . the only intrinsic evil is lack of love." Dr. Alex Comfort, poet and former conscientious objector, appeared in a BBC series advocating sexual freedom and the following year published the best-selling *The Joy of Sex: A Gourmet Guide to Lovemaking*, which presented sex not as holy communion but as healthy recreation. The miniskirt was christened by Mary Quant. The opinion poll rating of the Prime Minister, Harold Macmillan, collapsed and he resigned in October, being briefly succeeded by the self-effacing Lord Home.

In October 1964 Labour won the general election, and Harold Wilson became Prime Minister. The government, with the key role played by the Home Secretary, Roy Jenkins, backed an unparalleled series of reforms, some through private members' bills. In 1965 hanging was abolished. Anthony Crosland, Minister of Education and Science, "requested" Local Education Authorities to adopt comprehensive education, telling his wife that "if it's the last thing I do I'm going to destroy every fucking grammar school in England": within ten years 90 percent of secondary schools were comprehensive.[11] The Sexual Offences Act (1966) decriminalized homosexuality. Theatre censorship by the Lord Chamberlain—dating back to Sir Robert Walpole—was abolished in 1968. The divorce laws were relaxed (1969). There were Acts on Family Planning (1967), Abortion

(1967), Race Relations (1965 and 1968) and Equal Pay (1970). This was "the beginning of the end for the era of class and party. The mould in which popular politics had been set since the First World War began to crack as class divisions blurred and the major parties struggled to maintain the loyalty of voters."[12]

In 1965 the critic Kenneth Tynan said "fuck" on television, to widespread consternation. In 1966 England won the World Cup, the first fashion "boutique" opened in Carnaby Street, and Antonioni's film *Blow Up* portrayed an international vision of "swinging London"—a term popularized by *Time* magazine. A wave of student protests began, first at the London School of Economics and more fatefully with the creation of a Catholic civil-rights movement in Northern Ireland. Enoch Powell made his so-called rivers of blood speech, predicting conflict resulting from immigration—in the short term a self-fulfilling prophecy.[13] In 1969 "Je t'aime moi non plus," a song largely consisting of the whispered endearments and ecstatic sighs of Jane Birkin and a French singer, Serge Gainsbourg, was banned by the BBC, was denounced by the Vatican, and reached number 2 on the pop charts. In 1970 Germaine Greer published *The Female Eunuch*, urging the sexual and social liberation of women. The *Sun* began its regular topless "page three girl"; and Kenneth Tynan's musical, *Oh! Calcutta!*, opened, featuring nakedness and simulated sex on stage—a leading headmistress, Dame Mary Green, praised its "healthy freshness," though the (gay) Bishop of Southwark found it "boring as a boarding school bath night."[14] For the first time since the days of Byron, English men and women—the model Jean Shrimpton, the singer Mick Jagger, the actors Terence Stamp and Diana Rigg, and Christine Keeler—were seen as the most beautiful and exciting in the world, though only a generation away from the decent, repressed world represented by stars of the 1940s such as Celia Johnson and Trevor Howard.

The Tory MP Norman St. John Stevas called this "a permissive society," a good term: what these changes had in common was the abolition of a rather stern, self-disciplined, prudish, male-dominated culture. The family became less important; so, perhaps surprisingly, did sex, which came to carry less "emotional, economic and symbolic weight" and could instead become a commercialized entertainment.[15] Women were the main bearers of change: the idea of femininity centred on marriage, home and church was being replaced by a new idea of femininity based on work, romantic adventure, equality and socializing. Only in the 1960s did female novelists—Doris Lessing, Margaret Forster, Jackie Collins, Fay Weldon—begin showing unmarried women enjoying sex without guilt or retribution. The novelist Margaret Drabble proclaimed in the *Guardian* in

1967 "a sexual revolution . . . connected to that other major revolution in our society, the emancipation of women."[16] Women had for centuries been the bedrock of church-going, and when many abandoned it Christianity in England lost much of its substance. The nuclear family began changing into an extended and fluid grouping. Divorce tripled in the ten years from the early 1960s, mainly initiated by wives. Children whose births were registered by only one parent increased from under 4 percent in the 1960s to 24 percent in the 1990s.[17]

Similar changes were happening in other countries of north-western Europe, and in this broad context England's experience was unexceptional.[18] In the long run—still unfolding in the twenty-first century—all this amounted to a cultural, social and intellectual transformation of profound importance, creating a gulf separating modern experience of life from that of previous centuries. Secularization, in the broadest sense, was at the heart of it. First and most affected were predominantly Protestant countries whose churches in modern times permitted a more individualistic and critical approach to religion, and where religion was no longer a focus of national identity or indeed of social life. What seems characteristic of England was that the transformation took place, not without pain and controversy—far from it—but with the active encouragement of much of what the historian A. J. P. Taylor in 1953 first christened "the Establishment": the metropolitan political class, the BBC, the education system, the Church of England, "the whole matrix of official and social relations within which power is exercised."[19] There ceased to be a consensus among authorities, and no moral code was any longer seen as upheld by society as a whole.[20] This explains why there were marked differences from other English-speaking countries, notably Ireland and the United States. The Established Church, and its educated, middle-class clergy (and the BBC, its secular equivalent), played their traditional conciliatory role: they were not, and did not wish to be, a bulwark of cultural conservatism. They themselves first proclaimed that England had become "a secularized society"—even though most of its people considered themselves believers—and indeed radical theologians, impatient with "institutionalized religion," believed that this was God's will.[21] The Bishop of Woolwich, John Robinson, the most famous radical, was not a maverick outsider, but the son and grandson of canons of Canterbury, with six ordained uncles. His *Honest to God* sold a million copies, and was read twice by the Prime Minister, Harold Macmillan. In Ireland and the United States it was the most conservative religious groups, Catholic and Evangelical, that dominated and constituted an effective traditionalist front, whereas cultural and moral counter-revolutionaries in England, most famously the campaigner for television respectability Mary Whitehouse, were outsiders, figures of fun.

"Swinging London" and Liverpool became the world capitals of youth culture, and in this area England gained a lasting pre-eminence little noticed (or disapproved of) by adults, but recognized by adolescents the world over. At their best the 1960s brought new vitality and expressiveness to popular culture. Not all agreed with the opinion attributed to the music critic of *The Times*, William Mann (who admired their "pandiatonic clusters"), that the Beatles were the best songwriters since Schubert— a view that speaks volumes about the zeitgeist. Still, for the first time since the fifteenth century, England was leading the world in musical fashion. The Beatles, the Rolling Stones and their contemporaries were followed by prog rock, heavy metal, punk rock, new wave, and later Britpop, disseminating lasting and inventive European youth sub-cultures.

A crucial characteristic of the English cultural revolution was that it began as overseas power shrank, epitomized by the Wilson government's decision to withdraw from "East of Suez" in 1967—a sensible rationalization but the cause of much hand-wringing.[22] What linked cultural change with "declinism" is obvious—the humiliation of the Establishment, its loss of self-confidence, and the breakdown of authority and convention. Osborne's *Look Back in Anger*, as noted earlier, opened in the same year as the Suez Crisis, and "those who were anti-Suez also tended to be supporters of Look Back in Anger . . . while smoke bombs were bursting in Downing Street and mounted police charged the crowds in Whitehall."[23] Disenchanted mockery more than overt anger was the weapon of the satire craze. Parodies of Establishment symbols, including the mannered Macmillan, an outwardly "unflappable" but inwardly troubled and rather vulnerable person, showed the men in authority as repressed, inept and irremediably old-fashioned, seemingly oblivious to their own and the country's shortcomings. Satire's running theme was the absurdity of the pretensions and institutions of a nation fallen on hard times. The leading satirists were themselves dissident junior members of the Establishment, overwhelmingly from public schools and Oxbridge, who expressed the bitter disillusionment of "declinism" in the form of embarrassed self-deprecation. "England" and the characteristics of "Englishness" became the butt of exasperated scorn.

These years saw visible change in collective behaviour, with the rejection of long-established legal or social rules in favour of self-assertion. The outcome was inevitably mixed, most easily quantifiable when things went dramatically wrong, as in crime or family breakdown; happiness and freedom are harder to quantify. Crime may serve as an indicator of more general social rule-breaking, and the long-term changes here are immense. The period of greatest social peace and stability—or authority and conformity—is, despite two world wars, the period from the 1890s to the 1950s. Drunkenness, violence, crime and imprisonment all reached probably their lowest levels in history, and during the interwar years twenty-four prisons were closed.[24] George Orwell was not being controversial in commenting in 1940 on the "gentleness of English civilization . . . You notice it the instant you set foot on English soil."[25] It seemed no less obvious in 1955 to the influential anthropologist Geoffrey Gorer that the English were "gentle, courteous and orderly . . . you hardly ever see a fight in a bar (a not uncommon spectacle in the rest of Europe or the USA) . . . football crowds are as orderly as church meetings."[26] Gorer considered this rather too repressed: but from around 1960 things certainly changed. Recorded crime doubled between 1957 and 1967, and it doubled again by 1977. There were 200 robberies in 1937; 1,200 in 1957; 14,000 by 1977. Some of this was due to different recording, but not all: in 1937 there were only 800 criminals serving sentences of over three years in England and Wales; by 1997 there were 23,000.[27] Football hooliganism, though not entirely new, now became a national and international scandal, largely the doing of young working-class men no longer under the influence of older men, families and communities, dispersed by mass rehousing and economic change. The nadir came in Brussels in 1985, when thirty-eight Belgian and Italian spectators died due to drunken violence by Liverpool supporters. In England this territorial displacement and withdrawal of adult supervision may have gone further than in most countries, and was perhaps aggravated by vague resentment at the perceived diminution of Britain's place in the world, with football a substitute for patriotism among poorly educated white working-class youth,[28] encouraged by business interests and populist politicians.

The sixties cultural revolution and its aftermath were particularly good for "women, the young, and the fit."[29] "Women's lib," despite its historic triumphs, proved a hard slog, placing many women under a double stress of (often single) parenthood and career, and, if it had considerable success in feminizing public culture, it also had the paradoxical effect of making many women behave more like men in their public demeanour (girls getting drunk more than in most other countries[30]) and private behaviour (girls having casual sex). The sixties may have initiated more "classless" styles (clothing, leisure, accents), but they also helped to open a new gulf between the socially mobile and a new sub-proletariat. Among the inheritors of the libertarian sixties drug and sex culture—in a debased and destructive form—were ghettoized, vulnerable and marginal groups, often living in those unloved embodiments of 1960s utopianism, tower blocks.

The 1960s–1970s were not only libertarian: they also began a time of gradually increasing controls and pressures concerning speed limits, seat belts, drink-driving, smoking, drugs, violence, speech and certain kinds of sexual behaviour (with stricter definitions of rape and paedophilia). Some of this may have been a reaction against "permissiveness." Much of it came from a new acceptance of increasing state powers. Some—dubbed "political correctness"—came from the triumph of the new ideas and their crystallization into conventions and laws making what had recently been normal beliefs, prejudices, words and behaviour unacceptable, immoral, even criminal. This seems to have been taken much further in England than in most European countries, as if the old "Nonconformist conscience" had revived in secular guise.

"The Establishment," after faltering, proved remarkably resilient and adaptive. It would have been hard to imagine during the 1960s that, half a century on, the monarchy would be revered, the public schools booming, gentlemen's clubs expanding, the armed forces almost above criticism, the Prime Minister an Etonian, and Cambridge and Oxford hailed as Europe's leading universities. Like much in England, they changed and remained the same.

## THE "SICK MAN OF EUROPE"?

Alarm about decline from as early as the 1950s was increasingly fixed on economic performance, seen as the leading indicator of the nation's health—or rather, sickness. In the early postwar period, there had been no cause for alarm. Trade boomed while Continental competitors struggled to recover. In steel, power, aircraft and cars Britain was a world leader, accounting for 50 percent of world car exports.[31] The Volkswagen "beetle," offered in reparation for war damage, was turned down by the industry as inferior to British products such as the Morris Minor. Disquiet first appeared in the late 1950s and early 1960s, marshalled by Labour to undermine Tory claims of economic success. Economic growth figures, which now for the first time permitted international comparisons, seemed to show Britain lagging behind Continental competitors, especially Germany and France. An official report in 1953 warned of "relegation of the UK to the second division."[32] Over the next thirty years there was a swelling chorus of dismay—and sometimes glee—about the "the sick man of Europe," the "sub-ordinary nation state of ever shabbier suits and abominable footwear, Europe's crowned Skid-Row of the Third Millennium," and denunciation of supposed culprits, above all A. J. P. Taylor's "Establishment"—"aristocracy, public schools and Oxbridge which still dominate government."[33] Clearly, even when commentators spoke of "Britain" or "the UK," the failure was identified as really that of England: its elite culture, institutions and traditions.

What was the reality? By 1950 the English economy had narrowed the late-nineteenth-century productivity gap with America, and was far ahead of the Continent. However, European countries were rebuilding and modernizing after the devastation of the war, benefiting from America's Marshall Plan of financial assistance. They were powerfully motivated by acute deprivation not experienced in Britain—or in Canada, New Zealand, Australia and the United States, which also had comparatively slow growth. Keynes had joked that if the U.S. Air Force ("it is too late now to hope for much from the enemy") accidentally bombed "every factory on the North-East Coast and in Lancashire . . . when the directors were sitting there" it would greatly have promoted economic success.[34] But the biggest cause of faster Continental growth was not the changes forced by war, but a more fundamental structural modernization: the large agricultural workforce in France, Germany and Italy, displaced by mechanization, rapidly shifted into more productive industrial employment.[35] This catching-up process, which took place broadly from the mid-1940s to the early 1970s, gave them "windfall growth" at a higher rate than was possible in England, which had no large agricultural sector to convert. But once that catching up was finished, by the early 1970s, European growth rates became the same as, or slightly lower than, England's. There was, in short, no relative English economic "decline" over the second half of the twentieth century.

In fact, the English economy was developing further into services—not a sign of decline, but of modernization. Critics, however, invariably focused on manufacturing, which showed England's world share declining. Service industries were often dismissed as insubstantial, not least by manufacturers: "We will supply the Beefeaters round the Tower of London. We will become a curiosity."[36] England was regularly compared unfavourably with the best-performing manufacturing countries, whichever they were at the time—by definition, those experiencing "catch-up": Germany, France, later Japan, then Malaysia, China, etc. England's only unambiguous failure was the car industry, due to a combination of fragmentation, labour militancy (the German and French car industries used more pliable immigrant workers) and poor management: so from the 1970s to 2012 Britain became a net importer of cars, with a huge effect on the trade balance and employment. But other English manufacturing industries (chemicals, pharmaceutics, aero-engines,

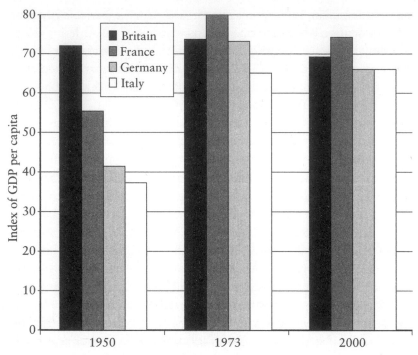

Figure 5: Index of GDP per capita, 1950, 1973 and 2000:
Britain, France, Germany and Italy

armaments) were highly successful. Overall, the postwar English economy was growing strongly, increasing people's prosperity, and maintaining a high level of employment.

This is not to say that all was perfect. For example, labour productivity in manufacturing between 1951 and 1989 grew by an average of 3.8 percent per year in Germany and 3.4 percent in Britain.[37] It might be argued that given certain advantages—victory in 1945, technological leadership in important industries, close economic and cultural links with the United States and the Commonwealth, global use of English, proximity to rapidly growing Continental markets—Britain should have been in the lead. But it had inherited problems, such as worn infrastructure and regionally concentrated older industries. It also had newer weaknesses: a shortage of professional industrial managers; a sometimes obstructive trade union movement; weaknesses in its education system, particularly in technical fields; balance-of-payments problems due to loss of overseas investments and the international role of sterling; postwar debts; and high defence costs. Labour's nationalization of public utilities and other industries were overall a failed experiment,[38] subject to political interference, delayed decisions, shortage of capital, passive management and market insensitivity. For example, the nationalized electricity industry insisted on ordering over-sophisticated equipment from British suppliers that was then too expensive to compete in export markets—"technical arrogance" that damaged manu-facturing.[39] The aircraft and aero-engine industries were undermined by the successive commissioning and cancellation of too many highly sophisti-cated and expensive military projects—the Saunders Roe P.177 fighter, the Blue Streak missile, the TSR-2 bomber—reducing the ability of a world-leading industry to produce for export. It has often been argued that unusu-ally high defence spending was more generally an economic drag, the cost being largely saved from welfare spending, including by charges for spec-tacles and false teeth: in the 1950s and 1960s Britain had proportionately a higher defence budget and a lower social-security budget than other Euro-pean states. It is also widely accepted that maintaining sterling's prestigious role as a reserve currency, used for nearly half the world's trading transac-tions in the 1950s, often meant that the pound, and hence British exports, were too expensive. The efforts of governments of both parties, obsessed with economic underperformance, to force growth by constant fiddling seems to have created repeated bouts of inflation, sterling crises (1961–62,

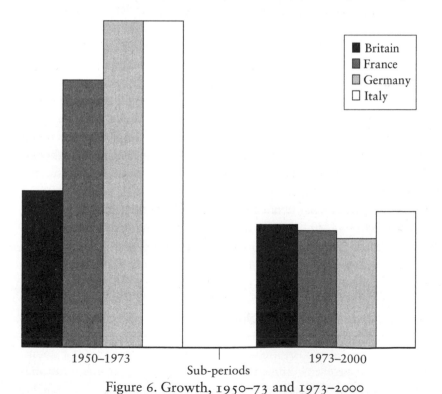

Figure 6. Growth, 1950–73 and 1973–2000

1965, 1966, 1967), and then inevitable spending cuts—so-called stop-go. However, this long list of problems, though real, had limited effect on the performance of the whole economy: when measured over the long term—from 1950 to 2000—Britain's economic performance was no different from the European norm. "Declinists" forgot that other countries too had their problems.

So a multitude of publications set out to diagnose England's supposedly unique economic decadence as part of some general vision of national dis-function: *The Stagnant Society*, *The Establishment*, *What's Wrong with Britain?*, *Is Britain Dying?*, even *Suicide of a Nation*. A distorted narrative of continuous economic failure from the 1870s was constructed, and then explained as due to deep-seated political and cultural failures. Two of the most sophisticated and influential declinists were academic historians: a military historian, Corelli Barnett, in *The Collapse of British Power* (1972), *The Audit of War* (1986) and *The Lost Victory* (1995), and an American cultural historian, Martin J. Wiener, in *English Culture and the Decline of the Industrial Spirit* (1981), begun during the miners' strike and three-day week in 1973–74. Wiener declared that "the leading problem of modern British history is the explanation of economic decline."[40] Both agreed that the explanation was cultural. Barnett, from a right-wing perspective, blamed the "liberal establishment," the public schools and Oxbridge, the Welfare State ("the broad scenario for Britain's postwar descent"), and the compla-cency of a victorious nation unwilling to recognize that the world did not owe it a living. Wiener, from the left, blamed a "quasi-aristocratic elite, which nurtured both the rustic and nostalgic myth of an 'English way of life,'" making the English "suspicious of change . . . energetic only in maintaining the status quo."[41] The views of Barnett and Wiener, some of them congenial to the left, also became a central Thatcherite theme in the 1980s. Although they have long since been intellectually demolished,[42] they seem to survive unchallenged in the public mind.

Declinism gives the political rhetoric of "modernization," attractive to radicals of right and left, its force and meaning. Declinist theories took it as axiomatic that England was uniquely unsuccessful, but never employed rigorous international comparisons. E. P. Thompson aptly termed this "inverted Podsnappery"—"*other* countries" (unspecified) were "in Every Respect Better."[43] Declinism, in short, was a characteristic feature of the 1960s and 1970s, part of the English cultural revolution. The damage it did—and perhaps still does—should not be underestimated: by tying together miscellaneous phenomena as part of a continuing tale of doom, it obscured real problems and indeed real successes, and made rational understanding more difficult.

## THE SINKING *TITANIC*

Declinism affected foreign policy profoundly. As we have seen, in the immediate postwar period politicians of all parties agreed that Britain must continue as a major global power. The story is commonly told as one of self-delusion, distracting Britain from its true destiny, integration into Europe. As Tony Blair put it, "British politicians surveying Europe then, in those almost unrecognisable days of powdered egg and Empire, failed the test . . . clutching at irrelevant assumptions and forgotten shibboleths."[44] This has remained a declinist commonplace. One prominent journalist wrote lugubriously in 2011 of "the country's lamentable failure to find a comfortable role for itself in the world," which he thought had something to do with the empire.[45]

British politicians were never indifferent to Europe, however, and 1950s polls showed public support for European unity. Bevin's problem was over-ambition, aiming to create an independent European super-power. These visions were dispelled by the Cold War, as we have seen, and then by the beginnings of economic integration through the European Coal and Steel Community. Britain's policy now focused on ensuring a continuing American commitment to European security through NATO. Behind the scenes, there was unprecedented sharing of secret intelligence with the United States under a 1947 treaty, which also included Canada, Australia and New Zealand, and which still applies. The relationship with America ("special," as the British saw it) was not a barrier to integration with the Continent—far from it, as the Americans were eager backers of European unity. But it is often argued that the "special relationship" encouraged British politicians and public opinion to cling to global ambitions rather than accepting a humbler role as a pioneer European partner. It has often been pointed out how unequal this "special relationship" is, and how prone British politicians have been to exaggerate it. It can thus be seen as another aspect of "declinism"—a simultaneous acceptance of and yet a wish to remedy or at least conceal supposedly dwindling power. Yet, rhetoric apart, it is not self-evident that the relationship has worked to Britain's overall disadvantage. The cost to Britain of its effort to keep America and Europe together was the maintenance of a relatively high defence budget (higher than that of Germany, comparable with that of France, but lower than that of the USA) and the acquisition of a nuclear deterrent. By 1958 the cost of development caused Britain to rely in part on American technology, signing a nuclear cooperation agreement. Macmillan's Nassau Agreement with President John F. Kennedy in 1963 provided an affordable submarine-based nuclear force using Polaris missiles.

The other main pillar of Britain's foreign policy came to be Europe. The old dream of European unity had been revived during the interwar period. The Labour intellectual Harold Laski predicted in 1944 that "the age of the nation state is over ... economically, it is the continent that counts: America, Russia, later China and India, eventually Africa ... the true lesson of this war is that we shall federate the Continent or suffocate." The need to rebuild European economies, resist Communism, and prevent a possible resurgence of German nationalism turned rhetoric into policy. The Schuman Plan (put forward with American encouragement by the French foreign minister, Robert Schuman, in 1950) provided for supranational control of the coal and steel industries of Germany, France and the Benelux countries. It also advocated a council of ministers, a court and an assembly. The Treaty of Paris (April 1951) duly set up the European Coal and Steel Community, with an explicit commitment to political unity.

The Schuman Plan was deliberately presented to Britain without consultation, as a *fait accompli*, which it was given forty-eight hours to accept in principle. Bevin would not take on "obligations" in Europe that restricted Britain's interests elsewhere, and he was suspicious of supranationality—"a Pandora's box full of trojan horses," in his attributed phrase. Labour's recent nationalization of coal and steel meant that government and unions were unwilling to hand control to an unaccountable body in Luxembourg—as Herbert Morrison, Bevin's successor at the Foreign Office, put it, "the Durham miners won't wear it."[46] Because of the Great Depression, the Second World War and the devastation of Europe, British trade had moved elsewhere, especially to the "Old Commonwealth" countries, from which it imported cheap food and to which it exported manufactured goods. In retrospect, and even for some at the time, it is clear that this was an unusual and temporary circumstance. It is nevertheless understandable that Labour backed colonial development and Commonwealth ties, for reasons both of sentiment and of self-interest. In 1950 Europe took only 10 percent of British exports. Australia was economically as important to Britain as "the Six" (members of the Coal and Steel Community) combined, and New Zealand more important than Germany. As Keynes put it, "What suits our exporters is to have the whole world as their playground."[47] So Labour's refusal to join the ECSC was inevitable. After the Suez debacle, the French, let down as they saw it by the Anglo-Saxons, turned towards Europe and Germany as alternative sources of Great Power status. The Treaty of Rome was signed in March 1957 setting up a European Economic Community committed to "ever closer union."

It is commonly asserted that had Britain joined in early, during the 1950s, its moral stature and political weight could have enabled it to lead

Europe, shaping developments in its own interests. This notion of Britain taking the helm is, in the view of the official historian of Britain's European policy, "shot through with nationalistic assumptions . . . as great as and more misguided" than those underlying its world-power pretensions.[48] This was dramatically demonstrated when in 1958 Britain tried to negotiate a free-trade agreement with the EEC. General de Gaulle, newly installed in power, stopped the negotiations in November 1958—the first and most damaging of his three vetoes. Although the German finance minister, Ludwig Erhard, architect of its "economic miracle," was in favour, the chancellor, Konrad Adenauer, would not oppose France. So Britain set up the European Free Trade Association in 1959, with Sweden, Denmark, Norway, Iceland, Finland, Switzerland, Austria, Ireland and Portugal.

Britain soon abandoned this policy, however. Here "declinism" played a crucial role, creating a desperate hope that joining the EEC could both remedy supposed economic failure and buttress influence in Washington and the Commonwealth. Washington disliked EFTA and put pressure on London to apply to join the EEC. "If we try to remain aloof," a Cabinet committee warned in 1960, "bearing in mind that this will be happening simultaneously with the contraction of our overseas possessions, we shall run the risk of [losing] any real claim to be a world Power." The Foreign Office feared that "at the best, we should remain a minor power in an alliance dominated by the United States." Macmillan formally applied to join in 1961. "The question," thought the Foreign Secretary, Selwyn Lloyd, "is how to live with the Common Market economically and turn its political effects into channels harmless to us."[49] This question would continue to exercise politicians of several generations.

The main problem was France, newly ascendent and ambitious under Charles de Gaulle, elected first president of the new Fifth Republic in December 1958, and an old man in a hurry. He intended to make France the leader of Europe, and wanted "to be the cock on a small dunghill instead of having two cocks on a larger one," as Macmillan put it to a sympathetic President John F. Kennedy in 1963.[50] Macmillan's frustration stemmed from a televised press conference on 14 January when de Gaulle, after long and wearisome negotiations, summarily vetoed the British application for membership on the grounds that "England is an island, sea-going, bound up by its trade, its markets, its food supplies, with the most varied and often the most distant countries." This would disrupt what he called a truly "European Europe."[51] The humiliation of de Gaulle's veto further weakened Macmillan at home, where he was beset by the Profumo scandal, and he resigned, ostensibly on health grounds, that October.

The Labour Party had been led since 1963 by Harold Wilson. He was the most brilliant politician of his day, prototype of a new grammar-school-educated North Country professionalism that seemed to be elbowing aside the effete public-school upper class, embodied by Macmillan and his successor as Tory party leader, the honourable, inoffensive, but emphatically not modern 14th Earl of Home, probably Britain's last aristocratic Prime Minister, who held office (renouncing his earldom) from 1963 to 1964—his mother was said to have remarked that "it was very good of Alec to have taken the job on." Wilson, Prime Minister from 1964 to 1970, was thus an embodiment of the social and cultural changes of the 1960s. He was an economist praising "pragmatism" and embodying the new concept of "meritocracy." In retrospect he seems an oddly insubstantial figure with no defining ideas, mainly remembered for his dictum that "a week is a long time in politics." Like most of his party, he was suspicious of European membership and urged support for Commonwealth trade: "We are not entitled to sell our friends and kinsmen down the river for a problematical and marginal advantage in selling washing machines in Düsseldorf."[52] Once in power in 1964, Wilson found that plans for galvanizing Commonwealth trade were a pipedream. He renewed the application to the EEC, reflecting that Britain was like a faded beauty, and Europe a go-ahead young man with good prospects: if not a love match, it could be Britain's last chance for a comfortable settlement.[53] But de Gaulle pronounced a third veto on 16 May 1967, using language of "quite exceptional bitterness, hostility and scorn."[54] Britain, he said, was economically incapable of membership, and its desire for accession was driven by desperation. The English, he told his entourage, "are a worn-out people."[55]

After de Gaulle had retired in 1969, following his humiliation by rioting students in Paris, Edward Heath's 1970 Conservative government seized the opportunity to pursue the application. Belief that membership at any price was the only remedy for Britain's diplomatic, economic and political "decline" had become the orthodoxy: Britain was "the sinking Titanic," as one of Heath's advisers put it, and Europe the lifeboat.[56] Heath, the most "pro-European" Prime Minister Britain has ever had, assured the French that the British were now ready to "give priority to [Europe] over their other interests in the world," though he grumbled privately that the Europeans "are constantly barging ahead with regulations drawn up to suit themselves and then coming along, more or less with a take-it-or-leave-it attitude, to present them to us."[57] Sir Con O'Neill, the chief official negotiator, was clear that the EEC was about power: "None of its policies was essential to us; many of them were objectionable." But, outside, Britain would decline into "a greater Sweden"—something Whitehall regarded as a fate worse than death. The terms for entry were tough, including sharing Britain's vast fishing grounds, accepting the Common Agricultural Policy to protect farming by raising prices and penalizing imports, and a large British financial contribution to common funds; but O'Neill decided to "swallow the lot."[58] Public support had collapsed since the first failed attempt to join, so the government mounted the biggest state publicity campaign since the war with vociferous support from business and most of the intelligentsia. The issue was carefully depoliticized: "The Community . . . hasn't made the French eat German food or the Dutch drink Italian beer." The EEC's faster economic growth was the main theme, represented on the front of an official pamphlet, *The British European*, by a page three girl in a skimpy Union Jack bikini proclaiming "EUROPE IS FUN! More Work But More Play Too!"[59] Politicians and diplomats concealed—perhaps from themselves—the commitment to "ever closer union" clearly spelled out in the founding treaties, which they dismissed as verbiage. The European Communities Act (1972), the legal basis of membership, declared that all present or future "rights, liabilities, obligations and restrictions" created by European law automatically applied in the United Kingdom "without further enactment" by Parliament, and with supremacy over English (and Scottish) law. High legal authorities debated whether this had ended, or could end, parliamentary sovereignty, without reaching clear conclusions. The public too was confused, tending to notice when picturesque cases emerged, such as that of the "metric martyrs," Sunderland market traders summonsed in 2003 for selling their greengrocery in pounds.[60]

If Britain's rulers had not been so panicky about "decline," would they have followed a different policy? Would a longer game, and less eagerness to "swallow the lot," have secured a better and less troubled relationship with Europe? It is commonly said that Britain joined the Common Market too late. Perhaps, on the contrary, it joined too early—just before the European economies entered a period of stagnation, and before it had faced up to its own economic shortcomings. In their haste, politicians avoided the question of what membership ultimately involved in terms of shifts of power and sovereignty. It turned out that de Gaulle had been right in fearing "England" as a disruptive presence.

# CHAPTER 20

# Storm and Stress

*We used to think that you could spend your way out of recession and increase employment by cutting taxes and boosting government expenditure. I tell you in all candour: that option no longer exists ... The cosy world ... where full employment would be guaranteed by the stroke of the Chancellor's pen, is gone for ever.*

James Callaghan to the Labour Party conference,
September 1976

*It seems to me that, while in the past, history was determined largely by the personalities and ambitions of the rulers of the people, in future it will be decided much more by the character of the people.*

Margaret Thatcher, 1990[1]

England experienced States of Emergency eleven times during the twentieth century. Five of them were between 1970 and 1974. It had only four full years of economic contraction from 1945 to 2008, all of them between 1974 and 1981.[2] During this disastrous decade, the post-war consensus on economic policy—"Butskellism"—unravelled. Some staple industries, both private and nationalized, faced intense competition from new producers, such as Japanese shipbuilders and European car-makers. Sterling was chronically vulnerable after the collapse in 1971 of the 1944 Bretton Woods system of fixed currency exchange rates, which initiated a long period of currency instability and attempts in all Western countries to apply "monetarism"—preventing inflation by controlling the money supply.[3] Edward Heath's Conservative government, elected in 1970, nationalized bankrupt industries such as Rolls-Royce and Upper Clyde Shipbuilders and attempted to boost growth by slashing taxes and interest rates, which caused an inflationary boom with prices rising by 9 percent a year and wages by 14 percent.[4] The British economy, and those who ran it at every level, did not know how to adapt. The most visible sign of trouble was strikes: total days lost were already reaching 70 million a year—no worse than Italy, but much worse than Germany, now the favourite model of economic virtue. The government passed an Industrial Relations Act (1971), to try to reduce strikes by some regulation of trade unions, and by making collective agreements legally binding through a National Industrial Relations Court. This was strongly opposed by the trade unions. The National Union of Mineworkers went on strike in January 1972, demanding a 25 percent pay rise, backed up by sending "flying pickets" to blockade power stations and fuel depots. The most famous incident was at the Saltley coke depot in Birmingham, which was forced to close by thousands of bussed-in pickets and sympathizers mobilized by a young Yorkshireman, Arthur Scargill. The police stood by helpless, and the government, noted Heath's political secretary, Douglas Hurd, in his diary, were left "wandering vaguely over [the] battlefield looking for someone to surrender to."[5]

Northern Ireland was the scene of another crisis.[6] During the late 1960s a civil-rights movement on the American model had been created to demand equality for Catholics. The Stormont government made only limited concessions, the police resorted to brutality, and Protestant "Loyalists" responded with violence. In August 1969 bloody communal rioting in Belfast and Londonderry had forced Wilson to send the army to keep order while a "new deal" for Catholics was worked out. "Loyalists" killed the first policeman and first fired at the army. A new "Provisional" IRA (which had broken away from the moribund "Official" IRA) added to the mayhem. In August 1971, after a bombing campaign in Belfast, the Heath government approved the administrative "internment"— imprisonment without trial—of 1,500 suspects. This proved both ineffective and inflammatory. On 30 January 1972, at a march against internment in Londonderry, paratroopers sent in to arrest rioters opened fire and killed fourteen people. The British embassy in Dublin was set on fire in protest. This was to be the deadliest year of the whole "Troubles," as Irish violence was quaintly and traditionally termed. From March, Northern Ireland's devolved government was suspended and the province ruled by a Secretary of State, the first being the dutiful William Whitelaw. He brokered an agreement at Sunningdale in December 1973 that gave Catholics an equal role in government and closer ties with Dublin, while reassuring Protestants that the Union was safe. However, when Labour returned to power in 1974, Harold Wilson gave in to Loyalists after a general strike and abandoned the agreement, bringing the first peace process to an end.[7]

The Royal Ulster Constabulary and the Ulster Defence Regiment (the local territorial force) largely took over security duties from the British army. In 1974 both sides began using car bombs in both parts of Ireland, and the IRA planted a series of bombs in England. Two in Birmingham pubs in November killed twenty-one people. A long war of attrition, marked by occasional spectacular outbursts, secret negotiations and periodic truces, began between the security forces and small Republican and Loyalist terrorist gangs. Many of these lived on welfare benefits—"the first war in history in which a single government paid and housed both sides."[8] They vied with each other in murder, torture, mutilation, extortion, drug-dealing and robbery. Yet people round the world, and most importantly in America, viewed the Republican struggle as "progressive": one Oxford undergraduate, Tony Blair, asked his college to subscribe to *An Phoblacht* ("The Republic"), the Provisional IRA newspaper.[9]

On 1 January 1973 Britain (with Ireland and Denmark) formally entered the EEC, officially celebrated with a "Fanfare to Europe," including pop and classical concerts and poetry readings. In October, on the festival of Yom Kippur, war broke out between Egypt and Israel, leading to cuts in the supply and huge increases in the price of Middle Eastern oil. This ended the halcyon period of postwar European growth and caused economic havoc across the industrialized world. So Britain's accession to a stricken EEC did not provide the hoped-for stimulus, and it experienced two full years of recession. The Community's Common Agricultural Policy (which supported farmers by keeping prices above world levels) increased British food costs by 40 percent, and its Value Added Tax further raised consumer prices. But not everyone suffered. Agriculture was boosted by the CAP, even returning to its 1870s acreage, with cereal prices rising 350 percent: in East Anglia a local joke was that the new crop rotation was "barley, barley, world cruise, barley." Coal mining benefited from dear oil. But the overall result was "stagflation," the debilitating combination of economic stagnation, rising inflation and rising unemployment. Some commentators warned that this was leading Britain towards South American levels of economic, and perhaps political, instability. Both parties saw the only alternative to mass unemployment and runaway inflation as an "incomes policy" to hold down wages, either agreed with or forced on the unions—the political equivalent of herding cats. Though all western Europe suffered, England alone experienced what many called "the English disease," a seemingly incurable condition threatening the breakdown not only of the economy, but of society and the state.

Four days after Yom Kippur, the National Union of Mineworkers

(NUM) demanded a 31 percent pay rise: its president, Joe Gormley, predicted that "If the country doesn't see the sense of our argument, it's woe betide them for the future."[10] An overtime ban caused the Heath government to declare a State of Emergency and order a three-day working week in December. Power cuts led to people shopping by candlelight. Inquiries about emigrating to New Zealand tripled. On 5 February 1974 the NUM voted overwhelmingly for a full-scale strike, and the following day Heath called a general election, on the issue "Who governs Britain?" On television Heath told the country, "It is time for you to say to the extremists, the militants . . . we've had enough."[11] The electorate was not in the mood for decision, and there was a sizeable swing to the Liberals from both Tory and Labour, giving a hung Parliament.

Harold Wilson formed a minority Labour government in March 1974, and it scrapped the Tory Industrial Relations Act, froze council house rents, and increased food subsidies and pensions. Michael Foot, Minister of Employment, bought off the miners with a large pay increase. Thus "the trail was laid for an enormous wage explosion; union leaders simply lit the matches."[12] Pay rises came to average nearly 30 percent. Tony Benn, Minister for Industry and then for Energy, urged an "alternative economic strategy" of wide nationalizations, controls over industry and restrictions on imports. This involved the "rescue" of a string of loss-making industries, subsidized cooperatives, ill-fated "restructuring" and the "picking of winners" who fell at the last fence, and sometimes the first. It is hard to imagine such mastodons as the British Leyland Motor Corporation, cobbled together by Benn from 100 companies, surviving even with £3.5bn of subsidy anywhere west of the Elbe—and not for long east of it. Ideas for trade protectionism contradicted Britain's membership of the EEC, which had a common-tariff policy. Labour insisted on "renegotiating or denegotiating" the terms of accession and putting the result to a referendum. Renegotiation—supposed to resolve, among other things, the CAP, Britain's budget contribution and Commonwealth access to Europe's market—had no significant outcome, but it was represented as "a New Deal in Europe." The Cabinet voted sixteen to seven (with mainly the left opposing) to accept the deal.[13]

On 5 June 1975 a referendum asked: "Do you think that the United Kingdom should stay in the European Community (the Common Market)?" The Yes campaign compared the Community with the United Nations and NATO, skirting round the fact that, unlike any other treaty organization, its rules were not fixed and that it could legislate independently of Parliament. Those who voted yes were apparently most concerned by security and Britain's future place in the world; the noes—urged on by the exotic alliance of Enoch Powell, Tony Benn and the Ulster Loyalist leader, the Rev. Ian Paisley—by food prices and the Commonwealth.[14] Least keen on Europe were Scottish islanders, Ulstermen and the left. The English, especially Tory voters from the prosperous south, were keenest: 64.6 percent of the English electorate voted; of those, 68.7 percent voted yes. Yet even this was acquiescence rather than enthusiasm: only 44 percent of the whole electorate voted yes, and without being sure what "yes" meant. Margaret Thatcher, the new Leader of the Opposition, hailed "this excellent result."

In April 1976 Harold Wilson bowed out, for unexplained reasons probably concerning his health. His replacement, James "Jim" Callaghan, was an avuncular-looking stalwart in the Bevin mould, described by one historian of the Labour Party as "a classic working-class conservative" who had "held the three highest offices in government without making a success of any of them" and who was "a wildly unsuitable leader" for a party influenced by the progressive ideas of the 1960s and infiltrated by the "hard left."[15] In his defence, he undeniably inherited a mess. Industry was floundering. Public spending had been rising since the 1960s. Taxes reached confiscatory levels—with the standard rate of income tax nudging 40 percent during the early 1970s, and the higher rate around 80 percent—even 98 percent on the top level of "unearned income." The cost of government borrowing rose faster in 1974 than in 1797, when Pitt had been forced to abandon gold. Wage inflation—which peaked at 27 percent in 1975, a level rarely seen in a developed country—was hitting exports, the balance of payments and sterling. All the economic indicators were bad: unemployment over 1,000,000, the balance of payments £1bn in the red, inflation stuck in double figures and a record budget deficit. During September 1976 sterling plunged by over 7 percent against the dollar and continued downwards—the chancellor, Dennis Healey, remembered it as "like the end of the world."[16] In one day, the twenty-eighth, it lost over 2 percent, and Callaghan gave his famous warning to the Labour Party conference in Blackpool that "the cosy world . . . is gone forever." He was coldly received, and the conference demanded more nationalization. Callaghan even warned on television of the danger of "a totalitarian government" in Britain. The government's credit was by this time very poor, and it had to negotiate six-month loans from European central banks, after which another short-term loan was required, this time $3.9bn from the International Monetary Fund—the biggest loan it had ever been asked for, and the first by an industrialized country. The IMF insisted on reductions in the budget deficit, and negotiations were tough (and at times bizarre, one secret meeting taking place in the cutting room of a London tailor).[17] The government had no real choice, though Benn and other left-wing ministers argued for an exit from the Common Market and a siege economy—evidently the road to ruin. Cuts were made in job-creation schemes, defence, housing and subsidies to loss-making industries. The Chief Secretary to the Treasury, Edmund Dell, recalled that "everyone I knew" regarded this crisis as "the worst period of their lives."[18] Over the next year, the financial situation stabilized, sterling strengthened, inflation and unemployment fell. This was aided by the first flow of North Sea oil, discovered in 1974, which alleviated balance-of-payments problems.

Was this a new dawn? It has been argued that the worst was over: that Labour, led firmly but kindly by "Uncle Jim" and the chancellor, Healey, had reduced inflation and administered the nasty medicine—including the biggest-ever postwar cut in public spending. At this time, 1977, poll results on "happiness" and measures of economic and social equality reached their best-ever levels. Britain's economic state was no worse than that of Italy. Stagnation was infantilizing: there was nothing ordinary people could do. Things not working properly was normal. Shopping by candlelight could be fun. Going on strike was a laugh. To be young was very heaven, as the 1960s revolution became the norm across the country. The Kinks' song "Lazing on a Sunny Afternoon" caught the mood (1976 had a memorably hot summer). Britain, suggested an American journalist, was leading the world towards a "post-industrial age."[19]

But the summer ended and the post-industrial age meant a decrease in unskilled factory work: in 1951 manual workers had been over 60 percent of the population; by 1991 they were under 40 percent, and falling rapidly. Hence, a future of chronic unemployment of the poorly educated, growing income inequality and family instability. Hence, growing industrial conflict and racial tension, and widespread violence in cities, at their worst between the mid-1970s and mid-1980s. The bell-bottoms and Laura Ashley dresses of the sixties were spurned by the skinheads' proletarian style and the "theatricalized poverty"[20] of punk rock, which appeared in 1976, expressing generalized and nihilistic anger. Healey allowed public spending to rise again once the IMF officials had left (an event he referred to as "Sod Off Day").[21] Unions were tired of exhortations to be responsible. At one "beer and sandwiches" meeting in Downing Street, the General Secretary of the huge Transport and General Workers' Union banged the Cabinet table and said, "Jim, it's my job to get 18 percent for my members, it's your job to get inflation down to 2 percent." Similarly, the miners' leader, Joe Gormley, proclaimed that "our role in society is to look after our members, not run the country."[22] Even the

Police Federation demanded a pay rise of between 78 and 104 percent, and threatened industrial action. Callaghan, nearing despair, decided against an early election in the autumn of 1978, which he would probably have won, and thus perhaps consigned the seemingly lightweight Margaret Thatcher to political oblivion.

Then from November 1978 to March 1979 Britain went through its notorious "Winter of Discontent," a paroxysm of strikes in a range of industries and occupations, especially in the public sector. It was the widest industrial conflict since the 1926 General Strike, and perhaps the most spectacular outburst of social disruption since the 1840s. The government's policy of a 5 percent limit on pay rises was defied by unions and even rejected by the Labour Party conference. Lorry drivers, hospital workers, teachers, rubbish collectors, House of Commons caterers, even gravediggers went on strike, demanding wage increases of up to 40 percent. "If it means that lives have to be lost," declared the leader of the London ambulancemen, "that is how it must be."[23] The outburst was a combination of opportunism and fear of missing out in the industrial equivalent of the January sales at a time when people had become used to high inflation and the need for constant wage rises subsidized by the taxpayer. Trade unions had reached the zenith of their power, after Michael Foot had given them legal privileges unknown since 1906, including the right to enforce a "closed shop"—that is, to force workers to join. Membership reached an all-time peak of over 13 million members in 1979.[24] There may also have been less tangible causes of the chaos. As we have seen, the 1960s began a general weakening of authority, and recent events made governments seem feeble, even contemptible. Extreme leftism was a presence among trade union militants, for many of whom the Communist world still provided inspiration. There was also a widespread culture of irresponsible individualism, in which actions seemed to have no consequences—the popular catchphrase "I'm all right, Jack," sums it up.

This "Winter of Discontent" humiliated the Labour government, but without at first doing much for the Tories, whose record with the unions had swung between provocation and surrender. On 7 January 1979 Margaret Thatcher gave a television interview in which she promised to "grasp this nettle" and end trade union immunity from the law. On 10 January a bronzed Callaghan returned from a summit meeting of the four principal Western leaders in Guadeloupe and commented that "I don't think that other people in the world would take the view that there is mounting chaos"—which the popular tabloid the *Sun* headlined as "Crisis? What Crisis?" The strike wave ended with wage increases and another government "concordat" with the unions, but something had snapped. One of the Prime Minister's aides recalled "a deadly calm in No. 10, a sort of quiet despair." The end came after proposals for devolution in Wales and Scotland were defeated in referendums on 1 March 1979. On thetwenty-eighth the government, deserted by the Scottish nationalists, was defeated in a motion of no confidence by one vote—the first time such a thing had happened since 1924. Two days later, the Tory MP Airey Neave, a close ally of Margaret Thatcher, was murdered by Irish terrorists in the precincts of the Palace of Westminster—reminder of another lowering crisis.

Opinion polls placed the reassuring Callaghan ahead of his little-known female opponent. Callaghan thought otherwise, musing that "perhaps once every thirty years . . . there is a sea-change in politics. It then does not matter what you say or what you do. There is a shift in what the public wants and what it approves of. I suspect there is now such a sea-change—and it is for Mrs. Thatcher."[25] On polling day, 3 May 1979, the Tory vote rose by 8 percent, mainly from the Liberals and thanks to a higher turnout. They won a majority of forty-three seats, with 43.9 percent of the vote to Labour's 36.9. They gained among women (attracted by Thatcher's adroit housewifely image[26]), the young, and skilled workers, especially in the Midlands and south. On 4 May Britain's first woman Prime Minister took office, proclaiming in Downing Street, not very convincingly, that "where there is discord, may we bring harmony."

Margaret Thatcher was the most admired and most hated—indeed, the only deeply admired and genuinely hated—Prime Minister since 1940. She was the most important peacetime holder of the office since Gladstone, the only one to leave an individual stamp on the country—something which, for all his virtues, could not be said of Attlee, the leader of a team running with the political tide. Her progress from Grantham corner shop to Downing Street became literally a legend in her own lifetime, with Hollywood gloss. The conflicting versions—the dauntless Boadicea who conquered national decline versus the malignant harpy who shattered the working class—magnify her personal importance. They have remoulded modern political identities into Thatcherite and anti-Thatcherite—a personalization of political ideas not seen since Sir Robert Peel.

Her rise within the Tory party in the circumstances of the time was extraordinary. When she was first adopted as a candidate in 1949, one MP grumbled that "a young girl of twenty-three" had been selected: "Could they not have got some prominent businessman?"[27] She was one of only seven Tory women MPs in 1966; she became party leader in 1975 and Prime Minister four years later. She is still the only woman who has risen from nowhere—not as the member of a political dynasty—to make a comparable political impact on any large state. The only European comparison more than three decades later is Angela Merkel, a political insider, not the conqueror of a sceptical party in which snobbery and sexism were standard (some of its staff used the acronym TBW—"that bloody woman"). She was well aware of this and sometimes enjoyed it: when sacking one patrician minister, she thought "he felt the natural order of things was being violated, [as if] being dismissed by his housemaid."[28] Her sex, while it could inspire real if exasperated chivalry in Tory ranks and among some civil servants, meant that she was always an outsider in those clubbable circles. Senior officials greeted her arrival, according to her Principal Private Secretary, "with some dismay."[29] She was continually in conflict with ministerial colleagues, especially at times of crisis: some grumbled in private and even rebelled in public, and one of her supporters criticized them in 1981 for "parading their consciences, frustrations, hysteria, snobberies, masculinities and ambitions before an audience."[30] Her personality aggravated the problem: in the words of one friend and admirer, "judged by the ordinary criteria of man-management, or of efficiency, or even those of Christian charity, she was often at fault," hectoring and humiliating.[31] More fundamental, and part of the explanation for her relentless combativeness, was the fact that she was usually isolated in the highest reaches of politics and officialdom, not expected to survive long, and at first not taken seriously. More than any Prime Minister since Gladstone (not the only resemblance), she relied on supporters outside Westminster and Whitehall.[32] To many on the left, especially feminists, her personality and her sex added to their loathing—how dare the pioneer woman be a hardline Tory reeking of suburbia! Moreover, she "shredded" the Labour Party ideologically[33]—the unkindest cut of all. Ever since, to the despair of many of its activists, the British left has been politically and intellectually on the defensive.

Her myth was invented by her enemies as much as by her admirers.[34] The term "Iron Lady" came from the Red Army newspaper. "Thatcherism" was identified by *Marxism Today*. "Victorian values" as a summary of her ideas was coined by a former Labour MP, the television interviewer Brian Walden. Her comment that "there is no such thing" as "society" was quoted out of context by her critics. Some of her most vehement supporters—born-again Thatcherites—were converts from the left, among them Alfred Sherman. Others who influenced her ideas were an odd collection of clever right-wing mavericks, including the Tory black sheep Enoch Powell and Sir Keith Joseph, a painfully self-critical and tactless intellectual described by a Labour opponent, Dennis Healey, as a mixture of "Hamlet, Rasputin and Tommy Cooper."[35] But she herself, although interested in ideas, was temperamental rather than ideological, using ideas rather than following them. Nigel Lawson, a Chancellor of the Exchequer and core Thatcherite who finally turned against her, summarized Thatcherism retrospectively as "a mixture of free markets, financial discipline, firm control over public expenditure, tax cuts, nationalism, 'Victorian values' . . . privatization and a dash of populism." But we should beware of attributing too much ideological coherence to the policies of one who combined basic principles with political pragmatism.[36] Thatcher's long period in office was one of constant and testing crises, but not always the same ones: inflation, strikes, Ireland, the Cold War, the Falklands, Europe. "Thatcherism" evolved as its circumstances changed.

Its main connecting thread was a patriotic version of declinism. One close adviser, John Hoskyns, spent a year preparing a huge diagram showing how all aspects of decline were connected.[37] Given the importance of economic failure to the declinist narrative, the economy was at the centre of Thatcher's concerns: "Everything we wished to do had to fit into the overall strategy of reversing Britain's economic decline, for without an end to decline there was no hope of success for our other objectives." But economics was not the sole end, and the market was only the means towards a restoration of social and political order: "Economics are the method; the object is to change the heart and soul."[38] The market was the way to escape from the political quagmire of the 1970s, in which governments loaded themselves with economic responsibilities they could not manage. "Unless we change our ways and our direction, our glories as a nation will soon be a footnote in the history books, a distant memory of an offshore island . . . remembered kindly for its noble past."[39]

Conflict was never far away during the Thatcher years. On the same day in August 1979 the IRA murdered Lord Mountbatten and two teenagers, and ambushed and killed eighteen soldiers. In 1980 came the Iranian embassy siege, in which the SAS rescued hostages with chilling efficiency—almost a sign of things to come. The same year there were several riots in provincial cities and a major strike in the nationalized British Steel Corporation. Hunger strikes were pursued in 1980–82 among convicted Irish terrorists demanding to be treated as political prisoners, and several starved themselves to death. And there was another coal strike.

The government's first economic aim was to bring down inflation. Contrary to what admirers and critics have supposed, there was no very clear strategy for doing this. Monetarism (limiting the money supply) was one idea which had been attempted previously by Labour, and indeed

was the orthodoxy followed by most central banks.[40] It proved more difficult and more destructive than expected: interest rates were raised to
bring down inflation, but this increased the value of sterling, also boosted
by oil revenues. So export competitiveness fell by 25 percent from 1979 to
1981. Subsidies to loss-making nationalized industries were cut. The
economy shrank disastrously by 4 percent in the second half of 1980.[41]
Uncompetitive businesses collapsed, unemployment doubled from
around 6 to 12 percent, and yet government borrowing was shooting up
uncontrollably, forcing up interest rates still further. On 10 October
1980, at the party conference at Brighton, Mrs. Thatcher proclaimed that
"the lady's not for turning," and that "there is no alternative." The chancellor, Geoffrey Howe, introduced a budget in March 1981 which flouted
orthodoxy by increasing taxation and cutting state spending during a
slump with the aim of reducing inflation and the government deficit,
increasing financial confidence, lowering interest rates, and cheapening
sterling. To admirers, this was a stroke of genius; to critics, an act of
lunacy. Several ministers thought of resigning.[42] BBC newsreaders provided a daily litany of job losses. A phalanx of 364 economists published
a declaration condemning the government and insisting that there were
"alternative policies"—not specified. A distinguished Cambridge signa-
tory predicted "apocalypse."[43] There were outbreaks of rioting in twelve
cities, causing one minister to predict "the decline and fall of the Tory
party." But the economy immediately began to improve, with reduced
public borrowing, lower inflation and interest rates, cheaper sterling, and
not least the impression that the government was determined to get a
grip on the economy. All this was not at first apparent: some ministers
continued to criticize and the *Guardian* announced on 3 December
1981 that an "obituary of Thatcherism is now in order."[44] The economy
grew by 3.7 percent per year from 1984 to 1988, one of the sharpest
expansions since 1945, and unemployment began to fall. The corporation of economists has never entirely recovered.

They still do not agree about exactly what happened. Critics insist that
the government's policy inflicted an unnecessarily deep recession,
destroyed swathes of the old heavy industry of northern England, Wales
and Scotland, wrought permanent social damage, and generated lasting
political resentment, while growth was merely due to North Sea oil and a
cyclical upturn. The bitterest critics imply that this was some deliberate
strategy to destroy industries—shipbuilding, coal, steel—that could have
been maintained, presumably by permanent subsidy and some sort of
protectionism, logically after leaving the European Community. Admirers
insist that the policy was a decisive way of reducing inflation, introducing

financial discipline, facing economic reality, and paving the way for growth. The difference is not one that can easily be bridged, not least because it shaped rival political dogmas. It may be that the Thatcher government acted precipitately. But something had to be done. The profits of private firms were collapsing. The great nationalized industries had mostly become bottomless pits for subsidy—in 1980–81 British Steel, for example, spent £4bn to make steel worth only £3bn, which it even then failed to sell.[45] They were subject to incoherent political meddling and reckless shop-floor militancy, and had developed an internal culture of fatalism or indifference. Those with which the public came most into contact—British Railways, British Airways, the Post Office, British Leyland—were bywords for poor quality and bad service. (When Callaghan had tried out his brand-new official car, the window had fallen out onto his lap.[46]) In the long run, the effect of the Thatcher government's policy was to turn off the life support system for the inanimate and rehabilitate the nationalized sector for privatization. This transformed some of them. British Steel's improvement over the 1980s has been described as "one of the most impressive on record in any business in any country at any time," overtaking American, Japanese and European rivals in productivity. Rolls-Royce went from bankruptcy to being the world's leading aero-engine-maker.[47] New investment began: 19,000 new firms, often "high tech," were set up between 1980 and 1986. Nissan's Sunderland car factory, built in 1985, became the most efficient in the world.

The price was cutting the workforce: between 1977 and 1983 British Steel lost 61 percent; British Leyland, 53 percent; British Shipbuilders, 28 percent.[48] As one industrialist commented wryly, unemployment had moved off the shop floor and into the street. The first tentative steps were taken towards reducing the power of trade unions. Norman Tebbit, Secretary of State for Employment, introduced the 1980 and 1982 Employment Acts, giving employers the right to sue trade unions for damages if they were involved (by "secondary picketing") in a strike not directly concerning their own employees, and it exposed trade unions to fines and their assets to seizure. The 1984 Trade Union Act required secret ballots for union leaders and exposed unions to legal action for damages if they held strikes without a vote by their members. From the mid-1980s the level of unemployment fell faster than in France, Germany or Italy, though without falling to its 1970s levels. A watershed in overall economic performance was 1985: before then, the British economy had grown more slowly than those of France and Germany; afterwards, it grew more quickly.[49]

A bolt from the blue came in the last week of March 1982, when

Argentinian forces suddenly seized the long-disputed Falkland Islands colony, inhabited by 1,800 British subjects.* The ensuing war would be one of the most important since 1945, the first time since then that the Royal Navy had been at war and had lost ships, the first sustained combat of modern aircraft against sophisticated surface ships,[50] and only the third time in history that Britain's main fleet had sailed so far from home—the others being to the Caribbean in 1782 and to the Pacific in 1945. The Argentinian government regarded the capture of the Falklands as a way to win domestic popularity, encouraged by repeated signs, both military and diplomatic, that Britain was indifferent. But a territory that had symbolic importance for the Argentinians turned out to have no less for the British. The First Sea Lord, Sir Henry Leach, put it bluntly to the Cabinet: "If we pussyfoot, if we don't move very fast and are not entirely successful, in a very few months' time we shall be living in a different country whose word will count for very little."[51] This was not a "Thatcherite" response: leading Thatcherites, including ministers John Biffen and Nicholas Ridley, fixated on economics and contemptuous of imperial nostalgia, sought a cheap resolution. Thatcher's favourite economic adviser, Alan Walters, suggested asking Buenos Aires to make the islanders a financial offer they could not refuse.[52] But for Thatcher herself, determined to reverse national decline, and regarding economics as ultimately secondary, the humiliation of yielding to an unprovoked attack was unpalatable, and she seized on the First Sea Lord's confidence: "Can we do it?" "We can, Prime Minister, and . . . we must."[53] This reaction was supported by the public and for a time by cross-party political opinion. Critics have accused her of using war as "a spectator sport—just another element in a consumer culture"[54] to remedy domestic unpopularity. But it was an equally possible route to political demise. Leading members of the Cabinet—including three holders of the Military Cross, and all with memories of the political wreckage of Suez—were very chary of military adventure, and this placed a heavy burden of responsibility on Thatcher personally.[55] The risks of a seaborne expedition 8,000 miles away, exposed to winter weather and air attack, were evident. The danger of major losses of ships and men was real: naval and military commanders were prepared for them, but it was unclear whether politicians and the public were. At stake for Britain was its claim to be a Great Power and one of the principal underwriters of international order.[56]

* During the eighteenth century, the then uninhabited islands were disputed by the British, French and Spanish, leading to a serious crisis in 1770, in which the British prevailed, finally annexing the islands in the 1830s. Settlers arrived from the 1840s. Argentina claimed to have inherited the disputed Spanish claim. The legal position is discussed in Lawrence Freedman, *The Official History of the Falklands Campaign* (rev. edn, 2 vols.; London, Routledge, 2007).

Foreign opinion was divided. Argentina was undeniably the aggressor, but claimed anti-colonial justification. Fortunately for Britain, the government in Buenos Aires was a right-wing dictatorship and proved diplomatically inept. The United Nations condemned Argentina's invasion—legally, Britain had an undoubted right to resist aggression—but urged negotiation. Many countries professed to see the dispute as trivial; but how they would have regarded Britain had it acquiesced in such an unprovoked attack is another matter.[57] Most of the Commonwealth, and in particular New Zealand, supported Britain; so did Norway, France and Chile. President Reagan and a divided American government vacillated. They feared annoying South America, tried repeatedly to broker a compromise, but also gave intelligence and logistical assistance to Britain and supplied Sidewinder air-to-air missiles.[58] The European Community was reluctant to back Britain or apply sanctions against Argentina, though it agreed to a temporary import ban and used the opportunity to overrule Britain's veto on agricultural price rises. Thatcher's stance was not to present Britain as a victim pleading for help, but as acting on behalf of the world order in resisting blatant aggression. Yet the crisis showed that even (or especially) in a world dominated by the rhetoric of multilateralism and collaboration, in a serious crisis a government or a country could find itself ultimately alone.[59]

The position of France was delicate: it had sold arms to Argentina, including modern aircraft and air-launched Exocet anti-ship missiles, five of which were operational. They were a serious threat: one of them was to sink the destroyer HMS *Sheffield*. The Argentinians had ordered fifty more Exocets, but the French halted shipments and found excuses to delay deliveries to Peru, in case they reached Argentina. The French air force flew a Mirage and a Super-Étendard over to East Anglia so that RAF pilots could get to know their capacities.[60]

Negotiations continued after the task force—100 ships and 30,000 men—sailed in April, but compromise, urged from all sides, proved elusive: the British government demanded evacuation of the invasion force before beginning negotiations; the Argentinians demanded that troops should remain and their sovereignty be conceded before negotiating. Various third-party interventions, including ill-judged American attempts, led nowhere. The Labour Party began to call for delay, the practical consequences of which would have been the loss of the islands due to the onset of winter.[61] The first shots were fired when an SAS force landed on remote South Georgia on 26 April. Real hostilities began in May after Argentina rejected a final British peace proposal. On the first the RAF bombed Port Stanley airfield, and Argentinian aircraft attacked the task force. On the second came the most controversial single action of the war, when the submarine HMS *Conqueror* torpedoed the cruiser *General Belgrano*, and 321 of its crew died. That the loss of life would have been far smaller if the Argentinian navy had been quicker to pick up survivors did not lessen the outcry both on the British left and abroad. An accusation was later made by the Labour MP Tam Dalyell that Thatcher "coldly and deliberately gave the orders to sink the *Belgrano*" outside the proclaimed maritime exclusion zone while the ship was sailing home, "in the knowledge that an honourable peace was on offer," so as to sabotage negotiations and precipitate a war for her domestic political advantage.[62] This astonishing accusation subsequently spawned a clutch of conspiracy theories in the *Daily Mirror*, the *Observer*, the *New Statesman*, stage plays, books and television documentaries, all marked (in the words of the campaign's official historian) by "fevered speculation and sheer irresponsibility."[63] The military considerations had been unambiguous: the *Belgrano* was known to be part of a planned naval attack, it constituted a serious threat, and permission to torpedo was given by the War Cabinet on the strong advice of the naval commanders. Two days later, on 4 May, HMS *Sheffield* was hit by an Exocet and sunk, killing twenty men. This brought mounting foreign and domestic calls for a cease-fire, and strong pressure from the Americans to accept a series of compromise plans, to which Thatcher reluctantly acceded[64]—but which the Argentinians then turned down.

The conflict was therefore fought out. The task force fought off courageous air attacks, inflicting and sustaining serious but not crippling casualties. RAF Harrier jump jets flying off two aircraft carriers outmatched the most modern conventional aircraft in manoeuvrability, and tactics were devised for avoiding Exocets, which included luring them away with helicopters, one piloted by the Duke of York. Marines and soldiers were landed on the main island on 21 May and fought their way to its single town, Port Stanley, where on 14 June the Argentinians surrendered. British casualties were lower than many had predicted: 255 killed and 777 wounded, with the loss of four warships and two supply ships; over 600 Argentinians had died. Thatcher's injunction to "Rejoice" (in fact, said at a much earlier stage, after the bloodless recapture of South Georgia) was used to paint her as heartless.

The conflict had varied international consequences. The Argentinian regime collapsed, an opportunity for democracy. The reaction of "world opinion," that amorphous concept, was mixed. It was commonly asserted that the war had been an unnecessary and archaic folly—"the empire strikes back." But it showed that Britain could act independently and even use force without the skies falling in. The "lesson of Suez" became less of a constraint.[65] There was grudging respect, including in Russia, for an expedition that no other country except the two superpowers would have been capable of, and the editor of the Italian daily *La Repubblica* thought that it showed Britain as "politically aggressive and influential," even "restored . . . to its prewar mover-and-shaker status."[66] It strengthened Anglo-American relations and greatly increased Thatcher's international standing, not least with Ronald Reagan, who after the Falklands victory conceded to her considerable moral and personal authority which had some importance in the final resolution of the Cold War.[67]

Did victory in the Falklands transform the national mood? Thatcher herself had no doubts: "We have learned something about ourselves—a lesson which we desperately needed to learn . . . This generation can match their fathers and grandfathers in ability, in courage, and in resolution . . . We have ceased to be a nation in retreat."[68] Her position within the Tory party was for the first time unassailable: "the Lady" was no longer the shrill interloper, but the warrior queen. Support for the war had been steady at around 80 percent—support in America had even reached 83 percent—and an opinion poll showed 80 percent to be "quite proud" or "very proud" to be British.[69] A 1979 Gallup poll had shown the British to be the most pessimistic of thirty-one countries surveyed; in 1983 they were the eighth most optimistic.[70] If there was one event that loosened the grip of declinism, it was surely this.

The Falklands victory did not, however, mean a new spirit of national unity. It won vilification as well as praise for Thatcher. The mainly left-wing minority (with a few dissident Tories and Liberals) who had opposed the war were bitter at what they saw as the whipping up of militaristic nationalism by "an absolutely Victorian jingoist." Tony Benn found it "embarrassing to live in Britain at the moment." Intellectuals mostly agreed and expressed their feelings in films, works of art and documentaries. The writer Alan Bennett described it as "the Last Night of the Proms erected into a policy." The historian E. P. Thompson predicted that Britain would suffer "for a long time, in rapes and muggings . . . in international ill will, and in the stirring up of ugly nationalist sentiment." The feminist journal *Spare Rib* denounced Thatcher's display of "male power." The Established Church had to be pressed hard to hold a service of "thanksgiving" rather than "reconciliation" at St. Paul's. For some their alienation from a country whose mood they disliked was deepened— better a country in decline than one revived by the "Falklands factor" and the tabloid *Sun*. R. W. Johnson in the *New Statesman* (17 June 1982) dissented, echoing Orwell in 1940: the left "have always proclaimed their hatred of military aggression and of fascism . . . But when it comes to the crunch they find they hate a right-wing Tory prime minister even more." Left-wing historians produced works deconstructing British and English national identity and what they saw as the malign legacy of empire and "Churchillism." Some realized that they had fundamentally misjudged how most people felt. The Marxist historian Eric Hobsbawm thought there had been "a public sentiment that could actually be felt" and "anyone of the Left who was not aware of this grassroots feeling . . . ought seriously to consider his or her capacity to assess politics."[71]

The war was relatively little referred to explicitly during the 1983 general election campaign. It was nevertheless important in the Tory victory, with a majority increased from 43 to 144, and Labour's vote falling to its lowest since 1931. Certainly, serious setbacks in the war would have damaged or destroyed the government, whereas success enhanced Thatcher's reputation for winning. She had other major advantages, however. The economy was improving. Labour had for years been shifting chaotically to the left, led by the hapless Michael Foot. Its election manifesto, "the longest suicide note in history,"[72] called for unilateral nuclear disarmament, massive nationalization, abolition of the House of Lords, and withdrawal from the European Community. Only 49 percent of manual workers voted Labour, compared with 70 percent in 1964. Bitter internal rows had led in 1981 to a secession of Labour moderates, who formed the Social Democratic Party led by the progressive Europhile Roy Jenkins, which split the Labour vote and in 1988 merged with the Liberals. Labour became practically a regional party, as before the First World War, centred in Scotland and the north, and winning only 17 percent of the vote in the south.[73] "Most Labour Party activists I knew," wrote one sympathizer, "worked in the public sector and were surrounded by like-minded people, only read the *Guardian* and were simply not aware that the rest of the country thought we were stark staring bonkers."[74] After its victory, the government speeded up the privatization of miscellaneous state-owned industries in a bold and original policy which included cheap sale of shares to public and to employees: they included British Telecom (1984), British Gas (1986), British Airways (1987), and water and electricity generating boards. A different kind of privatization was that of over 2 million council houses on favourable terms to their tenants—the British state had previously been the biggest landlord in the non-Communist world.

No less a part of the Thatcher saga than the Falklands war, and no less controversial, was the miners' strike of 1984–85. Miners occupied a special place in English life and in the mystique of the left—the Durham Miners' Gala was an annual ritual of banners and brass bands attended by Labour notables. Miners, always among the best paid of manual work-

ers, had also long been among the most militant: the General Strike of
1926 had started, and most wartime strikes had taken place, in the coalfields. Labour and particularly Tory governments had repeatedly been
humiliated by coal strikes. Mighty trade unions and strikers were not
popular, but the miners, largely because of the dangers they faced, enjoyed
unique public sympathy. The industry had boomed in the late nineteenth
century as a huge exporter, absorbing new workers from agriculture. Like
other staple industries, it had lost overseas markets, and the rise of oil,
nuclear power and natural gas further displaced coal. The amount mined
had fallen, as had the number of miners, from 700,000 in 1957 to
300,000 in 1970. Miners fought to maintain or improve their wages and
working conditions: Joe Gormley dreamed of a day when every miner
could have "a Jaguar out front to take him to work and a Mini at the side
to take his wife to the shops."[75] Equally important was keeping open the
pits on which small communities depended. Miners insisted that pits
should only be closed when they were exhausted, not when they were
uneconomic—a policy that required a subsidized and protected nationalized industry. One form of protection was using English coal in power
stations: this increased the miners' power in the short run (they could
force power cuts), but made them vulnerable in the long run (oil and gas
could be used instead). The ability to inflict rapid power cuts required
more than merely refusing to mine coal: as Arthur Scargill had shown in
1972, it meant preventing the movement of existing coal and coke stocks.

A trial of strength was predictable. Scargill, president of the NUM
since 1981, a Primitive Methodist transmuted into a Marxist class warrior, and his deputy, the Scottish Communist Mick McGahey, were spoil-
ing for a fight. Nicholas Ridley (one of Thatcher's stalwarts) had written
a report in 1977 which included tactics in case of a national coal strike—
a document subsequently claimed to prove a conspiracy. But the report
had little circulation and seems to have been forgotten. Besides, Ridley
and other senior Tories thought the miners would probably win. In
1981 the government had given in to miners' demands with alacrity. Since
then preparations had been made to withstand a coal strike. When in
March 1984 the Cortonwood pit in Yorkshire was scheduled to close on
economic grounds, Scargill took up the cudgels with remarkable assurance. The government was newly re-elected and determined. Summer was
coming on and coal stocks had been built up. Thatcher was determined
not to give in, and Scargill refused to negotiate. So it became a matter of
breaking the government or breaking the NUM.

Scargill refused to hold a national strike ballot, which he would probably have lost, and his bombastic charisma, while enthusing the most

combative, mainly in Yorkshire, Scotland and Kent, alienated others. Many miners voted against a strike (70 percent in Nottinghamshire), continued to work and left the NUM. Key allies, such as railwaymen, kept out. Scargill tried to close down the power industry by mass flying pickets and strong-arm tactics. This led to pitched battles between thousands of pickets and police, violence on a scale not seen since the nineteenth century. Over 11,000 people were arrested—possibly a peacetime record for England. Serious casualties, however, were few: certain inhibitions still applied. By early 1985 miners were returning to work. Many were house-owners and mortgage-payers, and their families were suffering badly. In March the strike ended. But the government's victory was not popular: its approval ratings collapsed.[76]

The outcome might have been unpredictably different but for chance. The IRA had planted a delayed-action bomb in the Grand Hotel, Brighton, where Thatcher and much of her government were staying during the party conference of October 1984. The bomb wrecked the hotel during the early hours of the twelfth: five people were killed, including the Deputy Chief Whip, Sir Anthony Berry, and others seriously injured, including Norman Tebbit, Secretary of State for Trade and Industry, and his wife, Margaret, who was permanently disabled. This was the narrowest escape of a British government since Guy Fawkes. Thatcher enhanced her reputation for courage, determination—and luck, by insisting that the conference continue as usual. The attack had aimed to sabotage discreet negotiations between the British and Irish governments, which led to the Anglo-Irish Agreement of 15 November 1985.

The miners' strike created deep loathing, perhaps more than anything else in the Thatcher years. It became for some a grim epic, celebrated in films and stage plays lamenting the loss of mining communities, and expressing a broader nostalgia for a golden age of brass bands and banners. Tebbit, a Thatcherite loyalist, said that she had broken "not just a strike, but a spell." It has been called the last great battle of the Industrial Revolution: "When it stopped the idea of the forward march of Labour stopped with it."[77] But unease was felt among paternalistic Tories, most famously the retired Harold Macmillan, who recalled coal miners serving in the trenches. Much indeed disappeared during the 1970s and 1980s: a patriarchal working-class society, neighbourly communities, chapel-going, decent men with polished boots and medals in the back of a drawer, family stability, self-respect. Whole landscapes—the Victorian landscapes of textile mills, tall chimneys, docks, pitheads, shipyards and terraced houses—were obliterated;[78] a few were preserved as museums, employing former workers to demonstrate the skills of a lost age. But the reasons for that loss were many: cultural, technological and social, as well as economic; and they were international. Similar stories could be told about Pittsburgh, Bilbao, Liège, Essen, Kharkov and Saint-Étienne—the last French coal mine closed in 2004. What is unique in the English story? England had been the country with the highest proportion of industrial workers and the most international economy, so it was uniquely affected by change. Thatcher and Scargill perhaps envenomed and accelerated a process that was taking place in many societies and under many political regimes. Yet the decline in the numbers employed in industry was not significantly greater during the Thatcher years (1.9 percent per year, 1979–1990) than subsequently under Labour (1.8 percent per year, 1997–2005).[79]

The Anglo-Irish Agreement of 15 November 1985 was a first step towards pacification, giving a symbolic role in Northern Ireland politics to Dublin, which in turn accepted Ulster's right to self-determination. But it dissatisfied many on both sides. The Ulster leader the Rev. Ian Paisley prayed to the Almighty "to take vengeance on this wicked, treacherous, lying woman."[80] Behind the scenes, the security forces were increasingly effective, including by penetrating the terrorist organizations. This required a degree of complicity in the activities of terrorist informers. Small special-forces units, part of a vast security infrastructure, were ambushing and often killing terrorists—denounced by some as a "shoot to kill" policy. Loyalist terrorists too were killing IRA members and supporters, sometimes with the collusion of some of the security forces, and for the first time membership in the IRA became a dangerous occupation. The IRA turned to soft civilian targets (such as pubs, fish and chip shops, and retail stores) in Northern Ireland and England in the 1990s.[81]

The Thatcherite "revolution" made a sustained effort to undermine what it saw as cosy and hostile vested interests: in the Civil Service (this was the hey-day of the satirical television series *Yes, Minister*), in trade unions, in academia, the BBC, the NHS ("the closest thing the English have to a religion," said Nigel Lawson, "with those who practise in it regarding themselves as a priesthood"), and in local government—especially spendthrift "loony left" local authorities. The favoured instrument was marketization to increase "consumer choice" and the disciplines of competition. Large parts of the Civil Service were turned into semi-autonomous "executive agencies" to implement government policies, it was hoped more efficiently: soon after Thatcher left office there were fifty such agencies, with 200,000 officials.[82] But when consumer choice did not work or seemed too risky, the government centralized (as in the capping of local-authority taxation), regulated (as in the National Curriculum), and created more appointed "quangos"* (for example, to regulate priva-

---

* "Quasi-autonomous non-governmental organizations."

tized utilities). This originated a bizarre quasi-sovietization by quotas and targets, which Sir Humphrey was keen to elaborate, and it created a new nomenklatura.

Thatcher played an active role in the last stages of the Cold War in the early 1980s. She gave public encouragement to domestic opponents of Communist regimes. She persuaded President Reagan to limit his Strategic Defense Initiative ("Star Wars") anti-missile programme, which alarmed the Soviet and many European governments, to the level of experimentation. She also supported the introduction of medium-range American nuclear missiles into Europe to balance similar Soviet weapons, in the face of considerable public opposition in Britain and on the Continent. Most importantly, advised by an idealistic KGB officer, Colonel Oleg Gordievsky, who had offered his services to MI6, Mrs. Thatcher had in 1984 identified in Mikhail Gorbachev a man with whom the West "could do business."[83] Her role in providing a Western response, when American diplomacy lost direction during Reagan's second term, was important, and included public support for Gorbachev and later Yeltsin, accompanied by frank private exchanges.[84] This was the beginning of the end of the Cold War and, to general surprise, of Soviet Communism and its empire. Chinese Communism kept political power—crushing demonstrations in Tiananmen Square in 1989 to do so—but abandoned socialism. If this evaporation of the main historical alternative to liberal capitalism did not mark the end of history, as influential voices proclaimed,[85] it certainly marked the end of an era, with consequences that are still developing.

One of them was "globalization"—the dismantling of many trade and political barriers, permitting freer and faster movement of goods, capital, people and communications—which put the world back onto its pre-1914 trajectory. The City of London's part was its "Big Bang" in October 1986, which removed traditional restrictive practices and opened trading to foreign banks. The City's activities as an international centre hugely expanded, partly balancing the loss of manufacturing. The cost of globalization included repeated crises in the world economy: a U.S. stock market crash in 1987, the "dotcom bubble" of the 1990s, an Asian crisis in 1997, a Russian crisis in 1998 and, above all, the world financial crash of 2008. For a time, it seemed that the consequences of the 1987 crash would be serious, and they were aggravated by over-reaction. The chancellor, Nigel Lawson, cut interest rates, causing a runaway boom in house prices. In an attempt to control inflation, he decided, without announcement, to link the value of the pound to that of the German mark. He also favoured joining the European Exchange Rate Mechanism (ERM), one of several schemes aiming to stabilize the exchange values of European currencies. This occasioned the last of Margaret Thatcher's many battles, this time against the "European super-state."

Tory Euroscepticism is a recent phenomenon, not a hangover of imperial nostalgia. The Tories, under Macmillan, Home, Heath and initially Thatcher, were the most strongly "European" party. Sovereignty was declared to be a theoretical issue that would not arise in practice: but it did inevitably arise when policies clashed. First, and most obviously, the entry of Britain and most other EFTA members began a process of indefinite enlargement of the EEC that Britain supported, but which made existing Community policies and institutions sources of tension. The Common Agricultural Policy (which took 70–80 percent of Community spending) and the prolonged and acrimonious wrangling over Britain's financial contribution to Community funds—over £1bn by the early 1980s—reflected not only economic divergence, but political, ideological and even cultural differences between an overwhelmingly urban society with a free-trading history and those (most obviously France) with an economic and emotional stake in agriculture. Mrs. Thatcher's "handbagging" (as it came to be known) of President François Mitterrand at Fontainebleau in June 1984 won a 66 percent rebate of "our money," but dramatized antagonism between Britain and the Continent, where Thatcher's style of open polemic—especially from a woman—raised hackles. It was also a departure from British diplomatic culture, tending always to support international organizations to secure "influence."[86] On the other hand, she and Mitterrand finally agreed to build a Channel Tunnel that December, and it opened in 1994, after more than a century of false starts.

Britain's recovered economic dynamism permitted it new initiative. A Whitehall paper, "Europe—the Future" (1984) originated the 1986 Single European Act, which created a European Union with a Single Market "in which the free movement of goods, peoples, services, and capital is assured." This was the first general liberalizing measure since the Common Market had been created, and it became a Community priority at Thatcher's behest.[87] Barriers to trade, including in public contracts, state aid, financial regulation and discriminatory standards, were to be gradually dismantled. This has been described as "perhaps the greatest single contribution ever made to the construction of Europe," with Margaret Thatcher the "founding mother of the new Europe."[88] She would assert that a "Community of sovereign states . . . a lightly regulated free market, and international free trade does not need a Commission in its present form."[89] As it lost its functions, the Brussels bureaucracy in a Thatcherite

"Europe" would thus wither away. This was just what de Gaulle had feared when he had blocked British entry: that "England" opposed a true European union and wanted only "a vast free trade zone."[90]

Thatcher's free-market European vision had many enemies. It conflicted with the romanticized view that saw "ever-closer union" as Europe's historic destiny, dispelling ancient conflicts and warding off external threats. The formidable president of the European Commission, Jacques Delors, formerly France's socialist finance minister, wanted Europe to be "a shelter in a world turned upside down by globalization"[91]—in other words, a haven from Thatcherism. This was an attractive message, which converted Labour and the trade unions from their visceral anti-Europeanism—Delors was given an ovation at the 1988 TUC conference. He argued that the Single Market required the Commission's powers to be extended into the environmental, social, monetary and regional fields to create an "organized space" rather than a "free trade zone."[92] His aim, he told the European parliament in 1988, was a federation by 2000 in which national parliaments would be subordinated and 80 percent of economic legislation come from Strasbourg. Thatcher dissented in a widely publicized speech in Bruges in September 1988:[93]

> We British are as much heirs to the legacy of European culture as any other nation . . . We have fought and we have died for her freedom . . . The European Community is *one* manifestation of that European identity, but it is not the only one . . . We shall always look on Warsaw, Prague and Budapest as great European cities . . . We have not successfully rolled back the frontiers of the state in Britain, only to see them re-imposed [by] a European super-state . . . Certainly we want to see Europe more united . . . But it must be in a way which preserves the different traditions, parliamentary powers and sense of national pride in one's own country; for these have been the source of Europe's vitality through the centuries.

The dispute was given urgency by the gradual ending of the Cold War in the late 1980s and the prospect of German reunification, which would create a potentially very powerful state. This worried several European leaders, among them Thatcher and Mitterrand, who consulted on how to slow unification down. But Mitterrand and Delors astutely did a deal with the West German chancellor, Helmut Kohl: he agreed as a quid pro quo for unification to tie a united Germany into Delors's plan for integrated economic and political structures, above all a European central bank and a single currency, of which Thatcher had always been suspicious and which she thought would inevitably be dominated by Germany. She was left with no effective German policy and an appearance of sterile xenophobia; and this brought her into conflict with the chancellor, Nigel

Lawson, and the Foreign Secretary, Geoffrey Howe. Their joint threats to resign on the eve of the Madrid European Council in June 1989 forced her to agree in Madrid to the first stage of Delors's plan and commit Britain to joining the ERM by the end of 1992. She subsequently removed Howe from the Foreign Office, and continuing tension over policy with Lawson led to his resignation in October. John Major, the new chancellor, would take sterling into the ERM the following year.

The postwar world structure was rapidly being transformed. Over the summer of 1989, Communist Europe collapsed. Closed borders were opened by the spontaneous action of millions of people. The Soviet Union began to disintegrate. In August the Iraqi dictator, Saddam Hussein, invaded Kuwait, and America and Britain began to plan his ejection. In November the Berlin Wall was pulled down, and on 3 October 1990 Germany was formally united. Two days later Britain joined the ERM at the rate of 2.95 deutschmarks to the pound—agreed with hindsight to have been too high, but insisted on by the other member states and backed by Labour and the Liberals.[94] Sterling had to be maintained at this rate by means of high interest rates during a recession. On 30 October, Thatcher reported to the Commons on the recent meeting of the European Council in Rome:[95]

> We would not be prepared to have a single currency imposed upon us . . . we are determined to retain our fundamental ability to govern ourselves through Parliament . . . Mr. Delors said . . . he wanted the European Parliament to be the democratic body of the Community, he wanted the Commission to be the Executive and he wanted the Council of Ministers to be the Senate. No. No. No.

The leader of the Labour Party, Neil Kinnock, retorted that "her tantrum tactics will not stop the process of change . . . All they do is strand Britain in a European second division." Geoffrey Howe, now Deputy Prime Minister, agreed with Kinnock and resigned on 1 November. Thatcher's stance was regarded by Europhiles such as Howe as destructive, nationalistic and embarrassingly crude. She had recently been weakened by a token challenge for the party leadership by an eccentric Europhile MP, Sir Anthony Meyer (who described a meeting with Thatcher supporters as like having "strayed into the servants' hall").[96] Furthermore, vociferous public opposition had emerged to the ill-conceived "poll tax," an attempt, strongly favoured by Thatcher, to levy a flat-rate "community charge" on all residents to make them more sensitive to the costs of local government. This provoked large-scale riots and vandalism in London, convincing many Tories that she had become an electoral liability.[97]

The coup de grâce was Howe's resignation statement in the Commons on 13 November. Dennis Healey had described being attacked by the former barrister as "like being savaged by a dead sheep," but now Howe's quiet monotone was more lethal than the rowdiest invective. Flourishing the declinist banner, he lamented Britain's delay in entering the EC and further delay in entering the ERM: it was "essential . . . not to cut ourselves off from the realities of power; not to retreat into a ghetto of sentimentality about our past . . . We dare not let that happen again." He lamented that "people throughout Europe see our Prime Minister's finger-wagging and hear her passionate, No, No, No . . . maximising our chances of being once again shut out." He ended with a polite call to rebellion.[98] The following day, another pro-European ex-minister, Michael Heseltine, challenged Thatcher for the party leadership and denied her an absolute majority in the first ballot, held on 20 November while she was in Paris to sign a "Charter for a New Europe" marking the end of the Cold War. The proof of waning support within her party caused her to withdraw in favour of John Major, a protégé, who was elected party leader and became Prime Minister after Thatcher's tearful resignation on 28 November.

So ended the eleven-year reign of England's most prominent non-royal female politician. For many people she personifies a market culture caring only for profit, blamed for everything from bankers' bonuses to football hooliganism (though at the same time there was also a steep increase in charitable giving and volunteering).[99] This is largely shooting the admittedly rather hectoring messenger. World political and economic changes were effectively irresistible in a country forced to earn its living by trade. Their impact in Britain was magnified by the fiasco of the policies of the 1970s. Thatcherite criticisms and attacks (many of them ineffective) on institutions and corporate interests—universities, the BBC, the civil service, nationalized industries, the professions—were animated by the obsession with decline nurtured for a generation by both left and right, though in her case with a determination to reverse and not simply manage it. For all these reasons, the United Kingdom under Margaret Thatcher changed more than any other western European country, affecting not only its economic structures but the very way its people think and behave. The strike culture disappeared. State spending was held down and the national debt shrank. Class boundaries became blurred, as politicians tried to appeal to "ordinary, hard-working people,"[100] yet economic inequality increased as old industries died and new businesses boomed. Thatcher's style—aggressive, argumentative, non-consensual, and conveying the impression that her tough decisions had been reached without much hand-wringing—made her actions a cause of bitterness, even when their necessity was grudgingly accepted. The effect was "smashing icons of British national identity more dramatically than she was able to build up patriotic feeling."[101] The ancient sectarianism of English politics was reignited, and ancient divisions between England (especially its southern core) and Scotland and Wales were widened. She mobilized public opinion to ensure that European integration could not happen by stealth. The Tory share of the vote fell at every election. So was "Thatcherism" worth it? Economists and economic historians are as divided as politicians and the public, and much depends on which statistics are chosen and for which years, and on assumptions about underlying trends. But no one subsequently advocated returning to the policies pursued by Heath, Wilson or Benn. Britain no longer seemed economically moribund and politically impotent.

John Major's government was inevitably seen as a lengthy postscript. Die-hard Thatcherites did not forgive what they saw as treason, and the Tory party remained divided, especially over Europe. Nevertheless, Major won another election in April 1992, partly by default, as Labour and its leader Neil Kinnock were still mistrusted. Major seemed "the old-fashioned English ideal of a thoroughly nice man,"[102] and as such he was commonly described as "grey" and gave an easy target to satirists. He introduced a National Lottery in 1993, whose funding of a wide range of cultural and sports activities would become an important part of national life. Privatization continued. But Major inherited four problems that would haunt his successors too: Europe, the Persian Gulf, Ireland and the Balkans.

The Maastricht Treaty on European Union (February 1992) formally tied the Single Market to Economic and Monetary Union, with a future single currency, the euro, whose coins and notes would enter circulation on 1 January 2002. The treaty also contained a "Social Charter" on employment conditions and workers' rights. Britain opted out from the Social Charter and from commitment to a single currency—in retrospect, a momentous decision. Two countries, Denmark and France, held referendums to approve the treaty. Amid the uncertainty thus created, speculative assaults were launched on the currencies of several members of the already creaking ERM. The Germans repeatedly refused to reduce their interest rates to take pressure off their partners. Finland, Sweden, Italy and Spain were all forced to devalue. The climax came when sterling too, after increasingly panicky attempts by John Major and the chancellor, Norman Lamont, to hold back the speculative tide, was forced out of the system on "Black Wednesday" (16 September 1992).[103] Four days later the French referendum narrowly approved Maastricht. The return to the familiar saga of sterling crises was a lethal blow to Tory claims of competence: the fall in Major's poll rating was the worst ever suffered in a single month by any Prime Minister, and Labour's lead rose from 2.5 percent to 17.8.[104] Euroscepticism within the Tory party strengthened. The government had wasted £3bn–4bn—about £50 per head of the population. But economically the fiasco proved a valuable stimulus: with a flexible currency, the British economy would by every measure outperform its peers on the Continent for the rest of the decade, and indeed until the crash of 2008.

British forces joined the Americans—with most of the EU disapproving—in what turned out to be an easy and crushing victory in February 1991 over the Iraqi army, liberating Kuwait after an eighteen-month occupation. But Saddam Hussein's continuation in power and resistance to United Nations instructions to disarm were the seeds of future conflict, as will be seen in the next chapter. In Ireland the "peace process" was decisively pushed forward. In December 1993 Major and the Irish prime minister, Albert Reynolds, signed a Downing Street Declaration agreeing on self-determination in Ireland on the basis of consensus, and the Irish Republic's constitutional claim to "the Six Counties" was subsequently dropped. The IRA announced a cease-fire in August 1994, and the Loyalists followed in October.

Far more difficult was the crisis arising from the break-up of Yugoslavia, which set Serbs, Croats and Bosnians at each other's throats. The president of the European Council, Jacques Poos, proclaimed in May 1991 that the crisis was "the Hour of Europe," showing that the European Union could regulate the Continent's post–Cold War affairs unaided.[105] France and Britain were eager to take charge, the latter with the intention of demonstrating a new spirit of commitment. "Defence in Europe is not an opt-out subject for us," declared the Foreign Secretary, Douglas Hurd.[106] However, neither Britain nor France wanted serious conflict. They refused to take sides, accepting only a humanitarian role, and pressed for a compromise that would necessarily favour Serbian nationalists. The worst fighting in Europe since 1945 became increasingly atrocious, with massacre, mass rape and "ethnic cleansing." Hurd admitted in his diary in August 1992 that "our prudent stance looks feeble and inhumane." By late 1994 Britain's policy was "falling to bits around us."[107] Dénouement came in 1995. Serb shelling of the Bosnian capital, Sarajevo, caused a new British commander to order air strikes against their ammunition dumps, the first such action of the war. The Serbs responded by seizing UN soldiers—including thirty British—as hostages. In July 1995 Serbs overran the "safe haven" of Srebrenica and slaughtered several thousand Bosnian men and boys. A small Franco-British Rapid Reaction Force, created some months earlier, was dispatched. American air-power supported counter-attacks by Croatian and Bosnian forces. The Serbs retreated rapidly, and a compromise agreement was signed at Dayton, Ohio, in November 1995. But this was not the end of the conflict.

As the 1990s wore on, another "sea change" affected British politics. Thatcher's party had served a purpose in crisis: many had voted for her and it without much liking either. But the crises were over: the Cold War was won, economic chaos quelled, state authority strengthened. The beneficiaries were not to be her Tory successors. What came to be called "sleaze"—a series of sexual and financial scandals more demeaning than heinous—crystallized public distaste for the Tories. The 1992 currency debacle destroyed their reputation for financial competence. Their ascendancy, the longest since the mid-nineteenth century, was ending: by 1994 they were 23 percent behind Labour in the polls, as women and middle-class voters bolted. The electorate wanted an end to upheavals but without regressing to the pre-Thatcher chaos. The Labour Party, under a new, smiling and articulate leader who proclaimed himself "a modern man from the rock and roll generation," offered just that in a pop song slogan: "Things can only get better."

# CHAPTER 21

# Things Can Only Get Better,
## 1997–c.2014

*I am a British patriot. Britain in my vision is not Britain turning its back on the world . . . We are a leader of nations or nothing.*

Tony Blair, 1997[1]

*Mine is the first generation able to contemplate the possibility that we may lead our entire lives without going to war or sending our children to war.*

Tony Blair, 1997[2]

Things could hardly have *been* better than in May 1997. No government since that of Disraeli in 1874 had come to power in anything like such favourable circumstances. With the end of the Cold War Britain faced no external threat for the first time since the 1890s. For the first time since the 1860s, it was outperforming not only Germany and the United States, but every large economy.[3] There were no significant internal challenges: the "Irish question," following the 1994 cease-fire, showed the best prospect of being answered since Gladstone's failure with Home Rule; the Tories were demoralized after their worst-ever defeat; the Liberals were keen on a pact; the far left and the trade unions were beaten; and the media were sycophantic. Not since Palmerston's heyday had a single party so dominated the landscape. The electorate was not asking much more than a quiet life to enjoy its prosperity. Blair won elections in 2001 and 2005 and enjoyed an uninterrupted ten years in Downing Street—the only Prime Minister other than Margaret Thatcher to do so since Lord Liverpool. The problems the country was to face were largely of the government's own making.

"New Labour," as it was now called, was embodied above all in Tony Blair, Gordon Brown, Chancellor of the Exchequer, and Peter Mandelson, its theorist and tactician, who was appointed Cabinet Office Minister. It was a synthesis of recent history, both a reaction against the rigours of Thatcherism and an acceptance of it as "the most thoroughgoing attempt at modernization Britain has yet experienced."[4] "Old" Labour's thread-bare attachment to Fabian socialism was ostentatiously jettisoned with the abolition of "Clause 4" of the party constitution (see p. 635) at Blair's behest at a special party conference in 1995. New Labour combined market economics with "proper progressive attitudes such as equality for women, gays, blacks and Asians."[5] "Modernization" was its key word, best defined as whatever the government favoured. Only 13 percent of its MPs had working-class backgrounds.[6] Unlike Thatcher, who in Gladstonian fashion had seen the market as moralizing, New Labour saw it, as Marx had, as radicalizing: it would thrust aside musty "Victorian values" and replace them with those of what Blair called "Cool Britannia," a culturally and socially modern society.

In contrast with Thatcherite individualism, New Labour took a managerial view of "social justice with the state as its main agent," as Blair wrote in 1998. Generous state spending—always called "investment"—would be managed by applying business methods to public services. There was a centralizing, even authoritarian side: "target culture" (in which institutional behaviour was dictated by sets of centrally imposed targets), Anti-Social Behaviour Orders, attempts to ban fox-hunting, more police with greater powers, more prisoners, a mass of repressive legislation (over 3,000 new criminal offences during their period in office), more surveillance cameras than anywhere in the world, and unusually high spending on law and order by international standards. One left-wing historian has attacked this "hard-nosed modernity" as "the most shameful episode in the history of the Labour Party."[7] An opposition MP was arrested inside the Palace of Westminster in 2008—something that Charles I had not managed. Emblematic of the clash between the liberal and the illiberal was that alcohol was made more freely available, and then attempts were made to control the inevitable results by increasing police powers. (In this case, the drunks won: town centres across the land were regularly taken over by the shambling hordes of the tipsy.)

Capitalism laid New Labour's golden eggs. By 2007 nearly a million people were working in the City and Docklands. New Labour's leaders had the enthusiasm of the newly converted for the miracles of free enterprise. As Mandelson put it, they were "intensely relaxed" at the prospect of people getting "filthy rich."[8] Many such people from around the world found this congenial—a high proportion of England's super-rich were now immigrants. The total wealth of the richest thousand people in the country is estimated to have risen during the Blair years from £99bn to £360bn, much held far beyond England's shores.[9]

The dominating figures were Tony Blair, Labour's most successful vote-winner, and Gordon Brown, who turned out to be one of its least. They were the products of a generation (not confined to Britain) in which politics had become a complete profession, and parties became increasingly detached from civil society. Ministers or MPs with some other major activity, such as trade unionism, the professions or business, became a rare species. Leading politicians were younger than at any time since the heyday of aristocracy in the eighteenth century; indeed, age now became a near disqualification for high office. They had similar backgrounds, dressed plainly, spoke blandly (gentrified "Estuary English," Scottish or northern), knew each other, intermarried, and in some notable cases were related.[10] Not coincidentally, New Labour MPs were described by one of their elder statesmen as "the most supine Members of Parliament in British history."[11] Yet the worm was capable of turning: "Old" and "New" Labour collided over the Iraq war in March 2003, when their parliamentary rebellion was the biggest in a governing party since the Tory split over the Corn Laws.

During the 1990s grass-roots membership of the main parties declined more than anywhere else in Europe, making them increasingly reliant on rich donors. Party loyalties frayed; voting became less predictable and more impulsive. Electoral turnout fell to the lowest level since the First World War—only 59 percent in 2001, compared with an earlier norm of over 70 percent and peaks of over 80 percent. This was an international trend, particularly marked in north-western Europe, though also in Canada, Australia and New Zealand. The fading of mobilizing ideologies, the blurring of class and religious identities, the professionalization of politics, economic globalization, the delegation of government powers to unelected regulatory bodies both domestic and international, and the strategy of competing for the "centre ground" made many voters feel that there was little at stake and/or that politicians were "out of touch," powerless or untrustworthy.[12] In contrast, activism outside the main parties increased, as in the Green Party, the Countryside Alliance and many local pressure groups. Also, from the 1990s onwards, anti-Establishment protest parties appeared in many European countries, including England, with the Eurosceptic United Kingdom Independence Party (UKIP).[13] In short, New Labour and its successor, the Conservative–Liberal Democrat coalition, were functioning in a new and shifting political environment.

Despite his uninhibited personal memoirs,[14] Blair remains an enigma—

possibly, in Victor Hugo's phrase, a sphinx without a riddle. He became Prime Minister at the age of forty-three without having held previous ministerial office. Unlike most if not all successful prime ministers, he had little interest in what he dismissed as "process"—the tedious business of actually governing. He saw his talents as persuading, inspiring, and communicating. His religious faith gave him invincible moral assurance. He radiated optimism, adopted an unpompous style ("Call me Tony"), which became *de rigueur* in government and the civil service. His informal method of "sofa government" operated through a small and motley entourage of friends and advisers, subverting normal administrative methods (such as taking minutes of meetings), and tending to politicize or by-pass civil servants. Hardly any other ministers had experience of running anything, few lasted long, and the few "Blairites" who did were shuttled from job to job, as were senior officials.[15] A recent historian of the Labour Party has condemned him as unprincipled, "with almost no knowledge of [Labour's] history, and even less respect for its values and traditions," merely a "non-political Conservative" in Labour guise.[16] But there was nothing Tory in his equal indifference to national history and tradition ("I'm naturally attracted by iconoclasm"), and in his metropolitan rootlessness. He spoke nostalgically of his childhood devotion to Newcastle United (football was an important populist shibboleth) but few were convinced.

Yet Blair, with his youthful optimism, might have been an excellent leader for untroubled times. "Something tolerant, something amiable, something humorous, some lightness of spirit in his own nature has marked his premiership and left its mark on British life," commented a liberal Tory.[17] He showed his best when dealing with the death of Diana, Princess of Wales, in a car accident in Paris on 31 August 1997. Her death and funeral had produced an astonishing outburst of public emotion, showing both the power of royalty in an age of celebrity and the unpredictable nature of the feelings it inspired. Momentarily, the monarchy as an institution, the Prince of Wales and the Queen herself were publicly criticized to a degree unseen since the 1860s in the belief that Diana—who inspired widespread affection, even adulation—had been badly treated during her marriage and after her divorce in July 1996. Blair handled the crisis deftly, both in his own comments praising "the people's princess" and in his advice to the Queen.

Economics were left to Blair's old friend Gordon Brown, the heir apparent, who uniquely remained chancellor for the whole of Blair's premiership, following a prior agreement between them that he would not challenge Blair for the leadership. Brown was a very different personality, driven and mercurial, drowning in detail and indecisive. Like Blair, he used a small entourage outside the Treasury hierarchy, most importantly Ed Balls, who rose from special adviser to minister. Lauded as a financial wizard, Brown too was impatient of routine and complexity; said a senior Treasury official: "I don't think he was terribly interested in the regulation of financial services," which became dangerously weak in an increasingly unstable financial system. When at last Prime Minister from June 2007— soon facing financial and political crisis—he found it hard to cope (an official contemplating a job in Downing Street was asked if he could accept "extreme verbal abuse").[18]

New Labour's strength was campaigning. It paid unprecedented attention to the media and those who owned them, most importantly Rupert Murdoch, proprietor of *The Times* and the *Sunday Times*, the *Sun* and Sky television. After leaving office, Blair became a godparent to one of Murdoch's children and established an unusually close relationship with Murdoch's wife.[19] The press was used as an instrument of politics, by "leaks," off-the-record "briefings," interviews and announcements by-passing Parliament.[20] Alastair Campbell, a talented and forceful former journalist and Blair's "Director of Strategic Communications," was one of the most powerful officials in recent history, equally detached from Parliament and from the civil service tradition of service to the Crown. Government revolved round headlines and "initiatives"—nearly 200 "task forces," inquiries and royal commissions were set up in the first twelve months.[21] *Yes, Minister* had satirized government in the 1970s and 1980s; the new equivalent was *The Thick of It* (2005), a black comedy of incompetence, chaos, bullying and "spin," as the primacy of presentation over substance became universally known.

In four broad areas New Labour's actions have historic importance and will long continue to be felt: the state, the population, foreign policy and the economy. At the time of writing this book, their consequences were still unfolding, and in this final chapter I shall try to indicate this unfinished story by discussing them thematically and at times departing from strict chronology.


## CHANGING THE STATE

Britain is unusual, perhaps unique, among democratic countries in allowing a government to use its parliamentary majority to alter the constitution as it sees fit. Several relatively minor reforms were introduced, and several abandoned, such as regionalization. Most hereditary peers lost their seats in the House of Lords in 1999, but there was no final reform of the Upper House, which was left as a mainly nominated body due to the unexpected difficulty of agreeing on what it should do or how it should be chosen. But the cumulative effects of constitutional reform, which once begun was difficult to limit, grew into the greatest change in the system of government of the United Kingdom since Irish independence in 1921. The most far-reaching change was national devolution. In 1998 a Scottish parliament was re-established for the first time since 1707, as were Welsh and Northern Ireland assemblies, with considerable powers of internal self-government, though with limited fiscal authority. Earlier devolution measures, from Gladstone to Callaghan, had failed. Scottish nationalism had re-emerged in the 1960s, growing in reaction to post-1945 centralization and later to Thatcherism, and it was encouraged by European integration and the benign post–Cold War climate. The first political losers were the Tories, who suffered an electoral Bannockburn in the 1997 elections, losing all their Scottish seats—a rout not stemmed by Major's conciliatory gesture of returning the Stone of Scone in 1996 after 700 years in England (see p. 108). The Tories thus resumed their Victorian position as an essentially English party: in the 1860s, for example, they had had only eight Scottish seats out of sixty, and in the 1880s two Welsh seats out of thirty. Labour faced a worse long-term danger, however, as it needed its Scottish seats to balance the Tory predominance in England. Devolution was seen as a way to kill nationalism by kindness and preserve Labour dominance in Scotland and Wales. But devolution was effectively irreversible, and could predictably ratchet towards self-government.

In Northern Ireland devolution was a way to end "the Troubles." British intelligence had penetrated the battered Republican movement in Belfast and knew that its leaders, Gerry Adams and Martin McGuinness, wanted a way out of the conflict and a legal political role through the Sinn Fein party. Huge IRA bombs in London and Manchester in 1996 and riots and violence in Ulster were part of a ruthless negotiating process and a product of factional conflict in the Republican ranks. The "Good Friday Agreement" of April 1998, doggedly pushed through by Blair in person, required Unionists to accept power-sharing and sit in government with former terrorists, and required Republicans to accept the Union de facto— at least for the time being, as many believed that a united Ireland would emerge gradually. A similar solution had first been proposed in the 1970s, and before that in 1920. It was now resoundingly endorsed by referendums in both Northern Ireland and the Republic in May 1998. In August the "Real IRA," a dissident group that rejected the settlement, murdered twenty-nine people with a bomb in Omagh, the worst of the many atrocities of the conflict. There followed a tense stalemate, revolving round the reluctance of the Provisional IRA formally to disarm—a symbolic semi-surrender—not to mention its involvement in spying, torture and (like the "Loyalist" gangs) in organized crime. Blair gambled on pushing through an agreement between the two most intransigent groups, Ian Paisley's hardline Democratic Unionists and the Sinn Fein leaders. At St. Andrews in October 2006, he succeeded. Admirers praised his statesmanship—as he himself had said in April 1998, "I feel the hand of history upon our shoulders." However, there was a cost. Blair was too worried that the IRA would return to violence to put pressure on them to disarm and formally renounce terrorism. The resulting tensions polarized opinion, fatally undermining the moderate nationalist SDLP and moderate Ulster Unionist Party, both of whom had always rejected violence, and increasing the political power of both Sinn Fein and the Paisleyites. These groups would dominate the new and lavishly funded power-sharing authority—hardly a model of liberal democracy. Gangsterism continued in Ulster's sectarian ghettos, but England could resume its normal indifference to Irish affairs, and Blair show off the solution as an example to the world of how to bring peace to a divided society. In all, some 3,500 people had been killed during the whole period of the Troubles, about 2,000 of them by the Republicans, 1,000 by Loyalists, and 500 by the security forces.[22]

New Labour thus set in motion profound changes in the British constitution mostly as a response to political problems outside England, but without having any precise end in view.[23] What had in Asquith's day been called "home rule all round" met—as it had then—the problem of England, and what was named the "West Lothian question," after the Westminster member for that constituency, Tam Dalyell. He had argued that the principle of allowing "my voting on issues affecting West Bromwich but not West Lothian" was in the long run unsustainable. English MPs would cease to share in the domestic government of Scotland, Wales and Northern Ireland, but Scottish, Welsh and Ulster MPs would continue to share in the domestic government of England, and might hold the balance of power between parties.[24] At first the problem was ignored by the English public. But as the Scots mysteriously acquired much-trumpeted advantages in health care and university education—with over 20 percent more being spent on public services per head—the disadvantages of being a nation without a state began to dawn. The idea of a self-governing England was bizarre, even alarming. But it became a possibility that the English might have to face if the Scots so decided.

This problem was inherited by New Labour's successors, the 2010 coalition government. In 2011 the Scottish National Party won an overall majority in the Scottish parliament and announced a referendum on full independence in 2014, the terms of which were agreed with the Conservative Prime Minister, David Cameron, by the SNP leader and Scottish First Minister, Alex Salmond. Whether this would produce a bold vote for independence or lead to further negotiations for autonomy within the United Kingdom (dubbed "devo-max"), it would inevitably have historic consequences for England too, in finance, law, defence, citizenship, the economy, foreign affairs and party politics—all subjects that remained politically taboo in Westminster, where politicians hoped that if ignored Scottish independence might go away.

The operations of the state were also being changed over a longer term by the implications of binding European commitments, especially under the European Convention on Human Rights and under European Union law. These have changed the role of the courts, causing them to apply broad principles, balancing "competing values," and making "value choices"[25] in the Roman law tradition, rather than invoking precedent, scrutinizing the precise wording of legislation, or interpreting "the will of Parliament" as sovereign, as in the Common Law approach. The European Communities Act (1972) had stated that all existing and future Community law was in certain areas binding on United Kingdom courts, with supremacy over domestic law if the two conflicted. Courts are required (except in areas where the United Kingdom has negotiated an "opt-out") to interpret Acts of Parliament in a manner consistent with European Union law. Judges have in effect ordered the government to disobey an Act of Parliament where they considered that it clashed with EU law.[26] In 1998 Labour passed the Human Rights Act, making the European Convention on Human Rights (initiated by the Tories at the end of the Second World War and reluctantly ratified by a suspicious Attlee government in 1951) part of domestic law. British courts were given powers to interpret British statutes in accordance with the Convention, to "take into account" judgments of the European Court of Human Rights at Strasbourg, and if necessary declare British statutes "incompatible" with the Convention, while, as a compromise with parliamentary sovereignty, leaving the final authority at Westminster—at least nominally.[27] Although not entirely clear in their constitutional implications, these two Acts fundamentally challenged the unquestioned sovereignty of "the Crown in Parliament" and the ancient principle that no parliament could bind its successors. Some legal experts even argue that the law (in practice the courts), not Parliament, is sovereign in some areas,[28] and that the Human Rights Act cannot legally be overruled or repealed. It has therefore been called "the cornerstone of the new constitution."[29] In the words of an Appeal Court judgment:

> Our constitution is dominated by the sovereignty of Parliament. But Parliamentary sovereignty is no longer, if it ever was, absolute . . . Step by step, gradually but surely, the English principle of the absolute legislative sovereignty of Parliament which Dicey derived from Coke and Blackstone is being qualified.[30]

The public became most aware of these developments in some highly publicized human rights cases, where Strasbourg or British judges ruled that some foreign criminal or suspected terrorist could neither be expelled nor detained. At a lower and more day-to-day level, civil servants cooperated directly and often informally with institutions in other EU countries. So did local authorities, especially those seeking EU funds. So did universities. This has been called "the Europeanization of UK government" and has quietly "transformed" its character by the adoption of EU criteria and regulations.[31]

Europhilia was Blair's instinctive position: "Europe is today the only route through which Britain can . . . maintain its historic role as a global player."[32] Like some earlier prime ministers, he wanted to be both a "bridge" between America and Europe and part of the inner core of European leadership. Consequently, Economic and Monetary Union (EMU), leading to a single currency, was a natural step—"not just about our economy, but our destiny." Giving greater independence to the Bank of England to control inflation and set interest rates soon after it took office—one of New Labour's most significant economic reforms—was aimed at preparing the way. However, as previous prime ministers had discovered, the European "route" contained unexpected twists. The next important stage in European integration was the single currency, the euro, agreed formally by EU governments in 1999, with money in circulation from 1 January 2002, and with a European Central Bank established in 1998 by the Amsterdam Treaty. But in 1997 the decision about whether Britain would adopt the euro had been put off, and the Treasury drew up "five economic tests" which effectively gave Brown a veto over membership—one of his most important decisions, though seemingly an unpremeditated one. By staying outside the Eurozone, which after the 2007 financial crash entered a long-term slump, Britain was put on a diverging path from the EU "core," with some future renegotiation of Britain's position inevitable.

## RAINBOW NATION

*We have the chance in this century to achieve an open world, an open economy, and an open global society with unprecedented opportunity for people and business.*

Tony Blair, January 2000

*Labour must change its approach to immigration . . . we were too dazzled by globalisation and too sanguine about its price.*

Ed Miliband, Labour leader, June 2012

After 2004 occurred the biggest influx of immigration in English history, causing the fastest increase in population ever recorded.[33] Blair told the Confederation of British Industry in April 2004 that "there are half a million vacancies in our job market and our strong and growing economy needs migration to fill these vacancies." The number of foreign-born workers doubled between 1997 and 2007 to 3.8 million as Britain fuelled an economic boom by borrowing people cheaply from abroad just as it was borrowing money. However, the economic effect of immigration is broadly neutral: the population and hence what is usually called "the size of the economy" is increased, but not per capita wealth.[34] New arrivals were running at about 500,000 a year in the early 2000s, those from outside the EU mostly with student visas. By 2008 there were over a million EU immigrant workers in Britain, and about 2 million from the rest of the world. It is mostly an English, not a British, phenomenon: over 90 percent of immigrants came to England. It is also mainly an urban, and above all a London, phenomenon: 38 percent of all immigrants lived there, and in 2010 nearly two-thirds of children born in London had one or both parents born overseas.[35] A different kind of concentration was in the industrial towns of the Midlands and north, where manual workers, typically from rural Pakistan and Bangladesh, had arrived to work in factories and service occupations from the 1960s onwards. They formed relatively poor and socially excluded—and self-excluding—Muslim communities.[36] Much of rural and small-town England was little affected apart from acquiring a new variety of ethnic restaurants and shops. But the overall statistics are eloquent. By 2008 one in nine of the UK population—around 7 million people—and one in three of the population of London had been born overseas; about a quarter of all state school children were from ethnic minorities.[37] England became as ethnically diverse as America or France, though the change happened much more quickly than in other EU countries except Spain and Italy, whose experience was comparable with that of Britain.[38]

From the eighteenth century until the 1980s, more people had left England than had arrived, with enormous impact on several parts of the world. The only large-scale immigration into England in modern times, apart from the brief Huguenot influx in the 1680s, was from other parts of the British Isles (such as the Irish in Liverpool). Immigration from further afield since the Second World War has led to great cultural enrichment, and some social problems. From the 1950s there was a growing trickle from Commonwealth countries, mainly from the Caribbean and the Indian sub-continent, and a small influx of about 27,000 Asian refugees from Kenya in the 1970s—one of the empire diasporas. This caused predictable friction, occasional violence and some political controversy, of which that surrounding Enoch Powell in 1966 was the most notorious. A sign of change in the opposite direction came in the 1990s in the case of Stephen Lawrence, an eighteen-year-old Londoner of Caribbean family murdered by racist thugs in April 1993, and whose family's long pursuit of justice and criticism of the Metropolitan Police won public sympathy and official recognition.

The social realities of immigration in England were little different from those elsewhere: hard work and rapid social mobility for some; persistent inequality for others; some xenophobic conflict at the grass roots marked by sporadic outbreaks of alarming disorder. Although the state education system, based on neighbourhood comprehensive schools, was not well conceived for promoting social integration or mobility, several ethnic groups (such as Hong Kong Chinese and Kenyan Asians) were more successful at school than the native average; others were on a level with the unskilled white working class.[39] Indians, Chinese and Pakistanis matched or exceeded the native population in buying their own homes.[40]

Most immigrants until the 1980s had historic and cultural connections with Britain—language, sports culture, and for West Indians Christianity. This facilitated integration—there were no "substantive moral and political conditions attached to becoming 'British.'"[41] Even the English language (most obviously an issue for Asian women) was not required. When the Home Office suggested in 2001 that this might be a condition of citizenship, the Joint Council for the Welfare of Immigrants dismissed it as "linguistic colonialism."[42] The middle-class left became instinctive supporters of immigration and multiculturalism. Business agreed. Legal equality was accepted, discrimination was outlawed, and—unlike in France, for example—the standing of minority "communities" and their "leaders" was recognized in a pragmatic attempt to create what has been called multicultural nationalism based on Britishness—though, as we shall see, self-contained identities are rapidly breaking down.[43] The multi-cultural approach, drawing on traditional ideas of individual liberty, religious pluralism and symbolic loyalty to the Crown, has been accused of perpetuating and even creating ethnic divisions, while others have regarded it as a necessary and humane form of integration. France, in contrast, saw interminable political and legal battles over women's dress, in which issues of national identity, political doctrines, race, religion and gender were entangled—questions that the English largely ignored.

By the late 1980s net immigration was at fairly low levels, roughly 50,000 per year. Anti-immigrant politics remained marginal, unlike in several other European countries. By the early 1990s only 5 percent of the population considered it a major problem. In the early 2000s ethnic minorities described themselves as "British," a political identity, rather than adopting the cultural identities of English, Scottish or Welsh, though this too may be changing as the growing number of mixed-race adults are more likely to see themselves as "English."[44]

British governments had long supported "enlargement" of the EU for diplomatic, economic and political reasons—it was hoped it would lead to a looser union. The British public was keener on it than the German or the French. So when eastern European states acceded in 2004, the British government agreed to free movement into Britain, unlike France and Germany, whose more vocal Europeanism did not extend to encouraging immigration. The right to free movement and settlement within the EU led to an unprecedented two-way movement. Many retired or semi-retired Britons confidently bought property in Spain, Portugal, Italy and France, where thousands unashamedly claimed social-security benefits. There were also over 300,000 with jobs in other EU countries. Far more came in the other direction, mainly young workers, from potato-pickers to post-doctoral researchers. Officials predicted 5,000–13,000 per year from eastern Europe: over 600,000 came in five years; by 2012 there were some 700,000 Poles resident in the U.K.[45] From some western European countries the rise was comparable: the number of French in England tripled in a decade, reaching some 300,000 by 2004, and there were roughly as many Germans.[46] At least one young French woman was delighted to discover that in London she could hold two undeclared jobs and receive housing benefit and free language lessons.[47] Some nationalities were present in a range of occupations from waiters to bankers, and established an institutional presence. The French in London had clubs, shops, newspapers, a radio station and a growing number of schools. The Poles were visible by sheer numbers, and Polish groceries and church services became familiar in many cities. The French and the Poles were the most industrious (85 and 86 percent, respectively, had jobs, though the Poles earned less); the Americans and Old Commonwealth citizens were the richest; the 100,000 Somali refugees the poorest (and although only slightly poorer than the Poles, ten times more dependent on social housing).[48]

The biggest sustained new element in immigration—about two-thirds of the total, and over 80 percent of net migration—came from outside the EU.[49] The government increased the number of work permits from about 20,000 per year in 1994 to around 150,000 per year (including renewals) from 2007–8.[50] It also relaxed controls on people applying to come to marry or study, many of whom remained and were then entitled to bring in dependants. In a later reversal of policy, legal non-EU immigration was severely cut between 2008 and 2009. But embarkation controls (recording those leaving the country) had been phased out between 1994 and 1998, making it impossible to keep track of whether those admitted for a fixed period had left.

Migrants into the EU made their way towards those countries offering economic betterment, of which England was at this time the most attractive, due to its booming economy, use of the main international language and loose regulation. The boldest congregated in a shanty town at Sangatte, near Calais, to stow away on Eurostar trains. No government proved capable of controlling, or even counting, such illegal entry: in 2005 the government "guessed" that it totalled between 300,000 and 600,000 people.[51] Several were working at the Home Office's immigration department in 2007, and others guarding official cars for the Metropolitan Police—even, it was reported, the Prime Minister's.[52]

Between 1999 and 2005 asylum-seekers added a further element. Many came from the disturbed Muslim regions of the Horn of Africa, Iraq and Afghanistan, and arrived "poor, unskilled, shell-shocked, and unable to speak English"; many were illiterate in their own languages.[53] Asylum was a tempting route for economic migrants too, for it gave strong legal protection. Blair promised to introduce identity cards and claimed that "significant numbers of economic migrants have been arriving in the UK, destroying their documentation and then trying to claim asylum—often by pretending to be from a different country to that from which they have actually come."[54] The annual number of asylum-seekers peaked in 2002 at 84,000—comparable with the level in Holland, Sweden and Germany. By 2010 applications in Britain had fallen to 23,000—though people granted asylum elsewhere in the EU (for example, Somalis in the Netherlands) could subsequently move to England.

The less skilled among the native population experienced competition for jobs, and wages were kept down. Between 2005 and 2007, 540,000 incomers found jobs and 270,000 British workers lost them.[55] There is no direct connection: foreign workers often had superior skills, education, flexibility and motivation, and accepted work either beyond the reach of or unattractive to natives. Yet the ability to import skills lessened the need to improve education and training for the poor, one of England's worst social and economic failures, generator of multiracial ghettoes of poverty and alienation.

The effects of immigration—whether of billionaire Russians or penniless Somalis—on house prices, levels of inequality, school performance and crime are difficult to assess, for there are clearly contradictory effects. Young urban blacks are disproportionately involved in gang violence, and hence are disproportionately in prison; but poor whites are overall more criminal.[56] Some new crimes appeared, including domestic slavery, "people trafficking," "honour killings," "sexual grooming," a few atrocious murders of child "witches" and of course terrorist conspiracies. Some groups, especially from the Balkans, acquired a fearsome reputation for organized crime. On the other hand, religious practice, including Evangelical and Pentecostal Christianity, was boosted by immigrant communities, especially in London: 57 percent of all young British church-goers were Londoners.[57] There are many unquantifiable advantages of diversity, making England and particularly London a unique microcosm of world cultures, fertile ground for innovation, and creating or renewing valuable international links. In terms of youth culture, it has been suggested, some part of being young and English was about being black.[58] The accent of cool youth took on a Caribbean lilt—a comparable phenomenon could be heard in Paris and Berlin. Seen from abroad, the capital for some was a dangerous "Londonistan"; for others it was the model of the successful global city of the future, the most exciting place on the planet.

The advantages and disadvantages of immigration were unevenly shared. The middle classes, both employers and consumers, gained: official pronouncements stressed the role of immigrants in restaurants and the arts. The poor, in areas of high immigration, felt a sense of injustice and dispossession—notoriously dismissed by Gordon Brown as "bigoted." A study of the East End found that the main grievance was a sense of unfairness, as local resources, especially housing, were disposed of by higher authority indifferent to existing local claims.[59] In political terms, many poor whites tended to drop out, or some drifted towards thuggish fringe parties such as the British National Party and the English Defence League. Far larger numbers, from all parties, started voting for UKIP, which began to base its campaign on uncontrolled immigration from the EU. Immigrant groups, especially Muslims, overwhelmingly supported

Labour, which had 68 percent of all ethnic minority votes. The upwardly mobile entrepreneurial elements, especially those with Chinese, Indian or Kenyan Asian roots, shifted slowly towards the Conservatives; Sikhs and Hindus were the most evenly divided between Labour and Tory.[60]

Muslim religious dissidence was first signalled by demonstrations in 1989 against blasphemy in a novel by the London-based Salman Rushdie—a dramatic challenge to multiculturalism from the respectable older generation of Pakistani immigrants. A different kind of alienation among younger Muslims grew during the 1990s and 2000s out of tensions between generations, between men and women, and with a host society seen as bewildering, decadent and tempting.[61] For self-obsessed young men, born-again religious extremism gave an escape from failure, frustration, guilt and complexity. It provided a glamorous identity, and a way of breaking the trammels of family and community, not least arranged marriages.[62] Gaols, as in all Western countries, became hotbeds of conversion to a religion offering uncomplicated male comradeship: in France, over 60 percent of prisoners are Muslims; in Holland, 20 percent; in Britain, 11 percent.[63] Student Islamic societies too were recruiting grounds: hardcore terrorists had qualifications in such subjects as computer science, business studies, engineering and medicine—vocational subjects posing no intellectual challenge to fundamentalism.[64] Anger was stoked by external events: wars in the Balkans, Chechnya, Afghanistan, Iraq and Somalia, and by vicious sectarian conflicts between Shia and Sunni and liberals and reactionaries which spread across much of the Muslim world. These were intensified by the "Arab Spring," beginning in Tunisia in December 2010 and spreading to Egypt and Libya. It degenerated into festering conflict in North Africa and a terrible civil war in Syria, beginning in March–April 2011, which devastated the country and drew in foreign religious fanatics. While many British Muslims became involved in providing medical and welfare assistance, thousands of others—British-born, immigrants and converts—joined well-funded extremist movements at home and abroad. Hundreds went to fight for jihadi groups in Africa and Syria. Many more were ambivalent in their attitudes to English society and the state.

The official response had long been to hope that multiculturalism and tolerance would defuse conflict. Nothing was done to prevent militant groups from organizing around certain mosques, cultural centres, student societies and newspapers. Foreign critics decried "Londonistan," but much of this activity was legitimate and accorded with the English tradition of political asylum. But there was a terrorist penumbra. British participation in the invasions of Afghanistan and Iraq, seen as attacks on

Muslims, increased the danger: "Anyone who is voting for Tony Blair," said one convert, "would be a legitimate target."[65] Plotters included refugees from Eritrea, Somalia and Ethiopia, an Iraqi doctor from Cambridge, a would-be male model, an aspiring cricketer and two dim-witted converts who failed to blow themselves up on an aircraft and in a café. Thus proliferated over a generation an underworld of violent religious conspiracy unseen since the Stuarts. Over several generations, English society will have to struggle to make communities now significantly penetrated by such radicalism fully part of itself.

The more general picture, however, is one of ethnic and racial mixing in social and family relations. Education is one factor, especially for young people of Indian and Pakistani origin: those with degrees are tending increasingly to marry into the white middle class and move into the commuter suburbs of London and the other great cities. Among those officially designated "Caribbean," between a half and a third have white partners, especially in the younger age groups: consequently, there are now twice as many children of Caribbean and white parents as of two Caribbean parents. Similar trends are emerging among newer immigrant groups: a considerable minority of children of Polish mothers have African or Asian fathers. In short, Britain already has about the same proportion of mixed-race children as the United States, despite the latter's much longer multi-racial history. Moreover, surveys indicate that adults of mixed parentage tend to see themselves not as part of a minority community, or even as British, but as English—"the identity of the comfortably assimilated."[66]

## BITTER WARS OF PEACE

*We have learned twice before in this century that appeasement does not work . . . War is an imperfect instrument for righting humanitarian distress; but armed force is sometimes the only means of dealing with dictators.*

Tony Blair, Chicago, April 1999

*I've had two wars—Kosovo and Afghanistan—and I think I can claim we got it right.*

Tony Blair, July 2002[67]

New Labour's foreign policy was intended to be more principled, assertive and effective than that of Major's Tories, restoring relations with the

United States shaken by failures in the Balkans, and standing at the centre of European affairs. Blair announced a new ethical, post-modern strategy freed from traditional national interest: "In the end values and interests merge . . . The spread of our values makes us safer."[68] The aim was to do good and feel good. Aid to Africa and action on climate change were emphasized. Blair has claimed the legacy of Gladstone, but he was more the heir of Palmerston, combining idealism, bombast and military action— five times in six years. Lacking Palmerston's gunboats, he tried "positioning," staying close to America as "a friend and an ally that will stand with you, work with you, fashion with you the design of a future."[69] Britain participated in a U.S.-led bombing campaign in Iraq in November 1998, to damage the country's weapons-manufacturing ability. In March 1999, following Serb aggression in Kosovo, mainly American NATO forces began bombing Serbia, and ground forces, led by Britain, France and Russia, occupied Kosovo to impose peace. The process was far from bloodless, yet it was generally regarded as a success for "humanitarian intervention." A small British force sent to Sierra Leone helped to stop atrocious civil conflict in 2000. Blair had succeeded by boldness, overruling the caution of experts.

The "Twin Towers" outrage in New York on 11 September 2001, organized by an Islamist organization, al-Qaeda, killed almost 3,000 people, and precipitated a "war on terrorism." Blair expressed British solidarity with the United States, and British forces joined an American attack on terrorist camps in Afghanistan. The Taliban religious dictatorship in Afghanistan was overthrown and al-Qaeda leaders dispersed. Blair worried that "rogue states" might arm terrorists with "weapons of mass destruction" (WMDs): "Post-9/11 . . . you no longer wait for the thing to happen. You go out actively and try to stop it." He feared being booed in the streets as "the Stanley Baldwin who did nothing."[70] The official view was that in combating terrorists it was better to fight "in their backyard than in ours, at a time and place of our choosing, not theirs."[71]

Iraq's Baathist regime under Saddam Hussein had a loathsome record of aggression and domestic atrocity, including the use of chemical weapons. There was evidence that it wanted to develop nuclear weapons. United Nations sanctions, aimed at preventing Iraqi rearmament, were breaking down. Following the 9/11 attacks, America was ready to act against "rogue states" and hoped that this would facilitate a general solution to the problems of the Middle East. In April 2002 Blair privately assured President George W. Bush that Britain would support American military action to remove the Iraqi dictator, Saddam Hussein, if America sought United Nations approval.[72]

This was the most controversial foreign-policy decision since Suez, and with hindsight the most gratuitous blunder since the Boer War. Policy was made by Blair and his entourage in a whirl of boldness, fantasy, incompetence and "spin." The ambition, as usual, was to be the bridge between America and Europe, internationalizing the operation, and urging progress towards an Israeli-Palestinian peace. Decisions were made in daily phone calls to Washington. The Foreign Office was by-passed and its legal advice given short shrift. In stark contrast with the Falklands war, the Cabinet was docile, reassured by occasional "unscripted" briefings.[73] Between April and September 2002 it did not discuss the matter. Its Defence and Overseas Policy Committee and its Intelligence Committee did not meet. Blair later suggested that Cabinet ministers must have known what was going on from reading the newspapers.[74]

Most intelligence services and some United Nations weapons inspectors believed that Iraq had been trying to develop new weapons, though no one knew how successful they had been. Evidence—aptly described as "sexed up"—was published in September 2002 from a variety of sources to persuade the public that there was a "current, serious and growing threat." The process later led to the suicide on 17 July 2003 of a civil servant, David Kelly, who had communicated his misgivings to a young BBC journalist, Andrew Gilligan. Blair assured the House of Commons that some WMDs could be ready for use in forty-five minutes; newspapers reported that they threatened British forces in Cyprus ("Brits 45 Minutes from Doom"[75]). Most of the press and broadcast media accepted the government's case. "Blair was a sincere deceiver," concluded a close observer. "He told the truth about what he believed; he lied about the strength of the evidence for that belief."[76] After the invasion, no such weapons were ever found: the Iraqi regime had stopped production and destroyed stocks, but had kept this secret for reasons of prestige and security.

In January 2003, 400,000 American and 46,000 British troops began assembling in the Persian Gulf; of the front-line troops, about one-third were British.[77] Unless Saddam Hussein permitted unlimited freedom to United Nations weapons inspectors to search for his WMDs, these troops would inevitably be used. The main European allies opposed invasion. The French, at first wavering, came under strong German and Russian pressure, and turned into the most vocal opponents of the war, engaging in a struggle with Britain to influence the UN Security Council over the justification for military action. On 30 January 2003 a public letter of support for American policy was signed by Blair and seven, and eventually fifteen, European prime ministers, splitting the EU. A French commentator described the declaration as being "written on English dictation."[78] On

10 March the French president, Jacques Chirac, announced that "whatever the circumstances" France would veto any UN resolution for military action "because there are no grounds for waging war in order to . . . disarm Iraq."[79] Whitehall seized on this as a way of escaping a UN vote, arguing that if the French had decided in advance to veto any resolution, then the process was nullified—an argument the Attorney General advised was without any basis in law.[80] The Americans, aware of Blair's domestic political difficulties, suggested that Britain might stay out of the fight, but he insisted on taking part in the invasion.

The war aroused impassioned and variegated domestic opposition. In February 2003 as many as a million people of all ages and backgrounds marched in London to protest. A third of Labour MPs rebelled in a Commons vote on 18 March, eventually won by the government with Conservative support. The Liberal Democrats denounced the war as illegal because the UN Security Council had not explicitly authorized an invasion. Yet two-thirds of the public trusted Blair's arguments, as did the Tories. Hostilities began on 20 March. Euphoria created by a quick victory in April 2003, when the coalition forces were greeted as liberators, soon dissipated. Iraq descended into violent sectarian chaos, for which the liberators were unprepared. British troops, intending to win over "hearts and minds" and hand out sweets to children, found themselves under attack, and over the whole intervention 179 lost their lives. Scandals concerning serious mistreatment of Iraqi prisoners, mostly by Americans but some by British troops, tarnished claims to moral rectitude, and years later led to embarrassing and controversial prosecutions of British soldiers. The cost in Iraqi lives due to direct Western military action, and even more to the internecine violence that followed, was undeniably huge: serious estimates suggested between 110,000 and 120,000 over eight years, with some estimates of "excess deaths" much higher.[81] This does not prove that it would have been better to leave Saddam Hussein triumphant, as he had already been a cause of even greater loss of life. Policy is frequently a choice between evils. Yet the least that can be said is that Blair personally incited, and attached Britain to, an ill-conceived and ill-executed American policy with terrible human consequences; and that he persuaded Parliament and the public to support him by arguments that were, to put it mildly, disingenuous. The perils of "sofa government," and New Labour's addiction to "spin," were patent. The best that can be said of Blair's conduct is that it was no worse than the reckless and illegal conduct of Eden in 1956 over Suez, in the heyday of Establishment policy-making. Significantly, unlike Eden, he did not resign: Labour MPs would growl but not bite.

British forces fought simultaneously in Iraq and Afghanistan, where operations, expected to be mere peacekeeping, became bitter, intractable and lengthy. The aim in Afghanistan had been to replace a Taliban dictatorship with a progressive democratic government. The ambition was steadily eroded to that of establishing any kind of government that would not actively harbour terrorists so that troops and equipment could be withdrawn during 2013–14, and politicians claim success. Leaving aside arguments about wisdom and morality, the British force proved to be overstretched and underequipped. Casualties were very low by the standards of most wars—446 deaths between 2001 and November 2013—but were very present in the public mind. Emotions were externalized in a spontaneous public ritual that developed in 2007 in the small town of Wootton Bassett, where people stood in silent tribute as coffins flown back from Afghanistan were driven away from nearby RAF Lyneham. Defence was one part of the public sector in which Labour was parsimonious, cutting the budget by over 20 percent during the 1990s to 2.5 percent of GDP—the lowest proportion since 1930. This was still high by European standards, but no comparable country was militarily so active. Men died due to lack of armoured vehicles and helicopters. A coroner described this as "inexcusable," and senior officers criticized the government publicly—unheard of since Lloyd George was attacked during the First World War. The Iraq and Afghanistan wars were estimated to have cost Britain over £40bn by 2013—several thousand pounds per family.[82] Some of the cost was covered by raising money by Private Finance Initiative contracts, a disguised form of loan, "the true costs of which will become apparent only in years to come."[83] The army, with a large part of its strength diverted to Afghanistan, by 2006 had lost control of its main Iraqi position in Basra to Shia "militias"—at one point it had only 500 infantrymen in a city of 2 million and signed an unpublicized truce with the militants. It had to be urgently supported by the Americans, some of whom made little secret of their impatience. In Helmand province in Afghanistan, where around 10,000 men were deployed—far more than in any of the Victorian campaigns—the army barely held its own in a Sisyphean struggle against an omnipresent and largely invisible enemy. It was like trying to cultivate an allotment in the jungle, said one disillusioned diplomat.[84] A symbol of its efforts might be the huge hydro-electric turbine laboriously convoyed through hostile territory to the Kajaki dam in 2008 but which could not be installed because of continued enemy presence. Uniquely in Europe, the British public—perhaps hardened by history—remained gloomily accepting of the human and financial costs: more British soldiers were killed than the combined total from all the other European contingents serving in Afghanistan, most of which remained in support roles. Yet the Iraq and Afghanistan tribulations destroyed the habitual trust in government honesty and competence among the British people. It also weakened the "special relationship" with America that Blair had intended to strengthen by making the public far more reluctant to endorse it. A later sign of this was the cross-party refusal of the House of Commons in August 2013 to support the coalition government in taking military action in Syria—a decision attracting general public approval. This vote in effect prevented a joint British, American and French retaliatory strike against the Assad regime for using chemical weapons against rebels, and caused some commentators to wonder whether the British public had turned permanently against what a former Foreign Secretary, Douglas Hurd, had famously called "punching above our weight in the world."[85]

The Afghan and Iraq interventions, as some had warned, made Britain not safer from terrorism but more exposed to it. On 7 July 2005 (as the G8 international summit was in session in Scotland, and the day after the 2012 Olympic Games had been assigned to London) four suicide bombs were exploded in the London Tube and on a bus, killing or injuring over 750 people. Three of the killers, all born in England, were from the same Pakistani suburb of Leeds and had qualifications in business studies or sports science; the fourth was a part-Jamaican convert. There followed several loosely connected bomb attempts, some only days after "7/7." All were aimed at ordinary people: on buses, in a nightclub (to kill "slags"), at shopping centres and at Glasgow airport. All failed in their object or were prevented by MI5 and the police (who mistakenly shot an innocent Brazilian in the London Tube a fortnight after the July bombing). Although similar conspiracies were widespread in Europe, England had become their centre: in 2007, 203 people were arrested on suspicion of terrorist offences, compared with 201 for the whole Continent. Most had links with Pakistan.[86] Despite fears of an anti-Muslim backlash, the English took all this phlegmatically. Many were troubled by plans for identity cards and restrictions such as "control orders" (a form of house arrest), which the courts in any case were reluctant to enforce. Common Law systems gave governments fewer powers than Roman law systems such as in France, Italy and Germany. MI5 and MI6 expanded their staffs and widened their activities, but were pursued by accusations of complicity in mistreatment of terrorist prisoners abroad. In the medium term, England's tranquillity depends in large part on events in the Arab world, Iran, Afghanistan, Africa and Pakistan, and their impact on Muslim communities here. On 22 May 2013 an off-duty soldier, Fusilier Lee Rigby, was publicly murdered in Woolwich, in the presence of shocked passers-by and partly shown on television. The killers were two Londoners of lower-middle-class Nigerian Christian origin, with a history of drugs, gangs and alienation—typical converts to Muslim extremism.[87] They posed as "soldiers of Allah" punishing Britain for its wars against Muslims. As new conflicts involving Muslims as aggressors or victims were breaking out from West Africa to Burma, the prospect was not reassuring.

### GOING FOR BROKE

*The spending plans that we set must ensure sustainable finances over the whole economic cycle—rigorous financial discipline that, together with monetary stability, ends once and for all the boom and bust that for 30 years has undermined stability.*
Gordon Brown, House of Commons, 11 June 1998[88]

The period from the mid-1990s to 2007 was a classic "boom and bust," creating the worst financial crisis since 1929, a world recession, disaster for several countries, and financial and political crisis for the Eurozone. Britain was exceptionally hard hit: after a period of growth that made it the richest large country in Europe, its bank losses due to the crisis were equivalent to 20.9 percent of GDP—more than three times the United States figure and nearly ten times the EU average. The immediate charge to the taxpayer was £117bn, though the final net loss was predicted as anywhere between £140bn (around £2,300 per head of the population) and £2.4bn (only £40 per head).[89] A later estimate of the total damage suggested that Britain had suffered considerably more than France and America and twice as badly as Germany, though less than the weakest Eurozone countries, Greece, Ireland and Italy.[90] Responsibility for the crisis, and responses to it, became the principal subject of politics.

The roots of the 2007 crash went back two decades, to the end of the Cold War, to China's sudden embrace of globalization, and the trade and financial imbalances that resulted from its huge export surpluses, due in part to its authoritarian domestic system which limited home consumption. Britain, America and several other countries ran large trade deficits, covered by cheap loans from China's surpluses—a classic forerunner of banking crises. Regularly at meetings of politicians and central bankers, worries were expressed that this imbalance was unsustainable in the long run. But, as Keynes had sagely remarked, in the long run we are all dead. In the meantime, banks, businesses, governments and ordinary citizens in many countries wallowed in cheap money.

The crash exposed the special risks run by countries with large financial sectors. None was larger than the City of London, which had built on its three-century dominance, rejuvenated by the 1986 "Big Bang," and benefiting from its openness to foreign participation and dominance of the European time zone. Gordon Brown boasted that over 40 percent of the world's foreign equities were traded in London, and over 30 percent of the world's currency exchanges took place there—more than in New York and Tokyo combined. By 2007 it had 550 international banks and 170 global securities houses. London bankers' bonuses tripled from 2001 to 2008, reaching £16bn, equal to half the defence budget.

Britain was increasingly consuming more than it produced, as public spending and borrowing shot up, and jobs moved away from exporting sectors and industry and into the public sector and construction. Industrial employment fell faster between 1997 and 2005 in Britain than anywhere else in Europe. The high rate of sterling since the mid-1990s made exports expensive and imports cheap.[91] Part of the huge resulting trade deficit was covered by invisible earnings from the financial and professional sector (banking, insurance, law, accountancy, consultancy), the great success of the boom years. But much of the gap was bridged by borrowing, whether buying Chinese electronics on credit cards or villas in Tuscany on second mortgages. Much of the money ultimately came from foreign banks. A symbol of the age was the diamond-encrusted skull manufactured in 2007 by the entrepreneurial artist and celebrity Damien Hirst, denizen of Blair's "Cool Britannia."[92]

New Labour's claim to public gratitude was its huge increase in spending: it was determined to remedy "underfunding" in the NHS, build new schools, create jobs, expand university education, and reduce poverty. More than 70 percent of the gains from tax changes and benefit increases went to the bottom half of the income distribution, and the incomes of the very poorest rose by over 10 percent.[93] In the north of England, growth in employment was mostly owed to public spending, which accounted for some 60 percent of economic output and 75 percent of new jobs.[94] This contrasted spectacularly with unpopular "Tory cuts," which had stabilized public spending, projected a balanced budget, but allowed inequality to grow. New Labour had a different feeling about public "investment," beginning with the Millennium Dome (over £800m, mostly from the Lottery[95]), and ending with the Olympic Games (over £9bn). Gordon Brown was hailed as a new Gladstone, but policy was the opposite of Gladstonian: it regarded increasing spending as desirable in itself. Blair announced he wanted to raise it to average EU levels—the first government to define success by cost rather than outcome. He boasted to the European parliament on 23 June 2005 that he had "increased investment in our public services more than any other European country"—no empty boast, for spending rose ten times faster than in Germany.[96] Much of this "investment" money went on increasing public-sector numbers, pay and pensions. By 2007, 28 percent of all workers (7.5 million people, 70 percent of them women) were directly or indirectly paid by the state.[97] Subsidies to the arts increased. Even academic stipends rose gratifyingly. This was popular and painless at a time of boom. The Tory opposition, fearing to be what one of its leaders called "the nasty party," promised to match Labour's spending if re-elected. The budget deficit rose rapidly towards 3 percent—the maximum permitted under EU rules—and more was concealed by the Private Finance Initiative, a system of disguised loans by which public projects (such as hospitals and schools) were paid for by private funding and then leased to the public, sometimes on onerous terms. The French president, Jacques Chirac, scoffed in 2005 that "over the years the English have wrecked their agriculture and then their industry. Now they only survive due to property inflation, financial speculation and their oil and gas."[98]

The government spent much on relieving poverty. Child poverty was brought below the OECD average, despite a high level of single-parent families.[99] Yet England remained unequal, even increasingly so. There were several reasons. In times of economic expansion, inequality grows. Paradoxically, stagnation, recession and war are good for equality. The boom in house prices from the mid-1990s, faster than in any other country, created a huge disparity in wealth between house-owners and the rest. Inequality was worst in what came to be called, in quasi-Victorian language, the "underclass," ravaged by generations of unemployment, broken families, teenage pregnancies, poor education, and lamentable health and life expectancy, including a level of obesity that by 2011 made the British the fattest people in Europe.[100] A cause of persistent inequality was the proportion of single mothers without jobs—four times the EU average.[101]

The debate yet again echoed that in the nineteenth century over the Poor Law: were handouts merely encouraging fecklessness and creating dependency? This was because England's welfare system, shaped by the heritage of the Poor Law, was based on universal entitlement. If it offered less it also demanded less than in Continental systems, where benefits were related to contributions, limited in time and conditional on strict tests. In Germany, for example, sickness benefits required approval by state medical officers, unemployment benefits were conditional on retraining, and jobseekers could be directed to employment in other parts of the country.

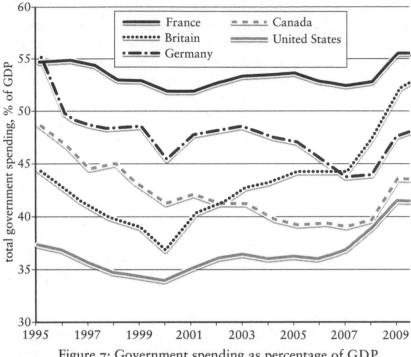

Figure 7: Government spending as percentage of GDP

Inequality was presented—sometimes confusing cause and effect—as the root of nearly all English evils, from obesity and on through teenage pregnancy to carbon emissions.[102] Yet the broad level of income inequality in England, which fell sharply between 1914 and the 1970s, seems to have been fairly stable since,[103] despite an unprecedented influx of poor immigrants on one hand and of the super-rich on the other—London was reported to contain the highest number of multi-millionaires in the world (over 4,000), many of them foreign. The English level of inequality is little different from that in comparable countries. None of the fifty richest people in the world in 2014 was British, though several lived in London.[104] Markedly greater equality, unsurprisingly, is found in small and/or homogeneous countries—Slovenia, Denmark, Finland, Norway, Japan. Diverse, open, undisciplined societies, such as England, Ireland, Italy, France, Australia and the United States, are unequal; but most figure highly in other measures of well-being, such as the Human Development Index.

In these societies, equality depends on levels of employment, and on the effectiveness of state education.[105] Here England had a serious problem by every measure. An Italian think-tank in 2007 placed Britain at the bottom of the list of developed countries in child well-being—admittedly, this was partly on the grounds that they were not more like Italians.[106] Though much money was spent on education by international standards— spending per primary-school pupil increased by over 30 percent from 2000 to 2008—and English children generally enjoyed school, their attainment was at best stagnant while other countries were improving. Labour spent on new buildings, reducing class sizes (popular but ineffective), and increasing numbers and pay of staff (79 percent of the total budget).[107] But poor teaching and ineffective methods remained widespread. Standards had improved only slightly since the 1960s, when the comprehensive system was established.[108] In international comparisons, England was actually regressing. More than one in ten of fifteen- to nineteen-year-olds were not in school, training or employment—comparable with Italy, Turkey and Mexico. Literacy and numeracy were mediocre—17 percent of school leavers were semi-literate and 22 percent innumerate in 2010. The country relied on private education or on immigration for many of its most highly trained people. Four top independent schools sent more pupils to Oxbridge than 2,000 mediocre comprehensives. Only one student from an Anglo-Caribbean family gained an undergraduate place at Oxford in 2009—worse, only seventy-one such students in the whole country achieved three grade As at A Level. Children from poor white families were in the same plight—a less visible scandal: of 80,000 children receiving free school meals, only forty got Oxbridge places in 2011, despite persistent "outreach" efforts by admissions tutors. The most excluded group in English society were poor white boys, of whom only about 12 percent obtained five good GCSEs.[109] Yet there was little public outcry, and teachers' representatives and Labour politicians minimized or even denied the system's failings.[110]

Education was one of the shibboleths that brought out the deep sectarian strain in English politics, making rational discussion almost impossible and reform difficult. Public debate was stuck in the 1950s, revolving round grammar schools and the 11-plus high school entrance examination, oblivious of other countries' experience. Blairite and later Tory reformers tried to subvert the state system by making more schools independent of local-authority and trade union control as "city technology colleges," "specialist schools," "academies," "trust schools" and "free schools." Many of these reintroduced traditional teaching, discipline and academic standards in place of 1960s progressive methods, to give poorer children "the education our richest children receive."[111] Nevertheless, more parents than ever—20 percent in wealthy cosmopolitan London—scrimped to send their children to independent schools, "a huge vote of no confidence in the state."[112]

The National Health Service was the biggest single recipient of new money. It was proverbially described as the world's biggest employer after the Indian railways—in fact, it employed more than the Indian railways and is by far the largest non-military public organization in the world.* Blair promised in 2000 to raise spending to the EU average, beginning with a 30 percent increase over five years. But the NHS had "a very weak capacity to manage or to use new funds in an effective way."[113] For example, an ambitious computerized record system (a pet project of Blair's) failed to work after costing £12bn—more than the Iraq war.[114] The government's political priority was to reduce waiting times for treatment—for example, for cancer, an important and very visible issue: when they came to power, some patients had to wait eighteen months for treatment, and the average was brought down to eighteen weeks during the Labour years, probably their principal achievement. Setting "targets" in such matters, however, risked entrenching a so-called target culture, by which efforts to meet prescribed targets led to neglect of other activities. More fundamental was the problem of managing a vast and sprawling organization, for whose perceived successes and failures politicians were held responsible. Labour ministers repeatedly quoted Bevan's quip about the "dropped bedpan" (see p. 773) and followed contradictory policies on decentralizing administration—creating autonomous "foundation trust" hospitals, for example, but then trying to monitor them in detail. They abolished Tory internal competition (an attempt to manage the NHS by market mechanisms), then reintroduced it under another name. New hospitals, popular with voters, were built using the Private Finance Initiative (PFI), which speeded up the process, but left expensive long-term liabilities: moreover, the NHS had always been too much based on hospitals, and the pressing need was to improve primary care and home care of the growing elderly population. Labour faced particular dilemmas, as creating the NHS was its proudest achievement, and politically it was the representative of the vast NHS workforce, which disliked criticism and interference, abhorred "privatization" (though doctors had always, of course, been private contractors), and saw the only real problem as "underfunding." In 2004, fearing a clash with doctors during the 2005 election campaign, the government blundered into new contracts with general practitioners that abolished their out-of-hours duties and made them the highest paid in Europe—the richest GP received £475,000 per year. By 2010 more than 26,000 NHS employees were paid over £100,000.[115] There were unplanned staff increases of 120,000. Hospital

---

* Exceeded in numbers in 2012 only by the American and Chinese military establishments and the international retailer Walmart, the world's largest company.

consultants increased by 67 percent in ten years, and their average basic pay reached £100,000 (often tripled by extra payments). So of the huge total funding increase nearly half went on pay and increased costs. Productivity fell by over 20 percent. By the end of Labour's term, parts of the NHS were insolvent despite a doubling of their budget. The largesse was popular with voters, who begrudged the NHS nothing. Yet there were repeated scandals. Official inquiries in 2010 and 2013 found that perhaps 600 patients (some estimates were much higher) died needlessly between 2005 and 2008 in Stafford Hospital due to "appalling" and "chaotic" conditions of filth and neglect under a management obsessed with "statistics, benchmarks and action plans": "all those who were present at oral hearings were deeply affected by what they heard"—an echo of the Andover Workhouse scandal in 1845.[116] The complicated emotions that could be aroused were shown when the woman who had exposed the Stafford Hospital's failings after her mother had died there suffered intimidation, her mother's grave was desecrated, and local people demonstrated in support of the hospital.[117] A succession of reports on other hospitals caused public unease concerning safety, yet most people remained suspicious of any attempts to change the system—a tricky political conundrum for later governments. Judged overall, the NHS in some ways improved over the Labour years (new facilities, shorter waiting times) and it provides relatively egalitarian access to treatment—far more so than in France, Germany or Italy.[118] But it also became one of the most expensive primary-care-led health services in the world, over-funded by comparison with similar systems such as in New Zealand, Finland or Spain, which also produced better results.[119]

Increased government spending was managed without raising income tax levels. Brown developed indirect "stealth taxes," as critics called them, such as increasing the tax liability of pension funds; and, wishing to dispel Labour's "tax and spend" reputation, he borrowed and spent instead. He had announced a "golden rule": that "over the [economic] cycle, current spending is covered by revenues," while "investment" could be financed by borrowing.[120] This proved less constraining in practice than it sounded, because the Treasury defined the terms. For the first three years of Labour, Brown kept to a manifesto promise to remain within the Major government's spending and borrowing limits. During Labour's second term, spending and borrowing shot up—indeed, Britain was the only OECD country to increase government borrowing during this period of strong growth, creating a "structural deficit."[121] Furthermore, spiralling Private Finance Initiative liabilities—estimated at several hundred billion pounds—and public-sector pension liabilities did not figure as part of government debt at all.

Cheap money, private and public, was corrupting—not only, of course, in England, which remained (and was recognized abroad as being) relatively, if decreasingly, honest.[122] There had never been a golden age of purity, and national heroes of the past—Gladstone, Lloyd George and Churchill for example—did things as a matter of course that would now seem shady (such as selling honours and accepting gifts). Though MPs were unpaid until 1911, nineteenth-century ministerial salaries were in real terms much higher than today. Nevertheless there was a slipping of standards as people got "filthy rich" not only by private business and banking, in which top salaries and bonuses multiplied, but—rather a novelty, at least since the mid-eighteenth century—by public office. Politicians increased their salaries and allowances, and found other ways of raising their incomes. A succession of ministers and MPs were found to have abused their positions. Resignation under a cloud was nothing new; but return to office thereafter was. Often there was no resignation at all in circumstances where it would once have been obligatory. Civil servants and senior officers moved sideways into well-paid positions with firms they had previously dealt with. MPs, former ministers and local councillors engaged in public relations and paid consultancy; Blair himself set a dazzling example after leaving office. Publicly funded bodies—the BBC, the NHS, government agencies, universities, local government, various "quangos" and even charities—decided they were duty bound to pay senior administrators at or above private-sector rates: the top 5 percent of public-sector earners had pay increases of 51 percent over ten years, and by 2010 some 9,000 earned more than the Prime Minister.[123] Political parties raised money—a murky business in most countries—by "gifts" and "loans" which often implied a quid pro quo. Blair was forced to protest that he was "a pretty straight kind of guy" after giving privileged treatment to an industry that was a large party donor; and later he (along with various advisers) was investigated by the police during a long-drawn-out scandal concerning the selling of honours—the first time a Prime Minister had been questioned in Downing Street, though not of course the first time one had been suspected of this old-established abuse. Vast numbers of honours were given to political allies—all but one of Labour's big donors became lords[124]—and high office was given to unelected people, which Blair explained as due to a dearth of talent among Labour MPs. In short, the dividing line between public office and private interest, first established in the late eighteenth century (see p. 364) faded, in a new political class whose status and livelihood derived almost entirely from political power.

Deference towards politicians had long gone, and now trust went too.

Electoral turnout plummeted. But anger and contempt for politicians as a whole only appeared when details of money previously claimed by MPs in expenses were leaked to the *Daily Telegraph* in May 2009. By the standards of most countries these were trivial (members of the French and European parliaments, for example, automatically received large tax-free allowances regardless of actual expenses). The British public, which clung to high expectations of public conduct, did not think so, and worked itself up into one of its periodic fits of morality over moat-cleaning, duck houses, packets of biscuits, dog food, pornography and, more substantially, taxpayer-funded property speculation.[125] The Speaker of the House of Commons was forced to resign for the first time since 1695. Many ministers and MPs returned money they had claimed. Several careers ended ignominiously; a few genuine cheats from both Houses went to prison. Some honourable MPs decided they had had enough and left politics. A further blow to political reputations came with the Leveson Inquiry (2011–13) into press standards, which discovered not only widespread lawbreaking by journalists and corruption among the police, but embarrassingly close relations between the Murdoch media empire and both the Labour and the Tory elites.

Much of this had taken place during the laxity of economic boom. A complacent assumption that "boom and bust" was a thing of the past led governments, as well as banks, investors and ordinary consumers, to indulge in financial recklessness on an unprecedented scale. In England, house prices had increased by 130 percent between 1998 and 2004. Individuals stopped saving, and borrowed to buy houses and finance consumption. In 1996 people had saved a tenth of their incomes. By 2007 they were spending more than they were earning, and owed the equivalent of 83 percent of GDP in mortgages, increasingly easy to obtain. Home ownership, usually lauded as a source of stability, had become the opposite. The British became the world's most indebted people. The current-account deficit peaked at minus 3.8 percent of GDP in 2007. In Ireland, Spain, Portugal, Italy, France, Greece and Cyprus, where Eurozone interest rates were low, the bubbles, and the deficits, also grew. World stock markets too were rising, reaching a peak in 2007.

In several countries—notably England, Scotland, the United States, Ireland and Iceland—the financial sector had ballooned in comparison with the rest of the economy. In Britain, it accounted for over 10 percent of GDP in 2007, and paid over 27 percent of all business taxes.[126] Few people remarked publicly on these alarming signs, or realized quite how dangerous the situation had become. Key figures were making too much money to worry. The head of the Royal Bank of Scotland, Sir Fred Good-

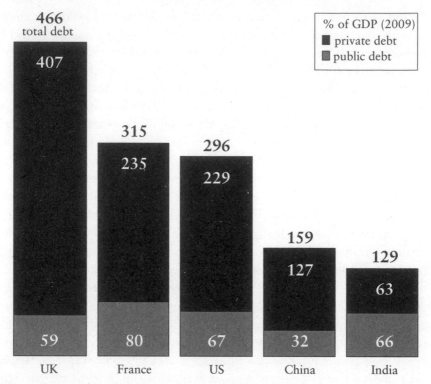

Figure 8: Combined public and private debt, 2009, as a percentage of GDP

win, knighted for "services to banking" in 2004, received over $26m in 2007 (he was stripped of his knighthood in 2012). The head of Lehman Brothers received $73m that same year, months before his firm went bankrupt. Pessimists had long expected a financial crash: but saying when was not so easy. Brown warned the Cabinet in July 2004 of "what would happen from 2008 onwards, of 1.9 percent average growth, how dreadful things were going to be"—they laughed.[127] Blair later commented on the crash with remarkable aplomb: "The failure was one of understanding. We didn't spot it."[128]

The disaster began in the United States early in 2007, with a series of collapses of mortgage-lenders. It spread to France in August 2007, then to Germany, Switzerland, England, Scotland, Belgium, Holland and Iceland. In September 2007 the first serious run on an English bank since 1866 began when people queued outside Northern Rock branches to withdraw their savings. The colossal failure of the Wall Street investment bank Lehman Brothers a year later, in September 2008, began a worldwide financial panic. In the City, 734 second-hand Ferraris went on sale in a week.[129]

What had happened? Fundamental causes of financial crashes include national overspending (current-account deficits and borrowing by both governments and people) and bloated property prices, both of which several countries, including America and Britain, had embarked on. American banks had extended easy credit to poorer people and this had rapidly created a huge "sub-prime" market in house mortgages, 20 percent of all new loans, worth some $1,300,000,000,000 by 2006, the equivalent of several million house purchases. House inflation, fuelled by this cheap and plentiful credit, proved to be the most unstable element of the world financial system. Many people had bought houses as a speculative investment, in the hope of cashing in from price rises; and by 2010 half of all new sub-prime borrowers had defaulted—an easy process in American law. To spread the risk, sub-prime mortgages had been resold to banks across the world in various packages ("derivatives") for huge sums of money, and buyers often did not understand what they had bought, or its potential worthlessness.

When the housing bubble burst, mortgage companies and banks found the value of their assets evaporating by trillions of dollars. Banks across the world—in Paris, Frankfurt, Zurich, Edinburgh and London—which had bought huge amounts of sub-prime assets found them literally valueless. Credit dried up, as no one knew who was facing bankruptcy. World stock markets collapsed, losing half their value in a few months. The amounts of money involved were stupendous, and almost meaningless: stock market losses were over $30,000,000,000,000. Small countries such as Iceland and Ireland had lost more than enough money to bankrupt the whole nation, and British deposits lost in Icelandic banks cost the British taxpayer £8bn—£26,000 for every Icelander. In Edinburgh, the Royal Bank of Scotland, which had become the biggest bank in the world on paper, with assets valued at £2.2 trillion (150 percent of Britain's annual GDP) suddenly lost $44bn—£8,500 for every Scot—and the British government had to buy shares worth £45bn with public money—an investment of £740 per head, which by 2013 had lost nearly half its value.[130] Never in financial history was so much owed by so many due to the recklessness of so few.

In England, the first to be hit in 2007 were mortgage-lenders, Northern Rock (which had developed its own form of sub-prime mortgages) and Bradford and Bingley. Both subsequently had to be nationalized. Governments round the world took defensive action. Gordon Brown, to his credit, backed a rescue operation put together by the Bank of England and the Treasury, and later copied by other countries, among them the United States. Some banks were "too big to fail," as their collapse would destroy others, so they were partly nationalized and pumped with new money. Taking over Northern Rock alone incurred liabilities of £100bn and pushed up the national debt from 37 to 45 percent of GNP.[131] The state became the owner of £57bn of bank shares of uncertain value: "Every UK household will have more than £3,000 invested in shares in RBS and Lloyds," said one official reassuringly.[132] Depositors had their money guaranteed by the state to prevent further panic. Among developed countries, Britain's budget deficit became second only to that of Ireland. In 2008 there was a plunge in total domestic expenditure as the economy slumped. Sterling was allowed to fall to stimulate exports and restrain imports. Interest rates were brought right down, and the Bank of England also began creating vast sums of money and propagated a new euphemism— "quantitative easing." This was only possible because Britain—as much by luck as by judgement—still had its own currency. The Bank of England warned that "we are facing very large deficits." The chancellor, Alistair Darling, confirmed in his 2009 budget that borrowing was at a peacetime record, and that there would have to be years of spending cuts and high taxes. Even so, the Institute of Fiscal Studies said that there remained a £45bn hole in the public accounts.[133]

In these circumstances, the New Labour experiment ended in "the passing of the era of free stuff."[134] Blair had resigned in June 2007, a delayed consequence of the mistrust generated by Iraq, aggravated by a succession of scandals, and hastened by the intrigues of Gordon Brown. Brown proved a startlingly inept Prime Minister. He faced a general election in May 2010. In these circumstances, decisive defeat and a Tory landslide, as in 1979, might have seemed logical. But it did not quite happen, and the result was a hung Parliament: 307 Conservatives (a gain of 97), 258 Labour (a loss of 94), and 57 Liberal Democrats (a gain of 8). Labour's 29 percent of the vote was its lowest since 1983: 40 percent of those attracted by Blair in 1997 had abandoned the party, half moving to the Conservatives or Lib Dems, and half going to the far right or not voting at all.[135] There was a 5 percent swing from Labour to the Tories— bigger than when Thatcher won in 1979. The Tories also gained votes from the Liberal Democrats. They won most English seats—297 to Labour's 191. But they won only 9 seats outside England, including only 1 of the 59 Scottish seats, 41 of which went to Labour. The Labour core vote held up in its heartlands, especially London, and in Scotland it even gained.

Even allowing for an unfavourable electoral system (Blair had won a majority in 2005 with fewer votes than the Tories in 2010), this was strange. David Cameron, Tory leader from 2005, had set out to "modernize" the party in the Blairite manner, but the Tory image still suffered from a post-Thatcher reaction. Moreover, it was hard to denounce economic and foreign policies that the Conservatives had supported. No party dared to be clear about the scale of public-spending cuts that would be required. The electorate was split down the middle on their necessity, and was partly convinced by Labour's accusation that the crisis was all due to "greedy bankers," while Gordon Brown had, as he incautiously put it, "saved the world."[136] The Tories did less well in constituencies with large ethnic minorities (most obviously, inner London), and those with a large public sector and heavy dependence on welfare.[137] Labour was the main party of the public sector, both workers (especially in local government, education and health) and consumers.[138] Public-sector employment and spending had grown most in Labour areas, replacing heavy industry. Labour supporters feared "Tory cuts": this outweighed moral outrage over the Iraq war and the unattractiveness of Brown. In contrast, in London and the south of England most new jobs were in the private sector.[139] So an ancient pattern of voting—originally religious, then socio-economic—was now reinforced by a public-private sector divide. Consequently, the map of party support still resembled that of the nineteenth century.

After some hesitation, as no one knew quite what the rules were, a Tory-Liberal Democrat coalition took office on 12 May 2010, with David Cameron as Prime Minister (at forty-four, the youngest since Lord Liverpool in 1812), and the leader of the Liberal Democrats, Nick Clegg (aged forty-three), as Lord President of the Council—that is, Deputy Prime Minister. This was the first peacetime coalition since 1931, the last big economic crisis. The Lib Dem leadership seized the opportunity to become a party of government, and hoped that electoral reform might make them permanently so. This hope was dashed when, after an unedifying campaign, a referendum on 5 May 2011 voted to keep the "first past the post" system, and in 2012 Tory backbenchers blocked a proposal for a fully elected House of Lords, or "Senate." In revenge, Lib Dems refused in January 2013 to support House of Commons constituency boundary changes, which would have benefited the Tories.

Tory ministers set out Thatcherite/Blairite remedies for the financial crisis: limitation of state spending, decentralization, competition, choice, efficiency—for the NHS (to place "purchasing power" in the hands of GPs), the schools (to give more power to parents and head teachers), the police (elected police commissioners) and the universities (raising fees to make universities compete). But Tory reformers found it as hard going as the Blairites had, and they proved at least as accident prone, as change was unpopular and unintended consequences abounded: the government amassed a list of U-turns and failures (on health, immigration, university fees, taxation, forests, school examinations, police commissioners) so rapidly that it "may possibly turn out to be the most blunder-prone government of modern times."[140] There was a short, cautious, lucky and successful military adventure in Libya comparable to Blair's early "humanitarian interventions." Key air and naval forces used were about to be scrapped to save money; ammunition had to be borrowed; the French did most of the bombing; and the Americans had to destroy Libyan air defences first. There was no change in Afghan policy, which was aligned with that of America, meaning a reduction of combat operations and a steady withdrawal of troops accompanied by optimistic declarations of success. Highly controversial long-term reforms were begun in education (including "free schools") by Michael Gove, and in welfare by Iain Duncan Smith, aiming at a "Universal Credit" scheme to make a transition from welfare to work easier by lessening the "poverty trap" in which gains from work were cancelled out by losses in benefit. Both these reforms at the time of writing were teetering between failure and success; but if carried out would amount to fundamental, even historic, changes.

Everything was overshadowed by the alarming state of public finances and the economy, on which ultimately all depended, including the political fortunes of the government. The new government inherited a budget deficit of £149bn—10.1 percent of GDP,[141] over three times the maximum permitted by the EU Stability and Growth Pact (1999). The "nasty party" was again there to administer bitter economic medicine in a crisis. An Office of Budget Responsibility was created in 2010, to act as a restraint on government by checking its books, potentially as important as Brown's grant of independence to the Bank of England. In the longer term, the crisis raised serious questions concerning three decades of economic policy. The left saw it as the collapse of the Thatcher/Blair experiment in "modernization," and a crisis of global capitalism. For economic liberals, it was the implosion of the Blair/Brown period of high state spending, and even the death knell of the "European social model" in the face of global competition. Perhaps both were right, which if so raised troubling questions about England's economic future.

The parties, of course, tried to blame each other for the financial disaster. The coalition government pointed to earlier Labour profligacy and emphasized the need to maintain financial confidence by controlling long-term expenditure and debt. Labour, at first unabashedly unrepentant, adopted Keynesian rhetoric, urging more spending and borrowing to stimulate growth, and criticizing the government for cutting "too far, too fast." Cameron, a carefully bland Etonian, proved oddly difficult to hate, or indeed to love; and his coalition with the Liberals gave the "nasty party" some protection at first, however frustrating for its backbenchers. Cameron also angered many rank-and-file Tories by supporting progressive cultural reforms, notably the Marriage (Same Sex Couples) Act in July 2013, and expressing support for women bishops. The financial crisis caused considerable upheaval and real hardship: there were repeated attempts to cut social spending, there were redundancies in the public sector, the retirement age and pension contributions were raised, and public-sector salaries were frozen—particularly important in restraining the cost of the NHS. Remarkably, public opinion seemed to accept, however grudgingly, some need for austerity, partly because the private sector was already being squeezed, and most people suffered cuts in their real wages. These at least had the effect of limiting job losses. The impact was inevitably uneven, given the regional disparities in poverty, unemployment and public-sector spending, which further emphasized the old north-south Labour-Tory divide. Opinion polls showed both a sudden rise in suspicion of business and the structure of power in society (including among conservatives), and at the same time a general and continuing fall in support for higher taxation and state spending.[142]

An alarming early sign of social and political trouble was evident in the extraordinary riots of August 2011, which began in London and were copied in other cities and even small towns. Nothing on this scale, with violence, looting and arson, had been seen in the capital since the 1783 Gordon Riots. As then, feeble policing was one element. But the riots were less a consequence of "Tory cuts" than of a deeper problem: they showed luridly the existence of a young multi-racial underclass in the richest city in Europe, marked out less by poverty than by an indifference to and alienation from the obligations of a civil society—obligations that many in high places had also very visibly ignored. Up to 20 percent of those aged sixteen to twenty-four were not in education, training or employment—the notorious "NEETs." It showed, even if economic circumstances improved, how far England had to go to rebuild a cohesive and inclusive nation.

It was necessary to "rebalance" the economy, as the jargon went: to reduce debt; to move resources from the public sector and construction to the exporting private sector; to reduce the relative importance of the financial sector by encouraging other industries; to invest in new domestic energy sources as North Sea oil ran out and old power stations closed—it is unclear at the time of writing how important shale gas might be as a contentious windfall. This "rebalancing" was a highly optimistic scenario; and it had to be done at a time when the Western economies, and particularly the Eurozone, were stagnant and financially unstable. The Governor of the Bank of England, Sir Mervyn King, predicted a tough period over ten or fifteen years. The pound depreciated by over 25 percent for a time, helping some export industries. Having its own currency permitted the Bank of England to continue to print vast quantities of money in the hope of sustaining economic activity—"quantitative easing" became almost an everyday expression, however obscure its meaning. Arguably, all this enabled Britain to avoid the sharp general fall in incomes and huge rates of unemployment that ravaged Ireland, Italy, Spain, Portugal and Greece.

England's problems were throughout complicated by the state of the Eurozone, the customer for some 40 percent of its exports. Membership of the euro meant that crisis-hit countries could not devalue to gain competitiveness and encourage economic growth, but were forced into severe austerity—wage cuts, welfare cuts, job losses—to reduce their costs. The very existence of the Eurozone seemed periodically threatened by the recurring prospect of a member state defaulting or leaving the euro, and no solution presented itself other than muddling through a succession of crises and last-minute improvisations. Though England's domestic economy was fairly resilient—especially the level of private-sector employment—its exports to Europe fell steeply. In 2012 its banks were owed £190bn by Ireland (the biggest debtor), Spain, Italy, Portugal and Greece, and £90bn more by France and Germany—a serious risk if the Eurozone failed.[143]

Government policy led by the Chancellor of the Exchequer, George Osborne, was cautious, even timid: neither slashing government spending and cutting taxes, as some economic liberals wanted, nor borrowing cheaply to finance nationwide infrastructure modernization, as many other economists urged. The first modest round of "Tory cuts" aimed to save £6bn a year (much less than the cost of the Olympic Games), reducing total spending only by 0.4 percent of GDP. The initial hope was to hold down state spending as the economy returned to growth so that by 2015–16 it would have fallen by 7.5 percent of GNP (even though in cash terms it would rise slightly), thus eliminating the "structural deficit." This would be a return to the 2004 level of spending—a fairly modest reduction by international standards.[144] Even this proved both difficult and unpopular, and was blamed by political opponents and some prominent economists for making the crisis worse.[145] But the amount actually "consumed" by the state (largely the NHS and schools) continued to rise although tax receipts fell. So government borrowing continued to increase and was predicted to peak as late as 2017, despite attempts to reduce the vast welfare budget and encourage, or impel, beneficiaries into jobs. Fortunately, the government was still able to borrow cheaply—another benefit of keeping sterling—and little of its long-term debt was due for early repayment. Interest rates, thanks in part to "quantitative easing," were kept down to 0.5 percent (minus 2–3 percent in real terms), transferring vast wealth from savers to borrowers, the biggest borrower of all being the government.

Many of the cuts in public spending came from capital investment, a less visible and unpopular form of economy, though economically a counter-productive one. The defence budget was also hit. The Royal Navy was left without aircraft carriers or aircraft, and dependent on sharing with the French, who seemed set to be stronger at sea for the first time since the seventeenth century. By December 2013 the French defence minister felt able to boast that "France has and will keep the top armed forces in Europe . . . in 2019 we will have 187,000 military personnel while Britain will only have 145,000."[146] On the stimulus side, a scheme to encourage house-buying—deplored by most economists—was introduced, presumably as the easiest and most popular way of encouraging economic optimism at the risk of encouraging another house prices bubble. The politically explosive question of airport expansion was postponed, but a dubious Keynesian project inherited from Labour for a high-speed rail connection between London and the north, "HS2," was pushed forward as an expensive modern public-works scheme, purporting to close the "north-south gap." There were convincing arguments that spending on more, smaller projects, whether in railways, cheap housing or energy, would have been a better use of money; but HS2 had the advantages of being spectacular and already in the planning stage. In the midst of a global crisis, the least that can be said is that worse disaster was avoided and markets reassured. By 2013 there were signs of economic recovery fuelled mainly by domestic consumption. Exports, in a generally weak global economy, gave little stimulus, despite successes in a few areas such as luxury cars and aero engines, and so "rebalancing" remained elusive. England was doing better than most of the Eurozone, but fundamental problems of debt and productivity remained, and it was uncertain how strong growth would be once interest rates ceased to be held down.

The travails of the Eurozone exploded the assumptions that had originally governed English attitudes to European integration: that it was a fount of prosperity, a pillar of national power, and anyway was historically inevitable. No English politician now espoused the view, still the official orthodoxy on the Continent, that Britain should adopt the euro as a token of full participation in the "European project." A paper by the European Council on Foreign Relations admitted that "Euroscepticism . . . once seen as a British disease . . . has now spread across the continent like a virus . . . Everyone in the EU has been losing faith in the project." Britain, once "the Eurosceptic outlier," now looked like the leader of a generally growing trend.[147] A now predominantly Eurosceptic Tory party forced the government to pass a European Union Act (March 2011) requiring a referendum before any new power was given to "an EU institution or body . . . to impose a requirement or obligation on the United Kingdom." It also declared that "only by virtue of an Act of Parliament" could "directly applicable or directly effective EU law" be recognized in the United Kingdom—a restatement of what was already the case. Cameron was forced to go further and promise an "in–out referendum" if he won the next election, following an attempt to renegotiate Britain's relations with the Eurozone. The rising vote attracted by the U.K. Independence Party put increased Eurosceptic pressure on all parties, especially the Conservatives, most directly threatened by UKIP competition at the polls. Immigration, a sensitive issue in a time of crisis, rose up the political agenda, especially as the citizens of new European member countries, including Romania, were acquiring rights of free movement. This, and the question of welfare rights of immigrants, caused friction between Westminster and Brussels and made it impossible to dismiss the European issue as the obsession of an eccentric minority. An EU opinion poll in 2013 showed that a majority of people in Britain (53 percent) thought the country would be better placed to face the future outside the Union, and only 36 percent took the opposite view.[148] The simultaneous Europe-wide elections to the European Parliament in May 2014 saw a surge of opposition to "Europe" almost everywhere outside Germany, usually expressed by anti-Establishment parties of the left and right. In Britain, UKIP topped the poll, with 27.5 percent of the vote, while support for the Liberal Democrats, the most Europhile party, collapsed. Moreover, the crisis had forced the Eurozone to agree to greater central control of public finances and banking, which made it inevitable that connections with Britain would to some extent have to be recast. It would take a foolhardy prophet to predict the outcome of a referendum on EU membership (if there is to be one), or its long-term consequences.

Despite the problems and uncertainties, and unusually bad weather too, 2012 was a year of celebration. The Queen's Diamond Jubilee saw both organized and spontaneous festivity on a huge scale over the summer, and a reassertion of consciously British identity symbolized by the Crown. It was even arranged for the Queen to shake hands with Martin McGuinness, former IRA commander and Deputy First Minister in Ulster—unthinkable until recently. This followed a historic royal visit to Dublin in May 2011, the first for a century, and the first to an independent Ireland. This carefully managed event was taken, far more than the visit of any politician, as symbolizing the end of centuries of conflict—a remarkable example of the power of monarchy to represent not merely a government, but a nation. The Jubilee demonstrated the long-accumulated prestige of Elizabeth II herself, who, like Victoria, had been on the throne for longer than most of her subjects could remember, and whose tireless activity had enabled the monarchy to reach into every corner of the kingdom as what Walter Bagehot in the 1860s had superciliously described as "a visible symbol of unity to those still so imperfectly educated as to need a symbol."[149] There must have been few British people who had never seen her in person, and relatively few people in the world who would not recognize her; an international opinion poll in 2014 picked her as the world's most admired woman.[150]

At first popular as a pretty and innocent queen, during the iconoclastic 1960s and 1970s she had often been mocked as remote and old-fashioned. She had even encountered unpopularity at the time of the death of Princess Diana in 1997, although her conduct during that ephemeral crisis of the monarchy had later been romanticized in a widely admired film.[151] Some long-term damage was certainly done by that crisis, especially to the Prince of Wales, above all among traditionalists and women, usually pillars of monarchical loyalty. His position was difficult. Though he was more active—for example, through the charitable Prince's Trust—and more seriously engaged in national issues than any heir to the throne since the eighteenth century, this did not placate all his critics, who seemed more affronted by an intellectually active prince than they would have been by a playboy.[152] Yet the Queen, in her vigorous old age, was now universally respected as a model of public duty, steering clear of the perilous vagaries of celebrity, somehow able during thousands of public engagements to combine personal charm with unforced dignity—even in a riskily jokey role in the 2012 Olympic opening ceremony, pretending to parachute into the arena accompanied by "James Bond." She personified what Walter Bagehot had called "the dignified part of the constitution," which "consecrates our whole state,"[153] and also provided a distinctive national and international symbol of Britain at a time when most large states were republics—all things that monarchists approved, and a republican minority tended to deplore. A discreet, even enigmatic figure, whose opinions could only be guessed at—"the Crown is of no party," Bagehot had declared—she gave the impression of unchanging permanence during seven decades of rapid cultural, social and political change. This permanence enabled four generations of one family, despite the various ills the flesh is heir to, somehow to represent both continuities and changes in

British society; and the birth on 22 July 2013 of a son, George, to a very modern couple, the Duke and Duchess of Cambridge (known almost universally as "Kate and William"), was taken as projecting the monarchy far into the future. In England, at least: the monarchy too would be unpredictably affected if Scotland became independent, while in Commonwealth monarchies, most obviously Australia, it is possible that Elizabeth II would be the last royal head of state—though a successful visit by "Kate and William" and little George in April 2014 was credited with postponing such an outcome indefinitely.

The spontaneous homemade jollifications of Jubilee street parties contrasted with the hyper-organized glitter of the London Olympics. But both showed a nation eager to celebrate itself in the midst of crisis in an inclusive and apolitical show of Britishness. Ten million people reportedly turned out to watch the Olympic torch carried round the country. Lavish disbursement of lottery money produced an opening ceremony to impress the world—a somewhat opaque, sentimentalized and yet dazzling historical pageant—followed by a gratifying crop of medal-winners. The stiff upper lip was consigned to oblivion amid copious tears of triumph or disappointment—British athletes were calculated to be twice as tearful as Americans. This multi-racial and multi-class festival gave the nation a flattering image of itself in contrast with the riots exactly a year before, and crime was reported to have dropped in London by 5 percent.

It was easy to object, as some did, that these national celebrations were self-deluding escapism, the national story made into a fairy tale, symbolizing neither a real past nor a real future. Perhaps. But they showed a nation eager to assert its existence as what the French philosopher Ernest Renan had called "a great solidarity." Reports of national demise, it seemed, had been exaggerated. England and Britain were facing daunting problems, continuing divisions and perhaps major upheavals. Yet the public mood, if one of discontent, was not one of resignation or despair: the shadow of declinism was long gone.

The death of Margaret Thatcher on 8 April 2013 and her funeral at St. Paul's Cathedral showed a different but equally characteristic face of England—its political sectarianism. Admirers mourned and the state paid tribute, as the Queen attended a Prime Minister's funeral for the first time since that of Churchill in 1965. But a few publicly celebrated that "the witch is dead"—this last spectacle perhaps unseen since the death of Castlereagh in 1822. On the other hand, verbal extremism did not carry over into physical violence at the time of the funeral, and no one had thought it would. But two fundamentally conflicting narratives of recent history re-emerged round Thatcher's formidable image: that she was the heroine who had saved the nation from imminent collapse, or that she had maliciously ravaged a harmonious and humane society.[154] It had long been commonplace to assert that party differences were disappearing in a morass of centrism, but Thatcher's death showed that in terms of emotion, if not of policy, England retained two antagonistic political sensibilities with historical roots stretching back at least two centuries.

The 2014 referendum on Scottish independence was bound to open a new phase in English as well as British history. After a campaign that turned in a few days from torpor to hysteria, the pro-union parties, Conservative, Labour and Liberal Democrats, hastily promised much greater autonomy for Scotland. On 18 September the Scots voted decisively by 55 percent to 45 percent (in a poll with an 84 percent turnout) to remain part of the United Kingdom, thus sparing the English, as well as themselves, the perilous thrills of total separation. But as soon as the result was announced, David Cameron pledged "a new and fair" constitutional settlement for the whole Kingdom, in which the "millions of voices of England must also be heard" and "a decisive answer" found to the West Lothian question. Greater self-government for England would have implications for the political balance in England and throughout the Kingdom. The Conservatives were generally the largest party in England—only in 1945, 1966 and 1997 did Labour win a majority there. But too solid a Tory predominance might create opposing pressure to fragment England into regions (already suggested in 1910), or encourage the alliance of anti-Tory groups (as in the nineteenth century), revive demands for proportional representation, or perhaps facilitate an erosion of Toryism with the rise of UKIP. As had happened after devolution in the other British nations, there would also surely be greater English self-consciousness and more debate about what kind of country England was and wanted to be. Many recalled G. K. Chesterton's ominous line: "But we are the people of England; and we have not spoken yet." No one had the faintest idea what they might say.

# Conclusion:
# The English and Their History

*Nothing ever stands still. We must add to our heritage or lose it,
we must grow greater or grow less, we must go forward or backward. I believe in England, and I believe that we shall go forward.*

George Orwell[1]

… Ingratitude
still gets to me, the unfairness
and waste of survival; a nation
with so many memorials but no memory.

Geoffrey Hill[2]

N ations resemble each other like a street of houses: of different sizes,
with different occupants, and different furnishings, but sharing many
basic characteristics. England is a rambling old property with ancient
foundations, a large Victorian extension, a 1960s garage, and some annoying leaks and draughts balancing its period charm. Some historians believe
England to be the prototype of the nation-state: "The birth of the English
nation was not the birth of a nation; it was the birth of the nations."[3] Some
English institutions are unusual not because nothing similar existed elsewhere—for example trial by jury, parliament, monarchy—but because
they survived here while disappearing elsewhere. Why this nation has
lasted so long, why its people have managed to retain a sense of identity
(both outside and inside the United Kingdom), how it has retained so
many unusual and ancient yet changing institutions, while yet being deeply
engaged in the world's epoch-making economic, cultural and political
transformations, are questions with a range of answers. They involve
England's particular geographical situation, its connections (and discon-
nections) with the "near abroad" and with the wider world, and the continuities and discontinuities of its internal politics. Choices and struggles

over the centuries by rulers and ruled are the connecting thread of the story; but we should not forget David Hume's sceptical verdict in 1757 that the outcome was due to "a great measure of accident with a small ingredient of wisdom and foresight." On a few occasions, however, that "small ingredient" has been crucial.

## CONNECTIONS AND DISCONNECTIONS

England is an island, as has often been said, inaccurately yet truthfully. One of those who pronounced this thumping commonplace was Charles de Gaulle, when he vetoed British membership of the Common Market in 1963. He concluded that "England" (as he thought of it) could not truly be part of Europe, not because it was isolated, but because it was too connected with the rest of the world: it would never agree to "shut itself up" in Europe.[4] He was right in realizing that the sea is the greatest highway, and that England's connections with others through the ages are central to its history. Contacts have often been hostile—though probably not more so than those between most of the rest of humanity. What became England was a tempting target for people from more crowded or less hospitable lands, including other parts of the archipelago. The centuries until 1066 are marked by frequent incursions and repeated conquests which successively attached the country to the Roman world, later Scandinavia and then France. The Norman conquest, the last and also the most durable, connected the country with the close Continent and led to further conquests in Wales, Ireland and (almost) Scotland. Was this the beginning of a thousand-year English Reich (see p. 104), in which Celtic neighbours provided the training ground for future imperialism? The reality is less simple and one-sided, with medieval England more often the target than the perpetrator of invasion. Security—from Alfred's burhs to the Trident submarines—had been a continual preoccupation. External danger first brought the kingdom of the English into existence, and over the centuries the recurring need to mobilize money and people for defence (and sometimes for aggression) created a powerful and coherent polity. This has always been one of the characteristics of the kingdom, and a prominent part of being English has been paying a lot of tax. The efficiency of its governmental system made England and then Britain more formidable at making war than its mere size warranted. However many defeats it suffered abroad, never since Hastings has it been vanquished on its own soil—the only time when the survival of an English identity and culture was uncertain. This is the simplest explanation of the longevity of its institutions and identity.

   The defeat at Hastings meant that for nearly a third of its total history,

England was linked to the western fringe of the Continent—for 400 years, as long as it has been linked with Scotland. Security and trade always forced it to take an interest in who controlled its "near abroad," and on several occasions nearly caused it to unite politically with France or the Netherlands (as in 1688 for a time it did). For nearly a thousand years after the kingdom's creation, England's close political and trading contacts were confined to its nearest neighbours. It was slower than other European coastal peoples such as the Norwegians, Portuguese and Spanish to make more distant forays. From the sixteenth century onwards, when its sailors ventured further, they were aiming mostly at its European enemies' overseas trade and possessions, leading in the sixteenth and seventeenth centuries to its first minor and insecure territorial acquisitions in the Caribbean, the Mediterranean, India and North America. The deadly post-1688 conflict with France—the "Second Hundred Years' War" that ended at Waterloo—transformed England and its place in the world. It motivated the creation of a United Kingdom with Scotland and later Ireland and inaugurated exactly two centuries of global empire—between the Seven Years' War (1756–63) and the rapid decolonization of the 1960s—the height of England's global promiscuity. This expanding power was seaborne, motivated by deadly rivalry with France, and galvanized by a rapidly growing population and by epoch-making economic change.

England's long, complex and changing connections with the overseas world have been important in both directions. This is not unique. Rome, of course, and more recently Portugal, Spain and France have marked, and been marked by, their colonial possessions and post-colonial relationships. England, like them, was profoundly affected by both the outflow and inflow of people. The English imperial experience was unique for the rapid growth, enormous size and short-lived existence of the British Empire. At its greatest extent it lasted barely a single lifetime, which in some ways limited its significance. To assess its overall consequences is no easy thing, and they have been discussed at some length in Chapters 9, 14 and 18. English power and wealth during these two centuries had both stabilizing and destabilizing effects on the world. There is some truth in the idea of a "Pax Britannica," in that British hegemony prevented the recurrence between 1815 and 1914 of global wars as in the eighteenth century. British police actions (themselves, of course, constantly using violence or its threat) probably lessened conflict in certain areas, and gradually suppressed some chronic sources of violence and suffering such as the Atlantic and Arab slave trades. What was characteristic of the British Empire, and what gave it lasting consequences, was its combination of global maritime power, the commercial and technological dynamism of the Industrial Revolution, and the mass migration it encouraged (not only from Britain, but from other European countries, India and China). The resulting globalization, which also affected the "informal" empire and independent states, gave rise to enrichment and impoverishment, stability and instability, opportunity and exploitation. British power facilitated these changes and failed to control them; though whether there were better alternatives is questionable. The impact was undeniably profound, and it included widespread adoption of English-style political, commercial and legal institutions, the emulation of cultural practices (such as sport) and the spread of English as the first global language.

There was never any possibility—and not much of an ambition either—of making this maritime empire into a global federation, and it proved ephemeral, like earlier links with Scandinavia, France, Holland, Hanover and Ireland. It has been forcefully argued that the end of empire also weakened the links holding England, Scotland and Wales together.[5] English hegemony sowed the seeds of its own downfall: internally, by provoking nationalist resistance from Ireland to India, and externally, by provoking challenges from rivals—France, Russia, Germany, Japan and the United States. The two world wars were in part wars against the British Empire. The most dangerous of these challenges, from an alliance of German, Japanese and Italian Fascists, threatened to create a new and deadly form of imperialism across Europe, Asia, Africa and the Middle East. The role of England, Britain and the empire in defeating this danger was certainly one of their most important historic actions. Though many in England had believed—or had said they believed—that colonies should naturally become self-governing in time, the rapid end of empire and of world hegemony created a corrosive sense of national decline in the post-1945 decades. This was largely an illusion (see pp. 767–69), but it was no less important for that, for it distorted and envenomed politics and damaged cultural self-confidence. Despite the difficulties and uncertainties faced by England and Britain today, declinism no longer casts such a debilitating shadow. On the contrary, it appears to be peace, security and confidence that are leading to increasing political independence for the British nations, so far with limited effects on England.

England has long been a powerful political, cultural and economic entity. But, oddly, it has rarely been a self-contained and autonomous nation—only between Alfred and Cnut, and again (though by then including Wales) under the Tudors. It has rarely shown much appetite for isolation, including today. Perhaps it is characteristic of an island nation close to a continent to have multiple but impermanent political relationships; as recently as 1956 the idea of forming a political union with France was officially raised, and the end of empire immediately motivated a rush to join the European Community. England's changing attachments to its neighbours have resulted today in a rare political phenomenon: a nation without a state. Until recently it shared this ambivalence with Scotland, Wales and Northern Ireland, but since devolution England has attained a special place in Europe: as the largest nation without its own political institutions. It therefore resembles in some ways a much bigger Flanders, Catalonia or Castile,[6] though hitherto without nationalist resentment, due to the willingness of the English to identify themselves simultaneously as British, espousing the multi-national political creation of which they were the dominant political and cultural element.[7] British identity was, and is, officially plugged—"British values," for example, are enjoined on us by politicians. This still affects twenty-first-century immigrants, who seem to find the "British" label easier to assume (p. 849). Yet, as an American historian sees it, Britishness "is more redolent of . . . Westminster than Hackney, 'Rule Britannia' than 'The Roast Beef of Old England,' swaggering John Bull than egalitarian Robin Hood."[8] The feeling for "England" was and is more emotive, human and earthy: "old England," "England expects," "Speak for England," even "traditional English Christmas" and "full English breakfast." "Oh to be in Britain / Now that April's there," or "in UK's green and pleasant land" would be utterly incongruous.

Though long passive about their rights within a devolving if not dissolving United Kingdom, the English are uniquely sensitive to the encroachments of the European Union. "Euroscepticism" is certainly one characteristic facet of English consciousness today, even if comparable feelings are now present across Europe. In all countries, attitudes to European integration are shaped by history: an attraction of "Europe" was that it appeared to offer every country an escape from its historic failures—defeat, occupation, foreign domination, dictatorship, aggression, civil war. In England's case, the escape was from "decline." The persistence and growth of English Euroscepticism are usually put down to a different experience of the Second World War (or indeed to a mythologized vision of that war) and to nostalgia for the empire, the Commonwealth and the "Special Relationship" with America. In fact, these things were powerful motives to join in European integration, at least for the elites, who feared becoming merely "a greater Sweden" (see p. 809). They hoped to create a new and special link with both the United States and with Europe, hoping to act as a "bridge" between them. Yet empire had, as General de Gaulle observed, left England with a level of global connectedness which distinguished it from Continental nations. Its people had more intimate family and cultural connections with North America, Australasia or the Indian subcontinent than with Belgium, Luxembourg or Bavaria.

The English, it seems, are uncomfortable at the prospect of being on their own, which they fear would make them less important and perhaps poorer, but they are even less eager for full commitment to a single relationship. For a nation less desperate than most to escape its recent history, the glories and benefits of "ever-closer" European union have seemed less evident and its results, including large-scale immigration, less worthwhile.* Moreover, Euroscepticism is just as likely to be fuelled by a suspicion of distant and unaccountable political power in a nation with ambivalent feelings about state interference, mistrust of politicians foreign as well as domestic, and an ingrained tradition of representative government. There is a curious paradox. Euroscepticism is mostly expressed in political terms, concerning sovereignty and law; yet it is strongest in England, which is not of course a sovereign nation. There is little correlation between Euroscepticism (a fairly broad phenomenon) and English nationalism (a tiny splinter). In other words, Euroscepticism is a form of British nationalism, mostly confined to the most "British" island nation, the English.

The English face important decisions. Their economic assumptions were severely dented by the 2007–8 crash, and it is meagre consolation to see from some neighbouring countries that things could be worse. Their political class is tolerated without enthusiasm. Historically, this is probably not exceptional, and it is arguably healthy that people do not look to politicians for magic solutions. Nevertheless, there is an uneasy sense of an incipient crisis of democracy, common to much of the Western world. But by far the greatest questions about England's future have been posed from outside, by processes set in motion in Scotland and the Eurozone. Whether the British political class will muster the vision and strength of purpose to create a new constitutional settlement for the United Kingdom and negotiate a relationship with the European Union able to win the genuine support of the people of England are subjects for future historians.

## CONTINUITIES AND DISCONTINUITIES

While the sea has always been the highway linking England with the outside world, it has also paradoxically been Shakespeare's "moat defensive," a physical and psychological boundary making access easy but large-scale invasion difficult. This combination, during the long period of Viking

---

* Europe-wide opinion polls have consistently shown the British as the most resistant to European integration: *Eurobarometer* 79 (July 2013) showed only 15 percent in favour of "economic and monetary union"—the lowest in the EU; and it was the only country in which a majority (53 percent) thought that they could face the modern world more effectively outside the EU. Figures for England alone would probably be higher.

raids, brought the early development of a single powerful kingdom able to defend the land, and to command its people's obedience and even their willing loyalty as taxpayers, law enforcers, soldiers and sailors. England was frequently invaded, but not subjugated for nearly a thousand years—since 1066, the only time when its political and social systems were permanently overthrown. Insularity had to be fought for and paid for over many centuries, with security finally gained by commanding the surrounding seas, and this demanded an immense and prolonged effort. Only from the 1780s onwards has invading England been a truly formidable enterprise—perhaps, in reality, an impossible one, as Napoleon and Hitler were both forced to accept. So England has not for many centuries been fought over, devastated and terrorized, the repeated fate of much of the Continent as recently as the 1940s. Few things have been as important in our history as a few miles of sea. This seems to have changed, or at least our awareness of it has done so. A recent profound historical break which has gone largely unremarked is the waning of the maritime dimension in national life: England now scarcely has a fishing fleet, a shipbuilding industry, a merchant marine, or sailors; and in 2013 the British government announced that England would no longer build warships. As a member of a permanent North Atlantic alliance, and of a friendly European Union, for the first time since it lost its Continental territories in the fifteenth century, the sea is no longer England's front line.

It has above all been the immunity of this strongly governed island nation to the transforming catastrophes of invasion, war and revolution that explains the survival not only of the ancient buildings and cultural treasures with which England is crammed,[9] but also of defining national institutions. Pre-eminent among these are the Crown and Parliament—such fundamental institutions are very rarely overturned unless undermined from without, usually by invasion and defeat. For the same reason, many subordinate autonomous bodies have also had remarkably long continuous existences—shires, boroughs, the Church and its parishes, universities, schools, charitable foundations, voluntary associations, political parties, regiments and of course identifiable families. The legal system can be traced back in detail for eight centuries, and in outline even longer. Whether such survivals are treasures to be safeguarded or encumbrances to be modernized is a matter of sentiment, opinion and sometimes keen controversy. For many centuries their longevity was a source of pride, and antiquity gave institutions protection and prestige, still often displayed in ancient or pseudo-ancient costumes and ceremonies. Perhaps because of our limited knowledge of history, and because of cultural changes that have tended to devalue the ancient, much of that prestige has faded. In some ways this may be beneficial—a gain for rationality. But there are dangers in careless forgetfulness for a country which long relied on conventions and traditions as safeguards for its rights and liberties, and even for a sense of its own identity, its civic morality and its solidarity. Informal understandings now have to be written down: a sign of the times was the need to hold an official inquiry in 1994 into "standards in public life"—a death knell of the "gentlemanly ethic" by which people instinctively knew what was done and not done—even if they sometimes disobeyed it.[10] What would even recently have been regarded as untouchable individual liberties—concerning speech, privacy, jury trial, arrest and detention—are commonly questioned and even transgressed, sometimes with little public reaction. Where sovereignty lies has become increasingly doubtful and controversial. Hasty and repeated constitutional tinkering by governments means that "we no longer have a constitution, in the sense of a set of conventions which set the bounds of executive power."[11]

Given such changes, is it really meaningful to talk about England and its institutions continuing or surviving over the centuries? National history assumes as its starting point some real continuity over time: that many generations of people, with different cultures, beliefs and ways of life, who have inhabited the same geographical area are somehow related by more than mere genes—if even by those. It presumes that institutions that bear the same name and inhabit roughly the same places (the House of Commons, let us say, or the University of Cambridge) are in some sense the same as centuries ago. George Orwell's view was typically trenchant: "What can the England of 1940 have in common with the England of 1840? But then, what have you in common with the child of five whose photograph your mother keeps on the mantelpiece? Nothing, except that you happen to be the same person."[12] The connection, he said, was that "it is *your* civilization, it is *you* . . . the suet puddings and the red pillar boxes have entered into your soul."

England's history, thought Orwell, to some extent determined how things developed: "Certain alternatives are possible and others not. A seed may grow or not grow, but at any rate a turnip seed never grows into a parsnip."[13] Striking metaphors are impermeable to analysis, but we would probably agree with the general point. As long as its present civilization lasts, England will not have a violent revolution, or a military coup, or a religious civil war. We often assume that other nations will behave in the same way as we do, and are sometimes surprised when they do not, or cannot. In both cases, history makes it so. How exactly does this "history" operate? If, to pursue my smaller example, we were to ask how exactly the present and future of Cambridge University are shaped by its history, we would probably point to its internal self-government, its ancient collegiate structure, its financial endowments, its established prestige, and its consequent ability to attract talent and inspire loyalty—a mixture of structure and culture that can incorporate and mould even rapid and extensive changes.

Structure and culture carry continuity in a nation's history too. On England's structure, we might point to long-established administrative unity (never being divided into autonomous regions), a powerful central government, an ancient and rarely questioned tradition of participation and representation in that government, an early and effective common law, a three-century history of legally guaranteed toleration of diversity, an even longer principle of power being restrained by law, and yet in potential conflict with this a sovereign Parliament which can (as Jean-Jacques Rousseau observed as early as the eighteenth century) become an elected dictatorship. Also fundamental, as we have noted, are many centuries of links with a great variety of other countries. It is not only very ancient structures that affect our lives. Our particular kind of Welfare State, deeply influenced by the Poor Law's relatively open-ended and unconditional right to benefits, is very different from American or European equivalents that confer more limited rights or make greater demands, and this has had important social consequences. A final example: England, uniquely, possesses simultaneously one of the world's largest capitalist entities, the City of London, and also one of its largest socialist institutions, the National Health Service—a difficult duality created by past wars (see pp. 310 and 773–74).

"Culture" is harder to define. There have been official attempts to list "British values," which turn out to be not very different from everyone else's.[14] More fundamental are the conscious and unconscious beliefs and habits of thought and behaviour arising from the particular experiences of a nation's history—what Burke called "prejudices" and Orwell "your civilization." Ideas about what these might be will inevitably vary, but several seem to emerge in preceding chapters as important. An early linguistic homogeneity which survived even repeated conquest, and made possible a sense of cultural kinship—the "felawschip" of "Inglysch" (see p. 129). An early transition to the "European marriage pattern" of nuclear families, involving greater economic and social autonomy, and relative gender equality (see p. 373). A flattering self-image of ancient freedom most famously expressed in Magna Carta and in the myth it inspired: "The English have been at all times extremely jealous of their liberties."[15] A simultaneous tradition of obedience (even grudging) to constituted authority and "some reverence" (in Tennyson's words) for "the laws ourselves have made,"[16] proved by the rarity of major rebellion. A suspicion of extremes in word or deed learned painfully during the religious and party conflicts of the seventeenth and eighteenth centuries, yet combined with a continuation of sectarian political divisions. A certain self-importance, which we might discern as long ago as the Anglo-Saxons ("a glorious and splendid people," in the words of a medieval charter), in the expansionary ambitions of the post-Conquest monarchs, in literature (such as the Arthurian legends and Shakespeare), in ancient claims to primacy within the British Isles, and more recently in pride in "the greatest empire the world has ever seen." A show of stoicism or stubbornness that takes a kind of pleasure in adversity, combined with a complacent and often apathetic assumption bred by a fortunate history that nothing seriously bad can happen (this irritated Orwell in 1940). An obsession with class, commonly said to be central to English culture (though France and India to name only two would be comparable): this seems to lie in the ability of its people to size each other up in subtle ways that do not depend merely on power, money, race and the display of material status symbols; and here long mutual familiarity and the absence of great upheavals seem important. Perhaps resentment of class is also an ancient English characteristic. Finally, of course, there is a long-established if undefined sense of English "identity," recognized over many centuries since first formulated by Bede, that feeling, as Orwell put it, of being "a family," even though "the wrong members" may be in control.[17]

Many observers over the years, English and non-English, have tried to pin Englishness down in more detail, often shrewdly and amusingly.[18] But much of what they think they observe changes substantially over time. If we do have distinctive common traits of feeling or behaviour—for example, some of those mentioned above, to which we might add a pervasive social awkwardness alternatively displayed in politeness, rudeness and a characteristic type of humour[19]—not many are much older than the later years of Queen Victoria. Even those began to change soon after the queen died, and were eroded by two world wars and the cultural revolution of the sixties, as if to turn English mores back to the pre-Victorian rough and tumble. Over the generations, a whole range of different and even contradictory characteristics have been recognized and caricatured as "typically English": both conformity and eccentricity, bluntness and reticence, deference and assertiveness, honesty and hypocrisy, community spirit and privacy, and so on. If we agree with Hume's view about liberty creating individuality, perhaps these different characteristics are indeed all "typically English." Some once-fundamental common features, however, have changed beyond recognition, perhaps most obviously self-consciousness as a Christian, and after the sixteenth century as a Protestant, nation. As in other parts of Protestant Europe, this has mutated fairly smoothly into the secularization, individualism and moral pluralism that are characteristic of Englishness today. As one historian of religion has observed (see p. 793) the 1960s generation may have differed from their parents more than any generation in history. It is possible to trace some of the roots of this change back to the eighteenth century, yet from the 1960s it accelerated at a dizzying rate, transforming mainstream views of gender, race, class, sexuality and behaviour, and turning a disciplined, decent, prudish England into a more raucous society that Hogarth and Gillray might have found not wholly unfamiliar.

The "Cool Britannia" of the late 1990s was a much-mocked slogan, yet it was accurate in evoking the plethora of cultural novelties that characterize today's England as much as its traditions. Today, if England inspires admiration, or at least curiosity, it is as likely to be for its modernity in music, art, consumerism and not least the cosmopolitan ferment of London, and the supposed ability of English society to accommodate continuity and discontinuity in tandem. For many at home and abroad, Arsenal and Radiohead are at least as typically English as Beefeaters and bowler hats, and London is the epitome of global modernity. Change has been fuelled by globalization, by the alarming dynamism of the City of London, and by consequent mass immigration. However new these things seem, they have grown out of England's global and imperial past: its present multi-ethnicity is as much a part of its heritage as thatched cottages and cream teas.

## HISTORY AND IDENTITY

Whatever elements, old and new, characterize England's national "civilization" today, taken as a whole it has retained an unusual characteristic: the English have long been "nonchalant" about nationhood and reluctant since the eighteenth century to assert English national rights, even denying that there was such a thing as English nationalism.[20] This is because as the core nation in a multinational state, and then in a global empire, it was neither desirable nor necessary to beat the "nationalist drum." Flag-waving came to seem embarrassingly or absurdly un-English—mocked by Dickens in the person of Mr. Podsnap—and to most English people it remains so. Also perhaps, like Macaulay (see p. 590), they did not greatly care what others thought of them. National identity was defined by what the nation was doing—spreading Christianity, European civilization, free trade, empire. Englishness therefore was not based on notions of ethnic purity or cultural uniqueness, which meant that nationhood was shaped not by "exclusion and opposition" but by "inclusion and expansion."[21] So it easily merged into Britishness, shown by the interchangeable use of "Britain" and "England."

Some commentators have seen it as a problem for the English today that, with empire long gone and Britishness unravelling, no very clear or positive sense of "Englishness" exists, as if it were only what is left over when the other things are taken away. England's lack of any avowed sense of national cohesion or purpose is often contrasted with enthusiastic yet respectable Scottish nationalism: the Cross of St. George, though more commonly displayed than in the past, is mostly confined to sporting events and is somewhat tarnished by association with political extremism. But there is something to be said for national nonchalance. It contrasts with France's unending quarrels about Muslim dress and recent polemics about gay marriage; with Germany's problems about naturalizing ethnic minorities; with America's ancient obsession with race; and with the sharp rise in xenophobic politics even in progressive Holland and Scandinavia. In recent decades the English have largely accommodated the shifts brought by changing moralities and multi-ethnicity, incorporating them into new varieties of Englishness. Who could be more English today than Rita Ora and Dizzee Rascal, Jessica Ennis and Rio Ferdinand?[22]

How important national identity is in people's lives depends on circumstance. We all have many forms of belonging: a nation is only one of them, and rarely among the most prominent except at times of external danger or sporting contests. England's successive incorporation into James VI and I's "Great Britain," the United Kingdom, the empire, the European Community, and a multi-cultural global society added ever more layers of identity, some of which subsequently fell away again. It has been suggested that "there is considerable evidence that people in England feel less and less of a national identity of any kind."[23] This would be nothing new. In the eighteenth century Daniel Defoe, with his sarcastic description of the "mongrel race,"[24] and David Hume, believing that English liberty created individuality, not uniformity,[25] took comparable views. But opinion polls suggest that English feelings of national identity today are strong, and very similar to those of their close European neighbours.[26] According to one critical observer, "It is necessary for peoples to trust each other, and somehow the English still do."[27] They show it in public outrage when trust is betrayed by politicians. This, however little boasted about, is a quality beyond price.

Despite their demise being regularly announced, nations remain the main focus of the political order and the primary guardians of the rights and safety of their citizens. For a nation to work as what Ernest Renan in 1882 called "a great solidarity," he believed that a shared heritage of memories must create a willingness "to continue living together" and to "fructify the heritage"—to make a go of the relationship. Edmund Burke in 1790 had expressed a similar, though more robust, view: all must accept that none had the right to "separate and tear asunder" the common heritage. Without such solidarity, he thought that political systems could rely only on compulsion. Less dramatically, they can just work badly, with high rates of alienation, shown by unwillingness to accept the more altruistic aspects of citizenship such as obeying the law, paying taxes, and voting, instead regarding fraud, nepotism, corruption and apathy as normal. Or they might hesitate on the brink of disintegration, like Belgium, Spain and the United Kingdom, in which the heritage of memories has to some extent been divided up among the constituent parts.

Nations might, Renan suggested, deliberately cultivate a positive shared history to buttress solidarity—an aim that some regard as evidently desirable, and others as an opium of the masses. He also thought that they must deliberately "forget" the divisive parts of their history.[28] This is not only undesirable but ultimately impossible: history does not obediently unite us, and it cannot forever be censored. It should enable us to examine our own assumptions about the past and its meanings for the present—the national stories we tell about ourselves. Knowledge and understanding seem to me the only honest and effective ways of preventing history from being abused—something that I imagine most professional historians believe, or at least hope.

In many countries, and certainly in England, history is often a source of division, an unlocked armoury of partisan weapons. We have a taste for histories of conflict and oppression. At a simple level, this is perhaps due to a naïve fascination with the horrors, cruelties and hardships of the past, which among other things reassure us of our own superiority. At a more sophisticated level, it is a reflection of "Whig history" and its offshoots, a story of progress through conflict that was originally the propaganda of a party, but which largely took over the history of the nation (see pp. 272–73). This story emphasizes struggle, giving the Whig party, its adopted ancestors and its successors the glorious leading roles. In the more radical versions of this myth, England's history is one of oppression, exploitation and conflict, in which every meagre advance in rights had to be seized by popular revolt, usually led by a heroic vanguard. For some this is an inspiring saga, regrettable only in that there was not more of it. When combined with the prevailing declinism of the postwar period, it created a negative overall view of England's history: ten centuries of conflict ending in failure. Hence the gloomy self-image of "inverted Podsnappery"—"*other* Countries" (unspecified) were "in Every Respect Better."

If England's history were indeed such a dark one, we would have to accept it and try to do better in future. But it is a distortion of perspective amounting often to the opposite of the truth. The English have never suffered—not, at least, since the worst periods of the Viking invasions or perhaps "the Anarchy" of the 1140s—prolonged state collapse and general violence comparable, for example, with the terrible ordeals widespread in central Africa since the 1970s. The country has never suffered as vicious a civil war as that in Syria at the time of writing, and has never experienced revolutionary terror anywhere near the scale of eighteenth-century France or twentieth-century Russia, China or Cambodia. Centuries passed without major outbreaks of political violence, primarily because government was strong and the territory relatively secure, preventing catastrophic breakdown and a Hobbesian conflict in which "every man is Enemy to every man." The clashes between "the community of the realm" and some of its monarchs were short and not very lethal. The disappearance of serfdom featured only the brief and unusual episode of the Peasants' Revolt of 1381 and sporadic local struggles. The Wars of the Roses amounted to occasional bursts of warfare involving a small part of the population. Even the religious upheavals of the Tudor and Stuart period avoided the prolonged and bloody wars suffered on the Continent, beside which the English Civil War, the worst internal conflict in the nation's history, pales. Unprecedented social and political changes were accommodated in the eighteenth and nineteenth centuries without revolutionary upheaval, and events such as Luddism and Peterloo were notorious because of their rarity. Compare the religious wars in the Netherlands and Germany, the gory end of absolutism in France in 1789, or the horrific conflicts over peasant land ownership in Russia in the nineteenth and twentieth centuries, in which millions were slaughtered or starved.

It is hard to think of any major improvement since Magna Carta brought about in England by violence. The bloodshed of the Civil War brought not freedom, but religious and military dictatorship. Many of the things we consider pillars of liberty—the Common Law, trial by jury, habeas corpus, religious toleration—came not from popular protest but from policies of the Crown developed by royal judges. Perhaps the only recent example of violence bringing significant change would be the riots preceding the 1832 Reform Act, though that was in some ways a backward step (see pp. 442–43). Democracy arrived between 1867 and 1928 within the existing political system, which could accommodate a wider franchise because it had long been representative before being democratic. Votes for women were ushered in not so much by the Suffragettes as by the First World War, and fully introduced by a Tory Prime Minister, Stanley Baldwin. The modern Welfare State grew out of the common needs and solidarities created by both world wars. Should not this historic predominance of domestic peace be a memory to cherish?

Some object, however, that these undramatic processes of change have meant that England's democracy and liberty are incomplete and uncertain, lacking constitutional guarantees, dependent on the concessions of rulers, and with power and privilege perpetuated in ancient institutions, not least Parliament itself. Yet it is hard to identify countries in which violence has brought about a superior system. France? Russia? China? We are more likely today to seek examples of good government from ancient nations whose histories have shown similar continuity to our own, such as in Scandinavia. However, England is too close to Europe's core, and too much astride its ocean highways, to have developed a comparably harmonious and homogeneous society: a Scandinavian-type England has probably been out of reach since 1066, when the country was politically attached to the near Continent. Political and cultural unity, slowly re-established by the 1400s, evaporated for good a century later in what I have called our religious "Great Divide." England's stormy rise to European and global power beginning in the seventeenth century and completed in the eighteenth made it part of a United Kingdom and a global empire, with economic, cultural and political consequences that are still working themselves out, and creating challenges with which today and in the future the English will have to cope.

Some of our problems are legacies of more recent history, however. Abandonment of age-old characteristics of English governance—decentralization of power under a strong but limited central government, wide participation in local administration and a high level of political involvement—dates only from the mid-twentieth century. A recent study identifies a serious deterioration in the quality of government in Britain only from the 1980s, and it lists many convincing reasons, including the institutional weakness of the Prime Minister, feeble scrutiny by Parliament, fragmentation of policy-making and political pressure to act hastily.[29] As always, we have to assess these things comparatively. In the quality of its government, it is difficult to say whether Britain is worse than other democracies of comparable size. Simple observation suggests that generally it is not. Many of its problems and discontents are shared by other societies wallowing in the luxury of seven decades of unsurpassed peace and prosperity, and having jettisoned the ideological and religious divisions, the utopian visions and the social stratification that once impelled most people to vote. A collapse of political participation, cynicism (sometimes justified) about the professional political class and the consequent rise of anti-establishment movements are phenomena occurring across the Western world.[30]

Where England is very unusual, however, is in having become one of the biggest centralized administrative units in the world, and managing this is a perennial, and perhaps insoluble, contemporary political problem. The growth of the state is a Europe-wide phenomenon arising from the extension of welfare democracy, but rarely in such a centralized form: the proportion of our public spending controlled from the centre is roughly twice that in France, Japan and Italy, and more than three times that in Germany.[31] This concentration of power and responsibility in Whitehall is largely a consequence of the Second World War. The judgement of the historian José Harris bears repeating: war changed Britain "from one of the most localized and voluntaristic countries in Europe to one of the most centralized and bureaucratic."[32] Centralization and bureaucracy were deliberately embraced in the 1940s and 1950s as a means to efficiency and equality. The resulting decline of local government, whose last great age was the 1930s, was further and deliberately accelerated during the political conflicts of the 1970s and 1980s. When economic controls proved counter-productive in peacetime, privatization in the 1980s eventually removed direct political control of industry, but not the political odium when trains run late or energy prices rise. In addition, the clatter of dropped hospital bedpans (see p. 773), GCSE results in Norfolk, teenage stabbings in Brixton, university fee levels, floods in Somerset—a never-ending conveyor belt of everyday problems—create a political and administrative burden that Whitehall and Westminster can neither manage nor surrender. Devolution of power to Edinburgh, Cardiff and Belfast has made England's position all the more stark. We rarely observe how different this is from how most other populous countries manage their affairs: local, regional or state governments, or non-political authorities, have autonomous responsibilities and (in the best cases) democratic accountability. So issues that dominate contemporary English politics—most obviously the endless micromanagement of "schools and hospitals"—are not matters for central government in comparable democratic countries. But centralization is a seventy-year habit we cannot, or will not, break. We may prefer it that way; but it has its price.

Centralization reacts with and is complicated by another English characteristic with a much longer history: the perpetuation of what I have called sectarianism in politics, which originated during the Great Divide. England is not unusual in having had prolonged religious conflict—far from it. Though spared the worst excesses of violence, it nevertheless suffered grievously during the sixteenth and seventeenth centuries; and stability was eventually brought only by the intervention of the Dutch in 1688 as part of a Europe-wide geo-political struggle. This Glorious Revolution legalized religious toleration for practical reasons of state—an important step towards not only religious but also political pluralism. Other countries too developed political systems shaped by religious differences: for example, the familiar duo of religious right and secular left in France and Spain, and of Christian Democrats and Socialists in several other European countries. But England is different. The Glorious Revolution sanctioned the permanent existence of two legally recognized and fairly balanced religious cultures, Anglican and Nonconformist, unlike in those countries (such as France, Italy, Spain, Russia, Prussia, Austria and Scandinavia) in which a single religion formed the overwhelming majority, whether by choice or by compulsion.

So England's major political division was not formed between a religious party of the right and a secularist party of the left, as was usually the case elsewhere, but between rival religious parties. England's opposition tendency (what I have called the "religious left") was more fundamentalist than its Establishment rival. The "Good Old Cause" of Commonwealth men, Whigs, Liberals and finally Labour—all were founded on Dissent, with strong Welsh and Scottish reinforcement. Methodism, as is commonly observed, was more important to this tradition than Marxism. It created a counter-culture determined to bring down the English Establishment as a matter of principle. The religious division took on geographical, social and cultural characteristics (Ambridge versus Coronation Street) still evident today. Economic changes did not efface, but, on the contrary, deepened, them. English politics, particularly on the left, absorbed the style and mentality of religious revivalism, stressing the morality of its causes and not infrequently the wickedness of its opponents ("lower than vermin," in Aneurin Bevan's pithy phrase). This religious fervour provided an inexhaustible dynamism in campaigning for virtue, for rights, for justice, for equality, for self-improvement; and it certainly prevented English political life from descending into a complacent torpor. Tireless campaigns for religious equality, for the abolition of slavery, against alcohol and prostitution, for the rights of women, for human rights abroad and in the empire would have been unimaginable without this restless and demanding conscience. Partly for this reason, issues in our highly centralized system that in many other European countries hardly figure as ideological controversies—welfare, health care, the education system,* even the school curriculum—in England still today take on symbolic importance in which differences of opinion become moral shibboleths solemnly pronounced on by bishops.

It would, however, be a travesty to suggest that our long history has bequeathed us only divisions and problems. By the standards of humanity as a whole, England over the centuries has been among the richest, safest and best governed places on earth, as periodical influxes of people testify. A royal government was developed, with many ups and downs, that was relatively participatory and efficient at maintaining stability and security. Living standards in the fourteenth century were higher than in much of the world in the twentieth.[33] Over the centuries, vast material and cultural investment created a "heritage" that we still admire, and an infrastructure much of which we still use. There has never since the seventeenth century been a government that could by most standards be considered despotic. A political and administrative culture was created that, at least since the later eighteenth century, has been generally honest and public-spirited, and this (with some recent lapses) still survives as a defence against the cancer of corruption. We who have lived in England since 1945 have been among the luckiest people in the existence of *Homo sapiens*, rich, peaceful and healthy. Not uniquely so: the lot of the whole Western world has been comparable, and in several countries slightly better. But for that, too, the people of England over the last 400 years can take a share of credit: for their economic and technological labours; for their long pioneering of the rule of law, of accountability and representation in government, of religious toleration and of civil institutions; and for their determined role in the defeat of modern tyrannies. Whatever its shortcomings, we live comfortably and safely on this legacy, amassed through the labours of many past generations and what Edmund Burke aptly called the wisdom of unlettered men.

I have tried to draw some conclusions, even some lessons, from our united and divided history. But history is more than a sounding-board for our present preoccupations. Like literature and art, it enriches our understanding, expands our sympathies, and simply gives us pleasure. Just as we preserve great buildings and ancient sites, so we seek to know about those

---

* In France the bitter rivalry between state and independent schools was defused in the 1960s by the taxpayer meeting the running costs of the latter in return for contracts with the state; while in Germany the system on which the detested English division of grammar, secondary modern and technical schools was based still exists—without arousing controversy.

who made them. History, like travel, "broadens the mind." The differences we encounter are precious in reminding us that our ways are not the only ways, and that other cultures and other generations have achievements as great as or greater than ours. Yet in the past, as in other countries, only some things are different and much is the same—a reminder of common humanity as well as of cultural diversity.[34]

We owe respect to the past, as we do to other societies today, not for the sake of our predecessors, who are beyond caring, but for our own sake. Treating the past as grotesque and inferior is the attitude of the tourist who can see nothing "Abroad" but dirt and bad plumbing. Recognizing the qualities of past societies with resources a fraction of ours may at least deflate our own complacency, and remind us that we have little excuse for our present social and political failings. Some people debate whether we should feel pride or shame in England's history. Logically, one is impossible without the other. Neither makes much sense unless we feel that something of our predecessors' culture is still alive in us, whether to be cherished or eradicated. Better than either pride or shame, it seems to me, would be to accept responsibility: both for repairing and compensating for the failings of past generations, and for preserving and handing on their achievements. No country and people have had their history more thoroughly explored, debated and retold both by themselves and by others. This is one of the principal ways in which a culture perpetuates and renews itself. It forms our ideas of who and what we once were, now are, and wish some day to become. I hope that a knowledge of history can help us to respect the past, understand the present, and be sensitive to the future. This book is my small contribution, a brick for our common house.

# Notes

ABBREVIATIONS

| | |
|---|---|
| *CEHMB* | *The Cambridge Economic History of Modern Britain*, eds. Roderick Floud and Paul Johnson (3 vols.; Cambridge UP, 2004) |
| *CIHBE* | *The Cambridge Illustrated History of the British Empire*, ed. P. J. Marshall (Cambridge UP, 2011) |
| *CHMEL* | *The Cambridge History of Medieval English Literature*, ed. David Wallace (Cambridge UP, 1999) |
| *CSHB* | *The Cambridge Social History of Britain, 1750–1950*, ed. F. M. L. Thompson (3 vols.; Cambridge UP, 1990) |
| HC Deb | House of Commons Debates |
| *HJ* | *The Historical Journal* |
| *LRB* | *London Review of Books* |
| MDA | "Mémoires et Documents: Angleterre," French Foreign Ministry Archives |
| MTF | Margaret Thatcher Foundation |
| *ODNB* | *Oxford Dictionary of National Biography* (Oxford UP, 2004–9) |
| OECD | Organisation of Economic Cooperation and Development |
| *OHBE* | *The Oxford History of the British Empire*, ed. Wm. Roger Louis et al. (5 vols.; Oxford UP, 1999–2002) |
| ONS | Office of National Statistics |
| *P&P* | *Past & Present* |
| *TLS* | *The Times Literary Supplement* |
| UP | University Press |

## Introduction: Who Do We Think We Are?

1. Benjamin Disraeli, in *Sybil; or, the Two Nations* (1845). 2. Pioneering theorists were John Stuart Mill, "Of Nationality, as Connected with Representative Government," in *Considerations on Representative Government* (1861), and Ernest Renan in an 1882 lecture, "Qu'est-ce qu'une nation?" In recent times, there have been influential works of scholarship both by "modernists" (arguing that nations are recent inventions) and by "primordialists" (arguing that nations have ancient

origins). Notable among the former are Ernest Gellner, *Nations and Nationalism* (Oxford, Blackwell, 1983), and Benedict Anderson, *Imagined Communities: Reflections on the Origins and Spread of Nationalism* (London, Verso, 1983); among the latter, Adrian Hastings, *The Construction of Nationhood: Ethnicity, Religion and Nationalism* (Cambridge UP, 1997).   3. Gellner, *Nations and Nationalism*, p. 138. Other ancient nations (by various criteria) include Denmark, Ireland, Norway and, as Hastings points out (pp. 150–51), Ethiopia.   4. The intellectual pioneer of "British history" was the historian of ideas John Pocock in the 1970s, in "British history: a plea for a new subject," *Journal of Modern History* 47 (1975), pp. 601–21. 5. Norman Davies, *The Isles: A History* (Basingstoke, Macmillan, 2000), p. xxvi. 6. In the famous phrase of William Faulkner.   7. Ernest Renan, *"Qu'est-ce qu'une nation?,"* ed. Philippe Forest (Paris, Bordas, 1991), p. 41 (my translation).   8. The great and somewhat controversial modern monument in this field of scholarship is Pierre Nora, ed., *Les Lieux de mémoire* (3 vols.; Paris, Gallimard, 1984–92), an attempt to catalogue France's national memory; parts translated as *Realms of Memory* (New York, Columbia UP, 1996–8) and *Rethinking France* (Chicago UP, 2001).   9. No work on England or Britain matches the scale and ambition of Nora's project; but approaching the subject is Alexander Grant and Keith Stringer, eds., *Uniting the Kingdom? The Making of British History* (London, Routledge, 1995), and Raphael Samuel et al., *Theatres of Memory* (2 vols.; London, Verso, 1994–8).   10. For example, Paul Langford, *Englishness Identified: Manners and Character, 1650–1850* (Oxford UP, 2000); Robert Colls, *Identity of England* (Oxford UP, 2002); Krishan Kumar, *The Making of English National Identity* (Cambridge UP, 2003); and, in a different register, Peter Mandler, *The English National Character* (New Haven, Conn., Yale UP, 2006).   11. "Of the Life and History of Thucydides" (1629).

## Prelude: The Dreamtime

1. Barry Cunliffe, *Britain Begins* (Oxford UP, 2013), pp. 38, 42, 47, 56–8; Chris Stringer, *Homo Britannicus: The Incredible Story of Human Life in Britain* (London, Allen Lane, 2006), pp. 8–11, 160–63, 231.   2. Cunliffe, *Britain Begins*, pp. 182–93.   3. Marcus Cunliffe, *Iron Age Communities in Britain: An Account of England, Scotland and Wales from the Seventh Century* BC *Until the Roman Conquest* (3rd edn; London, Routledge, 1991), pp. 28–9, 36–41, 58, 114–15; Oliver Rackham, *The History of the Countryside* (London, Phoenix, 2000), pp. xiv, 183, 197; Catherine Hills, *Origins of the English* (London, Duckworth, 2003), ch. 6. 4. Diodorus Siculus, quoted in Cunliffe, *Britain Begins*, p. 320.   5. Cunliffe, *Britain Begins*, pp. 352–4.   6. Ibid., pp. 4, 60–62.   7. Jonathan Scott, *England's Troubles* (Cambridge UP, 2000), p. 10.   8. Geoffrey of Monmouth, *The History of the Kings of Britain* (London, Penguin Books, 1966), pp. 71–3.   9. Cunliffe, *Iron Age*, p. 129. 10. David Mattingley, *An Imperial Possession: Britain in the Roman Empire, 54* BC–AD *409* (London, Allen Lane, 2006), p. 96.   11. Tacitus, *The Annals* (AD 110–20), book XIV.   12. Mattingley, *An Imperial Possession*, pp. 24–5.   13. Ibid.,

pp. 154–7. **14.** Ibid., pp. 157–8, 356, 368–75. **15.** James Campbell et al., *The Anglo-Saxons* (Oxford, Phaidon, 1982), p. 13. **16.** Mattingley, *An Imperial Possession*, p. 530. **17.** Julia M. H. Smith, *Europe After Rome: A New Cultural History, 500–1000* (Oxford UP, 2005), p. 162. **18.** Mattingley, *An Imperial Possession*, p. 534. **19.** Guy Halsall, *Worlds of Arthur: Fact and Fictions of the Dark Ages* (Oxford UP, 2013), p. 15. **20.** Gildas, *De excidio Britanniae: Ad fidem codicum manuscriptorum recensuit Josephus Stevenson* (London, English Historical Society, 1838), pp. 30–31 (my translation). **21.** See Halsall, *Worlds of Arthur*, p. 298. **22.** Cunliffe, *Britain Begins*, pp. 422–4. **23.** Ibid., p. 425. **24.** Smith, *Europe After Rome*, p. 175. **25.** Ibid., pp. 66–72. **26.** Geoffrey, *History*, p. 222. **27.** Antonia Gransden, "The growth of the Glastonbury traditions and legends in the twelfth century," *Journal of Ecclesiastical History* 27 (1976), pp. 337–58. **28.** For an up-to-date scholarly study of the evidence and the myths, see Halsall, *Worlds of Arthur*.

## PART ONE: THE BIRTH OF A NATION

**1.** Patrick Wormald, *The Times of Bede. Studies in Early English Christian Society and Its Historian*, ed. Stephen Baxter (Oxford, Blackwell, 2006), p. 106.

## 1. This Earth, This Realm *c.*600–1066

**1.** Patrick Wormald, in James Campbell et al., *The Anglo-Saxons* (Oxford, Phaidon, 1982), p. 119. **2.** Sarah Foot, "The making of Angelcynn: English identity before the Norman Conquest," *Transactions of the Royal Historical Society*, 6th series, VI (1996), pp. 42–3. **3.** Patrick Wormald, *The Times of Bede: Studies in Early English Christian Society and Its Historian*, ed. Stephen Baxter (Oxford, Blackwell, 2006), pp. 120–21. **4.** Barbara Yorke, *The Conversion of Britain: Religion, Politics and Society in Britain, c.600–800* (Harlow, Pearson, 2006), p. 178. **5.** Gildas, *De excidio Britanniae: Ad fidem codicum manuscriptorum recensuit Josephus Stevenson* (London, English Historical Society, 1838), p. 36. **6.** *Beowulf*, trans. Michael Alexander (London, Penguin Books, 2006), p. 117. **7.** Jonathan Clark, ed., *A World by Itself: A History of the British Isles* (London, Heinemann, 2010), p. 82. **8.** Eric John, in Campbell, *Anglo-Saxons*, p. 160. **9.** See James Campbell, *The Anglo-Saxon State* (London, Hambledon, 2000). **10.** Alfred P. Smyth, *Alfred the Great* (Oxford UP, 1995), pp. 325–8. **11.** *The Anglo-Saxon Chronicle*, trans. and ed. M. J. Swanton (London, Dent, 1996), p. 77. **12.** Eric John, in Campbell, *Anglo-Saxons*, p. 160. **13.** *Anglo-Saxon Chronicle*, p. 81. **14.** Foot, "Angelcynn," pp. 27, 32–3. **15.** Julia Crick and Elizabeth van Houts, eds., *A Social History of England, 900–1200* (Cambridge UP, 2011), p. 341. **16.** See Simon Keynes, "Anglo-Saxon Chronicle," in *The Wiley Blackwell Encyclopedia of Anglo Saxon England*, ed. Michael Lapidge et al. (2nd edn; Chichester, Wiley Blackwell, 2014), pp. 37–8; Campbell, *Anglo-Saxons*, pp. 221–2, 253. **17.** Campbell, *Anglo-Saxons*, pp. 346 7. **18.** Patrick Wormald, in Campbell, *Anglo-Saxons*, p. 157. **19.** E. A. Freeman, in

Sarah Foot, *Aethelstan: The First King of England* (New Haven, Conn., Yale UP, 2011), p. 242; see also David Horspool, *Why Alfred Burned the Cakes: A King and His Eleven-Hundred-Year Afterlife* (London, Profile, 2006), pp. 172–5, 198–203. **20.** *Anglo-Saxon Chronicle*, p. 108. **21.** Foot, *Aethelstan*, pp. 26–7, 216. **22.** Ibid., pp. 227–30. **23.** Patrick Wormald, *Legal Culture in the Early Medieval West: Law as Text, Image and Experience* (London, Hambledon, 1999), p. 260. **24.** Crick and van Houts, *Social History*, p. 121. **25.** Julia Smith, *Europe After Rome: A New Cultural History, 500–1000* (Oxford UP, 2005), p. 157. **26.** Wormald, *Legal Culture*, p. 366. **27.** J. R. Maddicott, *The Origins of the English Parliament, 924–1327* (Oxford UP, 2010), pp. 46–51. **28.** The Icelandic Althing, still existing, dates from the same period, but of course related to a much smaller community. **29.** M. K. Lawson, in Campbell, *Anglo-Saxons*, p. 170. **30.** Hugh M. Thomas, *The English and the Normans: Ethnic Hostility, Assimilation, and Identity, 1066–c.1220* (Oxford UP, 2003), p. 24. **31.** Wormald, *Legal Culture*, p. 381. **32.** Clark, *A World by Itself*, p. 29. **33.** Byrhtferth, in Campbell, *Anglo-Saxons*, p. 192. **34.** Thomas, *English and Normans*, p. 24. **35.** See Donald Scragg, ed., *The Battle of Maldon, AD 991* (Oxford, Blackwell, 1991). **36.** Kevin Crossley-Holland, *The Anglo-Saxon World* (Woodbridge, Boydell, 2002), p. 11. **37.** Maddicott, *Origins of the English Parliament*, p. 438. **38.** Henry of Huntingdon, *The History of the English People, 1000–1154*, trans. Diana Greenway (Oxford UP, 2002), p. 8. **39.** *Anglo-Saxon Chronicle*, p. 142. **40.** Henry of Huntingdon, *History*, p. 13. **41.** Ibid., p. 15. **42.** Barry Cunliffe, *Britain Begins* (Oxford UP, 2013), p. 486. **43.** Maddicott, *Origins of the English Parliament*, pp. 53–4. **44.** Henry of Huntingdon, *History*, p. 18. **45.** Ibid., p. 19. **46.** Simon Thurley, *The Building of England: How the History of England Has Shaped Our Buildings* (London, William Collins, 2013), pp. 65–6. **47.** Richard Mortimer, ed., *Edward the Confessor: The Man and the Legend* (Woodbridge, Boydell, 2009), p. 107. **48.** Paul Hill, *The Road to Hastings: The Politics of Power in Anglo-Saxon England* (Stroud, Tempus, 2005), p. 153. **49.** Bernard Cottret, *Histoire de l'Angleterre* (Paris, Tallandier, 2007), p. 20. **50.** Robert Bartlett, *The Making of Europe* (London, Penguin Books, 1994), p. 41. The non-Frankish kings were the Swedish, Danish and Polish. **51.** *Anglo-Saxon Chronicle*, p. 199. This, the Worcester manuscript, is the only contemporary English account of the battle. **52.** Guillaume de Poitiers, in Pierre Bouet, *Hastings, 14 octobre 1066* (Paris, Tallandier, 2014), p. 128. **53.** Guillaume de Poitiers, in Cottret, *Histoire de l'Angleterre*, p. 22. **54.** Bouet, *Hastings*, pp. 141–3. **55.** Guy of Amiens, in ibid., p. 142. **56.** *Anglo-Saxon Chronicle*, in Crick and van Houts, *Social History*, p. 108. **57.** William of Poitiers, *Gesta Guillelmi*, in Hugh M. Thomas, *The English and the Normans: Ethnic Hostility, Assimilation, and Identity, 1066–c.1220* (Oxford UP, 2003), p. 3. **58.** *Anglo-Saxon Chronicle*, p. 204. **59.** Ann Williams, *The English and the Norman Conquest* (Woodbridge, Boydell, 1995), p. 37. **60.** David Bates, *William the Conqueror* (Stroud, Tempus, 2004), p. 128. **61.** Elaine Treharne, *Living Through Conquest: The Politics of Early English, 1020–1220* (Oxford UP, 2012), p. 122. **62.** Elizabeth van Houts, *Memory and Gender in Medieval Europe, 900–1200* (London, Macmillan, 1999), p. 123. **63.** An eleventh-century charter, in

Thomas, *English and Normans*, p. 20.   **64.** Orderic Vitalis, in M. T. Clanchy, *England and Its Rulers*, *1066–1307* (3rd edn; Oxford, Blackwell, 2006), p. 16. **65.** Crick and van Houts, *Social History*, pp. 227, 253.   **66.** Thomas, *English and Normans*, p. 60; van Houts, *Memory and Gender*, p. 140; Williams, *English and the Norman Conquest*, p. 121.   **67.** Eadmer, monk of Canterbury, in Thomas, *English and Normans*, p. 288.   **68.** Bartlett, *Making of Europe*, p. 272.   **69.** *Anglo-Saxon Chronicle*, p. 215.   **70.** George Garnett, *The Norman Conquest* (Oxford UP, 2009), pp. 6–7.   **71.** F. W. Maitland, "English Law," *Encyclopaedia Britannica* (11th edn; Cambridge UP, 1911), vol. IX, p. 602.   **72.** John Hudson, *The Formation of the English Common Law: Law and Society in England from the Norman Conquest to Magna Carta* (London, Longman, 1996), p. 39.   **73.** Maddicott, *Origins of the English Parliament*, pp. 57–86.

## 2. The Conqueror's Kingdom

**1.** See James Campbell, in Jonathan Clark, ed., *A World by Itself: A History of the British Isles* (London, Heinemann, 2010), p. 108.   **2.** J. R. Maddicott, *The Origins of the English Parliament*, *924–1327* (Oxford UP, 2010), pp. 74–6.   **3.** Ibid., p. 443.   **4.** J. C. Holt, *Colonial England*, *1066–1215* (London, Hambledon, 1997), p. 25.   **5.** George Garnett, *Norman Conquest* (Oxford UP, 2009), p. 125.   **6.** Ann Williams, *The English and the Norman Conquest* (Woodbridge, Boydell, 1995), p. 79.   **7.** M. T. Clanchy, *England and Its Rulers*, *1066–1307* (3rd edn; Oxford, Blackwell, 2006), pp. 45, 92–3; Hugh M. Thomas, *The English and the Normans: Ethnic Hostility, Assimilation, and Identity*, *1066–c.1220* (Oxford UP, 2003), p. 107, who gives details of surviving English lineages.   **8.** J. G. A. Pocock, *The Ancient Constitution and the Feudal Law* (Cambridge UP, 1957), p. 249. **9.** Henry of Huntingdon, *The History of the English People*, *1000–1154*, trans. Diana Greenway (Oxford UP, 2002), p. 31.   **10.** John Gillingham, in Clark, *A World by Itself*, p. 116.   **11.** Clanchy, *England and Its Rulers*, p. 264.   **12.** Bernard Cottret, *Histoire de l'Angleterre* (Paris, Tallandier, 2007), p. 54.   **13.** Thomas, *English and Normans*, pp. 167, 178–9.   **14.** B. R. O'Brien, "From morðor to murdrum: the preconquest origin and Norman revival of the murder fine," *Speculum* 71:2 (1996), pp. 321–57, at p. 322.   **15.** David Carpenter, *The Struggle for Mastery: Britain*, *1066–1284* (London, Penguin Books, 2004), pp. 15, 127.   **16.** Simon Thurley, *The Building of England: How the History of England Has Shaped Our Buildings* (London, William Collins, 2013), p. 84; Holt, *Colonial England*, p. 6. **17.** Garnett, *Norman Conquest*, p. 109.   **18.** Julia Crick and Elizabeth van Houts, eds., *A Social History of England 900–1200* (Cambridge UP, 2011), pp. 368–9. **19.** M. T. Clanchy, *From Memory to Written Record: England 1066–1307* (3rd ed., Chichester, Wiley-Blackwell, 2013), p. 18.   **20.** Ibid., p. 19.   **21.** Thorlac Turville-Petre, *England the Nation: Language, Literature and National Identity*, *1290–1340* (Oxford, Clarendon Press, 2002), p. 95.   **22.** Elaine Treharne, *Living Through Conquest: The Politics of Early English*, *1020–1220* (Oxford UP, 2012), pp. 104–7, 123.   **23.** Jeremy Catto, "Written English: the making of the language,

1370–1400," *P&P* 179 (May 2003), p. 26.   **24.** Treharne, *Living Through Conquest*, pp. 104, 123, 149–51, 187; Elaine Treharne, "Textual communities (vernacular)," in Crick and van Houts, *Social History*, pp. 348–51.   **25.** See Clanchy, *From Memory to Written Record*, pp. 217–25   **26.** John Gillingham, *The English in the Twelfth Century: Imperialism, National Identity and Political Values* (Woodbridge, Boydell, 2000), pp. xvii, 96, 115, 192–3.   **27.** Thomas, *English and Normans*, p. 352.   **28.** Richard Taruskin, *The Oxford History of Western Music*, vol. I: *The Earliest Notations to the Sixteenth Century* (Oxford UP, 2005), p. 387.   **29.** Henry of Huntingdon, *History*, p. 35.   **30.** Ibid., p. 6.   **31.** Holt, *Colonial England*, p. 4; and see Rudyard Kipling, "The Tree of Justice," in *Rewards and Fairies* (London, Macmillan, 1910).   **32.** Gillingham, *The English*, p. xxi.   **33.** Thomas, *English and Normans*, p. 241.   **34.** Henry of Huntingdon, *History*, p. 31.   **35.** Laura Ashe, *Fiction and History in England, 1066–1200* (Cambridge UP, 2007), p. 6; Williams, *English and Norman Conquest*, p. 1.   **36.** Henry of Huntingdon, *History*, p. 89.   **37.** Dauvit Broun, *Scottish Independence and Ideas of Britain: From the Picts to Alexander III* (Edinburgh UP, 2007), pp. 41, 281.   **38.** The complexities are minutely analysed in Pocock, *Ancient Constitution*.   **39.** Benjamin Disraeli, *Sybil; or, The Two Nations* (1845), bk. 3, ch. 5.   **40.** Based on a study at the University of California, *Daily Telegraph* (3 April 2011).   **41.** Pocock, *Ancient Constitution*, pp. 53–4.   **42.** William Stubbs, *The Constitutional History of England* (5th edn; Oxford UP, 1891), vol. 1, pp. 584–5.   **43.** *The Life of Frederick the Great*, in *The Works of Thomas Carlyle* (Cambridge UP, 1897), vol. 3, p. 346.   **44.** J. M. Burrow, *A Liberal Descent: Victorian Historians and the English Past* (Cambridge UP, 1981), p. 147.   **45.** Rudyard Kipling, "Sir Richard's Song," *Puck of Pook's Hill* (1906).   **46.** See, for example, Holt, *Colonial England*.   **47.** See, for example, John Gillingham, in Alexander Grant and Keith J. Stringer, eds., *Uniting the Kingdom? The Making of British History* (London, Routledge, 1995), p. 51.   **48.** Maddicott, *Origins of the English Parliament*, p. 445—an authoritative modern account. **49.** Gillingham, *The English*, pp. 54–5.   **50.** Broun, *Scottish Independence*, pp. 7–21.   **51.** Richard of Hexham, 1138, in Gillingham, *The English*, p. 11. **52.** According to Henry of Huntingdon, *History*, p. 64.   **53.** *Peterborough Chronicle*, in Michael Jones and Malcolm Vale, eds., *England and Her Neighbours, 1066–1453* (London, Hambledon, 1989), p. 8.   **54.** Cottret, *Histoire*, p. 42.   **55.** See Bruce O'Brien, *Reversing Babel: Translation Among the English During an Age of Conquest, c.800–c.1200* (Newark, Delaware UP, 2011).   **56.** W. L. Warren, *Henry II* (new edn; New Haven, Conn., Yale UP, 2000), p. 208. For a concise summary, see Thomas K. Keefe, "Henry II (1133–1189)," *ODNB*.   **57.** Cottret, *Histoire*, p. 44.   **58.** Crick and van Houts, *Social History*, p. 121.   **59.** John Hudson, *The Formation of the English Common Law: Law and Society in England from the Norman Conquest to Magna Carta* (London, Longman, 1996), pp. 159–60. **60.** Jean-Philippe Genet, *La genèse de l'état moderne: Culture et société politique en Angleterre* (Paris, Presses Universitaires de France, 2003), pp. 71–9.   **61.** See John Hudson, *The Oxford History of the Laws of England*, vol. II: *871–1216* (Oxford UP, 2012), pp. 663–7, 754–5, 764–8.   **62.** F. W. Maitland, *The Forms of Action at Common Law* (Cambridge UP, 1936), p. 13.   **63.** See R. C. Van Caenegem, "English Law and the Continent," in *The Birth of the English Common Law* (2nd edn; Cambridge UP, 1988), p. 88.   **64.** A classic summary is F. W. Maitland and F. C. Montague, *A Sketch of English Legal History* (New York, Putnam, 1915).   **65.** On what Henry probably said, see Warren, *Henry II*, pp. 508–9.   **66.** Ibid., p. 112.   **67.** Ibid., p. 627.   **68.** "Chronicon Sancti Martini Turonensis," in John Baldwin, *The Government of Philip Augustus: Foundations of French Royal Power in the Middle Ages* (Berkeley, California UP, 1986), p. 356.   **69.** "Ménestrel de Rheims," in Jean Flori, *Richard the Lionheart: King and Knight* (Edinburgh UP, 2006), p. 412.   **70.** Carpenter, *Struggle for Mastery*, pp. 271, 280, 284.   **71.** F. F. C. Milsom, *Historical Foundations of the Common Law* (2nd edn; London, Butterworth, 1981), p. 410.   **72.** Tom Bingham, *The Rule of Law* (London, Allen Lane, 2010), p. 13.   **73.** Susan Reynolds, *Kingdoms and Communities in Western Europe, 900–1300* (2nd edn; Oxford, Clarendon Press, 1987), p. 268.   **74.** Anne Pallister, *Magna Carta: The Heritage of Liberty* (Oxford, Clarendon Press, 1971), pp. 101–14.   **75.** Carpenter, *Struggle for Mastery*, p. 23.   **76.** Clanchy, *England and Its Rulers*, p. 190.   **77.** Thomas, *English and Normans*, p. 339.   **78.** Carpenter, *Struggle for Mastery*, p. 307.   **79.** Clanchy, *England and Its Rulers*, p. 2. This section owes much to chs. 11 and 13.   **80.** Turville-Petre, *England the Nation*, p. 9.   **81.** Clanchy, *England and Its Rulers*, p. 259.   **82.** Reynolds, *Kingdoms and Communities*, pp. 149, 272; Michael Wood, *The Story of England* (London, Penguin Books, 2012), p. 153.   **83.** Maddicott, *Origins of the English Parliament*, pp. 389, 444–6.

## Five Centuries After Bede

**1.** Clanchy, *England and Its Rulers*, p. 1.   **2.** Peter of Blois, in Thomas, *English and Normans*, p. 301.   **3.** Thomas, *English and Normans*, p. 391.   **4.** Ibid., p. 392.   **5.** James Campbell, in Clark, *A World by Itself*, p. 88.   **6.** Van Caenegem, *Birth of the English Common Law*, p. 5.   **7.** Clanchy, *England and Its Rulers*, p. 245.   **8.** See, for example, Adrian Hastings, *The Construction of Nationhood: Ethnicity, Religion and Nationalism* (Cambridge UP, 1997), p. 4.   **9.** J. H. Baker, *An Introduction to English Legal History* (London, Butterworth, 2002), p. 1.   **10.** Ibid., pp. 28–9.

## PART TWO: THE ENGLISH UNLEASHED
## 3. A Well Good Land

**1.** Draft letter, in Michael Prestwich, *Plantagenet England, 1225–1360* (Oxford UP, 2005), p. 124.   **2.** Rosemary Horrox and W. Mark Ormrod, *A Social History of England, 1200–1500* (Cambridge UP, 2006), pp. 184, 188–90.   **3.** See John Steane, *The Archaeology of Medieval England and Wales* (London, Croom Helm, 1985), p. 107; Paul Hindle, *Roads and Tracks of the Lake District* (Milnthorpe, Cicerone, 1998), p. 58; John Langdon, *Horses, Oxen and Technological Innovation: The Use of Draught Animals in English Farming, 1066 to 1500* (Cambridge UP, 1986).   **4.** See T. Williamson, "Field systems," in *The Wiley Blackwell Encyclopedia of*

*Anglo-Saxon England*, eds. Michael Lapidge et al. (2nd edn; Chichester, Wiley Blackwell, 2014), pp. 188–90.    5. Oliver Rackham, *The History of the Countryside* (London, Phoenix, 2000), pp. 4–15, 172.    6. Ibid., pp. 194–7.    7. Christopher Dyer, *Making a Living in the Middle Ages: The People of Britain, 850–1520* (London, Penguin Books, 2003), pp. 101, 156, 235.    8. Charlotte Roberts and Margaret Cox, *Health and Disease in Britain: From Prehistory to the Present Day* (Stroud, Sutton, 2003), pp. 233–39, 242–48, 265–71.    9. Dyer, *Making a Living*, pp. 158–9, 164–5, 187–225; see also Richard Britnell, "Town life," in Horrox and Ormrod, *Social History*, pp. 134–78.    10. Britnell, "Town life," in Horrox and Ormrod, *Social History*, p. 136.    11. Horrox and Ormrod, *Social History*, p. 43.    12. Ibid., p. 39.    13. John Gillingham, *Richard I* (New Haven, Conn., Yale UP, 1999), pp. 108–9; Nicholas Vincent, "Two papal letters on the wearing of the Jewish badge, 1221 and 1229," *Jewish Historical Studies* 34 (1994–6), p. 209.    14. I. M. W. Harvey, "Was there popular politics in fifteenth-century England?," in R. H. Britnell and A. J. Pollard, eds., *The McFarlane Legacy: Studies in Late Medieval Politics and Society* (Stroud, Sutton, 1995), p. 155.    15. Bruce M. S. Campbell, in Horrox and Ormrod, *Social History*, pp. 188, 223, 225.    16. See Andy Wood, *The Memory of the People: Custom and Popular Senses of the Past in Early Modern England* (Cambridge UP, 2013), ch. 1.    17. Prestwich, *Plantagenet England*, p. 444.    18. Horrox and Ormrod, *Social History*, pp. 417–18.    19. Campbell, in ibid., p. 188.    20. See Mark Bailey, *The English Manor c.1200 to c.1500* (Manchester UP, 2002), and John Hudson, *The Oxford History of the Laws of England*, vol. II: *871–1216* (Oxford UP, 2012), pp. 663–7, 754–5, 764–8.    21. M. T. Clanchy, *England and Its Rulers, 1066–1307* (3rd edn; Oxford, Blackwell, 2006), pp. 273–7; Dyer, *Making a Living*, pp. 178–82; Miri Rubin, *The Hollow Crown: A History of Britain in the Late Middle Ages* (London, Penguin Books, 2005), p. 296.    22. Christopher Dyer, "The ineffectiveness of lordship in England, 1200–1400," *P&P* (2007), supplement 2, pp. 74–5.    23. *Mirror of Justices*, ed. William Joseph Whittaker, Publications of the Selden Society, 7 (London, Quaritch, 1895), p. 125.    24. Horrox and Ormrod, *Social History*, p. 206.    25. Ibid., p. 201.    26. *Sir Gawain and the Green Knight*, ed. and trans. W. S. Merwin (Tarset, Bloodaxe, 2003), p. 64.    27. Gerald Harris, *Shaping the Nation: England, 1360–1461* (Oxford UP, 2005), p. 132; K. B. McFarlane, *England in the Fifteenth Century: Collected Essays* (London, Hambledon, 1981), p. 243n.    28. Virginia Davis, *William Wykeham: A Life* (London, Hambledon Continuum, 2007), p. 201, n.24.    29. Simon Thurley, *The Building of England: How the History of England Has Shaped Our Buildings* (London, William Collins, 2013), pp. 116, 149.    30. Horrox and Ormrod, *Social History*, pp. 143, 176–8.    31. For statistics, see S. H. Rigby, ed., *A Companion to Britain in the Later Middle Ages* (Oxford, Blackwell, 2003), pp. 360–69.    32. See N. M. Trenholme, *The English Monastic Boroughs: A Study in Medieval History* (Columbia, Missouri UP, 1927), pp. 50–55.    33. Christine Carpenter, "Henry VI and the deskilling of the royal bureaucracy," *The Fifteenth Century*, 9 (2010).    34. J. H. Baker, *An Introduction to English Legal History* (4th edn; London, Butterworth, 2002), p. 146; Paul D. Halliday, *Habeas Corpus: From England to Empire* (Cambridge, Mass., Harvard UP, 2010).    35. John Watts, "The pressure of the public in late medieval politics," in Linda Clark and Christine Carpenter, eds., *The Fifteenth Century*, vol. IV: *Political Culture in Late Medieval Britain* (Woodbridge, Boydell, 2004), p. 172. **36.** G. O. Sayles, *The Functions of the Medieval Parliament of England* (London, Hambledon, 1987), vol. I, pp. 12, 15, 17, 23. **37.** Shakespeare, *Henry V*, act IV, scene i. **38.** Christine Carpenter, *The Wars of the Roses: Politics and the Constitution in England, c.1437–1509* (Cambridge UP, 1997), p. 68. **39.** Ibid., p. 39. **40.** Steane, *Archaeology of Medieval England and Wales*, p. 106. **41.** Shakespeare, *Richard II*, act IV, scene i. **42.** J. R. Maddicott, *The Origins of the English Parliament, 924–1327* (Oxford UP, 2010), pp. 388–9. **43.** Julia Crick and Elizabeth van Houts, eds., *A Social History of England, 900–1200* (Cambridge UP, 2011), p. 117 for village homicide; estimates for London suggest a rate between 36 and 52 per 100,000 population: Prestwich, *Plantagenet England*, pp. 507–8. Detroit in 2002 had 41.79 (see Crimeorg statistics) and the Western Cape Province in 2006–7 had 60.7 (Institute of Security Studies statistics). **44.** J. G. Bellamy, "The Coterel gang: an anatomy of a band of fourteenth-century criminals," *English Historical Review* LXXIX (1964), pp. 698–717. **45.** Prestwich, *Plantagenet England*, p. 561. **46.** Table 24, in Stephen Broadberry et al., "British economic growth, 1270–1870" (10 Jan. 2011; draft paper available online); 1990 international dollars (adjusted for purchasing power) are an accepted measure for such comparisons. **47.** Rackham, *History of the Countryside*, p. 88. **48.** Campbell, in Horrox and Ormrod, *Social History*, p. 183; Campbell in Rigby, *Companion*, p. 20. **49.** Bruce M. S. Campbell, "The Great Transition: climate, disease and society in the 13th and 14th centuries," Cambridge, The Ellen McArthur Lectures, February 2013. **50.** Clive Oppenheimer, *Eruptions That Shook the World* (Cambridge UP, 2011), pp. 261–7. **51.** John Gillingham, in Alexander Grant and Keith J. Singer, *Uniting the Kingdom? The Making of British History* (London, Routledge, 1995), p. 51; see also Clanchy, *England and Its Rulers*, p. 306, final sentence. **52.** Broun, *Scottish Independence*, p. 106. **53.** For a summary of the extreme complexity of these relations, see ibid., pp. 12–14. **54.** Colm McNamee, *The Wars of the Bruces* (East Linton, Tuckwell, 1997), p. 20. **55.** George Minois, *La Guerre de cent ans: naissance de deux nations* (Paris, Perrin, 2008), p. 38. **56.** M. Brown, *The Wars of Scotland, 1214–1371* (Edinburgh UP, 2004), p. 26. **57.** Broun, *Scottish Independence*, p. 9. **58.** Christopher Allmand, *The Hundred Years War: England and France at War, c.1300–c.1450* (Cambridge UP, 2001), p. 84. **59.** McNamee, *Wars of the Bruces*, p. 74. **60.** "Annals of Connacht," in ibid., p. 168. **61.** Carpenter, *Wars of the Roses*, p. 40. **62.** W. M. Ormrod, *Edward III* (Stroud, Tempus, 2005), p. 12. **63.** Maddicott, *Origins of the English Parliament*, pp. 359–62, 450. **64.** Huw Price and John Watts, eds., *Power and Identity in the Middle Ages* (Oxford UP, 2007), p. 156. **65.** Prestwich, *Plantagenet England*, p. 309; Minois, *Guerre de cent ans*, pp. 56, 66–7. **66.** The principal modern general history is Jonathan Sumption, *The Hundred Years War* (3 vols.; London, Faber, 1990–2009). **67.** Minois, *Guerre de cent ans*, pp. 68, 70, 75. **68.** Ormrod, *Edward III*, p. 30. **69.** Sumption, *Hundred Years War*, vol. I, pp. 526–31. **70.** Minois, *Guerre de cent ans*, pp. 102, 143. **71.** Harris, *Shaping the Nation*, p. 433. **72.** Froissart's chronicle, in Minois, *Guerre de cent ans*, p. 214. **73.** A

*Parisian Journal, 1405–1449*, trans. Janet Shirley (Oxford, Clarendon Press, 1968), p. 147. **74.** James Sherborne, *War, Politics and Culture in Fourteenth-Century England* (London, Hambledon, 1994), p. 4. **75.** *Sir Gawain and the Green Knight*, pp. 15, 81. **76.** Sir Thomas Malory, *Le Morte Darthur: The Winchester Manuscript*, ed. Helen Cooper (Oxford UP, 1998), p. xii. **77.** Roger Ascham (Elizabeth I's tutor), 1570, in Michael Alexander, *Medievalism: The Middle Ages in Modern England* (New Haven, Conn., Yale UP, 2007), p. 111. **78.** Brother John Clyn, of Kilkenny, in Ole J. Benedictow, *The Black Death, 1346–1353: The Complete History* (Woodbridge, Boydell, 2004), p. 144. **79.** Campbell, "The Great Transition," lecture 4. **80.** Benedictow, *Black Death*, p. 27. **81.** Estimates inevitably vary: see Horrox and Ormrod, *Social History*, pp. 14, 185; Benedictow, *Black Death*, pp. 382–3.

## 4. "The world is changed and overthrown"

**1.** Richard Marks and Paul Williamson, eds., *Gothic Art for England, 1400–1547* (London, V&A, 2003), p. 327; Rosemary Horrox and W. Mark Ormrod, *A Social History of England, 1200–1500* (Cambridge UP, 2006), pp. 248–9, 398–9. **2.** *Piers Ploughman*, in Horrox and Ormrod, *Social History*, p. 186. **3.** Alastair Dunn, *The Great Rising of 1381* (Stroud, Tempus, 2002), p. 34; S. H. Rigby, ed., *A Companion to Britain in the Middle Ages* (Oxford, Blackwell, 2003), p. 76. **4.** Virginia Davis, *William Wykeham: A Life* (London, Hambledon Continuum, 2007), p. 123. **5.** Samuel K. Cohn Jr., "Popular insurrection and the Black Death: a comparative view," *P&P* (2007), supplement 2, pp. 194–204. **6.** R. B. Dobson, *The Peasants' Revolt of 1381* (London, Macmillan, 1983), p. 18; Christopher Dyer, *Making a Living in the Middle Ages: The People of Britain, 850–1520* (London, Penguin Books, 2003), p. 288. **7.** John Gower, *Mirour de l'omme* (c.1377), in Dobson, *Peasants' Revolt*, p. 98. **8.** Ibid., p. xxxvi. **9.** Ibid., p. xxxvii. **10.** Rigby, *Companion*, p. 71. **11.** Ibid., p. 130; R. H. Britnell and A. J. Pollard, eds., *The McFarlane Legacy: Studies in Late Medieval Politics and Society* (Stroud, Sutton, 1995), pp. 156–8. **12.** Dobson, *Peasants' Revolt*, pp. 303–4. **13.** Britnell and Pollard, *McFarlane Legacy*, pp. 159–61. **14.** Dobson, *Peasants' Revolt*, p. 381; Dunn, *Great Rising*, p. 61. I have combined their slightly different renderings with modernized spelling. **15.** Gerald Harris, *Shaping the Nation: England, 1360–1461* (Oxford UP, 2005), p. 448. **16.** Dobson, *Peasants' Revolt*, p. xxxv. **17.** Andy Wood, *The Memory of the People: Custom and Popular Senses of the Past in Early Modern England* (Cambridge UP, 2013), p. 53. **18.** Dyer, *Making a Living*, pp. 298, 332. **19.** Wood, *Memory of the People*, p. 45. **20.** Ibid., pp. 50, 59. **21.** It can be heard, for example, on the CD *Music for Henry V and the House of Lancaster*, by the Binchois Consort (London, Hyperion Records, 2010). **22.** Richard Taruskin, *The Oxford History of Western Music*, vol. I: *The Earliest Notations to the Sixteenth Century* (Oxford UP, 2005), pp. 421–3, 433. **23.** Marks and Williamson, *Gothic Art for England*, pp. 126, 165. **24.** Dyer, *Making a Living*, p. 355; Maryanne Kowaleski, in Horrox and Ormrod, *Social History*, p. 256. **25.** Simon

Thurley, *The Building of England: How the History of England Has Shaped Our Buildings* (London, William Collins, 2013), pp. 157–63. **26.** John H. Harvey, *Henry Yevele: The Life of an English Architect* (London, Batsford, 1944). **27.** Ibid., p. 76. **28.** Marks and Williamson, *Gothic Art for England*, p. 130. **29.** Calculated in 1990 international dollars. Bruce M. S. Campbell, "The Great Transition: climate, disease and society in the thirteenth and fourteenth centuries," Cambridge, The Ellen McArthur Lectures, February 2013, lecture 4. **30.** Horrox and Ormrod, *Social History*, pp. 219, 242. **31.** Robert Tittler and Norman Jones, eds., *A Companion to Tudor Britain* (Oxford, Blackwell, 2004), p. 216. **32.** Jan de Vries, *The Industrious Revolution: Consumer Behaviour and the Household Economy, 1650 to the Present* (Cambridge UP, 2008), p. 87; Jonathan Clark, ed., *A World by Itself: A History of the British Isles* (London, Heinemann, 2010), pp. 139–40, 143. **33.** Thorlac Turville-Petre, *England the Nation: Language, Literature and National Identity, 1290–1340* (Oxford, Clarendon Press, 2002), p. 181. **34.** Ibid., pp. 9, 34–5, 71–5, 98–9. **35.** John of Trevisa (1385), in Charles Barber et al., *The English Language: A Historical Introduction* (2nd edn; Cambridge UP, 2009), p. 153. **36.** Jeremy Catto, "Written English: the making of the language 1370–1400," *P&P* 179 (May 2003), p. 27. **37.** Richard J. Watts, *Language Myths and the History of English* (Oxford UP, 2011), pp. 30–34. **38.** David Crystal, *The Stories of English* (London, Penguin Books, 2005), pp. 149–53, 162. **39.** Aude Mairey, *Une Angleterre entre rêve et réalité: Littérature et société dans l'Angleterre du XIVe siècle* (Paris, Sorbonne, 2007), pp. 70–74, 415–19. **40.** Crystal, *Stories of English*, p. 176; G. Olson, "Geoffrey Chaucer," in *CHMEL*, pp. 580, 582. **41.** See Barber, *English Language*, pp. 201–10. **42.** Catto, "Written English," pp. 40–41. **43.** Miri Rubin, *The Hollow Crown: A History of Britain in the Late Middle Ages* (London, Penguin Books, 2005), p. 150. **44.** A. L. Brown and Henry Summerson, "Henry IV (1367–1413)," in *ODNB*. **45.** Steven Justice, "Lollardy," in *CHMEL*, p. 676. **46.** See Anne Hudson and Anthony Kenny, "Wyclif, John (d. 1384)," in *ODNB*. **47.** Michael Alexander, *Medievalism: The Middle Ages in Modern England* (New Haven, Conn., Yale UP, 2007), p. 123. **48.** Sir Thomas Malory, *Le Morte Darthur: The Winchester Manuscript*, ed. Helen Cooper (Oxford UP, 1998), p. xii. See also P. J. C. Field, "Malory, Sir Thomas," in *ODNB*. **49.** *CHMEL*, pp. 725, 821. **50.** Harris, *Shaping the Nation*, pp. 451–2. A different explanation of Richard's policy is given by Christopher Fletcher, *Richard II: Manhood, Youth and Politics, 1377–99* (Oxford UP, 2008), who stresses Richard's determination to assert his authority on leaving childhood. **51.** W. M. Ormrod, *Political Life in Medieval England, 1300–1450* (London, Macmillan, 1995), p. 97. **52.** Harris, *Shaping the Nation*, p. 481. **53.** Parliamentary records, in Fletcher, *Richard II*, p. 271. **54.** *Chronical of Adam Usk*, in Gwilym Dodd and Douglas Biggs, eds., *The Reign of Henry IV: Rebellion and Survival, 1403–13* (York, Medieval Press, 2008), p. 48. **55.** George Minois, *La Guerre de cent ans: naissance de deux nations* (Paris, Perrin, 2008), p. 294. **56.** Harris, *Shaping the Nation*, p. 587. **57.** Ibid., p. 594. **58.** *Gesta Henrici Quinti*, in ibid., p. 543. **59.** Minois, *Guerre de cent ans*, p. 305. **60.** Anne Curry and Michael Hughes, eds., *Arms, Armies and Fortifications in the Hundred Years War* (Woodbridge, Boydell,

1994), pp. 161–81.   **61.** Minois, *Guerre de cent ans*, p. 311.   **62.** D. McCullock and E. D. Jones, "The Lancastrian politics, the French war, and the rise of the popular element," *Speculum* 58 (1983), p. 99.   **63.** See Jean Favier, *Pierre Cauchon: comment on devient le juge de Jeanne d'Arc* (Paris, Fayard, 2010).   **64.** Minois, *Guerre de cent ans*, p. 323.   **65.** Ibid., p. 342.   **66.** Jules Michelet, *Histoire de France* (5 vols.; Paris, Hachette, 1833), vol. 2, p. 113.   **67.** *Parisian Journal*, p. 272.   **68.** John Watts, "The pressure of the public in late medieval politics," in Linda Clark and Christine Carpenter, eds., *The Fifteenth Century*, vol. IV: *Political Culture in Late Medieval Britain* (Woodbridge, Boydell, 2004), pp. 160, 162; Brendan Simms, *Europe: The Struggle for Supremacy, 1453 to the Present* (London, Allen Lane, 2013), p. 22.   **69.** Paston letters, in Helen Castor, *Blood and Roses: The Paston Family and the Wars of the Roses* (London, Faber, 2004), p. 61.   **70.** Ibid., p. 97.   **71.** See Simms, *Europe*, pp. 7–8.   **72.** John Watts, *Henry VI and the Politics of Kingship* (Cambridge UP, 1996), p. 364; Carpenter, *Wars of the Roses*, pp. 254–7.   **73.** See Veronica Fiorato et al., eds., *Blood Red Roses: The Archaeology of a Mass Grave from the Battle of Towton* (Oxford, Oxbow, 2000).   **74.** Carpenter, *Wars of the Roses*, p. 205. See also Hannes Kleinecke, *Edward IV* (London, Routledge, 2009), pp. 208–9.   **75.** Carpenter, *Wars of the Roses*, p. 204.   **76.** Anthony Goodman, *The Wars of the Roses: Military Activity and English Society, 1452–97* (London, Routledge, 1981), p. 93; Michael K. Jones, "The myth of 1485: did France really put Henry Tudor on the throne?," in David Crummitt, ed., *The English Experience in France, c.1450–1588* (Aldershot, Ashgate, 2002), pp. 103–5.   **77.** Thomas Penn, *Winter King: The Dawn of Tudor England* (London, Allen Lane, 2011), p. 10.   **78.** Clifford S. L. Davies, "A rose by another name," *TLS* (13 June 2008), pp. 14–15.   **79.** Carpenter, *Wars of the Roses*, p. 247.   **80.** K. B. McFarlane, *England in the Fifteenth Century: Collected Essays* (London, Hambledon, 1981), pp. 243–4; Colin Richmond, "Identity and morality: power and politics during the Wars of the Roses," in Huw Pryce and John Watts, *Power and Identity in the Middle Ages* (Oxford UP, 2007), pp. 226–41.   **81.** Castor, *Blood and Roses*, chap 10.   **82.** Christine Carpenter, "Henry VI and the deskilling of the royal bureaucracy," *The Fifteenth Century* 9 (2010), pp. 36–7; Carpenter, *Wars of the Roses*, pp. 264–8.   **83.** Penn, *Winter King*, p. xx; Carpenter, *Wars of the Roses*, pp. 250–51, 266–8.   **84.** I. Harvey, in Britnell and Pollard, *McFarlane Legacy*, p. 158.   **85.** Harris, *Shaping the Nation*, p. 650.

## Writing the Middle Ages: Shakespeare and Lesser Historians

**1.** Neil MacGregor, *Shakespeare's Restless World* (London, Allen Lane, 2012), pp. 84–5.   **2.** The rarely performed *Edward III* was probably partly by Shakespeare.   **3.** Stuart Hampton-Reeves, "Theatrical afterlives," in Michael Hattaway, ed., *The Cambridge Companion to Shakespeare's History Plays* (Cambridge UP, 2002), p. 242.   **4.** John Kerrigan, *Archipelagic English: Literature, History and Politics, 1503–1707* (Oxford UP, 2008), pp. 13–21.   **5.** Richard Helgerson, *Forms of Nationhood: The Elizabethan Writing of England* (Chicago UP, 1994); Peter

Mandler, *The English National Character* (New Haven, Conn., Yale UP, 2006), p. 12. **6.** Shakespeare, *Henry VI*, I, act IV, scene vii.

## PART THREE: THE GREAT DIVIDE, *c.* 1500–*c.* 1700

**1.** Diarmaid MacCulloch, *A History of Christianity: The First Three Thousand Years* (London, Allen Lane, 2009), p. 594. **2.** For example, ibid., p. 596. **3.** Eamon Duffy, *The Stripping of the Altars: Traditional Religion in England, c.1400–c.1580* (New Haven, Conn., Yale UP, 2005), part I. **4.** Priscilla Martin, *William Tyndale's New Testament* (Ware, Wordsworth, 2002), pp. xii, xvii.

## 5. Reformation

**1.** Catrina Banks Whitley and Kyra Kramer, "A new explanation for the reproductive woes and midlife decline of Henry VIII," *HJ* 53 (2010), pp. 827–48. **2.** G. W. Bernard, *The King's Reformation: Henry VIII and the Remaking of the English Church* (New Haven, Conn., Yale UP, 2005), p. 17. **3.** Eric Ives, *The Life and Death of Anne Boleyn* (Oxford, Blackwell, 2004), pp. 161, 171; Bernard, *King's Reformation*, pp. 6–8. **4.** Diarmaid MacCulloch, *Reformation: Europe's House Divided, 1490–1700* (London, Allen Lane, 2003), p. xx. **5.** John Guy, *Tudor England* (Oxford UP, 1988), p. 126. **6.** Bernard, *King's Reformation*, p. 145. **7.** David Edwards et al., eds., *Age of Atrocity: Violence and Political Conflict in Early Modern Ireland* (Dublin, Four Courts, 2010), pp. 10, 53–4. **8.** Draft proclamation, 1539, in G. W. Bernard, "The making of religious policy, 1533–1546: Henry VIII and the search for the middle way," *HJ* 41 (June 1998), p. 332. **9.** Norman Cohn, *The Pursuit of the Millennium: Revolutionary Millenarians and Mystical Anarchists of the Middle Ages* (London, Paladin, 1970), ch. 13. **10.** Diarmaid MacCulloch, *Thomas Cranmer: A Life* (New Haven, Conn., Yale UP, 1996), pp. 169, 316. **11.** Guy, *Tudor England*, p. 146. **12.** Greg Walker, "Rethinking the fall of Anne Boleyn," *HJ* 45 (March 2002), pp. 1–29. **13.** Ives, *Anne Boleyn*, p. 344. **14.** Walker, "Rethinking," p. 11. **15.** Bernard, *King's Reformation*, p. 374; see also Alison Wall, *Power and Protest in England, 1525–1640* (London, Arnold, 2000), pp. 132, 170–72. **16.** See N. A. M. Rodger, *The Safeguard of the Sea: A Naval History of Britain, 660–1649* (London, Penguin Books, 2004), ch. 13. **17.** William Underwood, "Thomas Cromwell and William Marshall's Protestant books," *HJ* 47 (2004), pp. 537. **18.** Guy, *Tudor England*, p. 188; Bernard, *King's Reformation*, pp. 516–21. **19.** Bernard, *King's Reformation*, pp. 565–75; Bernard, "Making of religious policy," p. 340. **20.** MacCulloch, *Cranmer*, pp. 287–8. **21.** Ibid., pp. 312–13, 323. **22.** Elaine V. Beilin, ed., *The Examinations of Anne Askew* (Oxford UP, 1996), p. 127. **23.** Faramerz Dabhoiwala, *The Origins of Sex: A History of the First Sexual Revolution* (London, Allen Lane, 2012), pp. 13–16. **24.** Guy, *Tudor England*, p. 225. **25.** MacCulloch, *Cranmer*, pp. 410–20. **26.** Anna Whitelock and Diarmaid MacCulloch, "Princess Mary's household and the succession crisis, July 1553," *HJ* 50 (2007), p. 285.

27. MacCulloch, *Cranmer*, p. 546.   28. Eamon Duffy, *The Stripping of the Altars: Traditional Religion in England, c.1400–c.1580* (New Haven, Conn., Yale UP, 2005), part I, p. 562.   29. Eamon Duffy, *Fires of Faith: Catholic England under Mary Tudor* (New Haven, Conn., Yale UP, 2009), p. 7.   30. Duffy, *Stripping*, p. 528.   31. Duffy, *Fires of Faith*, p. 156.   32. MacCulloch, *Cranmer*, pp. 56, 572–605.   33. Duffy, *Stripping*, p. 565.   34. Guy, *Tudor England*, p. 239.   35. Duffy, *Stripping*, p. 477; and see Alexandra Walsham, *The Reformation of the Landscape: Religion, Identity and Memory in Early Modern Britain and Ireland* (Oxford UP, 2011).   36. Brad S. Gregory, *Salvation at Stake: Christian Martyrdom in Early Modern Europe* (Cambridge, Mass., Harvard UP, 1999), p. 9.   37. David Daniell, *Tyndale: A Biography* (New Haven, Conn., Yale UP, 1994), p. 277; Guy, *Tudor England*, p. 135; John Guy, *A Daughter's Love* (London, Fourth Estate, 2008), pp. 196–7.   38. F. W. Maitland, "English Law," *Encyclopaedia Britannica* (11th edn; Cambridge UP, 1911), p. 604.   39. Alexandra Walsham, "History, memory and the English Reformation," *HJ* 55 (2012), p. 904.   40. Guy, *Tudor England*, p. 251.   41. R. Bowers, "The Chapel Royal, the first Edwardian Prayer Book, and Elizabeth's settlement of religion, 1559," *HJ* 43 (2000), pp. 317–44.   42. By Christopher Haigh.   43. Conrad Russell, "The Reformation and the creation of the Church of England, 1550–1640," in John Morrill, ed., *The Oxford Illustrated History of Tudor and Stuart Britain* (Oxford UP, 1996), p. 280.   44. J. Sanderson, ed., *Change Ringing: The History of an English Art* (Cheltenham, Central Council of Church Bell Ringers, 1987), vol. I, pp. 34–8.   45. Richard Taruskin, *The Oxford History of Western Music*, vol. I: *The Earliest Notations to the Sixteenth Century* (Oxford UP, 2005), pp. 670–78.   46. Richard Rex, *Elizabeth: Fortune's Bastard?* (Stroud, Tempus, 2007), p. 68.   47. Christopher Haigh, *Elizabeth I* (2nd edn, Harlow, Pearson, 1998), p. 42.   48. See Ethan H. Shagan, "The English inquisition: constitutional conflict and ecclesiastical law in the 1590s," *HJ* 47 (2004).   49. Duffy, *Stripping*, p. 593.   50. Robert Tittler and Norman Jones, eds., *A Companion to Tudor Britain* (Oxford, Blackwell, 2004), p. 454.   51. Ibid., pp. 477–80, 483–5.   52. M. J. Rodriguez-Salgado, "The Anglo-Spanish war: the final episode in 'the Wars of the Roses'?," in M. J. Rodriguez-Salgado and Simon Adams, eds., *England, Spain and the Gran Armada, 1585–1604* (Edinburgh, John Donald, 1991), pp. 2–4.   53. Allan I. Macinnes and Jane Ohlmeyer, eds., *The Stuart Kingdoms in the Seventeenth Century: Awkward Neighbours* (Dublin, Four Courts Press, 2002), p. 76.   54. Cecil, in Stephen Alford, *Burghley: William Cecil at the Court of Elizabeth I* (New Haven, Conn., Yale UP, 2008), p. 106.   55. Rodger, *Safeguard of the Sea*, pp. 244–5.   56. Alford, *Burghley*, pp. 105, 174, 188.   57. Ibid., p. 199.   58. Edwards et al., *Age of Atrocity*, pp. 83–5.   59. Alford, *Burghley*, p. 249. See the vivid memoirs of a Jesuit missionary, *John Gerard: Autobiography of an Elizabethan*, ed. P. Caraman (Oxford, Family Publications, 2006).   60. Alexandra Walsham, "Miracles and the counter-reformation mission to England," *HJ* 46 (2003), pp. 812–13.   61. Patrick McGrath, *Papists and Puritans Under Elizabeth I* (London, Blandford, 1967), p. 173.   62. Walsham, "Miracles," p. 806.   63. Rex, *Elizabeth*, pp. 171–2.   64. McGrath, *Papists*, p. 193; John Morrill, "Dungeon, fire and sword" (paper given to St. John's College History

Society, 27 Jan. 2011). 65. John H. Langbein, *Torture and the Law of Proof: Europe and England in the Ancien Regime* (Chicago UP, 1977); William Richardson, "Richard Topcliffe," in *ODNB*; Alford, *Burghley*, p. 241. 66. Ibid., p. 242. 67. Ibid., p. 254. 68. Retha M. Warnicke, *Mary Queen of Scots* (London, Routledge, 2006), p. 232; Rodriguez-Salgado, "Anglo-Spanish war," pp. 9–10. 69. Alford, *Burghley*, p. 262. 70. Rodriguez-Salgado, "Anglo-Spanish war," pp. 12–17. 71. Rodriguez-Salgado and Adams, *England, Spain*, p. 272. 72. Alford, *Burghley*, p. 306; Rodger, *Safeguard of the Sea*, p. 253. 73. Ibid., pp. 248, 255. 74. Rodriguez-Salgado and Adams, *England, Spain*, p. 264. 75. Ibid., pp. 22, 273, 277; Rodger, *Safeguard of the Sea*, p. 259. 76. Colin Martin and Geoffrey Parker, *The Spanish Armada* (2nd edn, Manchester UP, 1999), p. 37. 77. Rodger, *Safeguard of the Sea*, p. 264. 78. Martin and Parker, *Spanish Armada*, pp. 187, 241. 79. Ibid., p. 236. 80. Garrett Mattingly, *The Defeat of the Spanish Armada* (London, Jonathan Cape, 1959), p. 295. 81. Martin and Parker, *Spanish Armada*, p. 242. 82. Rodger, *Safeguard of the Sea*, p. 296. 83. Keith Thomas, *The Ends of Life: Roads to Fulfilment in Early Modern England* (Oxford UP, 2009), p. 61. 84. Steve Hindle, "County government in England," in Tittler and Jones, *Companion to Tudor Britain*, p. 98. 85. "Homily against disobedience and wilful rebellion," in Rex, *Elizabeth*, p. 211. 86. Concepts formulated by the American cultural anthropologist Ruth Benedict, in *Patterns of Culture* (Boston, Houghton Mifflin, 1934). 87. David Norton, *The King James Bible: A Short History from Tyndale to Today* (Cambridge UP, 2011), p. 101; John T. Day et al., eds., *Word, Church and State: Tyndale Quincentenary Essays* (Washington, D.C., Catholic University of America Press, 1998), p. 17. 88. Andrew Boorde (traveller and physician), *c.*1550, in David Crystal, *The Stories of English* (London, Penguin Books, 2005), p. 287. 89. In Janel L. Mueller, *The Native Tongue and the Word: Developments in English Prose Style, 1380–1580* (Chicago UP, 1984), p. 166. 90. Gerald Hammond, "How they brought the good news to Halifax: Tyndale's Bible and the emergence of the English nation state," *Reformation*, 1 (1996), p. 14; Patrick Collinson, "William Tyndale and the course of the English Reformation," ibid., p. 77; Daniell, *Tyndale*, pp. 3, 280; Patrick Collinson, in Michael Hattaway, ed., *Companion to English Renaissance Literature and Culture* (Oxford, Blackwell, 2000), p. 30. 91. Collinson, in Hattaway, *Companion*, p. 30. See also Gordon Jackson, "The poetics of Tyndale's translation," and David Norton, "Buttons and ribbons, hartgoats and hedgehogs," *Reformation*, 1 (1996). 92. Stella Brooke, *The Language of the Book of Common Prayer* (London, André Deutsch, 1965), p. 20. 93. Norton, "Buttons," p. 132. 94. Mueller, *Native Tongue*, pp. 220–22. 95. He receives barely more space in the *Oxford Companion to English Literature* (2009) than the previous entry, Kenneth Tynan. 96. Gerald Hammond, in Hattaway, *Companion*, p. 167. 97. Norton, *King James Bible*, p. 84; Adam Nicolson, *Power and Glory: Jacobean England and the Making of the King James Bible* (London, HarperCollins, 2003), p. 58. 98. Miles Smith, in Nicolson, *Power and Glory*, p. 224. 99. Ibid., p. 211. 100. Ibid., pp. 192–3. I have modernized the spelling. 101. Hattaway, *Companion*, p. 33; Hilary Larkin, "The measure of Englishness in the Early Modern era" (Cambridge PhD thesis, 2007).

102. Norton, *King James Bible*, p. 191.   103. See Eugen Weber, *Peasants into Frenchmen: The Modernization of Rural France, 1870–1914* (London, Chatto & Windus, 1977), pp. 67–94.   104. See Benedict Anderson, *Imagined Communities: Reflections on the Origins and Spread of Nationalism* (London, 1991).   105. Patrick Collinson, in Hattaway, *Companion*, p. 33.   106. Ibid., p. 431.   107. See Lynn Enterline, *Shakespeare's Classroom: Rhetoric, Discipline, Emotion* (Philadelphia, Pennsylvania UP, 2013).   108. See Neil MacGregor, *Shakespeare's Restless World* (London, Allen Lane, 2012).   109. A. D. Nuttall, *Shakespeare the Thinker* (New Haven, Conn., Yale UP, 2007), pp. 17–22, 88, 94–9, 235; Jonathan Bate, *Soul of the Age: The Life, Mind and World of William Shakespeare* (London, Penguin Books, 2009), pp. 30–35.   110. See Richard Helgerson, *Forms of Nationhood: The Elizabethan Writing of England* (Chicago UP, 1992).   111. John Pemble, *Shakespeare Goes to Paris: How the Bard Conquered France* (London, Hambledon, 2005).   112. Nuttall, *Shakespeare the Thinker*, p. 88.   113. Berowne, in *Love's Labour's Lost*, act V, scene ii.   114. *Romeo and Juliet*, act III, scene ii.   115. François-Marie Arouet de Voltaire, "Du théâtre anglais (Appel à toutes les nations d'Europe)," *Œuvres Complètes de Voltaire* (92 vols.; Kehl, Société littéraire-typographique, 1785), vol. 61, pp. 350–76 (my translation).   116. Pemble, *Shakespeare*, pp. 105–6.   117. See Crystal, *Stories of English*, pp. 330–31.   118. David Crystal, *"Think on my words": Exploring Shakespeare's Language* (Cambridge UP, 2008), pp. 104, 230.

# 6. Revolution

1. Samuel R. Gardiner, *History of the Great Civil War, 1642–1649* (3 vols.; London, Longman Green, 1886–91), vol. 1, pp. 196–7.   2. Mark Kishlansky, *A Monarchy Transformed: Britain, 1603–1714* (London, Penguin Books, 1997), p. 78.   3. John Kerrigan, *Archipelagic English: Literature, History and Politics, 1503–1707* (Oxford UP, 2008), pp. 13–21.   4. *Journal of the House of Commons*, vol. I (22 March 1604).   5. Ezechiel 37:22.   6. J. G. A. Pocock, *The Ancient Constitution and the Feudal Law: A Study of English Historical Thought in the Seventeenth Century* (Cambridge UP, 1987), p. 237.   7. F. W. Maitland, "English Law," *Encyclopaedia Britannica* (11th edn; Cambridge UP, 1911), vol. IX, p. 605.   8. Anne Pallister, *Magna Carta: The Heritage of Liberty* (Oxford, Clarendon Press, 1971), p. 10.   9. Tom Bingham, *The Rule of Law* (London, Allen Lane, 2010), p. 17.   10. Jenny Wormald, "James VI and I (1566–1625)," in *ODNB*.   11. Mark Nicholls, *Investigating Gunpowder Plot* (Manchester UP, 1991), pp. 214–21.   12. It has been suggested that much of the powder had deteriorated and was harmless. This underestimates the military expertise of the plotters: detonation of part of it would have set off the rest.   13. Paper given by John Morrill at St. John's College History Society, 27 Jan. 2011.   14. Ronald Hutton, *Debates in Stuart History* (Basingstoke, Palgrave Macmillan, 2004), p. 80.   15. John Morrill, *The Nature of the English Revolution* (London, Longman, 1993), p. 8.   16. Kevin Sharpe, *The Personal Rule of Charles I* (New Haven, Conn., Yale UP, 1992), p. 56.   17. Ibid., pp. 656–7.   18. Hutton, *Debates*, pp. 78–9.   19. Alison Wall, *Power and Protest*

*in England, 1525–1640* (London, Arnold, 2000), p. 181. 20. Hutton, *Debates*, pp. 67–8. 21. Michael Braddick, *God's Fury, England's Fire: A New History of the English Civil Wars* (London, Allen Lane, 2008), p. 56. 22. "The Declaration of Sports," in Samuel Rawson Gardiner, *The Constitutional Documents of the Puritan Revolution, 1628–1660* (Oxford, Clarendon Press, 1889), pp. 31–5; Sharp, *Personal Rule*, p. 355. 23. Patrick Collinson, "Antipuritanism," in John Coffey and Paul C. H. Lim, eds., *The Cambridge Companion to Puritanism* (Cambridge UP, 2008), p. 23. 24. Patrick Collinson, quoted. in Sharp, *Personal Rule*, p. 731. 25. Christopher Hill, *Society and Puritanism in Pre-Revolutionary England* (London, Panther, 1969), p. 230. See also David Underdown, *Fire from Heaven: Life in an English Town in the Seventeenth Century* (New Haven, Conn., Yale UP, 1994). 26. A Whig tract (1720), in J. C. D. Clark, *English Society, 1688–1832* (Cambridge UP, 1985), p. 289. 27. Francis Rous (stepbrother of the prominent parliamentarian John Pym), in Diane Purkiss, *The English Civil War: A People's History* (London, Harper Perennial, 2007), p. 100. 28. Sharp, *Personal Rule*, pp. 758–63. 29. Wall, *Power and Protest*, pp. 93, 180; Charles Carlton, *Going to the Wars: The Experience of the British Civil Wars, 1638–1651* (London, Routledge, 1992), pp. 10–12. In Essex, offences tried as murder were 0.83 per 100,000 population; recorded homicides in 2004–5 were 0.8 per 100,000. 30. Morrill, *Nature*, p. 5; Sharp, *Personal Rule*, p. 610. 31. Ibid., pp. 792–5; Kishlansky, *Monarchy Transformed*, p. 49; Purkiss, *English Civil War*, p. 76. 32. Sir Henry Slingsby's diary, in Sharp, *Personal Rule*, p. 844. 33. Braddick, *God's Fury*, pp. 82–5. 34. Ibid., p. 95; Bingham, *Rule of Law*, p. 16. 35. Purkiss, *English Civil War*, p. 117. 36. John Reeve, "Secret alliance and Protestant agitation in two kingdoms: the early Caroline background to the Irish rebellion of 1641," in Ian Gentles et al., *Soldiers, Writers and Statesmen of the English Revolution* (Cambridge UP, 1998), p. 34. 37. David Edwards et al., *Age of Atrocity: Violence and Political Conflict in Early Modern Ireland* (Dublin, Four Courts, 2010), pp. 154–91; Braddick, *God's Fury*, p. 175; Purkiss, *English Civil War*, pp. 110–12. 38. Mark Stoyle, "English 'nationalism,' Celtic particularism, and the English civil war," *HJ* 43 (2000), p. 1116. 39. "The Grand Remonstrance" (1 Dec. 1641), in Gardiner, *Constitutional Documents*, pp. 127–54. 40. Purkiss, *English Civil War*, p. 122. 41. "A Declaration of the House of Commons" (17 Jan. 1642), in Gardiner, *Constitutional Documents*, pp. 159–63. 42. Anthony Fletcher, *The Outbreak of the English Civil War* (London, Arnold, 1981), p. 182. 43. Sharp, *Personal Rule*, pp. 180–83; and see Francis Haskell, *The King's Pictures* (New Haven, Conn., Yale UP, 2013). 44. See Hutton, *Debates*, pp. 86–7, 90. 45. Edward, Earl of Clarendon, *The History of the Rebellion and Civil Wars in England*, ed. W. Dunn Macray (6 vols.; Oxford, Clarendon Press, 1888; repub. 1992), vol. 4, p. 490. 46. See Sharp, *Personal Rule*, p. 954. 47. Braddick, *God's Fury*, pp. 209, 219–20. 48. Letter of 24 June 1642, *Letters of the Lady Brilliana Harley*, ed. Thomas Taylor Lewis (London, Camden Society, 1854), p. 172. 49. Fletcher, *Outbreak*, p. 360; Morrill, *Nature*, p. 15. 50. Fletcher, *Outbreak*, p. 372; Keith Thomas, *The Ends of Life: Roads to Fulfilment in Early Modern England* (Oxford UP, 2009), p. 62. 51. John Walter, *Understanding Popular Violence in the English Revolution: The Colchester*

*Plunderers* (Cambridge UP, 1999). **52.** Gardiner, *History of the Great Civil War*, vol. 1, p. 197. **53.** Charles Carlton, *This Seat of Mars: War and the British Isles, 1485–1746* (New Haven, Conn., Yale UP, 2011), p. 262. **54.** The standard "Whig" interpretation, see pp. 264–73. **55.** The quasi-Marxist view famously expressed by Christopher Hill: for example, in *Society and Puritanism*. **56.** See, for example, David Underdown, *Revel, Riot and Rebellion: Popular Politics and Culture in England, 1603–1660* (Oxford UP, 1985). For a discussion of the various interpretations, see Hutton, *Debates*. **57.** Sharp, *Personal Rule*, p. 934. **58.** Ibid., p. 935; Morrill, *Nature*, p. 13. On the loyalities of the peerage, see John Adamson, *The Noble Revolt: The Overthrow of Charles I* (London, Phoenix, 2007), and for a revised view, Richard Cust, *Charles I and the Aristocracy, 1625–1642* (Cambridge UP, 2013). **59.** Stoyle, "English 'nationalism,' Celtic particularism," p. 1120. **60.** Morrill, *Nature*, pp. 281–2. **61.** Fletcher, *Outbreak*, pp. 358, 419. **62.** Braddick, *God's Fury*, pp. 226–7, 232; Purkiss, *English Civil War*, pp. 164–6; and see Adrian Tinniswood, *The Verneys: A True Story of Love, War and Madness in Seventeenth-Century England* (London, Jonathan Cape, 2007). **63.** Barbara Donagan, *War in England, 1642–1649* (Oxford UP, 2008), p. 261. **64.** Ian Gentles, "The iconograpy of revolution: England, 1642–1649," in Gentles et al., *Soldiers, Writers and Statesmen*, pp. 91–113; Purkiss, *English Civil War*, p. 357. **65.** Purkiss, *English Civil War*, pp. 189, 228. **66.** Letter, 28 Jan. [1643], *Letters of The Lady Brilliana Harley*, p. 187. **67.** "Solemn League and Covenant," 25 Sept. 1643, in Gardiner, *Constitutional Documents*, pp. 187–8. **68.** Gardiner, *History of the Great Civil War*, vol. 2, pp. 58–9. **69.** "The Propositions of the Houses presented to the King at Oxford . . ." (24 Nov. 1644), in Gardiner, *Constitutional Documents*, pp. 193–204. **70.** Donagan, *War in England*, pp. 40–50; Carlton, *Seat of Mars*, pp. 90, 283. **71.** Stoyle, "English 'nationalism,' Celtic particularism," p. 1127. **72.** Ian Gentles, *The New Model Army in England, Ireland and Scotland, 1645–1653* (Oxford, Blackwell, 1992), p. 108. **73.** See Carlton, *Seat of Mars*, pp. 131–2, 138–9. **74.** Gentles, *New Model Army*, p. 95. **75.** Braddick, *God's Fury*, p. 387. **76.** See Barbara Donagan, "The casualties of war: treatment of the dead and wounded in the English civil war," in Gentles et al., *Soldiers, Writers and Statesmen*, pp. 114–32; and Barbara Donagan, "The web of honour: soldiers, Christians and gentlemen in the English civil war," *HJ* 44 (2001), pp. 365–89. **77.** Donagan, *War in England*, pp. 201, 209–10; Braddick, *God's Fury*, p. 378. **78.** Malcolm Gaskill, "Witchcraft and evidence in early modern England," *P&P* 198 (2008), pp. 33–70. **79.** Morrill, *Nature*, p. 320. **80.** Ibid., p. 184. **81.** Ibid., p. 209. **82.** Ian Gentles, "Thomas Rainborowe," in *ODNB*. **83.** Derek Hirst, *The Representative of the People? Voters and Voting in England Under the Early Stuarts* (Cambridge UP, 1975), pp. 104–5. **84.** Morrill, *Nature*, pp. 249, 384–8; Andrew Sharp, "John Lilburne," in *ODNB*; J. C. Davis, "The Levellers and Christianity," in Peter Gaunt, ed., *The English Civil War: The Essential Readings* (Oxford, Blackwell, 2000), pp. 289–99. **85.** "The Parliaments Reformation" (1646), in Braddick, *God's Fury*, p. 456. **86.** Gentles, *New Model Army*, p. 292. **87.** Ibid., p. 245. **88.** Ibid., p. 278. **89.** Gardiner, *History of the Great Civil War*, vol. 3, p. 561. **90.** Ibid., p. 569. **91.** "The charge against the king" (20 Jan. 1649), in Gardiner, *Constitutional Documents*, pp. 282–4; Sean Kelsey, "The death of Charles I," *HJ* 45 (2002),

p. 744. 92. Gardiner, *History of the Great Civil War*, vol. 3, p. 572. 93. Ibid., p. 573. 94. Jonathan Scott, *England's Troubles: Seventeenth-Century English Instability in European Context* (Cambridge UP, 2000), p. 50; Kelsey, "Death of Charles I," pp. 733, 748–9. 95. Gardiner, *History of the Great Civil War*, vol. 3, p. 596. 96. Clarendon, *History*, vol. 4, p. 492. 97. David L. Smith, *A History of the Modern British Isles, 1603–1707: The Double Crown* (Oxford, Blackwell, 1998), pp. 163–4. 98. Ibid., p. 171. 99. Morrill, *Nature*, pp. 384–5; Coffey and Lim, *Cambridge Companion to Puritanism*, pp. 79, 263–8. 100. Gentles, *New Model Army*, pp. 319, 322, 337–45. 101. John Morrill, "The Drogheda massacre in Cromwellian context," in Edwards et al., *Age of Atrocity*, pp. 242–65; Gentles, *New Model Army*, p. 361. 102. Micheál Ó Siochrú, *God's Executioner: Oliver Cromwell and the Conquest of Ireland* (London, Faber, 2008), pp. 221–50. 103. Carlton, *Seat of Mars*, pp. 147–51. 104. Morrill, *Nature*, pp. 380–82. 105. "Act appointing a Council of State," in Gardiner, *Constitutional Documents*, pp. 291–2. 106. Thomas Hobbes, *Leviathan* [1651] (Cambridge UP, 2008), pp. 89, 149, 152. 107. Richard Tuck, "Introduction" to ibid., p. ix. 108. Braddick, *God's Fury*, pp. 342–3. 109. Blair Worden, *Literature and Politics in Cromwellian England: John Milton, Andrew Marvell, Marchamont Nedham* (Oxford UP, 2007), pp. 8, 105–15, 343–7. 110. Accounts of Algernon Sidney, Bulstrode Whitelock (both present), and Colonel Edmund Ludlow, MP, quoted in *The Writings and Speeches of Oliver Cromwell*, ed. Wilbur C. Abbott (4 vols.; Cambridge, Mass., Harvard UP, 1938–48), vol. 2, pp. 641–4. 111. Smith, *Double Crown*, pp. 183–4. 112. Ian Woolrych, quoted in Hutton, *Debates*, p. 111. 113. A Leveller, quoted in Hutton, *Debates*, p. 113. 114. John Rogers, a Fifth Monarchist, during a confrontation in 1655, in *Writings and Speeches of Oliver Cromwell*, vol. 3, p. 613. 115. Smith, *Double Crown*, p. 189. 116. Hutton, *Debates*, pp. 129, 131. 117. Morrill, *Nature*, p. 84. 118. Hutton, *Debates*, p. 110. 119. Jonathan Scott, *When the Waves Ruled Britannia: Geography and Political Identities, 1500–1800* (Cambridge UP, 2011), pp. 73–5. 120. Ibid., p. 75. 121. Hutton, *Debates*, pp. 107–8. 122. Christopher Durston, *Cromwell's Major-Generals: Godly Government During the English Revolution* (Manchester UP, 2001), p. 155. 123. Faramerz Dabhoiwala, *The Origins of Sex: A History of the First Sexual Revolution* (London, Allen Lane, 2012), pp. 47–9. 124. Jan de Vries, *The Industrious Revolution: Consumer Behaviour and the Household Economy, 1650 to the Present* (Cambridge UP, 2008), pp. 89–90. 125. Durston, *Cromwell's Major-Generals*, pp. 160, 178. 126. Smith, *Double Crown*, p. 190. 127. 7 Feb. 1660, in *The Shorter Pepys*, ed. Robert Latham (London, Guild, 1986), p. 14. 128. 25 May 1660, in ibid., pp. 50–51. 129. *The Diary of John Evelyn*, ed. Guy de la Bédoyère (Woodbridge, Boydell, 1995), p. 113. 130. Ibid., p. 275. 131. See Kevin Sharpe, *Rebranding Rule: The Restoration and Revolution Monarchy, 1660–1714* (New Haven, Conn., Yale UP, 2013). 132. *Diary of John Evelyn*, p. 114. 133. John Wilmot, 2nd Lord Rochester, "A Satyr on Charles II." 134. Daniel Defoe, *The True Born Englishman and Other Writings*, eds. P. N. Furbank and W. R. Owens (London, Penguin Books, 1997), p. 34. 135. *Shorter Pepys*, p. 86; *Diary of John Evelyn*, p. 115. 136. The bitter quip attributed to Talleyrand. 137. Stephen Taylor and David L. Wykes, eds., *Parliament and Dissent* (Edinburgh UP, 2005), pp. 1–2; Blair Worden, *Roundhead Reputations: The English Civil Wars and the Passions of Posterity* (London, Allen Lane, 2001), pp. 3–4. **138.** *Shorter Pepys*, p. 662. **139.** Jenny Uglow, *A Gambling Man: Charles II and the Restoration* (London, Faber & Faber, 2009), p. 371. **140.** 14 June 1667, *Shorter Pepys*, p. 791. **141.** Scott, *England's Troubles*, p. 171. **142.** Uglow, *A Gambling Man*, p. 376. **143.** Mark S. Dawson, "Histories and texts: reconfiguring the diary of Samuel Pepys," *HJ* 43 (2000), pp. 407–31. **144.** Scott, *England's Troubles*, p. 170. **145.** Jean-Christian Petitfils, *Louis XIV* (Paris, Perrin, 1995), p. 330. **146.** Scott, *England's Troubles*, p. 176. **147.** Steven C. A. Pincus, "From butterboxes to wooden shoes: the shift in English popular sentiment from anti-Dutch to anti-French in the 1670s," *HJ* 38 (1995), p. 333. **148.** Scott, *England's Troubles*, p. 65. **149.** Pincus, "From butterboxes," pp. 352–3. **150.** Tony Claydon, *Europe and the Making of England, 1660–1760* (Cambridge UP, 2007), p. 226. **151.** Scott, *England's Troubles*, p. 180. **152.** Paul D. Halliday, *Habeas Corpus: From England to Empire* (Cambridge, Mass., Harvard UP, 2010), pp. 34, 213. **153.** Smith, *Double Crown*, p. 255. **154.** Report by Barillon, in H. D. Traill, *Shaftesbury, the first Earl* (London, Longman, 1888), p. 179. **155.** Scott, *England's Troubles*, p. 27; Smith, *Double Crown*, p. 258. **156.** Declaration, in Scott, *England's Troubles*, p. 201. **157.** J. G. A. Pocock, *The Discovery of Islands: Essays in British History* (Cambridge UP, 2005), p. 117. **158.** Smith, *Double Crown*, p. 262. **159.** Ibid., p. 265. **160.** Pocock, *Discovery of Islands*, p. 118. **161.** Smith, *Double Crown*, p. 275. **162.** J. R. Jones, "James II's revolution," in Jonathan I. Israel, ed., *The Anglo-Dutch Moment: Essays on the Glorious Revolution and Its World Impact* (Cambridge UP, 1991), pp. 47, 51, 70–71. **163.** Petitfils, *Louis XIV*, p. 485. **164.** Charles-Édouard Levillain, *Vaincre Louis XIV: Angleterre, Hollande, France: Histoire d'une relation triangulaire* (Paris, Champ Vallon, 2010), pp. 341, 346. **165.** Julian Hoppit, *A Land of Liberty? England, 1689–1727* (Oxford, Clarendon Press, 2000), pp. 17–18. **166.** For details, see Steve Pincus, *1688: The First Modern Revolution* (New Haven, Conn., Yale UP, 2009), pp. 166–70, 193–7. **167.** *Diary of John Evelyn*, p. 311. **168.** Jean-Philippe Cénat, "Le ravage du Palatinat: politique de destruction, stratégie de cabinet et propagande au début de la guerre de la Ligue d'Augsbourg," *Revue Historique* 307 (2005), pp. 97–132. **169.** Scott, *England's Troubles*, p. 217. See also Pincus, *1688*, p. 240. **170.** Brendan Simms, *Three Victories and a Defeat: The Rise and Fall of the First British Empire, 1714–1783* (London, Allen Lane, 2007), p. 40. **171.** Pocock, *Discovery of Islands*, p. 119. **172.** One of my reasons for writing this book was a conversation with a distinguished scientific colleague, who mentioned that he knew nothing about them. **173.** Dabhoiwala, *Origins of Sex*, pp. 53–5.

## The Civil War and "Whig History"

**1.** See Matthew Neufeld, *The Civil Wars After 1660: Public Remembering in Late Stuart England* (Woodbridge, Boydell and Brewer, 2013). **2.** John Oldmixon, *The*

*Critical History of England, ecclesiastical and civil* (London, Pemberton, 1726), in R. C. Richardson, *The Debate on the English Revolution* (3rd edn; Manchester UP, 1998), p. 46.   3. [Paul] de Rapin Thoyras, *Histoire d'Angleterre* (8 vols.; The Hague, A. de Rogissart, 1724–5), vol. 8, p. 119.   4. Ibid., vol. 1, pp. iv, vii, x, xiii, xvi; vol. 8, p. 724 (my translation).   5. Ernest Campbell Mossner, *The Life of David Hume* (2nd edn; Oxford, Clarendon Press, 1980), pp. 303, 307, 310; Nicholas Phillipson, *David Hume: The Philosopher as Historian* (London, Penguin Books, 2011).   6. David Hume, *The History of England* (6 vols.; London, A. Millar, 1757), vol. 6, p. 443.   7. Ibid., vol. 1, pp. 2, 145–6, 148, 163, 409–10, 424; vol. 2, pp. 30, 50, 305, 345, 347.   8. Phillipson, *David Hume*, p. 117.   9. Hume, *History of England*, vol. 2, pp. 445, 443; vol. 3, pp. 279–80; vol. 4, p. 737; vol. 5, pp. 260, 381.   10. Phillipson, *David Hume*, p. 128.   11. Hume, *History of England*, vol. 2, p. 446.   12. M. G. Sullivan, "Rapin, Hume and the identity of the historian in eighteenth-century England," *History of European Ideas* 28 (2002), pp. 153, 157.   13. Edmund Burke, *Reflections on the Revolution in France* (London, Penguin Books, 1986), pp. 102, 106, 116–19, 148, 178, 181–4, 194–5, 342.   14. Worden, *Roundhead Reputations*, pp. 207–8.   15. Ibid., p. 231.   16. Richardson, *Debate*, p. 80.   17. Thomas Babington Macaulay, *The History of England from the Accession of James the Second*, ed. C. H. Firth (6 vols.; London, Macmillan, 1913), vol. 1, p. 22.   18. François Guizot, *Histoire de la Civilisation en Europe* (new edn; Paris, Didier, 1854 [1840]), p. 311.   19. Worden, *Roundhead Reputations*, pp. 252, 264.   20. Gardiner, *History of the Great Civil War*, vol. I, p. 11; vol. 3, p. 605.   21. Worden, *Roundhead Reputations*, p. 257.   22. Eugenio F. Biagini, *Liberty, Retrenchment and Reform: Popular Liberalism in the Age of Gladstone, 1860–1880* (Cambridge UP, 1992), p. 383.   23. Worden, *Roundhead Reputations*, p. 229.   24. Quoted by Simon Green in his Birkbeck Lecture "The making and breaking of a Puritan progressive consensus," Cambridge, 28 Nov. 2013.   25. *The Expansion of England* (1883), in J. W. Burrow, *A Liberal Descent: Victorian Historians and the English Past* (Cambridge UP, 1981), p. 295.   26. David Cannadine, *G. M. Trevelyan: A Life in History* (London, HarperCollins, 1992), p. 18.   27. G. M. Trevelyan, *A Shortened History of England* (London, Penguin Books, 1987 [1942]), pp. 13–16, 558.   28. Cannadine, *Trevelyan*, p. 111.   29. Ibid., p. 113.   30. Herbert Butterfield, *The Whig Interpretation of History* (New York, Norton, 1965 [1931]), pp. v, 4, 12, 13, 63. See also Keith C. Sewell, *Herbert Butterfield and the Interpretation of History* (Basingstoke, Palgrave Macmillan, 2005), pp. 181–2; Michael Bentley, *Modernizing England's Past: English Historiography in the Age of Modernism* (Cambridge UP, 2006), ch. 6; and John Kenyon, *The History Men: The Historical Profession in England Since the Renaissance* (London, Weidenfeld & Nicolson, 1983), ch. 6.   31. See Geoff Eley and William Hunt, eds., *Reviving the English Revolution: Reflections and Elaborations on the Work of Christopher Hill* (London, Verso, 1988).   32. Christopher Hill, *Some Intellectual Consequences of the English Revolution* (1980), in Richardson, *Debate*, p. 248.   33. Andrew Bradstock, ed., *Winstanley and the Diggers, 1649–1999* (London, Frank Cass, 2000); Mark Kishlansky, "Madd Men," *LRB* (17 Feb. 2011), pp. 20–21.   34. Bentley, *Modernizing*, pp. 109–10.   35. *The Devil's Whore*, Channel 4 (2008).   36. Worden, *Roundhead Reputations*, p. 7.

PART FOUR: MAKING A NEW WORLD, *c.1660–c.1815*

1. David Hume, *Political Essays*, ed. Knut Haakonssen (Cambridge UP, 1994), p. 85.   2. Mark Goldie and Robert Wokler, eds., *The Cambridge History of Eighteenth-Century Political Thought* (Cambridge UP, 2006), p. 40.   3. Tony Claydon, *Europe and the Making of England, 1660–1760* (Cambridge UP, 2007), p. 363. 4. Claydon, *Europe*, p. 362. See also Ole Peter Grell and Roy Porter, eds., *Toleration in Enlightenment Europe* (Cambridge UP, 2000), pp. 42–3.   5. Voltaire, *Lettres philosophiques*, ed. F. A. Taylor (Oxford UP, 1946), p. 22 (my translation). 6. Jonathan Scott's phrase, in *England's Troubles: Seventeenth-Century English Instability in European Context* (Cambridge UP, 2000), p. 7.

## 7. And All Was Light

1. Martin Fitzpatrick et al., eds., *The Enlightenment World* (London, Routledge, 2004), p. 87.   2. J. G. A. Pocock, *The Machiavellian Moment: Florentine Political Thought and the Atlantic Republican Tradition* (Princeton UP, 1975), p. 451. 3. Fitzpatrick et al., *Enlightenment World*, p. 10.   4. T. Sprat, *The History of the Royal Society of London* (1667), in Fitzpatrick, *Enlightenment World*, p. 18. 5. *Novum Organum Scientarum* (1620), in Fitzpatrick, *Enlightenment World*, p. 7.   6. Margaret C. Jacob, *The Newtonians and the English Revolution, 1689– 1720* (Hassocks, Harvester Press, 1976), p. 18.   7. Fitzpatrick, *Enlightenment World*, p. 22.   8. John Spurr, "'Latitudinarianism' and the Restoration Church," *HJ* 31 (1988), p. 82.   9. Jacob, *Newtonians*, pp. 58, 116, 132–3.   10. John Locke, *An Essay Concerning Human Understanding*, ed. Kenneth P. Winkler (Indianapolis, Ind., Hackett, 1996 [1689]), p. 327.   11. For examples of Locke-worship, see Mark Goldie, ed., *The Reception of Locke's Politics* (6 vols.; London, Pickering and Chatto, 1999), vol. 1, pp. ix–x.   12. Locke, *Essay*, pp. 3, 33, 323.   13. John W. Yolton, *A Locke Dictionary* (Oxford, Blackwell, 1993), p. 219.   14. See Sylvana Tomaselli, in Grell and Porter, *Toleration*, p. 86.   15. John Locke, *Two Treatises of Government*, ed. P. Laslett (Cambridge UP, 2009), pp. 335, 366–7, 370.   16. Ibid., pp. 336, 412.   17. Quentin Skinner, *The Foundations of Modern Political Thought* (Cambridge UP, 1978), vol. 2, p. 239.   18. William Gibson, *The Church of England, 1688–1832: Unity and Accord* (London, Routledge, 2001), p. 81. 19. Ibid., p. 159.   20. Julian Hoppit, *A Land of Liberty: England, 1689–1727* (Oxford UP, 2000), p. 33.   21. Stephen Taylor and David L. Wykes, eds., *Parliament and Dissent* (Edinburgh UP, 2005), p. 57.   22. Gertrude Himmelfarb, *The Roads to Modernity: The British, French and American Enlightenments* (London, Vintage, 2008), pp. 27–8.   23. Roy Porter, *Enlightenment: Britain and the Creation of the Modern World* (London, Allen Lane, 2000), p. 160; Himmelfarb, *Roads to Modernity*, p. 38.   24. Daniel Mornet, "Les enseignements des bibliothèques privées, 1750–1780," *Revue d'Histoire Littéraire de la France* (July–September 1910), pp. 458–62.   25. James Boswell, *Life of Johnson*, ed. R. W. Chapman (Oxford UP, 1970), p. 509.   26. Ibid., p. 188.   27. Vic Gatrell, *City of Laughter: Sex and Satire in Eighteenth-Century London* (London, Atlantic, 2006), p. 9. See

also Thomas Keymer, "Freaks, dwarfs and boors," *LRB* (2 August 2012), pp. 17–18. **28.** Porter, *Enlightenment*, p. 326. **29.** Jean-Bernard Le Blanc, *Lettres d'un François* (The Hague, Neaulme, 1745), my translation. **30.** See Simon Macdonald, "Identifying Mrs. Meeke: another Burney family novelist," *Review of English Studies*, new series, 64 (2013), pp. 367–85. **31.** Susan E. Whyman, *The Pen and the People: English Letter Writers, 1660–1800* (Oxford UP, 2009), pp. 4, 20, 27, 218, 222, 224, 228, 230–31. **32.** David Hempton, *Methodism: Empire of the Spirit* (New Haven, Conn., Yale UP, 2005), pp. 30, 52. **33.** Ibid., pp. 2,187. **34.** Ibid., pp. 5, 20, 63, 78, 137. **35.** Paul Langford, *A Polite and Commercial People: England, 1727–1783* (Oxford UP, 1989), p. 246. **36.** Hempton, *Methodism*, pp. 89–92, 128; Langford, *Polite and Commercial*, p. 278. **37.** See Michael Hunter, "The decline of magic: challenge and response in early Enlightenment England," *HJ* 55 (2012), pp. 399–425. **38.** Porter, *Enlightenment*, p. 300. **39.** David Watkin, *The English Vision: The Picturesque in Architecture, Landscape and Garden Design* (London, John Murray, 1982), p. vii. **40.** Nikolaus Pevsner, *The Englishness of English Art* (London, Penguin Books, 1997), p. 157. **41.** Rev. William Gilpin, in Watkin, *English Vision*, p. 75. **42.** Ibid., p. 14. **43.** Daniel Defoe, *Robinson Crusoe* [1719], ed. Michael Shinagel (2nd edn; New York, Norton, 1994), p. 124; Anne Salmond, *The Trial of the Cannibal Dog: The Remarkable Story of Captain Cook's Encounters in the South Seas* (New Haven, Conn., Yale UP, 2003), p. 57. **44.** Faramerz Dabhoiwala, *The Origins of Sex: A History of the First Sexual Revolution* (London, Allen Lane, 2012), p. 104. **45.** John Robson, ed., *The Captain Cook Encyclopædia* (London, Chatham, 2004), p. 68. **46.** Porter, *Enlightenment*, p. 173. **47.** Roy Porter and Marie M. Roberts, eds., *Pleasure in the Eighteenth Century* (Houndmills, Macmillan, 1996), p. 1. **48.** Dabhoiwala, *Origins of Sex*, p. 81. **49.** Ibid., p. 364. **50.** Ibid., p. 119. **51.** Ibid., p. 350. **52.** C. P. Courtney, *Montesquieu and Burke* (Westport, Conn., Greenwood Press, 1975), pp. 275–6. **53.** David Hume, *Political Essays*, ed. Knut Haakonssen (Cambridge UP, 1994), p. 85. **54.** Adam Smith, *The Wealth of Nations* (London, Everyman, 1991), vol. 1, pp. 14–15. **55.** Fitzpatrick, *Enlightenment World*, p. 83. **56.** Porter, *Enlightenment*, p. 73. **57.** Whyman, *Pen and the People*, p. 81. **58.** Gatrell, *City of Laughter*, p. 7. **59.** Gibson, *Church of England*, pp. 159–64. **60.** Whyman, *Pen and the People*, pp. 75, 79. **61.** Richard D. Altick, *The English Common Reader: A Social History of the Mass Reading Public, 1800–1900* (Chicago UP, 1957), pp. 36–7. **62.** Porter, *Enlightenment*, pp. 77, 85–6, 206. **63.** Ibid., p. 79. **64.** James Boswell, *Life of Johnson*, ed. R. W. Chapman (Oxford UP, 1970), p. 185. **65.** Hempton, *Methodism*, p. 51; Jenny Uglow, *The Lunar Men: The Friends Who Made the Future* (London, Faber, 2002). **66.** Boswell, *Life of Johnson*, p. 615 (7 April 1775). **67.** John Brewer, *The Pleasures of the Imagination: English Culture in the Eighteenth Century* (London, HarperCollins, 1997), p. 154. **68.** Boswell, *Life of Johnson*, p. 859 (20 Sept. 1777). **69.** Brewer, *Pleasures of the Imagination*, pp. 44–9. **70.** Porter, *Enlightenment*, p. 22. **71.** Courtney, *Montesquieu and Burke*, pp. 286–7. **72.** Josephine Grieder, *Anglomania in France, 1740–1789* (Geneva, Droz, 1985), p. 109. **73.** See Hannah Greig, "All Together and All Distinct: Public Sociability and Social Exclusivity in London's Pleasure Gardens, c.1740–1800," *Journal of*

*British Studies* 51 (Jan. 2012). 74. Gatrell, *City of Laughter*, pp. 204–8.
75. [Jean-Bernard Le Blanc,] *Lettres de Monsieur l'Abbé Le Blanc, historiographe des bastiments du Roi* (Amsterdam, 1751), passim (my translation). 76. John Styles, *The Dress of the People: Everyday Fashion in Eighteenth-Century England* (New Haven, Conn., Yale UP, 2007), pp. 94–5, 181–2, 192–3. 77. Keith Thomas, *The Ends of Life: Roads to Fulfilment in Early Modern England* (Oxford UP, 2009), p. 65. 78. Charles Barber et al., *The English Language: A Historical Introduction* (2nd edn; Cambridge UP, 2009), pp. 218–19. 79. Gatrell, *City of Laughter*, p. 8. 80. Claydon, *Europe*, pp. 24–7, 33, 44–61. 81. Le Blanc, *Lettres*, p. 50. 82. *Letters of the Earl of Chesterfield to His Son*, ed. Charles Strachey (London, Methuen, 1932), vol. I, pp. 329–30. 83. Jeremy Black, *The British Abroad: The Grand Tour in the Eighteenth Century* (London, Sandpiper, 1992), p. 98. 84. *The French Journals of Mrs. Thrale and Dr. Johnson*, eds. Moses Tyson and Henry Guppy (Manchester UP, 1932), p. 149. 85. Brewer, *Pleasures of the Imagination*, p. 256. 86. Robin Eagles, *Francophilia in English Society, 1748–1815* (London, Macmillan, 2000), pp. 63–5. 87. Jack Lynch and Anne McDermott, eds., *Anniversary Essays on Johnson's Dictionary* (Cambridge UP, 2005), p. 33. 88. Ian McIntyre, *Garrick* (London, Penguin Books, 2000), p. 432. 89. *Letters of Horace Walpole*, ed. C. B. Lucas (London, Newnes, 1904), p. 523. 90. Patrick Parrinder, *Nation and Novel: The English Novel from Its Origins to the Present Day* (Oxford UP, 2006), p. 135. 91. Georges Grente and François Moureau, eds., *Dictionnaire des lettres françaises: le XVIIIe siècle* (Paris, Fayard, 1995), p. 62 (my translation). 92. Mary Wortley Montagu, *Letters* (London, Everyman, 1992), p. 466. 93. "Of national characters" (1748), Hume, *Political Essays*, p. 78. 94. Ibid., pp. 85–6. 95. Daniel Defoe, *The True-Born Englishman and other writings*, eds. P. N. Furband and W. R. Owens (London, Penguin Books, 1997), pp. 31–2. 96. Henry Fielding, *The History of Tom Jones* (London, Penguin Books, 1966), p. 874; and see Parrinder, *Nation and Novel*, p. 101.

## 8. A Free Country?

1. C. P. Courtney, *Montesquieu and Burke* (Westport, Conn., Greenwood Press, 1975), pp. 275–6. 2. 1690 pamphlet, in Julian Hoppit, *A Land of Liberty: England, 1689–1727* (Oxford UP, 2000), p. 2. 3. Stephen Taylor and David L. Wykes, eds., *Parliament and Dissent* (Edinburgh UP, 2005), p. 92. 4. Ibid., pp. 44–5. 5. Paul Kléber Monod, *Jacobitism and the English People, 1688–1788* (Cambridge UP, 1989), p. 171. 6. William Gibson, *The Church of England, 1688–1832: Unity and Accord* (London, Routledge, 2001), p. 5. 7. "A Trip to the Vaux-Hall" (1737), ibid., p. 158. 8. Ibid., p. 235. 9. See J. C. D. Clark, *English Society, 1688–1832: Ideology, Social Structure and Political Practice During the Ancien Régime* (Cambridge UP, 1985), ch. 5. 10. Mark Goldie, ed., *The Reception of Locke's Politics* (London, Pickering & Chatto, 1999), vol. 1, p. xlii. 11. Monod, *Jacobitism*, pp. 168, 194. 12. Gibson, *Church of England*, p. 166. 13. Susan E. Whyman, *The Pen and the People: English Letter Writers, 1660–1800* (Oxford UP,

2009), pp. 100–101.    **14.** Tony Claydon, *Europe and the Making of England, 1660–1760* (Cambridge UP, 2007), p. 285.    **15.** Based principally on war deaths: see Niall Ferguson, *The Cash Nexus: Money and Power in the Modern World, 1700–2000* (London, Allen Lane, 2001), pp. 29–37, 426.    **16.** J. G. A. Pocock, *The Discovery of Islands: Essays in British History* (Cambridge UP, 2005), p. 123.    **17.** Craig Rose, *England in the 1690s: Revolution, Religion and War* (Oxford, Blackwell, 1999), p. 63.    **18.** Hoppit, *Land of Liberty*, p. 93.    **19.** The "xenophobic" school includes Gerald Newman, *The Rise of English Nationalism: A Cultural History, 1740–1830* (London, Weidenfeld & Nicolson, 1987); Linda Colley, *Britons: Forging the Nation, 1707–1837* (New Haven, Conn., Yale UP, 1992); and Paul Langford, *Englishness Identified: Manners and Character, 1650–1850* (Oxford UP, 2000). More nuanced views include Claydon, *Europe*; Jonathan Scott, *England's Troubles: Seventeenth-Century English Political Instability in European Context* (Cambridge UP, 2000); Brendan Simms, *Three Victories and a Defeat: The Rise and Fall of the First British Empire, 1714–1783* (London, Allen Lane, 2007); and Robin Eagles, *Francophilia in English Society, 1748–1815* (London, Macmillan, 2000).    **20.** On this point, see Claydon, *Europe*, pp. 11–12, 123–4.    **21.** Ibid., ch. 3.    **22.** Ibid., pp. 11–12; Simms, *Three Victories*, p. 86.    **23.** Philip T. Hoffman and Kathryn Norberg, eds., *Fiscal Crises, Liberty and Representative Government, 1450–1789* (Stanford UP, 1994), p. 89.    **24.** John Brewer, *The Sinews of Power: War, Money and the English State, 1688–1783* (Cambridge, Mass., Harvard UP, 1988), pp. 70–79.    **25.** J. H. Plumb, *Sir Robert Walpole* (2 vols.; London, Allen Lane, 1972), vol. 2, p. 237.    **26.** Donald Winch and Patrick O'Brien, eds., *The Political Economy of British Historical Experience, 1688–1914* (Oxford UP, 2002), p. 258.    **27.** Scott, *England's Troubles*, p. 487.    **28.** Richard Middleton, *The Bells of Victory: The Pitt-Newcastle Ministry and the Conduct of the Seven Years' War, 1757–1762* (Cambridge UP, 1985), p. 153.    **29.** Robert Beddard, ed., *The Revolutions of 1688* (Oxford, Clarendon Press, 1991), p. 242.    **30.** See Kevin Sharpe, *Rebranding Rule: The Restoration and Revolution Monarchy, 1660–1714* (New Haven, Conn., Yale UP, 2013).    **31.** Clyve Jones, ed., *A Short History of Parliament: England, Great Britain, the United Kingdom, Ireland and Scotland* (Woodbridge, Boydell, 2009), p. 183.    **32.** Ibid., p. 170. For an interesting non-British view, see Denis Baranger, *Écrire la constitution non-écrite: Une introduction au droit politique britannique* (Paris, Presses Universitaires de France, 2008), pp. 278–82.    **33.** Monod, *Jacobitism*, p. 171.    **34.** See Hoppit, *Land of Liberty*, pp. 436–8.    **35.** Paul Langford, *A Polite and Commercial People: England, 1727–1783* (Oxford UP, 1989), p. 12.    **36.** A. V. Dicey, *The Law of the Constitution* (1885), in Colin Turpin and Adam Tomkins, *British Government and the Constitution* (Cambridge UP, 2011), pp. 58–9.    **37.** Hoppit, *Land of Liberty*, p. 43.    **38.** Jones, *Short History of Parliament*, p. 183.    **39.** Monod, *Jacobitism*, pp. 172, 195.    **40.** P. M. G. Dickson, *The Financial Revolution in England: A Study of the Development of Public Credit, 1688–1756* (London, Macmillan, 1967), p. 198.    **41.** Leandro Prados de la Escosura, ed., *Exceptionalism and Industrialisation: Britain and Its European Rivals, 1688–1815* (Cambridge UP, 2004), p. 185.    **42.** See Hoppit, *Land of Liberty*, pp. 408–11.    **43.** Jones, *Short History of Parliament*, p. 174.    **44.** According to Lord Hervey's memoirs, in Langford, *Polite and Commercial*, pp. 49–50. **45.** Simms, *Three Victories*, p. 253. **46.** Robert Shackleton, *Montesquieu: A Critical Biography* (Oxford UP, 1961), p. 301. **47.** Oliver J. W. Cox, "Frederick Prince of Wales and the first performance of 'Rule Britannia!,'" *HJ* 56 (2013), pp. 931–54. **48.** James Boswell, *Life of Johnson*, ed. R. W. Chapman (Oxford UP, 1970), p. 405; and see Vic Gatrell, *City of Laughter: Sex and Satire in Eighteenth-Century London* (London, Atlantic, 2006), pp. 38–40. **49.** Langford, *Polite and Commercial*, p. 185. **50.** French Foreign Ministry archives, *Mémoires et documents: Angleterre*, vol. 78, fos 73–4 (13 June 1745). **51.** John L. Roberts, *The Jacobite Wars: Scotland and the Military Campaigns of 1715 and 1745* (Edinburgh, Polygon, 2002), p. 112. **52.** Monod, *Jacobitism*, pp. 334–41. **53.** Geoffrey Plank, *Rebellion and Savagery: The Jacobite Rising of 1745 and the British Empire* (Philadelphia, Pennsylvania UP, 2006), pp. 87–91. **54.** Henry Fielding, *The History of Tom Jones* (London, Penguin Books, 1966), p. 336. **55.** Monod, *Jacobitism*, pp. 198–9. **56.** *A Journey to the Western Islands of Scotland* (1775), in John Styles, *The Dress of the People: Everyday Fashion in Eighteenth-Century England* (New Haven, Conn., Yale UP, 2007), pp. 185–6. **57.** Example kindly provided by Clarissa Campbell-Orr. **58.** Jones, *Short History of Parliament*, p. 183; Derek Hirst, *The Representative of the People? Voters and Voting in England Under the Early Stuarts* (Cambridge UP, 1975), pp. 104–5. **59.** Edmund Burke, *On Empire, Liberty, and Reform: Speeches and Letters*, ed. David Bromwich (New Haven, Conn., Yale UP, 2000), p. 55. **60.** Paul Langford, "Property and 'virtual representation' in eighteenth-century England," *HJ* 31 (1988), pp. 83–115; Jones, *Short History of Parliament*, pp. 172–90; Porter, *Enlightenment*, pp. 22–3. **61.** George Monbiot, *Guardian*, 24 Feb. 2009, and repeated in a television programme criticizing the National Trust, 7 Sept. 2009. Oddly, Monbiot thinks that this view of the past has been "airbrushed" out of history. **62.** James Sharpe, *Dick Turpin: The Myth of the English Highwayman* (London, Profile, 2004), pp. 77–8. **63.** E. P. Thompson, *The Making of the English Working Class* (London, Penguin Books, 1968), p. 66. **64.** Ibid., p. 99. **65.** Hoppit, *Land of Liberty*, p. 482; House of Commons Research Paper 99/56: Homicide Statistics (May 1999), table 1. **66.** Daniel Defoe, *The Fortunes and Misfortunes of the Famous Moll Flanders* (Ware, Wordsworth, 1993), p. 187. **67.** Sharpe, *Dick Turpin*, p. 89. **68.** John Hudson, *The Formation of the English Common Law: Law and Society in England from the Norman Conquest to Magna Carta* (London, Longman, 1996), pp. 512–18. **69.** Ibid., p. 510. **70.** Sharpe, *Dick Turpin*, p. 98. **71.** Richard Evans, *Rituals of Retribution: Capital Punishment in Germany, 1600–1987* (London, Penguin Books, 1997), pp. 42–7, 215. **72.** Fielding, *Tom Jones*, p. 552. **73.** Langford, *Polite and Commercial*, p. 301. **74.** Paul Slack, *The English Poor Law, 1531–1782* (London, Macmillan, 1990), p. 57. **75.** Ron Harris, in *CEHMB*, vol. I, p. 224. **76.** Olwen H. Hufton, *The Poor of Eighteenth-Century France, 1750–1789* (Oxford UP, 1974), p. 176. **77.** K. D. M. Snell, *Annals of the Labouring Poor: Social Change and Agrarian England, 1660–1900* (Cambridge UP, 1985), pp. 104–6; R. P. Hastings, "Poverty and the poor law in the North Riding of Yorkshire, c.1780–1837," Borthwick Papers No. 61 (University of York, 1982), p. 15. **78.** Styles, *Dress of the People*, pp. 16, 19–20.   79. Joel Mokyr, in *CEHMB*, vol. I, p. 2.   80. On this point, see Krishan Kumar, *The Making of English National Identity* (Cambridge UP, 2003), ch. 1.   81. Colley, *Britons*, is the major study of the formation of this kind of eighteenth-century Britishness.   82. Adrian Hastings, *The Construction of Nation-hood: Ethnicity, Religion and Nationalism* (Cambridge UP, 1997), p. 65.   83. Simms, *Three Victories* p. 86.   84. Christopher Clark, *Iron Kingdom: The Rise and Down-fall of Prussia, 1600–1947* (London, Allen Lane, 2006), is an interesting compara-tor: after 1871, it becomes a brief history of Prussia's transformation from kingdom to province.

## 9. The Rise and Fall of the Atlantic Nation

1. Piers Mackesy, *War Without Victory: The Downfall of Pitt, 1799–1802* (Oxford, Clarendon Press, 1984), p. 13.   2. Craig Rose, *England in the 1690s: Revolution, Religion and War* (Oxford, Blackwell, 1999), p. 105.   3. Brendan Simms, *Three Victories and a Defeat: The Rise and Fall of the First British Empire, 1714–1783* (London, Allen Lane, 2007), p. 79.   4. Most influentially by Montesquieu: "De la Constitution d'Angleterre," in *De l'esprit des lois* (1748), bk. 11, ch. 6.   5. Letters, 1726, in *Voltaire and the English* (Oxford, Voltaire Foundation, 1979), pp. 11–12.   6. Tony Claydon, *Europe and the Making of England, 1660–1760* (Cambridge UP, 2007), pp. 127–32.   7. *The History of John Bull* (1712).   8. Pamphlet, 1719, in Julian Hoppit, *A Land of Liberty: England, 1689–1727* (Oxford UP, 2000), p. 5. 9. P. J. Marshall, *The Making and Unmaking of Empires: Britain, India, and Amer-ica, c.1750–1783* (Oxford UP, 2005), p. 6.   10. James Thomson, "Liberty" (1735).   11. Philip D. Morgan, in Colin G. Calloway, *The Scratch of a Pen: 1763 and the Transformation of North America* (Oxford UP, 2006), p. 32.   12. Mar-shall, *Making and Unmaking*, p. 44.   13. See, for example, HM Treasury, "UK and EU trade" (2004), pp. 17–18, 23.   14. Michael Duffy, *Soldiers, Sugar and Seapower: The British Expeditions to the West Indies and the War Against Revolutionary France* (Oxford, Clarendon Press, 1987), pp. 385, 371.   15. French Foreign Minis-try report, 1779, in MDA, vol. 55, folio 74 (my translation).   16. Sudipta Das, *Myths and Realities of French Imperialism in India, 1763–1783* (New York, Peter Lang, 1992), p. 7.   17. *CEHMB*, vol. I, p. 230; vol. II, pp. 440–42.   18. Hugh Thomas, *The Slave Trade: History of the Atlantic Slave Trade, 1440–1870* (London, Picador, 1997), p. 249; Duffy, *Soldiers, Sugar* (1987), pp. 12–13.   19. In Marshall, *Making and Unmaking*, p. 363.   20. Ibid., pp. 15–16.   21. Das, *Myths and Reali-ties*, p. 7; Marshall, *Making and Unmaking*, p. 135.   22. Ibid., p. 44.   23. Philip D. Morgan, in Martin Daunton and Rick Halpern, eds., *Empire and Others: British Encounters with Indigenous Peoples, 1600–1850* (London, UCL Press, 1999), p. 51.   24. Marshall, *Making and Unmaking*, p. 130.   25. Duke of Newcastle, in Simms, *Three Victories*, p. 390.   26. Marshall, *Making and Unmaking*, p. 83; Frank W. Brecher, *Losing a Continent: France's North American Policy, 1753–1763* (London, Greenwood Press, 1998), p. 60.   27. Fred Anderson, *Crucible of War: The Seven Years' War and the Fate of Empire in British North America, 1754–1766*

(London, Faber & Faber, 2000), pp. 5–7. **28.** Pierre Pluchon, *Histoire de la colonisation française: des origines à la Restauration* (Paris, Fayard, 1991), p. 248. **29.** Earl of Chesterfield, in John D. Woodbridge, *Revolt in Prerevolutionary France: The Prince de Conti's Conspiracy Against Louis XV, 1755–1757* (Baltimore, Md., Johns Hopkins UP, 1995), p. 94. **30.** Kathleen Wilson, *The Sense of the People: Politics, Culture and Imperialism in England, 1715–1785* (Cambridge UP, 1995), pp. 178–205. **31.** Linda Colley, *Britons: Forging the Nation, 1707–1837* (New Haven, Conn., Yale UP, 1992), pp. 87–98; Wilson, *Sense of the People*, pp. 185–93. **32.** Wilson, *Sense of the People*, p. 193. **33.** Marie Peters, *Pitt and Popularity: The Patriot Minister and London Opinion During the Seven Years' War* (Oxford, Clarendon Press, 1980), p. 104. **34.** Stephen Brumwell, *Redcoats: The British Soldier and War in the Americas, 1755–1763* (Cambridge UP, 2002), p. 51; Lee Kennett, *The French Forces in America, 1780–1783* (London, Greenwood Press, 1977), p. xiv. **35.** Peter Padfield, *Maritime Supremacy and the Opening of the Western Mind* (London, Pimlico, 2000), p. 212. **36.** Richard Farmer, Fellow of Emmanuel, in J. C. D. Clark, *English Society, 1688–1832* (Cambridge UP, 1985), p. 188. **37.** Peters, *Pitt and Popularity*, p. 11. **38.** Clark, *English Society*, pp. 188, 237. **39.** James Boswell, *The Life of Johnson*, ed. R. W. Chapman (Oxford UP, 1970), p. 515. **40.** Edmund Burke, *On Empire, Liberty and Reform: Speeches and Letters*, ed. David Bromwich (New Haven, Conn., Yale UP, 2000), p. 466. **41.** S. M. Farrell, "Charles Watson-Wentworth, 2nd Marquess of Rockingham," in *ODNB*. **42.** Wilson, *Sense of the People*, p. 218. **43.** Anderson, *Crucible of War*, p. 507. **44.** Jeremy Black, *America or Europe? British Foreign Policy, 1739–63* (London, UCL Press, 1998), pp. 181–2. **45.** "Mémoire de M. de Choiseul remis au roi en 1765," *Journal des Savants* (1881), pp. 178, 253 (my translation). **46.** Paul Langford, *A Polite and Commercial People: England, 1727–1783* (Oxford UP, 1989), p. 377. **47.** Simms, *Three Victories*, p. 463. **48.** Marshall, *Making and Unmaking*, p. 104. **49.** Lance E. Davis and Robert A. Huttenback, *Mammon and the Pursuit of Empire: The Economics of British Imperialism* (Cambridge UP, 1988), p. 277; Calloway, *Scratch of a Pen*, p. 12. **50.** Max M. Mintz, *Seeds of Empire: The American Revolutionary Conquest of the Iroquois* (New York UP, 1999), pp. 5–7; Calloway, *Scratch of a Pen*, pp. 92–100; Marshall, *Making and Unmaking*, p. 191. **51.** Marshall, *Making and Unmaking*, p. 168. **52.** Calloway, *Scratch of a Pen*, pp. 28, 60, 90–91. **53.** Simms, *Three Victories*, p. 680. **54.** Samuel Foote, *The Works* (Hildesheim, Georg Olms, 1974), vol. 3, p. 187. **55.** Langford, *Polite and Commercial*, p. 534. **56.** Quotations in Marshall, *Making and Unmaking*, pp. 198–202. **57.** Samuel Johnson, *The Major Works*, ed. D. Greene (Oxford UP, 2000), p. 585; Boswell, *Life of Johnson*, p. 615. **58.** Marshall, *Making and Unmaking*, p. 332. **59.** Simms, *Three Victories*, p. 584. **60.** Speech, 22 March 1775, in Burke, *On Empire, Liberty and Reform*, pp. 72, 92. **61.** Simms, *Three Victories*, p. 588. **62.** "Mémoire" (1777), MDA, vol. 52, folio 230 (my translation). **63.** Stephen Conway, *The British Isles and the War of American Independence* (Oxford UP, 2000), p. 145. **64.** Langford, *Polite and Commercial*, pp. 547–8. **65.** Wilson, *Sense of the People*, p. 279. **66.** Simms, *Three Victories*, p. 598. **67.** Wilson, *Sense of the People*, p. 240. **68.** Thomas Paine, *Political Writ-*

*ings*, ed. Bruce Kuklick (Cambridge UP, 1989), pp. vii–viii.   69. Ibid., pp. 23, 24.
70. Marshall, *Making and Unmaking*, p. 65.   71. Daunton and Halpern, *Empire and Others*, p. 8.   72. Christopher Moore, *The Loyalists: Revolution, Exile, Settlement* (Toronto, Ont., McClelland & Stewart, 1994), pp. 34, 137.   73. Paine, *Common Sense*, p. 29.   74. MDA, vol. 52, folio 233.   75. A. Temple Patterson, *The Other Armada: The Franco-Spanish Attempt to Invade Britain in 1779* (Manchester UP, 1960), p. 154.   76. Conway, *British Isles*, pp. 22, 198–9.   77. Georges Lacour-Gayet, *La marine militaire de la France sous le règne de Louis XVI* (Paris, Champion, 1905), p. 232.   78. Ibid., pp. 256, 274; Claude Manceron, *The Wind from America, 1778–1781* (London, Eyre Methuen, 1979), p. 175.   79. Piers Mackesy, *The War for America, 1775–1783* (London, Longman, 1964), pp. 460–61; Simms, *Three Victories*, pp. 629–30.   80. Conway, *British Isles*, pp. 24, 32–4, 51–4.   81. Clark, *English Society*, p. 339.   82. Ian Haywood and John Seed, eds., *The Gordon Riots: Politics, Culture and Insurrection in Late Eighteenth-Century Britain* (Cambridge UP, 2012), p. 83.   83. George Rudé, *The Crowd in History: A Study in Popular Disturbances in France and England, 1730–1848* (New York, Wiley, 1964), p. 59; Haywood and Seed, *Gordon Riots*, pp. 3, 77–88; "Lord George Gordon," in *ODNB*.   84. Samuel Johnson, letter to Hester Thrale, in Boswell, *Life of Johnson*, p. 1055.   85. Haywood and Seed, *Gordon Riots*, pp. 73, 248.
86. Ibid., pp. 54–5, 73–88, 248.   87. Nicholas Rogers, *Crowds, Culture and Politics in Georgian Britain* (Oxford, Clarendon Press, 1998), p. 152; Rudé, *Crowd in History*, pp. 60–61.   88. Boswell, *Life of Johnson*, pp. 1053–4.   89. Haywood and Seed, *Gordon Riots*, pp. 218–19.   90. E. P. Thompson, *The Making of the English Working Class* (Harmondsworth, Penguin Books, 1968), p. 75.   91. Wilson, *Sense of the People*, p. 265.   92. Thompson gives them two pages out of over 900 in his classic *Making of the English Working Class*.   93. Langford, *Polite and Commercial*, p. 721.   94. Conway, *British Isles*, p. 223.   95. John Ferling, *A Leap in the Dark: The Struggle to Create the American Republic* (Oxford UP, 2003), p. 224.
96. Mackesy, *War for America*, p. 385.   97. Simms, *Three Victories*, pp. 589–90.
98. Mackesy, *War for America* p. 385.   99. Jonathan R. Dull, *A Diplomatic History of the American Revolution* (New Haven, Conn., Yale UP, 1985), pp. 109–10.
100. Conway, *British Isles*, p. 129.   101. Simms, *Three Victories*, p. 659.
102. Marshall, *Making and Unmaking*, p. 365.   103. Max M. Mintz, *Seeds of Empire: The American Revolutionary Conquest of the Iroquois* (New York UP, 1999), p. 173.   104. Albert Sorel, *Europe and the French Revolution: The Political Traditions of the Old Regime* (London, Collins, 1969), p. 382.   105. Mackesy, *War for America*, p. 518.   106. Wilson, *Sense of the People* p. 435.   107. Adam Smith, *The Wealth of Nations* (London, Everyman, 1991 [1776]), bk. IV, vol. II, p. 121.
108. Simms, *Three Victories*, pp. 660–61.   109. Roger Morriss, *The Foundations of British Maritime Ascendancy: Resources, Logistics and the State, 1755–1815* (Cambridge UP, 2011), pp. 14–20, 400–403.   110. Leandro Prados de la Escosura, ed., *Exceptionalism and Industrialisation: Britain and Its European Rivals, 1688–1815* (Cambridge UP, 2004), p. 53.   111. Ronald Finlay and Kevin H. O'Rourke, *Power and Plenty: Trade, War and the World Economy in the Second Millennium* (Princeton UP, 2007), p. 352.   112. Trevor Burnard and Richard Follett,

"Caribbean slavery, British anti-slavery, and the cultural politics of venereal disease," *HJ* 55 (2012), pp. 427–51.   113. William Cowper, 1788, in Chris Brooks and Peter Faulkner, *The White Man's Burdens: An Anthology of British Poetry of the Empire* (Exeter, Exeter UP, 1996), p. 114.   114. Thomas, *Slave Trade*, pp. 303–4, 340.   115. John Robinson, secretary to the Treasury, 1781, in Marshall, *Making and Unmaking*, p. 368.   116. P. J. Marshall, "Warren Hastings," in *ODNB*.   117. Burke's opening speech in the impeachment, 15 Feb. 1788, in Burke, *On Empire, Liberty and Reform*, p. 388.   118. Letter, 1786, in J. J. Sack, "The memory of Burke and the memory of Pitt: English conservatism confronts its past, 1806–1829," *HJ* 30 (1987), p. 640.   119. Miles Ogborn, *Global Lives: Britain and the World, 1550–1800* (Cambridge UP, 2008); Stephen Wheeler, "Skinner, James," in *ODNB*; see also Linda Colley, *Captives: Britain, Empire and the World, 1600–1850* (London, Pimlico, 2002).   120. P. J. Marshall, *"A Free Though Conquering People"*: *Eighteenth-Century Britain and Its Empire* (Aldershot, Ashgate, 2003), p. 3.

## 10. The First Industrial Nation

1. Chris Brooks and Peter Faulkner, *The White Man's Burdens: An Anthology of British Poetry of the Empire* (Exeter UP, 1996), p. 83.   2. Leandro Prados de la Escosura, ed., *Exceptionalism and Industrialisation: Britain and Its European Rivals, 1688–1815* (Cambridge UP, 2004), p. 15.   3. There is a vast historical literature on this topic, beginning with Arnold Toynbee, *Lectures on the Industrial Revolution of the 18th Century in England: Popular Addresses, Notes and Other Fragments* (London, Rivington, 1887), and J. and L. Hammond's even more negative picture, *The Bleak Age* (London, Longmans, 1934). David Cannadine examines in detail chronological changes in historical approaches in "The present and the past in the English industrial revolution, 1880–1980," *P&P* 103 (1984), pp. 131–72. Peter Mathias, *The First Industrial Nation: An Economic History of Britain, 1700–1914* (London, Methuen, 1969), was a pioneering effort to argue a less negative case, as, explicitly, was D. C. Coleman, *Myth, History and the Industrial Revolution: The Creighton Trust Lecture 1989, delivered before the University of London on Monday, 30 October 1989* (University of London, 1989). On recent academic research, a concise yet comprehensive introduction is Emma Griffin, *A Short History of the Industrial Revolution* (Houndmills, Palgrave Macmillan, 2010).   4. Robert C. Allen, *The British Industrial Revolution in Global Perspective* (Cambridge UP, 2009), p. 25.   5. Stephen Broadberry et al., "British economic growth, 1270–1870" (10 Jan. 2011), draft paper available online.   6. *CEHMB*, vol. I, p. 269.   7. Ronald Findlay and Kevin H. O'Rourke, *Power and Plenty: Trade, War and the World Economy in the Second Millennium* (Princeton UP, 2007), p. 362. This, the prevailing academic view, is disputed by Prasannan Parthasarati, *Why Europe Grew Rich and Asia Did Not* (Cambridge UP, 2011), pp. 39–46.   8. Jan de Vries, *The Industrious Revolution: Consumer Behaviour and the Household Economy, 1650 to the Present* (Cambridge UP, 2008).   9. A range of detailed research is summarized in ibid., pp. 123–33.   10. John Styles, *The Dress of the People: Everyday Fashion in*

*Eighteenth-Century England* (New Haven, Conn., Yale UP, 2007), p. 58. 11. Vries, *Industrious Revolution*, p. 23. 12. Ibid., p. 165. See also Craig Muldrew, *Food, Energy and the Creation of Industriousness: Work and Material Culture in Agrarian England, 1550–1780* (Cambridge UP, 2011). 13. *CEHMB*, vol. I, p. 277. 14. Vries, *Industrious Revolution*, p. 123. 15. Styles, *Dress of the People*, ch. 6. 16. T. De Moor and J. L. van Zanden, "Girl power: the European marriage pattern and labour markets in the North Sea region in the late medieval and early modern periods," cited in Allen, *British Industrial Revolution*, p. 14. 17. Usually termed the "European Marriage Pattern." 18. Paul Slack, *The English Poor Law, 1531–1782* (London, Macmillan, 1990), p. 55. 19. Vries, *Industrious Revolution*, pp. 103–4, 179; Emma Griffin, *Liberty's Dawn: A People's History of the Industrial Revolution* (New Haven, Conn., Yale UP, 2013), ch. 6. 20. *CEHMB*, vol. I, p. 120. 21. Ibid., p. 270. 22. Allen, *British Industrial Revolution*, p. 12. 23. Ibid., p. 55; *CEHMB*, vol. I, pp. 236, 354. 24. On the historiographical debates, see Griffin, *Short History*, chs. 6, 7 and 8. 25. Eric Williams, *Capitalism and Slavery* (Chapel Hill, North Carolina UP, 1944). 26. David Landes, *The Wealth and Poverty of Nations* (London, Little, Brown, 1998), p. xxi. 27. For example, C. Knick Harley, in *CEHMB*, vol. I, pp. 194, 198. 28. David Eltis and Stanley Engerman, "The importance of slavery and the slave trade to industrializing Britain," *Journal of Economic History* 60 (2000), pp. 123, 141. 29. P. K. O'Brien, "European economic development: the contribution of the periphery," *Economic History Review* 100, pp. 773–800, quoted in ibid., p. 198. 30. Findlay and O'Rourke, *Power and Plenty*, pp. 329–30. 31. See Prados de la Escosura, *Exceptionalism and Industrialisation*, pp. 59–60, 280. 32. Allen, *British Industrial Revolution*, ch. 10. 33. Ibid., p. 194. 34. Robert and Isabelle Tombs, *That Sweet Enemy: The French and the British from the Sun King to the Present* (London, Heinemann, 2006), pp. 183–4. 35. Adam Smith, *The Wealth of Nations* ([1776] London, Everyman, 1991), vol. I, p. 13; vol. II, p. 180. 36. *CEHMB*, vol. I, pp. 269–71. 37. Vries, *Industrious Revolution*, pp. 113–16, Styles, *Dress of the People*, pp. 324–5. 38. Allen, *British Industrial Revolution*, p. 48; Vries, *Industrious Revolution*, pp. 113, 118–19, 179–80. 39. On ordinary people's perceptions of the changes they were experiencing, see Griffin, *Liberty's Dawn*. 40. *CEHMB*, vol. I, p. 64; B. R. Mitchell and P. Deane, *Abstract of British Historical Statistics* (Cambridge UP, 1962), p. 6. 41. Findlay and O'Rourke, *Power and Plenty*, p. 315; *CEHMB*, vol. I, p. 60. 42. E. A. Wrigley and R. Schofield, quoted in Findlay and O'Rourke, *Power and Plenty*, p. 314. 43. Clive Oppenheimer, *Eruptions That Shook the World* (Cambridge UP, 2011), pp. 295, 306–19.

## 11. Wars of Dreams

1. Thomas Philip Schofield, "Conservative political thought in Britain in response to the French Revolution," *HJ* 29 (1986), p. 603. 2. Oscar Browning, ed., *Despatches from Paris, 1784–1790* (2 vols.; London, Camden Society, 1909–10), vol. 2, p. 243. 3. John Ehrman, *The Younger Pitt* (3 vols.; London, Constable, 1983),

vol. II, p. 4.   4. Jennifer Mori, *Britain in the Age of the French Revolution* (Harlow, Longman, 2000), p. 188.   5. Iain McCalman, *Radical Underworld: Prophets, Revolutionaries and Pornographers in London, 1795–1840* (Oxford, Clarendon Press, 1988), p. 63.   6. Emma Vincent Macleod, *A War of Ideas: British Attitudes to the Wars against Revolutionary France, 1792–1802* (Aldershot, Ashgate, 1998), pp. 153–4.   7. Stuart Andrews, *Unitarian Radicalism: Political Rhetoric, 1770–1814* (Basingstoke, Palgrave Macmillan, 2003), pp. 31–6; Gertrude Himmelfarb, *The Roads to Modernity: The British, French and American Enlightenments* (London, Vintage, 2008), pp. 104–5.   8. Edmund Burke, *Reflections on the Revolution in France*, ed. J. C. D. Clark (Stanford UP, 2001), pp. 63–5.   9. J. G. A. Pocock, *The Discovery of Islands: Essays in British History* (Cambridge UP, 2005), p. 121.   10. Burke, *Reflections*, passim; Edmund Burke, *On Empire, Liberty and Reform: Speeches and Letters*, ed. David Bromwich (New Haven, Conn., Yale UP, 2000), p. 36; letter, 1795, in J. J. Sack, "The memory of Burke and the memory of Pitt: English conservatism confronts its past, 1806–1829," *HJ* 30 (1987), p. 622. See also "Edmund Burke's Enlightenment," in Himmelfarb, *Roads to Modernity*, pp. 71–92.   11. Blair Worden, *Roundhead Reputations: The English Civil Wars and the Passions of Posterity* (London, Allen Lane, 2001), p. 207.   12. Andrews, *Unitarian Radicalism*, pp. 85–94.   13. Thomas Paine, *Political Writings*, ed. Bruce Kuklick (Cambridge UP, 1989), pp. 85, 97, 119, 120, 123, 125, 141, 142.   14. E. P. Thompson, *The Making of the English Working Class* (London, Penguin Books, 1968), pp. 100, 103.   15. Richard D. Altick, *The English Common Reader: A Social History of the Mass Reading Public, 1800–1900* (Chicago UP, 1957), p. 71; Thompson, *Making*, p. 118.   16. H. T. Dickinson, ed., *Britain and the French Revolution, 1789–1815* (London, Palgrave Macmillan, 1989), p. 29.   17. R. B. Rose, "The Priestley riots of 1791," *P&P* 18 (1960), pp. 68–88.   18. Dickinson, *Britain and the French Revolution*, pp. 36, 103. See also Macleod, *War of Ideas*, pp. 179–87.   19. Paine, *Political Writings*, p. 100.   20. Sack, "The memory of Burke and the memory of Pitt," p. 627; Stuart Semmel, *Napoleon and the British* (New Haven, Conn., Yale UP, 2004), p. 247.   21. Hadva Ben-Israel, *English Historians on the French Revolution* (Cambridge UP, 1968), p. 278.   22. H. T. Dickinson, *British Radicalism and the French Revolution, 1789–1815* (Oxford, Blackwell, 1985), pp. 234–9; Thompson, *Making*, p. 49; McCalman, *Radical Underworld*, ch. 2.   23. John Rule, "Edward Palmer Thompson," in *ODNB*.   24. Thompson, *Making*, pp. 13, 44, 914–15.   25. Mori, *Britain in the Age*, p. 127.   26. Andrews, *Unitarian Radicalism*, p. 37.   27. Boyd Hilton, *A Mad, Bad, and Dangerous People? England, 1783–1846* (Oxford, Clarendon Press, 2006), p. 460.   28. T. C. W. Blanning, *Origins of the French Revolutionary Wars* (London, Longman, 1986), p. 133; Dickinson, *Britain and the French Revolution*, p. 128.   29. Blanning, *Origins*, p. 149; Macleod, *War of Ideas*, p. 184.   30. Ibid., p. 37.   31. William Pitt, *Orations on the French War, to the Peace of Amiens* (London, J. M. Dent, n.d.), pp. 32–3.   32. Eric J. Evans, *William Pitt the Younger* (London, Routledge, 1999), p. 74.   33. Jean-Yves Guiomar, *L'Invention de la guerre totale, XVIIIe–XXe siècles* (Paris, Le Félin, 2004).   34. Ehrman, *The Younger Pitt*, vol. 2, p. 389.   35. Hugues Marquis, *Agents de l'ennemi: Les espions à la solde de l'Angleterre dans une France en révolution* (Paris, Vendémiaire, 2014), pp. 104–6. **36.** Clarke Garrett, *Respectable Folly: Millenarians and the French Revolution in France and England* (Baltimore, Md., Johns Hopkins UP, 1975), p. 139. **37.** G. E. Bentley, *Stranger from Paradise: A Biography of William Blake* (New Haven, Conn., Yale UP, 2001), p. 196; Garrett, *Respectable Folly*, pp. 212–13. **38.** Macleod, *War of Ideas*, p. 153. **39.** Mori, *Britain in the Age*, p. 100. **40.** Roger Knight, *Britain Against Napoleon: The Organization of Victory, 1793–1815* (London, Allen Lane, 2013), p. 157. **41.** Ibid., pp. 157–8. **42.** Paul D. Halliday, *Habeas Corpus: From England to Empire* (Cambridge, Mass., Harvard UP, 2010), pp. 253–6, 315. **43.** Thompson, *Making*, p. 21. **44.** E. H. Stuart Jones, *The Last Invasion of Britain* (Cardiff, Wales UP, 1950), p. 119; Roland Quinault, "The French invasion of Pembrokeshire in 1797: a bicentennial assessment," *Welsh History Review* 19 (1999), pp. 618–41. **45.** Mori, *Britain in the Age*, p. 168. **46.** Thompson, *Making*, p. 184. **47.** N. A. M. Rodger, *The Command of the Ocean* (London, Allen Lane, 2004), pp. 442–53; in contrast, Roger Wells, *Insurrection: The British Experience, 1795–1803* (Gloucester, Alan Sutton, 1983), pp. 79–109, argues for Irish involvement and political motivation. **48.** Edward Cooke and Josiah Tucker, *Arguments for and Against an Union Between Great Britain and Ireland Considered* (London, Stockdale, 1798), p. 9. **49.** J. C. D. Clark, *English Society, 1688–1832* (Cambridge UP, 1985), p. 345; Mori, *Britain in the Age*, pp. 117–18. **50.** Knight, *Britain Against Napoleon*, p. 388. **51.** Samantha Williams, *Poverty, Gender and Life-Cycle Under the English Poor Law, 1760–1834* (Woodbridge, Boydell, 2011), pp. 53–6. **52.** See Macleod, *War of Ideas*, for a survey of public opinion. **53.** Marquis, *Agents de l'ennemi*, pp. 175–7. **54.** Ehrman, *The Younger Pitt*, vol. 2, pp. 607, 624. **55.** Albert Sorel, *Europe and the French Revolution: The Political Traditions of the Old Regime*, ed. and trans. A. Cobban and J. W. Hunt (London, Collins, 1969), p. 362. **56.** George Canning, in Piers Mackesy, *War Without Victory: The Downfall of Pitt, 1799–1802* (Oxford, Clarendon Press, 1984), p. 43. **57.** Mackesy, *War Without Victory*, pp. 124–5, 132. **58.** Pitt, *Orations*, p. 430. **59.** Clive Emsley, *British Society and the French Wars, 1793–1815* (London, Macmillan, 1979), p. 96; Macleod, *War of Ideas*, pp. 109, 192–6. **60.** Knight, *Britain Against Napoleon*, pp. 220–21. **61.** Mackesy, *War Without Victory* p. 209. **62.** See Pierre Branda and Thierry Lentz, *Napoléon, l'esclavage et les colonies* (Paris, Fayard, 2006). **63.** George Canning, 1807, in Paul W. Schroeder, *The Transformation of European Politics, 1763–1848* (Oxford, Clarendon Press, 1994), p. 330. **64.** Thompson, *Making*, p. 495. **65.** William Wordsworth, "England! the time is come when thou shouldst wean" (1803). **66.** Semmel, *Napoleon and the British*, p. 95. **67.** McCalman, *Radical Underworld*, p. 1. **68.** Macleod, *War of Ideas*, p. 204. **69.** Lucian Regenbogen, *Napoléon a dit* (Paris, Belles Lettres, 1998), p. 114; Michèle Battesti, *Trafalgar: les aléas de la stratégie navale de Napoléon* (Paris, Napoléon 1er Éditions, 2004), p. 38. **70.** Knight, *Britain Against Napoleon*, pp. 253–4. **71.** J. E. Cookson, *The British Armed Nation, 1793–1815* (Oxford, Clarendon Press, 1997), p. 66. See also Austin Gee, *The British Volunteer Movement, 1794–1815* (Oxford, Clarendon Press, 2003). **72.** Knight, *Britain Against Napoleon*, pp. 81, 271–2. **73.** Charles Esdaile, *The Wars of Napoleon* (London, Longman, 1995), pp. 144–5.

74. Cookson, *British Armed Nation*, pp. 95–6; slightly different figures are given by Knight, *Britain Against Napoleon*, pp. 154–5, 259–60.   75. Roger Morriss, *The Foundations of British Maritime Ascendancy: Resources, Logistics and the State, 1755–1815* (Cambridge UP, 2011), ch. 3, and Knight, *Britain Against Napoleon*, passim.   76. Frank J. Klingberg and Sigurd B. Hustvedt, *The Warning Drum: The British Home Front Faces Napoleon: Broadsides of 1803* (Berkeley, California UP, 1944), p. 193. See also Semmel, *Napoleon and the British*, ch. 2.   77. Macleod, *War of Ideas*, pp. 163–73.   78. Linda Colley, *Britons: Forging the Nation, 1707–1837* (New Haven, Conn., Yale UP, 1992), p. 306.   79. Cookson, *British Armed Nation*, pp. 38–52; Knight, *Britain Against Napoleon*, ch. 9.   80. J. Christopher Herold, ed., *The Mind of Napoleon: A Selection from His Written and Spoken Words* (New York, Columbia UP, 1955), pp. 191–2; John Keane, *Tom Paine: A Political Life* (London, Bloomsbury, 1995), p. 441.   81. Letter, 4 Aug. 1805, *Correspondance de Napoléon I<sup>er</sup>* (32 vols., Paris, Imprimerie Impériale, 1858–69), vol. 11, p. 71.   82. Michael Lewis, *A Social History of the Navy, 1793–1815* (London, Allen & Unwin, 1960), pp. 361–70; Jean-Marcel Humbert and Bruno Ponsonnet, eds., *Napoléon et la mer: un rêve d'empire* (Paris, Seuil, 2004), pp. 128–9; Peter Padfield, *Guns at Sea* (London, Hugh Evelyn, 1973), p. 133.   83. Knight, *Britain Against Napoleon*, pp. xxii, 100.   84. Ehrman, *The Younger Pitt*, vol. 1, p. 108; vol. 4, pp. 808, 850–52.   85. Knight, *Britain Against Napoleon*, ch. 8.   86. 1813 figures, in Morriss, *Foundations of British Maritime Ascendancy*, pp. 71–3 ; annual costs, H. V. Bowen, *War and British Society, 1688–1815* (Cambridge UP, 1998), p. 17.   87. N. A. M. Rodger, *The Wooden World* (London, Fontana, 1988), p. 11; Rodger, *Command of the Ocean*, p. lxv.   88. Robert Greenhalgh Albion, *Forests and Sea Power: The Timber Problem of the Royal Navy* (new edn; Annapolis, Md., Naval Institute Press, 2000), pp. 9, 20, 86, 93; Bowen, *War and British Society*, p. 17.   89. Daniel Baugh, "Naval power: what gave the British naval superiority?," in Leandro Prados de la Escosura, ed., *Exceptionalism and Industrialisation: Britain and Its European Rivals, 1688–1815* (Cambridge UP, 2004), pp. 249–57.   90. Lewis, *Social History of the Navy*, pp. 361–70; Humbert and Ponsonnet, *Napoléon et la mer*, pp. 128–9; Padfield, *Guns at Sea*, p. 133. I am grateful to the military historian Dennis Showalter for his assessment.   91. Rodger, *Wooden World*, pp. 174–6, 181–2.   92. Ibid., p. 136.   93. Ibid., pp. 13, 208–9.   94. Morriss, *Foundations of British Maritime Ascendancy*, p. 26.   95. Knight, *Britain Against Napoleon*, pp. 174–5; and see Janet Macdonald, *Feeding Nelson's Navy: The True Story of Food at Sea in the Georgian Era* (London, Chatham, 2004).   96. Battesti, *Trafalgar*, p. 333.   97. Jean Tulard, *Napoléon, ou le mythe du sauveur* (Paris, Fayard, 1977), p. 206.   98. David B. Gaspar and David D. Geggus, *A Turbulent Time: The French Revolution and the Greater Caribbean* (Bloomington, Indiana UP, 1997), p. 89.   99. Roger Anstey, *The Atlantic Slave Trade and British Abolition, 1760–1810* (London, Macmillan, 1975), pp. 372, 407–8.   100. Alain Guéry, "Les comptes de la mort: pertes de guerre et conjoncture du phénomène guerre," *Histoire et Mesure* 6 (1991), p. 301.   101. Mori, *Britain in the Age*, p. 183, 174.   102. Brigadier-General Charles Stewart, in Knight, *Britain Against Napoleon*, p. 417.   103. Notably Thompson, *Making*, p. 604.   104. Mori, *Britain in the*

*Age*, p. 150.   **105.** Knight, *Britain Against Napoleon*, pp. 248–9, 264.   **106.** Ibid., p. 249.   **107.** Steven Englund, *Napoleon: A Political Life* (New York, Scribner, 2004), p. 517.   **108.** John M. Sherwig, *Guineas and Gunpowder: British Foreign Aid in the Wars with France, 1793–1815* (Cambridge, Mass., Harvard UP, 1969), pp. 4, 11, 338, 350; see also Knight, *Britain Against Napoleon*, ch. 13.   **109.** Schroeder, *Transformation*, p. 330.   **110.** John Bew, *Castlereagh: Enlightenment, War and Tyranny* (London, Quercus, 2011), p. 346.   **111.** Pierre Migliorini and Jean Quatre Vieux, *Batailles de Napoléon dans le Sud-Ouest* (Biarritz, Atlantica, 2002), pp. 199–202; Nicole Gotteri, *Soult: Maréchal d'Empire et homme d'État* (Besançon, Éditions la Manufacture, 1991), pp. 466–7.   **112.** [Blakiston,] *Twelve Years' Military Adventures in three Quarters of the Globe* (2 vols.; London, Henry Colburn, 1829), vol. 2, p. 338.   **113.** Gotteri, *Soult*, p. 467.   **114.** Emsley, *British Society*, p. 167; Knight, *Britain Against Napoleon*, pp. 451–3; Semmel, *Napoleon and the British*, pp. 148, 155, 290.   **115.** Jacques Logie, *Waterloo: The 1815 Campaign* (Stroud, Spellmount, 2006), p. 17.   **116.** Semmel, *Napoleon and the British*, pp. 160–66.   **117.** Philip Shaw, *Waterloo and the Romantic Imagination* (Houndmills, Palgrave Macmillan, 2002), p. 4; Victor Hugo, *The Wretched*, trans. Christine Donougher (London, Penguin Books, 2013), p. 315.   **118.** Quotations in Brent Nosworthy, *Battle Tactics of Napoleon and His Enemies* (London, Constable, 1995), pp. 237–8.   **119.** Shaw, *Waterloo*, p. 2.   **120.** Catriona Kennedy, *Narratives of the Revolutionary and Napoleonic Wars: Military and Civilian Experience in Britain and Ireland* (Houndmills, Palgrave Macmillan, 2013), p. 180.   **121.** Morriss, *Foundations of British Maritime Ascendancy*, p. 401.   **122.** Knight, *Britain Against Napoleon*, pp. xxii, xxxviii, 431, 465; see also Morriss, *Foundations of British Maritime Ascendancy*, passim.   **123.** Semmel, *Napoleon and the British*, p. 169.   **124.** Shaw, *Waterloo*, pp. 4, 37.   **125.** Burke, *Reflections*, p. 291.

## PART FIVE: THE ENGLISH CENTURY

**1.** *Selected Speeches of the Late Right Honourable the Earl of Beaconsfield*, ed. T. E. Kebbel (2 vols.; London, Longman Green, 1882), vol. 2, p. 534.   **2.** Ibid.   **3.** See Paul W. Schroeder, *The Transformation of European Politics, 1763–1848* (Oxford, Clarendon Press, 1994).   **4.** See C. A. Bayly, *The Birth of the Modern World, 1780–1914: Global Connections and Comparisons* (Oxford, Blackwell, 2004).   **5.** Alphonse de Lamartine, in *Voyage en Orient*, ed. Sophie Basch (Paris, Gallimard, 2011 [1835]), p. 420.

## 12. Dickensian England, *c.*1815–*c.*1850

**1.** K. J. Fielding and Anne Smith, "*Hard Times* and the factory controversy: Dickens vs Harriet Martineau," *Nineteenth-Century Fiction* 24 (1970), p. 405.   **2.** Patrick Parrinder, *Nation & Novel: The English Novel from Its Origins to the Present Day* (Oxford UP, 2006), p. 214.   **3.** Joanna Innes, in David Feldman and Jon Lawrence, eds., *Structures and Transformations in Modern British History* (Cambridge UP,

2011), p. 90. Dietary regulations provided 19,000 calories a week—about a third more than a typical agricultural labourer would have had, and roughly what is considered adequate for a manual worker today. **4.** Paul Johnson, in Martin Daunton, ed., *Charity, Self-Interest and Welfare in the English Past* (London, UCL Press, 1996), p. 245, and José Harris, in Donald Winch and Patrick O'Brien, eds., *The Political Economy of British Historical Experience, 1688–1914* (Oxford UP, 2002), pp. 416–17. **5.** Gertrude Himmelfarb, *The Idea of Poverty: England in the Early Industrial Age* (London, Faber, 1984), p. 454. **6.** Ibid., p. 202. **7.** David Newsome, *The Victorian World Picture* (London, Fontana, 1998), p. 167. **8.** Andrew Sanders, *Charles Dickens* (Oxford UP, 2003), p. 79. **9.** Michael Mason, *The Making of Victorian Sexual Attitudes* (Oxford UP, 1994), p. 108. **10.** Tim Parks, "How does he come to be mine?," *LRB*, 8 August 2013, pp. 9–14. **11.** *Hard Times*, quoted in Himmelfarb, *Idea of Poverty*, p. 484. **12.** *Blackwood's Edinburgh Magazine*, in ibid., p. 458. **13.** Ibid., p. 465. **14.** *Christian Remembrancer* (Jan. 1845), p. 301; Himmelfarb, *Idea of Poverty*, pp. 458, 465. **15.** Jonathan Rose, *The Intellectual Life of the British Working Classes* (Yale UP, 2001), pp. 111–15. **16.** Kathleen Tillotson, *Novels of the Eighteen-Forties* (Oxford UP, 1954), p. 110. See also Humphry House, *The Dickens World* (Oxford UP, 1942), pp. 18–34. **17.** Sanders, *Charles Dickens*, p. 53. **18.** *Household Words*, June 1853, in ibid., p. 66. **19.** James Mill, in William Thomas, *The Quarrel of Macaulay and Coker: Politics and History in the Age of Reform* (Oxford UP, 2000), p. 228. **20.** Fielding and Smith, "*Hard Times* and the factory controversy," pp. 404–27; Himmelfarb, *Idea of Poverty*, p. 485. **21.** G. M. Young, *Portrait of an Age* (Oxford UP, 1960), p. 29. **22.** *Blackwood's Edinburgh Magazine* (June 1871), p. 677. **23.** Ibid., p. 695. **24.** [Hannah Lawrance,] "The works of Charles Dickens," *British Quarterly Review* 35 (January 1862), p. 137; Richard D. Altick, *The English Common Reader: A Social History of the Mass Reading Public 1800–1900* (Chicago UP, 1957), pp. 383–4. **25.** [Lawrance,] "Works," p. 155. **26.** George Orwell, "Charles Dickens," in *Essays* (London, Penguin Books, 2000), p. 36. **27.** *Blackwood's Edinburgh Magazine*, June 1871, p. 690. **28.** Orwell, "Charles Dickens," p. 67. **29.** George Gissing, in Parrinder, *Nation & Novel*, p. 213. **30.** See Boyd Hilton, *A Mad, Bad, and Dangerous People? England, 1783–1846* (Oxford, Clarendon Press, 2006). **31.** E. A. Wrigley, "British population during the long eighteenth century, 1680–1840," in *CEHMB*, vol. I, p. 64. For an overview of population research, see Emma Griffin, *A Short History of the British Industrial Revolution* (Houndmills, Palgrave Macmillan, 2010), ch. 2. **32.** David Philips, "A new engine of power and authority: the institutionalization of law-enforcement in England, 1780–1830," in V. A. C. Gatrell, Bruce Lenman and Geoffrey Parker, eds., *Crime and the Law: The Social History of Crime in Western Europe Since 1500* (London, Europa, 1980), pp. 182–3. **33.** B. R. Mitchell and Phyllis Deane, *Abstract of British Historical Statistics* (Cambridge UP, 1962), pp. 8–10, 366, 388, 402–3. **34.** Rohan McWilliam, *Popular Politics in Nineteenth-Century England* (London, Routledge, 1998), p. 40. **35.** M. J. D. Roberts, *Making English Morals: Voluntary Association and Moral Reform in England, 1878–1886* (Cambridge UP, 2004), p. 101; David Taylor, *Crime, Policing and Punishment in*

*England, 1750–1914* (Houndmills, Palgrave Macmillan, 1998), pp. 20–21; Clive Oppenheimer, *Eruptions That Shook the World* (Cambridge UP, 2011), pp. 295, 306–19. **36.** Gareth Stedman Jones, *An End to Poverty? A Historical Debate* (London, Profile, 2004), pp. 89–109. **37.** House, *Dickens World*, p. 76. **38.** Boyd Hilton, *The Age of Atonement: The Influence of Evangelicalism on Social and Economic Thought, 1795–1865* (Oxford, Clarendon Press, 1988), p. 65. **39.** Hilton, *Mad, Bad*, p. 313. **40.** Jeremy Bentham, *A Fragment on Government* (1776), Preface, para. 2. **41.** Jeremy Bentham, *An Introduction to the Principles of Morals and Legislation* (2nd edn, 1823), ch. 1, para. 4. **42.** Young, *Portrait*, p. 68. **43.** Thomas, *Quarrel*, p. 228. **44.** Himmelfarb, *Idea of Poverty*, pp. 79–83. **45.** Juliet Barker, *Wordsworth: A Life* (London, Penguin Books, 2001), pp. 357–8. **46.** See Hilton, *Mad, Bad*, pp. 195–6. **47.** Henry Drummond, MP, in Hilton, *Mad, Bad*, p. 406. **48.** Ibid., pp. 221–2. **49.** Ronald Findlay and Kevin H. O'Rourke, *Power and Plenty: Trade, War and the World Economy in the Second Millennium* (Princeton UP, 2007), p. 315; E. A. Wrigley, "Coping with rapid population growth," in Feldman and Lawrence, *Structures and Transformations*, pp. 49–50. **50.** *Guardian* (24 July 2013); see also *CEHMB*, vol. I, p. 285. **51.** Benjamin Disraeli, *Sybil; or, The Two Nations* (1845), bk. 3, ch. 4; Jacques Gury, *Le voyage Outre-Manche: Anthologie de voyageurs français* (Paris, Robert Laffont, 1999), pp. 520, 522. **52.** F. M. L. Thompson, *The Rise of Respectable Society: A Social History of Victorian Britain, 1830–1900* (London, Fontana, 1988), p. 181. **53.** *CSHB*, vol. 2, p. 2. **54.** B. R. Mitchell, *European Historical Statistics, 1750–1970* (London, Macmillan, 1978), p. 39 (deaths of infants under one year). Cholera deaths: Norman Longmate, *King Cholera* (London, Hamish Hamilton, 1966), pp. 95–6; Alfred Fierro, *Histoire et Dictionnaire de Paris* (Paris, Robert Laffont, 1996), p. 774; Quentin Deluermoz, *Le Crépuscule des révolutions, 1848–1871* (Paris, Seuil, 2012), p. 147. **55.** House, *Dickens World*, p. 66. **56.** Dorothy Thompson, *The Chartists: Popular Politics in the Industrial Revolution* (New York, Pantheon, 1984), p. 250. **57.** K. Theodore Hoppen, *The Mid-Victorian Generation, 1846–1886* (Oxford UP, 1998), p. 96. **58.** Emma Griffin, *Liberty's Dawn: A People's History of the Industrial Revolution* (Yale UP, 2013), p. 161; J. K. Walton, in *CSHB*, vol. 1, p. 368. **59.** *Sybil*, bk. 3, ch. 4. **60.** Sheila M. Smith, "Willenhall and Wodgate: Disraeli's use of Blue Book evidence," *Review of English Studies*, new series, 13 (1962), pp. 368–84. **61.** Michael Mason, *The Making of Victorian Sexuality* (Oxford UP, 1994), p. 153. **62.** Taylor, *Crime, Policing and Punishment*, p. 28. **63.** Griffin, *Liberty's Dawn*, p. 242. **64.** Hilton, *Mad, Bad*, p. 432. **65.** For details, see ibid., ch. 6. **66.** For example, Antonia Fraser, *Perilous Question: The Drama of the Great Reform Bill 1832* (London, Weidenfeld & Nicolson, 2013). **67.** Hilton, *Mad, Bad*, pp. 411, 432. **68.** Thompson, *Chartists*, pp. 265–6. **69.** Hilton, *Mad, Bad*, pp. 417–20. **70.** J. C. D. Clark, *English Society, 1688–1832* (Cambridge UP, 1985), p. 404. **71.** Letter to *The Times* (9 Dec. 1830), in E. J. Hobsbawm and George Rudé, *Captain Swing* (London, Lawrence & Wishart, 1970), p. 236. **72.** Nick Clegg, speech in May 2010. **73.** Clyve Jones, ed., *A Short History of Parliament* (Woodbridge, Boydell, 2009), p. 262. **74.** Winch and O'Brien, *Political Economy*, p. 356. **75.** Hilton, *Mad, Bad*, pp. 354, 498.

Unmarried female property owners had voted in these elections.   76. Hobsbawm and Rudé, *Captain Swing*, pp. 262–3.   77. Hilton, *Mad, Bad*, p. 608.   78. Peter Mandler, "Chadwick, Sir Edwin," in *ODNB*.   79. R. P. Hastings, "Poverty and the Poor Law in the North Riding of Yorkshire, *c*.1780–1837," University of York, Borthwick Papers no. 61 (1982), p. 33.   80. Alexis de Tocqueville, *Memoir on Pauperism*, trans. Seymour Drescher (London, Institute of Economic Affairs, 1997), pp. 17, 24, 32, 35.   81. Snell, *Annals of the Labouring Poor*, p. 133; Himmelfarb, *Idea of Poverty*, p. 165; Winch and O'Brien, *Political Economy*, pp. 359–60. 82. Himmelfarb, *Idea of Poverty*, p. 182.   83. Samantha Williams, *Poverty, Gender and Life-Cycle Under the English Poor Law, 1760–1834* (Woodbridge, Boydell, 2011), pp. 66–8.   84. Martin Daunton, *Wealth and Welfare: An Economic and Social History of Britain, 1851–1951* (Oxford UP, 2007), pp. 525–6.   85. Winch and O'Brien, *Political Economy*, pp. 436–7.   86. Himmelfarb, *Idea of Poverty*, p. 188.   87. Thompson, *Chartists*, p. 30.   88. "Poor Man's Guardian," ibid., p. 29. 89. Himmelfarb, *Idea of Poverty*, p. 257.   90. Malcolm Chase, *Chartism: A New History* (Manchester UP, 2007), pp. 283–4.   91. Simon Morgan, "The Anti–Corn Law League and British anti-slavery in Atlantic perspective, 1838–1846," *HJ* 52 (2009), p. 90.   92. Frank Trentmann, *Free Trade Nation: Commerce, Consumption, and Civil Society in Modern Britain* (Oxford UP, 2008), p. 2; Hilton, *Mad, Bad*, p. 504.   93. Morgan, "Anti-Corn Law League," p. 91.   94. Hilton, *Mad, Bad*, p. 557.   95. John Prest, "Sir Robert Peel," in *ODNB*.   96. Young, *Portrait*, p. 44n; Hilton, *Mad, Bad*, p. 318.   97. Robert Peel, *Sir Robert Peel, and his era: being a synoptical view of the chief events and measures of his life and time* (London, N. H. Cotes, 1843), p. 10.   98. Roger Knight, *Britain Against Napoleon: The Organization of Victory, 1793–1815* (London, Allen Lane, 2013), p. xxix.   99. Denis Le Marchant, quoted in Clark, *English Society*, p. 394.   100. Tillotson, *Novels of the Eighteen-Forties*, p. 89.   101. Peter Gray, *The Irish Famine* (London, Thames & Hudson, 1995), p. 34.   102. Paul Bew, *Ireland: The Politics of Enmity, 1789–2006* (Oxford UP, 2007), pp. 177–8.   103. Ibid., pp. 187, 198–9.   104. Mary Daly, *The Famine in Ireland* (Dublin Historical Association, 1986), p. 97; Cormac Ó Gráda, *Black '47 and Beyond* (Princeton UP, 1999), p. 77.   105. Ó Gráda, *Black '47 and Beyond*, p. 8; see also Daly, *The Famine*, p. 113.   106. Cormac Ó Gráda, "Was the Great Famine Just Like Modern Famines?," in Helen O'Neill and John Toye, eds., *A World Without Famine? New Approaches to Aid and Development* (London, Macmillan, 1998), pp. 57–8; Ó Gráda, *Black '47*, p. 124.   107. H. F. Kearney, in Bew, *Ireland*, pp. 211–12.   108. Daly, *The Famine*, pp. 115, 123.   109. Bew, *Ireland*, p. 193.   110. *The Spectator* (20 Nov. 1847), in ibid., p. 200.   111. Bew, *Ireland*, pp. 202–5, 213.   112. Robert Blake, *Disraeli* (London, Methuen, 1969), pp. 232, 233, 237.   113. Prest, "Peel," in *ODNB*.   114. Blake, *Disraeli*, pp. 229, 234. 115. J. P. Parry, "Disraeli and England," *HJ* 43 (Sept. 2000), pp. 700, 703. 116. Hilton, *Mad, Bad*, p. 513.   117. *CSHB*, vol. 2, pp. 5, 132–3.   118. J. B. Leno, in Thompson, *Chartists*, p. 321.   119. Quotations from Thompson, *Chartists*, pp. 321–2, and John Saville, *1848: The British State and the Chartist Movement* (Cambridge UP, 1987), pp. 281–2.   120. For example, Chase, *Chartism*, p. 302; Hoppen, *Mid-Victorian Generation*, p. 130.   121. Hoppen, *Mid-Victorian*

*Generation*, pp. 201–4.  **122.** Robert J. Goldstein, *Political Repression in 19th Century Europe* (London, Croom Helm, 1983), p. 65.  **123.** Saville, *1848*, p. 164.  **124.** See Clark, *English Society*, p. 419.  **125.** Martin J. Wiener, *English Culture and the Decline of the Industrial Spirit, 1850–1980* (Cambridge UP, 1981), p. 46.  **126.** Gareth Stedman Jones, "National bankruptcy and social revolution: European Observers on Britain, 1813–1844," in Winch and O'Brien, *Political Economy*, p. 62; D. C. Coleman, *Myth, History and the Industrial Revolution* (London, Hambledon, 1992), p. 23.  **127.** See Tristram Hunt, in Feldman and Lawrence, *Structures and Transformations*, p. 143.  **128.** Frederick Engels, *The Condition of the Working Class in England*, ed. Eric Hobsbawm (London, Panther, 1969 [1844]), pp. 321–2.  **129.** Stedman Jones, "National bankruptcy," pp. 90–91.  **130.** *CSHB*, vol. 1, p. 371.  **131.** Mason, *Making of Victorian Sexuality*, p. 293.  **132.** Teresa Javurek, "A new Liberal descent: the 'Labourer' trilogy by Lawrence and Barbara Hammond," *Twentieth Century British History* 10 (1999), pp. 383, 397.  **133.** J. L. Hammond and Barbara Hammond, *The Labourer, 1760–1832* (new edn; Gloucester, Alan Sutton, 1995), p. 332.  **134.** Javurek, "New Liberal descent," pp. 378, 382, 388, 397.  **135.** Timothy Boon, "Industrialisation and catastrophe: the Victorian economy in British film documentary, 1930–50," in Miles Taylor and Michael Wolff, eds., *The Victorians Since 1901: Histories, Representations and Revisions* (Manchester UP, 2004), pp. 107–20.

## 13. Victorian England

**1.** The *Oxford English Dictionary* gives the first use ("Victorian era") in a literary work of 1875. On the idea of "Victorianism," Michael Mason, *The Making of Victorian Sexuality* (Oxford UP, 1994), pp. 8–20.  **2.** From the most successful modern "Victorian" spoof, George MacDonald Fraser's Flashman series—*Royal Flash* (London, Fontana, 1989), p. 11.  **3.** G. M. Young, *Victorian England: Portrait of an Age* (Oxford UP, 1960), p. vi.  **4.** The novelist Bulwer Lytton, in David Newsome, *The Victorian World Picture* (London, Fontana, 1998), p. 1.  **5.** Henry Blyth, *Skittles: The Last Victorian Courtesan* (London, Rupert Hart-Davis, 1970), pp. 76–7.  **6.** Jonathan Conlin, *Tales of Two Cities: Paris, London and the Birth of the Modern City* (London, Atlantic Books, 2013), p. 131.  **7.** Newsome, *Victorian World Picture*, p. 266.  **8.** W. L. Burn, in ibid., p. 10.  **9.** Young, *Victorian England*, p. 181.  **10.** Ibid., p. 141.  **11.** K. D. M. Snell and Paul S. Ell, *Rival Jerusalems: The Geography of Victorian Religion* (Cambridge UP, 2000), pp. 265, 325, 423; Callum G. Brown, *The Death of Christian Britain* (London, Routledge, 2001), p. 3. Gallup polls in 2008–10 indicated 42 to 43 percent of frequent church attenders in the USA, and 20 percent never attending.  **12.** Snell and Ell, *Rival Jerusalems*, pp. 118–20; David Hepton, *Methodism: Empire of the Spirit* (New Haven, Conn., Yale UP, 2005), pp. 212–16.  **13.** Census figures showed 5.3 million attending Anglican services; the next largest were the Wesleyan Methodists (1.5 million) and the Independents, heirs of the Puritans (1.2 million).  **14.** Eugenio Biagini, *Liberty, Retrenchment and Reform: Popular Liberalism in the Age of Gladstone, 1860–1880* (Cambridge

UP, 1992), p. 245. **15.** Snell and Ell, *Rival Jerusalems*, pp. 130, 399. **16.** M. J. D. Roberts, *Making English Morals: Voluntary Association and Moral Reform in England, 1787–1886* (Cambridge UP, 2004), p. 124. **17.** F. M. L. Thompson, *The Rise of Respectable Society: A Social History of Victorian Britain, 1830–1900* (London, Fontana, 1988), pp. 250–52, 260. **18.** Roberts, *Making English Morals*, pp. 228–30. **19.** John Henry Newman, *Apologia Pro Vita Sua*, ed. Ian Ker (London, Penguin Books, 1994 [1864]), pp. 93, 131, 259–62. **20.** Peter Mandler, ed., *Liberty and Authority in Victorian Britain* (Oxford UP, 2006), p. 190; Simon Green, "The rise and fall of the faithful city: Christianisation and dechristianisation in England, 1850–1950," Birkbeck Lectures, Cambridge, Nov.–Dec. 2013. **21.** Snell and Ell, *Rival Jerusalems*, p. 417. **22.** Christopher Clark and Wolfram Kaiser, eds., *Culture Wars: Secular-Catholic Conflict in Nineteenth-Century Europe* (Cambridge UP, 2003), pp. 162, 178. **23.** Biagini, *Liberty*, pp. 241, 252. **24.** Boyd Hilton, *A Mad, Bad, and Dangerous People? England, 1783–1846* (Oxford, Clarendon Press, 2006), pp. 632–4. **25.** Alfred Tennyson, *In Memoriam* (1850), LVI. **26.** Mandler, *Liberty and Authority*, p. 245. **27.** Hilton, *Mad, Bad*, p. 474. **28.** Richard D. Altick, *The English Common Reader: A Social History of the Mass Reading Public* (Chicago UP, 1957), p. 101. **29.** Snell and Ell, *Rival Jerusalems*, pp. 277–8. **30.** Newsome, *Victorian World Picture*, p. 8. **31.** Macaulay, in ibid., p. 172. **32.** François Guizot, *Histoire de la Civilisation en Europe depuis la chute de l'Empire romain jusqu'à la Révolution française* (Paris, Didier, 1847), p. 344. **33.** John Burrow, *A History of Histories: Epics, Chronicles, Romances and Inquiries from Herodotus and Thucydides to the Twentieth Century* (London, Penguin Books, 2009), p. 331. **34.** Thomas Carlyle, *Sartor Resartus*, eds. K. McSweeney and P. Sabor (Oxford UP, 1999), p. 4. **35.** Mandler, *Liberty and Authority*, pp. 227, 245. **36.** Alfred Tennyson, "You Ask Me, Why, Tho' Ill at Ease," 1833. **37.** Krishan Kumar, *The Making of English National Identity* (Cambridge UP, 2003), p. 193. **38.** Newsome, *Victorian World Picture*, pp. 47, 50, 51. **39.** Alfred Tennyson, "Maud" (1855). **40.** Constable Educational Series, 1860, in Suzanne Baudemont, *L'Histoire et la légende dans l'école élémentaire victorienne* (Paris, Klincksieck, 1980), p. 157. **41.** Samuel Smiles, *Self Help* (London, Sphere Books, 1968), pp. 149, 151. **42.** Matthew Arnold, *Culture and Anarchy*, ed. J. Dover Wilson (Cambridge UP, 1960), pp. 52, 101–2. **43.** Fiona MacCarthy, "Morris, William (1834–1896)," in *ODNB*. **44.** Robert Hewison, "Ruskin, John (1819–1900)," in *ODNB*. **45.** Jon Parry, "Liberalism and liberty," in Mandler, *Liberty and Authority*, p. 78. **46.** H. C. G. Matthew, "Gladstone, William Ewart," in *ODNB*. **47.** Mandler, *Liberty and Authority*, p. 53. **48.** Ibid., p. 41. **49.** Ibid., pp. 56–9. **50.** Harriet Ritvo, *The Animal Estate: The English and Other Creatures in the Victorian Age* (London, Penguin Books, 1990), pp. 125–6. **51.** Ibid., p. 135. **52.** Roberts, *Making English Morals*, p. 245. **53.** Mandler, *Liberty and Authority*, pp. 27, 85. **54.** Alexander Herzen, *My Past and Thoughts*, in ibid., pp. 19–20. **55.** Ibid., p. 17. See also Martin Francis, "The domestication of the male? Recent research on nineteenth- and twentieth-century British masculinity," *HJ* 45 (2002), pp. 637–52. **56.** Thompson, *Rise of Respectable Society*, p. 197. **57.** Martin Wiener, *Men of Blood: Violence, Manliness and Criminal*

*Justice in Victorian England* (Cambridge UP, 2004), p. 29.   **58.** Emma Griffin, *Liberty's Dawn: A People's History of the Industrial Revolution* (Yale UP, 2013), p. 104.   **59.** Jan de Vries, *The Industrious Revolution: Consumer Behaviour and the Household Economy, 1650 to the Present* (Cambridge UP, 2008), ch. 5.   **60.** Helen Bosanquet in Elizabeth Roberts, *A Woman's Place: An Oral History of Working-Class Women, 1890–1940* (Oxford, Blackwell, 1984), p. 112.   **61.** Vries, *Industrious Revolution*, p. 197; Young, *Victorian England*, p. 24.   **62.** José Harris, "From poor law to welfare state? A European perspective," in Donald Winch and Patrick O'Brien, eds., *The Political Economy of British Historical Experience, 1688–1914* (Oxford UP, 2002), p. 433.   **63.** Paul Johnson, "Risk, redistribution and social welfare in Britain from the poor law to Beveridge," in Martin Daunton, ed., *Charity, Self-Interest and Welfare in the English Past* (London, UCL Press, 1996), pp. 232–7, 244–6; *CEHMB*, vol. II, p. 306.   **64.** Jon Lawrence, *Speaking for the People: Party, Language and Popular Politics in England, 1867–1914* (Cambridge UP, 1998), p. 235.   **65.** Ibid., p. 265; Vries, *Industrious Revolution*, pp. 234–5.   **66.** *CSHB*, vol. 2, p. 35 (fig. 1.6).   **67.** Mason, *Making of Victorian Sexuality*, pp. 195–7, 200–203; Lucy Bland, *Banishing the Beast: English Feminism and Sexual Morality, 1885–1914* (London, Penguin Books, 1995), p. 56.   **68.** Simon Szreter, "Victorian Britain, 1831–1963: towards a social history of sexuality," *Journal of Victorian Culture* I (Spring 1996), p. 139.   **69.** Peter Gay, *The Bourgeois Experience: Victoria to Freud*, vol. II: *The Tender Passion* (Oxford UP, 1986), pp. 298–310.   **70.** G. R. Searle, *A New England? Peace and War, 1886–1918* (Oxford, Clarendon Press, 2004), p. 47; Mason, *Making of Victorian Sexuality*, pp. 64–6, 153.   **71.** Szreter, "Victorian Britain," pp. 141–2; and see Roberts, *A Woman's Place*, pp. 83–8.   **72.** Michael Mason, *The Making of Victorian Sexual Attitudes* (Oxford UP, 1994), pp. 124, 162.   **73.** Ibid., p. 132.   **74.** Judith R. Walkowitz, *City of Dreadful Delight: Narratives of Sexual Danger in Late-Victorian London* (London, Virago, 1992), p. 93.   **75.** Ibid., pp. 101–2; see also Judith R. Walkowitz, *Prostitution in Victorian Society: Women, Class and the State* (Cambridge UP, 1980).   **76.** Mandler, *Liberty and Authority*, pp. 125–55.   **77.** Bland, *Banishing the Beast*, pp. xiv–xvi, 51; Roberts, *Making English Morals*, pp. 263–72.   **78.** Edward J. Bristow, *Vice and Vigilance: Purity Movements in Britain since 1700* (Dublin, Gill & Macmillan, 1977), p. 202.   **79.** For the cultural atmosphere, see Walkowitz, *City of Dreadful Delight*.   **80.** *Vigilance Record*, April 1889, in Bland, *Banishing the Beast*, p. 106.   **81.** Bland, *Banishing the Beast*, p. 288.   **82.** Hera Cook, *The Long Sexual Revolution: English Women, Sex and Contraception, 1880–1975* (Oxford UP, 2004), pp. 81–2, 100–101, 105.   **83.** Mason, *Making of Victorian Sexuality*, pp. 43, 54–9, 77.   **84.** This paragraph draws on Simon Green's Birkbeck Lectures, "The rise and fall of the faithful city."   **85.** B. R. Mitchell and P. Deane, *Abstract of British Historical Statistics* (Cambridge UP, 1962), pp. 218, 225, 239, 271, 427–8.   **86.** Graham Robb, *Rimbaud* (London, Picador, 2000), pp. 184, 194.   **87.** B. R. Mitchell, *European Historical Statistics, 1750–1970* (London, Macmillan, 1978), pp. 16–33, 39–43.   **88.** *CSHB*, vol. 2, p. 197; Jay Winter and Jean-Louis Robert, eds., *Capital Cities at War: Paris, London, Berlin, 1914–1919* (Cambridge UP, 1997), p. 493.   **89.** *CEHMB*, vol. II, pp. 283, 295, 313;

J. C. Drummond, Tom Pocock and Anne Wilbraham, *The Englishman's Food: Five Centuries of English Diet* (rev. edn, London, Pimlico, 1991), ch. 19.  90. Mandler, *Liberty and Authority*, p. 47.  91. Mason, *Making of Victorian Sexuality*, p. 294.  92. *CSHB*, vol. 2, p. 196.  93. Ibid., p. 198.  94. Mitchell and Deane, *Abstract*, pp. 333–5; Martin Daunton, *Wealth and Welfare: An Economic and Social History of Britain, 1851–1951* (Oxford UP, 2007), pp. 226, 229.  95. W. D. Rubinstein, ed., *Wealth and the Wealthy in the Modern World* (London, Croom Helm, 1980), p. 60.  96. Daunton, *Wealth and Welfare*, p. 410; *Guardian*, 6 Dec. 2006; *FT Financial Adviser*, 15 April 2010; Office for National Statistics (ONS), *Social Trends* (Houndmills, Palgrave Macmillan, 2010), pp. 62–3; ONS Wealth and Assets Survey (press release, 3 Dec. 2012).  97. Rubinstein, *Wealth and the Wealthy*, pp. 18–19.  98. Gillian Sutherland, in *CSHB*, vol. 2, p. 158.  99. Donald J. Olsen, *The Growth of Victorian London* (London, Batsford, 1976), p. 23.  100. Thompson, *Rise of Respectable Society*, pp. 182–8, 195; Peter Clarke and Clive Trebilcock, eds., *Understanding Decline: Perceptions and Realities of British Economic Performance* (Cambridge UP, 1997), p. 115.  101. George and Weedon Grossmith, *The Diary of a Nobody* (London, Everyman, 1968 [1892]), pp. 27, 29.  102. Thompson, *Rise of Respectable Society*, pp. 210–11.  103. *CEHMB*, vol. II, p. 93.  104. Thompson, *Rise of Respectable Society*, p. 204.  105. Clive Emsley, *Hard Men: The English and Violence Since 1750* (London, Hambledon, 2005), pp. 39–41.  106. Thompson, *Rise of Respectable Society*, pp. 271–2, 287.  107. Ibid., p. 289.  108. George Puttenham, *The Arte of English Poesie*, in the *Encyclopaedia Britannica*, 1911, p. 598.  109. James Boswell, *Life of Johnson*, ed. R. W. Chapman (Oxford UP, 1970), pp. 469–70, 707.  110. Preface to *Pygmalion*, in *Collected Plays* (London, Bodley Head, 1972), vol. 4, p. 659.  111. Richard Shannon, *Gladstone: Heroic Minister, 1865–1898* (London, Allen Lane, 1999), p. 97.  112. Charles Barber et al., *The English Language: A Historical Introduction* (2nd edn, Cambridge UP, 2009), pp. 227, 238.  113. F. M. L. Thompson, *English Landed Society in the Nineteenth Century* (London, Routledge & Kegan Paul, 1963), pp. 27, 28, 109; K. Theodore Hoppen, *The Mid-Victorian Generation, 1846–1886* (Oxford UP, 1998), p. 16; Barry Reay, *Rural Englands: Labouring Lives in the Nineteenth Century* (London, Palgrave Macmillan, 2004), p. xi.  114. *CEHMB*, vol. II, p. 137.  115. *CSHB*, vol. 2, p. 260.  116. Hoppen, *Mid-Victorian Generation*, p. 22; *CEHMB*, vol. II, pp. 133, 281; Daunton, *Wealth and Welfare*, p. 216; "Food security in the UK: an evidence and analysis paper," Food Chain Analysis Group, DEFRA, 2006, p. 16; "Self Sufficiency in Food," from Agriculture in the United Kingdom, DEFRA, 25 March 2010.  117. See Andy Wood, *The Memory of the People: Custom and Popular Senses of the Past in Early Modern England* (Cambridge UP, 2013), Epilogue.  118. Thompson, *English Landed Society*, p. 290.  119. Hoppen, *Mid-Victorian Generation*, p. 22; David Cannadine, *The Decline and Fall of the British Aristocracy* (Yale UP, 1990), p. 31.  120. Ibid., p. 110.  121. Ibid. ch. 6.  122. Robert Colls, *Identity of England* (Oxford UP, 2002), p. 176.  123. Jeremy Burchardt, *Paradise Lost: Rural Idyll and Social Change since 1800* (London, Tauris, 2002), pp. 93–8.  124. J. Mordaunt Crook, "Arcadia to Subtopia," *TLS* (22 June 2012), p. 7.  125. Alan Howkins, "The commons, enclosure and radical histories," in David Feldman and Jon Lawrence, eds., *Structures and Transformations in Modern British History* (Cambridge UP, 2011), pp. 113–14. **126.** Alan Powers, "Up at a villa," *TLS* (25 March 2011), p. 5. **127.** *CEHMB*, vol. II, p. 313. **128.** Burchardt, *Paradise Lost*, ch. 5. **129.** The architects Raymond Unwin and Baillie Scott, 1909, in David Watkin, *The English Vision: The Picturesque in Architecture, Landscape and Garden Design* (London, John Murray, 1982), p. 194. **130.** See Colls, *Identity*, chs. 18–19. **131.** Reay, *Rural Englands*, pp. 1, 3, 180. **132.** Tim Barringer, "Broken pastoral: art and music in Britain, Gothic Revival to punk rock," Slade Lectures, Cambridge, 2009. **133.** *CEHMB*, vol. II, p. 168. **134.** Ibid., p. 127. **135.** Ibid., pp. 244–5. **136.** Ibid., pp. 72, 244–5. **137.** Jonathan Parry, "The decline of institutional reform in nineteenth-century Britain," in Feldman and Lawrence, *Structures and Transformations*, pp. 166–7, 170. **138.** See Mitchell, *European Historical Statistics*, pp. 373–5. **139.** Feldman and Lawrence, *Structures and Transformations*, p. 176. **140.** Hoppen, *Mid-Victorian Generation*, pp. 45, 63. **141.** Robert Blake, *Disraeli* (London, Methuen, 1969), p. 311. **142.** For a "history from below," see Peter Linehan, ed., *St. John's College, Cambridge: A History* (Woodbridge, Boydell, 2011), pp. 274–91. **143.** T. G. Otte, *The Foreign Office Mind: The Making of British Foreign Policy, 1865–1914* (Cambridge UP, 2011), pp. 14–15. **144.** Sir James Fergusson, in ibid., pp. 14–15. **145.** For details, see Cannadine, *Decline and Fall*, pp. 290–95. **146.** Walter Bagehot, *The English Constitution*, ed. Miles Taylor (Oxford UP, 2001 [1867]), p. 64. **147.** Shannon, *Gladstone: Heroic Minister*, p. 92. **148.** Prosper Mérimée, *Lettres à une Inconnue* (Paris, Calmann-Lévy, 1874), p. 214. **149.** Clare A. P. Willsdon, *Mural Painting in Britain, 1840–1940: Image and Meaning* (Oxford, Clarendon Press, 2000), p. 35. **150.** Ibid., p. 51. **151.** Clyve Jones, ed., *A Short History of Parliament* (Woodbridge, Boydell, 2009), pp. 256–67. **152.** Ibid., p. 204. **153.** H. J. Hanham, *Elections and Party Management: Politics in the Time of Disraeli and Gladstone* (Hassocks, Harvester, 1978), p. 4. **154.** Hoppen, *Mid-Victorian Generation*, p. 24. **155.** Hanham, *Elections and Party Management*, p. 4. **156.** *Bentley's Quarterly Review* 1 (1859), p. 355. **157.** John Vincent, *The Formation of the Liberal Party, 1857–1868* (London, Constable, 1866), pp. 3, 24, 38–9. **158.** Hanham, *Elections and Party Management*, pp. 54–5, 313; Vincent, *Formation of the Liberal Party*, pp. 38–9. **159.** Hoppen, *Mid-Victorian Generation*, p. 138. **160.** H. Taine, *Notes sur l'Angleterre* (12th edn, Paris, Hachette, 1903), p. 26. **161.** Hoppen, *Mid-Victorian Generation*, pp. 131–4. **162.** Mandler, *Liberty and Authority*, p. 91. **163.** Jonathan Parry, "Disraeli, Benjamin," in *ODNB*. **164.** For reassessment of Disraeli's ideas, see Jonathan Parry's entry in *ODNB* and his "Disraeli and England," *HJ* 43 (September 2000), pp. 699–728. The most recent large-scale biography is Robert O'Kell, *Disraeli: The Romance of Politics* (Toronto UP, 2013). **165.** Blake, *Disraeli*, p. 747. **166.** The novel was unfinished. Ibid., pp. 739–40. **167.** Matthew, "Gladstone, William Ewart," in *ODNB*. **168.** *The Gladstone Diaries*, ed. M. R. D. Foot et al. (14 vols.; Oxford, Clarendon Press, 1968–94), vol. I, p. xix. **169.** *Gladstone Diaries*, vol. IX, p. 103. **170.** See Gay, *Bourgeois Experience*, vol. 2, pp. 384–8. **171.** Lady Waldegrave, in J. P. Parry, *Democracy and Religion: Glad-*

*stone and the Liberal Party, 1867–1875* (Cambridge UP, 1986), p. 141n. 172. *Gladstone Diaries*, vol. IX, pp. 497 (2.iv.1880) and 499 (8.iv.1880). 173. Parry, "Disraeli," in *ODNB*. 174. Biagini, *Liberty*, pp. 389–91, 420, 424. 175. Hanham, *Elections and Party Management*, pp. 204–5. 176. Hoppen, *Mid-Victorian Generation*, p. 141. 177. Roberts, *Making English Morals*, p. 190. 178. David Taylor, *Crime, Policing and Punishment in England, 1750–1914* (Houndmills, Palgrave Macmillan, 1998), p. 53. 179. Shannon, *Gladstone: Heroic Minister*, p. 138. 180. Lawrence, *Speaking for the People*, p. 265. 181. Martin Pugh, *The Making of Modern British Politics, 1867–1939* (Oxford, Blackwell, 1982), p. 4. 182. Hoppen, *Mid-Victorian Generation*, p. 245. 183. Lowe (March 1866), quoted in ibid., p. 247. 184. Parry, "Decline of institutional reform," p. 175. 185. Hanham, *Elections and Party Management*, chs. 12 and 13. 186. Henry Pelling, *Social Geography of British Elections, 1885–1910* (London, Macmillan, 1967), p. 82. 187. Parry, "Decline of institutional reform," p. 186. 188. Cannadine, *Decline and Fall*, pp. 310–14. 189. Ben Griffin, *The Politics of Gender in Victorian Britain: Masculinity, Political Culture and the Struggle for Women's Rights* (Cambridge UP, 2012), ch. 8. 190. See Hoppen, *Mid-Victorian Generation*, chs. 15 and 17. 191. Matthew, "Gladstone," in *ODNB*, p. 32. 192. Parry, *Democracy and Religion*, p. 181. 193. Matthew, "Gladstone," in *ODNB*, p. 33. 194. Hanham, *Elections and Party Mangement*, p. xxx. 195. Ben Clements and Nick Spencer, *Voting and Values in Britain: Does Religion Count?* (London, Theos, 2014), pp. 10, 37–8. 196. Hilton, *Mad, Bad*, p. 519. 197. Mike Ashley, *Taking Liberties: The Struggle for Britain's Freedoms and Rights* (London, British Library, 2008), p. 9—a quasi-official example, being the catalogue of a British Library exhibition on the history of liberty since Magna Carta. For spirited variations on this theme, see Frank McLynn, *The Road Not Taken: How Britain Narrowly Missed a Revolution* (London, Bodley Head, 2012), and David Horspool, *The English Rebel: One Thousand Years of Troublemaking from the Normans to the Nineties* (London, Viking, 2009). 198. Aneuran Bevan's description of Tories in a speech at Manchester, July 1948. 199. Vincent, *Making of the Liberal Party*, p. xxix. 200. Judith Keeling, "What Makes the British?," *Oxford Today* 25, 2 (2013), pp. 27–8. 201. Snell and Ell, *Rival Jerusalems*, pp. 13, 77, 171. 202. Biagini, *Liberty*, p. 105; Vincent, *Making of the Liberal Party*, pp. xiv, xxii. 203. Clements and Spencer, *Voting and Values*, pp. 13, 19. 204. Élie Halévy, *A History of the English People* (5 vols.; London, T. Fisher Unwin/Ernest Benn, 1924–34), vol. 1, p. 339. 205. E. P. Thompson, *The Making of the English Working Class* (London, Penguin Books, 1968), p. 385. 206. V. A. C. Gatrell, "The decline in theft and violence in Victorian and Edwardian England," in V. A. C. Gatrell, Bruce Lenman and Geoffrey Parker, eds., *Crime and the Law: The Social History of Crime in Western Europe since 1500* (London, Europa, 1980), p. 241. 207. David Reynolds, *Britannia Overruled: British Policy and World Power in the Twentieth Century* (London, Longman, 1991), p. 232. 208. Neil Tranter, *Sport, Economy and Society in Britain, 1750–1914* (Cambridge UP, 1998), p. 37. 209. Tony Collins, *A Social History of English Rugby Union* (London, Routledge, 2009), pp. 3, 5. 210. William Acton (1857), in Collins, *English Rugby*

*Union*, p. 84; Richard Holt, *Sport and the British: A Modern History* (Oxford, Clarendon Press, 1992), p. 91.   **211.** Quoted by Richard Holt in his Sir Derek Birley Memorial Lecture, April 2003.   **212.** George Orwell, "Boys' Weeklies" (1939), in *Essays* (London, Penguin Classics, 2000), p. 83.   **213.** Jonathan Rose, *The Intellectual Life of the British Working Classes* (New Haven, Conn., Yale UP, 2001), p. 329.   **214.** Ibid., pp. 155–6.   **215.** David Vincent, *The Rise of Mass Literacy: Reading and Writing in Modern Europe* (Cambridge, Polity Press, 2000), pp. 9–10.   **216.** Holt, *Sport and the British*, p. 118; and see Gillian Sutherland, in *CSHB*, vol. 3, p. 124.   **217.** Collins, *English Rugby Union*, pp. 13–16. **218.** Tranter, *Sport, Economy and Society*, pp. 13, 17, and ch. 3 passim; Holt, *Sport and the British*, pp. 138, 152, 167, 171–2.   **219.** Thompson, *Rise of Respectable Society*, pp. 296–7.   **220.** Collins, *English Rugby Union*, p. 26; Tony Collins, *Rugby League in Twentieth Century Britain: A Social and Cultural History* (London, Routledge, 2006), pp. 2–5.   **221.** Holt, *Sport and the British*, pp. 264–5. **222.** Ibid., pp. 99–100.   **223.** Tranter, *Sport, Economy and Society*, pp. 49, 67; Holt, *Sport and the British*, pp. 101–2.   **224.** Tranter, *Sport, Economy and Society*, p. 47.   **225.** Ibid., p. 1.   **226.** Taylor, *Crime, Policing and Punishment*, pp. 21–8; Hera Cook, *The Long Sexual Revolution: English Women, Sex and Contraception, 1880–1975* (Oxford UP, 2004), p. 101; Winter and Robert, *Capital Cities at War*, p. 491.   **227.** Wiener, *Men of Blood*, p. 6.   **228.** *Tom Brown's Schooldays* (Oxford UP, 1999), p. 282; Wiener, *Men of Blood*, p. 53 (quoting *The Times*, 10 April 1875), pp. 58–9.   **229.** Taylor, *Crime, Policing and Punishment*, pp. 30–31; Robert B. Shoemaker, "The taming of the duel: masculinity, honour and ritual violence in London, 1660–1800," *HJ* 45 (2002), pp. 525–45; Wiener, *Men of Blood*, pp. 43–6, 51–3.   **230.** Wiener, *Men of Blood*, p. 289; see also Emsley, *Hard Men*, p. 40–41. **231.** Taylor, *Crime, Policing and Punishment*, pp. 50, 69; Gatrell, "Decline in theft and violence," p. 327.   **232.** "There goes the neighbourhood," *The Economist* (4 May 2006).   **233.** Taylor, *Crime, Policing and Punishment*, pp. 44–5. **234.** Gatrell, "Decline in theft and violence," p. 276; Taylor, *Crime, Policing and Punishment*, ch. 5; Emsley, *Hard Men*, ch. 8.   **235.** Gatrell, "Decline in theft and violence," p. 278.   **236.** Taylor, *Crime, Policing and Punishment*, pp. 150–54, 158–9; Emsley, *Hard Men*, pp. 180–81.   **237.** Gatrell, "Decline in theft and violence," pp. 269, 275, 278; Taylor, *Crime, Policing and Punishment*, p. 104; Home Office statistics, "Police manpower by type" (2002); Wiener, *Men of Blood*, pp. 19–20.   **238.** See Emsley, *Hard Men*, pp. 158–60, 163–9.   **239.** Wiener, *Men of Blood*, pp. 289–91.   **240.** Gareth Stedman Jones, "Working-class culture and working-class politics in London, 1870–1900: notes on the remaking of a working class," *Journal of Social History*, 7 (1974), p. 498.   **241.** Kate Fox, *Watching the English: The Hidden Rules of English Behaviour* (London, Hodder, 2004), pp. 62–3.   **242.** George Dangerfield, *The Strange Death of Liberal England* (London, Paladin, 1970), pp. 14, 358.   **243.** Roberts, *Making English Morals*, p. 287; see also Christian Topolov, *Naissance du chômeur, 1880–1910* (Paris, Albin Michel, 1994), ch. 7.   **244.** Bentley B. Gilbert, "Winston Churchill versus the Webbs: the origins of British employment insurance," *American Historical Review* 71 (April 1966), p. 847.   **245.** George K. Behlmer and Fred M. Leventhal, eds., *Singular*

*Continuities: Tradition, Nostalgia and Identity in Modern British Culture* (Stanford UP, 2000), p. 64. **246.** *In Darkest England and the Way Out* (1890), in Feldman and Lawrence, *Structures and Transformations*, p. 157. **247.** Daunton, *Wealth and Welfare*, pp. 532, 541, 544; Harris, "From poor law to welfare state?," pp. 424–32. **248.** Lawrence, *Speaking for the People*, p. 148. **249.** Henry Pelling, *Popular Politics and Society in Late Victorian Britain* (London, Macmillan, 1968), pp. 149–50, 159–60. **250.** Searle, *New England?*, p. 443. **251.** Lawrence, *Speaking for the People*, pp. 160, 262. **252.** Tranter, *Sport, Economy and Society*, p. 66; Mitchell, *European Historical Statistics*, pp. 27, 28, 32, 42–3; Winter and Robert, *Capital Cities at War*, p. 492. **253.** Gareth Stedman Jones, *Outcast London: A Study in the Relationship Between Classes in Victorian Society* (London, Penguin Books, 1984) , p. 331. **254.** Bland, *Banishing the Beast*, pp. 222–5. **255.** Daunton, *Wealth and Welfare*, pp. 101–2. **256.** Searle, *New England?*, pp. 353–4; Rose, *Intellectual Life*, p. 42. **257.** Searle, *New England?*, p. 351. **258.** Martin Pugh, "Working-class experience and state social welfare, 1908–1914: old age pensions reconsidered," *HJ* 45 (2002), pp. 777–90. **259.** Ibid., p. 794. **260.** Gilbert, "Winston Churchill versus the Webbs," p. 846. **261.** Ibid., p. 856; see also Topolov, *Naissance du chômeur*, pp. 407–12. **262.** Gilbert, "Winston Churchill versus the Webbs," p. 861. **263.** Searle, *New England?*, pp. 56, 61–2, 381. **264.** Holt, *Sport and the British*, p. 123. **265.** Bland, *Banishing the Beast*, pp. 312, 245. **266.** Martin Pugh, "Disraeli," *TLS* (25 Oct. 2013), p. 6. **267.** Griffin, *Politics of Gender*, p. 283. **268.** Esther Roper (1906), in Searle, *New England?*, p. 458. **269.** Ibid., p. 463. **270.** Ibid., p. 468. **271.** "Proclamation" (24 Sept. 1913). The only known surviving copy of this poster was recently auctioned by Bonhams, and was shown on their website. **272.** David Fitzpatrick, "Militarism in Ireland, 1900–1922," in Thomas Bartlett and Keith Jeffery, eds., *A Military History of Ireland* (Cambridge UP, 1996), pp. 383–6. **273.** Paul Bew, *Ireland: The Politics of Enmity, 1789–2006* (Oxford UP, 2007), p. 369. **274.** Pelling, *Popular Politics*, p. 161.

## 14. Imperial England, 1815–1918

**1.** Roger Morriss, *The Foundations of British Maritime Ascendancy: Resources, Logistics and the State, 1755–1815* (Cambridge UP, 2011), p. 77. **2.** John Bew, *Castlereagh: Enlightenment, War and Tyranny* (London, Quercus, 2011), p. 407. **3.** Emmanuel de Las Cases, *Mémorial de Sainte-Hélène* (Paris, Seuil, 1968), vol. 2, p. 1208 (my translation). **4.** Roger Knight, *Britain Against Napoleon: The Organization of Victory, 1793–1815* (London, Allen Lane, 2013), p. 468. **5.** Richard Shannon, *Gladstone: Heroic Minister, 1865–1898* (London, Allen Lane, 1999), p. 86. **6.** G. C. Peden, "From cheap government to efficient government: the political economy of government expenditure in the United Kingdom, 1832–1914," in Donald Winch and Patrick K. O'Brien, *The Political Economy of British Historical Experience* (Oxford UP, 2002), p. 356. **7.** G. R. Searle, *A New England? Peace and War, 1886–1918* (Oxford UP, 2004), p. 302. **8.** John Darwin, *Unfinished Empire: The Global Expansion of Britain* (London, Penguin Books, 2012), p. 189;

T. G. Otte, *The Foreign Office Mind: The Making of British Foreign Policy, 1865–1914* (Cambridge UP, 2011), p. 7. **9.** Paul M. Kennedy, *The Rise and Fall of British Naval Mastery* (London, Allen Lane, 1976), p. 168. **10.** Ibid., pp. 208–9; *OHBE*, vol. 3, p. 338. **11.** Ronald Findlay and Kevin H. O'Rourke, *Power and Plenty: Trade, War and the World Economy in the Second Millennium* (Princeton UP, 2007), pp. 377, 379, 407. **12.** C. A. Bayly, *The Birth of the Modern World, 1780–1914* (Oxford, Blackwell, 2004), esp. chs. 3 and 4. **13.** Philip D. Morgan, in Martin Daunton and Rick Halpern, eds., *Empire and Others: British Encounters with Indigenous Peoples, 1600–1850* (London, UCL Press, 1999), pp. 45–6. **14.** Jonathan Parry, *The Politics of Patriotism: English Liberalism, National Identity and Europe, 1830–1886* (Cambridge UP, 2006), p. 21. **15.** Ronald Hyam, *Understanding the British Empire* (Cambridge UP, 2010), pp. 73–4. **16.** Parry, *Politics of Patriotism*, p. 4. **17.** Ibid., p. 37. **18.** Ibid., p. 20. **19.** See Paul W. Schroeder, *The Transformation of European Politics, 1763–1848* (Oxford, Clarendon Press, 1994), ch. 11. **20.** Bew, *Castlereagh*, p. 411. **21.** Kennedy, *Rise and Fall*, p. 168. **22.** Hyam, *Understanding*, p. 83. **23.** Peter T. Marsh, *Bargaining on Europe: Britain and the First Common Market* (New York, Conn., Yale UP, 1999). **24.** Jacques Gury, *Le Voyage Outre-Manche: Anthologie de voyageurs français de Voltaire à Mac Orlan* (Paris, Robert Laffont, 1999), p. 939 (my translation). **25.** Knight, *Britain Against Napoleon*, p. 474. **26.** Lance E. Davis and Robert A. Huttenback, *Mammon and the Pursuit of Empire: The Political Economy of British Imperialism, 1860–1912* (Cambridge UP, 1986), pp. 315–16. **27.** Speech at Crystal Palace, 1872, in *Selected Speeches of the Late Right Honourable the Earl of Beaconsfield*, ed. T. E. Kebbel (2 vols.; London, Longman Green, 1882), vol. 2, pp. 529–34. **28.** *CEHMB*, vol. II, p. 467. **29.** J. R. Seeley, *The Expansion of England* (London, Macmillan, 1919), pp. 205, 213. **30.** Darwin, *Unfinished Empire*, p. 343. **31.** Hyam, *Understanding*, p. 79. **32.** Christopher Bayly, in Daunton and Halpern, *Empire and Others*, p. 25. **33.** William Thomas, *The Quarrel of Macaulay and Croker: Politics and History in the Age of Reform* (Oxford UP, 2000), p. 151. **34.** *OHBE*, vol. 3, p. 104. **35.** Seymour Drescher, "Whose abolition? Popular pressure and the ending of the British slave trade," *P&P* 143 (May 1994), p. 164. **36.** "Slavery in diplomacy: the Foreign Office and the suppression of the transatlantic slave trade" (Foreign and Commonwealth Office Historians: History Note no. 17, n.d.), p. 6. **37.** David Brion Davis, *Inhuman Bondage: The Rise and Fall of Slavery in the New World* (Oxford UP, 2006), p. 238. **38.** John Iliffe, *Africans: The History of a Continent* (Cambridge UP, 2007), p. 182. **39.** "Slavery in diplomacy," pp. 95–100. **40.** Ibid., p. 15; and see Keith Hamilton and Patrick Salmon, eds., *Slavery, Diplomacy and Empire: Britain and the Suppression of the Slave Trade, 1807–1975* (Brighton, Sussex Academic Press, 2009), p. 56. The *Amistad* incident became the subject of a film (1997). **41.** Iliffe, *Africans*, p. 153. **42.** Hugh Thomas, *The Slave Trade: The History of the Atlantic Slave Trade, 1440–1870* (London, Picador, 1997), p. 784 ; Davis, *Inhuman Bondage*, p. 244. **43.** Hamilton and Salmon, *Slavery, Diplomacy and Empire*, pp. 67–73; Thomas, *Slave Trade*, pp. 740–46. **44.** Palmerston to U.S. minister in London, 27 Jan. 1841, "Slavery in Diplomacy," p. 103. **45.** William St. Clair, *The*

*Grand Slave Emporium: Cape Coast Castle and the British Slave Trade* (London, Profile, 2006), p. 256.  **46.** Findlay and O'Rourke, *Power and Plenty*, pp. 340–41; Davis, *Inhuman Bondage*, pp. 247–8.  **47.** Olivier Pétré-Grenouilleau, *Les Traites négrières* (Paris, Gallimard, 2006), pp. 178–89.  **48.** Stephen Tomkins, *David Livingstone: The Unexplored Story* (Oxford, Lion Hudson, 2013), pp. 207, 145–6. **49.** Hamilton and Salmon, *Slavery, Diplomacy and Empire*, pp. 98–9.  **50.** Ibid., pp. 93–124; Guillemette Crouzet, "'A sea of blood and plunder': lutte contre la traite et politique impériale britannique dans l'océan indien vers 1820–1880," *Monde(s)* 1 (2012), pp. 213–35.  **51.** Francis Bertie, in Hamilton and Salmon, *Slavery, Diplomacy and Empire*, p. 115.  **52.** John Iliffe, *Honour in African Society* (Cambridge UP, 2005), p. 202; Sir F. D. Lugard, *The Dual Mandate in British Tropical Africa* (Edinburgh, Blackwood, 1926), p. 376.  **53.** Iliffe, *Honour*, pp. 203, 217, 220; Iliffe, *Africans*, p. 214.  **54.** Chris Brooks and Peter Faulkner, eds., *The White Man's Burdens: An Anthology of British Poetry of the Empire* (Exeter UP, 1996), p. 177.  **55.** Eric Richards, *Britannia's Children: Emigration from England, Scotland, Wales and Ireland Since 1600* (London, Hambledon, 2004), p. 2.  **56.** Judy Campbell, *Invisible Invaders: Smallpox and Other Diseases in Aboriginal Australia, 1780–1880* (Melbourne UP, 2002), pp. 81–6, 216–27. **57.** Richards, *Britannia's Children*, pp. 4–6. See also Tristram Hunt, *The Cities That Made an Empire* (London, Allen Lane, 2014).  **58.** Peter N. Carroll and David W. Noble, *The Free and the Unfree: A New History of the United States* (London, Penguin Books, 1988), p. 248.  **59.** Christopher Bayly, in Daunton and Halpern, *Empire and Others*, pp. 35–6; Ronald Hyam, *Britain's Declining Empire: The Road to Decolonisation, 1918–1968* (Cambridge UP, 2006), pp. 54–5.  **60.** David Day, *Claiming a Continent: A New History of Australia* (Sydney, Angus & Robertson, 1997), pp. 122, 129.  **61.** Frank Trentmann, *Free Trade Nation: Commerce, Consumption, and Civil Society in Modern Britain* (Oxford UP, 2008), p. 2.  **62.** Parry, *Politics of Patriotism*, p. 159; *OHBE*, vol. 3, p. 104.  **63.** *The World's Fair; or, Children's Prize Book of the Great Exhibition of 1851* (1851), in Bernard Porter, *The Absent-Minded Imperialists: Empire, Society and Culture in Britain* (Oxford UP, 2004), p. 92.  **64.** *CEHMB*, vol. I, p. 202.  **65.** Trentmann, *Free Trade Nation*, pp. 13–20; Parry, *Politics of Patriotism*, p. 160.  **66.** *CEHMB*, vol. I, pp. 190, 199.  **67.** Findlay and O'Rourke, *Power and Plenty*, p. 332.  **68.** Martin Daunton, *Wealth and Welfare: An Economic and Social History of Britain, 1851–1951* (Oxford UP, 2007), pp. 217–19.  **69.** A Professor Flower, speaking at the British Association, 1863, in Parry, *Politics of Patriotism*, pp. 22–3.  **70.** Glenn Melancon, *Britain's China Policy and the Opium Crisis: Balancing Drugs, Violence and National Honour, 1833–1840* (Aldershot, Ashgate, 2003), p. 72; *OHBE*, vol. 3, p. 107.  **71.** Christopher Hibbert, *The Dragon Wakes: China and the West, 1793–1911* (London, Penguin Books, 1984), p. 135.  **72.** Ibid., p. 147.  **73.** Jonathan Spence, *God's Chinese Son: The Taiping Heavenly Kingdom of Hong Xiuquan* (London, HarperCollins, 1996), pp. 230–32.  **74.** Dorothy Thompson, *The Chartists* (New York, Pantheon, 1984), p. 318.  **75.** Parry, *Politics of Patriotism*, p. 152. **76.** See Christopher A. Bayly, *The Birth of the Modern World, 1780–1914* (Oxford, Blackwell, 2004).  **77.** Miles Taylor, "The 1848 revolutions and the British empire," *P&P* 166 (2000), pp. 146–80.  **78.** Though seemingly not for the right reasons. See

Lynn McDonald, "Wonderful adventures: how did Mary Seacole come to be viewed as a pioneer of modern nursing?," *TLS* (6 Dec. 2013), pp. 14–15. 79. Seema Alavi, *The Sepoys and the Company: Tradition and Transition in Northern India, 1770–1830* (New Delhi, Oxford UP, 1995), p. 296. 80. Christopher Bayly, in Daunton and Halpern, *Empire and Others*, p. 34. 81. William Dalrymple, *The Last Mughal: The Fall of a Dynasty, Delhi, 1857* (New Delhi, Viking, 2006), p. 220. 82. Major Bingham's diary, in Saul David, *The Indian Mutiny 1857* (London, Penguin Books, 2003), p. 255. 83. David, *Indian Mutiny*, p. 259. 84. Thomas Lowe, in ibid., p. 281. 85. *Letters and Journal of James, Eighth Earl of Elgin*, ed. T. Walrond (London, John Murray, 1872), p. 325. 86. Letter to Canning, 9 Nov. 1857, in David, *Indian Mutiny*, p. 239. 87. Letter from Edward Vibart to his uncle, in Dalrymple, *Last Mughal*, p. 386. 88. Eric Stokes, *The Peasant Armed: The Indian Revolt of 1857* (Oxford, Clarendon Press, 1986), pp. 86–99. 89. Dalrymple, *Last Mughal*, p. 364. 90. *Ghalib: Life and Letters*, eds. R. Russell and K. Islam (New Delhi, Oxford UP, 1994), pp. 153, 158. 91. Alfred Comyn Lyall, a member of the India Council, "Badminton" (1876), in Brooks and Faulkner, *White Man's Burdens*, p. 221. 92. *CIHBE*, p. 49. 93. Robert C. Allen, *The British Industrial Revolution in Global Perspective* (Cambridge UP, 2009), pp. 182–3, 187, 193–4, 212–14; Findlay and O'Rourke, *Power and Plenty*, pp. 381, 421–3, 426; David Landes, *The Unbound Prometheus: Technological Change and Industrial Development in Western Europe from 1750 to the Present* (Cambridge UP, 1969), p. 240; Davis and Huttenback, *Mammon and the Pursuit of Empire*, pp. 228–9. 94. Mike Davis, *Late Victorian Holocausts: El Niño Famines and the Making of the Third World* (London, Verso, 2001), p. 37. 95. Helen O'Neill and John Toye, eds. *A World Without Famine? New Approaches to Aid and Development* (London, Macmillan, 1998), pp. 107–27, 134. 96. See David Hall-Matthews, *Peasants, Famine and the State in Colonial Western India* (Basingstoke, Palgrave Macmillan, 2005), passim. 97. Bernard Porter, *The Refugee Question in Mid-Victorian Politics* (Cambridge UP, 1979), pp. 192–4. 98. C. I. Hamilton, *Anglo-French Naval Rivalry, 1840–1870* (Oxford, Clarendon Press, 1993), p. 84. 99. Parry, *Politics of Patriotism*, p. 223. 100. Derek Beales, *England and Italy, 1959–60* (London, Nelson, 1961), p. 20. 101. Marsh, *Bargaining on Europe*, passim. 102. Beales, *England and Italy*, p. 142. 103. Hugh Cunningham, *The Volunteer Force: A Social and Political History, 1859–1908* (London, Croom Helm, 1975). 104. Parry, *Politics of Patriotism*, p. 230. 105. Elgin, *Letters and Journals*, pp. 205, 212, 325; see also Hibbert, *Dragon Wakes*, p. 224. 106. Francis Hastings Doyle, "The Private of the Buffs" (1866), in Brooks and Faulkner, *White Man's Burdens*, pp. 204–5. 107. Lytton Strachey, *Eminent Victorians* (London, Penguin Books, 1971), p. 191. 108. *OHBE*, vol. 3, p. 156. 109. Jonathan Rose, *The Intellectual Life of the British Working Classes* (New Haven, Conn., Yale UP, 2001), pp. 382–4. 110. See Amanda Foreman, *A World on Fire: An Epic History of Two Nations Divided* (London, Penguin Books, 2010), passim. 111. Rose, *Intellectual Life*, pp. 382–3. 112. James McPherson, *Battle Cry of Freedom* (New York, Ballantine, 1988), p. 384. 113. Foreman, *A World on Fire*, p. 170. 114. Richard Shannon, *Gladstone: Peel's Inheritor, 1809–1865* (London, Penguin Books, 1999), pp. 466–8. 115. E. D. Steele, *Palmerston and Liberalism,*

*1855–1865* (Cambridge UP, 1991), pp. 300–301. **116.** Gad Heuman, *"The Killing Time": The Morant Bay Rebellion in Jamaica* (London, Macmillan, 1994), pp. 90, 95, 137. **117.** Alistair Horne, *The Fall of Paris* (London, Macmillan, 1965), p. 165. **118.** Steele, *Palmerston and Liberalism*, pp. 259–61. **119.** Hannah Pakula, *An Uncommon Woman: The Empress Frederick* (London, Phoenix, 1996), p. 271. **120.** Richard Millman, *British Foreign Policy and the Coming of the Franco-Prussian War* (Oxford, Clarendon Press, 1965), p. 216. **121.** Edward Blount, *Memoirs* (London, Longman, 1902), pp. 218–19. **122.** Karina Urbach, *Bismarck's Favourite Englishman: Lord Odo Russell's Mission to Berlin* (London, Tauris, 1999), p. 208. **123.** Shannon, *Gladstone: Heroic Minister*, p. 90; see also Brendan Simms, *Europe: The Struggle for Supremacy, 1453 to the Present* (London, Allen Lane, 2013), pp. 245–7. **124.** Speech in 1866, in John K. Walton, *Disraeli* (London, Routledge, 1990), p. 39. **125.** Raoul Girardet, *L'Idée coloniale en France* (Paris, 1972), p. 78 (my translation). **126.** Jonathan Parry, "Disraeli, Benjamin," in *ODNB*. **127.** Ronald Robinson and John Gallagher with Alice Denny, *Africa and the Victorians: The Official Mind of Imperialism* (London, Macmillan, 1961), p. 163. **128.** Iliffe, *Africans*, pp. 156–7; Hyam, *Understanding*, p. 84. **129.** Iliffe, *Africans*, p. 176. **130.** *OHBE*, vol. 3, p. 349; Hyam, *Understanding*, p. 75. **131.** Hamilton and Salmon, *Slavery, Diplomacy and Empire*, p. 113. **132.** Brooks and Faulkner, *White Man's Burdens*, p. 237. **133.** Letter to John Bright, 14 July 1882, *Gladstone Diaries*, vol. X, p. 298. **134.** K. Theodore Hoppen, *The Mid-Victorian Generation, 1846–1886* (Oxford UP, 1998), p. 661; Michael Howard, *War and the Liberal Conscience* (Oxford UP, 1981), p. 56. **135.** Anthony Webster, "Business and empire: a reassessment of the British conquest of Burma in 1885," *HJ* 43 (2000), pp. 1003–25. **136.** Strachey, *Eminent Victorians*, p. 207. **137.** *Gladstone Diaries*, vol. X, p. 25 (28 Feb. 1881). **138.** Keith M. Wilson, ed., *The International Importance of the Boer War* (Chesham, Acumen, 2001), p. 14. **139.** Ibid., p. 22. **140.** Donal Lowry, ed., *The South African War Reappraised* (Manchester UP, 2000), p. 26. **141.** Martin Pugh, *Speak for Britain: A New History of the Labour Party* (London, Vintage, 2011), p. 56. **142.** Wilson, *Boer War*, p. 160. **143.** Zara S. Steiner, *Britain and the Origins of the First World War* (London, Macmillan, 1977), p. 23. **144.** *OHBE*, vol. 4, p. 50. **145.** Wilson, *Boer War*, p. 161. **146.** Darwin, *Unfinished Empire*, p. 329. **147.** Sebastian Walsh, "Britain, Morocco and the development of the Anglo-French entente" (Cambridge PhD, 2011). **148.** T. G. Otte, *The Foreign Office Mind: The Making of British Foreign Policy, 1865–1914* (Cambridge UP, 2011), p. 375. **149.** F. H. Hinsley, ed., *British Foreign Policy under Sir Edward Grey* (Cambridge UP, 1977), p. 324; Keith M. Wilson, ed., *Decisions for War, 1914* (London, UCL Press. 1995), p. 90.

## Englishness in the English Century

**1.** Boyd Hilton, *A Mad, Bad, and Dangerous People? England 1783–1846* (Oxford, Clarendon Press, 2006), p. 238. **2.** Bernard Porter, *The Absent-Minded Imperialists: Empire, Society and Culture in Britain* (Oxford UP, 2004), p. 314. **3.** Edward

Said, *Culture and Imperialism* (London, Vintage, 1994), p. 8.   4. Porter, *Absent-Minded Imperialists*, p. vii.   5. Details in *CEHMB*, vol. II, p. 194.   6. Lance E. Davis and Robert A. Huttenback, *Mammon and the Pursuit of Empire: The Political Economy of British Imperialism, 1860–1912* (Cambridge UP, 1986), p. 306.   7. Ibid.   8. Ronald Findlay and Kevin H. O'Rourke, *Power and Plenty: Trade, War and the World Economy in the Second Millennium* (Princeton UP, 2007), pp. 414–15, 422–3.   9. Said, *Culture and Imperialism*, p. 164.   10. Ibid., pp. 75, 98, 114.   11. Richard D. Altick, *The English Common Reader: A Social History of the Mass Reading Public, 1800–1900* (Chicago UP, 1957), p. 301; Jonathan Rose, *The Intellectual Life of the British Working Classes* (New Haven, Conn., Yale UP, 2001), p. 383.   12. The leading sceptic is Porter, *Absent-Minded Imperialists*.   13. J. R. Seeley, *The Expansion of England* (London, Macmillan, 1919), p. 10.   14. Rose, *Intellectual Life*, p. 338.   15. Said, *Culture and Imperialism*, p. 188.   16. Peter Mandler, *The English National Character: The History of an Idea from Edmund Burke to Tony Blair* (New Haven, Conn., Yale UP, 2006), pp. 41, 43, 51–8.   17. *Puck of Pook's Hill* (1906) and *Rewards and Fairies* (1910).   18. David Gilmour, *The Long Recessional: The Imperial Life of Rudyard Kipling* (London, John Murray, 2002), p. 171.   19. Lucy Delap, "'Thus does man prove his fitness to be the master of things": Shipwrecks and Chivalry in Edwardian Britain," *Cultural and Social History* 3 (2006).   20. *British Wreck Commissioner's Inquiry* (London, HMSO, 1912), final report: "Account of the Saving and Rescue of those who Survived: Numbers Saved."   21. H. G. R. King, "Scott, Robert Falcon (1868–1912)," in *ODNB*.

## PART SIX: THE NEW DARK AGE, 1914–1945

1. G. P. Gooch, *The History of Our Time* (London, Williams and Norgate, 1911), pp. 232, 248–9.   2. Michael Howard, *War and the Liberal Conscience* (Oxford UP, 1981), p. 53.   3. John Darwin, *The Empire Project: The Rise and Fall of the British World System, 1830–1970* (Cambridge UP, 2009), p. 580; David Reynolds, *Britannia Overruled: British Policy and World Power in the Twentieth Century* (London, Longman, 1991), p. 18.

## 15. The War to End War

1. Adrian Gregory, *The Last Great War: British Society and the First World War* (Cambridge UP, 2008), p. 2.   2. G. R. Searle, *A New England? Peace and War, 1886–1918* (Oxford UP, 2004), pp. 747, 779.   3. Richard Aldington, *Death of a Hero* (1929), in George Robb, *British Culture and the First World War* (Houndmills, Palgrave Macmillan, 2002), p. 155.   4. Wilfred Owen, "Dulce et Decorum est," drafted October 1917; *The Poems of Wilfred Owen*, ed. Jon Stallworthy (London, Chatto & Windus, 1990), p. 117.   5. Gregory, *Last Great War*, p. 2.   6. For details of that fateful day, see Christopher Clark, *The Sleepwalkers: How Europe Went to War in 1914* (London, Allen Lane, 2012), pp. 367–76.   7. Zara S. Steiner,

*Britain and the Origins of the First World War* (London, Macmillan, 1977), p. 31; Nicholas A. Lambert, *Planning Armageddon: British Economic Warfare and the First World War* (Cambridge, Mass., Harvard UP, 2012), p. 35.   8. Rolf Hobson, *Imperialism at Sea: Naval Strategic Thought, the Ideology of Sea Power, and the Tirpitz Plan, 1875–1914* (Boston, Mass., Brill, 2002), pp. 243–60; T. G. Otte, *The Foreign Office Mind: The Making of British Foreign Policy, 1865–1914* (Cambridge UP, 2011), pp. 347–9.   9. Letter, 16 April 1911, in Annika Mombauer, ed., *The Origins of the First World War: Diplomatic and Military Documents* (Manchester UP, 2013) p. 44.   10. Christopher M. Bell, *Churchill and Sea Power* (Oxford UP, 2013), pp. 17–35.   11. Richard Cobb, in R. J. W. Evans and H. Pogge von Strandmann, *The Coming of the First World War* (Oxford, Clarendon Press, 1988), p. 126.   12. T. G. Otte, "Détente 1914: Sir William Tyrrell's secret mission to Germany," *HJ* 56 (2013), pp. 182, 186. See also William Mulligan, *The Origins of the First World War* (Cambridge UP, 2010), pp. 84–91.   13. Otte, *Foreign Office Mind*, p. 372.   14. For a vivid account, see Clark, *Sleepwalkers*, parts I and II. 15. Patricia Clavin, *The Great Depression in Europe, 1929–1939* (Houndmills, Macmillan, 2000), p. 14.   16. David G. Herrmann, *The Arming of Europe and the Making of the First World War* (Princeton UP, 1996), p. 213.   17. Richard F. Hamilton and Holger H. Herwig, eds., *War Planning 1914* (Cambridge UP, 2010), p. 253.   18. The "Plan" has long been a source of controversy. For a recent judicious summary, see Annika Mombauer, "Of war plans and war guilt: the debate surrounding the Schlieffen Plan," *Journal of Strategic Studies* 28 (2005), pp. 857–85. 19. David Stevenson, *1914–1918: The History of the First World War* (London, Allen Lane, 2004), p. 41.   20. Keith Wilson, ed., *Decisions for War, 1914* (London, UCL Press, 1995), pp. 45–6; Herrmann, *Arming of Europe*, p. 218.   21. Clark, *Sleepwalkers*, p. 332.   22. Immanuel Geiss, ed., *July 1914: The Outbreak of the First World War: Selected Documents* (London, Batsford, 1967), p. 64.   23. Sir Arthur Nicolson (permanent under-secretary), 9 July, in Otte, *Foreign Office Mind*, pp. 388–9.   24. Catriona Pennell, *A Kingdom United: Popular Responses to the Outbreak of the First World War in Britain and Ireland* (Oxford UP, 2012), p. 26.   25. Ibid., p. 28.   26. Clark, *Sleepwalkers*, pp. 490, 493.   27. Steiner, *Britain and the Origins*, p. 223; Searle, *New England?*, pp. 519, 522.   28. Lambert, *Planning Armageddon*, p. 193.   29. Gregory, *Last Great War*, p. 17.   30. In John Keiger, "Crossed wires, 1904–1914," in Robert Tombs and Émile Chabal, eds., *Britain and France in Two World Wars: Truth, Myth and Memory* (London, Bloomsbury, 2013), pp. 32–3.   31. Otte, *Foreign Office Mind*, p. 390.   32. Pennell, *A Kingdom United*, p. 29.   33. Ibid., p. 34.   34. Geiss, *July 1914*, pp. 215, 359; Keith Wilson, *Problems and Possibilities: Exercises in Statesmanship, 1814–1918* (Stroud, Tempus, 2003), p. 202; Lambert, *Planning Armageddon*, p. 193; Clark, *Sleepwalkers*, pp. 528–31, 494, 528, 531, 535.   35. Wilson, *Decisions for War*, p. 177; Niall Ferguson, *The Pity of War* (London, Penguin Books, 1999), p. 173; Gerd Hardach, *The First World War, 1914–1918* (London, Allen Lane, 1977), p. 77.   36. Keiger, "Crossed wires," p. 33.   37. Fritz Fischer, *Germany's Aims in the First World War* (London, Chatto & Windus, 1967), pp. 99, 199; Matthew Stibbe, *German Anglophobia and the Great War, 1914–1918* (Cambridge UP,

2001), p. 208. **38.** Ferguson, *Pity of War*, pp. 168–73, 458; Richard J. Evans in the *Guardian* (13 July 2013 and 6 Jan. 2014), and *New Statesman* (23 Jan. 2014). **39.** Geiss, *July 1914*, pp. 232, 300, 373. **40.** Fischer, *Germany's Aims*, pp. 113, 221, 421. **41.** Stibbe, *German Anglophobia*, p. 18 and passim. **42.** "September Programme," 1914, in Fischer, *Germany's Aims*, pp. 98–107; see comments by Geiss, *July 1914*, p. 367. **43.** Stibbe, *German Anglophobia*, p. 207; Holger H. Herwig, *The First World War: Germany and Austria-Hungary, 1914–1918* (London, Arnold, 1997), p. 406. **44.** Stevenson, *1914–1918*, p. 42. **45.** Otte, *Foreign Office Mind*, p. 391. **46.** Gregory, *Last Great War*, p. 34. **47.** Letter of 31 July, in David Boyd Haycock, *A Crisis of Brilliance: Five Young British Artists and the Great War* (London, Old Street, 2009), p. 211. **48.** Pennell, *A Kingdom United*, p. 30. **49.** Lambert, *Planning Armageddon*, pp. 186–91. **50.** Pennell, *A Kingdom United*, p. 35. **51.** Haycock, *Crisis*, pp. 211–12. **52.** Quoted in Brendan Simms, *Europe: The Struggle for Supremacy, 1453 to the Present* (London, Allen Lane, 2013), p. 304. **53.** Howard, *War and the Liberal Conscience*, pp. 75–7; Jonathan Atkin, *A War of Individuals: Bloomsbury Attitudes to the Great War* (Manchester UP, 2002). **54.** Searle, *New England?*, p. 794. **55.** Hew Strachan, *The First World War*, vol. I: *To Arms* (Oxford UP, 2001), p. 200. **56.** Gregory, *Last Great War*, pp. 30–33. **57.** Stevenson, *1914–1918*, pp. 59, 92–3. **58.** Based on Ferguson, *Pity of War*, pp. 295, 336–7, 445. **59.** David Stevenson, *With Our Backs to the Wall: Victory and Defeat in 1918* (London, Allen Lane, 2011), p. 9. **60.** Sir Henry Wilson, in Peter Simkins, *Kitchener's Army: The Raising of the New Armies, 1914–1916* (Barnsley, Pen & Sword, 2007), p. 316. **61.** Robin Neillands, *The Great War Generals on the Western Front, 1914–1918* (London, Robinson, 1999), p. 133. **62.** See Gregory, *Last Great War*, ch. 3, and his "Lost generations," in Jay Winter and Jean-Louis Robert, eds., *Capital Cities at War: Paris, London, Berlin, 1914–1919* (Cambridge UP, 1997); see also P. E. Dewey, "Military recruiting and the British labour force during the First World War," *HJ* 27 (1984), pp. 199–223. **63.** J. M. Winter, *The Great War and the British People* (2nd edn; London, Palgrave Macmillan, 2003), p. 99. **64.** Gregory, "Lost generations," pp. 84–5, 102–3; Searle, *New England?*, p. 797. **65.** General Ivor Maxse, in Simkins, *Kitchener's Army*, p. 316. **66.** Alexander Watson, *Enduring the Great War: Combat, Morale and Collapse in the German and British Armies, 1914–1918* (Cambridge UP, 2008), pp. 142–3. On discipline, see Simkins, *Kitchener's Army*, p. 317; G. D. Sheffield, *Leadership in the Trenches: Officer-Man Relations, Morale and Discipline in the British Army in the Era of the First World War* (Houndmills, Macmillan, 2000), p. 157; and for regular army attitudes, amusingly caricatured, Robert Graves, *Goodbye to All That* (London, Penguin Books, 1960), pp. 149–50. **67.** Gregory, *Last Great War*, p. 71. **68.** Searle, *New England?*, pp. 752–4; Winter, *Great War*, p. 28; David Fitzpatrick, "Militarism in Ireland, 1900–1922," in Thomas Bartlett and Keith Jeffery, eds., *A Military History of Ireland* (Cambridge UP, 1996), p. 388. **69.** Searle, *New England?*, p. 757. **70.** David Reynolds, *The Long Shadow: The Great War in the Twentieth Century* (London, Simon & Schuster, 2013), p. 107. **71.** Graves, *Goodbye to All That*, p. 71. **72.** Jean Moorcroft Wilson, *Siegfried Sassoon: The Making of a War Poet* (London, Duckworth, 1998),

p. 295. 73. Searle, *New England?*, p. 767. 74. Gregory, *Last Great War*, pp. 79–80; Simkins, *Kitchener's Army*, p. 92. 75. Sheffield, *Leadership*, pp. 104–14; Watson, *Enduring the Great War*, pp. 117, 121–2. 76. Christopher Duffy, *Through German Eyes: The British and the Somme, 1916* (London, Weidenfeld & Nicolson, 2006), p. 68. 77. Gregory, *Last Great War*, pp. 101–3, 154–5; Searle, *New England?*, p. 766. 78. Published in 1954–5. See John Garth, *Tolkien and the Great War: The Threshold of Middle-Earth* (London, HarperCollins, 2004). 79. See Simkins, *Kitchener's Army*, and Ian F. W. Beckett and Keith Simpson, eds., *A Nation in Arms: A Social Study of the British Army in the First World War* (Manchester UP, 1985). 80. Stevenson, *Backs to the Wall*, p. 208; Maurice Pearton, *The Knowledgeable State: Diplomacy, War and Technology Since 1830* (London, Burnett, 1982), p. 156; Watson, *Enduring the Great War*, p. 29; Robb, *British Culture*, pp. 191, 201. 81. Searle, *New England?*, p. 671. 82. Winston Churchill, *The World Crisis* (abridged edn; London, Thornton Butterworth, 1931), p. 522. 83. Robin Prior, *Gallipoli: The End of the Myth* (New Haven, Conn., Yale UP, 2009), pp. 242–3, 249–52. 84. William Philpott, *Anglo-French Relations and Strategy on the Western Front, 1914–1918* (London, Macmillan, 1996), p. 112. 85. Robert T. Foley, *German Strategy and the Road to Verdun: Erich von Falkenhayn and the Development of Attrition, 1870–1916* (Cambridge UP, 2005), pp. 187–92. 86. John Horne and Edward Madigan, eds., *Towards Commemoration: Ireland in War and Revolution, 1912–1923* (Dublin, Royal Irish Academy, 2013), p. 33. 87. Research by Niamh Gallagher in Cambridge is exploring the remarkable extent of this support. 88. Desmond FitzGerald, quoted in Horne and Madigan, *Towards Commemoration*, pp. 26–7, and see 50–51. 89. I am indebted for these points to Eugenio Biagini and Niamh Gallagher. For a summary, see Fitzpatrick, "Militarism in Ireland," pp. 386–97. 90. Niamh Gallagher, "Orange and Green united: this is Ireland's war: the Irish Canadian Rangers' visit to Dublin, Armagh, Belfast, Cork and Limerick in January 1917," unpublished paper given at the Modern British History Seminar, Cambridge, 20 Jan. 2014, cited by permission of the author. 91. Paul Bew, *Ireland: The Politics of Enmity, 1789–2006* (Oxford UP, 2007), pp. 371–89; Horne and Madigan, *Towards Commemoration*, p. 39. 92. William Philpott, *Bloody Victory: The Sacrifice on the Somme and the Making of the Twentieth Century* (London, Little, Brown, 2009), pp. 166–7. 93. Ibid., p. 129. 94. Ibid., pp. 178–80; Wilson, *Siegfried Sassoon*, p. 268. 95. Philpott, *Bloody Victory*, pp. 186–7, 191–3, 205, 207; Duffy, *Through German Eyes*, p. 166; Dan Todman, *The Great War: Myth and Memory* (London, Hambledon Continuum, 2005), p. 19. 96. Watson, *Enduring the Great War*, pp. 11, 167; Herwig, *First World War*, pp. 203–4. 97. J. P. Harris, *Douglas Haig and the First World War* (Cambridge UP, 2008), p. 540; Gary Sheffield, *Forgotten Victory: The First World War: Myths and Realities* (London, Headline, 2001), pp. 167–83; Watson, *Enduring the Great War*, pp. 144, 151. 98. Duffy, *Through German Eyes*, p. 328. 99. Harris, *Douglas Haig*, pp. 236, 515–16, 539. See also Tim Travers, *The Killing Ground: The British Army, the Western Front and the Emergence of Modern Warfare, 1900–1918* (London, Unwin Hyman, 1987), esp. chs. 6 and 7. 100. Jonathan Boff, *Winning and Losing on the Western Front: The British Third Army and the Defeat of Germany in 1918* (Cambridge UP, 2012), pp. 240–42. 101. Searle, *New England?*, p. 705. 102. Alan Clark, *The Donkeys* (1961); for the popularization of the phrase, see Reynolds, *Long Shadow*, pp. 330–31. 103. Brian Bond, *The Unquiet Western Front: Britain's Role in Literature and History* (Cambridge UP, 2002), p. 95. 104. Martin Kitchen, *The German Offensives of 1918* (Stroud, Tempus, 2001), p. 78. 105. Harris, *Douglas Haig*, p. 511; Stevenson, *Backs to the Wall*, p. 264. 106. For a comparison of the three high commands, see Travers, *Killing Ground*, pp. 250–62; and for the now widely held view that the British did adapt successfully, see Sheffield, *Forgotten Victory*. 107. J. G. Fuller, *Troop Morale and Popular Culture in the British and Dominion Armies, 1914–1918* (Oxford, Clarendon Press, 1990), p. 135. 108. Boff, *Winning and Losing*, p. 249. 109. Stéphane Audoin-Rouzeau and Jean-Jacques Becker, eds., *Encyclopédie de la Grande Guerre 1914–1918* (2 vols.; Paris, Perrin, 2012), vol. 1, p. 417. 110. John Keegan, quoted in Searle, *New England?*, p. 695. 111. Edwin Campion Vaughan, *Some Desperate Glory: The Diary of a Young Officer, 1917* (London, Frederick Warne, 1981), pp. 223–4. 112. Ibid., p. 228. 113. Robin Prior and Trevor Wilson, *Passchendaele: The Untold Story* (New Haven, Conn., Yale UP, 1996), p. 195; Harris, *Douglas Haig*, pp. 370–71; Watson, *Enduring the Great War*, p. 153. 114. Ibid., pp. 150, 155. 115. Searle, *New England?*, pp. 747, 779. 116. John Horne, ed., *State, Society and Mobilization in Europe During the First World War* (Cambridge UP, 1997), p. 170. 117. Watson, *Enduring the Great War*, pp. 7, 37, 43; Audoin-Rouzeau and Becker, *Encyclopédie de la Grande Guerre*, vol. 1, p. 421. 118. Todman, *Great War*, pp. 4–5; Wilson, *Siegfried Sassoon*, p. 2. 119. "The New Church Times, with which is incorporated the Wipers Times" (1 May 1916), in *The Wipers Times: The Famous First World War Trench Newspaper*, ed. C. Westhorp (London, Conway, 2013), p. 64. 120. J. C. Dunn, *The War the Infantry Knew* (1938), quoted in Searle, *New England?*, p. 747. See also Craig Gibson, *Behind the Front: British Soldiers and French Civilians, 1914–1918* (Cambridge UP, 2014). 121. Vaughan, *Some Desperate Glory*, p. 90. 122. Dunn, *The War the Infantry Knew*, quoted in Searle, *New England?*, p. 748. 123. Wilson, *Siegfried Sassoon*, p. 269. 124. Gerard Oram, *Military Executions During World War I* (Houndmills, Palgrave Macmillan, 2003), pp. 18, 24, 32; Watson, *Enduring the Great War*, p. 42. 125. Horne, *State, Society*, pp. 134–5, 142. 126. Based on Ferguson, *Pity of War*, p. 295. 127. Watson, *Enduring the Great War*, p. 83. 128. Gregory, *Last Great War*, p. 131. 129. Ibid., p. 133; Audoin-Rouzeau and Becker, *Encyclopédie de la Grande Guerre*, vol. 1, p. 431. 130. Reynolds, *Long Shadow*, p. 341. 131. Wilson, *Siegfried Sassoon*, pp. 372–86. 132. See Christopher Andrew, *The Defence of the Realm: The Authorized History of MI5* (London, Allen Lane, 2009), p. 102. 133. Roger Chickering and Stig Förster, eds., *Great War, Total War: Combat and Mobilization on the Western Front, 1914–1918*, pp. 180, 189, 200; Herwig, *First World War*, p. 284; Searle, *New England?*, pp. 817–18. 134. Ibid., pp. 778, 783, 788, 793. 135. Gregory, *Last Great War*, p. 147. 136. John Burnett, *Liquid Pleasures: A Social History of Drinks in Modern Britain* (London, Routledge, 1999), pp. 132–4. 137. F. M. L. Thompson, *English Landed Society in the Nineteenth Century* (London, Routledge, 1963), pp. 327–33; see also David Cannadine,

*The Decline and Fall of the British Aristocracy* (New Haven, Conn., Yale UP, 1990), pp. 97–8. **138.** Searle, *New England?*, p. 792. **139.** Ibid., pp. 828–9. **140.** Gregory, *Last Great War*, pp. 266–7. **141.** Ibid., p. 218. **142.** Jason Tomes, *Balfour and Foreign Policy: The International Thought of a Conservative Statesman* (Cambridge UP, 1997), pp. 198, 212–14. **143.** Lambert, *Planning Armageddon*, pp. 238–40. **144.** Herwig, *First World War*, p. 285. **145.** C. I. Hamilton, *The Making of the Modern Admiralty: British Naval Policy-Making, 1805–1927* (Cambridge UP, 2011), pp. 248–9; N. J. M. Campbell, *Jutland: An Analysis of the Fighting* (London, Conway Maritime Press, 1987), pp. 2, 338, 365, 374–8, 386. **146.** Hamilton, *The Making*, p. 12. **147.** Arthur Turner, *The Cost of War: British Policy on French War Debts* (Brighton, Sussex Academic Press, 1998), pp. 4–5; Ferguson, *Pity of War*, pp. 322–6; Gerd Hardach, *The First World War 1914–1918* (London, Allen Lane, 1977), pp. 289–90. **148.** Lambert, *Planning Armageddon*, chs. 5, 6, 8. **149.** Herwig, *First World War*, pp. 288–9. **150.** Ibid., pp. 283–96; Stevenson, *Backs to the Wall*, pp. 224–5, 370–73, 420–37; Audoin-Rouzeau and Becker, *Encyclopédie de la Grande Guerre*, vol. 2, p. 725. **151.** Paul Kennedy, in Jay Winter et al., eds., *La Première Guerre mondiale*, vol. I: *Combats* (Paris, Fayard, 2013), p. 376. **152.** Chickering and Förster, *Great War, Total War*, p. 191. **153.** I. F. Clark, *Voices Prophesying War: Future Wars, 1763–3749* (2nd edn; Oxford UP, 1992), p. 91. **154.** Winston S. Churchill, *The World Crisis* (abridged edn; London, Thornton Butterworth, 1931), p. 723. **155.** Chickering and Förster, *Great War, Total War*, pp. 199–206; Audoin-Rouzeau and Becker, *Encyclopédie de la Grande Guerre*, vol. 1, pp. 576, 578–9. **156.** David T. Zabecki, *The German 1918 Offensives: A Case Study in the Operational Level of War* (London, Routledge, 2006), p. 76; Stevenson, *Backs to the Wall*, p. 33; Martin Kitchen, *The German Offensives of 1918* (Stroud: Tempus, 2001), pp. 203–4. **157.** Kitchen, *German Offensives*, p. 16; Zabecki, *German 1918 Offensives*, pp. 5, 95. **158.** Zabecki, *German 1918 Offensives*, pp. 95, 99. **159.** Harris, *Douglas Haig*, pp. 433, 437–8, 447; Kitchen, *German Offensives*, p. 74; Zabecki, *German 1918 Offensives*, pp. 160–61. **160.** Sheffield, *Forgotten Victory*, pp. 226–7, 232; Kitchen, *German Offensives*, p. 85; Watson, *Enduring the Great War*, p. 182. **161.** Watson, *Enduring the Great War*, pp. 74, 77, 85. **162.** Zabecki, *German 1918 Offensives*, pp. 84–6, 168, 170, 312. **163.** Watson, *Enduring the Great War*, p. 235. **164.** Zabecki, *German 1918 Offensives*, p. 204. **165.** John Darwin, *Unfinished Empire: The Global Expansion of Britain* (London, Penguin Books, 2012), p. 332. **166.** General von Lossberg, quoted in Tombs and Chabal, *Britain and France*, p. 70. **167.** Erich von Ludendorff, *My War Memoirs* (2 vols.; London, Hutchinson, n.d.), vol. 2, pp. 680, 684. **168.** Boff, *Winning and Losing*, p. 98. **169.** Jackson Hughes, "The battle for the Hindenburg Line," *War and Society* 17 (Oct. 1999), p. 56. **170.** Boff, *Winning and Losing*, pp. 36–7, 232–3. **171.** *Statistics of the Military Effort of the British Empire During the Great War, 1914–1920* (London, HMSO, 1922), p. 757. **172.** Stevenson, *1914–1918*, pp. 476–81. **173.** Robb, *British Culture*, p. 223. **174.** Ibid., pp. 208–20. See also Reynolds, *Long Shadow*, pp. 179–85. **175.** Rudyard Kipling, "London Stone: Nov. 11 1923." **176.** See particularly Bond, *Unquiet Western Front*; and see

Todman, *Great War*; and Reynolds, *Long Shadow*.   **177.** See Jay Winter, in Tombs and Chabal, *Britain and France*, p. 167.   **178.** Howard, *War and the Liberal Conscience*, p. 84.   **179.** Winston S. Churchill, *The World Crisis* (6 vols.; London, Butterworth, 1923–31).   **180.** David Lloyd George, *War Memoirs* (6 vols.; London, Nicholson and Watson, 1933–6).   **181.** Bond, *Unquiet Western Front*, pp. 47–8; Todman, *Great War*.   **182.** Gregory, *Last Great War*, p. 41.   **183.** Arthur Ponsonby, *Falsehood in War-Time* (New York, Dutton, 1928), pp. 9, 25–6.   **184.** John Horne and Alan Kramer, *German Atrocities 1914: A History of Denial* (New Haven, Conn., Yale UP, 2001).   **185.** Reynolds, *Long Shadow*, p. 209.   **186.** Richard Overy, *The Morbid Age: Britain and the Crisis of Civilization* (London, Penguin, 2010), pp. 184–5, 425 n. 36.   **187.** For details, see Reynolds, *Long Shadow*, pp. 343–6.   **188.** *The Wipers Times* (20 March 1916), p. 45.   **189.** Wilfred Owen, "1914" (written 1914, revised 1917–18), *Poems of Wilfred Owen*, p. 93.   **190.** Siegfried Sassoon, "A Night Attack," *The War Poems*, ed. Rupert Hart-Davis (London, Faber, 1983), p. 43.   **191.** "On Seeing a Piece of Our Heavy Artillery Brought into Action," written 1917–18, *Poems of Wilfred Owen*, p. 128.   **192.** Reynolds, *Long Shadow*, pp. 172–9.   **193.** Horne and Madigan, *Towards Commemoration*, p. 134.   **194.** Todman, *Great War*, ch. 5; Reynolds, *Long Shadow*, pp. 345–8.   **195.** J. M. Keynes, *The Economic Consequences of the Peace* (London, Macmillan, 1919), p. 133.   **196.** *The Times* (21 March 1963), in Todman, *Great War*, p. 109; and see Reynolds, *Long Shadow*, pp. 330–42.   **197.** Todman, *Great War*, p. 68.   **198.** For example, the assertion by the education secretary, Michael Gove, that it was "a just war . . . defending the western liberal order," *Daily Mail* (2 Jan. 2014), and responses to it, including that of his Labour shadow, Tristram Hunt, *Observer* (5 Jan. 2014).

# 16. The Twenty-Year Truce

**1.** David Stevenson, *With Our Backs to the Wall: Victory and Defeat in 1918* (London, Allen Lane, 2011), p. 1.   **2.** Winston Churchill, *The Second World War* (6 vols.; London, Cassell, 1948–54), vol. 1, p. 7.   **3.** Margaret MacMillan, *Peacemakers: The Paris Conference of 1919 and Its Attempt to End War* (London, John Murray, 2001), pp. 35, 53–4, 156–8.   **4.** Zara Steiner, *The Lights That Failed: European International History, 1919–1933* (Oxford UP, 2005), p. 48.   **5.** Ibid., p. 18.   **6.** MacMillan, *Peacemakers*, pp. 43, 53–4, 156–8; Anthony Lentin, *Lloyd George and the Lost Peace: From Versailles to Hitler* (Basingstoke, Palgrave Macmillan, 2001), p. 4.   **7.** Manfred F. Boemeke et al., *The Treaty of Versailles: A Reassessment After 75 Years* (Cambridge UP, 1998), p. 351.   **8.** MacMillan, *Peacemakers*, pp. 169–70.   **9.** Though not all: notably Stefan Schmidt, *Frankreichs Außenpolitik in der Julikrise 1914* (Munich, Oldenbourg, 2009), and Christopher Clark, *The Sleepwalkers: How Europe Went to War in 1914* (London, Allen Lane, 2012). For the more orthodox view, see Annika Mombauer, *The Origins of the First World War: Controversies and Consensus* (London, Longman, 2002), and Gerd Krumeich, *Juli 1914: Eine Bilanz* (Paderborn, Schoeningh, 2013).   **10.** The issue roused debate in

Germany as the centenary dawned. For example, the newspaper *Die Welt* (4 Jan. 2014) welcomed historical studies denying Germany's prime responsibility for the war, hoping this would facilitate a less inhibited and less altruistic German foreign policy. 11. "Reply of the Allies and Associated Powers," 16 June 1919, in Étienne Mantoux, *The Carthaginian Peace; or, The Economic Consequences of Mr. Keynes* (Oxford UP, 1946), p. 94. 12. Note, 18 March 1919, in Jason Tomes, *Balfour and Foreign Policy: The International Thought of a Conservative Statesman* (Cambridge UP, 1997), p. 158. 13. Harold Nicolson, in Lentin, *Lloyd George*, p. 74. 14. John Maynard Keynes, *The Economic Consequences of the Peace* (London, Macmillan, 1919), pp. 31, 33, 38, 51, 56, 59, 133, 135. 15. Robert Skidelsky, *John Maynard Keynes: A Biography* (3 vols.; London, Macmillan, 1983–2000), vol. 2, p. 4. 16. Keynes, *Economic Consequences*, pp. 209, 215, 250. 17. Skidelsky, *Keynes*, vol. 2, pp. 34, 251. 18. Patricia Clavin, *The Great Depression in Europe, 1929–1939* (Houndmills, Macmillan, 2000), p. 9; Gerd Hardach, *The First World War, 1914–1918* (London, Allen Lane, 1977), p. 153. 19. Stephen A. Shuker, *The End of French Predominance in Europe* (Chapel Hill, North Carolina UP, 1976), p. 14. 20. Cash and goods to the value of 21.5 billion gold marks. Boemeke, *Treaty of Versailles*, p. 367. 21. Ibid. 22. Michael Howard, *War and the Liberal Conscience* (Oxford UP, 1981), p. 84. 23. Memorandum, 1935, in David Dutton, *Neville Chamberlain* (London, Arnold, 2001), p. 201. 24. Howard, *War and the Liberal Conscience*, p. 86. 25. Steiner, *Lights That Failed*, p. 67. 26. *The Economist* (31 Dec. 1999); Jacques Bainville, in Steiner, *Lights That Failed*, p. 68. 27. Ronald Hyam, *Britain's Declining Empire: The Road to Decolonisation, 1918–1968* (Cambridge UP, 2006), pp. 19, 74. 28. Ibid., pp. 31, 32, 34, 70. 29. Paul Bew, *Ireland: The Politics of Enmity, 1789–2006* (Oxford UP, 2007), p. 409. 30. John Horne and Edward Madigan, eds., *Towards Commemoration: Ireland in War and Revolution, 1912–1923* (Dublin, Royal Irish Academy, 2013), p. 60; Bew, *Ireland*, p. 443. The precise number of Irish casualties, long a controversial subject, is complicated by the fact that not all soldiers in Irish regiments were Irish, and on the other hand by whether or how to count Irish emigrants in Britain and other parts of the empire. See David Fitzpatrick, "Militarism in Ireland, 1900–1922," in Thomas Bartlett and Keith Jeffery, eds., *A Military History of Ireland* (Cambridge UP, 1996), pp. 392, 501. 31. Hyam, *Britain's Declining Empire*, pp. 5, 34, 49–59. 32. See Malvika Singh and Rudrangshu Mukherjee, *New Delhi: Making of a Capital* (New Delhi, Roli Books, 2009). 33. David Reynolds, *The Long Shadow: The Great War in the Twentieth Century* (London, Simon & Schuster, 2013), pp. 116–17. 34. Hyam, *Britain's Declining Empire*, pp. 35, 41; John Darwin, *Unfinished Empire: The Global Expansion of Britain* (London, Penguin Books, 2012), pp. 344–5. 35. Hyam, *Britain's Declining Empire*, p. 74. 36. *CEHMB*, vol. II, pp. 357–8; Daunton, *Wealth and Welfare*, p. 556. 37. Bernard Harris, *The Origins of the British Welfare State: Social Welfare in England and Wales, 1800–1954* (Houndmills, Palgrave Macmillan, 2004), pp. 220–24. 38. *CEHMB*, vol. II, p. 462. 39. Simon Green, "The evolution of modern indigenous paganism," Birkbeck Lecture, Cambridge, 5 Dec. 2013. 40. See, for example, Kenneth E. Silver, *Esprit de Corps: The Art of the Parisian Avant-Garde and the First World War, 1914–1925* (London, Thames &

Hudson, 1989). 41. Alexandra Harris, *Romantic Moderns: English Writers, Artists and the Imagination from Virginia Woolf to John Piper* (London, Thames & Hudson, 2010), p. 10. 42. Ibid., pp. 14, 15, 184–6, 207–9, 214–21. 43. See Ross McKibbin, *Classes and Cultures: England 1918–1951* (Oxford UP, 1998), ch. 10, "Music for the people." 44. Ibid., p. 400. 45. Philip Williamson, *Stanley Baldwin: Conservative Leadership and National Values* (Cambridge UP, 1999), pp. 83–5. 46. Clavin, *Great Depression*, p. 33. 47. *CEHMB*, vol. II, p. 462; Martin Daunton, *Wealth and Welfare: An Economic and Social History of Britain, 1851–1951* (Oxford UP, 2007), p. 229. 48. Clavin, *Great Depression*, p. 72; *CEHMB*, vol. II, p. 380. 49. *CEHMB*, vol. II, p. 329; Daunton, *Wealth and Welfare*, p. 177. 50. Clive Emsley, *Hard Men: The English and Violence Since 1750* (London, Hambledon, 2005), p. 110. 51. Daunton, *Wealth and Welfare*, pp. 180, 231. 52. J. M. Winter, *The Great War and the British People* (London, Palgrave Macmillan, 2003), p. 251. 53. Daunton, *Wealth and Welfare*, p. 556. 54. Ibid., p. 288; Jim Tomlinson, "Thrice denied: 'declinism' as a recurrent theme in British history in the long twentieth century," *Twentieth Century British History* 20 (2009), p. 243. 55. See Charles P. Kindleberger, *The World in Depression, 1929–1939* (London, Allen Lane, 1973), pp. 291–301. 56. Daunton, *Wealth and Welfare*, pp. 180–81; Clavin, *Great Depression*, p. 112. 57. Williamson, *Stanley Baldwin*, p. 302. 58. Ibid. 59. Emsley, *Hard Men*, p. 127. 60. Richard Overy, *The Morbid Age: Britain and the Crisis of Civilization* (London, Penguin Books, 2010), p. 267. 61. *CEHMB*, vol. II, p. 468. 62. Overy, *Morbid Age*, pp. 72–4. 63. Ibid., pp. 52–5, 58; Stanley Weintraub, "Shaw and the strongman," *TLS* (29 July 2011), pp. 13–15. 64. Overy, *Morbid Age*, pp. 80, 283–8, 291, 296. 65. Sidney and Beatrice Webb, *Soviet Communism: A New Civilisation?* (University Labour Federation, [1936?]), pp. 339, 423–4, 426, 432. 66. *CEHMB*, vol. II, pp. 327, 350; Overy, *Morbid Age*, p. 68. 67. Daunton, *Wealth and Welfare*, pp. 232, 235, 253; Reynolds, *Long Shadow*, p. 67. 68. A. F. Lucas, "Industrial reconstruction and the control of competition" (1937), in *CEHMB*, vol. II, p. 340; see also pp. 320, 338, 365–9. 69. Barry Eichengreen, in *CEHMB*, vol. II, p. 337. Keynes's idea of using state spending to increase demand had not influenced policy. 70. Peter Mangold, *Success and Failure in British Foreign Policy: Evaluating the Record, 1900–2000* (London, Palgrave Macmillan, 2001), p. 147. 71. Winston S. Churchill, *While England Slept: A Survey of World Affairs, 1932–1938* (New York, Putnam, 1938), p. 403. 72. P. M. H. Bell, *France and Britain, 1900–1940: Entente and Estrangement* (London, Longman, 1996), p. 150. 73. Darwin, *Unfinished Empire*, p. 334. 74. Steiner, *The Lights That Failed*, p. 573. 75. R. A. C. Parker, *Churchill and Appeasement* (London, Macmillan, 2000), p. 14. 76. Reynolds, *Long Shadow*, pp. 223–4. 77. Steiner, *The Lights That Failed*, pp. 776, 792. 78. Dutton, *Neville Chamberlain*, p. 198; Howard, *War and the Liberal Conscience*, p. 97. 79. Bell, *France and Britain*, p. 175. 80. Howard, *War and the Liberal Conscience*, pp. 88–9; Parker, *Churchill and Appeasement*, p. 31; David Edgerton, *Warfare State: Britain, 1920–1970* (Cambridge UP, 2006), p. 15. 81. Churchill in the House of Commons, 14 March 1933, in David Cannadine and Ronald Quinault, eds., *Winston Churchill in the Twenty-First Century* (Cambridge UP, 2004), p. 170. 82. Parker, *Churchill and*

*Appeasement*, p. 87. For Hitler's tactics, see Ian Kershaw, *Hitler* (2 vols., London, Penguin Books, 1998–2000), vol. 1, pp. 582–9.    83. Anthony Adamthwaite, *Grandeur and Misery: France's Bid for Power in Europe, 1914–1940* (London, Arnold, 1995), p. 203.    84. Zara Steiner, *The Triumph of the Dark: European International History, 1933–1939* (Oxford UP, 2011), pp. 149, 222.    85. Ibid., p. 217.    86. Overy, *Morbid Age*, pp. 321–2, 326.    87. Ibid., ch. 6.    88. Steiner, *Triumph of the Dark*, p. 169.    89. John Shepherd, *George Lansbury: At the Heart of Old Labour* (Oxford UP, 2002), pp. 325–7.    90. Steiner, *Triumph of the Dark*, p. 296; Andrew David Stedman, *Alternatives to Appeasement: Neville Chamberlain and Hitler's Germany* (London, Tauris, 2011), p. 177; Alison Appleby, "The British left intelligentsia and France: perceptions and interactions, 1930–1944" (PhD, Royal Holloway, 2013), pp. 50–54, 90–95.    91. Uri Bialer, *The Shadow of the Bomber: The Fear of Air Attack and British Politics, 1932–1939* (London, Royal Historical Society, 1980), pp. 47, 56–7; I. F. Clark, *Voices Prophesying War: Future Wars, 1763–3749* (2nd edn; Oxford UP, 1992), pp. 153–60.    92. B. Russell, "Which way to peace?" (1936), in Dutton, *Neville Chamberlain*, p. 170.    93. *People of Britain*, dir. Paul Rotha (1936).    94. Reynolds, *Long Shadow*, p. 225.    95. Williamson, *Stanley Baldwin*, pp. 47–9; Overy, *Morbid Age*, p. 341; Bernard Harris, *The Origins of the British Welfare State: Social Welfare in England and Wales, 1800–1945* (Houndmills, Palgrave Macmillan, 2004), pp. 285–7.    96. Note, First Sea Lord, 1937, in Christopher M. Bell, *The Royal Navy, Sea Power and Strategy Between the Wars* (Houndmills, Macmillan, 2000), p. 109.    97. Edgerton, *Warfare State*, pp. 32–3, 43; G. C. Peden, *Arms, Economics and British Strategy: From Dreadnoughts to Hydrogen Bombs* (Cambridge UP, 2007), pp. 110–12.    98. Steiner, *Triumph of the Dark*, p. 299.    99. Ibid., pp. 21–2; Overy, *Morbid Age*, pp. 271–4.    100. Ibid., p. 271.    101. Richard Toye, *Lloyd George and Churchill: Rivals for Greatness* (London, Pan Macmillan, 2008), p. 317; George Lansbury, *My Quest for Peace* (London, Michael Joseph, 1938), pp. 141, 143, 145.    102. Talbot C. Imlay, *Facing the Second World War: Strategy, Politics and Economics in Britain and France, 1938–1940* (Oxford UP, 2003), p. 199; Steiner, *Triumph of the Dark*, pp. 22–4.    103. Dutton, *Neville Chamberlain*, p. 201.    104. Steiner, *Triumph of the Dark*, pp. 337–40.    105. Ibid., pp. 557–60, 573.    106. *The Diaries of Sir Alexander Cadogan, O. M., 1938–1945*, ed. David Dilks (London, Cassell, 1971), pp. 72–3; Elisabeth du Réau, *Édouard Daladier, 1884–1970* (Paris, Fayard, 1993), p. 95.    107. Imlay, *Facing the Second World War*, p. 79.    108. Mangold, *Success and Failure*, p. 56.    109. Steiner, *Triumph of the Dark*, p. 580.    110. Ibid., p. 610.    111. Alan Sharp and Glyn Stone, eds., *Anglo-French Relations in the Twentieth Century* (London, Routledge, 2000), p. 193; Steiner, *Triumph of the Dark*, pp. 607, 632–3.    112. Michael Dockrill, "British official perceptions of France and the French," in Philippe Chassaigne and Michael Dockrill, eds., *Anglo-French Relations, 1898–1998* (London, Palgrave Macmillan, 2002), p. 99.    113. Steiner, *Triumph of the Dark*, pp. 607, 632; Overy, *Morbid Age*, p. 345.    114. Letter to sister, 23 July 1939, in Dutton, *Neville Chamberlain*, p. 210.    115. Neville Thompson, *The Anti-Appeasers: Conservative Opposition to Appeasement in the 1930s* (Oxford, Clarendon Press, 1971), p. 27.    116. Kershaw, *Hitler*, vol. 2, pp. 123, 164.    117. Dutton, *Neville Chamberlain*, p. 206.    118. Peden, *Arms, Economics*,

p. 111. **119.** Adam Tooze, *Wages of Destruction: The Making and Breaking of the Nazi Economy* (London, Allen Lane, 2006), ch. 8. **120.** Ibid., p. 274. **121.** Henry Channon, *Chips: The Diaries of Sir Henry Channon*, ed. Robert Rhodes James (London, Weidenfeld & Nicolson, 1967), p. 177. **122.** Parker, *Churchill and Appeasement*, p. 223. **123.** Imlay, *Facing the Second World War*, pp. 200–201. **124.** Stedman, *Alternatives to Appeasement*, p. 191; Channon, *Chips*, p. 194; Dutton, *Neville Chamberlain*, p. 132. **125.** Steiner, *Triumph of the Dark*, p. 296; Stedman, *Alternatives to Appeasement*, p. 177; Appleby, "The British left intelligentsia and France," pp. 90–95. **126.** Stedman, *Alternatives to Appeasement*, p. 187. **127.** Edgerton, *Warfare State*, pp. 3–45. **128.** Harold Nicolson, *Diaries and Letters 1930–1964*, ed. S. Olsen (London, Collins, 1980), p. 145. **129.** Donald Cameron Watt, *How War Came* (London, Pimlico, 2001), pp. 99–108, 164; Steiner, *Triumph of the Dark*, p. 725. **130.** Watt, *How War Came*, p. 185. **131.** According to Blanche Dugdale, who was in the public gallery, quoted in ibid., p. 580. **132.** Watt, *How War Came*, pp. 579–80. **133.** Overy, *Morbid Age*, p. 221. **134.** "Cato" (Michael Foot, Peter Howard, Frank Owen), *Guilty Men* (London, Gollancz, 1940), pp. 20–21, 31, 34, 57, 125. See Dutton, *Neville Chamberlain*, ch. 3, and Philip Williamson, "Baldwin's reputation: politics and history, 1937–1967," *HJ* 47 (2004), pp. 127–68. **135.** Richard Weight, *Patriots: National Identity in Britain, 1940–2000* (London, Macmillan, 2002), p. 115. **136.** Steiner, *Triumph of the Dark*, p. 1053; see also Tooze, *Wages of Destruction*, ch. 8. **137.** Stedman, *Alternatives to Appeasement*, p. 233. **138.** Tom Harrison, *Living Through the Blitz* (London, Penguin Books, 1978), p. 29. **139.** Watt, *How War Came*, p. 622. **140.** Imlay, *Facing the Second World War*, p. 229.

# 17. The Edge of the Abyss, 1939–1945

**1.** Tobias Jersak, "Blitzkrieg revisited: a new look at Nazi war and extermination planning," *HJ* 43, 2 (June 2000), p. 578. **2.** John Welshman, *Churchill's Children: The Evacuee Experience in Wartime Britain* (Oxford UP, 2010), pp. 5–7, 13. **3.** Angus Calder, *The People's War: Britain, 1939–45* (London, Jonathan Cape, 1969), pp. 34–6, 54–5. **4.** Jersak, "Blitzkrieg," pp. 566–7. **5.** Christopher Hill, *Cabinet Decisions on Foreign Policy: The British Experience, October 1938–June 1941* (Cambridge UP, 1991), p. 313. **6.** Adam Tooze, *The Wages of Destruction: The Making and Breaking of the Nazi Economy* (London, Allen Lane, 2006), p. 327. **7.** Ibid., pp. 332, 384. **8.** I. C. B. Dear and M. R. D. Foot, eds., *The Oxford Companion to World War II* (Oxford UP, 2005), p. 324. Slightly different figures are given in G. C. Peden, *Arms, Economics and British Strategy: From Dreadnoughts to Hydrogen Bombs* (Cambridge UP, 2007), p. 203. **9.** Winston S. Churchill, *The Second World War*, abridged edn by Denis Kelly (London, Penguin Books, 1989), p. 220. **10.** John Colville, in David Dutton, *Neville Chamberlain* (London, Arnold, 2001), p. 119; Ben Pimlott, *Hugh Dalton* (London, Jonathan Cape, 1985), pp. 273–6. **11.** John Lukacs, *The Last European War: September 1939–December 1941* (London, Routledge, 1977), p. 95; Paul Addison and Jeremy A. Crang, eds., *Listening to Britain: Home Intelligence Reports on Britain's*

*Finest Hour, May to September 1940* (London, Vintage, 2011), p. 16.　**12.** Jersak, "Blitzkrieg," p. 568.　**13.** P. M. H. Bell, *A Certain Eventuality: Britain and the Fall of France* (Farnborough, Saxon House, 1974), p. 32.　**14.** Churchill, *Second World War*, pp. 242–4; Eleanor M. Gates, *End of the Affair: The Collapse of the Anglo-French Alliance, 1939–40* (London, Allen & Unwin, 1981), pp. 77–9.　**15.** *The Diary of a Staff Officer (Air Intelligence Liaison Officer) at Advanced Headquarters North BAAF, 1940* (London, Methuen, 1941), p. 26.　**16.** Jersak, "Blitzkrieg," p. 568.　**17.** David Edgerton, *Britain's War Machine: Weapons, Resources and Experts in the Second World War* (London, Penguin Books, 2012), p. 62. **18.** Peden, *Arms, Economics*, p. 124.　**19.** Dear and Foot, *World War II*, p. 130. **20.** Marc Bloch, *Strange Defeat* (Oxford UP, 1949), p. 75.　**21.** Robert Tombs and Émile Chabal, eds., *Britain and France in Two World Wars: Truth, Myth and Memory* (London, Bloomsbury, 2013), p. 96.　**22.** Field Marshal Lord Alanbrooke, *War Diaries 1939–1945*, ed. Alex Danchev and Daniel Todman (London, Phoenix, 2001), pp. 67–8.　**23.** Martin S. Alexander, "Dunkirk in military operations, myths and memories," in Tombs and Chabal, *Britain and France*, pp. 96–8.　**24.** John Lukacs, *The Duel: Hitler vs. Churchill, 10 May to 31 July 1940* (Oxford UP, 1990), pp. 100–111; Bell, *A Certain Eventuality*, pp. 34–48.　**25.** Lukacs, *Duel*, p. 101. **26.** Ibid., p. 102.　**27.** Peter Clarke, *Hope and Glory: Britain 1900–1990* (London, Allen Lane, 1996), p. 186.　**28.** For a detailed analysis, see Hill, *Cabinet Decisions*, ch. 6, and for a dramatic narrative, Lukacs, *Duel*, pp. 95–111.　**29.** Alexander, in Tombs and Chabal, *Britain and France*, p. 97; Jean-Louis Crémieux-Brilhac, *Les Français de l'an 40* (2 vols.; Paris, Gallimard, 1990), vol. 2, pp. 631–2.　**30.** Diary entry, 27 May, in Hill, *Cabinet Decisions*, p. 162.　**31.** Bell, *A Certain Eventuality*, p. 43.　**32.** Cabinet minutes, 28 May, in Hill, *Cabinet Decisions*, p. 163.　**33.** Hugh Dalton, *The Second World War Diary of Hugh Dalton, 1940–45*, ed. Ben Pimlott (London, Jonathan Cape, 1986), pp. 27–8; David Reynolds, *In Command of History: Churchill Fighting and Writing the Second World War* (London, Allen Lane, 2004), p. 172.　**34.** Statistics in Dear and Foot, *World War II*, p. 243. There are differing estimates of numbers evacuated, depending mainly on whether they include non-combatants who had left earlier.　**35.** Calder, *People's War*, pp. 108–9. **36.** Lukacs, *Duel*, p. 111.　**37.** Denis Richards, *Royal Air Force, 1939–1945*, vol. I: *The Fight at Odds* (London, HMSO, 1974), pp. 120, 150.　**38.** See Robert and Isabelle Tombs, *That Sweet Enemy: The French and the British from the Sun King to the Present* (London, Heinemann, 2006), pp. 559–60.　**39.** Cabinet minutes, 16 June, in Hill, *Cabinet Decisions*, p. 183.　**40.** T. S. Eliot, "Little Gidding" (1942).　**41.** Published in 1941 in the paper *France Libre*, it was not republished for over sixty years until it appeared in *Le Nouvel Observateur* (20–26 June 2002), pp. 4–8 (my translation).　**42.** Tom Harrison, *Living Through the Blitz* (London, Penguin Books, 1978), p. 127.　**43.** Calder, *People's War*, p. 111.　**44.** Tombs and Chabal, *Britain and France*, p. 101.　**45.** George Orwell, *Essays* (London, Penguin Books, 2000), pp. 140–50.　**46.** Peter Fleming, *Operation Sealion* (London, Pan, 1975), pp. 192–3; Gerhard L. Weinberg, *Visions of Victory: The Hopes of Eight World War II Leaders* (Cambridge UP, 2005), p. 11.　**47.** Diary entry, in Lukacs, *Last European War*, p. 98.　**48.** See Richard Toye, *Lloyd George and Churchill:*

*Rivals for Greatness* (London, Pan Macmillan, 2008), pp. 369–72. **49.** Alison Appleby, "The British left intelligentsia and France: perceptions and interactions, 1930–1944" (PhD, Royal Holloway College, 2013), p. 100. **50.** T. D. Burridge, *British Labour and Hitler's War* (London, André Deutsch, 1976), pp. 26, 55–6. **51.** On Hitler's strategy, see Brendan Simms, *Europe: The Struggle for Supremacy, 1453 to the Present* (London, Allen Lane, 2013), pp. 349–80. **52.** Jochen Thies, *Hitler's Plans for Global Domination: Nazi Architecture and Ultimate War Aims* (Oxford, Berghahn, 2012), pp. 161–3. **53.** Ibid., pp. 161–2. **54.** Lukacs, *Last European War*, p. 419. **55.** Addison and Crang, *Listening*, pp. 126, 232. **56.** Clarke, *Hope and Glory*, p. 195. **57.** Speech at Westminster Hall, 30 Nov. 1954, in Richard Toye, *The Roar of the Lion: The Making of Churchill's World War II Speeches* (Oxford UP, 2013), introduction. **58.** David Cannadine, *In Churchill's Shadow: Confronting the Past in Modern Britain* (London, Allen Lane, 2002), pp. 34–5, 86–7. **59.** Clarke, *Hope and Glory*, p. 208; Reynolds, *In Command of History*, ch. 13; Toye, *Roar of the Lion*, passim. **60.** Alanbrooke, *War Diaries*, p. 590 (10 Sept. 1944). **61.** Edmund Burke speaking of Pitt the Elder. **62.** Calder, *People's War*, pp. 123, 126–7. **63.** Ibid., pp. 51–4. **64.** Gordon Martel, ed., *The World War Two Reader* (London, Routledge, 2004), pp. 251–8. **65.** Dear and Foot, *World War II*, pp. 124–7. **66.** Home Intelligence Report, 16 Aug. 1940, in Addison and Crang, *Listening*, pp. 231, 336. **67.** Tooze, *Wages of Destruction*, pp. 400–405. **68.** Dear and Foot, *World War II*, p. 127. **69.** Home Intelligence Report, 21 Aug., 1940, in Addison and Crang, *Listening*, p. 348. **70.** Addison and Crang, *Listening*, pp. 234, 313. **71.** For how these worked, see "electronic navigation systems" in Dear and Foot, *World War II*, pp. 256–8. **72.** Richard Overy, *Why the Allies Won* (London, Pimlico, 1995), p. 109. **73.** Lukacs, *Last European War*, p. 403. **74.** See note 41. **75.** Addison and Crang, *Listening*, pp. 164, 420, 336. **76.** See, for example, Angus Calder, *The Myth of the Blitz* (London, Jonathan Cape, 1991); Clive Ponting, *1940: Myth and Reality* (London, Hamish Hamilton, 1990). **77.** Helen Jones, *British Civilians in the Front Line: Air Raids, Productivity and Wartime Culture, 1939–45* (Manchester UP, 2006), p. 197. **78.** Harrison, *Living Through the Blitz*, pp. 80–82, 97, quoting three London women; John Strachey, in Calder, *People's War*, p. 171. **79.** Jones, *British Civilians*, pp. 145, 146, 156; Harrison, *Living Through the Blitz*, p. 58; *Nella Last's War: The Second World War Diaries of Housewife, 49*, eds. R. Broad and S. Fleming (London, Profile, 2006), p. 73. **80.** Jones, *British Civilians*, pp. 155, 160, 196, 201, 203. **81.** Addison and Crang, *Listening*, p. 329. **82.** Calder, *People's War*, pp. 223, 226. **83.** Jones, *British Civilians*, p. 158; Harrison, *Living Through the Blitz*, pp. 103, 111. **84.** Mary Clayton, diary, in James Hinton, *Nine Wartime Lives: Mass-Observation and the Making of the Modern Self* (Oxford UP, 2010), p. 76. **85.** Jones, *British Civilians*, pp. 158–9. See also Calder, *People's War*, pp. 182–5. **86.** Jones, *British Civilians*, pp. 149–50, 179. **87.** House of Commons, 22 June 1940, in Calder, *People's War*, p. 107. **88.** *CEHMB*, vol. III, p. 1. Statistics also from this source. **89.** For statistics, see *What Britain Has Done, 1939–1945* (new edn; London, Atlantic, 2007 [Ministry of Information, 1945]), pp. 13–14. **90.** See, for example, Hinton, *Nine Wartime Lives*, pp. 97–100, 117–20.

91. Martel, *World War Two*, p. 318; Calder, *People's War*, p. 107. 92. Richard Toye, *Churchill's Empire: The World That Made Him and the World He Made* (London, Macmillan, 2010), p. 238. 93. *CEHMB*, vol. III, p. 16. 94. Calder, *People's War*, pp. 117–18, 267–70, 328, 335, 345, 390. 95. Alan Bullock, *Ernest Bevin: Foreign Secretary 1945–1951* (London, Heinemann, 1983), p. 854. See also *What Britain Has Done*, pp. 12–13; Neil Stammers, *Civil Liberties in Britain During the Second World War: A Political Study* (London, Croom Helm, 1983). 96. *CEHMB*, vol. III, p. 10; Peden, *Arms, Economics*, pp. 178, 186. 97. Calder, *People's War*, p. 323. 98. Ina Zweiniger-Bargielowska, *Austerity in Britain: Rationing, Controls, and Consumption, 1939–1955* (Oxford UP, 2002), pp. 60, 65–6. 99. Calder, *People's War*, pp. 277, 387. 100. Tooze, *Wages of Destruction*, p. 419. 101. Calder, *People's War*, pp. 393–6. 102. José Harris, in Martel, *World War Two*, p. 330. 103. James Chapman, *The British at War: Cinema, State and Propaganda, 1939–1945* (London, Tauris, 1998), p. 3. 104. Peter Mandler, *The English National Character: The History of an Idea from Edmund Burke to Tony Blair* (New Haven, Conn., Yale UP, 2006), pp. 190–92. 105. Chapman, *British at War*, pp. 83–4, 161, 180–84; Robert Murphy, *British Cinema in the Second World War* (London, Continuum, 2000), pp. 64, 67. 106. Chapman, *British at War*, pp. 247–8. 107. Calder, *People's War*, p. 524. 108. Bernard Harris, *The Origins of the British Welfare State: Social Welfare in England and Wales, 1800–1954* (Houndmills, Palgrave Macmillan, 2004), p. 283. 109. Welshman, *Churchill's Children*, pp. 87–8, 90–94, 276–7. 110. Martin Daunton, *Wealth and Welfare: An Economic and Social History of Britain, 1851–1951* (Oxford UP, 2007), p. 560. 111. Clarke and Trebilcock, *Understanding Decline*, p. 174; Calder, *People's War*, p. 528; Harris, *Origins*, p. 300; José Harris, "Beveridge, William Henry, Baron Beveridge (1879–1963)," in *ODNB*. 112. *Nella Last's War*, p. 219. 113. Nicholas Timmins, *The Five Giants: A Biography of the Welfare State* (new edn; London, HarperCollins, 2001), p. 43. 114. Ibid., p. 47. 115. Robin Harris, *The Conservatives: A History* (London, Bantam, 2011), p. 365. 116. Timmins, *Five Giants*, p. 76. 117. Ibid., pp. 76–8, 87–8, 92, 98–9. 118. R. S. Wood, deputy secretary of the Board of Education, in Harris, *Origins*, p. 289. 119. On this famous phrase, see Richard Toye, "The 'gentleman in Whitehall' reconsidered: the evolution of Douglas Jay's views on economic planning and consumer choice, 1937–1947," *Labour History Review* 67 (2002), pp. 185–202. 120. Harris, in Martel, *World War Two*, p. 325. 121. Keith Douglas, *The Complete Poems*, ed. Desmond Graham (3rd edn, London, Faber, 1998), p. 117. 122. Talbot C. Imlay, *Facing the Second World War: Strategy, Politics and Economics in Britain and France, 1938–1940* (Oxford UP, 2003), p. 16. 123. Sönke Neitzel and Harald Welzer, *Soldaten: On Fighting, Killing, and Dying: The World War II Tapes of German POWs*, trans. Jefferson Chase (London, Simon & Schuster, 2012), p. 195. 124. Edgerton, *Britain's War Machine*, p. 3. 125. Statistics in Dear and Foot, *World War II*, pp. 65–7, 145–7, 622–5, 896. 126. Ibid., pp. 370, 931–6, 965. 127. Ronald Hyam, *Britain's Declining Empire: The Road to Decolonisation, 1918–1968* (Cambridge UP, 2006), p. 90; Toye, *Churchill's Empire*, p. 262. 128. Matthew Stibbe, *German Anglophobia and the Great War, 1914–1918* (Cambridge UP, 2001), pp. 196,

200–204; Lukacs, *Last European War*, pp. 401–2. **129.** Neitzel and Welzer, *Soldaten*, p. 196. **130.** Stibbe, *German Anglophobia*, p. 196. **131.** Lukacs, *Last European War*, pp. 204, 493, 515—a mine of fascinating reflections. **132.** BBC broadcast, 18 June 1940. It was not recorded because the BBC required twenty-four hours' notice (information provided by the late M. R. D. Foot). **133.** Toye, *Lloyd George and Churchill*, p. 382. **134.** Lukacs, *Last European War*, pp. 394, 403. **135.** Ibid., p. 386. **136.** Stibbe, *German Anglophobia*, p. 204. **137.** Richard Overy, *The Bombing War: Europe, 1939–1945* (London, Allen Lane, 2013), p. 319. **138.** Hinton, *Nine Wartime Lives*, p. 57. See also David Reynolds, *Rich Relations: The American Occupation of Britain, 1942–1945* (London, HarperCollins, 1995). **139.** Kathleen Burk, *Old World, New World: The Story of Britain and America* (London, Little, Brown, 2007), pp. 556–9. **140.** Harris, in Martel, *World War Two*, p. 332. **141.** Overy, *Why the Allies Won*, p. 32; Tooze, *Wages of Destruction*, p. 404. **142.** Ibid., pp. 410–12, 418–20. **143.** Peter Elliott, *The Cross and the Ensign: A Naval History of Malta, 1789–1979* (London, HarperCollins, 1994), pp. 148, 184. **144.** Overy, *Why the Allies Won*, p. 26. **145.** Dear and Foot, *World War II*, p. 49; Tooze, *Wages of Destruction*, pp. 399–400; Max Hastings, *All Hell Let Loose: The World at War, 1939–1945* (London, HarperPress, 2012), pp. 274, 284. **146.** Overy, *Why the Allies Won*, pp. 32, 46–7; Dear and Foot, *World War II*, pp. 53–4. **147.** Ronald Lewin, *Ultra Goes to War: The Secret Story* (London, Arrow, 1980), p. 18. **148.** Details in David Kahn, *Seizing the Enigma: The Race to Break the German U-Boat Codes, 1939–1943* (London, Frontline, 2012), pp. 262–6. **149.** Stibbe, *German Anglophobia*, p. 204. **150.** Tooze, *Wages of Destruction*, pp. 423–4. **151.** Army high command instructions, May 1941, in ibid., p. 480. **152.** Weinberg, *Visions of Victory*, p. 36. **153.** Overy, *Bombing War*, p. 280. **154.** C. M. Turnbull, *A History of Singapore, 1819–1988* (Oxford UP, 1989), p. 182. **155.** Christopher Bayly and Tim Harper, *Forgotten Armies: The Fall of British Asia, 1941–1945* (London, Allen Lane, 2004), p. 106. **156.** Peden, *Arms, Economics*, pp. 213–15. **157.** Bayly and Harper, *Forgotten Armies*, p. 118. **158.** Information later given secretly by Churchill in the Commons, 23 April 1942, *Secret Session Speeches*, ed. Charles Eade (London, Cassell, 1946), pp. 49–50. **159.** Alanbrooke, *War Diaries*, p. 210. **160.** Bayly and Harper, *Forgotten Armies*, pp. 120, 123, 128, 130. **161.** Churchill, *Second World War*, p. 518. **162.** Bayly and Harper, *Forgotten Armies*, p. 146. **163.** Turnbull, *History of Singapore*, p. 184; Dear and Foot, *World War II*, p. 139. **164.** Lizzie Collingham, *The Taste of War: World War Two and the Battle for Food* (London, Penguin Books, 2011), pp. 146–54; Hastings, *All Hell Let Loose*, p. 227. I am grateful to Professor N. A. M. Rodger for his expert opinion on shipping shortages. **165.** Edgerton, *Britain's War Machine*, p. xvi. **166.** Nicolson, *Diaries and Letters*, pp. 207, 210–11. **167.** Alanbrooke, *War Diaries*, pp. 228–9, 231. **168.** Churchill, *Second World War*, pp. 601, 606. **169.** Lukacs, *Last European War*, pp. 412–13. **170.** Orwell, *Essays*, p. 142. **171.** Martel, *World War Two*, pp. 180–81. **172.** Ivor Rowberry, aged twenty-two, South Staffordshire Regt., in Hastings, *All Hell Let Loose*, pp. 582–3. **173.** A gritty yet moving fictionalized portrayal by an infantry corporal, first published in 1948, is Alexander Baron, *From the City, from the*

*Plough* (London, Black Spring Press, 2010); comparably powerful in non-fiction is Peter White, *With the Jocks: A Soldier's Struggle for Europe, 1944–45* (Stroud, History Press, 2002). **174.** Lukacs, *Last European War*, p. 404. **175.** Neitzel and Welzer, *Soldaten*, p. 267. **176.** Alanbrooke, *War Diaries*, p. 206 (3 December 1941). **177.** On the long and often fraught Anglo-American discussions, see Andrew Roberts, *Masters and Commanders: The Military Geniuses Who Led the West to Victory in World War II* (London, Allen Lane, 2008), esp. ch. 12. **178.** Dear and Foot, *World War II*, p. 35; *What Britain Has Done*, p. 34. **179.** Pitt in the House of Commons in 1757. **180.** Alanbrooke, *War Diaries*, p. xxvi. **181.** Dear and Foot, *World War II*, p. 912. **182.** Tooze, *Wages of Destruction*, p. 592. **183.** Paul Kennedy, *Engineers of Victory: The Problem Solvers Who Turned the Tide in the Second World War* (London, Allen Lane, 2013), pp. 43–50. **184.** Overy, *Why the Allies Won*, pp. 53–62; *What Britain Has Done*, pp. 33, 36. **185.** Overy, *Bombing War*, p. 403. **186.** Bernard Wasserstein, *Britain and the Jews of Europe, 1939–1945* (2nd edn; Leicester UP, 1999), pp. 8–9. **187.** David Reynolds, *The Long Shadow: The Great War in the Twentieth Century* (London, Simon & Schuster, 2013), p. 286. **188.** See William D. Rubinstein, *The Myth of Rescue: Why the Democracies Could Not Have Saved More Jews from the Nazis* (London, Routledge, 1997). **189.** Robin Neillands, *The Bomber War: Arthur Harris and the Allied Bomber Offensive, 1939–1945* (London, John Murray, 2001), p. 14. **190.** Churchill, *Second World War*, p. 602. **191.** Overy, *Bombing War*, p. 297. **192.** Churchill, *Second World War*, p. 186. **193.** Ibid. **194.** Calder, *People's War*, pp. 491–4. **195.** This view has recently been authoritatively restated in Overy, *Bombing War*; for a critical response, see Edward Luttwak, "Opportunity Costs," *LRB* (21 Nov. 2013), pp. 23–4. **196.** Edgerton, *Britain's War Machine*, p. 216. **197.** Peden, *Arms, Economics*, p. 218. **198.** Richard J. Evans, *The Third Reich at War, 1939–1945* (London, Allen Lane, 2008), pp. 443–9; Overy, *Bombing War*, pp. 327–9. **199.** Ibid., pp. 324–5. **200.** Evans, *Third Reich at War*, pp. 442, 446; Luttwak, "Opportunity Costs," p. 23. **201.** Tooze, *Wages of Destruction*, pp. 597, 600, 625. **202.** Neillands, *Bomber War*, p. 189; Tooze, *Wages of Destruction*, p. 602. **203.** See Overy, *Bombing War*, pp. 353–5. **204.** Airey Neave, *Saturday at MI9: A History of Underground Escape Lines in North-West Europe in 1940–5* (London, Hodder and Stoughton, 1969), passim; S. G. Ottis, *Silent Heroes: Downed Airmen and the French Underground* (Lexington, Kentucky UP, 2001), pp. 22, 44–6. **205.** Phillips P. O'Brien, "East versus west in the defeat of Nazi Germany," *Journal of Strategic Studies* 23 (June 2000), p. 98; Evan Mawdsley, *Thunder in the East: The Nazi-Soviet War, 1941–45* (London, Hodder Arnold, 2005), p. 203. **206.** Tooze, *Wages of Destruction*, p. 599; Evans, *Third Reich at War*, p. 461; Neillands, *Bomber War*, pp. 384–5, 396; Overy, *Why the Allies Won*, pp. 118, 129–33; O'Brien, "East versus west," pp. 93–4; Hastings, *All Hell Let Loose*, pp. 486–8. **207.** Neil Gregor, "A *Schiksalsgemeinschaft*? Allied bombing, civilian morale, and social dissolution in Nuremberg, 1942–1945," *HJ* 43 (2000), pp. 1051–70; Tooze, *Wages of Destruction*, pp. 603–5; Evans, *Third Reich at War*, pp. 459, 703–6. **208.** Douglas, *Complete Poems*, p. 125. **209.** Louis Allen, in Dear and Foot, *World War II*, p. 138. For a vivid soldier's-eye view, see George

Macdonald Fraser, *Quartered Safe Out Here: A Recollection of the War in Burma* (London, HarperCollins, 2000). **210.** Weinberg, *Visions of Victory*, p. 108. **211.** Tooze, *Wages of Destruction*, pp. 648–51. **212.** See Christopher Andrew, *The Defence of the Realm: The Authorized History of MI5* (London, Allen Lane, 2009), pp. 296–305. **213.** M. R. D. Foot, *SOE in France: An Account of the Work of the British Special Operations Executive in France, 1939–1944* (2nd edn; London, Frank Cass, 2004), pp. 349–50, and information given to the author by the late M. R. D. Foot. **214.** Olivier Wieviorka, *Histoire du débarquement en Normandie: Des origines à la libération de Paris* (Paris, Seuil, 2007), pp. 228, 233, 235; for statistics, see Dear and Foot, *World War II*, p. 667, and Portsmouth D-Day Museum website. **215.** Hastings, *All Hell Let Loose*, p. 585. **216.** Sgt. Trevor Greenwood, *D-Day to Victory: The Diaries of a British Tank Commander* (London, Simon & Schuster, 2012), p. 114. **217.** Ibid., p. 68. **218.** Tombs and Chabal, *Britain and France*, p. 142. **219.** John Keegan, *Six Armies in Normandy: From D-Day to the Liberation of Paris* (London, Penguin Books, 1983), p. 188. **220.** Greenwood, *D-Day to Victory*, p. 89. **221.** Foot, *SOE in France*, pp. 357–9, 362–3. **222.** Olivier Wieviorka, in Tombs and Chabal, *Britain and France*, p. 150. **223.** Max Hastings, *Overlord: D-Day and the Battle for Normandy* (London, Michael Joseph, 1984), p. 147. **224.** Baron, *From the City*, p. 128. **225.** Neitzel and Welzer, *Soldaten*, p. 206. **226.** David French, " 'Tommy is no soldier': The morale of the Second British Army in Normandy, June–August 1944," *Journal of Strategic Studies* 19 (December 1996), pp. 154–78; Neitzel and Wetzler, *Soldaten*, pp. 267–8. **227.** Lord [Peter] Carrington, *Reflect on Things Past* (London, Collins, 1988), p. 57. **228.** Dear and Foot, *World War II*, pp. 761–3. For a gripping account of this largely forgotten war by a young English officer, see White, *With the Jocks*. **229.** Hastings, *All Hell Let Loose*, p. 493. **230.** Overy, *Bombing War*, pp. 380–82. **231.** Dear and Foot, *World War II*, pp. 102, 832–3, from which many of the statistics in this section are taken, and Neillands, *The Bomber War*, pp. 348, 379–80, who gives slightly different figures. **232.** Reynolds, *Long Shadow*, pp. 282, 285–6. **233.** Dear and Foot, *World War II*, p. 965. **234.** Louis Allen, "Burma Campaign," in ibid., p. 139. **235.** Harris, *Conservatives*, p. 362. **236.** See Laura Beers, "Labour's Britain, fight for it now!," *HJ* 52 (2009), pp. 667–95. **237.** Hinton, *Nine Wartime Lives*, p. 59. **238.** Kevin Jeffreys, *Politics and the People: A History of British Democracy Since 1918* (London, Atlantic, 2007), p. 78; Clarke, *Hope and Glory*, p. 215. **239.** Clarke, *Hope and Glory*, p. 215; Harris, *Conservatives*, pp. 362–73; David Butler and Anne Sloman, *British Political Facts* (5th edn; London, Macmillan, 1980), p. 213. **240.** José Harris, in Martel, *World War Two*, p. 325. **241.** Dear and Foot, *World War II*, p. 54.

## Memory, History and Myth

**1.** See Reynolds, *In Command of History*. **2.** Interviews with ABC and Sky News, 21 July 2010. **3.** See Hyam, *Britain's Declining Empire*, p. 92. **4.** Mawdsley, *Thunder in the East*, p. 245. **5.** Above all Tooze, *Wages of Destruction*; and see note 206 above.    6. Wendy Webster, *Englishness and Empire, 1939–1965* (Oxford UP, 2005), pp. 194–6.    7. Notably Corelli Barnett, *The Audit of War: The Illusion and Reality of Britain as a Great Nation* (London, Macmillan, 1986); Calder, *The Myth of the Blitz*; Ponting, *1940: Myth and Reality*.    8. Calder, *Myth of the Blitz*, introduction.    9. As shown magisterially in Calder's earlier book, *The People's War*, and more recently in works such as Jones, *British Civilians*, and, from a different angle, Mark Roodhouse, *Black Market Britain, 1939–1955* (Oxford UP, 2013).    10. Hinton, *Nine Wartime Lives*, p. 127 and passim.    11. Notably David Edgerton, *Warfare State: Britain, 1920–1970* (Cambridge UP, 2006), and his *Britain's War Machine*; and Peden, *Arms, Economics*. The range of research on the wartime economy is summarized in *CEHMB*, vol. III, ch. 1.    12. Ross McKibbin, *Classes and Cultures: England, 1918–1951* (Oxford UP, 1998), p. 419.    13. Murphy, *British Cinema*, pp. 235–6.    14. John Ramsden, " 'The People's War': British war films of the 1950s," *Journal of Contemporary History* 33 (1998), pp. 40–42, 48–9.    15. For example, *Yanks* (1979), *Hope and Glory* (1987), *Land Girls* (1998).    16. Abby Waldman, "The role of government in the presentation of national history in England and France, c.1980–2007" (Cambridge PhD, 2011), pp. 224–6. For a recent discussion of miscellaneous themes, see also Lucy Noakes and Juliette Pattinson, eds., *British Cultural Memory and the Second World War* (London, Bloomsbury, 2014).    17. Edgerton, *Britain's War Machine*, pp. 1–2.    18. Harris, in Martel, *World War Two*, p. 317.    19. Ibid., p. 324.    20. Ibid., p. 331.

PART SEVEN: AN AGE OF DECLINE?

1. Peter Clarke and Clive Trebilcock, eds., *Understanding Decline: Perceptions and Realities of British Economic Performance* (Cambridge UP, 1997), p. 149    2. Matthew Parris and Andrew Bryson, eds., *Parting Shots* (London, Viking, 2010), pp. 205–13.    3. Polly Toynbee, *Guardian* (16 July 2004), p. 27.    4. Jim Tomlinson, "Inventing 'decline': the falling behind of the British economy in the postwar years," *Economic History Review* XLIX (1996), p. 731.    5. Wendy Webster, *Englishness and Empire, 1939–1965* (Oxford UP, 2005), pp. 140–41.    6. World Bank figures of gross national income per head in 2008. The only country with a larger population to rank higher than the U.K. was the USA; all the other richer countries but one—including Luxembourg, Norway and Switzerland—had populations smaller than that of Greater London.

18. Postwar

1. Richard Vinen, *Thatcher's Britain: The Politics and Social Upheaval of the 1980s* (London, Simon & Schuster, 2009), p. 292.    2. Kevin Jefferys, *Politics and the People: A History of British Democracy since 1918* (London, Atlantic, 2007), pp. 91–3, 121, 125, 153, 156–7.    3. Peter Clarke, *Hope and Glory: Britain 1900–1990* (London, Allen Lane, 1996), p. 199.    4. G. C. Peden, *Arms, Economics and British Strategy: From Dreadnoughts to Hydrogen Bombs* (Cambridge UP, 2007),

p. 346.  5. *CEHMB*, vol. III, p. 16.  6. Kathleen Burk, *Old World, New World: The Story of Britain and America* (London, Little, Brown, 2007), pp. 564–8. 7. John Darwin, *Unfinished Empire: The Global Expansion of Britain* (London, Penguin Books, 2012), p. 357; John Darwin, *The Empire Project: The Rise and Fall of the British World System, 1830–1970* (Cambridge UP, 2009), pp. 531, 544; Peden, *Arms, Economics*, pp. 245–7, 250; Martin Daunton, *Wealth and Welfare: An Economic and Social History of Britain, 1851–1951* (Oxford UP, 2007), p. 384.  8. Ronald Hyam, *Britain's Declining Empire: The Road to Decolonization, 1918–1968* (Cambridge UP, 2006), p. 131.  9. Bernard Harris, *The Origins of the British Welfare State: Social Welfare in England and Wales, 1800–1954* (Houndmills, Palgrave Macmillan, 2004), p. 300.  10. Nicholas Timmins, *The Five Giants: A Biography of the Welfare State* (new edn; London, HarperCollins, 2006), p. 41.  11. José Harris, "From poor law to welfare state? A European perspective," in Donald Winch and Patrick O'Brien, eds., *The Political Economy of British Historical Experience, 1688–1914* (Oxford UP, 2002), pp. 434–7.  12. David Edgerton, *Warfare State: Britain, 1920–1970* (Cambridge UP, 2006), pp. 65–7; *LRB* (3 March 2011), p. 34; Daunton, *Wealth and Welfare*, pp. 548–9.  13. Gavin Stamp, *Britain's Lost Cities* (London, Aurum, 2007). See also Robert Colls, *Identity of England* (Oxford UP, 2002), pp. 344–7.  14. Timmins, *Five Giants*, p. 145. 15. Anne Orde, *The Eclipse of Great Britain: The United States and British Imperial Decline, 1895–1956* (Houndmills, Macmillan, 1996), p. 163.  16. Peter Hennessy, *Muddling Through: Power, Politics and the Quality of Government in Postwar Britain* (London, Gollancz, 1996), p. 99.  17. Alan Sharp and Glyn Stone, eds., *Anglo-French Relations in the Twentieth Century: Rivalry and Cooperation* (London, Routledge, 2000), p. 259; Hyam, *Britain's Declining Empire*, pp. 136–8. 18. Minute of meeting on 5 Jan. 1949; and memo of meeting of 23 Aug. 1950, in Robert Tombs and Émile Chabal, eds., *Britain and France in Two World Wars: Truth, Myth and Memory* (London, Continuum, 2013), p. 206.  19. See Darwin, *Unfinished Empire*, pp. 339–41, for a slightly different analysis.  20. Hyam, *Britain's Declining Empire*, pp. 106, 113.  21. Ibid., p. 110.  22. Ibid., p. 109. 23. The views of Ronald Hyam, in ibid., p. 111; and Perry Anderson, "Why Partition?," *LRB* (19 July 2012), pp. 11–19.  24. Clarke and Trebilcock, *Understanding Decline*, p. 217.  25. Paul Addison, *No Turning Back: The Peacetime Revolutions of Post-War Britain* (Oxford UP, 2010), pp. 121–2.  26. Darwin, *Unfinished Empire*, p. 353.  27. Hyam, *Britain's Declining Empire*, pp. 124, 127.  28. Anne Applebaum, *Iron Curtain: The Crushing of Eastern Europe* (London, Penguin Books, 2013), p. 152.  29. Benny Morris, *1948: A History of the First Arab-Israeli War* (New Haven, Conn., Yale UP, 2008), p. 38.  30. Edgerton, *Warfare State*, p. 68.  31. Orde, *Eclipse*, p. 184.  32. Jefferys, *Politics and the People*, p. 90.  33. Ibid., pp. 114–21. See also Peter Hennessy, *Having It So Good: Britain in the Fifties* (London, Allen Lane, 2006), p. 9.  34. E. Shils and M. Young, "The meaning of the coronation," *Sociological Review* (1953), in Addison, *No Turning Back*, p. 112.  35. Doris Lessing, in Addison, *No Turning Back*, p. 112.  36. Wm. Roger Louis and Roger Owen, eds., *Suez 1956: The Crisis and Its Consequences* (Oxford, Clarendon Press, 1989), pp. 123, 220.  37. Ibid., pp. 225, 228.  38. For a modern assessment, see G. C. Peden, "Suez and Britain's decline as a world power," *HJ* 55 (2012), pp. 1073–96. 39. Ronald Hyam, *Understanding the British Empire* (Cambridge UP, 2010), p. 89. 40. Christopher Andrew, *The Defence of the Realm: The Authorized History of MI5* (London, Allen Lane, 2009), pp. 442–3. 41. Louis and Owen, *Suez*, p. 130. 42. Hyam, *Britain's Declining Empire*, p. 267. 43. Darwin, *Unfinished Empire*, pp. 358–9, 366–71. 44. Hyam, *Understanding*, p. 89. 45. Hyam, *Britain's Declining Empire*, p. 189. 46. Hennessy, *Having It So Good*, p. 302. 47. David Anderson, *Histories of the Hanged: Britain's Dirty War in Kenya and the End of Empire* (London, Weidenfeld & Nicolson, 2005), p. 7. 48. Hyam, *Britain's Declining Empire*, p. 263. 49. BBC News, 6 June 2013. 50. For such accusations, see Caroline Elkins, *Britain's Gulag: The Brutal End of Empire in Kenya* (London, Jonathan Cape, 2005), esp. p. 366. 51. John Blacker, "The demography of Mau-Mau: fertility and mortality in Kenya in the 1950s: a demographer's viewpoint," *African Affairs* 106 (April 2007), pp. 205–27. 52. Anderson, *Histories of the Hanged*, pp. 13–28. 53. Chris Brooks and Peter Faulkner, eds., *The White Man's Burdens: An Anthology of British Poetry of the Empire* (Exeter UP, 1996), p. 265. 54. An oral comment made at a Franco-British Council conference at the Institut Singer, Paris, 28 Jan. 2009. 55. See, for example, Jennifer Pitts, *A Turn to Empire: The Rise of Liberal Imperialism in Britain and France* (Princeton UP, 2005). 56. John Ehrman, *The Younger Pitt: The Years of Acclaim* (London, Constable, 1984), p. 401 (speech in April 1792). Blair merely expressed "deep sorrow that [the slave trade] could ever have happened," BBC News, 27 Nov. 2006. 57. Niall Ferguson, *Empire: How Britain Made the Modern World* (London, Penguin Books, 2004). Vehement exponents of the contrary view include John Newsinger, *The Blood Never Dried: A People's History of the British Empire* (London, Bookmarks, 2013), and Richard Gott, *Britain's Empire: Resistance, Repression and Revolt* (London, Verso, 2011). 58. E. Said, *Orientalism: Western Conceptions of the Orient* (London, Penguin Books, 1977); and *Culture and Imperialism* (London, Vintage, 1994). 59. David Hall-Matthews, "Famines in (South) Asia," *History Compass* 2 (2004), p. 1. 60. Hyam, *Britain's Declining Empire*, p. 132. 61. *CIHBE*, p. 357. 62. As in sex, colourfully documented in Hyam, *Understanding*, part V. 63. John Iliffe, *Honour in African Society* (Cambridge UP, 2005), p. 203. 64. Hyam, *Understanding*, p. 192. 65. Hyam, *Britain's Declining Empire*, p. 3. 66. George Orwell, "The Lion and the Unicorn," in *Essays* (London, Penguin Books, 2000), p. 152. 67. Said, *Culture and Imperialism*, p. 47. 68. For a pointed discussion, see Mahmood Mamdani, "Lessons of Zimbabwe," and ensuing correspondence, in *LRB* (4 and 18 Dec. 2008 and 1 Jan. 2009). 69. Hyam, *Britain's Declining Empire*, p. 4. 70. See Christopher A. Bayly, *The Birth of the Modern World, 1780–1914* (Oxford, Blackwell, 2004). 71. See, for example, Jeremy Paxman, *Empire: What Ruling the World Did to the British* (London, Viking, 2011), pp. 5, 285. 72. Important exponents of these opposing views are John M. MacKenzie, *Imperialism and Popular Culture* (Manchester UP, 1986); Bill Schwarz, *Memories of Empire*, vol. I: *The White Man's World* (Oxford UP, 2011); Wendy Webster, *Englishness and Empire, 1939–1965* (Oxford UP, 2005); and Bernard Porter, *The Absent-Minded Imperialists: Empire, Society and*

*Culture in Britain* (Oxford UP, 2004). 73. Porter, *Absent-Minded Imperialists*, ch. 12, suggests hypothetical ways in which a non-imperial Britain might have developed differently. 74. Stephen Howe, in Ben Jackson and Robert Saunders, eds., *Making Thatcher's Britain* (Cambridge UP, 2012), p. 251. 75. George Orwell, "Shooting an elephant," in *Essays*, p. 22. 76. Orwell, "Lion and the Unicorn," p. 152. 77. C. Knick Harley, in *CEHMB*, vol. I, p. 202. 78. See Michael Fry, *The Scottish Empire* (Phantassie, Tuckwell Press, 2001). 79. Said, *Culture and Imperialism*, p. 4.

## 19. England's Cultural Revolutions

1. Callum Brown, *The Death of Christian Britain* (London, Routledge, 2001), p. 9. 2. Ibid., p. 190. 3. Hera Cook, *The Long Sexual Revolution* (Oxford UP, 2004), p. 321; Brown, *Death of Christian Britain*, pp. 171, 175, 187–8. 4. Richard Holt, *Sport and the British: A Modern History* (Oxford, Clarendon Press, 1989), p. 335. 5. Adrian Bingham, *Family Newspapers? Sex, Private Life, and the British Popular Press, 1918–1978* (Oxford UP, 2009); Kate Fisher, *Birth Control, Sex and Marriage in England, 1918–1960* (Oxford UP, 2008). 6. Brown, *Death of Christian Britain*, p. 176; Paul Addison, *No Turning Back: The Peacetime Revolutions of Post-War Britain* (Oxford UP, 2010), pp. 213–14. 7. Brown, *Death of Christian Britain*, p. 188; Simon Green, "The evolution of modern indigenous paganism," Birkbeck Lecture, Cambridge, 5 Dec. 2013. 8. See Peter Hennessy, *Having It So Good: Britain in the Fifties* (London, Allen Lane, 2006), pp. 497–501. 9. C. H. Rolphe, ed., *The Trial of Lady Chatterley* (London, Penguin Books, 1990), pp. 17, 70–71. 10. Bingham, *Family Newspapers*, p. 257. 11. Nicholas Timmins, *The Five Giants: A Biography of the Welfare State* (new edn; London, HarperCollins, 2001), pp. 236–7. 12. Kevin Jefferys, *Politics and the People: A History of British Democracy Since 1918* (London, Atlantic, 2007), p. 160. 13. See Camilla Schofield, *Enoch Powell and the Making of Postcolonial Britain* (Cambridge UP, 2013). 14. Addison, *No Turning Back*, p. 203. 15. Cook, *Long Sexual Revolution*, p. 340; Addison, *No Turning Back*, p. 214. 16. Ibid., pp. 239–40, 271. 17. Ibid., pp. 338–9; A. H. Halsey and Josephine Webb, eds., *Twentieth-Century British Social Trends* (Houndmills, Macmillan, 2000), p. 62. 18. By the early 2000s, for example, basic levels of religious belief in Britain were rather higher than in Scandinavia, the Netherlands and France, slightly lower than in Belgium, and much lower than in Catholic Europe. Special Eurobarometer, *Social Values, Science and Technology* (European Commission, June 2005), p. 9. 19. Henry Fairlie elaborated the concept in an article in the *Spectator* in 1955; see Peter Oborne, *The Triumph of the Political Class* (London, Simon & Schuster, 2007), p. 26. 20. Cook, *Long Sexual Revolution*, p. 286. 21. Sam Brewitt-Taylor, "The invention of a 'secular society'? Christianity and the sudden appearance of secularization discourses in the British national media, 1961–1964," *Twentieth-Century British History* 21 (2013), pp. 327–50. 22. G. C. Peden, *Arms, Economics and British Strategy: From Dreadnoughts to Hydrogen Bombs* (Cambridge UP, 2007),

pp. 331–8; Gill Bennett, *Six Moments of Crisis: Inside British Foreign Policy* (Oxford UP, 2013), ch. 4.   23. Kenneth Tynan, in Stuart Ward, ed., *British Culture and the End of Empire* (Manchester UP, 2001), p. 74.   24. Clive Emsley, *Hard Men: The English and Violence Since 1750* (London, Hambledon, 2005), p. 4.   25. George Orwell, "The Lion and the Unicorn," in *Essays* (London, Penguin Books, 2000), p. 142.   26. Geoffrey Gorer, in Christie Davies, *The Strange Death of Moral Britain* (New Brunswick, N.J., Transaction, 2004), p. 19. See also Peter Mandler, *The English National Character: The History of an Idea from Edmund Burke to Tony Blair* (New Haven, Conn., Yale UP, 2006), pp. 198–205.   27. Halsey and Webb, *Twentieth-Century British Social Trends*, pp. 682–4, 697–8.   28. Holt, *Sport and the British*, pp. 335, 337, 343.   29. Halsey and Webb, *Twentieth-Century British Social Trends*, p. 22.   30. "Health at a Glance, 2013" (OECD, November 2013) found that of thirty-three member countries only in the UK, Finland, Sweden and Spain did girls appear to get drunk more often than boys, p. 46. Only in Denmark were teenage girls bigger drinkers than in Britain; in France girls drank less than half as much as in Britain. *Daily Telegraph*, 30 Nov. 2013.   31. *CEHMB*, vol. III, p. 66.   32. Jim Tomlinson, "Inventing 'decline': the falling behind of the British economy in the postwar years," *Economic History Review* 49 (1996), p. 742.   33. Jim Tomlinson, *The Politics of Decline: Understanding Post-War Britain* (Harlow, Longman, 2000), pp. 23, 44.   34. Peter Clarke and Clive Trebilcock, eds., *Understanding Decline: Perceptions and Realities of British Economic Performance* (Cambridge UP, 1997), p. 150.   35. The classic account of this process for France, where the effects were particularly striking, is Jean Fourastié, *Les Trente Glorieuses ou la révolution invisible de 1946 à 1975* (Paris, Fayard, 1979).   36. Lord (Arnold) Weinstock, 1985, in Clarke and Trebilcock, *Understanding Decline*, pp. 21–2.   37. Jim Tomlinson, "Thrice denied: 'declinism' as a recurrent theme in British history in the long twentieth century," *Twentieth Century British History* 20 (2009), p. 239.   38. *CEHMB*, vol. III, ch. 4.   39. Francis Tombs, *Power Politics: Political Encounters in Industry and Engineering* (London, Tauris, 2011), pp. 36–7, 107.   40. Martin J. Wiener, *English Culture and the Decline of the Industrial Spirit, 1850–1980* (Cambridge UP, 1981), p. 3.   41. Ibid., p. 154.   42. See especially Barry Supple, "Fear of failing: economic history and the decline of Britain," *Economic History Review* 47 (1994), pp. 441–58; Clarke and Trebilcock, *Understanding Decline*; Tomlinson, *Politics of Decline*; Nicholas Crafts, "The golden age of economic growth in Western Europe, 1950–1973," *Economic History Review* 48 (1995), pp. 429–47.   43. E. P. Thompson, "The peculiarities of the English," *The Socialist Register* (1965), p. 312.   44. Speech to the European Research Institute, Birmingham, 23 Nov. 2001.   45. Jeremy Paxman, *Empire: What Ruling the World Did to the British* (London, Viking, 2011), p. 286.   46. Alan Bullock, *Ernest Bevin: Foreign Secretary, 1945–1951* (London, Heinemann, 1983), pp. 768–74; Alan S. Milward, *The UK and the European Community*, vol. I: *The Rise and Fall of a National Strategy, 1945–1963* (London, Frank Cass, 2002), p. 71.   47. Tomlinson, "Thrice denied," p. 244.   48. Milward, *UK and the European Community*, vol. I, p. 3.   49. Ibid., pp. 317–18.   50. Telephone conversation, 19 Jan. 1963, in Stephen Wall, *The Official History of Britain and the*

*European Community*, vol. II: *From Rejection to Referendum, 1963–1975* (London, Routledge, 2013), p. 7.   51. Robert and Isabelle Tombs, *That Sweet Enemy: The French and the British from the Sun King to the Present* (London, Heinemann, 2006), pp. 622–6.   52. Jim Tomlinson, "The decline of the empire and the economic 'decline' of Britain," *Twentieth Century British History* 14 (2003), p. 210. 53. Helen Parr, *British Policy Towards the European Community: Harold Wilson and Britain's World Role, 1964–67* (London, Routledge, 2005), ch. 1.   54. *Britain's Entry into the European Community: Report by Sir Con O'Neill on the Negotiations of 1970–1972*, ed. D. Hannay (London, Frank Cass, 2000), p. 11. 55. Alain Peyrefitte, *C'était de Gaulle* (2 vols.; Paris, Fayard, 1994), vol. 2, p. 311. 56. Roy Denman, *Missed Chances* (London, Indigo, 1996), p. 233. Denman was an adviser to both Wilson and Heath.   57. Minute of 21 Nov. 1971, in Wall, *Official History*, p. 421.   58. O'Neill, *Britain's Entry*, pp. 39, 40, 355, 358–9. See also Wall, *Official History*, p. 81.   59. Richard Weight, *Patriots: National Identity in Britain, 1940–2000* (London, Macmillan, 2002), pp. 477–82.   60. Colin Turpin and Adam Tomkins, *British Government and the Constitution* (Cambridge UP, 2011), pp. 339–61.

## 20. Storm and Stress

1. Annotation on document, March 1990, Foreign and Commonwealth Office, *Documents on British Policy Overseas*, series III, vol. VII (London, Routledge, 2010), p. 503.   2. Richard Vinen, *Thatcher's Britain: The Politics and Social Upheaval of the 1980s* (London, Simon & Schuster, 2009), p. 36; Peter Clarke, *Hope and Glory: Britain, 1900–1940* (London, Allen Lane, 1996), p. 402.   3. See Duncan Needham, *Monetary Policy from Devaluation to Thatcher, 1967–82* (London, Palgrave Macmillan, 2014).   4. Clarke, *Hope and Glory*, p. 332.   5. Douglas Hurd, in Andy Beckett, *When the Lights Went Out: What Really Happened to Britain in the Seventies* (London, Faber & Faber, 2009), p. 86.   6. See Simon Prince and Geoffrey Warner, *Belfast and Derry in Revolt: A New History of the Start of the Troubles* (Dublin, Irish Academic Press, 2011).   7. See Michael Kerr, *The Destructors: The Story of Northern Ireland's Lost Peace Process* (Dublin, Irish Academic Press, 2011).   8. Paul Bew, *Ireland: The Politics of Enmity, 1789–2006* (Oxford UP, 2007), p. 555.   9. *Independent* (19 July 2006).   10. Beckett, *When the Lights Went Out*, pp. 130–31.   11. Ibid., p. 146.   12. Clarke, *Hope and Glory*, p. 348.   13. Stephen Wall, *The Official History of Britain and the European Community*, vol. II: *From Rejection to Referendum, 1963–1975* (London, Routledge, 2013), pp. 578–84.   14. Ibid., pp. 585–90.   15. Martin Pugh, *Speak for Britain: A New History of the Labour Party* (London, Vintage, 2011), p. 354.   16. Beckett, *When the Lights Went Out*, pp. 331–9.   17. Ibid., pp. 347–8.   18. Vinen, *Thatcher's Britain*, p. 75.   19. Beckett, *When the Lights Went Out*, pp. 409, 415–16. Generally on this period, see Dominic Sandbrook, *State of Emergency: The Way We Were: Britain, 1970–1974* (London, Allen Lane, 2010), and *Seasons in the Sun: The Battle for Britain, 1974–1979* (London, Allen Lane, 2012).   20. Paul Addison, *No*

*Turning Back: The Peacetime Revolutions of Post-War Britain* (Oxford UP, 2010), p. 326.   **21.** Recollection of Lord (Nigel) Lawson, at "The 1981 Budget: Facts and Fallacies" (conference held at The Grocers' Hall, 27 Sept. 2011, transcript ed. Duncan Needham et al.), p. 23: https://www.chu.cam.ac.uk/media/uploads/files/1981 _Budget.pdf (consulted 4 May 2014).   **22.** Recollection of Sir Tim Lankester (then Callaghan's private secretary), ibid., pp. 14–15; Gormley, quoted in Beckett, *When the Lights Went Out*, p. 437.   **23.** Addison, *No Turning Back*, p. 274.   **24.** Clarke, *Hope and Glory*, p. 355.   **25.** Kenneth O. Morgan, *Callaghan: A Life* (Oxford UP, 1997), p. 697.   **26.** Ben Jackson and Robert Saunders, eds., *Making Thatcher's Britain* (Cambridge UP, 2012), p. 131.   **27.** Vinen, *Thatcher's Britain*, p. 22. **28.** Margaret Thatcher, *The Downing Street Years* (London, HarperCollins, 1993), p. 151.   **29.** Charles Moore, *Margaret Thatcher: The Authorized Biography* (London, Allen Lane, 2013), vol. I, p. 406.   **30.** Charles Douglas-Home, in ibid., p. 640.   **31.** Robin Harris, *Not for Turning: The Life of Margaret Thatcher* (London, Bantam, 2013), p. 161.   **32.** Jackson and Saunders, *Making Thatcher's Britain*, p. 11.   **33.** Pugh, *Speak for Britain*, p. 387.   **34.** The most trenchant analysis by an admirer—who also has much to say about enemies—is Shirley Robin Letwin, *The Anatomy of Thatcherism* (London, Fontana, 1992).   **35.** Denis Healey, *The Time of My Life* (London, Penguin Books, 1990), p. 488.   **36.** Clarke, *Hope and Glory*, p. 367; Vinen, *Thatcher's Britain*, p. 273.   **37.** Vinen, *Thatcher's Britain*, p. 82.   **38.** Thatcher, *Downing Street Years*, p. 15; interview in *The Sunday Times*, 3 May 1981, MTF website.   **39.** Peter Clarke and Clive Trebilcock, eds., *Understanding Decline: Perceptions and Realities of British Economic Performance* (Cambridge UP, 1997), p. 277.   **40.** See Needham, *Monetary Policy*.   **41.** Alan Booth, *The British Economy in the Twentieth Century* (Houndmills, Palgrave Macmillan, 2001), pp. 180–81.   **42.** Moore, *Margaret Thatcher*, vol. I, pp. 628–30. **43.** See Philip Booth, ed., *Were 364 Economists All Wrong?* (London, Institute of Economic Affairs, 2006), and "The 1981 Budget: Facts and Fallacies."   **44.** Moore, *Margaret Thatcher*, vol. I, pp. 637, 651.   **45.** *CEHMB*, vol. III, p. 99.   **46.** Sandbrook, *Seasons in the Sun*, p. 262.   **47.** *CEHMB*, vol. III, p. 99; Francis Tombs, *Power Politics: Political Encounters in Industry and Engineering* (London, Tauris, 2011), chs. 7–8.   **48.** Addison, *No Turning Back*, p. 331; Clarke and Trebilcock, *Understanding Decline*, p. 23.   **49.** David Card and Richard B. Freeman, "What have two decades of British economic reform delivered?" (Washington, D.C., National Bureau of Economic Research, Working Paper 8801, 2002), pp. 20, 70; *CEHMB*, vol. III, p. 294.   **50.** Nigel West, *The Secret War for the Falklands* (London, Little, Brown, 1997), pp. xvii, 12.   **51.** Vinen, *Thatcher's Britain*, p. 139. **52.** Ibid., pp. 148–9.   **53.** Moore, *Margaret Thatcher*, vol. I, p. 667.   **54.** Michael Paris, *Warrior Nation: Images of War in British Popular Culture* (London, Reaktion, 2000), p. 245.   **55.** Robin Harris, *Not for Turning*, pp. 206–9; Moore, *Margaret Thatcher*, vol. I, p. 697.   **56.** Paul Sharp, in T. G. Otte, ed., *The Makers of British Foreign Policy: From Pitt to Thatcher* (Houndmills, Palgrave Macmillan, 2002), p. 265.   **57.** Paul Sharp, *Thatcher's Diplomacy: The Revival of British Foreign Policy* (Houndmills, Macmillan, 1999), p. 67.   **58.** Kathleen Burk, *Old World, New World: The Story of Britain and America* (London, Little, Brown, 2007), pp. 633–7. 59. Sharp, *Thatcher's Diplomacy*, pp. 98, 99. 60. Lawrence Freedman, *The Official History of the Falklands Campaign* (rev. edn, 2 vols.; London, Routledge, 2007), vol. II, pp. 71, 281. 61. Sharp, *Thatcher's Diplomacy*, pp. 80–83, 86. 62. Hansard, HC Deb 21 December 1982, vol. 34, col. 900. 63. Freedman, *Falklands Campaign*, vol. II, pp. 289–98, 750–52. 64. On this complex story, see Moore, *Margaret Thatcher*, vol. I, pp. 717–31. 65. Sharp, *Thatcher's Diplomacy*, p. 100; Otte, *Makers*, p. 266; Freedman, *Falklands Campaign*, vol. II, p. 730. 66. Richard Weight, *Patriots: National Identity in Britain, 1940–2000* (London, Macmillan, 2002), p. 626. 67. Sharp, *Thatcher's Diplomacy*, p. 107; Burk, *Old World, New World*, p. 638. 68. Speech to Conservative rally, Cheltenham, 3 July 1982, MTF website. 69. Weight, *Patriots*, p. 626; Burk, *Old World, New World*, p. 636. 70. Vernon Bogdanor, "Clever hopes," *TLS* (22 March 2013), p. 25. 71. Paris, *Warrior Nation*, pp. 247–50; Weight, *Patriots*, pp. 614, 619–21; Sharp, *Thatcher's Diplomacy*, p. 95; Stephen Howe, "Internal decolonization? British politics since Thatcher as post-colonial trauma," *Twentieth Century British History* 14 (2003), pp. 293–4; Moore, *Margaret Thatcher*, vol. I, pp. 756–7; Vinen, *Thatcher's Britain*, p. 153. 72. A witticism attributed to the Labour MP Gerald Kaufman. 73. Addison, *No Turning Back*, p. 336; Pugh, *Speak for Britain*, p. 373. 74. Kevin Jefferys, *Politics and the People: A History of British Democracy Since 1918* (London, Atlantic, 2007), p. 238. 75. Vinen, *Thatcher's Britain*, p. 158. 76. Jackson and Saunders, *Making Thatcher's Britain*, p. 8; Harris, *Not for Turning*, pp. 227–34. 77. Robert Colls, *Identity of England* (Oxford UP, 2002), p. 156. 78. Ibid., p. 341. 79. Ken Coutts, Andrew Glyn, and Bob Rowthorn, "Structural change under New Labour," *Cambridge Journal of Economics* 31 (2007), pp. 845–61. 80. Bew, *Ireland*, pp. 532–5. 81. Michael Burleigh, *Blood and Rage: A Cultural History of Terrorism* (London, Harper Perennial, 2009), pp. 301, 325–30, 336. 82. Peter Hennessy, *Muddling Through: Power, Politics and the Quality of Government in Postwar Britain* (London, Gollancz, 1996), p. 295. 83. Christopher Andrew, *The Defence of the Realm: The Authorized History of MI5* (London, Allen Lane, 2009), pp. 724–5; Robin Renwick, *A Journey with Margaret Thatcher: Foreign Policy Under the Iron Lady* (London, Biteback, 2013), ch. 11. 84. Sharp, *Thatcher's Diplomacy*, p. 235; Renwick, *Journey*, ch. 11. 85. Famously Francis Fukayama, *The End of History and the Last Man* (New York, Free Press, 1992). 86. Sharp, *Thatcher's Diplomacy*, p. 157. 87. Stephen Wall, *A Stranger in Europe: Britain and the EU from Thatcher to Blair* (Oxford UP, 2008), p. 25. 88. John Gillingham, *European Integration, 1950–2003: Superstate or New Market Economy?* (Cambridge UP, 2003), pp. 136, 146, 231. 89. Speech to Global Panel, The Hague, 15 May 1992, MTF website. 90. Robert and Isabelle Tombs, *That Sweet Enemy: The French and the British from the Sun King to the Present* (London, Heinemann, 2006), pp. 618–26. 91. Interview in *Le Nouvel Observateur* (20–26 March 1997), p. 26 (my translation). 92. Stockholm speech, 1988, in George Ross, *Jacques Delors and European Integration* (Cambridge, Polity Press, 1995), p. 43. 93. Speech to the College of Europe, MTF website. 94. Kevin Jefferys, *Finest and Darkest Hours: The Decisive Events in British Politics from Churchill to Blair* (London, Atlantic, 2003), p. 262. 95. Hansard, HC Deb, vol. 178, cols. 869–92.

96. Vinen, *Thatcher's Britain*, p. 263.   97. For details, see Harris, *Not for Turning*, pp. 288–95, and Anthony King and Ivor Crewe, *The Blunders of Our Governments* (London, Oneworld, 2013), ch. 4.   98. Hansard, HC Deb, 13 Nov. 1990, vol. 180, cols. 461–5.   99. David Marquand, *Britain Since 1918: The Strange Career of British Democracy* (London, Weidenfeld & Nicolson, 2008), p. 320.   100. See Jackson and Saunders, *Making Thatcher's Britain*, ch. 7.   101. Peter Mandler, *The English National Character: The History of an Idea from Edmund Burke to Tony Blair* (New Haven, Conn., Yale UP, 2006), p. 233.   102. Addison, *No Turning Back*, p. 312.   103. For details, see Gillingham, *European Integration*, pp. 288–9, and for the Whitehall perspective, King and Crewe, *Blunders*, ch. 7.   104. Jefferys, *Finest and Darkest Hours*, p. 276.   105. See Morton Abramowitz et al., *The Western Balkans and the EU: "The Hour of Europe"* (Paris, EUISS, 2011).   106. Brendan Simms, *Unfinest Hour: Britain and the Destruction of Bosnia* (London, Penguin Books, 2003), p. 111.   107. Douglas Hurd, *Memoirs* (London, Little, Brown, 2003), pp. 455, 471.

## 21. Things Can Only Get Better, 1997–c.2014

1. John Kampfner, *Blair's Wars* (London, Simon & Schuster, 2003), p. 3   2. "The Blair years," *Evening Standard* (n.d.).   3. Anthony Seldon, ed., *Blair's Britain, 1997–2007* (Cambridge UP, 2007), pp. 187–8.   4. Peter Mandelson and Roger Liddle, *The Blair Revolution: Can New Labour Deliver?* (London, Faber, 1996), p. 10.   5. Tony Blair, *A Journey* (London, Hutchinson, 2010), p. 90.   6. Martin Pugh, *Speak for Britain: A New History of the Labour Party* (London, Vintage, 2011), p. 397.   7. Ross McKibbin, in *LRB* (10 June 2010), p. 13.   8. Said during a visit to businesses in California, reported in the *Financial Times*, 23 Oct. 1998.   9. See the *Sunday Times* Rich List, annually.   10. For example, the Miliband brothers (rival candidates for leadership of the Labour Party, September 2010); the Eagle twins, Angela and Maria (in the 2010 Shadow Cabinet), and the married couple Yvette Cooper and Ed Balls (in the Labour Cabinet 2008–10, and the subsequent Shadow Cabinet).   11. Roy Hattersley, in Seldon, *Blair's Britain*, p. 25.   12. For a concise analysis, see Peter Mair, *Ruling the Void: The Hollowing of Western Democracy* (London, Verso, 2013), and comparative statistics, pp. 28, 35, 40–41.   13. Kevin Jefferys, *Politics and the People: A History of British Democracy Since 1918* (London, Atlantic, 2007), pp. 250–63.   14. Blair, *Journey* (London, Hutchinson, 2010).   15. Jefferys, *Politics and the People*, p. 401; for the broader context, see Anthony King and Ivor Crewe, *The Blunders of Our Governments* (London, Oneworld, 2013), esp. chs. 18, 19, 20, 23.   16. Pugh, *Speak for Britain*, pp. 387–91.   17. Matthew Parris, in Andrew Rawnsley, *The End of the Party* (London, Viking, 2010), p. 451.   18. Rawnsley, *End of the Party*, pp. 483, 521.   19. *Guardian*, 5 Sept. 2011.   20. Pugh, *Speak for Britain*, p. 402; Peter Oborne, *The Triumph of the Political Class* (London, Simon & Schuster, 2007), ch. 11.   21. Rawnsley, *End of the Party*, pp. 204, 132–9; Seldon, *Blair's Britain*, p. 5.   22. Paul Bew, *Ireland: The Politics of Enmity, 1789–2006* (Oxford UP, 2007), pp. 547–55; Michael

Burleigh, *Blood and Rage: A Cultural History of Terrorism* (London, Harper Perrennial, 2009), p. 345; Martyn Frampton, *Legion of the Rearguard: Dissident Irish Republicanism* (Dublin, Irish Academic Press, 2010), pp. 201–78.   **23.** Philip Norton, "The Constitution," in Seldon, *Blair's Britain*, p. 122.   **24.** Hansard, HC Deb., 14 Nov. 1977, vol. 939, col. 122.   **25.** Francis G. Jacobs, *The Sovereignty of Law: The European Way* (Cambridge UP, 2007), pp. 1–2.   **26.** For example, in the famous (among lawyers) Factortame case (1989–91). See Colin Turpin and Adam Tomkins, *British Government and the Constitution* (Cambridge UP, 2011), pp. 347–53.   **27.** See opinion of Lord Sumption in the Supreme Court, Michaelmas Term 2013, UKSC 63, pp. 55–6, in *R (Chester) v Secretary of State for Justice*. **28.** Jacobs, *The Sovereignty of Law*, p. 2.   **29.** Vernon Bogdanor, *The New British Constitution* (Oxford, Hart, 2009), p 53.   **30.** Lord Hope of Craighead, in *R (Jackson) v Attorney-General* (2006).   **31.** Simon Bulmer and Martin Burch, "The 'Europeanization' of central government: the UK and Germany in historical institutionalist perspective," in Gerald Schneider and Mark Aspinall, *The Rules of Integration* (Manchester UP, 2001), p. 93.   **32.** Seldon, *Blair's Britain*, p. 533. **33.** John Salt, director of Migration Research Unit, UCL, quoted in *The Economist*, 26 Aug. 2006, p. 25; 2011 census results, *The Times*, 16 July 2012.   **34.** House of Lords Select Committee on Economic Affairs, 1st Report of Session 2007–8: *The Economic Impact of Immigration* (1 April 2008), vol. I, p. 26.   **35.** Office of National Statistics (ONS), *Total International Migration*, Time Series 1991–2007, table 2.01a; *Migrant Workers*, table 2, "Births in England and Wales by parents' country of birth."   **36.** See A. H. Halsey and Josephine Webb, eds., *Twentieth-Century British Social Trends* (Houndmills, Macmillan, 2000), pp. 152–7. **37.** *Guardian*, 22 June 2011.   **38.** ONS, *Population Trends*, no. 135, p. 28; *Migration Statistics* (House of Commons Library, Standard Note 06077, 2011), p. 12. **39.** *Economist*, 24 Oct. 2009, p. 33.   **40.** Ivan Reid, *Class in Britain* (Cambridge, Polity Press, 1998), pp. 26–7; *Economist*, 20 Oct. 2007, p. 44.   **41.** Adrian Favell, *Philosophies of Integration: Immigration and the Idea of Citizenship in France and Britain* (Houndmills, Macmillan, 1998), p. 113.   **42.** Robert Colls, *Identity of England* (Oxford UP, 2002), p. 161.   **43.** Ibid., pp. 115, 131.   **44.** Institute for Public Policy Research study, cited in the *Sunday Times*, 18 Feb. 2007, p. 7; "Into the melting pot," *The Economist*, 8 Feb. 2014, p. 23.   **45.** "Mobility within the EU," Discussion Paper 379, National Institute of Economic and Social Research (April 2011); ONS, *Population by Country of Birth and Nationality Report*, *August 2013*, fig. 5.   **46.** Richard Mayne et al. eds., *Cross Channel Currents: 100 Years of the Entente Cordiale* (London, Routledge, 2004), p. 272.   **47.** Personal communication to the author.   **48.** *The Economist*, 20 Oct. 2007, p. 44. **49.** ONS, *Migration Statistics*, table 3c, p. 9.   **50.** *Daily Telegraph*, 23 Jan. 2009.   **51.** Seldon, *Blair's Britain*, p. 355.   **52.** *Guardian*, 13 Nov. 2007; *Daily Telegraph*, 12 Nov. 2007.   **53.** *The Economist*, 3 March 2012, p. 35.   **54.** Speech to CBI, 27 April 2004.   **55.** *The Economist*, 3 Nov. 2007, p. 33.   **56.** Ibid., 28 Oct. 2006, p. 34.   **57.** Ibid., 23 Sept. 2006, p. 33.   **58.** Colls, *Identity*, p. 166.   **59.** Geoff Dench, Kate Gavron and Michael Young, *The New East End: Kinship, Race and Conflict* (London, Profile, 2006), pp. 225–7.   **60.** "The colour of votes," *The Economist* (2 Feb 2013); Runnymede Trust press release (26 Oct. 2011); Ben Clements and Nick Spencer, *Voting and Values in Britain: Does Religion Count?* (London, Theos, 2014), pp. 11, 41.  **61.** Burleigh, *Blood and Rage*, p. 441.  **62.** Shiv Malik, "My brother the bomber," *Prospect Magazine*, 135 (30 June 2007).  **63.** Burleigh, *Blood and Rage*, p. 507.  **64.** Ibid., p. 376.  **65.** Ibid., p. 470.  **66.** "Into the melting pot," *The Economist*, 8 Feb. 2014, pp. 23–4.  **67.** Chris Mullins, *The Diaries of Chris Mullins*, vol. 1: *A View from the Foothills*, ed. Ruth Winstone (London, Profile, 2009), p. 302.  **68.** Speech to Chicago Economic Club, 22 April 1999.  **69.** Ibid.  **70.** Rawnsley, *End of the Party*, p. 89.  **71.** Strategic Defence Review (July 2002), quoted in Seldon, *Blair's Britain*, p. 626.  **72.** Blair's statement to the Chilcot Inquiry, 21 Jan. 2011, pp. 8–9. The Iraq Inquiry website: Evidence.  **73.** Robin, Lord Butler of Brockwell, "Review of Intelligence on Weapons of Mass Destruction: Report of a Committee of Privy Counsellors," House of Commons paper 898 (2004), para. 610.  **74.** Statement to Chilcot Inquiry, 21 Jan. 2011, p. 18.  **75.** *Sun*, 25 Sept. 2002.  **76.** Rawnsley, *End of the Party*, p. 121.  **77.** Figure given by Gen. Sir M. Jackson, in the *Sunday Telegraph* (10 May 2013), p. 18.  **78.** Nicolas Bavarez, *La France qui tombe* (Paris, Perrin, 2003), p. 57.  **79.** See Robert and Isabelle Tombs, *That Sweet Enemy: The French and the British from the Sun King to the Present* (London, Heinemann, 2006), pp. 681–6.  **80.** The Iraq Inquiry: Declassified Documents: 14 Jan. 2003 Attorney General's draft advice to Prime Minister ("Iraq: interpretation of resolution 1441" annotated "As handed to Prime Minister on 14 Jan. 2003"), para. 18.  **81.** *Daily Telegraph* (15 March 2013).  **82.** By 2013 the Afghan war was estimated to be costing Britain about £15m per day, and the total cost was variously estimated at between £25bn and £37bn (*Guardian*, 30 May 2013); the Iraq war was officially stated to have cost £9.24bn (BBC News, 14 Dec. 2011).  **83.** *The Economist*, 13 Jan. 2007, p. 29.  **84.** Sherard Cowper-Coles, on Radio 4's *Today* programme, 18 June 2013.  **85.** Douglas Hurd, "Making the world a safer place" (Jan. 1992).  **86.** Burleigh, *Blood and Rage*, pp. 477–9, 505.  **87.** For details, see, for example, *The Times* (20 Dec. 2013), pp. 6–7.  **88.** Hansard, HC Deb, 11 June 1998, vol. 313, col. 1195.  **89.** Johan A. Lybeck, *A Global History of the Financial Crash of 2007–2010* (Cambridge UP, 2011), pp. 10, 161, 310–11.  **90.** Carmen Reinhart and Kenneth Rogoff, *The Economist* (11 Jan. 2014), p. 64.  **91.** Seldon, *Blair's Britain*, p. 279; Ken Coutts, Andrew Glyn and Bob Rowthorn, "Structural change under New Labour," *Cambridge Journal of Economics* 31 (May 2007), pp. 3, 12–13.  **92.** Rawnsley, *End of the Party*, p. 482.  **93.** For a broadly positive assessment arguing that Labour should have done more, see Polly Toynbee and David Walker, *The Verdict: Did Labour Change Britain?* (London, Granta, 2010); see also Nicholas Timmins, *The Five Giants: A Biography of the Welfare State* (new edn; London, HarperCollins, 2001), p. 613.  **94.** Coutts et al., "Structural change under New Labour," pp. 845–61; University of Oxford, Department of Economics, Economics Series Working Papers, 312 (Feb. 2007).  **95.** Anthony King and Ivor Crewe, *The Blunders of Our Governments* (London, Oneworld, 2013), ch. 8. The basics of the project had been initiated by the Tory Michael Heseltine.  **96.** European Commission figures, in Ludger Schuknecht,

*Booms, Busts and Fiscal Policy: Public Finances in the Future* (London, Politeia, 2009), p. 9. **97.** Michael Moran, Sukhdev Johal and Karel Williams, "The financial crisis and its consequences," in Nicholas Allen and John Bartle, eds., *Britain at the Polls, 2010* (London, Sage, 2011), pp. 104, 107. **98.** *Le Canard Enchaîné* (15 June 2005), p. 2. **99.** OECD report, "Doing Better for Families" (2011). **100.** OECD report, "Health at a Glance 2013" (2013), p. 59. **101.** *The Economist*, 17 June 2006, p. 31, and 29 July 2006, p. 30. **102.** Richard Wilkinson and Kate Pickett, *The Spirit Level: Why Equality is Better for Everyone* (London, Penguin Books, 2010). **103.** See the *Financial Times* (24/25 May 2014), p. 5, questioning statistics in Thomas Piketty, *Capital in the Twenty-First Century* (Cambridge, Mass., Harvard UP, 2014), purporting to show a long-term increase in concentration of wealth. **104.** "The Super Rich List" (*Sunday Times Magazine*, 11 May 2014), p. 40. **105.** OECD report, "Divided We Stand: Why Inequality Keeps Rising" (December 2011). **106.** Among the criteria for well-being were having communal family meals; drinking, smoking and sex were deplored. Innocenti Research Centre, "An Overview of Child Well Being" (Unicef 2007). **107.** OECD report, "A Family Affair: Intergenerational Social Mobility," in *Going for Growth* (2010), p. 12. **108.** Sammy Rashid and Greg Brooks, "The levels of attainment in literacy and numeracy of 13- to 19-year-olds in England, 1948–2009," NRDC report, 2010. See also *The Economist*, 5 Dec. 2009, p. 38. **109.** OECD report, "Doing Better for Children" (2009); *Guardian*, 25 Sept. 2010, p. 26; *Daily Telegraph*, 16 October 2010; *The Economist*, 5 Dec. 2009, p. 38; Katherine Birbalsingh, "Is the British education system broken?," Sir John Cass's Foundation Lecture 2011, pp. 8–9, 10, 11, 18. **110.** Robert Taylor, in Seldon, *Blair's Britain*, p. 234. **111.** Birbalsingh, "Is the British education system broken?," p. 14. **112.** *The Economist*, 25 June 2011, p. 39. **113.** Nick Bosanquet, "The health and welfare legacy," in Seldon, *Blair's Britain*, p. 388. **114.** King and Crewe, *Blunders*, pp. 285–6. **115.** BBC News report (20 Sept. 2010); OECD report, "Health at a Glance, 2013" (2013), p. 75. **116.** *Independent Inquiry into Care Provided by Mid Staffordshire NHS Foundation Trust: January 2005 to March 2009* (2010), chairman's comments, vol. I, p. 10. **117.** Wolverhampton *Express & Star* (27 May 2013). **118.** OECD report, "Health at a Glance, 2013," p. 145. **119.** Bosanquet, "Health and welfare," pp. 397–9, 404–5; *The Economist*, 15 Sept. 2007, p. 38; Ellen Nolte and Martin McKee, "Measuring the health of nations: updating an earlier analysis," *Health Affairs* 27, 1 (2008), p. 65; OECD report, "Health at a Glance, 2013," p. 25. **120.** Hansard, HC Deb, 11 June 1998, vol. 313, col. 1195. **121.** *The Economist*, 14 Oct. 2006, p. 129; 19 March 2011, p. 93. **122.** Transparency International: in the "corruption perceptions index" it fell from eleventh in 1998 to sixteenth in 2011 (behind Australia—perhaps a little oddly—Canada, Germany and Japan). **123.** BBC1, *Panorama*, "Because We're Worth It," 20 Sept. 2010. **124.** Pugh, *Speak for Britain*, p. 401. **125.** *Daily Telegraph*, "The Complete Expenses File" (n.d.). **126.** Lybeck, *Global History*, pp. 7, 95–6, 104, 107, 117. **127.** David Blunkett. *The Blunkett Tapes: My Life in the Bear Pit* (London, Bloomsbury, 2006), p. 666. **128.** Blair, *Journey*, pp. 664, 667. **129.** Rawnsley, *End of the Party*, p. 581. **130.** *The Economist* (15 June 2013), p. 30; Lybeck,

*Global History*, pp. 169, 198.   **131.** Ibid., p. 226.   **132.** Moran et al., "Financial crisis," p. 110.   **133.** Rawnsley, *End of the Party*, p. 641.   **134.** *The Economist*, 10 April 2010, p. 37.   **135.** Andrew Geddes and Jonathan Tonge, eds., *Britain Votes 2010* (Oxford UP, 2010), p. 71.   **136.** Hansard, HC Deb, Prime Minister's Questions, 10 Dec. 2008, vol. 485, col. 527; and see Moran et al., "Financial crisis," pp. 110–14, and Geddes and Tonge, *Britain Votes 2010*, pp. 7–24.   **137.** Dennis Kavanagh and Philip Cowley, *The British General Election of 2010* (Houndmills, Palgrave Macmillan, 2010).   **138.** Moran et al., "Financial crisis," p. 100; David Denver, *Elections and Voters in Britain* (2nd edn; Houndmills, Palgrave Macmillan, 2007), p. 77.   **139.** Moran et al., "Financial crisis," pp. 106–7.   **140.** King and Crewe, *Blunders*, pp. 399–415.   **141.** *New Statesman* (14–20 March 2014), p. 23.   **142.** British Social Attitude surveys, interpreted by Clements and Spencer, *Voting and Values in Britain*, pp. 70–75.   **143.** *The Economist* (23 June 2012), p. 34.   **144.** *The Economist* (14 Aug. 2010), pp. 18–19.   **145.** A concise statement of this view is Robert Skidelsky, "The economic consequences of Mr. Osborne: What have we learned from four years of austerity?," *New Statesman* (14–20 March 2014), pp. 23–9.   **146.** *The Times* (20 Dec. 2013), p. 2.   **147.** Jose Ignacio Torreblanca, Mark Leonard et al., "The Continent-wide rise of Euroscepticism" (London, ECFR, May 2013), p. 1. For a fuller analysis of the roots of Euroscepticism, see Mair, *Ruling the Void*, ch. 4.   **148.** Eurobaromètre standard 79 (printemps 2013), p. 69.   **149.** Walter Bagehot, *The English Constitution*, ed. Miles Taylor (Oxford UP, 2001 [1867]), p. 45.   **150.** A poll of 14,000 people in thirteen countries, *The Times* (11 Jan. 2014), p. 4.   **151.** *The Queen* (2006), dir. Stephen Frears.   **152.** See, for example, comments by Vernon Bogdanor in the *Guardian* (5 Sept. 2013), and A. N. Wilson, "Why Prince Charles should not remain silent," *Sunday Telegraph* (25 May 2014), p. 23.   **153.** Bagehot, *English Constitution*, pp. 7, 45.   **154.** A *Guardian*/ICM opinion poll showed 50 percent believing that Thatcher's achievement had been "positive" for Britain, and 62 percent that she had changed social attitudes to women; 20 percent thought her influence had been "very bad": *Guardian* (9 April 2013), p. 2.

## Conclusion: The English and Their History

**1.** George Orwell, "The Lion and the Unicorn," in *Essays* (London, Penguin Books, 2000 [1940]), p. 188.   **2.** Geoffrey Hill, *The Triumph of Love: A Poem* (London, Penguin Books, 1999), p. 40.   **3.** Liah Greenfeld, *Nationalism: Five Roads to Modernity* (Cambridge, Mass., Harvard UP, 1993), p. 23; see also Adrian Hastings, *The Construction of Nationhood: Ethnicity, Religion and Nationalism* (Cambridge UP, 1997)   **4.** Charles de Gaulle, *Mémoires d'espoir* (2 vols.; Paris, Plon, 1970), vol. 2, pp. 203, 236; Alain Peyrefitte, *C'était de Gaulle* (2 vols.; Paris, Fayard, 1994), vol. 1, p. 63.   **5.** Linda Colley, *Britons: Forging the Nation 1707–1837* (New Haven, Conn., Yale UP, 1992), pp. 6–7.   **6.** Though they of course do have certain autonomous political institutions.   **7.** Colley, *Britons*, is the most influential account of the making of British identity.   **8.** Philip D. Morgan, in Martin Daunton and Rick Halpern, eds., *Empire and Others: British Encounters with Indigenous Peoples 1600–1850* (London, UCL Press, 1999), pp. 43–4    9. See, for example, Simon Jenkins, *England's Thousand Best Churches* (London, Penguin Books, 2002), and *England's Thousand Best Houses* (London, Penguin Books, 2004).    10. Robert Colls, *Identity of England* (Oxford UP, 2002), p. 178.    11. Sir John Baker, in Colin Turpin and Adam Tomkins, *British Government and the Constitution* (Cambridge UP, 2011), p. 10.    12. Orwell, "Lion and the Unicorn," p. 139.    13. Ibid.    14. For the British citizenship test, they are listed as democracy, individual liberty, tolerance, etc. The BBC's PM programme (10 June 2014) featured a very rapid international survey, in which more characteristic ideas—obedience to the rules, fair play, the rule of law, respect for tradition—appeared to be widely identified with Britishness.    15. A theme of the pioneer Whig historian Paul de Rapin (see pp. 264–65).    16. "The Princess: Conclusion" (1847).    17. Orwell, "Lion and the Unicorn," p. 150. See also David Cannadine, *Class in Britain* (London, Penguin Books, 2000).    18. A recent example that is both shrewd and amusing is Kate Fox, *Watching the English: The Hidden Rules of English Behaviour* (London, Hodder & Stoughton, 2004).    19. Emphasized by Fox, *Watching the English*, pp. 401–9.    20. Krishan Kumar, *The Making of English National Identity* (Cambridge UP, 2003), pp. 30–32, 176, 273.    21. Ibid., pp. ix–xii.    22. Or in a different cultural and generational register, Lord (William) Waldegrave's "ideal of Englishness . . . a Latvian, Jewish, German, Italian mixture of all the cultures of Europe . . . Isaiah Berlin." Michael Ignatieff, *Isaiah Berlin: A Life* (London, Vintage, 2000), p. 300    23. Peter Mandler, *The English National Character: The History of an Idea from Edmund Burke to Tony Blair* (New Haven, Conn., Yale UP, 2006), p. 238.    24. Daniel Defoe, *The True-Born Englishman and Other Writings*, ed. P. N. Furband and W. R. Owens (London, Penguin Books, 1997).    25. David Hume, "Of national characters" (1748), in *Political Essays*, ed. Knut Haakonssen (Cambridge UP, 1994), pp. 85–6.    26. See *Eurobarometer 71* (Jan. 2010), pp. 35–7.    27. Colls, *Identity of England*, p. 381.    28. Ernest Renan, "*Qu'est-ce qu'une nation?*," ed. Philippe Forest (Paris, Bordas, 1991), p. 34.    29. Anthony King and Ivor Crewe, *The Blunders of Our Governments* (London, Oneworld, 2013), p. x and passim.    30. For a concise summary, see Peter Mair, *Ruling the Void: The Hollowing of Western Democracy* (London, Verso, 2013).    31. *The Economist* (14 Aug. 2010), p. 19. See on this point Simon Jenkins, *Thatcher and Sons: A Revolution in Three Acts* (London, Penguin Books, 2007).    32. José Harris, in Gordon Martel, ed., *The World War Two Reader* (London, Routledge, 2004), p. 331.    33. See, for example, Angus Maddison, *The World Economy: Historical Statistics* (Paris, OECD, 2003).    34. See David Cannadine, *The Undivided Past: History Beyond Our Differences* (London, Penguin Books, 2014).

# Further Reading

In attempting to prepare a guide to this immense subject that will not be dauntingly long, I have not tried to list every major or outstanding work. Rather, I am giving principal modern works of reference and research—all of which of course have extensive bibliographies—and also suggesting works that I have found particularly valuable and stimulating, again giving preference where possible to modern works. I have rarely chosen anecdotal books with aspirations to local colour ("The morning dawned cold and rainy," etc.), largely because I confess to finding them unreadable. The best way to get a "feel" for the past is through its own literature, art, diaries and letters, and so a few familiar and less familiar examples of these are suggested in each section. Many modern authors of fiction try to re-create the past, and a few even succeed. Among those who—in very different ways—do so brilliantly are Hilary Mantel, in *Wolf Hall* (London, Fourth Estate, 2009) and *Bring Up the Bodies* (London, Fourth Estate, 2012), a modern representation of the court of Henry VIII; Patrick O'Brian, in his meticulously imagined twenty novels on the naval war against Napoleon beginning with *Master and Commander* (London, Collins, 1970) and ending with *Blue at the Mizzen* (London, HarperCollins, 1999); and George Macdonald Fraser, in his comic satire on Victorianism, the twelve Flashman novels, beginning with *Flashman* (London, Collins, 1969).

## REFERENCE AND GENERAL WORKS

The obvious starting points are the monumental *New Oxford History of England* (Oxford, Clarendon Press, 1995–2011), ten weighty volumes so far by distinguished historians, and *The Penguin History of Britain* (London, Penguin Books, 1997–2011), nine somewhat slimmer volumes by a no less distinguished cohort. Several individual volumes of these series are also mentioned under later headings. For the early-modern and modern periods, see *The Cambridge Social History of Britain, 1750–1950*, ed. F. M. L. Thompson (3 vols.; Cambridge UP, 1990), *The Cambridge Economic History of Modern Britain*, eds. Roderick Floud and Paul Johnson (3 vols.; Cambridge UP, 2004), and *The Oxford History of the British Empire* (5 vols.; Oxford UP, 1998–9). *The Oxford Dictionary of National Biography* (Oxford UP, 2004–9, also available online) is indispensable for the whole of our history. *Blackwell Companions to British History* (Oxford, Blackwell), of which nine chronological volumes have appeared or are planned, give detailed introductions to important themes. An astonishing individual achievement as well as an invaluable guide is Charles Arnold-Baker, *The Companion to British History* (3rd edn, Longcross Denham Press, 2008). *The Oxford Companion to English Literature*, ed. Dinah Birch et al. (7th edn, Oxford UP, 2009), is a comprehensive concise guide to authors and major works; and *The Oxford English Literary History*—with thirteen volumes planned and gradually being published—will eventually satisfy most curiosities. *The Oxford History of English Art* (9 vols.; Oxford, Clarendon Press, 1949–78) covers not only individual artists and their works, but styles, movements and conditions of production.

On fundamental general themes: Oliver Rackham, *The History of the Countryside* (London, Phoenix, 2000); Simon Thurley, *The Building of England: How the History of England Has Shaped Our Buildings* (London, William Collins, 2013); Charles Barber, Joan C. Beal and Philip A. Shaw, *The English Language: A Historical Introduction* (2nd edn, Cambridge UP, 2009); David Crystal, *The Stories of English* (London, Penguin Books, 2005); Tom Pocock and Anne Wilbraham, *The Englishman's Food: Five Centuries of English Diet* (rev. edn, London, Pimlico, 1991); Charlotte Roberts and Margaret Cox, *Health and Disease in Britain: From Prehistory to the Present Day* (Stroud, Sutton, 2003); Clyve Jones, ed., *A Short History of Parliament: England, Great Britain, the United Kingdom, Ireland & Scotland* (Woodbridge, Boydell, 2009); Sheridan Gillie and W. J. Shields, eds., *A History of Religion in Britain: Practice and Belief from Pre-Roman Times to the Present* (Oxford, Blackwell, 1994). On national identity in several of its aspects: Adrian Hastings, *The Construction of Nationhood: Ethnicity, Religion and Nationalism* (Cambridge UP, 1997); Krishan Kumar, *The Making of English National Identity* (Cambridge UP, 2003); Robert Colls, *Identity of England* (Oxford UP, 2002); Paul Langford, *Englishness Identified: Manners and Character, 1650–1850* (Oxford UP, 2000); Peter Mandler, *The English National Character: The History of an Idea from Edmund Burke to Tony Blair* (New Haven and London, Yale UP, 2006); and Kate Fox, *Watching the English: The Hidden Rules of English Behaviour* (London, Hodder, 2004). For an acute and timely analysis of today's political challenges, see Michael Kenny, *The Politics of English Nationhood* (Oxford UP, 2014).

## PRELUDE AND PART I: THE BIRTH OF A NATION

On origins and early context, Barry Cunliffe, *Britain Begins* (Oxford UP, 2013), and on the Roman connection and its aftermath, David Mattingley, *An Imperial Possession: Britain in the Roman Empire, 54 BC–AD 409* (London, Allen Lane, 2006); Julia M. H. Smith, *Europe After Rome: A New Cultural History, 500–1000* (Oxford UP, 2005); and Robert Bartlett, *The Making of Europe* (London, Penguin Books, 1994). On the beginnings of the English and their kingdom, Catherine Hills, *Origins of the English* (London, Duckworth, 2003); James Campbell et al., *The Anglo-Saxons* (Oxford, Phaidon, 1982); and Sarah Foot, "The making of *Angelcynn*: English identity before the Norman Conquest," *Transactions of the Royal Historical Society*, 6th series, VI (1996). On myth, Guy Halsall, *Worlds of Arthur: Fact and Fictions of the Dark Ages* (Oxford UP, 2013). *The Wiley Blackwell*

*Encyclopedia of Anglo-Saxon England*, eds. Michael Lapidge et al. (Chichester, Wiley-Blackwell, 2014), provides a modern and accessible scholarly guide.

On late Anglo-Saxon and post-Conquest England: Julia Crick and Elizabeth van Houts, eds., *A Social History of England, 900–1200* (Cambridge UP, 2011); Frank Barlow, *The Godwins: The Rise and Fall of a Noble Dynasty* (Harlow, Longman, 2002); Ann Williams, *The English and the Norman Conquest* (Woodbridge, Boydell, 1995); J. C. Holt, *Colonial England, 1066–1215* (London, Hambledon, 1997); Hugh M. Thomas, *The English and the Normans: Ethnic Hostility, Assimilation, and Identity, 1066–c.1220* (Oxford UP, 2003); M. T. Clanchy, *England and Its Rulers, 1066–1307* (3rd edn, Oxford, Blackwell); and W. L. Warren, *Henry II* (new edn, New Haven and London, Yale UP, 2000).

On crucial political developments, see J. R. Maddicott's magisterial *Origins of the English Parliament, 924–1327* (Oxford UP, 2010) and J. H. Baker, *An Introduction to English Legal History* (London, Butterworth, 2002).

A major survey of the high Middle Ages is Michael Prestwich, *Plantagenet England, 1225–1360* (Oxford UP, 2005). For introductions to a vast subject, see F. Donald Logan, *A History of the Church in the Middle Ages* (2nd edn, Abingdon, Routledge, 2013); Henry Mayr-Harting, *Religion, Politics and Society in Britain, 1066–1272* (Harlow, Longman, 2011); and Frank Barlow, *The English Church* (2 vols.; London, Longman, 1979).

N. A. M. Rodger, *The Safeguard of the Sea: A Naval History of Britain, 660–1649* (London, Penguin Books, 2004) has brought one of the most fundamental aspects of our history to scholarly prominence.

To experience these centuries in their own words—or at least in words as close as most of us can get to them—see *Beowulf*, tr. Michael Alexander (London, Penguin Books, 2001); Bede, *The Ecclesiastical History of the English People*, eds. J. McCure and R. Collins (Oxford UP, 1999); *The Anglo-Saxon Chronicle*, tr. and ed. Michael Swanton (London, J. M. Dent, 1996); Henry of Huntingdon, *The History of the English People, 1000–1154*, tr. Diana Greenway (Oxford UP, 2002); Geoffrey of Monmouth, *The History of the Kings of Britain*, tr. L. Thorpe (London, Penguin Books, 1966); *Sir Gawain and the Green Knight*, tr. W. S. Merwin (Highgreen, Bloodaxe, 2003).

## PART II: THE ENGLISH UNLEASHED

Lively and authoritative introductions to later-medieval history are Rosemary Horrox and W. Mark Ormrod, *A Social History of England, 1200–1500* (Cambridge UP, 2006); W. M. Ormrod, *Political Life in Medieval England, 1300–1450* (London, Macmillan, 1995); and Miri Rubin, *The Hollow Crown: A History of Britain in the Late Middle Ages* (London, Penguin Books, 2005). A fine work of synthesis is Gerald Harriss, *Shaping the Nation: England, 1360–1461* (Oxford, Clarendon Press, 2005).

A concise socio-economic overview by a leading authority is Christopher Dyer, *Making a Living in the Middle Ages: The People of Britain, 850–1520* (London,

Penguin Books, 2003); see also R. H. Britnell, *The Commercialization of English Society, 1000–1500* (2nd edn, Manchester UP, 1996). On the great transforming disaster, C. Platt, *King Death: The Black Death and Its Aftermath in England* (London, UCL Press, 1996). A classic work in popular culture and politics is R. B. Dobson, *The Peasants' Revolt of 1381* (London, Macmillan, 1983). On women, see Henrietta Leyser, *Medieval Women: A Social History of Women in England, 450–1500* (London, Phoenix, 2001), and Mavis E. Mate, *Women in Medieval English Society* (Cambridge UP, 1999); and on queens, Helen Castor, *She-Wolves: The Women Who Ruled England Before Elizabeth* (London, Faber, 2010).

On foreign and domestic political upheavals, Michael Prestwich, *Armies and Warfare in the Middle Ages: The English Experience* (New Haven and London, Yale UP, 1996); Christopher Allmand, *The Hundred Years War: England and France at War, c.1300–c.1450* (Cambridge UP, 2001); Jonathan Sumption, *The Hundred Years War*, (3 vols.; London, Faber, 1990–2009); Jim Bradbury, *The Medieval Archer* (Woodbridge, Boydell, 1985); Malcolm Vale, *War and Chivalry: Warfare and Aristocratic Culture in England, France and Burgundy at the End of the Middle Ages* (London, Duckworth, 1981); Christine Carpenter, *The Wars of the Roses: Politics and the Constitution in England, c.1437–1509* (Cambridge UP, 1997); A. J. Pollard, "The tyranny of Richard III," *Journal of Medieval History*, 3 (1977); and for a grass-roots view, Helen Castor, *Blood and Roses: The Paston Family and the Wars of the Roses* (London, Faber, 2004).

On religion, Peter Heath, *Church and Realm, 1272–1461: Conflict and Collaboration in an Age of Crisis* (London, Fontana, 1988); and Christopher Harper-Bill, *The Pre-Reformation Church in England, 1400–1530* (London, Longman, 1996). On English language and literature, Elaine Treharne, *Living Through Conquest: The Politics of Early English, 1020–1220* (Oxford UP, 2012); M. T. Clanchy, *From Memory to Written Record: England, 1066–1307* (3rd edn, Chichester, Wiley-Blackwell, 2013); Thorlac Turville-Petre, *England the Nation: Language, Literature and National Identity, 1290–1340* (Oxford, Clarendon, 2002); Jeremy Catto, "Written English: the making of the language, 1370–1400," *Past & Present* 179 (May 2003); and David Wallace, ed., *The Cambridge History of Medieval English Literature* (Cambridge UP, 1999).

The most famous and accessible examples of that language and literature are Geoffrey Chaucer, *The Canterbury Tales*, tr. N. Coghill (London, Penguin Books, 2003); Sir Thomas Malory, *Le Morte Darthur: The Winchester Manuscript*, ed. Helen Cooper (Oxford UP, 1998); and *The Paston Letters: A Selection in Modern Spelling*, ed. N. Davis (Oxford UP, 1983).

## PART III: THE GREAT DIVIDE, c.1500–c.1700

An introduction to political, social and cultural themes is Robert Tittler and Norman Jones, eds., *A Companion to Tudor Britain* (Oxford, Blackwell, 2004), and a concise chronological survey is John Guy, *Tudor England* (Oxford UP, 1988). On government, see David Starkey et al., *The English Court: From the Wars of the*

*Roses to the Civil War* (London, Longman, 1987). Diarmaid MacCulloch, *Reformation: Europe's House Divided, 1490–1700* (London, Allen Lane, 2003), and Eamon Duffy, *The Stripping of the Altars: Traditional Religion in England, c.1400–c.1580* (New Haven and London, Yale UP, 2005), are vivid accounts of what was changing and what was being lost. On reactions, Ethan H. Shagan, *Popular Politics and the English Reformation* (Cambridge UP, 2003). The key figures in England's largely top-down religious revolution are scrutinized in G. W. Bernard, *The King's Reformation: Henry VIII and the Remaking of the English Church* (New Haven and London, Yale UP, 2005); Diarmaid MacCulloch, *Thomas Cranmer: A Life* (New Haven and London, Yale UP, 1996); Richard Rex, *Elizabeth: Fortune's Bastard?* (Stroud, Tempus, 2007); and Stephen Alford, *Burghley: William Cecil at the Court of Elizabeth I* (New Haven and London, Yale UP, 2008). On external politics and war, Wallace MacCaffrey, *Elizabeth I: War and Politics, 1588–1603* (Princeton UP, 1992); a vivid fresco of the European context is Garrett Mattingley, *The Defeat of the Spanish Armada* (London, Cape, 1959).

On the great cultural phenomena, see Neil MacGregor, *Shakespeare's Restless World* (London, Allen Lane, 2012); A. D. Nuttall, *Shakespeare the Thinker* (New Haven and London, Yale UP, 2007); David Daniell, *William Tyndale: A Biography* (New Haven and London, Yale UP, 1994); David Norton, *The King James Bible: A Short History from Tyndale to Today* (Cambridge UP, 2011); Adam Nicolson, *Power and Glory: Jacobean England and the Making of the King James Bible* (London, HarperCollins, 2003).

For insightful one-volume surveys of the whole Stuart period, see David L. Smith, *A History of the Modern British Isles, 1603–1707: The Double Crown* (Oxford, Blackwell, 1998), and Mark Kishlansky, *A Monarchy Transformed: Britain, 1603–1714* (London, Penguin Books, 1997). Jonathan Scott, *England's Troubles: Seventeenth-Century English Instability in European Context* (Cambridge UP, 2000), is a brilliant interpretation of England's experience as part of a wider European crisis. On the Stuarts' first narrow escape, Mark Nicholls, *Investigating Gunpowder Plot* (Manchester UP, 1991). On the crucial religious conflict, John Coffey and Paul C. H. Lim, eds., *The Cambridge Companion to Puritanism* (Cambridge UP, 2008), and John Morrill, "The religious context of the English Civil War," *Transactions of the Royal Historical Society* 34 (1984). On wider questions of belief and behaviour, Alexandra Walsham, *Charitable Hatred: Tolerance and Intolerance in England, 1500–1700* (Manchester UP, 2009), and Keith Thomas, *The Ends of Life: Roads to Fulfilment in Early Modern England* (Oxford UP, 2009).

For the global context of the Civil War, see Geoffrey Parker, *Global Crisis: War, Climate Change and Catastrophe in the Seventeenth Century* (New Haven and London, Yale UP, 2013). Michael Braddick, *God's Fury, England's Fire: A New History of the English Civil Wars* (London, Allen Lane, 2008), is a gripping and comprehensive survey. On its beginnings, indispensable are Kevin Sharpe, *The Personal Rule of Charles I* (New Haven and London, Yale UP, 1992), and Anthony Fletcher, *The Outbreak of the English Civil War* (London, Arnold, 1981). On the experience of the conflict, Barbara Donegan, *War in England, 1642–1649* (Oxford UP, 2008); and on its meanings John Morrill, *The Nature of the English Revolution* (London,

Longman, 1993), and Ronald Hutton, *Debates in Stuart History* (Basingstoke, Palgrave Macmillan, 2004).

Ian Gentles, *The New Model Army in England, Ireland and Scotland, 1645–1653* (Oxford, Blackwell, 1992), is crucial for the parliamentary side. On politics and ideas, Ian Gentles et al., *Soldiers, Writers and Statesmen of the English Revolution* (Cambridge UP, 1998), and Derek Hirst, *The Representative of the People? Voters and Voting in England Under the Early Stuarts* (Cambridge UP, 1975). On the Lord Protector, Ian Gentles, *Oliver Cromwell: God's Warrior and the English Revolution* (Houndmills, Palgrave Macmillan, 2011). On later understandings, Blair Worden, *Roundhead Reputations: The English Civil Wars and the Passions of Posterity* (London, Allen Lane, 2001).

Jenny Uglow, *A Gambling Man: Charles II and the Restoration* (London, Faber, 2009) is a lively portrayal of the man and the period; Tim Harris, *Restoration: Charles II and His Kingdoms, 1660–1685* (London, Penguin Books, 2006), provides the broader picture. John Bunyan's *The Pilgrim's Progress*, ed. W. R. Owens (Oxford UP, 2008), evokes the mental world of Dissent, and the diaries of Samuel Pepys its dissolution—see *The Shorter Pepys*, ed. Robert Latham (London, Penguin Books, 1987).

PART IV: MAKING A NEW WORLD, *c.*1660–*c.*1815

Julian Hoppit, *A Land of Liberty? England, 1689–1727* (Oxford, Clarendon Press, 2000), and Paul Langford, *A Polite and Commercial People: England, 1727–1783* (Oxford UP, 1989), are major works of synthesis, and J. C. D. Clark, *English Society, 1688–1832* (Cambridge UP, 1985), is a provocative interpretation stressing the centrality of religion and characterizing England as a traditional *ancien régime*.

Craig Rose, *England in the 1690s: Revolution, Religion and War* (Oxford, Blackwell, 1999), and Tony Claydon, *Europe and the Making of England, 1660–1760* (Cambridge UP, 2007), both show England's political changes as part of a European drama. On domestic politics, W. A. Speck, *Reluctant Revolutionaries: Englishmen and the Revolution of 1688* (Oxford UP, 1988); Frank O'Gorman, *Voters, Patrons and Parties: The Unreformed Electoral System of Hanoverian England, 1734–1832* (Oxford, Clarendon, 1989); Paul Langford, *Public Life and the Propertied Englishman, 1689–1798* (Oxford, Clarendon, 1991); and the classic J. H. Plumb, *Sir Robert Walpole* (2 vols.; London, Cresset, 1956–60).

England began its bumpy rise to global power. See John Brewer, *The Sinews of Power: War, Money and the English State, 1688–1783* (Cambridge, Mass., Harvard UP, 1988); Brendan Simms, *Three Victories and a Defeat: The Rise and Fall of the First British Empire, 1714–1783* (London, Allen Lane, 2007); Jeremy Black, *A System of Ambition: British Foreign Policy, 1660–1793* (Harlow, Longman, 1991); Elizabeth Mancke and Carole Shammas, eds., *The Creation of the British Atlantic World* (Baltimore, Johns Hopkins UP, 2005); and P. J. Marshall, *The Making and Unmaking of Empires: Britain, India, and America, c.1750–1783* (Oxford UP, 2005). Bruce Lenman, *Britain's Colonial Wars, 1688–1783* (Harlow, Longman,

2001), is comprehensive and concise. A dramatic account of the turning point of the Seven Years' War is Frank McLynn, *1759: The Year Britain Became Master of the World* (London, Jonathan Cape, 2004), and Piers Mackesy, *The War for America, 1775–1783* (London, Longman, 1964), shows how it was knocked off the perch. For the effects at home, Kathleen Wilson, *The Sense of the People: Politics, Culture and Imperialism in England, 1715–1785* (Cambridge UP, 1995); Stephen Conway, *The British Isles and the War of American Independence* (Oxford UP, 2000); and Ian Haywood and John Seed, eds., *The Gordon Riots: Politics, Culture and Insurrection in Late Eighteenth-Century Britain* (Cambridge UP, 2012). For the view from the sharp end, Stephen Brumwell, *Redcoats: The British Soldier and War in the Americas, 1755–1763* (Cambridge UP, 2002), and N. A. M. Rodger, *The Wooden World: An Anatomy of the Georgian Navy* (London, Fontana, 1988). Linda Colley, *Britons: Forging the Nation, 1707–1837* (New Haven and London, Yale UP, 1992), argues that this period sees the emergence of British identity.

Not all was conflict and conquest. Roy Porter, *Enlightenment: Britain and the Creation of the Modern World* (London, Allen Lane, 2000), shows the crucial English and British dimensions of a European cultural revolution. John Brewer, *The Pleasures of the Imagination: English Culture in the Eighteenth Century* (London, HarperCollins, 1997), surveys artistic and intellectual novelties. Other English pleasures are unveiled in Vic Gatrell, *City of Laughter: Sex and Satire in Eighteenth-Century London* (London, Atlantic Books, 2006); John Styles, *The Dress of the People: Everyday Fashion in Eighteenth-Century England* (New Haven and London, Yale UP, 2007); and Faramerz Dabhoiwala, *The Origins of Sex: The First Sexual Revolution* (London, Allen Lane, 2012).

However, the Age of Enlightenment was no less an age of belief: see Nigel Yates, *Eighteenth-Century Britain: Religion, Politics, and Society, 1745–1815* (Harlow, Longman, 2008); William Gibson's concise and lucid *The Church of England, 1688–1832: Unity and Accord* (London, Routledge, 2001); and David Hempton's vivid *Methodism: Empire of the Spirit* (New Haven and London, Yale UP, 2005).

It was also an age of liberty in reading, writing and talking. See Patrick Parrinder, *Nation and Novel: The English Novel from Its Origins to the Present Day* (Oxford UP, 2006); David Vincent, *Literacy and Popular Culture: England, 1750–1914* (Cambridge UP, 1989); Susan E. Whyman, *The Pen and the People: English Letter Writers, 1660–1800* (Oxford UP, 2009); Jenny Uglow, *The Lunar Men: The Friends Who Made the Future* (London, Faber, 2002); and the same author's *Dr. Johnson, His Club and Other Friends* (London, National Portrait Gallery, 1998). On what they wrote and said: Daniel Defoe, *Robinson Crusoe* and *Moll Flanders* (many editions); Lord Chesterfield, *Letters to His Son,* ed. James Harding (London, Folio Society, 1973), for an inimitable and unintentionally funny guide to polite manners; James Boswell, *Life of Johnson,* ed. R. W. Chapman (Oxford UP, 1970); Henry Fielding, *Tom Jones,* ed. R. Mutter (London, Penguin Books, 1966); Lawrence Sterne, *The Life and Opinions of Tristram Shandy, Gentleman,* ed. G. Petrie (London, Penguin Books, 1967); and anything and everything by Jane Austen (on whom, see Peter Knox-Shaw, *Jane Austen and the Enlightenment,* Cambridge UP, 2004).

This was also a time of economic and social transformation. Jan de Vries, *The*

*Industrious Revolution: Consumer Behaviour and the Household Economy, 1650 to the Present* (Cambridge UP, 2008), is an influential interpretation. On England's experience in a wider context, see Ronald Finlay and Kevin H. O'Rourke, *Power and Plenty: Trade, War and the World Economy in the Second Millennium* (Princeton UP, 2007); L. Prados de la Escosura, ed., *Exceptionalism and Industrialisation: Britain and Its European Rivals, 1688–1815* (Cambridge UP, 2004); and Robert C. Allen, *The British Industrial Revolution in Global Perspective* (Cambridge UP, 2009). *The Cambridge Economic History of Modern Britain*, eds. Roderick Floud and Paul Johnson, vol. 1 (Cambridge UP, 2004), synthesizes modern research at length, as does Emma Griffin more concisely in *A Short History of the British Industrial Revolution* (Houndmills, Palgrave Macmillan, 2010). On an important aspect of the general story, see Edward H. Hunt, *British Labour History, 1815–1914* (London, Weidenfeld & Nicolson, 1981); Deborah M. Valenze, *The First Industrial Woman* (Oxford UP, 1995); and Jane Humphries, *Childhood and Child Labour in the British Industrial Revolution* (Cambridge UP, 2010).

On the epoch-making struggles of the turn of the century, Paul W. Schroeder, *The Transformation of European Politics, 1763–1848* (Oxford, Clarendon Press, 1994), provides the indispensable broad view. Jennifer Mori, *Britain in the Age of the French Revolution* (London, Pearson, 2000); Clive Emsley, *British Society and the French Wars, 1793–1815* (London, Macmillan, 1979); and H. T. Dickinson, ed., *Britain and the French Revolution, 1789–1815* (London, Macmillan, 1989) are incisive summaries. Emma Vincent Macleod, *A War of Ideas: British Attitudes to the Wars Against Revolutionary France, 1792–1802* (Aldershot, Ashgate, 1998), is a brilliant overview; Stuart Andrews, *Unitarian Radicalism: Political Rhetoric, 1770–1814* (Basingstoke, Palgrave, 2003), and Clarke Garrett, *Respectable Folly: Millenarians and the French Revolution in France and England* (Baltimore, Johns Hopkins UP, 1975), re-create the religious underpinnings of English radicalism. E. P. Thompson, *The Making of the English Working Class* (London, Penguin Books, 1968), is a classic: vivid and moving though no longer convincing. Edmund Burke, *Reflections on the Revolution in France*, ed. J. C. D. Clark (Stanford UP, 2001), and Thomas Paine, *Political Writings*, ed. Bruce Kuklick (Cambridge UP, 1989), are the indispensable and still compelling contemporary tracts.

Charles Esdaile, *The Wars of Napoleon* (London, Longman, 1995), is a lucid summary. John Ehrman, *The Younger Pitt* (3 vols.; London, Constable, 1983), and Roger Knight, *Britain Against Napoleon: The Organization of Victory, 1793–1815* (London, Allen Lane, 2013), both monuments of scholarship, show in detail how and why Britain was victorious. J. E. Cookson, *The British Armed Nation, 1793–1815* (Oxford, Clarendon Press, 1997), and Austin Gee, *The British Volunteer Movement, 1794–1815* (Oxford, Clarendon Press, 2003), show the grass-roots effort. On the greatest British overseas commitment, David Gates, *The Spanish Ulcer: A History of the Peninsular War* (London, Pimlico, 2002), concentrates on military detail; Charles Esdaile, *The Peninsular War: A New History* (London, Allen Lane, 2002), takes a broader perspective. N. A. M. Rodger, *The Command of the Ocean* (London, Allen Lane, 2004), and Roger Morriss, *The Foundations of British Maritime Ascendancy: Resources, Logistics and the State, 1755–1815* (Cambridge

UP, 2011), illuminate one crucial facet of English power; and John M. Sherwig, *Guineas and Gunpowder: British Foreign Aid in the Wars with France, 1793–1815* (Cambridge, Mass., Harvard UP, 1969), illuminates the other—financial muscle. On the diplomatic brain behind the victory, John Bew, *Castlereagh: Enlightenment, War and Tyranny* (London, Quercus, 2011), and on its military brain, Rory Muir, *Wellington: The Path to Victory* (New Haven and London, Yale UP, 2013)—the first part of the most recent biography of the great general. Stuart Semmel, *Napoleon and the British* (Yale UP, 2004), discovers unexpected fondness for the former enemy. Roger Anstey, *The Atlantic Slave Trade and British Abolition, 1760–1810* (London, Macmillan, 1975), recounts one of the greatest by-products of the conflict.

### PART V: THE ENGLISH CENTURY

The global changes that framed England's hegemony are analysed in C. A. Bayly, *The Birth of the Modern World, 1780–1914: Global Connections and Comparisons* (Oxford, Blackwell, 2004). Fundamental changes at home are covered in *The Cambridge Economic History of Modern Britain*, eds. Roderick Floud and Paul Johnson (3 vols.; Cambridge University Press, 2004), vol. 1, and *The Cambridge Social History of Britain, 1750–1950*, ed. F. M. L. Thompson (3 vols.; Cambridge UP, 1990). The political tremors are dazzlingly analysed in Boyd Hilton, *A Mad, Bad and Dangerous People? England, 1783–1846* (Oxford, Clarendon Press, 2006). On social problems and the responses to them, Gertrude Himmelfarb, *The Idea of Poverty: England in the Early Industrial Age* (London, Faber and Faber, 1984), and Ursula Henriques, *Before the Welfare State: Social Administration in Early Industrial Britain* (London, Longman, 1979); over the longer term, Martin Daunton, *Wealth and Welfare: An Economic and Social History of Britain, 1851–1951* (Oxford UP, 2007), and Jose Harris, "From poor law to welfare state? A European perspective," in Donald Winch and Patrick K. O'Brien, *The Political Economy of British Historical Experience, 1688–1914* (Oxford UP, 2002). Radical responses are narrated in E. J. Hobsbawm and George Rudé, *Captain Swing* (London, Lawrence & Wishart, 1970), a classic; Malcolm Chase, *Chartism: A New History* (Manchester UP, 2007); and Dorothy Thompson, *The Chartists: Popular Politics in the Industrial Revolution* (New York, Pantheon, 1984). Important are Gareth Stedman Jones, *Outcast London, A Study in the Relationship Between Classes in Victorian Society* (London, Penguin Books, 1984), and his influentially revisionist *Languages of Class* (Cambridge UP, 1983). An optimistic picture of change is given in Emma Griffin, *Liberty's Dawn: A People's History of the Industrial Revolution* (New Haven and London, Yale UP, 2013).

Social, economic and intellectual uncertainties produced an intellectual and literary response of unparalleled importance, including the works of Dickens, the Brontës, George Eliot, Elizabeth Gaskell, Disraeli, Thackeray, Trollope and many others, concisely analysed in the still valuable work by Kathleen Tillotson, *Novels of the Eighteen-Forties* (Oxford, Clarendon Press, 1954). Thomas Hughes, *Tom Brown's Schooldays* (Oxford UP, 1999 [1857]) had wide influence on "muscular

Christianity." A very different voice of Victorian England was Alfred Tennyson: see Christopher Ricks, *Tennyson* (Basingstoke, Macmillan, 1989). Philip Davis, *The Victorians* (vol. 8 of *The Oxford English Literary History*, Oxford UP, 2002), covers literary genres, their intellectual context, and their conditions of production. An approving study of prominent figures is Simon Heffer, *High Minds: The Victorians and the Birth of Modern Britain* (London, Cornerstone, 2013). On readers, see Richard D. Altick, *The English Common Reader: A Social History of the Mass Reading Public, 1800–1900* (Chicago UP, 1957), and Jonathan Rose, *The Intellectual Life of the British Working Classes* (New Haven and London, Yale UP, 2001).

The high-Victorian period is sketched in G. M. Young's sparkling *Portrait of an Age* (Oxford UP, 1960) and no less vividly by David Newsome, *The Victorian World Picture* (London, Fontana, 1998). A. N. Wilson, *The Victorians* (London, Hutchinson, 2002), is readably mordant. Key developments are covered in F. M. L. Thompson, *The Rise of Respectable Society: A Social History of Victorian Britain, 1830–1900* (London, Fontana, 1988); José Harris, *Private Lives, Public Spirit: A Social History of Britain, 1870–1914* (Oxford UP, 1993); and K. Theodore Hoppen's acute *The Mid-Victorian Generation, 1846–1886* (Oxford UP, 1998). The still-powerful old world is analysed in F. M. L. Thompson, *English Landed Society in the Nineteenth Century* (London, Routledge & Kegan Paul, 1963); its waning in David Cannadine, *The Decline and Fall of the British Aristocracy* (New Haven and London, Yale UP, 1990), and Jeremy Burchardt, *Paradise Lost: Rural Idyll and Social Change Since 1800* (London, Tauris, 2002). Pioneering works that did much to rescue the Victorians from the condescension of posterity are Asa Briggs, *Victorian Cities* (London, Penguin Books, 1963), *Victorian People: A Reassessment of Persons and Themes, 1851–67* (London, Penguin Books, 1965), and *Victorian Things* (London, Penguin Books, 1990). Fascinating comparative studies are Donald J. Olsen, *The City of a Work of Art: London, Paris, Vienna* (New Haven and London, Yale UP, 1986), and Jonathan Conlin, *Tales of Two Cities: Paris, London and the Birth of the Modern City* (London, Atlantic Books, 2013).

Religion, manners and morality and the changes they underwent lie at the heart of Victorian England. Important works are K. D. M. Snell and Paul S. Ell, *Rival Jerusalems: The Geography of Victorian Religion* (Cambridge UP, 2000); David Newsome, *Godliness and Good Learning: Four Studies on a Victorian Ideal* (London, Murray, 1961); M. J. D. Roberts, *Making English Morals: Voluntary Association and Moral Reform in England, 1878–1886* (Cambridge UP, 2004); David Taylor, *Crime, Policing and Punishment in England, 1750–1914* (Houndmills, Palgrave Macmillan, 1998); Clive Emsley, *Hard Men: The English and Violence Since 1750* (London, Hambledon, 2005); Deborah Gorham, *The Victorian Girl and the Feminine Ideal* (London, Croom Helm, 1982); Michael Mason, *The Making of Victorian Sexuality* (Oxford UP, 1994), and *The Making of Victorian Sexual Attitudes* (Oxford UP, 1994); Hera Cook, *The Long Sexual Revolution: English Women, Sex, and Contraception, 1800–1975* (Oxford UP, 2004); Edward J. Bristow, *Vice and Vigilance: Purity Movements in Britain Since 1700* (Dublin, Gill & Macmillan, 1977); Judith R. Walkowitz, *City of Dreadful Delight: Narratives of Sexual Danger in Late-Victorian London* (London, Virago, 1992); Sean Brady, *Masculinity and Male Homosexuality in Britain, 1861–1913* (Basingstoke,

Palgrave Macmillan, 2005); and Lucy Bland, *Banishing the Beast: English Feminism and Sexual Morality, 1885–1914* (London, Penguin Books, 1995). The pioneering work on a new popular culture is Richard Holt, *Sport and the British: A Modern History* (Oxford, Clarendon, 1992).

Victorian politics went from oligarchy to democracy—at least in appearance. Michael Bentley, *Politics Without Democracy, 1815–1914* (London, Fontana, 1984), and Martin Pugh, *The Making of Modern British Politics, 1867–1939* (Oxford, Blackwell, 1982), trace the process. H. J. Hanham, *Elections and Party Management: Politics in the Time of Disraeli and Gladstone* (Hassocks, Harvester, 1978), is a fascinating and at times comical description of how it was done. On political parties: Jon Lawrence, *Speaking for the People: Party, Language and Popular Politics in England, 1867–1914* (Cambridge UP, 1998); John Vincent, *The Formation of the Liberal Party, 1857–1868* (London, Constable, 1966), still valuable; Eugenio Biagini, *Liberty, Retrenchment and Reform: Popular Liberalism in the Age of Gladstone, 1860–1880* (Cambridge UP, 1992); Robin Harris, *The Conservatives: A History* (London, Bantam, 2011), a modern single-volume history; and Martin Pugh, *Speak for Britain: A New History of the Labour Party* (London, Vintage, 2011). Gladstone and Disraeli are of course crucial: see Eugenio F. Biagini, *Gladstone* (Basingstoke, Macmillan, 2000); Richard Shannon, *Gladstone* (2 vols.; London, Allen Lane, 1999); J. P. Parry, *Democracy and Religion: Gladstone and the Liberal Party, 1867–1875* (Cambridge UP, 1986); and *The Gladstone Diaries*, ed. M. R. D. Foot et al. (14 vols.; Oxford, Clarendon Press, 1968–94); on his great rival, Jonathan Parry, "Disraeli and England," *HJ* 43 (September 2000), and his *Benjamin Disraeli* (Oxford UP, 2007); Robert Blake's classic *Disraeli* (London, Methuen, 1969) is still highly readable. On the queen and monarchy generally, Christopher Hibbert, *Queen Victoria: A Personal History* (London, HarperCollins, 2001); in different style, Dorothy Thompson, *Queen Victoria: Gender and Power* (London, Virago, 2001), and Frank Prochaska, *Royal Bounty: The Making of a Welfare Monarchy* (New Haven and London, Yale UP, 1995). On other women, Kathryn Gleadle, *Borderline Citizens: Women, Gender and Political Culture in Britain, 1815–1867* (Oxford UP, 2009). On the financial bedrock of government, Martin J. Daunton, *Trusting Leviathan: The Politics of Taxation in Britain, 1799–1914* (Cambridge UP, 2001).

Three great interconnected political themes were foreign policy, free trade and empire. Outstanding are Jonathan Parry, *The Politics of Patriotism: English Liberalism, National Identity and Europe, 1830–1886* (Cambridge UP, 2006), and Frank Trentmann, *Free Trade Nation: Commerce, Consumption, and Civil Society in Modern Britain* (Oxford UP, 2008). More broadly on foreign policy, Keith Robbins, *Britain and Europe, 1789–2005* (London, Hodder Arnold, 2005); Kenneth Bourne, *Foreign Policy of Victorian England, 1830–1902* (Oxford, 1970). On those responsible, T. G. Otte, ed., *The Makers of British Foreign Policy: From Pitt to Thatcher* (Houndmills, Palgrave Macmillan, 2002), and on the most famous of them, David Brown, *Palmerston and the Politics of Foreign Policy, 1846–55* (Manchester UP, 2002). On execution, T. G. Otte, *The Foreign Office Mind: The Making of British Foreign Policy, 1865–1914* (Cambridge UP, 2011).

The other great theme is empire: see John Darwin, *Unfinished Empire: The*

*Global Expansion of Britain* (London, Penguin Books, 2012), and *The Empire Project: The Rise and Fall of the British World System, 1830–1970* (Cambridge UP, 2009); James Belich, *Replenishing the Earth: The Settler Revolution and the Rise of the Anglo-World, 1783–1939* (Oxford UP, 2009); Gary B. Magee and Andrew S. Thompson, *Empire and Globalisation: Networks of People, Goods and Capital in the British World, c.1850–1914* (Cambridge UP, 2010); and Ronald Hyam, *Understanding the British Empire* (Cambridge UP, 2010). On India, Eric Stokes, *The Peasant Armed: The Indian Revolt of 1857* (Oxford, Clarendon, 1986); Saul David, *The Indian Mutiny, 1857* (London, Penguin Books, 2003); and William Dalrymple, *The Last Mughal: The Fall of a Dynasty, Delhi, 1857* (New Delhi, Viking, 2006). On late-Victorian expansion, the classic is Ronald Robinson and John Gallagher with Alice Denny, *Africa and the Victorians: The Official Mind of Imperialism* (London, Macmillan, 1961). On what it cost, Lance E. Davis and Robert A. Huttenback, *Mammon and the Pursuit of Empire: The Political Economy of British Imperialism, 1860–1912* (Cambridge UP, 1986). On effects at home, Bernard Porter, *The Absent-Minded Imperialists: Empire, Society and Culture in Britain* (Oxford UP, 2004), argues that they were few.

On the *fin de siècle*, see George Dangerfield's lively, influential and erroneous *Strange Death of Liberal England* (London, Paladin, 1970 [1936]), and for a weighty corrective, G. R. Searle, *A New England? Peace and War, 1886–1918* (Oxford, Clarendon Press, 2004). On crucial aspects of these years, Ben Griffin, *The Politics of Gender in Victorian Britain: Masculinity, Political Culture and the Struggle for Women's Rights* (Cambridge UP, 2012); Sandra S. Holton, *Feminism and Democracy: Women's Suffrage and Reform Politics in Britain, 1900–1918* (Cambridge UP, 1986); and Peter F. Clark, *Lancashire and the New Liberalism* (Cambridge UP, 1971).

## PART VI: THE NEW DARK AGE, 1914–1945

On the beginnings of the disaster there is a large literature: of particular relevance are Zara S. Steiner, *Britain and the Origins of the First World War* (London, Macmillan, 1977); T. G. Otte, *July Crisis: The World's Descent into War, Summer 1914* (Cambridge UP, 2014); and Catriona Pennell, *A Kingdom United: Popular Responses to the Outbreak of the First World War in Britain and Ireland* (Oxford UP, 2012). On the nation at war, Adrian Gregory, *The Last Great War: British Society and the First World War* (Cambridge UP, 2008), is a searching and sensitive study; J. M. Winter, *The Great War and the British People* (London, Palgrave Macmillan, 2nd edn, 2003), has become a classic. Jay Winter and Jean-Louis Robert, eds., *Capital Cities at War: Paris, London, Berlin, 1914–1919* (Cambridge UP, 1997), provide enlightening comparisons.

On the conduct of the war and the experiences of the combatants there is a vast and uneven literature. Among the most reliable works are Peter Simkins, *Kitchener's Army: The Raising of the New Armies, 1914–1916* (Barnsley, Pen & Sword, 2007); Ian F. W. Beckett and Keith Simpson, eds., *A Nation in Arms: A Social Study of the*

*British Army in the First World War* (Manchester UP, 1985); Willliam Philpott, *Bloody Victory: The Sacrifice on the Somme and the Making of the Twentieth Century* (London, Little, Brown, 2009); Gary Sheffield, *Forgotten Victory: The First World War: Myths and Realities* (London, Headline, 2001); Alexander Watson, *Enduring the Great War: Combat, Morale and Collapse in the German and British Armies, 1914–1918* (Cambridge UP, 2008); and Jonathan Boff, *Winning and Losing on the Western Front: The British Third Army and the Defeat of Germany in 1918* (Cambridge UP, 2012). On the war at sea, the definitive work is still Arthur J. Marder, *From the Dreadnought to Scapa Flow: The Royal Navy in the Fisher Era, 1904–1919* (5 vols.; Oxford UP, 1961–70).

On the varied experiences of men serving abroad, see Richard Holmes, *Tommy: The British Soldier on the Western Front, 1914–1918* (London, HarperCollins, 2004), and Craig Gibson, *Behind the Front: British Soldiers and French Civilians, 1914–1918* (Cambridge UP, 2014). Among many memoirs by soldiers, Private Frank Richards's chatty *Old Soldiers Never Die*, ed. H. J. Krijnan and D. E. Langley (Peterborough, Krijnan & Langley, 2004); the terse and immediate *General Jack's Diary: The Trench Diary of Brigadier-General J. L. Jack, D.S.O.*, ed. John Terraine (London, Eyre & Spottiswoode, 1964); Edwin Campion Vaughan, *Some Desperate Glory: The Diary of a Young Officer, 1917* (London, Frederick Warne, 1981); and James C. Dunn, *The War the Infantry Knew: A Chronicle of Service in France and Belgium*, ed. Keith Simpson (London, Jane's, 1987). See also Jean Moorcroft Wilson, *Siegfried Sassoon: The Making of a War Poet, 1886–1918* (London, Duckworth, 1998).

On the aftermath of the war and its memory, David Reynolds, *The Long Shadow: The Great War in the Twentieth Century* (London, Simon & Schuster, 2013), is now the key work; see also Brian Bond, *The Unquiet Western Front: Britain's Role in Literature and History* (Cambridge UP, 2002), and Dan Todman, *The Great War: Myth and Memory* (London, Hambledon Continuum, 2005).

On the unabating disaster of the interwar period, the magisterial works are now Zara Steiner, *The Lights That Failed: European International History, 1919–1933* (Oxford UP, 2005), and *The Triumph of the Dark: European International History, 1933–1939* (Oxford UP, 2011). See also Margaret MacMillan, *Peacemakers: The Paris Conference of 1919 and Its Attempt to End War* (London, John Murray, 2001), and David Reynolds, *Britannia Overruled: British Policy and World Power in the Twentieth Century* (London, Longman, 1991). On the travails of empire, Ronald Hyam, *Britain's Declining Empire: The Road to Decolonisation, 1918–1968* (Cambridge UP, 2006).

On domestic developments, see Ross McKibbin, *Classes and Cultures: England, 1918–1951* (Oxford UP, 1998); Peter Clarke, *Hope and Glory: Britain, 1900–1990* (London, Allen Lane, 1996); and Kevin Jeffreys, *Politics and the People: A History of British Democracy Since 1918* (London, Atlantic, 2007), p. 78. On social and economic issues, Ina Zweiniger-Bargielowska, ed., *Women in Twentieth-Century Britain: Social, Cultural and Political Change* (Harlow, Longman, 2001); Patricia Clavin, *The Great Depression in Europe, 1929–1939* (Houndmills, Macmillan, 2000); and Bernard Harris, *The Origins of the British Welfare State: Social Welfare in England and Wales, 1800–1945* (Houndmills, Palgrave Macmillan, 2004). Richard Overy, *The Morbid Age: Britain and the Crisis of Civilization* (London, Penguin Books, 2010), is a brilliant evocation of interwar pessimism. A concise introduction to attitudes to war is Michael Howard, *War and the Liberal Conscience* (Oxford UP, 1981). On appeasement, see Martin Ceadel, *Pacifism in Britain, 1914–1945: The Defining of a Faith* (Oxford UP, 1980); David Dutton, *Neville Chamberlain* (London, Arnold, 2001); and Andrew David Stedman's thought-provoking *Alternatives to Appeasement: Neville Chamberlain and Hitler's Germany* (London, Tauris, 2011). For a refutation of traditionally pessimistic accounts of British weakness, see David Edgerton, *Warfare State: Britain, 1920–1970* (Cambridge UP, 2006), and G. C. Peden, *Arms, Economics and British Strategy: From Dreadnoughts to Hydrogen Bombs* (Cambridge UP, 2007).

Gripping evocations of the onset of the Second World War are Donald Cameron Watt, *How War Came* (London, Pimlico, 2001), and John Lukacs, *The Last European War: September 1939–December 1941* (London, Routledge, 1977). Talbot C. Imlay, *Facing the Second World War: Strategy, Politics and Economics in Britain and France, 1938–1940* (Oxford UP, 2003), analyses Allied dilemmas; Tobias Jersak, "Blitzkrieg revisited: a new look at Nazi war and extermination planning," *HJ* 43, 2 (June 2000), contains essential correctives to the traditional narrative of the 1940 catastrophe and its aftermath. I. C. B. Dear and M. R. D. Foot, eds., *The Oxford Companion to World War II* (Oxford UP, 2005), is an essential work of reference, as in narrative form is Gerhard L. Weinberg, *A World at Arms: A Global History of World War II* (Cambridge UP, 1994). There is of course an immense and continually expanding literature on the war: a vivid recent synthesis is Max Hastings, *All Hell Let Loose: The World at War, 1939–1945* (London, HarperPress, 2011).

On Churchill and his entourage, his own account is a classic: Winston S. Churchill, *The Second World War*, single-volume abridged edition by Denis Kelly (London, Penguin Books, 1989), and see David Reynolds's gloss, *In Command of History: Churchill Fighting and Writing the Second World War* (London, Allen Lane, 2004); also Andrew Roberts, *Masters and Commanders: How Roosevelt, Churchill, Marshall and Alanbrooke Won the War in the West* (London, Allen Lane, 2008). A key aspect of Churchill's leadership is covered by Richard Toye, *The Roar of the Lion: The Making of Churchill's World War II Speeches* (Oxford UP, 2013). Field Marshal Lord Alanbrooke, *War Diaries, 1939–1945*, eds. Alex Danchev and Daniel Todman (London, Phoenix, 2001), gives the sometimes jaundiced view of an over-worked general.

Important and authoritative analyses of decisive aspects of the war are Richard Overy, *Why the Allies Won* (London, Pimlico, 1995), and *The Bombing War: Europe, 1939–1945* (London, Allen Lane, 2013); Adam Tooze, *Wages of Destruction: The Making and Breaking of the Nazi Economy* (London, Allen Lane, 2006); Phillips P. O'Brien, "East versus West in the defeat of Nazi Germany," *Journal of Strategic Studies* 23 (June 2000); and on the crucial maritime struggle, the standard work is still Stephen Roskill, *The War at Sea* (3 vols.; London, HMSO, 1954–61).

On the Home Front, Angus Calder, *The People's War: Britain, 1939–45* (London, Literary Guild, 1969), is a moving and magisterial account. Tom Harrison,

*Living Through the Blitz* (London, Penguin, 1978), relates individual experiences. On public responses, see Paul Addison and Jeremy A. Crang, eds., *Listening to Britain: Home Intelligence Reports on Britain's Finest Hour, May to September 1940* (London, Vintage, 2011). An insightful study of people's behaviour under fire is Helen Jones, *British Civilians in the Front Line: Air Raids, Productivity and Wartime Culture, 1939–45* (Manchester UP, 2006). Other important aspects are covered in Ina Zweiniger-Bargielowska, *Austerity in Britain: Rationing, Controls, and Consumption, 1939–1955* (Oxford UP, 2000); Bernard Harris, *The Origins of the British Welfare State: Social Welfare in England and Wales, 1800–1954* (Houndmills, Palgrave Macmillan, 2004); Nicholas Timmins, *The Five Giants: A Biography of the Welfare State* (new edn, London, HarperCollins, 2001); and José Harris, "War and social history: Britain and the home front during the Second World War," in Gordon Martel, ed., *The World War Two Reader* (London, Routledge, 2004).

The literature of the Second World War is less celebrated than that of the First. A personal selection of the writings of participants (the first two of whom were killed): Richard Hillary, *The Last Enemy* (London, Vintage, 2010 [1942]); Keith Douglas, *The Complete Poems*, ed. Desmond Graham (3rd edn, London, Faber, 1998), and his memoir as a tank commander, *Alamein to Zem Zem* (London, Faber & Faber, 2008 [1946]); Peter White, *With the Jocks: A Soldier's Struggle for Europe, 1944–45* (Stroud, History Press, 2002); and a later memoir, George Macdonald Fraser, *Quartered Safe Out Here: A Recollection of the War in Burma* (London, HarperCollins, 2000). Evocative novels of the war are Alexander Baron, *From the City, from the Plough* (London, Black Spring Press, 2010); and Evelyn Waugh, *Put Out More Flags* (London, Penguin Books, 2011 [1943]), and *The Sword of Honour* (London, Penguin Books, 2011 [1965]), all with clear autobiographical elements.

## PART VII: AN AGE OF DECLINE?

On the crucial theme of decline, see Peter Clarke and Clive Trebilcock, eds., *Understanding Decline: Perceptions and Realities of British Economic Performance* (Cambridge UP, 1997); and revisionist works by Jim Tomlinson, "Thrice denied: 'declinism' as a recurrent theme in British history in the long twentieth century," *Twentieth Century British History* 20 (2009), "Inventing 'decline': the falling behind of the British economy in the postwar years," *Economic History Review* XLIX (1996), and *The Politics of Decline: Understanding Post-War Britain* (Harlow, Longman, 2000).

On the postwar period there is a large literature, prominent within it Paul Addison, *No Turning Back: The Peacetime Revolutions of Post-War Britain* (Oxford UP, 2010); and Peter Hennessy, *Never Again: Britain, 1945–51* (London, Cape, 1992), and *Having It So Good: Britain in the Fifties* (London, Allen Lane, 2006); see also the voluminous treatment by David Kynaston, *Austerity Britain, 1945–51* (London, Bloomsbury, 2007), and *Family Britain, 1951–57* (London, Bloomsbury, 2009). On the 1970s and 1980s, Dominic Sandbrook, *State of Emergency: The Way We Were;*

Britain, 1970–1974 (London, Allen Lane, 2010), and *Seasons in the Sun: The Battle for Britain, 1974–1979* (London, Allen Lane, 2012); and for recent reconsideration, Lawrence Black et al., *Reassessing 1970s Britain* (Manchester UP, 2013).

On cultural transformation, Callum Brown's influential and controversial *The Death of Christian Britain* (London, Routledge, 2001); Hera Cook, *The Long Sexual Revolution: English Women, Sex and Contraception, 1880–1975* (Oxford UP, 2004); J. Garland et al., "Youth Culture, Popular Music and the End of 'Consensus' in Post-War Britain," *Contemporary British History* (2012); and Hugh McLeod, *The Religious Crisis of the 1960s* (Oxford UP, 2007).

On the end of empire, Ronald Hyam, *Britain's Declining Empire: The Road to Decolonisation, 1918–1968* (Cambridge UP, 2006); Peter Clark, *The Last Thousand Days of the British Empire: The Demise of a Superpower, 1944–47* (London, Penguin Books, 2008); John Darwin, *Britain and Decolonisation: The Retreat from Empire in the Post-War World* (Basingstoke, Macmillan, 1988); and David Anderson, *Histories of the Hanged: Britain's Dirty War in Kenya and the End of Empire* (London, Weidenfeld & Nicolson, 2005).

Policy towards European integration has been analysed authoritatively and at length: Alan S. Milward, *The UK and the European Community*, vol. I: *The Rise and Fall of a National Strategy, 1945–1963* (London, Frank Cass, 2002); Stephen Wall, *The Official History of Britain and the European Community*, vol. 2: *From Rejection to Referendum, 1963–1975* (London, Routledge, 2013); Helen Parr, *Britain's Policy Towards the European Community: Harold Wilson and Britain's World Role, 1964–67* (London, Routledge, 2006); and Stephen Wall, *A Stranger in Europe: Britain and the EU from Thatcher to Blair* (Oxford UP, 2008). A detailed and iconoclastic study of the context is John Gillingham, *European Integration, 1950–2003: Superstate or New Market Economy?* (Cambridge UP, 2003).

The Thatcher period is now being thoroughly scrutinized: see Richard Vinen's incisive *Thatcher's Britain: The Politics and Social Upheaval of the 1980s* (London, Simon & Schuster, 2009); Graham Stewart, *Bang! A History of Britain in the 1980s* (London, Atlantic, 2013); Ben Jackson and Robert Saunders, eds., *Making Thatcher's Britain* (Cambridge UP, 2012); Charles Moore, *Margaret Thatcher: The Authorized Biography*, vol. 1: *Not for Turning* (London, Allen Lane, 2013); and Robin Harris's astringent insider's view, *Not for Turning: The Life of Margaret Thatcher* (London, Bantam, 2013). On foreign policy, Paul Sharp, *Thatcher's Diplomacy: The Revival of British Foreign Policy* (Houndmills, Macmillan, 1999), and Lawrence Freedman, *The Official History of the Falklands Campaign* (rev. edn, 2 vols.; London, Routledge, 2007). On her mixed legacy, Simon Jenkins, *Thatcher and Sons: A Revolution in Three Acts* (London, Penguin Books, 2007).

On the New Labour period, Anthony Seldon, ed., *Blair's Britain, 1997–2007* (Cambridge UP, 2007); John Kampfner, *Blair's Wars* (London, Simon & Schuster, 2003); Andrew Rawnsley, *The End of the Party* (London, Viking, 2010); and, more favourably, Polly Toynbee and David Walker, *The Verdict: Did Labour Change Britain?* (London, Granta, 2010). The end of the story is clearly analysed by Johan A. Lybeck, *A Global History of the Financial Crash of 2007–2010* (Cambridge UP, 2011).

These years have led to uneasy questioning of the political system, noteworthy essays being Anthony King and Ivor Crewe, *The Blunders of Our Governments* (London, Oneworld, 2013), and Peter Oborne, *The Triumph of the Political Class* (London, Simon & Schuster, 2007). Peter Mair, *Ruling the Void: The Hollowing of Western Democracy* (London, Verso, 2013), sketches the international context.

# Acknowledgements

When beginning this book, I admit I felt some trepidation concerning the reaction of my colleagues in the Cambridge History Faculty, who I thought might tell me I should stick to my own patch. If they did think this, they never let on, and on the contrary gave generous encouragement and advice for which I am sincerely grateful. From first-year undergraduate to regius professor, they were willing to share ideas and provide information, whether in casual conversations in corridors and over meals or in more sustained discussions. Many were willing to answer questions and comment on a paragraph or two. Some were generous enough to read and reflect on longer passages, even whole chapters: and here I wish to express particular thanks to Eugenio Biagini, Christine Carpenter, John Morrill, Richard Rex and Tom Stammers. I am also grateful for advice and information to Nora Berend, Lucy Delap, Richard Evans, Niamh Gallagher, Mark Goldie, Boyd Hilton, Liesbeth van Houts, Jon Parry, Anne-Isabelle Richard-Picchi and Brendan Simms. My colleagues in the Modern European Subject Group also supported my request for a term's sabbatical leave.

I was fortunate in having the help at an early stage of several outstanding young scholars, who advised on the literature, read drafts, and made valuable suggestions and corrections: they were Elma Brenner, Ben Dabby, Hilary Larkin, Laura Napran, Lucy Rhymer, Daniel Robinson, Angus Vine and Faridah Zaman.

As far as my college, St. John's, was concerned, I fear I became a social menace, subjecting its members, Ancient Mariner fashion, to questions and impromptu discussions for which I would like to express both thanks and apologies. The extended community of fellows and former fellows, honorary fellows, research associates, and present and former students were unfailingly tolerant and helpful. Some were kind enough to express an interest in what I was doing and on one occasion even turn up to hear me talk about it. Several read and made valuable comments on extracts of the text, particularly Richard Aikens, Richard Butler, Jeevan Deol, Petra Geraats, Ben Griffin, Liz Gunnion, Iain Hamilton, John Iliffe, Hamish McLaren, Máire Ní Mhaonaigh, Christopher Moule, Philip Murray, Richard Nolan, Siân Pooley, Simon Prince, Katherine Reggler, Frank Salmon, Sylvana Tomaselli and Esther-Miriam Wagner. Spontaneous advice, often over lunch or dinner, was given by Graeme Barker, Richard Beadle, Partha Dasgupta, Keith Jeffery, John Kerrigan, Anne-Louise Kinmonth, Peter Linehan, Nick Manton, Mark Nicholls, Ulinka Rublack, Simon Szreter, Rebecca Thomas and the late George Watson. Thanks to all for authoritative opinions on a vast range of topics from Anglo-Saxon linguistics to contemporary constitutional law, and from Hobbesian conflict to jihadi terrorism.

I would like to thank scholars in other fields, from other faculties or other institutions, some of them friends and acquaintances, but several of whom I have never met, who kindly responded to questions concerning their own research, which I had encountered and admired: Paul Bew, Clarissa Campbell-Orr, David French, Keith Hamilton, Richard Holt, John Keiger, Gerd Krumeich, Edward Lee-Six, Charles-Édouard Levillain, Clive Oppenheimer, William Philpott, Nicholas Rodger, Dennis Showalter and Richard Toye. I owe particular thanks to James Campbell, who kindly read and commented in meticulous detail on the medieval sections of the book.

Alison Appleby, Hilary Larkin, Simon MacDonald, Abby Waldman and Sebastian Walsh gave me permission to cite their unpublished doctoral dissertations. The Newton Trust kindly provided grants to assist with research expenses.

All the above contributed immensely to this book, and made its writing a constant adventure. They have also saved me from committing many errors. I am grateful to the assiduous readers of the first edition who kindly wrote to me to point out some others, now corrected in this edition. Those that doubtless remain, and the opinions expressed, are entirely mine. If there are people whose advice or writings I have omitted to acknowledge, here or in the footnotes, I hope that they will accept my apologies and thanks.

Finally, I wish to acknowledge my great debt to Bill Hamilton, my agent, and to Stuart Proffitt, Publishing Director at Penguin Books, and all the team at Penguin, for their unfailing support for and confidence in a project that some (including at certain moments its author) might easily have concluded was eccentric and unrealistic. Stuart devoted a vast amount of care and attention to editing the text—though that phrase is inadequate to describe his contribution, which was like nothing so much as that of an ideal Oxbridge supervisor, erudite, scrupulous, critical and encouraging. But perhaps my biggest debt is to my wife, Isabelle, *presqu'aussi anglaise que moi*, who has had to put up with this book invading so many weekends and evenings: I hope she thinks it was worth it, and I am sure she is pleased it is over.

# Index

on by the exotic alliance of Enoch Powell, Tony Benn and the Ulster Loyalist leader, the Rev. Ian Paisley—by food prices and the Commonwealth.[14] Least keen on Europe were Scottish islanders, Ulstermen and the left. The English, especially Tory voters from the prosperous south, were keenest: 64.6 percent of the English electorate voted; of those, 68.7 percent voted yes. Yet even this was acquiescence rather than enthusiasm: only 44 percent of the whole electorate voted yes, and without being sure what "yes" meant. Margaret Thatcher, the new Leader of the Opposition, hailed "this excellent result."

In April 1976 Harold Wilson bowed out, for unexplained reasons probably concerning his health. His replacement, James "Jim" Callaghan, was an avuncular-looking stalwart in the Bevin mould, described by one historian of the Labour Party as "a classic working-class conservative" who had "held the three highest offices in government without making a success of any of them" and who was "a wildly unsuitable leader" for a party influenced by the progressive ideas of the 1960s and infiltrated by the "hard left."[15] In his defence, he undeniably inherited a mess. Industry was floundering. Public spending had been rising since the 1960s. Taxes reached confiscatory levels—with the standard rate of income tax nudging 40 percent during the early 1970s, and the higher rate around 80 percent—even 98 percent on the top level of "unearned income." The cost of government borrowing rose faster in 1974 than in 1797, when Pitt had been forced to abandon gold. Wage inflation—which peaked at 27 percent in 1975, a level rarely seen in a developed country—was hitting exports, the balance of payments and sterling. All the economic indicators were bad: unemployment over 1,000,000, the balance of payments £1bn in the red, inflation stuck in double figures and a record budget deficit. During September 1976 sterling plunged by over 7 percent against the dollar and continued downwards—the chancellor, Dennis Healey, remembered it as "like the end of the world."[16] In one day, the twenty-eighth, it lost over 2 percent, and Callaghan gave his famous warning to the Labour Party conference in Blackpool that "the cosy world . . . is gone forever." He was coldly received, and the conference demanded more nationalization. Callaghan even warned on television of the danger of "a totalitarian government" in Britain. The government's credit was by this time very poor, and it had to negotiate six-month loans from European central banks, after which another short-term loan was required, this time $3.9bn from the International Monetary Fund—the biggest loan it had ever been asked for, and the first by an industrialized country. The IMF insisted on reductions in the budget deficit, and negotiations were tough (and at times bizarre, one secret meeting taking place in the cutting room of a London